T&T Clark Handbook of Christian Theology and Climate Change

T&T Clark Handbook of Christian Theology and Climate Change

EDITED BY
Ernst M. Conradie and Hilda P. Koster

t&tclark

T&T CLARK
Bloomsbury Publishing Plc
50 Bedford Square, London, WC1B 3DP, UK
1385 Broadway, New York, NY 10018, USA
29 Earlsfort Terrace, Dublin 2, Ireland

BLOOMSBURY, T&T CLARK and the T&T Clark logo are trademarks of
Bloomsbury Publishing Plc

First published in Great Britain 2020
This paperback edition published in 2022

Copyright © Ernst M. Conradie, Hilda P. Koster and contributors, 2020

Ernst M. Conradie and Hilda P. Koster have asserted their right under the Copyright, Designs and Patents Act, 1988, to be identified as Editors of this work.

For legal purposes the Acknowledgements on p. xiii constitute an extension of this copyright page.

Cover design: Terry Woodley
Cover image © mauritius images GmbH / Alamy Stock Photo

All rights reserved. No part of this publication may be reproduced or transmitted in any form or by any means, electronic or mechanical, including photocopying, recording, or any information storage or retrieval system, without prior permission in writing from the publishers.

Bloomsbury Publishing Plc does not have any control over, or responsibility for, any third-party websites referred to or in this book. All internet addresses given in this book were correct at the time of going to press. The author and publisher regret any inconvenience caused if addresses have changed or sites have ceased to exist, but can accept no responsibility for any such changes.

A catalogue record for this book is available from the British Library.

Library of Congress Control Number: 2019946179

ISBN: HB: 978-0-5676-7515-6
PB: 978-1-3503-2039-0
ePDF: 978-0-5676-7517-0
ePUB: 978-0-5676-7516-3

Typeset by Deanta Global Publishing Services, Chennai, India

To find out more about our authors and books visit www.bloomsbury.com and sign up for our newsletters.

Dedicated to

Vítor Westhelle (1952–2018)

&

Denis Edwards (1943–2019)

Their sustained and deeply rooted contributions, as reflected in this volume, changed the climate within and beyond Christian theology.

Contents

List of figures		xii
Acknowledgements		xiii
Introduction: Christian theology and climate change in the North Atlantic context *Ernst M. Conradie and Hilda P. Koster*		1

PART I WORKING WITH OTHERS: THE NEED FOR MULTIDISCIPLINARY COLLABORATION

Introduction *Ernst M. Conradie*		13
1.1	Working with climate scientists *Heather Eaton*	15
	A response to Heather Eaton *Katharine Hayhoe and W. Douglas Hayhoe*	27
1.2	Working with evolutionary biologists *Lisa H. Sideris*	31
	A response to Lisa Sideris *Vidyanand Nanjundiah*	48
1.3	Working with environmental economists *Annika Rieger and Joerg Rieger*	53
	A response to Annika and Joerg Rieger *Terra Schwerin Rowe*	65
1.4	Working with politics *Willis Jenkins*	70
	A response to Willis Jenkins *Tinyiko Maluleke*	83
1.5	Working with climate engineers *Forrest Clingerman*	90
	A response to Forrest Clingerman *Asfawossen Asrat*	103
1.6	Working with artists *Nancy Rakoczy*	107
1.7	Working with climate activists in civil society *Todd LeVasseur and Bernard Zaleha*	120
	A Southern African response to Todd LeVasseur and Bernard Zaleha *Kate Davies and Ngonidzashe Edward*	132
1.8	Working with climate activists in other religious traditions *Paul O. Ingram*	136
	A response to Paul Ingram *Allan Samuel Palanna*	147

PART II FINDING COMMON MORAL GROUND IN WORKING WITH OTHERS

Introduction: A moral Anthropocene *Larry Rasmussen* 153

2.1 Finding common ground on a moral vision for the good society
Cynthia Moe-Lobeda 157

    A response from a Latinx/Latin American perspective *Raimundo C. Barreto* 174

2.2 Finding common ground on ecological virtues *Steven Bouma-Prediger* 178

    An Islamic response to Steven Bouma-Prediger *Yasien Mohamed* 189

2.3 Finding common ground on appropriate values, goals, policies and middle axioms *James B. Martin-Schramm* 193

    A response to James Martin-Schramm *Philipp Pattberg* 206

2.4 Finding common ground on environmental rights and responsibilities
Kevin J. O'Brien 211

    A response to Kevin O'Brien *Flávio Conrado* 222

PART III WORKING WITH AND AGAINST OTHERS FROM WITHIN

Introduction *Ernst M. Conradie* 227

3.1 Working with Orthodox forms of Christianity *John Chryssavgis and Frederick Krueger* 229

    A response to John Chryssavgis and Frederick Krueger *George Zachariah* 240

3.2 Working with Catholic forms of Christianity *Celia Deane-Drummond* 244

    A response to Celia Deane-Drummond *María Pilar Aquino* 255

3.3 Working with Anglican forms of Christianity *Rachel Mash* 259

    A response to Rachel Mash *Kapya Kaoma* 270

3.4 Working with Lutheran forms of Christianity *Vítor Westhelle* 277

    A Tanzanian response to Vítor Westhelle *Gwamaka Ephraim Mwankenja* 288

3.5 Working with Reformed forms of Christianity *Nadia Marais* 291

    A response to Nadia Marais *August Corneles Tamawiwy* 303

3.6 Working with Anabaptist forms of Christianity *Nathanael L. Inglis* 308

    A response to Nathanael L. Inglis *Paulus S. Widjaja* 320

3.7	Working with Pentecostal and Evangelical forms of Christianity *Christopher J. Vena*	324
	An African response to Christopher Vena *Loreen Maseno*	336
3.8	Climate change and the ecumenical movement *Wesley Granberg-Michaelson*	340
	A response to Wesley Granberg-Michaelson *Guillermo Kerber*	351

PART IV THE CHRISTIAN STORY OF GOD'S WORK

	Introduction: On telling the story *Ernst M. Conradie*	359
4.1	God's initial and ongoing creating *Thomas Jay Oord*	362
4.2	God's work through the emergence of humanity *Peter Manley Scott*	373
4.3	The emergence of human sin *Ernst M. Conradie*	384
4.4	God's continued providence *Clive Pearson*	395
4.5	God's acts of salvation for us *Ernst M. Conradie*	406
4.6	God's work of salvation in and through us *Hilda P. Koster*	417
4.7	God's work through the church *Karen L. Bloomquist*	431
4.8	God's work of consummation *Geiko Müller-Fahrenholz*	440
4.9	Climate change and God's work of election *Gijsbert van den Brink and Eva van Urk*	451
4.10	The story of God's work: An open-ended narrative *Ernst M. Conradie*	462
	The Christian story of God's work – a Brazilian response *Ivone Gebara*	467
	The Christian story of God's work – an African American response *Willie James Jennings*	474
	The Christian story of God's work – a Chinese Christian response *Lai Pan-chiu*	480

PART V THE CHRISTIAN NOTION OF GOD'S IDENTITY AND CHARACTER

	Introduction *Ernst M. Conradie and Hilda P. Koster*	493
5.1	The Spirit and climate change *Sigurd Bergmann*	497
	An African eco-woman's response to Sigurd Bergmann *Fulata L. Moyo*	509

5.2	Jesus the Christ and climate change *Sallie McFague*	513
	An African response to Sallie McFague *Robert Owusu Agyarko*	524
5.3	God as Father: Patriarchy and climate change *Susan Rakoczy*	528
	A response to Susan Rakoczy *Whitney A. Bauman*	540
5.4	The triune God and climate change *Denis Edwards*	545
	A response to Denis Edwards *Teddy C. Sakupapa*	556

PART VI THE PROMISE AND PERILS OF ECCLESIAL PRAXIS

	Introduction *Hilda P. Koster*	563
6.1	Climate change and liturgical praxis *Christina M. Gschwandtner*	566
	A response to Christina Gschwandtner *Ezra Chitando*	576
6.2	Climate change and exegetical, hermeneutical and homiletical praxis *Barbara R. Rossing*	579
	A response to Barbara Rossing from South Asia *Monica Jyotsna Melanchthon*	593
6.3	Climate change and Christian fellowship *Erin Lothes Biviano*	597
	A response to Erin Lothes *Kuzipa Nalwamba*	611
6.4	Climate change and pastoral theology *Storm Swain*	615
	A response to Storm Swain from the Philippines *Elizabeth Tapia*	627
6.5	Climate change, ecclesial praxis and social teaching *Seán McDonagh, SSC*	631
	A response to Seán McDonagh, SSC *Meehyun Chung*	642

PART VII CONCLUDING OBSERVATIONS

	Introduction *Hilda P. Koster*	649
7.1	Doing justice to issues of class? *Kwok Pui-lan*	651
7.2	Doing justice to issues of gender? *Sharon A. Bong*	655
7.3	Doing justice to issues of race? *Melanie L. Harris*	659
7.4	Doing justice to religious diversity? *Kim Yong-Bock*	663
7.5	Doing justice to animals? *David L. Clough*	674

7.6 Doing justice to geographic divides? *Jesse N. K. Mugambi*   677

7.7 Doing justice to carbon mitigation? *Hans Diefenbacher*   684

Select bibliography   689

Index   700

Figures

1.5.1	Types of climate engineering proposals under discussion. Image used with permission from the Institute for Advanced Sustainability Studies, Potsdam, Germany	94
1.6.1	*Desert Walk Series: Desert Power Plant in the Sacred Land,* Yoon Cho, 2011–16, www.yooncho.com	111
1.6.2	*Kill Me or Change*, Chin Chih Yang, performance at the Queens Museum of Art, 28–9 July 2012, https://vimeo.com/46775357	113
1.6.3	New York Biennale Art 2009: *Carry Water* – Chin Chih Yang, 16 October 2009, posted by Lu, http://newyorkbiennaleart2009.blogspot.com/2009/10/carry-water-chin-chih.html (accessed 8 January 2019)	115
2.I.1	Diagram of present moral responsibility, used with permission from *From Bible and Ethics: A New Conversation* © Fortress Press 2018	154
2.I.2	Diagram of moral responsibility coterminous with planetary, or ecosphere, boundaries, used with permission from *From Bible and Ethics: A New Conversation* © Fortress Press 2018	155

Acknowledgements

A large multi-authored book project like this is by its very nature a collaborative endeavour. It requires dedication, commitment and support from a community of scholars, friends and family. We are grateful therefore to everyone who shared our vision for this project and encouraged us to bring together this handbook on 'Christian Theology and Climate Change' that we hope will be a welcome resource for students, teachers, pastors and scholars.

There are several people whom we wish to acknowledge specifically. We are first and foremost grateful to the scholars in the field of ecotheology who, when we first approached them with the plan for this book, gave us constructive feedback and much inspiration. We are tremendously encouraged, moreover, that so many scholars, from different geographical locations, disciplines, religious persuasions and theological traditions, agreed to be part of this volume. They contributed their erudition, energy and scholarly passion to this project, recognizing the need to gather our collective knowledge and wisdom for engaging with this critical moment in Earth's history. This book would not have been possible without their dedication and commitment.

We are grateful to Anna Turton, senior commissioning editor for theology at T&T Clark/Bloomsbury Publishing, who enthusiastically shared our rather unorthodox vision for this handbook. Her enthusiasm and unwavering support has made it so much easier for us to work, edit and complete it on time.

We also thank our individual institutions, the University of the Western Cape (Cape Town, South Africa) and Concordia College (Moorhead, Minnesota), that gave support and encouragement for this volume. In particular, Hilda thanks Concordia College for awarding her a Centennial Research Grant that allowed her to work on this project during the summer of 2018. Ernst acknowledges that this work is supported in part by the National Research Foundation of South Africa (grant-specific unique reference number 85,944). As the grant holder, he acknowledges that the opinions, findings and conclusions or recommendations expressed in any publication generated by NRF-supported research are those of the authors and that the NRF accepts no liability whatsoever in this regard.

We are greatly indebted to our colleagues, friends and families. Ernst is thankful to several UWC colleagues who agreed to contribute to this volume, for a fellowship on 'The Ethics of the Anthropocene' at the Vrije Universiteit in Amsterdam in 2018 that facilitated work on the project, drawing in more contributors, and to Concordia College for inviting him to offer the Oen Lecture in November 2018 that also allowed for the opportunity to do some crucial planning for this book. Ernst is especially grateful for the

Acknowledgements

unwavering support of Marietjie Pauw, his partner for more than thirty years, not least in being with their children, Pieter Conradie and Hildegard Conradie, during his frequent absences from home while sustaining her own postdoctoral work in artistic research with a focus on decolonial aesthesis.

Hilda thanks her husband, Jan Pranger, and her daughter, Emma Rachel Pranger, for supporting her work on this project in so many ways. Jan's own work on political theology, extraction industries and world Christianity continues to be an inspiration. Hilda is grateful to the Collegeville Institute at St. John's University (Collegeville, MN) for the opportunity to participate in the 2018 August writing retreat 'Apart and yet A Part'. Friends and colleagues at Concordia College in Moorhead continue to be a closely knit network of support. Special thanks go to Ellen Aho and Richard Gilmore for shared meals and conversation and to Alfhild Ingberg for the gift of proofreading and stimulating feedback. Thanks also to Arnfríður Guðmundsdóttir of the University of Iceland for the invitation to speak at the 2018 Arctic Circle conference in Reykjavik, but mostly for being a tremendously supportive friend and sojourner in feminist theology and all things academic for more years than either one of us cares to remember.

As co-editors it is our hope that this handbook will find its way to graduate and undergraduate classrooms, church groups and into research papers. We hope it will inspire deep conversation and bold action on behalf of a fragile and endangered planet.

We dedicate this work to our esteemed colleagues Vítor Westhelle (1952–2018) and Denis Edwards (1943–2019). Their sustained and deeply rooted contributions, as reflected in this volume, changed the climate within and beyond Christian theology. Vítor completed his essay titled 'Working with Lutherans' in the week before his death as a kairotic message, – and not only to Lutherans – while Denis's essay on the Triune God and climate change constitutes a doxological culmination of his life and work in Christian ecotheology.

Ernst Conradie
Hilda Koster
30 March 2019

Introduction: Christian theology and climate change in the North Atlantic context

Ernst M. Conradie[1] and Hilda P. Koster[2]

North Atlantic Christianity

Any comprehensive engagement with Christian theology and climate change must acknowledge that climate change is a multifaceted, global problem that requires the collaboration of role players in multiple social contexts, from various disciplines.

For Christian theology to contribute to such forms of collaboration it must also recognize that what is described in this volume as 'North Atlantic Christianity' is as much part of the problem as it may be part of the solution. This term obviously requires clarification but provisionally it may refer to Christians and Christian communities whose ancestors lived predominantly in Europe by the advent of modernity and may have emigrated elsewhere since then.

Not only have countries situated in the North Atlantic contributed the vast proportion of historic carbon emissions, North Atlantic Christianity arguably has legitimized the rise of industrial capitalism and clearly has been unable to stem the tide of increasing carbon emissions. This *companion* addresses these concerns by creating a wide-ranging conversation between North Atlantic theologians, theologians in the Global South and non-theological scholars, representing the fields of climate science, political science, economics and environmental activism. Given the complicity of North Atlantic Christianity in the current crisis, the main essays are written by theologians situated within that context. Such essays are followed by responses from contributors from outside North Atlantic Christian theology – because they are situated in other geographic regions, or because they are not standing in the Christian tradition, or because their main discipline is not theology, or because they represent minority voices where North

---

[1] Ernst M. Conradie is Senior Professor in the Department of Religion and Theology at the University of the Western Cape in South Africa, the leading historically black university in the country. He is situated in the Reformed tradition, teaches systematic theology and ethics and specializes in Christian ecotheology.

[2] Hilda P. Koster is Associate Professor of Religion, Environmental and Sustainability Studies at Concordia College (Moorhead, MN, USA), a college of the Evangelical Lutheran Church of America. Originally from the Netherlands, she teaches and writes on ecological theology and environmental ethics with a focus on gender.

Atlantic Christianity is predominant. Unfortunately, there is one case, namely Nancy Rakoczy's essay on 'Working with Artists', where we were unable to include such a response. In Part Four, three responses are included but then to the section as a whole and not to individual essays.

The question that is addressed throughout this volume is how Christians might find common ground across confessional traditions as well as divisions due to differences of race and class, gender and sexual orientation, language and culture. It thus allows Christians to come together and critically engage the ecological wisdom in the deepest roots of their traditions in order to collaborate with others in the face of global climate distortions.

An ecological critique of North Atlantic Christianity

This *handbook* will be published in the North Atlantic context and is aimed primarily at students situated in the same context, although it would hopefully also be used by pastors and academics, English-speaking Christians in other parts of the world and by those engaged in climate justice in civil society outside of the Christian tradition. This recognition poses serious challenges for approaching and then structuring such a volume. Most Christians in the North Atlantic context would hopefully maintain that a retrieval of the Christian scriptures, spiritualities, beliefs, values, missions and practices may help to address concerns over anthropogenic climate change. This would account for the need for such a volume. However, for many others, North Atlantic Christian theology is as much (or more!) part of the problem than it may be part of the solution.

This suspicion is based on three core observations: First, there is the obvious reality that countries situated in the North Atlantic have contributed the vast proportion of historic carbon emissions. Second, Christianity was the dominant form of religion in the North Atlantic context at the advent of the Industrial Revolution and clearly has been unable to stem the tide of increasing carbon emissions in such countries since then. If Christianity did not provide ideological legitimation for industrialized capitalism, its critique of the associated ecological destruction remained ineffective enough that, in the eyes of outsiders, it is implausible that North Atlantic Christianity would now provide the main source of inspiration to address climate change. This is exacerbated by the alleged allegiances between right-wing Evangelicalism and global capitalism. Third, the shifting centre of gravity in global Christianity suggests that the North Atlantic region is no longer necessarily the locus where creative responses to a challenge such as climate change are to be expected. Fourth, there are lasting concerns over the environmental impact of academic forms of doing theology (given the carbon footprint of institutions, guilds, conferences, travelling and publications) as well as over its effectiveness in providing transformative resources for an ecological spirituality, ethos and praxis. What, one may ask, is the actual impact of producing academic theology? Accordingly, if Christian theology is to play any significant role in mitigating climate change, the voices of those marginalized by climate change should be privileged – climate refugees, Indigenous peoples, the poor, women, children and species facing extinction.

A counter-intuitive strategy

Given such considerations, what strategy should be employed to approach such a volume on Christian theology and climate change? Consider the options: One may simply ignore the challenge and muster the considerable expertise available to produce a volume that would provide excellent resources for students but would constitute a form of sustained theological imperialism – that is, offering theological reflections for and on behalf of everyone else. One may also seek to widen the network of contributing authors to include voices outside of North Atlantic Christian theology. Given the role of English as medium of communication this would be open to criticisms of co-option within an already established framework. Such efforts towards being representative may be sincere and aimed at acknowledging an ecumenical diversity in terms of race, gender, confessional tradition and geographic context but almost always remains skewed if the point of departure is from within a dominant context. One may also opt to include only voices from the margins, but this would fail to see that such publications on climate change already exist – to which the editors of this volume have contributed.[3] Such voices are already heard and they can speak for themselves. One may even opt to publish such a volume elsewhere, also to ensure affordability and availability, but this is scarcely feasible given distribution networks. Finally, one may simply give up and refuse to produce any such a volume – but that would deprive students of much-needed resources on a crucial contemporary issue.

In this volume we have opted for another rather risky and counter-intuitive strategy. We asked contributors to engage self-consciously in a form of North Atlantic contextual theology. This means that the contributors invited to write the main essays are all situated within North Atlantic Christianity, typically within a 'high-carbon footprint' context. This is of course tricky since there are many voices from the margins in countries with

---

[3] See, e.g. Ernst M. Conradie, Sipho Mtetwa and Andrew Warmback (eds), *The Land is Crying for Justice: A Discussion Document on Christianity and Environmental Justice in South Africa* (Stellenbosch: Ecumenical Foundation of Southern Africa, 2002); Ernst M. Conradie, 'Epilogue: Theological Reflections on Ecumenical Action and Advocacy on Climate Change', in Grace Ji-Sun Kim (ed.), *Making Peace with the Earth: Action and Advocacy for Climate Justice* (Geneva: WCC, 2016), 234–47; Ezra Chitando and Ernst M. Conradie (eds), 'Praying for Rain? African Perspectives on Religion and Climate Change', *The Ecumenical Review* 69:3 (2017), 311–435; also South African Council of Churches, Climate Change Committee, *Climate Change – a Challenge to the Churches in South Africa* (Marshalltown: SACC, 2009); Grace Ji-Sun Kim and Hilda Koster, *Planetary Solidarity: Global Women's Voices on Christian Doctrine and Climate Justice* (Minneapolis: Fortress, 2017).

a high per capita carbon footprint, while there are also individuals with a high-carbon footprint in centres of power that are otherwise on the periphery of the global economy. As editors we asked contributors to attend to especially three general considerations.

First, each contributor was asked to take seriously the suspicion that North Atlantic Christian theology may be as much part of the problem in mitigating climate change as it may be of the solution. Depending on the particular theme addressed, this requires a foregrounding of those issues that may exacerbate anthropogenic climate change.

Secondly, we asked contributors to assume that the implied readers are Christian students coming predominantly from a high-carbon-footprint context. What resources can be provided for such students (implying the need for authors not to focus merely on their own interests and positions)? What would one need to say to such students that would enable them to address the underlying challenges adequately in their own contexts? Arguably, this form of self-critique follows the pattern of liberation theology for the wealthy, feminist theology for men, black theology for whites and ecological theology for humans.[4]

Thirdly and crucially, the contributors were asked to assume that whatever they are saying to such students will be overheard by others outside of North Atlantic Christian theology – because they are not students, not situated in the North Atlantic context, do not belong to one of the Christian traditions or work within other disciplines. To make this concrete, we invited respondents from such contexts for each of the essays. Respondents were asked to address the question whether such a contribution speaks effectively to the suspicion that North Atlantic Christian theology is more part of the problem than it may be of the solution. We hope that this strategy would stimulate some lively debate that would indeed provide a valuable set of critical resources for students of theology, especially but not only in the North Atlantic.

Working with others to address climate change

Another set of questions concerns how such a volume should be structured. There may be strong arguments on intra-Christian grounds to focus on the available theological resources in such a way that their authenticity can be ensured. Accordingly, one has to depart from the substantive claims of the Christian faith and their dependence upon the biblical texts. If so, one could include (in this order) sections on the biblical texts, biblical hermeneutics, the Christian tradition, Christian doctrine, Christian ethics, ecclesial governance, liturgical practices, ecclesial praxis, Christian mission, dialogue with other religious traditions and collaboration with other role players in civil society working for climate justice.

---

[4] See Jürgen Moltmann, *Experiences in Theology: Ways and Forms of Christian Theology* (Minneapolis: Fortress, 2000).

Such a more 'deductive' approach may be theologically authentic but runs several other risks: To start with a retrieval of the best that Christian doctrine has to offer and then to appropriate such resources to address climate change may well avoid the challenge sketched above. It would also underestimate the internal contestation over the interpretation of core theological concepts. Moreover, climate change is by definition a multifaceted global problem that requires the collaboration of role players in multiple social contexts, from various disciplines, in many walks of life and across divisions of geography, religious affiliation, class, race, gender and sexual orientation. To use Christian particularity as a point of departure may well undermine the ability to address the actual challenges associated with climate change. The 'and' used in the title of this volume to connect Christian theology and climate change is therefore as elusive as the other terms may be.

In order to structure this volume we have opted for the inverse strategy – namely, to undermine Christian particularity and authenticity – despite the risks that this may pose. The point of departure is to recognize that Christians seeking to address the challenges associated with anthropogenic climate change will need to collaborate with others for the common good to address what is by definition a global challenge. Such multidisciplinary collaboration requires attention to several considerations.

First, some working definition of the common good and a rationale for such collaboration is required. This will not be offered upfront but, provisionally, Dietrich Bonhoeffer's famous distinction between the ultimate and the penultimate may be helpful.[5] Christians can and do find it possible to work with others towards the common good by gathering sufficient consensus on moral visions, goals, values, virtues, rights and obligations that are certainly highly significant but not necessarily of ultimate concern. Ironically, there is much less consensus on what is truly ultimate. This applies not only between religious traditions but also among Christians. This does not mean that the category of the ultimate is not significant; convictions about what is ultimate may help to guard against unhelpful compromises.

Secondly, such collaboration requires a spirit of humility, a willingness to learn from others and from other disciplines and some restraint in not taking over ongoing dialogue. The mere presence of Christians in such forms of collaboration is already an important witness. If anything, the role of Christians in such forms of collaboration would be to help ensure that marginalized voices are heeded.

Thirdly, there is a need to address suspicions that such collaboration is endangered by the presence of Christianity, that Christianity is actually part of the problem. As will be indicated below, this has important implications for particular forms of collaboration in specific spheres of society.

Finally, in such forms of collaboration, Christians should be ready to explain to themselves (and if need be to others) what the particular contribution may be that they can bring to the table. In some cases this can be a contribution that only (some branches of) Christianity can make. If so, to merely reiterate what others say and do would fail

---

[5] See Dietrich Bonhoeffer, *Ethics* (Minneapolis: Fortress, 2005), 146–70.

to act responsibly. Indeed, given their own carbon emissions, Christians in general and North Atlantic Christians in particular may have more of an impact on mitigating climate change than any other religious group. However, such a contribution would only be authentic and liberative if they can retrieve the ecological wisdom in the deepest roots of their own traditions.

The main sections of the volume

The first main section of this volume includes essays that explore the promises and perils embedded in multidisciplinary forms of collaboration to address anthropogenic climate change. In each case the focus is on ways in which some aspects of North Atlantic Christianity may undermine such collaboration. This section includes essays and responses on collaboration with (a) climate scientists, (b) evolutionary biologists, (c) environmental economists, (d) political theorists, (e) geoengineers, (f) artists, (g) climate activists in civil society and (h) climate activists in other religious traditions.

In each of these essays on working with others the general societal challenges around mitigation and adaptation as well as a range of cross-cutting ethical issues related to climate change come into play. These include concerns over animal well-being, biodiversity, biotechnology, consumerism, debt, deforestation, education, farming, finances, food security, gender, geoengineering, health, human rights, inequality, justice, peacemaking, population, poverty, reproductive health, sexuality, taxation, technology transfer, unemployment, water, wetlands and so forth, as well as the formation of appropriate virtues such as wisdom, justice, resilience and frugality. Since these ethical issues cut across almost any conversation on climate change, they are not thematized individually – also since these are themes to which whole volumes can be dedicated. They are regarded here as transversals in the sense that all contributions have to do justice to such concerns in one way or another.

Such collaboration with others will, sooner rather than later, require an ad hoc understanding of the common good, a common vision, common values and principles. All participants will come to the table with assumptions in this regard, but reflection on the underlying issues will only be possible on the basis of collaborative praxis. For this reason it is not regarded as the first step but as one that flows from such collaboration.

The second main section of this volume will therefore focus on what is of penultimate concern: the possibilities for common moral ground without seeking to occupy the moral high ground. Following the mapping of the moral landscape proposed by Larry Rasmussen,[6] this section includes essays on (a) prophetic visions for the good

---

[6] See Larry Rasmussen, *Earth-Honoring Faith: Religious Ethics in a New Key* (Oxford: Oxford University Press, 2013), 127–59.

(sustainable) society, (b) ecological virtues, (c) appropriate values, goals, policies and middle axioms, and (d) environmental principles, rights and responsibilities. In each of these essays that task is threefold, namely to reflect on ways in which Christian praxis may have undermined efforts to find common ground, to reflect on the possibilities and prospects for finding such common ground, and to consider what North Atlantic Christianity can contribute in this regard, especially in areas in which others cannot.

The recognition of the need for working with others in the public sphere, also those standing outside the Christian tradition, may hide the inability of those within the wider Christian tradition to work with and alongside each other. Despite considerable ecumenical efforts towards a common witness, especially over the last century or so, Christianity remains deeply divided on many crucial ethical issues, including climate change. These divisions run along various long-standing confessional traditions (with many debates on what constitutes orthodoxy) but also across differences of race and class, gender and sexual orientation, language and culture, geography, worldviews (in dialogue with modern science or not) and so forth. It would be grossly inappropriate not to bring such divides into play in an exploration of Christian theology and climate change. The most appropriate strategy may be to focus on the long-standing confessional traditions since all the other divides then come into play in any case. This poses a different challenge, namely that adherents to these traditions typically believe that the best resources to address climate change may be found within that particular tradition, while others outside may see some blind spots more readily. The question that therefore has to be addressed is whether and to what extent each of these traditions may be regarded as part of the problem in mitigating carbon emissions.

The third main section of this volume therefore focuses on 'working with and against others from within'. It includes essays on what may arguably be identified as the main branches that constitute the 'tree' of the wider Christian tradition, especially within the North Atlantic context. On this basis there are essays on (a) Orthodox forms of Christianity, (b) Catholic forms of Christianity, (c) Anglican forms of Christianity, (d) Lutheran forms of Christianity, (e) Reformed forms of Christianity, (f) Anabaptist forms of Christianity, (g) Pentecostal and Evangelical forms of Christianity and (h) ecumenical fellowships that seek to (but often fail to) overcome confessional divides but may well remain part of the problem too. In each case a two-edged question needs to be raised: to what extent does this particular branch of Christianity offer solutions to the problems that no one else offers, and to what extent does this tradition also remain part of the problem? In each essay ethical themes such as patriarchy, environmental racism, the marginalization of Indigenous peoples, debates on reproductive health and sexual orientation have to be taken into account insofar as they are relevant for responding to climate change.

There is no way in which it would be possible for Christians to work together with others outside and within the Christian tradition to address the challenges associated with anthropogenic climate change without coming to terms with the heart of the Christian faith. Some may sense the need to underplay or even to shy away from

Christian particularity for the sake of finding common ground. This would constitute a false dilemma, not least because of the inclusive impulse in the story that Christians tell about the path that they have travelled with God – from a wandering nomad in Abraham, to runaway slaves in Egypt, to exiles in Babylon, to a new-born messiah who was a refugee in Egypt, to the radically inclusive ministry of Jesus of Nazareth, to the One who was crucified, to the saints and martyrs of the church. There is of course a diversity of ways in which the story of God's work is told, already indicated by the four canonical gospels. There is no need to or possibility of finding consensus as to how this story is to be told. This is partly because the ongoing story of God's work remains incomplete and is now confronted with a new chapter in an ominous, changing climate. It is also because of a multiplicity of voices, clustered together in diverging schools of thought, within contemporary Christian theology (and ecotheology) that each recognize insights that are indeed authentically Christian but cannot be readily harmonized with each other. However, there are ways in which this story is being told that can only undermine any Christian efforts to address climate change. Such distortions have to be addressed or else Christianity would remain part of the problem.

The fourth section of this volume will explore such distortions in the ways in which the story of God's work is told in the context of North Atlantic Christian theology. This is a complex task, not only because the story is incomplete but also because the plot of the narrative implies that every episode is influenced by other episodes. Although it remains a single narrative, this is not a story that can be told in one session; it is always told in fragments and from within particular locations. The task to address distortions in the story will be divided in a number of essays, including ones on (a) God's work of creation and ongoing creation, (b) the emergence of humanity, (c) the emergence of human sin, (d) God's continued providence, (e) God's acts of salvation for us (liberation, healing, reconciliation, guidance, etc.), (f) God's work of justification and sanctification in us and through us, (g) the formation of the church with its many ministries and mission, (h) the consummation of God's work and (i) God's election of Israel as a 'light' and a 'balm' for the nations as the 'inner secret' of God's work.

It is impossible to tell the story of God's work without a sense of God's identity and character. For Christians, this constitutes the deepest mystery of history and offers the best available clues as to how a changing climate is to be interpreted. This is also where the Christian confession of faith in the Triune God is most contested amidst a changing climate so that other rubrics such as religion, ultimate reality, culture or spirituality are preferred by some in order to refrain from giving offence and to facilitate collaboration with others. This cannot be a way forward if only because that would leave the suspicions that Christianity remains part of the problem unexplored. For those inside the Christian tradition the Triune confession is nothing but the doxological conclusion of their faith.

The fifth section of this volume therefore includes essays on the Christian faith in God as Father, Son and Spirit. The traditional terms are maintained here deliberately precisely because they raise so many suspicions that Christianity remains part of the problem and far from the solution. However, in order to stimulate some reflection, the traditional order is reversed. Instead of the logic of confession, a logic of coming to this confession is followed, starting (a) with experiences of God the Spirit, moving (b) to the ways in which the identity of this Spirit is exemplified in the Spirit of Christ and then (c) to reflections on the 'Father' of whom we know mainly through the ministry of Jesus the Christ. In bringing this threefold confession together, this section concludes with (d) a reflection on faith in the Triune God in the context of a changing climate.

Following the model of theological reflection on ecclesial praxis (involving an ongoing spiral of acting, seeing, judging and acting) it remains important to return to the original question – namely, whether North Atlantic Christians can really work with others to address anthropogenic climate change. Or do they remain part of the problem? If not, what can they contribute that others, including Christians elsewhere in the world, cannot?

This set of questions is addressed in the final main section of this volume, with specific reference to various aspects of ecclesial praxis. This includes essays on (a) liturgical praxis, (b) exegetical, hermeneutical and homiletical praxis, (c) Christian fellowship, (d) pastoral praxis, and (e) ecclesial praxis in terms of the ministries and missions of the church, as guided by social teaching.

Finally, there is a need to consider whether such a volume did justice to a range of considerations – in terms of class, gender, race, religious diversity, the lives of other animals and geographic divides. The crucial question, though, is what difference a volume of this nature could make to carbon mitigation. Given the carbon footprint of the volume itself – which far exceeds its weight in paper – one has to ask whether it indeed helps to reduce carbon emissions, at least within the circles of what is called North Atlantic Christianity and more specifically Christian theology. This is a question that can only be answered by the readers of this volume!

PART I

Working with others: The need for multidisciplinary collaboration

Introduction

Ernst M. Conradie

Climate change is by definition a global challenge that has to be addressed collaboratively. Christians who are concerned about climate change therefore have to work with others in a multidisciplinary way. There is no other way. In this section of the volume it is suggested that such collaboration will involve at least climate scientists, evolutionary biologists, environmental economists, political role players, geoengineers, social scientists, artists, climate activists in civil society and in other religious traditions. Other role players could easily be added.

Such collaborative opportunities could and should be readily regarded as a form of Christian witness and should therefore be welcomed from within Christian traditions. However, there are two challenges that confront and may well undermine such collaborative work.

On the one hand, it should not be taken for granted that such others may wish to work with Christians in addressing climate change. Experts and practitioners in such fields may well regard Christianity, at least North Atlantic Christianity, to be part of the problem. They may carry some injuries and harbour scepticism over the very possibility of such collaboration.

This is easy to understand. Consider the climate denialism fostered in forms of right-wing Christianity in the North Atlantic and how that would be received by scientists contributing to the Intergovernmental Panel on Climate Change (IPCC), especially those located in other continents. They may well find it difficult to differentiate between various branches of Protestantism. At the same time, climate scientists, strangely enough, seem to have become latter-day prophets, against their own methodological inclinations, issuing all sorts of warnings that few seem to heed. What opportunities may that hold for collaboration?

Similar comments may be made regarding evolutionary biology while geoengineers may wish to avoid any moralizing in seeking solutions to complex problems. Political scholars, economists and social scientists may harbour different reservations that relate to methodologies in their fields – where religious practitioners may be an object of research but are not readily regarded as a resource for research collaboration. Artists and activists in civil society and in other religious traditions may be willing to work with anyone committed to their cause. However, they would be mindful of the tragic history of iconoclasm and of Christian Crusades and heresy trials. They may well resist attempts from Christians to take the lead in addressing climate change.

On the other hand, Christians may agree on the pragmatic need to work with others in addressing climate change. However, they would tend to have diverging theological explanations as to how such collaboration is to be understood. Consider endless debates on the multiple challenges posed by evolutionary biology to an understanding of the Christian faith (that is, the role of chance versus divine intentionality, human descent versus claims for human uniqueness, coming to terms with pain and suffering, the origins of human sin, natural selection versus divine election). Likewise, diverging positions are adopted in global Christianity on a theology of religions and on what interfaith and multifaith dialogue entails.

In short, there is an obvious need for multidisciplinary collaboration in addressing climate change but that is easier said than done. This section will explore the promise and perils of such collaboration and will do so upfront.

Chapter 1.1
Working with climate scientists

Heather Eaton[1]

Science without religion is lame, religion without science is blind.

– Albert Einstein

Introduction: Climate sciences, changes and challenges

Climate scientists continue to present data about current changes to planetary climate patterns and dynamics. They observe myriad specific climate processes and track the transformations and deviations from the norm. They insist that the stability of Earth's climate systems is compromised and that such instability could jeopardize a large range of human activities from local survival to global economic, agriculture and political processes. Specific predictions must remain vague, as climate processes and the consequences of both major and minor changes are difficult to know with accuracy. Of methodological necessity, climate science is empirical, cautious, value free and operates with consensus.

Christians cannot escape grappling with climate change, although the range of responses is large. The intersections between the realities of climate change and a host of Christian beliefs, commitments, teleologies, ethics and imperatives are multiple. The manner, depth and significance of these exchanges also vary greatly. Within this spectrum there are specific groups of Christians who refuse to accept climate science or are climate change deniers. In April 2018 evangelical Christians in the United States discussed concerns around climate change and environmental protection, revealing the debates and disputes. This is well covered in an online documentary, 'The Climate

---

[1] Heather Eaton is Professor in Conflict Studies at Saint Paul University, Ottawa, Canada. She is informed by Catholic intellectual traditions. She teaches and writes on ecology, feminism and theology, religion and ecology; ethics, eco-justice, animal studies and non-violence.

and the Cross'.[2] Thus there is no consensus on how Christians could or should address climate change, or whether such a consensus is fathomable.

Yet, in a basic manner both science and theology seek and claim truths. Each addresses questions of knowledge of the world (Earth) and its purposes. If we refuse to adopt Stephen Jay Gould's view that science and religion are non-overlapping magisteria (NOMA),[3] then it is necessary to probe some exchanges between the two. What must be recognized is that neither scientific societies nor Christian communities are well positioned to confront the political powers and economic players and practices that are mainly determining decisions on climate change. Perhaps a collaboration between the two, with other disciplines and movements, could have traction and transformative capacity.

This essay explores different aspects of what is important to consider from climate scientists, and why it is worthwhile for Christians to listen to and collaborate with them. My comments are based on several convictions:

- the dynamics of the biosphere remain largely unknown;
- theologians should care deeply about the Earth;
- humans emerged from and are embedded in evolutionary processes and fully dependent upon ecological processes;
- there is an intimate relationship between social, spiritual and ecological health;
- religious imagination and commitments are shaped by current realities more than by traditions and histories;
- we live in a divine milieu: that is, the Divine is embedded in and involved with the cosmos and the Earth;
- climate change is occurring, is anthropogenic and we have a moral and spiritual responsibility to respond.

It is important to consider why some might ignore climate change and reject what scientists are learning. Those who are climate change deniers or refuse to understand the anthropogenic causes, be they Christians or otherwise, can act as obstacles to collective action to reduce the impacts. The reasons for such recklessness need to be unpacked. People can, and do, believe what they want and what keeps them comfortable, and ignore or dismiss as false what is challenging. Some Christians may put more emphasis on their beliefs, or on a future next life, than attending to the current political, economic, social and ecological conditions. People can also ignore something as serious and complex as climate disturbances for other reasons: the costs of change will be high, politicians are doing little, affluent lifestyles must end, poverty

---

[2] See 'The Climate and the Cross', https://www.theguardian.com/environment/ng-interactive/2018/apr/13/the-climate-and-the-cross-us-evangelical-christians-tussle-with-climate-change (accessed 20 August 2018).
[3] Stephen Jay Gould, 'Nonoverlapping Magisteria', *Natural History* 106 (March 1997), 16–22.

is already oppressive, the effects are elsewhere, the greatest impacts may be in the future, there is no easy path forward, a lack of concern for the common good, or a generalized apathy.

We do not have the luxury of passivity in front of climate change. One way to address this is to learn from and work with climate scientists, and understand what science is saying about climate changes.

To know the world

To search, ponder, know and interpret the parameters of existence is an ongoing human activity, although the inclination is not shared by all and resources are not available to many. Nevertheless, it is a perennial quest. It is an outward quest, to know *where we are*, an inner quest of *who we are*, and the ongoing interpretative quest of *why we are, why life is* and *how to live*. Of course, each of these has a vast array of responses. To seek, perceive and understand, as far as human sensibilities can stretch, is, in my view, at the core of many scientific and theological themes.

While sciences and theology can be influenced by distinct agendas, the desire to know the world remains a core driver. Within branches of science and theology, there is a deep quest to know and understand the Earth and the natural world. To know the Earth, from subatomic physics and microbiology, to evolution and planetary patterns, including climate science, can be appreciated as an inner, psychic drive. These efforts are a collective force that conveys meaning to contexts, orientations and purpose to the lifeworld and to human life. The search for knowledge, insights, wisdom, coherence and intelligibility are shared by the best of both science and theology.

The epistemological tools for science and theology are both similar and very different. They are similar in the desire to understand the world and to make claims about the nature of reality. They share this deep quest to comprehend the micro, meso and macro aspects of what humans can *detect* and *discern* from the breadth, depth and expanse of reality. Both science and theology include quantitative and qualitative data gathered and gleaned from numerous sources and methods. This shared quest, even if lofty, is a horizon both can agree upon and is a starting point of why theologians should take scientific pursuits seriously. Furthermore, it is urgent that we integrate what climate scientists are understanding of climate changes – not only for human survival but also because it will shape the human imagination, ethics, spirituality, core beliefs and social structures for ages to come. The next section surveys climate sciences and changes, recommending to Christians and those studying theology what must be learned and why and where theology can participate and contribute.

Scientific methods, climate sciences and the biosphere

Scientific knowledge is gained through empirical modes of inquiry. This is the general method of science in the pursuit to know the world, in this case the Earth. While there are multiple kinds of sciences, each with nuances, limited foci, specific agenda, interpretations and even biases, as a general claim the goals of science are to understand the world in empirical terms. The methods of inquiries tend to be specific and the findings precise, verifiable and describable. Often the results must be replicated.

The natural sciences require verifiable data or predictable patterns within a cause-and-effect paradigm. They are cautious about certainties or even probabilities, and are therefore open to revision with new methods or data. What is static is more comprehensible than what is dynamic. Anomalies, transformations, the unexpected and interactions can be difficult to evaluate. However, whole systems thinking and theories of emergent complexities, entanglement and new materialisms have disrupted or expanded frameworks. The cause-and-effect paradigms are insufficient to explain data that indicates interconnected, energetic and transforming actualities. They are changing scientific paradigms, because such theories best explain new observations from active interdependent environments, such as climate systems.

To understand climate changes, one needs to understand climate systems. In order to comprehend climate systems one needs to perceive that these are integrated into the biosphere. For this, scientists were required to consider scientific paradigms beyond cause and effect, such as whole systems thinking. For example, it took considerable effort for the Gaia hypothesis, a whole systems approach that recognizes that the Earth functions as a vital ensemble, to be accepted. The Earth is best considered as a biosphere, organic and living rather than mechanistic and governed by predictable laws. The biosphere consists of intensely interactive systems, within continual exchanges from subatomic physics to climate dynamics. The processes of the biosphere flow actively through biochemical interactions, molecular activities, exchanges between inorganic and organic forms, and through the subtle, sensitive and mutually influential interactions within bioregions, ecosystems, air, water, plant and animal lives.

One theme within ecotheology is that of creation. A core focus has been to affirm the goodness of creation, that it has integrity as a whole, and that God is implicated, involved, within or a dynamic of *creation*. To understand Earth sciences informs and strengthens an awareness of processes of the natural world, which affirms the integrity of creation. The sources to claim a *theology* of creation come from elsewhere. However, to learn Earth sciences expands ones ecological knowledge, which can infuse ecological theology with insights and ecological literacy.

Climate changes

The term *climate* is rarely unpacked sufficiently to grasp that there are countless relationships, best understood as dynamic, intermingled and embedded processes of the biosphere. Climate systems don't exist 'out there'. They are planetary processes embedded in the whole of life ways. Realizing that climate changes means disrupting countless biospheric and climatic systems is a first step in comprehending what is and will occur.

To refer to *climate change* is excessively broad and almost meaningless without addressing specifics. Most people know little of the meaning of climate change, even if the term is in global and public discourses. Climate changes are generating ecological and biospheric problems, yet in uneven and often uncertain ways. The most obvious are the destabilized weather patterns and intensified tornadoes, hurricanes, rains and droughts. But this is a small portion of what is and will occur, and the full impacts are uncertain and overall unknowable. Consequences impacting the biosphere will be most significant, as this affects countless interconnected living Earth communities. Thus for theologians to understand climate changes means paying attention, regularly, to what is being learnt and what could be the implications.

Climate changes are studied from numerous scientific disciplines. The Intergovernmental Panel on Climate Change produces copious reports and types of data, as do many other scientific disciplines and agencies. The assertion *that* the climate systems are changing and that these changes are affecting weather patterns, ice caps, and ocean and wind currents in unpredictable ways required extensive study and was only the beginning. To understand *how* the climate systems are changing and how to measure this, and to grasp something of causes and effects, required more years of intensive and extensive studies. To recognize the impacts of climate changes on countless dynamics of and relationships within the biosphere involves many disciplines and considerable focus and resources. All this – climate sciences and changes – must be appreciated as a complex, intricate and indeed a massive scientific mission. Without understanding this fundamental scientific project – to know enough about the intricacies, complexities and interactions of climate systems, and how they are changing – mitigating, adapting to and preparing for climate change are severely limited. We all need to learn the basics.

Some, perhaps most, natural scientists are deeply concerned about the consequences of climate changes, especially on human populations. One aspect, often ignored by social sciences, environmental humanities, ecotheology and religious studies, is the effect on multiple species. Many species are diminishing or becoming extinct due to rapid changes affecting migration, habitat, food systems and plant–insect relations, as well as other aspects of their ecological niche. Furthermore, climate change impacts countless interacting life forms in the natural world in unpredictable ways: plants, trees, animals, insects, birds, fish, waterways, oceans and the list goes on. The myriad interconnected processes within the biosphere are barely perceived and understood, and the consequences of climate changes will be interactive, immense and immeasurable.

The nature of climatic systems and climate changes make projecting into and preparing for the future difficult. In the short term, for humans, there is much to be anxious about: food and water insecurities, coastal communities, weather patterns, migrations and inequities. In the long term, there are issues of when and how the biosphere will adapt or not, tipping points, extinctions and evolutionary pathways, and the likely termination of the Cenozoic era (the last sixty-five million years). The short-term impact is of concern within many Christian contexts. For example, church communities must deal with weather issues, water shortages, food insecurities in places, migrations and environmental refugees and more. Some churches are active in addressing these issues in their communities, in their countries, internationally and within their traditions. Eco-justice programmes are a good example of educational, supportive, activist and collaborative efforts. A further question is how theologians are reflecting on the long-term projections and what this means. If the biosphere and the natural world diminish significantly, what would this mean for theological frameworks, claims and commitments?

The importance and limits of climate sciences

Climate science has many facets, and it is urgent that climate changes be addressed, owing to the biospheric impacts. There is no way forward without grasping what the sciences are ascertaining. In addition, scientists make climate knowledge available and obtainable. It is not private or esoteric, and it belongs to human communities. It is also important to understand some of the limits to such science, and how and why climate changes sprawl into many social and natural systems.

Climate sciences cannot forecast climate changes. Understanding is one aspect; predictions are another. Climate systems do not function only in a cause-and-effect manner, and they have many moving parts, so to speak. These parts have dissimilar influences and impacts, in distinct and seemingly unrelated regions. The effects of disruptions on one part, such as increased temperatures and CO_2 in ocean currents, are unpredictable on another, such as increased drought because winds are warmer and cannot hold sufficient precipitation. While we need what the sciences provide, including their approaches, caution and observations, we cannot make assumptions that scientific knowledge is all we need. There are measurements, assessments and estimates, and all of this fall short of understanding the full effects of climate changes. For example, in the summer of 2018, thousands of wildfires occurred in dozens of countries, with catastrophic consequences to all manner of life. Climate sciences forecast that it would be warmer and dryer this year. The amount, spread and intensities of the fires, and the incalculable consequences were unpredictable.

Scientific assertions are often circumspect. While this is laudable and increases creditability, it has some noteworthy limits. For example, in order to understand something in depth it often must be isolated from contextual dynamics and interactions, and is both disembedded and displaced. An illustration may help. Water analysis may detect multiple chemicals within a water way. However, chemicals and toxins are carried by water, air, plants and animals. They move in different concentrations from the basin to the top layer of water, as well as around shorelines and with perennial or ephemeral currents. While analysis reveals the presence of chemicals at the test site, it reveals little else. Furthermore, no analyses are able to detect the constant and fast molecular interactions that occur with H_2O molecules (approximately 590 miles per second). Water is the basic Earth solvent and can bond readily with just about everything. Chemicals are continuously intermingling, bonding with water and creating new molecular forms. It is impossible to know the influence of chemicals and toxins in waterways and on related life forms. Thus, to understand something precisely in Earth sciences, reductionism and often isolation are needed to make studies manageable. Thus, while these approaches to complex observations can be seen as necessary, and the conclusions cautious, this can also limit comprehension.

A further limit is that what is known of the effects of climate changes are known only after the fact. For example, rapid climate changes force ecosystems and bioregions to adapt and re-establish equilibrium, or a relative homeostasis. The sequences of alterations are usually understood after they have occurred. For example, honey bees are declining. Habitat loss, shifting temperatures and diseases are determined to be related to climate changes. Other causes, such as neonicotinoid pesticides, are also involved in the catastrophic decline is bees. Yet, one third of the food produced in North America and Europe, the fruits, nuts and vegetables, requires pollination by bees. Food production will decline with the decimation of bees. Such knowledge is (somewhat) mainstream news, but only now that bee colonies are collapsing. The point is that many of the details of the effects of climate changes are only seen after the fact.

Climate changes: Ecological and social systems

Often the public or popular depiction of climate change is of dramatic weather patterns and disruptions, and their consequences to human populations. Of course, many problems are, and will be, the multiple impacts of weather patterns on human lives. Yet, weather is too simplistic and inadequate a category to grasp climate changes. While hurricanes, tornadoes, storms and flooding are devastating in multiple ways, disaster preparedness is only one necessary adaptation. To see climate changes as predominantly related to intense weather disasters is to ignore other facets that may be equally devastating.

For example, one realization is (re)dawning, slowly: that human lives and livelihoods are ultimately and fundamentally dependent on ecological health and a vibrant natural world. Humans are fully embedded within the biosphere. When planetary health and flourishing diminish and the natural world deteriorates, so does human health and flourishing. This is a difficult perception for many in the North Atlantic prosperous regions, as we live, think, organize and communicate in ways detached from an awareness of our radical ecological dependence. Ecologically, dependency is obvious to most who study evolution and some of the Earth sciences. Of course, throughout human histories this dependency was self-evident and still is to many Indigenous and farming societies. Many religious and spiritual traditions have had this awareness and some continue to teach the necessity of living within the rhythms and limits of the natural world. However, such a realization is only beginning to be taken seriously in the affluent, urban, industrialized parts of the world.

Nonetheless, politics, economics, transportation and governance carry on as if climate change is connected to weather and there is an *environment* extraneous to human life. It is as if there are human communities, surrounded by an independent and external *environment* that influences our lives, for better or worse. What is correct is that humans emerged from and are embedded in and fully dependent upon the natural world. Humans live within an Earth community.

Some Christians, and others, may choose not to 'believe' in evolutionary processes. They may claim that humans have some other origin and destiny than that of the biosphere. They may consider that all of the Earth is simply a set of resources for human use and that they are irrelevant in terms of intrinsic value and spiritual presence. However these views are uninformed by science and are merely opinions, beliefs or declarations. For example, creationism is not an alternative theory to evolution. It is a belief, against vast and substantial scientific evidence. Creationist or other anti-evolution or anti-science views have been forcefully influenced by long traditions and theological worldviews and structures that support them. There is much evaluation of these within ecological theology.[4] Several forms of ecotheology are integrating evolution and allowing their worldviews to be shaped and transformed by the natural sciences.

It is noteworthy that most North Atlantic urbanites are unable to explain specifically how their food is grown, what it needs to thrive or what ecosystem it comes from, let alone know the economic, political, transportation and justice issues around food production. Yet, food insecurities are increasing in tandem with climate changes. This lack of ecological knowledge will cause much harm. The natural sciences are needed to understand something as basic and vital as food, and the foundational and fundamental elements of ecological dependency. Climate sciences are needed to see the integrative

---

[4] The list is long. For references until 1996 see a list compiled by John Cobb at http://www.cep.unt.edu/ecotheo.html (accessed 31 August 2018). The National Centre for Science Education developed a bibliography on theology and evolution. See https://ncse.com/library-resource/bibliography-theology-evolution (accessed 31 August 2018). Discussions between theology and evolution or the natural sciences are distinct across theological traditions, such as process or sacramental theologies, incarnational frameworks or biblical studies, or whether the starting point is evolution and cosmology or theology.

and dynamic functioning of the biosphere. Climate changes affect the whole, albeit unevenly.

In addition to ecological dependency, human communities live within interconnected social systems, including those of education, economics, political processes, security, transportation and food production. And these societies, throughout the world, are structured, or patterned, with inequities and inequalities. Systems of affluence and poverty, racism or ethnocentrism, gender discrimination and unequal resources access – and the intersectionality of such injustices and/or oppressions – exist in every society. These inequities and inequalities are structured and sustained within the operative social systems (education, economics, governance and so on). The dynamics and impacts of geophysical climate changes – for example, that bees are declining or that a hurricane will affect whatever is in its path – are not determined by these inequities and inequalities. However, the responses and resources are mobilized within these patterns. Thus, those with more privilege, power, assets, influence, social mobility and the ability to adapt to climate destabilizations will fare better than those with less. These social, political and moral dimensions of climate change are substantial. It is too simplistic to suggest that Christian theologians and communities from affluent and ecologically stable contexts are less concerned about climate changes and eco-justice than those from places of ecological degradation and scarcity, economic deprivation and consistent and crippling injustices. But at times this is true.

The point is that a reliance only on science is insufficient and will not reveal significant and influential social, political, economic or justice dimensions. It is equally true that some scientists may be loath to extrapolate from the data, to forecast, to discuss related issues or deliberate implications for economics, ethics, social changes or aesthetics, or to ponder theological considerations. However, many are interested in, anxious about and motivated by them. Here too is a place for dialogue.

Climate sciences cannot offer a prognosis. While there is a virtual consensus that climate change is occurring and that it is anthropogenic, there is a range of views on its causes, consequences, timelines, tipping points, and mitigations and adaptations. Prominent and careful scientists disagree with each other, or change their minds, or say it is urgent that we act immediately, that there is time or that it is too late, or that no one really knows. These discrepancies are considered, or used, by some to indicate a lack of agreement on key realizations. Climate change deniers, energy moguls, duplicitous politicians and some Christian traditions revel in these discrepancies. On the other side, fervent climate change activists are emboldened to protest and campaign more, as well as bombard the media with warnings and dire predictions. Here is where listening carefully, understanding the disagreements, discerning any bias and taking a measured position is important.

My view is that these disagreements are due to the complexities of climate sciences and the immense difficulties of assessing the consequences. We should not expect scientists to act as prophets of what is to come, or assume that they have full agreement on what is occurring now. However we should learn enough to understanding the seriousness of the warnings, even and especially when the consequences are not known. Climate changes are destabilizing, intricate, ingenious life ways already, and causing a precariousness within the biosphere affecting countless species and life ways. Much of this is a result of human actions, ignorance, arrogance and apathy. Studying minor disagreements among scientists or contesting climate deniers are a distraction from these elements.

Some challenges to and insights from theology

From my vantage point, theology must be understood as plural in every way. Christian traditions and histories have internal divergences, particular emphases and dissimilar hermeneutics and interpretations. Institutions and religious bodies have unique teaching and leadership styles, structures and authorities, with distinct weight to texts, doctrines, teachings, signs, symbols, imagery, rituals and so on. No two Christians, even from the same tradition and community, will be Christian in the same way, with the same views and priorities. Individual differences and plurality is the norm. Of course plurality can be used politically. In some countries the policy is that of a melting pot, or a mosaic, or as a social policy to maintain systemic inequalities based on race or ethnicity, class or other ideological reasons. My point is simply that to use the term *Christianity* or *Christian* suggests unanimity, cohesion and uniformity, which does not exist within or between Christian traditions or among those within the same group.

One of the most important distinctions between science and theology is method. As mentioned, scientific methods are systematic, empirical, detectible and repeatable, and intended to be value free. There are thousands of scientific techniques, but overall the method is consistent. Theological methods are multiple with multidisciplinary interpretations, and can be unverifiable and value-laden. Methodological differences across theological foci – doctrine, biblical, spirituality, ethics and inter-religious exchanges – are extensive. Theological priorities depend upon the historical moment, Christian tradition, theological orientation and the context, convictions and commitments of the interpreter. This does not make theological claims fallacious. Rather it means that theology does not have definable or agreed-upon methods. Thus theology and science cannot be readily compared in terms of methods.

The differences cannot be easily categorized either. It is important not to consider science and theology in dichotomous terms, such that science is objective, empirical, observative, factual, collective and public while theology is subjective, hypothetical, unobservable, inscrutable, personalist and private. Nor is it correct to claim that science deals with facts and theology is concerned about values. These categories simply do not apply. The facile claim that religion and science are non-overlapping magisterium, as suggested by Stephen Gould, avoids the epistemological questions raised by exchanges between science and theology, and limits the potential richness of dialogue.

There are tomes written about theological methods. Without going into detail about specific challenges, a few comments are needed in terms of working with scientists. One is that theology, whether done in seminaries, universities or worshipping communities, is often unclear or not transparent about presuppositions, analyses and methods. The rationale for positions, beliefs or assertions may not be demonstrable or verifiable. Such epistemological frailties hamper multidisciplinary exchanges and make theological insights vulnerable and dubious.

Nevertheless, theologians are distinctive, and among themselves they do not share the same concerns and are not asking the same questions. These differences are important, and among ecotheologians there are disagreements about priorities in an era of climate changes. It could be confusing and disheartening for scientists to wade through these differences and distinctions. This is yet another reason that theologians need to learn to work with climate scientists and understand climate changes, as this is the starting point for dialogue and constructive transformations.

In order for climate scientists to talk with and listen to theologians, there needs to be clarity of both epistemology and method, as well as intelligibility and transparency on what content theology can contribute to the climate changes discussions. Otherwise theological insights will be reduced to a 'faith perspective' and not perceived to be politically or socially relevant. Although theological and religious languages are highly symbolic, there are crucial insights and analyses about justice, greed, sin, integrity, right relations, sacrifice, solidarity, resistance, hope, goodness, beauty, wisdom, wonder and more. The symbols, related experiences and myriad discernments need to be lucid and coherent, as they are essential concerns within the many issues involved in climate changes.

Contemporary ecotheologies have many dialogue partners: religious studies, philosophy, social sciences, Earth sciences and cosmology. The Forum on Religion and Ecology maintains an in-depth website with ample resources. The European Forum on the Study of Religion and the Environment has a specific section on climate change.[5] There are handbooks, encyclopaedias and countless books and articles on religion and ecology, ecotheology and the need to address climate changes. Many other excellent websites, syllabi, essays and other resources exist from the Global South and the North Atlantic regions. Each of these theological trajectories is following distinct inquiries and methods. Within these pursuits, some are concerned primarily with morality, ethics and eco-justice. Some liberation ecotheologies address systemic inequalities and inequities, oppressions and often economics. In some Christian contexts, theology is addressing creation, revelation and redemption in response to sin. In other contexts creation is predominantly informed by cosmology, evolutionary and natural sciences. Others follow

---

[5] Forum on Religion and Ecology: http://fore.yale.edu/religion/christianity/; European Forum for the Study of Religion and the Environment: http://www.hf.ntnu.no/relnateur/index.php?lenke=ridecc.php; Environment and Ecology: also http://environment-ecology.com/religion-and-ecology/321-ecotheology.html (accessed 24 August 2018).

religious experiences, and creation in this context may be about spiritual sensibilities of wonder, wisdom and awe. In each of these ecotheologies, ecological literacy is crucial.

Conclusion

In an era of uneven, unpredictable and yet consequential climate changes, the best responses to mitigate, prepare or adapt will be well informed by climate science. To be a dialogue partner, theologians need to do some epistemological homework in order to be seen as more than offering quaint, esoteric, personalist or in-group perspectives. Those in the North Atlantic or other affluent regions must address their massive ecological footprint and patterns of apathy and injustices. Theology may need to translate the religious impulses, spiritual sensibilities and theological insights to be a part of a larger global effort to address the causes and consequences of climate changes of the present and to prepare for a viable future. It is the call of our times.

A response to Heather Eaton

Katharine Hayhoe[1] and W. Douglas Hayhoe[2]

Climate change is an environmental issue, some argue, relevant only to those who worship creation rather than the Creator. It's a distant issue, many more believe, that only matters to faraway plants and animals or future generations, not to us. But as Heather Eaton's essay clearly shows, neither of these perspectives are true.

Climate change already affects us today, in the places where we live. We care about it because it impacts what's already at the top of our priority list: our own health and welfare, that of our family and our community, the economy, our safety and security and, in the most profound and fundamental way, the natural environment that supplies every resource that makes life possible on this planet. Not only that, but these impacts are profoundly unjust. They fall disproportionately on those who have done the least to contribute to the problem, the poor and the vulnerable, the very people Christians are called to love and to care for.

Eaton's essay connects the dots directly between these impacts and the work of the church. She highlights how 'church communities must deal with weather issues, water shortages, food insecurities in places, migrations and environmental refugees, and more.' To address this issue, she argues, Christian theologians should interact more closely with climate scientists. She delineates the challenges, chief among them the significant differences between 'systematic, empirical, and repeatable' scientific methods versus the symbolism that theology uses to express 'crucial insights ... about justice, greed, sin, integrity, right relations, solidarity, resistance, hope, goodness, beauty, wisdom, wonder, and more'. At the same time, however, she also emphasizes the benefits. Most people do not want to separate the science from what they believe, 'the outward quest to know *where we are*' (i.e. the Earth and how it functions) from 'an inner quest of *who we are,* and the outgoing interpretative questions of *why we are, why life is,* and *how to live*'. If we are to act on what science tells us, we want this action to be a natural outgrowth of our identity.

---

[1] Katharine Hayhoe is an atmospheric scientist whose research focuses on quantifying climate impacts on human systems and the natural environment. She is a professor at Texas Tech University, hosts the PBS digital series Global Weirding, and has been named one of TIME's 100 Most Influential People and Christianity Today's 50 Women to Watch.

[2] Doug Hayhoe has worked as a science teacher, K–12 science coordinator and as Professor of Science Education. He is Research Professor at Tyndale University College and Seminary in Toronto, Canada. His research focuses on environmental education, and science and Christianity.

As scientists and educators, we wholeheartedly agree with this premise. While science is the map we use to navigate creation, it's faith that provides the compass. To tackle massive, thorny, complex issues like climate change, we need to integrate our facts and our data with our faith and our values. Today more than ever, those connections between theologians and scientists need to be built up and strengthened. And we propose that even Eaton's essay would benefit from such a conversation, as it would allow it to reference the substantial body of social science research that unpacks exactly why and how people reject climate science, as well as allowing it to convey an accurate understanding of how it is human-based (and therefore value-based) uncertainty that dominates our calculations of how much climate will change and how bad it will be.

While we live in a world that is governed by empirical science, our response to that science is strongly determined by our philosophical, ideological, political and religious values, and nowhere is this more evident than in the area of climate change. 'America's new Weather Religion … don't be another government idiot', was one man's comment on a recent interview in which Katharine explained how her faith motivated her work on climate science. 'If she read her Bible, [she'd know that] all these things are going to happen in the end times,' claimed another on Twitter.

These seemingly religiously motivated objections lead some, including Eaton, to speculate on various causes, including a fundamental aspect of Christian theology or culture that may lead people to reject climate science. Yet social science analyses clearly show that such arguments are typically smokescreens for the genuine objections, which are best characterized as solution aversion and originate primarily from people's political ideology. It's true that public opinion polls consistently show US white Evangelicals and white Catholics to be least in agreement with the science and least concerned about the impacts of a changing climate. But it's not their theology or their religious affiliation that drives their opinions: it's their politics, specifically their adherence to the tenets of the Republican Party over and above those of their faith.

When it comes to climate change communication, research-based messaging finds that the four most important things to know are: it's real; it's us; it's bad; there are solutions and the future is in our hands.[3] In Eaton's essay, there is a repeated tendency to emphasize uncertainty in a way that diminishes these key, clear messages we all need to know. Throughout the essay, there are many references to how the complexity of the climate system can only lead to 'vague predictions' when in fact the science is clear: while some amount of change is inevitable, 'the magnitude of [future] climate change depends primarily on cumulative emissions of greenhouse gases and aerosols and the sensitivity of the climate system to those emissions'.[4] In addition, repeated use of the

---

[3] National Academies of Sciences, Engineering and Medicine (NASEM), 'The Science of Science Communication', https://www.nap.edu/read/18478/chapter/4 (accessed 3 March 2019).

[4] Katharine Hayhoe et al., 'Climate Models, Scenarios, and Projections', in *Climate Science Special Report: Fourth National Climate Assessment, Volume I*, Donald J. Wuebbles et al. (eds) (Washington, DC: U.S. Global Change Research Program, 2017), 133–60.

phrase 'climate sciences' (three times more often than the phrase 'climate science', as is standard in both popular and academic dialogue) minimizes the *bonding* between the various branches of climate science that all contribute to a single common understanding of the fact that our climate is changing, that this change is caused by humans, and that it presents a serious threat to our society.

While Eaton accepts the 'virtual consensus that climate change is occurring, and that it is anthropogenic', a conclusion to which the most recent scientific study assigns only a 1-in-3.5 million chance of error,[5] she nevertheless states that 'there is a range of views on the causes, consequences, timelines, tipping points, and mitigations and adaptations. Prominent and careful scientists disagree with each other, or change their minds, or say it is urgent that we act immediately, that there is time or that it is too late, and that no one really knows.' In reality, scientific uncertainty regarding human attribution ranges from whether human activities are causing *nearly all* of the observed warming (a minimum of 93 per cent) to *more than all* of the observed warming (up to 123 per cent), given that natural factors are known to be exerting a cooling influence on the earth's climate over the last few decades.[6]

Scientists furthermore agree that, while some amount of change is inevitable, it is not too late to avoid the most serious and dangerous impacts. A host of reports, from the IPCC's 'Global Warming of 1.5°C' report[7] to the US National Climate Assessment,[8] clearly quantify how impacts scale with carbon emissions, emissions which are in turn a product of the choices we as a society are making now and in the future. There is room for uncertainty, as humans have never before conducted such a massive and unprecedented experiment with the only planet we have; but all indications are that such uncertainty points in one direction: the possibility of greater, rather than lesser, amounts of change than anticipated.[9]

Finally, Eaton's essay accurately presents the serious social catastrophes that might result from climate change. At the same time, however, it consistently downplays the accuracy or usefulness of climate projections from models, instead emphasizing the unpredictability of what may happen. The essay begins by stating that '[s]pecific predictions must remain vague, as climate processes and the consequences of both

---

[5] Benjamin D. Santer et al., 'Celebrating the Anniversary of Three Key Events in Climate Change Science', *Nature Climate Science* 9 (2019), 180–2.

[6] Thomas Knutson et al., 'Detection and Attribution of Climate Change', in *Climate Science Special Report: Fourth National Climate Assessment, Volume I*, 114–32.

[7] IPCC, 'Summary for Policymakers', in *Global Warming of 1.5°C* (Geneva: World Meteorological Organization, 2018). This is an IPCC Special Report on the impacts of global warming of 1.5°C above pre-industrial levels and related global greenhouse gas emission pathways, in the context of strengthening the global response to the threat of climate change, sustainable development and efforts to eradicate poverty.

[8] David R. Reidmiller et al. (eds), *Impacts, Risks, and Adaptation in the United States: Fourth National Climate Assessment, Volume II* (Washington DC: U.S. Global Change Research Program, 2018).

[9] Robert E. Kopp et al., 'Potential Surprises – Compound Extremes and Tipping Elements', in *Climate Science Special Report: Fourth National Climate Assessment, Volume I*, 411–29.

major and minor changes are difficult to know with accuracy.' It continues, '[c]limate sciences cannot forecast climate changes. Understanding is one aspect; predictions are another,' and then adds, 'These disagreements [regarding the consequences that may happen] are due to the complexities of climate sciences, and the immense difficulties of assessing the consequences.'

We are fully cognizant of the massive complexity involved in modelling and understanding the response of our planet's climate system to this unprecedented experiment. However, what Eaton's essay fails to communicate is the fact that the greatest uncertainty in predicting future climate conditions and their attendant consequences comes not from uncertainty in the climate science itself or its computer models but from the uncertainty regarding the human decisions that will be made by individuals, governments and political parties and leaders over the coming years. Will the world's countries achieve the goals of the Paris Agreement, or will they blow past these targets, doubling or even tripling levels of carbon dioxide in the atmosphere? The answer to this question is not a matter of scientific uncertainty. Rather, it will be determined by the politics and economics and ideologies that drive our nations.

This is why climate model outputs should not be referred to as predictions, as they are in Eaton's essay. Predictions are forecasts of the future that include a quantifiable scientific uncertainty, such as 'there is a 40 percent chance of rain in the next 24 hours.' Projections, on the other hand, are more of an *if-then* statement. They show what will happen depending on the choices we make, choices that are fundamentally unpredictable from a scientific perspective. A climate projection says, '*if* humans emit X gigatons of carbon, *then* the world will warm by at least Y°C.' Svante Arrhenius, a Swedish scientist who won the Nobel Prize for his work in physical chemistry in 1903, was the first to fill in these blanks, accurately calculating how much the planet would warm as carbon dioxide built up in the atmosphere, using nothing more than the science known at that time. Today, modelling efforts primarily focus on understanding the implications of these changes for the interconnected physical, natural and socio-economic systems that support life on this planet.

Eaton's essay fills a critical need, stimulating us to think more deeply about how to engage Christian leaders and theologians with climate scientists to generate the transformative actions needed for us as individuals, as well as for our communities and global society, to avoid the most serious and even dangerous impacts of climate change. Long-term, hopeful action can only be maintained by the knowledge that our actions and our choices matter, and that knowledge is what scientists can bring to the conversation.

Chapter 1.2
Working with evolutionary biologists

Lisa H. Sideris[1]

Introduction

Christians seeking to address climate change need to work with others, including evolutionary biologists. This cooperative spirit is prompted by concerns over the havoc wreaked by climate change in terms of species extinction and biodiversity loss. It is also prompted by efforts to find synergy between cosmic, biological and human (cultural) evolution and the normative, meaning-making narratives of religion. Calls for dialogue and convergence between evolutionary and Christian perspectives often entail an implicit assumption that locating common ground will engender the desired ethical attitudes and behaviours towards the natural world. However, it is also possible that scientists and religionists may converge on a shared language, or speak in the same narrative voice, but in ways that do not advance but potentially hinder concern for issues like climate change. In the midst of calls for common ground, there is a need for circumspection in the articulation of meaning-making narratives that bear the imprimatur of science while implicitly or explicitly performing a theological function. Evolutionary perspectives can be invoked to preserve, rather than challenge, claims to human exceptionalism and uniqueness, and by doing so, they may perpetuate a hubristic agenda of planetary management.

A case in point centres on the emergence of 'new' paradigm in biology known as the Extended Evolutionary Synthesis (EES) and the attendant idea of niche constructors, that is, the power of organisms to shape their environments in ways that alter the direction and dynamic of evolution. The EES aims to counter the focus of the so-called modern synthesis (or 'neo-Darwinism') in biology on genes and genetic programming.[2] The new synthesis proposes a more organism-centred perspective, arguing that organisms both shape and are shaped by their selective and developmental environments. The EES broadens traditional concepts like heredity, extending it beyond genes to encompass

---

[1] Lisa H. Sideris is Professor of Religious Studies at Indiana University, a large public research university in Bloomington, Indiana. Her research interests include environmental ethics at the intersection of science and religion, Anthropocene narratives, and the ways in which science and technology function religiously.

[2] It is questionable whether the terms 'neo-Darwinism' and the 'modern synthesis' should be considered synonymous, as some scholars would argue that features of a neo-Darwinian perspective were shed long ago.

myriad forms of inheritance: epigenetic, physiological, ecological, social and cultural. With its broader understanding of heredity, the EES has fostered conceptions of organisms as playing an active role in shaping their environments. Organisms inherit not only genes but also behaviours and environments. This understanding of the role of organisms in shaping their environments can be interpreted as evidence of *continuity* among all life forms, human and non-human alike. But according to several prominent advocates of EES, this account also underscores important *dis*continuities that mark humans off as an extraordinary species whose world-shaping capacities are without precedent or parallel in the non-human natural world.

These claims for discontinuity and human distinctiveness clearly impinge upon environmental ethics and discourse. They lend support to a particular account of the human species and frame debates about the way in which creatures like us interact with the wider natural world. In what follows, I explore some key features of the EES and an accompanying portrait of humans as the *supreme* niche-constructing species. I consider a cluster of related questions and concerns: What does the EES and the image of humans as powerful niche constructors portend for human responsibility for the environment? Does the idea that humans have been modifying and recreating their environments throughout evolutionary history serve to naturalize recent alterations like climate change? If so, what prescriptions for the future are implied by this account? Throughout the discussion that follows, I draw particular attention to the way in which this 'new' evolutionary perspective is proffered as a compelling narrative of creative, innovative and adaptable humans in an age of unprecedented environmental change. This narrative functions as a form of theological anthropology, even among 'secular' theorists of niche construction theory.

The EES and niche construction: An evolutionary rethink?

Claims regarding the need for a new evolutionary paradigm came to wider attention with the publication of a high-profile debate in the journal *Nature* in 2014. The article spells out both pro and con positions on the proposition that evolutionary theory is in need of a 'rethink'.[3] This piece was followed by others, notably a multi-authored article titled 'The Extended Evolutionary Synthesis: Its Structure, Assumptions, and Predictions' published in 2015. The latter calls for a new conceptual framework for evolutionary

---

[3] Kevin Laland et al., 'Does Evolutionary Theory Need a Re-think? Researchers are Divided over What Processes Should be Considered Fundamental', *Nature: International Weekly Journal of Science* 514:7521 (8 October 2014), 161–4; and the side-by-side comment by Gregory Wray and Hopi Hoestra et al., 'Does Evolutionary Theory Need a Re-think', *Nature: International Weekly Journal of Science* 514:7521 (9 October 2014), 161–4.

biology that incorporates insights derived from areas of biology that, the authors claim, are marginalized by the standard account.[4] These include the following: evolutionary developmental biology ('evo-devo'; the field of study that compares developmental processes of different organisms in order to gain insights about ancestral relationships between them and to better understand how developmental processes evolved); developmental plasticity (an organism's capacity to change its phenotype in response to its environment); and inclusive inheritance (a broadened account of inheritance that incorporates all processes of inheritance, whether genetic or non-genetic); as well as an all-important concept of niche construction theory (NCT; activities and choices of organisms, through which they alter or stabilize environmental states – more on this concept below). Taken as a whole, proponents argue, these insights support the conclusion that organisms are not just products but also *causes* of evolution. Moreover, organisms act as generators and refiners of novelty and innovation when confronted with environmental challenges. Through niche construction, organisms can even change environments to suit themselves.

Leading the charge in favour of a rethink is biologist and animal behaviourist Kevin Laland. In the pro/con piece published in *Nature*, Laland and colleagues contend that the debate over the EES is no mere 'storm in an academic tearoom' but entails a 'struggle for the very soul of the discipline'[5] (though elsewhere Laland appears to walk back on this somewhat dramatic claim[6]). Laland and colleagues maintain that in its standard form, evolutionary theory retains an inordinate focus on classic gene-centred processes, at the expense of others. Defenders of standard evolutionary theory (SET), they allege, hew to a narrow version of evolution that posits organisms as passive, programmed entities. By contrast, Laland and others claim that 'living things do not evolve to fit into pre-existing environments, but co-construct and coevolve with their environments, in the process changing the structure of ecosystems'.[7] Defenders of the SET respond that those pushing for the EES present a straw-man version of the standard evolutionary account. They further contend that processes touted by EES proponents are already given appropriate emphasis in standard evolutionary theory and argue that the evidence, at present, does not warrant giving them greater attention.

It is important to gain a fuller sense of what is included within the category of niche construction and why the concept is appealing to a number of scholars both within and beyond the sciences. A signature example of NCT is the profound modification of natural

---

[4] Kevin Laland et al., 'The Extended Evolutionary Synthesis: Its Structure, Assumptions, and Predictions', *Proceedings of the Royal Society B: Biological Sciences* 282 (2015), 1–14.

[5] Laland et al., 'Does Evolutionary Theory Need a Re-think?', 162.

[6] In an interview with evolutionary biologist David Sloan Wilson – an avid enthusiast of the EES, NCT and multilevel selection – Laland states that bold rhetoric of new paradigms, revolution and/or replacement of the existing theory is counterproductive. See David Sloan Wilson and Kevin Laland, 'Empowering the Extended Evolutionary Synthesis', https://evolution-institute.org/empowering-the-extended-evolutionary-synthesis/ (accessed 1 October 2018).

[7] Ibid.

environments introduced by beavers, through cutting down trees and building dams. By living in the environments they create, beavers in turn affect their own future evolution. Another well-known example is earthworms whose burrowing behaviour changes the make-up of soil. The altered soil, in turn, creates a feedback dynamic, influencing future generations of earthworms and placing *new* selection pressures on them. In order for a behaviour to count as genuine niche construction, some would argue, this feedback is essential: the constructing activity must demonstrably influence the evolution of the 'constructor' organism or the evolution of other species.[8] As with debates about the EES more generally, scientists disagree about whether niche construction has been neglected in standard evolutionary theory, with some arguing that it has already been 'extensively incorporated in both ecological and evolutionary studies for at least over a century'.[9] Critics of an evolutionary overhaul further charge that the overly broad definition of niche construction is problematic, consisting of a whole suite of processes whereby organisms alter their own and others' environments. For example, in a classic formulation, niche construction is the process whereby organisms, through their metabolism, activities, and choices, modify their own and / or each other's niches.[10] To critics, this definition is so capacious as to be virtually meaningless: 'Given that everything an organism does, including living or dying, affects the environment, NC would appear to be a synonym of biology, in which case, we fail to see how it could be "neglected."'[11]

Often at the crux of this debate is Darwin's all-important concept of natural selection. Those favouring an evolutionary rethink are not tossing out natural selection, but they understand it to be constrained or biased in particular directions by developmental processes. Variation, on this account, is not wholly random; certain forms may be more readily produced than others. An example frequently cited by advocates of the EES is a case of evolutionary convergence among cichlid fishes from Lake Malawi and Lake Tanganyika. These organisms show remarkable similarities in body shape, even though they are more closely related to species in their *own* lake than to those in the other lake.[12] These similarities cannot merely be coincidental, Laland and others argue, but suggest that developmental processes play an active and creative role, guiding gene pathways in specific directions. Similarly with processes of niche construction, the EES proposes that organisms can modify their environmental states in non-random ways that impose a bias on selection pressures. In short, niche construction is seen by proponents of the EES as a process that influences selection, directing evolution by non-random alterations of selective environments and enabling organisms and their environments to co-evolve.

---

[8] Kevin Laland, *Darwin's Unfinished Symphony: How Culture Made the Human Mind* (Princeton: Princeton University Press, 2017), 194.

[9] Manan Gupta et al., 'Niche Construction in Evolutionary Theory: The Construction of an Academic Niche?', *Journal of Genetics* 96:3 (2017), 491–504 (493).

[10] John Odling-Smee et al., 'Niche Construction', *The American Naturalist* 147:4 (1996), 641–8.

[11] Gupta et al., 'Niche Construction in Evolutionary Theory', 493.

[12] Laland et al., 'The Extended Evolutionary Synthesis'.

As a religion scholar and non-scientist, it is not my place to pronounce on the scientific merits, or lack thereof, of these duelling proposals. What interests me is the way in which the EES and especially the related concept of niche construction – in various forms – is being taken up as a powerful new image of the human in an age of climate change and the Anthropocene. The concept of niche construction has taken on a vigorous life of its own, due in part to a handful of science popularizers who discern in NCT a new way of looking at life, notably human life. I discuss the work of a few such advocates of NCT in what follows, while acknowledging that their views do not necessarily represent the broader study of niche construction and the EES.

The numinous appeal of the extended synthesis?

In considering what is appealing about the EES and NCT to scientists and non-scientists alike, it is important to note that terms such as *directional* or *non-random* or *guiding* commonly appear in discussions of what makes the EES approach different. While these words may have carefully delineated meanings to evolutionary biologists, to others they may suggest the possibility that evolution proceeds in purposive, progressive or providential ways. Niche construction can thus serve as a revised theological anthropology to counter non-directional secular theories of naturalistic evolution.[13] Recently, controversy ensued when the John Templeton Foundation, which promotes science–religion dialogue, provided significant funding to Laland and a team of researchers (both scientists and philosophers), whose ambition it is to test the viability of the EES. Representatives of the foundation had followed the debate in *Nature* and its intimations of an emerging evolutionary overhaul with keen interest, as well as the months of dialogue that followed. Laland and a team of nearly fifty scholars were awarded $8.7 million to put the EES to the test.

Some scholars worry that the EES might give solace to creationists or proponents of intelligent design: 'Suggestions that something is missing from [the standard evolutionary] picture – for example, that evolution is somehow directed or that genetic changes can't fully explain it – play into the hands of creationists, who leap on them as evidence against evolution itself.'[14] Similarly, biologist and atheist blogger Jerry Coyne (who closely monitors the Templeton Foundation's funding decisions and blogs about

---

[13] Celia Deane-Drummond who has both theological and scientific training explicitly develops niche construction as a promising theological anthropology, whereas secular proponents of NCT may be unaware of the implicit theological dimensions of the popular narratives they construct. See Celia Deane-Drummond, 'Evolution: A Theology of Niche Construction for the Twenty-First Century', in *Theology and Ecology across the Disciplines: On Care for Our Common Home*, Celia Deane-Drummond and Rebecca Artinian-Kaiser (eds) (London: T&T Clark, 2019), 241–56.

[14] Elizabeth Pennisi, 'Templeton Grant Funds Evolution Rethink', *Science* 22 (April 2016), http://science.sciencemag.org/content/352/6284/394.full (accessed 1 October 2018).

them with great rancour) has speculated that Templeton's interest in the EES and NCT stems from an abiding anti-evolution bias. On this account, calls for an evolutionary rethink might be read as signalling ominous (or, for some, auspicious) cracks in the Darwinian façade. In lashing out against the EES and the generous funding it has garnered, Coyne gestures towards a certain 'numinous' quality that lurks within the EES – something suggestive of organisms wielding agential power or perhaps even shades of purposive design in evolution.[15] As a thoroughgoing rationalist, Coyne means to impugn the EES by associating it with anything vaguely *numinous*; but such numinosity, if indeed it exists, need not entail or encourage creationist or intelligent design aspirations.

This debate is fascinating in its own right, but especially for what it suggests about the role of science in shaping or even becoming a new theological anthropology that influences our discernment of humans' place within nature and our ethical relationship thereto. However, I see little reason to suspect that the Templeton-funded team – many of whom focus on organisms like dung beetles and green algae – harbours any such crypto-religious or subversive agenda. That does not mean, however, that evolutionary narratives spawned by the EES function in a wholly secular fashion. In fact the EES has *also* struck a chord with Christian theologians and theologically minded scholars.

Whether they are expressly interested in theology or not, many scholars see something refreshing, even something distinctly hopeful or reassuring, in an EES view of life. Where the standard evolutionary account appears inimical to conceptions of animal agency – insofar as organisms have at times been caricatured as genetically programmed survival machines – the EES potentially opens up a new appreciation for animals as participants in evolutionary processes and as actors in the drama of human evolution. Understandably, NCT appeals to Christians who resist reductive, gene-centred interpretations of evolution. Theologian Celia Deane-Drummond and anthropologist Agustín Fuentes, who collaborated on a Templeton-funded project on human distinctiveness,[16] argue that in its attention to the 'mutual malleability' of organisms and their environments, as well as to shared social and biological kinship of humans and animals, NCT sheds new light on how humans evolved to be the unique species that we are.[17] They insist that the evolutionary process of becoming human was and is a *multispecies* endeavour. Non-human beings that play a significant role in the human community niche must 'be considered as agential factors in the investigation

---

[15] See Jerry Coyne, 'Templeton Wastes $11 Million in Attempt to Change Evolutionary Biology', https://whyevolutionistrue.wordpress.com/2016/04/08/templeton-wastes-11-million-in-attempt-to-corrupt-evolutionary-biology/ (accessed 1 October 2018).

[16] See 'Human Distinctiveness', Center for Theology, Science, and Human Flourishing, https://ctshf.nd.edu/research/human-distinctiveness/ (accessed 1 October 2018).

[17] Celia Deane-Drummond and Agustín Fuentes, 'Human Being and Becoming: Situating Theological Anthropology in Interspecies Relationships in an Evolutionary Context', *Philosophy, Theology, and the Sciences* 1 (2014), 251–75 (255).

of the evolutionary and social processes involved in being and becoming human in community'.[18]

Another 'hopeful' aspect of the EES and NCT, for some, is the alternative it presents to evolutionary psychology. NCT often depicts humans as remarkably plastic and adaptable, not rigidly defined by biology, countering an image advanced by evolutionary psychologists and in popular science writing of humans 'trapped in the past by an outdated biological legacy', struggling to adapt to modern conditions with stone-age brains.[19] Our minds are not atavistic Swiss Army knives, comprised of special-purpose modules, proponents of EES insist. We are flexible problem solvers, creatures who adapt and innovate. Moreover, niche-constructing processes enable a more rapid response to environmental challenges than is the case with strictly genetic adaptations that take place slowly over generations. There is a certain solace in this vision of humans as a resourceful species that has always, one way or another, creatively responded to challenging conditions.

Some of these aspects of NCT may account for its appeal to scholars across disciplines; these features are also relevant to an articulation of an implicit theological account of the human. In the context of our own species, niche construction entails that humans not only adapt to their environments through processes such as natural selection but *actively re-make their worlds*. In other words, this conception of humans as a uniquely powerful, world-making species functions as a kind of theological anthropology, even for those who do not see themselves as engaged in a theological enterprise. This image of the human has special resonance across a range of contemporary issues and fields of study, including Anthropocene studies and discourse, climate ethics and even astrobiology.

Laland is a case in point of a scientist invested in spreading the good news of the EES and NCT, beyond the scientific community. While this portrait of the human offers a refreshing alternative to evolutionary psychology, it also risks perpetuating a mode of human interaction with nature that is creative (and reflects our adaptability) but *also* demonstrably destructive. Put differently, the rhetoric of NCT may make it difficult to critique human–nature interactions that fall under 'successful' niche construction. These interactions include large-scale transformations of the planet such as climate change.

Hopeful narratives of niche construction

For many scholars who discuss NCT in the context of humans, the theory often functions to sharply delineate human forms of environmental modification, innovation, adaptability and creativity from the activities of non-humans. While earthworms or beavers engage in significant alterations of their environments, the argument goes that

---

[18] Ibid., 256.
[19] Laland, *Darwin's Unfinished Symphony*, 232.

humans recreate their worlds in truly exceptional ways. Our presumed capacities for self-conscious transformation, our boundless creativity, or our 'ultra-sociality' (more on this below) set us apart. This portrait of the human as *the* niche-constructing species is often couched in hyperbolic, superlative language and in tones that are congratulatory and even reverential. Our species' evolutionary innovations and accomplishments are marked as 'unprecedented' and 'unrivaled'. Similarities between humans and animals are 'superficial', Laland believes, and accordingly, the 'intellectual credentials' of other animals have been inflated.[20]

Accounts of the human in NCT highlight our 'successful' history of adaptation, where success is lauded irrespective of the long-term, negative impacts on the broader spectrum of life, and in ways that prophesy a continuing pattern of success into the future. There is something oddly short-sighted and even tautologous, I am suggesting, in these pronouncements of human evolutionary success, as if an evaluation of how humans interact with their environments is reducible to crude, survival-of-the-fittest criteria. Our success as a species is correlated with an assumed capacity to outpace, to 'beat' the strategies of other organisms, as if we are rivals in a grand evolutionary competition. Humans' capacity to work around limits and constraints, through intensified innovation and scaling up of our modifications, is seen as a hallmark of success, despite the disaster our creations spell for other organisms, as well as for ourselves, down the road.

For example, in *Darwin's Unfinished Symphony* (2017), Laland presents the human species as 'champion' niche constructors, repeatedly invoking the word *potent* to characterize qualities unique to the human species and its cultural evolution. Humans manifest an 'extraordinarily potent capacity to modify the circumstances of our lives', he writes.[21] 'A uniquely potent innovativeness and enhanced capability for high-fidelity social learning has allowed our species to devise means of exploiting our environments with extraordinary efficiency.'[22] 'Our species' extraordinary accomplishments can be attributed to our uniquely potent capability for culture.'[23] Examples of our potent niche construction include widespread agriculture, deforestation, urbanization, climate alterations and similar dramatic planetary transformations. These descriptions of human power exalt humans as victors in a thrilling evolutionary contest. Note this language: 'Our potent culture and the feedback it generated, switched on the evolutionary afterburners and allowed our cognition to race ahead of that of other species, thereby generating a major gulf between the intellectual capabilities of humans and other animals.'[24]

What does Laland mean by 'potent' niche construction? What does 'racing ahead' look like? Potency often signals sheer scale – no other organism has transformed an entire *planet*. At other times, our potency is a function of our *self-conscious, self-aware*

---

[20] Ibid., 15.
[21] Ibid., 229.
[22] Ibid., 263.
[23] Ibid., 7.
[24] Ibid., 231.

remaking of the environment. Humans alone reconstruct their worlds knowingly, proponents of NCT stress, and this *knowingness* is taken to suggest that we can direct our powers towards constructive rather than destructive world-making. Other capacities alleged to be uniquely human come into play as well: powers of symbolic communication or tool manufacture: 'Our ancestors constructed a world sufficiently rich in symbolism to generate evolutionary feedback in the form of self-modified selection pressures that favored structures in the mind functioning to manipulate and use those symbols with efficiency.'[25] Feedback mechanisms involved in symbolic communication also shaped the evolution of human tool-making, allowing skills to be transmitted rapidly through teaching. Our ancestors' reliance on these technologies generated selection for increasingly complex forms of communication, which, in turn, generated an increasingly effective spread of tool-making methods. Genes and culture co-evolving in this way enabled our species to build environments that benefitted themselves, and to then adapt to life within those environments in an iterative fashion. Laland concludes his inventory of humans' superlative qualities with this flourish: 'human minds and human environments have been engaged in a long-standing, intimate exchange of information, mediated by reciprocal bouts of niche construction and natural selection, leaving each *beautifully fashioned in the other's image.*'[26]

The strong current of optimism running through discussions of niche construction may obviate the need for more sober reflection on the damage we have wrought, the sort of reflection that might allow a genuine reappraisal of our interactions with the environment. Proponents of niche construction tend to gloss over its darker side, as if deforested landscapes or climate change were minor collateral damage, an acceptable side effect of our increasing evolutionary 'fitness' and 'adaptiveness'. Positively valenced terms – fitness, adaptation, creativity, novelty, success and so on – make it difficult to view our niche-constructing powers in anything but a positive light.

This is not to say Laland and others ignore such dangers and downsides altogether. Most acknowledge that humans' potency in transforming the environment may ultimately inflict harm on other species, the environment and even – given enough time – themselves. All organisms can have both positive and negative impacts on their selective environments. However, the tendency is to present human niche construction and the activities that comprise as if, by definition, they constitute evolutionary success. Our behaviour remains 'largely adaptive', Laland argues, 'in spite of the radical transformations brought about in the environment'.[27] Even the onset of climate change does little to alter this confident appraisal: 'Eventually', Laland concedes, 'human habitat degradation, most obviously anthropogenic climate change, may well negatively influence human fitness. However, for the time being, other species bear the brunt of our

---

[25] Ibid., 194.
[26] Ibid., 233 (my emphasis).
[27] Ibid., 232.

activities, for whom the consequences are rarely so positive.'[28] Laland lists widespread species endangerment and extinction among the negative consequences of human niche construction but proceeds with a largely untroubled assessment:

> In the meantime, the human species thrives and our numbers rise relentlessly, a clear sign that in the short term humanity benefits from our niche construction. Contrary to popularized narratives of environmental exploitation leading to cultural collapse, recent studies demonstrate that agricultural and other cultural practices shifted human carrying capacity upward.[29]

Contra evolutionary psychology, humans are not chained to our evolutionary past, but free agents of our own – and others' – futures: 'Characterized by a remarkable plasticity', humans alone are empowered to correct mismatches between our biological adaptations and the world around us. No other animal exhibits 'anything approaching the remarkable flexibility and problem-solving capabilities conferred by human culture'.[30]

But to return to Laland's claim: have humans left our environments *beautifully fashioned* in our image? Any number of stunning scenes from around the planet testify against this verdict: cities devastated by superstorms, exhausted animals searching for places to rest in the absence of sea ice, recording-breaking wildfires engulfing the Western United States, beaches covered in plastics that wind up in the digestive tract of 90 per cent of the world's seabirds. Do such alterations count as a form of niche construction? Plastic wastes provide an interesting case. These wastes do not merely endanger sea creatures and other non-human animals. Endocrine disrupting chemicals – xenoestrogens – found in plastics may be exerting directional evolutionary pressures on future generations of humans owing to oestrogenic effects on both men (possible lowered sperm counts) and women (possible early onset menopause). In this respect, we have systematically changed our environments in ways that change the selection pressures to which future generations are exposed, thus biasing selection.[31] This behaviour meets the criteria for niche construction, though it hardly warrants descriptors like 'adaptive' or 'successful'.

Indeed, climate change is a prime example of human niche construction because it induces evolutionary change in other species. Erle Ellis, an environmental scientist and 'eco-modernist', writes extensively about the Anthropocene and human–environment interactions and promotes a particular version of niche construction in which climate transformation figures prominently. 'How and why', Ellis asks, 'did humans gain such

---

[28] Ibid.
[29] Ibid., 232–3.
[30] Ibid., 232.
[31] For more on this, see Greg Downey, 'Plastics, Tiny Penises and Human Evolution', http://blogs.plos.org/neuroanthropology/2015/04/19/plastics-and-human-evolution/54 (accessed 1 October 2018).

exceptional capacities to reshape planet Earth?'³² For Ellis our exceptionality lies in our ultra-sociality: 'The capacity of behaviourally modern humans for social learning is unrivaled among species – even human sociality itself is socially learned.'³³ When NCT is combined with a full understanding of humans' exceptional sociality, the picture that emerges is what Ellis calls 'sociocultural niche construction'. This portrait renders humans 'unlike any other species in Earth's history', the only one with the capacity to 'transform an entire planet'.³⁴

Ellis echoes Laland's appeal to NCT as offering an alternative to depressing narratives that posit humans as 'environmental destroyers'.³⁵ Like others who endorse NCT, Ellis argues that many organisms actively engage in changing their environments. Humans, however, represent earth's 'ultimate ecosystem engineer' who have long used their powers to, for example, clear land, domesticate plants and animals and create settlements. Humans are no mere destroyers of nature, he reminds us, for our societies have also

> reduced and eliminated pollution, have protected and restored endangered species and their habitats and may even now be undergoing a massive shift in energy systems that could prevent catastrophic global climate change. The boom in Anthropocene discussions might itself indicate that societies are *waking up* to the realities of becoming a global force in the Earth system.³⁶

In an essay titled 'Evolving the Anthropocene', Ellis and colleagues present a similar upbeat account of humans meeting challenge after challenge with the engineering acumen and extra-genetic inheritances that characterize our species: 'Over time, human capacities to engineer ecosystems evolved to support larger and larger populations, producing ecological inheritances with both beneficial and harmful adaptive consequences through evolutionary processes of niche construction.'³⁷ Note the intriguing phrase 'harmful adaptive consequences'. Ellis and his co-authors do not explain how harmful adaptive consequences differ from beneficial ones. Their examples of exceptional engineering skew towards developments deemed beneficial insofar as they produce 'upscaling' events in human societies. Successive upscaling

---

³² Erle Ellis, 'Why is Human Niche Construction Reshaping Planet Earth?', *Extended Evolutionary Synthesis* (17 April 2017), http://extendedevolutionarysynthesis.com/why-is-human-niche-construction-reshaping-planet-earth/ (accessed 1 October 2018).

³³ Erle Ellis, 'Evolving toward a Better Anthropocene', *Future Earth* (29 March 2016), http://www.futureearth.org/blog/2016-mar-29/evolving-toward-better-anthropocene (accessed 1 October 2018).

³⁴ Erle Ellis et al. 'Evolving the Anthropocene: Linking Multi-Level Selection with Long-Term Social-Ecological Change', *Sustainability Science* 13:119 (2018), https://doi.org/10.1007/s11625-017-0513-6.

³⁵ Erle Ellis, 'Why Is Human Niche Construction Transforming Planet Earth?', in 'Molding the Planet: Human Niche Construction at Work', Maurits W. Ertzen, Christof Mauch, and Edmund Russell (eds), *Rachel Carson Center Perspectives: Transformations in Environment and Society* 16:5 (2016), 63–70 (65).

³⁶ Ellis et al. 'Evolving toward a Better Anthropocene' (my emphasis).

³⁷ Ellis et al. 'Evolving the Anthropocene'.

events are presented as 'major societal regime shifts', beginning with hunter–gatherer societies, moving through agrarian, industrial and post-industrial societies. As humans enter the industrial and post-industrial era, ecological inheritances include such innovations as GMOs, toxic pollution and climate change. Material inheritances include plastics and electronics, while cultural inheritances include scientific specialization, telecommunication and robotics. Through niche construction, humans have, in a favourite phrase of Ellis's, *evolved the Anthropocene*: 'human societies gained the capacity to transform a planet, without intending to, through a runaway evolutionary process of sociocultural niche construction which caused societal upscaling and niche construction intensity to increase together.'[38] These runaway processes lock society into 'long-term cycles of adaptation in their sociocultural niche, as [humans] work harder to sustain ever more demanding societies'.[39] Ellis pronounces these trends generally progressive, even if not always straightforwardly so. 'Times have never been better' for most people, he argues, though like Laland he concedes that the same cannot be said for non-human beings with whom we share our transformed planet.[40]

There is a peculiar way in which these sweeping perspectives on the human species, for all of their investment in the *longue durée*,[41] remain astonishingly short-sighted. Humans are succeeding remarkably, indeed 'relentlessly' – for now – as indicated in our growing numbers, our extra-genetic transmission of culture, and the upscaling and intensification of our transformations. Success in the immediate term is defined as little more than reproductive success. Never mind that our 'ecological' inheritances include climate change and toxic waste.

Can humans sustain current trends? At times, Ellis and co-authors leave the question open. But elsewhere, Ellis invokes NCT as grounds for anticipating and ushering in a good Anthropocene. The key to this brighter future lies in fully embracing our world-transforming powers and turning them towards good: 'By engaging with, not against, the processes of sociocultural niche construction, we might guide this new "great force of nature" toward better outcomes for both humanity and nonhuman nature.'[42] Thus, responding to the Anthropocene entails doing more of the same, doing what makes us human (that is, niche construction) but with a mysterious infusion of greater *wisdom*. How this new wisdom will emerge – enabling us to 'intentionally build better societies and cultures of nature' rather than destructive ones – is never explained.[43] The assumption seems to be that wise stewardship will itself evolve out of the current positive trends Ellis's narrative cites.

---

[38] Ibid.

[39] Ellis et al. 'Why Is Human Niche Construction Transforming Planet Earth?'.

[40] Ibid., 69.

[41] 'Behaviourally modern human societies', Ellis writes, 'have always engineered ecosystems to sustain themselves.' See Ellis et al., 'Evolving toward a Better Anthropocene'.

[42] Ellis et al., 'Evolving toward a Better Anthropocene'.

[43] Ibid.

Indeed, as the motif of humans *waking up* to full self-awareness suggests, the basic narrative offered by these popularizers of NCT is akin to a (secularized) Irenaean theology. An Irenaean account, named after the theologian Irenaeus of Lyon (130–202 CE), holds that humans are not so much evil as immature and that through encountering obstacles in the world, we develop – or in this case collectively evolve – into more perfect beings. In contrast to accounts of humans as created in a perfect state from which they subsequently fell, an Irenaean narrative holds that our perfection lies in the future rather than the past.[44] Climate change is not in itself a moral failing, on this view, but a manageable by-product, one of the growing pains of our species' evolution towards mature planetary oversight.[45] Our adaptability and powers of innovation inspire a liberatory tale that contrasts with the pessimism of evolutionary psychology and the declensionist worldview of environmentalism.

'Go forth and create'

Clearly, these accounts of our niche-constructing species are not merely descriptive. They perform a normative, even quasi-mythic function, as we look towards a future increasingly defined by climate change and other large-scale planetary transformations. The narrative aspect is taken even further in the work of Agustín Fuentes who, more so than Laland and Ellis, explicitly frames niche construction as a powerful new, quasi-theological narrative.[46] Fuentes offers a 'new story of human evolution' centred on NCT, where a niche encompasses the individual, the group and the community (both human and non-human members). Niche construction constitutes 'the epic tale of all epic tales', an exciting new 'grand narrative'.[47] Fuentes believes that an up-to-date understanding of evolution, provided by the EES and NCT, can help us to navigate the challenges of climate change and the Anthropocene. As he argues in his popular book-length treatment of the subject, *The Creative Spark: How Imagination Made Humans*

---

[44] An Irenaean account is often contrasted with an Augustinian account of evil. See John Hick, *Evil and the God of Love* (New York: Macmillan, 1966).

[45] Clive Hamilton makes a similar argument about eco-modernists such as Erle Ellis's vision of the good Anthropocene. See 'The Theodicy of the "Good Anthropocene"', *Environmental Humanities* 7 (2015), 233–8.

[46] Some of Fuentes's work moves back and forth between secular and (occasionally) theological territory, but all of it functions as theological anthropology.

[47] Agustín Fuentes, *The Creative Spark: How Imagination Made Humans Exceptional* (New York: Dutton, 2017), 4–5, 16. Deane-Drummond seeks to maintain a line between descriptive accounts of niche construction, as one finds among anthropologists and biologists, and grand narrative varieties proffered by Anthropocene boosters like Ellis. However, it is quite clear that Fuentes, as an anthropologist, is engaged in a grand narrative project. See Deane-Drummond, 'Evolution', 251.

Exceptional, the hallmark of human niche construction and the defining feature of our evolutionary success is *creativity*.

Like Laland and Ellis (and despite Fuentes's own emphasis elsewhere on human 'becoming' as a multispecies project), Fuentes is enormously invested in the exceptional nature of humans. He acknowledges the niche-constructing behaviours of beavers and earthworms but insists that humans are 'in a class all our own' when it comes to reshaping our surroundings.[48] Discontinuities interest him most, for they 'tell us more about who we are as a species than do the similarities'.[49] Like others, Fuentes understands tool use and symbolic communication as pivotal (and intertwined) developments in human evolution. Humans took the 'creative spark' to new levels 'constructing an entirely new way of making a living on this planet – a way that would eventually *beat everything else, ever*'.[50] In keeping with a rhetorical framing common to popularizers of NCT, Fuentes concedes that our alterations of the planet have created a perilous situation for the long term: 'It is possible that we may have constructed our way into a non-manageable scenario.'[51] But by and large, his narrative is one of linear progression; lines of the genus *Homo* that faded into obscurity, such as Neanderthals, are assumed to have lacked our unique creativity. He calls upon continued cultivation of human powers of becoming – innovation, collaboration and creation – as key to shaping the future of our species and the environment.

Thus, our way forward in the Anthropocene involves making the most of our creative capacities. For inspiration, Fuentes urges us to recall that the human species has successfully overcome huge challenges in our past: 'When the cards are against us we dream big and then we act,' he writes. 'If we succeed and make the twenty-first century a beneficially creative era, the stories our descendants tell about us will emphasize our creativity and collaboration, not our blunders and disunity.'[52] The book ends with a benediction of sorts: 'Go Forth and Be Creative'.[53]

Niche construction and its attendant vision of the human are marshalled in these narratives as a kind of pep talk for our species not in the sense of inspiring *difficult change* in behaviour but as a reminder of past successes and an exhortation to draw more deeply upon the reservoir of creativity and adaptability that advanced our species to this point. To wit: 'Let's meet those challenges head on and shoot for another 2 million years of creativity,' Fuentes urges at the close of his book.[54] Yet, this heavy investment in our adaptability and creativity may act as a disincentive to genuine, positive change. While

---

[48] Ibid., 10.
[49] Ibid., 11.
[50] Ibid., 23 (my emphasis).
[51] Fuentes, 'Becoming Human in the Anthropocene', in *Religion in the Anthropocene*, Celia Deane-Drummond et al. (eds) (Eugene: Wipf and Stock, 2017), 103–18 (109).
[52] Fuentes, *The Creative Spark*, 273.
[53] Ibid., 292.
[54] Ibid., 292.

this may not be what Fuentes intends, my concern is that a focus on these essential human qualities acts as a kind of insurance policy *against* having to undertake the difficult work of accommodating ourselves to planetary limits, rather than further modifying the environment to suit our own needs.

A similarly upbeat niche-constructing narrative has found its way into perspectives from astrobiology (the study of planets in the universe and their habitability). From an astrobiological perspective, we can perceive our planet to be one of many potential life-generating planets in the universe. If indeed earth shows parallels with these 'exoplanets', in terms of its origin and stages of evolution, then we might expect that even the emergence of climate change marks a universal planetary stage, a predictable outcome of any planet with technologically 'successful' life forms. This is the dubious claim made by astrobiologist Adam Frank, who frequently engages in public outreach through popular books, blogs and public radio segments. On Frank's account, climate change is just the latest transformation of the planet by a species that has been 'building civilizations out of whatever we could get our hands on for at least 8,000 years'. Understood in the context of our species' ancient penchant for world-building, climate change is not our 'fault' but simply 'how we roll'.[55]

Frank has collaborated with an urban planner named Marina Alberti who analyses cities as a form of evolutionary niche construction. Rapid expansion of urbanization may be driving a turning point for our planet, insofar as urbanization contributes to the positive feedbacks involved in climate change.[56] These feedbacks may trigger planetary disruptions akin to the Great Oxidation Event of over 2 billion years ago that engendered an entirely new kind of planet. But as Frank sees it, these dramatic transformations tell an exciting rather than terrifying story, not one of looming catastrophe but of 'the unique opportunity that humans have in shaping the earth'.[57] Just as Laland and others embrace a liberating story of adaptable, flexible humans unbound from their evolutionary past, Frank's account stresses the saving power of innovation. Frank argues: 'Evolution has always been about innovation in the endless exploration of new niches.'[58] Elsewhere he and Alberti conclude that climate change and the Anthropocene may be 'a generic consequence of any planet evolving a *successful technological species*'.[59] Claims for human exceptionalism are here somewhat muted (in the sense that *any* intelligent species in the universe might evolve an Anthropocene), but the treatment of climate change as remediable side effect of innovation and adaptive success holds. In keeping with Irenaean tropes, Frank's embrace of niche construction entails that humans are not

---

[55] Adam Frank, 'Climate Change is Not Our Fault', *13.7 Cosmos and Culture* (16 October 2015), https://www.npr.org/sections/13.7/2015/10/06/446109168/climate-change-is-not-our-fault (accessed 1 October 2018).

[56] 'Positive' feedback here refers to processes that *amplify* climate change.

[57] Frank, 'Can Cities Change Earth's Evolution?', *13.7 Cosmos and Culture* (3 March 2015), https://www.npr.org/sections/13.7/2015/03/03/390349330/can-cities-change-earths-evolution (accessed 21 October 2018).

[58] Ibid.

[59] Adam Frank et al., 'Earth as a Hybrid Planet: The Anthropocene in an Evolutionary Astrobiological Context', *Anthropocene* 19:13 (2017), 13–21 (my emphasis).

greedy or evil but immature cosmic teenagers. Indeed, climate change is itself a hallmark of incipient maturity, our 'coming of age as a true planetary species'.[60] Rather than despair we should remember that 'we human beings have done some pretty awesome things'.[61]

Nuancing the narrative

In these accounts of the human species 'successfully' evolving climate change and the Anthropocene, we see a blend of naturalizing and normative/prescriptive narratives. Zev Trachtenberg, a philosopher who blogs about the Anthropocene, understands that naturalizing human niche construction raises a 'profound moral question':

> If it is 'only natural' for human beings to alter the landscape to suit their own standards of habitability – i.e., if in doing so they are doing what, in a sense, they cannot but do as natural beings – what is the basis for moral evaluation of their niche construction activities? If we don't blame beavers for making dams, even if the resulting ponds damage other creatures, how can we blame human beings for doing in essence the same thing, albeit at a wider scale?[62]

Trachtenberg finds NCT attractive in the prospect it offers for a naturalized morality. That is, he believes, the theory has the distinct virtue of bringing humans fully into nature by underscoring continuity between ourselves and all other living things. But if we wish to critique human activities that are transforming the planet and endangering other life forms – notably, climate change – then we must articulate a normative standard that requires humans (unlike beavers) to police behaviours that come 'naturally' to us. How and where do we locate this normative standard? And if we locate it, does it not simply reintroduce discontinuities and binaries between humans and nature? Trachtenberg holds out hope that, properly articulated, NCT can provide a naturalized ethic that nevertheless supports a critique of certain forms of niche construction as counter-adaptive.

An ethically nuanced and critical account, such as Trachtenberg seeks, may yet be developed. Such an account will need to be explicitly normative, rather than smuggling in normative and prescriptive assumptions under the pretence of doing objective science. For now, the problem remains that niche construction, as advanced by Laland, Ellis, Fuentes and others, denies such continuities but without articulating evaluative criteria

---

[60] Adam Frank, 'Climate Change and the Astrobiology of the Anthropocene', *13.7 Cosmos and Culture* (1 October 2016), https://www.npr.org/sections/13.7/2016/10/01/495437158/climate-change-and-the-astrobiology-of-the-anthropocene (accessed 21 October 2018).
[61] Frank, 'Climate Change Is Not Our Fault'.
[62] Zev Trachtenberg, 'Niche Construction', https://inhabitingtheanthropocene.com/2014/07/07/niche-construction/ (accessed 1 October 2018).

for good and bad forms of human niche construction. NCT, as articulated by these thinkers, fails to fully recognize our niche-constructing behaviours – arguably, the most prominent of such behaviours – as counter-adaptive. Moreover, the centrality of tools and technology, the metaphors of engineering and world-building that figure prominently in these narratives, lend support to grand techno-fixes like climate engineering as our next big innovation. If, for these theorists, none of humanity's current transformations of the planet – not climate change, not a sixth extinction – serve to overturn the verdict of humans' adaptive success, it is difficult to imagine what developments could. Perhaps nothing short of a precipitous decline in human population, and all the chaos and suffering that would entail, will register as indicators that our way of adapting is, in fact, maladaptive. Our non-human kin are already suffering this fate while we flatter ourselves with tales of our unrivalled power, our remarkable capacity to dream big, to engineer ourselves and our worlds, to 'beat everything else, ever'.

Much hinges on how the story of human evolution is told. It is easy to see why both scientists and theologians are attracted to the liberating storyline of the EES and niche construction. But the development of this evolutionary perspective in the direction of ethics and theology (implicit or otherwise) must be undertaken carefully, so as not to reproduce or exacerbate aspects of Christian theology that undermine environmental values, notably an inordinate preoccupation with human exceptionalism, anthropocentric manipulation and management of the natural world, and an overriding quest to transcend earthly limits. The insights of niche construction need not play into a progressive, all-too-liberating narrative of extraordinary humans and their adaptive success. As anthropologist Greg Downey astutely observes, niche construction can be read in precisely the opposite way, as 'draw[ing] attention *away* from progressive accounts of human evolution' that confidently assume 'our future will be determined by our intentions and aspirations, made manifest in technological advances'.[63] Many examples of niche construction illustrate that our innovations neither straightforwardly confer 'advancement' nor successfully enact our best intentions. Rather, they contain within them cultural processes that impact future evolution in deleterious ways, as with the endocrine disrupting properties of plastic waste. However, this may not be the story proponents of NCT are interested in telling. With their rehearsal of success stories of the past, present and near-term human future; with their reminders that humans maintain a robust presence, even now on our rapidly warming planet, these storytellers reassure us that salvation lies in doubling down on the behaviours that brought us to this perilous point.

---

[63] Downey, 'Plastics, Tiny Penises and Human Evolution' (my emphasis).

A response to Lisa Sideris

Vidyanand Nanjundiah[1]

'Working with evolutionary biologists' deals with implications sought to be drawn from niche construction theory.[2] The theory itself is an aspect of contemporary evolutionary thinking, situated by some within a larger body of ideas referred to as the Extended Evolutionary Synthesis (EES). The EES seeks to broaden the range of explanations for evolution provided for in the neo-Darwinian or modern synthesis.[3] Lisa Sideris urges caution on those who, drawing from niche construction, would seek to make value judgements. For example, people have sought to find support from niche construction theory for their view that 'evolution proceeds in purposive, progressive or providential ways'. Carrying on, they have inferred that humans have become caring and sustaining occupants of the biosphere. Is the inference valid? On the ground that human activities (presumably to be counted part of niche construction) rather obviously have also contributed to environmental damage, her answer is no. She points out that niche construction theory can be misused to reach two opposite conclusions. One can say that human benevolence towards the physical and biological environment is an expected outcome; one can also say that environmental damage and climate change are expected outcomes. That apart, 'niche construction – in various forms – is being taken up as a powerful new image of the human in an age of climate change and the Anthropocene'. The concept of niche

---

[1] Vidyanand Nanjundiah is Honorary Professor at the Centre for Human Genetics in Bangalore, India. After studying physics in St. Xavier's College, Bombay, and the University of Chicago, he worked on problems of developmental and evolutionary biology. Although not religious, he is intrigued by religious beliefs and practices as they appear from an evolutionary standpoint.

[2] It deals with other matters as well. Fortunately they do not appear to be central, because I am not competent to engage with them. I do not understand what 'convergence between evolutionary and Christian perspectives' might entail or how niche construction theory could be developed (as it is said to have been, by Celia Deane-Drummond) 'as a promising theological anthropology'. Similarly, it is not clear to me in what sense the EES can be said to exert a 'numinous appeal', except in a very personal sense, one that – by definition – is impossible to contest. My view on these matters is that natural science has nothing to say about religious belief other than to suggest plausible neurobiological, psychological, behavioural and sociological perspectives through which it might be viewed. See also note 10.

[3] The correct dating of the modern synthesis has been debated. It is convenient to locate it at 1942 because that was the year Julian Huxley's influential book *Evolution: The Modern Synthesis* was published. The 2010 MIT Press publication *Evolution – the Extended Synthesis*, Massimo Pigliucci and Gerd B. Müller (eds), plays an analogous role with regard to the EES.

construction has been put forward as a 'refreshing counter' to natural selection-based evolutionary explanations of psychology.

Sideris deserves thanks for drawing attention to the overblown rhetoric with which some supporters of niche construction theory seek to buttress its claims: always a sign that belief in a theory may be less than firm. At the same time, I wish an implicit message in her essay had been made explicitly: natural science cannot be used to support, or counter, value judgements based on ethical considerations. Similarly, the implications of a theory in natural science may console one, but that is irrelevant when it comes to assessing the theory's validity. Before analysing these and related statements, one needs to situate the idea of niche construction within the larger body of evolutionary theory.

The Darwin–Wallace theory of evolution by natural selection explains *why* it is that living forms appear to be the products of engineering design: that is, why they often possess features that are suited to the circumstances of their life.[4] The explanation rests on a set of testable assumptions. In brief, 'natural selection' is the term used to refer to a process whereby certain traits spread through a population over time. The traits are displayed by individuals, exhibit inter-individual differences and heritability,[5] and are correlated with differential reproductive success. As examples of relevant traits one can think of the ability to find and utilize resources, to convert food to useful energy, to evade predators, to build a nest, to find a mate, to raise offspring, etc. Evolution by natural selection will continue as long as heritable variation persists and is correlated with differential reproduction. The outcome of the process is that the traits in question become progressively better. Here 'better' implies continuous improvements in the means through which organisms engage with the world, improvements in an engineering sense. This consequence of natural selection, known as adaptation, makes them resemble the products of intelligent design.[6]

Where do genes come in? Genes are chemical molecules that are copied and the copies are (usually) passed on from generation to generation. Also, genes are essential participants in chemical processes that result in the synthesis of specific proteins – in the synthesis of the raw materials required for building bodies. Genes change on account of a variety of accidents (and today, can also be changed intentionally by human design). Accidents result from the inherently unpredictable ('stochastic') nature of molecular interactions; unforeseeable external causes such as radioactivity can also be a cause, as can the mobility exhibited by DNA sequences. Genetic differences translate

---

[4] The claim is that the theory does address the 'why' question.
[5] The traits themselves are not heritable, but the capacity to develop them is. Reproductive success is meant in a relative sense: living longer, or leaving behind more offspring, than the average member of the population. For a fuller account of evolutionary theory in general and natural selection in particular, see John Maynard Smith, *The Theory of Evolution* (Cambridge: Cambridge University Press, 1993).
[6] Relative to the chances of the average individual in the population, a well-adapted individual has a higher chance of leaving behind progeny that, in turn, possess a similar advantage. Lewontin defines adaptation as 'the manifest fit between organisms and their environment' and discusses the subtleties necessary in dealing with the concept. See Richard C. Lewontin, 'Adaptation', *Scientific American* (September 1978), 213–29.

into differences in proteins, which translate into differences in traits. For these reasons, natural selection can be thought of as the unfolding of a series of events that begins with random genetic change and through which, indirectly and gradually, the genetic composition of a population changes.

According to the standard picture, evolution by natural selection takes place in an external world – the environment – whose characteristics are either stable or change very slowly. The environment is in part physical (light, air, water), in part chemical (food, acidity) and in part biotic (predators, prey, members of the same species). Metaphorically speaking, the environment confronts organisms with the problem of coming to terms with it. Natural selection enables generations of descendants to approach, in incremental steps, ever closer to a solution to the problem. If a solution is actually reached, the organism has found its niche in the environment; it has found 'a comfortable or suitable position',[7] perhaps the most suitable position possible.

This line of reasoning implies that the environment, and so the niche, is something 'out there'. It is a given: quite distinct from the organisms and the problem solvers, as well as, to a good approximation, unchanged during the course of the evolving adaptation.[8] Niche construction theory holds that that is simply not true, at least not universally, and perhaps never. It asserts that organisms can have a hand in choosing, or constructing, the environments in which they live; they carve a niche for themselves. Beaver dams are much-cited examples, to which can be added bird nests and, in the case of humans, the myriad ways in which they try to modify environments for personal ends. In such situations, adaptation to the environment is no longer a puzzle, because the environment has been shaped by the organism so as to serve an adaptive role. Organisms and their environments co-evolve. No wonder, then, that adaptations are rife: organisms mould their own environments and carve niches for themselves. Niche construction must be distinguished from 'niche differentiation', the idea that a niche can be subdivided or partitioned into smaller niches, each occupied by individuals adapted to that sub-niche. For instance, a niche that is occupied by a 'generalist' species can also exhibit differentiation if several 'specialist' species are adapted to parts of it.

Two observations are in order. First, even though niche construction theory tends to be presented as an alternative to standard evolutionary thinking, the notion of niche construction is not opposed to natural selection.[9] On the contrary, it advances a

---

[7] The second definition is found in https://en.oxforddictionaries.com/definition/niche (accessed 16 October 2018).

[8] In mathematical language, this description of evolution by natural selection resembles approaching the solution of a boundary-value problem via successive approximations.

[9] The EES has many elements, niche construction being one of them. Some of the elements were known to the architects of the modern synthesis but their importance vis-à-vis natural selection was downplayed. See Veena Rao and Vidyanand Nanjundiah, 'Haldane's View of Natural Selection', *Journal of Genetics* 96:5

selectionist explanation, albeit one in which the environment is elevated from passive bystander to active participant. In fact, much before the expression 'niche construction' was coined, evolutionary biologists (including Darwin) had considered situations in which environments co-evolved with organisms. A classic example is the evolution of group behaviour: traits of one member impinge on those of others and each forms part of everyone else's environment. Second, all said and done, if there is a role for niche construction in evolution, it is in individual-level adaptation. As with any trait that evolves by natural selection, the ability to construct its own niche is a trait too. If it continues, the result is to make some individuals in a descendant population more successful at leaving behind offspring than others. The hypothesis of niche construction does not concern itself with whether different species end up living in peaceful coexistence, or one species eliminates the rest. We may consider one of the outcomes more desirable than the other, but our feelings cannot be used to pass judgement on an evolutionary theory. As a component of evolutionary thinking, niche construction has nothing to do with whether the relationship of humans to air, water, plant and animal life is that of nurturing caregivers or mindless despoilers. To be sure, there is an important concomitant of niche construction theory that standard natural selection lacks, namely an element of positive feedback. This is most obvious in the context of a biotic environment, because niche construction amounts to saying that the traits of an organism depend not only on its own genes but on the genes of the organisms with which it interacts and which, in turn, interact with it. Feedback would permit more rapid evolutionary change than possible in its absence.[10]

To conclude, the 'success' of human beings, as shown by 'growing numbers, ... extra-genetic transmission of culture, and the upscaling and intensification of our transformations', cannot be related to natural selection. Natural selection would apply only when one human enjoyed a net reproductive advantage *over another human being* on account of the possession of heritable traits. Time will show whether the EES will turn out to be a major extension of neo-Darwinian thinking, but there is no legitimate way in which it could 'give solace to creationists or proponents of intelligent design'. The worry is unwarranted even though that cannot prevent creationists or believers in intelligent design from insisting that it does provide them solace. Niche construction theory should be considered on its own terms, whether as part of standard evolutionary theory or of the EES. It constitutes no more than a component of naturalistic explanations of the living world; its validity has to be tested empirically, case by case. It has neither a 'darker side' nor a 'lighter side'. At a personal level, niche construction theory may offer 'a certain solace in this vision of humans as a resourceful species that has always, in one way or another, creatively responded to challenging conditions', not as 'trapped in the

---

(2017), 765–72. The hypothesis of niche construction can be discussed independently of other strands of the EES.

[10] See Vidyanand Nanjundiah and Santosh Sathe, 'Social Selection in the Cellular Slime Moulds', in *Dictyostelids*, Maria Romeralo et al. (eds) (Berlin: Springer-Verlag, 2013).

past by an outdated biological legacy';[11] once again, the sentiment is disconnected from the theory. Whether they accept the validity of niche construction theory or not, many evolutionary biologists do feel that 'reductive, gene-centred interpretations of evolution' oversimplify things. There may be Christians – biologists or otherwise – who resist such interpretations too. But the fact that they do is independent of whether the theory is valid or not.

---

[11] Kevin Laland, *Darwin's Unfinished Symphony: How Culture Made the Human Mind* (Princeton: Princeton University Press, 2017), 232 is cited by Sideris as the source. As Sideris aptly remarks, 'This portrait of the human as the niche-constructing species is often couched in hyperbolic, superlative language, and in tones that are congratulatory and even reverential.'

Chapter 1.3
Working with environmental economists

Annika Rieger[1] and Joerg Rieger[2]

Introduction

Awareness of environmental degradation, culminating in the broad global transformations of human-caused climate change, is no longer a peripheral issue. And while there may be some debate of climate change, a simple denial is no longer an option in light of the data and the agreement of 97 per cent of scientists.[3] In light of the sheer magnitude of the challenge, which has the potential to threaten human survival, much of what we know must be rethought, including traditional academic disciplines. In this essay, an environmental sociologist and a theologian enter into a conversation with environmental economists and others concerned about the relation of ecology, economics and religion for the sake of developing constructive proposals for the way forward.

While the role of economics in environmental degradation is hard to dispute, in this essay we will also take a look at the role of religion, with a particular concern for the role of Christianity. As historian Lynn White argued in his classic 1967 article in *Science*, Western Christianity in its Latin forms has been part of the problem, and so it will need to become part of the solution as well. According to White, Western Christianity is 'the

---

[1] Annika Rieger is currently a doctoral student in sociology at Boston College. Her research focuses on the intersections of economics and the environment, the impact of the international business climate on emissions, and the sustainability of traditional and alternative businesses types.
[2] Joerg Rieger is Distinguished Professor of Theology, Cal Turner Chancellor's Chair in Wesleyan Studies, and Founding Director of the Religion and Justice Program at Vanderbilt University. His work deals with matters of religion and power, related in particular to economics, drawing on a wide range of historical and contemporary traditions.
[3] In the confrontation of climate-change science and climate-change denial, we are not dealing with two ideas of equal value, not simply because of a lack of science on one side of the debate but also because of clear ideological commitments and disproportionate funding on the side of those who deny climate change. See the discussion of the problematic role of ideas in the debates around climate change in Laurel Kearns, 'Climate Change', in *Grounding Religion: A Field Guide to the Study of Religion and Ecology*, Whitney Bauman, Richard Bohannon and Kevin J. O'Brien (eds) (London: Routledge, 2nd edn, 2017), 141–6.

most anthropocentric religion the world has seen',[4] playing off humanity and the natural world and leading to the devaluation and destruction of the latter on a grand scale. White argues that this attitude has shaped Western culture to the core, influencing even modern science to such a degree that it cannot solve the problems by itself, and post-Christian Western culture continues to be shaped by this disregard for nature. Today, the denial of climate change might be considered a blatant example of such disregard, and religion has played a role in this denial as well.

In the past five decades, theologians have picked up White's call to reclaim alternative theological traditions in various ways. At the core of this call was developing a closer relationship between the Divine and nature, a matter that is more common in the history of Christianity than White realized and that today is widely emphasized in ecotheology circles.

Nevertheless, a great deal of work still needs to be done in regard to the economics of modern capitalism, an area of concern that White did not address. For White, there seems to be no qualitative difference between the economics of the early Middle Ages and later capitalist developments. Yet, as we will show, it makes a difference whether we define the current age as the 'Anthropocene' or as the 'Capitalocene'.

Moreover, bringing ecology and religion (or nature and God) closer together is one thing; what kinds of images of God are at work is another matter, especially when God is often envisioned in top-down and hierarchical ways that resemble not only the workings of medieval feudal systems but also neoliberal capitalism where winner takes all. The question thus is how ecology and religion are tied to capitalist economics, both for good and for ill, and what deeper encounters between these fields might accomplish as we address environmental degradation and climate change.

Classical positions in ecological social science and parallels in theology

Since religious and theological studies tend to employ the history of ideas even when engaging environmental and economic concerns, a closer look at social–scientific and economic paradigms is imperative before engaging in conversation. Most ecological social science work has been developed since the 1960s, and the two main theoretical paradigms arose in the 1980s: the treadmill of production (ToP)[5] and ecological modernization (EM).[6]

---

[4] Lynn White, Jr, 'The Historical Roots of Our Ecologic Crisis', *Science* 155:3767 (March 1967), 1203–7 (1205).

[5] Allan Schnaiberg, *The Environment: From Surplus to Scarcity* (New York: Oxford University Press, 1980).

[6] Udo Ernst Simonis, 'Ecological Modernization of Industrial Society: Three Strategic Elements', *International Social Science Journal* 121 (1989), 347–61; Gert Spaargarden and Arthur P. J. Mol, 'Sociology,

In both paradigms economics is the central concern, recognizing that the current capitalist economic system of production and consumption is the main contributor to environmental degradation, culminating in climate change. Similar to efforts that seek to bring together ecology and religion, environmental economists seek to bring together ecology and economics, based on the insight that economics which neglects ecology becomes destructive of it, just like religion that neglects ecology. Despite this agreement the two perspectives are often seen as polarizing and in conflict with one another, since EM sees the current economic system as salvageable with modifications, while ToP sees the current economic system as the unequivocal source of the problem and the solution its overthrow and replacement with a new system. Similar disagreements about the role of economics can be found in theological approaches dealing with the environment, as we shall see.

Ecological modernization theory argues that capitalism can become more 'green' and that societies can become more sustainable and reduce their environmental impact by utilizing the progress of technology, supported by pressure from interest groups that push corporations and dominant institutions to prioritize the environment. While the environment has been seen as an 'externality' in economics and has not been factored into accounting costs and benefits, giving ecological resources as well as degradation a monetary value factors them into business considerations.[7] Basically, EM theorists argue that rather than thinking of the environment as external to economic concerns, it should be brought into the equation and adequately accounted for. This process will force corporations to face the true costs of business and encourage them to invest in 'greening' their production. The political process is of special importance to this model because politics is seen as the institution that is most likely to be able to implement pressure and encourage changes towards sustainability.[8] Suggestions for policy are important to most EM studies, either to help mitigate current damage or to prevent future degradation.[9] Sustainability is important to the theory in both senses – EM asks how economic institutions can become environmentally sustainable in order for the institutions themselves to be sustainable and continue their existence.

Christian mainline opinions often fit with this approach, as they share the concern for continuing the existence of institutions as well as institutionalized ideas of God. This can be seen, for instance, in common efforts to divest endowments from funds linked to carbon emissions without challenging the capitalist logic of growth, often assumed to be sanctioned by God. Theological approaches that support capitalism, trying to make it

---

Environment, and Modernity: Ecological Modernization as a Theory of Social Change', *Society & Natural Resources* 5:4 (1992), 323–44.

[7] Spaargarden and Mol, 'Sociology, Environment, and Modernity', 334–6.
[8] Frederick H. Buttel, 'Ecological Modernization as Social Theory', *Geoforum* 31 (2000), 57–65.
[9] Spaargarden and Mol, 'Sociology, Environment, and Modernity', 338–41.

more just, can also be found in agreement with EM. Images of God in these approaches tend to envision God in terms of the sustainer and reformer of the status quo.[10]

The ToP theory, on the other hand, targets an institutional system that prioritizes economic growth encouraged by increasing industrialization, which results in environmentally detrimental outcomes.[11] The economic system in question, regarded as the root of environmental degradation, is capitalism, because it requires increasing levels of production and consumption of material goods to promote economic growth and ensure its continuing existence.[12] This is perhaps the most problematic aspect of capitalism: the system depends on growth, profits, innovation and investment, efficiency and constantly increasing industrial production.[13] Any progress – whether innovation or growth – is likely to increase resource extraction, hazardous waste, pollution and other forms of environmental degradation, culminating in climate change. ToP theorists argue that the continuation of a capitalist economy will only result in further environmental degradation and that a new economic order is necessary to end the cycle of environmental harm.[14] ToP presents an encompassing critique of the economic status quo, which makes solutions more difficult to identify but also opens up the possibility of cooperation with other social justice movements that present similar critiques and work towards shared goals. While this approach finds fewer parallels in Christian communities than EM, it finds kindred spirits in the work of many ecologically minded theologians who are engaging matters of economics.[15] These approaches tend to envision God as a fundamental challenge to the economic status quo and linked to emerging alternatives.

The ToP and EM theories have engaged in tennis-match-like critiques of one another. The originator of ToP, Allan Schnaiberg, is critical of ecological modernization's faith in the capitalist system he sees as the source of environmental destruction. He also challenges EM's main solution, the idea that technology is the key to environmental sustainability: no matter how much technology improves it will never be enough to assuage the constant production and consumption of capitalism.[16] Another common

---

[10] See, for instance, Brent Waters, *Just Capitalism: A Christian Ethic of Economic Globalization* (Louisville: Westminster John Knox, 2016).

[11] Allan Schnaiberg, 'Sustainable Development and the Treadmill of Production', in *The Politics of Sustainable Development: Theory, Policy and Practice within the European Union*, Susan Baker et al. (eds) (London: Routledge, 1997), 72–88 (75).

[12] Allan Schnaiberg, David N. Pellow and Adam Weinberg, 'The Treadmill of Production and the Environmental State', in *The Environmental State Under Pressure*, Arthur P. J. Mol and Frederick H. Buttel (eds) (London: JAI/Elsevier, 2000), 15–32.

[13] Schnaiberg, Pellow and Weinberg, 'The Treadmill of Production'.

[14] Richard York, 'The Treadmill of (Diversifying) Production', *Organization & Environment* 17:3 (2004), 355–62 (360).

[15] See, for instance, from a Christian perspective, John B. Cobb, Jr, and Herman E. Daly, *For the Common Good: Redirecting the Economy toward Community, the Environment, and a Sustainable Future* (Boston: Beacon Press, 2nd edn, 1994), and from a Buddhist perspective Ernst F. Schumacher, *Small is Beautiful: Economics as if People Mattered* (San Francisco: Harper&Row, 1973).

[16] Schnaiberg, 'Sustainable Development and the Treadmill of Production', 76–7.

critique of EM is that it cherry picks case studies,[17] usually selecting industries from Northern Europe that have implemented diverse technologies and instigated their own efforts at environmental protection. EM theorists acknowledge this focus, but they do not see it as a failing of their theory. They argue that the Netherlands and Germany, the countries from which most EM case studies are drawn, are simply the current countries that are best implementing the ideals of ecological modernization.[18] However, ToP theorists see this issue as a sign of a deeper flaw: they argue that EM theorists have failed to provide sufficient empirical support for their theory because their case studies are isolated and show no proof that modernization *as a whole* is encouraging sustainability at any level.[19] EM theorists defend their reliance on case studies as focusing on best practices and showing the potential ways in which capitalist industrialization can be environmentally beneficial.[20]

The defence that Mol and Spaargarden, the theorists best known for their contributions to EM, give for their theory is that the ToP is more concerned with 'academic debates' about 'philosophy' than the actual 'questions raised by activists and policy makers'.[21] They see ToP as having limited value because it cannot provide real-world solutions. This is a common critique of ToP.[22] The solutions that it does provide are seen as idealistic and utopian because they call for systemic change. EM theorists argue that their theory can provide practical and applicable solutions to environmental problems that utilize pre-existing tools such as development, modernization and innovation.[23] By focusing on reform rather than replacement, EM theorists argue that working within the economic system can solve the current environmental crisis.

Similar tensions between fundamental critiques of capitalism and efforts to ameliorate it can also be found in theological debates, even though the focus is typically more on intellectual disagreements than actual empirical studies. Still, the observation that climate change is not effectively addressed and may well spin out of control quicker than assumed is now also an important part of the debate.[24] The urgency of the situation does not allow any of the positions to claim victory in the debates at this time, pushing for a closer look at the problems and more creative reflections.

---

[17] Richard York and Eugene A. Rosa, 'Key Challenges to Ecological Modernization Theory', *Organization & Environment* 16:3 (2003), 273–88 (280–1).
[18] Spaargarden and Mol, 'Sociology, Environment, and Modernity', 324.
[19] York and Rosa, 'Key Challenges', 382.
[20] Buttel, 'Ecological Modernization as Social Theory', 39.
[21] Arthur P. J. Mol and Gert Spaargarden, 'Ecological Modernisation Theory in Debate: A Review', *Environmental Politics* 9:1 (2000), 17–49 (39).
[22] Buttel, 'Ecological Modernization as Social Theory', 60–1.
[23] Mol and Spaargarden, 'Ecological Modernisation Theory in Debate', 334–8.
[24] Kearns, 'Climate Change', 137–57.

The tension between production and consumption

The divergence between the theories of ToP and EM begins with what they identify as the source of environmental degradation and climate change, and whether more damage to the environment comes from the production or the consumption of material goods. At the heart of the debate are their opposing conclusions on the role of industrial capitalism as a solution or problem. For example, both theories have opposing views of the role of information and communication technologies (ICTs). The two theories interpret the effectiveness of a potential solution based on whether it can adequately tackle the problematic side of the production/consumption dynamic. For EM theorists who focus on consumption, ICTs are a good solution because they are easily consumed, promise increased efficiency and could potentially decrease the overall amount of material resources consumed.[25] ToP theorists focusing on production see ICTs as problematic because their implementation in industry increases efficiency, lowering the costs of production and ultimately increasing consumption and emissions.[26]

When theologians have engaged economic underpinnings of ecological destruction, consumption is often the primary target. Sallie McFague, for instance, has focused on consumerism, arguing that the problem is not a lack a love of nature (an earlier assumption of hers) but the temptations of consumption.[27] An argument that religious engagements of economics need to pay more attention to production – and that problems of consumption are linked to the demands of production (often mediated through the advertising industry) – was made by Rieger.[28] If consumerism is seen as closely related to the capitalist imperative to constantly increase production, a more profound analysis and critique of capitalism is required.

As the ICT example showed, the disagreement as to from which side of the production/consumption dynamic environmental degradation originates results in solutions targeting different sides of the dynamic. While EM theory recognizes that industrialization has created ecological problems, they see the further development of industry as the only path towards solving those problems.[29] This understanding of the problem encourages solutions that often focus on consumption: that is, the introduction of new technologies, changing consumer patterns to be more ecologically minded, and incorporating environmental and sustainability values into society. Innovation – in the form of new regulations, industrial processes, technologies and consumer demands, to

---

[25] Lorenz M. Hilty and Thomas F. Ruddy, 'Sustainable Development and ICT Interpreted in a Natural Science Context', *Information, Communication, and Society* 13:1 (2010), 7–22 (12–18).

[26] Kenneth A. Gould, David N. Pellow and Allan Schnaiberg, *The Treadmill of Production: Injustice and Unsustainability in the Global Economy* (Boulder: Paradigm, 2008), 101–4.

[27] Sallie McFague, *Life Abundant: Rethinking Theology and Economy for Planet in Peril* (Minneapolis: Fortress, 2001), xi, 33.

[28] Joerg Rieger, *No Rising Tide: Theology, Economics, and the Future* (Minneapolis: Fortress, 2009).

[29] York and Rosa, 'Key Challenges', 274.

name a few areas – is seen as our best hope for dealing with ecological degradation, and capitalism is seen as the economic system best suited to encourage these innovations.

One of the potential solutions often proffered by EM theorists is implementing technology in as many realms possible. ICTs, for instance, might have the potential to decouple consumption and material goods, given the correct incentives. This decoupling would allow for growth with limited environmental effects because consumption levels could remain stable but would require less material resources. The dematerialization of consumption would solve the 'sustainability dilemma': the paradox that arises when the adoption of the consumption levels of developed countries by 'developing' countries presents an irreconcilable ecological burden on the future.[30] If consumption were decoupled from material goods, 'developing' countries could adopt the consumption levels of 'developed' countries without burdening the environment. Even without the possibility of dematerialization, the implementation of technology to increase the efficiency of production would enable more goods to be produced with less resource and less waste.

ToP theorists see the suggestions offered by EM theorists as short-term solutions to a long-term problem, and this lack of long-term vision is rooted in EM as focusing on the wrong 'end' of the economic equation: consumption rather than production. ToP theorists focus on the production side of the dynamic because they argue that production is driven not by consumer demand but rather by the demands of capitalism.[31] Thus, the only way to stop environmentally harmful practices is to target the root of the problem – the capitalist production system. As such, most of the solutions that treadmill theorists offer can seem idealistic in that they call for sweeping economic reforms. However, these theorists see global social movements such as the Landless Movement, the World Social Forum and others as offering a chance to enact solutions. These social movements call for broad social change, especially economic change, and have been able to mobilize diverse groups of people, not only to call on institutions to enact these changes but also to start making small-scale changes to their own lives. One aspect of ICTs that ToP theorists do approve of is their ability to connect global communities and facilitate the growth of transnational social movements.[32] These groups coalesce around different social problems, but by mobilizing large groups of people they are able to wield bottom-up, democratic power. By calling for widespread social equality and disrupting business as usual, these movements are challenging the basis of the global capitalist ToP system that produces climate change.

In the field of academic theology, more profound critiques of capitalism and support for ToP's emphasis on social movements can be found in approaches belonging to the diverse family of liberation theologies. While liberation theologies have often

---

[30] Hilty and Ruddy, 'Sustainable Development', 8–12.
[31] Gould, Pellow and Schnaiberg, *The Treadmill of Production*, 19–24; in theology, a similar argument has been made by Rieger, *No Rising Tide*, Chapter 4.
[32] Gould, Pellow and Schnaiberg, *The Treadmill of Production*, Chapter 7.

been considered to be primarily concerned with human oppression and exploitation, broader awareness of the range of oppression and exploitation has long been part of the conversation, including matters of ecology. The work of Brazilian liberation theologians Leonardo Boff and Ivone Gebara may serve as examples.[33] The ecofeminist work of Gebara, in particular, is deeply connected to poor people's movements, especially the everyday experiences of women in the poorer neighbourhoods of Brazil, where she resides. In these theologies, images of God are located in the midst of the struggle, with the Divine not only inhabiting the world in general (as most ecological theologians agree) but at work in specific contexts, in solidarity with struggling humanity and the earth and movements for liberation.[34]

Where do we go from here: Ecological thinking and next steps

In more recent debates, the arguments of the two camps have sometimes been put in conversation. Some traits of ToP and EM are combined in the work of Juliet Schor and others who are working at the intersection of environmental sociology and economics. While Schor challenges consumerism (like EM), she is also attuned to the underlying economic challenges that come from business as usual (like ToP).

Charting a way forward, Schor and some of her collaborators suggest a new economic model that takes its cues from both emerging grass roots movements and ecological models. Here, ecological thinking is not subordinated to economic thinking but put in conversation with it. These approaches resonate with the work of theologian John Cobb and others who are adding theological reflection to the conversation. Cobb, for instance, is promoting images of God as caring for all creatures, suffering and rejoicing with them, and appreciating diversity.[35] Putting ecological, economic and theological conversations in conversation is particularly important in light of the fact that all of these factors have contributed to the problems leading to climate change – yet how might these various perspectives reshape each other?

Juliet Schor and Craig Thompson make the interesting observation that the fathers of neoliberal economics such as Friedrich von Hayek also draw on ecological models. In this case, a specific interpretation of biological evolution provides the basis for the

---

[33] Leonardo Boff, *Cry of the Earth, Cry of the Poor* (Maryknoll: Orbis, 1997); Ivone Gebara, *Longing for Running Water: Ecofeminism and Liberation* (Minneapolis: Fortress, 1999).

[34] Gebara, *Longing for Running Water*, 103–4, identifies God in terms of 'relatedness as a continual presence that is made explicitly in different ways in different beings', uniting immanence and transcendence (reference to Sallie McFague).

[35] John B. Cobb, 'Christianity, Economics, and Ecology', in *Christianity and Ecology*, Dieter T. Hessel and Rosemary Radford Ruether (eds) (Cambridge: Harvard, 2000), 497–511 (508).

neoliberal economic emphasis of competition as natural and necessary for flourishing. Here, the often-referenced principle of 'survival of the fittest' is taken to mean competition of all against all. In contrast, Schor and Thompson point out that more recent understandings of biological evolution have developed a sense of cooperation and symbiotic relationships.[36] This sort of cooperation does not diminish diversity but supports it, as it is built on various specializations and adaptations to harsh environments.

While this kind of ecological thinking can still bear some resemblances with neoliberal economic thinking – decentralized rather than centralized approaches, appreciation for markets rather than planned economies – it also defies neoliberal economics by redefining success and emphasizing interconnectedness rather than individualism. Markets, in the new paradigm, are not defined by individualized competition but by forms of cooperative networks that might be described as 'rhizomatic'. Schor and Thompson suggest the trope of the rhizome – complex root systems that spread and thrive underground and that are hard to uproot.[37] Some theologians have gone even further, arguing that humans need to understand themselves as inextricable parts of the ecology, 'becoming plant, animal, mineral',[38] because human bodies include all these realities at all times, whether we are aware of it or not. In this model, the Divine, finds its place within ecology as well, as part of the world rather than separate from it.

In these ecological models agency is found not in individuals (whether human or Divine) but in organized cooperatives that are interconnected, allowing for broader connections with other social networks that tie into social movements. Here, a different sort of bottom-up economy develops: the heart of ecological economics is not individual agency (with all the problems that this has created in the corporate system, where some individual actors are exponentially more powerful than others) but collective forms of agency that shape up in worker and consumer cooperatives, community-supported agriculture, communal networks and alternative communities.[39] This kind of agency goes easier on the planet and counteracts human-caused climate change, as its primary goal is not growth (and the maximization of profits) at all cost but 'a commitment to live within the limits of the biosphere'.[40] In parallel, theologians also have argued for broadened notions of agency that resist the modern capitalist ideal of the individual as the supreme agent. Bauman, for instance, talks about agency in relation to our 'biohistories', and, in a different vein, the collective agency of working people has also

---

[36] Juliet B. Schor and Craig J. Thompson, 'Introduction: Practicing Plenitude', in *Sustainable Lifestyles and the Quest for Plenitude: Case Studies of the New Economy*, Juliet B. Schor and Craig J. Thompson (eds) (New Haven: Yale University Press, 2014), 240–1.

[37] Thompson and Schor, 'Introduction', 245, with reference to Gilles Deleuze and Félix Guattari.

[38] Whitney A. Bauman, *Religion and Ecology: Developing a Planetary Ethic* (New York: Columbia Press, 2014), 155, also referencing Deleuze and Guattari.

[39] See the case studies in Schor and Thompson, *Sustainable Lifestyles*.

[40] Schor and Thompson, 'Introduction: Practicing Plenitude', 7.

been emphasized by theologians.[41] In the big picture, this emerging agency could be extended to non-human agency.

Another result of ecological economics is resistance to extreme inequalities by advocating shared ownership of economic and ecological means and shared productivity. At the core is a new productive base of the economy, composed of small-scale green enterprises, community trusts, local businesses and popular access to capital.[42] This brings together three concerns: production of wealth, restoration of ecosystems and local empowerment. According to Schor, the basic principles of the new economy are to work and spend less as well as to create and connect more – the latter being enhanced by new communication technologies (ICTs). In this context, Schor talks about 'true materialism', pushing beyond dominant materialisms that are interested in material things mostly for symbolic qualities.[43] True materialism is linked to providing opportunities for economically struggling communities. In theology, materialism is currently being reclaimed as well, based on an understanding that the Abrahamic religions share a strong concern for the flourishing of life on this earth.[44]

Diversity is a trademark of models that draw their cues from emergent ecological thinking, accounting for their resilience and adaptability as well as a different kind of efficiency. This diversity also undergirds a 'networked revolution' and 'deep solidarity' that was not yet part of earlier conversations.[45] The result is alternative economies and consumption patterns, embodied for instance in the parallels between consumer and worker co-ops. In this context, the economic concern for production and productivity is fundamentally transformed.

Journalist Naomi Klein has also argued for networks of resistance, drawing connections between seemingly disparate struggles because 'the logic that would cut pensions, food stamps, and health care before increasing taxes on the rich is the same logic that would blast the bedrock of the earth to get the last vapors of gas and the last drops of oil'.[46] This serves as another reminder of why economics is so crucial when discussing the large-scale ecological exploitation and climate change. While conservatives have long used economic arguments to stop climate action, Klein challenges progressives to

---

[41] Bauman, *Religion and Ecology*, 165. For the agency of working people see Joerg Rieger and Rosemarie Henkel-Rieger, *Unified We Are a Force: How Faith and Labor Can Overcome America's Inequalities* (St. Louis: Chalice Press, 2016), and Cobb and Daly, *For the Common Good*, 298–314.

[42] Schor and Thompson, 'Introduction: Practicing Plenitude', 8, referencing the work of Gar Alperovitz.

[43] Schor and Thompson, 'Introduction: Practicing Plenitude', 10, 13; see also Juliet Schor, *Plenitude: The New Economics of True Wealth* (New York: Penguin Press, 2010).

[44] See, for instance, Joerg Rieger and Edward Waggoner (eds), *Religious Experience and New Materialism: Movement Matters* (New York: Palgrave Macmillan, 2016).

[45] Schor and Thompson, 'Introduction: Practicing Plenitude', 22, networks were, for instance, not yet on the horizon in Schumacher's *Small is Beautiful*. For the term 'deep solidarity', see Rieger and Henkel-Rieger, *Unified We Are a Force*.

[46] Naomi Klein, *The Changes Everything: Capitalism vs. the Climate* (New York: Simon and Schuster, 2014), 61.

do the same. The climate crisis can be addressed by challenging economic exploitation by developing alternative models of strengthening the economy and building more equitable systems that empower the public square and generate better work and working conditions.[47]

The economic perspective also broadens our sense of the importance of the resistance that is building. Opposition to fracking or high-risk pipelines, for instance, is not merely a matter of environmental concern but also of participation in the decision-making process in both politics and economics.[48] This opposition is intersectional, interracial and intergenerational, uniting people at the local level as well as at the global. Like many progressive theologians of the present, Klein finds hope in social movements that address the unfinished business of the liberation movements of the past two centuries, noting that victories on the legal front were mostly lost on the economic front.[49] The good news is that the urgency of climate change can help us turn this around. In a reversal of the shock doctrine, the impending disasters add urgency and move us beyond ethics and morality as the primary motivation.[50] This matches some of the underlying sensitivities of liberation theologies, where God-talk is focused not so much on ethics and morality (a frequent misunderstanding) but on broader historical developments that lead to liberation and the energy and motivation that is found there.

Klein reminds us that solidarity is built into the resistance of climate change, because we are less isolated than a decade ago: social media, worker co-ops, farmer's markets and neighbourhood sharing banks.[51] A growing sense of solidarity is emerging in theology as well, pushing beyond forms of identity politics that kept progressives in silos.[52]

Conclusion

As we have seen in the fight against environmental degradation and climate change, there is a good deal of synergy between ecology, economics and theology – what has been part of the problem can become part of the solution. This is true both for economics and for theology.

In this context, theological approaches add a critique of economics that pushes beyond the approaches of environmental sociologists and economists discussed and

---

[47] Ibid., 125.
[48] Ibid., 295.
[49] Ibid., 458.
[50] See Naomi Klein, *The Shock Doctrine: The Rise of Disaster Capitalism* (New York: Metropolitan Books, 2007); Klein, *This Changes Everything*, 406, 417.
[51] Klein, *This Changes Everything*, 466.
[52] One example is the experience of the working group on class, religion and theology at the annual American Academy of Religion. This group has been heavily engaged in co-sponsoring sessions with groups that work on topics of race, ethnicity, gender and culture.

could be useful in further conversations with ecology. Parallel to White's critique of Christianity as disconnected from nature, there is broad agreement among all theorists discussed in this essay that economics is disconnected as well, both from nature and from people. As economist Robert Nelson has observed, the task of top economists is to keep the big ideas of neoliberalism before people rather than to perform empirical studies and to analyse data. In this way, it seems, economics comes to resemble a certain kind of religion that is also mostly about big ideas.[53] This kind of religion is also characteristic of much of North Atlantic Christianity, which may be the reason why neoliberal economics and conservative Christianity display certain affinities.

However, things do not need to be this way and alternatives exist: instead of relegating itself to the promotion of big ideas (that have too often not materialized), economics can be reconstructed from the ground up, in touch with the ecological, sociological and political dynamics described in this essay. The same is true for religion. Instead of relegating itself to the promotion of big ideas and problematic images of the Divine that continue to do tremendous damage (much resistance against climate science is currently supported by religion), religion can be and has been reconstructed from the ground up. Unexpected experiences of the Divine involved in the material world and in liberation communities – particularly in struggles for survival and flourishing – are motivating people not only to resist but also to develop alternatives.[54]

The theological battle is, thus, not merely about ideas and images of the Divine but about engagements with the Divine in places where life is promoted, be it in nature's resilience or in people's resistance and production of alternatives. The future engagement of climate change bears some promise when it moves from the realm of big ideas to actual struggles on the ground.

---

[53] Robert H. Nelson, *Economics as Religion: From Samuelson to Chicago and beyond* (University Park: Pennsylvania State University Press, 2001). See also the critique of economics in Rieger, *No Rising Tide*.

[54] For descriptions of economic alternatives developed in relation to religious communities see Rieger and Henkel-Rieger, *Unified We Are a Force*, and Joerg Rieger and Kwok Pui-lan, *Occupy Religion: Theology of the Multitude* (Lanham: Rowman & Littlefield, 2012).

A response to Annika and Joerg Rieger

Terra Schwerin Rowe[1]

A rising tide lifts all boats.

– attributed to President John F. Kennedy[2]

To stand nearly naked and heavy from winter on the water's edge, wade awkwardly into the shallows, dive under the first cold wave, taste first salt, surface and dive again to reach the calmer waters beyond, floating there until water and skin become the same temperature – this is the best way I know to belong again, body and soul, to some larger part of the planet.

– Kristin Dombek, 'Swimming against the Rising Tide'[3]

Annika and Joerg Rieger have offered us a gift in their essay on Christianity and ecological economics. I'd like to offer an expression of gratitude for this gift by extending some of their arguments and insights based on my experience and research.

Although I research and teach full time now, in 2014 I proposed and received grant funding to start a new trans-congregational, interfaith ministry.[4] We decided to call it the Hudson Valley Cooperative, intentionally employing the economic designator 'cooperative' to reference an alternative mode of economic relations instead of a more recognizably religious or traditional ministry term. The goal of the ministry was to address issues at the intersection of social, economic and ecological justice through trans-congregational and interfaith cooperative efforts. We decided to focus on food, faith and community building in our local Hudson Valley, New York neighbourhoods. While the particular shape of the ministry developed in conversation with many partners and participants, my initial desire to start such a ministry was a direct overflow of the

---

[1] Terra Schwerin Rowe is Assistant Professor at the University of North Texas, Philosophy and Religion Department, home to the journal *Environmental Ethics* and a leading PhD program in environmental philosophy. Her work focuses on critical and constructive approaches to the Protestant tradition from the perspective of environmental and feminist concerns.
[2] According to JFK's speech writer, though, he got it from the New England regional chamber of commerce. See Ted Sorensen, *Counselor: A Life at the Edge of History* (New York: HarperCollins, 2008), 140.
[3] Kristin Dombek, 'Swimming against the Rising Tide: Secular Climate-Change Activists Can Learn from Evangelical Christians', *New York Times,* 9 August 2014.
[4] Many thanks to the 'Sower's Project' of the Metro NY Synod (ELCA) for giving me the grant.

theological conclusions I was drawing while working on my book, *Toward a Better Worldliness: Economy, Ecology and the Protestant Tradition.*[5]

Kristin Dombek's 2014 Op Ed in the *New York Times* helped me articulate the kind of amorphous aims I wanted to address in the ministry and the book. Dombek attends to a key issue for us as we face the reality of climate change: How do we learn (again) that we belong, body and soul, to this planet? So much of the Western religions, philosophies and economics have trained us to believe and live as though we do not belong here, as if this were not our true home. Drawing on her ambiguous (and now disavowed) childhood faith in Evangelical Christianity, Dombek made, what seems to me, a remarkable observation about the Christian tradition and its relationship to environmental concerns. While Lynn White, Jr, and a host of others have rightfully emphasized the negative environmental impacts of the Christian tradition, Dombek highlighted its *affective* strength: it is a tradition, in her experience, that might teach people how to belong body and soul to something larger than themselves – to see themselves as a small piece of a larger, interconnected whole that requires our trust and calls forth our responsibility.

Yet, many of us in the West (especially the United States) have also been trained – at least affectively, at a gut-knowing kind of level, if not intellectually – to believe the article of faith expressed by JFK, that the rising tide of economic growth will eventually lift all boats. The relationship between Christianity and environmental issues has been severely complicated by the interconnection of the religion with neoliberal capitalism. This complexity is exacerbated to the point of crisis in the case of climate change.

Fuelling climate change

Theories of a resonance between capitalism and Christianity have an extended history.[6] Rather than competing with one another, these contrasting theories can be seen to create a multifaceted picture of the complex ways that Christian beliefs and values have often

---

[5] Terra Schwerin Rowe, *Toward a Better Worldliness: Ecology, Economy, and the Protestant Tradition* (Minneapolis: Fortress, 2017).

[6] Max Weber's is likely the most well-known argument connecting Protestantism and capitalism, but even his argument in 1905 was adding to an already existing debate. R. H. Tawney follows in Weber's trajectory. Responding to Lynn White, Jr, William Coleman turned attention to economics rather than technology while John Cobb and Hermann Daly along with Sallie McFague turned theological attention to these issues. Joerg Rieger also highlights early and important contributions from Latin American theologians and economists in *No Rising Tide: Theology, Economics, and the Future* (Minneapolis: Fortress, 2009). More recently, political theorist William Connolly has focused on the particularities of and resonance between American-style capitalism and American evangelicalism, while Indian novelist and essayist Amitav Ghosh has argued that our Protestant-influenced, rationalized, accounting, demystified modern bourgeoisie minds have been trained to exclude the impossible, the improbable and thus cannot think, cannot comprehend the realities of climate change in all of its probability defying realities.

unintentionally or unwittingly contributed to and supported capitalism. In light of the Riegers's well-placed emphasis on the value of growth and production as the most pernicious aspects of capitalism, none of the most well-known arguments seem to hit this particular nail on the head. As far as economic-growth-induced climate change is concerned, the key theological accelerant is not predestination (Weber), providence (Coleman), human anthropology and sin (Cobb and Daly), nor demystification / rationalization of the world (Weber and Ghosh) but the cherished and theologically central Christian doctrine of resurrection.

This connection is not well known so I will outline it briefly. Where economic growth functions by returns on investments, capitalism emerges as the ultimate expression of a Christian economy because it functions by a principle of resurrection: ideally every investment dies only to return – redeemed, resurrected as a capital gain. This, at least, is the insight Jacques Derrida and Georges Bataille arrive at in reading Hegel's symbolic economy in *The Phenomenology of the Spirit* – itself significantly influenced and inspired at the time by Adam Smith's recently released economic treatise.[7] My sense is that the appeal of a basic resonance between Christianity and capitalism on an affective, gut-knowing level is what inspired Hegel to amplify the gesture of growth-based capitalism in spite of his concerns with its social dynamics.[8] While we may grant that Hegel was not uncritical of the social effects of capitalism, what seems clear is that for Hegel both material and symbolic/religious economies ideally function 'by securing a return on every investment'.[9]

Where climate change, capitalism and Christianity have become so imbricated, as Annika and Joerg point out, it is not enough to simply bring ecology and religion or nature and God closer together. The task of critically re-examining our models of God – and especially our models of redemption – remains key. The crucial question now becomes, what kind of Christianity – what models of God and articulations of redemption – might swim counter to the rising sea levels of climate change rather than ride the rising tide of capitalism that falsely promises to raise all boats?

---

[7] Georges Bataille, *The Accursed Share: An Essay on General Economy, Vol. 1: Consumption*, trans. Robert Hurley (New York: Zone Books, 1991) and Jacques Derrida, 'From Restricted to General Economy: A Hegelianism without Reserve', in *Writing and Difference* (Chicago: University of Chicago Press, 1978), 251–77.

[8] See Andrew Buchwalter (ed.), *Hegel and Capitalism* (Albany: State University of New York Press, 2015).

[9] Mark C. Taylor, 'Capitalizing (on) Gifting', in *The Enigma of Gift and Sacrifice*, Edith Wyschogrod, Jean-Joseph Goux and Eric Boynton (eds) (New York: Fordham University Press, 2002), 50–74 (55). Taylor also notes here that Bataille and Derrida find 'in Hegelianism a transparent translation of the foundational principles of a capitalistic market economy'(53). Where Hegelianism seems compelled to account for every expenditure and ensure a return on every investment, Derrida notes that 'the force of this imperative: that there must be meaning, that nothing must be definitely lost in death'. See 'From Restricted to General Economy', 256–7. This argument connecting resurrection and capitalism is more fully articulated in Rowe, *Toward a 'Better Worldliness'*.

Swimming counter to a rising tide

> The future engagement of climate change bears some promise when it moves from the realm of big ideas to actual struggles on the ground.
>
> – Annika and Joerg Rieger

While it is tempting to look for anti-economic or anti-exchangist models of redemption to counter our growth-based models, this ultimately only undermines our ecological concerns. After all, the ecological systems that sustain life also function by human and other-than-human economies of exchange.[10] Gracefully, Christian faith does offer powerful alternative models of exchange. Building from the more radical interpretations of the *communicatio idiomatum* (the redemptive exchange of creaturely and divine attributes in Christ), soteriologically extended from Christ to the sacramental elements, to the believer, to the neighbour and finally to the world, this is what I have called 'communicating grace'. Here grace emerges as much as a table blessing (we 'say grace' after all) for all of us 'messmates' (Donna Haraway) as a mode of divine forgiveness of sins. Such a circulation of divine and creaturely gifts communicates a sense of belonging both to Christ and the world, enticing us to feel more profoundly that we belong to a vast ocean of interdependence – a communion that holds us up, that we come to trust and for which we become responsible.

Where competition remains the engine of Smith's growth-based economics, with communicating grace symbiosis becomes the key principle of exchange relations. Annika and Joerg helpfully point out that recent models of evolution emphasize cooperation and symbiosis rather than zero sum competition. This is significant since, along with Christian redemption, capitalism and Darwinian evolution are also mutually influential.[11] Often, neoliberal capitalists point to competition – supposedly the engine of the evolutionary process – as justification for capitalist competition. Therefore, counter-models of evolution, such as Lynn Margulis's symbiogenesis, offer disruptive models not only in biology but in economics as well. Since the primary goal of symbiotic economics is not growth but a 'commitment to live within the limits of the biosphere' (Klein), our socio-economic justice concerns and climate concerns are also inextricably, symbiotically interconnected.

Christians might add models of redemption to this list of interconnections. This is why I felt compelled to start a ministry like the Hudson Valley Cooperative. Here, symbiogenesis became our mode of ministry. Recognizing that food issues lay at the nexus of environmental (including climate change), economic and social justice concerns, we decided to reach out to a local historical community-supported agriculture (CSA; hey

---

[10] See Rowe, *Toward a Better Worldliness*.
[11] Adrian Desmond and James Moore, *Darwin: The Life of a Tormented Evolutionist* (New York: W.W. Norton & Company, 1991).

Phillies Bridge Farm!) and began to build relationships of trust and mutual benefits. We started with service events (mundanely sacramental things like hauling, weed pulling and egg gathering) concluding with picnics ('communion' for Christians) at the farm where we would share insights into the connections between farming/gardening and our spiritual lives. Soon the farm was supplying our meals with heaps of veggies and sun-warmed watermelon, then we were organizing family fun day fundraisers for the farm, and then we were writing grants together to supply free or highly subsidized CSA shares to families in the food desert neighbourhoods of our congregations and synagogues.

Living in the Capitalocene,[12] Christian communities must find ways to articulate and enact models of redemption as symbiotic and cooperative. In the face of climate change we must be clear about one thing – our interdependence might as easily be our undoing as our redemption. But the sacralization of our economic and ecological interdependence – a sanctification of the mutual interpenetration of our lives with those of others, a communication of self to other and other to self, in, with and through Christ – might just allow such vulnerability to become our redemption rather than our downfall.

---

[12] Donna Haraway, Andreas Malm and Jason Moore all started to use the term independently – and now collaboratively. See Donna Haraway, 'Anthropocene, Capitalocene, Plantationocene, Chthulucene: Making Kin', *Environmental Humanities* 6 (2015), 159–65.

Chapter 1.4
Working with politics

Willis Jenkins[1]

The United States as corrupting political context for Christian theology

Repudiation of the Paris Agreement by the US government has revealed a crisis within North Atlantic Christian theology. The US president's break with the Agreement did not itself cause this crisis but merely brought to light a theological fissure that made it possible. Over the past decade, US theological engagements with the politics of climate change have followed paths so divergent that it is no longer clear how they can all belong to the same confession of faith.

Sometimes it is the task of theology to explain a dogmatic unity that underlies and fosters different expressions of Christianity even amidst their political conflict. At other times it is the task of theology to intensify the dogmatic significance of political conflict, explaining the basic incompatibility of certain positions. In the United States, where white ethno-nationalism allies itself with extractivist energy politics and expresses Christianized contempt for the very idea of climate change, even amidst dwindling atmospheric space for the material effluent of our North Atlantic ways of life, it seems to me that theology's task in regard of climate change must take the latter form. Perhaps it is nearing time for the church catholic to explain why, at least for those living in high polluting societies, integrating climate-mediated relations into responsibilities of the faith has become a *status confessionis* – a matter on which the Christian faith stands or falls.

Of course, Christian faith requires no particular climate politics and is fully compatible with principled rejection of certain policy instruments, including the 2015 Paris Agreement. Christian faith does not stand or fall over endorsement of any one form of climate politics. It does, however, require bearing responsibility *in some way* for relations with others – neighbours, enemies and all creatures. It requires responsibility for the conditions of politics. Insofar as the relations involved in climate change mediate

---

[1] Willis Jenkins is Professor of Religious Studies at the University of Virginia (USA), a public university located on unceded Monacan territory in the Rivanna River watershed of the Chesapeake Bay bioregion. Trained in Christian theology, Jenkins works in religious ethics and environmental humanities.

life-jeopardizing harms, acknowledging participation in them – the condition for any politics – is prerequisite for Christians to live their faith into every part of their life. Failing to do so while political arrangements enlist residents of high-carbon societies into imposing the costs of their way of life on others would be theologically negligent. At the very least, moralizing political violence with Christian ideas should be excluded by the church catholic as a plausible theological option.

When so rudimentary an exclusion must be drawn, it signals that theology is in danger of being corrupted by its context. It is similar to holding that, while Christian faith does not stand or fall with one political form of responding to the needs of the vulnerable, faith does require working with politics in some way to affirm their belovedness in God. At any rate, the faith altogether rules out any theological moralization of political contempt for vulnerable persons. Needing to say such a thing signals that political relations are corrupting basic possibilities for theology. For example, any form of Christianity that explicitly allies itself with the politics of white supremacy ceases, in the regard of the church catholic, to hold a plausible theological claim to the body of faith. Nonetheless, theological communities have repeatedly had to clarify that incompatibility – as recently as 2017 in the United States.[2]

In fact, white nationalism seems entangled with the climate politics of US Christianity. Repudiation of the Paris Agreement was made possible by contempt for any talk of climate responsibility among a certain faction of American Christianity. US citizens who identify as white and Evangelical are significantly less likely than other demographics to show concern about climate change. Is it the whiteness, the US citizenship or the Evangelicalism that is more explanatory? That remains difficult for sociologists to prise apart, but whatever drives the entanglement, it helps explain the evident racial disparity in climate concern that runs through US churches: white Catholics are more sceptical than Latinx Catholics, white Protestants more sceptical than black Protestants. White US Evangelicals (WUSE) are the most sceptical demographic and it is a crucial shift within that constituency that seems to have given moral cover to the effort of the US government to turn away from international cooperation and to dismantle domestic climate policies. Whereas only a decade before WUSE leaders supported some action on climate change, by 2016 the WUSE faction had turned hostile towards *any* form of political attention to climate change and began enlisting theology to depict the very idea of climate relations as inimical to Christianity.

How can theology work with such politics? It would seem grossly insufficient to merely voice preference for a different climate policy because WUSE denialism runs deeper than policy differences; it nullifies membership in any *polis* that includes climate-mediated relations. Theology in this context must work instead to establish the conditions for politics, by clarifying what relations constitute the contemporary *polis*

---

[2] See The Boston Declaration, https://thebostondeclaration.com/ (accessed 10 April 2018), which was developed amidst relative silence from white US Evangelicals regarding the rise of white nationalism in the United States, including several instances of white terrorist violence.

and how they are theologically significant. If one faction of Christianity, in service to ethno-nationalist powers, refuses to acknowledge its enfleshment in life-jeopardizing relations, then it may be time to draw a rudimentary exclusion. Perhaps the church catholic will regard this faction as losing plausible claim to belong to the body of faith.

However, even those US theologians who recognize climate-mediated relations as part of their *polis* find themselves poorly disposed to truthfully articulate their theological significance due to corrupting features of the US political context. Those features are much more daunting than the obstructive denialism of one demographic. In fact, scapegoating WUSE denialism might conceal forms of political negligence running through North Atlantic Christianity, including those theologies in favour of a climate politics.

I therefore focus this essay on describing how US political conditions corrupt conditions for truthful political theology. In his *Perfect Moral Storm* Stephen Gardiner analyses three general features of climate change that lure interpreters towards 'moral corruption'. Among the political consequences of that corruption he lists distraction, hypocrisy, complacency, unreasonable doubt and false witness.[3] In this essay I explain how US political conditions intensify those features and add several more, which in aggregate make US political theologies – including 'progressive' and 'eco-justice' ones – extremely vulnerable to forms of moral corruption. In cumulative argument, Christian theology within the expanded *polis* made by North Atlantic atmospheric powers may be regarded by the global church as barely possible, and then only under narrow conditions set through confessional accountability and political solidarity – like passing through the eye of a needle.

Wickedness

Climate change is a 'wicked problem', in the sense that any way of organizing its complexity into a problem admissible of redress involves controversial interpretations. It is not the sort of problem that can be solved in ways either true or false; rather, human responses will be better or worse depending on the ideas and values that interpret it. Unavoidable controversies over interpretation do not imply empty relativism or allow anti-science constructivism; all ways of making sense of climate change (including denial of its existence) carry biophysical consequences, and some ways of making sense of climate change are better than others. 'Wickedness' here simply means that there will be argument over criteria of better and worse ways to respond, with accountability to reliable knowledge about biophysical consequences of their interpretations being one condition of meaningful argument.

---

[3] Stephen Gardiner, *A Perfect Moral Storm: The Ethical Tragedy of Climate Change* (New York: Oxford University Press, 2011), Chapter 9.

Responsibility for wicked problems is therefore vulnerable to certain weaknesses in political culture. Inability to assess the reliability of knowledges, impatience with complexity, distrust of other stakeholders, alienation from institutions of mutual governance, structural unfairness among groups of citizens, embittered factionalism – each of those weaknesses undermines the culture of argument needed to develop responsibility for a wicked problem. Each has become prevalent in US political culture and each threatens to erode theological capacities of US communities to helpfully contribute to interpreting wicked problems. One implication of wickedness: theologies that focus on establishing the general significance of the problem without descending to political interpretation of its particular relations may further weaken, rather than bolster, political capacities to respond well.[4]

Quotidian complicity

Because the energy and transportation infrastructure of most of the United States is so heavily invested in fossil-fuel energy, nearly everyone participates in the systemic production of a planetary problem, no matter their own intentions or desires. Causes of climate change emerge from everyday activities like cooking breakfast and lighting a classroom. Moreover, many of these everyday activities were never intrinsically wrong and would remain innocent if performed under different conditions; they are now caught up in wrong only because their aggregation with trillions of other acts contributes – in a non-linear way across vast scales of time and space – to cumulative dangers. Now, as US residents inherit a basic form of life entangled with an epoch-shaping predicament, almost no activity, however quotidian or innocent, escapes complicity with wrongdoing.

US residents who care about climate change and recognize the rudiments of its causes therefore seem to face dire political options. Extricating ourselves from the causes of anthropogenic climate change would effectively entail removing ourselves from material forms of shared relation – so alienating ourselves from the polity altogether. On the other hand, working to develop responsibility from within the polity seems to require indicting its structure of everyday life, which may imply judging the historical development of those conditions as a terrible mistake – perhaps on the order of founding a free nation in genocide and slavery and therefore requiring similar theological politics of dissent.[5]

Either way, facing climate change in the United States with a realistic appreciation of its causes seems to require seeing everyday activity as complicit with structural

---

[4] Willis Jenkins, *The Future of Ethics: Sustainability, Social Justice, and Religious Creativity* (Washington DC: Georgetown Press, 2013).
[5] Kevin J. O'Brien, *The Violence of Climate Change: Lessons of Resistance from Nonviolent Activists* (Washington DC: Georgetown Press, 2017).

violence.[6] Theological communities who already hold a negative view of US political history may incorporate climate complicity into their critique, but for communities with ambivalent or positive views of the material form of life in the United States, the incentive is high to elide the political challenge of climate change by presenting it in terms other than complicity, violence or structural evil.

Historical emissions

Precisely because of its historical investment in fossil energy, membership in US society creates high stakes for a thorny political question in global climate negotiations: whether and how past pollution creates present responsibilities. Anthropogenic climate change is dangerous now because the spike in fossil-fuel use from the beginning of the industrial era deposited a great stock of GHGs in the atmosphere. Even if few people in the first century of North Atlantic industrialism could have foreseen connections of fossil energy and planetary ecology, should not the present inhabitants of the countries most responsible for those emissions shoulder a proportionately greater share of the burdens for addressing climate change now?

Requiring polluters to pay the costs of harmful actions, even if unintentional, satisfies a basic intuition of fairness. While ignorance or innocent intention might reduce grounds for punitive consequences, those who cause bad consequences should generally take responsibility for them.[7] However, as one might expect, negotiators from the United States often reject that view of fairness for a much different one. Sometimes called the 'fair teamwork' approach, this view holds that everyone should bear equal burdens of participating in a solution. Since the United States is so heavily invested in fossil energy, its costs to draw down emissions are relatively higher than those of less industrialized societies; therefore, the United States should be compensated or otherwise induced to participate in mitigation.[8] On this view, historical investment in fossil fuels *reduces* burdens of responsibility.

The discourse of fair teamwork shapes a significant element of official US political resistance to any climate agreement. Legislators and administrators in the United States are acutely sensitive to any possibility that they might concede economic advantages to late-industrializing countries just because those countries did not get around to polluting sooner – although they seem correlatively dim about the implications of carbon-fuelled economic advantages for the relative unfairness of the United States' historic relations with 'less developed' countries.

---

[6] Cynthia Moe-Lobeda, *Resisting Structural Evil: Love as Ecological-Economic Vocation* (Minneapolis: Fortress, 2013).

[7] Henry Shue, 'Global Environment and International Inequality', *International Affairs* 75:3 (1999), 531–45.

[8] Eric Posner and Cass Sunstein, 'Climate Change Justice', *Georgetown Law Journal* 96 (2008), 1566–612.

Views about fair allocations of responsibility for climate change thus shape views about the moral significance of history. How should US theological communities regard material advantages gained through activities that at the time seemed acceptable but in hindsight seem disastrous? Is our inheritance of privilege sufficiently fair, or do we actually live in ways that have run up a massive ecological debt?

This feature of climate change thus opens onto analogous matters of reparative justice – and analogous asymmetries of moral sensitivity. While there is a strong case that the United States owes reparations for slavery to black Americans, white ears (which disproportionately appear on the heads of our political leaders) seem deaf to it. Refusing to account for history in matters of fairness permits white US citizens to regard as fair our general advantages over a group that was historically exploited in ways now regarded as paradigmatically unjust. Because it is difficult to think clearly about fairness from within relations shaped by histories of world-making injustice, US theological communities – especially white US theological communities – have an incentive to depoliticize history altogether.

Global asymmetry and non-accountability

North Atlantic incentives to avoid reckoning with historical emissions are exacerbated by perverse global asymmetries in the distribution of causes and consequences of climate change. Many of the societies most vulnerable to consequences of climate change have contributed the least to its causes, while the societies most responsible for it tend to be less vulnerable to its consequences. In general, the industrialized North Atlantic faces less severe threats and is more capable of adapting to them, while, in general, Global South societies face worse threats with less adaptive capacity for problems that, perversely, they did little to cause.

That asymmetry confounds climate politics because the interests of those most vulnerable to climate change do not align with the interests of those most responsible for its causes, and there are no effective institutions of accountability. It is important to note, however, that the asymmetry here does not map exactly onto the geopolitical bifurcation inherited from Kyoto (Annex 1 and non-Annex 1 countries). Seeing the political geography of climate change is, in fact, one of its difficulties. The economies of Brazil, India and China have become major emitters and no longer map onto North or South, while some of the largest historic emitters are corporate entities located outside the North Atlantic. Moreover, carbon-intensive lifestyles are pursued by an affluent elite within every country. Meanwhile, within the North Atlantic and especially within the United States there are significant populations of climate-vulnerable people, often living in geographies corresponding to political exclusion. So the asymmetry of causes and consequences that confounds climate politics runs along multiple axes and without strict regard for national borders.

Nonetheless, it is generally fair to say that the carbon-intensive ways of life of the North Atlantic are comparatively less vulnerable to their consequences and so generally misaligned with interest in actions to prevent dangerous climate change. The political misalignment incentivizes a particular form of environmental misperception: people living in the North Atlantic are encouraged to see differential climate vulnerabilities as tragic misfortune rather than political distribution. Especially as our regions take adaptive measures, it becomes easier to see impacts elsewhere as the result of natural vulnerabilities.

That concealment may be exacerbated by devolution of climate politics to regional scales. As federal US climate policy shifts from aspirational to antagonistic, many look to cities and regions to take responsibility. The scalar shift may intensify misperception in some ways, since local climate initiatives tend to focus more on adaptation than mitigation, on resilience rather than reduction. For example, as most of the $19 billion in New York City's climate plan is deployed to defend the city against rising sea levels, it will come to seem normal that storm waters stop against its elevated defences but engulf the coastal communities in the Global South – as if New York were located on higher ground. Local climate politics thus conspire to naturalize unequal vulnerabilities at the global scale, perversely multiplying North Atlantic advantages over the South. Indeed, structural advantage welcomes the sort of climate pragmatism that, by seeking local solutions, suppresses critical attention to global inequalities. Intensifying management of climate impacts thus 'launders inequality to the point of invisibility', writes legal scholar Jedediah Purdy, because it inscribes the advantages of the wealthy into landscapes subsequently read as natural.[9] Flooding in Dhaka will appear to New Yorkers as a 'natural disaster'.

The context of North Atlantic theological communities within the global relations of climate change thus incentivizes political actions that intensify global inequalities by prioritizing adaptation over mitigation, thus covering overall negligence with the appearance of responsible action while further concealing North Atlantic production of climate vulnerability.

Economic inequality

The issues of the preceding two sections, on historical emissions and geopolitical asymmetries of cause and effect, are often interpreted through views about wealth inequalities, which are themselves shaped by different background assessments of market capitalism and the world history it has shaped. While global wealth inequalities do not always align with historical emissions or with geopolitical distributions of causes

---

[9] Jedediah Purdy, *After Nature: A Politics for the Anthropocene* (Cambridge: Harvard University Press, 2015), 47–8.

and impacts – for quite poor people live in high emitting nations and quite wealthy in less industrialized countries – they do so regularly enough to influence interpretations of the relation between political economy and climate change.

Starkly differing views of global economic history create distrust among representatives from wealthier and poorer societies.[10] Wealthier societies have an incentive to view the economic history from which their advantage emerges as fair and indeed beneficial for all. Poorer societies, especially those which have been enmeshed in colonial and neocolonial relations with wealthier ones, are more likely to view the same economic history as structurally exploitative.

Insofar as entering global arguments over climate change involves encountering criticism of shared economic relations, many theological communities in the United States have an incentive to avoid climate arguments or to minimize the connection of climate change with an assessment of market capitalism, in order to continue regarding our own wealth as fairly obtained. If a political condition for the possibility of fair global arguments over climate change entails restructuring the background allocations of wealth currently undermining cooperation, then wealthy theological communities may prefer not to engage the issue at all, or to do so in ways that remain superficial to underlying political economy – symbolic installation of solar panels rather than economic restructuring. Meanwhile, US theologies aligned with the poor and the precarious may call for economic justice in ways that regard climate change as a secondary symptom of capitalism, with the effect of excusing themselves from political attention to climate-mediated relations and perhaps thereby contributing to unreasonable delay.

Settler colonialism

Perverse asymmetry in distributions of cause and effect are especially unjust in regard of Indigenous peoples, constituting a new wave of displacement brought about by atmospheric consequences of the settler ways of life that displaced them in the first place. Moreover, as Kyle Powys Whyte argues, the sensitivity of Indigenous peoples to climate impacts is often itself a product of settler colonialism, which immobilizes and contains Indigenous peoples in order to facilitate resource extraction, thereby undermining their long-held strategies for adapting to environmental change. So 'the settler colonial strategies that impede adaptation today are the ones that were originally designed to facilitate carbon-intensive economic activities'.[11]

---

[10] J. Timmons Roberts and Bradley Parks, *A Climate of Injustice: Global Inequality, North-South Politics, and Climate Policy* (Cambridge: MIT Press, 2006).

[11] Kyle Powys Whyte, 'Is It Colonial Déjà Vu? Indigenous Peoples and Climate Justice', in *Humanities for the Environment*, Joni Adamson and Michael Davis (eds) (New York: Routledge, 2018), 88–105 (102).

One reason why Indigenous peoples have been so politically engaged with climate change is that, insofar as their ways of life depend on ecological relations that are being stressed, they interpret anthropogenic climate change as a new chapter in the settler colonialism. Whereas their territories were previously appropriated by invasion and broken treaty, they are now taken through imposed environmental change – and sometimes by dominant-culture *remedies* for those changes. For example, Indigenous representatives may regard carbon trading schemes as devices that allow settler societies to continue violating Indigenous rights to subsistence, development and self-determination, while reproducing a settler political ecology that commodifies relations that should be held sacred.

Climate change thus puts new questions to the way of life developed by settler peoples in North America. Indeed, one explanation for climate denialism among WUSE may be their moral investment in the white settler project: perhaps they sense that the role of extractivist land politics in US nation-building must be protected from delegitimizing entanglements. Identification with settler colonialism may be less intense among other US Christianities, yet in most churches there remains a strong incentive to avoid remembering that their altars are built in places still claimed as territories of Indigenous peoples. The incentive to avoid letting climate politics put the political question of Indigenous sovereignty to them may impede non-Indigenous theologians who join Indigenous opposition to fossil energy (in new pipelines, for example) from understanding why the same Indigenous communities may also oppose instruments for managing climate change (like REDD+, for example).[12] Understanding the climate politics of Indigenous peoples would, for theology, require reckoning with Indigenous political theologians that insist on the territorial specificity of liberation.[13]

Future generations

The perverse asymmetry between causes, consequences and political agency appears in a different way across time: future generations are vulnerable to climate actions taken now, yet they have no political voice in the present generation, which finds itself with the prospect of steep costs to avoid harms to the future and no accountability to those most vulnerable to the decision. The present generation thus has an incentive to defer costly action to the silent future and continues to take the benefits of an energy policy

---

[12] REDD+ refers to the UNFCC initiative for 'Reducing Emissions from Deforestation and Degradation', first introduced in 2005 and renegotiated in 2015 ('+'). It is basically a way of integrating forest management in less-developed countries into global climate partnerships. Some Indigenous peoples object that it further erodes their sovereignty over territory and/or ecological relations.

[13] George E. Tinker, *American Indian Liberation: A Theology of Sovereignty* (Maryknoll: Orbis, 2008).

whose greatest costs will be borne by future generations.[14] Moreover, each generation rising into agency inherits this disincentive, perhaps along with rising cost of actions from the previous generation's deferral, thus iterating the problem over time.

The timescales involved in climate change strain the temporal imaginaries of democratic politics. What is dizzyingly fast in geological time appears so slow to election cycles that it hardly registers. While liturgical communities curate modalities of time that would seem to allow them to listen to the future and break out of short-term mindsets, the evidence that North Atlantic churches actually do so is disappointing.[15] For theological communities living in societies whose ways of life are organized to distribute their burdens to future generations, the incentive to think with the future or in any unconventional temporality (like that of the communion of saints) is actually low. Because North Atlantic economies are organized on expectations of steady GDP growth, they discount risks of climate disruption to future generations – and do so at rates set by current economic behaviour, which is unaccountable to the interests of future generations. Participants in those economies are therefore disciplined to think of their lives in financialized terms, including a certain kind of relation to the future.[16]

Politics as human exceptionalism

The perverse asymmetry between causes, consequences and political agency reproduces itself in still a different way across species. While as much as half of Earth's biodiversity may be at risk of extinction due to anthropogenic climate change, only one species has standing and voice in political arenas. The consequences of climate change threaten other species with diminishment and annihilation, consequently disrupting and disturbing biotic communities in unforeseen ways. Indeed, the current regime of life on Earth may be at risk, but Earth has no voice in US political processes.

Despite evidence that the ecological consequences restricting politics to humans seem disastrous, and despite the counterfactual existence of contemporary polities that recognize legal standing for forms of non-human life, the anthropocentric exclusion of politics is taken as such common sense in most North Atlantic political theologies that they can proceed with it as untroubled premise as to what constitutes a political domain. If 'nature has been the thing without politics', as Purdy puts it, then climate change presents a crisis.[17] In fact, argues Bruno Latour, the crisis is at once theological and the greatest geopolitical conflict of our time: responses to climate

---

[14] Gardiner, *A Perfect Moral Storm*, Chapter 5.
[15] Michael Northcott, *A Political Theology of Climate Change* (Grand Rapids: Eerdmans, 2013).
[16] Jenkins, *The Future of Ethics*, Chapter 7.
[17] Purdy, *After Nature*, 21.

change reveal a cosmological rift between those letting Gaia reshape the politics of belonging and those whose politics continues to construct 'human' belonging from silenced 'nature'.[18] The practical point for theological response to climate change – if politics happens only among humans, then accountability for climate-mediated harms to other forms of life will remain weakly optional and then, if considered at all – must be articulated within a political membership organized on the assumption that creation is politically silent.

Political myths of nature

Basic interpretative rules in modern North Atlantic worldviews seem challenged by climate change. No longer can nature appear as an inert stage for politics, a thing without politics itself, for now basic ecological conditions appear politically produced while Earth systems seem to become political actants. As the modern North Atlantic sense of 'nature' as antonym to 'culture' appears dysfunctional, it becomes more evident that making sense of climate change requires thinking without or beyond the inherited North Atlantic concepts. Seeing the way its complexity also frustrates received notions of responsibility and justice, political philosophers debate whether modern thought is competent to interpret climate change.[19]

There is reason to doubt, therefore, whether North Atlantic theological communities even have the concepts to say something politically truthful about climate change. In that case, the first work of climate politics must be cosmological repair. Michael Northcott holds something like this view, arguing that, because 'the foundational Enlightenment separation between nature and culture, and hence between natural history and the history of the earth, is the core conundrum of climate change', political communities heir to the Enlightenment will not be able form an adequate climate politics until the roots of their political cosmology are repaired.[20] Northcott thinks repair can be undertaken by North Atlantic theology working with premodern sources, but his argument implies that North Atlantic theologians may rather need to attend to political cosmologies operating without the North Atlantic nature/culture schema. Indigenous cosmovisions in which non-human persons make political claims would seem especially apt. In any case, non-Indigenous North Atlantic theological communities may not have anything to say about climate change until we are trained into the myths and virtues of a different way of life.

---

[18] Bruno Latour, *Facing Gaia: Eight Lectures on the Climactic Regime* (New York: Polity, 2017).
[19] Dale Jamieson, *Reason in a Dark Time* (New York: Oxford Press, 2014).
[20] Northcott, *A Political Theology of Climate Change*, 188.

Cynical deception

As if it were not already difficult enough to overcome all those impediments to climate politics, the US public in general and US Christian churches in particular have been the target of intentional disinformation campaigns. It is becoming clear that fossil-fuel companies have hidden information about climate change while funding efforts to sow confusion and undermine trust in climate science – all in order to reduce prospects for political action.[21] Here the fundamental mismatch between the fossil reserves owned by those companies and the atmospheric space remaining to humanity produces the most difficult asymmetry, driving a carbon politics that represents disaster to the current regime of life on Earth.

Fossil-fuel propaganda efforts include specific targeting of key Christian constituencies. After many Evangelical leaders signed a call to climate action in 2006, a well-funded campaign successfully split their alliance by narrating concern for climate change as part of an anti-Christian conspiracy. The ruse was shockingly successful as many WUSE leaders went silent on climate change. Meanwhile, a separate fossil-funded effort targets black churches through a programme that, among other things, organizes gospel music events that promote the benefits of cheap fossil energy to low-income communities and associate renewable energy with white elitism.[22]

Conclusion

Political conditions for interpreting climate change in the United States seem extraordinarily liable to corrupt theological witness. Where they do not lead theological communities to explicit denialism or confused silence, they tempt Christian political thought towards misdirected measures, symbolic gestures, unintentional complicity or incompetent interpretations. The inadequacy of US Christian responses to climate change illustrates the peril that climate change poses to the US way of life and to the association of US Christianity with that way of life.

It may therefore be nearing the time for the church catholic to make a rudimentary exclusion; it may be time to explain how central theological confessions of the Christian faith are at stake in the relations involved in climate change, such that those who repudiate or abandon those relations can no longer be regarded as having a plausible claim to the body of faith. Impetus for that move, however, must come from without, through discernment of the church beyond the North Atlantic. If and when it becomes time, there is a wide ecumenical witness to the confessional significance of the political

---

[21] Naomi Oreskes and Erik Conway, *Merchants of Doubt* (New York: Bloomsbury, 2011).
[22] Kenya Downs, 'The Koch Brothers Vs. God', *Grist* (14 March 2018), https://grist.org/article/koch-brothers-preached-the-fossil-fuel-gospel-in-virginia-then-black-churches-fought-back/ (accessed 10 April 2018).

relations involved in climate change, including major doctrinal statements from the first Global South pope of the Roman Catholic Church, the Eastern Orthodox Church, the World Council of Churches and the Evangelical Lausanne Movement, in addition to the witness of a number of North Atlantic prophets, the witness of Indigenous peoples (including some Christian Indigenous communities) and, for those with ears to hear, the witness of Earth.[23]

---

[23] I am indebted to Lucila Crena for helpful comments here.

A response to Willis Jenkins

Tinyiko Maluleke[1]

Turning and turning in the widening gyre
The falcon cannot hear the falconer;
Things fall apart; the centre cannot hold;
Mere anarchy is loosed upon the world.

– William Butler Yeats[2]

Before things fall apart, come let us search of an ecologically responsible theology

When my dog Bruno died in February 2015, my sense of loss was so unbearable[3] that I wrote an opinion piece about it. Writing about my loss became an important outlet for my raw emotions at the time. Through it, I was able to voice my disappointment with and disapproval of former South African president Jacob Zuma's exclusionary anthropocentric politics. In December 2012, Zuma delivered a wide-ranging speech on the need for building a caring society and for 'decolonizing' the African mind. In the speech, among other things, Zuma controversially advised the nation 'not to elevate our love for our animals above our love for other human beings'.[4]

Ordinarily, one would assume that the construction of a caring society necessarily includes care for the environment and for creatures other than humankind. However, in the banal and race-laden political battles of South Africa, even animals have been assigned sides. One commonly held stereotype, in that regard, is that black people love

---

[1] Tinyiko Maluleke is Professor of Theology, Senior Research Fellow and Deputy Director of the University of Pretoria's Centre for the Advancement of Scholarship. His expertise lies in the intersection of politics, religion and culture. He has been involved in University executive management and is a prominent public intellectual who has written many opinion pieces in the mainstream media.

[2] These are the first four lines of William Butler Yeats's 1921 poem 'The Second Coming', included in William Butler Yeats, *Michael Robartes and the Dancer* (1921), now available on Kindle Books.

[3] Tinyiko Maluleke, 'I Am African and I Mourn for My Dog Bruno' (6 March 2015), https://mg.co.za/article/2015-03-06-i-am-an-african-and-i-grieve-for-my-dog-bruno (accessed 8 January 2019).

[4] Quoted in Ibid.

humans more than they love animals while white people are supposed to love animals more than they love humans. Therein lay the sting of Jacob Zuma's project for a caring society and a decolonized African mind. It seems that according to Zuma, a caring society is one that excludes animals from the realm of human affection, so that affection can only be expressed between and among humans. Though Zuma may have taken the point to the extreme in his 2012 speech, he is not an exception. His view is reflective of the prevailing views among his compatriots. Therein lay my real disappointment – not only and not merely with Zuma and his utterances.

While the Apartheid regime valorized the lives of white people, it seems that the post-Apartheid ANC government has been looking for ways of redress through policies and rhetoric designed to demonstrate the worth of the lives of black people. Both approaches are essentially anthropocentric. They envisage a humans-first-other-life-forms-later hierarchy. Given the 350 years of colonial and Apartheid history, it is at one level understandable that South African politics – like similar nation-state politics – have been and remain human-centred.

Accordingly, the preamble to our constitution seems to place human beings at the centre while the country as such is framed in terms of its human ownership:

> We, the people of South Africa,
> Recognise the injustices of our past;
> Honour those who suffered for justice and freedom in our land;
> Respect those who have worked to build and develop our country; and
> Believe that South Africa belongs to all who live in it, united in our diversity.[5]

For many South Africans, the crucial political questions pertain to the reparation and enhancement of race relations. Though more famous for its Apartheid policies of racial segregation, South Africa has the distinction of hosting one of the world's oldest race relations institutions, the South African Institute for Race Relations, now nearly ninety years old. Such has been the importance of race and social engineering in South Africa that the issues of human relations have long preoccupied both politicians and theologians.

Ironically, the scars and festering wounds of slavery, colonialism and Apartheid are evident not only on the lives of human beings but also on other animals. Our landscape itself has been variously and indelibly marked by the effects of slavery, colonialism and Apartheid. For instance, the discovery of gold in Johannesburg 130 years ago has affected the terrain, landscape and the entire ecosystem of the area. Evidently, human beings were not the only victims of colonialism and its 'civilizing' agenda,[6] but the rivers, mountains, forests and animals were equally affected.

---

[5] Preamble to the South African Constitution.
[6] See Patrick Harries, *Butterflies and Barbarians: Swiss Missionaries and Systems of Knowledge in South-East Africa* (Oxford: James Currey, 2007).

The Apartheid system separated people through forced removals such as when black people were forcibly removed from Sophiatown.[7] Similarly, in order to create homelands for various black ethnic groups and in order to rid whites-only areas of all 'black spots', people had to be moved from one area to another, often with devastating ecological consequences. We often neglect the impact of such contrived human influxes on new environments and on animals – domestic and non-domestic – alike.

More than 130 later, the discovery of gold in Johannesburg and of diamonds in Kimberley, combined with the migratory labour system has not just strained human relations but also has had disastrous environmental impacts ranging from polluted drinking water to periodic earth tremors. The primary commitment of Dutch and British settlers was to serve the interests of their colonial principals back home. Who would represent the interests of the marine life in the two oceans wrapped around South Africa's coastline? Who would care for the seas? The National Party looked after the interests of the Afrikaners. Who would look after the interests of the lakes and the rivers? From the time of its establishment 107 years ago, the African National Congress sought to defend the rights of the marginalized and the disenfranchised African majority. But who would defend the elephants, the dogs and the rhinos? Even when animals[8] were brought into the equation, it would be on human terms or they would be collateral in the war between and among humans.[9]

On closer scrutiny, there is evidence to suggest that the humans in question on both sides are heterosexual males. Neither the liberation movements nor the Apartheid regime considered women as full humans alongside men.[10] The intersection between ecological justice and gender justice has been lost to many theologians and politicians. Except in the negative, pejorative and condescending sense in terms of which countries and territories are routinely feminized into 'virgins' to be 'conquered'.

Whereas Apartheid society was characterized by racial hierarchies with ecological issues as distant appendages, few metaphors have seized the post-Apartheid era more than those of reconciliation and forgiveness. Inspired by the example of Chilean Truth and Reconciliation Commission of the early 1990s, South Africa established a similar commission chaired by Archbishop Desmond Tutu.[11]

---

[7] Bloke Modisane, *Blame Me on History* (Johannesburg: Jonathan Ball, 1987).

[8] Terence Ranger, *Voices from the Rocks: Nature, Culture and History in the Matopos Hills of Zimbabwe* (Oxford: James Curry, 1999).

[9] Jane Carruthers, *The Kruger National Park: A Social Political History* (Pietermaritzburg: UKZN Press, 1995).

[10] Tinyiko Maluleke, 'Of Wounded Killers and "Failed Men": Broadening the Search for Liberating African Masculinities', *Journal of Gender and Religion in Africa* 24:1 (2018), 33–78. See also Mmatshilo Motsei, *The Kanga and the Kangaroo Court: Reflections on the Jacob Zuma Rape Trial* (Johannesburg: Jacana, 2007).

[11] See Tinyiko Maluleke, 'Truth, National Unity and Reconciliation in South Africa', *Missionalia* 25:1 (1997), 59–86.

The model was premised on the assumption that individual truth-telling and disclosure would lead not only to the healing of individuals but also to national healing and national forgiveness. The jury is still out as to whether these lofty goals have been reached.[12] Even so, the South African reconciliation project is only one of a series of anthropocentric interventions – social, political and economic – aimed at 'building a new nation'.

The notions of 'rainbow nation' and 'transformation' are significant for the envisaged national ideal. Theologically speaking, reconciliation, when viewed from a biblical perspective, particularly, has cosmic implications. After all, has creation not been groaning in anticipation of God's intervention (see Rom. 8.22)? Do the heavens not declare the glory of God? Do the skies not proclaim the work of his hands (Ps. 19.1-2)? And yet, in the two and half decades of South African quarrels, experiments and reflections about reconciliation and transformation, the Earth has been conspicuous by its omission from the debates. Even significant theological publications from South Africa, such as the otherwise groundbreaking book by David Bosch,[13] seem to have had a blind spot when it comes to ecological perspectives. In this book, as in several others of comparable stature, there is little awareness of the global ecological disaster that often went hand in hand with the discharging of the 'white man's burden' as it related to mission and evangelization,[14] which sometimes included large-scale reforestation projects and the reorientation of human relations with and perceptions of nature. African theologies of liberation have equally not managed to emerge from their anthropocentric cocoons.

A few theologians, such as Ernst Conradie, have focused on Christian ecotheology for a sustained period. Laurenti Magesa[15] has convincingly argued that in African religion, almost everything – animate and inanimate – is sacred. Itumeleng Mosala sought to extend the notion of reconciliation so that it includes more than humans when he wrote:

> Reconciliation must have something to do with the reversal of our alienation; and our alienation is not from white people first and foremost; our alienation is from our land, our cattle, our labour which is objectified in industrial machine.[16]

Similarly, Marthinus Daneel has tracked the earthkeeping traditions and practices of some Zimbabwean Independent Churches.[17] Several problems are discernible even in the works of those who have consciously delved into ecological issues. The approaches either tend to be parallel to political theologies and theologies of liberation or attempt

---

[12] See, Tinyiko Maluleke, 'Perhaps We Are Too Ready to Forgive', https://mg.co.za/article/2015-02-05-perhaps-we-are-too-ready-to-forgive (accessed 11 January 2019).

[13] David Bosch, *Transforming Mission: Paradigm Shifts in Theology of Mission* (Maryknoll: Orbis, 1991).

[14] See Harries, *Barbarians and Butterflies*.

[15] Laurenti Magesa, *What is Not Sacred?: African Spirituality* (Maryknoll: Orbis, 2013).

[16] Itumeleng Mosala, 'The Meaning of Reconciliation: A Black Perspective', *Journal of Theology for Southern Africa* 59 (1987), 19–25.

[17] Marthinus Daneel, *African Earthkeepers,* vols. 1 and 2 (Maryknoll: Orbis, 2001).

to replace them. Theologians need to find the connections between Christian mission theologies and ecology, and between political theologies and ecology. Furthermore, theologians who delve into ecological issues should seek kindred spirits among the likes of Mosala, Magesa and several African (eco)feminists. Instead, many ecotheologians located in Africa tend to seek dialogue partners from Europe and North America, almost exclusively. In this regard, Jenkins is correct to call for Christian theology to come to a 'reckoning with Indigenous political theologians'.

What Willis Jenkins's essay amply demonstrates, is how inhibitive the Euro-American political space is for ecologically responsible theology to flourish.

Engaging Jenkins

Without airbrushing the fissures between and within various South African theological orientations, I have argued that most of them tend to negate the plight of the Earth as a legitimate theological quest. In this context, theological contempt for climate change manifests through silence and exclusion rather than overt theological polemics of the kind that Jenkins accuses of propping up 'extractivist energy politics' in the United States.

Contextual and liberationist South African theology declared a *kairos* moment to deal with Apartheid policies through the declaration of Apartheid as a heresy and the publication of the Kairos Document in 1986. The latter had great impact within South Africa and beyond. By way of contrast, the 2009 South African Council of Churches' document on climate change, which aligned itself with a climate *kairos*, did not have nearly the same impact.[18] Nor did it mobilize the same levels of participation from the theological community. This is, in part, because theologians and politicians have yet to break the code that links South Africa's most 'wicked problems' to the ecological crisis.

South Africa's 'wicked problems' are well known. They include inequality, unemployment, poverty, a comatose economy and a dire lack of social cohesion. What we seem to have failed to do is to make the connections between these challenges and the current looming ecological disaster. As a result, the thought of a *status confessionis* around theological recalcitrance vis-à-vis climate change seems far-fetched in our context. Jenkins repeatedly calls for the 'church catholic' to consider excluding those theological actors who are either sceptical or contemptuous of the climate crisis we face and to declare them strangers to the faith community. In this way he emphasizes the critical stage in which the Earth is at this point in time.

In our context, the reticence towards environmental degradation is not so much scepticism about the science of climate change or disdain for ecological issues. It is

---

[18] See South African Council of Churches, *Climate Change – A Challenge to the Churches in South Africa* (Marshalltown: SACC, 2009).

rather the lack of discernment which prevents African theological communities from cross-referencing and seeing the connectedness between the challenges faced by the Earth and the well-known wicked problems of our time.

Jenkins correctly notes that quotidian complicity aggravates climate change through routine, yet indispensable, acts such as cooking and travelling. Closely linked to this point is the burden of history and how we are all entangled in the effects of the atmospheric and ecological actions of previous generations. A point which Jenkins almost makes, but not quite, is that the pervasive nature of climate change means it cannot be tackled at nation state or even regional block levels, for reasons which Jenkins articulates rather well.

The point Jenkins makes about the need for ecotheologians to operate on a transfigured time scale is important. Theologians not only need to see the connections between ecology and their current theological agendas but also need to work to the rhythm of a different time scale than the five-, ten- or fifteen-year plans of conventional politics. The harming of ecological biodiversity takes longer than the term of a president. Sometimes the full ecological impact is felt a century later. To conclude his essay, Jenkins calls for 'cosmological repair' aimed at helping us to unlearn some of the ecologically disastrous consequences of the Enlightenment. Once again he recommends engagement with 'premodern sources' or what he calls 'Indigenous cosmovisions' so as to access 'myths and virtues of a different way of life'. Jenkins locates the ecological myopia or ecological blindness of our times in the realm of epistemology and cognition, hence his call for transcending the Enlightenment framework by reconnecting with Indigenous worldviews.

My sense is that we need to do more than merely refresh and revise the dominant but culpable Euro-American intellectual and theological traditions. In fact, one of the first things we must abandon is the idea that all we need to do is to access 'premodern sources' and 'Indigenous cosmovisions'. Until we valorize the humanity of the bearers of these 'cosmovisions' as well as their past and present experiences, it will be neither sufficient nor possible to artificially access Indigenous knowledge and worldviews. Even if it were possible to access these cosmovisions, to do so without dealing with the reality of the knowledge bearers' inherited and contemporary suffering at the hands of political, academic and commercial merchants of (white) human superiority would be farcical. The South African Department of Science and Technology has established and advocated a knowledge domain called the Indigenous Knowledge Systems (IKS). But can the IKS of despised Indigenous communities, that remain marginalized, be sustainably appreciated?

If Jenkins's 'cosmological repair' project is to stand a chance of succeeding, it must begin with a reparation project for the humanity of those whose intrinsic worth was questioned alongside that of the fauna and flora – the people whom 'science' relegated to the realm of 'things'. Latin American liberation theology was on the right path when it identified the 'non-human' as its primary interlocutor, in place of white middle-class males. Unfortunately, even liberation theology seems to have failed to include the environment and the Earth among the oppressed. The acts that enslaved and colonized people are the same acts that have brought the Earth to the point of ecological implosion. The challenge we face is therefore primarily one of integration. We need to stop excluding the Earth from our discussions of forgiveness, reconciliation and transformation, and from the ranks of the oppressed, marginalized and vulnerable.

Concluding thoughts

I began this essay by referencing my opinion piece about the death of my dog Bruno. Towards the end of the opinion piece, I referred to the famous verse, 'for God so loved the world' (John 3.16). It seems to me that there is nothing exclusively anthropocentric about God's love. If God loves the world, then Jesus Christ did not die for human beings alone or a section thereof. He died for the entire world, which God so loves. In light of this, I suggested that when Jesus comes again, my dog Bruno and I will dance with him. My inspiration for this seemingly outrageous claim was a popular Xitsonga language call-and-response chorus we sing in South African churches. The chorus paints a picture of people dancing with Jesus on occasion of his arrival at the Second Coming:

Call: *Siku rin'wana Hosi Yesu u ta vuya.* (One day, the Lord Jesus will come again.)
Response: *Siku rin'wana Hosi Yesu u ta vuya.*
Call: *Hina hi ta cina-cina, hi ta cina-cina na Yesu.* (And we shall dance, and dance with Jesus.)
Response: *Hina hi ta cina-cina, hi ta cina-cina na Yesu.*

Assuming that the Second Coming has environmental and ecological consequences, I couldn't bear the thought of excluding my beloved dog, in the anticipated dance with Jesus.

And yet I fear that the spectre of chaos and confusion that came to Europe in the aftermath of the First World War, which was so eloquently captured by William Butler Yeats in 'The Second Coming', may come to pass yet again, though this time with planetary consequences.

Ironically, Yeats's lines, 'things fall apart; the centre cannot hold; mere anarchy is loosed upon the world', inspired Africa's second English novel, Chinua Achebe's *Things Fall Apart*[19] – a novel that speaks to the chaos visited upon Africa in the wake of colonialism. If slavery, colonialism and the two world wars occasioned 'things fall apart' moments for human beings, indications are that the ecological disaster which human beings are driving is threatening the Earth with utter extinction. There may be no dancing when Jesus returns, after all. Instead, his Second Coming may signal the end.

---

[19] Chinua Achebe, *Things Fall Apart* (London: Heinemann, 1958).

Chapter 1.5
Working with climate engineers

Forrest Clingerman[1]

Climate engineering[2] and Christian theology after Paris

If it is true that 'climate change changes theology',[3] then it might be time for a 'theology after Paris'. In 2015 the Paris Agreement clarified the international response to greenhouse gas emissions and anthropogenic climate change. One of its most important objectives is '[h]olding the increase in the global average temperature to well below 2°C above pre-industrial levels and pursuing efforts to limit the temperature increase to 1.5°C above pre-industrial levels, recognizing that this would significantly reduce the risks and impacts of climate change'.[4] Increasingly, researchers wonder whether this is possible without research into and implementation of climate engineering, the deliberate manipulation of Earth systems to limit anthropogenic climate change. Should humanity domesticate the climate, moving from the image of God to 'playing God'?

This essay starts with the claim that climate engineering and Christian climate theologies must be in conversation with one another. One task in this conversation is to show how theology impacts societal understanding of climate engineering. As Kevin O'Brien and I suggest, theologians should explain to the scientific community how religion provides meaning to many; how religion challenges or builds up scientific authority; how religion offers narratives and symbols for understanding; and how religion provides useful

---

[1] Forrest Clingerman is Professor of Religion and Philosophy at Ohio Northern University (Ohio, USA), a United Methodist institution. Indebted to the continental philosophical tradition, he teaches and researches environmental theology and philosophy from a Protestant background.
[2] Among scientific researchers and policy analysts there is discussion over the most appropriate term to use: climate engineering, geoengineering or climate intervention. The present essay will use these terms interchangeably.
[3] Sigurd Bergmann, 'Climate Change Changes Religion: Space, Spirit, Ritual, Technology – Through a Theological Lens', *Studia Theologica* 63 (2009), 98–118.
[4] United Nations, *Paris Agreement* (2015), 3. https://unfccc.int/sites/default/files/english_paris_agreement.pdf (accessed 26 May 2018).

moral tools to aid our public deliberation.[5] The present essay suggests the other side of the conversation: climate engineering research should impact theology and the self-understanding of Christian communities. To put this more strongly, Christian climate theologies cannot avoid, ignore or misrepresent the different forms of geoengineering but instead must seek dialogue with the scientific community in order to understand the challenges and possibilities that the idea of climate engineering represents. I first provide a description of climate engineering, noting a few theological questions that arise. Second, I uncover why theology is open to a range of possible interpretations of climate engineering. Finally, I illustrate a theological case study – reconciliation, sin and justice – that shows how climate engineering complicates theological reflection.

What does it mean to engineer the climate?
Defining climate engineering

The Paris targets require more than small efforts at emissions reductions. For instance, in the heavily publicized IPCC Special Report on meeting the 1.5°C target, some form of climate engineering has a role in at least three of the four pathways studied.[6] But what is climate engineering? There are debates over the definition of climate engineering,[7] but the Royal Society's influential 2009 report is a good place to start: 'the deliberate large-scale manipulation of the planetary environment to counteract anthropogenic climate change'.[8] Indeed, as Rob Bellamy and Javier Lezaun suggest, this definition has become almost canonical (though they convincingly argue it is also problematic), insofar as it 'carved out geoengineering as a specific and relatively self-contained object of public debate', concretized the two-sided taxonomy of carbon dioxide reduction and solar radiation management, and highlighted the governance dilemmas of climate engineering.[9]

---

[5] Forrest Clingerman and Kevin J. O'Brien, 'Playing God: Why Religion Belongs in the Geoengineering Debate', *Bulletin of the Atomic Scientists* 70 (2014), 27–37.

[6] IPCC, Global warming of 1.5°C. An IPCC Special Report on the impacts of global warming of 1.5°C above pre-industrial levels and related global greenhouse gas emission pathways, in the context of strengthening the global response to the threat of climate change, sustainable development and efforts to eradicate poverty (Geneva: World Meteorological Association, 2018).

[7] For instance, see Paula Curvelo and Ângela Guimarães Pereira, 'Geoengineering: Reflections on Current Debates', *International Journal of Science in Society* 4 (2013), 1–21; National Research Council, *Climate Intervention: Carbon Dioxide Removal and Reliable Sequestration* (Washington, DC: The National Academies Press, 2015), viii.

[8] Royal Society, *Geoengineering the Climate: Science, Governance and Uncertainty* (London: The Royal Society, 2009), 1.

[9] Rob Bellamy and Javier Lezaun, 'Crafting a Public for Geoengineering', *Public Understanding of Science* 26 (2017), 402–17 (404).

Theological reflection should pay close attention to four elements of the Royal Society's definition. First, climate engineering *intentionally* changes Earth systems to address the effects (rather than the causes) of climate change – we are in the 'realm of intentionality'.[10] Regardless of justifications put forward (to 'buy time', avert climate emergencies, ensure climate justice, etc.), the goal always is to counteract the anticipated effects of anthropogenic climate change. So while some argue 'humans have always engineered the climate', past emissions aren't forms of climate engineering, because anthropogenic climate change is an *unintentional* consequence of using fossil fuels. Theologians should ask about this intentionality: Is climate engineering the atmospheric manifestation of the Anthropocene? Is this a fearful or hopeful Anthropocene?

Second, climate engineering is a manipulation of Earth systems through *technological* means. It is necessary to discuss technologies in the plural rather than the singular and perhaps to challenge absolute distinctions between artefact and nature. The humanly guided techniques of climate engineering are different than mitigation projects such as forest protection, ethical calls for frugality or resource redistribution, or social policies designed to reduce greenhouse gas emissions. For theologians, this technological intentionality is a key area of reflection, since this muddles our sense of 'self-in-creation', as well as the perceived boundary between humanity and the rest of creation.

Third, climate engineering is *large-scale* in orientation and impact. Geoengineering is not local weather modification – its impacts are not geographically small or temporally short term. Instead researchers envision affecting larger, even global, scales. This is part of the reason that forms of climate engineering that fall under the category of 'negative emissions technologies' (NETs) are considered essential for reaching the Paris targets. Can theology accept the good of the Paris Agreement, if it requires forms of large-scale responses of climate engineering? What forms of knowledge, guidance and consent are ethically needed?

Finally, the purpose of climate engineering is to overturn the *effects* of climate change, without necessarily requiring mechanisms to address its causes. Climate engineering defines its objective differently than other responses to climate change. Mitigation proposals are concerned with the *causes* of climate change, insofar as '[m]itigation is a human intervention to reduce the sources or enhance the sinks of greenhouse gases.'[11] Vaughan and Lenton remark, '[t]he difference between mitigation activities and climate geoengineering can be likened to prevention versus medicine.'[12] Adaptation also has a different objective. Adaptation seeks to acclimatize individuals and society to climate

---

[10] Christopher J. Preston, 'Beyond the End of Nature: SRM and Two Tales of Artificiality for the Anthropocene', *Ethics, Policy and Environment* 15 (2012), 188–201 (191).

[11] IPCC, 'Summary for Policymakers', Climate Change 2014: Mitigation of Climate Change. Contribution of Working Group III to the Fifth Assessment Report of the Intergovernmental Panel on Climate Change (New York: Cambridge University Press, 2014), 4.

[12] Naomi E. Vaughn and Timothy M. Lenton, 'A Review of Climate Geoengineering Proposals', *Climatic Change* 109 (2011), 746–90 (746).

change impacts. Like climate engineering, adaptation proposals are oriented toward the effects of climate change. Yet unlike climate engineering, adaptation focuses on 'living with' the effects, not masking them.

Beyond the material and social differences between climate engineering, adaptation and mitigation, there is a more fundamental difference: climate engineering dissociates causes and effects. This raises one of the many ethical questions of climate engineering.[13] A pressing issue for Christian communities is to understand whether climate engineering can express a global love of the neighbour. Currently, the unequal distribution of benefits foreseen is not necessarily balanced in a way that aligns with the fact that particular regions are historically to blame for climate change (the United States and Europe). Indeed, Duncan McLaren notes that climate engineering proposals are often framed on a 'clean sheet', 'where impacts of and responsibilities for climate change were not already unevenly distributed and contested'.[14] This clean sheet means climate engineering raises unique issues of justice, temptation and responsibility. Theological approaches to climate engineering are faithful to the Christian message only insofar as they respond to the historical and cultural causes of climate injustice; this is especially important for advocating for the marginalized and voiceless on issues of consent and representation. Because climate engineering addresses the effects of climate change and not its causes, Christian theologians and ethicists must address the ways that climate engineering has the potential to replicate the inequities and ongoing structural violence of anthropogenic climate change.

Forms of climate engineering

Researchers identify two categories of climate engineering proposals (see Figure 1.5.1): solar radiation management and carbon dioxide removal. The first category, 'solar radiation management' (SRM), alters the planet's solar radiation budget. Nearly all SRM proposals suggest ways to manipulate the planetary reflectivity to counteract the increased radiation retained due to greenhouse gases. Proposals include marine cloud brightening, cirrus cloud thinning and stratospheric aerosol injection (SAI). Marine cloud brightening focuses on spraying particles in order to increase the cover of low-lying, highly reflective clouds over the ocean. The particles need not be exotic: fine

---

[13] Philosophical ethical literature on climate engineering is expanding rapidly. A sample includes Mike Hulme, *Can Science Fix Climate Change?* (Malden: Polity, 2014); David W. Keith, *A Case for Climate Engineering* (Cambridge: MIT Press, 2013); Christopher Preston, *Engineering the Climate: The Ethics of Solar Radiation Management* (Lanham: Lexington, 2012); and Alan Robock, '20 Reasons Why Geoengineering May Be a Bad Idea', *Bulletin of the Atomic Scientists* 64 (2008), 14–18, 59.

[14] Duncan McLaren, 'Framing Out Justice: The Post-politics of Climate Engineering Discourses', in *Climate Justice and Geoengineering: Ethics and Policy in the Atmospheric Anthropocene*, Christopher J. Preston (ed.) (Lanham: Lexington, 2016), 139–60 (146).

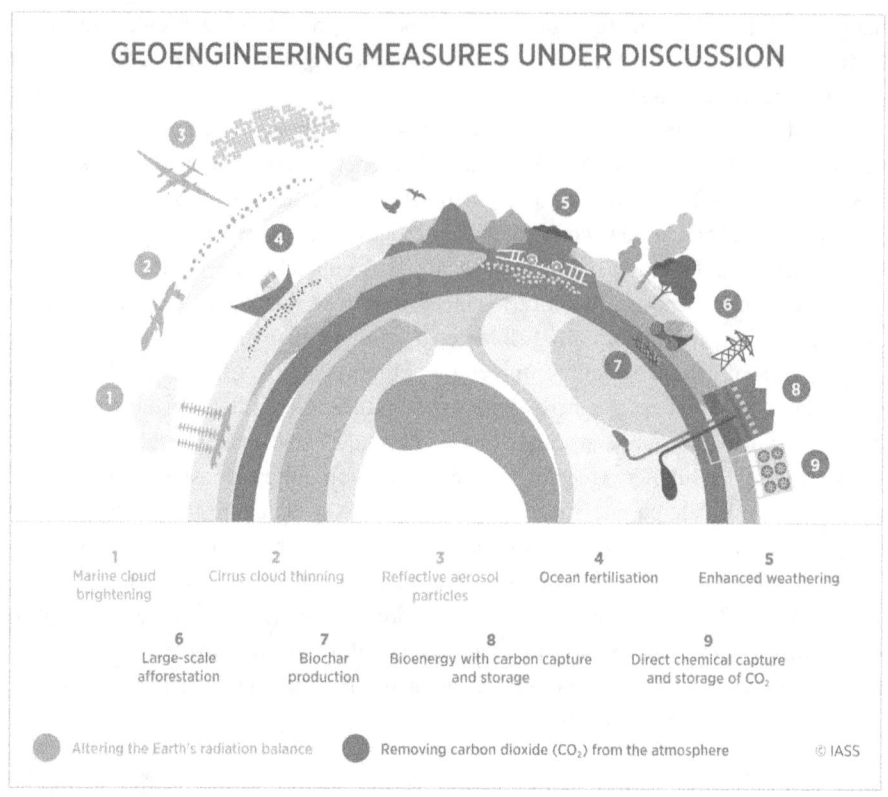

Figure 1.5.1 Types of climate engineering proposals under discussion. Image used with permission from the Institute for Advanced Sustainability Studies, Potsdam (©IASS).

mists of saltwater could be adequate to effectively seed clouds. In contrast, cirrus cloud thinning attempts to reduce certain forms of heat-trapping cloud cover, specifically the high-altitude cirrus clouds. Finally, SAI proposals are perhaps the most discussed SRM proposals. SAI proposals advocate the introduction of particles into the stratosphere to reflect solar radiation, as an analogue to how volcanic eruptions have influenced global temperatures. SRM is not a reversal of the process of anthropogenic climate change but a reversal of one or more effects; this is why 'cocktail engineering' (using several types simultaneously) might be required.[15] While research started with a focus on overall global temperature reduction, recent research has expanded to understand other environmental impacts, such as precipitation change, will occur when 'dimming the sun'.

---

[15] Long Cao, Lei Duan, Govindasamy Bala and Ken Caldeira, 'Simultaneous Stabilization of Global Temperature and Precipitation through Cocktail Geoengineering', *Geophysical Research Letters* 44 (2017), doi: 10.1002/2017GLO74281.

The second category of climate engineering proposals, 'carbon dioxide removal' (CDR), focuses on large-scale removal of greenhouse gases. There are several forms of CDR: land-based processes (industrial afforestation and bioenergy with carbon capture and storage (BECCS) are the two forms discussed in the IPCC Special Report on 1.5°C), ocean-based processes (e.g. iron fertilization), or chemical processes (e.g. 'enhanced weathering' of substances that naturally bind with carbon dioxide or direct air capture processes [DAC]). Some of these techniques (e.g. afforestation and iron fertilization) upscale and industrialize otherwise natural processes of carbon capture. Others (e.g. BECCS and DAC) depend on creating technologies to remove carbon dioxide or other greenhouse gases from the atmosphere. Increasingly, CDR proposals are separated from SRM, with the former being normalized as the 'negative emissions technologies' (NETs) required to meet the Paris targets.[16]

Even though SRM and CDR are placed together in discussions of responding to climate change, there are also distinctions to be made. Most obviously, while SRM modifies Earth's radiation budget, CDR attempts to modify the carbon budget. Furthermore, SRM is often discussed as an emergency response to runaway climate change; in models it reduces global temperatures quickly. Yet SRM lacks the robustness needed to be the main response to climate change since '[t]he use of SRM is strongly dependent on the magnitude of its side-effects and their persistency through time'.[17] CDR, on the other hand, appears as a more gradual and long-term way to address climate change and is perceived as more aligned with 'natural' or less-invasive approaches. Indeed, some proponents see CDR as related to the emissions reduction techniques of mitigation. The availability of technologies exposes other differences between SRM and CDR. SRM (especially SAI) proposals often are seen as adapting current technologies, which is part of the reason it is 'fast, cheap, and imperfect'.[18] In contrast, many CDR proposals require new technological processes or the radical scaling up of existing technologies. Recently, proponents have attempted to separate CDR from SRM in the public imagination, perhaps in order to avoid any negative response to SAI from being applied to NETs. Furthermore, there are uncertainties and potential environmental side effects unique to each.[19]

---

[16] Jan X. Minx, William F. Lamb and Max W. Callaghan et al., 'Fast Growing Research on Negative Emissions', *Environmental Research Letters* 12 (2017), 035007; National Academies of Sciences, Engineering, and Medicine, *Negative Emissions Technologies and Reliable Sequestration: A Research Agenda* (Washington DC: The National Academies Press, 2018).

[17] Olivier Bahn, Marc Chesney and Jonathan Gheyssens et al., 'Is There Room for Geoengineering in the Optimal Climate Policy Mix?' *Environmental Science & Policy* 48 (2015), 67–76 (74).

[18] David W. Keith, Edward Parson and M. Granger Morgan, 'Research on Global Sun Block Needed Now', *Nature* 463 (28 January 2010), 426–7 (426).

[19] David P. Keller, Ellias Y. Feng and Andreas Oschlies, 'Potential Climate Engineering Effectiveness and Side Effects During a High Carbon Dioxide-Emissions Scenario', *Nature Communications* 5 (2014), 3304, doi: 10.1038/ncomms4304

Clarifying these differences, and seeing the efficacy of climate engineering more generally, is necessary for work in the ethics and policy of geoengineering, in both forms of CDR and SRM. Some of the claims made about the benefits and impacts of specific proposals have been exaggerated or underplayed; the 'unknown unknowns' are (predictably) not known. This has led to the elision of scientific, political and moral claims. In an assessment of scientific work, Caldeira and Bala write, 'physical scientists often fail to distinguish between neutral empirical statements and value-driven normative and prescriptive statements ... [O]n the part of both scientists and scholars there has been a little too much presentation of opinions as if they were facts and exhortations as if there were conclusions of empirical studies.'[20] Given the fundamental differences between proposals, it might not be possible to construct a single 'theology of climate engineering'. Are SRM and CDR morally, politically, economically, socially and conceptually so different that they require different theological assessments? How can theologians navigate empirical research and the implicit value statements made by different geoengineers?

Most importantly, while it might be tempting to assume ill intentions, it is important to recognize that climate engineering researchers advocate mitigation and adaptation before all else. This is a point on which people of faith undoubtedly will agree. Advocating research and – if necessary – deployment of climate engineering is nearly always framed as a matter of preparedness in a world that seems resistant to addressing the problem. The call for preparation was a pivotal reason for the Nobel laureate Paul Crutzen's 2006 influential essay, where he writes, 'the very best would be if emissions of the greenhouse gases could be reduced so much that the [geoengineering] would not need to take place.' But he continues, 'Currently this looks like a pious wish.'[21] As Mike Hulme argues, there are political, economic and social dynamics to climate change.[22] These dimensions have created tragic obstacles to mitigation and adaptation. If we cannot overcome these obstacles, what happens if climate geoengineering is the only alternative left on the road to Paris?

Theological reflection and climate engineering

Since Crutzen's essay, people beyond the 'geo-clique' (the nickname given to prominent geoengineering researchers) have debated geoengineering. Even among climate

---

[20] Ken Caldeira and Govindasamy Bala, 'Reflecting on 50 Years of Geoengineering Research', *Earth's Future* 5 (2017), 10–17 (13).
[21] Paul J. Crutzen, 'Albedo Enhancement by Stratospheric Sulfur Injections: A Contribution to Resolve a Policy Dilemma?' *Climatic Change* 77 (2006), 211–19 (217).
[22] Mike Hulme, *Why We Disagree about Climate Change: Understanding Controversy, Inaction and Opportunity* (New York: Cambridge University Press, 2009).

sceptics, discussions about climate engineering have been happening: the 2017 US House of Representatives Committee on Science, Space, and Technology (chaired by climate sceptic Lamar Smith) hearing on 'Geoengineering: Innovation, Research, and Technology' comes a decade after the conservative Heartland Institute newsletter *Environment and Climate News* published David Schnare's article 'Geo-Engineering Seen as a Practical, Cost-Effective Global Warming Strategy'. If sceptics, researchers, policy analysts and political leaders all wrestle with climate engineering as a response strategy, then public climate theologies must similarly ponder its importance.

Conversations among the lay public (and, by extension, members of faith communities) on geoengineering are beginning from a lack of knowledge. Yet studies show that the public already is willing to form a variety of responses, which include opposition, scepticism or concern, and cautious engagement.[23] In other words, we readily find a diversity of responses and a deeply held ambivalence to the topic emerging from a general lack of knowledge about climate engineering.

Just as the discussion of climate engineering in the public square is just beginning, theological reflection on climate engineering is extremely preliminary. Of course, communities of faith should not immediately turn to moralizing without adequate knowledge of the topic. Already Christians mirror the responses of the public at large, debating whether the appropriate theological response is opposition, concern or cautious engagement. In an essay elsewhere, I suggested that this continuum emerges from competing narratives – symbolized by a new Tower of Babel and an optimistic Pelagian impulse.[24] For some theologians, Christians should oppose climate engineering completely, treating geoengineering researchers with suspicion. For example, Sharon Delgado argues that climate engineering is a technological response supposedly created and controlled by 'a small group of powerful people based on what is profitable and will further their ends'. According to Delgado, geoengineering advocates ignore calls for justice and reverence for the earth, instead jumping past the only appropriate response – robust and far-reaching mitigation – to embrace a dangerous technofix.[25] Delgado represents a position that identifies climate engineering as morally bankrupt and unjust. For others, these technologies are not evil per se but nonetheless materially reiterate the ideological and economic structures that caused anthropogenic climate change. Ethicist Michael

---

[23] Adam Corner, Nick Pidgeon and Karen Parkhill, 'Perceptions of Geoengineering: Public Attitudes, Stakeholder Perspectives, and the Challenge of "Upstream" Engagement', *WIREs Climate Change* 3 (2012), 451–66; Phil Macnaghten and Bronislaw Szerszynski, 'Living the Global Social Experiment: An Analysis of Public Discourse on Geoengineering and Its Implications for Governance', *Global Environmental Change* 23 (2013), 165–74; Victoria Wilbeck, Anders Hansson and Jonas Anshelm et al., 'Making Sense of Climate Engineering: A Focus Group Study of Lay Publics in Four Countries', *Climatic Change* 145 (2017), 1–14. These studies also show how social–scientific researchers initially concentrated on public perception in the United States and Europe, but more recently have sought to analyse a more global public perception.

[24] Forrest Clingerman, 'Between Babel and Pelagius: Religion, Theology and Geoengineering', in *Engineering the Climate*, 201–19.

[25] Sharon Delgado, *Love in the Time of Climate Change* (Minneapolis: Fortress, 2017), 84–5.

Northcott, for instance, draws on a more nuanced understanding of geoengineering than Delgado to argue that climate engineering fits into the modern narrative of human mastery of nature.[26] Theologians should follow Northcott to seriously investigate how geoengineering shares the same ideological framework as the origins of climate change. Finally, some theologians and ethicists, such as Sarah Fredericks[27] and Laura Hartman, studied the moral complexity at the heart of climate engineering, suggesting how it can participate in repentance and justice, but equally in hubris and suffering.[28] These positions suggest a cautious engagement, which starts by identifying the boundaries that faith communities should construct to define responsible research and implementation.

What underlies this diversity is not a tepid uncertainty but a recognition of an important theological task. Indeed, Christians cannot turn their backs on climate engineering: since climate change is multileveled, complex and intractable – that is, a wicked – problem, theologians must critically evaluate social interpretations of the climate, including the debate over climate engineering that we are confronted with after Paris. In other words, 'as a discipline [theology] highlights the conflict of interpretations that define our changing hermeneutics of the climate, because theologians are experts at asking and reflecting on what serves to ground the wickedness of the problem.'[29] This reflection becomes pivotal when researchers ask: how do individuals and communities create meaning 'in the absence of strong related opinions, predispositions, and given framings'?[30]

The creation of meaning in the face of new circumstances develops in a complicated way for religious and other groups alike. For Christian communities, everyday theological reflection becomes part of the process, guiding individuals and groups in making normative and existential evaluations. As Thomas Bruhn, Stefan Schäfer and Mark G. Lawrence found in a focus group on faith and climate engineering in Germany, '[p]articipants did not see the church's mandate as making concrete technological suggestions or assessing specific technologies proposed by others. The church's mandate was rather considered as a contribution to an 'ethical engineering', as, for example, reflected in the statement, 'If our attitude does not change, all technology will not help.'[31] Adherents can see Christian faith as a framework for defining individual responsibility, assessing

---

[26] Michael S. Northcott, *A Political Theology of Climate Change* (Grand Rapids: Eerdmans, 2013), 92–100.

[27] Sarah Fredericks, 'Ritual Responses to Climate Engineering', in *Theological and Ethical Responses to Climate Engineering*, Forrest Clingerman and Kevin J. O'Brien (eds) (Lanham: Lexington, 2016), 165–85.

[28] Laura M. Hartman, 'Healing the Climate? Christian Ethics and Medical Models for Climate Engineering', in *Theological and Ethical Responses to Climate Engineering*, Forrest Clingerman and Kevin J. O'Brien (eds) (Lanham: Lexington, 2016), 129–48.

[29] Forrest Clingerman, 'Theologians as Interpreters – Not Prophets – in a Changing Climate', *Journal of the American Academy of Religion* 83 (2015), 336–55 (345).

[30] Wilbeck, 'Making Sense of Climate Engineering', 2.

[31] Thomas Bruhn, Stefan Schäfer and Mark G. Lawrence, 'From the Guardian of Eden to Eden's Gardener? Experiences from Dialogues with Religious Groups on Climate Engineering and Possible Implications for Transdisciplinarity', in *Theological and Ethical Responses to Climate Engineering*, Forrest Clingerman and Kevin J. O'Brien (eds) (Lanham: Lexington, 2016), 17–36 (29).

proposals of climate engineering and ultimately making recommendations.[32] Through this work, religion offers a unique vantage point on climate engineering: faith relativizes questions of scientific feasibility and maximizes questions of what theologian David E. Klemm and ethicist William Schweiker call 'the integrity of life before God'.[33]

Reconciled in climate engineering?

If religious faith is where we use concepts, morals, stories, rituals and other practices to encounter what Paul Tillich called our 'ultimate concern', then theology is the systematic and critical engagement on the everyday experience of faith. In the light of climate change, theologians have the 'role of mediator, helping different constituencies focus on the ambiguities that surround the ways we find meaning and value in the face of climate change'.[34] In the Anthropocene, theologians interrogate our climate technologies. The areas in which theology might be altered in this encounter are countless: anthropology, eschatology, atonement, ethics, Christology and many other areas of theological reflection are challenged by climate engineering. The remainder of the essay will provide one illustration of this: climate engineering complicates theological discussions of sin, repentance and reconciliation.

Sin, repentance and reconciliation

Anglican bishop David Atkinson writes, '[t]echnology can be a marvelous servant, but becomes a destructive master.'[35] This expresses a lens through which to see the conflicting desires of climate engineering. CDR and SRM are technological servants: they have the potential to limit the effects of anthropogenic warming, remove the risk of overshoot, and provide needed time to implement mitigation and adaptation plans in a climate emergency. But they also threaten to be destructive masters: easily replicating secular global economic structures, empowering tendencies of Empire and colonialism, and unreflectively fostering a logic of consumerism and technoscientific optimism. Furthermore, this ambivalence takes unique forms within different geoengineering programmes. CDR is either a moderating, measured technique to wean ourselves from an overindulgence of fossil fuels or a scientific means to render the conversation of responsible energy use unnecessary. SRM is either deploying technology to limit the

---

[32] Ibid., 27–9.
[33] David E. Klemm and William Schweiker, *Religion and the Human Future* (Malden: Blackwell, 2009), 35–8.
[34] Clingerman, 'Theologians as Interpreters', 337.
[35] David Atkinson, *Renewing the Face of the Earth* (Norwich: Canterbury Press, 2008), 90.

worst crisis points of a rapidly changing climate on behalf of climate victims or a hubristic gamble for the global elite, based on the Enlightenment's ideological mistakes. Do some geoengineering proposals emerge as a means to assist in healing and wholeness, as Hartman suggests? Or, do they fit with the strain of theological logic that perpetuates domination and mastery of the Earth, as Northcott argues?

One theological context for the technological gambit of climate engineering, then, is the need to reframe our sense of sin and reconciliation, for, as philosopher Christopher Preston writes, 'another defining feature of the Anthropocene would be the change in our moral responsibilities'.[36] Christians might see a dilemma here: is climate engineering made up of technologies that reiterate the individual and structural sins of modernity, *as well as* technologies that assist in our reconciliation of broken relationships between each other and the Earth itself?

We can understand climate engineering and individual sin through Neil Messer's Barthian suggestion that climate sins are related to idolatry.[37] For Messer, individual climate sins are apparent in cases of climate denial through falsehood (in the denial of climate change, cognitive evasion and/or moral corruption). But we also find sin in the acceptance of climate change, when we fall prey to sloth (in the form of political inertia and the like) or, most relevant to the present discussion, pride. Pride occurs in the possibility of technological solutions, confusing the ultimate and penultimate, and presumptions of self-reliance. Theological assessments of forms of climate engineering require discerning how specific climate techniques fit within these idolatrous frames: is the acceptance of a proposal predicated on sloth or hubris, or does it force us to re-envision the past climate inertia and technological optimism?

Similarly, climate engineering proposals can be interpreted to reiterate the structural sin of modernity. Theologian Cynthia Moe-Lobeda suggests that climate change is a sin of structural violence, which 'refers to the physical, psychological, and spiritual harm that certain groups of people experience as a result of unequal distribution of power and privilege'.[38] Structural violence has two components. First, 'structural violence degrades, dehumanizes, damages, and kills people by limiting or preventing their access to the necessities for life or for its flourishing.'[39] The aims of climate engineering force us to rethink how technology works to alleviate the effects of anthropogenic climate change. One could argue that it is paradoxical technology, which restores the victims of our past mastery of nature by seeking *more* overwhelming mastery and control. Climate engineering proposals possibly suggest that a further anthropogenic domestication of the climate can enhance access to life's flourishing. But Moe-Lobeda posits a second

---

[36] Preston, 'Beyond the End of Nature: SRM and Two Tales of Artificity for the Anthropocene', 198.

[37] Neil Messer, 'Sin and Salvation', in *Systematic Theology and Climate Change: Ecumenical Perspectives*, Michael Northcott and Peter M. Scott (eds) (New York: Routledge, 2014), 124–40 (132–4). See also the essay on the emergence of sin elsewhere in this volume.

[38] Cynthia Moe-Lobeda, *Resisting Structural Evil: Love as Ecological-Economic Vocation* (Minneapolis: Fortress, 2013), 72.

[39] Ibid., 73.

dimension to structural violence: 'the complicity or silent acquiescence of those who fail to take responsibility for it and challenge it'.[40] On this score, some (or all) forms of climate engineering might perpetuate the violence of climate change by hiding its harm from view. By dissociating our historical and present emissions with the technologies intended as a response, climate engineering might tempt us to avoid responsibility or even to efface the voice of climate victims. In this vein, Bronislaw Szerszynski and his colleagues have questioned whether SRM can ever be made compatible with democratic forms of governance.[41] On individual and societal levels, climate engineering requires theological reflection to redefine responsibility for one's alteration of the climate – that is, whether geoengineering reinforces or reduces climate sin.

It should be clear that climate engineering is not itself a climate sin but instead leads to responsibility or temptation. Dane Scott uses the work of social ethicist Reinhold Niebuhr to argue for the ways some of our frames for climate engineering (specifically, talk of SRM) can lead to temptation. Niebuhr's understanding of sin and temptation, for Scott, is a more useful ethical term that the more frequently used 'moral hazard' argument. Two common frames for SRM are (1) SRM as 'Plan B', needed if we must buy time for mitigation and adaptation plans to be implemented or take effect and (2) SRM as 'Insurance Policy', something that should be researched in order to have insurance in case of a climate emergency or runaway climate change. Niebuhr's ethics saw how a significant flaw in humanity often manifests itself through pride and overreach. According to Scott, these frames 'create, in Niebuhr's terms, temptations for sin'.[42] Acknowledging this does not mean that we should avoid climate engineering altogether but instead be wary of the temptations that climate engineering poses. In fact, naming the temptation of climate engineering is a way to avoid 'the unfortunate fate ... [that climate engineering becomes] a political tool of moral crusaders and cynical realists', and instead asserts the need to respond to structural violence with a spirit of repentance.

If climate engineering creates a theological debate over sin and temptation, so too do we see the need to reflect on repentance. True repentance suggests a life-changing contrition, rather than a modest apology or guilt. Seeing repentance in this way has a long history: 'Late medieval theologians made a distinction between perfect sorrow for sin (contrition) and imperfect sorrow for sin (attrition). Contrition was sorrow for sin out of love of God; attrition sorrow for sin out of fear of punishment.'[43] Connecting the spirit of contrition with climate engineering, Kevin O'Brien advocates that the Christian community recognizes not only how climate change is a structural sin but also that an

---

[40] Ibid.
[41] Bronislaw Szersynski, Matthew Kearnes, Phil Macnaghten, Richard Owen and Jack Stilgoe, 'Why Solar Radiation Management Geoengineering and Democracy Won't Mix', *Environment and Planning* A45 (2013), 2809–16.
[42] Dane Scott, 'The Temptations of Climate Engineering', in *Theological and Ethical Responses to Climate Engineering,* Forrest Clingerman and Kevin J. O'Brien (eds) (Lanham: Lexington, 2016), 39–58 (46).
[43] Ronald K. Rittgers, 'Penance, Penitence, Repentance', in *Dictionary of Luther and Lutheran Traditions*, Timothy J. Wengert (ed.) (Grand Rapids: Baker, 2017), 585–8 (585).

ethical response cannot be exclusively personal action and a feeling of guilt. Since it is imperative to respond to structural violence through repentance, this provides a way of understanding the promise and limits of climate engineering proposals: is a particular project or implementation an attempt at reconciliation or not?[44] Climate repentance must take certain steps: acknowledgement of the extent of the problem, apology for our complicity and a redress of the problem.[45] While this might appear like an uncomplicated process, Ernst Conradie points out numerous difficulties to confessing guilt that are applicable to geoengineering: Do we truly acknowledge the problem if we continue to contribute to it? Who should confess? To whom are we confessing? And how should we confess to truly respond to the problem?[46] Reconciliation and confession are necessary steps to climate justice, which O'Brien defines as 'accepting the fact that climate change is a reality but refusing to accept the mistakes that created it or the inequities and violence it causes'.[47] Climate engineering, whether in the form of CDR or SRM, can only fit within this definition of justice if it done within a pure spirit of sorrow and reconciliation.

Conclusion

Atkinson provides us with a way to sum up the theological dilemma presented by climate engineering: 'climate change forces us to reflect on our human creativity, not least in relation to technology. There are those who see technology as the source of our problems. It is the requirement of energy resources on such a scale, resulting from the industrialization of the world, which has caused the situation in which we find ourselves. There are those who believe that technology can also find us the answer.'[48] If climate engineering is problem and solution, does it participate in both sin and reconciliation, responsibility and temptation? Theologians must finally turn to the question of justice, especially when we confront divisions between who is most responsible for anthropogenic climate change, who is directing geoengineering research and policy discussions, who will 'control the thermostat' of the planet, and who is likely to suffer the consequences of global warming. In a theology after Paris, we must answer the questions of who we are and how we become reconciled with one another.

---

[44] Kevin J. O'Brien, '"First to be Reconciled": The Priority of Repentance in the Climate Engineering Debate', in *Theological and Ethical Responses to Climate Engineering*, Forrest Clingerman and Kevin J. O'Brien (eds) (Lanham: Lexington, 2016), 187–203 (192).

[45] Ibid., 195–7.

[46] Ernst M. Conradie, *The Church and Climate Change* (Pietermaritzburg, South Africa: Cluster Publications, 2008), 90–2.

[47] Kevin J. O'Brien, *The Violence of Climate Change: Lessons of Resistance From Nonviolent Activists* (Washington DC: Georgetown University Press, 2017), 5.

[48] Atkinson, *Renewing*, 22.

A response to Forrest Clingerman

Asfawossen Asrat[1]

Forrest Clingerman's essay argues that 'Christian climate theologies cannot avoid, ignore, or misrepresent the different forms of geoengineering, but instead must seek dialogue with the scientific community in order to understand the challenges and possibilities that the idea climate engineering represents' under the premise that 'climate engineering and Christian climate theologies must be in conversation with one another'. The essay reflects an excellent grasp of current climate change and climate engineering discourses. However, the 'Christian climate theologies' described in the essay, though possibly well argued, are not presented in such a way that a non-expert can easily follow them. This may be since the essay follows upon a previous publication article by the author which discussed how theology impacts societal understanding of climate engineering.[2]

The underlying assumption is that considering the role of some form of climate engineering in meeting the 1.5°C goal in the Paris Agreement is necessary. However, framing the role of climate engineering with the feasibility of the Paris Agreement without or before any background discussion of the climate-change mitigation measures is an oversimplification. The significant uncertainties of climate engineering should be discussed from the outset. The way climate engineering (geoengineering) is introduced at the beginning of the essay gives the wrong impression that it is an 'accepted' view. It has to be clearly shown that climate engineering is still a controversial proposal under discussion. In addition, since the Paris Agreement did not consider climate engineering as a possible means to achieve the stated goals this indicates that the mainstream climate-change community is yet to recognize the proposals. Discussion on climate engineering research should therefore be framed as part of the bigger discourse on climate change and the possible responses (mitigation and adaptation measures).

The core message of the essay is presented in the second section, 'What does it mean to engineer the climate?' In this section the author critically evaluates the Royal Society's definition of climate engineering.[3] His evaluation can be summarized as

---

[1] Asfawossen Asrat is Professor of Geology at the School of Earth Sciences, Addis Ababa University, Ethiopia. His research spans a wide range of the earth sciences, particularly reconstruction of the past climate of Eastern Africa using geological archives (speleothems, cave sediments, lake sediments, etc.) and geochemical proxies.

[2] Forrest Clingerman and Kevin J. O'Brien, 'Playing God: Why Religion Belongs in the Geoengineering Debate', *Bulletin of the Atomic Scientists* 70 (2014), 27–37.

[3] Royal Society, *Geoengineering the Climate: Science, Governance and Uncertainty* (London: The Royal Society, 2009), 1.

follows: climate engineering is an intentional, large-scale manipulation of the Earth system through technological means to overturn the effects of climate change. He further argues that though climate engineering defines its objectives differently (that is, to counter the effects of climate change and not to address the causes of it), climate theologians should reflect on climate engineering by placing it within the broader context of climate responses. The essay would have been clearer if it started with this assertion in order to avoid the 'oversimplification' I indicated in the previous paragraph.

The essay argues that one of the ethical issues related to climate engineering is that it dissociates causes and effects of climate change, which makes it fundamentally different from climate adaptation and mitigation. It is further argued that climate engineering has the potential to replicate the historical inequalities caused by climate change and that Christian theologians must address the historical causes of climate injustice and advocate for the consent and representation of the marginalized and voiceless. This argument is in line with several scientific studies which show strong regional difference in both long-term natural and anthropogenic climate change. One such study concluded that '[a]t multi-decadal to centennial scales, temperature variability shows distinctly different regional patterns, with more similarity within each hemisphere than between them'.[4] The effects of climate change are equally disparate in various parts of the world. The tropical and subtropical regions constituted by the economically lagging countries in Africa, Asia and Latin America, the least contributors to anthropogenic climate forcing, have been hard hit by the consequences of climate change due to their vulnerable economic bases. Such countries, which spend more than half of their income on food generated by largely rain-fed agriculture, will be severely affected by frequent extreme events (droughts and flooding), lower and erratic rainfall (Africa and Latin America) and by rising sea levels (Asia).[5] It is with such background that the uncertainties and potential benefits and/or harms of climate engineering should be framed in developing countries (the Global South). The Global South is at the frontline of climate-change-driven impacts and subsequently these countries have the most to gain or lose from climate engineering. However, the Global South is relatively under-represented in public deliberations about climate engineering.[6] This has to change and the Global South should play a stronger role in both climate engineering research and governance discussions in order to make its voice heard and to set and prioritize research agendas pertinent to the region. Climate researchers from the Global South recently emphasized that 'nations most vulnerable to climate change must drive modelling,

---

[4] PAGES 2k Consortium, 'Continental-scale Temperature Variability During the Past Two Millennia', *Nature Geoscience* (2013), doi: 10.1038/NGEO1797.

[5] IPCC, 2013: Summary for Policymakers. In: *Climate Change 2013: The Physical Science Basis: Contribution of Working Group I to the Fifth Assessment Report of the Intergovernmental Panel on Climate Change,* Thomas F. Stocker et al. (eds) (Cambridge and New York: Cambridge University Press, 2013), 3–29.

[6] David E. Winicoff, Jane Flegal and Asfawossen Asrat, 'Engaging the Global South on Climate Engineering Research', *Nature Climate Change* 5 (2015), 627–34.

ethics and governance discussions'[7] on climate (solar) geoengineering. Clingerman's emphasis on addressing historical climate injustice and advocating for the consent and representation of the marginalized is in perfect line with the arguments and actions of the growing climate engineering community in the Global South.

In the section on 'Forms of Climate Engineering' the author evaluates the ideas of previous workers on the political, economic and social obstacles against the feasibility of adaptation and mitigation measures, and questions, 'what will happen if climate engineering [would be] the only alternative left on the road to Paris?'. I challenge the framing of climate engineering as the 'only alternative'. Why is it easier to take this alternative than the mitigation and adaptation options? What if the same political, economic and social obstacles that made mitigation and adaptation efforts unsuccessful hinder climate engineering in the same way? What do theologians think about 'alternative scenarios'? If the only alternative left is to 'sin' for an ultimate good, would that be acceptable as the 'only alternative' to take? Would not this framing of alternative scenarios undermine the ongoing efforts on mitigation and adaptation?

The section 'Theological Reflection and Climate Engineering' presents a concise but informative discussion on public responses to climate engineering proposals, evaluated from a theological perspective. However, the bulk of the conversations happening in the Global North should be viewed as representing only a fraction of the world population. There is a need to incorporate the views of the Global South for a fuller appraisal of global public response. For instance, in many African societies including 'Christian' communities, where natural forces and processes such as weather and climate fluctuations are generally believed to be controlled by a supernatural (divine) force, and extreme climate events such as droughts and flooding are usually considered as punishment against human 'sin' and 'wickedness', intervention at a grand scale such as climate engineering ('moving from the image of God to "playing God"?') will be viewed in a different perspective than that of the Global North, to say the least. Framing the question whether climate engineering can even be considered as a means to tackle climate change requires serious thought, taking such global differences within the 'framework of belief, value, and meaning'.

The section on 'Reconciled in Climate Engineering?' offers an excellent discussion on climate engineering within the perspective of the theological concepts of sin, repentance and reconciliation. Though the theoretical basis of the theological discussion is beyond my expertise, I concur with the argument that climate change (and climate engineering) affects various parts of the world and various communities differently, in many cases at the expense of each other. This is well explained in terms of climate sin. However, I challenge the notion that we need to interpret 'climate engineering as both a technology with the potential to reiterate the individual and structural sins of modernity, as well as a technology that is poised to assist in our reconciliation of broken relationships

---

[7] Atiq Rahman, Paulo Artaxo, Asfawossen Asrat and Andy Parker, 'Developing Countries Must Lead on Solar Geoengineering Research', *Nature* 556 (2018), 22–4.

between each other and the Earth itself'. How can climate engineering be considered as assisting reconciliation with the Earth while it is basically breaking the natural cycle of the Earth to try to 'fix' the broken cycle due to anthropogenic forcing? How does climate engineering fit into the concept of climate repentance while it is framed as an alternative to mitigation?

In conclusion, the essay provides a broad overview of climate engineering and manages to show climate theologians can provide the theoretical basis to evaluate climate engineering in terms of sin, repentance and reconciliation. The last paragraph of the essay poses several crucial questions, which in my opinion should be dully addressed by both the climate science and climate theology communities alike.

Chapter 1.6
Working with artists

Nancy Rakoczy[1]

Climate artists have created a new genre, whose primary concerns and subject matters are global warming and climate change. These artists have attuned themselves to the devastation that has been wreaked upon the earth and, with passionate determination, have produced an avalanche of projects to save the earth from further damage. The variety of work ranges from performative to problem solving. Some artists seek to imagine a future without fossil fuels as a primary resource. Other works may be conceptual or subversive with a sly wit that challenges the received norms. Whether acting as part of a collective or alone, these artists demand that attention be given to our warming planet.

Visionaries, prophets and witnesses

Climate artists are visionaries, prophets and witnesses: with imagination and foresight, they warn of future devastation, catastrophe and imminent disasters. Native Americans and other Indigenous groups, especially, have warned for centuries that the earth, air and water are to be nurtured and managed as if they were living beings. Only now is the United States waking up to these prophetic voices alerting us to collective destruction. The projects of Eve S. Mosher, Sarah Cameron Sunde and Gideon Mandel warn of rising waters. Yoon Cho uses the backdrop of the harsh desert terrain to ask about the proper use of sacred lands. All are determined in their commitment to bring attention to climate change.

The West may regard environmental sins as a new category for repentance, but for centuries Native Americans, First Peoples and Inuit leaders have sounded the alarm about damage to the earth: 'It took generations of Western science to catch up to an understanding of the eco system that we have in our homelands ... we were the ones

---

[1] Nancy Rakoczy has been approved for ordination in the ELCA church (Lutheran). She is an exhibiting artist active in LICA Artists and NOMAA in New York City. Her work uses discarded plastics to comment on the intersection of spirituality and feminism, and the conflict of nature with the environment and politics.

who noticed the [climate] changes first.'² With global warming upping the stakes, their concerns about climate change have been amplified on film. Located in the Pacific Northwest, the Native American Film Academy, Climate Film Academy and Wisdom of the Elders (WOTE) sponsored the film *Roots of Tradition* (2016) which focused on the effects of climate change on the sacred, traditional foods of Nez Perce Indians. As roots, berries and salmon disappear, so do significant elements and traditions of the Nez Perce culture connecting them to the earth and water. As Lee Bourgeau, tribal elder reflects: 'I'm worried that all of our first foods are being threatened by the changes in the climate. And we won't have these foods anymore. They will be ancient history.'³ As the foods disappear and the rivers poisoned, the Nez Perce ponder their own survival. The film is a document of their struggle and ends with a wordless, haunting lament.

When a nation's economic self-interest is the engine that drives the country, it creates a kind of blindness that finds its consequences in global warming, a form of collective suicide. In contrast, to be an Inuit leader is to be a prophet, not just for one's people but for the global community as well.

Jens Danielsen of Qaanaaq, Greenland Delegate of the Inuit Circumpolar Council, arrived at the 2015 Paris Climate Accord, with a message about climate change to the international community: 'The world has a mortal fever. I am a witness to this sickness. I see our way of life, thousands of years old, facing storms we can no longer read.'⁴ Mel Chin, documentary film-maker showed his film *L'Artique est Paris* and stated, 'The Arctic drives the climate of the world, and it has changed, challenging this way of life.'⁵ To demonstrate the crisis, Chin filmed Danielsen and his team, who had trained seven French poodles to drive sleds through Paris, guided by Inuit leaders who wore the traditional garb of seal, polar bear and caribou skins. This performative statement was to drive home that not just the Artic is changing but all of our environments are being harmed, due to the neglect and degradation of the planet we share.

Another visionary and prophet, Eve S. Mosher, created the seminal *HighWaterLine* project as a wake-up call to communities that were at risk of flooding due to climate change. In 2007, five years before Superstorm Sandy hit New York City, she used a US geologic survey topographic map to chalk a continuous line around the 70 miles of New York City coastline and Brooklyn, to indicate a 10 feet line above sea level where flooding would most probably occur.⁶ Her project was predictive of more disastrous

---

² Rose High Bear, executive producer, Wisdom of the Elders, Climate Film Academy, *Roots of Tradition* (2016), https://www.nativeartsandcultures.org/native-american-film-acdemy-climate-film-festival (accessed 10 January 2018).
³ Ibid.
⁴ Mel Chin, *L'Artique est Paris* (2015), https://vimeo.com/207194660 (accessed 5 December 2017).
⁵ Ibid.
⁶ Eve S. Mosher, www.evemosher.com/2007/highwaterline (accessed 5 December 2017).

flooding: by 2020, floods that had occurred every one hundred years were projected to occur every forty-three, a disaster to individuals and local economies.

Mosher's 3-inch blue chalk line sliced across streets and divided neighbourhoods into 'wet' and 'dry'. The line was stark, with a minimalist's power. She said of the line, 'It helps people to visualize climate change. It helps localize it.'[7] Mosher's work was performative: wheeling her industrial-grade chalk device into underserved neighbourhoods served as a catalyst for conversations on climate change and carbon footprints. The chalk line prodded the imaginations of the community to imagine their homes under water, to see the water lapping at their doorsills. The work was collaborative as it sought to draw communities together to face these dangers and create solutions. In addition to New York City, Mosher also took the *HighWaterLine* project along the Delaware River; to Philadelphia, Miami and Bristol in the UK, where community organizers preceded her to educate residents who were also facing rising waters due to climate change.

Sarah Cameron Sunde's work is that of vigilant witness to the disasters of global warming and rising tides. Her *36.5 A Durational Performance with the Sea* (2013) was a performative response to Hurricane Sandy's devastation and also served as a comment on the difficulties of artists to survive.[8] Presented as a four-channel video installation, Sunde, dressed in a red wet suit, stood motionless as a sentinel in tidal pools for a full tidal cycle of twelve hours as the waters rose and fell to her neck. Fully dressed individuals in business attire joined her as the waters rose up to their chests. Her work registered as an extreme protest to the negligence that climate science has received until lately. Human scale, the measurement of the person in relation to the vast global issues around water, is another factor in her work. She performs our collective vulnerability overwhelmed by the rising waters.

Sunde's community of meditative watchers became more aware of water, stillness, movement, current, temperature and later discussed the ideas her work generated. This communal group shared the risks and dangers of rising waters. Sunde took her performance to Maine, Mexico and San Francisco over the course of 2013 and 2014. In 2015 the performance travelled to the Netherlands and to Bangladesh, countries that are currently experiencing the catastrophic effects of climate change.[9] For 2020, she plans simultaneous performances around New York City and the world.

Similar to Sunde's watchful witness of rising tides is the South African Gideon Mendel's photographic record, *Drowning World*. Beginning in 2007, Mendel set to photograph the rising tides in ten countries due to global warming. He's taken his camera to some of the poorest countries, which are among the most vulnerable. 'Chinta et Samundri Davi, *Village de Salempur près de Muzaffarpur, Bihar,*

---

[7] Ibid.
[8] Sarah Cameron Sunde, *36.5 A Durational Performance with the Sea*, http://www.365waterproject.org/ (accessed 5 December 2017).
[9] Sarah Cameron Sunde, *Portfolio,* http://www.sarahcameronsunde.com/portfolio_page/36-5/ (accessed 5 December 2017).

Inde, Aout' shows two Indian women, their homes collapsing in a flood behind, themselves chest deep in water.[10] One woman's face is resigned, the other anguished. His photos picture people of all nationalities knee or thigh deep in floodwaters. 'The victims often appear stoic, paralyzed, and numb. Yet, Mendel says, they often tell him they are grateful to have him bear witness.'[11] Like Sunde, Mendel's work sounds the alarm to a world, which can't quite grasp the enormity of the crisis in which we are immersed, and so immerses himself in the catastrophe along with the victims, adding to their collective witness.

Yoon Cho's performative – *Desert Power Plant in the Sacred Land* (2011–16), presented as photographs and a video installation – set herself the task of walking long distances as a way to witness and document the 'beauty, destruction and preservation of the land in Arizona'.[12] Like Mosher and Sunde, Yoon's work uses the unit of human scale against the backdrop of vast and stark landscapes to evoke awe, wonder and regret. Regret is evident at the destruction of not just natural spaces given over to a nuclear power plant but lands that are also sacred to the Native Americans who have inhabited these lands for millennia. Like Sunde, who risked the tides that rose to her chin, Cho faced overwhelming heat and vast distances as she walked and photographed the rugged terrain for her photographic statements about the poisoned, sacred landscapes. Whereas *Roots of Tradition* depicted the struggle of Native Americans to hold out against the juggernaut of Western progress that recognizes nothing in the natural world as sacred, in *Desert Power Plant in the Sacred Land* Cho's tiny figure was a witness almost lost against the backdrop of the nuclear power plant planted deep within the harsh desert (Figure 1.6.1).

Like Cameron and Cho, Chinese artist Cai Guo-Qiang's work was also that of witness and risk taker. Where regret was at work in Cho's work, dismay permeated Cai's retrospective, *The Ninth Wave* (2014). For this piece he ferried ostensibly sick animals, such as wolves, monkeys, camels and zebras, made of goat hide and synthetic materials, on a boat to demonstrate how fossil fuels poisoned the life around us. As *The New Yorker* reports, 'Cai's exhibit suggests an ironic thematic reversal: nature's state of helplessness in the face of modern man's relentless, Promethean drive to progress.'[13] Cai's work was politically risky for its critical stance. Only his international stature gave him some immunity from the Chinese government, which believed climate change a hoax.

---

[10] Gideon Mendel, http://www.artists4climate.com/en/artists/gideon-mendel/ (accessed 5 December 2017).

[11] Coburn Dukeheart, 'Gideon Mendel's Portraits from a Drowning World', *National Geographic* (15 January 2015), http://proof.nationalgeographic.com/2015/01/15/gideon-mendels-portraits-from-a-drowning-world/ (accessed 6 December 2017).

[12] Yoon Cho, *Desert Walk Series: Desert Power Plant in the Sacred Land,* 2011–16, www.yooncho.com.

[13] Orville Schell, *The New Yorker* (3 October 2014), http://www.newyorker.com/culture/cultural-comment/chinese-artist-confronts-environmental-disaster (accessed 5 December 2017).

Working with Artists

Figure 1.6.1 *Desert Walk Series: Desert Power Plant in the Sacred Land,* Yoon Cho, 2011–16, www.yooncho.com.

'Unless I see … and put my finger on … I will not believe': Art for the doubting Thomases

Both performance artists and filmmakers have created a new subgroup within the genre of climate art, devoted to documenting the melting Arctic and glaciers. Many artists have provided opportunities to touch and feel the melting glaciers as a way to witness the catastrophic event of global warming.

For the 2015 Paris Climate Talks, Danish-Icelandic artist Olafur Eliasson and geologist Minik Rosing brought melting glaciers to the people. For *Ice Watch* they arranged eight 11-tonne blocks of glacial ice from a fjord outside of Greenland, into a circle creating an ice clock. Eliasson's purpose was to galvanize people into action: 'Art has the ability to change our perceptions and perspectives on the world, and *Ice Watch* makes the climate challenges we are facing tangible. I hope it will inspire shared commitment to taking climate action.'[14]

Eliasson's *Your Waste of Time* (2013) placed 800-year-old chunks of ice broken from Icelandic glaciers into a refrigerated gallery space. Here time was visibly measured in

---

[14] Beckett Mufson, '90 Tons of Glacial Ice Melt in Front of the Paris Climate Talks', *Creators-Vice,* 2 (2 December 2015), https://creators.vice.com/en_us/article/xy4mjk/90-tons-of-glacial-ice-melt-in-front-of-the-paris-climate-talks (accessed 6 December 2017).

centuries, rather than in decades.¹⁵ These works served to confront our short attention spans with the irrefutable visual and tactile evidence of melting glaciers.

Among activist-artist collectives, few have been as inventive and successful as Liberate Tate of London in confronting limited imaginations with the reality of global warming. Beginning in 2010, they took their witty, subversive and provocative performance art to protest the museum's collaboration with British Petroleum. The collective's confrontations pointed to the destructive impact oil drilling has had on the planet, while their mission was to pressure the Tate to divest themselves of British Petroleum's sponsorship.

With *Floe Piece* (2012), members of the collective brought 55 kilograms of Arctic ice into the Tate on a stretcher, borne by four people dressed and veiled in funereal black, giving the performance an air of uneasy anonymity. The video's soundtrack was the crunching and grinding noises of glaciers melting in the Arctic.¹⁶ Terry Gosnell of Liberate Tate said, 'Arctic ice is melting at record rates as a result of climate change. The irony is that the same oil companies that carry a lot of responsibility for climate change, are using the melting ice as an opportunity to drill for more oil in previously inaccessible areas.'¹⁷ The ice was left to melt on the floor of the Tate Museum.

The artist as serious trickster and Christ figure

In their single-minded pursuit of profit, corporations and governments have undermined the health of the planet. In response, some artists like Liberate Tate have assumed the necessary role of trickster as a way to demonstrate our collective predicament. With *Kill Me or Change* (2012) climate artist Chin Chih Yang also assumed the role of serious trickster for the world. Called the 'Taiwanese Charlie Chaplin', the performance was by turns provocative, dangerous, serious and playful, as Yang stood outside the Queens Museum of Art in Flushing, Queens, New York, while a mesh net with 30,000 empty soda cans was suspended over his head.¹⁸ These cans were emblematic of an individual's lifetime consumption of soda. With an ambulance parked nearby, the cans were released and cascaded over Yang, almost completely covering him (Figure 1.6.2).

The power of the work was in its multiple shocks – chief among them was the possibility that Yang would be injured or killed. Another jolt was the massive collection of 30,000 cans: a lifetime of consumer waste exposed! Yang confronted us with a

---

[15] See Expo 1: New York, 'Olafur Eliasson: Your Waste of Time', http://www.momaps1.org/expo1/module/olafur-eliasson-your-waste-of-time/ (accessed 7 December 2017).

[16] See Floe Piece, Liberate Tate, 2012, https://vimeo.com/channels/360124/35078978.

[17] Steve Anderson, 'Art Collective Uses Arctic Ice to Protest at Gallery's BP Sponsorship' (16 January 2012), http://www.independent.co.uk/arts-entertainment/art/news/art-collective-liberate-tate-uses-arctic-ice-to-protest-at-gallerys-bp-sponsorship-6290448.html (accessed 7 December 2017).

[18] Chin Chih Yang, 'Face the Earth' (21 August 2017), https://vimeo.com/233323268.

Working with Artists

Figure 1.6.2 *Kill Me or Change*, Chin Chih Yang, performance at the Queens Museum of Art, 28–9 July 2012, https://vimeo.com/46775357.

spectacle to wake us out of our shared torpor where mass extinction threatens and looms over us like the mesh net.

Martha Wilson of Franklin Furnace said of Yang: 'It is the job of artists to change the way we see. Chin Chih Yang is asking us to change the way we see our responsibility for the planet. Basically he's willing to die for the planet. I believe art can change the world.'[19] The role of the trickster-artist is to provoke and sensitize the viewer to look again at the world through the artist's lens and take action.

---

[19] Chin Chih Yang, *Kill Me or Change,* performance at the Queens Museum of Art, 28–9 July 2012, https://vimeo.com/46775357.

To mark the first anniversary of the Gulf of Mexico disaster, Liberate Tate produced the iconic performance piece *Human Cost* (2011).[20] Evoking an ancient ritual gone awry, one performer lay naked and prostrate on the marble floor of the Tate Museum, as two others dressed in black, their faces veiled and anonymous, slowly poured a mixture of charcoal and sunflower oil over him from goose-neck oil containers. The performance elicited pity and dismay, as the actor lay helpless in a pool of black sludge, a reminder of oil tankers that heedlessly spewed their cargo into fragile ecosystems and their animal inhabitants.

With *Carry Water* (2009), Chin Chih Yang took on the role of a Christ figure as a way to demonstrate his concern for the melting ice caps, climate change, rising tides and the preciousness of water.[21] Over the course of five days, he set himself the task to laboriously carry buckets of water the length of Manhattan, deliberately echoing Christ's walk to Calvary. Yang dressed himself in a white tunic with a green fabric draped diagonally across one shoulder. He carried the water in two large, white industrial containers yoked across his shoulders (Figure 1.6.3). Companions witnessed Yang's muscle strain, sweat and fatigue. He would stop to rest along the thirty-block route and comment on how heavy the water was, how hard the task, and express concern if he would actually be able to finish the walk. In turn, we would offer him encouragement to keep going. Yang's performance was enacted as a way to try and awaken an indifferent world to action.

Artists: Turning the world right side up

Scripture – from the Beatitudes to the Magnificat – offers a view of how the world would look if we would surrender to God's grace. The meek would inherit the earth. The mighty would be pulled down from their thrones. In short, if the underprivileged had more power, the world would be turned right side up. At the heart of the community-based artists' collective, Ghana ThinkTank: Developing the First World, is the question, what would the world look like if people on the margins rather than the wealthy and well-connected were consulted? Located in Detroit, Michigan, they have set themselves the task to not just align themselves with the so-called Third World but to seek out representatives of the these parts of the world for insight and wisdom on projects, as a corrective to the corrosive effect of First World domination of our planet. By pursuing a deliberate reversal of the 'natural' order of Western supremacy, Ghana ThinkTank's projects also calls to attention that the First World's solutions to climate change can be problematic and harmful rather than beneficial.

---

[20] *Human Cost*, performance at the Tate Britain – First Anniversary of the Gulf of Mexico disaster, https://vimeo.com/channels/360124/22677737.

[21] *New York Biennale Art 2009: Carry Water – Chin Chih Yang* (16 October 2009), posted by Lu, http://newyorkbiennaleart2009.blogspot.com/2009/10/carry-water-chin-chih.html (accessed 8 January 2019).

Figure 1.6.3 New York Biennale Art 2009: *Carry Water* – Chin Chih Yang, 16 October 2009, posted by Lu, http://newyorkbiennaleart2009.blogspot.com/2009/10/carry-water-chin-chih.html (accessed 8 January 2019).

In regard to climate change, only 42 per cent of residents in Wayne County (Detroit) believe it will harm them personally.[22] As a response to this attitude, Williams College Museum of Art in Massachusetts commissioned Ghana ThinkTank in 2016 to reach out to think tanks in Indonesia and Morocco, two countries grappling with the immediacy of climate change and address the question, how does climate change affect you?[23] These

---

[22] Jennifer Marlon et al., 'Yale Climate Opinion Maps', *Yale Program on Climate Change Communication*, http://climatecommunication.yale.edu/visualizations-data/ycom-us-2016/?est=happening&type=value&geo=county&id=26163 (accessed 8 December 2017).

[23] See 'Climate Change' (11 October 2015), http://www.ghanathinktank.org/current-projects-2/ (accessed 6 December 2017).

thinkers then travelled to the United States in order to meet with the collective and discuss their solutions within the Detroit community, reversing the expectations that the flow of information and aid is from the top down.

Climate change has provoked some artists to use wind and light as their mediums, exposing our dependence on fossil fuels as not just ill-advised, but lacking some essence of beauty and inspiration. The Land Art Generator Initiative sponsors an international competition as a way to generate design solutions to replace fossil fuels with renewable energy.

Danish wind artists Laura Mesa Arango and Rafael Sanchez Herrera designed *The Sound of Denmark* (2014), a project that proposes to place twelve giant Viking horns along the harbour of Copenhagen. These horns would function not only as wind turbines generating energy but also as wind instruments. As the wind pushes through a complex series of apertures, the structures create a 'sound landscape'.[24] The shapes of these massive horns point to the past with an evocation of ancient Vikings' reliance on wind power, juxtaposed with the present need to harness wind for energy. This elegant solution underscores that there are more ingenious, stylish and efficient ways to meet our energy needs.

While the Danes played with wind, the Dutch architect-designer studio Roosegaarde played with both wind and light when it produced *Windlicht* (2016) at the Eneco windfarm at Sint Annaland in Zeeland in the Netherlands. As the windmill blades rotated, thin green lights jumped from one windmill to the other. The effect was especially beautiful at night and it 'looks like jumping rope with the wind'.[25] The Studio also designed a sustainable dance floor in Rotterdam in which the dancers' movement produced the club's music and lights: 'A dance floor can become one big generator, turning every movement into new power.'[26] These design solutions point to the availability of alternatives but also demonstrate how unnecessary our slavish dependence on fossil fuels is.

Artists as disturbers of the peace

Chin Chih Yang and Liberate Tate could have occupied the category of disturbers of peace as they countered corporate misdeeds and heedless consumerism with their provocative performances. The work of Lauren Bon and the Metabolic Studio are also disturbers of peace, as peace is determined by corporate entities. The mission of the

---

[24] See 'Horn Structures Produce Wind-Generated Sounds in Denmark for LAGI 2014', Designboom, https://www.designboom.com/architecture/the-sound-of-denmark-2014-land-art-generator-initiative-10-10-2014/ (accessed 7 December 2017).

[25] Studio Roosegaarde, *Windlicht*, https://www.studioroosegaarde.net/project/windlicht/ (accessed 7 December 2017).

[26] Studio Roosegaarde, Sustainable Dance Floor, https://www.studioroosegaarde.net/project/sustainable-dance-floor/ (accessed 7 December 2017).

Studio is rendered in tall neon letters on their exterior walls: 'Artists Need to Create on the Same Scale that Society Has the Capacity to Destroy.'[27] They were included in the Climate Change Arts Festival (2015) in Los Angeles, scheduled in tandem with the Paris Climate Talks.

Their project *Not a Cornfield* (2004-2005) sought to uncover and reconnect with the buried history beneath the anonymous concrete of downtown Los Angeles. Like Cho and Mosher, whose work dealt with vast land masses, the Metabolic Studio's mission is to 'create "devices of wonder" that are specific to land and water sites, positing new modalities in thinking and behaviour, with projects that are participatory and activist in nature'.[28]

This project consists of a 'metabolic sculpture' planted in an abandoned rail yard in downtown Los Angeles, transforming it into a 32-acre cornfield for one agricultural cycle.[29] Not a timid project, it involved

> 90 miles of irrigation stripping, 1,500 truckloads of clean soil, 30,000 lbs. of corn seed and 42 bails of corn fodder, the work signalled the beginning of a decade of experimentation on reconnecting land with water, engaging and collaborating with agencies and communities in the city, questioning and probing the edges of the permissible.[30]

Not a Cornfield had elements of both pathos and subversive humour. It prodded the viewer to remember who the original guardians of the land were, while also evoking the temporal nature of all ownership.

Not a Cornfield's disruptive nature was apparent in the expectations it upended: who expects a temporary cornfield growing in a metropolis? Memory was an essential element as the location bridged the past and present by subtly invoking memories of the First Peoples who had cultivated this parcel of land centuries before. With the restoration of the land to its original though temporary use, *Not a Cornfield* recalled the passage of time and layers of history contained within those acres, including reminders of colonialism and the violence inherent. With the cornfield's final disappearance, memory again played a crucial role; the viewer was challenged to remember its temporary restoration and the part it played in the layering of history at that location. Like Yoon Cho's *Desert Power Plant in the Sacred Land* and WOTE's *Roots of Tradition*, *Not a Cornfield* also invoked regret at the loss of the sacred and challenged assumptions about urban progress, which had roots in colonial exploitation.

Time was a crucial element for understanding some of these projects. *Not a Cornfield*, Sunde's watchful work, WOTE's film, Mendel's photographs and Mosher's minimalist

---

[27] See Lauren Bon and the Metabolic Studio, http://www.metabolicstudio.org/actions.

[28] Ibid.

[29] See Lauren Bon and the Metabolic Studio, http://www.metabolicstudio.org/section/actions/not-cornfield (accessed 7 December 2017).

[30] Ibid.

blue line, all included the passage of time as a way to understand our relationship to land, water and the climate. *Not a Cornfield* and *Roots of Tradition* measured time in millennia, as did all the glacier projects. *Kill Me or Die*, *Roots of Tradition* and the *HighWaterLine* project also evoked its scarcity: we're running out of time to take action in regard to global warming. Sunde's project invited others to lose track of time and meditate on the water's flow, temperature and wind, along with the shared risk of placing themselves in harm's way as the waters rise higher.

Cho, Mosher, Sunde, WOTE, Mendel, Liberate Tate and Yang also used the human figure in their work, as a unit of measurement against the behemoth of corporate misdeeds and consumerism, the cause of global warming and climate change. All evoked the vulnerability, isolation and fragility of the human species confronting disaster. It's as if they're saying, 'Look! Tides are rising up to this specific chin, these particular knees and thighs. Do you care?' For Yang, the message is directed to the consumer. Change or die: we may bury ourselves in an absurd cascade of soda cans, as we heedlessly consume and discard.

Got hope?

Where is the hope when our world seems bent on a global scale of self-destruction? The myth of the lone artist striking out on his or her own has been replaced by a new understanding that a collective of artists can have an outsize impact by creating public awareness and policy, and by engaging the public in ways unique to artists. Though some of the artists' work evoke isolation and vulnerability, their strength lies in collectives that are devoted to sounding the alarm. In the past decade, more and more artists and designers are added to the coterie of the concerned who are determined to use their creativity to generate new solutions. Says Nez Perce tribal elder James Holt, 'The people of today have a lot of power in their hands to enact policies to address climate change … I hope we can achieve that level of action necessary to protect our way of life.'[31] Artist Gustaff Harriman Iskandar explained that artists traditionally have a special status and social function in Indonesian society: 'The artist often has an important position in the community (sometimes as spiritual leader, or politician) and is expected to make a contribution to society.'[32] Artists' integrity is an overlooked yet essential quality in all societies. If we are to survive as a planet, it is critical that these voices not be ignored as prophets usually are but respected and paid attention to.

---

[31] Rose High Bear, executive producer, Wisdom of the Elders, Climate Film Academy, *Roots of Tradition*, https://www.nativeartsandcultures.org/native-american-film-academy-climate-film-festival (accessed 7 December 2017).

[32] Yasmine Ostendorf, 'Fresh Perspectives on Art and Ecology: Indonesia' (8 November 2017), http://ecohumanities.org/2017/11/08/fresh-perspectives-on-art-and-ecology-indonesia/ (accessed 6 December 2017).

In March of 2016, after six years of Liberate Tate's creative confrontations, the Tate Museum and British Petroleum came to a mutual agreement to terminate its twenty-six-year sponsorship. This victory proved that relentless, tactical pressure could create social change. Climate artists have shown that creativity, imagination and audacity are indispensable tools when confronting the evils of global warming.

Chapter 1.7
Working with climate activists in civil society

Todd LeVasseur[1] and Bernard Zaleha[2]

But let CO_2 roll on like a river, methane like a never-failing stream!
– Authors' rewriting of Amos 5.24 for a time of planetary regime shift, caused by the human animal

When Christ is maladaptive

This essay explores and then theorizes about potential collaborations between North Atlantic Christian groups and North Atlantic civil-sector climate activists, with a specific focus on actors in the United States. It utilizes a comparative perspective to very briefly investigate the theology and climate change work of a US Christian group working on climate-change issues with and as climate activists (Evangelical Environmental Network (EEN)) and a Christian group explicitly opposed to climate-change activism (Cornwall Alliance, CA). Overall, we argue that Christians in the United States, broadly speaking, are maladaptive in their theological teachings about and responses to climate change (as evidenced by CA and by polling numbers from a variety of polling sources), despite examples of some Christian groups who are working on climate change with civil society (as evidenced by EEN). Rather, the data suggests that Christian theology as formulated and put into practice by a variety of Christian groups in the United States has historically been and remains a key inhibitor for successful climate-change activist work. Given this, we remain dubious that, at least at a national level, US Christians

---

[1] Todd LeVasseur is Visiting Assistant Professor in Religious Studies and Environmental and Sustainability Studies at the College of Charleston in Charleston, South Carolina, where he also directs the Sustainability Literacy Institute. He has published widely in the environmental humanities.
[2] Bernard Daley Zaleha, an independent scholar, received his PhD in Sociology and Environmental Studies from the University of California, Santa Cruz. His research in the areas of environmental and political sociology, sociology of religion, currently focuses on the anti-environmental backlash within conservative American Christianity. He attends a Disciples of Christ congregation.

at large scales will actively partner with civil-society climate activists to address the sobering reality of human-induced climate change. A variety of literature, including religious studies, political ecology, sustainability studies, ecological hermeneutics and religion and nature theory, is used to craft this overall argument.

Readers should note that we are not Christian theologians or apologists, but rather we write this essay from the perspective of scholars who adopt a soft social constructionism grounded in the cognitive science of religion and that field's recognition that humans are neurologically predisposed to beliefs in non-material, non-empirical entities or forces. This leads many, perhaps most, humans to have experiences they deem 'religious' as commonly understood. Rather, prima facie we accept the scholarship that demonstrates that there is no universal Christianity; rather, there are multiple Christianities that have been shaped by multiple intersecting social, economic, political and ecological factors. Moreover, the Christianities of today are shaped by residues of multiple and often competing interpretations of multiple-authored texts strategically made sacred[3] that resulted from the eradication and suppression of pre-Christian traditions in Europe from the fourth to eighth centuries[4] and creation of a new nearly hegemonic Christian social identity.[5] As religious studies scholars standing in the framework of methodological naturalism, we recognize the traditional Christian understanding of Jesus as the divine creator of the cosmos who is simultaneously God and human as a social construction without empirical foundation. Most Christians, however, still embrace with varying degrees of certainty these traditional assumptions. Frustratingly, this understanding leads many US Christian believers of an Evangelical or fundamentalist ideology to deny the biophysical reality of our climate-changed planet, even though *Homo sapiens* itself is at risk as we rapidly approach 500 parts per million (ppm) of atmospheric carbon dioxide (CO_2) in the coming years. So how did we get here, and how do Christian views of anthropogenic climate change shape possible collaborative work with civil-society actors, especially in the United States?

Christianity and nature

In this essay we can only explore in broad strokes the interactions between contemporary Christianity, climate change and politics in the United States. To do so, however, we must situate our analysis within larger scholarly discussions about Christian views of the natural world. It is within this container that contemporary Christian stances on

---

[3] Bart D. Ehrman, *Lost Christianities: The Battles for Scripture and the Faiths We Never Knew* (New York: Oxford University Press, 2003).
[4] Ramsay MacMullen, *Christianity and Paganism in the Fourth to Eighth Centuries* (New Haven: Yale University Press, 1997).
[5] Burton L. Mack, *The Christian Myth: Origins, Logic, and Legacy* (New York: Continuum, 2001).

climate change are held, while this container is equally shaped by political identities and standpoints, especially in the US context. The major part of this essay undertakes this historical and theoretical work and creates the context of our claim that US Christianity, broadly speaking, is not currently amenable to working with civil-society climate activists.

We begin by pointing out that the ancient Israelites were an agrarian people living in a bioregion that supported pastoral, riverine, desert, maritime and farming lifeways.[6] The concern for receiving calories in a bioregion that suffered varying rainfall patterns, flooding and extreme dry heat shaped many early Israelite rituals, social customs and teachings. The patriarchal agrarian identity also shaped concepts of in-group identity, where knowing Hebrew and a culturally distinct devotion to Yahweh created a unique political-religio-cultural group located in the Palestinian/Israeli landbase of today (although the modern category of 'religion' was not known at this ancient time).[7] And it is precisely this place-specific religious identity that early Christians grappled with, both theologically and also bioculturally.

By a relaxing of Jewish laws and then wedding an emergent Christian identity and customs to Hellenic philosophies that privileged the rational and the human over the emotional and the physical,[8] a potential religion of empire was born. In addition, early Christianity was born in fervent apocalyptic expectation that persists in many Christian communities to this day. Jesus is depicted in both Matthew and Luke as saying he would return before that generation had passed. This 'end times' concept meant that with the expected deliverance, worldly affairs would be set right by God, the righteous would be resurrected and experience eternal life here on this earth. These early communities, inspired by Jesus but not yet called Christian (that would not occur until 112 CE), were incorporating the then-existing apocalyptic expectations in Judaism that had emerged around the Maccabean revolt in the 160s BCE. New Testament scholar Bart Ehrman calls the above 'horizontal dualism'. There is a past ruled by wickedness that is brought to a divine supernatural end, followed by an eternal reign of divine righteousness, all occurring here on this earth. During the first two centuries, this expectation persisted, but its non-occurrence eventually took a toll. Some communities began to embrace a new 'vertical' model of heaven and hell. Life on this planet was irredeemable and God's ultimate triumph would occur by redeeming the righteous into heaven and committing

---

[6] Daniel Hillel, *The Natural History of the Bible: An Environmental Exploration of the Hebrew Scriptures* (New York: Columbia University Press, 2006); Ellen Davis, *Scripture, Culture, and Agriculture: An Agrarian Reading of the Bible* (Cambridge: Cambridge University Press, 2008).

[7] Tomoko Masuzawa, *The Invention of World Religions, or, How European Universalism Was Preserved in the Language of Pluralism* (Chicago: University of Chicago Press, 2005); Brent Nongbri, *Before Religion: A History of a Modern Concept* (New Haven: Yale University Press, 2013).

[8] Frederic L. Bender, *The Culture of Extinction: Toward a Philosophy of Deep Ecology* (Amherst: Humanity Books, 2003).

the wicked to hell. This planet became a stage on which each individual's eternal fate, either in heaven or in hell, is determined.⁹

Both forms of 'end times' apocalyptic expectation – horizontal and vertical – have persisted in Evangelical to moderate forms of Christianity up to the present. In both forms our planet is not that significant and is ultimately slated for an abrupt (and, for many, imminent) end, either because it is abandoned and/or destroyed once divine judgement occurs and all people are either in heaven or hell, or because it has been miraculously transformed through divine power as the eternal home of the righteous. Within this mindset, catastrophic climate change and environmental deterioration do not effectively compete for concern with this expected cosmic drama. And as shown below, famed journalist Bill Moyers demonstrated that this mindset in the United States is leveraged into public policy advocacy resisting efforts to combat climate change.

The Australian biblical scholar Norman Habel comments that the Genesis creation stories, and the Old Testament (Hebrew Bible) broadly, gained further influence with the expansion of Christianity in the early centuries up to the present. This specifically includes the Priestly creation story in Genesis where humans, both male and female, are simultaneously created in the image of God, are then given the duty and privilege to dominate all other creatures created and are told to zealously subdue the earth.¹⁰ Habel's exegesis focuses in part on the Hebrew words *kabash* and *rada* – to subdue and rule¹¹ – and that it is this understanding of 'dominion' that suffuses the Genesis story and which Habel observes is willingly adopted by most Christians, past and present, as the basic cosmological understanding of the created order. In short, the mandate to subdue and dominate spread with Christianity's period of imperial/colonial expansion across the world,¹² often leading to overshoot and collapse. It is important to recognize that adherents of Christianity are not alone in this; it may be an inclination of a variety of religions, or even human nature, to impact ecosystems in ways that are almost always maladaptive.¹³

We do recognize that there were theological innovations in US Christianity in the late 1700s and 1800s leading to a nascent appreciation, even reverencing of the natural world.¹⁴ This then allowed for a synthesis among liberal Christians of post-

---

⁹ Bart D. Ehrman, *Jesus, Interrupted: Revealing the Hidden Contradictions in the Bible (and Why We Don't Know About Them)* (New York: HarperOne, 2009), 263–4.

¹⁰ Norman Habel, *An Inconvenient Text: Is a Green Reading of the Bible Possible* (Hindmarsh: ATF Press, 2009), 4.

¹¹ Ibid., 8.

¹² Robert Marks, *The Origins of the Modern World: A Global and Environmental Narrative from the Fifteenth to the Twenty-First Century, World Social Change* (Lanham: Rowman & Littlefield, 3rd ed., 2015).

¹³ Yi-Fu Tuan, 'Discrepancies between Environmental Attitude and Behaviour: Examples from Europe and China', *Canadian Geographer* 12:3 (1968), 176–91; Jared Diamond, *Collapse: How Societies Choose to Fail or Succeed* (New York: Viking, 2005).

¹⁴ Mark Stoll, *Inherit the Holy Mountain: Religion and the Rise of American Environmentalism* (Oxford and New York: Oxford University Press, 2015).

1859 Darwinian insights with a theocentric[15] perspective that supported an expansion of environmental concern in the 1960s and 1970s (recall the first Earth Day in 1970). Nonetheless, the resurgence in the United States of Christian fundamentalism effectively swamped these progressive impulses. Overall the dominant impulse of US Christianity has been to subdue and dominate the natural world and this impulse is today grafted in the United States to both vertical and horizontal dualisms, especially in the majority of Evangelical strains of US Christianity.

US Christian fundamentalism

The 1859 publication of Charles Darwin's *On the Origin of Species*[16] for the first time equipped humans with the option to base their cosmology and worldview on a naturalistic, scientific understanding of visible reality. The repercussions of Darwinian evolution, which removed a concept of telos and/or the anthropic principle from a credible understanding of observable reality, were seen by many US Christians as a threat to the hegemonic Christian understanding of reality found in Genesis and the New Testament. Contemporary evolutionary understandings of the origin and development of life depend on major gains in the natural sciences and technological instruments since the time of Darwin, so that today's climate-change models are tethered to supercomputer data modelling and data sets that result from the combined work of thousands of natural scientists the world over. This is seen most clearly in the Intergovernmental Panel on Climate Change reports. These provide an example of a thoroughly democratic and transparent process of better understanding the science behind how our planet works, especially in relation to anthropogenic climatic changes and the impacts of CO_2, methane, water vapour and other natural processes on the earth's atmosphere, lands, rivers and oceans.

However, the majority of US citizens from 1859 onwards, regardless of religious identity, have often, and at times quite proactively and aggressively, ridiculed Darwinian and neo-Darwinian evolution. While it is true that some religious leaders and bodies have accepted and even embraced evolution, there remains a vociferous and politically influential denunciation of evolutionary science in favour of the biblical creation story (or stories, as there are two different and contradictory myths laid out in Genesis 1 through 3). This dispute over how humans appeared on a planet that they did not create plays a unique role in US politics, including especially in Evangelical Christian responses to anthropogenic climate change.

---

[15] James M. Gustafson, *A Sense of the Divine: The Natural Environment from a Theocentric Perspective* (Cleveland: Pilgrim Press, 1994).

[16] Charles Darwin, *The Origin of Species by Means of Natural Selection* (Salt Lake City: The Project Gutenberg, 2009).

Christianity and climate change in the United States – from the 1960s to today

A key development in the discussion of the role of Christianity in American attitudes towards the environment was the publication in 1967 of Lynn White Jr's still-influential and widely cited essay 'The Historical Roots of Our Ecologic Crisis'. In this, recounting the separation of God from nature within Judaism and Christianity, White declared that 'in its Western form, Christianity is the most anthropocentric religion the world has seen', and opined that much environmental degradation is directly traceable to Christianity's radical anthropocentrism.[17]

The first major Christian response to White was from the then prominent and still widely cited thinker within Evangelical Christianity, Francis Schaeffer. In *Pollution and the Death of Man* (1970), Schaeffer acknowledges the intensifying problems of environmental pollution but denies that these problems stemmed from Christian arrogance and anthropocentrism.

Schaeffer was no doubt aware that more pantheistic reinterpretations of Christian doctrine were already well underway within mainline Christian denominations under the influence of the process philosophy of Alfred North Whitehead and the Christian process theology of Charles Hartshorne.[18] Thus, though he argued that human authority over God's creation was not unlimited, Schaeffer also cautioned throughout his book, faithful to Paul of Tarsus's creator/creation distinction and consistent with White's thesis, that humans must not let worries over environmental pollution tempt them into a more pantheistic understanding of nature. Faithful Christians must, according to Schaeffer, stay within the framework of humanity as the proper and rightful stewards of God's creation. While other Evangelical theorists and theologians such as Loren Wilkinson[19] and Calvin B. DeWitt[20] have further developed Schaeffer's foundational ideas, the basic framework of the stewardship model remains in place to the present, and stewardship is the main trope that is used by all Evangelicals and fundamentalists who discuss environmental issues.

The next significant development within Evangelical environmentalism was its move into policy advocacy. In 1993, the EEN formed as a subsidiary ministry of Evangelicals for Social Action,[21] a social justice advocacy organization founded in 1973. It formed

---

[17] Lynn White, 'The Historical Roots of Our Ecologic Crisis', *Science* 155:3767 (1967), 1203–7.

[18] John W. Cooper, *Panentheism, the Other God of the Philosophers: From Plato to the Present* (Grand Rapids: Baker Academic, 2006).

[19] Peter De Vos, Loren Wilkinson and Calvin Center for Christian Scholarship, *Earthkeeping, Christian Stewardship of Natural Resources* (Grand Rapids: Eerdmans, 1980).

[20] Calvin B. DeWitt, *Earth-Wise: A Biblical Response to Environmental Issues* (Grand Rapids: CRC Publications, 1994).

[21] David Larsen, 'Evangelical Evironmental Network', in *Encyclopedia of Religion and Nature*, Bron Taylor (ed.) (London and New York: Continuum International, 2005), 624–5.

in order to provide Evangelical participation in the then emerging National Religious Partnership for the Environment, a Jewish and Christian umbrella organization whose purpose was to 'promote environmental causes in church and temple teaching'.[22] Though primarily an educational organization formed to distribute environmental information to Evangelical congregations, the EEN also led a political campaign in 1996 to help fend off Republican efforts in Congress to weaken the federal Endangered Species Act.[23] In the course of that campaign, Evangelical lay theologian and environmental studies professor Calvin B. DeWitt declared that the federal Endangered Species Act was 'the Noah's ark of our day' and that 'Congress and special interests are trying to sink it'. As part of the campaign to protect the Act, DeWitt and other Evangelical leaders organized a network of Evangelical 'Noah' congregations who pledged to oppose congressional efforts to weaken federal species protection.[24] The campaign was successful, and Evangelical participation in the campaign was widely credited as a substantial factor in this political victory.[25]

The US political and social issue that caused Evangelicals and fundamentalists to re-engage in secular politics was abortion, which was made legal at the federal level in the *Roe v. Wade* US Supreme Court ruling of 1973. At the time of the ruling, the former president of the Southern Baptist Convention (the largest Protestant denomination in the United States) had praised the decision and the SBC had passed a resolution two years earlier calling for the liberalization of abortion laws. Evangelicals were generally indifferent or somewhat favourable towards the decision initially. Efforts to revoke the tax-exempt status, however, of the fundamentalist Bob Jones University in South Carolina due to its racially discriminatory policies was another matter. Operatives in the Republican Party sought a way to mobilize resentment of a federal clampdown on racist policies at conservative Christian colleges in favour of Republican candidates, and abortion ended up being an issue they could exploit.[26] Jerry Falwell's 'Moral

---

[22] Mick Womersley, 'National Religious Partnership for the Environment', in *Encyclopedia of Religion and Nature*, Bron Taylor (ed.) (London and New York: Continuum International, 2005), 1158–9.

[23] Larsen, 'Envangelical Evironmental Network', 625.

[24] Peter Steinfels, 'Evangelical Group Defends Laws Protecting Endangered Species as a Modern "Noah's Ark"', *New York Times* (31 January 1996), http://www.nytimes.com/1996/01/31/us/evangelical-group-defends-laws-protecting-endangered-species-amodern-noah-s-ark.html (accessed 15 August 2018).

[25] The work of EEN created the context for other Evangelical groups to emerge who are concerned about environmental/climate change issues. These include Christians and Climate (http://www.christiansandclimate.org/statement/; accessed 29 July 2018); the work of Evangelical climate scientist Katharine Hayhoe; and Young Evangelicals for Climate Action (https://www.yecaction.org/; accessed 29 July 2018), to name a few. A variety of Evangelical groups denounced the Trump administration's decision to withdraw the US from the Paris climate accords, but again, these are in the extreme minority of voices in US Evangelicalism. See Timothy Mclaughlin, 'US Evangelical Groups Pan Trump's Climate Accord Exit', https://www.reuters.com/article/us-usa-climatechange-right/u-s-evangelical-green-groups-pan-trumps-climate-accord-exit-idUSKBN18T301 (accessed 29 July 2018).

[26] Randall Balmer, 'Fundamentalism, the First Amendment, and the Rise of the Religious Right', *William & Mary Bill of Rights Journal* 18 (2010), 889–900.

Majority' advocacy group was one example. With a platform built upon fundamentalist and conservative views about abortion, evolution and women's rights, coupled with an emergent 'trickle down' economic orthodoxy of the Republican Party under Ronald Reagan, the stage was set for a resurgent Christian fundamentalism in US politics.[27] Over the past forty years there has flourished an anti-environmental, climate-change denying, anti-choice, pro-corporate tax breaks and business growth fusion of Christianity and Republican policy that began in the late 1970s and that still defines Republicanism through the Bush, Sr, Bush, Jr and now Trump eras.[28]

It is important to understand that even as mainstream branches of Christianity have come to accept evolution (the Catholic Church has stated that Catholic doctrine is compatible with evolution),[29] fundamentalist Evangelicals are still the 'gatekeepers' of political power in many states in the United States and, at least as of 2018, at the federal level. This means that fundamentalist Christian policymakers and their Evangelical voting base disproportionately impact, shape and determine US climate policy at the federal level, which under President Trump and his administration is strategically in denial of accepting that human behaviour is causing the Earth's climate to change. This position is at odds with science and is directly caused in part by a large number of Republican voters in the US holding fundamentalist Christian views about science, creation and eschatological expectations.

The history covered here helps one to recognize that conservative US Christians largely embrace an aggressive denial of biophysical reality when compared to Christians concerned about climate change in other parts of the North Atlantic. More so, this aggressive refutation of basic science makes it nearly impossible for civil-society actors

---

[27] Julie Zauzmer and Sarah Pulliam Bailey, 'After Trump and Moore, Some Evangelicals Are Finding Their Own Label Too Toxic to Use', *Washington Post* (14 December 2017), https://www.washingtonpost.com/local/social-issues/after-trump-and-moore-some-evangelicals-are-finding-their-own-label-too-toxic-to-use/2017/12/14/b034034c-e020-11e7-89e8-edec16379010_story.html (accessed 15 August 2018).

[28] See Todd LeVasseur, 'The Environment Contains No "Right" and "Left": Navigating Ideology, Religion, and Views of the Environment in Contemporary American Society', *Journal for the Study of Religions and Ideologies* 11:33 (2012), 62–88; Robin Globus Veldman, 'An Inconvenient Faith? Conservative Christianity, Climate Change and the End of the World' (PhD Dissertation, University of Florida, 2014); Bernard Daley Zaleha and Andrew Szasz, 'Keep Christianity Brown! Climate Denial on the Christian Right in the United States', in *How the World's Religions Are Responding to Climate Change: Social Scientific Investigations*, Robin Globus Veldman, Andrew Szasz and Randolph Haluza-DeLay (eds) (New York: Routledge, 2014), 209–28; Bernard Daley Zaleha and Andrew Szasz, 'Why Conservative Christians Don't Believe in Climate Change', *Bulletin of the Atomic Scientists* 71:5 (2015), 19–30; Randall Balmer, 'Fundamentalism, the First Amendment'.

[29] Gallup Inc., 'Evolution, Creationism, Intelligent Design', http://news.gallup.com/poll/21814/evolution-creationism-intelligent-design.aspx (accessed 1 April 2018). As of May 2017, Gallup's survey results report that 38 per cent of those polled believed that humans have evolved with God guiding such evolution; 19 per cent that humans evolved with God playing no part; and 38 per cent that God created humans in their present form (i.e. no belief in evolution); and 5 per cent having no opinion. For Pew survey results from 2014 on how US citizens view environmental issues through religious lenses, see http://www.pewforum.org/religious-landscape-study/views-about-environmental-regulation/ (accessed 1 April 2018).

to work with most US Evangelical Christians on policies devoted to either climate-change mitigation or adaptation.

For example, the political theorist Steven Cohen explains that in the US political system, and this is mirrored throughout the North Atlantic, political agendas are determined and acted upon by coalitions of stakeholders. These coalitions form around key policy questions that thus shape tactics and policy proposals. These policy questions include asking an issue's degree of legitimacy; the role the issue plays in electoral politics; whether the issue should be addressed at local, state or the federal level of government; and key for this essay asking, 'How does the scientific certainty or uncertainty related to the definition of the problem or its potential solution influence the politics of the issue?'[30] Of even more import is Cohen's insight that 'The political definition of [an] issue is critical in shaping how the issue is framed and ultimately addressed.'[31]

Cohen's exploration of these guiding questions about politics inform our analysis about the lack of coalition building we can expect in the United States between conservative Christians and civil-society actors working to adapt to climate change. This is because first and foremost various public polling of US Evangelical Christians, and the analysis shared throughout this essay, strongly suggest that climate change is for these voters simply not a legitimate political concern. More so, data suggests that for electoral politics in the United States, Republican politicians have strategically used climate change as a wedge and as a framing mechanism to attract and retain Evangelical voters; that these voters consistently claim that 'Big Government' at the federal level uses climate change as an excuse to infringe upon state's rights and the rights of business owners with unneeded regulations; and that the Republican Party has been successful in creating in their voting bloc (read: Evangelical Christians) a belief that there is extreme scientific uncertainty about the cause of current climate changes, let alone if the climate is even changing away from established geological baselines.

As explored below, this political framing of climate change by US Evangelical leaders has made it almost impossible for civil-society actors to build coalitions with majority-Christian voting blocs; rather, US Evangelical leaders and the Republican Party have framed climate change in such a way to vote out those who accept climate change and who want to use government to mitigate or adapt to it.[32] For example, the former South Carolina US House of Representatives, Bob Inglis (Republican), was asked during an interview why he lost his bid for re-election in 2010 in a heavily Republican state. He posited that 'I committed various heresies against the Republican orthodoxy … the most enduring heresy that I committed was saying the climate change is real, and let's do

---

[30] Steven Cohen, *Understanding Environmental Policy* (New York: Columbia University Press, 2006), 25–6.
[31] Ibid., 26.
[32] See, for example, Ben Adler, 'Most Republicans Who Accept Climate Science are Skipping Cleveland' (18 July 2016), about the Republican national convention for Trump winning that party's nomination for President. http://www.slate.com/articles/health_and_science/climate_desk/2016/07/the_few_republicans_who_accept_climate_change_are_largely_skipping_the_republican.html (accessed 22 April 2018).

something about it.'³³ If current Republican politicians are voted out by their own base for committing such a heresy, then how much harder for civil-society actors to make coalitions with US Evangelical Republican voters? We turn now to briefly explore why contemporary US Evangelical Republicans are so hostile to the reality of anthropogenic climate change.

A lack of concern for climate change in US Christianity

Famed journalist Bill Moyers produced a Public Broadcasting Service documentary airing in late 2006, 'Is God Green?', which explored the conflicts within Evangelical Christianity over climate change and environmental policy generally. Moyers was directed by prominent Evangelical leaders like James Dobson and Charles Colson to interview Calvin Beisner, founder of the Cornwall Alliance for the Stewardship of Creation, their designated pitchman for Evangelical climate change denial. Beisner's doctorate is in Scottish religious history. He is not a climate scientist.³⁴

In the course of his interview, the full, unabridged text of which is published on Moyers website,³⁵ Beisner explains that God directs humans to exercise 'forceful rule' over our planet. 'Quite frankly, if you are going to mine for precious metals, for fossil fuels, for anything else, you don't do that with a feather brush, you know. You don't do it by quietly blowing a breath on something as you would to blow out a candle.' When asked by Moyers if humans have 'a moral obligation to clean up the consequences of that force', Beisner said, 'as far as we are able to and, always, we also have a moral obligation to do rational, cost-benefit analysis, implying that the cost of clean-up might not be cost-beneficial'. Beisner also acknowledges that his work has received funding from ExxonMobil, but saw no conflict-of-interest in this, as it is to be expected that ExxonMobil would want voices such as his to be heard in public policy circles.

Finally, when pressed by Moyers whether he worried that he might be wrong about the unimportance and non-existence of global warming, Beisner said that even if it turns out to be real and harmful, it is of little ultimate importance, because where one is 'going to live [in either heaven or hell for] eternity' should be any reasonable human's primary concern. Here is an express dismissal of the earth's importance, by an ExxonMobil funded Evangelical fossil-fuel proponent. Conservative Christian activists

---

[33] Jason Breslo, 'Bob Inglis: Climate Change and the Republican Party' (23 October 2012), https://www.pbs.org/wgbh/frontline/article/bob-inglis-climate-change-and-the-republican-party/ (accessed 22 April 2018).

[34] Tom Casciato, 'Is God Green?', in *Moyers on America*, Felice Firestone and Judy Doctoroff O'Neill (eds) (USA: PBS, 2006).

[35] Bill Moyers and Calvin E. Beisner, 'Is God Green? (Moyers on America)' (New York: PBS.com), http://www.pbs.org/moyers/moyersonamerica/print/beisner_print.html (accessed 30 March 2018).

don't usually come right out and say this, but Beisner here illustrates how ancient apocalyptic expectations translate into present-day polemics against environmental regulation and displays how a fatalistic expectation of imminent divine rescue forms part of the bedrock of conservative Christian anti-environmentalism.

Beisner's understanding, together with many American Evangelicals, is captured in the lyrics of a popular Protestant folk hymn written by Albert Brumley during the Great Depression: 'This world is not my home. I'm just a passing through. If heaven's not my home, then Lord what will I do.'[36] A Pew study in 2006 reported that 20 per cent of Americans believe Jesus will return in their lifetimes.[37] By 2010, 41 per cent were saying Jesus would return by 2050.[38] Signs of this apocalyptic strain within conservative Protestantism pop up in various ways. A Baptist church near Boise, Idaho produced this bumper sticker: 'Forget "Save the Earth"; What About Your Soul? The Earth Is Going to Burn; What About You?'. A Christian bookseller sold bumper stickers and T-shirts emblazoned with 'Global Warming Is Nothing Next to Eternal Burning'. This fatalism is captured in another gospel classic, also written by Brumley, 'I'll Fly Away'. Indeed, this most recorded gospel song in American history[39] perfectly captures the world denial we have been discussing here that has so influenced much of conservative Christianity.[40]

This world denial comes up again in America's ongoing battles over evolution. Josh Rosenau in 2015 prepared a striking image of how starkly American Christianity is divided by attitudes about and belief in evolutionary science.[41] It depicts a near perfect trend line from liberal science-embracing Jews[42] in the upper right corner (down to the Assemblies of God in the lower left, who are widely regarded as America's most fundamentalist, most theologically conservative denomination). And, unsurprisingly, rejection of evolutionary science is closely tied to rejection of climate-change science – and those in this part of the graph overwhelmingly vote Republican.

---

[36] Albert E. Brumley, *Albert E. Brumley's Book of Radio Favorites: A Collection of Sacred, Sentimental, and Folk Songs* (Powell: Stamps-Baxter, 1938).

[37] Pew Forum on Religion & Public Life, 'Many Americans Uneasy with Mix of Religion and Politics' (2006), http://www.pewforum.org/Politics-and-Elections/Many-Americans-Uneasy-with-Mix-of-Religion-and-Politics.aspx (accessed 1 April 2018).

[38] Pew Research Center, 'Life in 2050: Amazing Science, Familiar Threats: Public See a Future Full of Promise and Peril' (22 June 2010), http://assets.pewresearch.org/wp-content/uploads/sites/5/legacy-pdf/625.pdf (accessed 30 March 2018).

[39] Kevin Donald Kehrberg, *"I'll Fly Away": The Music and Career of Albert E. Brumley* (Lexington: University of Kentucky, 2010), 10, https://uknowledge.uky.edu/gradschool_diss/49/

[40] William R. Inge, 'The Permanent Influence of Neoplatonism Upon Christianity', *The American Journal of Theology* 4:2 (1900), 328–44.

[41] Josh Rosenau, 'Evolution, the Environment, and Religion', in *NCSE Blog* (Oakland: National Center for Science Education, 2015), https://ncse.com/blog/2015/05/evolution-environment-religion-0016359/ (accessed 18 August 2018).

[42] Arthur Waskow, 'Rabbis against Climate Change' (2015), http://forward.com/opinion/national/309548/rabbis-against-climate-change/ (accessed 18 August 2018).

Conclusion

The influence of all wings of American Christianity is subject to the increase and decline of its various groups. Recent demographic reports are informative. The third American Religious Identity Survey released in March 2009[43] showed that the percentage of Americans who self-identify as Christian dropped to 76 per cent in 2008 compared to 86 per cent in 1990, a 11.6 per cent drop over eighteen years. The Pew Research Center recently documents that between 2007 and 2014, Christian self-identification dropped from 78.4 to 70.6 per cent, a 10 per cent decline over only seven years. This decline was accompanied by a jump in Americans unaffiliated with any particular religion from 16.1 to 22.8 per cent, a 42 per cent increase. Within Christianity, Evangelicals held more or less steady, experiencing a slight decline from 26.3 to 25.4 per cent.[44] Thus, the haemorrhaging within Christianity is within the more moderate to liberal wings. While this may be bad news for institutional forms at this end of the Christian spectrum, the fact that those exiting are moving outside traditional religions altogether is perhaps good news for environmental protection generally and the advancement of public policies addressing climate change. As we have laid out, the secular and the unaffiliated have some of the highest rates of environmental concern, perhaps showing that for them, planet earth really is their home. However, as long as Evangelical Christians of conservative and fundamentalist varieties deny anthropogenic climate change and aggressively advocate for policies that do nothing to help mitigate or adapt to such change, then working with other activists in civil society may be difficult because such activists may be suspicious of working with any Christians given the maladaptive attitudes of such evangelical Christians in the United States as outlined in this essay.[45]

---

[43] Barry A. Kosmin and Ariela Keysar, 'American Religious Identity Survey' (Hartford: Trinity College, Report, March 2009), https://commons.trincoll.edu/aris/files/2011/08/ARIS_Report_2008.pdf (accessed 18 August 2018).

[44] Pew Research Center: Religion & Public Life, 'America's Changing Religious Landscape: Christians Decline Sharply as Share of Population; Unaffiliated and Other Faiths Continue to Grow', http://www.pewforum.org/2015/05/12/americas-changing-religious-landscape// (accessed 18 August 2018).

[45] See Bernard Zaleha, 'A Tale of Two Christianities: The Religiopolitical Clash Over Climate Change Within America's Dominant Religion', (PhD dissertation, University of California, Santa Cruz, 2018).

A Southern African response to Todd LeVasseur and Bernard Zaleha

Kate Davies[1] and Ngonidzashe Edward[2]

In *Working with Climate Activists in Civil Society*, LeVasseur and Zaleha explore and discuss how US Christians have been 'maladaptive' in their theological teachings about and responses to climate change. They claim that Christian theology and the praxis of Christian groups in the United States have been and remain key inhibitors for successful climate-change activism. While this direct correlation between conservative theology and praxis may be true for the United States, the link between religion and climate activism is, in our opinion, more complex and nuanced in the Global South.

People in Southern Africa frequently encounter droughts, floods, fire, crop failure, hungry seasons and other climate-related challenges. Climate disruption is a lived experience. Although people may not have the language of science to define the problem, they experience it even if it does not have a name. We believe that, in general, a lack of response in the subcontinent is not due to conservative climate-change denialism, as is claimed to be the case among US Christians. We suggest, instead, that the absence of activism is because church leadership has not translated the problem into a theological framework which would elicit agency among Christian congregations, so that other social and economic issues take precedence over ecological ones.

How does the Christian landscape in South Africa compare with that of the United States? According to a 2010 survey on religious demography in South Africa, more than 80 per cent of the population have a Christian association.[3] A breakdown of denominational affiliation indicates that in 2001, nearly 41 per cent of Christians belong to one or other of the several thousand African Independent/Initiated/Indigenous Churches (AICs). Stemming from both Christian and African traditional religious roots, these groupings have a variety of organizational forms, many with no physical infrastructure. In spite of a historic relationship with nature (and the ancestors) and with a constituency that is disproportionately impacted by climate change, to our knowledge there has been no informed response from AICs regarding climate change. Our comments in this response

---

[1] Kate Davies is Co-founder of SAFCEI, the Southern African Faith Communities' Environment Institute, where she pursues a special interest in faith-based environmental learning.
[2] Ngonidzashe Edward is the Climate Justice Coordinator of the Jesuit Ecology and Development Program for Southern Africa. He is also a member of the Global Catholic Climate Movement.
[3] Willem Schoeman, 'South African Religious Demography: The 2013 General Household Survey', *HTS Theological Studies* 73:2 (2017), 1–7.

therefore exclude this not insignificant grouping of Christians. The 2010 religious survey also notes that more than 7.34 per cent of Christians belong to Pentecostal and charismatic churches – although this may well be underestimated. The absence in this constituency of a strong social justice agenda so characteristic of many of the mainline churches in South Africa suggests to us that these churches are likely to more closely follow the conservative approach to climate activism in the United States as described by LeVasseur and Zaleha.

Christianity has been charged with responsibility for environmental degradation. In his famous thesis on 'The Historical Roots of our Ecological Crisis' Lynn White, Jr, traces how environmental degradation is a direct consequence of Christianity's radical anthropocentrism.[4] According to LeVasseur and Zaleha, this radical anthropocentrism continues in the United States and is being propagated and taught by the majority of conservative Evangelical and fundamentalist Christians around the world.

The situation in Southern Africa is not dissimilar. LeVasseur and Zaleha emphasize that the 'mandate to subdue and dominate spread with Christianity's period of imperial/ colonial expansion across the world'. In Southern Africa, the situation was made worse by the 'unholy' alliance between Christianity, colonialism, Apartheid and poverty. Despite the tainted history, Christianity, which is a powerful social role player in Southern Africa, has the potential to play a crucial role in the reversal of the very ecological crisis for which it has been held responsible. In this regard, Kate Davies believes that Christianity can offer the necessary inspiration, spiritual vision, ecological wisdom, ethical discernment, moral power and hope to address environmental degradation and climate change.[5]

Why isn't this happening? Christians do not lack concern about how a changing climate is threatening human livelihoods and well-being. Many, particularly in rural contexts, are already vulnerable to the increased risks brought about by climate disruption. The link between environmental threats, socio-economic issues and climate disruption, and an effective response to these are, however, not obvious until there is an understanding of climate disruption drivers. According to the South African Council of Churches, there has been a failure to make the connection between climate change and immediate social issues because climate is viewed as a distant issue over which we have no control.[6] What is lacking in Southern Africa is informed Christian leadership and community. This would not only help people make the connection between social concerns and environmental issues but encourage critical reflection on how theological and ethical principles should guide and inform a Christian response to the crisis.

---

[4] Lynn White, Jr, 'The Historical Roots of our Ecological Crisis', *Science* 155 (1967), 1203–7.
[5] Kate Davies, 'Greening Christian Institutions and Practices An Emerging Ecclesial Reform Movement', in *Ecclesial Reform and Deform Movements in the South African Context,* Ernst M. Conradie and Miranda N. Pillay (eds) (Stellenbosch: Sun Press, 2015), 40–60.
[6] South African Council of Churches, *Climate Change – A Challenge to the Churches in South Africa* (Braamfontein: SACC, 2009).

Making these connections has become crucial in defining the contemporary justice struggle in South Africa.[7] In 'Seeking Eco-Justice in the South African Context', Conradie and others stress the link between ecological concerns and the problems that the poor and marginalized face in Southern Africa.[8] There is the need to help people understand that these issues are intertwined and therefore part of the same struggle. Awakening this realization through theology and Christian social teachings is the role church leadership needs to foster and institutionalize in order to grow climate activism.[9]

A spike in faith-based climate activism that took place at the COP 17 Climate talks in Durban in 2011 marked a shift in understanding and commitment among some Christian groups in Southern and Eastern Africa. For many, this was the first time climate change was connected to social justice. Prior to this, most of the activism had focused on a social agenda seeking to address issues of poverty, unemployment, the HIV and AIDS pandemic, gender-based and domestic violence, xenophobia, gangsterism, drugs, crime and corruption.[10] At COP 17 the two agendas of social justice and climate disruption were brought together under the same banner through the 'We Have Faith: Act Now for Climate Justice!' campaign. In the build-up to the conference, Christian leaders were called upon to explore and promote ecotheological and eco-justice principles as expressed in the Earth Charter.

Among so-called mainline churches in the Global South, Christian ecotheology is emerging as key to addressing the problems of environmental degradation and climate change. This gives a language and ethical framework which speaks to and promotes ideas and praxis that express environmental responsibility, stewardship and caring for creation (and in a few instances custodianship). In Southern Africa, ecotheology has not been sufficiently developed or mainstreamed. This is despite recognition of the need for a credible ecotheology that is culturally relevant and sensitive to African Christian communities. Developing such a theology would promote a purposeful ideological orientation for sustainable ecological engagement and praxis, finding expression in public worship, sermons, prayers and pilgrimages, becoming what Pope Francis calls 'ecological spirituality'.[11]

---

[7] During South Africa's liberation struggle, there was little or no consideration of environmental issues, because the focus was defined in a specific way, namely political liberation.

[8] See Ernst M. Conradie, Charity Majiza, Jim Cochrane, Welile T. Sigabi, Victor Molobi and David Field, 'Seeking Eco-justice in the South African Context', in *Earth Habitat: Eco-Injustice and the Church's Response,* Dieter T. Hessel and Larry L. Rasmussen (eds) (Minneapolis: Fortress, 2001), 135–57.

[9] See the 'olive agenda' proposed by Steve de Gruchy in *Keeping Body and Soul Together: Reflections by Steve de Gruchy on Theology and Development* (Pietermaritzburg: Cluster Publications, 2015); also Diakonia Council of Churches, *The Oikos Journey: A Theological Reflection on the Economic Crisis in South Africa* (Durban, 2006).

[10] The South African Faith Communities' Environment Institute (SAFCEI) and its partners organized the 'We Have Faith, Act Now for Climate Justice' campaign leading up to COP 17 in Durban in November/December 2011. Using the momentum that the COP created, several activities were carried out under the theme 'Act Now for Climate Change'. See the 'We Have Faith Campaign Report', available at http://safcei.org/resources/we-have-faith-campaign/ (accessed 1 February 2019).

[11] Pope Francis, *Laudato Si': On Care for Our Common Home* (Vatican City: Encyclical Letter, 2015).

Liturgical celebrations and exploring and embracing ecological spirituality are effective approaches to building an informed understanding of the faith–eco-justice nexus in Christian communities. However, it is more the exception than the rule that Southern African congregations hear an environmental message from the pulpit. Here, eco-justice is not high on the church agenda and in many cases it is not on the agenda at all, due to reasons described above. Greater numbers of Christians in Southern Africa would have knowledge about climate change if they were hearing it from the leadership they trust the most. Agency is not absent because people are apathetic or in denial. People are less likely to be activists and agents for change when leadership is seen to be ill-equipped and unprepared for the challenge.

Promoting ecotheology is one way of challenging the dominion theology that LeVasseur and Zaleha state is so pervasive among conservative and evangelical Christians in the United States. The dangerous theology of dominion has been used by President Trump and Christian fundamentalist groups to endorse the exploitation of the natural world and unsustainable policies and practices.

Consumerism has become a new global religion from which South Africa is not immune, but there are not many Christian groups in this region that overtly embrace radical anthropocentrism. We do, however, have our fair share of dangerous theologies, including mastery theology, escapist theologies, enculturation theologies in the context of consumerism, blaming theologies and the prosperity gospel.[12] They have been responsible for distorting or ignoring the climate message, discouraging people from paying attention to the issue or focusing exclusive attention on the hereafter.

Climate change is the most threatening environmental challenge of our time. There is an urgent need for social and community activism to work in partnership with science. Because the majority of Southern Africans are Christian and because churches are some of the most organized, widespread, well-connected and respected civil-society organizations, they are well-placed to play a key role in this process. They have also had experience in the social justice struggle and have a long history of providing humanitarian aid. While climate activism may not be considered core gospel business, it is an eco-social responsibility.

Why therefore have Christians not responded to the current crisis? In the Southern African context, we do not believe it is because of conservative denialism. We suggest it is in part because faith leadership does not operate in the epistemological framework of climate science. It is also because underpinning value systems with ecotheology is largely absent from current leadership training and thinking. Christian leadership has not yet been mandated to incorporate and embed ecological wisdom and concerns in daily faith praxis nor has the climate crisis discourse emerged in Christian policy frameworks.

---

[12] The South African Council of Churches discusses these theologies in great details. See *Climate Change – A Challenge to the Churches in South Africa*, 6.

Chapter 1.8
Working with climate activists in other religious traditions

Paul O. Ingram[1]

Introduction

Writing as a Quaker who practices Zen Buddhist disciplines of meditation and a leader in contemporary Buddhist–Christian dialogue, Sallie B. King describes three interdependent forms of inter-religious dialogue, sometimes called interfaith dialogue: conceptual dialogue, socially engaged dialogue and interior dialogue.[2] The focus of conceptual dialogue is doctrinal, theological and philosophical. It is concerned with a religious Way's collective self-understanding and worldview. Persons participating in conceptual dialogue compare doctrinal and philosophical formulations on such questions as ultimate reality, human nature, suffering and evil, the role of Jesus in Christian faith and practice with the roles of the historical Buddha, Muhammed or Confucius in the Buddhist, Islamic and Confucian Ways.

Since issues of social, economic, gender and ecological violence and injustice are systemic, global, interconnected and interdependent, they are neither religion-specific nor cultural-specific. This is the focus of socially engaged inter-religious dialogue. Accordingly, faithful human beings representing all religious Ways mutually apprehend common experiences of injustice along with resources for working together to liberate human beings, indeed, planet Earth itself, from the global forces of systemic oppression. Whenever socially engaged inter-religious dialogue focuses on ecological issues like global warming, the natural sciences are of necessity included in the conversation as a third partner. Since capitalism is the source of the economist's faith in growth and the consumerism that is the empowering force of global warming and other ecological issues, the social science discipline of economics must be brought into the discussion.

---

[1] Paul O. Ingram is Professor Emeritus of History of Religions at Pacific Lutheran University, Tacoma, Washington. His research interests include Buddhist–Christian dialogue, science–religion dialogue, process theology and Islamic–Christian dialogue.

[2] Sallie B. King, 'Conclusion: Buddhist Social Activism', in *Engaged Buddhism: Buddhist Liberation Movements in Asia*, Christopher S. Queen and Sallie B. King (eds) (Albany: State University of New York Press, 1996), 401–52.

I agree with John B. Cobb, Jr, that policies engendering sustainable development – where the economy serves the community and not vice versa – are not only feasible and economically sound but more faithfully represent the emphasis in the Christian Way, as well as in non-Christian religious Ways, on the dignity of the individual and the value of the common good.[3]

Finally, if the participants in interior dialogue are to be believed, within the common struggle for liberation from injustice an experiential referent or common ground emerges that enables them to hear one another and be mutually transformed in the process. This is so because interior dialogue concentrates on disciplines such as meditation, contemplative prayer, centering prayer, dance and music. Interior dialogue involves practising meditative and prayer disciplines in dialogue with one's dialogical partners. Interior dialogue is important because once we 'hear' the 'music' of a religious Way other than our own, we are enabled to achieve a deeper understanding of the 'lyrics' of the teachings and practices of that Way as well as our own religious Way. In fact, this is the goal of all three forms of inter-religious dialogue. Otherwise, dialogue becomes missionology whereby participants merely converse with their own faith traditions as 'superior' to all others.

Socially engaged inter-religious dialogue as resource for climate action

The remainder of this essay will focus on the practice of socially engaged inter-religious dialogue with the natural sciences as a third partner. My thesis is that socially engaged inter-religious dialogue focused on the global causes of climate change – free market capitalism – is the best resource human beings possess for rescuing planet Earth from environmental destruction 'before it's too late', as John Cobb has phrased it.[4] But it must be also kept in mind that socially engaged dialogue must be grounded in conceptual and interior dialogue and the natural sciences.

Human beings have been struggling to create just, compassionate communities inclusive of all sentient beings at least since shamans painted the shapes of animals in deep caves in Lascaux, France and Altamira, Spain, 18,500 to 14,000 years ago. In all times and in all places against all odds this struggle continues. It is humanity's religious Ways that everywhere took the lead in this struggle, often against conventionally

---

[3] See John B. Cobb, Jr, *Sustaining the Common Good: A Christian Perspective on the Global Economy* (Cleveland: Pilgrim Press, 1994), Preface, Chapter 1.

[4] See John B. Cobb, Jr, *Spiritual Bankruptcy: A Prophetic Call to Action* (Nashville: Abingdon Press, 2010), Chapter 1 and Jay B. McDaniel, 'Ten Ideas for Saving the Planet', in *Replanting Ourselves in Beauty: Toward an Ecological Civilization*, Jay B. McDaniel and Patricia Adams Farmer (eds) (Anoka: Process Century Press, 2015), 200–36.

religious human beings and institutions that populate all religious Ways. So, the call to live justly and compassionately in human community inclusive of the sentient life forms with whom we share this planet has come from a minority of powerful religious or should I say 'prophetic' voices throughout the histories of humanity's religious Ways.

Examples abound: the entire Mosaic tradition celebrated by Jews as interpreted through the oracles of the eighth-, seventh- and sixth-century BCE prophets; the historical Jesus whom Christians confess as the Christ of faith; Mohammed; Gautama the Buddha; the Daoist sages; Confucius; and aboriginal religious Ways. Contemporary examples abound as well: they include every rabbi I've ever met; Martin Luther King, Jr, Thomas Merton and Thomas Keating; Badsha Khan and Mohandas Gandhi; Wing-tzit Chan; process theologians John B. Cobb, Jr, Jay McDaniel and Patricia Adams Farmer; wise lay followers of all religious Ways struggling throughout their lives to live justly and compassionately in human communities inclusive of all sentient beings.[5]

Consequently, human resources for resisting free market economic practices and the political systems responsible for global environmental injustice are clearly available in humanity's religious Ways. This is also the opinion of Pope Francis. His third encyclical, *Laudato Si'* ('Praise Be To You'), calls all Roman Catholics, indeed all Christians, faithful followers of non-Christian religious Ways, secularists and scientists to engage in a global dialogue centred on climate change and on the basis of this dialogue take immediate and decisive action to address and redress its main cause: global warming.[6]

Of course, other important inter-religious voices and organizations are engaged in dialogical confrontation with environmental issues. Again, examples abound: the Dalai Lama; Elizabeth A. Eaton, the presiding bishop of the Evangelical Lutheran Church in America; the Lutheran World Federation; the United Methodist Church; the Presbyterian Church (USA); Justin Welby, Archbishop of Canterbury; the bishops of the American Episcopal Church; the membership of the Society for Buddhist-Christian Studies; the Religious Action Center of Reformed Judaism; the Forum on Religion and Ecology, founded by Mary Evelyn Tucker and John Grimm; the Buddhist Churches in America; the Center for Process Studies in Claremont, California; the Center for Theology and the Natural Sciences in Berkeley, California; online organizations such as Pondo Populus; and Muslim theologians like Farhan Shah, who is an important voice of protest against the government of Norway's expansion of oil rigs in the North Sea; the Islamic Declaration on Global Climate Change, issued in Istanbul, Turkey, on August 18, 2015; the Coalition on the Environment and Jewish Life (COEJI) – and the list could go on across the planet.

Every person and organization listed in the above paragraph is utterly devoted to calling us to a global socially engaged inter-religious dialogue that (1) insists that climate change is real and caused by human beings; (2) calls for rapid conversion of

---

[5] See Paul O. Ingram, *You Have Been Told What Is Good: Interreligious Dialogue and Climate Change* (Eugene: Cascade Books, 2016), Chapters 1–3.

[6] Pope Francis, *Laudato Si': On Care for Our Common Home* (San Francisco: Ignatius, 2015).

global economies from oil, coal and gas to renewable sources of energy such as solar and wind power; (3) insists that the first victims of global warming are the poor; and (4) keeps in mind that given the extent of the environmental damage human beings have already caused, we no longer have room for a slight shift from fossil fuels. We simply must make an immediate leap to renewable forms of energy because the life of all sentient beings is at stake.

The question is, what positive influence might socially engaged inter-religious dialogue with the natural sciences as a third partner have in combatting global warming? First, every religious Way, as specified by the teachings of each, calls us to create just, compassionate communities that seek the common good of people and the natural environment supporting all life. The goal of inter-religious dialogue is mutual creative transformation interdependent with the creative transformation of the environment. This is the primary obligation all faithful people share without exception. But entering inter-religious dialogue as a means of asserting the priority of our own religious Way over others is a monological prophylactic meant to protect us from whatever it is we reject. Forms of exclusivism, including Christian fundamentalism, are irrelevant when it comes to resolving environmental issues like global warming.

Second, socially engaged inter-religious dialogue assumes the interdependence of all things and events. Every religious Way I have encountered in my work as a historian of religions asserts that the foundations of justice, compassion, community and the common good rests on the interdependence of all things and events. Violence, injustice, the oppression of women and the poor, and the exploitation of the Earth's natural resources by the corporate and politically greedy tear this interdependence apart. Here lies the source of violence, injustice and the destruction of human community and our community with the environment.[7] All one need do to confirm this is read the daily newspapers, catch the daily news on television or bury one's attention in social media. Each of humanity's religious Ways has instructed human beings through their own distinctive teachings and practices about 'what is good', as Micah 6.6-8 has it. It is time to listen and act accordingly.

Third, there are millions of people on this planet whose collective resistance just might be the force necessary to compel the leaders of economic and political institutions to cease working for the good of the wealthy and powerful through 'top-down' economics and to propel them to work for the common good of all human and non-human beings on planet Earth through 'bottom-up' economics.[8] While socially engaged inter-religious dialogue does not require doctrinal agreement, it *does* require a focus on just, compassionate community for the common good inclusive of persons,

---

[7] See Herman E. Daly and John B. Cobb, Jr, *For the Common Good: Redirecting the Economy toward Community, the Environment, and a Sustainable Future* (Boston: Beacon Press, 1989), Introduction, Chapter 1.

[8] Philip Clayton and Justine Heinzekehr, *Organic Marxism: An Alternative to Capitalism and Ecological Catastrophe* (Claremont: Process Century Press, 2014), Chapter 1.

including those who identify themselves as secularists or atheists. For when it comes to environmental issues like global warming, water depletion or deforestation, we are all in this together. Doctrinal and philosophical differences fade away like snakes shedding skin as politicians and their corporate allies are forced to pay attention and change the ways economic systems work.

Perhaps the following example will clarify this: During July and August of 2015 hundreds of protesters surrounded a huge Royal Dutch Shell drilling platform scheduled to be towed from Portland, Oregon, to the Gulf of Alaska to begin exploratory oil drilling. Protesters surrounded the rig in hundreds of kayaks in an attempt to stop an icebreaker from towing it up the Willamette River to the Columbia River out to the Pacific Ocean and north to Alaska. A large number of protesters hung from a bridge crossing the Willamette River from ropes long enough to block the icebreaker. Protesters hung from these seats in shifts for three days until they were arrested. I can't really argue that the protest 'worked', because the icebreaker pulling the oil rig eventually arrived in the Gulf of Alaska. But on 28 September 2015, Royal Dutch Shell abandoned its quest to become the first company to produce oil in Alaska's Arctic waters because it 'failed to find enough oil to make drilling profitable'.

None of the protesters in Portland worried about the religious commitment of the persons sitting in kayaks carrying protest signs or hanging from a bridge. Yet the protesters included Christians from all denominations – Jews, Muslims and Buddhists from different traditions, as well as people who identified themselves as 'spiritual but not religious', along with committed secularists, agnostics and atheists. While informal and unplanned, conceptual and interior dialogical conversations occurred between the people surrounding the icebreaker and hanging from the bridge, so that, as the Qur'an affirms, people 'might know each other', the energizing force propelling this effort was the perception of a common humanity unifying religious differences in the struggle to create a just, compassionate community working for the common good and the truth of what climate scientists are revealing about global warming. In situations requiring justice and compassion, doctrinal differences and practices become, in the words of Nagarjuna, the Indian Buddhist logician, 'secondary truths'. Certainly, the defining 'secondary truths' of socially engaged religious Ways need to be understood by means of conceptual and interior dialogue so that 'we may know each other'. But the greater truth behind the diversity of religious teachings and practices is how secondary truths reveal our common humanity, as Confucius pointed out, that defines us as human. In our religious diversity we are one, or 'non-dual' as my Buddhist friends put it.

The scientific facts of global warming have been confirmed and are well known. And while scientific contributions to specific conceptual and interior dialogues are in their infancy, the contributions of the scientific community to socially engaged interreligious dialogue are taken with utmost seriousness.[9] According to climate scientist

---

[9] See Paul O. Ingram, *Buddhist-Christian Dialogue in an Age of Science* (New York: Rowman & Littlefield, 2008), Chapter 1.

James Hansen, the primary cause of global warming is over-reliance on fossil fuels.[10] Fossil-fuel reserves are at present declining, yet large oil corporations continue tearing the Earth apart to extract every last drop of oil and lump of coal. In this search, corporations like Exon, Shell and British Petroleum proudly advertise that they are drilling the depths of the oceans and exploring the most pristine environments to feed consumerist addiction to fossil fuels while increasing the profits of their stockholders. But this corporate greed is 'as insane as a drug addict trudging through an arctic blizzard in search of a fix'.[11]

Here's the major scientific fact: if humanity is to continue to survive on a planet similar to the one on which human civilization evolved thousands of years ago and to which all present life on Earth is biologically adapted, the ratio of carbon and oxygen (CO_2) must be reduced to at most 350 particles per million (ppm). Hansen estimates that peak CO_2 can be kept to about 445 ppm, with large estimates for remaining oil and gas reserves, if coal is phased out by 2030, although some 'peakists' believe that the planet is already at peak oil production because nearly half of the globe's readily extracted oil has already been consumed.

Consequently, Hansen argues that we must pursue a radically different direction premised on the possibility that achieving 350 ppm CO_2 or lower this century will minimize the possibility of passing tipping points that spiral out of control: continued global warming caused by the emission of greenhouse gases into the atmosphere, the complete disintegration of Arctic and Antarctic ice sheets and the rapid rise of sea levels, the acidification of oceans and the loss of coral reefs, and the mass extinction of countless species. The list goes on: rising temperatures coupled with an increase in dangerous weather-related events like hurricanes, abnormally heavy rainfall and flooding, interrupted by increasing periods of heat waves, and rising sea levels flooding coastal cities and farming communities. And the tragedy is all this planetary destruction is directly linked to current capitalist economic practices that sell consumerism like an addictive drug.

Accordingly, the future is grim indeed, and we had better act now to undertake the necessary steps to reverse global warming. As a matter of fact, the Chinese government arguably has taken the lead in resisting global climate change, and the Center for Process Studies under the leadership of process theologians John B. Cobb, Jr, and Jay McDaniel have engaged with the Chinese to encourage their efforts as an example of the possibilities of creative transformation. The government of China is revisiting the classical Chinese Religious Ways by placing Confucian and Daoist traditions in dialogue with the official Marxist political philosophy under which the Chinese people have been governed since 1948. The Confucian Way offers guidelines for living in harmony among people. Confucian teachings and practices encourage us to respect older people,

---

[10] James Hansen, 'Timeline for Irreversible Climate Change', Policy Innovations (22 April 2008), *Yale Global Online,* http//www.policyinnovations.org/ideas/commentary data/000049/ (accessed 10 January 2018).
[11] Ibid.

to practice the arts of politeness and peace, to work for the greater good of the whole, to cultivate our individual capacities for wisdom, to grow in compassion and thereby become fully human.

The Daoist Way encourages living in balanced harmony with the natural process of the Earth by living flexibly, simply and remaining sensitive to the life's energy (qi) coursing through all things and events, seeking balanced harmony within our own bodies, the very place where the Dao (Way) is incarnated in us, and living in balanced harmony with the ever-shifting energy of the polar forces in nature known in China as *yin* and *yang*. Process theologians also believe that harmony among people and harmony with the Earth are the best hope for humanity. Process theologians like me are encouraged by contemporary Chinese leaders who offer hope that, in future, China will continue evolving into an ecological civilization that embodies this sort of balanced harmony between *yin* and *yang* in both urban and rural settings.

Perhaps the most consistently ongoing inter-religious dialogue between the world's religious Ways is now occurring under the auspices of the World Parliament of Religions. The first meeting of the Parliament took place in Chicago during the 1893 World's Fair. In 2009, the Parliament met in Melbourne, Australia. The Melbourne Parliament focused on issues of sustainability and climate change through the lenses of aboriginal spiritualities. The Council for the Parliament at Melbourne concluded that economic practices, environmental degradation and religiously inspired violence are interconnected. Consequently, it is necessary that all persons of faith strive for global peace and justice by exploring the causes of religious conflict, creating cross-cultural networks for addressing issues of religious violence and finding ways to work together internationally to confront global environmental threats by reforming capitalist practices causing global warming.

Of course, different peoples will have different ways of creating ecological civilizations. An African 'ecological civilization', for example, will be uniquely African; an American ecological civilization, American. Each will have its own unique structures of existence. For process thinkers 'harmony' is not 'sameness'. It is the sort of harmony that respects and takes delight in differences. Furthermore, harmony is not static but fluid as it evolves over time. It includes a healthy dose of novelty and creativity, with dissonance as well as consonance, like jazz or some of my favourite Bach fugues. Most important, it is nonviolent togetherness, which can be objectively embodied in how we build cities and care for rural life. It can be enjoyed subjectively in acts of compassion. In its objective and subjective expressions, it embodies creative, postmodern sustainability.

Serious efforts are now underway to repair the ecological damage in China caused by its attempts to 'catch up with the West' as a means of achieving independence from Western imperialism. China's dialogue with its classical religious Ways and process theologians such as John Cobb, Catherine Keller, Zhihe Wang and Meijun Fan have concentrated on the development of sustainable communities, meaning communities that are creative, compassionate, participatory and ecologically wise with no one left behind. These communities are guided by three ideals: economic viability, ecological integrity and social well-being. Apart from economic viability no community is sustainable; it must offer jobs and livelihoods that give people a sense of dignity and satisfaction in work. Without ecological integrity, no community can survive because it will destroy is resource base, a problem now happening worldwide. Without social well-being, it will be miserably joyless and unjust. Process thinkers often refer to this as the 'holy trinity of sustainable communities'.[12]

Accordingly, the future looks bleak indeed and we better follow China's example and take the necessary steps to reverse global warming. Such collective action must begin by breaking our consumerist addiction to fossil fuels because a large fraction of CO_2 emissions will linger in the atmosphere for many centuries. In other words, 'we're not going to get back the planet we used to have, the one on which our civilization developed'.[13] Given this reality, what might the structure of a socially engaged inter-religious dialogue focused on climate change look like? And how might such a dialogue help human beings resist the consumerist causes of global warming? In the hope of energizing such dialogue, in what follows I shall add my voice to inter-religious discussions about how the religious Ways of the world might become a force to be reckoned with against consumerist economic and political systems rapidly pushing life on this planet to extinction.

Passing over and returning

For me, a convenient starting point in thinking about the structure and purpose of inter-religious dialogue is the process that John S. Dunne described as 'passing over and returning', which means that the structure of dialogue is Socratic.[14] Authentic dialogue reflects a twofold realization by those participating that (1) they are ignorant of the 'truth' and (2) they desire to undertake the search for this 'truth' which is, as Socrates believed, the first step towards wisdom. Once we experience this push, dialogue entails two *yin*- and *yang*-like movements: 'passing over' into the faith and experiences of persons dwelling in religious Ways other than our own and 'returning to the home' of one's own religious Way, hopefully with our creativity transformed by the odyssey of the encounter.

Of course, much depends on the worldview from which the odyssey begins. Normally, Christians pass over and return to a faith tradition within the Christian Way, a Muslim to a tradition of the Muslim Way, or a Buddhist to a school of the Buddhist Way such as

---

[12] See Jay B. McDaniel, 'The Tao of Sustainability', *Replanting Ourselves in Beauty: Toward an Ecological Civilization,* Jay McDaniel and Patricia Adams Farmer (eds) (Anoka: Process Century Press, 2015), 1–6.

[13] Bill McKibben, *Earth: Making Life on a Tough New Planet* (New York: St. Martin Griffin, 2010).

[14] John S. Dunne, *The Way of All the Earth: Experiments in Truth and Religion* (Notre Dame: University of Notre Dame Press, 1978), Preface and Chapter 1.

Zen or one of the many schools of the Tibetan or Chinese traditions. But many faithful people find themselves unable to return to the home of their original religious Way because they are either overwhelmed or deeply influenced by the reality of religious pluralism and the relativizing of religious faith and practice this reality occasions. They may wear the labels of a religious Way or they may be committed secularists. Some experience dual religious identities, for example, finding themselves both Roman Catholic and Zen Buddhist.[15] Engaging in the adventure inter-religious dialogue is not for the faint hearted. Many people, including me, end up being theological pluralists. But the consensus of those involved in inter-religious dialogue is that the goal is renewal and creative transformation. Otherwise, why bother with dialogue at all?

But before socially engaged inter-religious dialogue can evolve into something more than a conversation about religious teachings and doctrines between persons of different faith traditions, it must take on a prophetic character in its focus on global warming and its causes, blame for which lies primarily with large corporations whose only purpose seems to be to increase the consumption of the Earth's resources while lining the pockets of corporate executives in the process. This requires bringing the natural sciences into this dialogue as a 'third partner' as well as the discipline of economics because since the seventeenth century, a scientific cosmology has emerged about the physical processes at play in the universe – from subatomic quantum forces, to planets, to the universe itself in general, to the biological processes creating and sustaining live.[16]

All religious Ways, of course, have their own worldviews. These must not be merely abandoned but reinterpreted in light of what the natural sciences have discovered about the physical processes of the universe in general and planet Earth in particular. The physical causes of global warming must be understood before appropriate corrective actions can be undertaken. As far as I can tell, a prophetic, socially engaged inter-religious dialogue in partnership with the natural sciences might be the best hope human beings have for addressing ways of curtailing the global consumerism fuelling global warming.

Accordingly, socially engaged inter-religious dialogue is a powerful resource for developing strategies for directly confronting those corporations most directly responsible for creating consumerist addiction to 'things' most people do not need – that is literally eating this planet alive. The issues are systemic: capitalist economic practices need to be humanized. I agree with Philip Clayton that establishing a more just wealth distribution needs to be included on the agenda of any inter-religious dialogue focused on climate change.[17]

For example, those of us addicted to the automobile will be forced to rely on smaller, more fuel-efficient vehicles or electric vehicles. There will come a time in the near future when Earth's human population will need to rely on mass systems of transportation,

---

[15] Paul F. Knitter, *Without Buddha, I Would Not Be A Christian* (Oxford: One World, 2001).
[16] Ingram, *Buddhist-Christian Dialogue*, Chapter 1.
[17] See Clayton and Heinzekehr, *Organic Marxism*, Chapter 2.

which will necessitate the rebuilding of national infrastructures to accommodate the increasing reliance on trains and buses that will be required to transport massive numbers of people with rapid efficiency. Human beings will need to relearn how to live simply and efficiently in small self-sustaining communities producing most of what they need – food, shelter, schools, hospitals, police and fire departments, plus open spaces for communal gatherings – while relying on larger communities for obtaining what cannot be produced locally. The goal is sustainable living for the common good, which will require finding more efficient methods of recycling a community's waste while taking from the Earth only that which is necessary for the quality of human life as well as the non-human life.

All the above will require changes in economic policies that few CEOs and politicians – and the majority of ordinary people addicted to consumerism – will be willing to make unless they are forced to do so either by peaceful protest or an ever-warming and more damaged planet or both. Communal action cutting across religious, cultural, political and ideological boundaries must begin now before it is too late.

According to Pope Francis, 'human ecology is inseparable from the notion of the common good.'[18] The 'common good' refers to the totality of communal relationships that allow human beings and the sentient beings with whom we share life on this planet to achieve, as Whitehead would phrase it, an individual and communal 'wholeness greater than the sum of its parts'.[19] In the present context of economic globalization, where injustices abound everywhere so that growing numbers of human beings are deprived of the basic necessities of life and more and more species are driven to extinction and are even considered expendable according to current economic practices, the common good is most directly a summons to solidarity firmly based on a preferential option for the poor and oppressed. This entails a massive redistribution of the planet's goods more equitably, based on the recognition that human beings are forced into abject poverty and non-human beings into extinction. This creates the ethical imperative to work for the common good – a foundational imperative at the heart of the world's religious Ways.

Furthermore, the common good must be extended to future generations. As the current global economic crisis makes clear, working for the common good must not exclude those who come after us. Sustainable development is interdependent with intergenerational solidarity. My point is this: when we reflect on the kind of world we are leaving to future generations, we apprehend everything differently. Planet Earth is perceived as a gift freely received that we must share with others. The Earth can no longer be viewed in a utilitarian way as a place in which economic efficiency, production and consumption are the centre of human interest. Intergenerational solidarity is not an option. It is a requirement of compassionate, just community, as the Hebraic prophets

---

[18] Pope Francis, *Laudato Si'*, 108.
[19] Alfred North Whitehead, *Process and Reality: Corrected Edition*, David Ray Griffin and Donald W. Sherburne (eds) (New York: The Free Press, 1985), 346–9.

instruct us. Planet Earth is on loan to each generation and must be passed on to the next with minimal wear and tear.

Conclusion

I remain cautiously hopeful that it is possible to begin addressing the human causes of climate change. A socially engaged inter-religious dialogue focused on climate change with the natural sciences as a third partner just might be our best option for undertaking the necessary actions that slow global warming and perhaps even reverse the worst of it. But the reality is that the pace of consumption and environmental damage has so stretched planet Earth's capacity to sustain life that environmental catastrophes are likely to increase in both frequency and destructive power. The effects of the present imbalances caused by human activity can only be reduced by decisive collective action here and now.

The reality is this: the majority of human beings now living on this planet practice one of the world's religious Ways. All religious Ways call faithful persons to create communal structures that exhibit justice and compassion. Here rests the foundation for a planet-wide inter-religious dialogue seeking ways to protect the environment while defending the poor through networks of socially engaged faithful persons. Again, I must emphasize that this inter-religious dialogue should include the natural sciences as a third partner. The science underlying climate change must be understood before action can be taken to reverse the planet-wide damage that is now occurring. The shear gravity of the ecological crisis demands that every human being on planet Earth begin seeking the common good founded on compassionate justice for all human beings and sentient beings with whom we must share the resources of this planet.

A response to Paul Ingram

Allan Samuel Palanna[1]

Faith-based institutions and communities have a renewed role towards just engagement in the context of climate change. This also acknowledges the growing influence of faith communities to steer the conscience of governments and societies bent upon pursuing a destructive development path causing irreparable damage to the life systems of earth. Hence, Paul Ingram's article offers a welcome reminder, emphatically stressing the perusal of interfaith dialogue as a credible direction to be envisaged in order to address the grim reality of global warming. The core of this article may be summed up in Ingram's emphatic note: 'a prophetic socially engaged inter-religious dialogue in partnership with the natural sciences might be the best hope human beings have for addressing ways of curtailing the global consumerism fuelling global warming.' This affirmation is perhaps the most important contribution of this article. It suggests a realization that an intersectional, multilayered approach to dialogue is essential in knitting together a more realistic and viable approach to social issues in conversation with other faiths.

Ingram's encouraging emphasis on a trialogue including faith communities and the natural sciences as conversation partners augurs well amidst changing geopolitical and scientific advances in the context of climate change. Mutual suspicions in this regard have often led to a breakdown in communication. When faith representatives become open to the idea of integrating faith with the natural sciences, there is the immense possibility of seeking conversations outside the realm of theological deliberations. Addressing the need for theologians to be involved in conversation with the emerging strides in science, Robin Gill succinctly points out that 'moral discernment in the complex and fast changing world ... is possible only if theologians are prepared to listen carefully to their colleagues in science and moral philosophy'.[2] Celia Deane-Drummond's cautious approach also needs to be considered while conversing with science as she critically points out that current science is not value free.[3] Scientific deliberation on climate change has not been without problems. The issue of human-induced climate change

---

[1] Allan Samuel Palanna is Associate Professor in the Department of Theology and Ethics at the United Theological College (Bangalore, India). He is an ordained Presbyter in the Church of South India, Karnataka Southern Diocese. His area of interest has been health care ethics and Christian social ethics in India.
[2] Robin Gill, *Health Care and Christian Ethics* (Cambridge: Cambridge University Press, 2006), 57.
[3] Celia Deane-Drummond, *Theology and Biotechnology: Implications for a New Science* (London: Geffrey Chapman, 1997), 11.

has been debated with contrary sets of evidence, though extensive research points to human activity as the main cause of climate change. There has been speculation as to how multinational corporations fund scientific research for agreeable results. The growing dominance of the 'Anthropocene narrative' in natural science in relation to climate change must also be critically perceived, since it has the propensity to be overtly anthropocentric. Malm and Hornborg express concern about the dominant role of natural science in climate-change deliberations: 'we find it deeply paradoxical and disturbing that the growing acknowledgment of the impact of societal forces on the biosphere should be couched in terms of a narrative so completely dominated by natural science.'[4] In such a context, what may be of primary importance is the ability to listen to colleagues in the natural sciences and critically address the impact of climate change on the most vulnerable communities and life forms around the world through theological discernment.

Discussing faith affirmations are important since social engagement flows out of deeply held beliefs and theological sentiments. Perceiving that there is a marked difference between doctrinal claims and social motivations may not always be helpful. Any interfaith dialogue centred on ecological concerns must also delve deep into the faith resources of religious traditions in order to seek connections between doctrinal affirmations and social engagement. While examples of nature conservation among the world religions are important, it is crucial to perceive forms of spirituality and faiths other than the more recognizable world religions as a major focal point in seeking climate justice. Though contexts of dialogue such as the World Parliament of Religions are important, formal dialogue face some challenges. It continues to centre on dominant faith representatives and philosophical deliberations. While dialogue may sustain an enduring link between people and communities, it does not automatically result in meaningful change. A top-down approach to dialogue may not always be helpful since formal dialogue may not 'trickle down' to the lived experience of communities. Inter-religious dialogue often happens unnoticed in everyday exchanges in communities and these must be acknowledged.

It is important to address three areas of significance in understanding the role of religion in climate activism: earth affirmation in particular faiths and communities; the role of spirituality in conservation; and the place of spirituality in activism. The role of spirituality and religion in ways that reflect both *experience* and *institution* need to be addressed. They both may involve a sense of ultimate purpose, meaning and values; a sense of the holy or sacred; and/or a relationship with transcendent reality or higher power. Religion, in addition, involves a stronger institutional context; a shared set of beliefs, rituals or practice; and a more or less identifiable community of believers. Given these dynamics, it is a challenge to decipher the spiritual knowledge systems of marginalized religions or faiths rooted in the oral traditions present in ethnic or

---

[4] Andreas Malm and Alf Hornborg, 'The Geology of Mankind? A Critique of the Anthropocene Narrative', *The Anthropocene Review* 1:1 (2014), 62–9 (63).

Indigenous communities. Such communities, traditionally, have had strong bonds with nature. Given the threat to their traditional habitats due to the large-scale developments fuelled by multinational corporations, these communities have inspired resistance, informed by their spirituality. There needs to be a renewed focus on the spirituality and lived experiences of local as well as Indigenous communities since these have remarkably assured the preservation of ecosystems around the world. This is particularly important in the South Asian context where climate activists from the Indigenous *adivasi* communities are deeply engaged in transformative people's movements in seeking climate justice.[5] Many perspectives on religion either do not acknowledge the presence of Indigenous belief systems or, at best, only hint at it in passing. Forums must consider listening to Indigenous faith communities expressing their spiritualities which inform the sustenance of ecosystems in their contexts. Climate change must be addressed from the perspective of the poor who find themselves confronted with the adverse effects of climate change. It is in this context that religious communities need to converse with each other as Wendy Tyndale, commenting from the perspective of developmental change, suggests that faith groups 'are more firmly rooted or have better networks in poor communities than the non-religious ones and that religious leaders are trusted more than any others'.[6]

The narrative of sustainable development needs further exploration as to whether the term is itself an oxymoron. Can present development discourse indeed be sustainable? What are the possibilities of de-growth in the rhetoric of sustainable development? Industries and business houses have conveniently masked their destructive activities in the name of a loosely tailored, often ambiguous concept of sustainability without guaranteed, verifiable and time-bound interventions of replenishing fragile ecosystems. Michael Jacobs labelled the concept of sustainable development as a 'green washing' mentality that shrouds the real destructive nature of development.[7]

While the environment policies of companies are increasingly perceived as 'sustainable', the successes remain spotty and scattered, emblematic of what could be done with more consistency and commitment without the stock markets determining the environmental policies of companies. Regulations regarding environmental standards of industrial corporations are constantly revisited based on the change in government policy towards corporations and their 'positive' impact on the economy. The laxed approach to compliance with environmental guidelines and the flouting of regulations by industries have become a common scenario in South Asian countries. 'Humanizing'

---

[5] See George Zachariah, *Alternatives Unincorporated: Earth Ethics from the Grassroots* (New York: Routledge, 2015).

[6] Wendy Tyndale, 'Idealism and Practicality: The Role of Religion and Development', *Development* 46:4 (2003), 22–8 (26).

[7] Michael Jacobs, 'Sustainable Development as a Contested Concept', in *Fairness and Futurity*, Andrew Dobson (ed.) (Oxford University Press: Oxford, 1999), 21–45 (24).

the current capitalist domains may not be appropriate given the inherently anti-people and anti-environment framework of such domains.

All interfaith conversations offer hope, as Ingram emphasizes, especially when discerned with radical honesty. Frankness and sincerity are indeed values that must be deeply appreciated in conversations on climate change. But conversing in an atmosphere of *radical honesty* is something else. As Andrew Shanks puts it: 'to be frank is nothing more than truly to say what you think; and to be sincere is nothing more than truly to mean what you say. But what I would call "radical" honesty means being truly open to *what other people may have to say*.'[8] Further, to be radically honest means 'to love the prospect of the moral lessons to be learnt from your encounter with other people more even than you love the prospect of receiving their love and attention'.[9] What can be a way forward is to have interfaith practitioners grapple with the legitimate demands of climate justice as a focal narrative with radical honesty that can consciously circumvent contentious issues of doctrine and purposely privilege the voices of the most vulnerable communities for the sake of the future of the earth.

---

[8] Andrew Shanks, *Faith in Honesty: The Essential Nature of Theology* (Aldershot: Ashgate Publishing Limited, 2005), 2 (emphasis original).

[9] Ibid.

PART II

Finding common moral ground in working with others

Introduction: A moral Anthropocene

Larry Rasmussen[1]

Humanity needs to develop a moral membership that encompasses the scale of the problems it faces.[2]

And what scale would that be? If human agency is 'exercised cumulatively across generational time, aggregately through ecological systems, and non-intentionally over evolutionary futures',[3] if, in other words, Anthropocene agency is 'pervasive human influence throughout earth's systems'[4] and runs down the centuries into deep time, then appropriate 'moral membership' dictates comparable dimensions of human responsibility. The scale of human responsibility is planetary because the human imprint is planetary.

Clive Hamilton argues that this encompassing imprint means 'a new anthropocentrism' on the part of 'the world-making creature' we are.[5] 'New anthropocentrism' may not be the best phrase. But Hamilton's point, hammered home time and again in *Defiant Earth: The Fate of Humans in the Anthropocene*, is wholly valid: If we do not centre the collective, cumulative systemic powers we exercise, wittingly or unwittingly, then we fail responsibility itself. We fail to acknowledge we are a force of nature, which has become a geological force, exiting the late Holocene and climate stability to create the climate volatility of the early Anthropocene. Unless we recognize the unique scope and depth of our world-creating powers, accountability for our actions matches neither the spatial nor the temporal scale of the problems we generate. 'Moral membership' proper to the Anthropocene eludes us.

The needs of a moral Anthropocene can be graphed. Figure 2.I.1 captures the assumptions of present moral responsibility in much of the world. Armed with modern scientific and technological powers and a burgeoning human population (quadrupling in

---

[1] Larry L. Rasmussen is Reinhold Niebuhr Professor Emeritus of Social Ethics, Union Theological Seminary, New York City. From 1990 to 2000 he served as Co-moderator of the World Council of Churches unit, Justice, Peace, Creation. He is a member of the United Church of Santa Fe (UCC).
[2] Willis Jenkins, *The Future of Ethics: Sustainability, Social Justice, and Religious Creativity* (Washington, DC: Georgetown University Press, 2013), 111.
[3] Ibid., 1.
[4] Ibid.
[5] Clive Hamilton, *Defiant Earth: The Fate of Humans in the Anthropocene* (Malden: Polity Press, 2017), Table of Contents. 'A new anthropocentrism' and 'world-making creature' are used throughout the book and treated at length in Chapter 2, 'A New Anthropocentrism', 36–75.

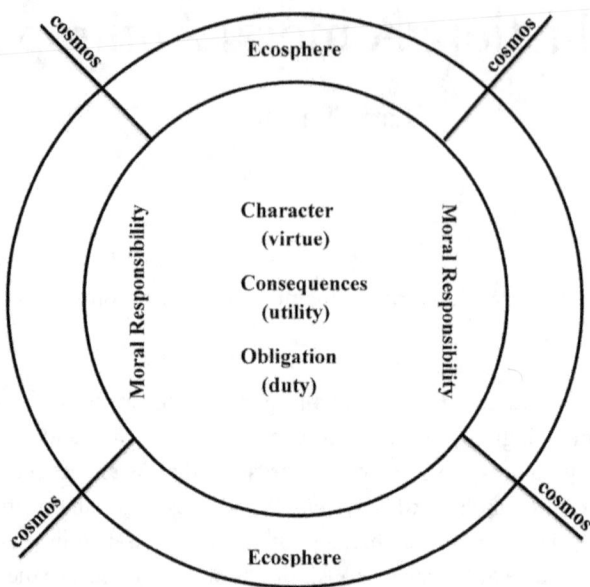

Figure 2.I.1 Diagram of present moral responsibility, used with permission from *From Bible and Ethics: A New Conversation* © Fortress Press 2018.

the last century alone), this is the world that, in the wake of the Industrial Revolution and globalization, generated and institutionalized human dominance everywhere. The moral universe itself, however, is the smaller circle of human society within the larger circle of the planet or ecosphere. The moral universe is human-to-human relationships and well-being only, just as key normative elements such as love and justice are intra-human alone. This leaves much of the ecosphere, whether the parental elements themselves (earth, air, fire and water) or the vast membership of the full community of life, outside the circle of moral attention and responsibility. They are moral externalities. The real world and its life are folded into the *Homo sapiens* world on its terms. The elements of any full-bodied Christian theological and social ethic thus shrink to the circle of human-to-human relationships, whether that be qualities of individual and collective character (virtue), the consequences of human agency (their utility for human life) or moral bottom lines (our baseline obligations or duties to others).

If this moral terrain is retained, responsibility matching the reach of our factual agency goes missing. Retaining the moral vision of this terrain and failing to move to the moral vision of Figure 2.I.2 leads to consequences that are criminal, if not death-dealing (e.g. species extinction).[6] It is not too much to say that Anthropocene citizens

---

[6] For a discussion of the notion of moral vision, see Larry L. Rasmussen, *Earth-Honoring Faith: Religious Ethics in a New Key* (Oxford: Oxford University Press, 2013), 143–50.

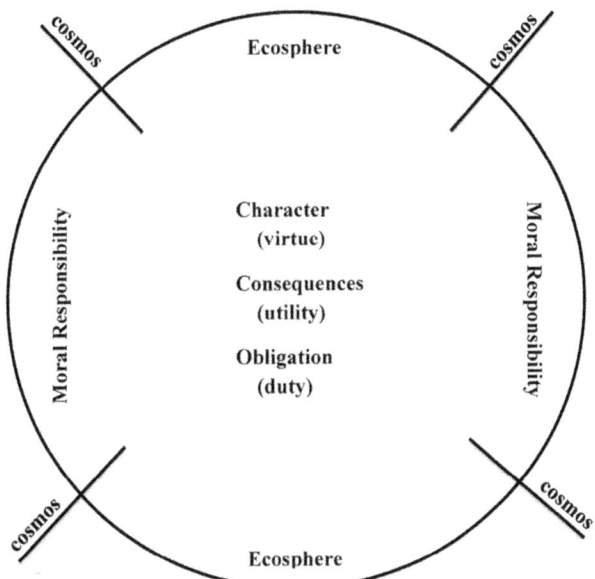

Figure 2.I.2 Diagram of moral responsibility coterminous with planetary, or ecosphere, boundaries, used with permission from *From Bible and Ethics: A New Conversation* © Fortress Press 2018.

living Holocene habits and exercising its 'responsibility' doom their children and their children's children unto the third and fourth generation.

Figure 2.I.2 reflects responsibility that is coterminous with planetary, or ecosphere, boundaries. The ecosphere as a whole, both present and future, is home to the responsibility that theological and social ethics articulate and embody. Responsibility here acknowledges that all natural systems are either already embedded in human systems or profoundly affected by them, whether humans inhabit these kingdoms of nature or not. Often they do not – for example, the high atmosphere, the deep oceans and the polar ice caps. The moral world of the Anthropocene matches planetary boundaries.

For Christian ethics the questions are these: What content of character and conduct belong to this expanded circle? What choices, actions, policies, institutions and systems generate consequences commensurate with a big human world on a small planet? What are we duty bound to do, or refrain from doing, as imperatives for a viable way of life? What yields a durable future, under conditions that have flipped for us and much of life? 'From the very beginning of the world, the other species were a lifeboat for the people,' writes Robin Wall Kimmerer. 'Now, we must be theirs.'[7]

---

[7] Robin Wall Kimmerer, *Braiding Sweetgrass: Indigenous Wisdom, Scientific Knowledge, and the Teachings of Plants* (Milkweed Editions, 2013), 8.

The essays that follow in this section take on these questions. It's a sound beginning. Yet it's only a beginning. This volume and numerous others are needed if we are to live into these questions and a full-bodied ethic. Suffice it for the moment to post them and to recognize those who have already flagged them and led the way. Hans Jonas did so in 1984 with *The Imperative of Responsibility: In Search of an Ethics for the Technological Age:* 'The altered nature of human action' and 'the lengthened reach of our deeds' 'moves *responsibility*, with no less than man's fate for its object, into the centre of the ethical stage'. Complicating it all is that extrapolation from available data and presently utilized ethical systems 'fall short of the causal pregnancy of our technological deeds'. Failing this 'causal pregnancy' we come up short both conceptually and in practice.[8]

With all due credit to Jonas for his leadership, it was Dietrich Bonhoeffer forty years earlier, in 1944, who posed the agenda specifically for Christian theology and ethics. In his uncanny anticipation of the Anthropocene, Bonhoeffer wrote of a new historical and civilizational era in which everything turns on humankind because of expanded and unprecedented human knowledge and powers. Long-standing notions of God as the rescuer God (*deus ex machina*) and God as a working hypothesis (the God-of-the-gaps) no longer avail. The centuries of Christian consciousness tied to these 'Gods' in fact subvert accountability and responsibility when world-creating powers rest in human hands, reside in human choice and extend across the whole of earthly life. Who is God, then, and who is Jesus Christ for us in this epoch? What do the elemental base points of theology mean in such a time as this – 'creation, fall, reconciliation, repentance, faith *vita nova*, last things'?[9] 'What does a church, a congregation, a sermon, a liturgy, a Christian life'[10] mean in this new dispensation? What creed would we write such that we'd stake our lives on it?[11] All this Bonhoeffer must rethink as chapters in a prospective new book, 'Taking Stock of Christianity' and 'What is Christian Faith, really?'[12] Only after this foundational work could Bonhoeffer return to work on *Ethics* and take up his intention there, nothing less than a comprehensive theory of responsibility.

Bonhoeffer had no chance to finish his work and volumes like this one pursue it in ways he could not. But the work is the same. The difference is that we know the urgency of his agenda even better than he did.

---

[8] Hans Jonas, *The Imperative of Responsibility: In Search of an Ethics for the Technological Age* (Chicago: University of Chicago Press, 1984), Preface, ix–x, emphasis Jonas's.

[9] Dietrich Bonhoeffer, 'Outline for a Book', in *Letters and Papers from Prison*, Dietrich Bonhoeffer Works, Vol. 8 (Minneapolis: Fortress, 2015), 502.

[10] Bonhoeffer, 'Letter of 30 April, 1944', in *Letters and Papers from Prison*, 364.

[11] Bonhoeffer, 'Outline for a Book', 502.

[12] See Ibid., 500.

Chapter 2.1
Finding common ground on a moral vision for the good society

Cynthia Moe-Lobeda[1]

Where there is no vision, the people perish.

– Prov. 29.18

While it is true that without vision the people perish, it is doubly true that without action the people and their vision perish as well.

– Johnnetta Cole[2]

Introduction

This splendid planetary home brings forth life abundant, even out of death. Life arising from death and destruction is Earth's song of hope and God's song of justice-seeking, Earth-relishing love.

Societies reshaped towards the great shalom in which all people have the necessities for life with justice and joy while Earth's ecosystems flourish are at the heart of a moral vision grounded in Christian traditions. According to this moral vision, people will strive to transform unjust or exploitative social structures into structures that foster justice, compassion, healing, joy and ecological sanity.

Yet, such a claim regarding moral vision rings hollow, even dangerously deceptive, from the mouth and heart of this author and any who like her are situated in the United States – a society historically most responsible for climate colonialism and still benefitting materially from the fossil-fuel-driven extractive economic systems that have generated it. This moral vision is yet more suspect when expressed from within

---

[1] Cynthia Moe-Lobeda is Professor of Christian Ethics at Pacific Lutheran Theological Seminary and is on the Doctoral Faculty of the Graduate Theological Union (Berkeley, California). She is situated in Lutheran traditions and her work addresses climate justice and climate colonialism, moral agency, economic justice, public church, ecofeminist theology and faith-based resistance to systemic oppression.
[2] Johnnetta B. Cole, *Conversations: Straight Talk with America's Sister President* (New York: Anchor, 1993), 75.

a religious tradition (Christianity) that has, in both beliefs and practices, undergirded exploitative ways of living.[3]

Much must transpire for this moral vision to be authentic in the twenty-first-century context of climate catastrophe and climate colonialism. Identifying that work is the task of this essay. It will grapple with what must transpire methodologically, theoretically and practically if this moral vision – articulated by Christianities in the United States – is to be: (1) worthy of being considered as common ground among people of diverse religious traditions, secular fields of inquiry, and varied social and geographic locations; (2) authentic in spite of being articulated by people of a society and religion that have betrayed the vision itself; and (3) capable of addressing the crises of climate change and climate justice. In the process, core elements of such a moral vision and guidelines for moral perception emerge.

In this essay, I first name the moral perils inherent in the quest for common ground on moral vision and then reframe the meaning of 'moral vision'. Next I pose two questions arising from those perils and that reframing, followed by two sections responding to these two questions. A final section sketches a path from moral vision to its enactment.

But first I must acknowledge the womb from which this moral vision emerges. It is born of a love story that is magnificent and all-encompassing far beyond human capacity to image. The great Mystery who called this creation into being, the reality whom Jews, Christians and Muslims call God – and whom other religious traditions know by other names – loves this creation and each one of us with a love that will never dim, a love more powerful than any force in heaven or earth. This sacred love is liberating and healing this good creation, and calls all of creation to receive this love – to relish it, revel in it and trust it. But that is not all. We human creatures are called to embody this life-giving and life-transforming love; we are called to give it social form.

Moral peril

In ecclesiological terms, if the church is the one universal body of Christ, this body of Christ is divided among active thieves, passive profiteers, and deprived victims.
– Peter Pero, in discussing the global economy[4]

Tremendous danger accompanies the quest for common ground or common moral vision when that quest is initiated by Christians within a society that has taken lands, water,

---

[3] Christianities are many and highly varied. Some Christian beliefs and practices have nurtured justice and Earth's well-being. Yet, on the larger scale, looking especially over the last 500 years, dominant Christian traditions have been theologically and practically wrapped up in the development and hegemony of capitalism and the ways of life that flow from and support it. I will not argue this point here. It has filled volumes.

[4] Albert Pero, Jr, 'The Church and Racism', in *Between Vision and Reality: Lutheran Churches in Transition*, Wolfgang Greive (ed.) (Geneva: Lutheran World Federation, 2001), 260–74 (262).

minerals and other priceless life-giving goods from other peoples, and has rationalized that theft as either historically necessary or morally good. The danger deepens if that theft and justification thereof continue, as they do.

North American Christian communities in sites of relative economic privilege regularly and sincerely declare a vision of God's love for the world. In song, chant, scripture and other means of theological declaration, we affirm that 'God so loved the world'. Many of us agree that the God revealed in Jesus calls the people of God to love others as God loves, and particularly to love the vulnerable neighbour. As a result, many Christians seek to shape lives that serve the common good and especially the vulnerable among us.

Yet, a haunting contradiction looms. Many caring, compassionate Christians (like many of this volume's authors and readers) unwittingly benefit from and comply with economic arrangements that enrich some by impoverishing many and consuming Earth's natural capital. Jesuit priest John Sobrino said it well: For many of the poor, he noted to a group of US citizens, 'poverty means death'. In El Salvador, he went on to say, people are not poor by chance; 'they are made poor by the systems that bring your material wealth'.[5] Sri Lankan theologian, Tissa Balasuriya, O.M.I., cries out: 'Why is it that … Christians … who proclaim eucharistic love and sharing deprive the poor people of the world of food, capital, employment, and even land … inequities grow … [and] the rich live like Dives in the Gospel story?'[6]

Today, climate change deepens the contradiction between the vision of God's love for the world and lived reality. Caused overwhelmingly by the world's high-consuming people, climate change is wreaking death and destruction first and foremost on impoverished people who also are disproportionately people of colour. The island nations that will be rendered unsuitable for human habitation by rising sea levels, subsistence farmers whose crops are undermined by climate change and coastal peoples without resources to protect against and recover from the fury of climate-related weather disaster are not the people largely responsible for greenhouse gas emissions.[7] Nor are they, for the most part, white.[8] The class and race dimensions of this moral travesty glare.

The mode of living characteristic in the United States depends on extraction and exploitation. Yet it has been seen as a 'good life', a fundamentally moral life. Children are raised to achieve and continue this way of life. The church has, for the most part, not led Christians to challenge or resist this way of life.

How can this be? How can a way of life that renders such danger to planetary viability and that requires exploitation be uncritically accepted? Vision of the moral good in

---

[5] Jesuit priest, Jon Sobrino, in conversation.

[6] Tissa Balasuriya, *The Eucharist and Human Liberation* (Maryknoll: Orbis, 1979), xi–xii.

[7] As recognized by the UN Conference on Sustainable Development, climate change 'represents the gravest of threats to the survival' of some island nations. See http://sustainabledevelopment.un.org/futurewewant.html (accessed 6 July 2018).

[8] Another example is the 40 per cent of the world's population whose lives depend upon water from the seven rivers fed by rapidly diminishing Himalayan glaciers.

any society is established by dominant sectors to uphold the power arrangements that maintain their dominance. Thus, the established moral vision rationalizes itself and is ill-equipped to assess itself. In colonial North America, for example, a moral vision was established by Northern European men who owned property. Slavery, therefore, was seen by slave-holding society as moral, and primary sources of moral authority such as the Bible sanctioned it. In similar manner, morally valuing maximizing profit – seeing it as good – makes extractive industries that save money and maximize profit appear to be good despite the devastation to workers, water systems or land that may result from the profit-maximizing moves.

The fact that a socially constructed moral vision is established to preserve dominant sectors' privilege has yet another shadow side: its dangers tend to be relatively invisible to those who are advantaged by the vision. White people in white dominant societies, such as the United States, tend not to realize that whiteness is 'normalized', receives privileges and colonizes white people's vision of the good. In like manner, the dangers inherent in a vision of the good embraced by a society that is, in fact, engaged in an ongoing consumption orgy are not evident to people engaged in that consumption orgy.

The point here is not that we who have lived this life are morally bad. In many aspects of our lives we may be tremendously compassionate, honest, generous and caretaking to others and the Earth. The point, rather, is that the moral vision of a people who have claimed as good a structure of life that devastates Earth's life systems and multitudes of people is suspect. Such a moral vision must be transformed with careful critical consciousness that cracks through the blinders of privilege. Moral vision, if it is to live up to its charge of enabling healing and liberation as manifestations of God's love, must reveal uncritically held assumptions regarding what is morally good that sanction 'the way things are'.

So, we tread on morally perilous ground.

Yet, the quest to articulate and embody a critical moral vision is morally and practically indispensable. It is requisite if humankind is to find its way into more equitable and ecologically viable ways of organizing our life together. 'Where there is no vision, the people perish' (Prov. 29.18). *So, in this essay, we enter a morally crucial quest fraught with moral peril.*

Two clarifications are vital. In probing matters of structural injustice, we are talking not about our intent but about the impact of our lives. And we are talking not about the impact of individual lives but about our collective impact.

Moral vision – a dual meaning

The fact that a people has seen as morally acceptable ways of life that have produced morally heinous consequences suggests that their *way of seeing* has been morally flawed.

We are beckoned to rethink how we perceive reality. Towards that end, this essay poses a dual meaning of the term 'moral vision'.

Its first and common meaning is the vision of the good that a people or a person holds, and that guides decisions and action. It is largely unconscious, assumed through the process of socialization into a particular group or society. Moral vision is shaped by the values, norms and practices of the society and significant groups in which our lives unfold. It is taught by the narratives of history, advertising, cultural 'heroes', religious traditions, news media and social structures assumed to be normal. A moral vision – conscious or not – tells us what is good, right and true.

A second connotation of 'moral vision' is intimately related to the first. 'Moral vision' also implies ways of seeing that are moral. More specifically, it implies ways of seeing worthy of being considered moral in the context of climate catastrophe and historic and contemporary normalization of exploitation, *for people who are* material beneficiaries of the economic systems that have perpetrated both and who have largely failed to acknowledge the moral unacceptability of both.

Each connotation of the term gives rise to a question.

- Regarding 'moral vision' in the first sense of the term, can Christianity in the high carbon-footprint world contribute anything to finding some common ground on moral vision?
- Regarding 'moral vision' in the second sense of the term, for a society that has held ways of organizing life – in particular economic life – that breed profound inequity and climate violence as a good life, how and what are we to see if our vision is to be moral and viable for building common ground?

Response to the first question

My response to the first is evident in this essay's opening paragraphs. The answer is yes; Christianity from the high carbon-footprint world can contribute to a common moral vision. Consider two grounds for this 'yes', namely the call to religion in this time of crisis and a paradoxical moral anthropology.

The call to religion

All wisdom and knowledge traditions are called upon to meet the crises of climate change and climate injustice. Earth's great religious traditions are gifts from the great and holy reality that many people call God. They are gifts to the Earth community to aid it in realizing God's vision of life in its fullness for all. All religious traditions are finite and fallible, for all are human endeavours; none offers complete wisdom in its own. Yet they are vital threads in the tapestry of human wisdom. Because they have wisdom to offer, religions bear tremendous moral responsibility to do so; if the people faithful to particular religious traditions do not uncover and draw upon the resources offered by their tradition and bring those resources to the great pan-human challenge of our time, then these life-saving and life-sustaining resources remain dormant. Tremendous gifts of power for life and for the good are left untapped.

Paradoxical moral anthropology

But, does not Christianity's complicity in climate atrocity and economic exploitation disqualify it as a source of spiritual and moral wisdom for climate justice? No. Nor does that complicity free Christianity from the obligation to contribute to a common moral vision.

Why? Any moral vision presupposes a moral anthropology – a sense, usually unconscious, of who the human creature is as a moral being. A moral vision for climate justice must face the confounding paradox at the heart of a Christian moral anthropology. While we are broken by sin – including climate sin – we also are body of Christ, bearers of God's love on Earth.

For fulfilling this second face of our being, the Spirit brings God's infinite and indomitable love to abide in us. The Bible teaches that the God whose passionate life-giving love is stronger than all else abides within and among humans. We are bearers of the divine Spirit – *Ruach* in ancient Hebrew – that force of God's being that God pours into the human creature despite whatever else we are. This is an ancient faith claim: God's love dwells in and among us is justice-making, self-respecting and earth-honouring love.

Thus, from a Christian moral perspective we humans are paradoxical and contradictory creatures. While we are broken by sin, especially structural sin, we are *simultaneously* precisely the opposite; human creatures are bearers of God's healing, liberating love that can be stopped by nothing. The one does not negate the other. Said differently, while our lives are entwined in structures of injustice, we are nevertheless called to resist and transform those structures.

What does this mean for the question at hand? Human beings from the high-carbon-footprint world are irrevocably wound up in what Christian theology calls climate sin, a form of structural sin; every moment of our lives is shaped by the material 'benefits' of the fossil-fuel orgy and 500 years of wealth transfer from the Global South to the Global North that produced those 'benefits' and produced the climate crisis. While we cannot *fully* relinquish that situation or gain freedom from that structural sin (because we cannot undo the past or fully dismantle the structures of the present), we are nevertheless called to live into a radically different reality. It is a reality in which our lives are not dependent on the exploitation of Earth or humans.

In short, Christianity's complicity in climate injustice does not release Christians or the church from the power and obligation to resist and transform that injustice. Yet, because of Christianity's historical and contemporary alignment with empire, Christians – more than members of any other religion – must be deeply self-critical and intentional about their contributions to addressing the climate crisis. This begins with intentionality in how we perceive reality. That intentionality brings us to the second of the two questions posed above.

Response to the second question: How and what are 'we' to perceive?

For a society that has held ways of organizing economic life that breed inequity and climate violence as a good life, how and what are we to see if our vision is to be moral and viable for building common ground? Consider six guideposts to a morally viable vision. Throughout this section of the essay, the first person pronoun 'we' takes on a more particular meaning. I use it to indicate citizens of the United States.

Moral–Spiritual vision: Four lenses

In the words of James Baldwin, 'Not everything that is faced can be changed, but nothing can be changed until it is faced', that is, until it is seen. Moral perception requires seeing 'what is going on', especially unmasking systemic injustice that masquerades as good or that hides from those who benefit from it. Seeing 'what is going on' is the first of four lenses.

In the context of climate crisis, seeing 'what is going on' includes recognizing three layers in the moral atrocity of climate change. First, the people most vulnerable to the ravages of climate change are – in general – not those most responsible for it. Second, climate-privileged societies and sectors may respond to climate change with policies and practices that enable them to survive with some degree of well-being under the limited conditions imposed by the planet's warming, while relegating the most climate-vulnerable societies to death or devastation as a result of those conditions.[9] And finally, measures to reduce carbon emissions designed by privileged sectors may further

---

[9] 'Climate vulnerable' refers to nations and sectors that are particularly vulnerable to the impacts of climate change. As defined by the IPCC, 'vulnerability' refers to 'the degree to which a system is susceptible to, or unable to cope with, adverse effects of climate change' (IPCC Working Group 2, 2001, Third Assessment Report, Annex B: Glossary of Terms). I use 'climate privilege' to indicate nations and sectors most able to adapt to or prevent those impacts, or less vulnerable to them.

endanger climate-vulnerable sectors. A team of Indian scholars points out that 'poor and marginalized communities in the developing countries often suffer more from ... climate mitigation schemes than from the impacts of actual physical changes in the climate.'[10] Many voices of the Global South recognize these dynamics as climate debt or climate colonialism. They situate it as a continuation of the colonialism that enabled the Global North to enrich itself for five centuries at the expense of Africa, Latin America, Indigenous North America and parts of Asia.

A grave danger accompanies the moral commitment to see what is. We may be overwhelmed by the magnitude and complexity of systemic injustice, by guilt or shame for our role in it, or by a sense of powerlessness. The forces of wrong may seem too powerful for human beings to impact. One's efforts may appear futile. A sense of inevitability and hopelessness may suck away at hope and moral agency. Therefore, *seeing what is – when the view is of systemic evil – must be accompanied by a second, third and fourth perceptual lens.*

The second lens sees what could and should be – that is, alternatives to the structures and practices that exploit and oppress people and Earth: 'People can be morally and emotionally disgusted with what the system is doing but still cooperate because they see no alternative.'[11] Seeing alternative modes of economic life and movements that are living into them is vital. A Chinese proverb cautions, 'Unless we change direction, we will get where we are going.' Changing direction begs first recognizing, even dimly, alternative viable destinations.

The third lens, I describe as 'mystical vision'. By this I mean acknowledgement of sacred powers at work in the cosmos enabling life and love ultimately to reign over death and destruction. Mystical vision confirms what Sallie McFague refers to as 'our hope against hope that our efforts on behalf of our planet are not ours alone but that the source and power of life in the universe is working *in and through us* for the well-being of all creation, including our tiny part in it'.[12]

For years, I taught this trifold vision, and then began to realize a missing element, a vital source of life and hope – namely, beauty. And so a fourth lens recognizes the extravagant beauty surrounding and imbuing this planet's living beings. A feast of sensuous delight – the touch of wind on naked skin, shimmering colours flooding eyesight, the astounding grey of a wintery sky, the feel of a hand caressing aching back, the sound of a bird singing its heart into the world, the scent of lilac, the glitter of leaf in wind, and infinitely more are glimpses of the Divine. They bring joy and strength. The exquisite sensuous beauty of this world is yet another revelation of God. It can propel and sustain the work towards climate justice.

---

[10] Soumya Dutta et al., *Climate Change and India* (New Delhi: Daanish Books, 2013), 12.
[11] Mary Hobgood, *Dismantling Privilege: An Ethics of Accountability* (Cleveland: Pilgrim Press, 2000), 151.
[12] Sallie McFague, *The Body of God: An Ecological Theology* (Minneapolis: Fortress, 1993), 212, emphasis added.

Moral–spiritual vision, then, is a term to signify the union of vision through four lenses at one time:

- seeing what is going on in whatever situation is at hand, especially unmasking systemic evil that masquerades as good;
- seeing what could be – that is, alternatives;
- seeing evermore fully the sacred Spirit of life coursing throughout creation and leading it, despite all evidence to the contrary, into abundant life for all; and
- seeing, in the midst of brutality, also the magnificent beauty that surrounds and imbues the ordinary everyday realities of life.

Moral perception will hold these four together in one lens. Vision of this sort is subversive because 'it keeps the present provisional and refuses to absolutize it'.[13] Moral–spiritual vision reveals a future in the making and breeds hope for moving into it.

Structural and communal

In order to see 'what is going on', moral vision will see beyond the private and interpersonal dimensions of life to the communal and social structural. This means that when we imagine who we are in the relationships that shape our lives, we will perceive the threads that bind us to people and ecosystems we will never actually see and whom we may not know exist: the underpaid farmworkers who pick our food and may be sprayed with chemicals in the process, the Indigenous people whose lives are lost or endangered while resisting the invasion of their homelands by the oil companies that supply our homes and vehicles with fuel, the underpaid labourers whose low wages reduce the cost of our consumer goods and so on. Moral vision does not simply see the homeless child in the streets of our cities. Moral vision sees also our functional relationship to that child and sees, in particular, whether or not our way of life and the public policies and corporate actions that make it possible are contributing to her poverty.

Similarly, structural and communal vision sees the moral good fostered by structural threads that bind us to people around the world and to other-than-human creatures: business practices that insist on a living wage, safe working conditions and healthy environments, or public policies protecting people and lands. In short, a moral vision must extend beyond immediate interpersonal relationships to social, structural and ecological relationships. This expansion of moral vision is crucial if we are to construct social structures that serve primarily the widespread good rather than primarily the

---

[13] Walter Brueggemann, *Prophetic Imagination* (Philadelphia: Fortress, 1978), 119, 44.

interests of wealth accumulation. Such vision contradicts dramatically the privatization of life characteristic of neoliberalism.

Whose eyes?

The content of a moral vision depends upon the company we keep. To whom we listen and whose perspective we seek out matters. Moral perception and moral deliberation are deeply flawed unless they seek out and prioritize perspectives from the margins of power and privilege. The life and death import of this commitment is evident in the movement within the United States to face and dismantle America's 'original sin' of racism. Until white people dare to see reality as it is experienced by people of colour, we are less likely to join that movement. In the context of climate colonialism, perspectives of climate-vulnerable people are an essential ingredient of moral vision.

A caveat is necessary: No person situated in privilege in any particular social category can claim to read reality accurately from the margins of that category. However, a critical perspective holds that one can and must make every effort to do so, always acknowledging the limitations of that effort. That is a central challenge and commitment of Christian ethics done from or addressed to positions of historically accrued privilege.

Clearly, complexity abounds in heeding this guideline. Climate-vulnerable people's perspectives are diverse and multiple. Gaining access to those perspectives may mean opening new lines of communication and building new relationships of trust. Yet, complexity does not diminish the imperative of seeking to see reality as experienced from the underside of power and privilege.

Encompassing Earth community[14]

A moral vision that is true to the God revealed in the Christian scriptures will encompass the full Earth community, not only humans. The scope of morality in the modern Western world – until the rise of contemporary ecological consciousness – has been bounded by the human. A moral future calls for an ecocentric and biocentric rather than anthropocentric moral vision.

By ecocentric I do *not* mean necessarily prioritizing the well-being of Earth over that of humans. Such prioritizing by people of the Global North is morally questionable, given that so many of Earth's human beings are still denied the basic necessities for human life. The shift from an anthropocentric to an ecocentric vision and consciousness does not refer to a shift in *what gets priority*. It means a shift in how we fundamentally

---

[14] This section is taken – with some small revisions – from Cynthia Moe-Lobeda, *Resisting Structural Evil: Love as Ecological-Economic Vocation* (Minneapolis: Fortress, 2013), Chapter 5.

see the human in relationship to the rest of creation. It is a move from assuming that all of life centres on the human, to recognizing that this is biologically not true. And it is a move to expand the moral universe beyond the human.

An ecocentric moral vision and consciousness will perceive the 'exquisite interconnectivity of all life' and its implications for morality.[15] That interconnectedness renders humankind first and foremost *a part of* nature and its economy, rather than *apart from* these. Moral obligation and even moral agency extend beyond the human to the greater community of life. The purpose of economic life is not only production and distribution of goods but also the well-being of Earth's ecosystems.

Wherein lies the necessity of this shift from anthropocentric to ecocentric moral vision? In the most pragmatic terms, self-interest as a species warrants the change. We, the human ones, are dependent, in every moment, on millions of other species without which we would die. Our lives depend on thousands of unseen organisms living on and in our bodies, thousands more in a foot of soil, the trees of the Amazon rainforest. Yet our numbers, consumption levels and disregard for the other-than-human are destroying species and life-support systems crucial to our health and survival as a species. To continue in this disregard may be to write our death sentence as a species.

Not only self-interest but also social justice demands the move to reinstate the human world into Earth's world (in particular, to resituate human economies in Earth's economy). Social degradation and ecological degradation are inextricably linked. Ecological degradation produces social inequity in the forms of climate injustice and environmental racism. Thus, social justice requires attention to the morality of humankind's relationship with the broader community of life.

Theological integrity, too, prompts this move to a non-anthropocentric moral framework. In the creation story in Genesis, God declares that creation is 'good' long before human creatures appear in the story. Moreover, a long-standing (but not universally held) Christian eschatological assumption is that the 'already and not-yet' reign of God includes the other-than-human parts of creation.

The shift to an ecocentric vision of reality goes further. The life web of which we are a part is not merely a system of connectedness and interdependence but also, in a sense, a system of ontological sameness. We, as every other thing, living and non-living, are offspring of the same parent that flared forth some 13.7 billion years ago in the cosmic process known as the big bang. We are 'distant cousins' to the stars and 'close relatives' of myriad species extant, extinct and yet to come.[16]

Grounding for an ecological shift in moral vision would be startling enough were it to stop here with humans sharing molecular composition, interdependence, intrinsic worth and ultimate salvation with the other-than-human, while retaining sole status as the species with agency. Yet the shift in morality extends even further. Ecotheology and ecological

---

[15] David Suzuki, *Sacred Balance: Rediscovering Our Place in Nature* (Seattle: Mountaineers Books, 2002), 3.
[16] These terms are often used by Larry Rasmussen.

ethics are recovering the *agency* of the other-than-human.[17] The Hebrew scriptures indicate the powerful agency of the wind, mountains, water and more. They too are called upon by God to undertake the crucial task of witnessing to the power and presence of God.

Moral vision expanded to include the other-than-human is fraught with complexity. To illustrate: How are we to understand moral subjectivity in the other-than-human? On what grounds do specific moral values and obligations apply differently to humans than to other-than-humans? What moral constraints ought to be placed on human beings in light of our sameness with and dependence upon otherkind? These and related conundrums illustrate crucial work to be done in Christian ethics and other fields if we are to develop a sense of morality that extends beyond the human.

Expanding the scope of morality has implications for the call to privilege perspectives from the underside of power discussed above. The Earth crisis expands the meaning of 'underside' and 'margins'. If moral wisdom is to be found on the underside of dominant power structures, then the other-than-human has wisdom to communicate.

How will we hear wisdom for living in sync with Earth's needs, from voices not human? How can we conceptualize perceiving and learning from other-than-human perspectives? A moral vision for a just and sustainable future will venture into this uncharted terrain of asking how human creatures may hear moral wisdom spoken in the 'languages' of other kind. The church is invited to explore more fully and bring to public use the biblical testimony that God calls upon the creatures and elements of Earth to 'testify', 'witness', 'minister' and convey God's message (Ps. 104.4) but also to praise God (Psalms 148).

Life-giving but not superior wisdom

A moral vision worthy of building common ground will eschew claims that Christianity holds moral wisdom superior to that of other religions or spiritual traditions, and will insist instead that all of Earth's great faith traditions have resources to contribute. A moral vision rooted in a particular religious tradition will cultivate, in the words of Rabbi Zalman Schachter-Shalomi, 'commitment to Earth's wellbeing and to right relationships among human beings' that 'surpasses my commitment to a particular ... belief system', while also drawing deeply from that particular belief system.

Paradox

Heeding these five guideposts calls forth a sixth. It is to accept and live with jolting paradox. Moral vision will embrace paradox and in particular the paradoxes of hope

---

[17] See, for example, Nancy Erhard, *Moral Habitat: Ethos and Agency for the Sake of Earth* (Albany: SUNY Press, 2007).

and despair, profound joy and equally profound sorrow, the possible and seemingly impossible, anger as a companion of love and as tutored by it, and religious traditions that both pass on and betray the heart of their message.

From a Christian theological perspective, there is good reason for such contradictions. They are rooted in a fundamental paradox of Christian faith. Christianity holds that life as God would have it, while apparently impossible, is indeed breaking into the world now. Human beings – and perhaps all of creation – are called to live according to this 'already and not yet' 'kingdom' of God.

How and what are we to perceive?

Christian traditions offer these six guideposts for how people of climate privilege who are citizens of the United States and grounded in Christian traditions may see and construct a moral vision that is authentic and viable for building common ground in the context of climate violence.

From vision to enactment

Articulating and agreeing upon a moral vision per se is not the most controversial or difficult dimension of developing a common moral vision. The controversy and complexity lie in (1) perception of what the vision means for the structures of society and for people's daily practices and (2) how we are to move towards that vision. A moral vision for life in which all people have the necessities of life with dignity and Earth's ecosystems flourish may be widely shared. But understandings of what policies, practices and social structures will lead to enacting that moral vision in law, public policy, corporate policy, other institutions, cultural norms and lifestyle practices may vary tremendously. As social theorist John Powell notes, 'visions must be reflected in social structures and institutions, or they remain merely dreams deferred.'[18] I would add not only deferred dreams but also deceptive blindfolds, distracting people from what is going on. Therefore articulating a moral vision must include articulating some sense of its embodiment in social structures, institutions and policies, and of what changes – especially in distribution of power and vital resources – would be entailed in realizing this moral vision.

The moral vision suggested herein is inherently an economic moral vision; it is a vision regarding how Earth's bounty – often referred to as resources or goods – is used and shared among all who depend for every moment of life on it. This economic

---

[18] John A. Powell, *Racing to Justice* (Bloomington: Indianapolis University Press, 2012), xix.

moral vision envisions economies in which all people have the necessities required for a healthy life, and Earth's life systems are sustained and regenerated. This would mean, by definition, that no people accumulate vast wealth at the cost of impoverishing others or Earth's life-support systems.

It is one thing to envision such an economy. It is another thing to admit what changes it requires and to move in that direction. One path for moving from a broad vision to its enactment proceeds through steps that become ever more concrete, leading finally to the enactment of the vision in actual practices. That path begins with the moral vision and moves to identify broad principles which, if heeded, would realize the vision. The next step is more concrete – namely to articulate goals that flow from and cohere with those principles. The final and most concrete step is to specify concrete policies and practices that would flow from and achieve these goals. In short, a moral vision will acknowledge its constituent principles, goals, public policies and resulting practices.

Elsewhere I have theorized four such constituent principles.[19] Widely recognized, they are ecological sustainability, environmental equity, economic equity and economic democracy, where democracy implies relatively distributed and accountable economic power.

None of these principles, or the vision articulated here, is compatible with advanced global capitalism and ways of life in accord with it.[20] This is not an ideological statement or a political or moral opinion. It is a statement about physical reality: *Earth as a biophysical system cannot continue to operate according to the defining features of capitalism as we know it.* Capitalism as it has developed from classical economic theory, through neoclassical theory and on to neoliberalism aims at and presupposes what Earth can no longer provide for:

- unlimited growth in production of goods and services;
- unlimited 'services' (required for unlimited growth) provided by Earth. These services include 'soil formation and erosion control, pollination, climate and atmosphere regulation, biological control of pests and diseases', and more;[21]
- unlimited 'resources' (required for unlimited growth), such as oil, timber, minerals, breathable air, cultivable soil, air with a CO_2 concentration of somewhere between 275 and 350 ppm, oceans with a balanced pH factor, the ocean's food chain, potable water and so on;
- an unregulated market in which the most powerful players are economic entities having a mandate to maximize profit, the legal and civil rights of a person, the legal right and resources to achieve a size larger than many nations; no accountability to bodies politic, be they cities, states/provinces or nations; and the right to privatize, own and sell goods long considered public; and

---

[19] See Moe-Lobeda, *Resisting Structural Evil*, Chapter 8.
[20] This and the following paragraphs draw heavily on Moe-Lobeda, *Resisting Structural Evil*, Chapter 2.
[21] See Janet Abramowitz, 'Putting a Value on Nature's "Free" Services', *World Watch Magazine* 11:1 (January/February 1998), 14–15.

- freedom of individuals to do as they please – within the limits of law – with economic assets (including unlimited carbon emissions and highly speculative investment).

The Earth can no longer provide or support these requirements of unregulated corporate and finance-driven global capitalism. Hence, carrying on indefinitely with it is not an option.[22] The option is something different.

(This is not a stand against business. It is a stand *for* business that is not dominated by mega-corporations, business that is not entitled to the rights of a citizen and is compelled by a mandate to maximize profit. And it is an appeal for business to become an active force of ecological sustainability and restoration. Moreover, it is a firm appeal to resituating the market as one instrument of society rather than as the determining actor in society.)

While humankind has no choice in *whether* or not economic life will change dramatically, we have considerable choice about the *nature* of that change. What, then, are the options for the economic order following corporate and finance-driven, fossil-fuelled global capitalism? This is a necessary question for any who would take seriously the moral vision proposed herein of a world in which all people have what they need to live with basic human dignity and Earth's life-support systems are maintained and replenished. Without asking this question, the vision is 'a dream deferred'. The default option is to try to carry on with the economy largely as it is while establishing modest voluntary limitations on carbon emissions. The consequence – relatively unchecked climate change – is horrific.

Another possibility would be serious concerted efforts to mitigate climate change, *without* also questioning some basic market norms, such as the assumption that certain rights (the right to drink potable water, access protein sources, eat non-toxic food, breath clean air, etc.) are based on the ability to pay. This option would continue to grant a few people disproportionate use of the atmosphere and oceans for absorbing carbon emissions. This group also would continue to have relatively greater protection from floods, hurricanes and other climate-related 'natural' disasters. As crops and water supplies diminish, this group would consume an increasingly disproportionate share of them. Where this option would lead, we do not know. We do know that it would produce millions of environmentally caused deaths in Asia, Africa, Latin America and among economically impoverished people of Europe and North America.

Or we could choose to move towards economic orders shaped by other norms.

Enter here the role of moral vision and its constituent principles. According to the moral vision articulated above and its principles, we would design and test the goals,

---

[22] Historically the question has been: 'Can capitalism as we know it change substantively?' The question no longer pertains, because capitalism as we know it cannot *not* change. The question has become, 'In what direction and by whose directives?'

policies and practices of governments (be they local, state or national), corporations and other business, and civil-society institutions based on whether or not they:

- operate within, rather than outside of, Earth's great economy (ecological sustainability);
- move towards more equitable 'environmental space' use (environmental equity);
- decrease the gap between the world's 'enriched' and 'impoverished' people and peoples, and prioritize need over wealth accumulation (economic equity); and
- are accountable to bodies politic (be they of localities, states, nations or other) and favour distributed power over concentrated power (economic democracy).

In short, for the moral vision articulated herein to be authentic, capable of addressing climate injustice and worthy of consideration as common ground, Christians of the Global North will commit ourselves to profound reorientation of economic life, on all levels of social organization.

At first glance, this may seem beyond the realm of the possible. However, that is not the case. Economies are produced by human actions and decisions. Anything constructed by human actions and decisions can be undone and redone by other actions and decisions. The most vital, widespread and diverse movement that the human world has known is now afoot in a multilingual and multifaceted effort to construct more socially equitable and ecologically viable modes of economic life. These paths are forged not through cognitive knowing alone but also through the knowing born of relationship, embodied practice and trust in a Spirit that indwells but also transcends the material and social dimensions of life.

Closing

A flock of birds flying gracefully through the sky presses forward in one direction. Then, in a flash and as a whole, a great swoop occurs and they are off in an utterly different direction. The radical change to which we are called is that dramatic. The birds have an ingrained mechanism enabling them to redirect themselves as a whole and with tremendous grace and apparent ease. We don't. We must forge an unknown path, step by step. The only way to get there is to go there. We will end up in the direction that we head. Moral vision is one vital ingredient in that reversal.

So we return to the moral vision grounded in Christian traditions articulated at the essay's outset. It is the vision of societies reshaped towards the great shalom in which all people have the necessities for life with justice and joy, and Earth's ecosystems flourish. According to this moral vision, human beings strive to transform unjust and exploitative social structures and the practices demanded by them into structures and practices that nourish justice, compassion, healing, joy and ecological sanity.

We asked: Given that both the United States as a nation and Christianity as a religion have betrayed this vision and contributed to climate injustice, can Christianities from this historically high-carbon-footprint part of the world contribute to a moral vision that is viable as common ground in the current context of climate catastrophe and climate colonialism?

We responded: Yes. But only if accompanied by moral vision in a second sense of the term (moral ways of perceiving reality). For this reason, we pursued a second question: For a society that has held ways of organizing life – in particular economic life – that breed profound inequity and climate violence as good, how and what are we to see if our vision is to be moral and viable for building common ground? Six guidelines emerged. The test for a moral vision is this: Does it nourish moral–spiritual power for imagining, recognizing, forging and adopting ways of life that enable justice among human beings, a sustainable relationship between the human species and our planetary home, and joy?[23] Whether the moral vision (in both senses of the term) proposed herein passes that test remains for the future to tell.

---

[23] By 'ways of life', I mean principles, policies and practices applied at the levels of household, business, institutions of civil society and government, as well as worldviews.

A response from a Latinx/Latin American perspective

Raimundo C. Barreto[1]

The essay by Cynthia Moe-Lobeda on the search for common ground on a moral vision for the good society must be affirmed. She mainly speaks from and to 'North American Christian communities in sites of relative economic privilege', exposing some of the contradictions in their faith statements on the love of God in Jesus for God's whole creation.

Moe-Lobeda denounces the flawed nature of an anthropocentric moral vision, debunking the possibility that such moral vision can provide the grounding for a sustainable world. In fact, she shows, even well-intentioned responses may end up reinforcing new forms of colonialism. Yet, her response to the question of whether 'Christianity from the high-carbon world (the carbon colonizing world)' can contribute anything to finding some common ground on a moral vision is indeed 'yes'. How can that be so?

Moe-Lobeda raises two fundamental questions in her essay. The first question relates to 'the vision of the good that a people or a person holds, and that guides decisions and action'. The second question addresses another meaning of moral vision, as 'ways of seeing or perceiving that are moral'. She asks, 'For a society that has held ways of organizing life – in particular economic life – that breed profound inequity and climate violence as a good life, how and what are we to see if our vision is to be moral and viable for building common ground?' She provides a thorough answer to this question based on a four-dimensional moral vision which sees what is going on, promotes a vision of what could and should be, acknowledges sacred powers at work in the cosmos, and understands beauty as a source of life and hope.

Furthermore, she prioritizes 'perspectives from the margins of power and privilege', and 'people of colour' to inform such subversive moral perception. This is, however, the point where the limits of her approach surface, particularly as she adds the important caveat that 'no person situated in privilege in any particular social category can claim

---

[1] Raimundo C. Barreto is a Brazilian scholar teaching world Christianity in the History and Ecumenics Department at Princeton Theological Seminary. He is one of the three conveners of the Princeton Theological Seminary World Christianity Conference and the general editor of the Fortress Press Series 'World Christianity and Public Religion'.

to read reality accurately from the margins of that category'. This response informs her answer to the first question, although it also has implications for the second.

Moe-Lobeda is not wrong in affirming that Western (carbon-colonizing) Christianity has something to contribute in finding common moral ground. She acknowledges, though, the contradiction ingrained in this form of Christianity, implying that any attempt to change the course of self-destruction requires that we also face other facets of structural injustice, including racism, colonialism and economic injustice. Furthermore, she eschews any attempt to portray Christianity as morally superior to other religions, insisting that 'all of Earth's great faith traditions have resources to contribute'. Yet, her language implies that Christians are morally capable of acknowledging their mistakes and making the changes necessary to shift the course towards a sustainable moral vision. She ends her essay by showing some confidence in a moral vision grounded in Christian traditions where 'human beings strive to transform unjust and exploitative social structures and the practices demanded by them into structures and practices that nourish justice, compassion, healing, joy, and ecological sanity'.

Considering the entanglement of Western Christianity with the modernity/coloniality[2] that has shaped the world in which we live for the past 500 years, such a vision, such a vision, although desirable, does not seem realistic. Christianity cannot save the world on its own; it cannot even save itself without the help of others. Salvation for the contemporary world can only be articulated interculturally and inter-religiously. But to attain such an intercultural approach, one is required to fully acknowledge the key role Western Christianity played in the creation of the worldview that enabled modernity/coloniality. For such a task, I turn to some analytical tools forged by Latin American scholars for an assessment of the deep impact of coloniality and racism, which privileges Indigenous, black and women responses. In other words, I approach Moe-Lodeba's first question through the lenses of an epistemic inversion which accentuates the subversive power of subjugated knowledges and agency.[3]

Enrique Dussel offers at least two contributions that are of great significance here. First, Dussel was one of the first thinkers of his generation to understand that modernity is not exclusively a European phenomenon. On the contrary, 'Modernity appears when Europe affirms itself as the "center" of a World History that it inaugurates; the "periphery" that surrounds this center is consequently part of its self-definition.'[4] The world system that emerged in the sixteenth century produced the values, norms and exploitative global economic system that is at the root of the ecological crisis we face today. Second, Dussel calls for a decolonization of Christian theology, to correct the

---

[2] See Anibal Quijano, 'Coloniality of Power, Eurocentrism, and Latin America', *Nepantla: Views from the South* 1:3 (2000), 533–80.

[3] See Raimundo C. Barreto, 'Brazil's Black Christianity and the Counter-hegemonic Production of Knowledge in World Christianity', *Studies in World Christianity* 25:1 (2019), 71–94.

[4] Enrique Dussel, 'Eurocentrism and Modernity (Introduction to the Frankfurt Lectures)', *Boundary* 2 20:3 (1993), 65–76 (65).

course of a Messianic Christianity turned into an imperial Christendom, which in the sixteenth century became the heart of the new world system, as it expanded to the Atlantic world, the centre of colonial Christendom.[5] In such a system, modernity and coloniality were intertwined. Colonial Christendom was formed through the negation of the non-European other, especially the Indigenous peoples of the Americas and millions of enslaved Africans.

If the centring of European cultures, of whiteness and of Christendom are at the root of the world system that has brought us to the brink of self-destruction, can Christianity reverse its inversions on its own? My answer is 'no'.

Christian theologians can make some contributions, as Moe-Lobeda proposes, on the basis of recovering important elements of transformation, repentance and conversion. Moreover, the recovery of the difference between Christianity and Christendom as well as of the distinction between Christianity and the West is also important. Christianity, always formed in the encounter between Gospel and culture can be understood as a dynamic and paradoxical religion, which relates in multiple ways to different cultures, sometimes working as a prophetic element within a given culture, sometimes being shaped ineradicably by them to the point of adopting cultural traits as its own tenets, as is the case with the intrinsic association between Christianity and whiteness in some contexts and with the adherence to the myth of Europe as the cradle of Christianity. Such self-assessment and criticism is important, but it cannot be done by Christians alone.

As it placed itself at the centre of the modern/colonial world system, Western Christianity denied the worth of Indigenous cultures and traditional religions in different parts of the world. Referring to the Mayan encounter with European Christianity as 'the invasion of Christianity into the world of the Mayas',[6] Vitalino Similox Salazar, a K'aqchiquel Maya theologian, affirms that without understanding Indigenous religion and theology, European missionaries wrote them off 'as pagan, idolatrous and polytheistic'.[7] They forced the Maya to relinquish their own culture and remain silent.[8] This applied to many other Indigenous encounters with Christianity around the world. Despite centuries of subjugation and suppression, Indigenous and African-derived religions have not only survived but also experienced a revitalization in the past few decades, both in their own right as traditional religions and in shaping some expressions of non-Western Christianity.

Many Indigenous peoples have refused to choose between their Indigenous traditions and their Christian identities. To stay with the case mentioned above, many Mayas today

---

[5] Enrique Dussel, 'The Epistemological Decolonization of Theology', *Postcolonial Theology, Concilium* 2 (2013), 21–31 (23).

[6] Vitalino Similox Salazar, 'The Invasion of Christianity into the World of the Mayas', in *Crosscurrents in Indigenous Spirituality, Interface of Maya, Catholic and Protestant Worldviews,* Guillermo Cook (ed.) (Leiden: Brill, 1997), 35.

[7] Ibid., 36.

[8] Ibid., 37.

are asking what it means to be a Mayan Christian – to be Mayan and Christian at the same time.

In her essay, Moe-Lodeba rightly points to the need to move from an anthropocentric moral vision to an ecocentric one. However, she does not engage traditional worldviews which have for thousands of years developed ways of life in which humans and other-than-human forms of life are deeply intertwined. Whereas contemporary Christians in high-carbon societies are beginning to speak about a shift in morality, Indigenous peoples who have resiliently survived colonization, slavery and cultural genocide continue to live among us, insisting in the value of a way of life which points to an alternative moral vision.

What is thus required from Christians in the West? First, we are called to listen to the prophetic criticism echoed by a number of Native Americans who point to the dangers of the Western Christian worldview.[9] Such listening, although prioritizing subaltern voices and Indigenous epistemologies, does not imply the eradication of Christian worldviews. A number of Indigenous thinkers are speaking nowadays from within Christian ranks. They are on the frontline of a radical transformation in world Christianity. The world Christianity that is thriving today in parts of the formerly colonized world is informed, among other things, by the revitalization of Indigenous religions. In such contexts, there is an understanding that 'the colonization of spiritual wealth went hand in hand with the destruction of ancestral knowledge, which the original colonizer and current neocolonizers have categorized as "superstitions"'.[10] Decolonial epistemologies and theologies help retrieve such silenced voices and knowledges. Panentheist epistemologies, ecotheologies and ecofeminist theories from the South have helped decentre Western Christianity, promoting a reformulation in Christianity's self-perception.[11] The relocation of theological voices to what used to be the peripheries of Eurocentric modern Christianity opens the window for other ways of being Christian,[12] particularly among those who are most directly impacted by climate change. It gives greater protagonism to those whose *cotidiano* is formed in conversation with other religious traditions, thus producing a liberative intercultural communication, which can potentially serve as a common ground for a moral vision for a good and sustainable society.

---

[9] Listening is key for learning and change, even when it means listening to a sharp Indigenous voice which turns the white world upside down as in the case of Sioux thinker Vine Deloria, Jr. For an overview of his life and thought, see George Tinker, 'Walking in the Shadow of Greatness: Vine Deloria Jr in Retrospect', *Wicazo Sa Review* 21:2 (2006), 167–77.

[10] Marilú Rojas Salazar, 'Decolonizing Theology: Panentheist Spiritualities and Proposals from the Ecofeminist Epistemologies of the South', *Journal of Feminist Studies in Religion* 34:2 (2018), 92–8 (93).

[11] Mario I. Aguilar, 'Public Theology from the Periphery: Victims and Theologians', *International Journal of Public Theology* 1 (2007), 321–37.

[12] Ibid., 324.

Chapter 2.2
Finding common ground on ecological virtues

Steven Bouma-Prediger[1]

But lacking the qualities of virtue, can we do the difficult things that will be necessary to live within the boundaries of the earth?

– David W. Orr[2]

Deafness, ignorance, indifference and denial

Climate change is real.[3] The earth is, on average, warming up and we humans are largely responsible. But some of us seem deaf or ignorant, indifferent or in denial. According to Thomas Berry, we are deaf. 'Our scientific inquiries into the natural world', he argues, 'have produced a certain atrophy in our human responses.' With respect to other creatures, he observes, 'we cannot hear the voices speak or speak in response.'[4] We are unable to perceive the wonder of the world around us or its ongoing destruction.

For others the problem is ignorance. If only people knew the scope and severity of the problems, some insist, they would take action. There is solid evidence for widespread ecological illiteracy. For example, the National Environmental Report

---

[1] Steven Bouma-Prediger is the Leonard and Marjorie Maas Professor of Reformed Theology and Director of the Environmental Studies Program at Hope College (Holland, Michigan). He is situated in both the evangelical and the Reformed traditions. He teaches philosophical, historical and constructive theology, and specializes in Christian ecological theology and ethics.
[2] David W. Orr, *Earth in Mind* (Washington DC: Island Press, 1994), 62.
[3] Many sources could be cited to support this claim. Two of the most highly respected and frequently cited sources are the Intergovernmental Panel on Climate Change (http://ipcc.ch/) and the NASA Goddard Institute of Space Studies (www.giss.nasa.gov).
[4] Thomas Berry, *The Dream of the Earth* (San Francisco: Sierra Club, 1988), 16–17.

Card consistently shows that most Americans fail a basic environmental literacy test: 'As the results of the most recent surveys make clear, Americans lack the basic knowledge and are unprepared to respond to the major environmental challenges we face in the 21st century.'[5]

Many people are apathetic. They simply don't care.[6] In response to an editorial I wrote in the local newspaper about the effects of global warming in Michigan, one person responded: 'Yawwwwwwwn, will someone please turn on the Cubs game and hand me a cold beer, please?' Whether adopting a hedonistic ethic of 'Eat, drink, and be merry for tomorrow we die' or overcome by the cynicism of our times, some people just don't care enough to move them to responsible action.

For others denial is the root problem. We know enough; we simply do not want to face the mess we have made. As Mark Lynas puts it: 'We live in a society consumed by denial' where 'politicians make the occasional speech about the gravity of the climate change crisis and then go right back to business' and citizens 'claim to be worried about global warming ... but we still do remarkably little to change our own habits and lifestyles'. Or we deny that we have any responsibility: 'it's someone else's problem and we vaguely hope that someone else will sort it out.'[7]

I hear nothing. I know nothing. I don't care. It's not that bad and not my problem. Deafness, ignorance, indifference and denial – a raft of reasons for why the earth is aching. But others of us feel our home is no longer fit for human habitation. Like Aldo Leopold, we are aware that we live in a world of wounds.[8] We are not deaf to the groans of the earth.[9] We know too much to claim ignorance. We care too much to be indifferent. And we reject denial, for the evidence is too hard to evade.[10] These four ways are not open to us.[11]

---

[5] See www.neetf.org/roper/roper.shtm, the website of the National Environmental Education and Training Foundation. For a trenchant critique of ecological illiteracy and a compelling alternative, see David Orr, *Ecological Literacy* (Albany: SUNY, 1992), especially part 2.

[6] For a number of years pollsters have tracked American attitudes regarding various environmental issues, for example, climate change and species extinction. While the results show some positive change, for example, from 2016 to 2017 an increase from 37 per cent to 45 per cent of Americans who say they 'worry a great deal' about climate change, the level of apathy remains quite high. See http://www.gallup.com/poll/206030/global-warming-concern-three-decade-high.aspx (accessed 12 March 2018).

[7] Mark Lynas, *High Tide: The Truth About Our Climate Crisis* (New York: Picador, 2004), 296.

[8] Aldo Leopold, *Sand County Almanac* (New York: Ballantine, 1966), 197.

[9] Peter Wohleben, *The Hidden Lives of Trees: What They Feel, How They Communicate – Discoveries from a Secret World* (Vancouver: Greystone Books, 2016).

[10] Barry Levy and Jonathan Patz (eds), *Climate Change and Public Health* (New York: Oxford University Press, 2015).

[11] See Steven Bouma-Prediger and Brian Walsh, *Beyond Homelessness: Christian Faith in a Culture of Displacement* (Grand Rapids: Eerdmans, 2008).

The complicity of North Atlantic Christianity in the climate crisis

There is not space here to dive deeply into the reasons why Christians and their theology and ethics have contributed to the climate crisis. I will merely mention and briefly comment on a number of important factors.[12]

First, our de facto theology has all too often been deistic – affirming that God exists and that God creates but denying that God is in any meaningful way really related to the created order. According to this view 'nature' is autonomous, operating like a self-sustaining machine, not needing divine assistance. The natural world is, furthermore, viewed merely as a repository of raw material or resource for human exploitation. As Wesley Granberg-Michaelson puts it, 'Christian faith in the West has been captive to the assumptions of modern culture which sever God from the creation and subject the creation to humanity's arrogant and unrestrained power.'[13] It is not difficult to see how such a materialistic worldview underwrites the pillage and plunder of the natural world.

The fact that the North Atlantic church has been captive to the modern Western worldview is well documented and that this captivity warrants critique is no less clear.[14] While scientific and/or technological examples are often given as evidence of 'humanity's arrogant and unrestrained power', many argue that the most pernicious examples of such abusive power are economic. That is, the captivity of the church to modernity is most malignant in its subservience to the gods of consumption and wealth. This critique is no more trenchant than in the words of Wendell Berry:

> Despite its protests to the contrary, modern Christianity has become willy-nilly the religion of the state and the economic status quo. Because it has so exclusively dedicated itself to incanting anemic souls into Heaven, it has been made the tool of much earthly villainy. It has, for the most part, stood silently by while a predatory economy has ravaged the world, destroyed its natural beauty and health, divided and plundered its human communities and households.[15]

Second, the North Atlantic church has accepted the anthropocentrism of modernity. In the words of Granberg-Michaelson, 'Modern cultural and theological assumptions have placed humanity at the center of purpose and meaning in the universe.'[16] Having rendered God harmless, we have enthroned ourselves at the centre of things. This human-centredness is evident in countless ways. We assume rights apply only to

---

[12] For a more in-depth exposition of these factors, see Steven Bouma-Prediger, *For the Beauty of the Earth* (Grand Rapids: Baker Academic, 2010), Chapter 3.

[13] Wesley Granberg-Michaelson, *Ecology and Life* (Waco: Word, 1988), 34.

[14] On the cultural captivity of the Church, especially with respect to environmental issues, see Norman Wirzba, *From Nature to Creation* (Grand Rapids: Baker Academic, 2015).

[15] Wendell Berry, *Sex, Economy, Freedom, Community* (New York: Pantheon, 1992), 114–15.

[16] Granberg-Michaelson, *Ecology and Life*, 35.

humans. Bioethics (the ethics of life) assumes the only important life is a human life. The earth is viewed as a stage on which humans perform. Land is of value only if human labour is mixed with it. It is not difficult to see how such a perspective legitimates the despoliation of creation.

Third, we have made technology into a god. Bhopal, Chernobyl, Exxon Valdez – the list of technological disasters grows with frightening frequency. And those are only the large-scale examples of our technological hubris: 'Our culture adheres to a blind faith in technological progress', Granberg-Michaelson observes, 'as the means to resolve environmental problems and the maldistribution of world resources.'[17] If you doubt the veracity of this claim, simply eavesdrop on a conversation about environmental degradation or world hunger. Without fail someone will opine that while we have serious problems, technology will save us. As one Chicago corporation unabashedly puts it, 'Science and technology must answer our problems. If they don't, nothing else will.'[18]

This is not a critique of technology per se. The power to shape and form culture is a God-given dimension of human existence. Technology is an inescapable feature of human life. The question is not whether we use technology, but what kind of technology, and how much, and for whom, and at what cost? As Langdon Gilkey insightfully observed years ago, technology is ambiguous.[19] It can be both blessing and bane. Insofar as we put our ultimate allegiance in technology, we have misplaced our faith and are engaging in idolatry.

Fourth, the North Atlantic church has forgotten creation.[20] We have forgotten that Genesis begins with creation and that Revelation ends with a renewed creation. We have forgotten that the Apostles' Creed begins with an affirmation of God as Creator of heaven and earth. We have forgotten that, in the words of St. Paul in Colossians 1, all things were created and hang together in Christ. While reading the book of Scripture, we have forgotten to read the book of nature.[21] As Granberg-Michaelson concludes, 'The Western Church's modern theology has fought between being personalized or politicized, and largely has forgotten the theology of creation as its starting point.'[22] Because of such forgetfulness we operate with a faith so focused on human redemption that we lose sight of the cosmic scope of God's work. Conversion is limited to individual people. The kingdom of God is reduced to church activities. By implication, 'in such a mind-set, environmental problems are at best nothing more than another issue over which Christians may have different opinions, all largely unrelated to the gospel'.[23]

---

[17] Ibid., 37.
[18] Quoted from Brian J. Walsh and J. Richard Middleton, *The Transforming Vision* (Downers Grove: Intervarsity, 1984), 135.
[19] Langdon Gilkey, *Society and the Sacred* (New York: Crossroad, 1981).
[20] Wirzba, *From Nature to Creation*, Chapters 1 and 3.
[21] See, for example, the Belgic Confession, article 2, where these two books are mentioned in response to the question of how God is known to us.
[22] Granberg-Michaelson, *Ecology and Life*, 40.
[23] Ibid., 41.

Finally, the North Atlantic church, especially the American church, has operated with an escapist eschatology. Many American Christians believe that in the future the earth will be destroyed, with Christians whisked off the earth to heaven. So why care for something that will (sooner rather than later) be destroyed? This otherworldliness has fostered, according to historian Roderick Nash, a view of the earth as 'a kind of halfway house of trial and testing from which one was released at death. … Christians expected that the earth would not be around for long. A vengeful God would destroy it, and all unredeemed nature, with floods or drought or fire.' Hence Nash concludes: 'Obviously this eschatology was a poor basis from which to argue for environmental ethics in any guise. Why take care of what you expected to be obliterated?'[24] This interpretation of the Bible has had deadly consequences, especially when paired with a dualistic anthropology that sees the human person as a soul trapped in a body. Neither an escapist eschatology nor a dualistic anthropology is truly biblical, but they are nonetheless pervasive in the American church.[25]

How Christian theology and virtue ethics can address the challenge of climate change

Christian theology, properly understood, provides a robust rationale and compelling motivation for caring for the earth, including addressing climate change. Indeed, as I argue at length elsewhere, earthkeeping is integral to Christian discipleship.[26] A properly biblical Christian theology reminds us that our human calling is to serve and protect the earth that is our home (Gen. 2.15). Such a theology reminds us that in God's good future, the New Jerusalem comes down from heaven to earth and all things are renewed and redeemed (Revelation 21–22). It reminds us that in the doxology 'all creatures here below' praise God, that in the Lord's Prayer we ask that God's will be done 'on earth as it is in heaven', and that in the second to last line of the Apostle's Creed we affirm 'the resurrection of the body'. A biblically based and historically rooted Christian theology calls us to care for creation.[27]

---

[24] Roderick Nash, *Rights of Nature* (Madison: University of Wisconsin Press, 1989), 91–2.
[25] Ernst M. Conradie, 'Reformed Perspectives from the South African Context on an Agenda for Ecological Theology', *Ecotheology: The Journal of Religion, Nature, and the Environment* 10:3 (2005), 281–314.
[26] See Bouma-Prediger, *For the Beauty of the Earth*.
[27] This claim is supported by many authors from across a broad spectrum of theological traditions, for example, mainline Protestant Larry L. Rasmussen, *Earth-Honoring Faith* (New York: Oxford, 2013), Evangelicals Daniel Brunner, Jennifer Butler and Aaron S. Swoboda, *Introducing Evangelical Ecotheology* (Grand Rapids: Baker Academic, 2014), Anabaptists Ryan Harker and Janeen Bertsche Johnson (eds), *Rooted and Grounded* (Eugene: Pickwick, 2016), Pentecostal Aaron J. Swoboda, *Blood Cries Out* (Eugene: Pickwick, 2014), Eastern Orthodox John Chryssavgis, *Cosmic Grace and Humble Prayer* (Grand Rapids:

This theology of earthkeeping generates an ethic in which certain virtues are prominent. In the Christian tradition there are seven cardinal or core virtues: temperance, courage, justice, wisdom, faith, hope and love.[28] This list of seven is a creative combination of the four virtues most important to Aristotle and the three theological virtues of St. Paul. It is important to recall that the Aristotelian tradition was kept alive by medieval Muslim scholars, thus allowing a Christian theologian such as Aquinas to benefit from the insights of Aristotle. That the Christian faith has a robust tradition of virtue ethics has only recently been rediscovered.[29] And as David Orr reminds us in the epigram at the beginning of this essay, in the face of climate change we need certain virtues. We need particular habitual dispositions to act excellently, to borrow Aristotle's definition, if we are to successfully meet the challenges of climate change.

Ronald Sandler insightfully observes that there are two factors about climate change that especially merit our attention: the increased rate and the increased uncertainty (and unpredictability) of ecological change.[30] As he argues, 'Because global warming accelerates the rate of change and exacerbates the information deficit and uncertainty about the ecological future, it makes biological and cultural adaptation to ecological changes more difficult, for both us and other species.'[31] Thus, given the need for openness and flexibility, Sandler highlights the following virtues as most needed in the face of climate change: humility, patience, restraint and reconciliation. In their discussion of climate change, Kathryn Blanchard and Kevin O'Brien argue that to combat feelings of helplessness we need faith: faithful personal transformation, faithful engagement in democracy and faithful use of technology.[32] And in his book on climate change Chris Doran emphasizes the virtue of hope.[33] Such is the range of virtues mentioned by thoughtful scholars seeking to successfully address the challenge of climate change.

In my view, the virtues we most need in this time of climate change are humility, wisdom, justice and hope. Given the brevity of this essay I do not have the space to elaborate on each of these – outline biblical roots, sketch historical development and

---

Eerdmans, 2013), and Pope Francis's widely read encyclical *Laudato Si': On Care For Our Common Home* (2015).

[28] For one insightful recent treatment of these virtues, see Karl Soderstrom, *The Cardinal and the Deadly: Reimagining the Seven Virtues and Seven Vices* (Eugene: Cascade, 2015).

[29] See, for example, Alasdair MacIntyre, *After Virtue*, 2nd edn (Notre Dame: University of Notre Dame, 1984).

[30] Ronald Sandler, 'Global Warming and Virtues of Ecological Restoration', in *Ethical Adaptation to Climate Change,* Allen Thompson and Jeremy Bendik-Keymer (eds) (Cambridge: MIT, 2012), 63.

[31] Ibid.

[32] Kathyrn Blanchard and Kevin O'Brien, *An Introduction to Christian Environmentalism* (Waco: Baylor, 2014), Chapter 6. Blanchard and O'Brien creatively pair different virtues with various environmental problems, for example, prudence with species extinction, temperance with food insecurity. In my approach I describe pairs of virtues for different features of the human condition, for example, wonder and humility for living as creatures, gratitude and self-control for living with enough.

[33] Chris Doran, *Hope in the Age of Climate Change* (Eugene: Cascade, 2017).

describe contemporary exemplars.[34] In what follows I will merely define and briefly elaborate on each of these virtues.

The virtue of humility is the settled disposition to accurately estimate our abilities or capacities. The virtue of humility thus implies self-knowledge and, especially, knowing the limits of our knowledge. It includes the acknowledgement that we are finite. But we are not just finite, we are faulted. The brokenness we know in ourselves (and the effects we see all around us) is something we acknowledge with regret and seek with God's grace to overcome. In short, finitude and fallenness give us more than ample reason to be humble. Aware of our ignorance, we do not claim to know more than we really know. Aware of our sins, we do not pretend to be perfect.

The vice of deficiency is hubris or overweening pride. Hubris is the failure to acknowledge our own limits and/or brokenness. When full of pride we overestimate our abilities and are vain and boastful. Thinking ourselves in control, we make foolish decisions that wreak havoc for ourselves and for others.

The vice of excess is self-deprecation. Aristotle speaks of those who belittle their authentic accomplishments as exhibiting undue humility or mock modesty. We play down our abilities and speak disparagingly of our legitimate achievements. We are unable to acknowledge our actual gifts and abilities or we refuse to properly accept our genuine strengths.

What then of *ecological humility*? The virtue of ecological humility is the settled disposition to act in such way that we know our place and fit harmoniously into it – whether our local community, our bioregion or our home planet. If ecologically humble, we acknowledge that we are finite and fallen. If ecologically humble, we have an accurate estimation of our abilities and capacities (for good and ill). This requires not only self-knowledge and knowledge of the world in which we live but also awareness of the limits of our knowledge. We frankly acknowledge our limited ability to know the future consequences of our actions and we have an honest awareness of our penchant for self-deception. Before making decisions, we survey as many consequences as possible. We explore alternatives, seek out blind spots and consider worst-case scenarios. If ecologically humble, we act cautiously. While this virtue applies to all people, it is especially relevant to those of us who are privileged North Atlantic citizens.

The vices corresponding to ecological humility are ecological arrogance and ecological self-deprecation. Ecological arrogance puts us, cocky and confident, at the centre of the universe. And so, despite the manifest evidence of both unforeseen and unintended consequences, we go too fast and cut corners. Thinking we know everything, we ignore opposing points of view. Always in a hurry, we do not exercise caution or go slow. And the natural world, of which we humans are an integral part, suffers.

Ecological self-deprecation diminishes the role of humans as earthkeepers. If captured by this vice, we undervalue the important place we humans have as caretakers

---

[34] For more, see Steven Bouma-Prediger, *Earthkeeping and Character: Exploring a Christian Ecological Virtue Ethic* (Grand Rapids: Baker Academic, 2019).

of creation and responsible agents of change for the good. We sometimes talk as if the world would be better off without us – that humans are a virus, a plague, a scourge upon the earth.[35] We fail to see how we have a legitimate and significant role to play in caring for the earth.

The virtue of wisdom is the settled disposition to make sound practical judgements, informed by the accumulated experience of the community and guided by keen discernment of what is good and right and true. The wise person, Aristotle writes, exhibits the 'capacity to act with regard to human goods'.[36] If we are wise, then we know what the truly greatest good is and also have the practical knowledge needed to attain it. The virtue of wisdom, furthermore, is shot through with an abiding awareness of life's precariousness, an understanding and prizing of the excellences of life and an unwavering sense of thanksgiving for the sheer giftedness of life. As a student once wrote in a paper, 'I realize now how fragile and delicate life really is, and that has helped me to appreciate it more. I also know that there are many things I cannot take for granted anymore.' Awareness, appreciation, gratitude – such is the grammar of wisdom.

There is only one vice contrary to wisdom, namely, foolishness or the propensity to act unwisely. Foolishness is the habitual absence of sound judgement. If foolish, we lack good sense. We show no discernment. We eschew learning from the past, shower scorn upon our elders and thus make the same mistakes again and again. We think cleverness is the same as intelligence.[37] The fool confuses 'the goods life' for the Good Life.

The virtue of *ecological wisdom* is the disposition to make insightful and discerning judgements about our common home, the earth. If ecologically wise, we plan ahead and take the long view. We exercise restraint and take our time. We take seriously the cycles and scales of the natural world. We see everything connected to everything else and so adopt the canoe camper's version of the Golden Rule: treat those downstream as you would have those upstream treat you. The ecologically wise remind a culture infatuated with the 'world-wide web' that the original and truly important worldwide web is biodiversity.

The vice of ecological foolishness is the disposition to act as if the earth is endlessly exploitable and expendable. Enslaved to this vice, ecological services such as the natural purification of water are invisible to us and ecological costs such as air pollution are viewed as 'externalities'. By living only for today we act as if the future does not matter. Valuing only short-term consequences or quarterly returns, we are blind to the future. We do not see our home planet as a holy mystery and thus cannot see 'prosperity' for what it truly is, namely, the long-term ruination and despoliation of God's good earth.

The virtue of justice is the habitual disposition to act fairly. Justice in whatever form – commutative, distributive or retributive – concerns fairness or equity. If we are just, then we do not play favourites. We are even-handed and impartial. But equity is not to

---

[35] For one example of this view, see Alan Weisman, *The World without Us* (New York: Picador, 2008).
[36] Aristotle, *Nicomachean Ethics*, 1140b, 20.
[37] Orr, *Earth in Mind*, Chapter 6.

be confused with equality. The virtue of justice involves the ability to discern when to treat equals equally and unequals differentially, and thus it implies having the virtue of wisdom. In our culture justice has to do with respect for people's rights.[38] As Nicholas Wolterstorff argues, justice is what due respect for the worth of someone requires. It is treating someone as befits her or his worth and thus involves respecting another person's rights.[39] So if we are just, we respect the rights of others, even when faced with competing rights.

In my view, the virtue of justice is not a mean and thus has only one vice, namely, injustice. If we are unjust, we exhibit the propensity to be partial. We play favourites for no good reason or, more perversely, for personal gain. If we are unjust, we are not inclined to be even-handed, impartial or fair-minded. We fail to respect the rights of others.

The virtue of *ecological justice* names the settled disposition to act fairly when faced with the recognized rights or legitimate claims of creatures both human and non-human. If we exhibit this virtue, then we not only respect the rights of all humans – women and men, racial and ethnic minorities, citizens and immigrants – but also show respect for the value of domestic animals and wild plants, endangered species and damaged ecosystems. We render with equity to human and non-human alike what their worth requires. One timely example of this eco-virtue is climate justice or the disposition to treat fairly those affected by climate change.[40]

Ecological injustice names the disposition to violate the rights of others and/or fail to respect the worth of others, including non-human creatures.[41] For non-human creatures that have rights, ecological injustice is our failure as moral agents to respect those rights. For non-human creatures without rights but whose intrinsic value generates duties for us, ecological injustice names our failure to exercise our duties.[42] We violate the rights of domestic animals. We fail to properly value wild landscapes. In either case, we treat other creatures – human and non-human – unjustly. In the case of climate change, injustice names the fact that those who contribute the least to carbon emissions are very often those who suffer the most from the negative consequences of climate change.

Last but not least, the virtue of hope. Hope is confident expectation of future good. It involves imagining some good future, believing that such a future is possible and acting in such a way as to bring this good future to fruition.[43] So hope involves doing three

---

[38] Lewis Smedes, *Choices* (San Francisco: Harper and Row, 1986), Chapter 4.
[39] Nicholas Wolterstorff, *Justice in Love* (Grand Rapids: Eerdmans, 2011), 85–7. For a brief mention of the rights of non-humans, see pp. 138, 146. For a more in-depth discussion of justice, see Nicholas Wolterstorff, *Justice: Rights and Wrongs* (Princeton: Princeton University Press, 2010).
[40] James B. Martin-Schramm, *Climate Justice: Ethics, Energy, and Public Policy* (Minneapolis: Fortress, 2010).
[41] Paul Haught, 'Environmental Virtues and Environmental Justice', *Environmental Ethics* 33:4 (2011), 357–75.
[42] Holmes Rolston, *Environmental Ethics* (Philadelphia: Temple University Press, 1988), Chapters 1 and 6.
[43] Lewis Smedes, *Standing on the Promises* (Nashville: Thomas Nelson, 1998), Chapters 2–4.

things – imagining, believing and acting. For Christians the expectation of a good future is based on God's promises and God's character as a keeper of promises.[44] We Christians hope for shalom or the reign of God because we worship a God who raised Jesus from the dead as a sign of the future restoration of all things. Thus the virtue of hope is the settled disposition to act with confidence to bring about some imagined good future – graduating from college, having a healthy baby, decreasing your carbon footprint and so forth. If we embody this virtue, then we are inclined to live in ways that make this desired good future real.

There are two vices that correspond to the virtue of hope. The vice of deficiency is despair. Despair is the absence of any expectation of a good future. As its etymology suggests, it is the loss of all hope (*de-sperare*). Despair is cynicism of a profound kind, for it signals a failure or inability to trust. Despair is the hopelessness that leads, as Søren Kierkegaard describes it, to the sickness unto death.[45] If despairing, we exhibit little or no confidence in the future.

The vice of excess is presumptuousness. In contrast to the confident expectation of genuine hope, overtaken by this kind of false hope we exude a brashness that takes the good future for granted. We have an unwarranted audacity of belief. We are unjustifiably overconfident about our hoped for good future.

The virtue of *ecological hope* names the settled disposition to yearn for and act to bring about God's good future of shalom for all the earth, rooted in confidence that such a future ultimately lies in God's good hands. If we embody this virtue, we remember the rainbow promise made to Noah, we celebrate the resurrection and we anticipate the New Jerusalem. We imagine our local lake purged of all invasive species and free of water contaminated by harmful bacteria and do whatever we can to make such a future come to be. We act in such a way that God's good future – a thriving neighbourhood, a healthy local watershed, a flourishing home planet – becomes a reality.

The vice of ecological despair names hopelessness in the face of our aching earth. In the face of pervasive ecological degradation, we cannot imagine that any liveable future on earth is possible. Aware of intractable ecological problems, we find it hard to believe there is any way out. Persistently pummelled by climate-change data, we abandon belief in any good future.

The vice of ecological presumptuousness is a disposition of overconfidence that presumes something – perhaps some new-fangled technology – will save us. If we fall victim to this vice, we fail to realize that there are pretenders to hope in our anxious world. We are taken in by prophets (profits?) of easy credulity. Or we presume that ecological healing will be pain free or won't demand much from us.

---

[44] Hope is different from optimism, since optimism is an inclination to put the most favourable face on actions or events, without adequate warrant or reason. See N. T. Wright, *Surprised by Hope* (New York: HarperCollins, 2008), Chapter 5.

[45] Søren Kierkegaard, *Sickness unto Death* (Princeton: Princeton University Press, 1941).

Embodying the ecological virtues faithfully

Climate change is real. And deafness, ignorance, indifference and denial are not viable options. Given our tendency to both overweening pride and self-deprecation, we need the virtue of humility to know our proper place and role in this world of wonders. Given our propensity to act foolishly, we need the virtue of wisdom to navigate our way to a world in which all flourish. Given our penchant for injustice, we need the virtue of justice to render with fairness to all creatures that which their worth requires. And given our inclination to despair, we need the virtue of hope to imagine God's good future of shalom, believe that it is possible and bear witness in all we do to that good future. In sum, to live more responsibly in a world of climate change we need these and other ecological virtues. Earthkeeping is woven throughout our theology and ethics, liturgy and hymnody, and creeds and confessions. In this time of climate change, may God grant us the habitual dispositions we need to do the difficult things that are necessary to live within the boundaries of the earth.

An Islamic response to Steven Bouma-Prediger

Yasien Mohamed[1]

In this response I will firstly provide a general Islamic perspective on virtue ethics and its relevance to climate change, and secondly respond to Steven Bouma-Prediger's essay. In my response I will try to identify some points of convergence and divergence in relation to Bouma-Prediger's own internal Christian critique of US churches' theological perspective on humankind and nature.

Islamic ethics is concerned with good character and the means of acquiring it, and took shape gradually from the seventh century, culminating in the eleventh century with the teachings of Miskawayh, al-Raghib al-Isfahani and al-Ghazali. These classical Islamic philosophers gave shape to Islamic virtue ethics, which combined Qur'anic teachings, the Traditions of Muhammad, the precedents of Islamic jurists and classical Greek ethical ideas. They were particularly inspired by the Arabic translation of Aristotle's *Nicomachean Ethics*.[2]

The eleventh-century Islamic philosophers framed their conception of virtue ethics within the paradigm of an Islamic cosmological view that saw humans as a microcosm of the world, which meant that humankind, both body and soul, is inherently connected to the cosmos, both physical and celestial. This idea was partly inspired by an earlier group of Islamic philosophers of the ninth century, the Brethren of Purity, who promoted a respectful attitude to nature with their notion of humankind as a microcosm, their emanationist view of creation and the way they illustrated the connectedness between humankind and nature. They showed that the natural environment has intrinsic value and so should be respected, not exploited for our superfluous wants.

Government policies and legislation are not enough to change our behaviour towards the natural environment. We need to change ourselves through the cultivation of virtues, for God states in the Qur'an that He will not change our conditions unless we change ourselves: 'Truly, God does not change the condition of a people, unless they change that which is within themselves' (Q. 13.11). In other words, the ecological crisis around us is a result of the spiritual crisis within us. We have become slaves to the concupiscent

---

[1] Yasien Mohamed is Senior Professor of Arabic and Islamic Philosophy in the Department Foreign Languages at the University of the Western Cape, South Africa. He is a founding member of the International Society of Islamic Philosophy and received an award from the Islamic Republic of Iran for his book *The Path to Virtue*.

[2] Yasien Mohamed, *The Path to Virtue: The Ethical Philosophy of al-Raghib al-Isfahani* (Kuala Lumpur: International Institute of Islamic Thought and Civilization, 2006), Chapter 1.

soul, hence our unbridled desire for material things and immoderate passion for consumerism. The 'corrupters' of the earth in the Qur'an are actually those who corrupt their own souls.

A central paradigm of Platonic and Aristotelian virtue ethics is the tripartite division of the soul into the rational, concupiscent and irascible faculties. The balance of these faculties leads to the four cardinal virtues of wisdom, temperance, courage and justice. This has been Islamised or Christianised by directing these virtues to the happiness of the hereafter and by adding theological virtues such as faith, hope and love. Through virtue ethics we learn to discipline the concupiscent soul, which leads to the virtue of temperance, an essential moral quality for frugal living and the moderate use of natural resources.

The message of virtue ethics is fundamentally important for our ethical behaviour towards the environment by teaching us to be responsible for our actions. The biological sciences have illustrated how human societies affect the earth's biodiversity. Scientific consensus indicates that modern climate change is driven by humans, linked largely to burning fossil fuels. This change is occurring at an unprecedented rate, with alarming environmental consequences. From this brief discussion it is clear that the problem is not purely environmental but also ethical and theological.

I will now briefly respond to Bouma-Prediger's essay on Christian virtue ethics and his critique of US churches. Much in his essay resonates with Islam, but due to limitations of space I will only touch on a few points of agreement and some points of difference.

Bouma-Prediger holds that the modern scientific attitude has made us indifferent to nature, promoting a materialistic conception of the world and failing to make us see the wonders of God's presence in nature. There are many verses in the Qur'an, including verse 17.44, which refer to the 'voices' or hymns from nature that glorify God: 'The seven heavens and the earth, and whosoever is in them glorify Him. And there is no thing, save that it hymns His praise, though you do not understand that praise' (Q. 17.44). This verse suggests that one should not disrespect any aspect of nature, for, whether we understand it or not, everything is possessed of spirit and praises God.

Bouma-Prediger presents an internal critique of Christian theology, which he believes to be partly responsible for the ecological crisis. However, he does not identify the root problem within the early history of Christianity. In his *Man and Nature*, Islamic philosopher Seyyed H. Nasr states: 'The type of nature which is profoundly Christian ... is ... associated more with the contemplative and metaphysical dimension of Christianity than with the theology. Theology is too rationalistic and man-orientated to be concerned with the spiritual essence and symbolism of cosmic phenomena.'[3] Max Weber's classic *The Protestant Ethic and the Spirit of Capitalism* attempts to demonstrate that it is the Protestant work ethic that contributed to the foundations of capitalist individualism,

---

[3] Seyyed Hossein Nasr, *Man and Nature: The Spiritual Crisis of Modern Man* (London: George Allen and Unwin, 1976), 60.

unrestrained by a theology that respects the link between nature and God. Thus, when people measure the value of their humanity in terms of material possessions, it will lead to unbridled consumerism and ecological destruction.

One of Bouma-Prediger's internal criticisms of US churches is that their teachings have become too deistic. Accordingly, God does not play a direct role in creation; 'nature' is autonomous, operating like a self-sustaining machine and has no need of divine assistance. Consequently, through the spread of deism, the hand of God was removed from creation. It is therefore no wonder that when Adam Smith, the father of capitalism, speaks of the Invisible Hand, he is not referring to God but to the economic forces governing human economic activity.

Thus, Protestantism, and the North Atlantic church in particular, partly contributed towards worldliness through its world-affirming theology and work ethic, while Catholic theology tended to espouse a more ascetic lifestyle and encouraged respect for the earth as a sign of God's wonder. Islam took a middle path between these two extremes: while it affirmed this world, it also treated it with due respect as a sign of God's power and beauty. As is evident from Pope Francis's encyclical on the environment *Laudato Si'*, the Catholic Church is more open to the reality of climate change and has connected contemporary science with theology. Catholic theology emphasizes that the created world is good and that humans have to be responsible stewards of the earth and its creatures.[4]

Amidst climate change, virtue ethics demands that we act with respect towards nature as a trust from God. Thus, everything in nature reverberates with the wonders of God, including plants. For example, a tree is not just a dead thing; it has intrinsic value, as Islam teaches. In a prophetic narration it was said that a tree was heard crying when the Prophet Muhammad left its stump in Medina. Like this tree, all of creation has inherent value. We have the right to eat from a plant or an animal, but we have no right to destroy them wantonly. Similar to the Catholic attitude, Islam understands the earth (and all of creation) from a theocentric perspective; the earth is a sign of God and a means of sustenance, so that humans can recognize God and live as His stewards in this world. As the vicegerents of God on earth, we therefore have an Islamic obligation to protect the natural environment.

Partly due to the contribution of Alasdair Macintyre and partly due to the failure of deontology and utilitarianism, virtue ethics has been revived in modern times. However, Macintyre fails to mention the contribution of Islamic philosophers and in his treatment of Thomas Aquinas makes no mention of the influence of al-Ghazali on Christian scholastic theology.[5] Bouma-Prediger, however, acknowledges the Islamic contribution and the fact that the Aristotelian ethical tradition was kept alive by medieval Muslim

---

[4] See Pope Francis, *Laudato Si': On Care for Our Common Home* (Vatican City: Encyclical Letter, 2015), Chapter 2.

[5] Alasdair MacIntyre, *A Short History of Ethics: A History of Moral Philosophy from the Homeric Age to the Twentieth Century* (New York: Macmillan Company, 1966), 117–19.

scholars. However, al-Ghazali not only helped to revive Aristotelian ethics but also presented a model of synthesis of the Greek and Islamic, which inspired the likes of Aquinas.

Islamic intellectual Imam Afroz Ali states: 'Global warming is a sign that the human soul is having a fever.'[6] Thus, we need to cure the feverish soul with virtues. Generally speaking, US churches hold that humankind has dominion over the earth. This leads to ecological arrogance and the exploitation of the natural environment. Biblical theology provides a compelling motivation for ecological humility (Gen. 2.15), and this resonates with the verse in the Quran: 'The servants of the Compassionate are those who walk humbly upon the earth, and when the ignorant address them, they say, "Peace"' (Q. 25.63). This should not be taken literally but means that we should be humble in this world and should adopt an attitude of peace. If we extend this into our relationship with the natural environment, we should cultivate ecological humility.

The dangers of climate change can be curtailed through the moral re-education of our souls. Ecology is a major moral challenge for Christians and Muslims in the twenty-first century, but the real challenge is how to link ethics, theology and science. Scientific knowledge, although changing, should inform theology and be informed by it in turn, so that we can live with justice and wisdom on the earth. We need to revitalize virtue ethics so that we can see the sacral value in nature again and work towards the re-enchantment of nature.

---

[6] Imam Afroz Ali, 'Environmental Ethics: The Quran's Signs of the Times', Ramadan Lecture Series, Al-Ikhlaas Academia Library and Resource Centre, 20 May 2018.

Chapter 2.3
Finding common ground on appropriate values, goals, policies and middle axioms

James B. Martin-Schramm[1]

Mind the gap: An ethical assessment of the Paris Agreement

This essay draws on resources I proposed in *Climate Justice: Ethics, Energy, and Public Policy*[2] to conduct an ethical assessment of the Paris Agreement that was adopted by 195 nations on 12 December 2015. I begin with a brief history of the ethic of ecological justice that grew out of the World Council of Churches and then explain how the ethic and its four moral norms (sustainability, sufficiency, participation and solidarity) pertain to the ethical assessment of climate policies in general. The bulk of the essay utilizes guidelines I proposed in *Climate Justice* to assess the temporal, structural and procedural dimensions of the Paris Agreement.

The ethic of ecological justice

Faced with the prospects of nuclear war, rapid population growth, deepening poverty and growing environmental degradation, members of the World Council of Churches (WCC) from all over the world began in the 1970s to grapple with the complicated and interconnected problems related to social justice and environmental well-being. Over time, four moral norms emerged from these vigorous deliberations (sustainability,

---

[1] James B. Martin-Schramm is Professor of Religion and Director of the Center for Sustainable Communities at Luther College (Decorah, Iowa). He is an ordained member of the Evangelical Lutheran Church of America. Most of his scholarship has focused on ethics and public policy.
[2] James B. Martin-Schramm, *Climate Justice: Ethics, Energy, and Public Policy* (Minneapolis: Fortress, 2010).

sufficiency, participation and solidarity) to better understand and flesh out what justice requires.[3] These norms were not imposed 'from above' but rather emerged from the 'ground up'.

Viewing these norms as a helpful source of collective moral wisdom, Presbyterian and Lutheran taskforces comprised of lay and ordained members have modified and applied these norms in various social statements about a wide range of issues over the last four decades. While some may characterize these social statements as dictums imposed from above, they have no binding moral force over members of these denominations. These statements and the norms that undergird them have been developed by committees of people who have worked together to produce practical resources to help members of both denominations grapple ethically with concrete problems 'on the ground' in their communities. They are not the only sources for ethical guidance, but they have offered ethical resources and a common moral vocabulary to critique the status quo and to assess proposals for change in civil society.

The ethic of ecological justice and its related moral norms can be utilized in general ways to conduct an ethical assessment of international and national climate policy proposals. For example, the norm of sustainability precludes short-sighted emphases on economic growth that fundamentally harm Earth's climate in the future, but it also excludes any approach to climate policy that doesn't address the suffering of over two billion people who are trapped in energy poverty today.[4] Sustainability emphasizes the importance of healthy, interdependent communities for the welfare of present and future generations.

The norm of sufficiency emphasizes that all of creation is entitled to share in the goods of creation. This means, most fundamentally, that all forms of life are entitled to those things that satisfy their basic needs and contribute to their fulfilment. Insofar as the norm of sufficiency repudiates wasteful and harmful consumption and emphasizes fairness, it represents one dimension of distributive justice. Many nations in the developing world are implicitly appealing to the norm of sufficiency as they demand the 'right to development' and insist they not be required to make the same rate or level of reductions in greenhouse gas (GHG) emissions as citizens of wealthy, developed nations.

---

[3] Paul Abrecht (ed.), *Faith, Science, and the Future* (Geneva: World Council of Churches, 1978); and Roger L. Shinn (ed.), *Faith and Science in an Unjust World* (Geneva: World Council of Churches, 1978). It is important to acknowledge, however, that a few years later the WCC replaced its references to sustainability and a 'sustainable society' with references to 'justice, peace, and the integrity of creation'. This is because '[s]ustainability had become a watchword for the interconnection of everything good – and ideological cover for some things bad'. See Willis Jenkins, *The Future of Ethics: Sustainability, Social Justice, and Religious Creativity* (Washington DC: Georgetown University Press, 2013), 137. While 'sustainability' can become a wax nose that is twisted to justify anything, that does not mean the term loses all value as a norm, hence I continue to employ it in my work, as does Jenkins in *The Future of Ethics*, 133–42.

[4] Jatin Nathwani, 'Empowering the Powerless – Let's End Energy Poverty', *Phys.org* https://phys.org/news/2018-01-empowering-powerlesslet-energy-poverty.html (accessed 24 March 2018).

The norm of participation stresses that the interests of all forms of life are important and must be heard and respected in decisions that affect their lives. There is little question that this norm is violated by fossil-fuel companies who fund research to cast doubt on the scientific consensus about climate change and global warming. It is also violated by the power their money buys in the halls of power through campaign contributions and other forms of corruption. Finally, the norm is violated by various economic relationships between nations that foster and perpetuate forms of neocolonialism.

The norm of solidarity highlights the kinship and interdependence of all forms of life and encourages support and assistance for those who suffer. Solidarity calls the powerful to share the plight of the powerless, the rich to listen to the poor and humanity to recognize its fundamental interdependence with the rest of nature. The norm of solidarity supports intra-generational transfers of resources from the rich to the poor so that they can adapt to climate change both now and in the future, but it also calls present generations to make sacrifices for future generations as a matter of intergenerational ethical responsibility.

Ethical guidelines and middle axioms

These four moral norms sketch the broad outline of an ethic of ecological justice and can be applied generally to debates about climate policy. Additional ethical guidelines are needed, however, to assess particular climate policy proposals. I developed the following guidelines to help expand and apply the ethic of ecological justice and its related moral norms to specific climate policy proposals.[5] These guidelines serve as middle axioms, which connect and apply Christian norms to concrete policy proposals and enable ethical deliberation with a diverse group of conversation partners. Viewed correctly, middle axioms are not bland expressions of political compromise or tools to foster incremental progress but rather are, in the words of James Nash, 'means of guiding us in designing and assessing specific answers to concrete problems in ways that promote the "best possible" approximation of Christian norms' in a religiously and philosophically diverse world.[6]

The following ethical guidelines can be used to assess the temporal, structural and procedural dimensions of climate policy proposals.

---

[5] Martin-Schramm, *Climate Justice*, 40–4.
[6] James A. Nash, *Loving Nature: Ecological Integrity and Christian Responsibility* (Nashville: Abingdon Press, 1991), 194.

Temporal dimensions

- *Current urgency:* Given the fact of global warming and the dire consequences associated with rapid climate change, climate policy proposals should be evaluated on the extent to which they address what Martin Luther King, Jr, famously termed 'the fierce urgency of Now'.[7]
- *Future adequacy:* The proposed level and timetable of reductions in GHG emissions must be sufficient to avoid catastrophic consequences associated with climate change.
- *Historical responsibility:* A greater and proportional share of the burden associated with reducing GHG emissions must fall on those who have been major emitters in the past.
- *Existing capacity:* Those with more financial and technological resources should bear a greater share of the cost associated with reducing emissions than those who have much less.
- *Political viability:* A morally praiseworthy climate proposal must have sufficient political support to make it realistic and viable.

Structural dimensions

- *Scientific integrity:* Climate policies must be based on the best current science and have the capacity to be revised in light of future scientific findings.
- *Sectoral comprehensiveness:* An ethically adequate climate policy should spread GHG reduction requirements over all sectors of an economy (agriculture, heavy industry, transportation, etc.), rather than lay the burden or blame on one or more particular industries.
- *International integration:* Since the planet's atmosphere does not recognize political boundaries, national climate policies must be consistent with international agreements and be integrated with them.
- *Resource sharing:* Morally praiseworthy climate proposals should contain mechanisms to transfer resources from the rich to the poor, so the poor can bear the cost and acquire the technologies necessary to mitigate emissions in the present and adapt to climate change in the future.
- *Economic efficiency:* Climate policies that achieve the greatest measures of ecological and social well-being at the least economic cost are morally preferred.

---

[7] Martin Luther King, Jr, 'I Have a Dream', 28 August 1963, http://www.americanrhetoric.com/speeches/mlkihaveadream.htm (accessed 27 March 2018).

Procedural dimensions

- *Policy transparency:* It is vital that all parties be able to comprehend the impact of a climate policy upon them and to discern how and by whom the policy will be implemented.
- *Emissions verifiability:* With several principal greenhouse gases and emission sources spread around the world, climate policies must identify ways to verify emission reductions with a high degree of confidence and accuracy.
- *Political incorruptibility:* The auctioning of emission allowances and/or the collection of taxes on GHG emissions will generate major fiscal obligations that the rich and powerful will seek to avoid, as well as enormous revenue streams that some will try to misappropriate. Climate policies must be designed so that they cannot easily be corrupted by the rich and abused by the powerful.
- *Implementational subsidiarity:* While the focus must be on global reductions of greenhouse gas concentrations, better climate policies will utilize the principle of subsidiarity to empower those closest to the source of the emissions to decide how best to achieve the reductions.

Many of these climate policy guidelines reflect different aspects of the eco-justice norms, but they also can be associated with particular norms. For example, the guidelines of current urgency and future adequacy clearly address the norm of sustainability. So too do the guidelines that emphasize the scientific integrity of climate policy proposals and the verification of emission reductions. The norm of sufficiency is addressed in part by the guidelines that emphasize economic efficiency and sectoral comprehensiveness. Sufficiency is also addressed when the guidelines of historical responsibility and existing capacity are employed to place more of the burden for reducing GHG emissions on those who have the most financial capacity to bear it. The norm of participation is fleshed out in the guidelines that emphasize policy transparency, political incorruptibility, international integration, implementational subsidiarity and political viability. Finally, the guidelines of resource sharing, historical responsibility and existing capacity all address the norm of solidarity and the equitable distribution of the financial burdens and moral responsibilities associated with reducing GHG emissions and adapting to climate change.

An ethical assessment of the Paris Agreement

On 12 December 2015, 196 parties to the United Nations Framework Convention on Climate Change (UNFCCC) reached a new legally binding framework for an internationally coordinated effort to address climate change. A similar 2009 Conference of the Parties in Copenhagen had failed miserably because developed and developing countries could not reach agreement about what their 'common but differentiated responsibilities and respective capabilities' should be when the first commitment period for the Kyoto Protocol concluded at the end of 2012.[8] Whereas the Kyoto Protocol had imposed *obligatory* emission reduction targets on industrialized countries and exempted developing countries from such obligations, the Paris Agreement invited all nations to make *voluntary* mitigation contributions that must be ratcheted up over time and reviewed by experts.

This new 'pledge and review' approach resulted in an unprecedented degree of international consensus on how to address climate change. For the first time, all signatory parties agreed to develop plans to contribute to climate-change mitigation from 2020 onward, though many developing countries made their commitments conditional on financial and technological support.[9] Developed countries offered absolute, economy-wide emission reduction targets, and developing countries took a range of approaches, including reductions in per capita emissions and emissions intensity. In addition, the parties agreed to a long-term temperature goal to hold global temperatures to 'well below 2°C above pre-industrial levels and to pursue efforts to limit the temperature increase to 1.5°C'.[10] The inclusion of this more stringent target was a major victory for a 'high ambition coalition' of more than 100 island states and 'less developed' countries who are already bearing the brunt of the impacts from global warming and climate change. Led by the Marshall Islands, this bloc called attention to their plight before and during the meeting in Paris with their slogan, '1.5 to Stay Alive'.[11] This new coalition

---

[8] United Nations Framework Convention on Climate Change, Preface and Article 4.1, *UNFCCC* http://unfccc.int/files/essential_background/convention/background/application/pdf/convention_text_with_annexes_english_for_posting.pdf (accessed 27 March 2018). On 25 July 1997, the US Senate unanimously passed Senate Resolution 98 (95-0), which opposed a resolution opposing any treaty that excluded developing countries from making mandated, scheduled emission reductions or resulted in serious harm to the US economy. See https://www.congress.gov/bill/105th-congress/senate-resolution/98 (accessed 27 March 2018). Needless to say, the exclusion of the world's two largest GHG emitters from obligations under the Kyoto Protocol meant the treaty made little impact on reducing global emissions.

[9] Key to the success in Paris was a joint statement about one year earlier between the president of the United States, Barack Obama, and the president of the People's Republic of China, Xi Jinping. Together, they 'announced their respective post-2020 actions on climate change, recognizing that these actions are part of the longer range effort to transition to low-carbon economies, mindful of the global temperature goal of 2°C. The United States intends to achieve an economy-wide target of reducing its emissions by 26%–28% below its 2005 level in 2025 and to make best efforts to reduce its emissions by 28%. China intends to achieve the peaking of CO_2 emissions around 2030 and to make best efforts to peak early and intends to increase the share of non-fossil fuels in primary energy consumption to around 20% by 2030. Both sides intend to continue to work to increase ambition over time.' The White House, 'U.S.-China Joint Announcement on Climate Change', 11 November 2014, https://obamawhitehouse.archives.gov/the-press-office/2014/11/11/us-china-joint-announcement-climate-change (accessed 27 March 2018).

[10] UNFCCC, Paris Agreement, Article 2.1 (a), http://unfccc.int/resource/docs/2015/cop21/eng/10a01.pdf#page=2 (accessed 25 March 2018).

[11] Chukwumerije Okereke and Philip Coventry, 'Climate Justice and the International Regime: Before, During, and After Paris', *WIREs Climate Change* 7 (2016), 839. DOI: 10.1002/wcc.419.

also fought successfully to make the Paris Agreement legally binding, to review national emission reduction commitments every five years and to develop a system to track and report progress towards these commitments.[12]

The Paris Agreement entered into legal force on 4 November 2016 when at least fifty-five parties representing at least 55 per cent of global greenhouse gas emissions had ratified the Agreement.[13] As of April 2018, 175 of the 195 signatories have ratified the Agreement[14] and 190 countries have submitted their initial intended nationally determined contributions accounting, which account for 99 per cent of global emissions.[15] The rest of this essay summarizes key aspects of the Paris Agreement and offers an ethical assessment of each by drawing on the climate policy guidelines described above.

Mitigation, transparency and accountability

Summary: The parties could not agree on a specific date when global emissions should peak, but the parties did agree (1) 'to reach global peaking of greenhouse gas emissions as soon as possible, recognizing that peaking will take longer for developing country Parties'; (2) 'to undertake rapid reductions thereafter in accordance with best available science'; and (3) 'to achieve a balance between anthropogenic emissions by sources and removals by sinks of greenhouse gases in the second half of this century, on the basis of equity, and in the context of sustainable development and efforts to eradicate poverty'.[16]

To achieve these mitigation goals, each country agreed to 'prepare, communicate and maintain successive nationally determined contributions' (NDCs) to reduce domestic emissions and to revise these at least every five years on the basis of their 'highest possible ambition, reflecting its common but differentiated responsibilities and respective capabilities, in the light of different national circumstances'.[17]

---

[12] Climate Focus, 'The Paris Agreement Summary', Briefing Note, December 2015, 2, http://www.climatefocus.com/sites/default/files/20151228%20COP%2021%20briefing%20FIN.pdf (accessed 25 March 2018).

[13] It is worth noting that the Paris Agreement actually consists of two documents – the Agreement itself and the Decision by the parties to approve it. The Paris Agreement is a legally binding executive agreement but it is not an international treaty. This nomenclature was necessary to secure agreement from the United States because an international treaty had little chance of being approved by the US Senate.

[14] United Nations, 'Paris Agreement-Status of Ratification', http://unfccc.int/paris_agreement/items/9444.php (accessed 24 March 2018).

[15] Center for Climate and Energy Solutions, 'Paris Climate Agreement Q&A', https://www.c2es.org/content/paris-climate-agreement-qa/ (accessed 24 March 2018).

[16] United Nations, 'Paris Agreement', Article 4.1, http://unfccc.int/resource/docs/2015/cop21/eng/10a01.pdf#page=2 (accessed 25 March 2018).

[17] Ibid., Article 4.2-3. Michael Northcott claims that the Intended Nationally Determined Contributions (INDCs) submitted in Paris 'can easily be avoided by importing carbon-intense goods and services from other domains'. He is right that the carbon footprint of developed countries would be much larger if the carbon footprint of imported goods from developing nations was included, but that does not mean the

The Paris Agreement allows parties to cooperate in achieving their mitigation goals through (1) joint NDCs within a regional economic integration organization (like the European Union);[18] (2) voluntary partnerships that can include the transfer of mitigation outcomes achieved through emissions trading or results-based payments;[19] and (3) investments made via a new Sustainable Development Mechanism that allows private and public entities to support mitigation projects that generate transferable emission reductions.[20]

The ultimate success of the Paris Agreement hinges on an 'enhanced transparency framework for action and support'.[21] As part of a 'global stocktake' process every five years, parties have to collect and make available information necessary to track progress made in implementing and achieving their NDCs and file national inventory reports.[22] This information is to be provided every two years, though an exception is provided for the 'least developed' and small island countries. Reviews of this information will be 'facilitative, non-intrusive, non-punitive [in] manner, [and] respectful of national sovereignty'.[23] In addition, to facilitate implementation and promote compliance, the Agreement establishes a committee that 'shall be expert-based and facilitative in nature and function in a manner that is transparent, non-adversarial and non-punitive'.[24] The parties gave themselves three years, until the twenty-fourth Conference of the Parties (COP 24) to be held in Poland in December, 2018, to negotiate detailed rules, guidelines and procedures for implementing the Agreement.

Ethical assessment: The Paris Agreement satisfies the current urgency guideline insofar as it strives to hold global temperatures to 'well below 2°C above pre-industrial levels and to pursue efforts to limit the temperature increase to 1.5°C'.[25] It satisfies the scientific integrity guideline by agreeing 'to undertake rapid reductions [after emissions have peaked] ... in accordance with best available science'. Most importantly, the Paris Agreement does a far better job than the Kyoto Protocol in terms of satisfying the historical responsibility, existing capacity and political viability guidelines because the new voluntary approach brought 'developed' and 'developing' nations together on the basis of their 'common but differentiated responsibilities and respective capabilities'

INDCs of developed countries can be 'avoided' entirely; their INDC obligations remain and pertain to domestic, economy-wide emission reduction commitments. See Michael Northcott, 'Climate Change and Christian Ethics', in *The Wiley Blackwell Companion to Religion and Ecology,* John Hart (ed.) (Chichester: Wiley Blackwell, 2017), 286–300 (291).

[18] Ibid., Article 4.16.
[19] Ibid., Article 6.2.
[20] Ibid., Article 6.4. The Agreement also seeks to avoid double counting of emission credits and other problems associated with the Clean Development Mechanism associated with the Kyoto Protocol.
[21] Ibid., Article 13.1.
[22] Ibid., Article 14.1.
[23] Ibid., Article 13.3.
[24] Ibid., Article 15.1-2.
[25] Ibid., Article 2.1 (a).

to address global warming and climate change.[26] 'Developed' countries agreed that they 'should continue taking the lead by undertaking economy-wide absolute emission reduction targets' while 'developing countries' agreed that they 'should continue enhancing their mitigation efforts ... towards economy-wide emission reduction or limitation targets in the light of different national circumstances'.[27]

The Paris Agreement fails, however, in terms of the future adequacy guideline. According to the non-partisan research group, Climate Interactive, if present trends continue, the concentrations of carbon dioxide will increase from around 403 ppm in 2018 to 850 ppm by 2100. As a result, the global average surface temperature will rise 4.2°C above pre-industrial levels by 2100.[28] The most recent edition of the annual *Emissions Gap Report* published by the United Nations Environment Programme (UNEP) concludes that '[t]he NDCs that form the foundation of the Paris Agreement cover only approximately one third of the emissions reductions needed to be on a least-cost pathway for the goal of staying well below 2°C'.[29] Climate Interactive projects the Paris NDCs will only limit warming to 3.3°C above pre-industrial levels by 2100 and that carbon dioxide concentrations will still climb to 660 ppm by the end of this century. Noting that this gap in ambition is 'alarmingly high', UNEP urges the signatories of the Paris Agreement not to wait until 2023 to ratchet up their NDCs but rather to use the facilitative dialogue taking place during 2018 to develop revised and far more ambitious emission reduction commitments.[30] Encouragingly, UNEP notes that much of the emissions gap can be closed by 2030 by aggressively adopting six cost-effective and proven emission reduction methods – 'solar and wind energy, efficient appliances, efficient passenger cars, afforestation and stopping deforestation'.[31]

Mitigation, transparency and accountability in relation to the emissions verifiability guideline are other areas where the Paris Agreement significantly falls short. While the Paris Decision that approves the Paris Agreement commits the parties to develop binding, procedural rules for the preparation and assessment of their NDCs, nothing in the Agreement or the Decision makes their execution and accomplishment legally binding. Nor is there any prescribed way to assess the equitable distribution of the mitigation burden on the basis of historical responsibility or existing capacity. While developed and developing countries are required to develop NDCs, they are not legally

---

[26] Ibid., Article 2.2.
[27] Ibid., Article 4.4.
[28] Climate Interactive, 'Climate Scoreboard: UN Climate Pledge Analysis', *Climate Interactive*, https://www.climateinteractive.org/programs/scoreboard/ (accessed 27 March 2018). The world is already about 1°C warmer compared to the pre-industrial era.
[29] United Nations Environment Programme, *The Emissions Gap Report 2017*, Executive Summary, xiv, https://wedocs.unep.org/bitstream/handle/20.500.11822/22101/EGR_2017_ES.pdf?sequence=1&isAllowed=y (accessed 25 March 2018).
[30] Ibid. As for achieving the 1.5°C goal, UNEP notes this will be very hard if not impossible if NDCs are not ratcheted up significantly by 2020.
[31] Ibid.

required to achieve them. This is a source of concern on all sides. Nevertheless, the political viability guideline would not have been satisfied otherwise. The reality is that members of the United Nations have found it very hard to force each other to comply with other international agreements. For example, the permanent members of the UN Security Council routinely veto proposals submitted by other permanent members. Compliance will have to be achieved another way. The Paris Agreement relies on public transparency as the primary means of holding countries accountable. With all parties now at the table, developed countries can hold each other accountable and developing countries can do likewise. Will it work? Not perfectly. Will it work fast enough? It clearly is not doing so yet. Can this new, non-punitive but morally accountable approach succeed? Only if it is employed with integrity by a new generation of leaders galvanized to address the perils posed by global warming and climate change – and only if those leaders have their feet held to the fire by their constituents.

Deforestation, adaptation and loss and damage

Summary: The Paris Agreement includes a short but exclusive section on carbon sinks and acknowledges the value of reducing emissions from deforestation and forest degradation (REDD+). It encourages all parties to 'take action to conserve and enhance, as appropriate, sinks and reservoirs of greenhouse gases'.[32] It also encourages all parties 'to take action to implement and support, including through results-based payments activities relating to reducing emissions from deforestation and forest degradation' as well as 'the role of conservation, sustainable management of forests, and enhancement of forest carbon stocks in developing countries'.[33]

Similarly, the Paris Agreement includes a new goal absent from previous UNFCCC agreements to enhance 'adaptive capacity, strengthening resilience, and reducing vulnerability to climate change'.[34] The Paris Agreement urges countries to put more emphasis on adaptation planning and to strengthen their cooperation by using a share of the proceeds from emissions trading via the Sustainable Development Mechanism to finance adaptation in developing countries. African countries succeeded in getting this qualitative goal included in the Agreement, but they failed to secure quantitative commitments of funding from developed countries to achieve this new adaptation goal.[35]

Small island countries also managed to have the Paris Agreement include a provision extending the Warsaw International Mechanism for Loss and Damage to adverse effects of climate change. The mechanism should be used to 'enhance understanding, action

---

[32] United Nations, 'Paris Agreement', Article 5.1.
[33] Ibid., Article 5.2.
[34] Ibid., Article 7.1.
[35] Climate Focus, 'The Paris Agreement Summary', 4.

and support' for vulnerable countries to cope with unavoidable impacts of climate change including extreme weather events as well as slow-onset impacts like rising sea levels.[36] Specific opportunities include developing early warning systems, engaging in comprehensive risk assessment and management, and improving the resilience of communities and ecosystems.

Ethical assessment: The inclusion of the section on carbon sinks and deforestation helps satisfy the sectoral comprehensiveness and international integration guidelines, but the Paris Agreement falls short in relation to both insofar as it does not address emissions from agriculture (nor aviation or shipping) in any significant way. A significant amount of deforestation is due to agriculture – especially the clearing of forests to graze animals for meat production or for biofuel production. Similarly, the addition of the adaptation goal and the Warsaw Loss and Damage provision begin to satisfy the historical responsibility, existing capacity and resource-sharing guidelines, but insofar as no funding commitments are required and no financial liability is incurred by developed countries, these guidelines are far from being met.

Finance, technology and capacity building

Summary: Under the Paris Agreement, developed country parties 'shall provide financial resources to assist developing country Parties with respect to both mitigation and adaptation in continuation of their existing obligations under the Convention'.[37] While developed countries are asked 'to take the lead in mobilizing climate finance', all parties are 'encouraged to provide or continue to provide such support voluntarily'.[38] The Agreement does require developed countries to submit biennial reports on levels of assistance and requires that these reports be 'transparent and consistent'.[39]

On technology transfer, the Agreement states the parties 'share a long-term vision on the importance of fully realizing technology development and transfer in order to improve resilience to climate change and to reduce greenhouse gas emissions'.[40] The Agreement goes on to establish a broad framework to provide guidance on a new Technology Mechanism with the goal of 'accelerating, encouraging and enabling innovation … for an effective, long-term global response to climate change and promoting economic growth and sustainable development'.[41]

---

[36] United Nations, Paris Agreement, Article 8.4.
[37] Ibid., Article 9.1. The phrase, 'in continuation of their existing obligations under the Convention', was a stipulation sought by the United States so as not to create new binding financial commitments requiring congressional approval.
[38] Ibid., Articles 2–3.
[39] Ibid., Article 9.7.
[40] Ibid., Article 10.1.
[41] Ibid., Article 10.3-5.

The Agreement also stresses the need for collaborative capacity building to help developing countries, 'in particular countries with the least capacity, such as the least developed countries, and those that are particularly vulnerable to the adverse effects of climate change, such as small island developing States, to take effective climate change action'.[42] While the Agreement states that all parties 'should cooperate to enhance the capacity of developing country parties to implement this Agreement', it indicates that 'developed country Parties should enhance support for capacity building actions in developing country Parties'.[43]

Ethical assessment: Money is always where the rubber hits the road. There is no question that the Paris Agreement falls far short in terms of the resource sharing and historical responsibility guidelines. In Copenhagen, developed countries pledged in 2009 to provide $30 billion in climate finance by 2010–12 and $100 billion per year in public and private resources by 2020.[44] In the end, no real progress was made on this front in Paris other than to establish a process to revisit the question every five years as part of the global stocktake process. In addition, the Paris Decision extends the $100 billion annual goal through 2025 and makes it a minimum funding floor for every year thereafter.[45]

As of January 2018, the Green Climate Fund has only raised $10.3 billion in pledges from forty-three state governments.[46] The United States has pledged $3 billion and has deposited $1 billion in cash. By way of comparison, Sweden has only pledged $581 million but it has deposited $4 billion.[47] The response of the United States and other wealthy countries is woefully inadequate, and it is not clear how it is going to get better. Without substantially increased funding commitments from developed countries, the injunctions in the Paris Agreement regarding climate financing, technology transfer and capacity building are mere lip service.

Conclusion

Clearly, despite much hype and hope, the Paris Agreement falls far short in terms of satisfying the ethical guidelines for evaluation of climate policies. Some point to President Trump's announcement to withdraw the United States from the Paris

---

[42] Ibid., Article 11.1.
[43] Ibid., Article 11.3.
[44] Okereke and Coventry, 'Climate Justice and the International Regime', 844.
[45] United Nations, Paris Decision, Item 53, 8.
[46] Green Climate Fund, 'Resource Mobilization', https://www.greenclimate.fund/how-we-work/resource-mobilization (accessed 28 March 2018).
[47] Green Climate Fund, 'Status of Pledges and Contributions to the Green Climate Fund', 29 January 2018, https://www.greenclimate.fund/documents/20182/24868/Status_of_Pledges.pdf/eef538d3-2987-4659-8c7c-5566ed6afd19 (accessed 28 March 2018).

Agreement as proof that the Agreement's voluntary approach is fatally flawed.[48] The reality is that the United States cannot legally withdraw until at least 4 November 2019, which is when the Agreement will have been in force for at least three years. To date, the United States is the only nation that has threatened to withdraw and President Trump's announcement to do so prompted two holdouts, Nicaragua and Syria, to decide to sign the Agreement.[49] No other nations have announced plans to withdraw. The United States stands alone. It is hard to imagine that this sort of international isolation will not have an eventual impact on US policy. No one likes being a moral pariah. Over time, moral force, rather than legal coercion, may well prove more effective in securing consensus and galvanizing political will to address climate change.

The collaborative approach of the Paris Agreement provides a sound basis for long term, international cooperation on climate change, but the situation is dire. The current slate of nationally determined contributions to mitigate emissions is far from sufficient, but it is a start. They include the first halting steps by many countries that have refused to take any steps up to now. One can hope, as costs for climate-change mitigation continue to decline rapidly and as more alternative energy systems support sustainable development in poor countries, that both 'developed' and 'developing' countries will ratchet up their commitments to hold global temperatures to 'well below 2°C above pre-industrial levels and to pursue efforts to limit the temperature increase to 1.5°C'.[50] In the end, though, hope is not enough. Those who want to avert catastrophic climate change must also take responsibility and act in various ways to address the climate crisis. That certainly includes Christian communities. One way, to be sure, is to challenge national leaders to work together to achieve the goals enshrined in the Paris Agreement. There are many other ways to act, however. These include making and implementing individual and institutional commitments to reduce greenhouse gas emissions at the necessary rate and scale based on our 'common but differentiated responsibilities and respective capabilities' and fully cognizant of the 'the fierce urgency of Now'.[51]

---

[48] Michael D. Shear, 'Trump Will Withdraw U.S. from Paris Climate Agreement', *New York Times*, 1 June 2017, https://www.nytimes.com/2017/06/01/climate/trump-paris-climate-agreement.html (accessed 27 March 2018).

[49] Brady Dennis, 'As Syria Embraces Paris Climate Deal, It's the United States against the World', *Washington Post*, 7 November 2017, https://www.washingtonpost.com/news/energy-environment/wp/2017/11/07/as-syria-embraces-paris-climate-deal-its-the-united-states-against-the-world/?utm_term=.26d594829295 (accessed 28 March 2018).

[50] UNFCC, Paris Agreement, Article 2.1 (a). http://unfccc.int/resource/docs/2015/cop21/eng/10a01.pdf#page=2 (accessed 25 March 2018).

[51] King, 'I Have a Dream'.

A response to James Martin-Schramm

Philipp Pattberg[1]

The ethics of disruptive change and the role of religion

Climate change represents a uniquely complex social justice challenge. Different from other cases of historical social (in)justice, climate change does not allow for an easy attribution of wrongdoing across time, space and class. Rather, 'victims, wrongdoers, and beneficiaries are dispersed (but unequally so) among different communities and generations'.[2] The emerging ethical questions that lie at the core of climate change are as follows: How do we balance historic responsibilities with current capacities in an interconnected world of competition for market and resource access? How do we balance rights and responsibilities of current and future generations under high sociotechnical uncertainties? And how can we best distribute costs and benefits of climate-change action across societies, groups and individuals? It is due to this immense challenge and the importance of ethical scholarship on climate change that an ecological justice approach to the Paris Agreement and ongoing climate actions is much needed. In this short response to James Martin-Schramm, I argue that the Paris Agreement indeed falls short not only in terms of satisfying ethical guidelines but also in terms of effectiveness. As a consequence, urgent additional actions are needed to raise the ambition level to meet the 2°C target. In the context of the much-discussed non-state global action agenda – that is, the possible contributions of regions, cities, companies and civil society – I will focus on the ambiguous role of religious groups and individuals.

In 1992, when the international community agreed on the United Nations Framework Convention on Climate Change (UNFCCC), the science of climate change was still developing, greenhouse gases were predominantly emitted by developed countries and the concentrations of carbon dioxide in the atmosphere had just surpassed 350 ppm. Some twenty-seven years later, climate change is scientifically uncontested, China has overtaken the United States as the world's largest emitter of CO_2 and atmospheric

---

[1] Philipp Pattberg is Professor of Transnational Environmental Governance at Vrije Universiteit Amsterdam, Institute for Environmental Studies, the Netherlands. His research is concerned with institutional performance, complexity and change in issue areas ranging from climate change to biodiversity and oceans.

[2] Lukas H. Meyer and Dominic Roser, 'Climate Justice and Historical Emissions', *Critical Review of International Social and Political Philosophy* 13:1 (2010), 229–53.

concentrations are now measured above 410 ppm. Against this background, states have successfully concluded a new global agreement under the UNFCCC, the 2015 Paris Agreement.[3] Prior to the Paris Agreement, the climate regime focused on allocating emission reductions among (a group of) countries. The normative basis for allocating emission reduction requirements was the principle of common but differentiated responsibility, and it was interpreted as a clear distinction between North and South in terms of responsibilities for climate-change mitigation. The new agreement, however, has turned the climate regime on its feet by introducing a 'pledge and review' approach based on Nationally Determined Contributions (NDCs). Under this approach, states decide their ambition levels independently instead of engaging in negotiations about 'who does what'. The result is a more flexible system that for the first time includes all countries in the quest to reduce GHG emissions to keep temperature increase below 2°C compared to pre-industrial levels.

But while the Paris Agreement has been widely acknowledged as a breakthrough in climate diplomacy,[4] serious doubts remain about its ability to achieve the necessary fast transformation towards net zero emissions by 2050. We are not on track with regard to the necessary emissions reduction and political opposition, and climate denialism is mounting in a number of countries. Recent assessments of the effectiveness of the Paris Agreement have highlighted a number of challenges. Following Barrett,[5] analysts agree that a successful climate-change mitigation agreement must achieve three related goals:[6] broad participation of polluters, adequate levels of compliance and sufficient ambitions with regard to emissions reduction. While the Paris Agreement fulfils the participation criterion – as of 2019, the Paris Agreement has been signed by 197 parties and has been ratified by 184 with 181 submitted NDCs – it falls short on compliance and sufficient ambitions to reduce emissions. In the 2018 Emissions Gap Report by the United Nations Environment Program (UNEP 2018), the authors conclude that

> current commitments expressed in the NDCs are inadequate to bridge the emissions gap in 2030. Technically, it is still possible to bridge the gap to ensure global warming stays well below 2°C and 1.5°C, but if NDC ambitions are not increased before 2030, exceeding the 1.5 degree goal can no longer be avoided.[7]

In fact, to meet the 1.5°C target, the current ambition level contained in the NDCs would have to be increased fivefold by 2030. Much expectation is currently set on non-state

---

[3] Philipp Pattberg and Oscar Widerberg, 'The Climate Change Regime', *Oxford Research Encyclopedia* (2017), doi: 10.1093/acrefore/9780190228620.013.46.

[4] Radoslav Dimitrov et al., 'Institutional and Environmental Effectiveness: Will the Paris Agreement Work?' *WIREs Climate Change* (2019), doi: https://doi.org/10.1002/wcc.583.

[5] Scott Barrett, 'Climate Treaties and the Imperative of Enforcement', *Oxford Review of Economic Policy* 24:2 (2008), 239–58.

[6] Dimitrov et al., 'Institutional and Environmental Effectiveness'.

[7] UNEP, 'The Emissions Gap Report', United Nations Environment Programme, Nairobi (2018).

actors in bridging the ambition gap.[8] While some observers are cautiously optimistic about the potential of non-state actors to meaningfully contribute to climate-change mitigation,[9] others point to existing problems with accountability and transparency of non-state climate actions.[10]

In sum, evidence is accumulating that suggests that the Paris Agreement is falling short both in terms of justice and effectiveness. Consequently, disruptive change and transformative action are urgently required that need to gain speed and depth quickly over the next years. In the words of Martin-Schramm, 'those who want to avert catastrophic climate change must also take responsibility and act in various ways to address the climate crisis'. This brings me to the urgent and somewhat under-researched question: what is the role of religion in the process of rapid and disruptive transformation? The role of religion, in particular the role of the Judeo-Christian tradition, in the environmental crisis has been scrutinized ever since Lynn White's article of 1967.[11] Beyond the generic criticism, a more nuanced picture has emerged. This is not the space to review in detail the state of the art on religion and sustainability. However, I want to briefly mention a number of more recent studies that exemplify two fruitful questions to be asked in the context of the required transformation: In a situation of required rapid change, how useful is a Christian worldview? And, what strategic options exist for relating religious worldviews to sustainable behaviour?

Starting with the former question, a now classical attempt to replicate and broaden an earlier study on the relation between religious orientation and environmental concerns[12] finds that literal interpretations of the Bible, belief in God and Christian affiliations correlate negatively with environmental concerns (in this study, measured as favouring increased spending on the environment). Catholics are more likely to support spending than Protestants, but both groups are far less likely than non-believers or people who understand the Bible as a book of fables. An important implication of this line of research is that strategies to mobilize religious individuals and groups should vary. A more recent study by Koehrsen reveals that organized religion played a very minor role in the energy transition in the pioneering city of Emden, Germany. As Koehrsen states, 'In a highly environmentally active region, there are few indications that religion has a

---

[8] Sander Chan and Idil Boran et al., 'Promises and Risks of Non-state Action in Climate and Sustainability Governance', *WIREs Climate Change* (2018).

[9] Jale Tosun and Jonas Schoenefeld, 'Collective Climate Action and Networked Climate Governance', *WIREs Climate Change* 8:1 (2017), e440.

[10] Oscar Widerberg and Philipp Pattberg, 'Accountability Challenges in the Transnational Regime Complex for Climate Change', *Review of Policy Research* 34:1 (2017), 68–87.

[11] Philipp Pattberg, 'Conquest, Domination and Control: Europe's Mastery of Nature in Historic Perspective', *Journal of Political Ecology* 14:1 (2007), 1–14.

[12] See Douglas Lee Eckberg and T. Jean Blocker, 'Varieties of Religious Involvement in Environmental Concerns', *Journal for the Scientific Study of Religion* 28 (1989), 509–17; Andrew Greeley, 'Religion and Attitudes toward the Environment', *Journal for the Scientific Study of Religion* 31:1 (1993), 19–28.

specific function.'[13] One may conclude that ongoing transitions are possible without the involvement of religious actors and that there is little empirical evidence to suggest that religion has played a major role on climate-change-related transitions to date. Finally, a recent study on opinions about climate change comparing Muslims, Christians and secular groups in the UK reveals that both Muslim and Christian groups have low perceptions of urgency for environmental issues due to beliefs in afterlife and divine intervention.[14] On the other hand, scholars have pointed to the positive contribution that public theology can make to the climate-change crisis. Kjetil Fretheim argues that public theology can offer faith, hope and love by 'speaking with an inclusive, probing voice, searching for shared ground, compromise and collaboration, but also the use of a prophetic, critical and transformational language integral to the Christian tradition'.[15]

With regard to the second question, research by Mikusinski and colleagues on biodiversity and religion shows that biodiversity relevant areas are concentrated in countries with larger Catholic populations. Furthermore, the authors conclude that 'the Roman Catholic and Orthodox Churches appear to have the greatest per capita opportunity to influence discourses on biodiversity'.[16] This type of research opens up possibilities of developing conservation (and more general sustainable development) strategies by understanding religion as a source of influence in the governance of a particular environmental challenge.

To conclude, against the background of critical assessments of the Paris Agreement and related broader climate actions, Martin-Schramm's ethical framework is very timely and useful. By developing middle axioms, based on the four fundamental norms of sustainability, sufficiency, participation and solidarity, Martin-Schramm successfully connects Christian norms to concrete policies (along the temporal, structural and procedural dimensions). The framework, based on Christian ecological justice, relates smoothly to broader debates about climate justice and thereby feeds into the emerging social justice movement around climate change.[17] What seems to be a relevant way forward when it comes to the ecological justice framework presented by Martin-Schramm is to use the framework for guiding the transformative process that lies ahead. For example, the necessary transformation of the global energy system will require ethical assessment and guidance in order to succeed. A Christian-inspired

---

[13] Jens Koehrsen, 'Does Religion Promote Environmental Sustainability? Exploring the Role of Religion in Local Energy Transitions', *Social Compass* 62:3 (2015), 296–310 (306).

[14] Aimie L. B. Hope and Christopher R. Jones, 'The Impact of Religious Faith on Attitudes to Environmental Issues and Carbon Capture and Storage (CCS) Technologies: A Mixed Method Study', *Technology in Society* 38 (2014), 48–59 (48).

[15] Kjetil Fretheim, 'Democracy and Climate Justice: Public Theology in the Anthropocene', *International Journal of Public Theology* 12 (2018), 56–72 (72).

[16] Grzegorz Mikusinski, Hugh P. Possingham and Malgorzata Blicharska, 'Biodiversity Priority Areas and Religions – a Global Analysis of Spatial Overlap', *Oryx* 48:1 (2013), 17–22 (17).

[17] See Ashley Dawson, 'Climate Justice: The Emerging Movement against Green Capitalism', *South Atlantic Quarterly* 109:2 (2010), 313–38.

framework could provide important inputs into the broader multicultural and diverse debate about possible energy futures by enabling, in the words of Martin-Schramm, 'ethical deliberations with a diverse group of conversation partners'. However, Christian theology can inspire frameworks for climate justice but is limited in its acceptance of urgency and agency. As the short critical reflections on the agency of religion show, to move from ethical assessments to transformative practices will require more careful analysis of the opportunities and limitations of religion in addressing the climate-change challenge.

Chapter 2.4
Finding common ground on environmental rights and responsibilities

Kevin J. O'Brien[1]

Introduction

Lucia Quispe, a farmer in the rural community of Khapi, Bolivia, knows that the climate is changing and fears what this means for herself and her two children. She explained to a group of Oxfam researchers: 'It does not rain when it should any more. At any moment, there might be clouds and the rainfalls. Before, there was a season for rain, and a season for frost and a period of winter. Now, it is not like that anymore ... we get more illnesses, more colds, more coughs, because of the sudden changes in the weather.' When asked how she felt about her children's future, she responded, 'Sad, and very worried. If we don't have water, what are we going to live from? There's no life without water.'[2]

Bolivia is home to 20 per cent of the world's tropical glaciers, which are rapidly shrinking as the global climate changes. This leads to both flooding and droughts, endangering livelihoods and food supplies. This is one of the poorest nations in Latin America, which means both that Bolivians have few economic resources to ease the transition to this new reality and that they bear relatively little responsibility for the problem of climate change causing it. Bolivia also has the highest percentage of Indigenous peoples on the continent, and they, too, are existentially threatened. Consider the Uru Chipaya, a community on the Lauca River that has maintained a consistent way of life for 4,000 years. They now face extinction because the river on which they have always lived, and by which they have always defined themselves, is drying up. The Uru

---

[1] Kevin J. O'Brien is Professor of Religion and Dean of Humanities at Pacific Lutheran University. His teaching and research focus on environmental ethics and climate change, stressing the intersections of science, ethics, religion, nonviolence and social justice.

[2] Oxfam, 'Bolivia: Climate Change, Poverty, and Adaptation' (2009), 39, https://www.oxfam.org/sites/ww w.oxfam.org/files/file_attachments/bolivia-climate-change-adaptation-0911_4.pdf (accessed 29 December 2015).

Chipaya insist that while individuals might survive and migrate elsewhere, their culture could not endure without the Lauca.

In 2009, the Bolivian ambassador to the World Trade Organization, Angélica Navarro Llanos, used such facts to argue that her nation is owed a debt.[3] Bolivia's economy, the traditional ways of life of its Indigenous peoples and the very lives of its citizens are threatened by climate change, a problem created and disproportionately caused by people in developed countries who emit the majority of the world's anthropogenic gases. She argued that Bolivians have a right to reparation, and the developed world has a responsibility to pay for the harm they have caused.

As an economically and socially secure citizen of the United States, I hear this as a call for my government – and perhaps for me personally – to pay for the harm that we have caused. In 2014, Bolivia was responsible for 0.1 per cent of the world's greenhouse gas emissions, while the United States was responsible for 14.4 per cent.[4] This disparity is just one example of the unjust distribution of wealth, power and authority that contributes to and exacerbates the damage of climate change. So, it is reasonable to insist that the poor and Indigenous peoples of Bolivia have a right to aid in dealing with a changing climate, and people like me have a responsibility to provide that aid.

How such rights and responsibilities might be enforced is an incredibly complicated question. This essay will not answer it, but will work towards an answer by arguing that a dialogue with Christian ethicists and theologians about rights and responsibilities can help to clarify what is at stake. I will first characterize these concepts in the abstract and then explore a globalist Christian perspective, exemplified by Pope Francis's *Laudato Si'*, on environmental rights and responsibilities. I will then consider a more particularist Christian perspective, exemplified by Brazilian theologian Ivone Gebara and Indian theologian George Zachariah. My argument will be that any moral discussion of rights and responsibility requires a complicated set of decisions about the scope of one's community, but that the basic right of our neighbours to our attention and care is nevertheless a straightforward duty that all Christians should embrace. More concretely, while the question of who owes what to Bolivia is an endlessly complicated one, the question of whether those who can afford it should help our Bolivian neighbours is not.

Rights, responsibilities and communities

Most simplistically, rights are that to which a person or community is entitled, and responsibilities are that which a person or community owes to others. The two generally go hand in hand: if I have a political right to free speech, my government has some

---

[3] Angélica Navarro Llanos, 'Climate Debt: The Basis of a Fair and Effective Solution to Climate Change', *Technical Briefing on Historical Responsibility*, 4 June 2009.

[4] CAIT Climate Data Explorer 2014, http://cait.wri.org/historical/ (accessed 25 March 2018).

responsibility to protect my capacity to speak; if you have a right to life, I have a responsibility not to threaten your survival.

Larry Rasmussen helpfully emphasizes that rights and responsibilities are never just about an individual; defining them is part of the formation and maintenance of community. What we deserve and what we owe each other tends to be written out in constitutions because these rights and responsibilities 'constitute' what it means to be a member of a group. At the political level, obligations and expectations 'comprise the basic bodywork for a nation as it grows and changes' and establish 'some minimum shared terms for getting along'.[5]

So, the first ten amendments to the US Constitution enumerate a Bill of Rights that constitutes citizenship in the nation: every citizen has a right to free speech, to bear arms, to a speedy and public trial and so on. These rights help to define what it means to be a citizen, and so the government spends considerable time determining what it means to honour them and working out what responsibilities are required to ensure that they endure. These are entitlements and obligations constitutive of the nation.

However, the rights enshrined in this constitution shed no real light on whether a wealthy, carbon-emitting citizen of the United States owes anything to a poor farmer in Bolivia suffering from climate-induced drought. The Bill of Rights is limited to the US context, constituting what US citizens deserve from one another and from our government; it does not address those outside that community. A wider set of rights and responsibilities is required to deal with questions of international rights. The United Nations General Assembly attempted to create this when it issued a 'Universal Declaration of Human Rights' in 1948. This declaration articulated rights and responsibilities for the human race, outlining the moral framework for a global community.[6] Its twenty-fifth article asserts that 'everyone has the right to a standard of living adequate for the health and well-being of himself and his family', which suggests that a farmer unable to feed her family has the right to aid. However, the document does not specify whose responsibility it is to ensure that right is enforced, and the United Nations as it currently exists is not equipped to take on that role. Furthermore, the declaration was written before climate change or environmental degradation were common concerns, so it would take considerable interpretation to determine how this right might apply today.

An even more universal declaration is found in the Earth Charter, written by an international commission and launched in June 2000. While the Declaration on Human Rights sought to constitute a species-wide community, this document seeks something even broader, declaring humanity's 'responsibility to one another, to the greater community of life, and to future generations'. Interestingly, the Charter asserts few rights, as the authors could not find widespread agreement on whether non-human

---

[5] Larry L. Rasmussen, *Earth-Honoring Faith: Religious Ethics in a New Key* (New York: Oxford University Press, 2013), 139.
[6] 'The Universal Declaration of Human Rights', http://www.un.org/en/universal-declaration-human-rights/ (accessed 19 February 2018).

creatures have rights.[7] However, it does assert 'the right of all, without discrimination, to a natural and social environment supportive of human dignity, bodily health, and spiritual well-being, with special attention to the rights of Indigenous peoples'.[8] This establishes basic rights for the Uru Chipaya of Bolivia. The wealthy world has failed its responsibility to prevent harm, and so owes something to those whose dignity, health and well-being have been endangered.

Mary Evelyn Tucker and John Grim write that the Earth Charter is a sign that 'the ethical compass of the human is expanding'.[9] This expansion of rights and responsibilities signals a truly global approach to a world of ecological interconnection and climate change. However, the Earth Charter is not a legal document, and no formal political entity accepts it as constitutive. There is, currently, no global community that legally enforces global obligations. This means that the question of 'common ground on environmental rights and responsibilities' is at least as much a question about 'common ground' as about rights and responsibilities. Can there be such common ground? Should there be?

Laudato Si' and universal human responsibility

Pope Francis's encyclical *Laudato Si'* attempts to establish a global common ground that includes the forceful articulation of rights and responsibilities. While it is most explicitly a letter to the Catholic community over which the pope has authority, this letter is addressed to 'every person living on this planet', hoping for 'dialogue with all people about our common home'. Because we share a single planet, he argues, we are called to think from a global perspective, to build *'one world with a common plan'*.[10] This document seeks to establish enough common ground that the rights of all will be acknowledged and every human being will feel responsible for the well-being of every other.

Language of duty and obligation is used in *Laudato Si'* primarily to assert the equality of all people. Pope Francis critiques vast inequities in the distribution of wealth and consumption that destroy the environment and lead to 'desperate and degrading poverty' alongside 'so much waste'. He notes that, in practice, global inequality suggests that 'some consider themselves more human than others, as if they had been born with

---

[7] Steven C. Rockefeller, 'Global Interdependence, the Earth Charter, and Christian Faith', in *Earth Habitat: Eco-Injustice and the Church's Response*, Dieter Hessel and Larry L. Rasmussen (eds) (Minneapolis: Fortress, 2001), 101–21.

[8] Earth Council, *The Earth Charter* (Costa Rica: Earth Council, 2000), 1.2.a.

[9] John Grim and Mary Evelyn Tucker, *Ecology and Religion* (Washington DC: Island Press, 2014), 157.

[10] Pope Francis, *Laudato Si': On Care for Our Common Home* (Vatican City: Encyclical Letter, 2015), §3, 164, emphasis in original.

greater rights'.[11] By contrast, he insists, true rights are universal, borne in equal share by every member of the global human community.

Constituting a community generally involves creating boundaries, including some by leaving others out. In its discussion of rights, *Laudato Si'* focuses on human beings, and it explicitly emphasizes that human beings have 'unique worth' and 'immense dignity' because 'every man and woman is created out of love and made in God's image'. These claims suggest that there are rights that go along with being human, rights to which other creatures and species and systems have no access. However, Pope Francis further suggests that the uniqueness of humanity includes 'tremendous responsibility' of care for the rest of creation and leaves 'no place for a tyrannical anthropocentrism unconcerned for other creatures'. As uniquely powerful and loved beings, humans are called to do more, not less, for the rest of the creation. Thus, while the document does not ascribe rights directly to other creatures or species, it explicitly laments extinction of thousands of species which 'will no longer give glory to God by their very existence', emphasizing that human beings 'have no such right'.[12] The right to determine the fate of other species, Pope Francis suggests, belongs only to God.

Similarly, only God has the right to ultimately control the earth's resources. For Pope Francis, human beings have no inviolable right to private property. Noting again that economic inequality and poverty are both a cause and a cost of environmental degradation, *Laudato Si'* insists that the resources of the earth belong to the Creator and have been given to the care of 'the whole human race'. No one has a right to do whatever they want with any piece of creation; instead, all property is to be used for the common good. This is demonstrated in a more positive statement of rights, when Pope Francis explicitly argues against the privatization of water by asserting that *'access to safe drinkable water is a basic and university human right, since it is essential to human survival and, as such, is a condition for the exercise of other human rights.* Our world has a grave social debt towards the poor who lack access to drinking water.'[13]

This right of access to water and the 'grave social debt' it incurs return us to the concrete needs of human beings in Bolivia. They face drought conditions as their glaciers shrink and their seasons become unpredictable. If we understand humanity as a singular, united community, and if we understand that every person in Bolivia is entitled to sufficient water, then it becomes the duty of the rest of us to ensure that they get sufficient water for their needs. The right creates a responsibility, suggesting that all who have overused water or taken it for granted owe a debt alongside all who have carelessly burned fossil fuels and contributed to shrinking glaciers. By this moral logic, the resources of humanity should be pooled to assist Bolivians and all others whose access to safe water is threatened by a changing climate. *Laudato Si'* seeks to

---

[11] Ibid., §90.

[12] Ibid., §90, 65, 68, 33. This approach is comparable to that of the Earth Charter, which *Laudato Si'* explicitly echoes (§207).

[13] Ibid., §93, 30, emphasis in original.

motivate us towards a global moral community that would establish and enforce that responsibility.

Postcolonial rights and the call of particularity

An alternative view pushes against the idea of a truly global community, at least as constituted by an authority like Pope Francis. Brazilian ecofeminist theologian Ivone Gebara, for example, acknowledges the value of *Laudato Si'* but argues that it is inevitably limited by the specific context from which it emerges. The Catholic Church, she asserts, is a hierarchical and patriarchal structure, and so there is reason to suspect any articulation of global community from its leader.

Pope Francis's care for the poor and for women, Gebara argues, is ultimately paternalistic, acknowledging that everyone has value but deriving and defending that value based on a 'patriarchal symbolic vision in which the male figure remains the center of the world's organization and of divine revelation'. For example, the pope writes about the particular struggles and rights of women in *Laudato Si'*, but 'women do not speak in their own voice about their life situations, their sufferings, and their demands' in the encyclical. This matters, Gebara argues, because true reflection on the plight of real women in a world of climate change requires ongoing reflection alongside women who are empowered to speak for themselves. *Laudato Si'* lacks such ongoing reflection; it seeks a global community without honouring the particularity of women's communities.[14]

The same point could be made about the poor and all other marginalized peoples, for whom Pope Francis advocates but to whom the encyclical does not provide direct voice. The encyclical itself acknowledges this need in one case, noting that 'Indigenous communities and their cultural traditions' should be 'principal dialogue partners'.[15] But *Laudato Si'* does not engage in that dialogue to justify or explore its core moral arguments. It speaks for rather than with Indigenous communities. Pope Francis writes generally, insisting that everyone should be treated equally with one voice, emphasizing common ground rather than diversity. Gebara, on the other hand, cautions that any centralized authority will always miss the nuanced experience and needs of the oppressed.

Gebara makes universal claims but even they insist upon particularity. She argues that the most common ground to be found in the human species is our diversity: every person always comes 'from within some concrete context', and so 'all knowing has a universal localness about it'. The human family should therefore not seek universal

---

[14] Ivone Gebara, 'Women's Suffering, Climate Injustice, God, and Pope Francis's Theology: Some Insights from Brazil', in *Planetary Solidarity: Global Women's Voices on Christian Doctrine and Climate Justice*, Grace Ji-Sun Kim and Hilda P. Koster (eds) (Minneapolis: Fortress, 2017), 67–79 (76).

[15] Pope Francis, *Laudato Si'*, §146.

truths but instead seek 'universal diversity'.¹⁶ Simplistic universals close off discussion, while openness to diversity and particularity makes discussion more possible. From this perspective, any generalizable 'human right' must be looked at with suspicion unless it includes careful attention to what those rights look like from the perspective of particular, concrete peoples in their own contexts.

Indian theologian George Zachariah offers a similar argument, critiquing most environmental ethics for assuming 'a view from nowhere'. The attempt to speak globally, to treat the earth as a single object floating in space, ignores the particularities and specificities of colonization, oppression and violence that lead different human communities to have vastly different experiences of this planet. Zachariah seeks a 'grassroots earth ethic' that prioritizes an 'oppositional gaze' over and against such globalist thinking.¹⁷ He argues that the task of Christian ethics is to critique anything 'detached and disembodied', and so his own constructive ethic focuses on the concrete claims and activism of a particular protest movement in India's Narmada Valley.¹⁸ The goal is not to find straightforward rights or responsibilities for all people but instead to find and explore 'alternatives' to the dominating and colonial systems that have for too long defined Christian morality.

Zachariah and Gebara share a suspicion of any claim that one person from one perspective can represent or capture a human universal, and so they seek to constitute community in particularist ways. Rights and responsibilities, in this perspective, are established differently by different peoples, and every community should have the right to such self-definitions. All knowledge comes from particular places and contexts, and so all articulations of rights and responsibilities will, inevitably, be located and partial. Zachariah insists that the communities of the Narmada Valley have the right to determine their land's future, but he does not seek to universalize that right to a global community. Gebara insists that the oppressed women of Brazil have the right to define their own liberation, but she does not assume that there is an easily translatable idea of liberation that will then apply to all people everywhere. To the extent they define a universal right, it is the right of every community to speak for itself and determine its own future. Thus, the primary responsibility that people like me owe those in other parts of the world is to allow them to live for themselves and to refrain from impeding their well-being or from attempting to define it.

This offers a different perspective on Bolivians' struggles with their changing climate. While it is important that individuals in Bolivia lack access to safe drinking water, a more primary focus would be the disruption of the culture of Bolivian farmers like Lucia Quispe and the Uru Chipaya. I suspect that Gebara and Zachariah would discourage me from assuming that there is a single remedy for both. The multiple cultures of Bolivia

---

¹⁶ Ivone Gebara, *Longing for Running Water: Ecofeminism and Liberation* (Minneapolis: Fortress, 1999), 62.
¹⁷ George Zachariah, *Alternatives Unincorporated: Earth Ethics from the Grassroots* (London: Equinox, 2011), 101.
¹⁸ Ibid., 133.

each have the right to determine their own futures, to live as they wish to live. The moral problem could not be fully defined by a universalizable right to water but instead by the particular struggles of peoples to raise their children and maintain their cultures.

From this perspective, it is worth noting that the Bolivian ambassador to the World Trade Organization did not ask the 'developed' world to fix Bolivia's problems. Instead, she asked that reparation be paid, that Bolivia be given the resources to do as it chooses in response to this problem that others have made for it. She did not seek the creation of a new global body to take responsibility for all human lives; instead, she asserted both the right of her government to take care of its people and the responsibility of the people who have degraded the climate to make reparation. Gebara and Zachariah would likely encourage us to ask whether the Bolivian government could adequately speak and advocate for the diverse cultures within the nation, but empowering Bolivia is certainly closer to the particular and local rights they advocate than a more abstract universal human community.

Framing the choices for environmental rights and responsibilities

Before further exploring the distinction between Gebara and Zachariah's position on the one hand and Pope Francis's on the other, it is worth noting a fundamental agreement between them. These perspectives all lead to the conclusion that Bolivians and all other human victims of the changing climate have had their rights violated, and a response is called for.

This is not a universal opinion. Responding to Angélica Navarro Llanos and representatives of other nations who had made similar requests, the United States' Special Envoy for Climate Change, Todd Stern, refused to accept responsibility for any suffering caused by a changing climate. He pled ignorance: 'I actually completely reject the notion of a debt or reparations or anything of the like. ... For most of the 200 years since the Industrial Revolution, people were blissfully ignorant of the fact that emissions caused a greenhouse effect.'[19] Because US citizens and officials did not realize the harm they were causing, he argued, they do not owe anyone anything. This argument is based on a tenuous moral assumption: if I don't *know* I am violating a right then I have no responsibility for redressing the harm. That idea is not part of any legal or moral system of which I am aware, and so, in my judgement, Stern's argument is bad ethics. However, because there is no legal regime governing climate negotiations – no community has been constituted that could enforce international

---

[19] Andrew C. Revkin and Tom Zeller, Jr, 'U.S. Negotiator Dismisses Reparations for Climate', *The New York Times*, 10 December 2009: A12.

climate rights and responsibilities – Todd Stern and the government he represents can make any argument that they like.

Another, more theoretical rejection of a claim for reparation comes from political philosophers Jonathan Pickering and Christian Barry. Unlike Stern, they concede that there is a moral logic to these claims – those who are suffering from climate change have a right to repair, while those who disproportionately caused the problem have a responsibility to provide it. However, Pickering and Barry suggest that it is not pragmatic to make this case in contemporary global discourse. They worry that calling for reparation will inspire defensiveness in the industrialized world; it will discourage the most economically powerful nations from participating in the global conversations necessary to respond to climate change.

Laudato Si's globalist ethic responds to both arguments by asserting a global moral community. 'All people of good will' should come to see that every human being has basic rights, such as the right to safe and drinkable water. When anyone lacks such access, everyone is responsible for doing something to help. This changes the subject away from Todd Stern's concern – can a nation that was unaware of the harm it was causing be held accountable? – and from Pickering and Barry's worry – will it drive wealthy nations away if they are asked to pay reparation? By emphasizing a single global community, Pope Francis insists that 'we' human beings are responsible for helping those who struggle in Bolivia. Because of *Laudato Si's* emphasis on overcoming economic inequality, it stands to reason that nations in the developed and consumptive world contribute substantially to help those who need it, but our 'debt' comes not primarily from our guilt but from our wealth. We currently control a larger share of the resources which God calls us to use for the benefit of all.[20]

By contrast, the particularist views of Gebara and Zachariah suggest that a singular moral community cannot be trusted to meet the needs of poor, oppressed and Indigenous communities in Bolivia or anywhere else. The specific nature of each community must be emphasized, and no global body could faithfully assess and meet the needs of a farmer like Lucia Quispe and the Uru Chipaya people. The only path to justice comes from empowering communities to speak for themselves and define their own rights. To reach this goal, wealthy communities in places like the United States need to admit the harm their colonization of the climate has caused, to cease the harm they have caused, and to begin to redress it while surrendering their own authority. This will require an admission of guilt and then genuine repentance. It will require direct argument against Todd Stern's moral logic and will risk the defensiveness that Pickering and Barry fear.

The limitation of the globalist position is that it too easily universalizes rights and responsibilities, missing the particularities of real human communities and therefore running the risk of continuing exclusive universalities. The limitation of the particularist position is that it calls wealthy people to responsibility without constituting a moral

---

[20] Pope Francis writes, 'We must continue to be aware that, regarding climate change, there are *differentiated responsibilities*' (§52, emphasis in original).

community that will justify, energize or enforce it. I know of no clear path to a compromise or synthesis position, and suspect that this is a choice that must be made when we advocate for environmental rights and responsibilities in a world of climate change. Is it more important to inspire people with the possibility of a global community where everyone has equal rights, or to defend the concrete rights of particular communities and peoples by emphasizing the dangers of universalism?

A Christian parable of climate responsibility

Rather than offer my own answer to that question, I will conclude by appealing to a parable, a long-standing way for Christians to avoid answering a straightforward question.[21]

In the Gospel of Luke, a lawyer 'tests' Jesus with a question. After establishing that one should 'love your neighbour as yourself', the lawyer asks, 'who is my neighbour?'. Jesus responds with a story: A man is robbed and left half dead on the side of the road. A priest and a Levite both pass by without stopping. A Samaritan, by contrast, cares for the injured man, takes him to an inn and ensures he has time and space to heal. Jesus concludes: 'Which of these three, do you think, was a neighbour to the man who fell into the hands of the robbers?' The lawyer replies, 'The one who showed him mercy', and Jesus instructs his interlocutor to 'Go and do likewise.'[22]

One lesson to be drawn from this parable is the moral principle it assumes: Christians should love their neighbours, and this means caring for them. In a world of climate change, our neighbours are suffering from droughts and floods and extreme weather, and all of these trends are almost certain to increase. The Gospels offer a clear responsibility: love your neighbours; show them mercy. It is worth emphasizing again that the Christian thinkers cited above seem to agree on this: Zachariah, Gebara and Pope Francis all insist that Christians have a responsibility to do something on behalf of those who suffer from environmental degradation. The peoples of Bolivia are neighbors to all the rest of us, and when we see them suffering, Christians should not turn our eyes; we should care for them and enlist others to do the same.

A second lesson comes from the fact that there is no clear answer to the lawyer's specific question in this parable. He asks 'who is my neighbour?' Jesus answers with a story that never uses the word, and then concludes by reframing the question. Parables are frustrating that way, but there is something to be learned from that frustration. Christians

---

[21] In case the reader is curious, I consider myself a particularist, and my scholarly arguments about climate change tend to focus on the actions members of my own community should take rather than making universal claims. See Kevin J. O'Brien, *The Violence of Climate Change: Lessons of Resistance From Nonviolent Activists* (Washington DC: Georgetown University Press, 2017).

[22] Lk. 10.25-38, NRSV.

are never promised clear answers to the moral complexities of life in the world. Rather, the Gospels give those who ask for clear answers confusing and unpredictable stories or aphorism that theologians have spent two millennia interpreting. We should ask the Christian tradition, 'What rights and responsibilities will help us to make sense of a world of climate change?' and 'Should we emphasize universal rights or particular responsibilities?' But we should not expect straightforward or simple answers to those questions. When the Christian moral tradition is healthy, it emphasizes the complex realities of parables rather than the easy answers of political slogans.

A third and final lesson, though, keeps us from being trapped by that ambiguity, because the parable insists on action despite complexity. The lawyer asks 'who is my neighbour?' – a question we might use the language of this essay to interpret as, 'Who has the right to my love?' Jesus concludes his story with 'who was a neighbour?', suggesting that the more important question is, 'Who carries out their responsibility to love others?' The central character in this parable is not the beaten and bloodied man but the Samaritan who helps him. The command that concludes the parable is 'Go and do likewise.' We have no easy answers along the roads of life, but we must, nevertheless, act mercifully to those who need our help.

The global community to which *Laudato Si'* aspires is a very different goal from the local communities that Zachariah and Gebara seek to empower. There is no easy answer to the question which one is a better expression of Christian environmental rights and responsibilities, and/or which one will build a world where our neighbours are more loved. As scholars, the debate should engage us, and its nuances are worth many years and many volumes of reflection. Engaging that work is a part of faithful life in the complex world of climate change. But Christians are also called to act, to find some way to advance one or both goals and to embrace the responsibility of honouring the rights of the poor, the marginalized, the drought-stricken and the refugee.

We must advocate for Lucia Quispe, the farmer who fears there will be no life for her children, and the Uru Chipaya, who will have no culture without the drying Lauca River. Whatever else we do, Christians should be moved to act. We have a responsibility to show these neighbours mercy.

A response to Kevin O'Brien

Flávio Conrado[1]

Over the last decades, Christian theologians and ethicists put forth a great effort to creatively respond to environmental problems, which have become increasingly urgent. Other social issues, such as urban life and its consequences, issues of economic inequality and conflicts related to intercultural coexistence, also deserve serious treatment in terms of responses from Christian theology and ethics. Climate change, however, poses a more fundamental problem. For the challenge now is to reflect properly and creatively on a subject that potentially threatens humanity with extinction. Accordingly, the challenge posed to Christian theology and ethics by climate change needs to take priority at this juncture. However, simply discussing arguments is not enough. It is necessary to create bold strategies for engaging, from a deeply rooted moral imagination, religious actors and public institutions, so as to articulate a public theology and a robust social practice. The urgency of climate change requires that we find altogether new answers and new practices. Simply putting new wine in old wineskins (Mk 2.18-22; Mt. 9.14-17) will not do.

In his essay, Kevin O'Brien draws on the contributions of the Brazilian ecofeminist theologian Ivone Gebara, who denounces the paternalistic and patriarchal symbolic vision that a global community might erect from a global document like Pope Francis's *Laudato Sí*. Similarly, O'Brien reiterates the Indian liberation ethicist George Zachariah's insistence that poor, local communities and marginalized people must speak for themselves, defining their rights, responsibilities and future life. A global vision that discounts the specificities and particularities of human communities and endangered species runs the risk of becoming a discourse that denies what it promises to deliver. At the same time, however, it is urgent that the argument of localism or particularism does not supplant solutions that consider broader aspects of the impacts of climate change on regions, biomes and large groups of people.

I appreciate O'Brien's in-situ and concrete starting point. He vividly contrasts the pains and cries of local Indigenous communities in Bolivia to the disparities in wealth, knowledge, and power of countries and communities in the Global North. I wonder, however, whether his way of opposing a globalist position to a more localized knowledge

---

[1] Flávio Conrado is an anthropologist, organizer and scholar-activist. He holds a PhD in Sociology and Anthropology from Federal University of Rio de Janeiro (2006). He works as Coordinator in Intersecções, a platform to promote courageous conversations on Evangelical faith and eco-justice issues, and as member of the international board of GreenFaith.

and experience ultimately does not disqualify both approaches and perspectives. What is called for is not so much an either/or perspective but rather a both/and approach.

Ignoring the local is indeed a real risk. It risks being caught up in the very elusive scope of decisions and definitions at the global level. This has too often led to infinite postponement of concrete action by global actors. It also takes away the capacity for articulating a contextual and local position for defining and struggling for rights and responsibilities.

O'Brien's essay raises the question whether it is 'more important to inspire people with possibility of a global community where everyone has equal rights, or to defend the concrete rights of particular communities and peoples by emphasizing the dangers of universalism?' My response is that we need to work dialectically with both positions in order to address such a complex problem. On the one hand, we should acknowledge the language of principles, rights and responsibilities as perhaps the best categories to foster environmental care and protection and to mediate social–environmental conflicts which impact local communities. On the other hand, however, we should recognize that it is exactly this language which puts us in a situation of a failure to respond when it comes to finding and developing concrete processes and comprehensive solutions. One must agree then with Gebara and Zechariah on the limitations of a detached and disembodied global ethic. At the same time it is necessary to widen our perspective and put local and global voices in dialogue. We need to consider both local and global voices when discussing solutions to a problem which is bigger than everyone involved.

Although a papal encyclical such as *Laudato Si'* serves as an important platform for providing a moral vision for Catholics in the world, and possibly also for other Christians – especially those of an ecumenical orientation – it is not a sufficient basis for advancing the dialogue that is needed among peoples, cultures and spiritualities for a sustainable future that prevents climate change. *Laudato Si'* serves as the basis for Catholics and help them to recognize themselves as part of an important paradigm shift in humanity – namely, to recognize in their own tradition the space for socioecologically responsible thinking and acting.

Thus, I understand that our common ground, its principles, rights and responsibilities must come from an inter-religious paradigm and an interconnected worldview. As an anthropologist and scholar-activist, acting in evangelical, ecumenical and inter-religious platforms in the Global South, as well as in human rights and environmental secular ones, I can see the importance of a perspective and an approach which not just joins together different religions and spiritualities but also recognizes the importance of science, politics and the marketplace for finding solutions. However, opportunities for broad-ranging conversations have to be created both at the global *and* the local level. Global, regional and local platforms are opportunities for dialogue and confrontation of ways of life, for sharing ideas about a new moral imagination, and for exchanging new practices of conservation, protection and environmental sustainability.

Here I want to highlight especially the significance of interfaith initiatives that places spiritualities and religious organizations in dialogue for the common good. The UN

Environment Programme mentions at least sixty different interfaith initiatives at the local, regional or global level, demonstrating that we are able to engage communities of faith, clergy and lay people at multiple levels and across faith traditions while searching for an innovative approach and a re-imaginative perspective to environmental ethics.

One interesting experience, involving and uniting important global interfaith organizations to protect rainforests and Indigenous people (who protect the forests), is the Interfaith Rainforest Initiative, a coalition of religious and Indigenous people, the scientific community and environmental and climate NGOs. Fostering dialogue between scientific knowledge, religious discourse and Indigenous wisdom is paramount to this initiative and brings to the table different but necessary assets, resources, living practices and moral imagination which is required for understanding the risks and for advocating better policies. Surely, this is not an easy task and requires negotiation, active listening, goodwill and a sense of urgency. There is no other way than this promising endeavour.

Maybe we could offer another parable of the Gospels to Christians concerned with climate change and who are searching for a way to engage our current disaster. After John the Baptist's disciples reached out to Jesus asking him if he was the true messiah, Jesus performed some miracles and gave testimony about his eccentric and transgressive cousin. He ends up talking about his own people who couldn't gather that the best way of discernment is paying attention to our actions: 'To what can I compare this generation? They are like children sitting in the marketplaces and calling out to others: "We played the pipe for you, and you did not dance; we sang a dirge, and you did not mourn." … But wisdom is proved right by her deeds' (Mt. 11.16-19).

If we can learn something from the recent COPs, climate campaigns and building movements, there is a surprising energy, passion and growing consciousness on climate change around the world. As Christians we should look for common ground to be expressed in the interfaith wager to pursue eco-justice and the integrity of creation, so that we may live out the virtues of encounter, hospitality, conversion and hope. Then we can join together as different languages, peoples, cultures and nations; we can dance like children in the forests to celebrate a renewed and reimagined planet earth.

PART III

Working with and against others from within

Introduction

Ernst M. Conradie

The previous two main sections of this volume on Christian theology and climate change are based on the assumption that climate change is a challenge that Christians cannot address on their own. They need to work alongside others in such a way that they typically would not take the lead. There is a need to find common moral ground in order to work with others. In particular, Christians in the North Atlantic context need to recognize that such others may well harbour the suspicion that Christianity as such remains part of the problem, even where they are able to work with individual Christians or Christian organizations.

This main section of the volume takes the argument one step further. Working with others in the public sphere, also those standing outside the Christian tradition, may hide the inability of those within the wider Christian tradition to work with and alongside each other. Despite considerable ecumenical efforts towards a common witness, especially over the last century or so, Christianity remains deeply divided on many crucial ethical issues, including climate change.

These divisions run along various long-standing confessional traditions (with many debates on what constitutes orthodoxy) but also across differences of race and class, gender and sexual orientation, language and culture, geography, worldviews (in dialogue with modern science or not) and so forth. One may mention the way in which climate denialism is fostered in some circles, while the popularity of the prosperity gospel plays a role in other contexts. The accusation is that so-called mainline churches are wedded to 'old money' and thus partly responsible for legitimizing historic carbon emissions. By contrast, Pentecostal and other independent churches may well be attracted to 'new money' and thus to the expansion of a consumerist culture throughout the world – with a widening carbon footprint.

It would be grossly inadequate not to bring such divides into play in an exploration of Christian theology and climate change but also impossible to bring each of these divides into thematic focus. The most appropriate strategy may be to focus on the long-standing confessional traditions since all the other divides will then come into play in any case. This poses a different challenge, namely that adherents to these traditions typically believe that the best resources to address climate change may be found within that particular tradition, while others outside may see some blind spots more readily. The question that therefore has to be addressed is whether and to what extent each of these traditions may be regarded as part of the problem in mitigating carbon emissions. Why may it be difficult for other Christians to work, for example, with Roman Catholics? Or with Southern Baptists? The same question applies to other traditions.

The third main section of this volume, then, will focus on 'working with and against others from within'. It will include essays on what may arguably be identified as the main branches that constitute the 'tree' of the wider Christian tradition, especially within the North Atlantic context. The identification of such main branches remain somewhat arbitrary, but the inclusion of essays on the Orthodox, Roman Catholic, Anglican, Lutheran, Reformed, Anabaptist and Pentecostal traditions should be obvious enough. We opted against adding essays on Methodist and evangelical forms of Christianity since the boundaries and distinctive differences with the traditions already listed are not that clear.

One further essay was added on ecumenical fellowships. Such fellowships have been established across many divides and this has strengthened the authenticity of Christian witness. The World Council of Churches, in particular, has played a leading advocacy role in civil-society debates on climate change. Yet, as is widely asserted in ecumenical studies the ecumenical movement is in a constant state of crisis, resulting in diverging notions of forms of ecumenicity.[1] Does this affect the ability of some Christians to work with other Christians in addressing climate change? What about the inner tensions within the Christian tradition, for example, between fundamentalists and liberals, evangelicals and ecumenicals and the so-called mainline churches and a wide array of 'independent' churches? How do these tensions affect an ability to work with (and not against) others from within?

It should be clear that the integrity of Christian witness (and indeed the unity of the church that forms part of the Christian confession) is at stake here. In working with secular activists, Christians concerned with the challenges posed by climate change will be reminded of their 'brothers' and 'sisters' who are climate denialists. While Christians concerned with climate change may wish to highlight internal differences among Christians, critics from outside Christianity may well prefer to focus on the similarities among Christians. Unless the distinctions among Christians can be clarified from within, it may well be easier for outsiders to regard Christianity in general to be 'part of the underlying problem'.

---

[1] See Ernst M. Conradie (ed.), *South African Perspectives on Notions and Forms of Ecumenicity* (Stellenbosch: SUN Press, 2013).

Chapter 3.1
Working with Orthodox forms of Christianity

John Chryssavgis[1] and Frederick Krueger[2]

Orthodox Christians have inherited a biblically based, traditional theology of creation that is capable of addressing the crisis of environmental degradation and the specific challenge of global climate change. Interpreted in accordance with scripture and worship of the church, the classics of patristic literature define a world in which the origin and destiny of the human person is to transform and transfigure God's creation. This occurs by remaining steadfastly focused on the Creator and by relentless struggle to transform the human person from the divine image into the divine likeness. Such transformation becomes a prerequisite and parallel for the transfiguration of the larger creation.

Despite this inheritance Orthodox communities often fail to fulfil their deep theology of creation and become champion earth healers. Part of the challenge, as G. K. Chesterton observes, is that 'Christianity has not been tried and found wanting; it has been found difficult and not tried.' In the modern application of Orthodox theology and practice of Orthodox spirituality, one serious problem is that the keys to the transformation of the individual and the whole of creation have frequently been left in the past, resulting in a reduction of the patristic mind, the role of the sacraments and the way of the ascetics.

This has also meant a fragmentation of the ability to maintain awareness of the sacred that fills all things in creation. The alternative vision proposed by the Enlightenment, which observed creation as markedly distinct from God, has further diminished the traditional vision of God and the world.

Just as the present degradations to creation are foretold in Isaiah's depiction of a suffering creation (Isa. 24-25), so also inspiration and resolution may be derived from the scriptural and patristic emphasis on the role and responsibility of humankind 'to serve and preserve the earth' (Gen. 2.15). This vocation is encapsulated in the prayer of

---

[1] John Chryssavgis is Archdeacon of the Ecumenical Patriarchate and serves as theological adviser to Ecumenical Patriarch Bartholomew on environmental issues. He has taught in Sydney (Australia) and Boston (United States) and is the author of numerous books on creation care in the Orthodox tradition.

[2] Frederick Krueger serves as Executive Director of the Orthodox Fellowship of the Transfiguration, Executive Coordinator for the National Religious Coalition on Creation Care, and Chairman of World Stewardship Institute. He previously served as linguist and Russian intelligence analyst for the National Security Agency, as campaign manager, editor, author and wilderness guide.

the Orthodox Liturgy: 'Thine own of Thine own, we offer to Thee, on behalf of all and for all.' Returning creation back to God in an act of thanksgiving and praise recalls the divine mandate in the first chapters of Genesis and restores a cosmological vision and sacramental relationship to the earth.

The Orthodox Christian vision of God in all things

Heavenly King, Comforter, and Spirit of Truth, everywhere present and filling all things .... Come and abide in us, cleanse us from all impurity and save our souls.

This prayer marks the opening of many liturgical services in the Orthodox Church. It invokes the Holy Spirit and captures the guiding Christian vision of God's presence everywhere, filling all things. The fundamental spiritual principle that Christ, through the Holy Spirit, is everywhere present[3] leads to the recognition that the whole creation is sacred, while every place is infused with the vitalizing sacredness of God (see Acts 17.28). Thus every location becomes a sacred point of human interaction and potential encounter with God.

When we awaken to this awareness, our relationship with nature becomes an introduction and entrance into a living, sacred space where nature, humankind and God meet as one. Consequently, a sacramental vision of creation emerges. This vision cultivates a respectful response to creation, an attitude of thanksgiving and a practice of self-discipline. The Orthodox Church has always emphasized these qualities as a proper ethical response to creation.[4] This vision also calls us to a series of applications that honour God's presence and restrain human behaviour so that God is honoured and creation is transformed.

The technical theological phrase for this approach is *a Eucharistic ethos*. It implies a cosmically thankful perspective, the conviction that creation is not our possession or property. In this perspective, the world is filled with divine grace, a gift of wonder, goodness and beauty that is offered back by God in an act of gratitude and love. In the process of thankful offering, human beings serve as priests of creation, themselves changed by their offering. As individuals increasingly enter this spiritual practice of

---

[3] Athanasius of Alexandria writes, 'The Spirit of the Lord fills the universe.' Thus David sings, 'Where shall I go from thy Spirit?' (Ps. 139.7). The book of Wisdom observes, 'Your incorruptible Spirit is in all things' (Wis. 12.1). And 'the angels came to stand before the face of the Lord', as it is written in Job. And Jacob the patriarch dreamed: 'Behold! A ladder set up on the earth, and the top of it reached to heaven; and the angels of God ascended and descended upon it' (Gen. 28.12). See Athanasius, *Letter to Serapion, On the Holy Spirit*, 1.26.

[4] Clement of Alexandria writes, 'True food is thanksgiving. He who offers up thanks will not indulge excessively in pleasure.' See *Paedagogus*, Book II.1-2.

praise and thanksgiving, they also intuit the original blessedness of the world and experience divine energy in creation.

In response to the presence of God in all things, the Orthodox Church also calls its faithful to *an ascetic ethos*. This embodies a sense of discipline – of self-restraint and self-control – in order no longer to consume wantonly and wastefully but instead manifest an intentional frugality and individual restraint for the sake of valuing all things. Respect and restraint in turn becomes the doorway to caring for plants and animals, for trees and rivers, for mountains and seas, for all human beings and the entire cosmos. Then, human beings become instruments of peace and life. Then, everything assumes its divine purpose, as God originally intended for the universe.

The ascetic ethos further teaches the futility of the acquisitive mentality that underlies consumerism and is a major driver of climate change. A deliberately cultivated and renewed form of asceticism is essential if we are to limit our desires and increase respect for all creation. Humanity requires a refined lifestyle for the sake of a restored creation. Asceticism, however, is not a flight from the world. It is a counteractive or corrective practice that repents from and resists whatever degrades and diminishes creation. Indeed, asceticism awakens new possibilities for the healing of creation. For instance, it places technology in its proper context to address the invasion of electronic communications and scientific applications. The late Patriarch Ignatius IV of Antioch observed: 'Asceticism empowers us to fight, on behalf of truth and goodness, the temptation to construct the world as a closed system devoid of God.'[5]

Beyond a Eucharistic and ascetic ethos, the Orthodox Church also highlights *a liturgical ethos*, which emphasizes cooperation, connectivity and community within creation. The liturgical ethos is an amplification of the song of creation, which continually praises the creator. Moreover, it fosters associations that allow Christians to counter the social structures of sin with new structures of virtue, harmony and peace. It also fuels new forms of cooperation for food cultivation, economic cooperation and alternative clean energies.

Indeed, the liturgical ethos challenges the lie of individualism as a pillar of the consumer mentality. Individualism isolates people from one other and causes them to seek private gain, separate from and at the expense of other people and creation. By contrast, the liturgical ethos cultivates a new sense of inner, spiritual glory, beyond the tempting, passing glamour of this world. Through the liturgical ethos, Orthodox Christians join in an inspirational song of thanksgiving and cooperation, holding festivals that celebrate the goodness of life and acknowledging that we all share the same air, water and earthly resources.

---

[5] Patriarch Ignatius IV of Antioch, presentation to the Swiss Catholic Bishops and Swiss Conference of Churches, Lucerne, Switzerland, 12 March 1989.

The vision of God's presence in all things leads the classic writers of the church to speak of a cosmic liturgy. The Scriptures tell of the praise that trees and all creation have for their creator (see Ps. 96.12). All people are called to enter into that cosmic liturgy of praise and worship.[6] Gregory of Nyssa describes the Divine as everywhere present:

> For when he considers the universe, can any person be so simpleminded as not to believe that the Divine is present in every thing, pervading, embracing and penetrating it? For all things depend upon Him who is, and nothing can exist which does not have its being in Him who is.[7]

And in our own time, Ecumenical Patriarch Bartholomew echoes:

> The Lord fills all creation with His divine presence in one continuous connection from the substance of atoms to the mind of God. Let us renew the harmony between heaven and earth, and transfigure every detail, every particle of life. Let us love one another, and lovingly learn from one another, for the edification of God's people, for the sanctification of God's creation, and for the glorification of God's most holy name.[8]

In this enlarged vision of human life and all creation, our ecosystem becomes part and parcel of our spiritual life and aspiration for wholeness and salvation. In brief, the threefold ethos of Eucharist, ascesis and liturgy translates into a life of prayer, fasting and almsgiving.

Finally, this vision and ethos of the Orthodox Church combine into a cosmic movement of spiritual energy from God through humanity as priest of creation. In the midst of this grand circle of heaven on earth, Christians can recognize their place in the cosmic order. Then, each person consecrates all things through a priestly ministry or priesthood of all believers. This is the vision of Christ and the Holy Spirit filling all things, within which humanity is called to elicit the latent potentiality of all creation in order for the world to shine in all goodness and glory. This associates spiritual sensitivity and even *theosis* with art and poetry, science and technical knowledge. While we cannot yet discern all of the implications of such living, we are nonetheless able to foretaste and facilitate the process of cosmic transfiguration.

---

[6] The Liturgy of St. James affirms this cosmic awareness: 'The heavens declare the glory of heaven; the earth proclaims the sovereignty of God; the sea heralds the authority of the Lord; and every creature preaches the magnificence of God.'

[7] Quoted in Andrew Linzey, *Love the Animals: Meditations and Prayers* (New York: Crossroad Press, 1989), 8.

[8] Address in Manila (February 2000).

The theology of transfiguration

It is our responsibility as human beings to be stewards of God's created order. We are all called to be sensitive to the greatest risk to the survival of our planet – namely, the dramatic changes in our climate and in our environment. We reach out to you ... to set the example of respecting, nurturing, and preserving God's created order.[9]

To articulate a more comprehensive guide for Christian interaction with the environment, particularly global climate change, it is helpful to return to the scriptural sources. Like an operator's handbook for machinery, to adopt a medieval image and metaphor, the creator has provided detailed guidance for the right functioning of creation and humans upon the earth.[10]

According to the Judeo-Christian Scriptures, in the beginning, God created the heavens and earth, the sun and stars, the earth and waters, the grass and plants, and all its many creatures and features (see Gen. 1.1-31). Scripture unfolds the intricacy of creation, where the creator blesses the creatures on the sixth day, saying, 'Be fruitful and multiply and fill the earth' (Gen. 1.28). On the same day, in creating human beings, we read that Adam and Eve bear the divine image and likeness (see Gen. 1.26). The early Christian writers distinguished between image and likeness, noting that the 'image' relates to latent spiritual potential, while the 'likeness' represents the extent to which one actualizes the original blessing and potential.

In this context, then, God charges the first humans 'to replenish the earth ... and have dominion over the fish of the sea, the fowl of the air, and every living thing that is upon the earth' (see Gen. 1.28, KJV). Dominion, from the Hebrew 'râdâh', signifies the rule of a king. Since ancient royalty sought to rule in the place of the Lord, they also sought the attitudes and mind of the Lord. Thus, the command to dominion simultaneously imposes an obligation and vocation to treat creation as the Lord God would. This means that we should relate to the land with care and compassion, mercy and justice, as well as wisdom and regard for its ultimate end. After all, 'creation is the love of God for man-made visible'.[11]

An inner dimension of dominion is also essential in this regard. Each person must exert dominion over his or her 'human nature' as a precondition for any dominion over the rest of nature. The practice of dominion requires the suppression of attitudes that desacralize the land or desecrate the soul. Purification of heart and mind – by overcoming the vices of greed, gluttony, pride, insensitivity and other rapacious tendencies that defile the individual and the land – are fundamental to proper dominion.

---

[9] Address by Ecumenical Patriarch Bartholomew at the United Nations (26 October 2009).
[10] In exploring the scriptural texts of the New Revised Standard Version to prepare *The Green Bible* (New York: Harper Collins, 2008), Fred Krueger identified 2,476 verses related to the environment.
[11] Vincent Rossi, 'Climate Change: Desecrating the Icon of Creation', *Newsletter, Orthodox Fellowship of the Transfiguration* 2:2 (2010), 1.

Alongside scriptural dominion is the command to replenish the earth. The Hebrew word 'mâlê' is sometimes translated as 'fill', although no English word captures the original Hebrew completely. The word essentially means referring or returning to the beginning. Replenishing is only a partially adequate rendering. Just as dominion seeks the will of God and acts on behalf of the Lord, 'mâlê' consecrates creation back to God, seeking to preserve and promote the original balance, beauty and integrity of the world. On the surface, we can discern here the modern practice of recycling, but the deeper meaning goes further and conveys an offering of creation back to God in an act of thanksgiving and praise. The theology of the Orthodox Church preserves this original, scriptural meaning in its liturgy. At the epiclesis of the Divine Liturgy of St. John Chrysostom – namely, at the moment of the consecration of the bread and wine – the priest exclaims, 'Thine own of thine own, we offer unto thee, on behalf of all and for all.' Cosmologically, this action symbolizes a re-consecration of creation back to God in order that its primal integrity and beauty might be restored and renewed.

In the second chapter of Genesis, we read that God placed the human in the garden to 'dress and keep it' – or in a more ecologically sensitive rendering – 'serve and preserve it' (Gen. 2.15).[12] These archaic terms convey the meaning of the original Hebrew 'âbad' and 'shâmar'. To 'dress' the garden means to raise it up. This should be distinguished from a charge merely to improve it; after all, dressing means to cultivate something into fruition and fulfilment.

The Hebrew 'âbad' means to bring to completion, just as seeds follow an organic process of planting, nurturing and harvest. Adam is entrusted the garden as a living seed to be cultivated through service into flowering or perfection. In the fourth century, Basil the Great described this process as a mandate to raise the earth to its full cosmological potential. This implies a relationship to God based upon cooperation and participation leading to *theosis* (deification or divinization).

Furthermore, the word 'keep' conveys the Hebrew 'shâmar', which involves renewal or vigilance but especially protection from desecration. 'Shâmar' involves a vigilant watching and guarding against anything that would destroy that which is 'dressed'. The implication is that any destructive forces must be rooted out for the growth and flourishing of the garden. This applies not only outwardly to the earth but also inwardly to Adam's attitudes. The principle of 'shâmar' applies to climate change inasmuch as any force or energy disrupting the equilibrium of the world's atmosphere is prohibited.

Scripture then relates how God orders Adam to name the animals (Gen. 2.20). Naming the creatures is not an arbitrary exercise. It requires discernment of and connection to the spiritual purpose of each creature. This process is informed by the way each Hebrew letter or sound has a specific meaning that represents and reflects the quality and energy of God. Each consonant manifests the tangible attributes of G-d, the unwritten vowels in the divine name of JHVH. In the seventh century, Maximus the Confessor provided

---

[12] Alternatively translated as 'to till and keep it' (RSV) or 'to serve and protect'.

insightful guidance about discerning the energy of created things, which he called their 'inner essences':

> If, instead of stopping short at the outward appearance, which visible things present to the senses, you seek with your intellect to contemplate their inner essences, seeing them as images of spiritual realities or as the inward principles of sensible objects, you will be taught that nothing belonging to the visible world is unclean. For by nature all things were created good.[13]

Entry into the experience or knowledge of these inner essences (*logoi*) requires attention and contemplation to distinguish the interior or cosmic dimension of creation.

Indeed, the Psalms tell us that creation rejoices in spiritual wholeness: 'Worship the Lord in the beauty of holiness' (Ps. 96.9-11). Throughout Scripture, we discover numerous qualities that inform and inspire a right orientation towards creation. Some of these include the familiar affirmations that 'the earth is the Lord's and all that is in it' (Ps. 24.1; 1 Cor. 10.26) and that obeying God and His commandments brings blessings (Deut. 7.13), which in turn translate into prosperity (Deut. 2.7), a productive land (Deut. 6.11) and a fruitful life (Deut. 4.26). By contrast, disobedience and transgression of the divine commands brings 'curses' on people and their property (Deut. 28.29).

In this perspective, there emerges an intentional way of life, without which worship cannot be whole and the beauty of holiness is misplaced. Ecumenical Patriarch Bartholomew develops this same line of thought at a symposium on the Amazon River in July of 2006:

> We hear of air and water pollution, of global warming and the threatened extinction of numerous animal or plant species. How should we react? What do they mean for the ways we are accustomed to living? Every product we make and enjoy, from the paper we work with, to processed meat and the soy beans that sustain its industry, every tree we fell, every building we construct, every road we travel, definitively and permanently alters creation. We must be responsible and responsive citizens; we must be careful and caring pilgrims ... If we are not moved to compassion, bandaging the wounds of the earth, assuming personal care, and contributing to the painful costs, then we might easily be confronted with the question, which of these do you resemble: the Good Samaritan or the indifferent priest?[14]

Beyond the above biblical passages and principles, the themes of faithfulness and repentance are repeated admonitions in Scripture. The Book of Isaiah develops these themes from a particular angle, declaring that the sins of people are reflected in the creation:

> The earth mourneth and fadeth away ... The earth also is defiled under the inhabitants thereof; because they have transgressed the laws, changed the ordinance, broken the everlasting covenant. Therefore hath the curse devoured the earth, and they that dwell therein are desolate. (Is. 24.4-6, KJV)

---

[13] Maximus the Confessor, *The Philokalia* II, 185.
[14] 'The Fragile Beauty of the World', Opening Address in Manaus, Brazil.

When plague, poverty and pestilence ravish the land – or, as in our day, violent expressions of climate change and virulent examples of toxic wastes, as well as air and water pollution – Scripture determines that these are the inevitable consequences of disobedience. The sole remedy is a return to righteousness (see Is. 24.15; 25.1-6).

The New Testament is also replete with ecological messages and meanings, repeatedly presenting the charge and challenge of internal and external transformation. In brief, the Incarnation of the divine Word establishes the premise that the whole earth must be considered holy because 'God so loved the world' (Jn 3.16). In the Sermon on the Mount, Jesus declares the ways of heaven on earth, thereby inaugurating the first-fruits of the 'new heaven' on the 'new earth' (Rev. 21.1) and inspiring us to pray: 'Thy kingdom come; Thy will be done on earth as it is in heaven' (Mt. 6.10). And in Paul's Epistle to the Romans, we are enjoined not to be conformed to the world, 'but to be transformed by the renewing of our minds' (see Rom. 12.1-2).

Finally, even after narrating the plagues poured down upon the earth, the good angel in the book of Revelation provides a reassuring guidance that few have historically understood, capturing a right orientation towards creation can deflect all the plagues, including climate change: 'Hurt not the earth, neither the seas nor the trees' (see Rev. 7.3). When the time comes for the fearful and final judgement, the author of the book of Revelation provides an alarming caution:

> And the nations were angry, and thy wrath is come, and the time of the dead, that they should be judged, and that Thou should give reward unto thy servants, the prophets, and to the saints, and them that fear thy name, small and great, and should destroy them which destroy the earth. (Rev. 11.18, KJV)

Thus, in the biblical view, the ecological crisis is no accident. Scripture neither underestimates technology nor undermines economy. Instead, it addresses climate change as a moral decline of cosmic proportions. Reparation or restoration of this condition requires a repentant return to the way and will of God. An ecological repentance must engage and connect human beings to the deeper essence of 'dominion' as 'dressing and keeping' the earth. Such repentance involves a lifelong journey of working in community and reshaping societal structures.

The living pulse of the planet

The solution of the ecological problem is not only a matter of science, technology and politics but also, and perhaps primarily, a matter of radical change of mind, of new values, of a new ethos.[15]

---

[15] Ecumenical Patriarch Bartholomew, 'Building Bridges'. Address at Izmir University of Economics (9 February 2015).

The evidence is clear that carbon dioxide and other greenhouse gases are rising in the world's atmosphere.[16] This increase is due primarily to the burning of fossil fuels by humans, which constitutes the key factor 'forcing' climate change.[17] As a result, 'since 1900, the global average surface temperature has increased by about 1.41 degrees F'.[18]

What must be highlighted as the cause of these emerging climatic conditions is the burning of fossil fuels, particularly petroleum as fuel for transportation, coal for energy and natural gas for home heating and energy generation. In the past our grandparents never knew that the burning of fossil fuels was so dangerous. We have organized society around energy, but we are now realizing that it is lethal to the further advance of civilization. Already the Orthodox Church has examined these conditions and concludes that we must initiate major changes in human behaviour.

Over a decade ago, Ecumenical Patriarch expressed the following assessment of the responsibility of Orthodox Christians:

> Unless we take radical and immediate measures to reduce emissions stemming from unsustainable – in fact unjustifiable, if not simply unjust – excesses in the demands of our lifestyle, the impact will be both alarming and imminent ... Climate change is much more than environmental preservation. Insofar as it human-induced, it is a profoundly moral and spiritual problem.[19]

Similarly Orthodox bishops across the United States of America issued a formal declaration on the threat posed by climate change:

> Faithful to the responsibility given to us within God's good creation, it is prudent to listen to the world's scientific leaders as they describe changes occurring in the world's climate ... Immediate measures must be taken to reduce the impact of these changes to the world's climate. If we fail to act now, the changes that are already underway will intensify and create catastrophic conditions. A contributing root cause of these changes to our climate is a lifestyle that contains unintended, nevertheless destructive side effects ... The excessive use of fossil fuels is degrading and destroying the life of creation ... As Church leaders, it is our responsibility to speak to this condition inasmuch as it represents a grave moral and spiritual problem.[20]

---

[16] Statement by the Fifth Assessment of the Intergovernmental Panel on Climate Change (IPCC), World Meteorological Organization, Geneva, Switzerland, May 2014.

[17] US NASA Global Climate Change, Vital Signs of the Planet, Statement on the role of carbon dioxide, at https://climate.nasa.gov/causes/ (accessed 5 August 2017).

[18] 'Climate Change: An Overview from the Royal Society and the U.S. National Academy of Sciences' (Washington DC, 2014), 3.

[19] Ecumenical Patriarch Bartholomew, 'Statement on Climate Change', 12 August 2005.

[20] Standing Conference of the Canonical Orthodox Bishops in the Americas, 'Global Climate Change: A Moral and Spiritual Challenge', *New York City*, 25 May 2007. See http://assemblyofbishops.org/news/scoba/2007-05-25-global-climate-change (accessed 15 June 2017).

A five-step programme to address climate change

Unless we change the way we live; we cannot hope to avoid ecological damage. This means that – instead of solely depending on governments and experts for answers – each of us must become accountable for our slightest gesture and act in order to reverse the path that we are on, which will of course also include prevailing upon governments and leaders for the creation and application of collective policy and practice … Each believer and each leader, each field and each discipline, each institution and each individual must be touched by the call to change our greedy ways and destructive habits.[21]

At a recent scientific and religious gathering at the Vatican Pontifical Academy of Sciences, Pope Francis asked the gathered experts, 'Can humanity still survive, or is this the end?' Initially, the group did not provide a clear response, but after a full day of reflection and discussion, they came to a unanimous conclusion: 'Yes, humanity can make it, but only if we are very intentional about changing our behaviour and attitudes.'[22] In the United States, the Orthodox bishops also underlined the need for practical measures towards addressing and amending climate change.[23]

In the context, then, of an Orthodox theological response to climate change, the following are some fundamental steps to repent of an ecological wastefulness and recover an ecological worldview:

(i) Before considering or correcting our ways, we are called to pray for change in our personal attitudes and habits. Such is the depth of *metanoia* (repentance). It is also the fundamental acknowledgement and assertion that the world belongs to Someone larger than our own narrow concerns and petty interests. The problem is not merely our inadequate response to climate change but the failure to confess God as the loving creator of all.

(ii) We must live in a manner that is consistent with what we believe and how we pray, despite any attending inconvenience. At the very least, this means caring about the effect of our lives upon our neighbours, respecting the natural environment and demonstrating a willingness to live within our own means and the means of our planet. Otherwise, we cannot claim to care about anyone or anything beyond ourselves and our own.

(iii) Climate change inevitably demands a reduction and eventual elimination of our consumption of fossil fuels. However, it also requires a pursuit and acceptance of

---

[21] Ecumenical Patriarch Bartholomew at the UN Religions for Peace Interfaith Summit on Climate Change, 19 September 2014.

[22] Story narrated by Dr Charles Kennel, Scripps Institute of Oceanography in California during a panel discussion at COP-23 in Marrakesh, Morocco (November 2016).

[23] Statement by the Standing Conference of Canonical Orthodox Bishops in America.

alternative energy sources, such as solar or wind power, as well as other methods that minimize our impact upon the world. Again, this will require intentional and perhaps uncomfortable efforts from all people without exception. Humility and self-limitation is the permanent corrective to arrogance and greed.

(iv) We must continually learn all that we can about the emerging implications of climate change. Furthermore, we must analyse and advocate the consequences of climate change with family and friends, as well as public officials and elected representatives at the city, state and national levels. There is no single group of individuals or set of institutions – but also no region or religion, as well as no state or nation – that can be blamed for or excluded from the global crisis that we call climate change.

(v) We must set an example in the way that we choose to live, admitting that we are all responsible for the global crisis, while each of us has a vital role in responding to the challenge. We must express willingness to change whenever and wherever this is possible. We are called to promulgate this message and practice these principles in all areas of our life and work. This is not optional: the Judeo-Christian Scriptures bluntly tell us that we will be judged by the choices we make (see Rev. 11.18).

These guidelines are designed to correct the failures of Eastern Orthodox Church members to live out their faith. There has been too much tendency to blend into the consumer culture for Orthodox churches to live out the implications of their theological and spiritual worldview. Orthodox bishops, with only few notable exceptions, have not yet either caught or taught the need to address climate change. This has left clergy and laity without direction. As a result, some clergy have considered climate change a political issue and, therefore, avoided it. Others have been persuaded that the science remains either dubious or unsettled, and have waited for more conclusive declarations about the human impact on climate change and the need for a change of lifestyle. A love of comfort and ease is further cause because any necessary changes ultimately require sacrifice and education. However, all of these failures can be addressed. The theology that addresses climate change is clear. The framework exists. But the education necessary to mobilize Orthodox Christians has been sorely lacking.

Each generation faces certain tests that challenge the life of the world and integrity of its civilization. One of those issues, by which we shall be assessed by future generations, is whether we will adhere to the command and call to exercising self-restraint in our use of energy or whether we will ignore that command and call by pursuing the excessive gratification self-indulgence involved in over-reliance on fossil fuels. If we aspire to the first, then we shall 'perceive everything in the light of the Creator God'.[24]

---

[24] John Climacus, *Ladder of Divine Ascent*, Step 4, 58.

A response to John Chryssavgis and Frederick Krueger

George Zachariah[1]

John Chryssavgis and Frederick Krueger enable us to experience the ecological richness of Orthodox theology and its relevance for ministries of creation care. Their essay invites us to reflect on who we are vis-à-vis God's creation in order to become transformed so as to transform the world in the context of climate change. This response engages critically with their arguments and proposals, and shares some tentative ecotheological reflections informed by the subaltern communities from the ground zeroes of climate injustice.

Orthodox theology affirms creation as sacred. When we realize that creation is 'infused with the vitalizing sacredness of God', our understanding and attitude towards nature changes and we begin to practise a sacred relationship with nature. Nature, thus, becomes for us an epiphanic space, where we meet the Divine in our organic engagement with God's creation. Nature also offers us the possibility to reclaim and celebrate the primordial communion between the Divine, human beings and the rest of creation. The Orthodox ethical response to climate change emerges from this sacramental vision of creation. Chryssavgis and Krueger identify three forms of ethos that are characteristic of the Orthodox eco-ethical response: a Eucharistic ethos, an aesthetic ethos and a liturgical ethos. These forms of ethos are not just proposals for ethical action in the context of climate change; they also offer us a profound theological understanding of what it means to be human in relation to the rest of creation. Said differently, they summarize Orthodox theological anthropology, which is a bold critique of, and alternative to, the dominant greed-oriented anthropologies of our times.

In their articulation of Orthodox theological anthropology, the authors reiterate the need for a spirit of introspection and subsequent acts of *metanoia* to purify our minds and hearts so that we can abstain from the acts of desacralizing the earth. Ecological repentance is the starting point for the transfiguration of creation, and it requires intentional change in our behaviour and attitudes. The discernment that we are all responsible for the climate crisis should lead us to opt for an ecological worldview where we embrace self-restraint, humility and self-limitation. On the whole, the essay is

---

[1] George Zachariah is Lecturer in Theological Studies at the Trinity Methodist Theological College, Auckland, Aotearoa, New Zealand. Originally from India, he has also served at the United Theological College, Bangalore, India, as Professor and Chairperson of the Department of Theology and Ethics. A lay member of the Mar Thoma Church, he teaches and writes on ecotheology.

an altar-call in the wake of the climate crisis to repent and to mend our worldviews and lifestyles so that we will be able to 'preserve everything in the light of the Creator God'.

The objective of this volume, according to the editors, is to articulate how North Atlantic Christian theology could respond to the climate crisis drawing from its distinctive sources and to inspire readers from the same social location to engage in ministries of creation care. The responses by scholars from other social locations enhance the scope of this volume by initiating a critical interrogation of North Atlantic Christian theology and its interpretation of the hegemonic Judeo-Christian tradition which bears a 'huge burden of guilt' for the current ecological crisis. My response contributes to this overall aim by underscoring the need for contextual reformulations of Orthodox ecotheology informed by the cry of the earth and the cry of the subaltern communities, communities which are disproportionately affected by the climate crisis.

Claims of homogeneity and universality in theological discourses not only erase the voices of the subaltern communities but also canonize the perspectives of the dominant as the absolute truth for all. 'North Atlantic Christian theology', the nomenclature used in this volume, is therefore in itself problematic as it privileges the theological reflections emerging from locations of power and privilege within the North American context. The same criticism applies to Orthodox theology as well where the diverse voices within the Orthodox community are not taken into consideration. This calls for the political will to stay away from claims of homogeneity and universality and affirm the situatedness of God-talk in our particular locations that inform our theological reflections and articulations. Differently said, all theologies are contextual, and our reluctance to recognize that testifies to our power and privilege.

One of the profound ecological insights that we gather from Orthodox theology is its understanding of earth as sacred. As the essay explains, exploitation of the environment is nothing but the desacralization of the sacred earth, and hence, it is a sin against God. For St John of Damascus, 'the whole earth is a living icon of the face of God'.[2] He further brings a soteriological dimension to earth:

> I worship the Creator of matter who became matter for my sake, who willed to take His abode in matter, who worked out my salvation through matter. Never will I cease honoring the matter which wrought my salvation! I honor it, but not as God. Because of this I salute all remaining matter with reverence, because God has filled it with his grace and power. Through it my salvation has come to me.[3]

We don't come across such a powerful theological affirmation of earth in the salvific purpose of God in other strands of Christian theology. Panentheistic theological explorations are important in our contemporary context of ecological destruction. However, an engagement with the Indigenous religious traditions and their panentheistic reflections is missing in this essay.

---

[2] See https://anastpaul.wordpress.com/2016/12/04/quotes-of-the-day-4-december/ (accessed 2 August 2018).
[3] Ibid.

In addition, Orthodox theology contributes to ecotheology a non-anthropocentric theological anthropology. Orthodox theology envisions human beings as priests of creation. Here human beings are understood as a microcosm which rejects all dichotomies and sees all of nature reflected within the human and situates the human within the rest of nature. As the priests of creation, human beings serve as the mediators through whom God manifests Godself to creation and redeems it. Unfortunately, Chryssavgis and Krueger use the biblical concepts of 'dominion' and 'stewardship' to elaborate on the notion of priesthood. From an ecotheological perspective these concepts require critical interrogation. Ecotheological engagement with Scripture, as articulated in the eco-justice hermeneutical principles developed by the Earth Bible team,[4] is based on the hermeneutics of suspicion and retrieval. However, the biblical interpretation of Chryssavgis and Krueger does not recognize the presence of 'texts of terror' in the Scripture. Instead, the attempt is to 'redeem' inherently problematic texts and concepts such as 'dominion' and 'stewardship'.

The vocation of human beings expounded in the first creation story in the book of Genesis is to subdue the earth and to have dominion over the community of creation. As Lynn White, Jr, rightly observed, 'Christianity ... not only established a dualism of man and nature, but also insisted that it is God's will that man exploit nature for his proper ends.'[5] In other words, the Priestly account of the creation narrative offers a Christian axiom that nature has no reason for existence other than to serve humanity, and this sense of vocation is the theological rationale that inspires all imperial projects of conquest, occupation, rape and plunder of those commons and lives which do not matter to the dominant. Any attempt to 'redeem' the concepts of 'subdue' and 'dominion' is problematic as it legitimizes aggression and exploitation. Similarly, the concept of stewardship also requires critical interrogation. As the Indian Orthodox theologian Paulos Mar Gregorios observes, 'Replacing the concept of domination with the concept of stewardship will not lead us very far, for even in the latter there lies the hidden possibility of the objectification and alienation which are the root causes of the sickness of our civilization. Nature would remain some kind of property, owned not by us, of course, but by God, given into our hands for efficient and productive use.'[6]

Finally, Chryssavgis and Krueger observe that we are all affected by the climate crisis and propose that if we change our lifestyle and consumption pattern, we can solve the problem. First of all, such a diagnosis blaming human beings per se for the climate crisis is problematic as it absolves the sins of neoliberal capitalism. It is in this context that

---

[4] Norman C. Habel, *Reading from the Perspective of Earth* (Sheffield: Sheffield Academic Press, 2000), 38–53.

[5] Lynn White, Jr, 'The Historical Roots of Our Ecological Crisis', *Science* 155 (1967), 1203–7 (1203).

[6] Paulos Mar Gregorios, *The Human Presence: Ecological Spirituality and the Age of the Spirit* (New York: Amity, 1978), 87.

'Dancing with God in the Rainbow', the theological statement of the Ekalesia Kelisiano Tuvalu, becomes instructive:

> We are also wary of the capitalist wisdom which now proposes a new agenda of fixing the environment. We are wary of the impacts of sustainability proposals such as planting trees, changing light bulbs, tapping renewable energy sources and the likes. Are they aimed at protecting earth or safeguarding the prevailing exploitative economic model? We reject this capitalist deception.[7]

The responses to Nathaniel Rich's recent article[8] in the *New York Times Magazine* where he blamed 'human nature' which is 'incapable of sacrificing present convenience to forestall a penalty imposed on future generations' further reiterate this position: 'If they were serious about investigating what's gone so wrong, this would be about capitalism's inability to address the climate change catastrophe. Beyond capitalism, humankind is fully capable of organizing societies to thrive within ecological limits.'[9]

The North Atlantic Christian theology represented by Chryssavgis and Krueger does not seem to be cognizant about the environmental justice movement and the historic struggle of the Standing Rock Sioux Tribe. As Naomi Klein reminds us, 'we have to see how climate change, racism, austerity, deepening income inequality, mass incarceration are all deeply interconnected'.[10] The subaltern climate justice movement in India also echoes the same concern: 'It is time to say loudly that the crisis is not really about climate. … It is about us, our lives, and the planet – and the way in which the powerful and the rich of the earth have dominated and kept destroying us for centuries to accumulate private wealth.'[11] The challenge before Orthodox ecotheology is to become intentionally intersectional and to initiate theological reflections at the interface of class, race/caste and gender.

---

[7] 'Dancing with God in the Rainbow', theological statement by the Ekalesia Kelisiano Tuvalu, September 2016 (unpublished).

[8] See https://www.nytimes.com/interactive/2018/08/01/magazine/climate-change-losing-earth.html?action=click&contentCollection=magazine&region=rank&module=package&version=highlights&contentPlacement=1&pgtype=sectionfront (accessed 5 August 2018).

[9] See https://www.commondreams.org/views/2018/08/06/capitalism-killed-our-climate-momentum-not-human-nature (accessed 7 August 2018).

[10] See http://hub.jhu.edu/2016/02/24/naomi-klein-foreign-affairs-symposium (accessed 7 August 2018).

[11] See http://www.thecornerhouse.org.uk/sites/thecornerhouse.org.uk/files/Mausam_July-Sept2008.pdf (accessed 20 August 2018).

Chapter 3.2
Working with Catholic forms of Christianity

Celia Deane-Drummond[1]

Introduction

The Roman Catholic Church is at a critical moment with respect to its ability to work with those who are both inside and outside the church on matters related to climate change. Broader environmental concerns have been integral to Catholic social teaching since the early 1970s, even if that focus was not necessarily widely appreciated, either at the grass roots or the Vatican.[2] Prior to Pope Francis, anthropocentrism in Catholic social thought often seemed too deeply embedded to shift towards a more radical perspective.[3] Seán McDonagh notes the slow official endorsement of climate change, its marginalization in catechetical documents and its tendency even then to stress less controversial features of environmental degradation and social justice.[4] In 2007, when Pope Benedict XVI mentioned climate change, it was listed after a discussion of preservation of the environment and sustainable development as being of 'grave concern to the entire human family'.[5] That year a Vatican conference on Justice and

---

[1] Celia Deane-Drummond is Senior Research Fellow in Theology and Director of the Laudato Si' Research Institute at Campion Hall, Oxford University. As well as holding two doctorates in plant physiology and theology, she was Chair of the European Forum for the Study of Religion and Environment from 2011 to 2018.

[2] Celia Deane-Drummond, 'Joining in the Dance: Ecology in Roman Catholic Social Teaching', *New Blackfriars* 93:1044 (2012), 193–212.

[3] Donald Dorr argued anthropocentrism was still strongly wedged into Catholic social teaching and its central claim for integral humanism, even when proclaiming care for the environment. So, 'it is a pity that Benedict, who is so committed on environmental issues, did not locate everything he has to say about human responsibility and business activity in this time of *economic* crisis within the broader context of the *ecological* crisis of our time ... ecological issues are treated almost entirely in terms of human concerns'. Donald Dorr, 'Themes and Theologies in Catholic Social Teaching Over Fifty Years', *New Blackfriars* 93:1044 (2012), 137–54 (144). Pope Francis has made that shift, though my reading of both Pope Benedict XVI and Pope John Paul II is that they were already moving in this direction. See Deane-Drummond, 'Joining the Dance'.

[4] Seán McDonagh, 'Climate Change and Ecclesial Praxis: Ministries and Mission', this volume.

[5] Pope Benedict XVI, 'Letter to the Ecumenical Patriarch of Constantinople on the Occasion of the Seventh Symposium of the Religion, Science and the Environment Movement, September 1st, 2007'; extract

Peace included climate-change deniers, suggesting some confusion over climate-change science.⁶ By 2009 Pope Benedict XVI was prepared to acknowledge 'the disturbing data of the phenomenon of climate change'⁷, and following Pope John Paul II's world day message of peace ten years previous, his 2010 message included a stress on climate change as one of the 'realities' along with desertification and degradation of the natural environment.⁸

It was Pope Francis's *Laudato Si'* (*LS*) that finally removed any ambiguity about the official position of the Catholic Church on climate change, acknowledging not just its realities but also dedicating significant space to scientific results. Even though a number of Catholic grass roots movements and lay theologians had recognized climate change, official endorsement was significant. One of the strengths of *LS* is not just the attention it gives to climate change, but also its portrayal of a wider narrative that makes sense to Catholic and Christian communities and beyond. The ecological theme of interconnectedness is strong: shifting human ecology and integral humanism to integral ecology.⁹

The ecumenical significance of *Laudato Si'*

Although there have been many and diverse commentaries written on this encyclical since its release, its key significance in terms of promoting a Catholic contribution to ecumenical discussion on climate change is as follows:

1. *Climate matters to those who are the poorest and most vulnerable in global society.* Pope Francis's attention to the poorest of the poor¹⁰ is not particularly unusual given that one of the distinctive marks of Catholic social thought is solidarity with the marginalized. The difference is that it joins up concern for those who are in poverty with all other creatures on planet earth vulnerable to climate change. Various attempts to measure that vulnerability have been attempted, but the interconnection between different types

---

reprinted as 'The Arctic: Mirror of Life', in Pope Benedict XVI, *The Garden of God: Toward a Human Ecology* (Washington: Catholic University of America Press, 2014), 19–20.

⁶ McDonagh, 'Climate Change', this volume.

⁷ Pope Benedict XVI, 'Letter to Hon. Mr Silvio Berlusconi, Prime Minister of Italy, on the Occasion of the G8 Summit, July 1st 2009', reprinted in *The Garden of God*, 190.

⁸ Pope Benedict XI, Message for the Celebration of the World Day of Peace, January 2010, reprinted as 'If You Want to Cultivate Peace, Protect Creation', in *The Garden of God*, 41.

⁹ Integral ecology has been used for different purposes by secular scholars; the point here is to illustrate how Pope Francis is quite deliberately putting ecology to the fore, without losing the traditional Catholic stress on human dignity.

¹⁰ References to those that are poor appear multiple times in all its sections, often linked in a comparative way with the earth as equally vulnerable and oppressed, though interestingly characterized as 'nature' or 'earth', rather than as specific and named creatures.

of vulnerability is clear.[11] Ironically, transnational companies use calculated national vulnerability indices to decide whether or not to invest, leading to greater vulnerability.

2. *Climate matters to refugees.* This is relevant for those who are driven from their homes as a direct or indirect result of climate change. Pope Francis acknowledges the massive social issue associated with migration[12] and joins this up with climate impacts. There are no explicit international protection measures in place for those refugees fleeing as a direct result of climate impacts. While climate refugees are likely to become even more intense with rising sea levels, as in the Indian subcontinent, unpredictable temperature variation and weather patterns, extreme drought conditions in land masses such as many parts of sub-Saharan Africa, and shortages in basic resources of food and water can lead to conflict capable of triggering breakdown in peace and a mass exodus.

3. *Climate matters to the sciences.* The scientific discussion in the encyclical is arguably one of its most novel features in comparison with earlier official statements. Pope Francis has special words of encouragement for ecologists, conservationists and other scientists trying to understand climate impacts. It is also significant that a special issue of an academic biological journal was dedicated to the encyclical, and evangelical environmentalist Calvin de Witt's article on *Laudato Si'* was one of the five most downloaded documents in 2017.[13]

4. *Climate matters to vulnerable non-human species, ecosystems and the earth itself.* Pope Francis makes it clear that the theological basis for valuation of creation stems from the biblical affirmation of the goodness of creation, the loving affirmation of a Creator God, and recognition of the Earth as a precious gift, where God is present even in the smallest speck of life.[14] It is those aspects of creation that have not been given significant attention that Pope Francis calls out, the fungi and 'lower' forms of life like plankton in danger of being forgotten.[15] Stress on God as the *God of all life* broadens out

---

[11] Martina Grecequet, 'A New Era of Human and Non-human Migration', paper delivered at a conference on 'Radical Ecological Conversion After *Laudato Si'*: Discovering the Intrinsic Value of Creatures: Human and Non-Human', Gregorian University, Rome, 7 March 2018.

[12] Pope Francis links migration of both human and non-human species to climate change in *LS* §25, 35, 176. Subsequent to the encyclical, migration and the plight of refugees is an even more significant topic of discussion within the Catholic Church, though not always with attention to the interlaced environmental aspects.

[13] Calvin de Witt interprets *LS* as earth stewardship, but the real significance of his article is that a journal such as *The Quarterly Review of Biology* had four articles commenting on *LS*. See Calvin de Witt, 'Earth Stewardship and *Laudato Si''*, *Quarterly Review of Biology* 91:3 (2016), 271–84.

[14] On the goodness of creation, see *LS* §69, 77, 86; on the loving affirmation of God, see *LS* §77; the precious gift of the Creator, *LS* §155, 159; God is present in the smallest and most fleeting existence, so 'Even the fleeting life of the least of beings is the object of his love, and in its few seconds of existence, God enfolds it with his affection', *LS* §77.

[15] See *LS* §34; 40.

a traditional Catholic emphasis on the preservation of human life from the moment of conception until death, a position that is also represented in the encyclical.[16] The earth is 'among the most abandoned and maltreated of our poor'.[17]

5. *Climate matters to technology.* Pope Francis is certainly not against scientific and technological innovations or solutions, but he is insistent that they are not sufficient, and finding solutions to complex problems like climate change just in technologies is to fall into the unhelpful grip of the technological paradigm.[18]

6. *Climate matters to the economy.* Finding alternative ways of considering the global market economy is one of the main challenges once the roots of ecological devastation and climate change are attributed to unjust patterns of consumption and production.[19] Pope Benedict XVI also discusses the idea of an economy of gratuitousness in *Caritas in Veritate*,[20] but Pope Francis is much more strident in his criticism of the present structural global market arrangements.

7. *Climate matters to the city.* One of the striking features of the encyclical is the attention to pressures on lifestyles in urban communities.[21] The degradation and squalid conditions sit alongside small and close communities that still find a way to express hope in spite of dire circumstances. Paying proper attention to social structure of societies is just as important as political and international governance. It is also significant that the seventeen United Nations Sustainable Development Goals (SDGs) were published in 2015 very soon after *LS*, many of the goals resonate strongly with themes in the encyclical.[22]

---

[16] Protection of human embryos is mentioned in *LS* §117, 120, 136.

[17] *LS*, §2.

[18] The technological paradigm is discussed in *LS* §106–14.

[19] See, for example, *LS*, §5; 50–2, 161–4, 191–3.

[20] Pope Benedict XVI, *Caritas in Veritate*, 2009 §34–8. What is interesting here is that the theme of gratuitousness that builds on the work of Pope John Paul II in *Centesimus Annus* stems from an understanding that given that we are all sinners (§34), understanding ourselves as subject to original sin, then shapes how to think about the social and economic life. The superabundant and unmerited God-given gift of hope and charity even though all are sinners impacts on structures of society. *LS* also takes up the issue of sin but relates this to rupture in relationships with God, each other and the natural world, joining with the Orthodox Patriarchate in making such claims of *ecological* sin and with Latin American scholarship in naming *structural* sin. The concept of total dependence on God will have resonance with Protestant scholars, though pushing to include ecological sin and even sins of the economy will resonate particularly with those who are more ecologically conscious. See Ernst Conradie, '*Laudato Si'* and the Root Causes of Ecological Destruction', *Journal of Theology for Southern Africa* 157 (2017), 138–45.

[21] *LS*, §147–55.

[22] For the United Nations Sustainable Development Goals see http://www.un.org/sustainabledevelopment/. While the language of sustainable development can be challenged both in its claim for a truly ecological understanding of sustainability and its claim for development that can have colonial undertones, SDGs are an attempt, at least, to move away from crude economic growth measurements through national GDPs.

8. *Climate matters to families*. The attention that Pope Francis gives to healthy family life and the individual decisions made day by day[23] is a striking reminder that the Catholic Church is concerned with daily practices. Grounding ecological virtue in daily life takes away the overwhelming feeling of powerlessness that many experience when confronted with the immensity of climate-change issues. Indeed, Pope Francis is prepared to say that 'living our vocation to be protectors of God's handiwork is essential to a life of virtue; it is not an optional or a secondary aspect of our Christian experience.'[24]

9. *Climate matters to the church*. Reforming the church as part of a wider process of ecological conversion is one of the challenges that Pope Francis has set himself in his ministry. His understanding of what the Church means and its representation across theological scholarship that is sympathetic to liberation theology, but without losing contact with more traditional approaches, is one of the challenges. The Argentinian version of liberation theology with its stress on a theology of the people is arguably rather more able to mediate in this way between different conflicting schools of thought.[25]

10. *Climate matters in prayer*. The encyclical is embedded in a prayerful and pastoral approach to the problems at hand, not just by weaving in the praise poem of Pope Francis's exemplar, St Francis of Assisi, but also by offering examples of the kind of prayers and practices. When Pope Francis visited Washington, DC, in his state visit soon after the encyclical was released, he deliberately took time to pray with those of other religious traditions in order to show how the issues facing humanity are not limited to any particular church.[26] He encourages, then, in his role as the first Jesuit primate of the Church, an Ignatian spirituality that finds God in all things, that is capable of detachment from inordinate desires and is committed to seeking justice.

11. *Climate matters in worship*. Pope Francis concludes his encyclical with a strong message that joins up a distinctive Catholic focus on the Eucharist but widens this out to the idea of a cosmic liturgy, one that recognizes the theological significance of Creation but also the cosmic significance of Christ's action in history. The idea of sacramental transformation of the world is distinctly Catholic in its emphasis, but by touching on the heart of Catholic identity in this way, Pope Francis hopes to touch the hearts of those who are already invested in Catholic ways of thinking and acting.

12. *Climate matters to Indigenous communities*. Pope Francis is not content just to name those who are vulnerable and whose cultures are under threat due to climate change as

---

[23] *LS*, §213.
[24] *LS*, §217.
[25] Juan Carlos Scannone, 'Pope Francis and the Theology of the People', *Theological Studies* 77 (2016), 118–35.
[26] Michelle Boorstein, 'The Story Behind Pope Francis' Interfaith Service at Ground Zero', *Washington Post*, 25 September 2015.

those who need to trigger our sense of compassion and desire for greater justice, but he also insists that there are insights, especially from indigenous and other marginalized communities that need greater representation in current debates.[27]

While there are other issues as well that feed into the complex arguments for integral ecology that seeks to join together thinking across different disciplines, overall Pope Francis wants to generate a new kind of social imaginary that captures both hearts and minds in a way that leads to a profound and deep ecological conversion.[28] That conversion is not just about a turn to care for the natural world but also about a deeply integrated sense of the way human beings are bound up with the lives of other creatures: care for the natural world is an integral part of care for ourselves.

One of the reasons why Pope Francis has managed to elicit the response he has across a broad spectrum of the public is because he appeals to basic human psychology. An environmental psychology is one that seeks to identify the motivating factors in promoting change. In accordance with this approach, norms, values, attitudes, goals, emotions, cognitive bias, habits, social interactions, socio-demographic characteristics, personal experience, communication, personality, efficiency beliefs and knowledge all play a part in effective and lasting change.[29] *LS* resonates with virtually all these features, including the power of his own charismatic *persona* and abilities to communicate effectively with others. One difficulty in making changes is that those that wish for change can feel isolated. Pope Francis has provided a platform through which other Christians and not just Roman Catholics can come together and share in a common mission, especially through joining up spiritual, educational and conservation aspects of the church's work. Its potential to shift the sociopolitical landscape and global negotiations was clear at the 2015 Paris climate summit immediately after the release of the encyclical.[30] However, working towards lasting cultural change in the manner called for by the pope remains much more difficult.

Questions, therefore, arise as to how far and how effective this ecological conversion might actually be both within and beyond the church and where the points of resistance might lie. How radical can such ecological conversion become?

---

[27] *LS*, §146, 179.
[28] Pope John Paul II and Ecumenical Patriarchate Bartholomew I also refer to ecological conversion, but Pope Francis deepens the challenge of that call through greater attention to global structural change and some guidance as to the means to make those changes. See *LS*, §216–21.
[29] Katharina Beyerl, 'What Makes Us Think and Act Differently? Psychological Perspectives on Radical Ecological Conversion', paper delivered at a conference on 'Radical Ecological Conversion After *Laudato Si'*: Discovering the Intrinsic Value of Creatures: Human and Non-Human', Gregorian University, Rome, 8 March 2018.
[30] McDonagh, 'Climate Change', this volume.

Some concerns over *Laudato Si'*

There are specific areas that could have been given much more attention and so potentially lead to sharp criticism and even rejection of this message:

1. *Gender issues* are particularly obvious to those who have been working in this area for some time. A number of feminist scholars have pointed to the failure of Pope Francis to face squarely the disproportionate impact of climate change on women.[31] He notes both men and women are responsible actors, and unlike his predecessors avoids using 'men' to refer to humanity.[32] But this does not go far enough. Although Pope Francis frequently talks about the poor, he does not acknowledge that the majority of those that are poor are women and are more dependent on natural resources for survival, and so are disproportionately impacted by climate change. The lack of access of women who are poor to education and systems of power accentuates these problems further. On the other hand, where Pope Francis does refer to women, his idealization of the Virgin Mary[33] as a mother, with the traditional role of protector ascribed to Joseph, tends to convey an essentialist view of women with specific stereotypical roles to play in the family. His appeal to Mary will also resonate with many more traditional Catholics, and linking Mariology with ecological concern is likely to be new for that audience.[34] His stress on the loving care of God for creation at least points towards an ethic of care that moves away from a portrayal of God in terms of dominating hierarchies. His other gestures in this direction through references to 'mother earth' may smack of essentialism, but to expect more would, it seems to me, have alienated even further other more conservative constituents in the church. It is a pity, nonetheless, that Pope Francis failed to give any attention to women's grass roots movements that have been so powerful in initiating change, such as the *Conspirando* in Latin America or the *Chipko* movement in India and the *Greenbelt* movement in Kenya, with the iconic leadership of Wangari Maathai, all of which have showcased in an important way the empowerment of women in action to address climate change.

---

[31] See, for example, Lisa Cahill, 'The Environment, The Common Good and Women's Participation', in *Theology and Ecology across the Disciplines: On Care for Our Common Home*, Celia Deane-Drummond and Rebecca Artinian-Kaiser (eds) (London: Bloomsbury, 2018), 135–48; Rosemary Carbine, 'Imagining and Incarnating an Integral Ecology: A Critical Ecofeminist Public Theology', in *Planetary Solidarity: Global Women's Voices on Christian Doctrine and Climate Justice*, Grace Ji-Sun Kim and Hilda Koster (eds) (Minneapolis: Fortress, 2017), 47–66; Ivone Gebara, 'Women's Suffering, Climate Injustice, God, and Pope Francis' Theology: Some Insights from Brazil', in *Planetary Solidarity*, 67–79; Sharon A. Bong, 'Not Only for the Sake of Man: Asian Feminist Theological Responses to *Laudato Si*", in *Planetary Solidarity*, 81–96.

[32] For example, *LS*, §58, 60, 75, 103, 106, 127.

[33] *LS*, §241–2.

[34] To suggest, as Rosemary Carbine does, that a pontiff could be other than patriarchal in their theological approach is, it seems to me, unrealistic. However, he can, by appointing women advisers, show that it is possible to affirm women's leadership even within a system structured along broadly patriarchal lines.

2. *Population issues* are not really tackled responsibly in the encyclical. The pope is correct in suggesting that overconsumption by those with wealth across the globe, including those living in poorer nations, is among the most serious factors in creating the global anthropogenic carbon footprint[35] and that blaming population growth alone for leading to climate-change problems is a mistake.[36] Yet it is obvious also that given current rates of population growth the carrying capacity of the planet is not sufficient and that this would be the case even if all human beings living on the planet reduced their footprint to that needed for bare and minimal subsistence levels. It is easy to understand why the Catholic Church resists policies such as 'reproductive health', given its determination to defend the rights of the unborn. There may be other ways to promote ecological responsibility in relation to family size, especially in communities that are high consumers. Reducing consumption is a priority, but so is finding ways to promote responsible parenthood.[37]

3. *Philosophical consistency*: Pope Francis's description of the climate as a common good[38] is inconsistent with a more traditional definition of the principle of the common good that he adopts from Vatican II.[39] It would have been more precise to say that the climate is a good of the global commons. Although the anthropocentrism and human exceptionalism of his predecessors is corrected, the focus and priority given to human worth sits somewhat uneasily alongside attention to other creatures. It is not made clear how to adjudicate between these different demands. Pope Francis uses the term 'intrinsic value' on three occasions, with respect to widening its scope to creatures beyond the human community,[40] to ecosystems as such,[41] and to the world as a whole,[42] all of which are impacted by climate change. At the same time, he argues that human beings have a 'unique dignity' and in other places he is prepared to speak about the natural world in an instrumental way, so he uses 'ecosystem services' to describe the health of the ecosystem.[43] He also praises the achievements of medical science and other scientific research, which necessarily takes an instrumental perspective on other life forms, while strongly resisting instrumentalization of human life as ever permissible under any circumstances.[44] His account of evolutionary history is also

---

[35] *LS*, §172.
[36] *LS*, §50.
[37] It is significant that Pope Benedict XVI mentioned the idea of responsible parenthood in *Caritate in Veritate* (§44) following a discussion of population growth where 'due attention must obviously be given to responsible procreation'.
[38] *LS*, §23.
[39] *LS*, §156.
[40] *LS*, §118.
[41] *LS*, §140.
[42] *LS*, §115.
[43] *LS*, §25. He mentions agriculture, fishing and forestry.
[44] *LS*, §136.

surprisingly brief; affirming evolution as a process but rejecting the idea that human life is described adequately by evolutionary emergence. The difficult ethical questions of how to adjudicate between different life forms and the relationships between intrinsic and instrumental value are unresolved, except for an encouragement 'to live wisely, to think deeply and to love generously'.[45] Further, the difficult issue of how to navigate the tensions between evolutionary science and faith in creation is left unexplored. Given that, it is perhaps surprising that Pope Francis has achieved the acclaim he has among scientific communities, though his gesture towards dialogue is clearly appreciated.

4. *Political resistance*: Although he does not spell out his approach to the Vatican as such in the encyclical, it is well known that his style of leadership, his focus on practice and his consistency in gestures that express his commitment to live out what he claims are all ways of showing his commitment to reform from within have met with considerable resistance.[46] Such resistance is not confined to the Catholic curia; more conservative Catholics, especially in powerful nations such as the United States or Australia, have actively sought to undermine his message. There was an attempt to discredit the climate science in the encyclical by pointing to associations between his scientific advisers and anti-pro-life campaigns.[47] Other accusations that he is dabbling inappropriately in politics or being Marxist in his leanings as a result of his commitment to structural reform are also common. A further complication is that the message of *LS* itself can be interpreted in different ways in public discourse within the Catholic Church, especially in powerful nation states like the United States, and trying to work out ways in which that division might be navigated is a complex cultural task.[48]

---

[45] *LS*, §47.

[46] Christopher Lamb, 'Reforming Rome is like Cleaning the Egyptian Sphinx with a Toothbrush Says Pope', *The Tablet*, 21 December 2017.

[47] While the initial accusations were levelled at the way Pope Francis took advice from those scientists like Hans Joachim Shellnhuber from the Potsdam Institute for Climate Impact (PIK) who were thought to be associated with anti-pro-life campaigns, a more recent shift has been a direct attack on Pope Francis. By supporting the UN SDGs, he is accused of capitulation to its support of pro-abortion measures and so compromising the unambiguous stance of the Catholic Church towards all forms of contraception. Further unease has arisen through his approach to the family in *Amoris Laetitia*. Part of the problem is Pope Francis's attempt to reform on family matters may undermine his authority. See Staff Reporter, 'Pro-Life Leaders from 13 Countries Accuse Pope Francis of Failing to Uphold Church Teaching', *Catholic Herald*, 12 December 2017, http://www.catholicherald.co.uk/news/2017/12/12/pro-life-leaders-from-13-countries-accuse-pope-francis-of-failing-to-uphold-church-teaching/ (accessed 1 May 2018). Such accusations by association are weak at best but show the growing backlash within the more conservative constituency of the Catholic Church.

[48] Erin Lothes, for example, discusses the divisions within American Catholic groups in response to *LS*, using cultural analysis as a way of distinguishing different interpretations of his message. The tendency to read into this document's preconceived political positions is clearly articulated in her essay on 'Climate Change and Christian Fellowship', this volume.

5. *Non-human animals:* Given the message of *LS* with respect to climate change and the interconnectedness of all life, there is a surprising lack of attention to practical steps towards compassionate animal welfare and the significant contribution that agriculture makes to the global carbon footprint through methane production, along with the impact of concentrated feeding operations which also raise striking issues of social justice for those working in the community. Changing eating habits, promoting fair trade and refraining from eating meat, especially that arising from cruel methods of farming, is one area that would have been relatively easy to promote, especially given the excessive overconsumption and waste of food that Pope Francis points out. While he uses the language of interconnectedness and affirms Indigenous approaches to living, he does not take the next step and speak of the active agency and subjectivity of other animals.

6. *Natural suffering and evil:* Pope Francis is almost naïve in his positive appraisal of the natural world and his celebration of the joy of being in its presence, following inspiration from Francis of Assisi. While the suffering of animals and other species caused by anthropogenic climate change and mostly through loss of habitat is mentioned, he does not adequately consider the evolutionary and current history of natural predation and death. Although evolutionary biologists are now just as keen to point to collaboration at the root of evolutionary biology as much as nature 'red in tooth and claw', his failure to recognize natural suffering renders his message less convincing to those who have been heavily influenced by neo-Darwinian logic or who are faced with difficult choices about which species to protect.

7. *Biblical interpretation*: Given the attention given to collating the details of the scientific account, the interpretation of the Bible in *LS* is formulaic and lacks proper appreciation of hermeneutics or current biblical scholarship on passages of environmental significance. Paying proper attention to this area is particularly important when engaging in dialogue with Protestants, especially those who adhere to the authority of scripture.

8. *Economic challenges*: Accusing the market economy of being redundant without suggesting a clearly worked out framework for an alternative is bound to lead to frustration. Integral ecology attempts to do that, but there are complex economic systems to navigate and detailed political negotiations that are necessary in order to bring about the kind of changes that are pointed out in this encyclical. This also applies to other structural changes, which need more rigorous analysis, such as ways to tackle the corruption in governance that Pope Francis recognizes is part of the problem.

9. *Indigenous communities*: While these communities are flagged up for special treatment, it is not clear what role they might play in relation to the dominant political and social structure of the Global North. How can their example of living be translated into terms

that make sense to others outside these communities?[49] Are there dangers of idealizing ways of life that are animistic and thus not in keeping with Christian teaching? Why are considerations of the rural landscape left to a discussion of Indigenous lifestyles? How can a richer sense of the importance of slowing down, a de-rapidification as Pope Francis puts it,[50] be inspired by lives that are different from the frenetic pace of those living in the richer nations of the world? Such problems are not really addressed in the encyclical.

10. *Idealism and sacramentality*: The sacramental life of the Catholic Church is arguably its heart. But naming 'universal communion' and a Mass for the world, in common with other creatures and planet earth, as a goal is going to be a hard transition to make for those who view the Eucharist differently. There is much more work to be done to translate the vision of *LS* into practical steps that will promote genuine environmental responsibility and not just the 'green' rhetoric that Pope Francis rejects.[51]

A response to such problems and gaps in the argument opens up significant opportunities for Catholic theologians to work towards change in a way that takes up the spirit of what is proposed in *LS*. Working with a hierarchical institution that is as vast as the Catholic Church and that is socially, politically and culturally diverse is an immense challenge but also a huge responsibility.

---

[49] David Aftandilian, 'What other Americans Can and Cannot learn from Native American Environmental Ethics', *Worldviews* 15 (2011), 219–46.
[50] *LS*, §18.
[51] *LS*, §45, 49.

A response to Celia Deane-Drummond

María Pilar Aquino[1]

A distinctive characteristic of Celia Deane-Drummond's contribution to the study of climate change and environmental justice is her sustained commitment to develop constructive theological approaches in the complex interaction of religious faith, the natural sciences, ecological studies and Catholic social thought.[2] In today's global theological community, one seldom comes across a scholar who masters the research methods of the natural sciences and theology to unravel the complexities of interdisciplinary theological practice in relation to ecological concerns. Deane-Drummond has been able to do so because she holds the proper academic credentials[3] and has maintained a research agenda for more than three decades within a field of study that she has helped shape, namely ecotheology. From her earlier publications to the latest,[4] her work has sought to encourage Christian theologians to both take seriously ecological concerns and engage in dialogue with other religious traditions seeking shared intervention for constructive ecological transformation. I admire her sustained work and wish to honour her vision and contributions to ecotheology.

My response to Deane-Drummond's essay begins with appreciation of the conceptual framing for her approach to the Catholic position on climate change. She acknowledges a shift in Catholic social teaching from a traditional anthropocentric reductionism to

---

[1] María Pilar Aquino was born in Ixtlán del Río, Nayarit (Mexico). She is a feminist Catholic theologian and Professor Emerita of Theology and Religious Studies at the University of San Diego. A president of the Catholic Theological Society of America (2019–2020), she is a member of the International Advisory Committee of the World Forum on Theology and Liberation of the World Social Forum.

[2] I use the expressions 'Catholic social thought' with reference to a broad theological tradition on social concerns produced by Catholic actors beyond the official hierarchy of the Catholic Church and 'Catholic social teaching' in reference to the tradition of social teaching produced by members of the Catholic Church's hierarchical body.

[3] Deane-Drummond earned a PhD in plant physiology from the University of Reading (1980) and a PhD in theological studies from the University of Manchester (1992).

[4] The academic and pedagogical writings by Celia Deane-Drummond are extensive. Here, I simply wish to illustrate an evolving 'ecotheological' tradition that she has pioneered. See, for example, her *Gaia and Green Ethics: Implications of Ecological Theology* (Cambridge: Grove Books, 1993); *A Handbook in Theology and Ecology* (London: SCM Press, 1996); *Eco-Theology* (London: Darton, Longman and Todd, 2008); *A Primer in Ecotheology: Theology for a Fragile Earth* (Eugene: Cascade Books, 2017). Two of her edited books also exemplify this tradition: Celia Deane-Drummond and Heinrich Bedford-Strohm (eds), *Religion and Ecology in the Public Sphere* (London: Continuum, 2011), and Celia Deane-Drummond and Rebecca Artinian-Kaiser (eds), *Theology and Ecology Across Disciplines* (New York: Bloomsbury, 2018).

the notion of integral ecology, made possible by Pope Francis's encyclical *Laudato Si'* (*LS*). This framing is important because any theological discourse presupposes and entails a given theological anthropology. A shift from the supremacy of the human over the natural world to ecological interdependence or a shift from a utilitarian mindset to intergenerational solidarity and compassionate care does not obliterate the bases of Catholic social teaching but rather enrich them. Charles Curran asserts that this teaching 'rests on two fundamental anthropological principles: the dignity and sacredness of the human person and the social nature of the person'.[5] The understanding of the human as constituted not by isolated individualism but by relationality and interdependence with community and the planetary environment affirms a new anthropological epistemology in Catholic social teaching. This is an epistemological approach placed within the vision and framework of a religiously grounded integral ecology, which also provides support for the engagement of religious actors who seek alternatives to overcome the human roots of the ecological crisis.

A second response involves the usefulness of Deane-Drummond's evaluative approach to *LS*. The articulation of her essay by two reflective tracks allows the reader to identify clearly twelve categories that reveal the ecumenical significance of *LS* and ten categories that highlight insufficiently addressed concerns or unresolved issues present in *LS*. As for the first track, I value greatly the centrality given by Deane-Drummond to solidarity with the marginalized and the most vulnerable global population exposed to the harmful impact of climate change. Her approach gives visibility not only to the ecumenical intent of *LS* but also to the ecumenical grounding of the option for the poor and the oppressed. In addition to being an articulating principle of Catholic social teaching,[6] this option has become a distinctive hermeneutical principle shared by the ecumenical community of liberation theologians around the world.

Inspired by this option, both the Ecumenical Association of Third World Theologians (EATWOT) and the World Forum on Theology and Liberation (WFTL)[7] have declared a collective commitment to embrace the ecological paradigm by developing ecotheological perspectives to support social practices and religious spiritualities for intervention in the

---

[5] Charles E. Curran, *Catholic Social Teaching, 1891–Present: A Historical, Theological, and Ethical Analysis* (Washington DC: Georgetown University Press, 2002), 131.

[6] Donal Dorr, *Option for the Poor and for the Earth: Catholic Social Teaching* (Maryknoll: Orbis, 2012).

[7] See, for example, Rohan Silva, Marlene Perera and Shirley Lal Wijesinghe (eds), 'Eco-Crisis: Theological Visions', *Voices from the Third World* (June 2009), 1–135; Latin American Theological Commission (ed.), 'Ecology and Religion: In this Hour of Planetary Emergency', *Voices* 34:1 (2011), 1–326; Adam K. Arap Chekwony (ed.), 'Ecological Vision in a Groaning World', *Voices* 36:2–3 (2013), 1–147; José María Vigil (ed.), 'Deep Ecology: Spirituality and Liberation', *Voices* 37:2–3 (2014), 1–414; María Pilar Aquino (ed.), '*Laudato Si*' and Ecology', *Voices* 39:2 (2016), 1–199. These and other issues of *Voices,* the theological journal of the Ecumenical Association of Third World Theologians (EATWOT), are available to download from http://eatwot.net/VOICES/ (accessed 14 February 2019). See also Luis Carlos Susin and Joe Marçal G. dos Santos (eds), *Nosso Planeta Nossa Vida. Ecología e Teología* (São Paulo: Paulinas and World Forum on Theology and Liberation, 2011).

transformation of the climate crisis which further burdens systemic injustice against people and the earth. As a concerted endeavour, this commitment is illustrative of a deeper shift that is taking place at the core of Catholic social thought in moving the theological agenda from social concerns affecting the human alone to ecological concerns affecting the human and the environment together, both concerns linked to questions of justice. According to Jaime Tatay Nieto, a Jesuit scholar who specializes in the study of integral ecology in Catholic social teaching, the social question that was articulated at the end of the nineteenth century (*Rerum Novarum*, 1891) has become the socio-environmental question in the twenty-first century (*Laudato Si'*, 2015).[8] Today, Christian religious actors can no longer understand the social as separate from the environmental or the environmental as separate from justice for the poor and the excluded.

A third response relates to the positive value given by Deane-Drummond to the notion of ecological conversion in Pope Francis's effort to reform the church. I discern hope on her part about the opportunity that climate concerns offer to different theological traditions, such as liberation theology and the more 'traditional' approaches that she mentions, for working together on the challenges that the Catholic Church faces today. I tend to be sceptical about this. The current architecture of the church prevents a potential ethical or political compatibility of the theological agenda embraced by liberation theology and traditional theological approaches. On the one hand, taking into account contextual differentials, liberation theologies around the world share in common a theological method aimed at the radical transformation of unjust social systems and relationships. Grounded in a preferential option for the poor and guided by a vision of a global just society, liberation theology is informed by ethical values consistent with respect for human dignity, solidarity, peace with justice, universal common good, well-being for all and care for the integrity of the environment, among other life-affirming values. Latin American liberation theologians Guillermo Kerber and Olga Consuelo Vélez Caro have indicated the methodological convergence of liberation theology and Pope Francis's encyclical, *Laudato Si'*,[9] as well as the significance of this convergence for the global ecumenical movement. In this light, the more traditional theologies would need to adopt a liberation-oriented theological method if ecological conversion is to occur.

On the other hand, while Deane-Drummond does not explain her use of the term 'traditional approaches', an interpretation of this term may include theologies and spiritualities that over centuries of Catholic thought have fostered goodness in the relationship of the human with God, nature and other humans seen as neighbours in

---

[8] Jaime Tatay Nieto, SJ, 'De la "cuestión social" a la "cuestión socio-ambiental": Implicaciones de Laudato Si' para la DSI', in *Cuidar de la Tierra, cuidar de los pobres. Laudato Si' desde la teología y con la ciencia*, Enrique Sanz Giménez-Rico (ed.) (Maliaño: Editorial Sal Terrae, 2015), 169–84.

[9] Guillermo Kerber, 'Ecumenical Background and Reactions to Laudato Si", *Voices* 39:2 (2016), 63–75; Olga Consuelo Vélez Caro, 'The Ecological Conversion Encyclical and Its Accessibility to the Impoverished of this World', *Voices* 39:2 (2016), 38–49.

need. But it can also refer to theological traditions informed by philosophical and doctrinal frameworks that have provided legitimacy to the exploitation of humans and environmental destruction and continue to disregard the practices of religious actors for climate justice as valid theological locations. These are traditional or conservative theological approaches in which the interests, values and struggles of marginalized peoples for sustainable environments are deemed irrelevant for theological construction. Linked to the notion of ecological conversion, Deanne-Drummond appears to value the insights offered by the various theological traditions of the Catholic Church that promote constructive change in the interest of protecting people together with the environment in which they live. In this sense, critical discernment is required from those who are motivated by Catholic faith regarding the plurality of resources, values and symbols that they draw from the to inform their commitment to change the present and build a different, more just and sustainable future for all. The encyclical *Laudato Si'* has become a crucial resource for such discernment. In his splendid study of integral ecology in Catholic social teaching, Tatay[10] acknowledges that while *LS* does not provide resolution to the complexity of ecological matters, it does provide an initial response to the contemporary concerns about sustainability, climate change and integral ecology from the standpoint of magisterial teaching, a response that needs to be adopted in ecclesia, matured theologically, implemented in community and revised continually. The notion of ecological conversion becomes a process for all involved theological actors who find motivation and commonality in the vision of integral ecology.

A fourth and final response refers to gender issues as mentioned by Deane-Drummond in her second reflective track. She addresses critically the limitations of *LS* in three areas: neglecting the disproportionate impact of climate change on women, essentializing women in stereotypical roles as mothers and caregivers and disregarding the struggles of grass roots women for environmental justice. I am in full agreement with her and praise her criticism. Pope Francis declares a commitment to 'move forward in a bold cultural revolution' (*LS*, §114). This desired revolution must begin by radically eliminating patriarchal ideology from Catholic teaching and church power structure. Ecological conversion includes full recognition of women's human rights in society and church. Integral ecology cannot take place without justice for women within the Catholic Church. As a matter of climate change, Pope Francis can begin to make such a bold cultural revolution within the church by stopping to make ignorant, simplistic and demeaning comments about feminism.[11]

---

[10] Jaime Tatay, SJ, *Ecología Integral. La Recepción Católica del Reto de la Sostenibilidad: 1891 (RN) – 2015 (LS)* (Madrid: Biblioteca de Autores Cristianos, 2018).

[11] Pope Francis uses the term 'feminism' as a synonym of 'machismo', see *Vatican News*, 'Pope Francis: Woman is the Image of the Church that is Mother', *Vatican News*, 22 February 2019; 'Papa Francesco: "La donna è l'immagine della Chiesa che è donna, è sposa, è madre"', *Zenit Il Mondo Visto da Roma*, 22 February 2019, https://it.zenit.org/articles/papa-francesco-la-donna-e-limmagine-della-chiesa-che-e-donna-e-sposa-e-madre (accessed 24 February 2019).

Chapter 3.3
Working with Anglican forms of Christianity

Rachel Mash[1]

The Industrial Revolution and the Church of England

Climate Change has its roots in the Industrial Revolution, when a shift was made towards a rapid increase in the use of fossil fuels. The Industrial Revolution, which took place from the eighteenth to the nineteenth centuries, was a period when predominantly rural societies became industrial and urban, beginning with Britain in the late 1700s. Manufacturing was often done in people's homes, using hand tools or basic machines. Industrialization marked a shift to powered, special-purpose machinery, factories and mass production. There were several reasons why it began in Britain: British landlords had been able to push their peasants off the land – a process called 'enclosure'. Previously working-class people had been able to use tracts of lands known as 'the commons' for water, wood and grazing. Many of these people then moved to the cities in search of work and found poorly paid conditions at factories.

At the same time, because of the British Empire there was a great opportunity for trade, with raw materials coming from colonized countries and production taking place at factories in England. A strengthening middle class boosted by cheap labour was able to fund inventions and trade. The Industrial Revolution marked the beginning of the shift to fossil fuels and the rapid adoption of coal power for steam-powered machinery and railroads. Britain was able to lead the way due to their vast coal fields and river system which could be canalized for transportation.

As the state church, what was the role of the Church of England during the Industrial Revolution? In rural communities, the Church of England was the local church where farmworkers and landed class would worship together (albeit in different pews!). Once the rural working class moved to the city, many of them suffered great hardships and

---

[1] Rachel Mash is Environmental Coordinator for the Anglican Church of Southern Africa (South Africa, Lesotho, Namibia, Angola, Mozambique and Eswatini). She is also a steering member of the Anglican Communion Environmental Network and the Green Anglicans Movement.

found a home with churches such as the Methodist Church or other non-conformist churches which proved to be much more conscious of the needs of the new industrial working class. Landowners and business people found themselves more at home in the establishment Church of England. Often the interests of church leaders and business leaders dovetailed, for instance, the so-called Protestant work ethic of hard work and clean living. Profit tended to be seen as a moral positive, regardless of cost to the worker.

During the age of Enlightenment, science was impoverished by the lack of spiritual insights. Science could answer the question 'how' but not the question 'why'. God was seen at best as a 'clockmaker' leaving this machine for humans to control. Nature was no longer alive or permeated with spiritual presence; it was objectified and lost any rights. It was seen as simply matter to be manipulated to satisfy human need or greed. The Industrial Revolution primarily took place in Christian countries where the sense of the spiritual value of creation had been lost.

As the church turned inward and focused on personal salvation and debates about doctrine, the scientific community developed a parallel salvation story – the power of science and technology to save the world. Some of those dreams have turned into nightmares. The Christian world had moved from a theology of wonder to a theology of plunder. The scene was set for the tragedy to unfold.

The colonial period

During the colonial period of the nineteenth and twentieth centuries British missionaries played an ambiguous role. They were driven by a desire to serve humanity and improve its quality of life; however, they held to a moral self-righteousness that led to a disparagement of local cultures and values. They were closely tied with the values of the colonizing powers and enabled colonialism to take place.[2] I will focus on the impact of colonization on Southern Africa, but many of the principles are the same in other countries that were colonized.

In terms of climate change, colonialism affected land use, consumerism and the extractive industries.

In terms of land use, one of the longest lasting detrimental impacts of missionaries was the introduction of a dualistic theology. When they came into contact with Indigenous beliefs around the sacredness of nature they dismissed these beliefs as paganism. It could be argued that what they encountered was panentheism – the belief or doctrine that God is greater than the universe and includes and interpenetrates it – a belief in the sacredness of Creation. This they confused with pantheism and demonized as paganism.

---

[2] See http://www.sahistory.org.za/article/european-missionaries-southern-africa-role-missionaries (accessed 1 June 2018).

Converts had to change their relationship to nature and worship God within the four walls of the church.

The colonial era was also undergirded by dominion theology – with reference to Gen. 1.28, 'fill the earth and subdue it. Rule over the fish and the birds and every living creature'. Based on a dualism derived from the Enlightenment, missionaries and colonial powers defined 'civilization' as disconnecting oneself from the Earth and using natural goods as a source of economic profit. Instead of humans being seen as a part of the web of life and with a responsibility to preserve it to sustain future generations, people were taught that nature existed for humans to benefit from economically.

Local acceptance of early missionaries in the Eastern Cape was influenced by their technological ability to introduce furrow irrigation into an otherwise drought-stricken land. Missionaries from the Church of England tended to form 'mission stations' where farming and evangelization came hand in hand.[3] The London Missionary Society in 1800 recommended that missionaries 'should carry with them some acquaintance with agriculture or those branches of mechanics which admit of a useful application in uncivilized countries'.[4] David Livingstone is represented in his statue in Edinburgh with a Bible in one hand and the other resting upon an axe.

Some of these agricultural methodologies would have far-reaching impacts on climate change in Africa. Faced with brittle soil and barely fertile soil, Africans copied the missionaries and embraced the plough, designed for clay soil. African soil fell apart and lost its nutrients leading to erosion and a drop in soil fertility. And so Africa has become dependent on synthetic fertilizers leading to emissions of Nitrous Oxide. According to one study 5.2 million tonnes of CO_2 equivalent (CO_2-eq) emissions was produced from artificial fertilizers in South Africa in 2012.[5]

In terms of land ownership, European missionaries believed Africans were lazy and were not using their land adequately so it was in their 'best interests' for Europeans to use it. They even preached that salvation could only be obtained through formal work which meant one had to earn a pay check. The only people who paid for labour at the time were Europeans colonialists.

A newspaper editorial of March 1873, on the subject of local labour, among other things urged missionaries to 'single out all the unemployed young men they know of, at their various stations, and talk over the matter with them individually … The missionary's work is not done when the work of the pulpit and the duties of religious instruction are over. He must follow these up, by seeing how the young men growing

---

[3] See https://mg.co.za/article/2016-02-04-sa-farmers-find-alternatives-to-unsuitable-ploughing (accessed 1 June 2018).

[4] See https://www.sahistory.org.za/article/european-missionaries-southern-africa-role-missionaries (accessed 9 January 2019).

[5] See https://www.sciencedirect.com/science/article/pii/S2211464516300537 (accessed 1 June 2018).

up under his care, set themselves to the first duty of practical Christianity – which is to earn an honest livelihood.'[6]

In this way missionaries were complicit in aiding Europeans in taking land that belonged to Africans and then forcing them to work for a living so that they would pay taxes to the colonial power. As Archbishop Tutu often observed, 'When the missionaries came to Africa they had the Bible and we had the land. They said "Let us pray." We closed our eyes. When we opened them we had the Bible and they had the land.'

Apart from the huge injustice – in terms of climate change this meant a shift from small-scale sustainable use of the land to eventual large commercial farms. Organic farming methodologies that created carbon sinks were converted into carbon sources.

In terms of consumerism, the missionaries had strong links with traders. Livingstone, although a Congregationalist, came to Africa with the London Mission Society – which was interdenominational but with many evangelical Anglicans. He divided his ministry into three categories: commerce, Christianity and civilization. 'Christianity would provide principles for moral guidance, while legitimate commerce and education would encourage Africans to produce their own goods from their fertile soil to trade with Europeans.'[7] Both traders and missionaries believed that educating the population would lead to a spread of both commerce and Christianity, and missionaries had a role in co-opting Indigenous peoples into the market economy. People being forced to pay the hut tax in cash were also forced to leave their land in order to enter the cash economy of commerce. WG Cumming, Resident Magistrate of Xalanga, Transkei, commented in 1880 that

> In order that money might be obtained to pay the hut-tax, hundreds of young men have been sent into the Colony by their relatives to work in the town and among the farmers. The frequent recurring necessity of having to find the money for their friends, will gradually force the young men out of the groove in which they have been living ... By being brought more immediately in contact with civilisation, an alteration will be wrought in their character; and in process of time, habits which have been fostered by a mode of existence calculated to develop all the evil qualities in a man will, under new conditions of life, be, if not eradicated, at least held in check.[8]

Consumer goods were available at local trading stores. So the missionaries together with the traders helped to shift the community from a self-sustaining lifestyle to one dependent on external consumer goods. The seeds of environmental degradation were

---

[6] See http://www.sahistory.org.za/article/european-missionaries-southern-africa-role-missionaries (accessed 3 June 2018).

[7] See http://www.scielo.org.za/scielo.php?script=sci_arttext&pid=S1017-04992013000200016 (accessed 3 June 2018).

[8] See http://www.sahistory.org.za/article/european-missionaries-southern-africa-role-missionaries (accessed 3 June 2018).

being sown; Christianity and consumerism would go hand in hand, with the loss of the sacredness of the land.

In terms of the extractive industries, a factor which was to have a profound influence upon the long-term social and economic make-up of Southern Africa was the creation of a migrant labour system from the 1870s onwards. Forced by the hut tax to earn cash, young men were a ready source of cheap labour for the mining industry.

By 1895, at the height of his powers, Cecil John Rhodes, son of a Church of England priest, was the unquestioned economic master of South Africa, ruling over the destiny of the Cape and its white and African subjects, controlling nearly all of the world's diamonds and much of its gold, and effectively ruling over three colonial dependencies in the heart of Africa. In an April 1897 letter Olive Schreiner wrote:

> We fight Rhodes because he means so much of oppression, injustice, & moral degradation to South Africa; – but if he passed away tomorrow there still remains the terrible fact that *something in our society has formed the matrix which has fed, nourished, built up such a man!*[9]

The matrix which had fed, nourished and built up Cecil John Rhodes and the ideology of Empire and colonialism was undergirded by the teaching of the church. The Earth was no longer sacred – to see it as such was condemned as 'paganism'. God commanded us to take from the earth as our God-given right. The values of the extractive industries had been formulated – cheap fossil fuels would become available based on abuse of the environment and the workforce.

Signs of hope

In this section I will highlight some of the key moments in the history of the Anglican Church in terms of a recognition of environmental ministry and climate change.

(a) *The Fifth Mark of Mission:* A turning point in Anglican theology was at the Anglican Consultative Council (ACC) in 1990, when the ACC stated that having appreciated the missiological and biblical implications of the creation and environmental crisis, the ACC decided that a new mark of mission that captured this understanding was inevitable. The ACC stated, 'We now feel that our understanding of the ecological crisis, and indeed of the threats to the unity of all creation, mean that we have to add a fifth affirmation.'[10] And so a fifth mark on environmental sustainability was added to the four marks of mission. The Five Marks have won wide acceptance among Anglicans and among other

---

[9] See http://www.sahistory.org.za/people/cecil-john-rhodes (accessed 3 June 2018), emphasis added.

[10] See http://www.anglicancommunion.org/mission/marks-of-mission/history.aspx (accessed 7 June 2018).

Christian traditions, and have given parishes and dioceses around the world a practical and memorable 'checklist' for mission activities.

- To proclaim the Good News of the Kingdom;
- To teach, baptize and nurture new believers;
- To respond to human need by loving service;
- To seek to transform unjust structures of society; to challenge violence of every kind and to pursue peace and reconciliation;
- To strive to safeguard the integrity of creation and sustain and renew the life of the earth.

(b) *The Role of the Archbishop of Canterbury*: Although the role of the Archbishop of Canterbury is far from that of the pope – for he has no authority over the global Anglican Communion, he is however recognized as primus inter pares (first among equals) of bishops worldwide and as a spiritual leader. And so his attitude to the environment is influential. The Archbishop of Canterbury also has a leading role in nurturing Anglican relationships with other churches worldwide and at home.

Archbishop Rowan Williams (2002–12) was for a long time known as a committed environmentalist and had published frequent articles on the subject; for instance, in the *Guardian* he stated:

> Ecological questions are increasingly being defined as issues of justice; climate change has been characterised as a matter of justice both to those who now have no part in decision-making at the global level yet bear the heaviest burdens as a consequence of the irresponsibility of wealthier nations, and to those who will succeed us on this planet – justice to our children and grandchildren.[11]

Interestingly in 2002 he became a druid[12] which shows an appreciation of the Indigenous beliefs of his homeland, Wales. Needless to say this caused a bit of a flurry from the Evangelical Right accusing him of embracing paganism.

Since Archbishop Justin Welby (2013–) comes from a background in the oil industry it may have been harder for him initially to take up the challenge formulated by the fifth mark of mission, but at ACC in Lusaka he stated that the two greatest challenges facing us are climate change and inter-religious violence. He called for decisive action on religiously motivated violence and climate change, which he described as 'major, global conflicts with a very clear religious content'.[13]

More recently he wrote an article for the *New York Times* where he stated, 'Climate change is the human thumb on the scale, pushing us toward disaster. It is not a distant

---

[11] See https://www.theguardian.com/commentisfree/belief/2009/mar/26/religion-anglicanism (accessed 7 June 2018).

[12] See http://news.bbc.co.uk/2/hi/uk_news/wales/2172918.stm (accessed 7 June 2018).

[13] See https://livingchurch.org/2016/04/16/welby-time-act-climate-violence/ (accessed 8 June 2018).

danger – it is already with us. As we continue to burn fossil fuels, its effects will only grow.'[14]

The issue has also been highlighted at recent primates meetings – and it appears to be a subject that archbishops who are bitterly divided on the issue of homosexuality can agree on – so perhaps climate change may help to pull together a divided Anglican Communion.[15]

It is hoped that climate change will be high on the agenda for Lambeth 2020 – the global gathering of all Anglican bishops. All primates have been requested to prepare a 'Letter for Creation' to highlight the impact of climate change in their province, in preparation for Lambeth.[16]

(c) *Conferences*: In terms of ecumenical conferences, there are several that have been influential in the life of the Anglican Church.

First, the First International Congress on World Evangelization met in Lausanne, Switzerland, in 1974. It was organized in part by Billy Graham and was attended by some 2,700 participants and guests from over 150 nations who met here to discuss and promote evangelism. The second conference was held in Manila in 1989.

The third Lausanne conference was held in Cape Town in 2010. Four thousand Christian leaders representing 198 countries attended the Congress in Cape Town, South Africa, and influenced the more evangelical side of the Anglican Church. Creation care has become a priority for the Lausanne movement, as the Cape Town commitment stated, 'We are also commanded to care for the earth and all its creatures, because the earth belongs to God, not to us. We do this for the sake of the Lord Jesus Christ who is the creator, owner, sustainer, redeemer and heir of all creation.'[17]

Secondly, seventeen bishops with a concern for climate change from all six continents, from Australia to Zimbabwe met in Cape Town in 2015 to share their experiences and to formulate a way forward around climate change. The meeting resulted in the release of the declaration 'The World Is Our Host', which sets a new agenda on climate change for the 85-million-strong Anglican Communion:

> We accept the evidence of science concerning the contribution of human activity to the climate crisis and the disproportionate role played by fossil-fuel based economies. Although climate scientists have for many years warned of the consequences of inaction there is an alarming lack of global agreement about the way forward. We believe that the problem is spiritual as well as economic, scientific and political,

---

[14] See https://www.nytimes.com/2017/11/03/opinion/faith-climate-change-justin-welby.html (accessed 8 June 2018).

[15] See http://www.anglicannews.org/news/2017/10/anglican-primates-discuss-action-on-climate-change.aspx (accessed 9 June 2018).

[16] See http://www.churchcare.co.uk/about-us/campaigns/news/1074-anglican-primates-invited-to-create-a-picture-of-what-care-for-creation-means-2 (accessed 28 April 2018).

[17] See https://www.lausanne.org/content/ctc/ctcommitment (accessed 11 June 2018).

because the roadblock to effective action relates to basic existential issues of how human life is framed and valued: including the competing moral claims of present and future generations, human versus non-human interests, and how the lifestyle of wealthy countries is to be balanced against the basic needs of the developing world. For this reason the Church must urgently find its collective moral voice.[18]

The bishops called for churches to divest from industries 'involved primarily in the extraction or distribution of fossil fuels'.

Follow-up meetings of eco bishops are being planned in 2018 for Latin American bishops and African bishops.

(d) *Mission and Development Agencies*: There has been a significant shift in priorities by Mission and Development Agencies that work with the Anglican Church, as climate change is increasing its impact on countries they serve:

- The Global Anglican Alliance states, 'Climate change is not just an environmental problem. It is a humanitarian and development emergency, and it is already affecting vulnerable communities worldwide.'[19]
- Christian Aid says, 'Climate change – this is the biggest challenge we face.'[20]
- The United Society of Partners in the Gospel focuses on climate justice and has produced a booklet on advocacy and resources with stories from around the world: 'Faith in a changing climate: stories from the world church, ideas for prayer and action'.[21]
- Tearfund is committed to working with local churches helping poor communities to adapt to the impacts of climate change while speaking out to world leaders to reduce global emissions level.[22]
- The Australian Anglican Board of Mission states that 'the Anglican Communion's Marks of Mission emphasize our commitment to protect, care for and renew life on our planet. Many of ABM's partners are already dealing with the impacts of climate change, among them our closest neighbours.'[23]

(e) *Congregations*: Many congregations are now getting involved with eco-congregation programmes through either Anglican organizations such as the CoE 'Shrinking the Footprint' or ecumenicals such as Eco Church run by Arocha International or interfaith movements such as 'Interfaith Power and Light' in the United States. Here in Africa, the

---

[18] See http://acen.anglicancommunion.org/media/148818/The-World-is-our-Host-FINAL-TEXT.pdf (accessed 23 May 2018).
[19] See https://anglicanalliance.org/advocacy/climate-justice/at they serve (accessed 8 June 2018).
[20] See https://www.christianaid.org.uk/campaigns/climate-change-campaign (accessed 20 May 2018).
[21] See http://www.uspg.org.uk/docstore/175.pdf (accessed 22 April 2018).
[22] See https://www.tearfund.org/about_you/old_campaign_site/climatechange/ (accessed 20 May 2018).
[23] See https://www.abmission.org/pages/climate-change.html (accessed 8 June 2018).

Green Church movement of Diocese of Harare supports the work in Central Africa and partners with the Green Anglicans movement in Southern Africa.

These organizations help congregations to reduce the carbon footprint of the building, electricity, water, paper and look at use of church land. For example in the UK many Anglican churches are among the 5,500 churches which have shifted to green energy.[24]

(f) *Divestment:* Divestment from fossil fuels has been an important part of the response of the Anglican Church. Quite a number of dioceses and provinces have already shifted their money out of fossil fuels.

The Episcopal Church (USA) made a symbolic but very important move of a portion of their church holdings. This shows that use of fossil fuels is a moral issue. They also encouraged individual parishes and dioceses to move funds from coal, oil and gas.[25] It was also an important signal following the United States pulling out of the Paris Agreement that civil society was also able to take steps.

All the dioceses in New Zealand have divested – they are living the reality of the sea-level rise as the province includes Fiji and Polynesia this is one of the most active on climate change. The small island states are the hardest hit in terms of sea-level rise.[26]

The Anglican Church of Southern Africa voted at Synod in September 2016 to divest their reserve funds from fossil fuels.[27] Although there are currently no fossil-free portfolios listed on the Johannesburg Stock Exchange, part of the resolution was to put pressure on investment companies to provide alternative green portfolios. Archbishop Tutu has become one of the faces of the campaign of the NGO 350.org to divest.[28]

The Church of England has chosen a different route, that of shareholder activism, which has had some success. Through a $10 billion fund that finances the church's mission activities, cathedral costs and clergy pensions, the church has been quietly and successfully engaging with European companies in the energy and mining industries for the past few years. BP, BHP Billiton and Royal Dutch Shell have all voluntarily adopted to reveal the climate change impact of their companies.[29] In 2017 the church sponsored a resolution on 'climate risk' disclosure at ExxonMobil's AGM, which was passed in spite of opposition by the company.

---

[24] See https://www.theguardian.com/environment/2018/aug/03/5500-uk-churches-switch-to-renewable-energy (accessed 6 August 2018).
[25] See https://www.theguardian.com/world/2015/jul/03/episcopal-church-fossil-fuel-divestment (accessed 8 June 2018).
[26] See http://coalaction.org.nz/network/350/five-out-of-five-anglican-dioceses-vote-to-divest-from-fossil-fuels (accessed 23 May 2018).
[27] See http://www.greenanglicans.org/the-anglican-church-of-southern-africa-votes-to-divest-from-fossil-fuels/ (accessed 23 May 2018).
[28] See the homepage at https://350.org/
[29] See https://www.pressherald.com/2017/08/04/church-of-england-rallied-investors-in-successful-exxon-climate-fight/ (access 8 June 2018).

In 2017, the Church of England further joined the Environment Agency Pension Fund, the Grantham Institute (at the London School of Economics) and others to launch the Transition Pathway Initiative (TPI), an online tool to assess the progress of companies in the oil and gas industry (as well as other sectors) in preparing for the transition to a low-carbon economy. TPI is supported by asset owners with more than $7 trillion of assets under management. Companies are evaluated based on their management of greenhouse gas emissions.

However in 2018, the Diocese of Oxford, partly inspired by its twinning relationship with the Diocese of Kimberley and Kuruman in South Africa, brought a motion on divestment to General Synod. Their motion called for divestment by 2020 from companies not in line with the Paris Agreement. Although the motion was not successful it laid the way for an amendment which was passed calling on the Church of England to divest from companies not in line with the Paris Agreement by 2023.[30]

(g) *Liturgy:* An important liturgical action for the Anglican Church has been the inclusion of the Season of Creation in the church's liturgical calendar. This is a month-long season when churches preach, pray and teach about issues of the environment and climate change. It enables local speakers to address the issue and for parishioners to make commitments to lifestyle change. At ACC in 2012, provinces were requested to consider the inclusion in their liturgical calendar. The Anglican Church of Southern Africa and the Church of the Province of Central Africa have done so.[31]

Materials have also been widely distributed from the World Council of Churches (known as ' Time for Creation').[32]

In 2017 a partnership was formed between the Anglican Communion Environmental Network (ACEN), the Global Catholic Climate Movement (GCCM), the World Council of Churches and the 'Act Alliance' to promote a Season of Creation together. The Lutheran World Federation (LWF) also joined this alliance in 2018.[33]

(h) *Conferences of the Parties:* Various Anglican leaders have attended COP meeting as part of the NGO engagements: Archbishop Rowan Williams attended Copenhagen (2009); Archbishop Tutu led a rally in Durban (2011); bishops from the Church of England led a 'pilgrimage of hope' to Paris (2017); and Bishop Marc Andrus of the Episcopal Church (USA) attended the COP at Bonn (2018).

(i) *Diocesan and provincial initiatives*: There are many such initiatives around the world doing important work to encourage parishes to take up the challenge in three levels:

- spirituality of care for creation; services on environmental themes; celebration of Season of Creation; world water day; World Environment Day; Earth Day, etc;

---

[30] See https://www.ft.com/content/56291334-8e98-11e8-b639-7680cedcc421 (accessed 6 August 2018).
[31] See http://www.greenanglicans.org/resources/liturgical/ (accessed 5 August 2018).
[32] See https://www.oikoumene.org/en/what-we-do/climate-change/time-for-creation (accessed 9 June 2018).
[33] See the homepage at www.seasonofcreation.org

- local church action – reducing their environmental footprint;
- advocacy on renewable energy, environmental challenges, divestment, etc,

Some excellent examples include:

- Church of South India Department of Ecological Affairs, who celebrate World Environment Day across the country and have a very strong Green Schools movement;[34]
- Anglican Church of Southern Africa, who have successfully mobilized a strong youth movement. They focus on tree planting, local clean ups and organic farming as well as training clergy in theology of creation care;[35]
- Church of England, which has turned its focus on shrinking the footprint of church buildings and reducing carbon footprint as well as use of church land.[36]

Working with Anglicans

Generally Anglicans are committed to ecumenical work and are part of local minister fraternals and local councils of churches. Depending on which end of the church spectrum, evangelical churches will work happily with other evangelical churches, while high churches are happy to work with Catholic churches. It has been interesting to see how with the current pope there is a greater openness to work with Catholic churches. There is generally an openness to work with interfaith groups (though less so among evangelical Anglicans)

Anglicans have tended to have a strong commitment to social justice and care for the environment in terms of its impact on human social justice. We need to learn from our Indigenous brothers and sisters more about the sacredness of the earth and amplify their voices in the communion.

Through the diocesan links, churches have formed relationships with dioceses in other parts of the globe. This means that the issues of climate change in the Global South can be brought into the life of the high-carbon-emitting nations.

However, the Anglican Church is being challenged by the issue of homosexuality which threatens to split the church. The issue is taking up a lot of the time and energy of church leaders. It has divided the church and there is the danger that people will be judged based on where they stand on this issue even if they are discussing environmental issues. There is a tendency to put people in boxes, and teaching on climate change might be ignored if it comes from 'the other side' of the worldwide church.

---

[34] See http://www.csisynod.com/erec.php (accessed 22 May 2018).
[35] See the homepage at http://www.greenanglicans.org/
[36] See http://www.churchcare.co.uk/shrinking-the-footprint (accessed 8 June 2018).

A response to Rachel Mash

Kapya Kaoma[1]

'The Anglican Church's challenge of homosexuality', as Rachel Mash writes, has potential to 'split the church'. Without underestimating this threat, it is clear that the ecological crisis is uniting Anglicans across the globe. Lambeth 1998 and to some extent 2008 may be rebranded as being about homosexuality. But these conferences dedicated equal time to addressing the Anglican fifth mark of Christian mission: 'To strive to safeguard the integrity of creation, and sustain and renew the life of the earth.' Unlike sexuality, climate change knows no sexual orientation – it is a threat that demands communal responses. Land degradation, air and water pollution, clean water campaigns and deforestation are among the many issues that Anglicans are jointly working on.

When we speak of Anglicans, however, there is need to acknowledge that Anglicanism is informed by two distinct traditions – Anglo-Catholicism and Evangelicalism. The Anglican Communion, for example, is a member of the World Council of Churches, as well as the Lausanne Congress. The dual identity and the theological diversity of the Communion enable Anglicans to partner with various Christian traditions on earth care. Mash speaks to some of these initiatives, and in my response, I provide commentary on some of these issues.

Civilization, colonialism, Christianity and the death of nature

Mash makes an important point on what I term 'the death of nature'. She rightly points to the marriage between civilization, colonialism and Christianity in the commodification of nature. Lynn White, Jr's complaint against Christianity seems to fit Mash's observation about missionaries' dualistic dominion theology. Just as nature lost its rights, so did Africans.

---

[1] Kapya Kaoma is Visiting Researcher at Boston University Center for Global Christianity and Mission and Distinguished Visiting Professor at St. John's University in Zambia. Originally from Zambia he is an Anglican pastor and human right activist, noted for his pro-LBRT+ activism.

The growth of industrialization followed the exploitation of Africa's natural goods. In this regard, Mash is right in arguing that these factors distanced Africans from the world of nature. Since civilization was the direct opposite of the African lifeworld, Christianity was an instrument of colonialism and vice versa. Generally, missionaries worked side by side with colonial authorities in their vilification of nature-loving African rituals and customs.

It is nonetheless important to note that some missionaries had great sensitivity to nature. Mash identifies David Livingstone, the London Missionary Society (LMS) missionary, as an example of how three Cs – Christianity, civilization and commerce – led to the fourth C – the conquest of African lands. Yet, his writings were also critical of European civilization that robbed non-humans of their rights. Livingstone upheld the 'duty of a sacred regard to life' by which he opposed mass killings of animals or wanton waste of animal life through 'the ferocious but childlike, abuse of the instruments of destruction [guns]'.[2] To him, 'every form of life' was sacred, thus humanity had a duty to protect non-human life.

This attitude was not limited to Livingstone. Another LMS missionary, Albert Schweitzer, promoted the 'ethics of reverence for life'. Like Livingstone, Schweitzer advocated the rights of animal life. To him, humanity should always try 'as far as possible to refrain from destroying any life, regardless of its particular type'.[3] A similar sensitivity was shared by William Carey (the father of modern missions), whose name is associated with a number of plants in India.[4] In short, not all missionary lenses were ecologically bankrupt.

Land and the challenge of limitless growth

Although Mash attributes the saying on the missionaries' exchange of the Bible with African land to Desmond Tutu, the origin of this saying is still disputed. Nonetheless, it speaks to this injustice of colonialism – land grabs in which the church played an important role. To Africans, however, land is 'an ancestral commons, and not a commodity to be sold'.[5] To this day, landlessness is another driver of environmental degradation since it shifted population density elsewhere. Although churches are

---

[2] David Livingstone, 'Dr. John Kirk, Screw Steamship Pearl at Sea off Madeira', 18 March 1858, in *The Zambesi Doctors: David Livingstone's Letters to John Kirk 1858–1872*, Reginald Foskett (ed.) (Edinburgh: University Press, 1964), 44 (my emphasis).

[3] Albert Schweitzer, 'The Ethics of Reverence for Life', http://www1.chapman.edu/ schweitzer/sch/reading4/html (accessed 16 July 2018). Originally published in *Christendom* 1 (1936), 225–39.

[4] Dave Bookless, 'Jesus is Lord ... of All? Evangelicals, Earth Care and the Scope of the Gospel', in *Creation Care in Christian Mission*, Kapya J. Kaoma (ed.) (Oxford: Regnum Studies in Mission, 2016), 105–20 (106).

[5] Kapya John Kaoma, 'African Religion and Colonial Rebellion: The Contestation of Power in Colonial Zimbabwe's Chimurenga of 1896–1897', *Journal for the Study of Religion* 29:1 (2016), 57–84 (59).

working to resolve this colonial injustice, many mission stations are products of colonial land grabs.

In addition, Mash points to the historical role extractive industries play in distancing Africans from the land. Unfortunately, this process has continued in postcolonial Africa. Whereas colonial hut tax forced many Africans to abandon ancestral homes for cities, the uprooting of Africans continues in the name of development and unemployment. Across sub-Saharan Africa, mining interests overshadow people's claims to ancestral lands. Amidst uncontrolled unemployment and Africa's rapid population growth, millions of Africans live in urban areas or around mountains – contributing to landslides that are frequently claiming lives and creating environmental refugees. Besides, city life is one of the major drivers of pollution, land degradation and consumerism. Unfortunately, consumerism is built on the false premise of limitless growth, although the earth and its goods are limited.

This observation leads to another challenge – population growth and intensive farming. As the continent's population explodes, the need for hybrid seeds and intensive farming grows, compounding the ecological crisis. To resolve this problem, we need 'sustainable living' as opposed to sustainable development which, I argue, shares the myth of limitless growth. Although churches are divided on the issue of family planning,[6] I propose that the church addresses uncontrolled population growth and its implications for earth care.

The birth of eco-Anglicanism

In *The Church in God's Household,* Clive Ayre and Ernst Conradie argue that the ecological crisis has led to the ongoing reformation of Christianity.[7] Christian theologies and ethics are becoming ecological. Mash shows how Anglicanism is undergoing this ecological reformation – Anglican voices on climate change and ecotheologies are growing in number. The Anglicanism defined by sexuality is slowly being redefined as eco-Anglicanism. Anglican ecotheologians include Rowan Williams, Dave Bookless, Sallie McFague, Christopher Wright and Kwok Pui-lan, among many others. These theologians have called for ecologically informed Anglicanism and their efforts are paying off.

---

[6] Kapya J. Kaoma, *God's Family, God's Earth: Christian Ecological Ethics of Ubuntu* (Zomba: University of Malawi Kachere Press, 2013), 164-7.

[7] Clive W. Ayre and Ernst M. Conradie (eds), *The Church in God's Household: Protestant Perspectives on Ecclesiology and Ecology* (Pietermaritzburg: Cluster Publications, 2016).

New Anglican ecological identity

Mash shows that ecological awareness and the responsibility to address the mounting ecological crisis have taken hold of Anglicans – from Africa to Europe to Asia and to South America. Anglican bishops are encouraging creation care activities, while demanding earth-friendly policies in their nations and beyond.

The ecological reformation of the Anglican Communion dates back to the 1968 Lambeth Conference, when bishops called for 'living responsibly to all that God has given us includes caring for the physical world around us'.[8] In 1984 Anglicans adopted earth care as an important mark of Christian mission. Since then, successive Archbishops of Canterbury have advocated Earth care.

In 2009 former Archbishop of Canterbury Rowan Williams called Earth care 'a moral imperative'. As Mash shows, Williams has continued to campaign against climate change across the globe. And although Archbishop Welby's leadership has been challenged by disputes on sexuality, he has consistently advocated creation care and openly called for ecologically friendly policies.

It is clear that addressing climate change is an important issue of global Christian theology. It has also increased inter-religious partnership as people of faith work to influence global and local policies on climate change. Following his predecessor's 2009 *Lambeth Declaration*, Archbishop Welby issued a new interfaith *Lambeth Declaration* (2015) that called on 'the nations of the world urgently to limit the global rise in average temperatures to a maximum of less than 2°C'. Signed by religious leaders of different faiths, both declarations noted that climate change affects the poor the most. While Welby noted 'prayerful solidarity and compassion with victims and survivors of the recent extreme weather in many places around the world',[9] he also called for proactive measures to address global warming.

Ecological reformation has become the magnet of ecumenical earth care initiatives and actions. Whereas churches hold different theological positions on many issues, the ecological crisis has brought the Orthodox Church, World Council of Churches, the Evangelical Lausanne Movement, the Vatican and African Initiated Churches together. It has given birth not only to a liturgical 'Season of Creation',[10] but also to joint statements from global religious leaders. Following Pope Francis's encyclical *Laudato Si'*, Welby and the Ecumenical Patriarch Bartholomew of the Orthodox tradition jointly stated that the Earth 'is a gift to all living creatures and all living things. We must, therefore, ensure that the resources of our planet are – and continue to be – enough for all to live abundant

---

[8] Thabo Makgoba, 'Foreword', in *Creation Care in Christian Mission*, Kapya J. Kaoma (ed.) (Oxford: Regnum Studies in Mission, 2016), xi.
[9] Justin Welby, 'Our Moral Opportunity on Climate Change', https://www.nytimes.com/2017/11/03/opinion/faith-climate-change-justin-welby.html (accessed 3 December 2018).
[10] Ibid.

lives.'¹¹ On 3 November 2015, Patriarch Bartholomew spoke at Lambeth Palace, declaring creation care a 'sacred task and a common vocation'.¹² In 2017 Archbishop Welby called fighting climate change 'an opportunity to find purpose and joy, and to respond to our creator's charge. Reducing the causes of climate change is essential to the life of faith. It is a way to love our neighbour and to steward the gift of creation.'¹³

In Africa, Archbishop Desmond Tutu has emphasized earth care. In *God Has a Dream*, Tutu contrasts African attitudes towards nature with Enlightenment values. He writes,

> When Africans said, 'Oh, don't treat that tree like that, it feels pain', others used to say, 'Ah, they are pre-scientific; they're primitive.' It is wonderful now how we are beginning to discover that it is true – that that the tree does hurt, and if you hurt the tree, in an extraordinary way, you hurt yourself. Every shrub and by extension every creature has the ability to be a burning bush and to offer us an encounter with the transcendent.¹⁴

Archbishop Thabo Makgoba of Cape Town equally highlights earth care as an important aspect of Anglicanism. On Good Friday 2015 in Cape Town, Anglican bishops invited churches to urgently find 'the collective moral voice' in defence of God's creation.¹⁵

Anglican Evangelicals working on earth care in global Evangelicalism

It is important to note that the first Lausanne Congress on World Evangelization has Anglican roots too. Although Mash identifies Billy Graham as the founder, the leading Anglican Evangelical theologian John Stott was the co-founder of the 1974 Lausanne Congress. Stott addressed the ecological crisis as among the issues facing Christianity today as early as 1984 – the same year that Anglicans declared creation care as the fifth mark of Christian mission. In *The Radical Disciple,* Bookless observes, Stott put earth

---

[11] Patriarch Bartholomew and Justin Welby, 'Climate Change and Moral Responsibility', https://www.nytimes.com/2015/06/20/opinion/climate-change-and-moral-responsibility.html (accessed 4 December 2018).

[12] John Bingham, 'Science Alone Cannot Save the Planet, Insists Spiritual Leader of Orthodox Church', 3 November 2015, https://www.telegraph.co.uk/news/religion/11973107/Science-alone-cannot-save-the-planet-insists-spiritual-leader-of-Orthodox-Church.html (accessed 4 December 2018).

[13] Ibid.

[14] Desmond Tutu, *God Has a Dream: A Vision of Hope for our Time* (New York: Doubleday, 2004), 29.

[15] See Makgoba, 'Foreword'; also the Anglican Consultative Council and the Anglican Environmental Network, *The World Is Our Host: A Call to Urgent Action for Climate Justice* (Cape Town, 2015).

care among the 'eight characteristics of Christian discipleship which are often neglected and yet deserve to be taken seriously'.[16]

Eco-Anglicanism introduced by Stott continues to influence global Evangelicalism. While US Evangelicalism has overwhelmingly denied anthropogenic climate change,[17] prominent Anglican Evangelicals have consistently pushed for the acknowledgement of climate change as an evangelical issue. Although David Bookless rightly characterizes *The Lausanne Cape Town 2010* as 'a theological springboard for evangelical involvement in Creation care',[18] English evangelicals such Christopher Wright and David Bookless played an important role in ensuring that creation care is addressed at that conference.

Wright's evangelical theology of creation care is expounded in *The Mission of God*. Like Stott, Wright notes that earth care is an important element of Christian life. But he adds that creation's 'essential relatedness to God' makes nature sacred though not divine.[19] Wright concludes that 'creation care is an urgent issue in today's world'; thus to be indifferent 'is to be either desperately ignorant or irresponsibly callous'.[20] He characterizes climate change denying evangelicals as reading damaged Bibles. Wright writes,

> It is baffling to me that there are so many Christians, including sadly (and especially) those who claim to be evangelicals, for whom this matter of Creation care, or ecological concern and action. The Lordship of Christ over the earth also affects the way we think about the actual places where we and others live.[21]

No doubt, this theological perspective had a lasting effect on Lausanne Cape Town 2010, as well as *Lausanne Global Consultation on Creation Care and the Gospel* in Jamaica in 2012 and other Evangelical region conferences in Africa and South Asia.[22]

Working with Anglicans on creation care

Anglicanism is undergoing a transformation as it relates to Earth care and the impending ecological catastrophe. As Christians, we have an obligation to protect and defend

---

[16] Bookless, 'Jesus is Lord ... of All?', 112.
[17] See Ibid., 105–20.
[18] Ibid., 106.
[19] Christopher J. H. Wright, *The Mission of God: Unlocking the Bible's Grand Narrative* (Downers Grove: Inter-Varsity Press, 2006), 402.
[20] Ibid., 413.
[21] Christopher J. H. Wright, 'The Care of Creation: The Gospel and Our Mission', in *Creation Care in Christian Mission*, Kapya J. Kaoma (ed.) (Oxford: Regnum Studies in Mission, 2016), 183–97.
[22] Creation Care and the Gospel Conference: East and Central Africa, https://www.lausanne.org/gatherings/issue-gathering/creation-care-and-the-gospel-conference-east-and-central-africa (accessed 3 December 2018); Creation Care and the Gospel Conference: South Asia, https://www.lausanne.org/gatherings/creation-care-gospel-conference-south-asia (accessed 4 December 2018).

God's Earth. As Mash shows, Anglican missiological and theological responses to this crisis are encouraging. The ecclesiological structures of global Anglicanism make it possible to work with the Vatican, the World Council of Churches, the Orthodox Church, Independent Churches, other faiths, governments and nations on creation care. The Evangelical wing of Anglicanism allows Anglicans to influence global Evangelicalism. Working with Anglicans on creation care means working with all of God's people, participating in the mission of the Creator God.

Chapter 3.4
Working with Lutheran forms of Christianity

Vítor Westhelle[1]

An eco-conscious Lutheranism

Global climate change is a global problem, yet it does not affect the whole globe in the same manner and evokes different responses. Among these, of particular importance is the response of those who see nature as creation. Thus, what does climate change have to do with religion and for that matter, Lutheranism? It has everything to do with religion and especially Lutheranism. If the Lutheran Reformation came about as a theological response to the plea of the supplicant, then Lutheranism and Lutheran theology cannot but respond to cries of the Earth and the earthlings.

Though Lutheranism has its origins in the Global North, specifically Germany, after five hundred years it now has the majority of its followers in the Global South. Lutheranism, sadly, a little later in the game than the other confessional families, is now realizing that its future lies in the southern hemisphere. Yet, its theology and piety is still largely controlled by the North Atlantic axis, Northern Europe and the United States. The extent of influence the Global South will have in Lutheran theology will be significantly dependent on the impact of climate change that will drastically affect those places where the majority of Lutherans are and will growingly continue to be.

And, because it is precisely in these places that the ecological crisis is at its worst, the stark reality of ecological crisis cannot but be brought to the Lutheran theological agenda. To this end two strategies could be developed and implemented but in distinct ways for those in the southern hemisphere and the ones in the North (who for five hundred years have controlled Lutheranism):

(1) Awaken global Lutheranism to the awareness of the unequal impact of climate change that will affect adversely most of the communion, now in the Global South.

---

[1] Vítor Westhelle (1952–2018) was Professor of Systematic Theology at the Lutheran School of Theology at Chicago and Chair of Luther Research at Faculdades EST, São Leopoldo, Brazil. Born in Brazil and ordained in IECLB, he was a gifted teacher and served in several faculties of theology for the last quarter of a century. His voice has shaped the works of many a theologian over the years.

(2) Call upon Lutheran theology to buttress its piety and practice in the midst of this world, in a manner that responds to the environmental challenge.

A presentation of the Reformer's understanding of the spheres of public responsibility of Christians in the world follows the enhancement and implementation of these two strategies. The theological and ethical development of these spheres is Luther's original contribution to Christian ethics.[2]

This dual approach or strategy, working with the North–South divide, needs to be qualified in two important senses; one is geographic and the other symbolic. Geographically, the Global South is comprised of countries that have been colonized from the sixteenth century through the twentieth century by European and later North American powers. By this criterion, the Global South comprises the geographical places of the world affected by colonialism orchestrated mainly by the North Atlantic axis. But there is a second, symbolic, sense in which the Global South is defined. This does not coincide exactly with the geographical definition, but refers to subaltern people who are more concentrated in the geographical South but are equally present in the geographical North, and is created by race, class and sex, discrimination and exclusion. It is equally true that the reverse is also the case. The symbolic North finds itself in the geographical South. To exemplify with an extreme case, the deforestation of the Amazon is headed by a Brazilian elite of lumber entrepreneurs. The same reproduction of this symbolic divide is as true for Chicago as it is for São Paulo, Sri Lanka, Lagos and Shanghai.

Strategy I

The Lutheran World Federation (LWF), a global communion of churches in the Lutheran tradition (representing 95 per cent of those who claim a Lutheran confessional identity) has been engaged in raising eco-consciousness. Conferences,[3] declarations and resolutions[4] have been issued with increasing intensity during the last forty years by this organization that currently has a Nigerian president and a Chilean general secretary. One of the three themes of the LWF assembly in Namibia in May 2017, 'creation not for sale', speaks to this commitment. But the global communion of Lutherans seems to be unhurried in its efforts towards the same.

---

[2] Although it apparently relied on the medieval conception of the three estates, Luther's theory of the three public orders works in a very different way, as it will be shown.

[3] See, for example, Karen L. Bloomquist (ed.), *God, Creation and Climate Change: Spiritual and Ethical Perspectives* (Geneva: Lutheran World Federation, 2009).

[4] For the declarations and resolutions issued by the LWF since 1977, see https://www.lutheranworld.org/climate-justice/resolutions-statements-climate (accessed 28 March 2018).

The difficulty of raising eco-consciousness among Lutherans has some historical grounds. The Lutheran Reformation laid its most decisive argument against the Roman Church and its practices saying that no action of humans would earn them any merit in God's court. *Vita passiva* became the catch word for this understanding of faith that precludes any human agency in God's election. Grace is a pure gift, completely independent of our doing. As Luther carried his argument to its logical conclusion, in the celebrated *Bondage of the Will*,[5] even the best action carried out would amount to a deadly sin, insofar as it would be an attempt to negotiate one's divine election and earn salvation. Most of the efforts of the Reformer in the early fifteen years of the Reformation movement were concentrated on this particular theological agenda. Although our relationship to God (in *coram deo* perspective) represented only part of the theological task, the other part, our relationship to the world (in *coram mundo* perspective), our *vita activa*, received a short shrift. This one-sided emphasis was further stressed mostly by Lutheran orthodoxy as it developed from the second half of the sixteenth century. As a result, many Lutherans, unaware of these two perspectives in Luther's theology, transpose to our relationship to the world (the *coram mundo* perspective) the passive and the receptive attitude that belongs exclusively to our relationship to God (the *coram deo* perspective).

If the affirmation of the radical freedom God has in choosing the elect is only part of the story, why are Lutherans often associated with quietism and ethical inaction? The explanations can be myriad, the emphasis on the doctrine of justification being one of the reasons. But it could also be explained in part by the eighteenth-century Enlightenment that eclipsed the understanding of the *vita passiva* with the celebration of human accomplishments, leaving Lutheran orthodoxy in a defensive and reactive position.

The epistemic location of most Lutherans in the last five centuries along with Lutheran orthodoxy, and the reading of Luther out of context, can be attributed to the quietism and inaction that seem to be plaguing Lutherans. Lutherans, mainly in Europe and the United States, have been defined by their middle-class position in society, characterized by their conservative belief that the least done will preserve the privileges achieved. This is precisely what is changing with the demographic relocation of the Lutheran population and it is already being reflected in the Lutheran World Federation's pronouncements about the environment since the first assembly held in the Global South, in Dar es Salaam (1977). It is not a coincidence that the first statement by the communion regarding the environment was issued not in Geneva but in the capital of Tanzania. The statement was framed as a question of responsible use of energy in connection to justice and read thus:

---

[5] Martin Luther, *Works*, Jeroslav Pelikan and Helmut T. Lehman (eds), 55 vols (Philadelphia: Muehlenberg and Fortress; Saint Louis: Concordia, 1955–86), 33:15–295. Hereafter cited as *LW* followed by volume and page(s).

'The LWF make provision to include the energy issue within the context of the concern for the root causes of social and economic injustice.'[6]

Deforestation, privatization of freshwater supplies, pharaonic projects, like dams that deprive people of access to the land and destabilize the ecosystem, these, more than the effects of carbon emission, define the most immediate impact of environmental changes to the people in the Global South. It is primarily a question of social and economic justice in all that concerns our relation to the environment.

Global climate change is indeed already making an impact in the lives of people in the Global South with rising sea levels affecting coastal regions and the depletion of the ozone layer that affects people who live in the Tropics unequally, raising, for example, the incidence of skin cancer. However, this is not a front to be prioritized in the work with people in the Global South. As far as consequences of climate change are concerned, long-range planning is the way to go for the Global North but for the Global South the question of justice in the human relationship with the rest of nature here and now takes priority over the consequences of climate change for the coming generations. Hence a dual approach needs to be discerned.

Considering the double aspect of the North–South divide, the geographic and the symbolic, when addressing Lutherans in the Global North, priority should be given to issues concerning climate change as caused by carbon emission that will be drastically felt by the generations to come. When addressing the peoples in the South, what needs to be emphasized is their need for support in the struggle for justice, mainly as political issues that are presently at work, of which the lumber industry, the privatization of water supplies and governmental mega projects are just a few examples. The South does not need to be lectured on questions of carbon emission as much as it needs political support in the struggle with these other ecological factors that are part of our environmental crisis.

The recognition of this dual approach is important, not because carbon emission is inconsequential in the Global South but because there is a need to prioritize among different causes that compromise the environment, for the sake of achieving a certain level of justice.

In this dual approach what is required from Lutherans in the Global North is to be self-critical and look at its own carbon footprint and call for repentance and conversion. An instructive example of this is the 2014 *A Bishops' Letter about the Climate* issued by the Church of Sweden, still the single largest Lutheran church in the world.[7] This letter lifts up the church's confession, 'I have shared in the alienation of the world from God', and takes it to mean that the effects of our irresponsibility affect everyone in the world but also, and this is decisive, that everyone shares responsibility This confession of sin, therefore, does more than calling upon individuals and nations to change their ways according to their peculiar circumstances. It is issued in the name of the Church of

---

[6] See https://www.lutheranworld.org/climate-justice/resolutions-statements-climate (accessed 28 March 2018).
[7] Church of Sweden, *A Bishops' Letter about the Climate* (Uppsala: Ineko, 2014).

Sweden by its bishops, representing a single church in a particular country. This country, Sweden, has taken more measures than most countries in the world to address climate change and is also one of the countries that is likely to be the least affected by the consequences of human-caused climatic change and disasters. Yet, instead of pointing fingers at obvious culprits, the church's letter calls upon the very people it addresses to atone, not for the presumed amount of quantifiable shortcomings of Sweden but instead for being part of humanity that share the same household, the same *oikos*. It explicitly disavows a lack of repentance on account of others faring much worse in climatic awareness and responsibility indexes. It does not point fingers and yet acknowledges that the Global South, having contributed less to the damage, suffers more from the effects of the ecological damage and will increasingly do so.

This first strategy aims at raising awareness of the gravity of the situation, the different approaches to the ecological crisis in the Global North and the Global South, and the unequal impact that the destruction of the environment is causing. This inequality has a greater impact in the part of the world where most Lutherans are now to be found.

Strategy II

The second strategic move is explicitly theological. It goes to the theology of Martin Luther in order to disavow quietism and advocate for active engagement in the healing of the world. The Lutheran quietism and inaction is a misuse of Luther's conception of the *vita passiva*, which pertains exclusively to our relationship to God in receiving the gift of grace. This is only one of the two dimensions of human existence. The other entails our relationship to the world (the *coram mundo* perspective) in which our *vita activa* unfolds itself. The operational concept that regiments the first dimension is faith and grace, in the second it is love and reason.

This distinction between faith and love, grace and reason, is central to the understanding of Luther's ethics. In God we trust and God we fear, but the world is to be loved. Even if Luther is not very consistent in the use of language, strictly speaking, to love God is a category mistake. One can only love that which passes away, what is finite and transient. In this sense, Luther follows the Apostle Paul in his reduction of the double commandment, the love of God and of the neighbour (Mk. 12.29-31 and parallels), to a single one: 'The entire Law is fulfilled in a single decree: "Love your neighbour as yourself"' (Gal. 5.14). The reason for this, both in Paul and in Luther, is to protect faith from being confused with our work, even if it is a work of love. Love belongs to the active life, while faith is exclusively passive. And this active life is lived in the world that is finite and transient. Love, insofar as it belongs to the world, must function in the world with the tools employed in this world. This function engages reason for love to be effective. 'We must use our reason, or else give away to the fanatics,' said Luther in explaining the presence of Christ in the depth of everything created.[8] This love is not a sentiment; it is rational and aims at the achievement of equity.

Love is directed to the created order of things: nature, which the eyes of faith know as creation. When Luther says that 'only faith can see creation',[9] he is affirming that nature in the perspective of faith is a gift. Luther's view of nature as creation results from the belief that the Word became flesh; it is a gift given for the promotion of life. In its materiality it is majestic (*maiestate materiae*[10]). The unique point of Luther's Christology, the affirmation that the finite is capable of the infinite (*finitum capax infiniti*), allows him to interpret the Council of Chalcedon (451 CE) about the union of the two natures to imply that Christ 'is and can be wherever God is and that everything is full of Christ through and through'.[11] And 'you must place this existence of Christ, far beyond things created ... and ... place it as deep in and as near to all created things as God is in them'.[12]

Yet, nature has been damaged by our sin, and we fail to see it as beloved creature of God. Therefore, he can say boldly: 'Not only in the churches, therefore, do we hear ourselves charged with sin. All the fields, yes, almost the entire creation is full of such sermons reminding us of our sin.'[13] Again, as in Paul's letter to the Romans, nature is groaning due to human sinfulness: 'for creation was subjected to futility, not of its own will. ... We know that the whole creation has been groaning in labour pains until now' (Rom. 8. 20, 22).

The word 'ecology', which has been used since the nineteenth century in biology, came to refer to the human interaction with the rest of nature only in the 1950s, indicating that we have crossed a threshold in our relationship with nature. It is the coming into awareness that humans have a problematic relationship to the environment. Therefore, it is not surprising that Luther sees nature revealing our sinful condition. In fact, it is a conclusion Luther arrives at out of his Christology, not by a premature ecological awareness. The Christ that becomes flesh (read nature) for the redemption of the flesh is the One that humans tortured and put to death. Thus the framework for Luther's insight on ecological awareness is his theology of the cross, the cross of Christ and metaphorically the 'cross' of a nature in which Christ is present 'through and through', and also tortured and put to death.

---

[8] *LW* 37: 224.

[9] Martin Luther, *Martin Luthers Werke: Kritische Gesamtausgabe*, 73 vols (Weimar: Herman Böhlaus, 1883–2009), 38:53, 24–5. Hereafter quoted as *WA* followed by volume, page(s), and line(s).

[10] *WA* 39/II: 4, 32–3.

[11] *LW* 37: 218.

[12] *LW* 37: 223. Luther finds in the prophet Jeremiah corroboration for this affirmation in the rhetorical question: 'Do I not fill heaven and earth?' (Jer. 23. 24); *LW* 37: 216.

[13] *WA* 42: 156, 24–7.

Luther and the spheres of public responsibility: Church, politics and economy

According to Luther, amidst such nature we are charged with a threefold responsibility, exercised through institutions in which our public and active life finds its finite expression. Luther used the old medieval understanding of the orders or institutional estates that regulated life: the church (*ecclesia*), government (*politia*) and the household (*oeconomia*). Luther changed the static nature of these institutions by conceiving them as anthropological expressions of a human active life. All of us, as humans, exercise skills that manifest themselves as expressions of one of these public activities. Luther then reads the medieval estates as 'functions', not as stable institutions into which one belongs. These functions are interpreted as human faculties innate to all individuals. Hence everyone has a function in the church, in the government and in the household. Or, to phrase it in another way, the institutions or estates are the resulting factor of the human exercise of the three faculties that define the human. This resonates with what the Indian environmental activist and scientist Vandana Shiva calls 'Earth Democracy', where the freedom of nature and of humans as part of nature functions as a continuum and is lived out in our everyday thoughts and lives.[14]

Even though Luther never defined these anthropological faculties, he was likely relying on the Aristotelian distinction between *theoria*, *praxis* and *poiesis* to account for the grounding of church, government and household, respectively. Unyielding critic of Aristotle that the Reformer was, his criticism concerned the use of the philosopher for strict theological matters: 'Indeed, no one can become a theologian unless one becomes one without Aristotle.'[15] However, on matters that concerned the human relationship to the world, Aristotle and other philosophers 'treat this matter most admirably'.[16] And all these public spheres are encompassed by our relationship to the world and are not strictly theological in the sense of dealing with our relationship to God, including the church. When Luther speaks about church as *ecclesia*, he is referring to a humanly established institution distinguished from community. It belongs to the same class of public spheres as government and household.

Some brief remarks about the two first public realms mentioned above, church and government, are necessary as to their importance for issues concerning the environment. The third public sphere, the household or the economy is the one that pertains directly to our relationship with nature and thus its relevance for a Lutheran approach to ecology.

---

[14] Vandana Shiva, '*Swaraj*: From *Chipko* to *Navdanya*', in *Religion and Ecology,* John Hart (ed.) (Oxford: John Wiley & Sons, 2017), 12.
[15] *LW* 31: 12 (thesis 44).
[16] *WA* 40/III: 203, 24.

First, the church as an earthly institution is established at creation's seventh day, the *Sabbath*.[17] The emphasis here is that the church is to serve the fulfilling of the third commandment, the keeping of the day of rest for the *whole* of creation. In his *Genesis Commentary*, Luther finds the church already in paradise. An interesting image for the church comes when Luther discusses the tree of life and knowledge.[18] He takes this tree as the metaphor for the church, where Adam, Eve and *all* their descendants would come to worship. This tree would be their 'pulpit and altar'.[19] Living in a Christendom regime, it is remarkable that Luther would define *ecclesia* as this institution that belonged to the whole humanity.

Two conclusions follow from this. First, the Reformer, despite his inherited Christendom mentality, would identify the 'church' as a universal phenomenon (Adam and all his descendants). This easily leads to the logical implication that it would include all 'churches' in the world: shamanism, Buddhism, Islam, is Christianity and so on. 'Church' is the name we give to the spaces we elect to live our peace in and to be receptive to whatever the divine is communicating to us. This, in fact, is the definition of the Greek word *theoria*, a receptive attitude of contemplation. And, this is precisely why *theoria* becomes the human faculty through which *ecclesia* comes into being.

Second, this space is not only designed for humans but for the whole of creation that will rest on that day for its own restoration. Among Luther's criticism of the Greek philosophers, or of all philosophy, is that they can deduce the existence of a god, but they fail to recognize this as God, creator of the entire world and what is in it.[20] And, for Luther, what God creates is, of necessity, an expression of God's love: 'The love of God does not find, but creates, that which is pleasing to it.'[21]

Ecclesia should, therefore, be interpreted as 'religion', as a universal endowment of humans seeking to establish stable means of relating to the divine. This is legitimate as long as it is understood as a finite human institution created to open a space in which devotion to the divine and to the whole of creation, as God's work of love, is made possible.

The next sphere is *politia*, government. It not only refers to the state apparatuses but includes also what in modern times is known as civil society. In his Genesis commentary, Luther understands government as an institution to protect and care for the citizens of society, both in terms of defence against infringement of the rights and dignity of all that is by God created, and also to promote the common good.[22] That the latter includes nature beyond humanity can be inferred from the logic of the argument. If God loves

---

[17] *LW* 1: 80-82.

[18] Note that Luther does not distinguish between the tree of life and the tree of good and evil.

[19] *LW* 1: 94–5.

[20] *LW* 34: 138 (theses 13-14).

[21] *LW* 31: 41.

[22] *LW* 1: 104.

what God creates, including humans, then nothing of this creation should be left to pillage, destruction, torture, violations and ultimately death.

Praxis is the human faculty that regiments *politia* that includes all means used to organize our social life. *Praxis*, since Plato, is a noun to describe all human action that does not result in an objective product. In other words, it describes all intersubjective activities we are engaged in in organizing and legislating our social existence. Luther understood *politia* as a necessity, particularly, after Cain's assassination of his brother, according to the Genesis account. In his *Genesis* commentary, Luther identifies the emergence of the political sphere (*politia*) as resulting from Cain's assassination of his brother over the product of their labour offered to God as sacrifice. At least in the *Genesis* commentary, politics comes as a result of human sinfulness.[23] And it is also where corrections to the wrongdoings are to be carried out with the protection of the weak and the punishment of the wrongdoer.

Even if the Reformer did not see non-human nature as part of the most fragile and vulnerable that need protection, this step is also logically implied. To see nature as neighbour who we are called to love, protect and defend through political means available, through legislation, and persecution of abusers and explorers, is implied in Luther's reading of Chalcedon regarding the presence of Christ in all of nature 'through and through'. To understand the objective criteria by which the right of the other, human and non-human alike, is infringed, we need to proceed to the next sphere of public responsibility, the economy or the household.

In the first centuries of the Common Era when Latin became the dominant language in the West two Greek concepts that were kept distinctly apart, *praxis* and *poiesis*, received only one translation encompassing both, namely *actio*. With that, the distinction between production and socialization became fuzzy. *Poiesis*, or labour, is distinct from *praxis*, in that it describes a labour done that entails an objective result, something produced – a chair, a book (thus we have the etymology for 'poetry') or ploughing the land for sowing. But it goes farther; it accounts also for sexual reproduction, the generation of an offspring. As opposed to *praxis*, labour (as *poiesis*) describes the interaction of humans with the rest of nature, including human nature, shaping it, transforming it and bringing about something that was objectively not there before.

The process of exchange that happens between nature and the subject of *poiesis* is mutually transformative. It is not only external nature that is transformed by labour but the subject itself is transformed in the process. Labour implies a metabolism; properties of the object of labour as well as the subject are both transformed. An illustrative example is the second account of creation in Genesis 2. The human that is formed from the humus of the earth is called to be its cultivator, to produce a harvest and feed the same body made from it. This mutually effective relationship is damaged by human sin, in which our investment in the transformation of nature does not return to us in equitable

---

[23] Luther is not very consistent on the emergence of the political sphere. At other places in his writings he finds it as an arrangement of human sociability already in paradise.

proportion but is alienated and thus may be properly described by using the biological notion of metabolism.

This metabolism implied in the relationship between humans and the rest of nature is what Luther had in mind in describing the third public sphere that he called *oeconomia*, which is normally translated as household. At the time of the Reformation the household was the nucleus of the economy now. Indeed, before the Industrial Revolution of the eighteenth century, the household was the locus of the economy, the primary place of production by labour, including the labour of giving birth. By understanding the public spheres in a functional sense, as the expression of the exercise of the human faculties, Luther reintroduced the Greek distinction between praxis or action (*praxis*), on one hand, and labour (*poiesis*), on the other.

Creation: The crucified's presence in nature

The importance of reintroducing this distinction is to discern the factors at interplay in the production process in which the metabolism between the labourer and the external nature takes place, and political processes by which the result of the human intervention in nature is administered and allotted to different social actors. Keeping the two processes distinct allows us to examine the exploration of natural resources as an economic issue that produces destruction and alienation. With this alienation, the metabolic relationship is lost. However, here is where we move to *praxis*, to the political processes that legislate the accumulation of alienated products and their distribution. Hence tackling the issue of economic intervention in the natural world – which is part of all metabolic processes that happen in nature – and the political administration of the result of this intervention is a different matter altogether.

The above discourse of dealing with the economic process in which alienation takes place and creates social injustice is precisely the reason why, in the first strategy, it is necessary to differentiate between the ecological agendas of the North and the South. In the Global South this alienation expresses itself in present injustices that must be addressed and amended, while in the Global North where societies have achieved a certain level of equity for its members the question of justice is addressed taking the future, the generations to come, into consideration.

The Word become flesh; nature, the earth, has more than enough room for all of us. It is important to remember that we are humans only in alliance with and reliance on what is not human in creation. However, in the name of progress and our innate want for more than what is necessary we destroy the very same thing that is our ally and advocate. Our voices drown the voice of the earth that is crying out in various timbres and hues.

How long till we notice? How long till we awaken to this disaster in the wait? As the Earth Charter says, 'The choice is ours: form a global partnership to care for Earth and one another or risk the destruction of ourselves and the diversity of life. ... As never before in history, common destiny beckons us to seek a new beginning. This requires a change of mind and heart.'[24] It is our responsibility to this world.

The quote attributed to Luther that if he knew that the world would end tomorrow he would still plant a tree is possibly apocryphal, but it illustrates well Luther's approach to our responsibility towards the world. That the world would end is something that belongs exclusively to God: we cannot and should not do anything about it. Our responsibility is to love the world although and because it is transient.

It goes without saying that the Lutheran tradition has indeed contributed to the environmental problem. Lutheran teachings are both a boon and a blow in addressing climate change and environmental concerns. As I have explicated above, Luther's take on the spheres of life is a wake-up call to fulfil one's public responsibility, particularly the one concerning explicitly the human relationship with the rest of nature. In fact, there is one nugget of Luther that could cross ecumenical divides and help engage in this common call: Luther's third mode of Christ's presence, which postulates God's presence in the whole of nature. This nature has been created by the Word that resonates in it for as long as it lasts. Ergo, all we do to destroy the environment and all we do not do to prevent it puts us straight alongside of the executioners of Jesus, or else the passive crowd of bystanders.

---

[24] Taken from the Earth Charter, http://earthcharter.org/discover/the-earth-charter/ (accessed 4 April 2018).

A Tanzanian response to Vítor Westhelle

Gwamaka Ephraim Mwankenja[1]

I am sad to learn that Vítor Westhelle, professor of systematic theology at the Lutheran School of Theology at Chicago (LSTC), died on 13 May 2018. Though I did know him personally, it was a great pleasure to get the opportunity to respond to his essay 'Working with Lutheran Forms of Christianity'. In this way I also feel I have lost a colleague.

Westhelle asserts that climate change is a global problem and its impacts are wide, and evokes different responses to it, including a religious one. Thus, he points out the importance of tackling climate change problems from a religious point of view, particularly, from a Lutheran theological perspective. Furthermore, he argues that the future of Lutheranism lies in the Global South because that is where the majority of its members live, despite the fact that Lutheranism has its origin in the Global North and is theologically still largely controlled by the North. Along with this assertion, Westhelle points out that while the Global North is the main cause of climate change the Global South is most affected by its impact. Nevertheless Lutheranism in the North has not yet sufficiently responded to this challenge, perhaps due to its theological quietism. As such, Westhelle believes that Lutheranism is complicit in climate change. Therefore, in order to rectify the past mistakes, Westhelle aims at persuading his readers that climate change should be included in the Lutheran theological agenda.

To this end Westhelle adopts two strategies. The first strategy seeks to raise awareness about the impacts of climate change in a way that is proportional to the two contexts: the Global South and the Global North.

The second strategy is a theological perspective which seeks to address a traditional misuse of Luther's teaching on justification by faith which became the main cause of quietism and ethical inaction in order to advocate an active engagement in addressing ecological destruction.

According to Westhelle, such a dual approach in addressing climate change in the context of North–South divides is defined in two senses: the geographic and the symbolic. The geographic takes into consideration colonial history where the South had been victimized by the North, while the symbolic considers unjust tendencies in the South as well as in the North, despite differences in the degree of the injustices that are perpetrated.

---

[1] Gwamaka Mwankenja is an ordained Minister of the Evangelical Lutheran Church in Tanzania, Konde Diocese. He is the Diocesan Director for Education and Theology.

In terms of the first strategy, as indicated above, this approach serves the purpose of raising awareness of the unequal impacts of environmental destruction along the North–South divide, and how such problems should be addressed respectively.

Westhelle has succeeded in portraying the ecological crisis along North–South divides by presenting examples, even with minimal details, of the impacts of climate change in both the Global North and the Global South. For the North the main example is the problem of carbon emissions, while typical examples in the South include the problems caused by deforestation, the privatization of fresh water supplies and the huge infrastructural projects that destabilize the ecosystem.

Westhelle therefore suggests that the main concern of the North in relation to climate change is carbon emission and its impacts on the future generation, while the Global South is faced with environmental injustices that are of a more political nature. This leads Westhelle to conclude that 'The South does not need to be lectured on questions of carbon emission as much as it needs political support in the struggle with these other ecological factors that are part of our environmental crisis.'

However, Westhelle does not clearly indicate how this political support should be offered. This yields a temptation to define political support in terms of the North supporting the South according to a superior–inferior framework. It should also be noted that the Global South is as guilty as the Global North as far as environmental destruction is concerned despite the fact that it contributes less to the carbon emission. The dependency on wood and charcoal for energy is a typical example of ecological destruction in the African context.

What is important at this particular point in time is a mutual and reciprocal endeavour beyond the North–South divide to address the ecological crisis. This challenge has to be addressed by Lutherans, as one branch of global Christianity.

In terms of the second strategy, Westhelle concentrates on challenging quietism and advocate participation in addressing climate change. He argues that during the early fifteen years of Reformation movement Lutheran orthodoxy put much emphasis on the vertical relationship of humans to God, based on Luther's concept of the *vita passiva*, which explains the human relationship to God in receiving the gift of grace where faith alone is the requirement.

He maintains that this was a misunderstanding of what Luther meant when he affirmed that justification is by faith alone. He uses Luther's expressions of the difference between faith and love on the one hand and grace and reason on the other to challenge a Lutheran misconception concerning justification by faith. He points out the importance of taking the two dimensions of human relatedness, to God (in faith and grace) and relationships to nature or creation (in love and reason). This understanding leads to the perception of the impacts of climate change as resulting from human sinfulness.

In order to augment his thesis that the ecological crisis in general and climate change in particular should be included in the Lutheran theological agenda, Westhelle discusses Luther's understanding of Christian responsibility in and for the world, as expressed by way of Luther's distinction between *ecclesia, politia and oeconomia* as 'anthropological expressions of a human active life'.

He maintains that according to Luther these institutions are not static but are functions in which human skills are exercised, and that all three these institutions are concerned with human relationship to the world.

In the first place Luther defines ecclesia as being inclusive of the whole creation. In the second place, Luther defines *politia or* government not only as a state apparatus but as a civil society also. This is due to its function in relation to the protection of citizens. In addition, the function of *politia*/government is also to protect God's creation. In the third place, according to Luther the concept of *oeconomia* (household) is defined in the context of the relationship between humans and the rest of nature.

Westhelle maintains that Luther distinguished between the two Greek words *poiesis* and *praxis* in order to define the concept of *economia*. While labour or *poiesis* results in objective production, *praxis* refers to 'the political process that legislate the accumulation of the alienated products and their distribution'.

Westhelle maintains that, according to Luther, the distinction between *poiesis* and *praxis* helps us to clearly see the roles of each other and the relationship between the two, especially when Luther uses the analogy of metabolism to imply the relationship between humans and the rest of nature in relation to the public sphere, the *oeconomia* where the two complement each other. He propounds that Luther's theology on spheres of life can serve as a 'wake-up call' to human beings to fulfil their stewardship responsibility towards nature (creation) because it is God's creation, and human beings and the rest of nature are interrelated and interdependent.

This is what Westhelle names as 'an eco-conscious Lutheranism', seeking to advocate that nature has been created by God and that He resonates in it. Therefore, when we destroy the environment or when we fail to protect it from destruction we sin before God who is its creator.

Westhelle has succeeded in portraying the theological pitfalls which caused Lutheranism to remain inactive regarding the impacts of climate change. He rightly points out that 'The extent of influence the global South will have in Lutheran theology will be significantly dependent on the impacts of climate change that will drastically affect those places where the majority of Lutherans are and will growingly continue to be.'

This statement indicates that we are in need of a paradigm shift for doing theology. In a changing climate, a contextual perspective from the Global South needs to be systematically integrated in theology. One example may be the integration of elements of African philosophy, especially regarding the African metaphysical concepts of reality and being.

Chapter 3.5
Working with Reformed forms of Christianity

Nadia Marais[1]

Introduction

Can God forgive us for what we've done to this world? This is a key question in the film *First Reformed* (2017). Michael, a young environmental activist, confronts the minister of the local (Dutch) Reformed congregation in a conversation about his despair about the future. This, Michael explains, is a future into which his child will be born: a future deeply and irrevocably marked by climate change, in which ocean levels will have risen, extreme weather patterns will manifest, and food and water scarcity will become extreme. This future is not a distant future, he reminds the minister; since his own child will live to see the consequences of climate change.[2]

It is worth considering the 'us' of Michael's question. The 'us' of the above-mentioned question may refer to human beings. In the age of the Anthropocene humanity has the power to determine 'the fate of the earth and the future'.[3] The 'us', then, involves the perpetrators of climate change, those living and benefitting from the Anthropocene, the age of 'earth in human hands'.[4] The 'us' may be even more specific; however, 'us' may

---

[1] Nadia Marais is Lecturer in Systematic Theology at the Faculty of Theology, Stellenbosch University, South Africa. Her research focuses on ecological theology, theological anthropology and soteriology with specific reference to human and ecological flourishing. She is an ordained minister in the Dutch Reformed Church of South Africa and a Mandela Rhodes Scholar.

[2] This observation – namely, that the good life for current generations are not necessarily in the best interests of the survival of future generations – is echoed in the work of theologians who write about climate change. Ernst Conradie, for instance, observes that there is what he calls 'tension' between current and future generations: 'Although the impact of climate change is already visible, it will be far more significant in 50 years [*sic*] time. In a probably unprecedented way, our toxic waste products, our use of nuclear energy and our use of fossil fuels will have a direct impact on our grandchildren who will experience the daunting reality of climate change.' See Ernst M. Conradie, 'Confessing Guilt in the Context of Climate Change: Some South African Perspectives', *Scriptura* 103 (2010), 134–52 (145 in particular).

[3] See Michael S. Northcott, *A Political Theology of Climate Change* (Grand Rapids: Eerdmans, 2013), 22.

[4] See the book by the astrobiologist David Grinspoon, with the title *Earth in Human Hands: Shaping Our Planet's Future* (New York: Grand Central, 2016). This title is echoed by Michael Northcott who describes

refer to Christians and the specific contribution of Christianity to climate change.[5] As the South African theologian Ernst Conradie notes, 'Christianity has been as much part of the problem as of the solution.'[6]

The 'us' that is at fault – the 'us' that God needs to forgive – may, however, be applied even *more* particularly to a specific Christian tradition, namely the Reformed tradition. It is one thing to write about what human beings – broadly speaking – may need to change or do (or not do) in order to mitigate climate change. Considering the contribution of Christianity – both the harmful ways of living and thinking that contribute to climate change and possible Christian responses to climate change – is the focus of this volume. But to consider how one works with specifically *Reformed* forms of Christianity when Christian theology and climate change is in view requires careful theological consideration. If the 'us' that this essay must consider is Reformed Christianity, what is the particular theological logic in view here? Which appropriate and inappropriate responses, helpful and destructive theological interpretations, complicities and critiques does the Reformed Christian tradition offer in particular?

This 'us' is quite challenging because it requires asking, as Reformed theologians have often done, what the deeper theological dilemma is that we are faced with when confronted with climate change. How the theological dilemma of climate change is framed necessarily shapes which (Reformed) responses may be offered.

Climate change as theological dilemma

Theology is concerned with climate change, argues Clive Pearson, because '[t]he future well-being of life as we know it in the ecozoic era is seemingly at stake.'[7] As such, climate change should remain a high priority on the agenda of public theology, since no less than the earth itself is at stake, in that '[i]ts fragility and resilience press in upon us.'[8] *Reformed* theology, moreover, is concerned with 'the flourishing of all'.[9] This requires analysis of global warming or climate change as a theological problem,[10] or 'reading the

---

human beings as 'the strongest biological force on earth'. See Michael Northcott, *A Moral Climate: The Ethics of Global Warming* (London: Darton, Longman & Todd, 2007), 12.

[5] See the well-known essay by Lynn White, Jr, 'The Historical Roots of Our Ecological Crisis', *Science* 155 (1967), 1203–7.

[6] Conradie, 'Confessing Guilt', 137.

[7] See Clive Pearson, 'The Purpose and Practice of a Public Theology in a Time of Climate Change', *International Journal of Public Theology* 4 (2010), 356–72 (356).

[8] Ibid., 357.

[9] Ibid., 356, 361.

[10] See the chapter 'Global Warming: A Theological Problem' – in Sallie McFague's *A New Climate for Theology: God, the World, and Global Warming* (Minneapolis: Fortress, 2008), 27–40.

signs of the times'.¹¹ Michael Northcott and Peter Scott explain that the term 'climate change' is 'shorthand for the scientific realization that human industrial activities, especially burning fossil fuels, clearing or burning forests and making cement, are taking place on such a scale that they are changing the earth's climate. This is manifest in more extreme weather, drought, flood, melting ice, rising oceans and strengthening storms ... [It is t]he scientific prediction of momentous change in future atmospheres.'¹²

The Christian faith tradition offers an ambivalent witness with regard to climate change.¹³ Perhaps it may present, at best, 'ambiguous promise' in dealing with climate change.¹⁴ Christianity has contributed conflicting theological perspectives on the environment. Reformed forms of Christianity, in particular, have contributed to no small extent to this array of damaging attitudes and practices. Reformed theology prioritized the salvation of human beings – often salvation from the (old) earth and (physical) bodies – above all else, including the creation of all living beings. James Nash points out that the ecological crisis is also 'a theological-ethical crisis' for Christian traditions.¹⁵ Reformed theology may also offer a particularly Reformed response to climate change by asking the questions: What is the theological problem of climate change? Which specifically theological contribution(s) may assist in analysing climate change?

It may seem obvious that how this question regarding the theological dilemma of climate change is answered will provide an indication of the kind of contribution that Reformed forms of Christianity may make. Arguably, it is already in the framing of this question towards seeking *theological* grounds for the dilemma of climate change that Reformed theology could possibly make a contribution. Such a contribution includes contours of a hermeneutic from which this question may be asked – regarding the theological distortions and justifications that may have contributed to climate change – as it has also asked when faced with Arian ideology, Apartheid and globalization.

---

[11] Clive Pearson not only argues for 'a pressing imperative to discern the signs of the times' that includes dealing with 'the matter of climate change', but concludes that '[t]he rhetoric of global warming, rising sea levels, carbon trading schemes, and various timelines and projections point to the present being a *kairos* moment.' *Kairos* language emphasizes the urgency of theological response to climate change. Indeed, '[t]he current concern for global warming has attracted the language of *Kairos* ... Now climate change forces upon as "a moment of truth and opportunity where our collective response will have far-reaching consequences". What we say and do (and do not do) right now matters.' See Pearson, 'The Purpose and Practice of a Public Theology', 362–3.

[12] See Michael S. Northcott and Peter M. Scott, 'Introduction', in *Systematic Theology and Climate Change: Ecumenical Perspectives,* Michael S. Northcott and Peter M. Scott (eds) (New York: Routledge, 2014), 1–14 (1).

[13] Pearson, 'The Purpose and Practice of a Public Theology', 366–7.

[14] See H. Paul Santmire, *The Travail of Nature: The Ambiguous Ecological Promise of Christian Theology* (Minneapolis: Fortress Press, 1985).

[15] James A. Nash, 'Toward the Ecological Reformation of Christianity', *Interpretation* 50:1 (1996), 5–15.

Moreover, in each of these specific examples Reformed forms of Christianity have also gone beyond analysis, by not only articulating the perceived theological problem[16] but also confessing the Christian faith anew. The (Reformed) response to the theological dilemma in view – whether natural theology,[17] a theology of irreconcilability or a theology of ruthless consumerism – has taken the form of Reformed declarations and confessions of faith, such as the Barmen Declaration (1934), the Belhar Confession (1986) and the Accra Confession (2004). Stated somewhat differently, Reformed theology has opted for confessional language when confronted with systemic violence, particularly in situations where distortions of the gospel have offered theological justifications for such violence. This would typically also include an attempt to grapple not only with God's 'no' but also with God's 'yes' – and therefore also include the attempt to rethink and reformulate the good news of the gospel in a given situation and context.

In Reformed theology references to (the concept of) climate change have recently entered the theological grammar of Reformed confessions.[18] A small example to illustrate this point is the Accra Confession of the World Communion of Reformed Churches (2004), which describes 'the woundedness of creation itself' and the treatment of 'nature as a commodity' more broadly, but also specifically includes the term 'climate change' in its analysis of the theological problem of globalization.[19] It is worth noting that some Reformed forms of Christianity have opted to frame climate change

---

[16] Northcott and Scott describe this, with similar examples, as 'theology of crisis' and theologians such as Karl Barth – primary writer of the Barmen Declaration – as 'theologians of crisis'. Such theologians, they argue, 'called for the bold reassertion of the intellectual decisiveness of Christian confessional doctrines, and the cultural decisiveness of Christian moral and worshipping practices in the face of the crises of the twentieth century'. They argue that 'climate change provides a different and yet parallel crisis, and thereby an opportunity for theological development and the necessity for confession.' See Northcott and Scott, 'Introduction', 3.

[17] The matter of natural theology, and the wariness in the Reformed tradition of natural theology, is a complicated topic for discussion and cannot be dealt with thoroughly enough here. Not only does it require thoroughly contextual interpretations of Reformed dealings with natural theology – such as Karl Barth's opposition to natural theology in Germany, and Jaap Durand's opposition to natural theology in South Africa – but it also opens up the theological debate about the relationship between nature and grace. See Ernst M. Conradie, 'All Theology Is Natural Theology: The Hermeneutic Necessity of Natural Theology?,' *Nederduitse Gereformeerde Teologiese Tydskrif* 52:1&2 (2011), 58–65; 'The Necessity of Natural Theology? In Conversation with John Calvin on the Human Senses,' *Nederduitse Gereformeerde Teologiese Tydskrif* 52:1&2 (2011), 66–82.

[18] See Graham Ward, *How the Light Gets In* (Oxford: Oxford University Press, 2016), 8.

[19] It should be noted, however, that there is just one explicit reference to climate change in Accra – namely, in Article 8 of the Accra Confession, which criticizes 'the drive for profit of transnational corporations [that] have plundered the earth and severely damaged the environment'. Accra points out that '[i]n 1989, one species disappeared each day and by 2000 it was one every hour.' Climate change is listed, among others, as one of the consequences of '[t]he policy of unlimited economic growth among industrialized countries'. See *The Accra Confession: Covenanting for Justice in the Economy and the Earth* (Geneva: World Communion of Reformed Churches, 2004).

in terms of the metaphor of God's covenant with all living beings (Gen. 9.8-12).[20] In this covenant – initiated by God and upheld by God – creation is described as God's household, wherein an 'economy of grace' is operative.[21] And this covenant – which is itself 'a gift of grace' – is 'not for sale on the marketplace'.[22]

Reformed theologians have called for 'an ecological reformation of the Christian tradition', particularly in the wake of the theological complicity of Reformed forms of Christianity in varying degrees – ranging from outright justification of rule over the earth and exploitation of the earth's resources to less outright benefit drawn from global warming by association with countries that 'have a proportionally high per capita emission of greenhouse gases'.[23] What does such an ecological reformation entail?

Ecological reformation of Christian theology

The inadequacy of (traditional) theological traditions to reflect adequately, relevantly, effectively, constructively and faithfully on climate change has been noted by a number of theologians, including James Nash.[24] This includes, in particular, the tendency to frame the earth, or the ecosphere, as 'the scenery or stage for the divine-human drama', and therefore as 'theologically and ethically trivial'.[25] John Calvin, the father of

---

[20] See the excellent article in this regard by Old Testament scholar, Terence E. Fretheim, 'The God of the Flood Story and Natural Disasters', *Calvin Theological Journal* 43 (2008), 21–34. See also his *God and the World: A Relational Theology of Creation* (Nashville: Abingdon, 2005).

[21] WCRC, *The Accra Confession*, Article 20. Ernst Conradie has explored this metaphor – of the earth in God's household – in his inaugural lecture, entitled 'The Earth in God's Economy: Reflections on the Narrative on God's Work', *Scriptura* 97 (2008), 13–36. See also his research project on this topic, entitled *The Earth in God's Economy: Creation, Salvation and Consummation in Ecological Perspective* (Berlin: LIT Verlag, 2015). The notion of an economy of grace is also explored by Douglas M. Meeks, 'The Economy of Grace: Human Dignity in the Market System,' in *God and Human Dignity*, R. Kendall Soulen and Linda Woodhead (eds) (Minneapolis: Fortress Press, 2006), 196–214; Douglas M. Meeks, *God the Economist: The Doctrine of God and Political Economy* (Grand Rapids: Eerdmans, 1989); and Kathryn Tanner, *Economy of Grace* (Minneapolis: Fortress Press, 2005).

[22] WCRC, *The Accra Declaration*, Article 20. In 2017 the theme for the Lutheran World Federation's Assembly echoed exactly this view in the three sub-themes that articulated what they describe as Martin Luther's opposition to ecclesial practices of his time: (1) salvation – not for sale, (2) human beings – not for sale, and (3) creation – not for sale. The overarching theme of this assembly was 'Liberated by God's Grace'. See https://lwfassembly.org/en/liberated-gods-grace (accessed 1 March 2018). See also Hilda P. Koster, 'Tanner's Theology of God's Ongoing Gift-Giving as an Ecological Theology', in *The Gift of Theology: The Contribution of Kathryn Tanner*, Rosemary P. Carbine and Hilda P. Koster (eds) (Minneapolis: Fortress, 2015), 257–85.

[23] Pearson, 'The Purpose and Practice of a Public Theology', 367.

[24] Nash, 'Toward the Ecological Reformation of Christianity', 5. See also Ernst M. Conradie, *Christianity and Ecological Theology: Resources for Further Research* (Stellenbosch: SUN Press, 2007), 65–6.

[25] Nash, 'Toward the Ecological Reformation of Christianity', 6.

Reformed theology, is not named outright here, but it is perhaps worth noting that he describes creation (more than once!) as 'the theatre of God's glory', and it is exactly this metaphor – creation as stage or scene – that is criticized in this regard.[26]

John de Gruchy is not entirely convinced that this particular description of creation by John Calvin is to blame for ecological destruction. He acknowledges that 'Calvinism has sometimes been blamed for encouraging unrestrained human dominion of the earth's resources in fulfilment of what is called the "cultural mandate" (Gen 1.26)' but describes this as 'an unfair judgement' and 'certainly not what Calvin taught'.[27] However, although Nash does not regard Christianity as 'the prime cause of ecological degradation' or as an 'anti-nature faith', he does maintain that the ecological crisis calls for 'the ecological reformation of Christianity'.[28]

The ecological reformation in view here consists of (at least) four marks or signs of 'relevant reform': (1) ecotheological reinterpretations of doctrine; (2) ecological reconception of ethics; (3) ecological expansion of relevant values; and (4) coherence of theology and science.[29] For Nash, these four features may enable us to develop a capacity from our theological traditions to deal with the ecological crisis (and climate change in particular).[30] At the very least this requires much more than only (more) creation theology.[31]

James Nash notes that climate change, in particular, requires of us to consider consequences for not only present neighbours but also future generations – or what he calls 'the extension of justice to future peoples'.[32] The future becomes the site of theodicy once we have to seriously consider ways in which we may 'limit the future consequences of evil'.[33] Christian theological reflection on climate change is therefore deeply shaped by our perceptions and expectations of the future. How we speak about climate change is how we speak about the future.[34] Perhaps this will call for nothing

---

[26] John de Gruchy comes to a somewhat different conclusion than Nash with regard to the implications that such a view of the world may have for environmental responsibility: 'Invariably, in speaking about this, Calvin is calling on us to take delight in God's beautiful handiwork, for though it is not the main source of faith, it provides evidence of God's providential care. God is active in the world. This reminds us that Calvin's vision of a reformed Christianity was one that was world-affirming, not world-denying. ... But Calvin's world-affirming teaching is also a reminder that care for the world, for the created order, or what we now refer to as environmental responsibility, is an essential aspect of human and therefore Christian responsibility.' See John W. de Gruchy, *John Calvin: Christian Humanist and Evangelical Reformer* (Wellington: Lux Verbi.BM, 2009), 121.

[27] Ibid.

[28] Nash, 'Toward the Ecological Reformation of Christianity', 7.

[29] Ibid., 7–14.

[30] Ibid., 15.

[31] Ibid., 7. Nash adds that '[w]hile providing a strong, sustaining foundation for ecological integrity, an ecologically reformed Christian theology can remain loyal to the historical affirmations of the faith' (9).

[32] Nash, 'The Purpose and Practice of a Public Theology', 11.

[33] Conradie, 'The Salvation of the Earth', 130.

[34] Pearson, 'The Purpose and Practice of a Public Theology', 372; Conradie, 'The Salvation of the Earth', 122.

less than an eschatology that can carry the weight of climate change's apocalyptic dimensions.

Here too the Reformed tradition has often been guilty of advocating escapism, with a keen interest in a heavenly future (away from earth) and an accompanying disinterest in this earth's future.[35] If the coming generations are to inherit this future – a future marked by wars over scarce resources, widespread famine and drought, mass migration and climate refugees, and the death of entire species of living beings – then the future is a source of terror. We may work towards mitigating anthropogenic climate change, but the future remains threatening and terrifying if the consequences of climate change appear to be inevitable and unavoidable.[36]

Perhaps there is some pastoral potential in this kind of rhetoric. Perhaps the language of urgency, danger, desperation, despair and threat may yet inspire us – on individual and systemic bases alike – to do something drastic, something extraordinary, about climate change. Perhaps Reformed forms of Christianity can best contribute to such an attempt by speaking the language of guilt, sin, misery and evil.[37] Yet the same Reformed tradition has the theological resources to shape a Christian vision or imagination of an earthed future wherein all living beings flourish.[38] In his overview of Christian responses to climate change Ernst Conradie includes 'the role of apocalyptic forebodings' but also

> a sense of gratitude for the sacred gift of God's good creation, an emphasis on human equality, recognition of God's nourishing providence, the position of the church as an alternative community, a retrieval of virtue ethics, calls for an ethics of stewardship and the message of redemption from threats such as climate change.[39]

---

[35] In a section headed by the question 'What does God's future look like?', Steven Bouma-Prediger offers some reflection into the kind of theological assumptions of contemporary Christians regarding the future: 'Disembodied spirits floating in the clouds. Angels playing harps. The earth destroyed and immortal souls clinging to the bosom of Jesus. These are only a few ideas about the future found in the minds of contemporary Christians.' See Steven Bouma-Prediger, *For the Beauty of the Earth: A Christian Vision for Creation Care* (Grand Rapids: Baker Academic, 2007), 110–16 (110).

[36] For examples of this kind of rhetoric regarding climate change, see Clive Hamilton's *Requiem for a Species: Why We Resist the Truth about Climate Change* (Sydney: Allen & Unwin, 2010) and Michael Novacek's *Terra: Our 100-Million-Year-Old Ecosystem – and the Threats that Now Put it at Risk* (New York: Farrar, Straus & Giroux, 2007).

[37] Yet Conradie *also* calls specifically for more than confession of faith. He argues that 'a Christian confession of guilt – and not just a confession of faith – may be the more appropriate response' to the ecological ambiguity of Christianity, and particularly the destructive consequences of its contempt for the world (*contemptus mundi*). See Conradie, *Christianity and Ecological Theology*, 65.

[38] Conradie, 'Confessing Guilt', 136. Bouma-Prediger describes this future as 'a glorious future – of a renewed heavenly earth, with a crystal-pure river and healing trees; of a gardened city, gates open to receive the riches of the world; of God dwelling with us at home in creation. A world of shalom.' Bouma-Prediger, *For the Beauty of the Earth*, 116.

[39] Conradie, 'Confessing Guilt', 137.

John Calvin himself offers another potential way of speaking theologically about climate change. The very Calvin who is cited for his metaphor of creation as the theatre of God's glory[40] – 'the stage upon which the drama of human salvation is acted out'[41] – wrote about the beauty of the stars, sun, moon, clouds and weather drawing upon a rhetoric of wonder and awe.[42] This is highlighted by a number of Calvin scholars.[43] The theological potential of such 'alphabets of theology' for speaking about climate change is worth exploring more fully.

Astronomy as the alphabet of theology[44]

A recent article in the *New York Times* points out that beauty is leading biologists to rethink evolution, since beauty is often considered redundant to natural selection – and yet 'beauty itself can become an engine of evolution'.[45] It is interesting to note that this view is echoed in a number of recent publications on ecotheology, with such titles as *Toward a Theology of Beauty*,[46] *For the Beauty of the Earth*,[47] *Ravished by Beauty*[48] and *Saving Beauty*.[49]

For John Calvin creation is beautiful.[50] A small indication of his recognition of such beauty is his writings about the stars. For him, the patterns of planets and stars, clouds and weather were a source of wonder. He makes the remarkable observation that 'astronomy is the alphabet of theology'.[51] And he writes about the stars not only in his biblical commentary on the book of Jeremiah but in various biblical commentaries (including his commentaries on Isaiah, Amos, the Psalms and Genesis).

---

[40] See also Susan Schreiner's *The Theatre of His Glory: Nature and the Natural Order in the Thought of John Calvin,* Studies in Historical Theology 3 (Durham: Labyrinth Press, 1991).

[41] See Pearson, 'The Purpose and Practice of a Public Theology', 367.

[42] See Diane M. Yeager, '"Suspended in Wonderment": Beauty, Religious Affections, and Ecological Ethics', *Journal of the Society of Christian Ethics* 35:1 (2015), 121–45.

[43] See, for example, Randall C. Zachmann's *Reconsidering John Calvin* (Cambridge: Cambridge University Press, 2012) and Belden Lane, *Ravished by Beauty: The Surprising Legacy of Reformed Spirituality* (Oxford: Oxford University Press, 2011).

[44] A version of this section, entitled 'Theology for Stargazers? "Astronomy Is the Alphabet of Theology"', was presented at the Symposium on Planetary-Scale Thinking in Astrobiology, Ethics, and Sustainability Studies, which took place from 28 to 30 May 2018 in Stellenbosch, South Africa.

[45] See Ferrish Jabr, 'How Beauty Is Making Scientists Rethink Evolution', *New York Times*, 9 January 2019.

[46] John Navone, *Toward a Theology of Beauty* (Collegeville: Liturgical Press, 1997).

[47] Bouma-Prediger, *For the Beauty of the Earth*.

[48] Lane, *Ravished by Beauty*.

[49] Kathryn Alexander, *Saving Beauty: A Theological Aesthetics of Nature* (Minneapolis: Fortress, 2014).

[50] Bouma-Prediger, *For the Beauty of the Earth*, 178.

[51] In Latin, 'Et certe Astrologia potest merito vocari Alphabetum Theologiae.' This specific reference comes from Calvin's Commentary on Jeremiah 10:2, from the *Ioannis Calvini Opera Omnia: Opera Exegetica Volumen VI*, Nicole Gueunier (ed.) (Geneva: Librairie Droz, 2016), 386–7.

Here we encounter a Calvin interested in astronomy – not only did he 'give a pretty good detailed list of what astrology was doing in the sixteenth century'[52] or hold high regard for what 'astronomers investigate with great labor',[53] but he also appeals to biblical characters, for instance, Moses (who, he thought, would have learned Egyptian astronomy while living in Pharoah's household) and Daniel (who, he thought, would have learned Babylonian astronomy in the Babylonian court), to justify why theologians should study astronomy.[54] In short, Calvin 'thinks we can learn from these studies even if we ourselves cannot do them'.[55]

Randall Zachman has argued in a number of publications[56] that 'the stars, the planets, and the sun ... were an area of passionate interest to Calvin'.[57] The stars teach ordinary believers how to contemplate God's works.[58] Contemplation of the stars is a deeply theological endeavour – and part of Calvin's advice in reflecting on God's work, particularly God's work of creation – that invokes both wonder and terror.[59] Stargazers who take Calvin's advice, argues Zachman, cannot but realize that 'we are both at home and lost in a universe of unimaginable immensity and mystery'.[60]

But why, asks Zachman: 'What was it that Calvin saw in astronomy that he didn't see in, say, botany, or that he didn't see in biology or zoology? ... [W]hy was it astronomy that was the alphabet of theology?'[61] For Calvin the answer to this question lies in the beauty of the heavenly order, and in particular that 'everything is moving ... and yet they do not smash into each other.'[62] He distinguishes between the order of stars and the

---

[52] Zachman, *Reconsidering John Calvin*, 20. Zachman points out that what Calvin refers to as astrology we need to translate as astronomy, because it was astronomy that he had in mind when writing about the stars (16, 20–4). Indeed, 'Calvin is also aware of what he calls "natural astrology"' – and Zachman defines this as a 'Nancy Reagan kind of astrology' – and even though, in Calvin's time, 'all of it was astrology, the study of the stars'; what 'we now call ... astronomy' was called astrology 'in Calvin's day' (16).

[53] Ibid., 22.

[54] Ibid.

[55] Ibid., 17.

[56] See, in particular, Randall C. Zachman, 'The Universe as the Living Image of God: Calvin's Doctrine of Creation Reconsidered', *Concordia Theological Quarterly* 16:4 (1997), 299–312; 'The Generosity of God: The Witness of the Reformed Tradition', *Institute of Reformed Theology Bulletin* 1 (2006), 3–5; 'Contemplating the Living Image of God in Creation', in *Calvin Today: Reformed Theology and the Future of the Church*, Michael Welker, Michael Weinrich and Ulrich Möller (eds) (Edinburgh: T&T Clark, 2011), 33–45; and 'Astronomy is the Alphabet of Theology': Calvin and the Natural Sciences', *Uniting Church Studies: Calvin Quincentenary* 27:1 (2011), 23.

[57] Zachman, *Reconsidering John Calvin*, 6.

[58] Ibid., 28.

[59] L. Serene Jones, 'Glorious Creation, Beautiful Law', in *Feminist and Womanist Essays in Reformed Dogmatics*, Amy Plantinga Pauw and Serene Jones (eds) (Louisville: Westminster John Knox, 2006), 19–39.

[60] Zachman, *Reconsidering John Calvin*, 2.

[61] Ibid., 24. Zachman also mentions, in response to this question, that his wife is a biologist and would say that biology is the alphabet of theology, contra Calvin.

[62] Ibid., 24–5.

order of planets; but his point remains the same: '[y]ou cannot really be a theologian, you cannot spell in theology, unless you study astronomy.'[63]

Calvin's advice, argues Zachman, has profound theological and pastoral implications, for ultimately 'astronomy dislocates us'.[64] The stargazer becomes overwhelmed by 'the immensity of the heavens' – which points beyond itself, to 'the infinity of God' – and thereby cultivates awareness of 'our own nothingness' in the face of this overwhelming infinity.[65] Astronomy, as the alphabet of theology, makes us aware of God's transcendence, and thereby decentres us – for 'what we come to know makes our place in the universe very, very tenuous'.[66] Gazing at the stars, contemplating the stars, reduces us to nothing: it is 'the sense of being snatched outside of yourself in awe and simultaneously being reduced to nothing'.[67]

And so perhaps this is the crucial theological point of Calvin's advice – namely, that astronomy is 'central to theology … because the heavens are the closest image we have of the infinite nature of God'.[68] For John Calvin, God's glory is inscribed in the heavens, in the movement of stars and planets; and the purpose of this inscribed glory is to draw the world into 'taking delight' in God's beautiful work;[69] being 'ravished' by beauty and wonder at the universe's 'beauteous fabric'.[70] The created world thereby becomes both an indication of God's providential care and a testimony to God's beauty.[71] As such, it is not only the stars themselves – as part of the universe and therefore the scope of God's created work – that interest Calvin, but also what they do to their contemplators, as 'teachers of desire'.[72] This desire is 'a garden of the senses', which awakens yearning and longing for God,[73] and the glory of God.[74] Delighting in the night sky above Lake Geneva, he saw God's glory in these flashes of light, 'as if the stars themselves sang his praises with an audible voice'.[75]

In the patterns of stars and planets God's good work is on display. The night sky inspires and shapes our desires, because they overwhelm our small worlds and small ambitions, and thereby draws us towards – or shapes 'a desire toward' – the creative and beautiful God.[76] For Calvin, as for the ecotheologians who write about beauty, beauty in creation echoes the beautiful God. We can read the patterns of such beauty in stars,

---

[63] Ibid., 24.
[64] Ibid., 26.
[65] Ibid., 2.
[66] Ibid., 28.
[67] Ibid., 28–9.
[68] Ibid., 27.
[69] De Gruchy, *John Calvin*, 120–1.
[70] Lane, *Ravished by Beauty*, 58; Zachman, *Reconsidering John Calvin*, 11, 22.
[71] De Gruchy, *John Calvin*, 121; Zachman, *Reconsidering John Calvin*, 26.
[72] Lane, *Ravished by Beauty*, 74.
[73] Ibid., 69.
[74] Ibid., 74.
[75] Zachman, *Reconsidering John Calvin*, 15–16.
[76] Lane, *Ravished by Beauty*, 75.

planets, weather and climate because God's beauty is recognizable in Jesus Christ *and* the created world.⁷⁷ As the South African Reformed theologian John de Gruchy notes,

> [S]urely Calvin, who wrote about the beauty of flowers, the smells that waft around us, the lovely colours and precious metals and stones created for our enjoyment and not just our use, knew this well.⁷⁸

Calvin's argument for why he thinks theologians should study astronomy is 'an appeal to the experience of wonder'.⁷⁹ The experience of being overwhelmed by infinity has the potential to disorder and disrupt our imaginations. All of creation (including sun, moon and stars) are 'bound by great anxiety and held in suspense by a great longing', remarks Calvin in his commentary on Romans 8.⁸⁰ This anxiety and longing can, however, only be remedied by wonder. The wonder that the stars invoke in us – and Calvin's intended rhetorical effect of speaking the language of being 'ravished with wonder before the beauty, majesty, and goodness of God' – is a 'wonder [that] reduces us to nothing'.⁸¹

Conclusion

> Global warming is the earth's judgement on the global market empire, and on the heedless consumption it fosters.⁸²

It should be evident by now that this essay has made no attempt to do theological cartographical work by mapping Reformed approaches to climate change.⁸³ Neither have I suggested ethical or practical responses that Reformed forms of Christianity may

---

[77] De Gruchy, *John Calvin,* 199. John de Gruchy adds that 'Calvin's aesthetic sensibility had its origins in his humanist training ... Yet the concept of beauty is less evident in the *Institutes* than truth and goodness, as in Reformed theology generally ... [because Calvin] feared the seductive power of false beauty, which led to human pretension and away from the true beauty and simplicity of God's glory in creation and redemption ... In short, truth and goodness without beauty lack the power to convince and therefore to save.' De Gruchy, *John Calvin,* 199–201.

[78] Ibid., 203. The quote from Calvin in mind here reads: 'For the little birds that sing, sing of God; the beasts clamor for him; the elements dread him, the mountains echo him, the fountains and flowing waters cast their glances at him, and the grass and flowers laugh before him' (121).

[79] Zachman, *Reconsidering John Calvin,* 20.

[80] Lane, *Ravished by Beauty,* 75.

[81] Zachman, *Reconsidering John Calvin,* 1.

[82] See Northcott, *A Moral Climate,* 12.

[83] For examples of theological exercises in mapping climate change, see Ernst M. Conradie, *Church and Climate Change* (Pietermaritzburg: Cluster Publications, 2008); McFague's *A New Climate for Theology*; Michael S. Northcott and Peter M. Scott, entitled *Systematic Theology and Climate Change: Ecumenical Perspectives*; Ernst M. Conradie, Sigurd Bergmann, Celia Deane-Drummond and Denis Edwards (eds), *Christian Faith and the Earth: Current Paths and Emerging Horizons in Ecotheology* (New York: Bloomsbury T&T Clark, 2014).

offer in the face of the disastrous consequences of climate change. There may very well be fruitful ethical principles and perspectives of Reformed theologians and from the Reformed tradition to consider in this regard, such as the precautionary principle (Wolfgang Huber),[84] the security of expectations (Michael Welker)[85] and hoping on behalf of coming generations (Russel Botman).[86] These all remain options to explore further.

However, let us return to the young environmental activist's question that this essay started off with. Can God forgive us for what we've done to this world? This question is anything but a hypothetical question asked by a fictional character in a film. This is the question of young people like the then fifteen-year old Greta Thunberg, who addressed the Climate Change COP24 Conference in 2018 and reminded the meeting that the burden of climate change will fall onto the shoulders of children and coming generations.[87] The questions raised by and addressed to Christian theology when considering climate change are urgent. Michael's question reminds us, however, that the Reformed tradition itself is a tradition of faith seeking understanding. Questions and questioning, protest and reform is rooted in the very tradition itself.

But Michael's question also illustrates how deeply intertwined 'Christian theology' and 'climate change' are. Perhaps Reformed forms of Christianity may yet yield important fruits in considering climate change theologically. If John Calvin can find an alphabet for theology in the stars, planets and weather – perhaps we too can be taught theological alphabets that articulate our deepest comfort amidst the threats of climate change.

---

[84] Wolfgang Huber, 'After Fukushima: The Precautionary Principle Revisited', *Verbum et Ecclesia* 33:2 (2012), 1–6.
[85] Michael Welker, 'Security of Expectations: Reformulating the Theology of Law and Gospel,' *The Journal of Religion* 66:3 (1986), 237–60.
[86] H. Russel Botman, 'Dread, Hope and the African Dream: An Ecumenical Collage', in *The Kuyper Centre Review (Volume 5): Church and Academy,* Gordon Graham (ed.) (Grand Rapids: Eerdmans, 2015), 1–25.
[87] See Greta Thunberg's full speech on YouTube, entitled 'Greta Thunberg full speech at UN Climate Change COP24 Conference', https://www.youtube.com/watch?v=VFkQSGyeCWg (accessed 10 January 2019).

A response to Nadia Marais

August Corneles Tamawiwy[1]

Reformed theology in creatiocentric perspective

The essay by Nadia Marais is very inspiring and, at the same time, challenging. The point Marais makes is important to show that it is the Reformed tradition that has often been guilty in prioritizing the salvation of human beings above that of all living being, advocating escapism towards a heavenly future and an accompanying disinterest in this earth's future. Hence, the Reformed tradition has also been guilty for encouraging utilitarian anthropocentrism that regards human beings as the centre of creation and views non-human nature as something of purely instrumental value for use by human beings. This perspective emphasizes human power and dominion over nature. It is ironic that by dealing with ecological issues from a Christian perspective we are actually trying to help save ourselves from ourselves.

Responding to this problem, Marais correctly notes that the rhetoric of beauty, wonder and awe in the theological work of John Calvin, who is interested in astronomy, can offer an alphabet for theology in speaking about climate change. Marais asserts that if Calvin can find such an alphabet for theology in the stars, planets and weather, we too can be taught an alphabet that articulates our deepest comfort amidst the threats of climate change. Astronomy, as the alphabet of theology, makes us aware of God's transcendence, and thereby decentres us. This rhetoric of beauty, wonder and awe in creation is important for Reformed theology to address our blind spot, namely, a creatiocentric perspective. In creatiocentric perspective, we are de-centring ourselves as human species to offer a better opportunity 'to become open to God's intentions for humanity rather than to continue humanity's appropriation of a perceived divine justification for theoretical anthropocentrism in, and practical domination of, God's creation'.[2] By doing this, Reformed theology in a creatiocentric sense should move from 'a human monarchic superiority over creation to human integration with creation'.[3]

---

[1] August Corneles Tamawiwy graduated from Boston University School of Theology with a master's in Theology, Philosophy, and Ethics. Originally from Indonesia, he teaches constructive theology and specializes in Christian ethics at the Theological Faculty, Duta Wacana Christian University, Yogyakarta, Indonesia. He also serves as Vicar at the Protestant Church in the Western part of Indonesia (GPIB).
[2] John Hart, *What Are They Saying About Environmental Theology?* (New Jersey: Paulist Press, 2004), 103.
[3] Ibid., 104–5.

An ecological reformation of the Reformed tradition

Reformed theologians have surely called for an ecological reformation of the Christian tradition. Christian soteriology and eschatology should not be inimical to the environment by enchanting Christians with another world, while they believe that God's judgement will destroy this material one. Human beings are not the exclusive recipients of God's salvific work, since God's redemptive work is for the entire natural world as well. Reformed theology is concerned with 'the flourishing of all'. This idea is demonstrated in the sacraments where non-human elements, bread and wine, reveal God's glory and indicate what the eschatological renewal will be like. However, this idea of redemptive work for the entire natural world is also problematic. Why should the Earth need to be 'redeemed'? Why is it 'fallen' just because of the sin of humans? It is rather humans who are fallen, and need to be led away from that consciousness and what precipitated it. The world is God's creation, all 'very good'. It has not all become corrupt because of the act(s) of one species – that would be an extremely anthropocentric view. In the Reformed tradition we have to remember that the new earth is not beyond this material world, but rather the renewal of the earth in its present conditions. Encountering God does not mean that we have to go towards God; instead it is God who comes to us. The redemptive work of Christ reminds us that this material world will not be left as it is because it is subject to God's redemptive plan.[4] This idea should redirect humans back to Earth. In God's redemptive work, we are all, human and non-human, included.

As Sallie McFague puts it, 'if justice means, most basically, fairness, then ecology and justice are inextricably intertwined, for on a finite planet with limited resources to support its many different kinds of beings, both human and nonhuman, sharing fairly is an issue of the highest priority.'[5] If the most basic meaning of justice is fairness, then justice means sharing the limited resources of our common space and recognizing that all things in our ecosystem have rights. Rights do not belong only to humankind and to nations, but also to other beings in creation. There are human and social rights, what we call global rights, but there are also ecological and cosmic rights.[6] To fight socio-ecological injustice, Reformed tradition should now realize that 'All things in nature are citizens, have rights, and deserve respect and reverence, ... today, the common good is not exclusively human; it is the common good of all nature.'[7]

---

[4] Benjamin J. Burkholder, 'Christological Foundations for an Ecological Ethic: Learning from Bonhoeffer', *Scottish Journal of Theology* 66:3 (2013), 347.

[5] Sallie McFague, *The Body of God: An Ecological Theology* (Minneapolis: Fortress, 1993), 5.

[6] Hart, *What Are They Saying About Environmental Theology?*, 91.

[7] Ibid., 92.

Deep listening to the deep *demos*

To respond to socio-ecological injustice, what Reformed theology needs is not only 'the preferential option for the poor' in the anthropocentric idea of the poor, but the poor in Jacques Rancière's sense, that is, the excluded voices because of our false sense of who has a voice. Non-humans are the poor since they lack a voice. Following Rancière, I have called the non-human poor the 'deep *demos*'.[8] According to Rancière, politics is about the recognition of those who are considered full members of society with an equal share of parts and those who are excluded or those who have a part only in 'a part of no part'. Rancière used three classic group of Aristotle: *oligoi* (the wealth), *aristoi* (the virtuous) and *demos* (the people who demand freedom). The *demos* is a false count because the *demos*' freedom is only because it lacks the other value of the *oligoi* and *aristoi*. Both of these, by virtue of possessing the qualities that the *demos* lack – that is freedom – make up what Rancière calls, the rich. The *demos* then are the poor, those whose voice is merely a noise.

By using Rancière's idea as my framework to evaluate the idea of socio-ecological justice, I suspect that the idea of justice in the human perspective tends to exclude the non-human voices. The idea of which voices 'make sense' is limited only to our anthropocentric order. The non-human voice is now merely a noise 'of voices expressing pleasure or pain', not 'the expression of a logos, which not only is the inventory of a power struggle but constitutes a demonstration of their right, a manifestation of what is just that can be understood by the other party', that is the party of human beings. The non-humans then become the *demos*. I call them, deep *demos*. The notion of deep *demos* is my contribution to understanding nature as the excluded political subject. This is inspired by the notion of 'deep incarnation' (Niels Henrik Gregersen), 'deep ecology' (Arne Naess) and 'deep history' (Daniel Lord Smail). There is a connection between them extending beyond the adjective 'deep' that also includes the attempt to overcome the principal contrast between 'man' and 'nature'. If the *demos* are the poor whose voices are merely a noise because they lack rights, then non-human others are deep *demos* as a political subject struggling for its own freedom. The voices, 'the cries of the earth',[9] are not actually missing. They have always been already there, but we misheard them. These voices represent the suffering in which Christ becomes incarnate, the deep suffering of Christ.[10] All of the piercing cries of the non-human creations have only one purpose: they yearn to be heard.

Sallie McFague contrasts two different 'eyes' to see the natural world, namely, the arrogant eye and the loving eye. The arrogant eye is the oppressors' eye. Oppressors

---

[8] See Jacques Rancière, *Disagreement: Politics and Philosophy* (Minneapolis: University of Minnesota, 1999), 22–9.

[9] Leonardo Boff, *Cry of the Earth, Cry of the Poor* (Maryknoll: Orbis, 1997).

[10] Niels Henrik Gregersen, 'Cur Deus Caro: Jesus and the Cosmos Story', *Theology and Science* 11:4 (2013), 370–93 (386).

use an arrogant eye to manipulate, objectify and exploit the natural world. The loving eye, on the other hand, is the eye of the second naïveté, to help us embrace intimacy while recognizing difference.[11] McFague believes that the loving eye needs detachment in order to see difference or, more precisely, the uniqueness of the other. I couldn't agree more with McFague. However, even when we have already trained our loving eye to see the uniqueness of the other, we often don't really understand them. We think that we already care, but it turns out that we only care about ourselves. Here I want to move beyond Marais's essay to say that our Reformed tradition should put more emphasis on listening to creation. Gilbert C. Meilaender argues that

> An ethics of virtue is dominated by the eye, by metaphors of sight and vision. To know what traits of character qualify as virtues we must *see* our world and human nature rightly. To *see* rightly, in turn, requires that we have the virtues. Virtue enhances *vision*; vice darkens and finally *blinds*.[12]

My suspicion is that we, Reformed theologians, have underappreciated the importance of listening to nature. It is not hard to see (read: listen) why. Like McFague, Meilaender argues that when it comes to communication the eye is very important in Western culture. The eye communicates whether we are really present or not. In Indonesia, by contrast, looking directly into the eyes of people who are older than oneself is a sign of disrespect. We are dishonouring them. It is worse if the elder to whom we are talking has actually been angry with us. By looking down to the earth, we are practising repentance, telling them with our body language that we apologize, while, at the same time, still honouring them.

Let me offer another analogy about seeing and listening. In the process of reading, one is not merely seeing the words with one's eyes and understanding the reading. One needs to listen to inner voices, who read the words one sees. In reading one might not hear anything, but that it is just because one is not listening. How many times does one find that one has been skipping lines because one is merely looking at the words without really listening to the inner voices that are doing the reading?

Listening, in conflict transformation, according to Thomas W. Porter, is 'an art, a spiritual practice'.[13] It is the key to all conflict transformation. He believes that 'Listening acknowledges and honours the other's uniqueness'.[14] By mentioning Jonathan Sacks, he argues that even in biblical Hebrew, there is no word that means 'to obey' because 'it uses the word *shema*, which means to hear, to understand and to respond'.[15] The idea

---

[11] Sallie McFague, *Super, Natural Christians: How We Should Love Nature* (Minneapolis: Fortress, 1997), 116.

[12] Gilbert Meilaender, *The Theory and Practice of Virtue* (Notre Dame: University of Notre Dame, 1984), 17 (italics in original).

[13] Thomas W. Porter, *The Spirit and Art of Conflict Transformation: Creating a Culture of Just Peace* (Nashville: Upper Room Books, 2010), 40.

[14] Ibid., 41.

[15] Ibid. (italics in original).

of listening in conflict transformation is important in considering how to listen to the unheard voices, the deep *demos*. If Ellen Bernstein develops the idea of deep seeing as the practice of seeing with the light of our soul,[16] I argue that we also need a kind of 'deep listening'. To listen is to include not only our ears, but also our eyes and heart. In the analogy of reading, we use all of our being to understand the reading. This is the importance of listening, the deep listening, to listen to the unheard voices of the deep *demos*.

In listening to the deep *demos* we not only need the eyes to see with attentive compassion, as McFague and Meilaender argue, but also need ears, and a heart, to listen with empathy, authenticity, curiosity and caring. We need to listen beneath and beyond the voices we have already heard, to hear the earth's cries. To do that, we need to expand our limits. In deep listening, we will realize how quick and easy profits ignore the cost of the environmental damage caused by human selfishness.[17] Attending to deep listening is how we can extend justice to future peoples, as Marais suggests. Whenever we do damage to nature, we will hear our future generations, those who will come after us, retroactively crying because of us, disappointed with us because of our irresponsible actions today. Therefore, we have to listen in order to limit the future consequences of evil.

Deep listening demands from us to enter into the chaos of another.[18] Not stopping at the limit of listening to the crying of human suffering, but going beyond that, transcending limits to listen to the cries of non-human suffering. We need deep listening to really listen to something beyond what we regularly hear, beyond human voices. Opening our ears, eyes and heart now means opening our boundaries, to make room for something beyond, something that could surprise us. When the boundaries are opened, we will arrive at what Richard Rohr calls a liminal or a sacred space.[19] In that very space, we will become aware of the limits of our own voices in order to be ready to welcome other voices, the crying of the earth. To listen to Christ who suffers with us and becomes incarnate in the suffering of all creation is to listen to the cry of the earth: 'Why have you forsaken me?' (Mt. 27.46).

---

[16] Ellen Bernstein, *The Splendor of Creation: A Biblical Ecology* (Cleveland: Pilgrim, 2005), 13–14.
[17] Pope Francis, *Laudato Si': On Care for Our Common Home* (Vatican City: Encyclical Letter, 2015).
[18] Here, I compare listening with mercy, which is defined by Jesuit Father, James Keenan as quoted in: Meghan J. Clark, 'The Examined Life: Mercy in Chaos', *U.S. Catholic* 81:4 (2016), 8.
[19] Richard Rohr, 'Grieving as Sacred Space: How These Anxious and Ambiguous Days Might Offer up the Most Holy of Gifts', *Sojourners Magazine* 31:1 (2002), 21–2.

Chapter 3.6
Working with Anabaptist forms of Christianity

Nathanael L. Inglis[1]

Anabaptist forms of Christianity: A diversity of traditions

Anabaptist forms of Christianity include diverse families of traditions such as Mennonites, Amish, Brethren and Hutterites, many of whom look back to the sixteenth-century Radical Reformation as their point of origin. But simply distinguishing between these broad traditions does not fully account for the rich diversity of Anabaptism today. Within and across these families, there is a spectrum of life and practice, from sectarian, Old Order groups to ecumenical and politically engaged mainline denominational groups. Moreover, while many Anabaptists live in North America, there are also Anabaptists communities throughout Central and South America, as well as in Asia, Africa and Europe. For the purposes of this essay, the focus will remain primarily on North American Anabaptism, and the most relevant distinction will not be between the various denominational families like Mennonites or Brethren, but the degree to which these various groups have acculturated to the dominant social, cultural, economic or political norms of North American societies.

Understanding three common Anabaptist values

Despite the diversity in North American Anabaptism, many Anabaptists hold several core theological values in common. When considering climate change, three values that deserve attention are non-conformity, nonviolence and community. This section will briefly introduce these themes as they are understood in non-acculturated, Old

---

[1] Nathanael L. Inglis is Assistant Professor of Theological Studies at Bethany Theological Seminary (Richmond, Indiana), a seminary affiliated with the Church of the Brethren. He teaches and writes on ecological theology and environmental ethics from an Anabaptist perspective.

Order communities and how they have been adapted by more acculturated Anabaptist denominations.

The first value of non-conformity describes a variety of attitudes or practices among Anabaptist communities that shape a 'cautious social distance' to their surrounding culture.[2] Historically, non-conformity was rooted in a two kingdoms theology by which Anabaptists understood themselves to be in the world but not of the world. Many Amish communities continue non-conformity today through a variety of customs, like living in geographically isolated communities, educating children in private religious schools and avoiding some modern conveniences. Each of these is a way in which Amish communities seek to maintain a cultural and theological non-conformity from the influences of modern society.[3] While the particular characteristics of non-conformity vary widely today, in all its forms it is a selective separation from mainstream society.

Perhaps the most distinctive and enduring practice of non-conformity is plain dress. Even for Anabaptist groups that more or less embraced modern culture, traditional clothing was one of the last vestiges of non-conformity to remain. For instance, by the late nineteenth century, the rapidly acculturating Church of the Brethren still understood plain dress to be a maker of non-conformity, but the underlying rationale – that it was an external marker of Brethren unity, humility and separation from mainstream society – was largely forgotten. Eventually they abandoned any real notion of separation for a more culturally accommodating value of 'simple living'.[4]

Like non-conformity, nonviolence is a second and closely related value that is shared among Anabaptist communities. In many ways, some understanding of nonviolence or pacifism is the primary way that Anabaptists express non-conformity in a society that they observe to be perpetually engaged in conflict.[5] Traditionally, nonviolence was interpreted through the lens of non-resistance: believing that Christians can most effectively bear witness to peace by not participating in a violent system.[6]

Non-resistance is an ethic that seeks to take Jesus's teaching in the Sermon on the Mount to heart: to not resist an evildoer, turn the other cheek and love one's enemies.[7] Most conspicuously, non-resistance informs Anabaptist conscientious objection to serving in the military, but in a broader sense, non-resistant Anabaptists often disengage from a society that they see as irredeemable.[8] Through non-resistance, Anabaptists have

---

[2] Leo Dreidger and Donald B. Kraybill, *Mennonite Peacemaking: From Quietism to Activism* (Scottdale: Herald Press, 1994), 49.

[3] Donald B. Kraybill, *The Riddle of Amish Culture* (Baltimore: Johns Hopkins University Press, 2001), 44–6.

[4] Carl F. Bowman, *Brethren Society: The Cultural Transformation of a 'Peculiar People'* (Baltimore: Johns Hopkins University Press, 1995), 114–16, 344–9.

[5] Ibid., 349.

[6] Driedger and Kraybill, *Mennonite Peacemaking*, 75.

[7] Mt. 5.38-48.

[8] John R. Burkholder, 'Can We Make Sense of a Mennonite Peace Theology?', in *Mennonite Peace Theology: A Panorama of Types,* John R. Burkholder and Barbara N. Gingerich (eds) (Akron: Mennonite Central Committee Peace Office, 1991), 4–9 (6).

attempted to strike a tenuous balance between divine and human authority. Historically, they tended to obey state laws as long as they did not violate God's laws, but at the same time, they also refrained from direct participation in political life.[9] However, even in their most traditional forms, non-resistance and non-conformity have always had a variety of interpretations based on the needs and the interests of local Anabaptist communities. While some non-acculturated Anabaptists may refuse to swear oaths, serve on juries or hold public office, they are more likely to pay taxes and vote, especially in local elections and on issues that directly affect their communities.[10]

While non-resistance is a part of the theological inheritance of many contemporary Anabaptist churches, since the mid-twentieth century other forms of Anabaptist nonviolence have taken root that are more compatible with social engagement.[11] One early voice in this movement towards greater social involvement was Gordon Kaufman, who helped to reshape the Mennonite discourse about the church's mission. He rejected the long-held notion among some Mennonites that being a faithful disciple of Jesus necessitated separation from secular society and withdrawal from political life. Instead he argued that love does not retreat from an evil situation, but enters into it in order to redeem it.[12] His central concern was to affirm the practice of non-resistance, but in a way that expands the focus of Christian love beyond the individual to the well-being of society as a whole. In his later work, Kaufman extends his notion of Christian social responsibility to include ecology. He argues that the causes of climate change, which are threatening the very viability of life on Earth, should be the fundamental theological and ethical concern for Christians today.[13] Kaufman was one of a growing number of Anabaptists who ushered in a paradigm shift from socially disengaged non-resistance to socially engaged peacemaking.[14]

Today there are many Anabaptists perspectives on nonviolence: from those who continue to uphold a traditional understanding of non-resistance to those who are involved in peacebuilding efforts. Some Mennonites and Brethren, for instance, work with the World Council of Churches, and Anabaptists of all walks of life are deeply committed to volunteer work related to disaster relief and development.[15] These initiatives are important extensions of the Anabaptist peace witness beyond its narrow historical focus on pacifism and conscientious objection. However, when it comes to climate change,

---

[9] Calvin Redekop, *Mennonite Society* (Baltimore: Johns Hopkins University Press, 1989), 218.
[10] John A. Hostetler, *Amish Society* (Baltimore: Johns Hopkins University Press, 1993), 256–7; Redekop, *Mennonite Society*, 226.
[11] See Burkholder and Gingerich, *Mennonite Peace Theology*.
[12] Gordon D. Kaufman, *Nonresistance and Responsibility and Other Mennonite Essays* (Newton: Faith and Life Press, 1979), 64–5.
[13] Gordon D. Kaufman, *In the Beginning ... Creativity* (Minneapolis: Fortress, 2004), 38.
[14] See Driedger and Kraybill, *Mennonite Peacemaking*.
[15] See, for instance, Fernando Enns, Scott Holland and Ann K. Riggs (eds), *Seeking Cultures of Peace: A Peace Church Conversation* (Telford: Cascadia Publishing House, 2004); and Redekop, *Mennonite Society*, 250–4.

Anabaptists in North America face systemic forms of violence within which they are already entangled. Although benefitting from the causes of climate change while denouncing its consequences is not a uniquely Anabaptist problem in North America, if Anabaptists are to continue to take non-conformity and nonviolence seriously, it will be necessary to consider the systemic dimensions of these values as well.

The third value that is perhaps most threatened by the gravitational pull of North American society is the prioritization of the community over the individual. Like the other two values, the Anabaptist understanding of community has many gradations. In their most traditional forms, Anabaptist groups intentionally create conditions of interdependence and mutual support among their members through service to one another.[16] The Hutterites, for instance, hold property in common, and some non-acculturated Anabaptist communities have a ban to excommunicate members who fail to live up to the community's shared standards.[17] Individuals enter into the community voluntarily, but with the awareness that each person is responsible for the well-being of all others.[18]

In highly individualized North American cultures, however, this community-based mutualism is a value that has lost its obvious purpose in all but the most non-acculturated groups. As John Eicher observes in his study of Iowa Mennonite farmers, the shift in farming from a way of life to a business has undermined the role that land traditionally played as a place for communal labour and interdependence. With increasing specialization, mechanization and expansion of farming operations, not only is there less need for collective human labour, but in the agribusiness model, neighbours are now considered to be competitors. Eicher quotes one Mennonite farmer who wonders whether modern farming practices were a divine test of Anabaptists' resolve. But if that is true, the farmer noted, 'we've failed. And it's possible now that we don't need each other ... so our Mennonite communities ... don't work together like we used to.'[19]

Another factor affecting the decline of traditional Anabaptist communities is a significant demographic shift during the second half of the twentieth century among Anabaptists from rural areas to cities and suburbs. As ecclesial communities become increasingly disembedded from geographic communities, some Anabaptists have had to reimagine community beyond the boundaries of church membership to include their non-Anabaptist neighbours. As a result, Anabaptists expanded their service to others from an internal focus on other church members to wider social initiatives.[20] Overall,

---

[16] Robert Friedmann, *The Theology of Anabaptism: An Interpretation* (Scottdale: Herald Press, 1973), 61–74.

[17] Hostetler, *Hutterite Society*, 146–7; Hostetler, *Amish Society*, 85–7.

[18] Harold E. Bauman, 'Forms of Covenant Community', in *Kingdom, Cross and Community: Essays on Mennonite Themes in Honor of Guy F. Hershberger*, John R. Burkholder and Calvin Redekop (eds) (Scottdale: Herald Press, 1976), 123–4.

[19] John Eicher, '"Every family on their own"?: Iowa's Mennonite Farm Communities and the 1980's Farm Crisis', *Journal of Mennonite Studies* 35 (2017), 75–96 (83).

[20] Joseph Smucker, 'Religious Community and Individualism: Conceptual Adaptations by One Group of Mennonites', *Journal for the Scientific Study of Religion* 25:3 (1986), 273–91 (277).

these trends combined to create a feedback loop of increasing acculturation, especially among North American Mennonites and Brethren.

Non-conformity, nonviolence and community-focused ethics are radical, countercultural values that have led individuals and groups to maintain incredible resolve in the face of adversity, to form resilient subcultures and to respond to persecution in ways that strengthened their faith and their communities. When confronted with the reality of climate change, however, it becomes apparent that without a systemic vision, even well-intentioned people can participate in harmful practices towards the climate and other human beings without realizing it. The moral consequences of a community's way of life have less to do with their theological ideals, their intentions or even their actions than with the conditions of the society they live in.[21] The remainder of this essay will therefore consider challenges and possibilities for Anabaptists and for other Christians who seek to work with them when applying their values to a systemic problem like climate change.

Reimagining non-conformity for a persecuted people who are now privileged

It is important to note that these distinctive values of non-conformity, nonviolence and community were not created in a historical vacuum. Early Anabaptists were concerned about restoring a primitive Christianity based on living out the moral teachings of Jesus, but their radical and sometimes illegal religious practices, like adult baptism, made them subject to persecution. Many Anabaptists share founding narratives of fleeing religious repression as exiles and refugees.[22] For some groups that immigrated to Pennsylvania in the late seventeenth and early eighteenth centuries, this is now a distant memory, but for others, such as the Mennonites who emigrated from Russia to Canada and the United States in the twentieth century, the history of persecution is much more recent. Even in North America, Anabaptists communities have at times felt oppressed by the power of the state – the most notable example being military conscription in times of war.

Yet, despite their origins rooted in persecution and exile, there are very few Anabaptist communities in North America today that are involuntarily on the margins of society. Whether they recognize it or not, the reality is that acculturated and Old Order Anabaptists alike share the advantages of citizenship in liberal democracies and benefit economically from capitalist economies and global trade. As predominantly

---

[21] Héctor Samour, 'The Concept of Common Evil and the Critique of a Civilization of Capital', in *A Grammar of Justice: The Legacy of Ignacio Ellacuría*, J. Matthew Ashley, Kevin F. Burke, SJ and Rodolfo Cardenal, SJ (eds) (Maryknoll: Orbis, 2014), 205–13 (209).

[22] See, for example, Thieleman J. van Braght, *The Bloody Theater, Or, Martyr's Mirror*, 15th edn (Scottdale: Herald Press, 1987).

white, economically secure and Christian, the majority of North American Anabaptists can today be counted among the privileged, not the persecuted or oppressed.

The shift among North American Anabaptists from being persecuted to being privileged changes the context of their ethics. Cynthia Moe-Lobeda explains that structural injustices are characterized by a 'paradox of privilege'. They are relatively invisible to those who benefit from them, and they are unchanged by the virtue or the vice of individuals within the system. For instance, she explains that as a citizen of the United States, 'I belong to a group that "has an oppressive relationship with" other groups without being "an oppressive person who behaves in oppressive ways".'[23] This paradox that Moe-Lobeda describes lies at the heart of the ethical tension in North American Anabaptist ethics as well.

It is all too easy for Anabaptist communities to justify living within an economically exploitative and ecologically destructive social system and even benefitting from it as long as they are not forced to act personally against their consciences. Non-acculturated forms of Anabaptism have little incentive to change social structures and may even believe that attempting to do so is futile, since the world is corrupted by sin. Acculturated Anabaptists can have even less critical distance from social norms and customs, and their interpretation of non-resistance as simple living reduces a communal ethical response to a matter of individual choice. While both of these options may be effectively countercultural, on their own they do not have the critical consciousness to be culturally transformative.

For example, when Anabaptists arrived in North America as refugees fleeing religious persecution, they often sought and received privileges like exemption from military service, religious freedom and land. But their ability to settle freely on the land often came on the heels of the displacement of Indigenous communities. In other words, the quid pro quo of Anabaptist religious freedom in North America was cooperation with expansionist government agendas to displace Indigenous peoples and to secure frontiers through agricultural development. The bargain between Anabaptists and the US and Canadian governments had disastrous consequences for both Indigenous peoples and for the land itself. In recounting his childhood on a homestead in Montana during the 1930s, Calvin Redekop recalls the whole community agreeing that the Dust Bowl must have been God's punishment for their disobedience. But what he now recognizes is that it

> was not God's punishment for our spiritual misdeeds; rather, it was the result of terrible sins committed by my parents' generation. They had not only benefited by taking free land from the dispossessed Assiniboine and Sioux Indians, but also, with

---

[23] Cynthia D. Moe-Lobeda, *Resisting Structural Evil: Love as Ecological-Economic Vocation* (Minneapolis: Fortress, 2013), 62.

plows and tractors, destroyed forever the terribly sensitive several-inch membrane of plant and animal life that had maintained the prairies for thousands of years.[24]

Joseph Wiebe's study of Anabaptist settler colonialism in Canada offers another example. In Manitoba, the Canadian government settled Mennonite homesteaders on land that was already claimed and occupied by Indigenous Métis communities. Yet the most important point in Wiebe's history is that the Mennonites were not unwitting accomplices of the Canadian colonial project. Instead, he documents how the Mennonite settlers were aware, even before they left Russia, that they were colonizing a land that was not empty.

One of the challenges of structural violence is that individuals and communities can be oppressed by one form of violence, while simultaneously benefitting from another.[25] In the case of these Mennonite settlers, they were at once both religious refugees from Russia and colonizers of Indigenous land. But in their new Canadian context, the relative status of the Mennonite settlers changed. Wiebe notes, 'It is one of the ironies of Canadian democracy that it increased the religious freedom enjoyed by immigrants like the Mennonites by diminishing Indigenous sovereignty.'[26]

These are just two examples of a pervasive history of settler colonialism among Anabaptists and other European immigrants to North America. When Anabaptists settled new land they could justify their actions and knowingly exclude new neighbours from their communities by relying on a narrow interpretation of separatist non-conformity. Through selective disengagement from society, Anabaptist non-conformity can fail to see structural injustices that the community benefits from.[27]

The Old Colony Mennonites continue to take the identity of a religiously persecuted community of perpetual sojourners to heart. After immigrating from Russia to Canada, they still plant new colonies throughout Central and South America in search of government concessions that will allow them to continue their distinctive way of life undisturbed. Whether they settle in Mexico, Belize or Bolivia, they do their best to set up near identical settlements to the ones they left in Canada or Russia. As one Old Colony Mennonite settler said about his family's impending move from Chihuahua Mexico to a new colony they were establishing in Argentina, 'We're going to create exactly the same world there that we built here.'[28]

Through innovative farming techniques like land reclamation, crop rotation and more recently, intensive irrigation, these Mennonite farmers have a proud history of making

---

[24] Calvin Redekop (ed.), *Creation and the Environment: An Anabaptist Perspective on a Sustainable World* (Baltimore: Johns Hopkins University Press, 2000), xiv.

[25] Moe-Lobeda, *Resisting Structural Evil*, 74.

[26] Joseph R. Wiebe, 'On the Mennonite-Métis Borderland: Environment, Colonialism, and Settlement in Manitoba', *Journal of Mennonite Studies* 35 (2017), 111–26 (120).

[27] Ibid., 119.

[28] Victoria Burnett, 'Mennonite Farmers Prepare to Leave Mexico, and Competition for Water', *New York Times*, 16 November 2015, A6, https://nyti.ms/1S0iXvU.

seemingly unproductive land profitable. But they also have a history of relocating to evermore remote areas when governments revoke their religious concessions or when land is no longer affordable. In the case of Chihuahua, some Old Colony Mennonites are now leaving for another reason: through over-irrigation they have depleted the water supply.

While this sort of practice is not representative of all Old Colony Mennonites, it illustrates the ecological and humanitarian danger of a settler colonialism that hides itself under cultural preservation. Having a higher loyalty to their religious community than to a place, in a few short decades these Mennonites managed to exploit and discard land in a delicate ecosystem that Indigenous and Mexican farmers have been living on for generations. As one of their Mexican neighbours observed, 'Their world is everywhere. … They arrive, they work the earth and when they need more, they move on. This is my land. … My dead lie here. I won't leave.'[29]

Paradoxically perhaps, no matter how far to the ends of the earth the Old Colony Mennonites transplant themselves, their choice to farm commodities like soybeans and corn inevitably links them *agriculturally* to global markets.[30] Yet, *culturally*, Old Colony Mennonite communities remain isolated from their nearest neighbours.[31]

Since Anabaptism's distinctive values were forged through strategies of survival in face of oppression, Anabaptists of social and economic privilege will not be able to live into these values in the same way today unless they critically assess the ways their communities are entangled in systems of violence and begin to discern the ethics of survival that oppressed communities, such as environmental refugees, are currently using to resist death. While Anabaptist values could potentially be part of a radical Christian response to climate change, they will mean very little in a North American context if they do not involve making the cause and the fate of vulnerable people, animals and ecosystems one's own.[32]

Turning ploughshares into swords? Anabaptist nonviolence and the systemic violence of climate change

While many Anabaptist farmers in North America value their relationships to the land and see themselves as good caretakers of it, land is often valued primarily in terms of

---

[29] Ibid.
[30] Ben Nobbs-Thiessen, 'Cheese Is Culture and Soy Is Commodity: Environmental Change in a Bolivian Mennonite Colony', *Journal of Mennonite Studies* 35 (2017), 303–28.
[31] Burnett, 'Mennonite Farmers Prepare to Leave Mexico'.
[32] Leonardo Boff, 'Liberation Theology and Ecology: Alternative, Confrontation or Complementarity?' in *Ecology and Poverty: Cry of the Earth, Cry of the Poor,* Leonardo Boff and Virgilio P. Elizondo (eds), *Concilium*, 1995/5 (Maryknoll: Orbis, 1995), 67–77 (71).

its profitability to support human communities and families. This is not bad in and of itself, but there is less concern for the ways that farming practices affect the health of the ecosystem or the ways that Anabaptist farmers participate in a global economic system that affects the climate as a whole.

One especially evocative image for a historically pacifist and agrarian people is the biblical depiction of an idealized future when people 'beat their swords into plowshares and their spears into pruning hooks'.[33] Without a systemic vision, however, it can be easy to miss the ways that even seemingly benign farming tools and standard agricultural practices can be wielded as weapons that contribute to the destruction of the land and the climate. Walter Klaassen laments that despite their historic commitment to non-resistance, which he defines as 'living without weapons', his fellow Anabaptists often applied this ethic too narrowly. He says, we 'did not have a clear understanding of a God-given mandate to farm without weapons as we had a mandate to live without weapons with our fellow citizens'.[34]

Despite Klaassen's critique, it is important to emphasize that Anabaptist communities have always related to the natural world in multiple and sometimes conflicting ways.[35] Royden Loewen compares the views and practices of Mennonite farmers on their land and environment in Manitoba, Kansas and Belize. He illustrates how in each case, the Mennonites' relationship to their environment was complex and often contradictory: 'Each of these communities pressed the land to yield a bounty and linked agriculture with the creation of order in nature, with the drawing of straight lines on the land', because 'social harmony was ... believed to be a fruit ... of "order on the land"'.[36] In different ways, these three communities each linked agricultural success and profitability with good stewardship of the land. And despite many farmers' professed 'affection for the environment', they were also determined to subdue it through the clearing of forests in order to create more productive farmland.[37]

As these cases demonstrate, a narrowly construed definition of nonviolence can conceal ways that Anabaptists can wittingly or unwittingly adopt agricultural practices that destroy ecosystems and contribute to climate change, while displacing their neighbours through settlement, mechanization or depletion of the land. When ethical reflection is limited in its concern for communities or individuals, it can overly focus on the symptoms of injustice, while failing to identify the ways that Anabaptist production and consumption patterns are tied to larger agricultural or economic policies that

---

[33] See Isa. 2.4 and Micah 4.3 (NRSV); also Harold S. Bender, *The Anabaptist Vision* (Scottdale: Herald Press, 1944), 32.

[34] Walter Klaassen, 'Pacifism, Nonviolence, and the Peaceful Reign of God', in *Creation and the Environment: An Anabaptist Perspective on a Sustainable World,* Calvin Redekop (ed.) (Baltimore: Johns Hopkins University Press, 2000), 139–53 (143).

[35] Royden Loewen, 'The Quiet on the Land: The Environment in Mennonite Historiography', *Journal of Mennonite Studies* 23 (2005), 151–64 (156).

[36] Ibid., 160.

[37] Ibid., 157–8, 160.

not only impact the climate but also impact the character and moral vision of North American Anabaptist culture.

Climate change and the ecological community

The fundamental challenge for Anabaptists when responding to climate change is to discern how to apply ethical values like non-conformity or nonviolence to a systemic problem. This is true for an Anabaptist understanding of community as well. Since their values are often attuned to community life or individual conscience, Anabaptists can paradoxically be willing to make great sacrifices to address the consequences of climate change – like attending to the needs of disaster victims in hurricanes or floods – but fail to see how their ways of life are contributing to its root causes. Unless the ethical community is defined in terms larger than the religious community or even the human community as an abstract whole, North American Anabaptists will continue to find it difficult to resist benefitting from the causes of climate change, even as they lament its consequences.

Along these lines, some Anabaptists are beginning to rethink the boundaries of community in innovative and more ecologically holistic ways. Ched Meyers proposes 'watershed discipleship' as a new imaginative framework for community. He explains that this concept has three interrelated meanings: it suggests that the world is in a 'watershed moment' of crisis, it identifies the bioregion as the place that Christian discipleship should be focused, and it indicates that as disciples of their watersheds, Christians will need to learn more about their specific places in order to live responsibly in them.[38]

In contrast to the Mennonites that Loewen describes, who equated order in nature with the drawing of straight lines on the land, Myers draws on insights from bioregionalism and watershed mapping. He observes that while human-made boundaries are often straight, natural boundaries never are. 'Such straight lines', he says, 'are the first order of abstraction, alienating us from the topographical and hydrological realities sustaining us.'[39] A watershed ethic makes connections between the well-being of humans and the natural world, and it requires a commitment to restorative justice for those who were displaced in the past and those who continue to be marginalized today.

For instance, Myers says, 'The current health of the place must be assessed from the perspective of both land and people who have experienced degradation: poisoned agricultural fields and farmworkers; paved over strip malls and low-wage workers;

---

[38] Ched Myers, 'From "Creation Care" to "Watershed Discipleship": Re-Placing Ecological Theology and Practice', *Conrad Grebel Review* 32:3 (2014), 250–75 (266).

[39] Ibid., 261.

threatened riparian habitat and homeless people.'[40] By redrawing the boundaries of the ethical community ecologically to include all life and life systems within the permeable border of a watershed, this paradigm is a challenge to Anabaptist communities to do more than reconsider their relationship to the land. The human–ecological community of a watershed also raises intersections between ethical issues like food sovereignty, Indigenous rights, environmental racism and economic development.

Myers calls Christians in general and Anabaptists in particular to a journey of 're-place-ment', noting that justice and sustainability on a global level requires a deep knowledge of and commitment to the health of one's own bioregion. Watershed discipleship suggests one vision for what an Anabaptist community-oriented ethic might look like, and in a way that potentially reimagines how non-conformity could be practised in an age of global climate change as well. Whether Anabaptists are living on rural farms or in suburbs or cities, a watershed is an idea and a physical reality that can also 're-root' nonviolence in a particular 'basin of relations' by inspiring a new awareness of interdependence and responsibility for human and non-human lives.[41]

If extending the boundaries of the Anabaptist ethical community to include other species and ecosystems is to be more than an abstract ideal, then starting with deep knowledge and responsiveness to one's own bioregion is an essential first step. However, it is also necessary to confront the underlying causes of climate change, such as an economic system based on unlimited growth, dependence on fossil fuels, and a distorted standard of consumption that is unsustainable and unattainable for the majority of the world's population.

Conclusion

Despite their diversity, Anabaptists share several theological and ethical dispositions. This essay focused on the ways that North American Anabaptists value non-conformity, nonviolence and community, and how this informs their relationship to the land, to society and to the climate.

As other Christians who are concerned about climate change consider how they might work with Anabaptist forms of Christianity, it is important to avoid over-romanticizing these diverse traditions, but it is equally important not to underestimate the radical potential that these values have to challenge the entrenched systems that perpetuate climate change. Non-conformity has the potential to be redefined, not as a sectarian withdrawal from society, but as an engaged solidarity with those human and ecological communities that are the causalities of a changing climate.

---

[40] Ibid., 264.
[41] Ibid., 264, 273.

Nonviolence is a value that has at times inspired Anabaptists to make great personal sacrifices in order to love their neighbours, strangers and even enemies. However, climate change is a form of structural violence that affects the whole planet and disproportionately impacts already marginalized people and threatened species. In this context, a more holistic ethic of nonviolence could challenge Anabaptists and other Christians alike to love all of the interdependent relations in their bioregion as neighbours, while loving other bioregions and their inhabitants as strangers.

Finally, since human communities are always embedded in larger ecological communities, the communal focus of Anabaptist ethics is one that can also be reimagined. Anabaptist communities are strengthened by more points of connection between members. If Anabaptists extend their communal values of intentional interdependence and mutual support to the ecosystems in which they live, not only can the boundaries of their community be expanded to include their natural environment, but the bonds of the community may themselves be reinforced.

Through socially engaged non-conformity, a holistic nonviolence and an ecologically expansive community, Anabaptists values offer creative possibilities for addressing climate change. Yet, Anabaptists and other Christians of privilege in the North American context will only truly be able to understand the systemic dimension of their ethical responsibility when they enter into common cause with the humans, animals and ecosystems whose lives are being violated by the current social order.

A response to Nathanael L. Inglis

Paulus S. Widjaja[1]

Following Christ in the contemporary world

The essay of Nathanael L. Inglis is very inspiring and, at the same time, challenging. Inglis has correctly elaborated the three main virtues that have been held dear by Anabaptists since the inception of the movement in the sixteenth century, namely, non-conformity, nonviolence and community. Yet Inglis also shows the 'paradox of privilege' that has taken place among both the acculturated and the non-acculturated contemporary Anabaptists in North America. While the Anabaptists are still holding the virtue of community, for instance, they nevertheless ignore the fact that they escaped from religious persecution in Europe only to push out the Indigenous inhabitants in the new 'promised' land. While some Anabaptists disengage themselves from the global market in order to live simply as the manifestation of the virtue of non-conformity, the choice of soybeans and corn that they plant are inevitably linking them agriculturally with the global market. Inglis then calls on the Anabaptists to re-evaluate their ethics so that they can live out the Anabaptist virtues sincerely without participating in the structural oppression of others and the earth. '[W]ithout a systemic vision, even well-intentioned people can participate in harmful practices toward the climate and other human beings without realizing it,' says Inglis. He then proposes a watershed discipleship, which will enable Anabaptists to cross beyond the old concepts of non-conformity, nonviolence and community, to explore a new frontier of Christian ethics that embraces the earth and challenges the structural injustices on earth.

Inglis's views can easily be affirmed, even by the Anabaptists whom he criticizes, including me. However, it needs a balance that appreciates the efforts of Anabaptists in their journey to imitate Christ. It might be true that modern North American Anabaptists are entangled in the 'paradox of privilege'. But it is also true that there are Anabaptists, both acculturated and non-acculturated, who work seriously and sincerely to live out Anabaptist virtues so as to pursue social–structural transformation. Some of the work done by the Mennonite Central Committee (MCC) and Mennonite World Conference (MWC) are worth mentioning.

---

[1] Paulus S. Widjaja is Dean of the Faculty of Theology, Duta Wacana Christian University in Yogyakarta, Indonesia, an interdenominational university owned by twelve different church synods from the Reformed and Mennonite traditions. He is a Mennonite ordained-pastor and teaches courses in the area of peace theology and ethics.

The MCC, with national headquarters in Akron, Pennsylvania, for the United States and in Winnipeg, Manitoba, for Canada, is 'a global, non-profit organization that strives to share God's love and compassion for all through relief, development and peace'.[2] MCC tries to implement concretely the Anabaptist virtues as elaborated by Inglis. Interestingly enough, both acculturated and non-acculturated Anabaptists are involved in the MCC. In its Akron storage house and workshop, for instance, we can see members of Amish communities work side by side with more modern Mennonites. They even sent their members to serve in the MCC decision-making board. One example is the establishment of the MCC Washington and Ottawa Offices and MCC United Nations Office.[3] The purpose of the establishment of these offices is self-evident from their very locations, namely, to engage more directly with those in power, both in the United States and Canada, and in the United Nations. These offices are intentionally based on the virtues of non-conformity, nonviolence and community. These offices try to transform unjust social systems by means of persuasion. This is an intentional choice since persuasion is a kind of action that is morally better than violence, manipulation and even legislation. Persuasion is power mixed with communality. It treats the opponents as human beings, as reasoning persons, and hence it is even better than nonviolent action. It also minimizes evil as it requires a degree of humility and emphasizes the effort to listen to others and to speak to them in circumstances that permit them to respond freely.

As the manifestation of nonviolence, persuasion works through the power of storytelling. Stories are much better than blueprints or ideologies in pointing to the way towards a different kind of future. Stories invoke compassion, which starts with listening and, in turn, creates understanding. By listening to the stories of specific injustices done to people we can touch their lives. Such an encounter will create compassion and motivate us to commit to peace and justice. That forms an integral part of spiritual formation and educational programmes because it creates human dialogue and relationships that lead to creative new alternatives. It will change one's perspective and provide the spiritual foundation for social change. As Jim Wallis shows,

> Instead of television shows that celebrate 'the lifestyles of the rich and the famous', we should document the consequences of such living upon the ecosystem and 'the life struggles of the poor and powerless'. Rather than creating envy through media fascination with the salaries of sports stars, talk show hosts, and big corporate executives, we should generate a sense of emulation by profiling those who forgo lucrative rewards for social responsibility.[4]

Different from other Christian advocacy groups which offer theological, philosophical or ideological comment on political issues, the MCC Washington and Ottawa Offices, as

---

[2] Information about the MCC can be found at https://mcc.org/.
[3] While for many faith-based organizations to have such offices is not surprising, it is quite unique within Mennonite history to get so close to power.
[4] Jim Wallis, *The Soul of Politics* (San Diego: Harcourt Brace, 1995), 198.

well as the MCC UN Office provide stories from around the world about certain issues. They do not see themselves as policy experts to offer suggestions on political policy, rather as people of faith involved with those who are suffering around the world and bring their stories to be considered by the policymakers.

The same can be said about the Mennonite World Conference (MWC) – an international body of Anabaptist–Mennonite related churches.[5] During the 2015 MWC Assembly which was held in Harrisburg, Pennsylvania, Howard Good, the national coordinator of the assembly, said that the assembly organizers 'decided early on that we would attempt to make the conference environmentally friendly to the degree that it was economically possible'.[6] To manifest that commitment concretely the assembly was held in a manner that ensures sustainability. The Mennonite Creation Care Network encouraged the planning committee to make the extra investment in order that all plates, cutlery, napkins, cups, leftover food for the total of 39,000 meals, and even the communion cups for the Lord's Supper celebration at the end of the event, were compostable for only $0.60/meal.[7] Of course one can say that it is only a once-in-every-six-year event. Yet it does show the seriousness of North American Mennonites to care for creation. It might be only one step, but this is a necessary step in a long journey to be truthful and faithful to what Anabaptist Mennonites have believed for ages.

It is a bit surprising that Inglis says very little about Jesus Christ because all what the Anabaptists, old and new, acculturated and non-acculturated alike, believe and hold dearly as the centre of their lives and the most basic foundation for their theology and ethics focus on Jesus Christ. Anabaptists need to look once more to the belief that 'No one may truly know Christ except one who follows Him in life', as Hans Denck, one of the foremost sixteenth Anabaptist leaders, had said in the past.[8]

The watershed discipleship that Inglis proposes should also include a broader and deeper understanding of Jesus's incarnation. Incarnation should not be separated from the salvific works of God in the universe so that the universe can transcend towards its ultimate goal, namely, the union of the whole universe with and within Christ. In incarnation Christ has permeated into all aspects of universe that 'everything is physically "Christified"'.[9] Niels Henrik Gregersen speaks of the incarnation as an event within which God, 'conjoined the material conditions of creaturely existence ("all flesh"), shared and ennobled the fate of all biological life forms ("grass" and "lilies"), and experienced the pains of sensitive creatures ("sparrow" and "foxes") from inside'.[10]

---

[5] Information about MWC can be found at https://mwc-cmm.org/.

[6] Karla Braun, 'A Deeper Shade of Green: Waste Reduction Measures at PA 2015', https://mwc-cmm.org/content/deeper-shade-green-waste-reduction-measures-pa-2015. (accessed 4 June 2018).

[7] Ibid.

[8] See https://gameo.org/index.php?title=Denck,_Hans_(ca._1500-1527) (accessed 16 July 2018).

[9] Nindyo Sansongko, 'The Christified Universe and the Vanquished Creatures: The Perspectives of Ilia Delio and Elizabeth A. Johnson', *Dialog: A Journal of Theology* 56:1 (2017), 61–72 (65, 69).

[10] Niels Henrik Gregersen, 'Cur Deus Caro: Jesus and the Cosmos Story', in *Theology and Science* 11:4 (2013), 370–93 (375).

The Gospel of John witnesses that the flesh (σάρξ) within which form Jesus lived as God incarnated is not related only to the worldly body of Jesus but to all material world. Hence the material world can be transformed and infused by the Spirit of God precisely because that flesh has been embraced by and in the logos.[11] Incarnation does not only mean that the infinite God has embodied the finite form, but also means that God has accepted and embraced the whole aspects of the universe within himself so that He can transform the universe from within.[12]

In conclusion, should contemporary Anabaptists seek to be faithful to the fundamental Anabaptist values of non-conformity, non-violence and community, they have to follow Jesus in all things. It is only by firmly standing on this belief that they will embrace the earth wholeheartedly and challenge any structural injustice that endanger the earth, just like the One whom they claim they follow. '[W]hoever says, "I abide in him", ought to walk just as he walked' (1 Jn 2.6, NRS).

---

[11] Ibid., 376, 381–3.
[12] Ibid., 383.

Chapter 3.7
Working with Pentecostal and Evangelical forms of Christianity

Christopher J. Vena[1]

Introduction

According to a recent study, only 28 per cent of Evangelicals believe that human activity significantly affects the climate, despite ever-growing evidence to the contrary.[2] This minority view held by a culturally dominant group undergirds the tensions surrounding environmental issues in the United States. Evangelicals, along with Pentecostals, continue to be a major source of resistance to climate justice efforts. Together they form a significant part of a political base in the United States that actively opposes environmental legislation and vigorously supports environmentally damaging industries.[3] This is a problem.

Evangelicals and Pentecostals have had a long and complicated relationship with environmentalism and environmental concerns. As the United States' environmental consciousness emerged in the 1950s and rose in popularity in the 1960s, Evangelical and Pentecostal voices like Calvin DeWitt and John McConnell, Jr, contributed to the call to rethink how contemporary Western societies lived in the world. At the same time, Christian communities, especially conservative ones represented by these movements, went on the defensive as they found themselves the subject of harsh criticism. Critiques like the one given in historian Lynn White Jr's oft-cited essay even went so far as to lay the blame for environmental degradation squarely on the shoulders of Christian

---

[1] Christopher J. Vena is Associate Professor of Theology at Toccoa Falls College (Toccoa Falls, GA, USA), a college affiliated with the Christian and Missionary Alliance. Operating out of a Wesleyan-Holiness tradition, he teaches systematic theology, ecotheology and spiritual formation.

[2] Pew study, 'Religion and Views on Climate and Energy Issues', 22 October 2015, http://www.pewinternet.org/2015/10/22/religion-and-views-on-climate-and-energy-issues/ (accessed 28 December 2018). Around 70 per cent of evangelicals believe climate change is real and that humans contribute in some sense. The 28 per cent figure represents those who believe that humans are *significantly* responsible for climate change.

[3] While Evangelicalism and Pentecostalism have clear and distinct historical and theological differences, the two are being treated together here because they share many ideological similarities. In many ways these movements are cousins, emerging out of the heritage of conservative Protestant orthodoxy. Without minimizing the important differences, this essay will focus on their shared cultural ideas and practices.

theology and practice.⁴ While White's thesis has been widely criticized, Evangelicals and Pentecostals remain caught in the midst of polarized cultural forces.

The tensions that exist in these movements are highlighted by widely divergent responses to climate science and climate justice. On the one hand, scholars and leaders of both movements have made positive contributions to the growing body of literature in the area of ecotheology and environmental ethics. They have also been actively involved in the formation of organizations, networks and ministries with the focal purpose of working towards environmental justice. On the other hand, the political, cultural and theological patterns that have characterized the majority of Pentecostal and Evangelical communities have been emblematic of the North American resistance to environmental concerns.

This essay engages Pentecostals and Evangelicals with specific reference to the North American context – since both these movements have a different shape elsewhere in the world. It critiques the destructive patterns of thought and culture that deny anthropogenic climate change and oppose climate justice, but also highlights positive pathways within each movement. Most importantly, it seeks to explore the possibility that the barriers to cooperative action can be overcome and that the resources for Evangelicals and Pentecostals to support climate action and work towards climate justice are embedded in their traditions.

Problematic ideologies

At the heart of Pentecostal and Evangelical resistance is a theologically informed culture that views the world – and God's interaction with it – in such a way that ecological concerns are neither important nor valid. Considering the diverse nature of both traditions, it might be better to think of Pentecostals and Evangelicals operating out of a conglomerate of related cultures that share family characteristics.⁵ The factors that drive and shape these cultures are themselves diverse and complex, so this essay will look to identify key patterns in broad strokes. It will look at some common theological influences on the way that Evangelicals and Pentecostals understand the world, as well as explore some of the cultural and political realities that influence their living in it.

One factor that flavours all Evangelical and Pentecostal cultures is the authoritative role of the Bible in governing faith and life, and with it often comes a particular method of interpreting scripture. The method favours a 'literal' reading of the text that is too often literalistic rather than literary, which opens the door for misreading important passages

---

⁴ Lynn White, Jr, 'The Historical Roots of Our Ecological Crisis', *Science* 55 (1967), 1203–7.
⁵ See Craig Allert, *A High View of Scripture?* (Grand Rapids: Baker, 2007), 17–36. His chapter on Evangelicals and traditionalism helpfully illuminates the cultural and theological diversity that has always been characteristic of the movement.

relevant to God's interaction with creation.⁶ Some examples of this are evident in how these traditions view the place and role of humanity in the world, as well as the final destiny of all created things. Both of these are key building blocks of an Evangelical/Pentecostal worldview. The first gives ontological and ethical priority to human life and behaviour, while the second influences the way these communities look at the effects of human action on the natural world.⁷ In addition, an abiding trust in the sovereignty of God provides an ultimate safety net against premature destruction of the planet.

Theological issues

One of White's criticisms of Christianity is the fundamental assumption of the primacy of humanity in the created order. Biblical passages like the ones that affirm that humans were created 'a little lower than the angels' (Ps. 8.5) or that proclaim that humans 'are much more valuable than [the birds of the air]' (Mt. 6.26) have anchored a theological tradition of seeing humanity as the pinnacle of creation with the invested authority to rule over it. God 'made [them] ruler over' creation and 'put everything under [their] feet' (Ps. 8.6). The mandate to 'have dominion' or 'rule over' (Gen. 1.26-28) generates an ethical framework where humanity relates to the rest of creation in instrumental ways. Creation exists for humans and human concerns are the only ones that matter in the end. This anthropocentric attitude – bequeathed to Western societies via Christianity, says White – has led to unchecked, unquestioned growth of human culture and industry. For most of human history the effects on ecosystems were relatively minimal or isolated. However, when societal factors allowed for an explosion in human population, coupled with ever-increasing industrial capacities, the cumulative effect was an unprecedented ability for humans to disrupt and damage systems on a planetary scale.

This anthropocentrism, embedded deeply in Evangelical and Pentecostal communities, also makes it difficult to be critical of destructive human activity, especially when the destruction is not immediately evident or does not pose a direct threat to human well-being. Since human flourishing is the criterion determining which actions are considered moral, attempts to limit activities that benefit humans may be judged to be immoral, no matter what other deleterious effects they may have on non-human nature.

Another prominent, yet problematic, feature of many Evangelical and Pentecostal worldviews owes its influence to dispensational eschatology.⁸ This features a pessimism

---

⁶ Kevin Vanhoozer helpfully points out that a literalistic interpretation is not really faithful to the literary sense of the text. See Kevin Vanhoozer, *Pictures at a Theological Exhibition* (Downers Grove: IVP Academic, 2016), 72–94.

⁷ Philip Schadel and Erik Johnson, 'The Religious and Political Origins of Evangelical Protestants' Opposition to Environmental Spending', *Journal for the Scientific Study of Religion* 56 (2017), 179–98.

⁸ See, for example, Peter Althouse, '*Left Behind* – Fact or Fiction: Ecumenical Dilemmas of the Fundamentalist Millenarian Tensions within Pentecostalism', *Journal of Pentecostal Theology* 13:2 (2005), 187–207 (188).

about human culture and the fate of the natural world. Human societies are supposed to degenerate and the planet will eventually be destroyed in cataclysmic fire. God's ultimate plan is the destruction of creation before taking the faithful away to heaven and casting the wicked into hell. Furthermore, the final destruction of the world is signalled by human wickedness, so in a twisted sense, societies behaving badly is a positive thing, a sign of better things to come.

The implications of this pessimism are twofold. First, it downplays the value of creation. The purpose of the natural world is reduced to the context wherein human lives are lived. It exists to support human life and has value only in human use. Furthermore, the ultimate destiny of the natural world is destruction. Creation has little to no intrinsic value. Second, eschatological pessimism undermines any impetus to change human habits that threaten environmental sustainability. If destruction of creation is the final condition of this world anyway, then why should humans be concerned about saving it?

A final element of the Pentecostal and Evangelical theological framework is the staunch commitment to a particular notion of God's sovereignty. It is not uncommon for climate deniers to appeal to God's sovereign control of the world as a kind of safety net against human activity. As one congressman opined, 'As a Christian, I believe that there is a creator God who is much bigger than us ... and I am confident that, if there's a real problem, he can take care of it.'[9] Even if humans could destroy the planet, God would not allow it to happen – at least not until God determined it was time for it to happen. In fact, even raising the alarm that human activity is threatening the planet is seen as either ignorance or hubris. Together, these theological threads feature prominently in a religiously reified worldview that either rejects the reality of climate change or dangerously dismisses its effects.

While these theological positions represent common characteristics in Pentecostal and Evangelical worldviews, not all are essential to the identity of these movements. Furthermore, there is much disagreement within these traditions about the implications of core beliefs about the Bible, God and the destiny of the planet. However, theology alone is not the driving factor in resisting climate change initiatives.

Cultural issues

Evangelicals and Pentecostals also share cultural dynamics that generate consistent patterns of opposition to climate issues. In fact, it could be argued that these cultural and political factors play a larger role in a posture of resistance than the theological reasons given above. Although theology and culture cannot be meaningfully bifurcated, the cultural dynamics allow these theological beliefs to be manifested in ways that

---

[9] Quoted in Lisa Vox, 'Why Don't Christian Conservatives Worry about Climate Change God?', *Washington Post*, 2 June 2017, https://www.washingtonpost.com/posteverything/wp/2017/06/02/why-dont-christian-conservatives-worry-about-climate-change-god/?noredirect=on&utm_term=.86e268d157b7 (accessed 31 October 2018).

ultimately create barriers to cooperation. Common patterns in the Pentecostal and Evangelical psyche that shape these community's politics when community values and practices are questioned are fear, distrust and disposition to protest.

From the Reformation itself to contemporary 'culture wars', conservative Christians have seen themselves in a battle for truth and cultural influence. Pentecostalism and Evangelicalism were both born out of this broader tradition of protest and conservation, their identities forged in opposition to liberalism and secularism. As Christianity and conservatism's influence waned over the last twenty years, these communities have become increasingly combative and polemic, expressing laments of persecution and ratcheting up the rhetoric of winning back something that was lost.[10]

In the midst of this, environmentalism was linked together with other political issues of justice like feminism, LGBTQ rights, abortion and universal health care. For a religious community that already feels like it is losing ground, acquiescence on – let alone acceptance of – any of these issues is considered a costly defeat. Because environmental concern was seen as an enemy position by so many, it is difficult for people to simply flip their stance. It 'feels wrong' at a visceral level.

Furthermore, a community like Evangelicalism that perceives its identity and influence as under attack, and which also prides itself for holding the moral high ground, will go to great lengths to preserve the rightness of its political alignments, even in the face of evidence to the contrary. Despite increasingly clear evidence of anthropogenic climate change, an alarming number of people in Evangelical and Pentecostal communities simply refuse to accept the data. Instead, they attack the credibility of the science and the scientists themselves, suggesting that career concerns and liberal biases drive these false scientific conclusions.[11] And while the vast majority of scientific research supports an overwhelming consensus among scientists, appeal is made to the few studies that question it.

Another cultural factor is the deeply ingrained idea of thinking about ethics and morality solely through the lens of individual, personal responsibility. People are responsible for what they do individually. They may choose to extend their moral agency beyond personal concerns, but they are not morally responsible for things outside direct personal agency. This leads to a widespread lack of awareness of the way systems and institutions affect people and contribute to injustice. This is also seen in evangelical attitudes towards race and poverty and clearly carries over into discussions of environmental justice. Because white Evangelicals and Pentecostals have largely benefitted from cultural systems, it is harder for them to acknowledge this benefit, preferring instead narratives of individual hard work and achievement based on merit.

---

[10] This seems to be, in essence, the appeal of Donald Trump's 'Make America Great Again' slogan.

[11] See much of the literature connected to the Cornwall Alliance, an online network of theologians, scientists and economists. This network of scholars is led by Calvin Beisner and others devoted to promoting 'godly dominion', economic development for the poor and proclamation of the gospel. Their work decries 'climate alarmism', suggests that environmental policies harm the poor, and questions the legitimacy of the consensus of climate scientists. See the homepage at www.cornwallalliance.org

Likewise, there is a reluctance to see that Evangelicals and Pentecostals in the West contribute to climate injustice – and therefore bear moral responsibility for addressing it – simply by participating in Western society.

Effects

All of these factors have contributed to the formation of communities that resist prophetic voices for change, villainize opposing perspectives on climate matters and cultivate a wilful ignorance of ecological problems. Perhaps the most insidious element of this culture of resistance is the phenomenon of climate denial. More than just an ambivalence to the issues or ignorance about climate data, a significant number of Evangelicals and Pentecostals actively reject the idea that there is a problem in the first place.

This resistance takes on several forms. For some there is a simple rejection of climate science, either citing dishonest corruption among climate scientists or suggesting the concept of climate change is an elaborate political hoax. Others, bolstered by their apocalyptic eschatology and view of God's sovereignty over the world, argue that even if the science is true, it does not ultimately matter. Working to fight climate change might even entail working against God's ultimate plan for the planet!

A particularly troubling feature of resistance is the phenomenon of those who accept the reality of climate change but believe that climate *solutions* pose a greater threat than rising global temperatures. It is suggested that these solutions are threats to the economy, to individual freedoms, to personal comfort or to the poor themselves.[12]

Practically speaking, this resistance translates to broad support of anti-environmental industries (big energy corporations and large-scale consumer companies) and politics (typically funded by those industries). As long as environmentalism is seen as a liberal concept or affiliated primarily with the Democratic Party platform, ideological tribalism will continue to feed resistance to climate justice. Until this cultural resistance can be overcome, many Pentecostals and Evangelicals will continue to be blind to the ways they contribute to systemic environmental degradation.

Pathways to cooperation

If there is to be any hope that Pentecostals and Evangelicals will lay down their anti-climate arms, it must begin with a conscious effort to overcome the barriers to

---

[12] Troy H. Campbell and Arron C. Kay, 'Solution Aversion: On the Relation between Ideology and Motivated Disbelief', *Journal of Personality and Social Psychology* 107:5 (2014), 809–24.

cooperation. This will not be an easy task and it will not change attitudes overnight. Culture change takes time and there will be setbacks along the way.

What makes the task so daunting is the way that barriers are embedded in ideology and identity. Overcoming the barriers requires more than simply presenting factual arguments or arguing the data or appealing to popular consensus. Since one's ideology is shaped by more than epistemic factors, these other factors must be addressed if one's beliefs and values are to change.[13] Simply presenting factual data is not enough.

For Pentecostals and Evangelicals, the theological and psychological forces that shape a culture of resistance must be confronted in a way that minimizes defensiveness and polarization. It will not be effective to merely scorn or scoff these communities. New conceptual space needs to be created by which individuals and communities can move beyond the defensiveness that often prevents people from listening and changing. The good news is that there are examples from within these traditions that have already done heavy lifting towards this end. This section will focus on two areas: Evangelical/Pentecostal theology and psychology.

Overcoming theological barriers

A key theological feature for both Evangelical and Pentecostal traditions is the centrality of Scripture. Significant common ground is achieved if initiatives towards climate justice display a commitment to biblical veracity and authority. This does not require embracing a particular concept of inspiration or inerrancy or even biblical authority. It does require an acknowledgement that the Bible can be an authoritative source advocating for climate justice. Initiatives that find significant connections to biblical language and concepts, and which seek to consciously align with biblical teachings, will be received much more readily than those that do not. It will feel familiar and less threatening. Even more effective is to draw resources for eco-justice from within the traditions and doctrines of particular denominations. This will be especially helpful for those communities with strong confessional identities.

The next step is to connect Evangelical and Pentecostal praxis to eco-justice concerns. To see eco-justice as an essential feature of discipleship is to link it to practices that are already highly valued in these communities. If this can be accomplished, it will help them to see that eco-justice does not stand against discipleship, but as a part of what it means to be a follower of Jesus. Furthermore, this paves the way for concrete acts of environmental justice to be carried out as an implication of Christian ethics and not something exterior to or additional to it. To act in Christian ways involves the moral sphere of environmental degradation.

---

[13] Matthew J. Hornsey et al., 'Meta-analyses of the Determinants and Outcomes of Belief in Climate Change', *Nature Climate Change* 6 (2016), 622–6.

Overcoming psychological barriers

On the psychological front, overcoming barriers means overcoming fear and defensiveness. Pentecostals and Evangelicals share some common features in their collective psyche. Both communities often feel marginalized or persecuted by an evermore secularized culture. The identity of both traditions is forged by a history of polemics and protest, standing in opposition to modernity and its secularizing influences.[14] The resulting fear and defensiveness contributes to the resistance to change and the impulse to conserve and protect one's tradition.

In recent years, internal fracturing and the loss of cultural influence have driven more conservative Evangelicals and Pentecostals towards a frenzied defensive posture, especially among their white constituents. So much of their identity is rooted in the rightness of their morality and practices that to suggest that some of these practices are contributing to environmental problems is threatening. Challenges become another instance of persecution.

Much can be done to mitigate this fear through building common ground and rooting eco-justice in the language of scripture and tradition. If fear can be overcome, then perhaps the reactionary and combative tendencies of these communities will be reduced and in turn, cooperation with others can be considered without threat to identity and values. At the same time, there are limits to what strategies alone can accomplish. A person or community unwilling to listen or dialogue will not cooperate. Despite attempts to find common cause, a shared language and common values, there will be elements of these communities that will remain resistant to climate justice.

Evangelical and Pentecostal resources

Perhaps the best pathway for overcoming Evangelical and Pentecostal resistance to climate change is from within the traditions themselves. For both groups, there has always been a segment committed to caring for the environment. These minority voices recognized the truth of the ecological crisis and diligently worked to provide scientific, political and religious solutions. While the majority in these communities remain apathetic or antagonistic towards climate problems, the foundation has been laid to build climate solutions out of the resources these traditions provide. There is not nearly enough space here to give an exhaustive account of those resources, so brief highlights will have to suffice.

---

[14] For an assessment of this in Evangelicalism, see Allert, *A High View of Scripture?* 27–9.

Historical roots and organizations

Both traditions have produced key figures and movements that have worked to advocate for eco-justice. Environmental scientist Calvin DeWitt has long been a voice representing Evangelicals at the intersection of faith and environmental ethics. A co-founder of the Evangelical Environmental Network (EEN), he also directed the Au Sable Institute for over twenty-five years, an organization dedicated to training college students in both environmental studies and faith-based stewardship. Today, younger climate scientists like Katherine Hayhoe and Dorothy Boorse have taken up the mantle. Other prominent public figures in the United States include Richard Cizek, former lobbyist and spokesman for the National Association of Evangelicals; Matthew Sleeth, the surgeon-turned-author/speaker and founder of Blessed Earth; and mega church pastors like Joel Hunter, Leith Anderson and Rick Warren. Well-known Evangelical scholars who engage environmental themes in the United States include Douglas Moo, Loren Wilkinson, Steven Bouma-Prediger and Daniel Brunner.

On the Pentecostal side, peace activist John McConnell, Jr, was instrumental in establishing the original Earth Day in 1970 which is still celebrated by the United Nations.[15] Scholars in this tradition with significant work in ecotheology include Cheryl Bridges Johns, Aaron Swoboda, Jeffrey Lamp and Matthew Tallman.

In addition to EEN, organizations like Young Evangelicals for Climate Action, Blessed Earth and A Rocha (with networks in many countries) seek to equip Christians towards mobilization in practical ways. While no specifically Pentecostal organization has risen to the prominence as some of its Evangelical cousins, groups like Pentecostals and Charismatics for Peace and Justice attempt to provide a platform for scholarship and resources focused on justice issues, including creation care.

Evangelical theological resources

Thanks to the work of these organizations and individuals, much headway has been made into the development of an Evangelical ecotheology.[16] By connecting creation care perspectives to doctrinal beliefs that are already embraced within Evangelical communities, it helps members rethink the implications of their beliefs. Since another essay in this volume is devoted to working with Reformed forms of Christianity, this particular section will look at three resources derived from Evangelicalism's Wesleyan and Arminian branches.

---

[15] Not to be confused with the Earth Day celebrated annually on 22 April.

[16] See, for example, Daniel L. Bruner, Jennifer Butler and Aaron J. Swoboda, *Introduction to Evangelical Ecotheology* (Grand Rapids: Baker, 2014).

The first is a conviction that love constitutes the fundamental nature of God's essence or being. Not only does this say something about God's goodness and benevolent disposition towards creation, but also lays the groundwork for human identity and responsibility. As creatures created in God's image, humans were intended to reflect God's love, grace and glory within creation. Because God loves creation, so too should God's image bearers.

Love also forms the core of all Christian ethics, seen in Jesus's forthright command to 'love the Lord your God with all your heart, and with all your soul, and with all your strength, and with all your mind' and to love 'your neighbour as yourself'. In doing so, Jesus says, all the teaching of the Law and Prophets come to fulfilment.[17] Love is what rightly guides human behaviour to align with God's desire for the world. There is no greater command. This is true of human action in and towards creation no less than in social and spiritual interactions.[18]

Love in the sense that Jesus highlights in the Great Commandment is not mere affection or a certain disposition towards people and things. Love is a way of actively being in the world, both individually and communally, that is grounded in the very nature of God, who is love (1 Jn 4.7-8). As Paul exhorts, be imitators of God and 'live a life of love' (Eph. 5.1). It is a love modelled after Christ that intentionally and sacrificially acts to promote the well-being and flourishing of others – *even non-human others*. Each person and each thing is loved in an appropriate way, according to the kind of thing that it is. As a quality of human relationality, to love is to act in ways that give life and promote the full-functioning of God's created order.[19]

Another theological resource derives from Wesley's oft-quoted 'no holiness but social holiness'.[20] By this he meant that the transformation of human lives does not occur in isolation from others, but only within the context of community life. Life together creates the crucible in which humans learn to imitate God *together*.

This has implications to shape an Evangelical approach to environmental justice. Since climate problems are the result of human societies – and not merely individuals – the solutions will naturally be social as well. Humans must learn to live differently and love corporately as a community. What does this look like? It means working towards restoring shalom by pursuing right relationships between us and God, each other, and the rest of creation. The way people live together in a community ought to promote the well-being of both the people and the place of that community. Real change begins with the transformation of community life.

---

[17] See parallel passages Mt. 22.34-40 and Mk 12.28-34.
[18] I developed this in Christopher Vena, 'Beyond Stewardship: Toward an Agapeic Environmental Ethic' (PhD dissertation, Marquette University, 2009).
[19] Benjamin Lowe and Christopher Vena, 'Integrating Creation Care with Relief and Development', in *Hands: Stories and Lessons of Wholistic Development*, Buzz Maxey (ed.) (CAMA Services, 2019), 61–70.
[20] This quote comes from the preface to John Wesley, *Hymns and Sacred Poems* (1789).

Finally, for Wesley, God is working to redeem all of creation, not just the human parts of it.[21] Biblical salvation is not about the soul escaping from creation into a faraway realm. Rather, salvation is about the redemption and healing of all things, including the planet. The Bible begins with creation and ends with new creation, the uniting of heaven and earth. The destiny of the earth is intertwined with that of humans and that, like us, it too will be set free from its groaning and oppression to sin (Romans 8). The world is not just spiralling downward into despair and destruction. The biblical vision we have of the future is one where, by the love and power of God, creation will be refined and renewed, and where human civilization and the natural world will be reconciled to once again flourish in a rich and peaceful relationship with each other and God (Revelation 22).

Pentecostal theological resources

Pentecostalism has its own set of rich theological resources from which to draw.[22] At the heart of Pentecostalism's theological identity is a robust pneumatology, which in turn shapes important features of ecclesial and community life. The Holy Spirit is an abiding and active presence, not only in the life of believers but in the whole of creation. The Spirit's activity in the world is varied, though typically connected with healing, new life and empowerment for faithful living.

Pentecostal pneumatology teaches that God's presence to the world as Holy Spirit is a healing, life-giving presence. When humans live in tune with the Spirit's work, they are empowered to live in ways that fosters the flourishing of all life. Climate justice is imagined as a participation in the life and mission of God, joining with the divine initiative to nurture and sustain life. It becomes an extension of the spiritual life already practised in Pentecostal churches. Awakening to climate justice is not a matter of converting to a different form of spirituality; it is a matter of expanding the spirituality already practised by Pentecostals into ecological spheres.

Connected to this idea that God's Spirit is at work in the world is a conviction that the work has an ultimate *telos*. Beyond merely redeeming human souls, God is at work redeeming all of creation and drawing it towards its eschatological consummation. The end goal of the Spirit's mission is to perfect creation and draw it towards eternal participation in God's life.[23] The world then is not headed for imminent destruction but for eventual restoration. This is extremely helpful for countering a narrative of

---

[21] This idea is evident in sermons like 'Sermon 60: The Great Deliverance'. See *The Complete Works of John Wesley*, Vol. 2 (Delmarva Publications, 2014).

[22] Academic works on the topic of climate change include Aaron J. Swoboda (ed.), *Blood Cries Out: Pentecostals, Ecology, and the Groans of Creation* (Eugene: Pickwick, 2014) and Amos Yong, *Spirit Renews the Face of the Earth* (Eugene: Wipf and Stock, 2009).

[23] Steven M. Studebaker, 'The Spirit in Creation: A Unified Theology of Grace and Creation Care', *Zygon* 43:4 (2008), 943–60 (950).

annihilation or inherent worthlessness of the natural world, and flows as an implication from Pentecostalism's spirituality of renewal.

Finally, Pentecostalism can potentially contribute to the global conversation on climate change through its unique capacity to unite people of faith across racial and class lines. Because this movement is defined and driven along experiential rather than dogmatic vectors, it appeals to those who share an experience of the Spirit's renewal in their lives and community. The work of Pentecost explicitly demolishes old social barriers in favour of a unity born in shared spiritual experiences. This gives the movement a tremendous advantage in breaking down the social barriers to cooperation. In addition, the rapid and widespread growth of Pentecostal communities around the globe holds great potential for community mobilization, if those communities' religious imaginations can be directed to include climate justice.

Conclusion: Working with Evangelicals and Pentecostals

Working with Evangelical and Pentecostal forms of Christianity on climate change can be extremely frustrating. Moving communities beyond apathy is difficult enough; overcoming distrust, antagonism and defiance feels impossible. Too many communities in these traditions are entrenched in a culture of resistance.

And yet, there is hope. Not only did a minority of Pentecostals and Evangelicals join forces with those combatting climate problems early on, they have also done much work to change the hearts and minds of their fellow believers over the last five decades. New academic works are published each year making the case for the compatibility of faith and environmentalism. Activist networks continue to provide more and better resources for their communities, helping them understand the nature of the problem. More and more churches have opened their pulpits and programmes to learning about climate science and the roles they can play towards climate justice. As a result, a younger generation of Evangelicals and Pentecostals are growing into ecological consciousness and reject the scepticism of their parents and grandparents.[24] As this younger generation matures and settles into roles of influence in their Evangelical and Pentecostal communities, there is hope that they will use the resources of their traditions to overcome the culture of resistance so dominant there now.

---

[24] Pew Study cited in Alan Neuhauser, 'On Climate, Sharp Generational Divide within GOP', *U.S. News and World Report,* 14 May 2018.

An African response to Christopher Vena

Loreen Maseno[1]

The essay 'Working with Pentecostal and Evangelical forms of Christianity' provides a much-needed contribution. It submits that Pentecostal and Evangelical forms of Christianity form a major source of resistance to eco-justice efforts. It critiques patterns of culture, thought and action that oppose eco-justice within Pentecostal and Evangelical Christianity. Further, the essay highlights some positive pathways and resources within Pentecostal and Evangelical movements which could be tapped in order to shift the tide from within.

Vena rightly indicates that Evangelicalism and Pentecostalism have clear and distinct historical and theological differences. Merging the two in the essay perhaps was a disservice. Historical and theological matters from each of these forms play a big role in their response to eco-justice efforts. At the same time, there have been misrepresentations and stereotyping which calls for finer distinctions of groups for purposes of clarity and context.

Vena refers to Evangelicals and Pentecostals in North America in the essay. However, it is not clear how the politics of the United States relate to this. Perhaps further references to Evangelicals and Pentecostals elsewhere in the West would serve to concretize the essay more firmly.

According to Jeffrey Goins, Pentecostals express little concern about environmental problems as a result of the Pentecostal worldview, which values the supernatural and sees nature as subordinate, dependent and temporary. He asserts further that the environmental crisis is not a pressing issue for Pentecostals because they view the natural environment as only of relative value, ultimately due to be destroyed.[2] These are well summed up in the essay, which presents theological issues, cultural issues and their effects for eco-justice within these forms of Christianity. On the level of theological issues, anthropocentrism, dispensational eschatology and commitment to

---

[1] Loreen Maseno is Senior Lecturer in the Department of Religion, Theology and Philosophy at Maseno University, Kenya; Research Fellow in the Department of Biblical and Ancient Studies at the University of South Africa; and a Humboldt Fellow.

[2] Jeffrey Goins, 'Expendable Creation: Classical Pentecostalism and Environmental Disregard' (unpublished Master's thesis, University of North Texas, 2007), 8–21.

God's sovereignty are singled out as key issues which adversely affect the way both Pentecostals and Evangelicals relate to the environment.

Although the essay singles out dispensational eschatology as a theological issue for Pentecostals, dispensational eschatology could also be seen to derive more from their tradition and history rather than their theology. Goins asserts that the reasons Pentecostals lack concern about the eco-crisis can be found in the Pentecostal tradition, their views of human and natural history, and their interpretation of scripture.[3] Given the assertion by Vena that Evangelicalism and Pentecostalism have clear and distinct historical and theological differences, the adequate placement of dispensational eschatology might perhaps have been teased out better if the two forms of Christianity were treated in different essays.

Indeed, Pentecostalism is regarded as experiential in form and consequently, there has not been an emphasis on doctrines and systematic theology. As Clark and Lederle have argued, 'To be Pentecostal primarily presupposes that one partakes of the common Pentecostal experience, and only secondarily presupposes commitment to a common "confession" of doctrine.'[4] This also flows into the arena of ecotheology, such that Protestantism does not have a single ecotheology, neither does Pentecostalism.[5]

On the African continent, this lack of a single ecotheology opens room for several creative possibilities.[6] The question is what a Pentecostal ecotheology might actually look like. One position advanced is from a pneumatological perspective.[7] Vena excellently suggests some resources available within Evangelicalism and Protestantism for ecotheology, key figures who have started organizations which work in the area of ecological justice[8] and even a vigorous pneumatology.

Vena shows how Pentecostal pneumatology presents the Holy Spirit as an abiding and active presence in the whole of creation. Further, when humans live in tune with the Spirit's work, they are empowered to live in ways that fosters the flourishing of all created life. In what follows I will focus on a Pentecostal ecotheology for Africa, from such a pneumatological perspective.

---

[3] Ibid.

[4] Mathew S. Clark and Henry I. Lederle, *What Is Distinctive About Pentecostal Theology?* (Pretoria: University of South Africa, 1983), 17.

[5] Robert Fowler, *The Greening of Protestant Thought* (Chapel Hill: University of North Carolina Press, 1995), 3.

[6] Loreen Maseno, 'Prayer for Rain: A Pentecostal Perspective from Kenya', *The Ecumenical Review* 69 (2016), 436–41.

[7] Aaron J. Swoboda, 'Tongues and Trees: Towards a Green Pentecostal Pneumatology' (unpublished PhD thesis, University of Birmingham, 2011), 35.

[8] On cooperating with environmental organizations, see Ernst M. Conradie, *Christianity and Ecological Theology* (Stellenbosch: Sun Press, 2006), 177–8.

African cities have seen the concentration of Pentecostal churches more than double since the 1970.[9] Such huge growth has altered the religious landscape across the continent. In African cities and the farmlands, there is commonly an orientation referred to by Kalu, as the 'organic world view'. This organic worldview sacralizes all realms of life and considers that there is nothing in the visible world that has not been predetermined in the invisible realm. This worldview is important in that for the African person, it attends to the dimension of space to include (1) the sky, wherein the supreme being is manifested as the sun, thunder and lightning; (2) the earth, with the earth deity responsible for human, plant and animal fertility; and (3) ancestral spirits or the spirit world, in which physical nature such as rocks, streams and trees are imbued with divine power. This organic worldview in Africa, in which the three dimensions of space are bound together, generates a tendency to seek divine intervention, cure or diagnosis.[10]

A Pentecostal ecotheology from a pneumatological perspective in Africa can be pursued on different fronts. According to Aaron Swoboda, there are four key pneumatological themes and typologies which emerge from the Pentecostal tradition and utilize the framework of a Pentecostal ecological pneumatology.

Swoboda's typologies for ecotheology show that the Spirit-baptized life leads to an emphasis of personal piety, social piety and righteousness. Second, the spirit of charismatic community of creation where the Spirit is narrated as an event or happening and happens through the charismatic community, with creation and the church as the households of the Spirit.[11] Third, the holistic spirit embodies both humans and non-humans.[12] A pneumatological format is sought to bring healing not just to the victimized creation but to the victimizer and perpetrator, namely humanity. Fourth, the spirit of eschatological mission: Swoboda contends that, in light of our comprehension of the experiential drive of Pentecostal spirituality, one of these foci in experiential Pentecostal pneumatology must be seen in terms of eschatological missionary fervour.[13] Consequently, there is a need for Spirit-baptized communities to exhibit a more just and righteous relationship to the Spirit-baptized earth.[14]

The natural environment has been degraded continually by humans who consider it only of relative value. Utilitarian anthropocentrism sees human beings as the centre of creation and overwhelmingly views non-human nature as a 'thing' of purely instrumental value for use by human beings. This perspective emphasizes human power

---

[9] Gwyneth H. McClendon and Rachel Beatty Riedl, 'Individualism and Empowerment in Pentecostal Sermons: New Evidence from Nairobi, Kenya', *African Affairs* 115:458 (2015), 126.

[10] Ogba Kalu, 'Preserving a Worldview: Pentecostalism in the African Maps of the Universe', *PNEUMA: The Journal of the Society for Pentecostal Studies* 24:2 (2002), 119–22.

[11] Swoboda, 'Tongues and Trees', 292–6.

[12] A cosmic pneumatology broadens the Spirit's empowering work to non-human spheres. See Andrew R. Williams, 'Flame of Creation: Pentecostal Eco-theology in Dialogue with Clark Pinnock's Pneumatology', *Journal of Pentecostal Theology* 26:2 (2017), 272–85.

[13] Ibid., 265.

[14] Ibid., 355.

over and dominion over nature.[15] Another pneumatological perspective for a Pentecostal ecotheology emphasizes a reading of contemporary environmental concerns as a response to the prophetic voices of non-human nature, and in that sense as a movement of the Holy Spirit. In other words, the cry of the earth, heard in the Spirit, is seen as effective prophecy.[16] Ecologically speaking, the prophetic tradition seeks to restore justice within the created world.

Muers and Swoboda's suggestions provide resources to be developed further, for a Pentecostal ecotheology on the African continent. Both Muers and Swoboda emphasize a pneumatological imagination for Pentecostals and feature the prominence of the Holy Spirit. However, Muers heightens the prophetic, which is rather salient in the work by Swoboda, rightfully suggesting what would be called 'the spirit of prophecy'. On the African continent, this would serve as a fifth important typology following the typologies of spirit baptism, the spirit of charismatic community, the holistic spirit and the spirit of eschatological mission.

---

[15] Heinrich Bedford-Strohm, 'Tilling and Caring for the Earth: Public Theology and Ecology', *International Journal of Public Theology* 1 (2007), 230–48 (235–36).

[16] Rachel Muers, 'The Holy Spirit, the Voices of Nature and Environmental Prophecy', *Scottish Journal of Theology* 67:3 (2014), 323–39 (336–7).

Chapter 3.8
Climate change and the ecumenical movement

Wesley Granberg-Michaelson[1]

Introduction

Vancouver, British Columbia, was the site of the World Council of Churches' Sixth Assembly, held in 1983. With its theme, 'Jesus Christ the Life of the World', the Assembly sought to engage pressing global issues, such as the nuclear arms race, racial oppression and economic injustice in a framework of confessing the truth of Christian faith. In the plenary brought from the Pacific Islands, a moving speech was presented by Darlene Keju-Johnson describing the ongoing health and environmental effects from US testing of nuclear weapons on the Marshall Islands. It left a lasting impression on the 4,500 people, comprised of delegates, visitors, guests and press, at the Vancouver Assembly, especially as she shared about the three tumours in her own body and doubts about whether she should have a baby. The eighteen-minute address demonstrated the interconnection between the issues of the nuclear arms race, justice, environmental preservation and health.

The Assemblies of the World Council of Churches (WCC), held once every seven years, constitute the most important events gathering the constituency of its member churches and charting broad directions for future ecumenical work. Its official reports include programme guidelines outlining general priorities and points of focus in the coming years. One of those priorities found in the report of the Vancouver Assembly was this: 'To engage member churches in a conciliar process of mutual commitment (covenant) to justice, peace, and integrity of creation should be a priority for World Council programmes.'[2] This single sentence had a major influence on WCC programmes over the next two decades and more, and provided the foundation for ecumenical engagement around climate change.

---

[1] Wesley Granberg-Michaelson is General Secretary Emeritus of the Reformed Church in America. He also served as Director of Church and Society for the World Council of Churches and has long been active in ecumenical organizations. He lives in Santa Fe, New Mexico, USA.

[2] D. Preman Niles, 'Justice, Peace and the Integrity of Creation', in *Dictionary of the Ecumenical Movement*, Nicholas Losssy et al. (eds) (Geneva: WCC and Grand Rapids: Eerdmans, 1991), 557–9.

Three elements in this programme priority deserve attention. First, the call was for a 'conciliar process of mutual commitment (covenant)'. The dream of Vancouver was not simply for the WCC to continue work on justice and peace, with new attention to environmental care. Such programmatic work in the WCC would have gone on almost automatically; it was in the WCC's DNA. But calling for a 'conciliar process' was something new and radical. It meant that the WCC should engage its member churches, and those beyond if possible, in the tradition of an ecumenical church 'council', like those which framed historic creeds and confessions, to make commitments around the issues of justice, peace and integrity of creation that would be rooted in the confession of the church's one Faith. Therefore, this was not a matter of taking ethical principles derived from Christian understandings and then attempting to develop 'middle axioms' and engage public policy on this basis. Rather, it called for churches to shape and express commitments to justice, peace and integrity of creation as core to confessing faith together, in movements towards greater Christian unity.

Second, this programme priority from Vancouver linked justice, peace and integrity of creation together, as interdependent parts of one whole. As these words from Vancouver began to find expression in the WCC's life and in ecumenical organizations around the world, it became known as the 'JPIC process'. One of the key elements was the conviction that it was not possible to seek these ends in isolation from one another. Rather, the interconnections between working for justice, striving for peace and preserving the integrity of creation were essential to embrace and express in programmatic efforts. The isolated 'silos' were to be broken down, as demonstrated vividly in the address of Keju-Johnson.

Third, introducing the commitment to 'integrity of creation' as part of this process was novel and fresh. It's important to note that environmental concerns were not entirely new to the WCC's agenda. In its Fifth Assembly, held in Nairobi in 1975, a programmatic framework was affirmed as the search for a 'just, participatory, and sustainable society' (JPSS). Attention to environmental concerns was encompassed within this, but it's fair to say that these remained marginal in the overall WCC agenda and that of its ecumenical partners during this period. However, the JPSS framework certainly provided a strong background for the commitment at Vancouver to justice, peace and integrity of creation.

But what exactly was meant by 'integrity of creation'? The term was original, intriguing and evocative. But its actual content was unclear. That reflected the general lack of theological attention to issues of care for the creation during this period in the early 1980s. While the environmental movement found international expression at the United Nations Conference on the Human Environment, held in Stockholm in 1972, leading to the establishment of the United National Environmental Program, voices from the church and the ecumenical movement were largely absent. Further, a common critique was that the environmental movement was driven by northern, wealthier nations which had the luxury to care about such matters, evading the more concrete challenges of economic injustice in the Global South. Those concerns were echoed strongly in the corridors of the Ecumenical Centre in Geneva.

However, Vancouver's call for the Justice, Peace and Integrity of Creation (JPIC) process, integrating these concerns, gained resonance, but also focused attention on the need for an ecumenical, theological understanding of the integrity of creation. The result was a major WCC consultation addressing this need held in Granavollen, Norway, in February 1988. Demonstrating the strength of ecumenical methodology, a highly diverse gathering of voices, theologically, geographically and culturally, were gathered together to seek common perspectives in understanding the integrity of creation. Indigenous people, feminist theologians, youth, those from the 'faith and order' work of the WCC, Orthodox theologians, ethicists and biblical scholars all shared and joined in fruitful dialogue. The result was a report which began to demonstrate the potential for ecumenical theology to define and engage robustly the challenges to the integrity of creation.[3]

While climate change was not featured in the report from Granavollen, this consultation, more than any other ecumenical initiative in this time, set the theological framework for the WCC to address this specific threat. Further, the language of 'integrity of creation' was ideally suited for this task. As the threats from climate change were understood, these constituted an altering of how the delicate balance of the earth's atmospheric temperature was designed to function. Human-caused activity primarily through the increasing, excessive burning of carbon was, in fact, damaging creation's integrity. Thus, while not by design, the transition from a general commitment to preserve the integrity of creation as part of the JPIC process to specific actions to address the causes of climate change seemed natural.

The first major and specific engagement of those from the ecumenical world with the challenge of climate change came later in 1988. On October 16, Jeremy Rifkin, president of the Foundation on Economic Trends, convened a strategic consultation in Washington, DC, to establish Global Greenhouse Network. Those from thirty-five countries, including several from the Global South heading important environmental organizations were convened, along with scientific experts, political representatives from emerging Green Parties in Europe, and leaders of initiatives around climate change. However, Rifken worked closely with Wesley Granberg-Michaelson (the author of this contribution) to have important representatives from the ecumenical world involved in this consultation. At the time, Granberg-Michaelson had just been appointed as the new director of church and society for the WCC. The consultation included those like Milan Opochensky, who would shortly become the general secretary of the World Alliance of Reformed Churches, as well as representatives from the National Council of Churches in India, the All African Conference of Churches, the National Council of Churches of Indonesia, the Latin American Council of Churches, the European Council of Churches, the Pacific Council of Churches, the National Council of Churches of the United States, and David Hallman from the United Church of Canada, who would later become a key leader of the WCC's work on climate change.

---

[3] For a first-hand account, see Wesley Granberg-Michaelson, *Unexpected Destinations: An Evangelical Pilgrimage to World Christianity* (Grand Rapids: Eerdmans, 2011), 136–7.

Rifkin was a prophetic and effective advocate around the threats of climate change, identifying these before they gained widespread attention. His organization's ability to mobilize a wide range of grass roots environmental groups in effective action was impressive, and he had previously partnered with Granberg-Michaelson in mobilizing church and religious voices around climate change and other environmental threats. This Washington, DC, consultation, however, marked the first time that a wide range of global ecumenical leaders gathered together with environmental activists and other experts specifically addressing the issue of climate change. It proved to be a prescient occasion gathering ecumenical attention and alliances that would be crucial to the WCC's emerging commitment to focus on climate change as a key part of its JPIC process.

The WCC's work to address the integrity of creation as part of the JPIC process became the responsibility of the Subunit on Church and Society, with Granberg-Michaelson as its new director. Its work drew on diverse representation from the WCC's constituency, and study materials for the churches were developed. Theologically, the attempt was made to draw on the variety of voices and perspectives present at the Granavollen consultation, with some overarching commitments grounded in a biblical theology of creation, and its relationship to God and humanity.

At the same time the overall JPIC process was now moving forward in the institutional life of the WCC, under the direction of Preman Niles. The original dream of a 'conciliar process', however, was encountering objections about the model of a church 'council', with questions about who could call this and what authority it would carry. Moreover, the initial hope was that the Vatican would officially join the WCC in convening such a global council or major gathering of the churches. Negotiations to do so proved elusive and frustrating, with an eventual decision of the Vatican's Pontifical Council for Justice and Peace not to be a co-convener. Navigating through these challenges, the WCC convened a global 'Convocation' on justice, peace and integrity of creation, held in Seoul in 1990. Four specific commitments, or 'covenants', were made for the JPIC process to move forward through specific actions of the churches, together. One of these was for 'preserving the gift of the earth's atmosphere to nurture and sustain the world's life'.[4]

The WCC's commitment to addressing climate change, and the underlying theological framework, was further solidified at the Canberra Assembly, held in 1991. The theme for the Seventh Assembly of the WCC was 'Come Holy Spirit – Renew the Whole Creation'. It was striking in three respects. First, it was a prayer. Second, unlike previous assemblies, the focus was on the Holy Spirit. Third, it drew attention to the 'whole creation'. One of its sub-themes was 'Giver of Life – Restore your Creation'. The work on this sub-theme encompassed the WCC's emerging attention to integrity of creation, and the report officially underscored the priority of continuing efforts to engage the churches to address the causes and threats of climate change.

---

[4] Niles, 'Justice, Peace and the Integrity of Creation', 559.

Already, those efforts were well underway through work to create an ecumenical presence and contribution to the United Nations Conference on Environment and Development (UNCED), known as the 'Earth Summit', held in Rio de Janeiro in June 1992. This major global gathering, concluding with a 'summit' of over 100 heads of state, was designed to galvanize international commitment to environmental preservation. Included was a goal of adopting a treaty or convention on climate change. A widespread and lengthy preparatory process for UNCED included NGOs from around the world in addition to formal governmental negotiations through the United Nations.

The WCC played a pivotal role in convening religious groups as part of this preparatory process for the Earth Summit. A Working Group of Religious Groups on UNCED was established, including about twenty organizations outside of the WCC's formal structures. Over two years, attention was given to the whole UNCED agenda, with a particular focus on a proposed Earth Charter. Ecumenical advocacy work on climate change became very concrete as the WCC sent teams to the Intergovernmental Negotiating Committee for the Framework Convention on Climate Change, beginning in 1991 and continuing through UNCED. When the Convention was finally adopted and signed by 154 nations at the Earth Summit, the WCC regarded it as a first step, but not strong enough to address the threat. The subsequent UN process to gain further global commitments with specific targets and goals continued over the next two decades, culminating in the Paris Agreement, adopted in December 2015. Throughout that time, the WCC maintained a consistent presence, bringing marginalized voices and moral challenges into the global process to address the threats posed by climate change to the integrity of creation, and its consequences.

The Earth Summit provided another important and related gathering which advanced theological perspectives on the integrity of creation and further solidified commitments to issues on the UNCED agenda, including climate change. In addition to the normal meeting of governmental delegations in the typical style of the United Nations, the Earth Summit welcomed non-governmental organizations in the preparatory process, and at the event, an unprecedented 1,400 NGOs were officially accredited to participate. Moreover, the Earth Summit attracted even more participants and groups who comprised the 'Global Forum', where 7,000 organizations from around the globe were present.

In light of the potential of the Earth Summit, and the astonishing participation of groups representing civil society from all parts of the globe, the WCC decided to convene a major presence in Rio de Janeiro to represent the churches and the ecumenical community. 'Searching for the New Heavens and the New Earth' was the title for this gathering, bringing together 176 people from fifty-four countries representing over seventy different churches. It was held Biaxada Fluminense, on the north side of Rio de Janeiro, a location reflecting the realities of the city's social strife and economic inequality. The local archbishop from the Catholic Church, Dom Mauro Morelli, served as co-host. The intent was to focus ecumenical hopes and prayers for the agenda of the Earth Summit from a context in contrast to the Riocentro, the modern, isolated conference centre where the official government delegations met.[5]

The written result from the WCC gathering at Rio came not in the form of a report, but rather, as a 'Letter to the Churches'. Its content and style provided further guidance for the WCC's ongoing efforts on integrity of creation as part of the JPIC process and influenced the framework for work addressing climate change. Adopting a style reminiscent of the New Testament epistles, the letter did not have the normal declaratory rhetoric of WCC Reports, but rather was a pastoral and confessional appeal for churches to respond from the basis of their faith to the threats facing humanity's common earthly home. In so doing, the letter highlighted at points the complicity of the churches in the threats posed to the integrity of creation: 'We dare not deny our own role as churches in the crisis which now overwhelms us. We have not spoken the prophetic word ourselves. Indeed, we did not even hear it when it was spoken by others.'[6] Larry Rasmussen, who was then the Reinhold Niebuhr Professor of Christian Ethics at Union Theological Seminary in New York, and who had contributed to the WCC's work to carry forth the JPIC process, was one of the key drafters.

The 'Searching for the New Heavens and a New Earth' ecumenical gathering also produced an important document on theology. Kwok Pui-lan, at that time a young theologian from Hong Kong who had written about the connections between feminist theology and ecology, coordinated a reflection team which attempted to identify new theological themes and fresh biblical interpretations relevant to the perils facing creation. In part it declared:

> We affirm the goodness of God's creation and the intrinsic worth of all beings. Anthropocentric, hierarchical, and patriarchal understandings of creation lead to the alienation of human beings from each other, from nature, and from God. The current ecological crisis calls us to move towards an eco-centered theology of creation which emphasizes God's Spirit in creation (Genesis 1:2; Ps. 104), and human being as an integral part of nature.[7]

Such perspectives, which also echoed theological themes from Granavollen, Seoul and Canberra, came to undergird the WCC's ongoing work on integrity of creation and its efforts to address climate change.

This historical overview has focused on the background which gave rise to the ecumenical community's attention to integrity of creation. The first five years of the WCC's work on climate change, and the global, institutional and theological influences shaping those efforts, have been examined to see how the foundations for this work were put into place. Nearly twenty-five years of further work by the WCC on climate

---

[5] For a full account of the WCC's participation in the UNCED process, see Wesley Granberg-Michaelson, *Redeeming the Creation, The Rio Earth Summit: Challenges for the Churches* (Geneva: WCC, 1992).
[6] Ibid., 32.
[7] Ibid., 78.

change have developed, expanded and matured from that basis. But what lessons and conclusions might be drawn from three decades of ecumenical engagement with the threat of climate change? Four perspectives may be offered.

Four perspectives on ecumenical engagement with climate change

1. Ecumenical work addressing climate change was prescient.
At times, the ecumenical movement, and the WCC as its key global instrument, identifies issues not generally on the agenda of the churches but which require clear and sustained attention and witness. One could argue that this was the case with the struggle against apartheid, human rights violations by military regimes in Latin American countries, the pioneering pedagogy of Paulo Freire, and several other examples. This also was true for the WCC's work addressing climate change.

When climate change first began gaining the WCC's attention in 1988, it was barely on the radar of the churches. Global awareness was not much better. The Intergovernmental Panel on Climate Change (IPCC), which became the key global body for presenting assessments of the threats of climate change and won the Nobel Peace Prize, with Albert Gore, in 2007, was only established in 1988. It took four years of preparatory work, with the participation of the IPCC, to establish the UN Framework Convention on Climate Change, signed by 154 nations at the Earth Summit. This simply established the framework for ongoing international work addressing climate change. Yet, the WCC became engaged in this effort when the IPCC was founded and accompanied the preparatory process for the Framework Convention. At the time, we could not have imagined that this issue would eventually galvanize global attention and become recognized as the overarching threat to preserving the integrity of creation.

It's hard to say what accounted for this early, prophetic attention by the WCC. Sometimes it's just a matter of providential good fortune, and an unanticipated alignment of key events. Certainly, the drafting team for the report from the Vancouver Assembly which originated the term 'integrity of creation' as part of the JPIC process, which was most likely influenced by Darlene Keju-Johnson's address, created a rhetorical framework providing both the reason and justification for addressing climate change. Further, a confluence of major ecumenical events, from the Seoul JPIC Convocation to the Canberra Assembly and then the Earth Summit, over less than three years, solidified the WCC's commitment in ways that were never anticipated.

Beyond question, the WCC's work to bring the threats of climate change to the attention of the churches, with a theological and biblical rationale for responding, garnered positive results. Many churches which had never considered the question turned their attention to this new threat. As the JPIC process gained ecumenical attention and currency during those early years, with the inclusion of integrity of creation, climate change became a fresh issue, and began regularly to be embraced within the network of ecumenical organizations and groups. While scepticism among some remained, the WCC's efforts tried to stress the impact of climate change on the most vulnerable and marginalized groups, and the voices of Indigenous people were also being included and heard.

Therefore, in evaluating the ecumenical movement's engagement with climate change, both theologically and programmatically, it's fair to say this work was prescient. It opened awareness and created new opportunities for churches and ecumenical groups to engage a question which previously has not been on their agendas, and which would prove, in succeeding years, to be vital to the future sustainability of the planet.

2. Ecumenical work addressing climate change was persistent.
As already noted, UNCED's Framework Convention on Climate Change was no more, and no less, than that – a framework for ongoing negotiations and international agreements. However, from the time of the Earth Summit on, the WCC has brought its voices and those of its member churches to meetings of the ongoing negotiating committee and 'Conference of Parties' (COP), meaning the major, annual global conferences to evaluate progress, review and revise goals, and adopt commitments for the international community to address the threats and consequences of climate change.

Beyond the formal UN negotiating process, the WCC has issued countless statements, letters, formal addresses, media packets and other means of communication in carrying out its work of advocacy and education. The WCC's own compilation of such texts surpasses hundred documents. At crucial moments when the international community has attempted to reach binding commitments, such as Copenhagen (2009) and Paris (2015), the WCC had facilitated a major presence and voices of its churches and ecumenical partners.

Beyond this, the WCC has worked with others in holding a variety of events, seminars and conferences which continue to build awareness around the threats of climate change and to strengthen theological approaches for undergirding the churches' response. In October of 2017, for example, the WCC organized a conference on 'Just Peace with Earth' in conjunction with the international Arctic Assembly held in Iceland. Its title echoes strongly the JPIC language, and the conference emphasized theological themes rejecting anthropocentric approaches to creation and welcoming the voices of Indigenous and island peoples. A major address was given by the Ecumenical Patriarch Bartholomew I. The consequences of climate change experienced in regions such at the Arctic and the imperative of fresh approaches engaging the actions of the churches were strong themes. That event continued a legacy of WCC work that now has stretched over three decades.

3. *Ecumenical work addressing climate change was participatory, engaging widely diverse voices.*

Climate change was completely new on the ecumenical agenda when it was first engaged in 1988. There were no established constituencies. As a result, it was possible to start with a 'blank slate' and reach widely in building an ecumenical network to address this challenge. The groundwork to do so was established by the WCC's methodology in giving attention to the integrity of creation. As mentioned, a diverse group of theological, cultural and geographical voices were gathered at the initial WCC consultation in Granavollen, Norway, in 1988. It was natural to engage many of these as the WCC's work on climate change began to emerge.

Therefore, feminist theologians exploring ecotheology joined with Orthodox theologians, representatives of Indigenous people, Pacific Islanders, scientists and environmentalists in contributing their perspectives to ecumenical efforts beginning to address climate change. These were new coalitions. It took time for them to develop, and those efforts remained imperfect. But within the WCC, the intent was to build a widely participatory process to address this fresh issue that was entering the ecumenical agenda.

Obstacles remained, and in the early stages of the WCC's work on climate change, the overarching North–South divide particularly around challenges of global economic injustice created questions among some regarding the validity of this issue. Put simply, those in the ecumenical community with a long history and deep commitment in working for the economic liberation of oppressed and marginalized groups frequently wondered why the WCC should address an issue that seemed as detached from the daily suffering and struggles of people as climate change seemed to be. During its initial years, the WCC's efforts often lacked the participation of these ecumenical actors. However, the Earth Summit, with its huge participation of NGO's, was beginning to frame a fresh narrative which linked together in practical ways environmental sustainability and economic justice. This also was reverberating in the JPIC process of the ecumenical community. Over time, this led to greater participation by those in ecumenical circles from the Global South in climate change work.

Despite this initial limitation, the WCC's efforts addressing climate change, when viewed historically over three decades, demonstrate a remarkably broad range of participation from those in the ecumenical community. Most noteworthy are the ways in which, over time, the voices of those who were the most vulnerable to the effects of climate change and already its victims were given prominence in the process. Persons with no previous ecumenical involvement became deeply engaged as well. For example, Elias Abramides, a scientist from Argentina who is part of the Orthodox Church, was sent by the ecumenical patriarchate to represent it in the WCC's climate change work beginning in 1992, and he remained deeply involved in the WCC's advocacy work for the next twenty-five years. Overall, the breadth of participation in the ecumenical work addressing climate change welcomed new voices, created unique partnerships and provided space for fresh expressions of the WCC's advocacy work in the global arena.

4. Ecumenical work addressing climate change was partial, never fulfilling its founding hopes.

At its inception, the WCC's engagement addressing climate change, and the leadership it gave on this issue to the broader ecumenical community, was motivated by the desire for its advocacy to make a decisive difference. If churches from around the world could be united in raising urgent pleas to preserve the integrity of creation, the international community might listen. Providing a moral and religious framework, supported by inter-religious efforts, could galvanize the will of governments and negotiators in the UN system to make commitments of enough strength for reversing global warming and its devastating consequences.

Three decades later the picture is grim. Many see the enormous time lost in getting to the Paris Accord as creating nearly irreversible, worsening trends. Further that Accord, still viewed by many as not decisive enough, is now being undermined by the withdrawal of the United States. While promising local initiatives and research combatting climate change around the globe continue to multiply, many scientists and global experts say the best we can now do is to mitigate worse consequences of ongoing climate change.

Certainly, ecumenical voices have been heard through the years of this process. But have they been heeded? On the one hand, it's impossible to know the full effects of ecumenical statements, conferences, reports and private conversations on the threats of climate change and the imperatives to take action. It can be said that even as early as the Earth Summit, diplomats and UN leaders began using moral and spiritual language to frame the need for action. And over the years, the consistent presence and well-informed advocacy of ecumenical representatives within negotiating sessions gained respect and credibility.

Yet, the threats first identified by the ecumenical community thirty years ago not only remain but have escalated. Countless factors and failures contribute to this reality. But judged by this standard, ecumenical efforts addressing climate change have failed to have the decisive influence that was originally imagined.

Other more fundamental hopes have also not been realized. The original intent from the Vancouver Assembly was for a 'conciliar process of mutual commitment (covenant) to justice, peace, and integrity of creation'. For this to have happened, churches would have come to regard commitments to combat the threats of climate change as intrinsic parts of their search for Christian unity. Those commitments would be made together, mutually, as part of our common faith. Moreover, how churches would relate to one another around the responsibility, impact and consequences of climate change would impact our fellowship.

In other words, the unity of churches in the United States with churches in the Pacific would be tested by their ability (or inability) to make mutual commitments around climate change. Likewise, drought within regions of sub-Saharan Africa caused or accentuated by global warming would be a test of the unity between churches of millions of members within that region with churches in industrialized countries such as Germany or Russia, and their levels of greenhouse gas emissions. The reality of *koinonia* between such churches would require mutual commitments addressing root causes of climate change and its consequences.

Such examples could be multiplied expansively. The point is that the JPIC process imagined that these interrelated issues, such as climate change, would be the occasion for the churches to give fresh expression to the truth of their one Faith through common responses to threats facing God's creation. Few examples of this can be found. In part, this mirrored the larger failure of the JPIC vision and intention to be realized. For the most part, the WCC's work addressing climate change simply became another programme in the ecumenical agenda. Certainly, it had great merit and was fruitful in many respects. But it often remained captured by the programmatic framework of education and advocacy that characterized many of the WCC activities rather than exploring how this might be part of a conciliar process of mutual commitment around JPIC.

This critique raises the question of ecclesiology and ethics. The WCC did take up this challenge in 1993 through consultations between those involved in its Faith and Order work and those engaged in the WCC's JPIC process. Its first publication entitled 'Costly Unity' gained widespread attention, and others followed.[8] But this never got to the point of engaging issues such as climate change within the broader question of how ethical commitments relate to ecclesiology, *koinonia* and the search for unity.

In conclusion, the WCC's work addressing climate change wrote a new chapter in ecumenical history. It was groundbreaking, formative and exemplary in many respects, with effects that rippled throughout much of the global church. The legacy of this witness continues to this day, even as the crisis of climate change continues unabated. Yet the hopes of how this threat to the integrity of creation might both test and deepen the unity of the churches around their common expression of faith remain largely unrealized.

---

[8] Thomas E. Best and Wesley Granberg-Michaelson (eds), *Costly Unity: Koinonia and Justice, Peace and Creation* (Geneva: WCC, 1993).

A response to Wesley Granberg-Michaelson

Guillermo Kerber[1]

Expanding the ecumenical perspective

Wesley Granberg-Michaelson offered a most valuable history of the World Council of Churches' (WCC) involvement in climate change issues. Being not only an actor but also a WCC leader at the genesis of the Council's work on climate change, his perspective highlights some of the most important aspects of the WCC's early involvement on the topic as well as four lessons and conclusions from the three decades of ecumenical engagement with the threat of climate change.

In my response I will build on my personal experience, working on ecotheology since the late 1980s in my home country, Uruguay, which led to my doctoral thesis on the place of ecology in Latin American theology in the 1990s and my work at the WCC, from 2001 to 2016, coordinating, from 2006 to 2016, its work on care for creation and climate justice. I will focus especially on climate work done in the last decade.

The ecumenical movement is more than the WCC

The focus of Granberg-Michaelson's essay is almost exclusively on the WCC. While the WCC might be considered the 'broadest and most inclusive among the many organized expressions of the modern ecumenical movement' according to the WCC's homepage,[2] in my view it might be misleading to suggest that the work done on climate change within the ecumenical movement was mostly related to the WCC. Regional ecumenical organizations, national councils of churches, ecumenical organizations at the national or local level have played a significant role in addressing climate change and, indeed, in the preliminary work on environment and integrity of creation.

---

[1] Guillermo Kerber teaches at the Atelier Oecuménique de Théologie in Geneva, Switzerland. A Catholic, originally from Uruguay, he has been working on ecotheology since the late 1980s, having coordinated networks and ecumenical work on ecotheology and climate change, for example at the World Council of Churches.

[2] See https://www.oikoumene.org/en/about-us (accessed 27 October 2018).

For instance, we should not ignore that Christian leaders had a key influence in addressing environmental issues, especially since the 1980s. In my opinion the role of the ecumenical patriarchate should be highlighted. In September 1989 Ecumenical Patriarch Dimitrios issued a 'Message on the Day of Prayer for the Protection of Creation' in which he underlined the 'destruction of the natural environment which is caused by man', as well as the 'phenomena which are threatening the life of our planet, such as the so called "phenomenon of the greenhouse" whose first indications have already been noted'.[3] In this message he declared 1 September of each year, the first day of the ecclesiastical year in the Orthodox Church, to be the day of the protection of the natural environment. When Ecumenical Patriarch Bartholomew was elected in 1991, he took a leading role in addressing the ecological crisis to the extent he has been called the Green Patriarch.[4] A few months after Dimitrios's message, on 1 January 1990, Pope John Paul II entitled his Message for the World Day of Peace, 'Peace with God the Creator, Peace with All of Creation'.[5]

The role of Christian leaders received unprecedented media attention with the release of Pope Francis's encyclical *Laudato Si': On Care for Our Common Home* in 2015.[6] The first chapter of the encyclical identified climate change as one of the major threats to the earth today (together with pollution, water crisis and the loss of biodiversity) but perhaps the leitmotiv of the encyclical is that 'everything is interconnected, everything is related'.[7] The emphasis on hearing both the cry of the earth and the cry of the poor[8] has as a clear precedent in the work on JPIC that Granberg-Michaelson also stressed. In fact, the Final Document of the Seoul Convocation affirmed: 'We are confronted by new and complexly interwoven threats: by entrenched and deadly forms of injustice ... by universal violence in open and hidden conflicts and increasing violations of fundamental human rights ... by the rapid degradation of the environment. ... The real danger lies in the interaction of these threats. Together they represent a global crisis.'[9]

This shows that, on climate change, the work of the WCC was prescient. As Granberg-Michaelson affirms, 'while scepticism among some remained, the WCC's

---

[3] The Message is available at https://www.patriarchate.org/-/message-by-h-a-h-ecumenical-patriarch-dimitrios-upon-the-day-of-prayer-for-the-protection-of-creation-01-09-1989 (accessed 31 October 2018).

[4] See John Chryssavgis (ed.), *Cosmic Grace, Humble Prayer: The Ecological Vision of the Green Patriarch Bartholomew I* (Grand Rapids: Eerdmans, 2003).

[5] The Message is available at: https://w2.vatican.va/content/john-paul-ii/en/messages/peace/documents/hf_jp-ii_mes_19891208_xxiii-world-day-for-peace.html (accessed 31 October 2018).

[6] Pope Francis, *Laudato Si': On Care for Our Common Home* (Vatican City: Libreria Editrice Vaticana, 2015).

[7] See *Laudato Si'* §70, 92, 117, 120, 137, 142 and 240.

[8] Ibid., §14, 49, 53 and 117.

[9] See 'Final Document: Entering into Covenant Solidarity for Justice, Peace and the Integrity of Creation', in D. Preman Niles (ed.), *Between the Flood and the Rainbow* (Geneva: WCC, 1992), 164–5. A more detailed analysis of the ecumenical movement and *Laudato Si'* can be found in Guillermo Kerber, 'Ecumenical Background and Reactions to Laudato Si'", *Voices* 39 (2016–2), 63–76.

efforts stressed the impact of climate change on the most vulnerable and marginalized groups, including Indigenous peoples'.

Climate justice as following on the JPIC conciliar process

This articulation between environmental threats, and later climate change, with vulnerable and marginalized groups paved the way to the emphasis on climate justice which has been at the core of WCC's and ecumenical work on climate for the last decade.

The second conclusion of Granberg-Michaelson is that the 'ecumenical work addressing climate change was persistent'. This conclusion focuses on the advocacy work of the WCC at the Conference of Parties (COPs) of the United Nations Framework Convention on Climate Change (UNFCCC). This focus on climate justice in my view follows directly on the JPIC process. This focus is clear through the titles of the statements delivered at COPs, for instance, 'A Matter of Justice: An Interfaith Statement' (at COP 3 in Kyoto, 1997); 'Moving beyond Kyoto with Equity, Justice and Solidarity' (at COP 10 in Buenos Aires, 2004); 'Once More a Plea for Immediate Action: Climate Justice for All' (at COP 17 in Durban, 2011); and 'To Bonn and Beyond: Act Now with Justice and Peace' (at COP 23 in Bonn, 2017).[10]

Together with this advocacy work at the United Nations, at the local level, churches and religious communities have also focused on climate justice in their action.[11]

From ecumenical to interfaith collaboration

The advocacy work of the WCC at the various COPs has been done with others. These included universities, civil-society organizations and increasingly other religious and spiritual groups. While the WCC indeed played a pivotal role in convening religious groups as part of this preparatory process for the Earth Summit in 1992, as Granberg-Michaelson highlights, the interfaith component of the advocacy work of the WCC became more and more important over the years and was reflected in various actions

---

[10] For a comprehensive report of WCC activities organized at COPs until 2011, see Elias C. Abramides and Juan A. Taffi, 'WCC Participation in UN Conferences on Climate Change', *Spiritual Values for Earth Community,* David G. Hallman (ed.) (Geneva: WCC, 2012), 153–60.

[11] An overview of some of these actions in different regions of the world can be found in Grace Ji-Sun Kim (ed.), *Making Peace with the Earth: Action and Advocacy for Climate Justice* (Geneva: WCC, 2016).

and statements.[12] I think this interfaith, or 'macro-ecumenical'[13] move, galvanized a common ground and agenda which helped to recognize that advocacy is part of the mission of religious actors.

In these interfaith initiatives, Christian leaders played a key role in recent years. Archbishop Anders Wejryd, primate of the Church of Sweden, convened an Uppsala Interfaith Summit on Climate Change in 2008. In 2014 the WCC together with Religions for Peace organized an Interfaith Summit on Climate Change in New York in which thirty faith and spiritual leaders adopted the Interfaith Climate Statement presented to the UN Secretary General in the context of the UN Climate Summit. Several other interfaith activities were organized in the following years.

Such interfaith collaboration does not occur only at the international level. At the local and regional level common initiatives are developed by different Christian churches and other faith groups to stress the centrality and sacredness of life, the care for the earth and for the most vulnerable, and the critiques of exploitation and overconsumption.

Given the gravity of the climate change crisis and the complexity of international negotiations, it became clear to religious organizations that they could not effectively address climate threats alone. Therefore, in addition to their interfaith work, campaigns and events with other civil-society actors were implemented. Examples of this are the Global Call for Climate Action, 350.org and the divestment from fossil fuels movement.[14]

It is true, as Granberg-Michaelson indicates, that after three decades of ecumenical involvement on climate change, the picture remains grim. On the one hand, the international agreements reached at the global level are very far from effectively responding to the consequences of climate change at the community level. On the other hand, among the WCC member churches, those who have made climate change a priority in their mission remain a tiny minority.

Should this negative assessment lead us, as Granberg-Michaelson suggests, to conclude that ecumenical efforts in addressing climate change have failed to have the decisive influence that was originally imagined? I don't think so. Being aware of the risk of anachronism, I would say that over the decades the WCC, the ecumenical movement and other faith traditions (as well as civil society, the scientific community and others) have realized the complexity of the climate change crisis and the multiple

---

[12] For a collection of ecumenical and interfaith declarations see Christoph Stuckelberger and Guillermo Kerber (eds), *Religions for Climate Justice: International Interfaith Statements 2008–2014* (Geneva: Globethics, 2014).

[13] Macro-ecumenism is used by Bishop Pedro Casaldáliga from Brazil to refer to interfaith collaboration. For a theological perspective of macro-ecumenism see José Maria Vigil, 'Macro-ecumenism: Latin-American Theology of Religions', *Along the Many Paths of God*, José María Vigil, Luiza E. Tomita and Marcello Barros (eds) (Berlin: LIT Verlag, 2008), 137–52.

[14] For a more detailed analysis of interfaith advocacy on climate justice see Guillermo Kerber, 'International Advocacy for Climate Justice', in *How the World's Religions are Responding to Climate Change: Social Scientific Investigations*, Robin Globus Veldman, Andrew Szasz and Randolph Haluza-Delay (eds) (London/New York: Routledge, 2014), 278–93.

factors involved, affecting the decision-making process at the international, national and even community levels.

We might also ask whether the priority given to advocacy work by the WCC was appropriate. The WCC financial and human resources diminished dramatically over the last thirty years. This compelled the WCC to make some decisions and discontinue some programmes with the reaction from some churches that a specific programme that was ended was their priority. In a context of scarce resources, the relevance given to climate change, due to the leadership of churches from regions such as Northern Europe, the Pacific and Africa, should be recognized. However, the frustration of ecumenical delegations after every COP over more than twenty years raises the question whether more emphasis put on what member churches are doing to respond to climate change would have been more 'effective'.

The last paragraphs of Granberg-Michaelson essay may give the impression that what started in the late 1980s was abandoned or failed. I think that efforts, albeit insufficient, were made to continue and develop the JPIC legacy amidst a changing climate in the WCC, its member churches, the ecumenical movement and the world. Within the WCC, various initiatives have taken to address the climate challenge, especially the 'Pilgrimage of Justice and Peace' adopted at the last WCC Assembly in Busan. In 2015, climate was the focus of this pilgrimage. Furthermore, several thematic issues of *The Ecumenical Review* have reflected on these topics in the last decade, not only from an ethical perspective but including aspects of spirituality, mission and *diakonia*.[15] The interrelation between climate and unity of the churches remains, as far as I know, something unrealized at the WCC, as Granberg-Michaelson regrets.

To respond to the question on ecclesiology and ethics that Granberg-Michaelson raises, we need to look at a broader picture of the ecumenical movement. Various initiatives at the global level have on one hand deepened the theological reflection on issues related to environment and climate change in particular. Two relevant examples are the international conferences hosted by the Orthodox Academy of Crete on 'Ecological Theology and Environmental Ethics' (2008, 2011, 2013, 2015, 2017) and on 'Sustainable Alternatives for Poverty Reduction and Ecological Justice' (2012, 2014, 2016) and the discussions within the Ecumenical Association of Third World Theologians which has focused on ecology and climate in various issues of its journal *Voices*.[16] Various representatives of the WCC played an active role in such initiatives. At the local level, although a small percentage, the movement of green churches,

---

[15] See the editions of *The Ecumenical Review* on 'Churches Caring for Creation and Climate Justice' (July 2010); 'Peace on Earth, Peace with the Earth' (March 2011); Ecumenical and Ecological perspectives of the God of Life (March 2013); 'Praying for Rain? African Perspectives on Religion and Climate Change' (October 2017) and 'Theology of the Oikos' (December 2018). See also the edition of the *International Review of Mission* on 'Mission and Creation' (November 2010).

[16] See the editions of *Voices* on 'Eco-Crisis Theological Visions' (2009); 'Religion and Ecology in This Hour of Planetary Emergency' (2011–1); 'Ecological Vision in a Groaning World' (2013–2&3); 'Deep Ecology, Spirituality and Liberation' (2014–2&3) and 'Laudato Si' and Ecology' (2016–2).

eco-congregations and other ecumenical expressions have brought to the congregational life issues that twenty years ago were only discussed in much narrower ecumenical circles.

I am quite aware this is not enough to effectively respond as ecumenical movement to the climate crisis. But having been witness to how grass roots ecumenical initiatives respond to climate change in places such as Brazil, Cameroon, Fiji, Indonesia, Germany and the United States, to mention only a few countries, I believe that these are seeds of hope that will grow in years to come.

PART IV

The Christian story of God's work

Introduction: On telling the story

Ernst M. Conradie

Earth scientists, including those contributing to reports gathered by the Intergovernmental Panel on Climate Change, have been constructing a fascinating narrative of remarkable changes in the earth's climate. There is an obvious need to situate anthropogenic climate change since the Industrial Revolution against the background of climate fluctuations over a much longer period. More specifically, there is a need to correlate the concentration of greenhouse gases in various layers of the earth's atmospheres with variations in the average global surface temperature, taking account of more dramatic regional changes.

The best indicator remains the concentration of carbon dioxide that has been as low as 180–210 ppm during ice ages, increasing to 280–300 ppm during warmer interglacial periods over the last two million years. Since the last ice age levels of carbon dioxide hovered around 280 ppm up to the mid-eighteenth century and have increased steadily since then to reach 407 ppm by mid-2017. This is the story of a changing climate.

It is significant to note the time frames adopted for reconstructing this narrative. One may focus only on the period since 1956 when Charles Keeling commenced with observations at the Mauna Loa Observatory, or on the period since the advent of the Industrial Revolution. Scientific data allow for reconstructions since the last ice age 12,000 years ago, for fluctuations during the cycle of ice ages over the past 2.5 million years, or over hundreds of millions of years. Over billions of years there have been dramatic changes since the formation of the earth 4.6 billion years ago, but with a steady decline in carbon overall. This is fascinating given the markers of the Industrial Revolution, the agricultural revolution, the period of hominin evolution, the emergence of multicellular life and the emergence of bacterial life. There is little doubt that forms of life in general and human civilization in particular have been influencing the climate so that the present epoch of anthropogenic climate change has to be framed within the much longer narrative.

In this section of the volume this narrative of a changing climate will be viewed through the lens of the story of God's work as told within the Christian tradition and constructed, deconstructed and reconstructed in Christian theology. Could this lens help Christians to make sense, if only for themselves, of the implications of the data gathered by scientists? Could this lens even assist others in multidisciplinary discourse on climate change? This lens, like most others (contrast telescopes with microscopes or colour filters), will distort the picture even if it enables one to see some details better. Or is the lens so stained, as sceptics may suspect, that it is of no further use and should be discarded?

A few brief observations on the Christian narrative of God's work will have to suffice here:[1]

First, many modes of narrative theology have insisted that the Christian faith is best understood not as a belief system but as a story. This is not merely the his-story of Christianity, but is theologically interpreted as an account of what God has done, is doing and is expected to do, based on God's promises and with reference to witnesses to past events such as the Exodus and the resurrection of Christ.

Second, theological expositions of the story have often functioned as metanarratives – much maligned in postmodern discourse. Some would say that there are not only different versions of the Christian story, but also different stories and indeed different gods. Can this story still be held together as one narrative? This remains an open question but the Christian story is undoubtedly a mega-narrative – the implied timeframe of this story scarcely exceeds four thousand years, but there are hints towards the very origins of life, of the earth (the land) and indeed the entire cosmos. It is at least clear that the story of the universe, of the earth, of life on earth and of the earth's changing climate is indeed one narrative, albeit one with many twists and turns.

Third, the story remains incomplete. It is told from within the present by reconstructing the past and in anticipation of what the future may hold. This implies that no one has a definitive version of the story, that there is some suspense (as with any good story) and that the (ecological) moral of the story is highly significant.

Fourth, this story can be told in many different ways. There is no one way to begin the story. It can be told from the centre (e.g. Jesus Christ), from the present (Christian communities), from the anticipated end and even from the beginning – even if the storytellers were obviously not present then. The story can also be messed up in many ways. In particular, it can be messed up within a North Atlantic context so that the dominance of civilizations and empires emerging from within this region is theologically legitimized.

Fifth, for Christians this is primarily a story of God's work. This includes what God has done for us and our salvation and what God is doing through us (as humans or more specifically as Christians), but the story cannot be reduced to salvation only as that is situated within the tension between creation and eschatological consummation (or re-creation). This begs hard questions around divine action in the world though.[2] It also begs questions in conversation with other religious traditions as to who this God is (to be discussed in the next section of this volume).

---

[1] See also the essays in Ernst M. Conradie et al. (eds), *Christian Faith and the Earth: Current Paths and Emerging Horizons in Ecotheology* (London: T&T Clark, 2014). The essays in this section build on such earlier work.

[2] See, especially, Robert John Russell, Nancey Murphy and William R. Stoeger, *Scientific Perspectives on Divine Action: Twenty Years of Challenge and Progress* (Berkeley: Center for Theology and the Natural Sciences/Vatican City: Vatican Observatory Publications, 2008).

Sixth, although there are many ways to construct the story, it is not so hard to identify common episodes that are captured in the various versions of the story. In this volume we have opted for nine such episodes, dimensions or features of the story: (1) God's initial and ongoing creation; (2) God's work through the emergence of humanity; (3) The emergence of human sin; (4) God's continued providence; (5) God's work of election; (6) God's acts of salvation for us; (7) God's work of salvation in and through us; (8) God's work through the church; and (9) the consummation of God's work. Again, these may be contested, the sequence may be debated, some omitted and others added, but there need not be grave disputes on the ones identified here.

Seventh, it is worth reminding that the narrative character of the story is often underplayed in theological reflections on these themes. This can only undermine the story. A more pertinent danger is to subsume one episode under another, for instance to focus the whole story on humanity, to subsume creation under salvation, to reduce theology to theodicy, to either revolve the story around election or to omit that altogether, to see this as a story of the church, or to subsume everything under evolution (ongoing creation). This can only mess up the story. What is needed is an act of juggling, keeping all the cones in the air, not catching any one of them lest all the others may fall.[3]

Finally, the plausibility of this story obviously remains contested. The reasons for such contestation may be the moral character of the storytellers, the destructive legacy of Christianity (and its environmental track record), and its plausibility in terms of current scientific insight. The main question in this section of the volume, though, is to establish whether this story may illuminate the story of a changing climate. This remains a huge challenge. Others may readily concede the significance of the emergence of human sin, but what about the claims of salvation and consummation? Can God rescue us from self-destruction amidst a changing climate? How is that to be expected? Or is the Christian story of God's work irrelevant amidst climate change? Since Christians cannot easily concede that, the onus is on them to demonstrate the plausibility of the story.

---

[3] For a discussion, see Ernst M. Conradie, *The Earth in God's Economy: Creation, Salvation and Consummation in Ecological Perspective* (Berlin: LIT Verlag, 2015).

Chapter 4.1
God's initial and ongoing creating

Thomas Jay Oord[1]

Christians confess God to be Creator. They do so for many reasons, but most point to the witness of Christian scripture as the primary source of their confession. Scripture writers offer diverse metaphors, analogies and narratives to describe God's creating. Christians today interpret these writings in various ways, and this leads them to speculate on *how* and *why* God creates.[2] The results of this speculation matter for how Christians respond theologically to ecological crises and relate to creation more generally.[3]

In this essay, I address four issues at the centre of Christian theology's engagement with creation in general and issues like climate change, environmental degradation and species extinction in particular. Many more issues are worthy of consideration. I choose these four for what they say about God's power and love in relation to creation. Implicit in them are three questions: Does God's love entail plans, desires and purposes for creation? Does God have the power to control creation to accomplish those purposes? Do creaturely actions – for good or ill – ultimately matter to God's purposes?

Ex nihilo?

Since the third century, most Christians have said God initially created our universe from absolute nothingness (*creatio ex nihilo*).[4] The Bible doesn't explicitly support this

---

[1] Thomas Jay Oord is a theologian, philosopher and scholar of multidisciplinary studies in the Northwest United States. He's the award-winning author of more than twenty books and a leading researcher in open and relational theology, science and religion, and love studies.

[2] For a good overview, see Ernst M. Conradie, 'What on Earth Did God Create? Overtures to an Ecumenical Theology of Creation', *The Ecumenical Review* 6:4 (2014), 433–53.

[3] I am indebted to many for conversations on this essay. I thank especially Charles Christian, Gloria Coffin, Hans Deventer, Todd Erickson, Eric Folk, Roland Hearn, Max Johnson, Mark Karris, Richard Kauffman, Catherine Keller, Graden Kirksey, Craig Lamos, Michael Lodahl, Isaac Petty, Andre Rabe, Jason Roberts, Graeme Sharrock and Tara Hodges West.

[4] For essays focusing on particular advocates of *creatio ex nihilo* in history, see chapters in David B. Burrell et al., *Creation and the God of Abraham* (Cambridge: Cambridge University Press, 2010) and 'Creation "Ex Nihilo" and Modern Theology', in *Modern Theology* 29:2 (April 2013), 5–21.

claim as numerous biblical scholars have noted. Biblical writers speak of God creating out of or in relation to creation (water, invisible things, chaos [*tehom*], the deep, and more) rather than from nothing. Nevertheless, the doctrine of creation from nothing prevails among liberal and conservative Christians.

Historians argue about the origin of the creation from nothing view. Gerhard May's widely influential thesis is that two Gnostic leaders introduced the idea. Gnosticism typically regards matter as inherently evil, so Gnostics would understandably be averse to the idea that a holy God used unholy materials when creating. Most Christians reject the Gnostic belief that matter is inherently evil, but they retain the creation from nothing view.

In the second century, Irenaeus proved influential in establishing *creatio ex nihilo* among Christians. '[God] was influenced by no one but, rather, made all things by his own counsel and free will,' argues Irenaeus.[5] 'God made those things that were made in order that all things might exist out of things that did not exist, just as he willed, making use of matter by his own will and power.'[6] The sovereignty of God was especially important for Irenaeus's claim that God created from nothing. 'The will of God must rule and dominate in everything,' he argued, 'everything else must give way to it, be subordinated to it, and be a servant to it.'[7]

There are Christians who propose alternatives to *creatio ex nihilo*. Some of yesteryear and some today suggest that God creates from Godself or *ex Christi*.[8] The idea that God creates out of Godself seems to lead to pantheism, however. Most Christians want to distinguish between the transcendent Creator and creation, believing God differs in important ways from creation and alone is worthy of worship. Consequently, *creatio ex deo/christi* theory has few adherents.

Other Christians argue that God creates out of chaos, possibilities, profundity, love, previously created things, eternal matter and more.[9] The motivations they have for proposing these theories vary, but some appeal to their favourite theory for its fruitfulness for ecological concerns. These theories also often provide a middle way between an entirely transcendent or entirely immanent God. Labels such as 'panentheism', 'a sacramental universe', 'theo-cosmocentrism' or 'deep incarnation' describe this middle way.

Those who offer alternative theories to *creatio ex nihilo* note two problems that the traditional view presents for motivating Christians to care for creation. The first problem

---

[5] Irenaeus, *Against Heresies, Ancient Christian Writers Series*, Book 2, Vol. 64 (New York: Newman, 2012), 1:1.
[6] Ibid., 10:2.
[7] Ibid., 34:4.
[8] For biblical support for creation out of Christ, see 1 Cor. 8.6; Col. 1.15-20; John 1.1-3, and Heb. 1.2.
[9] Find arguments for these views in Thomas Jay Oord (ed.), *Theologies of Creation: Creation Ex Nihilo and Its New Rivals* (New York: Routledge, 2015). See also Catherine Keller, *Face of the Deep: A Theology of Becoming* (London: Routledge, 2003) and Jürgen Moltmann, *God in Creation: An Ecological Doctrine of Creation* (London: SCM Press, 1985).

is that creation from nothing implies creation is ultimately insignificant. That which comes from nothing is finally superfluous.

Proponents of *creatio ex nihilo* typically regard creation's lack of necessity as positive. *Creatio ex nihilo* tells us, they say, that creation is a free divine gift from a transcendent God. God could have decided not to create, and God could decide, at any moment, to send creation into non-existence. Creation is a wholly divine gift bestowed and supported by God's omnipotence.

Thinking God created the universe from nothing, however, easily leads to thinking creation does not *ultimately* matter. Michael Zbaraschuk puts it this way: 'If the world is created out of the nothing in a free expression of the divine power, its radical contingency means that it is, at the end of the day, not very important. If God made it once unilaterally, so God can make it again.'[10] It's understandably difficult for some Christians to feel motivated to care for and protect what ultimately doesn't matter. The lack of motivation becomes especially problematic when caring for and protecting creation requires considerable self-sacrifice.

Some respond to this charge by arguing that earthly oriented motivations ought to be secondary. Christians ought to be primarily concerned with what God commands, they say, not with whether creation is radically contingent. 'Who cares *how* the universe was created or if it ultimately matters,' they say, 'we must obey God and not worry about understanding our world.'[11]

Making a biblical case that God commands care for creation, however, requires interpretative moves not obvious to many Christians.[12] While important scholarly work has been done, much of the biblical witness seems unconcerned with creation care. Anthropocentrism reigns. Ecologically-oriented theology would find strong scriptural justification had Jesus said, 'Love all creatures great and small, care for the earth and its ecosystems, and learn to live sustainably with creation!' While biblical writers say God cares for non-human creatures, explicit commands that humans love animals, ecosystems and the planet are rare if present at all.

The traditional creation from nothing view implies a second problem: If God has the power to create something from nothing, it stands to reason God has the power to prevent ecological degradation singlehandedly. Such prevention might mean overpowering humans to stop them from harming creation, or it might mean creating

---

[10] Michael Zbaraschuk, '*Creatio Ex Deo*: Incarnation, Spirituality, Creation', in *Theologies of Creation: Creation Ex Nihilo and Its New Rivals*, Thomas Jay Oord (ed.) (New York: Routledge, 2015), 79–86 (85).

[11] The concept of place-making is key to understanding ecotheology, meaning that humankind is tasked with knowing and indwelling the earth as the primary 'context' in which God has placed us. According to Craig G. Bartholomew, this is the primary function of Genesis, which Bartholomew perceives as more of a 'place story' than an 'earth story'. For more, see *Where Mortals Dwell: A Christian View of Place for Today* (Grand Rapids: Baker Academic, 2011).

[12] For examinations of the biblical claims about creation care, see Richard Bauckham, *The Bible and Ecology: Rediscovering the Community of Creation* (London: Darton, Longman, and Todd, 2010), Norman Habel (ed.), *The Earth Story in Genesis* (Sheffield: Sheffield Academic, 2000).

from nothing obstacles to thwart such harm. If God has *creatio ex nihilo* power and yet allows environmental degradation, one might even assume God *wants* that degradation. If God *really* cared about creation, the God with *ex nihilo* power could prevent ecological disaster singlehandedly.

This problem leads some Christians to adopt noninterventionist theologies, whereby God either can't or won't interrupt natural processes or creaturely free will. The 'God won't intervene' option doesn't solve the problem, of course. After all, 'won't' retains the idea God *could* prevent ecological degradation unilaterally. The 'God can't intervene' view is conceptually stronger but requires a more radical reformulation of divine power. Theologians who believe God can't or won't prevent ecological degradation unilaterally, however, should find alternatives theories to *creatio ex nihilo* attractive.

I suggest Christians set aside the view that God created the universe from absolute nothingness. Rather than follow the logic of Irenaeus, Christians should follow the logic of biblical passages, which consistently speak of God creating through, with, and alongside creation. A more adequate creation theory might say God lovingly creates something new in each moment from that which God created previously, and God's creating has always been occurring. Our universe began at the Big Bang, but it was preceded by previous universes and will be followed by more.[13]

We might call this theory '*creatio ex creatione sempieternaliter en amore*' (God creates out of creation, everlastingly in love), if we thought the Latin mattered. The everlasting God who everlastingly creates, is the ever Creator. This view not only fits the dominant biblical views of God creating from creation, but also supports the idea God creates through self-giving, others-empowering and therefore uncontrolling love. And it says the God who creates from creation cannot prevent environmental evils singlehandedly.

Co-creators?

When creating the heavens and the earth by hovering over the face of the deep 'in the beginning', God called upon what had been created to 'bring forth' more creation (Gen. 1). Whether understood in terms of procreation or the fashioning of something new from something previous, God calls upon creatures to create.

In recent centuries, many stress the significance of history for understanding existence. Science plays an important role in this heightened awareness of time's flow. At the heart of the scientific contribution is evidence that the universe is very old, and complex creatures emerged slowly through a long evolutionary process. In recent

---

[13] Many argue that Big Bang Theory leads us away from anthropocentrism to a more 'sobered' perception of our importance in the created order. Sallie McFague makes this argument in 'An Earthly Theological Agenda', in *Ecofeminism and the Sacred*, Carol J. Adams (ed.) (New York: Continuum, 1993), 84–98.

decades, cosmological measurements showing the expansion of the universe further establishes the ancient universe view.

Given an old universe, the emergence of new species over long periods, and an expanding universe, many theologians today argue that God is an ongoing Creator (*creatio continua*). Given the role of procreation and the activity of creatures making the world, many speak of creatures as co-creating with God.[14] God not only created long ago and called creatures to 'bring forth' others, but God also creates today and empowers creatures to be created co-creators.

The role humans play in creation is often tied conceptually to the first chapter of Genesis. There we find that humans are made in God's image (*imago dei*). Although the text is silent about whether other creatures reflect that image, Christians often appeal to this claim when arguing that humans differ in kind from other creatures.[15] Some explicitly affirm that humans have spiritual souls and are the only creatures God deems worth saving; other Christians implicitly affirm the idea.

Genesis 1 states that humans are to 'subdue' the earth and have 'dominion' over it.[16] Some interpret the language of subduing and dominion as encouraging humans to dominate other creatures and ravage the earth.[17] 'The rise of modern science, the mastery of the world that it enabled, and the catastrophic consequences for the natural environment that ensued,' says historian of science, Peter Harrison, 'were intimately related to the new readings of the seminal Genesis text, "have dominion."'[18] Such readings led Lynn White Jr famously to argue that Christianity 'bears a huge burden of guilt' for the planet's environmental problems.[19]

But Christians also read scripture as saying humans should steward creation. God's command to let the land rest during Jubilee, for instance, has been interpreted in this way.[20] Rather than dominating the natural order, some texts support the claim that God calls humans to nurture the world's well-being. In other words, the Bible can be interpreted as supporting both domination over and care for creation. In assessing

---

[14] See especially, Philip Hefner, *The Human Factor: Evolution, Culture, and Religion* (Minneapolis: Fortress, 1993).

[15] Pope Francis addresses this argument in *Laudato Si'*. He says, 'Each of the various creatures, willed in its own being, reflects in its own way a ray of God's infinite wisdom and goodness.' In his discussion he cites the presence of this concept in the Roman Catholic Catechism. See Pope Francis, *Laudato Si': On Care for Our Common Home* (Maryland: The Word Among Us Press, 2015).

[16] Norman Wirzba points to Genesis 2.15, where scripture describes Adam as a farmer and keeper of the garden. This framing of humankind's role among creation is characterized by 'transformation and healing rather than control or exploitation'. See Norman Wirzba, *Paradise of God* (New York: Oxford University Press, 2003), 125.

[17] Norman Habel notes that 'subdue', on just about any interpretation, suggests that humans treat creation harshly. Cf. *The Earth Story in Genesis*, 47.

[18] Peter Harrison, 'Subduing the Earth: Genesis 1, Early Modern Science, and the Exploitation of Nature', *Journal of Religion* 79 (1999), 86–96.

[19] Lynn White, Jr, 'The Historical Roots of our Ecological Crisis', *Science* 155 (1967), 1203–7.

[20] See, for instance, Arthur Waskow, *Godwrestling – Round 2* (Philadelphia: Jewish Lights, 1996).

how theologians use scripture, H. Paul Santmire concludes that, 'as a whole, Christian theology is both promising and not promising for those who are seeking to find solid traditional foundations for a new theology of nature.'[21]

Appealing to creatures as co-creators raises important questions for climate change and other environmental concerns. First, it suggests that even if *creatio ex nihilo* were the correct view of initial creation, God did not singlehandedly create the current state of the world. Creatures also played a role – they acted to promote beauty and goodness, but also caused destruction and evil. Some creatures are morally responsible, and their actions in relation to creation may be worthy of praise or blame.

The co-creating idea, secondly, provides a theoretical framework for believing creatures might play a role in reversing actions, habits and policies that harm the planet and its inhabitants. If this framework includes the view either that God voluntarily creates alongside creation or does so necessarily, constructive creaturely co-creating may be seen as crucial to promoting the common good.[22] Rather than subduing or dominating, humans may work lovingly to restore, nurture and celebrate creation.

Here again, however, the question of God's omnipotence comes into play. Is human activity merely child's play supervised by an omnipotent Teacher able to guarantee everything will work out? Is creaturely co-creating ultimately unimportant to the work of a sovereign deity who can ensure redemption unilaterally? Or does co-creating *really* matter, such that God can't prevent ecological disaster without creaturely cooperation? Does the planet's future good rest, at least in part, on what we do? How one answers such questions can influence one's motivation to care for creation.

Evil in creation?

In the first chapter of Genesis, we read repeatedly that God regarded what was created 'good'. Long before humans enter creation's drama, the Creator blesses creation and identifies it as valuable. In other biblical texts, we find God creating through Wisdom (e.g. Prov. 8.22-31), caring for the broader community of creation (Ps. 104, 148) and working towards new creation (e.g. Is. 65; 2 Cor. 5.17; Rev. 21.5). Various texts suggest that creatures have intrinsic value apart from what they may contribute to human flourishing (e.g. Ps. 19, 89, 104). One might have wished that biblical authors had written more about the value of non-human creation, but some texts do exist.

The Bible accounts well for the immense beauty and goodness we see in the world, but we also encounter plenty of ugliness, evil and ecological destruction. Some aspects of the universe seem marvellously designed, while others persist in chaos and decay. It's

---

[21] H. Paul Santmire, *The Travail of Nature: The Ambiguous Ecological Promise of Christian Theology* (Minneapolis: Fortress, 1985), 9.
[22] See Ibid.

not hard to imagine a loving God inserting in creation possibilities for love, beauty, truth and goodness. But why would God create a world with the possibility of greed, sloth, lust, gluttony, recklessness, rape, genocide, murder, torture and ecological disaster?

One Christian answer blames Adam and Eve. In this view, the sin of the first human pair – whether historical or mythical – provides a metaphysical framework to explain our current problems. Their fall doomed all creation: humans, other creatures, even inanimate objects and ecosystems. In some mysterious way, moral creatures inherit a propensity to sin from this original pair. Various biblical passages and the early writings of Augustine influence some Christians to believe nature is depraved and the world inextricably linked to sin and evil.[23]

The Adam and Eve answer offers a much-debated account of sin and evil, but it doesn't address the 'why' question asked above. To phrase it again, why would God initially make a world with the possibility for evil, especially so *much* evil? Does the immensity of evil derive from an unfortunate design flaw?

Some Christians answer this 'why' question by saying God thought it important to create a stage for the drama of moral development. In particular, God wanted humans freely to cooperate with love and thereby become suited for eternal bliss. If humans are truly free and their choices really matter, the possibility for them not to cooperate – and the evil that would result – must also have been built into the creation system.

Less often considered is why other animals and forms of life need to suffer.[24] Massive non-human suffering occurs not only in the present but has occurred in evolutionary history long before humans arrived. Why would a loving God create a world in which *so many* creatures suffer, creatures apparently not capable of moral development?

From the earliest struggles for survival to the present-day political and social systems, we find structures that encourage domination. So-called structural evils encourage the domination of the few and mighty over the many and weak. Some systems encourage instantaneous gratification or quick fixes that exploit the most vulnerable creatures and health of the earth.[25] Why would a loving God create a world with structural evil?

The most vulnerable people on planet earth are often harmed by the most powerful and wealthy. Economic factors privilege the wealthy to the detriment of the poor. Sometimes, North Atlantic theologies contribute directly or indirectly to this harm. It's easy for the abused and impoverished around the world to believe an omnipotent God

---

[23] Many theologians criticize Augustinian theology for being ecologically destructive. Perhaps most famous is Matthew Fox's criticism in *Original Blessing: A Primer in Creation Spirituality* (Santa Fe: Bear and Company, 1983). Others defend Augustine, appealing to his later writings as celebrating rather than denigrating nature. See, for instance, Santmire, *The Travail of Nature,* Chapter 4.

[24] Larry L. Rasmussen notes that this lack of consideration for the suffering of animals is in part due to humankind's broken relationship with the natural world. Our interactions and affection for the creation are now vastly manufactured and manicured. See *Earth-Honoring Faith: Religious Ethics in a New Key* (New York: Oxford University Press, 2013).

[25] For more on these structural injustices, see Cynthia D. Moe-Loebeda, *Resisting Structural Evil: Love as Ecological-Economic Vocation* (Minneapolis: Fortress, 2013).

must want the status quo, which includes their mistreatment. After all, the God who could overturn economic realities singlehandedly fails to do so. Why would God never or rarely intervene to rescue those oppressed by ecologically destructive practices?[26]

Four questions noted above challenge traditional Christian creation views. Why would a loving God create a world with (1) the possibility for so much evil, (2) apparently pointless animal and other creaturely suffering today and in evolutionary history, (3) structures of evil that make possible and even sometimes contribute to ecological harm and (4) economic realities the powerful use to oppress their fellow creatures?

My own response to these questions not only denies the traditional *creatio ex nihilo* view but also says God's love is inherently uncontrolling in relation to creation at all levels of complexity. The God whose love makes controlling others impossible is not culpable for allowing so much evil, animal suffering or the structures of evil. Creatures at all levels of complexity and throughout evolutionary history have been acting in positive and negative ways towards one another. God creatively influences each through creative love, but God cannot control creatures who harm others in genuinely evil ways. This God doesn't allow or permit evil, as if preventing it singlehandedly were possible. God can't control creation because uncontrolling love comes logically first in God's nature.

The view that God's love is essentially uncontrolling and God can't stop evil singlehandedly, however, worries some Christians. This worry is tied, in part, to concerns about eschatology. I move to the fourth issue at the centre of Christian theology's engagement with creation, in general, and issues like climate change, environmental degradation and species extinction, in particular.

The purpose of creation?

The preceding might prompt us to speculate on the purpose of life. What might be God's purpose in creating and loving creation? And does our view of creation's purpose – especially at its eschatological end – affect how we respond to climate change, ecological harm and species extinction?

The Westminster Confession describes God's purposes primarily in terms of glory and power. The Confession says it 'pleased' God to create all things from nothing 'for the manifestation of the glory of His eternal power, wisdom, and goodness'. God's creating for His own glory, says this tradition, ought to prompt our worship. Thinking the purpose of life is divine self-glorification fits well with theologies that promote

---

[26] See Christopher Southgate, *The Groaning of Creation: God, Evolution, and the Problem of Evil* (Louisville: Westminster John Knox, 2008).

creation from nothing, absolute divine independence, an impassible God, creation's total depravity and controlling power.[27]

The Confession's logic that God creates to manifest sovereign glory raises many problems, some of which I've identified. Consequently, many today argue that God's purpose in creating derives more from love than power, more from self-giving altruism than self-aggrandizing egoism. God's purpose for creating comes from a particular Trinitarian logic, say some Christians. God expresses love within Trinity everlastingly, and this self-love 'spills over' so that God freely creates others with whom to give and receive love.

Some compare this outpouring of intra-Trinitarian love with the creative love of a happily married, fertile, heterosexual couple. While the couple's love for one another does not require them to procreate, they may do so voluntarily. Their procreative choice might be an expression of their love for one another, but they would also choose to love their offspring.[28] Analogously, God's creating the universe was an unnecessary expression of the love God necessarily expresses within Trinity. God's purpose for creating, then, was a free expression of love.

Although this analogy puts love as the primary purpose of God's creating, it fails in many ways. It provides no assurance that God consistently loves creation, for instance. There's no necessary reason God would love a creation that may not have existed in the first place. Saying 'it's God's nature to love creation' won't do. Married couples not only don't necessarily love one another, but they don't necessarily love their children. Child abuse is real. A God who does not by nature love creation could choose not to love creatures and even to abuse them.

Many who adopt the view that intra-Trinitarian love 'spills over' to create also affirm *creatio ex nihilo*. But this means the Triune God who creates *creatio ex nihilo* has controlling power. And because this God lacks essential relations to creation, this God has no internal reasons to love those created. This God could make good on a threat we sometimes hear from exasperated parents: 'I brought you into this world, and I can take you out of it!'

The idea of the Trinity, *per se*, is not the problem. The problem is the view of God's controlling power and arbitrary relations with creation many Trinitarian theologians embrace. By adopting *creatio ex nihilo* and insisting that God's relations to creation are radically contingent, the problems I note above emerge. A stronger way to affirm God's purpose for creating is to affirm the Triune God's creating and relating are uncontrolling and necessary.[29]

---

[27] For a criticism of Augustine's theology of love that supports the basic view of the Westminster Confession, see Thomas Jay Oord, *The Nature of Love: A Theology* (St. Louis: Chalice, 2010), Chapter 3.

[28] Clark H. Pinnock offers this analogy in *Most Moved Mover: A Theology of God's Openness* (Grand Rapids: Baker, 2001), 145.

[29] For an argument that we need not choose between a Triune God or a God who essentially relates to creation, see Oord, *The Nature of Love*, Chapter 4.

It's the 'I can take you out of [this world]' claim, however, that tempts some Christians to hold fast to believing that God ultimately is in control. They deem eschatological guarantees supremely valuable, and only a God who creates *ex nihilo* and can control creation guarantees complete victory at the end. Some who despair that the majority of humans will ever work with God to save the planet hope for divine coercion as a backup plan.

The God capable of control can singlehandedly restore all creation, overcome the degradation of the environment unilaterally, and by fiat restore creatures to full health. Not surprisingly, this controlling power is alluring! If God has the power to overcome evil at the end, however, one wonders why God doesn't use that power against evil now. The divine means to bring about the eschatological end must be the divine means at play today.

The Colossians vision of the cosmic Christ might serve as a framework for considering eschatological and teleological ends. Not only were 'all things ... created' in Christ, says the author of the letter, but through Christ God 'reconciles all things' (Col. 1.16, 20). Not clear in the passage is *how* God in Christ reconciles. Does this activity entail magnificent displays of overpowering omnipotence? Or does the work of Christ occur only through winsome expressions of uncontrolling love?

The eighteenth-century British theologian John Wesley pondered the possibility that God might singlehandedly restore all creation at the eschaton. 'Suppose the Almighty to act *irresistibly*, and the thing is done,' he writes. On this view, 'all difficulty that the world would be saved vanishes away'.[30] In this imagined unilateral reconstruction, we'd witness the ultimate creation makeover![31]

As quickly as Wesley posits the idea of God irresistibly saving creation, however, he dismisses it. God will not save in this unilateral way, he says, because 'then man would be man no longer; his inmost nature would be changed. He would no longer be a moral agent, any more than the sun or the wind, as he would no longer be endued with liberty, a power of choosing or self-determination. Consequently, he would no longer be capable of virtue or vice, of reward or punishment.'[32]

Wesley's logic is anthropocentric. God 'will not save us without ourselves' means that we play an essential role in salvation. Wesley's salvific vision includes broader creation, however.[33] While his emphasis may be anthropocentric, the implications are cosmologic.[34]

---

[30] John Wesley, 'The General Spread of the Gospel', *The Works of John Wesley* (Kansas City: Nazarene Publishing House, 1872 authorized editor of the Wesleyan Conference Office), 6:280.

[31] See Michael Lodahl's exploration of Wesley's thoughts in *Renewal in Love: Living Holy Lives in God's Good Creation* (Kansas City: Beacon Hill, 2014).

[32] Wesley, 'The General Spread of the Gospel', 6:280.

[33] On the relation between creation and salvation, see Ernst M. Conradie, *Saving the Earth? The Legacy of Reformed Views on "Re-creation"* (Berlin: LIT Verlag, 2013).

[34] Wesley, 'The General Spread of the Gospel', 6:281.

The rationale we find in the Apostle Paul's letter to Roman Christians shape's Wesley's cosmological view of salvation. 'We know that the whole creation has been groaning in labour pains until now,' Paul writes. And 'the creation waits with eager longing for the revealing of the children of God.' From Paul's perspective, 'the creation was subjected to futility … in hope that the creation itself will be set free from its bondage to decay and will obtain the freedom of the glory of the children of God' (Rom. 8.22, 19-21).[35]

The logic, therefore, is that human activity is essential for cosmological salvation. And if God's uncontrolling love is the primary means for salvation at individual, social and cosmological levels, we might argue that love is the primary purpose of existence. In fact, we might say the *how* of God's creating and saving is uncontrolling love in relation to creation. The *why* of this creating and saving is also love: God's love for all creation and God's desire that creatures love.[36]

God's purpose for creating and saving matters not only for understanding the environmental crisis. It also matters for understanding creaturely action in response to God and creaturely motivations for cooperating with God to overcome that crisis. Believing God's initial creating was *ex nihilo* and God's eschatological saving will be unilateral easily leads to thinking our ecological efforts are inconsequential. Why act self-sacrificially for climate change if God will unilaterally save at the end no matter what we do?

The traditional Christian view of divine power undermines our taking personal responsibility for environmental degradation. Those in vulnerable and less powerful positions – especially outside North Atlantic confines – may find that an alternative doctrine of divine power based on uncontrolling love makes better sense. It makes better sense of why a loving God has not already toppled North Atlantic institutions, political systems and ideas that either assume the status quo is what God wants or assume God will someday in the future fix all problems unilaterally.

Therefore, I suggest Christians reject the idea that God controls when creating, sustaining or saving. God's persuasive love operates at the beginning, middle and end. And God empowers creatures to join the work of love and promote the well-being of all creation.[37] The ends of creation, both the eschatological and teleological ends, coincide in the work of love.

---

[35] Of particular note is Paul's phrase 'the creation was subjected to futility, *not of its own will but by the will of the one who subjected it*' (Rm. 8.20b). Who is 'the one who subjected' creation to futility? Satan? Humans? Adam? The context does not clarify. The only interpretation I strongly oppose says God subjected creation to futility. See also Southgate, *The Groaning of Creation*.

[36] Richard Rohr calls upon Christians to look closely at how traditional Western theology has impacted human behaviour and in turn the current state of the planet. Richard Rohr, 'Creation as the Body of God', in *Spiritual Ecology: The Cry of the Earth* (Point Reyes: The Golden Sufi Center, 2014), 257–66.

[37] J. Phillip Newell argues that to be made in the image of God means that we must use our power to love creation. See *Echo of the Soul: The Sacredness of the Human Body* (Harrisburg: Morehouse Publishing, 2000).

Chapter 4.2
God's work through the emergence of humanity

Peter Manley Scott[1]

Beginning

In our 2014 introduction to the volume *Systematic Theology and Climate Change*, Michael Northcott and I made the following two claims.[2] First, that the experience of climate change is not directly empirical. Second, that Christian theology had survived through various political crises in the twentieth century and had done so by remaking its distinctiveness. Five years have passed since that writing and the two claims seem less secure now. Setting aside the relationship between climate and weather, and our experience of new weather patterns, there does seem to be a change in our wider environment: not least a decline in the number of insects and a reduction in bird song. It is as if we are revisiting Rachel Carson's silent spring.[3] As for the second, the move to theological distinctiveness, the intellectual context now features the Anthropocene and astrobiology in which the earth as system is presented. This raises very difficult issues for theology that may not be adequately addressed by the recovery of a distinctive Christianity.

What are these issues? Astrobiology and the Anthropocene raise the issue of the earth as a *system*. One definition of astrobiology is 'the study of life in a cosmic context'.[4] As such, with its emphasis on the ways in which life interacts with its environment, astrobiology may well suggest the decentring of the human: we move from a biocentrism to a geocentrism. The Anthropocene may appear to be anthropocentric – and indeed some, such as David Grinspoon, have called for a 'good' Anthropocene with the

---

[1] Peter Manley Scott is Samuel Ferguson Professor of Applied Theology and Director of the Lincoln Theological Institute at the University of Manchester. His teaching and research is to be found at the intersection of political theology and ecological theology.
[2] Michael Northcott and Peter M. Scott, 'Introduction', in *Systematic Theology and Climate Change* (London: Routledge, 2014), 1–14.
[3] Rachel Carson, *Silent Spring* (London: Penguin 2000 [1962]).
[4] David C. Catling, *Astrobiology* (Oxford: Oxford University Press, 2013), 2.

implication that this may be in human control[5] – yet the assertion of the human as a geological force suggests otherwise. For geological forces are blind, so to speak. At least, such is the case given the aversion to the consideration of teleology in the natural sciences. Even extinction studies – an emerging area of enquiry in the humanities[6] – raises the issue of the system's demise.

In light of these developments, I am not recommending that theology needs simply to adjust to these insights. Instead, theology may reconsider its contribution and could do so through exploring responses to the following three questions:

What is *God* doing in and through the emergence of humanity? Any response is a matter of perspective. Which perspective, however? It is possible to say that God is bringing creation to a culmination in humanity and that a changing climate does not require any revision to such a view. A second view would argue that theological traditions might with some revision be able to give an account of how God is working, despite the loss of biodiversity that may be sourced to human activity. A third option would be to set aside these theological traditions – not polemically but in the sense of finding them seriously deficient. For this third option, God is not working, so to speak.

What is God doing in and through the *emergence* of humanity? Again, any response is a matter of perspective. Which perspective, however? To focus on emergence is to present the evolutionary history of humanity as consequential for understanding humanity's activity, including the basis and practice of reasoning and morality. How is the historical – the evolutionary-biological – development of humanity to be understood theologically in relation to grasping the significance for Christianity of human emergence?

What is God doing in and through the emergence of *humanity*? Once again, any response is a matter of perspective. Which perspective, however? Here we are referred to the consideration of a set of critical relationships. First, the emergence of humanity occurs alongside and in interaction with the emergence of other creatures. (This fact alone should raise concerns as regards the loss of biodiversity.) Moreover, such relationality must also be understood as social. As Karl Marx puts the matter in criticism of Ludwig Feuerbach: 'But *man* is no abstract being squatting outside the world. Man is the *world of man*: state, society.'[7] To explore, then, the emergence of humanity is to come to a judgement about the significance of other creatures for human living and the social configuration of human activities (which some call capitalism).

One essay in theological anthropology in the context of climate change cannot cover all these themes. Therefore, I shall note that standard theological schemas that stress creation/fall/redemption or nature/grace seem to offer only further contributions to anthropocentrism. Any theological anthropology in the context of a changing climate

---

[5] David Grinspoon, *Earth in Human Hands: Shaping our Planet's Future* (New York: Grand Central, 2016).
[6] Deborah Bird Rose et al. (eds), *Extinction Studies: Stories of Time, Death and Generations* (New York: Columbia University Press, 2017).
[7] Karl Marx, 'Towards a Critique of Hegel's *Philosophy of Right*: Introduction' (1844), in *Karl Marx: Selected Writings*, David McLellan (ed.) (Oxford: Oxford University Press, 1977), 63.

will need to attend to such anthropocentrism. Additionally, the emergence of the discourse of the Anthropocene raises a further issue: not only human–nature relations (as in the critique of anthropocentrism) but also the identification of humanity as a planetary or geological force. Furthermore, astrobiology raises the issue of the relation of human life to planetary life.

In the light of this development, consideration needs to be given to understanding humanity along two trajectories of *bios* and *historia*. The first refers us to the conditions of life of humanity as a species and the second to the historical conditions of human life in which human beings are socially active and transform their conditions of life. The interactions between *bios* and *historia* now require sustained theological attention in order to provide an account of the further emergence of humanity. I say 'further' because human social activity now seems to offer – despite representations to the contrary – another undoing of creation, a *lapsus secundus*.

Method: *Lapsus Secundus*

In the previous section, I explored the concept of humanity theologically and anthropologically. The double nature of this exploration raises methodological issues. That is, climate change and the Anthropocene refer us to non-theological disciplines. If we then pose the question – 'What sort of contribution can theology make to this discussion?'– we are presented with the task of clarifying the relationship between theology and these other disciplines. There is a variety of ways of construing the relationship between theology and the natural sciences, as Neil Messer has helpfully explained.[8] Without exploring the options in detail, my position here is that theology does have something to contribute to this discussion and for a specific reason related to the topic.

The specific reason is as follows: the discussion of nature in the context of a warming climate raises a difficult hermeneutical issue. Within a human-framed phenomenology of nature, a tension in the concept of nature has often been noted.[9] Put briefly, does nature refer to that which includes the human or that which is other than the human?[10] We can see the same duality replicate itself in the doctrine of creation: by creation are we referred to a created unity or a distinction between humanity and nature (with different destinies in which humans are in some essential way different from the rest)? In astrobiology we can see the same issue: does 'planetary' in astrobiological discussion refer to the totality of the earth system that we are inside, so to speak, or to that part of

---

[8] Neil Messer, 'Evolution and Theodicy: How (not) to Do Science and Theology', *Zygon* 53:3 (2018), 821–35.
[9] Peter M. Scott, *Anti-human Theology* (London: SCM Press, 2010), 1–4.
[10] See Gordon Kaufman, 'A Problem for Theology: The Concept of Nature', *Harvard Theological Review* 65:3 (1972), 337–66 (341).

the biosphere which we are damaging and therefore in response ought to change our behaviour? Is Fredric Jameson correct that this duality is 'revelatory of some ontological rift or gap in the world itself'?[11]

If there is such an ontological rift or gap, it is important to stress that there is no reason intrinsic to the disciplines that requires theology to attend to the human side of the rift, and sciences to the nature side of the rift. The epistemological rift will manifest itself on both sides, with reference to the human and with reference to nature. Theology does not have a fault that the sciences then repair. Instead, we should expect that there will be evidence of the rift in all these disciplines. In what follows I shall briefly comment on the implications for theology by introducing the term, *lapsus secundus*. What is this second fall?

Lapsus secundus is an epistemological term and allows a theological response to the novelty of an anthropogenic warming of our climate. As such, it makes two points that are dialectically related. First, we are not able to draw upon the resources of the theological traditions in a straightforward way; such a manoeuvre is blocked by an epistemological fall. Both the novelty of our present situation and the impact of Christian anthropocentrism do not permit the easy deployment of theological resources. In this sense, *lapsus secundus* functions as an epistemological protocol that requires the theologian to be cautious about the prospect of repair emerging from within theology. Second, in that 'fall' finds its meaning in relation to creation and redemption, this is already thinking with theological traditions. *Lapsus secundus* is a term that secures its meaning only by reference to a theological schema. We are unable to think theologically, yet such a conclusion is already theological! Therefore, *lapsus secundus* is a dialectical notion: it suggests a break from the Christian past and yet also relies upon a Christian schema for its meaning. The *lapsus secundus* functions *doubly*: for its meaning, a second fall requires being related to a traditional Christian schema; simultaneously, such a relatedness, by reference to a rupture, is blocked.

A warming climate and the transition into the Anthropocene identify a practical and an epistemological fall. Such a fall has *cosmic* implications for theological epistemology. We may savour the deep irony: Christian distinctiveness is maintained by reference to the fall and yet appeal to distinctiveness is blocked by the same reference. As such, we may now recall the assessment at the opening of this essay regarding an appeal to Christian distinctiveness as a response to climate change. Based on the epistemological strictures of *lapsus secundus*, we are required to appeal to Christian distinctiveness and yet are unable to do so.

What does such a conclusion recommend for the consideration of God's work in the emergence of humanity? First, that whatever theological repair work is required, it will not be provided in any straightforward sense by the natural sciences. Second, that theology will need at least in part to turn to its own resources. Third, that these resources will not be adequate to the task. I suggest, in sum, that we shall need to draw

---

[11] Fredric Jameson, *Valences of the Dialectic* (London: Verso, 2009), 23.

on theological resources and yet differently. What guides theology in this traditioned and yet creative effort?

A common realm

I begin with a set of theological insights. To start, I note that the theological understanding of humanity is often presented after the doctrine of creation. In this way, the difference of humanity from the rest of creation may be stressed; the concept of *imago dei* may be recruited at this point to reinforce the difference. Next, the incarnation may be introduced and of the way that it behoves divinity to be unsurpassably present in human form, a human person. Then the creation/fall schema may be used to present the way in which human beings are at some distance from God and the way in which Christ may be understood to restore humanity's exemplary status. Attention to the redemption of the human – a personal eschatology – may then follow. We arrive at the matter of anthropocentrism in theology: its specific contours and direction. At this point, the stringency of *lapsus secundus* presents us with the discontinuity of rupture: how can we propose God's work as emergent in humanity by reference to these theological concepts?

We can further explore anthropocentrism or humanocentrism by noting some terms that have been proposed as criticism. In refusing anthropocentrism, we might affirm biocentrism or geocentrism or cosmocentrism. Biocentrism focuses on the concept of life but regionally understood. Geocentrism suggests reference to earth rather than to life; NASA's 'earthrise' image is a visual presentation of this concept. Cosmocentrism suggests an even broader perspective for considering the status of the human.

There are difficulties at every turn. If we stick with humanocentrism, we face the rejoinder that humanity is valued more highly than the non-human and the way is then open in imagination for the othering and instrumentalization of nature. Should the difference be marked by human reason, a gendered rendering of this duality has been common, in which the capacity of reason has been assigned to the male – and emotion to the female. (This has been a source of the view that 'woman' is closer to 'nature' than 'man'.) If we prefer to place the stress on biocentrism or geocentrism, there is the danger that a reductionism will emerge in which the human is understood from the perspective of natural processes to the detriment of the personal integrity of human beings.[12] Cosmocentrism introduces a different, and more expansive, scale and yet it remains unclear what the status of humanity is in this perspective. Certainly, the naturalistic options of bio-, geo-, and cosmocentrism stress the continuity between humanity and nature. We might call these options, following Luco van den Brom, a

---

[12] For a fuller discussion, see Peter M. Scott, *A Political Theology of* Nature (Cambridge: Cambridge University Press, 2003), 32–8.

type of monism.[13] It is not hard to see why these options are sometimes understood to be offering a mere reversal rather than a sophisticated *re*interpretation of the relations between humanity and nature.

By these options we are being presented with a contrast between humanity and nature. Can this tension between humanity and nature be overcome theologically? Whitney Bauman says not, at least not in the profile of Christianity as it is widely understood.[14] It is my position, however, that we cannot think with the schema and yet we must. Theologically, it is possible to accomplish the latter by referring to theocentrism: that cosmos, life, planet and human all should be decentred and related afresh to the concept of God. That is the way proposed here although much depends on the concept of God that is operative. I have developed two terms for thinking about this: 'common realm' and 'postnatural'. Let us consider these in turn in order to develop 'a new political theology of nature … which links human culture and the nature of the earth differently'.[15]

As I argued in *A Political Theology of Nature*, theological attention may be paid to the interactions between a natural humanity and a socialized nature as a way of identifying such a common realm.[16] In framing the issue this way, theological attention is directed to human activities or to specific praxes. At this point, however, we must rethink the scope of creation. Under ecological conditions, we may not refer only to *human* society. Instead, the doctrine of creation must be extended so that society encompasses creatures, human and non-human. Contemporary societies may be understood as plural: as sustained by a multiplicity of groups and corporations. Yet, along with this, nature is also to be understood as plural. Human societies are internally plural but externally plural also. Human societies are thereby sustained at least partly by a diverse set of relationships with a plural nature. (We can get a sense of plural nature if we note the multiplicity of the ways in which nature engages with the human: sometimes in support and sometimes in opposition.) I call this a 'greater society' in which nature is seen in diverse ways as internal to humanity. 'Greater' is to be understood in two senses: as referring to richer ways of understanding social plurality and as indicating a society that exceeds human society.[17]

Humanity is thereby given a greater ecological specification, which I call the postnatural, as a way of moving beyond anthropocentric options and their oppositions. The postnatural permits theology to think in fresh ways about the continuities and discontinuities between humanity and nature. Moreover, such fresh thinking is rooted in the doctrine of God in that the theocentric position being developed here is a theological

---

[13] See Luco van den Brom, 'The Art of a Theo-ecological Interpretation', *Nederlands Theologisch Tijdschrift* 51:4 (1997), 298–313 (304).

[14] See Whitney Bauman, *Theology, Creation and Environmental Ethics* (London: Routledge, 2014).

[15] Jürgen Moltmann, 'European Political Theology', in *The Cambridge Companion to Political Theology*, Craig Hovey and Elizabeth Philips (eds) (Cambridge: Cambridge University Press, 2015), 3–22 (15).

[16] Scott, *A Political Theology of Nature*, 30–60.

[17] Peter Manley Scott, 'Does Nature Pluralize? Towards a Greater Society', *Political Theology* 16:1 (2015), 5–19.

position. To put the issue crisply, we are dealing here with the issue of creation and differentiation: how are the differences of creation to be understood as constituted by the action of the creating God? This matter is deep in theological tradition and yet the requirement, warranted by *lapsus secundus*, emerges to think about creaturely differentiation differently.[18] We can get a sense of how difficult this will be if we ponder the worship performance at a Hillsong worship 'concert': the focus is clearly on the cosmic presence of God and the worshipping human.[19] The clever use of lighting, and the attraction of the songs, together with their lyrical content, foregrounds the individual before God. The effect here seems to be the differentiation of the worshipper from a wider context, including the human context; the presence of God is the establishment of individual relationship. Yet, if my promotion of the postnatural is correct, this form of differentiation cannot be the best option in the context of climate change.

I have already said that this theocentric move is an effort to push past humanocentrism and its oppositions. Yet there is no accepted way of doing this. One may identify three strategies that seem to offer a theocentric way of providing an account of the common realm in postnatural thought.

The first approach we might call 'natural' or 'philosophical' theology or possibly even 'fundamental' or 'correlational' theology. In this approach, the emphasis is on working with, at a fundamental and theoretical level, core interpretations of God and the world. The aim is emphatically not to offer some alien-to-the-gospel philosophical conceptuality to which theology must then conform. Instead, philosophical theology derives its strength from its ability to enable thinking about the world from the concept of God because it is the concept of God that enables thinking about the whole. How we think about God is therefore critically important for the ways in which we think about the world. Within this style of theological argumentation it is possible to explore both the unity and differentiation of God and world as qualitatively different and yet as related. From this perspective, an argument that is less concerned with the difference of humanity from the rest of creation may be developed.[20]

The second approach we might call 'systematic' theology in which the resources of doctrinal traditions are extended or amplified. For example, we might begin from the doctrine of the Trinity or a Trinitarian doctrine of creation by noting that such a systematic approach is already working with differentiation in God as three persons, Father, Son and Holy Spirit. Humanity may be interpreted in a Trinitarian fashion so that the creative activity of God is understood as not restricted to the human (Father), as joining the activity of humans with other creatures in a pattern or shaping (Son), and as recommending the Christian life as one of reinterpretation and new performance (Spirit). The direction of such a position is towards a postnatural theocentrism in which

---

[18] For the tradition, see Denys Turner, *Eros and Allegory* (Cistercian Publications, 1995).
[19] For an example of Hillsong worship, see https://www.youtube.com/watch?v=nQWFzMvCfLE (accessed 20 October 2018).
[20] Scott, *A Political Theology of Nature*, 38–42.

a fresh interpretation of human activities as always related to the activities of other, non-human creatures is maintained.

The third approach follows liberation theology in which the focus is on the ways in which theological concepts and arguments provide constellations of ideological power. That is, social and political arrangements are reinforced through theological discourses.[21] The liberation approach also explores ways in which such discursive power might be challenged. 'The symbol of God functions,' argues Elizabeth Johnson in a summary of this position.[22] How might such an approach assist us in thinking about humanity in the context of a changing climate? What needs critical attention here is the ways in which theology might support the options of humanocentrism, and its oppositions, as presented at the start of this section.

Clearly, none of these approaches tells us where we might end up in our consideration of the emergence of humanity. Nor should we be surprised by this finding for its indeterminacy is related to the epistemology of *lapsus secundus*; reference to Christian distinctiveness is required and yet the way to that distinctiveness is blocked. If we are to speak of humanity theologically in the context of a warming climate, we shall need to do so by reference to other non-human creatures, by reference to human *activities*, and by careful attention to the ways in which theological discourses reinforce human distinctiveness in unhelpful ways. One way of exploring the emergence of humanity in this way is through the contrast of *bios* and *historia*: God is the God of life as well as history and detailed specification must be given to this claim in which our understanding of human (re)productive activities and the human share of life are implicated.[23]

Unity and vocation of humanity

In the light of the call for a theocentric account of human distinctiveness might we think of the unity and vocation of humanity differently? I propose to respond by elaborating on the unity of all creatures and by gesturing briefly towards an interpretation of human vocation as representative of all creatures.

One way of exploring the unity of all creatures would be to expand the notion of human beings as *imago dei*. For example, the direction of Jürgen Moltmann's argument is to expand traditional conceptions of *imago dei* and offer theological reasons – rather than anthropological reasons – for his position. In other words, *imago dei* is best explicated theologically as a relation to God and, in developing that relation, Moltmann

---

[21] Peter M. Scott, *Theology, Ideology and Liberation* (Cambridge: Cambridge University Press, 1994).

[22] Elizabeth A. Johnson, *Quest for the Living God: Mapping the Frontiers in the Theology of God* (New York and London: Continuum, 2007), 98.

[23] This reveals the importance of astrobiology to theology: the former may offer to the latter an opportunity to relearn a planetary perspective and thereby a renewed perspective on the concept of life.

moves from substantialist to relational understandings of the human.[24] Thus *imago dei* is related to *imago mundi*, and to *imago Christi* in that Christ is the eschatological image of God on earth to which the believer is oriented.[25] Exploring the terms of image and likeness, Moltmann argues that human beings are God's representatives on earth (image) and also reflect God (likeness), and thereby indirectly reveal God in the world.[26] Moltmann summarizes thus:

> So as God's image and appearance on earth, human beings are involved in three fundamental relationships: they rule over other earthly creatures as God's representatives and in his name; they are God's counterpart on earth, the counterpart to whom he wants to talk, and who is intended to respond to him; and they are the appearance of God's splendour, and his glory on earth.[27]

Moltmann immediately counters the seeming anthropocentrism by arguing that there is no special characteristic in this constellation of ideas that separates the human from the non-human. Instead, the human (1) represents, (2) corresponds to and (3) reveals God through its *whole existence*. Moltmann argues that humans image God by reference to whole person, true human community and humanity 'bound up with nature' rather than by reference to soul, individual and lordship. We have here, if you like, the expansion of the image as the *totus homo*. This, we may assume, is one part of what Moltmann means by *imago mundi*: '[the human being] should first of all view himself as the product of nature and – theologically too – as *imago mundi*.'[28] Given this, how does the human being as *totus homo* represent, correspond to and reveal God?

Elsewhere, I have argued that the representation of nature is a curious case: the human representation of nature is irrevocable but not complete.[29] Such representation cannot be withdrawn but it is not totalizing: the human cannot represent all aspects of nature, either practically or theologically. Moltmann concedes this point by implication when he contends that humans are bound up with nature. Human beings may partially transcend nature but they do not do so in such a way as to offer a comprehensive representative performance.

The human corresponds to God also as *imago mundi* and *totus homo*. Such a conclusion suggests that the revelation of God as Creator requires and reinforces the embedded and entangled characterization of human beings. Moltmann notes as much when he identifies the principle of mutual interpenetration as one of his guiding ideas for an ecological doctrine of creation. Such a principle applies to God as well as to

---

[24] For these terms, see Marc Cortez, *Theological Anthropology* (London: T&T Clark, 2010).
[25] Jürgen Moltmann, *God in Creation: A New Theology of Creation and the Spirit of God* (London: SCM Press, 1985), 226.
[26] Ibid., 219.
[27] Ibid., 220–1.
[28] Ibid., 51.
[29] Scott, *Anti-human Theology*, 48–51.

creation: 'God is the mutuality and reciprocity of love.' Moltmann continues that all true relationships are analogous to God, including 'man and woman *in* the kingdom of unconditional and unconditioned love, freed to be true and complete human beings'.[30] Such mutuality and reciprocity is true more generally, applicable across a doctrine of creation: 'All living things – each in its own specific way – live in one another and with one another, from one another and for one another.'[31] Thus it seems that all living things – and not just human beings – to the extent that they enjoy mutuality and reciprocity, correspond to God.

Presented in this way, concepts of unity and vocation converge. We cannot speak of the unity of the human with other creatures without also speaking of the representative role of the human as part of its vocation. Moreover, Moltmann's position suggests that the human vocation is to love. Given this articulation of unity and vocation, we may appreciate why the consideration of stewardship has decreased as a way of treating human vocation. Jenkins, Berry and Kreider note that 'stewardship frameworks are liable to the criticism that they entrench anthropocentric arrogance and legitimate an exploitative ideal of global ecological control.'[32]

The creaturely and representative work of love may stand as a summary of the vocation of the human. Yet the epistemological force of *lapsus secundus* is evident once more. If, as the Anthropocene proposes, humans are a geological force, what is love's work? If humans are creatures and yet representatives, what is love's work? If the vocation of the human is active in the context of extinction, what is love's work? If the future is *without* the human, what is the impact of that ending on our understanding of God's work in humanity? In what ways is the world constituted by God's work in humanity?

The theological significance of our context, of a changing climate in the Anthropocene, emerges more clearly. The theological 'identity' of the human in relation to other creatures, including its calling and task, need to be reconsidered. In one perspective, God's work in the emergence of humanity looks ill-judged: humanity seems to be the destroyer of a world. Yet we may immediately see that such a conclusion is too abstract. What needs careful theological discussion is the sorts of activities that humans undertake, and their configuration, in order to appraise the social activities that are the source of anthropogenic climate change. Such an appraisal will be attentive to the full range of creaturely relations. It will also need to elaborate on the vocation of the human as representative and limited. And it will need to consider the meaning and nature of love in the Anthropocene. Such concerns may be summarized as the theocentric decentring of the human. God's work in the emergence of humanity refers us to God's work in and through other creatures and a planet. Perhaps we need something like a preferential option for the planet in theological interpretation?

---

[30] Moltmann, *God in Creation*, 17.

[31] Ibid.

[32] Willis Jenkins, Evan Berry and Luke Beck Kreider, 'Religion and Climate Change', *Annual Review of Environment and Resources* 43 (2018), 85–108 (95).

A final decentring emerges: the end of the human as a species through an extinction event to which the human in a specific society has contributed. We are invited to consider a world without the human. This takes us, I think, to the heart of Christian anthropocentrism. A theological response to such an invitation would need to consider God's purposes in creating and the destiny of creation – these are concerns taken up by other essays in this volume.

Conclusion: The work of God in the Anthropocene

In this undoing of creation, what is God's work in the emergence of humanity? Perhaps at the heart of this essay is a suggestion about love: that loving is God's work in the emergence of humanity. Yet we are having the discussion in the context of a second fall in which articulating such an insight is both imperative and yet profoundly difficult, as we have seen.

Chapter 4.3
The emergence of human sin

Ernst M. Conradie[1]

Introduction

There is something wrong with the current global economic order. That much should be obvious. The symptoms are evident from a changing climate. Such symptoms are widely discussed in climate change discourse. If these are the symptoms (to stay with medical metaphors), how may the underlying disease be diagnosed?

According to a widely discussed formula, environmental impact (I) results from three intertwined factors, namely overpopulation (P), overconsumption (A for affluence) and extractive technology (T). This formula may well be plausible but does not clarify the relative weight of each factor. An adequate diagnosis would require one to probe deeper. One would need to reckon with multiple layers of the underlying problem – technological, economic, political, cultural, moral and arguably also spiritual.

Some suggest that the problem is merely *technological* and look for the remedy in geoengineering to assist adaptation strategies. Others caution that the instruments that created the problem will not necessarily resolve that. Some suggest that the problem is of an *economic* nature and lies with late-modern, industrialized, neoliberal capitalism – which is premised upon infinite economic growth within a finite planet. This leads to both economic inequalities and ecological destruction that have to be addressed through 'development' and the allocation of sufficient finances to change the energy base of the global economy – without disturbing the growth paradigm. In response, others suggest a 'new economics' that would not only produce wealth (the strength of capitalism) and redistribute wealth (the strength of socialism) but will redefine how wealth is understood. Some suggest that climate change is a *political* problem that can best be addressed through negotiations, balancing global power blocks, formulating treaties and mustering political will. International peace is the key to addressing climate change. Others caution that justice, including climate justice is the key to peace. Some would observe that the main problem is of a *cultural* nature given patterns of consumption and focus on the fault lines within a consumerist society and the consumerist aspirations of

---

[1] Ernst M. Conradie is Senior Professor in the Department of Religion and Theology at the University of the Western Cape in South Africa, the leading historically black university in the country. He is situated in the reformed tradition, teaches systematic theology and ethics and specializes in Christian ecotheology.

the middle class and the global poor alike – which forms the dynamo that entices further economic growth. That may be so, but the remedy for consumerism is not so clear. One may follow strategies of education, apocalyptic warnings, media coverage, management or moral renewal, but whether any of these would transform the now global culture of consumerism is unlikely. Many would recognize that the problem is a *moral* one and argue that those who contributed least to climate change will suffer the consequences disproportionally. They would emphasize justice, equity, sustainability, frugality and wisdom. Others would say that underneath the moral problem lies a *spiritual* problem. This is indicated by the lack of moral energy, moral vision and moral leadership to do what should be done promptly enough. If one knows what to do, has the ability and resources to do so, but still finds oneself unable to do what is right, then he or she suffers from a spiritual problem, not only a moral problem. Arguably, this also applies to collective efforts to address climate change.

A Christian contribution to social diagnostics?

What can Christians contribute to this diagnosis of underlying layers of the problem that manifests itself in a changing climate? Many Christians would be inclined to take a shortcut at this point to capture the root cause of climate change with three letters: sin. This is obviously facile given the painstaking work done by scientists, economic analysts, political observers, sociologists, activists and the like. The danger is that the value of such work will be simply dismissed and that Christian contributions will become unconnected to those of others. Since climate change is by definition a global problem, it cannot be resolved by interest groups working independently.

Yet, the facile reference to sin should not be dismissed prematurely either. Embedded in the Christian tradition is a highly sophisticated set of conceptual tools (used for pastoral, prophetic and ethical purposes) that may be employed for the kind of social diagnostics needed here. This is already evident from the medieval vocabulary used for the seven deadly sins[2] but also from the body of theological scholarship on the many manifestations of sin. Let me mention six examples, each with secular equivalents:[3]

Some would say that the underlying problem is *anthropocentrism*, thinking that the whole world revolves around the interests of the human species, not recognizing our evolutionary continuity with other species. They would link that with an emphasis on anthropogenic climate change (generated by humans). Christians would bring to this diagnosis an understanding of sin as pride (or hubris), thinking too highly of ourselves,

---

[2] See Ted F. Peters, *Sin: Radical Evil in Soul and Society* (Grand Rapids: Eerdmans, 1994).
[3] For a discussion, see Larry L. Rasmussen, *Earth-Honoring Faith: Religious Ethics in a New Key* (Oxford: Oxford University Press, 2013), 89–100; Ernst M. Conradie, 'Penultimate Perspectives on the Root Causes of Environmental Destruction in Africa', *Scriptura* 115 (2016), 1–19.

leading to self-centredness, autonomy and eventually to rebellion. Instead, they would suggest some theocentric approach that decentralizes the role of humanity.

Some would emphasize *consumerist greed*, the escalation of needs, wants and desires that have become infectious. One may focus on 'conspicuous consumption', that is, the elitist desire to demonstrate superiority over others, or on 'keeping up with the Joneses', or on the consumerist desires of the global poor (endorsed through the prosperity gospel), seeking things that are paraded by others, but being frustrated in their dreams and aspirations. The argument is that it would not be sufficient to replace carbon-based energy sources with more sustainable alternatives if the underlying problem of expanding resource consumption is not addressed. We have to learn to live within planetary means. Christians would bring to this diagnosis a rich tradition of understanding the temptations associated with greed, expressed with reference to money, possessions, sexual encounters, food and drink, drugs, tourism, raving experiences, etc.[4]

Others may argue that the problem is what Christians would call *sloth*. We sin not only in what we do but in what we have left undone. One may therefore call on a sense of individual and collective responsibility to address the challenges associated with climate change. None can claim innocence; we all have to get our hands dirty. This emphasis on responsibility is easily corrupted by a capitalist emphasis on the virtues of productivity, entrepreneurship, efficiency, education, training and development. The argument is that climate mitigation and adaptation do not call for restraint but for innovation and transformation.

Yet others would insist that the underlying problem is one of *domination* in the name of differences of gender, class, race, sexual orientation, education and especially species. Such domination is reinforced by a set of interlocking binary oppositions, hierarchies and ideologies. It leads to injustice, oppression, structural violence and therefore to suffering, misery, deprivation and destruction.[5] In the biblical roots of Christianity there are vivid examples of such violence, epitomized by slavery in Egypt and the execution of Jesus of Nazareth under the Roman Empire. In response, there is a need for solidarity with the victims of climate change, including concerns over marginalized land and its biodiversity.

Some would frame the problem as one of *alienation*, especially alienation from the Earth as the only home that humans have. Here one may point to the disenchantment of nature, the loss of a sense of the sacred, the impact of urbanization, the role of industrialization in alienating workers from the means of production and the products of their labour, the breakdown of families, and the psychological side effects of modernity (loneliness, depression). This diagnosis is not often related to climate change, perhaps because it is impossible to become alienated from the earth's atmosphere (short of

---

[4] See also Ernst M. Conradie, *Christianity and a Critique of Consumerism: A Survey of Six Points of Entry* (Wellington: Bible Media, 2009).

[5] For a discussion, see Cynthia D. Moe-Lobeda, *Resisting Structural Evil: Love as Ecological-Economic Vocation* (Minneapolis: Fortress, 2013).

space travel). Yet, such alienation may also be evident from our strategies to adapt our immediate climate to cope with heat and cold, droughts and floods. Such adaptation is as necessary as it has become part of the destructive cycle leading to climate change. In response, there is a chorus of voices calling for a cosmology that recognizes that we are 'at home on earth'. This diagnosis may draw from the Christian notion of sin as the privation of the good, especially in the form of broken relationships with ancestral homes, traditional values, marriages, juvenile delinquency, gangsterism and within moral communities. For Christians, such alienation ultimately points towards a broken relationship with the triune God.

Finally, there are those who would recognize sin as *folly*. Here one may point to climate denial, deception (misinformation), falsity, callousness, hypocrisy, ignorance and senselessness. In response, one may emphasize the need for wisdom in responding to climate change, including practical wisdom needed for adaptation, but also a recognition of the precautionary principle (foresight), in-depth analysis and insight, deliberation, long-term planning and swiftness to act when needed. Indeed, wisdom may be understood as saying the appropriate word at the appropriate time, doing what is right at the right time. Christians have a body of wisdom literature that they can draw on in this regard, partially borrowed from other sources.

An (ecological) critique of North Atlantic Christian discourse on sin

The discussion above suggests that Christians can indeed contribute something to a collaborative exercise of depth diagnostics to uncover the layers of the underlying 'disease' that manifests itself in the 'symptoms' associated with climate change. Some may be concerned that translating such Christian vocabulary on sin into secular categories will water down Christian notions of sin and thus undermine the distinctive contribution Christians could offer. Is this not a slippery slope towards self-secularization, reducing the Christian faith to what is vaguely religious or merely to generalized ethical categories? However, the more particular a Christian understanding of sin becomes (e.g. a broken covenant with the triune God), the less relevant it seems to be in the public sphere.

Such an authentically Christian critique of discourse on sin would still miss the challenges posed by the inverse (ecological) critique of Christian discourse on sin, especially if coming from the North Atlantic context. The term 'North Atlantic' is open to debate, but may be used to include Christians with ancestors who emigrated from Europe since the advent of modernity (1652 in the case of South Africa). Put succinctly, North Atlantic Christian discourse on sin can hardly contribute to a collaborative diagnosis on climate change if others suspect that the outcome of the diagnostic process may be that the problem is caused mainly by the sins of North Atlantic Christians! This cannot but undermine the plausibility and the credibility of any such contribution in the public sphere.

Let us focus on three layers of such a critique of the credibility of Christian discourse on sin:

Firstly, especially Western Christian theology is premised on the notion of the universality of sin. All humans are sinners and have deviated from God's Way (Rom. 3.23). All are therefore in need of God's grace. Sin cannot be graded as if some are worse sinners than others. At times this has been a liberating message, inviting an open confession of sin. We need no longer keep up the pretence that we are not guilty. It breaks the spiral of endless accusations. We are all in the same boat and may find healing amidst broken relationships.

However, in other contexts this liberating message can become a tool for oppression. For the rapist to tell the rape victim that we are all sinners would be to condone rape. The same applies for torturers, white supremacists, slave owners, patriarchs, colonizers and oppressors. It comes as no surprise that numerous contemporary theological movements have called for a sharp distinction between those who are sinners and those who are sinned against. This distinction is typically used to address not only interpersonal violence but especially structural violence – associated with patriarchy, slavery, imperialism, colonialism, apartheid and, especially, Empire. In ecumenical discourse on climate change the same distinction may be used to refer to historic carbon emissions. It would be appropriate to say that we are in the mess together, but it would be hypocritical for those most responsible for historic carbon emissions to make that point.

In the eyes of others, including Christians from other parts of the world, the obvious observation is that those countries that bear the heaviest responsibility for historic carbon emissions were all predominantly Christian (mostly Protestant) in terms of the religious adherence of its population by the advent of the Industrial Revolution. If Protestant churches are not guilty in terms of providing a theological legitimation for industrialized capitalism (the Max Weber/Lynn White thesis), they may be guilty in terms of what was left undone: the failure to respond to the signs of things going wrong. From the perspective of other religious traditions this observation may refer not only to historic carbon emissions but also to current efforts at climate mitigation. The problem is not merely the apparent reluctance of the US and Canadian governments to accept responsibility for addressing climate change. The argument is that the forces of neoliberal capitalism with its emphasis on expanding economic growth are aligned with the most rapidly expanding contemporary religious movement, namely Pentecostalism, often aligned with right-wing evangelicalism and the prosperity gospel. This may be a sweeping statement that requires detailed critical investigation, but there is enough circumstantial evidence to raise suspicions from far away. Put provocatively: American Christians who wish to deny the accusation that they are the ones responsible for a changing climate would need to explain that to Muslims in Bangladesh faced with flooding. They would also need to explain the differences between various brands of

American Protestantism. Secularized citizens in Europe also cannot wash their hands in innocence as if ridding themselves of the embarrassment of Christian allegiance will absolve them from a multitude of sins.

Secondly, an ecological critique of Christian discourse on sin would need to recognize the danger of misunderstanding sin. There is the obvious temptation to personalize sin, to treat it as a list of do's and don'ts. At worst sin is reduced to sexuality. Often becoming pregnant out of wedlock is the only 'sin' warranting church discipline. Or one may grudgingly pay 'sin tax' on tobacco or alcohol products. Fatty and high-calorie food may be described as 'deliciously sinful'. In these ways sin is trivialized and rightly subjected to public ridicule. Does the same apply to carbon sins? Would one need to buy, willingly or unwillingly, 'indulgences' in the form of carbon tax in order to escape from the guilt of failing to contribute to mitigation efforts, hoping that others would make the difference somewhere else in the world? One may even fly around the world from one conference to the next in order to combat climate change!

It may be best for North Atlantic and other Christians to admit a failure to clarify what kind of category sin is. This allows utter confusion to reign. Consider this list of conflicting interpretations of sin:[6]

- Sin describes individual acts of human wrongdoing: what individuals do to others, to themselves and to nature.
- Sin is not just a matter of doing, but also of thinking and saying. It is about dispositions, attitudes, attachments – which provide the breeding ground for wrongdoing.
- Sin also refers to what is left undone, a failure to accept responsibility, duties not fulfilled.
- Sin describes the character of a person rather than particular things that a person may do. Being a sinner is way more important than sinning. Habitual sin is much harder to stop.
- Sin describes the quality of a (broken) relationship, not the dispositions or deeds of any one individual. If so, one cannot sin on one's own. To sin is to participate in broken personal relationships. Such broken relationships are embedded in wider networks of families, communities, clans, institutions and affiliations.
- Sin is best understood as structural violence; it describes systems of oppression such as patriarchy, slavery, colonialism, apartheid, castes, capitalism, ecological destruction, a situation in which individuals and organizations alike are caught up.
- Sin entails not only structural violence but also cultural violence. If so, the focus should be on the power of ideological distortions: sin is about classism, sexism, racism, elitism, homophobia, xenophobia, etc.

---

[6] For a more detailed discussion, see Ernst M. Conradie, *Redeeming Sin? Social Diagnostics amid Ecological Destruction* (Lanham: Lexington, 2017), 107–76.

- Sin cannot be reduced to something moral but is primarily something religious. It is about broken relationships but then a broken relationship with God, broken at least from our side.
- Sin is best understood as idolatry. If it is religious in nature, it is not merely about an individual's relationship with God but about unbelief, rebellion, idolatry, putting one's trust in principalities and powers that cannot save us.
- Sin is about heresy, about radically distorting the gospel to serve one's own interests.

One helpful way of gaining clarity in this regard is the contrast between sin as guilt and sin as power. Some would focus on sin as guilt and then attend to things that individuals, groups or organizations do. Others would focus on sin as power and then attend to how individuals are influenced by forces beyond their locus of control. We are caught up amidst evil forces that are more powerful than what we can cope with and from which we cannot escape. A one-sided emphasis on either is dangerous. To focus on individual actions is to trivialize sin, to look for particular instantiations of sin as if there are other actions, attitudes, dispositions and thoughts that are not contaminated by sin. To focus on sin as power only is to portray individuals and groups as victims of forces beyond their control for which they therefore ultimately do not need to accept responsibility. This can only undermine human agency, including the agency of victims.

It is possible to combine an understanding of sin as power and as guilt in order to avoid such excesses. Perhaps one may start with sin as power (structural violence). Accordingly, sin may be understood as 'pervasive perversity'. It is the mess that we find ourselves in – with the disastrous impact of climate change as an obvious example. One may then need to add, firstly, that this is a mess to which we (humans) and our predecessors have all contributed in one way or another to create or to worsen the mess. However, there is no need to argue that we have contributed equally. Consider the role of those in positions of political and economic power (who have to act as moral agents) but also the position of infants, the sick, the senile (i.e. moral patients) on whose behalf others act. The victims of history are never completely innocent either and may well become the perpetrators of tomorrow. Secondly, this is a mess that causes suffering to all of us, including other animals and plants, albeit again not equally so. The suffering of the victims may be obvious but tyrants and torturers also suffer the consequences of oppression. However, it would be obscene to equate the suffering of the rapist and the rape victim. It is therefore necessary to consider the proportionality of guilt, alongside the universality of sin.[7] Thirdly, one may add that this is a mess from which we cannot escape, at least not by ourselves. Our best efforts at moral renewal, reconstruction, transformation and social development remain flawed and often even exacerbate the problem. In short, sin describes the mess that we find ourselves in, to which we all have

---

[7] Ibid., 143–8.

contributed (but not equally so), under which we all suffer (again not equally so) and from which we cannot escape.

A third way the use of the Christian category of sin in the public sphere is undermined is by the plausibility of two related categories, namely the 'fall' of humanity and 'original sin'. The latter term is often confused with the origin of sin and with the (sexual) transmission of sin. In my view it is best understood in terms of the inescapability of sin (i.e. the consequences and not the origin of sin). Sin describes a situation in which we find ourselves that has been there before we were born and which we cannot overcome on our own. However, such sin is not 'original' – as the category of the fall of humanity indicates. Something went awry somewhere sometime. Things are not what they are supposed to be. My sense is that all observers could acknowledge that. To suggest that things are quite acceptable as they are would raise suspicions of ignorance, (climate) denial or of defending positions of power, comfort and luxury.

However, the plausibility of the 'fall' of humanity remains deeply contested, especially in the light of what we know about evolutionary history. This follows from the recognition that there was pain, suffering, anxiety, ageing, death and extinction on earth long before hominids arrive. Biological death cannot be the result of human sin only (contra Augustine and others), even though sin can of course exacerbate suffering and result in death (e.g. murder, poaching, famine). Moreover, there is no scientific evidence of some paradise on earth that was altered through the 'fall'. Indeed, there are many behavioural continuities between humans and other animals. The underlying problem is that humans share traits with other animals (denoted by words such as 'murder', 'theft', 'deceit', 'possessiveness') that would be regarded as 'sinful' if done by humans. Gijsbert van den Brink concludes that 'we human beings ourselves seem to have been aggressive savages from the very beginning of our existence. Rather than having fallen it seems that we were "created fallen".'[8] Or in the often quoted formulation of Arthur Peacocke:

> So there is no sense in which we can talk of a 'fall' from a past perfection. There was no golden age, no perfect past, no individuals, 'Adam' or 'Eve', from whom all human beings have now descended and declined and who were perfect in their relationships and behaviour. We appear to be rising beasts [rising from an a-moral and in that sense innocent state to the capability of moral and immoral action] rather than fallen angels![9]

Such insights prompt further reflection on the relationship between what is termed 'natural evil' and 'social evil'. It seems clear that all natural evil cannot be the result

---

[8] See Gijsbert van den Brink, 'Should we Drop the Fall? On Taking Evil Seriously', in *Strangers and Pilgrims*, Eddy Van der Borght and Paul van Geest (eds) (Leiden: Brill, 2011), 761–77.

[9] Arthur R. Peacocke, 'Biological Evolution – A Theological Appraisal', in *Evolutionary and Molecular Biology: Scientific Perspectives on Divine Action*, Robert John Russell, William R. Stoeger and Francisco J. Ayala (eds) (Vatican City: Vatican Observatory Publications / Berkeley: Center for Theology and the Natural Sciences), 357–76 (373).

of social evil. Is the inverse then true? This seems to be gist of popular phrases such as 'nature red in tooth and claw', the 'survival of the fittest' and the recognition that cooperation is often employed towards destructive ends (war, crime). However, to suggest that social evil is the 'necessary' result of human evolution would undermine human responsibility, moral education, legal accountability and policy making alike. Humans are not merely evolutionary victims of their own 'selfish' genes, but remain responsible for what has gone wrong.

It is not possible to resolve this complex debate on natural evil and social evil here.[10] It suffices to observe a parallel distinction between climate change and anthropogenic climate change. There can be no doubt that the earth's climate has changed continuously over its 4.5-billion-year history. Such changes have often been catastrophic and have caused mass extinctions in the past. At the same time, climate change has been a driver of the evolution of species. The extinction of some species (e.g. dinosaurs) created room for others (e.g. hominids) to flourish. There is nothing immoral about a changing climate. The recognition that climates have been in constant change can therefore readily be used by climate sceptics and denialists as an excuse to sustain current practices. The introduction of the term *anthropogenic* climate change is therefore important to indicate that such change is not necessary or inevitable, but is caused by burning fossil fuels, leading to rapid global warming with diverse effects on particular ecosystems.

In the context of North Atlantic Christianity the parallels between the two distinctions (natural evil and social evil; climate change and anthropogenic climate change) are admittedly not that obvious. Arguably, those Christians who resist evolutionary theory are also more likely to be climate sceptics while Christians who endorse evolution through natural selection may well recognize anthropogenic climate change. Either way, it seems that some homework is necessary to connect insights from the natural and the human sciences with each other.

Addressing the challenge

Such an ecological critique of North Atlantic Christian discourse on sin poses significant challenges for any contribution from North Atlantic theology in diagnosing the underlying problems associated with climate change. I suggest that it can contribute to ecumenical reflections and collaborative, interdisciplinary efforts only if three conditions are met.

---

[10] See especially Nancy Murphy, Robert John Russell and William R. Stoeger (eds), *Physics and Cosmology: Scientific Perspectives on the Problem of Natural Evil* (Vatican City: Vatican Observatory Publications/ Berkeley: CTNS, 2006); Christopher Southgate, *The Groaning of Creation: God, Evolution and the Problem of Evil* (Louisville: Westminster John Knox, 2008); Ernst M. Conradie, 'On Social Evil and Natural Evil: In Conversation with Christopher Southgate', *Zygon: Journal of Religion and Science* 53:3 (2018), 752–65.

Firstly, there is a need for North Atlantic Christians to confess their guilt in the context of a changing climate.[11] Such guilt is associated (a) with historic carbon emissions, (b) with failures at current mitigation efforts and (c) with the hubris of assuming that they would need to take the lead in addressing the problem. All three of these aspects of confessing guilt will be demanding:

- Politicians in countries from the Global North may not welcome it if Christians from such countries confess such guilt in international forums. How would Tories respond if the Archbishop of Canterbury confesses the sins of the Anglican Church with regard to its support of an expanding British Empire through the means of industrialization?
- In discourse on mitigation it is widely assumed that an 80 to 90 per cent reduction in the use of fossil fuels is required in industrialized countries of the Global North within five or six decades since 1990 – of which the first three decades were the most significant. In some countries the exponential expansion in carbon emissions has been curbed but a significant reduction is not yet in sight. This cannot be addressed without implications for the lifestyles of church members in such countries – and for their consumerist aspirations to live the good life with quality education, health care and pensions. Instead, the Trump administration is not shy of focusing primarily on the economic needs of American citizens in order to make America 'great' again.
- People in positions of power often assume that they have to take the lead in addressing any pressing problem. Anglo-Saxons have the added advantage of using English as a language for global communication so that they always seem to be quicker to articulate their understanding of the problem than others who are still struggling to find the right words. This poses severe temptations in confessing guilt – since such confession requires long periods of silence, awaiting a response from those to whom such a confession is addressed or who may overhear such a confession. Indeed, it is an arduous spiritual exercise to confess guilt to those ranked 'lower' than oneself, whatever the criterion may be.

Secondly, in order to address the challenges posed to discourse of sin in the context of climate change, it may also be necessary to acknowledge one's misunderstanding of what sin is. North Atlantic Christians have great traditions of theological scholarship and typically take the lead, globally, in academic research, publication, supervision and teaching. Christians from the global South come to the Global North to study theology, but hardly vice versa. It is therefore hard to admit that one's theology may be inadequate. Could this apply to an understanding of sin? In the discussion above there are some indications of where the problem may lie. This is not merely a matter of personalizing

---

[11] See Ernst M. Conradie, 'Confessing Guilt in the Context of Climate Change: Some South African Perspectives', *Scriptura* 103 (2010), 134–52.

or trivializing sin – as the great traditions of ideology criticism are readily available in the Global North. The greater danger is the removal of discourse on sin from the public sphere – as if it is too embarrassing to even mention. Indeed, one may well ask whatever happened with sin? The keen academic interest in what is called 'natural evil' is a case in point as this may easily replace sin-talk or subsume that under a discussion of the theodicy problem. In response, it may well be necessary to 'redeem' the category of sin in the public sphere.

Thirdly, and this maybe even harder to admit, there is the danger that misunderstanding sin may be related to a misunderstanding of God. The problem is that sin-talk is often reduced to a matter of morality, of doing something wrong. Sin certainly includes that, but what about sin as ideology, idolatry and heresy – as the theological critique of apartheid recognized?[12] The specifically religious dimension of sin becomes manifest in quasi-soteriologies – putting one's trust, in life and death, in false saviours. This is a matter of orthopraxy but also of orthodoxy. One may claim to maintain the right doctrine but still put one's trust in education, the market, pension funds, military defence structures, democracy, or the power of positive thinking. Ultimately, idolatry cannot be separated from misunderstanding God. Put concisely, the danger that Christians elsewhere in the world may need to raise is whether God is not somehow viewed as Coloniser and Landlord – with repercussions for understanding creation (in gated communities), providence (maintaining law and order), salvation (the earth providing resources for us humans), church and especially mission (centrifugally enlarging the sphere of jurisdiction of the Landlord). Accordingly, the God of Christianity commenced *His* work in Jerusalem but from there the message spread to conquer the whole earth, since the Earth is the Lord's. If so, such sin not only pollutes the whole earth but suffocates the global climate with carbon dioxide.

---

[12] See Murray H. Coetzee and Ernst M. Conradie, 'Apartheid as Quasi-soteriology: The Remaining Lure and Threat', *Journal of Theology for Southern Africa* 138 (2010), 112–23.

Chapter 4.4
God's continued providence

Clive Pearson[1]

Starting in the wrong place

For the inhabitants of the low-lying islands of Tuvalu and Kiribati the belief in a providential God professed by the Christian tradition is an ever-present companion. The cultural and existential location of these coral atolls ringed with lagoons and palm trees is far removed from the emergence of a liberal Western democracy and its tendency to disregard the existence of God (hence the removal of any hint of providence to some place of subliminal dislocation). These islands are frequently referred to as the 'canaries in the mine'. Along with the Marshall Islands and the Maldives they comprise the nation states most at immediate risk from rising sea levels and the prospect of no longer being able to sustain habitation. It is no surprise that in terms of the politics of climate change Tuvalu has become as iconic as the retreating glaciers of Greenland and the receding extent of Arctic Sea ice. What will transpire on Tuvalu is seen as a forerunner of what is likely to happen to other coastal and river delta sites exposed to the sea's incursion. For those who practice the discipline of a systematic theology out of a North Atlantic context, Tuvalu and other small island states on the opposite of the world pose a challenge to the doctrine of providence.

They do so on several grounds. The most substantive has to do with how the probable future of these lands and their Indigenous peoples can be reconciled with the core claims of a caring God who is more than a momentary creator. Is it still possible to subscribe to a doctrine of providence that surmises an ongoing concern of a God of grace and mercy who wills the good of creatures and creation itself? How is the divine capacity for foresight implicit in the Latin *pro + videre* to be reconciled with the distinct possibility of 'cultural extinction'? That is the term coined by Tafue Lusama, a local theologian, to describe a life lived elsewhere other than on the islands that have sustained his people for centuries.[2]

---

[1] Clive Pearson is Senior Research Fellow of the Public and Contextual Theology research centre (PaCT) in Charles Sturt University, Australia. He is the editor-in-chief of the *International Journal of Public Theology*, is based in Sydney and is a member of the Uniting Church in Australia.
[2] Tafue Lusama, 'Punishment of the Innocent: The Problem of Global Warming with Special Reference to Tuvalu' (unpublished Master's Thesis, Tainan Theological Seminary and College, 2004), 15.

What meaning can then be taken from the traditional threefold pattern of providence – *conservatio* (the preservation of creation), *gubernatio* (the governance of creation to a particular end) and *concursus* (the ongoing and cooperating accompaniment of the divine)? What happens to a doctrine of providence if the vitality of life for a particular people is lost and cannot be woven into the continuing care of a sustaining God? Does God care? Is it perhaps conceivable that some redemptive purpose lies hidden within the heart of the triune God?

These theological questions play themselves out not in abstraction but in everyday life. Matters of preservation and sustainability, for instance, come face to face with the inundation of king tides, the salinity of soils and the inability to grow crops, out of season and prolonged droughts associated with changes in the directions of prevailing winds, and more intense storms.

The peoples of Tuvalu and the i-Kiribati are overwhelmingly Christian. It is this received faith that establishes a framework for meaning and purpose. The irony lies in there being no word for providence in the local vernacular;[3] their *talanoa* (the sharing of stories) and *fatele* (the performance of dancing songs) are not performed under the auspices of some explicit rendering of this doctrinal claim. The islanders are, nevertheless, a Bible-conscious people. It is this textual witness that lends itself to an implicit belief in what a formal theology would constitute as a doctrine of providence. This Oceanic way of reading the purpose and will of God is situated alongside multiple scientific studies that rightly set out to explain what is happening to their islands, their way of life and why.

The scriptural text most commonly invoked is Gen. 9.8-17. The appeal of Yahweh's covenant with Noah and every living creature is obvious. With a little hermeneutical licence, the bow becomes a rainbow and a promissory sign of how there will be no flood in the future that will wipe out humanity. The text can then become a counter-narrative to the empirically researched picture of climate change and sea-level rise.[4] This hermeneutical line of resistance is not without its problems. Maina Talia has argued that the debate on global warming 'has been conducted in a foreign language that is beyond the understanding' of most inhabitants.[5] That foreign language is not simply English. The technical complexities of a planetary problem can be hard to grasp at the best of times. Both Talia and Lusama are troubled by the levels of denial that 'we have a problem':[6] the Noah covenant is complicit. The expectation rapidly devolves into one

---

[3] The words most likely to be used are *atafai* and *tauisi*. Both refer to the practice of taking care. In terms of its etymology *atafai* refers to the image, the picture or shadow that guides human endeavour.

[4] Wolfgang Kempf, 'The Rainbow's Power: Climate Change, Sea Level Rises and Reconfiguration of the Noah Story in Oceania', in *Pacific Voices. Local Governments and Climate Change*, Ropate Qalo (ed.) (Suva: USP Press, 2014), 68–84.

[5] Maina Talia, 'Towards a *Fatele* Theology: A Contextual Theological Response in Addressing Threats of Global Warming in Tuvalu' (unpublished Master's Thesis, Tainan Theological Seminary and College, 2009), 25.

[6] Ibid., 24–6.

of an interventionist God who will reset creation and thus 'save us'. The language of providence may not be used but this adherence to Noah, a 'rainbow' and a promise represents an implicit trust in divine providence. It is an understandable appeal to the way in which the doctrine holds out the hope of sustainability through its accent on *conservatio*.

These types of questions and responses are not far from the surface given the urgency of the situation and the received traditions of the Christian faith. The well-embedded understanding of faith is such that providence could readily be reconciled with the regularity of winds and rains and the provision of life's staple foods. Even without any familiarity with the Heidelberg Catechism of 1563, the Catechism's questions and answers concerning understanding the providence of God (Question 27) and the benefits of acknowledging of such (Question 28) would have made sense within the past lived experience of islanders. '[H]eaven and earth, together with all creatures' were upheld by '[t]he almighty and ever-present power of God' who rules in such a way that everything, including the most basic means of sustenance, 'come to us not by chance but by his fatherly hand'. The comfort and consolation of such belief was a discernment of how 'no creature shall separate us from [the] love [of God]'; the concomitant benefits were patience in adversity, gratitude in the midst of blessing and the call and capacity to 'trust our faithful God and Father for the future'. All these things were sealed in the knowledge that 'all creatures are so completely in his hand that without his will they cannot even move'.

The difficulties arising out of this way of understanding providence are readily discernible. For all its merits, the summons to trust and patience can so easily become an invitation to ignore the signs of the times being made plain in the climate science data. Writing on sinking cities of the Earth, Jeff Goodell simply observes 'the water will come'.[7] In the case of Tuvalu sea-level rise is at a rate of more than twice the global average. What this basic measure indicates is an inequity in timing and the level of impact of climate change. In terms of a doctrine of providence it raises the problem identified by Vernon White: what is the relationship of the particular to the universal? The tendency of providence is towards a teleological purpose. It assumes the coming together of that threefold pattern – *conservatio*, *gubernatio* and *concursus* – for the sake of a divinely ordered good. That resolution is established within the redemptive and universal story of Christ: where then might these 'sub-narratives of history' – like that of these small island states – 'ultimately connect to Christ'?[8]

For the sake of a plausible doctrine, Tuvalu and those other small island states must stand for more than just an icon of climate change. The metaphorical status Robert Jay

---

[7] Jeff Goodell, *The Water Will Come: Rising Seas, Sinking Cities, and the Remaking of the Civilized World* (New York: Little, Brown and Company, 2017).

[8] Vernon White, *Purpose and Providence: Taking Soundings in Western Thought, Literature and Theology* (London: T&T Clark, 2015), 98–9.

Lifton assigned to the Marshall Islands of being this 'Job of nations'[9] belongs to them all. Their imminent prospects weave together a knot of awkward questions for which there are no easy answers. On Tuvalu the recourse to the Noah covenant can turn cultural attention back to the reason for the rising waters in the text itself and provoke a theory of retribution. The covenant with all flesh becomes bound to a further lament – this time 'what have we done that God is angry with us?' That *cri de coeur* is itself a legacy of Western mission to these islands. Lusama now finds himself obliged to wrestle with how to deal with the cultural problem of the punishment of the innocent. Noah gives way to Job. The apparent failure of *conservatio* gives rise to a theodicy of protest.

Now it is widely recognized that there are 'extremes of experience which seem flatly to refuse all meaning, even deferred meaning'. White is wise: 'There is no interpretation, no theological justification, that will satisfy – not in this life and our current frame of reference. Theology may just have to accept its limits here.'[10] That conclusion is not peculiar to a time of climate change and its intersection with a reading of providence. What these island experiences bear witness to is a surd, a sense of the tragic that has not yet run its course. It is still in its beginnings and is presenting the difficulties of how to discern the governance, activity (*gubernatio*) of God. The difficulty of doing such recommends a note of caution.

The dilemma surrounding this doctrine does not disappear with a recognition for a need for modesty and humility. It can take on a most disquieting ethical turn for those who benefit from climate/environmental privilege. The debates surrounding the first effects of climate change note that the peoples most vulnerable to this unfolding scenario are those whose own ecological footprint is miniscule. These faraway islands practice a modified subsistence economy. Lusama wonders what it will take for island nations to be heard by international climate conventions. He pointedly asks: 'how long must we repeat the story?'[11] The underlying public claim weaves together the Christological and the ethical: 'are we not your neighbours?'

It is not unusual for a natural disaster or impending cataclysm to lend itself to serious theological endeavour. The Lisbon earthquake of 1755 and the Boxing Day earthquake and tsunami of 2004 posed the problem of theodicy quite starkly. The boundary line between the problem of theodicy and the doctrine of providence can, of course, be easily blurred. Confronted with the tragic and the surd, the providential care of God can be 'difficult to commend or receive.'[12] The temptation to put these natural events on the same platform as that of potentially vanishing islands should, nevertheless, be resisted. The point of difference is not simply temporal. The Lisbon earthquake and the 2004 tsunami that raced across the Indian Ocean are completed past events. From the

---

[9] Ibid., 23–7.
[10] Ibid., 149.
[11] Ibid., 11.
[12] John Webster, 'On the Theology of the Providence of God', in *The Providence of God,* Francesca Aran Murphy and Philip G. Ziegler (eds) (London and New York: T&T Clark, 2009), 158–78 (158).

perspective of cause the present threat to Tuvalu does not lie in shifting tectonic plates. Here anthropogenic climate change and consequential rising sea levels situates all these low-lying islands on the very brink of the emerging Anthropocene.

The planetary Earth system is now displaying the effects of anthropogenic change. Its birth is bound up with what has been identified as an age of great acceleration that has been marked by increased energy use, excessive greenhouse gas emissions and rapid population growth.[13] In terms of causality the Anthropocene depends upon the exercise then of human freedom regardless of any reference to the existence of God, let alone the sovereign will of a Creator God. Humanity has itself become a geologic agent, a telluric force comparable to volcanism and glaciation and the like. From this perspective these islands are caught within a global shift in climate and changes to the Earth system itself. In terms of the ongoing viability of human habitation they find themselves enmeshed in what had been described initially as a wicked problem that has now become super-wicked.

The difficulties with the doctrine of providence do not begin with Tuvalu and the Anthropocene, however. For some time its prognosis had not been promising. It is countercultural. The doctrine assumes a comprehensive master-story: that unfolding narrative concerns itself, firstly, with the doctrine of God both in terms of aseity and economy. It was already at risk within a regime of modernity with its linear views of history and its ambient sense of progress. This vulnerability has only increased in a time of postcolonialism and postmodernity where there is serious critique of any possibility of metanarratives. The horrors of war and genocide of the twentieth century have led to a 'loss of confidence in epic readings of history'.[14] The 'big stories' that include the possibility of divine transcendence 'have lost their explanatory power'.[15]

Has providence been lost – or can it still perform a role of purpose and meaning? It is, after all, a 'central article of faith', even though it is not a biblical word.[16] Its strength and resilience has lain in its being a confession of faith and, as such, a revelatory claim.

Starting from the proper place

The recent theological consensus is sceptical about assuming 'the divine rule of the world on the basis of empirical observation'. David Fergusson observes that there is '[t]oo much that happens [that] is unpredictable and contrary to the will of God for this to be attributed to providence'.[17] The underlying conviction is that the intention motivating

---

[13] John McNeill and Peter Engelke, *The Great Age of Acceleration: An Environmental History of the Anthropocene Since 1945* (Cambridge: Harvard University Press, 2016).

[14] Webster, 'On the Theology of Providence', 158.

[15] White, *Purpose and Providence,* 15.

[16] David Fergusson, 'The Theology of Providence', *Theology Today* 67 (2010), 261–78 (261).

[17] Ibid., 266.

the divine purpose, its *telos*, is good. The problem lies in the difficulty of attributing some form of direct correspondence between the outworking of the divine will and what happens within a world of linear history. The well-intentioned advice that there can be a pedagogical benefit through the divine permission (rather than imposition) of suffering is always a high-risk claim. Does that future realization of an inner good actually justify and redeem what was tragic or a source of lament? Where might lie the epistemological basis for any such claim?

Those kinds of questions are ones of subjective apprehension. They can also form the function of a bridge into how particular understandings of providence can affect the doctrine of God in an adverse manner. David Bentley Hart thus dismisses accounts of providence that are 'disastrous' and 'quite degenerate'.[18] John Webster notes that 'bad doctrines of providence abound'.[19]

The root of this problem lies in not properly respecting that providence is a doctrine about God. Katherine Sonderegger argues that the doctrine's primary intention is 'not principally a doctrine about the abiding order and property and telos of creatures'.[20] In a similar vein Webster believes those bad doctrines arise whenever the attempt is made to 'extricate knowledge of providence from corruptions of temporality'.[21] The doctrine is then composed in a manner that 'neglect[s] the believer's stance *in media res*' and distorts a proper reading of the doctrine by allowing events within an immanent history to determine its framework of understanding.

For those whose brief is with the dogmatic and apologetic functions of the doctrine there is a need then to establish its proper place in the theological schema. That is partly because of the doctrine's all-pervasive nature. Its subject matter has to do with the doctrine of God as well as the continuing relationship of the Triune God to creation. It must of necessity then be 'ubiquitous' and establish connections along the full range of doctrines. Webster refers to 'linkages across the system of Christian teaching'.[22]

Here Webster is establishing the case for the 'coherence of the doctrine' alongside of its being a 'distributed doctrine'. That claim to coherence is established on the imperative not to separate the doctrine of creation from the doctrine of God, including the aseity of God. It may seem as if the doctrine is primarily concerned with how God relates to the ongoing relationship and purpose of creation, but that is to ignore how this work of divine love and care itself originates from within the very being of God. There is a 'backward connection to the doctrine of God'.[23]

---

[18] David Bentley Hart, 'Providence and Causality: On Divine Innocence', in *The Providence of God*, Francesca Aran Murphy and Philip G. Ziegler (eds) (London: T&T Clark, 2009), 34–56 (34, 40).

[19] Webster, 'On the Theology of the Providence of God', 164.

[20] Katherine Sonderegger, 'The Doctrine of Providence', in *The Providence of God*, Francesca Aran Murphy and Philip G. Ziegler (eds) (London: T&T Clark, 2009), 144–58 (145).

[21] Webster, 'On the Theology of the Providence of God', 164.

[22] Ibid., 160.

[23] Ibid.

This emphasis on the proper place and coherence of the doctrine is the ground upon which Hart argues the case for divine innocence. So much depends upon preserving the logic of transcendence. Here Hart is keen to take a step back from the common practice to situate the rhetoric of God – being the primary cause behind the secondary causality of human freedom and action – within a linear framework of immanence. That logic fails to take seriously the qualitative difference between Creator and creature. It is inclined to regard primary causality in terms of a more direct correspondence of cause and effect. It does not make a satisfactory distinction between what the creator and redemptive God wills and permits. It does not then leave sufficient room for a genuine human freedom rather than one that is contrived. Further, it crowds in upon that element of mystery, the inscrutable dimension of any doctrine of providence that must always lie beyond the comprehension of the finite creature.

It is evident, then, that there are a number of discrete aspects within the life of this doctrine. It presumes that creation itself arises out of the nature and will of a generous and self-giving God. The act of creation itself is not simply an isolated act. Nor is providence merely an act of maintaining that which is created. It assumes that there is meaning and purpose, depth and direction to creaturely life. That assurance is established in the economy of God. It assumes that 'the history of creation serves the history of grace'.[24]

From one place in time to another

This brings us back to the matter of the ongoing providence of God in a time of climate change. The issue has become one of whether or not a systematic understanding of the Christian faith can cross over from one geologic period to another and how this is interwoven with belief in providence. The theological importance of starting in the proper place is made at a moment within history when there is seemingly a surface absence of the doctrine.

That emphasis on the logic of transcendence rightly established the connection between providence and the doctrine of God. At the very least that serves as a revelatory and confessional counterclaim that lies beyond empirical proof. The dilemma then passes into a consideration of how the doctrine plays itself out in the field of human freedom and the divine economy. The implication for this transition is that the doctrine becomes a public line of faith-based reasoning in a mix of transdisciplinary studies.

On the basis of past experience White has argued that the doctrine retains its resilience and relevance 'because under pressure it can always be reconfigured'.[25] The arrival of the Anthropocene posits a very different kind of pressure, however. The deep-seated changes made to the Earth system through human agency are initiating a period

---

[24] Ibid., 168.
[25] White, *Purpose and Providence*, 141.

in the life of the planet, hence creation, without precedent and evident analogue. The past nurture of human culture and great civilizations – including the emergence and flowering of the Christian faith – transpired within a period where the climate was relatively stable and allowed for such flourishing. The theological infrastructure of the Christian faith itself developed relatively late within the Holocene period and that period is now passing.

The classical discussions on the doctrine of providence never envisaged a created order where humankind as a species might be the most prominent driver of change in the whole Earth system. We have become 'Earthmasters'.[26] Clive Hamilton argues that what is needed is a new anthropology that recognizes our newly realized power over creation. This is not a time for either a false innocence or hubris.[27]

At face value Hamilton's thesis need not disturb a doctrine of providence. What this reset in anthropology might mean still lies within the domain of immanence and causality. The language of cause and who caused what, why and how is highly operative in debates surrounding policies of mitigation, adaptation and the ethics of climate justice. It would, nevertheless, be entirely inappropriate now to insert into this line of cause and consequences a direct and explicit covenantal link to the redemptive will of God. The logic of transcendence remains. Whether the Anthropocene turns out to be 'good, bad or ugly'[28] the human species remains on this side of creaturely existence in spite of any new-found capacity for geoengineering and discourses on being post-human and an extra-terrestrial life. The rigorous theological concerns previously identified, namely the qualitative difference between Creator and creature, the distinction between divine will and permission, as well as the dialectic of divine sovereignty and human freedom, are still valid. Nothing has altered this perspective.

There is nevertheless an *apophatic* function to the doctrine that becomes more urgent. The exercise of human freedom is performed within the constraints of moral value. According to Christian belief our lives and world are flawed and coloured with sin. Some things can be wrongly ascribed to the will of God and thus deemed to be providential. Fergusson cites past examples of 'imperialist and totalitarian projects'.[29] It has not been too difficult to reduce providence to a belief that God is with 'us' in matters of war and imperial expansion, and thus in the process allowing this doctrine to legitimize that action. It can so easily then become complicit in matters of racial supremacy.

---

[26] Clive Hamilton, *Earthmasters: The Dawn of the Age of Climate Engineering* (New Haven: Yale University Press, 2013).

[27] Clive Hamilton, *Defiant Earth: The Fate of Humans in the Anthropocene* (Sydney et al: Allen & Unwin, 2017).

[28] Simon Dalby, 'Framing the Anthropocene: The Good, the Bad, and the Ugly', *The Anthropocene Review* 3:1 (2016), 33–51.

[29] David Fergusson, 'Theology of Providence', in *The Providence of God*, Francesca Aran Murphy and Philip G. Ziegler (eds) (London: T&T Clark, 2009), 261–9.

In a time of climate change the risk of co-option is likely to develop a number of worrying variants. One of the most disturbing is the increasing rhetoric to do with energy security and the militarization of the environment. Robert Marzec describes the emergence of defence policies established on a 'combat-oriented stance' towards the likely effects of climate change. The simulated climate-change war games will be transformed into actual conflicts over the loss of food, water and energy through the disruption caused by disease and the mass migration of millions of climate-displaced people. The language of sustainability gives way to that of adaptation based on security.[30] That practice and the grim prospect it foretells is far removed from the call Pope Francis makes in his encyclical, *Laudato Si'*, to care for 'our common home' and regard climate itself as a 'common good'.

The case could conceivably be made for a just war on climate grounds. The criteria might be established on a desire to defend the rights of those who are most vulnerable to the loss of that common good and whose home is no longer secure. The tendency that Marzec has discerned in this process of the militarization of the environment is towards national security at present rather than an ethic of climate justice on behalf of the other, however. It becomes a means by which a nation looks first to its own self-interest in the bid to aggrandize itself.

Endings

In the past the doctrine of providence assumed the regularity of seasons and what was required for the sustenance of life (*conservatio*). It presupposed the wise governance and administration of continuing creation (*gubernatio*). In a somewhat hidden way the divine will worked in collaboration with human freedom for a teleological purpose (*concursus*). In the Anthropocene – in the 'age of humans' – each one of these three aspects still has a role to play, though the doctrine itself is often seemingly invisible. Its place has been taken by the apocalyptic and eschatology – and, then, more often than not, by the discourse surrounding future ethics and the rights of subsequent generations. The latter happens around much imagery of extinction – Clive Hamilton has already written a requiem for the species, that species being us.[31] Elizabeth Kolbert has popularized the idea that the accelerated loss of biological diversity and animal species constitutes a human-induced sixth mass extinction on the Earth.[32]

---

[30] Robert P. Marzec, *Militarizing the Environment: Climate Change and the Security State* (Minneapolis: University of Minnesota Press, 2015).

[31] Clive Hamilton, *Requiem for a Species: Why We Resist the Truth about Climate Change* (New York: Routledge, 2014).

[32] Elizabeth Kolbert, *The Sixth Extinction: An Unnatural History* (New York: Picador, 2014).

The threefold pattern of a doctrine of providence offers a foil. It holds out hope for a fellowship of an ordered good that is responding to the will and purpose of God. It is a vehicle for a belief that God is not absent in the midst of these threats to life – and, indeed, is present in the vulnerability. Sometimes that foil is apophatic: it is saying what the divine will and purpose is not and doing so from the perspective of a theology of the cross. Such is the nature of the doctrine that it is preserving the master narrative of the Christian faith.

What might that mean?

How are we to conceive of providence if it is to be overtaken by a catastrophic sense of the apocalyptic that differs from a biblical eschatology? The doctrine of providence presumes a divine act of creation and economy that somehow lends itself to the fulfilment of the good that was intended in the creation of humankind. It is an act of God, the will of God being seen through to its *telos*. It is redemptive. The apocalyptic shock that the birth of the Anthropocene presages is of a different order. It can present us with an ending of creaturely life as we know it on this small blue planet set in a 'fortunate universe'. The creature rather than the Creator has brought about this end.

There is a disturbing alternative. Eco-modernists welcome the arrival of the 'good' or 'great' Anthropocene. The absence of providence here is effectively complete. The theological rhetoric of what the divine wills and permits gives way to the human capacity 'to rise to a higher level of planetary significance', to be 'as gods', so we may as well 'get good at it', as is repeatedly suggested in eco-modernist literature. The sacramental moment of the present – and the self's abandonment to divine providence – associated with the life of Jean-Pierre de Caussade has become 'an amazing opportunity' for a 'grand new era' in which humanity can overcome the temporary setbacks of climate change through technological creativity. The good and great Anthropocene and the resolution of climatic disruptions is the work of human freedom.[33]

Into such a seemingly benevolent future enter the inhabitants of low-lying islands like Tuvalu. They do not use the term providence and are unfamiliar with the theological arguments to do with such. It is difficult to envisage, given the complexities of rising sea levels and the politics of climate change, how they will share in the eco-modernist vision that 'nearly all of us will be prosperous enough to live healthy, free and creative lives'.[34] They raise questions such as: What did we do to deserve this? Are we not your neighbours? and What are we to preach? The underlying assumption of the good Anthropocene is that any sufferings (and extinctions of cultures) in the present should be endured for the sake of what is to come.

The experience of Lifton's Job-like nations is a difficult reminder of how our discourse on providence always falls short. There is always a risk that providence can become no more than a call to endure. That should not be the way for a resilient understanding of providence for this new period of the Anthropocene. From the biblical

---

[33] Clive Hamilton, 'The Theodicy of the "Good Anthropocene"', *Environmental Humanities* 7 (2015), 233–8.
[34] Ibid., 235.

roots of Christianity the notion of God's providence allows for lament, bewilderment and cries of dereliction and betrayal. Confessional claims regarding providence can serve an apophatic function that critiques an abandonment of God and the hubris of excessive human freedom. Its logic of transcendence can lead those who live in situations of climate privilege to consider how we use our freedom and what has been permitted to us. The deepening climate change crisis bids us to reflect upon how we live our lives in the shadow of endings and to do so in ways that nevertheless express (as best we know) the providential care of God. In a time of rising sea levels and disappearing islands that intimation of the intended purpose of God's ongoing providence might even present itself in the form of the stranger to be found at Matthew 25.31-46.

Chapter 4.5
God's acts of salvation for us

Ernst M. Conradie[1]

Does the good news make any difference?

At the heart of the Christian faith lies a message, proclaimed as good news, namely a message of salvation in Jesus Christ. However that salvation may be understood, the question that will be addressed in this essay is whether such salvation can make any significant difference amidst the challenges associated with climate change. Or, to raise the stakes: might this message prove to be the *decisive* difference in responding to climate change?

Some Christians may be inclined to suggest that to even ask such a question is to misunderstand the religious and the specifically Christian nature of salvation. It is primarily about the relationship of individual human beings (or a people?) with God – and not aimed at any one social issue. However, this is clearly not a viable response given the biblical witnesses that portray salvation as addressing a wide range of concrete social issues – including (economic) justice, peace (reconciliation between people) and healing, also for the land. If the message of salvation cannot make a difference to climate change, what difference can it make? This line of argument would yield more and more exceptions so that the ever narrower claim of salvation will soon die the death of a thousand qualifications.

Admittedly, a number of clarifications are necessary to discuss such a question:

Firstly, almost everyone (with the possible exception of militant atheists) would acknowledge that the message of salvation in Jesus Christ may make at least some difference. Many would agree that at least his followers can draw inspiration from the ministry of Jesus of Nazareth through his example, leadership, provocative actions and wisdom. There is no need to deny such a possible source of inspiration – in the same way that Christians can draw wisdom from the Buddha or the Prophet Muhammad. The Christian claim is more than that though, namely that this message has indeed made the most significant difference for the salvation of humans and, by extension, for the whole earth.

---

[1] Ernst M. Conradie is Senior Professor in the Department of Religion and Theology at the University of the Western Cape in South Africa, the leading historically black university in the country. He is situated in the Reformed tradition, teaches systematic theology and ethics and specializes in Christian ecotheology.

Secondly and inversely, few Christians would think it is necessary to claim that Jesus Christ is the *only* source for the kind of 'salvation' required to address climate change. The Christian tradition, after all, also recognizes the role of prophets, priests, apostles and disciples, indeed a whole cloud of witnesses. Even Christian exclusivists who claim in inter-religious dialogue that 'Jesus is the only Way' would not extend that to suggest that the message of salvation in Jesus Christ is the one and only way to address climate change. Hence the need for qualifiers such as 'most significant', 'decisive' or 'foundational' to describe the kind of difference that salvation in Jesus Christ can make.

Thirdly, and this has been the argument of my essay on sin in this book, this message will be undermined by an unwillingness, specifically on the side of North Atlantic Christians, to confess their complicity in historic carbon emissions and current mitigation efforts. A confession of faith in God's salvation from the impact of sin cannot be separated from a confession of sin.

Fourthly, the Christian claim regarding the message of salvation in Jesus Christ cannot be separated from the work of the Holy Spirit in us and through us. What has been accomplished in Jesus Christ would make no difference without the Spirit appropriating that in history. This essay would therefore need to be read together with the one on God's work of salvation in us and through us.

Finally, that history of salvation is, according to the Christian confession, not yet completed. The creative tension between the 'already' and the 'not yet' in the history of salvation has to be maintained. Christians still expect the consummation of the redemption that is inaugurated in Jesus Christ. This essay would therefore also need to be read together with the one on the consummation of God's work.

Scepticism over such an audacious claim

The question of whether the message of salvation in Jesus Christ can make a difference given the challenges associated with climate change therefore needs to be formulated more precisely: Has God's work of salvation in Jesus Christ established a reliable foundation that could (should or would?) make a (or the?) decisive difference in confronting the challenges associated with climate change? For Christians to refrain from an affirmative answer to this question would be to acknowledge that they do not believe their own message. However, the audacious nature of such a claim should be recognized for what it is. Indeed, climate activists not aligned to the Christian tradition may be baffled to even contemplate such a claim, to hear the Christian message of salvation as relevant to climate change. Four aspects of such scepticism may be briefly identified:

First, anthropogenic climate change is widely regarded as one of the major challenges to be addressed in the twenty-first century. The impact is already evident but the future challenges are likely to become more severe. How can the life of any person living two thousand years ago in a pre-industrialized context make a decisive difference to any future challenges? This just sounds too good to be true!

Second, there is the scale of the challenges associated with climate change and the numerous levels at which billions of humans will need to be involved wherever fossil fuels are produced, distributed and used. The significance of the message of salvation in Jesus Christ for each particular case would need to be demonstrated for the claim to remain plausible. At best such significance will be indirect but what significance does such a message have for Buddhist, Confucian or Hindu efforts to address climate change? Would they first need to convert to Christianity before such salvation could become evident?

Third, there is the so-called scandal of particularity associated with Jesus of Nazareth – who died without possessions, writings or descendants, having been abandoned by even his closest followers. To make encompassing claims about the significance of any one person's life and work seems to be arrogant, at least from the perspective of outsiders. It cannot but undermine the kind of collaborative efforts needed to address climate change. The message of salvation in Jesus Christ may be appropriated by Christians, but to make universalist claims on this basis seems to be arrogant.

Fourth, the plausibility of the message of salvation is undermined by the track record of the witnesses to that message. There is no need to deny the good work of some Christian communities over the centuries. It has brought healing and wholeness to many. However, this is of course counterbalanced by the destructive trail of blood and tears left behind by many crusaders for Christ. This is vividly illustrated by the missionary movements over the past two centuries, aligned with slavery, imperialism, colonialism and industrialization. However, the problem does not lie only with the mixed bag of followers of Jesus, but with the *Wirkungsgeschichte* of the message itself. If this message is one that can make a decisive difference to something like climate change, one would expect to see evidence of the kind of difference that it can make in the past twenty centuries. Such evidence can be found on a small scale, for example in the lives of individuals or particular communities. However, when the scale is enlarged to refer to churches, countries or bioregions it seems that the destructive legacy of Christianity is at least as evident as the salvation promised. How would responding to the truly global challenges associated with climate change be any different?

How may North Atlantic Christians respond to such scepticism that their core message cannot make any decisive difference in the context of climate change?

Retrieving the message: Three models of atonement

What did Jesus do that brings salvation? Christian proclamation regarding salvation is littered with ossified metaphors. He saves us. He heals us. He rescues us. He overcomes the demons in and around us. He liberates us. He redeems us. He died for us. He paid for our sins. He is our mediator with God. He took the punishment that we deserve. He offers forgiveness of sin. He accepts us as we are. He is our friend. He inspires us to resist oppression. He offers a third way to address violence (alongside the standard options of fight or flight). Through his resurrection he overcame the powers of death and destruction.

Each of these sayings is derived from the biblical roots of Christianity. Each goes back to some specific experience of salvation. Each experience is metaphorically extended to capture a more comprehensive notion of salvation but in the process clouds the meaning of such salvation. In each case it then becomes necessary to explain what Christ has done 'for us and our salvation' (as the Nicene Creed holds) and how that could still make a difference today. This is the task of reflection on the doctrine of atonement. Such at-one-ment is best understood as restoring the relationship between Creator and creation, often narrowed down to 'us' and God.

Most theories of atonement make use of a famous if much-debated threefold typology offered by the Swedish theologian Gustaf Aulén in his book *Christus Victor*, first published in Swedish in 1931.[2] In what follows below I will improvise freely on his typology, making a distinction between three main models, each including a variety of root metaphors.[3] I will show why it is so difficult to make each model relevant for discourse on climate change and in the section that follows return to the implications for Christianity in the North Atlantic context.

Victory

The first model is focused on the need for a decisive victory over the powers of death and destruction. This is born from specific concrete experiences where such powers are so immediate and overwhelming that no well-being, often no future whatsoever, is possible without first addressing that. In apartheid South Africa it was widely recognized that constitutional change was required before many other social challenges (poverty, unemployment, education, health, crime) could be addressed adequately.

There are numerous examples of such experiences. One may think of the liberation of slaves, a ransom paid to release hijacked captives, healing amidst a life-threatening disease, poisoning or epidemic, a rescue operation amidst various threats to life (e.g. drowning, shipwreck, armed robbery, being buried under rubble after an earthquake), a military victory over vicious enemies, finding food amidst famine or water in the desert, the landless occupying a land of milk and honey, the end of tyranny, freedom from

---

[2] See Gustaf Aulén, *Christus Victor: An Historical Study of the Three Main Types of the Idea of Atonement* (Eugene: Wipf and Stock, 2002).

[3] For one overview in the context of ecotheology, see Ernst M. Conradie, 'The Salvation of the Earth from Anthropogenic Destruction: In Search of Appropriate Soteriological Concepts in an Age of Ecological Destruction', *Worldviews: Global Religions, Culture, Ecology* 14:2–3 (2010), 111–40.

political oppression, being able to breathe amidst suffocating air pollution, the exorcism of evil spirits and so forth. The biblical witnesses describe such experiences in rich and colourful ways. Typically, this allows for metaphoric extension so that one may speak of economic liberation, the healing of memories, food for thought, etc.

Such experiences are also common to the ministry of Jesus of Nazareth. This need not be disputed here. The question is what lasting difference such experiences of victory over the powers of death and destruction could still make, besides serving as a source of inspiration amidst similar experiences. After all, those whom Jesus healed are now long gone, the poor will always be with us and evil still abounds. With his execution on the cross the ministry of Jesus ended in failure. The problems that he then addressed so heroically still have not been resolved.

There are many rather crude attempts to explain how what Christ has done establishes a lasting victory. For Christians, victory over the powers of death and destruction is made possible by the resurrection of Christ (not so much the cross or the incarnation). In a famous North Atlantic simile the contrast between the landing of the Allied Forces in Normandy (D-Day) and the end of the Second World War (V-day) may be used to explain how that decisive battle did not yet bring an end to the war. The fighting continued but (in hindsight) it was now just a matter of time. Accordingly, the resurrection of Christ indicates that death has been conquered but some patience is required to establish victory everywhere else on that basis. Others have suggested that the resurrection may be likened to V-day. The war against the powers of evil is already won. Peace has been signed (with God). The problem is that not everyone has heard the good news that the war is over – so that senseless fighting still continues. This suggests the importance of Christian proclamation.

The plausibility of such attractive imagery twenty centuries later is of course another matter. Not only is the 'historicity' of the 'bodily' resurrection contested; the history of Christianity itself does not warrant confidence that such a decisive/final victory over the powers of death and destruction has already been established. If so, this model of atonement could hardly be relevant to address the looming catastrophes associated with climate change. True, the kind of overwhelming threats that have to be addressed before any future becomes possible are typical of climate change, perhaps epitomized by the submerging of Pacific islands such as Kiribati and Tuvalu. Rescue operations are still possible and certainly much needed, but how that builds on the foundation established by the resurrection of Christ is no longer obvious.

Reconciliation

The second model is focused on the need to bring reconciliation amidst (violent) conflict. This is born from experiences where it is only possible to establish a future if the lasting impact of the past is addressed. For example, it would not help much to do a clean-up operation amidst the immediate threat of toxic pollution if the sources of pollution are not addressed. The underlying problem is the guilt that one party in a current conflict bears for the mess in which all are still caught up. It matters whether such guilt is assigned on both sides (e.g. marriage conflict, family feuds), unevenly proportioned (e.g. revolutionary violence in response to oppression) or lies with one party only (e.g. rape, murder). Such guilt can only be addressed by ensuring that justice is done – whether through criminal prosecution, restitution or compensation. However, full justice is never possible since what has once happened in the past can never be undone, even if some of the effects can be ameliorated. Reconciliation is then only possible through the complex process of forgiveness – where the victim forgives the perpetrator for what cannot be given back.[4]

In the biblical roots of Christianity there are numerous examples of concrete experiences where reconciliation is required. Consider steps taken towards such reconciliation through satisfaction (doing enough to appease the aggrieved victim/ landlord), bringing sacrifices as a sign of good will, paying financial debts (if need be by selling oneself or one's children as slaves), accepting punishment for wrongdoing, blaming the conflict on some scapegoat, sending in a mediator to resolve conflict (albeit that the mediator may die in the crossfire), sending representatives to negotiate a settlement, asking and offering forgiveness (in interpersonal relationships) or amnesty (in a political context), or a hero who sacrifices his or her own life to avert a looming catastrophe where the enemy would destroy the whole group.

Each of these metaphors has been used to explain how what Christ has done 'for us and our salvation' has helped to bring reconciliation between 'us' and God. The focus here is almost always on the suffering and the cross of Jesus Christ (not on the resurrection or the incarnation). The meaning of metaphors such as he 'paid' for our sins, he was 'sacrificed' on our behalf, he became a 'scapegoat' and he 'mediates' between us and God still has to be unpacked to explain what difference the death of Christ makes in the long run. Often such explanations become extremely crude. Take the notion of penal substitution as one example. It may be heroic to accept punishment on behalf of others – as many stories from Nazi concentration camps suggest. However, why would a loving God insist on such harsh punishment? How does that really help perpetrators? And, how is this redemptive to their victims – those who are sinned against?[5] Is this not an abusive divine parent who first demands such punishment and then punishes an only son?

The further question is what the long-term significance of the execution of one rabbi in a remote Roman province could be. According to several biblical witnesses (e.g. Col. 1.20), this event is indeed the turning point in human history; it even has cosmic significance. If so, how could this be relevant to the concentration of carbon in the

---

[4] For one discussion of the complexity of the process of reconciliation, see Ernst M. Conradie (ed.), *Reconciliation as a Guiding Vision for South Africa?* (Stellenbosch: SUN Press, 2013).

[5] See especially Andrew Sung Park, *The Triune Atonement: Christ's Healing for Sinners, Victims, and the Whole Creation* (Louisville: Westminster John Knox, 2009).

earth's atmosphere? Again, the kind of experiences from which such metaphors emerged remain typical and topical amidst climate change. There is talk about historic carbon emissions, a common but differentiated responsibility, paying carbon tax, climate debt, climate refugees, climate justice and power blocks in climate negotiations. All these suggest a need to address the legacy of the past amidst current conflicts in order to face an uncertain future. The relevance of confessing guilt amidst climate change need not be doubted, even if this is hardly popular.[6] The difficulty that Christians face is to explain how the cross of Jesus Christ could make a decisive difference amidst current conflicts. This is exacerbated by allegations that Christians, especially North Atlantic Christians, are deeply complicit in causing climate change. This cannot but undermine the plausibility of their message.

Moral inspiration

The third model is focused on the moral influence of the example set by Jesus Christ. This too is born from experiences where an individual, community or whole society gets stuck without the ability of finding a way out. Consider the abuse of alcohol or drugs – on a slippery slope to addiction, experiences of internalizing loneliness making someone ever more socially unacceptable, extramarital flirtations leading to eventual divorce, a school, congregation or company in a downward spiral, increasing lawlessness where gangsters are taking over, escalating racial conflict, financial meltdown, ongoing pollution, overpopulation, spiralling urban development, exponential economic growth on a finite planet, ever-rising carbon emissions, etc. In each case humans seem to have an inability to find the moral energy, moral courage and moral leadership to start addressing the problem. The result may be a total collapse of the individual's life, the school, the company, the country's economy, a whole civilization. This is also pertinent to climate change discourse. It may be regarded as a spiritual problem given our collective human inability (thus far) to turn the tide, despite an awareness of the scale and gravity of the problem, the collection of ample scientific evidence, media coverage, annual political meetings of the parties concerned, the availability of sufficient financial resources and technological know-how.

Many observers have responded to such a lack of moral will by pointing to the moral resources available in religious communities. Religious traditions have the symbols, archetypes, sacred texts, stories of saints and martyrs, organizational structures, resilience over centuries, authoritative leadership, regular meetings and adherence of ordinary citizens that can and do inspire billions of people to get their house in order. Such resources can be employed for the planetary household (the word 'economy' is

---

[6] See Ernst M. Conradie, 'Confessing Guilt in the Context of Climate Change: Some South African Perspectives', in *Ecological Awareness: Exploring Religion, Ethics and Aesthetics*, Sigurd Bergmann and Heather Eaton (eds) (Berlin: LIT Verlag, 2011), 77–96.

derived from the Greek oikos-nomos – i.e. the *rules* of the household) on the condition that the ecological foundations of that household are recognized (the word 'ecology' is derived from the Greek oikos-logos – i.e. the underlying *logic* of the household).

On this basis one may readily recognize the significance of the moral example set by Jesus Christ. Christianity with its two billion nominal adherents is after all the largest single religious tradition. Its moral sources can also inspire others through collaborative efforts. In the biblical roots of Christianity there are ample stories to illustrate such potential. One may focus on stories of friendship, on ministry to the sick and traumatized, on remarkable spiritual wisdom expressed through sayings and parables, on solidarity with the marginalized, on including those who were excluded, especially through Jesus's infamous table fellowship, on a willingness to confront oppressive religious authorities, on non-violent resistance to political and economic oppression, on the courage to face persecution and a willingness to die for one's convictions or for a particular cause.

Clearly, such a source of inspiration could still be relevant in the context of contemporary discourse on climate change. Admittedly, this would necessarily have to be one significant source of inspiration alongside others. The particular examples would need to be extrapolated within very different circumstances but this can be done, as weekly preaching on ancient biblical texts suggests. The moral example set by Jesus Christ could hardly be regarded as making a (or the) decisive difference amidst anthropogenic climate change, but there is no need to eschew its possible significance.

The 'moral inspiration model' for understanding the work of Christ 'for us and our salvation' is usually described as the 'modern' theory of atonement, although it may be traced back to the influence of the medieval scholar Peter Abelard (1079–1142). It remains popular in a modern secular context mainly because of the focus on the life and ministry of Jesus of Nazareth, also proclaimed to be the Messiah (the Christ). It should be noted that there is then no need to confront the complex cosmology assumed in the notion of incarnation (according to the Nicene Creed 'the One through whom all things were made'), the bloodiness of the cross as sacrifice and the intellectual embarrassment associated with the 'historicity' of a 'bodily' resurrection. One may still speak of the courage to die for one's convictions but not of the cross as sacrifice for the sins of humanity. One may still say 'Long live Jesus!' and affirm the longevity of his message, his cause (the coming reign of God) and his following, but without reference to the resurrection as a victory over death itself (only the forces of destruction).

While popular in a modern secular context, this model of atonement is resisted by those Christians who consider this as a 'liberal' watering down of the Christian message that undermines its power and significance, also in the context of climate change. Nevertheless, at times, we do not only need to resolve immediate problems or address the destructive legacy of the past. We also need to put structures, policies and codes of conduct in place with a view to the future. This is born from a recognition that in this dispensation it will never be possible to eradicate evil completely. In fact, any attempt to do so may well exacerbate evil by the instruments developed and employed for that purpose. History is littered with examples of such inquisitions. Christians may also add that God seems to be more patient with evil than we are with others or ourselves. In order to curtail evil we do need vivid case studies so that we can follow best practice. This is obviously applicable amidst climate change. Especially in a consumerist society we need to learn what following Christ means.[7]

The message of/to North Atlantic Christians

There is an obvious danger that North Atlantic Christians may regard the message of salvation in Jesus Christ as 'their' message – that is, one for which they bear the primary responsibility as witnesses. Missiological discourse since the Edinburgh 1910 conference has amply indicated that, historically, North Atlantic Christians have been recipients of a message that originated in Jerusalem. They remain recipients of 'mission from the margins' – as the World Council of Churches' document *Together towards Life* suggests.[8] The message does not belong to anyone as it is addressed *to* us, indeed *for* us and 'our' salvation. In Christian ecotheology the 'us' is typically expanded to suggest that the gospel is good news for the whole earth and therefore for all forms of life (if perhaps not yet beyond that).

This has significant implications for the witnesses to the message who become the ones carrying the message. Christians are at best nothing but witnesses to the Way; they do not hold the Truth and are not responsible to establish its truthfulness. Christians cannot 'save the earth' either – as if they have the power within themselves to overcome evil. If the message is indeed true, it can and should establish its own authenticity. Christians are therefore not called to be the judge of other proposed ways or even to discern the best way forward. According to their own creeds, such judgement is something that they expect from Jesus, the Christ. This implies that they may expect God's mercy for the victims of history and, precisely for that reason, a concern for God's justice. Admittedly, they are also not called to witness to other proposed ways since they cannot speak authentically about that either. Neither are they in a position to affirm that there are indeed 'many paths to the top of the mountain'.

The message has always been a sharp two-edged sword, cutting both ways. The messengers have often become martyrs – as the Greek word *martyria* (witness) also suggests. What does that imply for North Atlantic Christians in particular – amidst a changing climate? Why does it seem as though martyrs nowadays come mainly from other parts of the world?

---

[7] See John Kavanaugh, *Following Christ in a Consumer Society: The Spirituality of Cultural Resistance* (Maryknoll: Orbis, 2006).

[8] See Jooseop Keum (ed.), *Together towards Life: Mission and Evangelism in Changing Landscapes with a Practical Guide* (Geneva: World Council of Churches, 2013).

Answers to this question needs to be discerned through study, analysis and prayer within Christians communities in specific contexts, standing in specific confessional traditions but always in ecumenical conversation with their neighbours, their fathers and mothers in the faith, their sisters and brothers elsewhere in the world, and their grandchildren. Perhaps the dog, the cat, the birds and frogs in the garden, the bees and the earthworms can contribute some wisdom too! Let me nevertheless offer some pointers for further discussion:

First, a confession of faith in the forgiveness of sins on the basis of what Christ has done implies a need for the confessions of sins. Some would observe that a confession of sin only becomes possible once the graciousness of God's forgiveness is grasped. Sins that are known are also known to be forgiven. The order of knowing is not that important here. Instead, there is a unity of mutual implication between a confession of faith and a confession of sin. In the context of climate change North Atlantic Christians have a lot to confess! There can be no room for (climate) denial since the plausibility of the message partially depends on the authenticity of the messengers.

Second, North Atlantic Christians have to keep asking themselves whether they believe their own message. This need not be expressed through the scepticism of militant atheism but should be part of a healthy process of self-examination in Christian communities. With reference to the threefold models of atonement this can be done by responding to three basic questions: Do we (in this Christian community) really trust that victory over evil can best come through the way of the cross? Do we really trust that conflicts are best resolved through the power of confession and forgiveness? Do we as followers of Christ embody and practice the inspiring but radical example offered by Jesus of Nazareth – or do we ultimately rather put our trust in life and death in education, health insurance, the power of positive thinking, the market or our democratic institutions?

Third, as the discussion above suggests, there is a lot of homework to be done here in order to retrieve ossified metaphors for salvation in Jesus Christ. It may help to understand the original real life context from which these metaphors are derived and to trace how they have been extended to explain the work of Jesus Christ 'for us and our salvation'. None of these metaphors will suffice on its own. Each needs to be complemented by others. All three of the models of atonement are necessary as they speak to different kinds of problems – a situation that demands an immediate resolution, coming to terms with the destructive legacy of the past and planning for the future in order to curtail the spread of evil. All three are needed in the context of climate change: the dramatic need for adaptation, the undeniable need to address climate debts and the difficult task of finding an appropriate way forward for an economy not based on fossil fuels.

My sense is that it is best to maintain the focus on the whole narrative of the incarnation, life, ministry, suffering, death, resurrection and ascension of Jesus Christ. The dialectical tension between the various Christological symbols needs to be maintained given the long-standing tendency to subsume the one under the other, focusing only on the incarnation (Catholics and Anglicans?), the cross (Lutherans?), the resurrection (the Orthodox?), Ascension (Pentecostalism?), sitting at the right hand of the Father (Reformed?) or the 'second' coming of Christ (Adventists?).

This is a narrative, many would agree, about the inauguration of the coming reign of God – at first just in Galilee. It demonstrates a new social order (or experiment), based on solidarity with the marginalized in society and their inclusion in the household of God. The key to such inclusion is a different understanding of God – as loving father and not as king, emperor or high priest. It does raise many further questions about the inclusion of those who exclude others, but this cannot be addressed here.[9]

This narrative, I would suggest, provides the foundation, pattern and paradigm on which the work of the Holy Spirit may build in different contexts and in different times. In the household of God a stable *foundation* is provided by its cornerstone (Eph. 2.20). The building does not extend the foundation but erects walls upon the *pattern* provided. One building sets a *paradigm* for others to improvise on elsewhere. The foundation is necessary but not sufficient.

How this may be done is illustrated in the New Testament through Paul's shocking ministry that included also the gentiles in the household of God throughout the then Roman Empire. In the history of Christianity this message spread to new contexts. Often the recipients understood the message better than the messengers. Arguably, that applies to (former) slaves and their slave owners, the colonized and their colonizers, the Dalits in India and their British landlords, the LGBTQIA and the straight. Perhaps the sparrows who nest in the temple (Psalm 84) also understand God's household better than human pilgrims coming to the temple!

Does the work of Christ establish a foundation for houses to be built amidst a changing climate? Given the challenges of droughts, floods, hurricanes and a collapse of biodiversity associated with climate change, thick walls, a stable roof and air conditioning would clearly not suffice. Indeed, some ingenuity, creativity and improvisation is required in the whole household of God. Come Creator Spirit!

---

[9] See Ernst M. Conradie, 'Conversion Towards Radical Inclusivity', in *Belhar Confession: The Embracing Confession of Faith for Church and Society*, Mary Anne Plaatjies-Van Huffel and Leepo Modise (eds) (Stellenbosch: Sun Press, 2017), 153–60.

Chapter 4.6
God's work of salvation in and through us

Hilda P. Koster[1]

Introduction

The Christian gospel is not just a message of God's saving work for us, but also a message of God's work of salvation *in* us and *through* us by way of the Holy Spirit.[2] Traditionally the work of God's saving grace is explained in a variety of ways, including regeneration, deification, redemption and vocation. This essay's focus is on justifying and sanctifying grace by way of the doctrine of justification. Broadly speaking the insight offered by the doctrine of justification is that in Christ we are radically forgiven, freed and made right before God through a sheer act of grace.[3] The *Joint Declaration on the Doctrine of Justification* (1999), an ecumenical document that emerged out of years of dialogue between the Roman Catholic Church and the Lutheran churches, states that it is '[B]y grace alone, in faith in Christ's saving work and not because of any merit on our part [that] we are accepted by God and receive the Holy Spirit, who renews our hearts while equipping and calling us to good works.'[4] Precisely because we are found favourable in God's eyes despite our sins and without regard for the degree to which the virtues of our lives would merit such consideration, God's justifying grace offers climate-privileged people[5] the possibility of 'repentance, assurance, reconciliation, and the

---

[1] Hilda P. Koster is Associate Professor of Religion, Environmental and Sustainability Studies at Concordia College (Moorhead, MN, USA), a college of the Evangelical Lutheran Church of America. Originally from The Netherlands, she teaches and writes on ecological theology and environmental ethics with a focus on gender.
[2] I am grateful to my former colleague Alfhild Ingberg, retired Professor of English Literature, for her careful and insightful reading of this essay.
[3] For a helpful overview of the doctrine of justification, including current issues, see Dawn DeVries, 'Justification', in *Oxford Handbook of Systematic Theology*, John Webster, Kathryn Tanner and Iain Torrance (eds) (Oxford: Oxford University Press, 2007), 197–211.
[4] *Joint Declaration on the Doctrine of Justification*, § 15. See also, DeVries 'Justification', 202.
[5] By 'climate-privileged people' I mean people who like myself live in a geographic area, mainly the Global North, that generally is less affected by global climate change and who, because of their race, gender, economic situation and background, are benefitting from (settler) colonialism, capitalism, white supremacy and/or patriarchy.

ability to start anew'.[6] As such it speaks to the guilt, powerlessness, existential anxieties and fear climate-privileged people often experience vis-à-vis our current climate crisis. Indeed, this essay argues that because of its rich experiential dimension justifying grace is an antidote against moral apathy, indifference and denial with which people of relative privilege typically respond to climate-change-related anxieties.

Yet because Christianity's vocabularies of grace have often been human-centred and individualistic, the choice to focus on grace, let alone justifying grace, in the context of climate change is not self-evident. Indeed, in his ecological critique of Christianity, Lynn White, Jr, casts soteriology, and, hence, the doctrine of grace as the linchpin of Christianity's anthropocentric, individualist, dualist and hierarchical cosmology.[7] The orthodox Protestant doctrine of grace stands especially accused since it has tended to focus on the righteousness of God of the individual believer before God, de facto relegating the rest of creation to a stage or background of God's redemptive relationship with humans. Even so, in his seminal study *Ecologies of Grace* (2008) Willis Jenkins argues that Christianity's concepts of grace are key for understanding the logic of religiously motivated environmental practices and for restoring 'our lost senses to earth'.[8] Jenkins suggests, and I concur, that ecotheologians engage soteriology head-on: 'challenging bad-legacies of salvation and revaluing nature'.[9]

When it comes to the retrieval of the doctrine of justification in the context of climate change some 'bad legacies' are serious obstacles, however. I will name four at the outset. First, and in addition to its alleged anthropocentrism, the Protestant critique of work-righteousness has often led to a strict separation between justification and sanctification, and, hence, ethics. Thus Lutheran theologian Vítor Westhelle observes that because in Orthodox Lutheranism justification came to mean that even the best action could be an attempt to negotiate one's divine election and earn salvation, Lutheran piety favoured a passive attitude towards the world. Or as Westhelle puts it, the focus was on Luther's *coram Deo* perspective, which came at the expense of Luther's *coram mundo* perspective.[10]

Second, the doctrine of justification has tended to relegate service in and to the world to the realm of charity. While the victims of climate change obviously require charitable aide, climate change is first and foremost a matter of social, political, economic and ecological justice. After all, those who are least responsible for the current climate catastrophe – subsistence farmers in the Global South, island nations and coastal people of impoverished low-lying countries, Indigenous peoples and the economically

---

[6] Sharon Delgado, *Love in a Time of Climate Change: Honoring Creation, Establishing Justice* (Minneapolis: Fortress, 2017), 65.

[7] Lynn White, Jr, 'The Historical Roots of Our Ecological Crisis', *Science* 155 (1967), 1203–7.

[8] Willis Jenkins, *Ecologies of Grace: Environmental Ethics and Christian Theology* (Oxford: Oxford University Press, 2008), 12. Jenkins does not think White's criticism of traditional salvation stories inaccurate, but takes issue with the fact that Christian environmental ethics, in the wake of White's essay, has discarded the discourse of grace altogether.

[9] Ibid., 13.

[10] Vítor Westhelle, 'Working with Lutheran forms of Christianity', in this volume.

marginalized – unjustly suffer its consequences. In the words of Cynthia Moe-Lobeda, 'climate change screams white privilege, class privilege, and environmental racism'.[11] A North Atlantic theology of justifying grace worth its salt, therefore, must demand a radical commitment to resist the injustice climate-privileged people commit. Dietrich Bonhoeffer's admonition that God's grace is not 'cheap' but calls us into radical discipleship, rings loud and clear.[12]

A further obstacle in retrieving the doctrine of justification is that it has re-inscribed hegemonic gender binaries in ways that have been detrimental to women. In an influential 1988 essay, 'Luther on the Self: A Feminist Critique', Daphne Hampson argued that Luther's theology cultivates insecurity for women, because in grace, the self is decentred – found only outside itself, leaving a void in the proper place of an organizing sense of self that contributes to women's agency.[13] Feminists have further criticized the model of love underlying justifying grace, namely the relational dynamic of an active God and receptive human. Such a passive/active binary may lead one to idealize abusive relations. For, as Catherine Keller observes, when 'love is seen as a matter of acting *upon*', it easily becomes a matter of domination and control.[14] Because climate change disproportionally affects poor women, who often have a lack of access to education and are dependent on male relatives for their security, despite being the ones responsible for the sustenance of the family, cultivating passivity and lack of agency will be detrimental for their survival in a time of increased climate catastrophes.[15]

Finally, ecotheologian Terra Rowe has demonstrated that any retrieval of the doctrine of grace in the context of climate change must engage the critique that the Protestant notion of free grace has contributed to the conceptual foundations of neoliberal capitalism, namely individualism and commodification of nature and labour.[16] Most

---

[11] Cynthia Moe-Lobeda, 'The Spirit as Moral-Spiritual Power for Earth-Honoring, Justice Seeking Ways of Shaping Our Life in Common', in *Planetary Solidarity: Global Women's Voices on Christian Doctrine and Climate Justice*, Grace Ji-Sun Kim and Hilda P. Koster (eds) (Minneapolis: Fortress, 2017), 249–73 (251).

[12] According to Dietrich Bonhoeffer 'cheap grace' is a grace that preaches 'forgiveness without requiring repentance ... grace without discipleship, grace without the cross, grace without Jesus Christ, living and incarnate'. See Dietrich Bonhoeffer, *The Cost of Discipleship* (excerpts) translated by R. H. Fuller (New York: Macmillan, 1963), 47.

[13] Daphne Hampson, 'Luther on the Self: A Feminist Critique', *Word and World* 8 (1988), 334–43 (338). Quoted in Terra S. Rowe, *Toward a Better Worldliness: Economy, Ecology and the Protestant Tradition* (Minneapolis: Fortress, 2017), xv.

[14] Catherine Keller, *From a Broken Web: Separation, Sexism and Self* (Boston: Beacon Press, 1988), 37. Quoted in Rowe, *Toward a Better Worldliness*, xv–xvi.

[15] On Climate Change and Gender Justice, see Irene Dankelman, *Gender and Climate Change: An Introduction* (London: Routledge, 2010); Susan Buckingham and Virginie Le Masson (eds), *Understanding Climate Change through Gender Relations* (London: Routledge, 2019). For inspiring stories about women and resilience in the context of climate-related catastrophe, see Mary Robinson, *Climate Justice: Hope, Resilience, and the Fight for a Sustainable Future* (London: Bloomsbury, 2018).

[16] See Terra S. Rowe, 'Grace and Climate Change: The Free Gift in Capitalism and Protestantism', in *Eco-Reformation: Grace and Hope for a Planet in Peril*, Lisa E. Dahill and James B. Martin-Schramm (eds) (Eugene: Cascade Books, 2016), 253–71. See also Rowe, *Toward a Better Worldliness*, Chapter 2.

notably, Anglo-Catholic theologian John Milbank and others associated with the Radical Orthodox School have argued that the Protestant notion of grace as an alienable gift gave rise to the modern binary of gift/exchange that they see as the root cause of the alienation of property and the rise of isolated individualism. Because gifts that were once extensions of the giver became mere objects, gift/exchange dualism laid the groundwork for the commodification of the world. Whereas, in premodern society, inalienable gifts created communal ties, in modern societies 'the alienable gift shuttles between isolated individuals leaving no necessary obligation to other members of the body'.[17] Obviously, climate change has brought home that there is no free ride and that all our lives are deeply interconnected.

This essay, then, retrieves the doctrine of justification against these obstacles and objections. Because the Protestant account of justification stands especially accused, yet offers a rich experiential dimension, I will mainly draw on new developments in Protestant interpretations of grace, in particular those offered by the Finnish school of Lutheran theology and the work done by theologians retrieving the radical political tradition of Lutheran theology.[18] In order to make the claim that the discourse of justification speaks powerfully to the anxieties, fear and injustices engendered by our anthropogenic climate disasters, I will first draw on the discourse of sin understood as structural violence or evil as a way to pinpoint what ails us.

Climate sin: Violence, guilt and anxiety

Ethicist Kevin O'Brien calls climate change 'a wicked problem of structural violence'.[19] Climate change, with other wicked problems such as global poverty, is complex, multifaceted and defies easy answers. Yet, O'Brien argues that while we typically acknowledge the complexity of climate change, we often do not recognize climate change as a problem of structural violence – that is, a problem that is the 'product of a destructive system that degrades human lives, other species, and the world upon which all living beings depends'.[20] Like other forms of structural violence with which climate change intersects, such as racism, classism, sexism and colonialism, climate change does not have one cause or actor but is 'the result of countless small decisions and developments in politics, economics, and technology ... and cannot be stopped by individual action'.[21]

---

[17] Rowe, 'Grace and Climate Change', 263.

[18] For instance Ulrich Duchrow, Daniel Beros, Martin Hofmann and Hans. G. Ulrich (eds), *Die Reformation radikalisieren/ Radicalizing Reformation* (six volumes) (Münster: LIT 2015–2016)

[19] Kevin J. O'Brien, *The Violence of Climate Change: Lessons of Resistance from Non-Violent Activists* (Washington, DC: Georgetown University Press, 2017), 12.

[20] Ibid., 4.

[21] Ibid., 2.

As an issue of structural violence, then, climate change transcends our individual moral agency. While we, climate-privileged people, contribute to climate change by living our fossil-fuel dependent lives, climate change cannot be solved by our individual actions nor do these actions seem to make a difference that truly matters. Addressing this conundrum, Moe-Lobeda, who uses structural violence (a sociological category) to talk about sin as structural evil (a theological category), writes that it is the 'paradox of privilege' that regardless of our individual virtue or vice we are contributing to and reaping 'the benefits of economic and ecological violence'.[22] Yet, while our actions vis-à-vis climate change may seem ineffective and immaterial, failing to act not only keeps destructive socio-economic structures in place but reinforces them. This is the case because structural violence always involves 'the complicity or silent acquiescence of those who fail to take responsibility for it and challenge it'.[23] Moe-Lobeda, therefore, reminds us that while structural violence does not have a direct actor, it is often deadly for its victims: 'structural violence degrades, dehumanizes, damages and kills people by limiting or preventing their access to the necessities for life or for its flourishing.'[24]

There are, I believe, two closely related, yet distinct aspects to this analysis of climate change as structural violence that are significant for the retrieval of justifying grace. First, as Moe-Lobeda points out, privileged people are guilty when it comes to climate violence. Indeed, she presses North Atlantic Christians to confess and repent their complicity in climate sin. The latter requires that we break the cycle of moral oblivion in which we have uncritically aligned ourselves with economic structures that are harmful to the planet and climate-vulnerable communities. Drawing on the Lutheran understanding of sin, Moe-Lobeda sees this as a collective manifestation of the self-turned in upon self (*incurvatus in se*): our proclivity to relentlessly put our own interest at the centre.[25] She observes that 'we have become a society so addicted to our-consumption-oriented ways that we close our hearts and minds to the death and destruction required to sustain them.'[26]

Besides confessing our complicity in climate sin, a second aspect of viewing climate change through the lens of structural violence is the acknowledgement that we cannot help participating in political-economic structures that harm others and creation. This is indeed the tragedy of our current historical moment. Ernst Conradie aptly calls this condition the 'pervasive perversity' of sin. It is 'the mess we find ourselves in … and from which we cannot escape'.[27] Even '[our] best efforts at moral renewal,

---

[22] Cynthia D. Moe-Lobeda, *Resisting Structural Evil: Love as Ecological and Economic Vocation* (Minneapolis: Fortress, 2013), 61.

[23] Ibid., 72.

[24] Ibid.

[25] Cynthia D. Moe-Lobeda, 'Re-radicalizing Justification', in *Befreiung zur Gerechtigkeit/ Liberation towards Justice*, Ulrich Duchrow and Carsten Jochum-Bortfeld (eds) (Münster, LIT, 2015), 219–60 (243); See also Moe-Lobeda, *Resisting Structural Evil*, 58–60.

[26] Moe-Lobeda, *Resisting Structural Evil*, 59.

[27] Ernst M. Conradie, 'The Emergence of Human Sin', in this volume.

reconstruction, transformation, and social development remain flawed and often even exacerbate the problem.'[28] In light of this tragic condition, and keeping in mind the threat to planetary life that climate change poses, it is perhaps no wonder that climate-privileged people feel morally paralysed and, hence, seem apathetic when faced with our current predicament.

As a form of structural violence, then, climate change poses significant challenges for our moral agency: not only is our will held hostage to the global market and its lure to continue to consume, but our agency is also hampered by the pervasive perversity of sin, characteristic of our current climate moment. It is important, however, not to confuse our moral inadequacy vis-à-vis climate change with indifference. According to the Finnish theologian Panu Pihkala, apathy vis-à-vis climate change often is a manifestation of eco-anxiety.[29] Eco-anxiety captures psychological, moral and existential impacts caused by environmental destruction and typically manifests itself indirectly in the form of depression, socio-ethical paralysis and general loss of well-being. Pihkala observes that in response people have developed psychological and social defences, including denial and 'socially constructed silence'.[30] Pihkala further points to a growing body of literature on the 'myth of apathy', which explains that apathy in the face of climate change does not indicate, as is often assumed, that 'people care *too* little or not at all, but rather that they care too much'.[31]

In other words, in addition to moral challenges posed by climate change, it is pertinent that we also attend to the psychological and, especially, existential dimensions. Pihkala's work suggests that appealing mainly to guilt while failing to address underlying emotions and existential questions is counterproductive and even dangerous. It may, for instance, strengthen the appeal of authoritarian leaders, who, by denying the problem of climate change and promising to make 'America great again', offer 'a false hope that the problem is not real' or that they can bring back a situation in which 'things were still good'.[32] More often, however, people cope with anxiety related to climate change by increasing patterns of unsustainable consumption. Pihkala refers here to psychological studies offering insight in the way people across cultures use 'symbolic immortality' to create continued meaning for their mortal lives. People typically see their mortal lives as having continued meaning not just through their offspring, accomplishments and religious narratives, but also through 'the feeling that life goes on in the world of

---

[28] Ibid.
[29] See Panu Pihkala, 'Eco-Anxiety, Tragedy, and Hope: Psychological and Spiritual Dimensions of Climate Change', *Zygon* 53:2 (2018), 545–69.
[30] Ibid., 549.
[31] Ibid., 528. Pihkala refers to the insightful work by Renee Lertzman, *Environmental Melancholia: Psychoanalytical Dimensions of Engagement* (London: Routledge, 2015). See also, Mary Pipher, *The Green Boat: Reviving Our Lives in Our Capsized Culture* (New York: Riverhead Books, 2013).
[32] Pihkala, 'Eco-Anxiety, Tragedy and Hope', 551.

nature'.³³ Obviously, climate change threatens these 'sources of meaning and types of symbolic immortality' in a most fundamental manner. According to Pihkala, the way we respond to this situation is with what Erich Fromm has famously called 'automaton-conformity': 'people try to be like everyone else and continue unsustainable behavior as in a collective hypnosis or trance, even when they know on some level that this is disastrous.'³⁴

Pihkala's analysis is helpful, then, because it reveals climate change as not just an ethical problem but also an existential crisis. In other words, whereas our addiction to consumption may reveal the colonization of our will by the global market – in theological parlance this indeed is a matter of 'the bondage of the will' – it also is a disease of the soul that requires spiritual medicine to heal. How may Christian discourses on grace speak to both the moral inadequacies and the existential questions raised by our climate crisis? How might the gift of justification bolster 'fragile souls' to live out 'God's justice making love' in face of the pervasive perversity of climate sin?

Justifying grace in an age of climate change-related anxiety and moral paralysis

As we saw in the introduction, drawing out the promise justifying grace holds in the context of climate change is not an easy task. In so far as the doctrine has instigated or reinforced modern anthropocentrism, gender inequality and the commodification of nature, it clearly has itself become part of the problem. For many centuries, moreover, the doctrine of justification has caused deep divisions between the main strands of Christianity – divisions that have been bridged only recently. The *Joint Declaration on the Doctrine of Justification* has been crucial in helping Lutherans and Catholics find common ground on justification and it has also drawn Reformed and Methodists theologians into the conversation.³⁵ While differences remain, the document's

---

[33] Ibid., 552. Pihkala draws here on Shierry Weber Nicholson's important book *The Love of Nature and The End of the World: The Unspoken Dimensions of Environmental Concerns* (Cambridge: MIT, 2002).

[34] See Eric Fromm, *Escape from Freedom* (New York: Rinehart & Co., 1941) quoted by Pihkala, 'Eco-Anxiety, Tragedy and Hope', 552. The exponential increase in international tourism may well be an indication of this symptom. Whereas in 2009 there were 8 million people taking international tourist trips involving air travel, in 2017 that number has grown to 1.3 milliard trips. In 2017, 23 per cent of all air travel was business related, the rest was for tourism or leisure. See https://www.volkskrant.nl/nieuws-achtergrond/help-de-st ad-verzuipt-in-de-toeristen-en-zo-lossen-we-dat-op-~b42a1c43/ (accessed 11 August 2018). See Elizabeth Becker, *Overbooked: The Exploding Business of Travel and Tourism* (New York: Simon & Schuster, 2016).

[35] See for instance *The Biblical Foundation of the Doctrine of Justification: An Ecumenical Follow-Up to the 'Joint Declaration on the Doctrine of Justification'*, presented by a taskforce from the Lutheran World Federation, the Pontifical Council for Promoting Christian Unity, the World Communion of Reformed Churches, and the World Methodist Council (New York: Paulist Press, 2012).

consensus is that in Christ we are radically forgiven, freed and made right before God as a sheer act of grace. Catholics, who traditionally viewed grace as working cooperatively with the human will to perform good works worthy of eternal merit, agree with Lutherans on the absolute priority of grace. Lutherans in turn acknowledge that in spite of the priority of grace, we are not simply passive vis-à-vis our own salvation. As Lutheran theologian Ted Peters observes: 'Lutherans and Catholics both agree that we *actively* appropriate Christ's atoning accomplishment in the faith that justifies, in justifying faith.'[36]

Another important ecumenical development in the study of justification has been offered by the Finnish school of Lutheran theology associated with Tuomo Mannermaa, which has led to extensive dialogues between Lutherans and the Eastern Orthodox Church.[37] According to the Finnish interpretation, Luther's understanding of salvation can no longer be expressed only in terms of justification; it can now on occasion also be expressed in terms of *deification* or *theosis*, a notion central to Orthodox soteriology. Most importantly, the Mannermaa school argues that justification means that Christ comes to dwell in the heart of the believer through the Spirit. Grace is not just *forensic*, as orthodox Lutheranism had claimed, but also effects an *ontic* change. Crucial for this interpretation is the translation of Luther's phrase *in ipsa fide Christus adest*, which Mannermaa reads as 'in faith itself Christ is really present.'[38] God's gift is no longer just a declaration from outside the human but is now also a gift of communion with Christ; in faith, which is inscribed on our hearts by the Holy Spirit, God gives Godself and has us share in the divine nature.

Finnish theologian Veli-Matti Kärkkäinen further explains that Luther distinguishes between two kinds of righteousness, namely, the righteousness of Christ and the righteousness of the human being.[39] The first type of righteousness is alien: it is the righteousness that we receive from Christ solely on the basis of grace (*sola gratia*). The second type of righteousness is our righteousness: it is the righteousness that is being perfected *in* us, after we have received Christ's (first) righteousness. Whereas this second type of righteousness still has Christ as its origin, and, hence, is strictly speaking not our own, it does allow us to overcome sin and transform our nature towards Christ. We are, in other words, becoming Christ-like or better 'a work of Christ'. Our holiness results in good deeds: we become a 'Christ' to the neighbour. Yet while we can distinguish between the two kinds of righteousness, they are in fact

---

[36] Ted Peters, *Sin Boldly! Justifying Faith for Fragile and Broken Souls* (Minneapolis: Fortress, 2015), 344 (italics added).

[37] For a helpful account of the Finnish interpretation of justification, see Veli-Matti Kärkäinen, 'Justification', in *Global Dictionary of Theology,* William A. Dyrness and Veli-Matti Kärkäinen (eds) (Westmont: Inter-Varsity Press, 2009), 447–53. See also Carl E. Braaten and Robert W. Jensen, *Union with Christ: The New Interpretation of Luther* (Grand Rapids: Eerdmans, 1998).

[38] Braaten and Jensen, *Union with Christ*, viii.

[39] Kärkkäinen, 'Justification', 451.

inseparable: 'they are inscribed together as on a tablet which always is before our eyes and which we use daily.'[40]

The significant differences between these ecumenical developments on justification fall outside the scope of this essay, but they do seem to soften the active/passive binary of justifying grace feminists deem problematic. Both documents moreover emphasize that justifying grace is a matter of transformation, though only the Finnish reading pushes a notion of justifying grace as becoming Christ-like. And, finally the Finnish interpretation moves away from grace as an alienable and unilateral gift, which, as we saw, was implemented in the rise of modern capitalism and its commodification of nature. Because Christ comes to dwell in us, 'Christ both *is* and *gives* God's gift, indicating a shift from an alienable to the inalienable gift.'[41] According to Terra Rowe, this shift implies a significant change in our understanding of God's gift-giving in Christ, namely a shift 'from transaction and commodification to communion'.[42] This conceptual change breaks with the isolated individualism of most Protestant discourses on grace and opens up a discourse of grace affirmative of our entanglement in and with the web of life.

The new interpretations of justifying grace further bridge the divide between justification and sanctification hampering orthodox Lutheran doctrine. Indeed, as the Finnish interpretation explains, Christ's first righteousness cannot be separated from Christ's second righteousness, or God's sanctifying grace. This emerging interpretation of grace articulates an activist account of justifying grace that sees service in and to the world as inseparable from being made right with God. Ethical inaction and private piety are not an option, therefore. Yet, and this is crucial, while emphasizing service to the world our actions do not carry the weight of our redemption. For, as the Finnish interpretation demonstrates, our holiness follows solely from the alien righteousness of Christ. This indeed is good news for those of us overwhelmed by the fact that because of the structural complexity of climate change even our most well-intentioned actions may end up contributing to our current climate crisis.

A second way, therefore, in which the doctrine of justification is helpful is through the notion that we are simultaneously justified and sinner (*simul iustus et peccator*). Whereas this notion has been central to the Lutheran understanding of justification (it was vehemently rejected by the Council of Trent (1554-63)), both parties to the *Joint Declaration* embrace the idea.[43] The Finns interpret the *simul iustus et peccator* in light of our deification by way of the indwelling Christ. It

---

[40] Martin Luther, 'The Sacrament of the Body and Blood of Christ – Against Fanatics', in *Martin Luther's Basic Theological Works,* Timothy Lull (ed.) (Minneapolis: Fortress, 1989), 324–39 (331), quoted in Moe-Lobeda, 'Re-radicalizing Justification', 243.

[41] Rowe, 'Grace and Climate Change', 264.

[42] Ibid., 267.

[43] The Council of Trent (1545–1563), which defined for many centuries the Roman Catholic view of justification, vehemently rejected the notion that we are simultaneously righteous and sinner after being justified by grace. According to Trent, justification is not 'just the forgiveness of sins but also the sanctification

is by way of the indwelling Christ and the power of the Spirit that we are united with Christ and are empowered to love our neighbour with the actual love of Christ within. Yet, because the transformative power of God's justifying love is a gradual process, our efforts in serving the neighbour are never morally perfect. Drawing on the Finnish interpretation, Cynthia Moe-Lobeda explains that according to Luther humans are 'rusty tools, being polished by God for as long as they live'.[44] We are, in other words, in the process of being perfected in love. And because our righteousness is not ours, we cannot lose it. Justifying grace maintains our relationship with God despite our own failings and despite our love and quest for justice being hampered by the pervasive perversity of climate sin.

Additional insights regarding the redemptive/healing power of justifying grace for our current moment of climate anxiety and guilt can be drawn from Lutheran theologian Ted Peters' important and wide-ranging work on the doctrine of justification. Peters distinguishes between fragile and broken souls. Fragile souls experience a disconnection between the inner-self and the moral universe. Fragile souls typically use self-justification as a strategy to pretend that the inner-self and the moral universe are in harmony. Self-justification is not innocent, however. Peters explains that when our self-justification falls short it may lead 'to scapegoating of others to maintain our self-image as the just ones'.[45] Thus in the case of climate change we blame others for causing the mess, or justify our excessive carbon footprint by purchasing a carbon offset. According to Peters' interpretation the alien righteousness of Christ placed within our faith by the Holy Spirit provides us with a 'cleanliness in our thinking' that allows us to confront our half-hearted attempts at self-justification and frees us from the intricate web of self-deceits.[46] Peters therefore reiterates Luther's counsel to 'sin boldly'. To sin boldly means that 'with a pure heart we pursue justice and peace, recognizing that we cannot control the negative exhaust (!) we emit in the process.'[47]

Yet while Christ's alien righteousness will nurture the fragile soul, it is not effective when it comes to the broken soul. The broken soul experiences a complete breakdown of the moral universe, akin to what Pihkala has described as the breakdown of our sense of symbolic immortality. Peters writes, '[b]ecause the centered self is so dependent upon the moral universe that forms its identity, the shattering of the latter leads to the loss of the former.'[48] The collapse of the moral universe typically is caused by collective or individual guilt-laden trauma such as is the case with climate change. The 'relational

---

and renewal of the inward being by a willing acceptance of the grace and gifts whereby someone from being unjust becomes just'. Council of Trent, Session 6 §7, quoted in Kärkkäinen, 'Justification', 448.

[44] Ibid.
[45] Peters, *Sin Boldly!*, 459, also 168–70.
[46] Ibid., 462, also, 319–20.
[47] Ibid., 460, exclamation mark added.
[48] Ibid., 462–3. For Peters' account of the fragile and broken soul, see Peters, *Sin Boldly!*, Chapters 1 and 2.

presence' of the suffering and risen Christ when it is being accepted in faith 'provides us with a spiritual accompaniment that coaxes a new robustness of soul to assert itself'.[49] In other words, the collapsed moral universe is replaced by the abiding presence of Christ in whom we live and have our being. And because the indwelling Christ is the risen Christ, the relational presence of Christ in the soul points to God's promised future of justice, and, hence, restores in us our hunger and thirst for justice. This is good news not only for people whose moral universe is shattered by climate change, but also for a world suffering the deteriorating effects of our carbon-intensive lifestyles. The restoration of our moral universe should therefore not be confused with a state of complacency. On the contrary, justifying faith restores the inner-self and makes an unself-protective, open and vulnerable disposition towards loving oneself and others possible. What this means is that we regain the ability to allow ourselves to be troubled by the state of the world. Indeed, the fact that we are troubled by climate change-related destruction is itself a sign of the Spirit at work in us.

Justifying grace and climate justice

But what is the kind of justice we are to be hungering and thirsting for? How, in a time of climate-related violence and injustice, are we to love our neighbour? Justification is about a just and loving relationship with the world for the sake of the world. Peters writes that the love that flows from God's justifying grace is a love 'for the sake of the other, not for the sake of one's own spiritual development or progress'.[50] God's love further demands that we go beyond charitable service and work for justice in solidarity with those, both known and unknown to us, who suffer because of systemic injustice and violence. According to Moe-Lobeda, Luther was adamant that the fruit of God's justifying grace included resistance to political-economic power arrangements that prevented the poor and marginalized 'to experience and trust God's gift of unconditional and unstoppable love'.[51] The Methodist ecotheologian Sharon Delgado explains that God's justifying grace calls us into 'social holiness': we are 'perfected in love' as we seek 'justice for poor and vulnerable members of our human family, other species, and future generations'.[52] Catholic feminist theologian Elizabeth Johnson argues that in a time of global climate disruption 'commitment to ecological wholeness in partnership with a more just social order is the vocation that corresponds best to God's own loving

---

[49] Ibid., 463.
[50] Peters, *Sin Boldly!*, 327.
[51] Moe-Lobeda, 'Re-radicalizing Justification', 239.
[52] Delgado, *Love in a Time of Climate Change*, 9.

intent for our corner of creation.'⁵³ Understood this way, God's justifying grace draws us into work on behalf of climate justice and planetary health in solidarity with those who suffer the consequences of our climate crisis most acutely yet are least responsible for it, poor women prominent among them.

Justifying grace, then, not only makes us love the world for the world's sake, but it throws us into the work of justice-making love in solidarity with those whom society has marginalized due to structural violence. The indwelling Christ is the key for understanding the direction and focus of neighbour love towards justice. Moe-Lobeda argues that when we take seriously the gift of Christ's indwelling presence, we embrace that 'the God of justice-making love – who, in the form of a Palestinian Jew, defied the norms of the Roman Empire – lives within us ... Standing up against exploitation of vulnerable neighbors becomes an act of Christic love breathing within us.'⁵⁴ Here we are reminded that the indwelling Christ is both the risen and the suffering Christ. As the suffering Christ, God's indwelling love is the subversive justice-making love of the historical Jesus who resisted the power structures of his day, sided with the victims of empire and died on a cross. The scope of God's justice-making love, moreover, includes both the human and more-than-human community. The Danish theologian Niels Gregersen suggests that we interpret the divine incarnation in the person of Jesus of Nazareth by way of the idea of 'deep incarnation'.⁵⁵ Deep incarnation signifies that by taking on human flesh, God becomes an earth creature, a sentient being that is part of the interconnected system of life. The implication of this breathtaking insight is that when, by way of God's life-giving Spirit, the humanity of Jesus is united with the divine Word, *all* of creation is united with the divine. Deep incarnation thus broadens and deepens the *scope* of God's love: the whole community of life, in all of its evolutionary complexity, is included in God's redemptive justice-making love. And because the incarnation unites all of creation with Christ, Christ's indwelling presence also restores our own broken connection with the more-than-human community of life.

Christians are thus called to a radically inclusive love in solidarity with the victims of exploitative economic and sociopolitical structures perpetuating structural violence and injustice. Yet where may we find the moral–spiritual courage and power for living into this calling? This question is particularly pressing not only because of our own apathy, but especially also given the enormously powerful economic interests and ideologies invested in maintaining 'worldviews, power structures, public policies, and life practices that suck us into climate horror'.⁵⁶ According to the understandings

---

[53] Elizabeth A. Johnson, *Ask the Beast: Darwin and the God of Love* (London: Bloomsbury, 2014), 285. Quoted in Peters, *Sin Boldly!*, 329.
[54] Moe-Lobeda, 'Re-radicalizing Justification', 257.
[55] Niels H. Gregersen, 'The Cross of Christ in an Evolutionary World', *Dialog: A Journal of Theology* 40 (2001), 200–15.
[56] Moe-Lobeda, 'The Spirit as Moral-Spiritual Power', 253.

of grace discussed here, the moral power for living out God's justice-making love is not a humanly generated virtue. It comes from Christ dwelling within us and is energized by the Holy Spirit who unites us with Christ in faith. Moe-Lobeda argues that according to both biblical testaments, it is the Spirit who 'leads people to walk according to the ways of life set out by God through the Torah, the Hebrew prophets, and Jesus of Nazareth'.[57] While the Spirit is often thwarted by our shortcomings and other realities of our human fallibility – most pressingly our moral oblivion to the structural evil of climate change – Her presence and power is a transformative, empowering force propelling us to heed God's will.[58] The Spirit moreover is poured out not just or primarily on the individual, but on the body of Christ. We are not alone when facing the work of climate justice. For the Spirit is calling us into 'Spirit-imbued communities of resistance and rebuilding' as we seek more 'just and sustainable ways of living within Earth's web of life'.[59] The divine grace countering the structural, social sin of anthropogenic climate destruction is being experienced in social movements of deep, planetary solidarity.

A brief conclusion

Terra Rowe observes that '[t]he doctrine of grace remains one of the most urgent areas in need of eco-theological engagement.'[60] This essay has sought to contribute to this task by relating recent ecumenical studies on God's justifying and sanctifying grace to the moral paralysis, anxiety and guilt that keeps climate-privileged people from engaging the structural violence of climate change in a manner that is compassionate and just. While the doctrine of justification itself has been a stumbling block for an earth-honouring, justice-seeking engagement with climate change, I argued that its vocabulary of grace is worth rescuing from its ecological despisers. This is the case not only or even primarily because it is the grammar of faith familiar to many faith communities, but most of all because its experiential dimension speaks to climate change-related anxiety and apathy in deep and meaningful ways. In an age of blatant climate injustice, however, it is vital that we retrieve the communal, subversive justice-seeking aim of God's justifying and sanctifying grace. After all the indwelling Christ is the suffering Christ who, as Jesus of Nazareth, resisted the exploitative violence of imperial power and whose Spirit was poured out, after his death, on the community of his followers empowering them for radical love. Obviously, much more can be said about justifying grace and climate change.

---

[57] Ibid., 257.
[58] Ibid., 265.
[59] Ibid., 272.
[60] Rowe 'Grace and Climate Change', 167.

The work done by Terra Rowe and others on the ecological/economic implications of the Finnish interpretation of God's grace as an inalienable, reciprocal and multilateral gift is especially promising in this regard.[61] More attention should further be paid to the very relation between justification and (ecological) justice. Ernst Conradie has explored this aspect in the context of a post-Apartheid South Africa.[62] Here I have simply sought to keep the liberating and healing power of justification together with God's loving aim towards justice. In a world where climate-vulnerable communities perish because of the overconsumption of a few, God's love cries out for justice.

---

[61] Rowe, *Toward a Better Worldliness*.

[62] Ernst M. Conradie, *Om Reg Te Stel: Oor Regverdiging én Geregtigheid* (Wellington: Bybelmedia, 2018).

Chapter 4.7
God's work through the church

Karen L. Bloomquist[1]

Under climate change (or 'disruption') the predicable order is changing. For thousands of years, Indigenous people have known when it will rain, when to plant and when to harvest, but those times are now becoming unpredictable. The natural order of things that people have depended on for millennia is changing. So too is the felt dependability of God: God's promise to Noah that that the earth will never again be flooded (Gen. 8) is now doubted. Some ask, is God angry at humankind? Others conclude that God may have left the scene.

Awareness of climate change is provoking old and not so old questions, such as the extent of human responsibility, the relations between human activity and the rest of creation, between God and nature and among humans globally. But it also challenges, revises and expands what it means to be church for the sake of the *whole* world and *all* of creation – in collaboration with others because the future of life on Earth is a stake.

Churches and other faith communities have been adopting and changing many practices that can help to counter or lessen climate change: recycling, promoting sustainable gardening, changing building and investment practices away from fossil fuels, and emphasizing care for all creation. Churches are challenged to be good stewards of land and water, and work with those of other faiths and civil society. Churches along with others are advocating for changes from economies based on fossil fuels to those that sustain creation. 'Green' businesses and also churches have become the trend, and often are profitable. All of these are important, but not sufficient. It is the whole meta-framework that needs to change – which is the distinctive calling of churches and other faith traditions.

The meta framework driving so much of what is occurring today is that of neoliberalism. From its beginning (especially in the 1970s) neoliberalism has been a project to restore class power,[2] which in turn has increased inequalities. Neoliberalism has come to mean untrammelled ruling-class power, and a vicious assault of the rich

---

[1] Karen Bloomquist is a Lutheran pastor/theologian/activist living in a cohousing community in Oakland, California, where she recently pastored an African American congregation. She has taught in several seminaries, also in Bangalore, India, and previously headed the theological department of the Lutheran World Federation.
[2] David Harvey, *A Brief History of Neoliberalism* (Oxford: Oxford University Press, 2005), 16.

against the poor, especially those most dependent on the land, water and air. This is achieved through market mechanisms, fiscal austerity and the penetration of capitalist relations into every possible facet of human life. The result is that we see all our relations as necessarily competitive, and the people around us as rivals for scarce goods. The earth is exploited for the sake of economic profit. The aim is to get rid of any regulations or institutions that get in the way of neoliberalism's 'free' flow.

Neoliberalism has resulted in intense industrialization, various quests for the highest possible profit, the increasing financializing ever more arenas of life and 'civilization progress' at any cost to the environment. Everything is turned into a market transaction, a form of buying and selling. This permeates *all* arenas of life, which is why this becomes a religious or theological challenge. 'If we are entering the danger zone of so transforming the global environment, particularly its climate, as to make the earth unfit for human habitation, then further embrace of the neoliberal ethic and of neoliberalizing practices will surely prove nothing short of deadly.'[3]

Alternative meta-frameworks or overall narratives and corresponding practices are what religious traditions and communities can provide – to undergird the long-term changes needed. Churches must challenge and develop alternative understandings and practices that move away from neoliberal assumptions that have been fuelling climate change, as manifest around the world. Resulting domination over nature, and over vulnerable communities have marked this, as well as disturbing aspects of the history of church, especially when it has been aligned with ruling powers and practices that have contributed to climate change. Churches have too often silently endorsed or gone along with neoliberal premises and practices, such as when what is 'profitable' becomes the driving force in congregations:

What is apparent in much of the climate change movement is its classism and racism. The number of immigrants and climate refugees is increasing at startling rates, as people flee from the adverse effects of climate change. In the United States climate change tends to be a primary concern not of poor or working-class congregations but of predominantly white, middle-class churches. They may acknowledge that those of different classes or races are most vulnerable to the effects of climate change, but are hesitant to address the underlying ideologies that are quite contrary to the faith the church confesses. These ideologies have benefitted especially those who are affluent; the gap with the rest has increased. Ideologies based on classism, racism and neoliberalism become apparent when the actual priorities of these communities are heard, seen and actually guide what is proposed and done. 'Environmental justice has become an important component of the movement for social justice, and in a city like Oakland (CA), where almost three-fourths of the population are people of colour, investing in the health and needs of the community is non-negotiable. …. As we work towards a greener, more equitable future,

---

[3] Ibid., 173.

we will have to address the historical dispossession of black, brown and Indigenous communities because race and the environment are inherently connected.'[4]

Climate change is a global *kairos* that is 'intersectional' – that is, it brings together many different oppressions, such as what has occurred under colonialism and racism, and what results in vast economic inequalities. But churches typically have only addressed the uncontroversial surface tip of this 'iceberg'.

Church as ecclesia challenges the meta-framework

The essential identity and meta-framework of the church directly counters the meta-framework and logic of neoliberalism that lies beneath the surface of this iceberg, and increasingly is being exposed by angry voices on the Right as well as the Left. The heart of what means to be church goes against this logic and its practices. What is emerging is theology that emphasizes, for example, how God is active, with human beings, in, with and through the whole creation. God is 'the breath that enlivens and energizes the living breathing planet …. in ways that are intimate and transcendent'.[5]

The climate change *kairos* not only is an ethical challenge but also calls for a new sense of what it means to be church today, not set apart from but in relation to others, especially those throughout the world who are most affected, especially by what the more affluent have done and continue doing. This is a *kairos* for what it means to be church, not so much as an institution but as a movement, an *ecclesia* or public assembly in which people come together with those of different cultures, religions and locations to speak and act freely on matters of environmental justice.

If the church is to be true to its calling, especially in an era of climate change, which crosses all kinds of borders, then the boundaries of the church need to be viewed in more flexible, less institutionalized and more expansive ways than they usually have been. Through much of church history, churches have defined and set themselves in distinction from those of other faiths. In contrast, the church as *ecclesia* is a 'place' or 'event' of seeing, remembering and connecting – of putting together what is fragmentary, pointing to what is true, enabling us to see and act, including in organized actions with others. *Ecclesia* is intentionally collaborative across boundaries of religion, geography and self-interest.[6] Through common practices, through what the church characteristically has long been doing – preaching, teaching, caring, community-formation organizing and

---

[4] Marisa Johnson, 'Undoing Oakland's History of Environmental Racism', www.greenline.org/blog (accessed 12 May 2017).

[5] Sallie McFague, *The Body of God: An Ecological Theology* (Minneapolis: Fortress, 1993), 145.

[6] Karen L. Bloomquist, *Seeing-Remembering-Connecting: Subversive Practices of Being Church* (Eugene: Wipf and Stock, 2016), 94.

so on – what begins to be countered are the illusions, amnesia and disconnectedess that further climate change.

This involves crossing some of the usual boundaries between sacred and secular, between 'us' and 'them', between local and global manifestations of climate change, between Christians and those of other faiths, between different classes and races/ethnicities, and between humans and the rest of nature – in ways that are trans-contextual and transformative – for the sake of the creation that God loves, redeems and continually is transforming.

The Church is One Holy Catholic Apostolic

The *kairos* of climate change today provokes us to reconsider the traditional marks of what it means to be the church. The traditional four marks of the Church[7] – that it is One Holy Catholic Apostolic – need to be revised and expanded. This means resituating church not as over and above others, but *with* others.

Holiness: Rather than set apart and removed from the world, all of creation is holy, the abode of God and thus of the church. Indigenous and other faith understandings are especially key here. Because all of creation is holy, it cannot be separated from what is 'of God'. Protecting and restoring creation against the effects of climate change, therefore, is a holy calling of the church.

Catholic: All the world is affected by climate change, especially those most vulnerable. The Church is truly catholic, existing not for its own sake but for the future of the world, yearning for it to be redeemed, reconciled or fulfilled at the close of the age.[8] The church catholic embodies 'a subversion of and a prophetic deliverance from the pathological individualism, polarization and sectionalism of our terminal society',[9] which has largely compounded and made invisible the effects of climate change.

The catholicity of the church implies that it is simultaneously local and universal – what happens locally is connected with what happens globally. More than a platitude, these connections need to be made explicit. What is occurring locally is an aspect of the whole problem. Terminals on the West coast of America shipping millions of tons of coal to China, not only adversely affects what for thousands of years have been native lands, but continue to devastate the health of communities in our day. This is especially the case in West Oakland, where I currently serve as a pastor. There may be intense

---

[7] David N. Field with inputs from Hilde Marie Movafagh, 'Where on Earth is the Church (*Ekklesia*)?', in *The Church in God's Household: Protestant Perspectives on Ecclesiology and Ecology*, Clive W. Ayre and Ernst M. Conradie (eds) (Pietermaritzburg: Cluster Publications, 2016), 116–36.
[8] Jürgen Moltmann, *The Church in the Power of the Spirit* (Minneapolis: Fortress, 1993), 364.
[9] Alan E. Lewis, *Between Cross and Resurrection* (Grand Rapids: Eerdmans, 2001), 350.

drought in some areas and very strong storms elsewhere. We are interconnected through what is occurring in climate change in ways we may have been previously unaware.

One: Global responses are required. We're all in this together. This is a logic that goes against what increasingly prevails today, when nationalism and tribalism may be on the rise. In contrast, coordinated international action is required for countering climate change. The international scope of what it is to be church here comes to the fore. International organizations that work to combat climate change, violence and poverty around the world are increasingly under attack, or underfunded. Here the advocacy voice of the church needs especially to be heard. Long term, interconnected approaches are needed on behalf of the whole world in ways that resist endless pursuit of profit.

Apostolic: Instead of an afterthought, apostolicity is what animates the other marks. It is the church's 'sent-ness' out into the world: 'Apostolicity must be understood in the original New Testament sense of being set out the bear witness to the eschatological future that break forth in the life, death and resurrection of Jesus Christ.'[10] Under the *kairos* of climate change, this bearing witness needs to be in relation not only to people but to all of creation, and the future of Earth itself.

This can occur more readily if the essential calling and tasks of the church are reconceived, as I propose, through the active verbs: seeing, remembering and connecting. These verbs actually summarize what the church has been about for a long time. As Jesus said, 'I came that those who do not see may see' (Jn. 9.39). He repeatedly called his followers to remember (e.g. Mark 8.18; Matt 16.9). This is a kind of seeing that evokes remembering, energizing people to connect with others – which is what the life of the church is about. This occurs as it becomes more engaged with what is actually occurring through climate change – seeing what is going on, remembering what has been and connecting for the sake of the future. In working with others who may not share its faith, the church transcends cultural patterns that are accelerating climate change.

Why seeing, remembering, connecting?[11]

The framework of seeing-remembering-connecting is more immediately accessible than are usual 'churchy' words – yet these verbs go to the core of what it means to be church. Seeing-remembering-connecting can open up some deeply theological insights that are critical, historical and relational. These verbs (through translation) are also more universally accessible across cultures, including globally. They are transcultural.

---

[10] Cheryl M. Peterson, 'The One Holy, Catholic and Apostolic Church in North America', in *One Holy, Catholic and Apostolic Church*, Hans Peter Grosshans (ed.) (Geneva: The Lutheran World Federation, 2009), 171–88 (181).

[11] Although significantly reworked for this essay, much of this section draws from Chapters six, seven and eight of my book *Seeing-Remembering-Connecting*.

The African Ubuntu saying, 'I am because we are' encapsulates this. Perspectives from other cultures help to wake up North Atlantic Christians when we are clouded over with illusions, forgetfulness and separateness.

When intentionally practiced by a community over time, the practices of seeing, remembering and connecting *together* become a subversive declaring of who and whose we are as Christians in the midst of those forces that dominate, oppress and compound climate change, and immobilize us from challenging what is occurring. To begin naming what we are up against signals that confessing faith in this kind of God clearly can be dangerous or at least risky, provoking reactions.

The church as the body of Christ is called to embody and live this out – if it is to be credible to secular sceptics who are doubtful that religious traditions are still relevant today, especially in the face of climate change. Together we are empowered to cooperate and organize with others to resist these powers reigning over our lives and world. From those who are most vulnerable, we begin to discern what seeing, remembering and connecting is like.

'Seeing' is exemplified in a climate change encounter that occurred near Puri, India, in 2008. Villagers there knew quite well the effects of climate change because they could *see* it all around them. With them we stood on the shore and looked out to the sea of the Bay of Bengal. Beside us on the beach were the shells of large turtles whose habitat had been destroyed due to climate change. A few hundred yards out to sea was a sandbar shining golden in the sun, which would be submerged by the rising water in another two months. Only a few years ago that shining sandbar was a lively fishing village. Due to this rising sea level, the village is gone. Like several other villages along the coast, the sea had inundated the coastline and swallowed all before it. Fifteen years ago, said one fisherman, the shoreline was five kilometres out; now it is only a few hundred metres away. Nearby, trees have been planted to help hold back the further encroachment of the sea into the land, as well as protecting the Hindu temple that has replaced the previous temple that disappeared into the sea.

'Remembering' was what the Lummi Nation in Washington state (United States) did, as they led what became effective opposition to construction of a large coal terminal that was to ship many millions of tons of coal from the United States to China. The Lummis invited many other, mostly white middle-class activists to this shoreline site that for thousands of years had been sacred to them. They remembered the stories of suffering from and after contact with the Europeans who had settled their land. They remembered their ancestors whose bones had been buried on this sacred land for many generations. They also remembered when fish were more plentiful. And through this remembering – and refusing to be brought out by a large corporation – they empowered a movement that eventually was successful in preventing the coal terminal from being built here.

'Connecting' is what villagers in Tanzania did. Elderly women there were being killed off, because with their red eyes in their culture they were suspected of being witches. Their eyes had become red because with few trees around, due to deforestation, the women were using cow dung to cook food in enclosed huts. When new low-energy earthen stoves were introduced and used outside these huts, not only did the killing stop, but the whole village became healthier. Connections were made between cultural assumptions related to gender, realities of poverty and climate change.

This triad of verbs – seeing, remembering, connecting – uncovers three of the major pathologies pervading the world today, especially by those who can still afford to ignore climate change: illusion, amnesia and individualism (or separateness). In this sense, they point to the inevitably subversive nature of the church, especially in the face of dominating forces.

Uncovering the illusions, amnesia and separateness

As the polar opposites of seeing, remembering and connecting it is also necessary to uncover illusions, amnesia and separateness.

Illusions: 'A public that can no longer distinguish between truth and fiction is left to interpret reality through illusion. The worse reality becomes, the more people seek refuge and comfort in illusions … lies and distortions become truth and people can believe what they want to believe,' including denying that human-caused climate change is occurring. '*Blind faith in illusions is our culture's secular version of being born again* … The culture of illusion, one of happy thoughts, manipulated emotions, and trust in the beneficence of those in power, means we sing along with the chorus or are instantly disappeared from view like the losers on a reality show.'[12]

Although much of this illusion is generated by advertising and other corporate powers that benefit from our deception, this has also taken over the political scene today, causing more and more to feel cynical and drop out, with the attitude, 'after all, what can we do about climate change?' Rather than trusting what we can actually see for ourselves – that seeing is believing – we are submerged instead in illusions that create our world, for example that progress is always good, even if it destroys creation.

Social amnesia: 'Historical consciousness and truth are now sacrificed to the spectacles of consumerism, celebrity culture, hyped-up violence and a market-driven obsession with the self … Public values and the public good have now been reduced to nostalgic reminders of another era.'[13] Market-driven values get normalized by erasing any viable understanding of history, memory, power, ideology and politics. Without the necessary formative culture or a metanarrative that can provide people with a language that enables them to recognize the political, economic and social causes of their problems, a politics of despair, anger and dissatisfaction can easily be channelled

---

[12] Chris Hedges, *Empire of Illusion: The End of Literacy and the Triumph of Spectacle* (New York: Nation Books, 2009), 10–15. For phrasing the problem of climate justice as a problem of moral oblivion, see Cynthia Moe-Lobeda, *Resisting Structural Evil: Love as Ecological-Economic Vocation* (Minneapolis: Fortress, 2013), Chapter 5.

[13] Henry A. Giroux, 'Living in the Age of Imposed Amnesia', www.truth-out.org (accessed 18 April 2018).

into a politics of violence, vengeance and corruption, feeding far right-wing movements willing to trade in bigotry, thuggery and brutality.

In remembering we (re)interpret what we see or discern in relationship to who or whose we are, and who or what has been forgotten or overlooked across time and space. Remembering is a present activity that draws from the past for the sake of the future, in contrast to a nostalgia that tends to idealize and get stuck in the past. Our focus here is on remembering that leads to questioning, to critique of what is generally accepted, and to empowering transformation of what is. In other words, remembering has political implications for the present and the future. Remembering also becomes a deeply theological matter, a dynamic process that makes present again and leans into the future.

Remembering the losers and their histories opens up a wider critical social analysis. It also opens up greater possibilities for solidarity with those 'left behind' in much of the rest of the world. It irrupts from below. It remembers the preferred interests of empire. It leads towards critiquing what is for the sake for the sake of our and God's future, rather than remaining in bondage to the closed system of 'this is all there is'.

Individualism: The master narrative of individualism is one that those in power, the dominant subjects, those who have succeeded, tell about themselves. It becomes the lens through which we see and interpret what is going on in our lives and that of others. 'Others' are feared because they have the power to unravel the subjectivity of those in power. In this sense, individualism helps to support empire and to further climate change. It leads to a separation of issues and of persons who are different from 'us'.

Seeing-remembering-connecting leads to a kind of turning about or conversion, from the separateness of individuals or issues, towards new ways of being and connecting with others, including those most different from ourselves. Through this framework, new kinds of solidarity can come alive in our communities as well as across the world – not as an end in itself, but for the transformation of systemic injustices, especially those resulting in the *kairos* of climate change, and a new sense of what it means to be the church today.

Furthermore, this is a shift towards people who are empowered by what lies outside themselves. Grace or the indwelling Christ is what brings about our being empowered to see, remember, connect. Seeing is active: because of what we see (what is wrong or unjust), we must act. When we continue to go along with illusions, of what appears to be but is not really the case, *then* we passively submit to climate injustices. We overlook, that is, we forget and become ever more disconnected from others, and from the life God intends for us.

Countering climate change through ongoing faith-based practices

Given the powers that do dominate our lives and realities under which we live, such a stance eventually – through ongoing faith-based practices – becomes subversive. If the kinds of domination and empire outlined above are to be subverted, what is needed is a different kind of seeing-remembering-connecting that goes against the grain of what currently prevails.

The interlocked powers that have generated and continue to compound climate change incorporate the entire world, in ways that counter what it means to be church. Those who are thus sacrificed to climate change tend to be deleted from the memory of those who succeed. Instead, their sufferings are misleadingly interpreted as necessary on the path to the hoped for 'salvation' or 'progress' that the powers of domination promise. The metanarrative generated by empire provides a basis for interpreting reality and imposes a never reached horizon.

To counter this kind of 'transcendence' a framework is required in which this sacrificial logic does not prevail, but through which we are empowered to work for a more human and just social order. Seeing-remembering-connecting embodies a sense of transcendence – a going beyond the surface givens, into what might be. This involves moving from a sense of powerlessness to empowered action for others, in community. Seeing-remembering-connecting are practices nurtured and carried out again and again, because new faces of systemic injustices are continually appearing. This is what it means to be church, in collaboration *with* those of other faith traditions rather than over and against others.

For Christians, the Eucharist leads to communion, interdependence and connection with those most different from ourselves. Eucharist makes communion happen. In communion we eat and drink together the body and blood of Christ. We commune with both the divine and the human, and with all of creation. We enter into communion with God but also into horizontal communion of all. Worldly time and space are invaded by the heavenly, resulting in the possibility of a different kind of society. We become one with others in past, present and future: The future fulfilment of the past governs the present, oriented by the past and straining towards the future.

This goes to the heart of what it means to be church in the midst of the *kairos* of climate change, namely faithfully bearing witness – making *public* – what people actually are seeing and remembering, and connecting this with the rest of the world, with those of other faiths, and with the whole creation. It points to the cosmic scope of faith and common church practices. In the midst of the long-term developments that have resulted in the dramatic climate change that is occurring today, the church embodies and lives out a much different narrative, for the sake of all creation.

Chapter 4.8
God's work of consummation

Geiko Müller-Fahrenholz[1]

Humankind is faced with three interconnected and mutually reinforcing threats. These are nuclear annihilation, massive species extinction, including humans, and economic destruction. This 'trinity of evil' is unprecedented in the history of the human species. Therefore, it calls into question the accustomed responses and attitudes of the Christian faith. This essay focuses on the challenges put to the Christian understanding of the 'end of times' by our historical moment. How does the Christian understanding of God's ultimate purpose relate to such anthropogenic 'negative eschatology'?

An orthodox understanding of the 'last things' refers to the second coming of Christ and the final judgement as the decisive end-point of world history, which then will result in a double eternity, that is, everlasting hell for the damned and everlasting bliss for the elect. By contrast, the essay takes up an 'unorthodox' eschatology, presented, among others, by Karl Barth and Jürgen Moltmann, according to which the final outcome of history consists in the triumph of the universality or the consummation of all things in the all-reconciling God. The aim is to show that this concept of 'Allversöhnung' presents a hopeful and creative countermovement to the existing threats.

'Unprecedented'

The bombing of Hiroshima and Nagasaki in August 1945 marked the beginning of the end-time of the human race. As Jürgen Moltmann states: 'Hiroshima 1945 fundamentally changes the quality of human history: Our time has become time with a time-limit. The age in which we exist is the last age of humanity, for we are living at a time when the end of humanity can be brought about at any minute.'[2] He refers to the awesome reality that the massive development and deployment of ABC weapons has resulted in an overkill

---

[1] Geiko Müller-Fahrenholz is a retired pastor of the Lutheran Church in Germany who taught ecumenical theology and ecological ethics in Costa Rica. He is especially interested in the relationships between ecotheology and socio-psychological conditions and implications.

[2] Jürgen Moltmann, *The Coming of God: Christian Eschatology* (Minneapolis: Fortress, 1996), 204.

capacity by which humankind and most of organic life on earth can be annihilated many times over. It is often argued that this massive threat has produced a system of deterrence by which an all-out atomic war has thus far been prevented. But the controversy between the United States and North Korea towards the end of 2017 indicates how brittle this consensus is. Hence the potential of mass extinction continues to exist. It constitutes an unprecedented increase in human power.

Under the shadow of the nuclear threat and propelled by the massive abuse of natural resources, oil and gas in particular, our planet has entered into a process of global warming, often, and somewhat euphemistically, called 'climate change'. It would be more adequate to speak of an overall war of attrition and abuse which will lead to the destruction of most of humankind and organic life on this planet if the present course of economic exploitation is not radically halted. Again, this is unprecedented in human history.

We need to complement this grim picture by pointing out that the already existing grave economic disparities between the peoples of this world are bound to deepen not only, and certainly not primarily, because of the growth of the earth's populations, but because of the overconsumption of goods by the Global North, the grave injustices in food distribution, the losses of arable land caused by flooding and/or desertification and the overfishing of the rivers and oceans. These threats are interconnected and mutually reinforcing. The salient point is that this 'trinity of evil' constitutes an increase of power which we humans have never known before. More precisely, this power is in fact in the hands of the 'elites' of the Global North which signifies that the vast majority of the human race is exposed to a massive powerlessness or, more correctly, to an extinction unheard of in the history of humankind. This syndrome of power and powerlessness calls for a massive increase of responsibility which we humans, especially those of us in the 'North', have not known before either.

This is what the term 'unprecedented' signifies: We humans have acquired a kind of power with which we do not know how to cope. It goes beyond our accustomed patterns of thinking and feeling. The frames and models by which we have learned to organize our lives do not equip us to adequately deal with the challenges before us. It virtually blows our minds and produces various forms of numbing.[3] This unwillingness to comprehend or, rather, this inability to feel, helps one to understand why it is so difficult to develop the 'new kind of thinking' which Albert Einstein called for as early as 1946. The question is: Can the Christian faith enable us to transcend the limitations of our traditional views? More directly, can Christian eschatology give us the energies to cope with a reality that 'passes our understanding'?

---

[3] See Geiko Müller-Fahrenholz, *God's Spirit: Transforming a World in Crisis* (New York: Continuum, 1995), 59–77.

The 'Orthodox' concepts of eschatology

Basically, eschatology is about power, God's power and what it does to our world and time, to human experiences of despair and hopelessness. In this sense it corresponds with protology, the understanding of how it all began. God's power is first and foremost the power of the Creator of heaven and earth, of space and time. This power is not blind and accidental, but caring and compassionate. God's original blessing sustains and enlivens all parts of creation. It encompasses the brokenness and failure that form part and parcel of the finiteness of all created things. This also applies to the reality of evil. In spite of its destructive force and murderous violence, evil is not eternal, but belongs to the created world.

Hence nothing happens without God's will. 'Are not sparrows two a penny? Yet without your Father's leave not one of them can fall to the ground,' affirms the Bible (Mt. 10.29). The Christian faith connects this universality of power with the universality of salvation brought about by Jesus, the Christ. And this connection which is at the heart of the Trinitarian understanding of God leads to varying concepts of salvation history. Their aim is to identify the course of God's reign within the vicissitudes of human history and thus to help the faithful to find their way under the pressures of evil. With inner logic this search leads to the question: How are the ends of God to be related to the end of history?

This has had enormous consequences for the ways in which Christian communities have understood their purpose in the midst of the torments and burdens of everyday life. The Second Advent of Christ was a constant source of hope and fear. Christians were called to lead their lives in faithful anticipation of this final judgement. Their hope for salvation was ceaselessly mixed up with the constant threat of eternal damnation. This profound uncertainty gave the Church immense power because she administered the means of salvation. The faith in the Advent of Christ also gave urgency to the missionary calling: to bring the Gospel to all corners of the earth was the fundamental raison d'être of the followers of Christ – because it was necessary to bring the Good News to all peoples in order to save them from eternal damnation and thus to accelerate the Second Coming.

Christian eschatology is therefore basically about hope and courage in the face of death (in all its forms) and about the purpose of Christian life in the light of injustice, temptation and evil. It is concerned with the ways in which Christians lead their lives. It is about being awake and watchful. This is what Jesus taught his disciples. And he was very clear in his warning not to get caught up in speculations about 'the hour of his Coming' (cf. Mk. 13.21; Mt. 24.23-27; Lk. 21.7, Acts 1.7). But in spite of this admonition there have been repeated attempts throughout church history to do exactly that: to find out the hour, to name the day, to imagine the Coming, to figure out the judgement, to divide the chosen few from the lost ones. The apocalyptic writings in the Bible, notably those in John's Revelation, have ignited this search. Christian art, especially in the Middle Ages, is full of it. Various dates for the end of the world have been suggested and caused widespread uproar. In recent times the establishment of the state of Israel – in reference to Romans 11.25 – has been interpreted as a sure sign that the final stage of history has begun.

Another important – and complicating – aspect of this relentless search has to do with the 'thousand years of Christ's reign', as mentioned in Revelations 20.1-7. It has provoked vivid discussions throughout the history of the churches.[4] It may suffice here to briefly indicate the direction of the argument: premillenialists argue that the second coming of Christ inaugurates the thousand years' reign of God while postmillenialists hold that this period will culminate in the final cataclysm and the second coming of Christ. A typical example of this tension can be found in the writings of John Walvoord. As a long-term president of Dallas Theological Seminary, Walvoord did not limit his studies to the biblical texts but went on to place his reading of the apocalyptic texts into the political and economic problems of his time.[5] He was among those who paved the way for crude fictionalizations. 'End-time-fiction' has become hugely successful not only in the United States, but also in countries of the Global South, though not in Western Europe. To mention but two examples: In 1970 Hal Lindsey published his book *The Late Great Planet Earth*. It went through various editions (with interesting alterations!) and sold more than twenty million copies. An even more drastic, and shockingly violent, fictionalization of the 'last times' was produced by Tim LaHaye and Jerry B. Jenkins. Their 'story' with the title *Left Behind* comprises sixteen books and led to the production of several movies, adaptations for children and related products.[6] Lindsey, LaHaye and Jenkins represent an astounding trend to turn traditional Christian eschatology into an openly divisive and potentially murderous spirituality with profound impacts among many fundamentalist churches and movements throughout the world. To be sure, it is difficult to measure the extent of its influence, but it appears urgent for theological scholars to engage in an ecumenical investigation of this phenomenon. It illustrates that eschatology is a dangerous topic, not least because of these recent radicalizations that further bitter conflicts and separatist antagonisms among Christian communities. It is even more dangerous because it is doubtful whether and to which extent this eschatology can help to cope with the unprecedented nature of our contemporary situation.

In order to approach this question it seems appropriate to highlight three interconnected *structural* elements.

---

[4] See Moltmann, *The Coming of God*, 146–235.
[5] When Walvoord published the second, revised version of his bestseller *Armageddon, Oil and the Middle East Crisis* (Grand Rapids: Zondervan, 1991) he received a call from the White House requesting a copy. It made a powerful impression; more copies were requested almost immediately. Members of President George H.W. Bush's White House staff read it to deepen their understanding of events in the Middle East.
[6] For further details, see Geiko Müller-Fahrenholz, *America's Battle for God* (Grand Rapids: Eerdmans, 2007), Chapter 2 entitled 'End-Time Religion in America', 23–48.

First, the most important feature of traditional eschatology and most notably of its recent fictionalizations is its *inherent dualism*. It sees the course of history as a relentless battle between heaven and hell, light and darkness, soul and body, good and evil, a battle that is destined to culminate in a final global war between the Antichrist and the coming Christ. This dualism is regarded as a 'natural' law established by the Almighty. Therefore the world is run by wars. This is the fruit of its sinfulness. This dualism is not interested in communities and nations living at peace with each other. Rather, it helps to accept if not to legitimize destructive antagonisms and wars.

A second structural element is its emphasis on *meta-historical agents*. In other words, the essential, though hidden, agents of world history are God and Christ on the one side and the forces of evil (Satan, the Antichrist) on the other. It is implied, therefore, that all the worldly powers are not as mighty as they claim to be. In fact, they are nothing but unconscious servants of God's overarching plans. Obviously, this notion does not help to assess the real possibilities and powers of human beings. It does not even begin to comprehend the unprecedented nature of today's world affairs. It also encourages many human beings to accept their powerlessness and poverty as a part of God's design which will be put right in the world to come.

A third element concerns the profound indifference to, if not *contempt for, God's creation*. It is considered 'old' and perverted because of the sinfulness of the human race. Hence it is destined to go up in flames as the final global war takes place. Consequently, biological degradation and species extinction can be viewed as inevitable side effects of the heightening end-time warfare.

In light of these three features it seems obvious that this kind of eschatology is not capable of dealing adequately with the situation in which humankind finds itself today. To the contrary, it is a dangerous form of escapism. There is its heavy emphasis on dualistic frames of thinking. To be sure, these are often justified by the argument that they are found in the Bible. But this is a biblicism which does not recognize that dualistic thought-forms in the Bible have been influenced by widespread non-biblical apocalyptic scenarios of that era. It suffices to mention the Zoroastrian religion. This dualism leads to a 'political theology', or rather a 'meta-political theology', that is bellicose in character and unable to critically challenge the kind of power which marks our time.

It is possible to use this 'trans-historical' perspective in such a way as to interpret our anthropogenic end-time as a part of God's design. Such a view would have it that God's final judgement has already begun. In this vain it is possible to interpret the 'trinity of evil' as the forces of the Antichrist that are bound to bring human history to its end. Then there is no hope for the humans to come to their senses. Sooner or later a nuclear war will be unleashed. Or climate change will take its destructive course because the big economic powers cannot but speed up the destruction of nature's integrity. In this view the massive species extinction, including that of the human race, is destined to take its gruesome course. The only hope offered by this view is that Christ will rescue the few who have remained faithful to him and grant them eternal peace while the multitudes that follow the ways of the hidden Antichrist will end up in eternal damnation.

It is possible to see eschatology in this way. But is this the interpretation that Christian communities should adopt in order to bring hope and courage to our world? Obviously not! Rather, it is a theory of hopelessness and despair that pretends to be faithful to the biblical texts yet hides itself behind a trans-historical view. It does not encourage Christian communities to develop critical and constructive positions vis-à-vis the enormous powers that govern our world. It is not interested in elaborating ethical standards for scientific research, for instance with regard to the weapons industry or the impasses of geoengineering. It does not encourage efforts to build up networks of resistance and renewal.

One might think that this kind of eschatology would flourish among Christian communities which find themselves in the midst of extreme poverty and powerlessness. Although this does occur it is revealing to observe that this eschatology is most influential in the Unites States, that is, in the very centre of unprecedented power. How is this to be understood?

Although it is impossible to arrive at a conclusive answer here, it may be in order to point out some elements that merit our attention. The first derives from an identification of 'America's Manifest Destiny' and God's design for world history.[7] This exceptionalism facilitates a dualistic perspective between the forces of good (with 'America' as their prime agent) and the forces of evil (with varying nations at the lead). It implies the legitimization of power – as long as it serves the perceived good. And this in turn implies that America's position and use of power can be interpreted as the hidden workings of God Almighty. Consequently, the ultimate responsibility for this power is God's, and God is beyond human criticism. This subtle identification of human and divine power blurs the unprecedented current situation. What is even more important, it devalues the notion of human responsibility, especially when it comes to its economic and political forms. On the other hand, it may also be necessary to note that the assumed superiority disguises a profound sense of helplessness and despair that finds its 'solution' in the apocalyptic fiction provided by Lindsey, LaHaye, Jenkins and others. For what can the proverbial 'person in the pew' actually do when faced with nuclear annihilation, climate change and global degradation? The little one can do appears to be insignificant and worthless.

Psychologically speaking, it is very tempting to evade such questions and to deny the responsibilities they provoke. In this manner, evasion, denial and escapism can easily hide themselves behind a blind consumerism. But they can also hide themselves behind a pious face. Consequently, apocalyptic fiction with all its supposed biblical grounding can and does become a way to strengthen denial and to evade responsibility.

---

[7] Ibid., Chapter 1: 'God bless America: The Messianic Experiment', 1–22.

An 'alternative eschatology' – universality of salvation

Origen of Alexandria (185/6–254) was one of the greatest theologians of the early church. Many of his positions have been hotly disputed. Among these is his conviction that at the end of time God's universal grace will overcome all evil and unite all things in his eternal reign. 'Apokatastasis panton' is the formula by which this eschatology became known. It does away with the traditional concept of the 'two eternities' of heaven and hell and affirms that the all-encompassing love of God will and must triumph in the end.

As the ancient Creeds indicate, Origen's position was rebuked and regarded as heretical. But it has not disappeared. Instead, it has led a somewhat obscure life at the edges of Christian theology and mysticism. In recent times a widespread discussion has begun. Much of it has been prompted by Karl Barth[8] who was himself deeply influenced by Johann Christoph Blumhardt (died 1880) and his son Christoph (died 1919). Jürgen Moltmann has discussed this concept in great detail.[9] He also deals carefully with the discussion based on the biblical evidence and whether it speaks pro or contra the universality of redemption. His conclusion is: 'Universal election *and* a double outcome of judgement are well attested biblically. So the decision for the one or the other cannot be made on the ground of scripture.'[10] But Moltmann does not leave the argument there. Instead of weighing one sentence against another, he explores the central importance of the cross: 'The true Christian foundation for the hope of universal salvation is the theology of the cross, and the realistic consequence of the theology of the cross can only be the restoration of all things.'[11] It is this Christological centrality that invites Christians to see the future in the light of the advent of a compassionate and all-merciful God. It is the foundation of unquenchable hope and courage. This Christological focus places eschatology at the centre of theology and gives it fresh urgency. It must also be noted that it leads to a cosmological understanding of salvation. Moltmann emphasizes that the cosmos, and not simply humankind, is the goal of God's salvific work. He refers to the Gospel of John, where the love of God for the 'cosmos' is underscored, as in John 3.16. He also points to the St. Paul's affirmation that in Christ God reconciled the 'cosmos' unto himself (2 Cor. 5.19). It is obvious, then, that the healing and restoration of creation is the goal. The Christological centrality corresponds with the universality of salvation. This is not to say that the 'judgement of the quick and the dead' is renounced. But it is the crucified who is the judge. The logic of the cross determines the verdict. The passion of Christ is rooted in compassion.

---

[8] See Karl Barth, *Church Dogmatics*, II:2 (Edinburgh: T&T Clark, 1957).
[9] Moltmann, *The Coming of God*, 257–96.
[10] Ibid., 241.
[11] Ibid., 251.

An 'alternative eschatology' amidst climate change

With these brief references we may now turn to the question: What is the significance of this 'alternative eschatology' for the challenges before us today? In which ways can it enable Christian communities to cope with the massive threats? The following comes to mind:

First, the consummation of all things is central to God, a *dualistic understanding of history loses its grounding*. If compassion is more powerful than evil and if this compassion includes all of creation, there is no room left for an all-consuming end-time war. The Armageddon imagery loses its relevance; the way is free for reconciliation and healing. The all too human tendency to think in dichotomies and divisions is undercut and replaced by the conviction that all divisions are temporal and all dichotomies reconcilable. Dualism is no longer regarded as an inevitable historical necessity or an eternal law. The deadly spell of an all-out destruction is broken.

It is this hope in universal salvation that releases liberating energies which enable Christian communities to elaborate a critical and constructive understanding of human power. It enables them to think the unthinkable and to anticipate scenarios that can help to cope with the unprecedented threats of today. As they approach these tasks their sense of responsibility will be sharpened. But the 'alternative eschatology' has a spiritual dimension that may well be at least as meaningful as fresh intellectual endeavours. It frees the soul from the hopelessness or, positively speaking, it creates a new courage of the heart – the courage to feel the sufferings that are about to come, to mourn over all the losses, but also to imagine alternative possibilities and to engage in steadfast resistance. The creation of such a spiritual solidarity may well be the most important task of Christian communities. For they need to help people to cultivate their 'courage of the heart' or, in less poetic parlance, the spirituality of hope, courage and perseverance. There is no direct link between research and action, no immediate connection between design and implementation. The decisive link is in the realm of motivation, encouragement, steadfastness and joy.

Second, if the ends of God converge in the reconciliation of all things, Christian communities are free to 'demythologize' the Armageddon imagery and to name the powers for what they are: human. Trans-historical figures such as the Antichrist only serve to blur the issues at hand. It is necessary to reduce the 'powers and principalities' to what they are, that is, earthly constructs, developed by humans and to be challenged and corrected by humans.

This is not to deny that there is evil in the world. At times humankind witnesses forms of violence and destructiveness that appear to have assumed a power beyond that of their initial instigators. As a German citizen one cannot but remember the dictatorship of Hitler that unleashed the murderous excesses of the Holocaust and the relentless cruelties of the Second World War. But German citizens can also affirm that these evil excesses are temporal. We have seen that a self-critical assessment of our past has opened ways for reconciliation. In a similar manner the European Union was a project of reconciliation, at least for the founding generation which had lived through two disastrous wars.

Whenever Christians put their hope in the Advent of the all-reconciling God they become committed to the opening up of time. Whereas traditional eschatology is fascinated with images of the end, the 'alternative eschatology' is dedicated to new beginnings. This is of critical importance because it is committed to saving and creatively using time in the midst of our limited end-time situation. Further, while the old eschatology tends to concentrate on the salvation of the chosen few, the 'alternative eschatology' is working relentlessly against the 'trinity of evil' mentioned at the beginning. How is this to be done?

Christian communities will be committed to working for alliances that help to contain the threats before us. Since it is impossible for humankind to simply 'forget' the ways in which nuclear weapons can be built, it is necessary to elaborate and uphold a 'cordon sanitaire', that is, the establishment of a global consciousness which makes the use of these murderous weapons politically unthinkable and economically worthless. Similar 'cordons sanitaires' are needed to mitigate the impact of climate change. It is important to join non-government organizations as they fight for the formation and establishment of economic standards, for instance regarding the reduction of CO_2 in the atmosphere. Campaigns against deforestation at the local, regional and national levels are necessary and possible.

But churches can and must supplement these activities by programmes of their own. A similar case can and must be made for the management of drinking water and the art of gardening, especially in the ever-growing cities around the world. Churches can use their grounds to create gardens and thus to encourage people to use whatever space they have to undertake similar efforts.

Third, these suggestions indicate that an 'alternative eschatology' will *further a deep compassion with all forms of life on this planet*. It finds the idea of an all-out destruction abhorrent. That there would be a 'new creation' is of little comfort since it would imply the death of the 'old' one. Since climate change also means massive species extinction, Christian communities will want to be recognized as guardians of the functioning integrity of the ecosystems of the world, beginning with the plots of land they hold. Again, campaigns against the abuse of animals and the overconsumption of meat and fish are possible at all levels. But they will find more acceptance once they are accompanied by positive examples of how people can live better with less meat.

Fourth, throughout this text there has been repeated reference to 'Christian communities'. In fact, what we are talking about are *communities committed to each other in strong ecumenical relationships and structures* – after all, there can be no doubt that the churches' answer to global threats is an ecumenical, that is, earth-encompassing movement. Globalization has become a fact, even though many neo-nationalist movements, not only in the North, derive their strength from its denial. Sadly enough, many churches are following this trend and reduce their activities to the local and parochial levels. The weakening of the World Council of Churches, for instance, is an alarming trend that stands to be corrected. But perhaps it has become too institutionalized. Therefore, it may well prove necessary for committed Christian groups to cooperate with each other outside established ecclesial structures by forming ecumenical networks of mutual encouragement and common action. Their insistence on courage and perseverance will have to face up to the heavy loads of frustration, boredom and nihilism. In other words, the 'alternative eschatology' we are describing here *embodies itself in Christian movements of resistance.*

Fifth, why is it that this alternative eschatology has remained a small voice from the margins of the churches and their theologies? At a deep and emotional level it may well be the feeling that the prospect of universal salvation is not just. No final judgement? No punishment for the evildoers? No gratification for the righteous? No vindication in heaven for all the sufferings endured on earth? Questions such as these cannot be dismissed easily. They speak of bitter sufferings, untold injustices and humiliations. And they reveal a very deep-seated urge that things must be put right. Evil must be punished. Good deeds merit their reward. Hence the question arises: Is this 'alternative eschatology' good news for the rich? And does it add bitterness to the sufferings of the poor? The answer must be no. The hope for the coming of a reconciling and all-merciful God does not undo the struggles for a just and sustainable ordering of the world's affairs.

There exists a deep, if not innate, urge of every human being to be treated justly. And that is not simply an egalitarian postulate. Christians affirm that all humans are created in God's image, endowed with the same dignity and therefore entitled to be treated with equal respect and worth. We are speaking of nothing less than *original dignity* that needs to be seen as a part of the original blessing with which God graces all of creation. Hence every humiliation is a betrayal, just as every abuse of power must be seen as a wilful transgression. Both stand to be corrected and set right. This is certainly one of the reasons why the urge for retaliation is so deep.

With this affirmation of original dignity in mind the question must be raised again: How does the 'alternative eschatology' relate to the quest for justice? A possible answer may be this: just as the original dignity is God's protological gift, so the ultimate reconciliation is God's eschatological promise. Both gift and promise remain God's, which is to say that they stay out of the reach of humans. But they constitute the realm in which human beings are meant to lead their lives. God's gift of dignity translates itself into the constructive struggles for justice which exclude the urge for revenge and retaliation, as St. Paul makes clear in his letter to the Romans (12. 19). Therefore, the work for justice continues to be the great civilizing project of humankind throughout the ages. It assumes new urgency under the pressures of our time. Thus far, the quest for justice has concentrated on justice among human beings. It has not yet developed reliable standards for economic transactions, notably in their international forms. Nor has it as yet found reliable ways to control the impacts of the flow of capital around the globe. Nor do we have the appropriate legal procedures for the protection of animals and plants at national and international levels.

The promise that God's mercy will triumph in the end does not undo the dimension of judgement, as mentioned before. Therefore it would be a gross misunderstanding to assume that all the evil in the world would be excused easily. How the crucified Lord is going to deal with it is not our business. Rather, it is our business to gratefully accept the energies which God's final mercy sets free in order to live up to the responsibilities that our respective powers demand of us.

Chapter 4.9
Climate change and God's work of election

Gijsbert van den Brink[1] and Eva van Urk[2]

Introduction

The doctrine of divine election is not the first theme that comes to mind when we examine Christian themes that might make a difference to one's attitude vis-à-vis climate change. In a recent volume on systematic theology and climate change, terms like 'election' and 'predestination' do not even occur in the index – let alone that a separate contribution on their roles has been included.[3] Yet, doctrines, notions and intuitions about God's work of election have become deeply engrained in the Christian mindset throughout the centuries, and it should not be ruled out that they interact – for better or for worse – with practical attitudes adopted towards all sorts of 'worldly affairs'.

In fact, that this is the case has already been hypothesized more than a century ago when Max Weber formulated his famous thesis about the causal connection between Calvinism and capitalism. Although this thesis was more subtle than has sometimes been perceived, Weber indeed posited a causal connection between John Calvin's doctrine of predestination (or rather, its effect on later generations of Calvinists) and the rise of a cultural climate in which the 'rational' pursuit of economic gain became dominant. His core idea was that Calvinistic believers who were anxious about their eternal destination came to consider a strong and ascetic dedication to their this-worldly vocational calling as a mark of their belonging to the elect.[4] Capitalism could then emerge since people

---

[1] Gijsbert van den Brink is Professor of Theology and Science at the Faculty of Religion and Theology, Vrije Universiteit Amsterdam. Previously he was a professor of Reformed theology. His current work is on (Reformed) theology and the sciences, especially evolutionary biology. He is white, male, heterosexual, married, European and Protestant – and he tries to be aware of all that.
[2] Eva van Urk is a PhD candidate at the Faculty of Religion and Theology, Vrije Universiteit Amsterdam. She works in the field of Christian ecotheology and investigates the potential of the concept of *imago Dei* for addressing human-caused extinction and stirring ecological responsibility.
[3] Michael S. Northcott and Peter M. Scott (eds), *Systematic Theology and Climate Change: Ecumenical Perspectives* (London et al.: Routledge, 2014).
[4] See Max Weber, *The Protestant Ethic and the Spirit of Capitalism with Other Writings on the Rise of the West*, 4th edn (New York: Oxford University Press, 2009), 124–5.

started to reinvest the money they had earned so as to maximize their profits. Weber's thesis has given rise to an enormous amount of scholarly debate ever since it saw the light of day.[5] Had it been substantiated, the doctrine of election would undoubtedly have been the most prominent theological factor fuelling climate change today, since late-modern capitalism is by far its most important driver.[6] However, although sociologists occasionally still feel attached to it, social and economic historians have shown since the late 1970s that Weber's thesis cannot stand the test of careful quantitative research. As Philip Hoffman concludes, 'years of research in history and the social sciences have disproved ... Weber's thesis about the Protestant ethic.'[7] The cultural causes of capitalism are much more complex and variegated than to coincide with the specifics of one religious tradition. Yet, Weber's pivotal insight that religious doctrines may have unintended psychological consequences that shape our cultural habits still stands. It is precisely this insight that is relevant in current discussions on religion and climate change.

In what follows we will first sketch the main contours of Western doctrines of election and predestination. Next, we investigate various ways in which such doctrines arguably have been detrimental to Christian attitudes towards the climate and climate change. We then explore some interpretations of divine election that may encourage a more responsible way of dealing with contemporary climate change. Finally, we summarize our main conclusions.

Doctrines of election and predestination in the West

Let us start with some terminological clarifications with regard to God's work of election as it has been interpreted in classical Western theology. *Election* is the act by which God chooses some people to live with God eternally, a life often conceived of as taking place 'in heaven'. It is the positive part of God's act of *predestination*: the foreordaining by which God has appointed all human beings from eternity to their final ends: eternal life or eternal death. Thus, predestination also has a negative part, which is why theologians speak about *double* predestination. This negative part is usually called *reprobation*: the eternal decree by means of which God surrenders certain people to eternal punishment, condemning them to life 'in hell'. This negative part can further be characterized as

---

[5] For a short survey, see Philip Benedict, 'Calvinism and the Making of the Modern Economic Mind', in *Calvinism and the Making of the European Mind*, Gijsbert van den Brink and Harro M. Höpfl (eds) (Leiden: Brill, 2014), 199–209.

[6] See Naomi Klein, *This Changes Everything: Capitalism vs. the Climate* (New York: Simon and Schuster, 2014).

[7] Philip T. Hoffman, 'The Church in Economy and Society', in *The Cambridge History of Christianity, Vol. VII: Enlightenment, Reawakening and Revolution 1660–1815*, Stewart J. Brown and Timothy Tackett (eds) (Cambridge: Cambridge University Press, 2006), 72–86 (84). See also Benedict, 'Calvinism', 202–4.

either *damnation* (i.e. the active rejection of certain people) or *preterition* (i.e. the passively leaving people in their sins, as a result of which they remain unsaved).

The decree of predestination is often seen as logically preceding God's decision to create human beings and to permit their fall into sin ('supralapsarianism'). In order to execute the predestination decree in a just and rightful way, God decides not to repudiate innocent people but only sinners. By contrast, the decree of predestination may also be seen as logically following upon God's decisions to create human beings and to allow them to fall into sin: it is because humans have become sinners that God has decided to elect and save at least some of them ('infralapsarianism'). For our purposes, it may suffice to observe that it is within such dialectics of time and eternity, sin and grace that the doctrine of election gradually received a key role in the Western tradition, considerably affecting the minds and ways of life of many believers.[8]

Surely, however, such disturbing ideas about God 'arbitrarily' accepting some and rejecting others are the hallmark of one specific Christian sect, namely *Calvinism*? Indeed, this is the popular perception – but as a matter of fact this nexus of ideas is part and parcel of the entire Western tradition. As to the Eastern part of the church, doctrines of election and predestination were not elaborated in any detail since more optimistic assessments about human capacities remained dominant. Even though the human will and capacities were seen as negatively impacted by sin (to such an extent that Pelagianism – the view that humans can escape sin if they make the necessary efforts – was declined in the East as it was in the West), human free will was not completely annihilated by sin. As a result, with the help of God's grace it remained humanly possible to attain eternal salvation. In the West, the consequences of human sin were valued more seriously. For instance, according to Cyprian (third century) human nature was entirely corrupted as a result of sin. In such a context, although the freedom of the will was not explicitly denied, it is clear that human beings were hardly considered free to do good.

It is beyond dispute that the fountainhead of the Western doctrine of predestination was Augustine. Based on his personal religious experiences as an unwilling convert, Augustine framed various earlier intuitions on the decisive role of God's grace in attaining salvation into a more or less systematic account. According to Augustine, if God's grace is fully free and undeserved, it follows that those who are saved are not morally (or otherwise) better than others; thus, these others form the *massa perditionis* (multitude of the lost) because for some reason, unfathomable to us, God leaves them in their sinful state. Augustine bequeathed these ideas to the subsequent Western church. From the early Middle Ages onwards more and less stringent ways of interpreting Augustine came to fight for priority. Despite the fact that such towering figures as Thomas Aquinas and Bonaventure favoured a more stringent reading, the milder ways (which accentuated the need for human cooperation in faith and works, and tended

---

[8] For a short survey of the traditional debates, see Katherine Sonderegger, 'Election', in *The Oxford Handbook of Systematic Theology*, John Webster, Kathryn Tanner and Iain Torrance (eds) (Oxford: Oxford University Press, 2007), 105–20.

to bind predestination to God's foreknowledge of these) ultimately took precedence. In accordance with Augustine's ecclesiology, the role of the church's sacraments in yielding assurance of one's election was emphasized.

The magisterial Reformation, then, meant the retrieval of Augustine's doctrine of grace at the cost of his ecclesiology. What we find in Calvin's theology and later at the Synod of Dordt (1618–19) is hardly anything more than a 'republication' of Augustine's views on the prevenience of God's grace vis-à-vis the corrupted human will. And whereas Calvin teased out these views with great trepidation, the Synod of Dordt opted for the milder infralapsarian position (though without condemning supralapsarianism).[9] Still, it was in particular in the Reformed tradition that notions of divine predestination and election became intensified as compared to other Christian denominations.[10]

Late-modern revisions of the doctrine of predestination often try to overcome its inherent dualism and individualism by considering humanity as a whole to be the object of God's eternal decree. Thus, predestination is identified with election, and reprobation is either denied or seen as a temporary stage in God's dealings with the man Jesus Christ – the One who was rejected in our place in order to become chosen by God (Karl Barth). The suggested universalism, however, amounted to a break with the tradition and therefore was not universally shared. From a contemporary perspective it is easy to dismiss this predestinarian tradition as primitive, unsensitive or even ruthlessly dehumanizing. Indeed, predestination has become a 'contentious doctrine', evoking fear and anxiety among many who became obsessed with it. Moreover, it deeply divided Christian communities on both sides of the Atlantic.[11] We should not forget, however, that, as Sonderegger notes,

> it would be a misreading of the tradition to call it unscriptural or, indeed, pitiless. All major systematicians of this doctrine appeal constantly and consistently to scripture, especially to 'golden texts' in Romans, Ephesians, and the Gospel of John. Heightened in their piety was the sense of divine holiness and creaturely need and fault, themselves both deep and biblical themes. These themes are muted in our day – at least in the academic, systematic theology of our day – yet cannot fall wholly

---

[9] On Calvin, see his *Institutes* III 21.1: 'if anyone with carefree assurance breaks into this place [viz. of God's eternal decree], he will not succeed in satisfying his curiosity and he will enter in a labyrinth from which he can find no exit.' As to the Canons of Dordt, see Gijsbert van den Brink, *Dordt in Context: Gereformeerde Accenten in Katholieke Theologie* (Heerenveen: Jongbloed, 2018), esp. 87–95. The critical part of Dordt's decisions was that, for the first time in history, a particular take on predestination was made mandatory and imposed on the entire (Dutch Reformed) church.

[10] See Gijsbert van den Brink and Johan Smits, 'The Reformed Stance: Distinctive Commitments and Concerns', *Journal of Reformed Theology* 4 (2015), 325–47 (341, 346).

[11] For the US, see Peter J. Thuesen, *Predestination: The American Career of a Contentious Doctrine* (Oxford: Oxford University Press, 2009); for the European scene, see C. Graafland, *Van Calvijn tot Barth* (Zoetermeer: Boekencentrum, 1987).

silent, as the uniqueness and majesty of God are the unshakeable reality confronting every creature.[12]

Election and climate change: The problems

On the issue of human-induced climate change, it is not hard to see that the doctrines of election and predestination can be criticized from this perspective as well, since arguably they have detrimental effects on our approach to the environment in general and climate issues in particular.

First, the traditional conceptions of predestination and election are thoroughly anthropocentric: it is the salvation of human beings alone which is deemed all-important. Indeed, up to this very day the salvation of humans from the world (rather than with the world) is central to the spirituality of many Christian believers. Even worse: it is only human *souls* that matter in this tradition (the soul being the immaterial, non-earthly part of human existence). Due to (neo-)platonic influences, human bodies, which link us to the earthly and material world of nature, were often judged corruptible and therefore less worthwhile, if not entirely devoid of value. Thus, the entire scheme of God's dealings with the world could be reduced to the single issue of 'how does my soul end up in heaven'? Of course it can be countered that this is a caricature of what can be found in the works of all great Western theologians. True as that may be, it will not let us off the hook since this is the way in which official doctrines of election have been perceived and have affected the spirituality of countless believers.

Second, the doctrine of election is typically also thoroughly individualistic. Surely, more communal notions of election are available in the Christian tradition. For example, the Heidelberg Catechism (1563) has only one reference to election, namely in its section on the church. When it is asked 'What do you believe concerning "the holy catholic church"?', it is answered: 'I believe that the Son of God ... gathers, protects, and preserves for himself a *community chosen for eternal life* ... And of this community I am and always will be a living member.'[13] The community precedes the individual here, and individual life is embedded and can only flourish within the community. Many earlier and later formulations of the doctrine of election, however, focus on the individual, dividing the world's population into 'a definite number of particular people' who are saved and 'others' who are passed by.[14] Combined with the fact that earthly existence often paled into insignificance as compared to heavenly life, it is not hard

---

[12] Sonderegger, 'Election', 112.

[13] Heidelberg Catechism, the Lord's Day 21, https://www.rca.org/resources/heidelbergcatechism (accessed 9 July 2019), italics added.

[14] Canons of Dordt, I 7; I 6, 15, https://www.crcna.org/sites/default/files/CanonsofDordt.pdf (accessed 9 July 2019).

to see how such individualism fostered an 'avertive' as opposed to a 'world-formative' spirituality.[15] In such an atmosphere, anthropogenic climate change will not be seen as a serious challenge but will rather be met with indifference.

Third, the strongly theocentric focus of the doctrine of election – it is God who determines it all and nobody can question God's doings – can easily become a model for human conduct. If humans are created in the image of God, should they not relate like this God to those who are at *their* mercy, and expect from them the same sort of submission that we owe to God? John de Gruchy captures the concerns of many contemporary theologians in this regard when he asks:

> If God is defined primarily in terms of dominant will and power ..., does it not inevitably mean that human beings are understood in precisely the same way, so that they see their worldly vocation as one of domination and even manipulation, or conversely as dominated servitude and submission? ... Does not such a God inevitably sanction similar social arrangements, legitimating unjust class structures, the domination of woman by men, and even tyranny?[16]

To such 'similar arrangements' we can add the exploitation of nature and the indifference towards human-induced climate change and its dire consequences. Indeed, Sallie McFague has influentially applied this concern about the image of God as the sovereign monarch to ecological issues. She argues that since the metaphor of God as sovereign king suggests an external relationship between God and the world, according to which God is spatially removed from the world instead of being intimately and caringly present to it, this metaphor is destructive of the environment.[17]

Fourth, as we saw the doctrine of election emerged first and foremost to safeguard the unconditional and undeserved character of the *grace* of God.[18] According to some, however, this notion of grace as not requiring anything in exchange has detrimental consequences, including ecological ones. Drawing on the seminal work of Marcel Mauss, John Milbank argues that premodern society was constituted by a system of gift exchange which preceded the later split between subject and object.[19] Gifts were

---

[15] See for these terms Nicholas P. Wolterstorff, *Until Justice and Peace Embrace* (Grand Rapids: Eerdmans, 1983), 5.

[16] John W. de Gruchy, *Liberating Reformed Theology: A South-African Contribution to an Ecumenical Debate* (Grand Rapids: Eerdmans, 1991), 111–12.

[17] Sallie McFague, *Models of God: Theology for an Ecological, Nuclear Age* (Philadelphia: Fortress, 1987), 63–9. In her later work, McFague focused more emphatically on climate change, which she sees as symptomatic of a deeper crisis: human alienation from the world.

[18] In what follows we are indebted to Terra S. Rowe, 'Grace and Climate Change: The Free Gift in Capitalism and Protestantism', in *Eco-Reformation: Grace and Hope for a Planet in Peril*, Lisa E. Dahill and James B. Martin-Schramm (eds) (Eugene: Cascade Books, 2016), 253–71. See more broadly Rowe's *Toward a Better Worldliness: Ecology, Economy, and the Protestant Tradition* (Minneapolis: Fortress, 2017).

[19] John Milbank, *Being Reconciled: Ontology and Pardon* (New York: Routledge, 2003); John Milbank, 'Can a Gift Be Given? Prolegomena to a Future Trinitarian Metaphysic', *Modern Theology* 11 (1995), 119–61. See Marcel Mauss, *The Gift: The Form and Reason for Exchange in Archaic Societies* (New York:

not just objects that could be exchanged for something else ('tit for tat') but extensions of the givers, who made themselves dependent on the recipient by their gift-giving. Thus, gifts participated in the personhood of the giver, and gift exchange was not about economics but about building intricate relational networks and living in communion. Theologically speaking, this communion included both God and creation. It was only when nominalism came to posit a strong divide between God and creation that the Reformation's notion of unilaterally bestowed grace could emerge. Gifts now became mere commodities, and grace came to be seen as an external gift, bestowed by an active Giver who does not expect anything in return from the recipient – as a result of which the recipient may remain passive. Milbank especially targets Protestant doctrines of grace in this connection, since these depict God's forgiveness as freely given, without a need to make reparation on the part of the human sinner.

Whereas Milbank's worries in this connection are mainly social, economic and ecclesial, others have started to see important ecological issues lurking here as well. It seems clear that the emerging ideal of human autonomy encouraged a conception of nature as passive and inert. Environmental ethicist Michael Northcott, for example, sees a connection between the nominalist divide between God and creation and the church's renouncement of its traditional prohibition of mining; now that the relationship between humans and the earth came to be conceptualized as an external one, mining (which functions as the material base of capitalist economies) was no longer experienced as a violation of the earth.[20] Thus, it seems that the very notion of grace which functioned as the primary motive and rationale behind Western notions of election is complicit in the objectification of nature that lies at the root of our contemporary ecological problems – including anthropogenic climate change.

All in all, it seems we have ample reason to discard theological notions of election and predestination because they aggravate the ecological crisis and fuel negligence with regard to as urgent a global problem as current climate change. Or could we distinguish aspects and interpretations that may be a help rather than a hindrance when it comes to addressing contemporary climate concerns?

Election and climate change: Some prospects

Although it would be an oversimplification to suggest that anthropogenic climate change might be resolved by correcting our theologies, climate change is not just a scientific problem either, since deeply ingrained cultural and social ways of thinking,

---

W.W. Norton, 1990; original French ed. 1925). Mauss's view was not a romantic one: he realized that premodern gift exchange practices were not free from self-interest; yet, a fostering of the other's well-being was involved as well.

[20] Michael S. Northcott, *A Political Theology of Climate Change* (Grand Rapids: Eerdmans, 2013), 55.

perceiving and behaving are involved.[21] There is no doubt that religious intuitions and perspectives play an important part here. It is the task of theology to analyse such intuitions and perspectives and if need be to 'reform or reinvent itself ... in the face of the unprecedented and unique nature of climate change'.[22] To what extent could and should doctrines of predestination and election be 'reformed or reinvented' in this connection? A couple of things might be put forward in addition to what we have seen in the previous section.

First, in response to Milbank's point summarized above, it is by no means clear that the notion of free grace involved in Protestant doctrines of election is indeed unilateral in the sense of being exclusive of exchange. For example, according to some (Finnish) interpretations of Luther's theology, there is a profound sense of interconnectedness in Luther's theology of grace. Grace is not just God's forgiveness declared to us from an external point of view (*extra nos*) but it includes union with Christ. In fact, *Christ himself* is the gift given to the sinner, not just some 'thing'. This suggests a participatory ontology that looks very much like Milbank's.[23] Reformed theology has often been more wary of concepts of human participation in the divine reality since the qualitative difference between Creator and creation was taken most seriously here. That is not to say, however, that the bestowal of divine grace was considered to remain without any response. In fact, on the contrary, the Heidelberg Catechism devotes most of its space to a lengthy elaboration of the notion of gratitude as the believer's spontaneous response to God's free gift of justification, spelling out in detail what sort of concrete attitudes are fit in return to (though not as a payment for!) God's gracious acquittal of sin and guilt. It is precisely the cruder ways of *quid-pro-quo* thinking, pervasive in the later Middle Ages, that are overcome here. Moreover, as we have seen, the Protestant doctrines of grace and election were not so much creative innovations as they were retrievals of Augustine's theology of grace. The rise of nominalism apparently did not form an unbridgeable gap here. Accordingly, experiencing and acknowledging God's free grace today might very well elicit in us the due response of, among other things, respecting the integrity of creation.

Second, the notion of divine sovereignty which is behind the Christian doctrines of election and predestination has never been intended to take human responsibility lightly; it rather served to ground and undergird such responsibility. If indeed we are to submit to God's sovereign will, this means that all our activities should be directed to what we can know about God's purposes.[24] To be sure, until recently these purposes have rarely been extended to the climate or even the well-being of non-human life forms;

---

[21] On the cultural dimensions of climate discourse see Mike Hulme, 'The Conquering of Climate: Discourses of Fear and Their Dissolution', *The Geographical Journal* 174 (2008), 5–16.

[22] Forrest Clingerman, 'Theologies of the Climate', *Religious Studies Review* 42:2 (2016), 71–6 (74).

[23] See Rowe, 'Grace and Climate Change', 264–7; and Carl Braaten and Robert Jenson (eds), *Union with Christ: The New Finnish Interpretation of Luther* (Grand Rapids: Eerdmans, 1998).

[24] See de Gruchy, *Liberating Reformed Theology*, 114–15.

the so-called cultural mandate was rather read as a carte blanche to exploit the earth.[25] Yet, if we are guided by the same orientation on God's will today, the global climate comes to mind quite naturally as a domain of special concern. Indeed, though there is still a long way to go (especially in terms of overcoming disinformation and sloth – that most underestimated of all sins), the awareness that the created world is God's – not ours – and therefore should be taken care of in responsible ways, seems to be gradually growing among Christians.[26] It has even been argued that *without a Creator* the earth becomes a warehouse from which everyone can take what one wants without restraint.[27] Addressing climate change from a theological perspective does not necessarily require a stronger emphasis on divine immanence at the expense of divine transcendence, as many hold.[28] Rather, what we need is a 'theocentric pragmatism' which starts from what is already going on in Christian communities (instead of pursuing revolutionary worldview changes), places God at the centre and makes us rethink our moral obligations towards the earth and future generations from God's point of view.[29]

Third, it should be kept in mind that divine election and predestination should never become isolated from the overall Christian doctrine of God, which is thoroughly Trinitarian in nature.[30] Where notions of God's sovereign and all-determining power are cut loose from the concrete revelation of God's love in Jesus Christ which is made known through the Holy Spirit, they should be criticized and rejected as sub-Christian. In the ordering of dogmatic themes, the doctrine of divine election might therefore best be situated at the end of our reflections on God's works in creation and redemption, not at the beginning, since otherwise it tends to obscure the significance of God's concrete salvific acts.[31] The electing God is the Redeemer who has encountered us in Jesus Christ, the suffering Servant, and who enlivens us through his Spirit. To quote De Gruchy one more time: 'Without the trinitarian and Christological qualifications which affirm that God's power is the power of grace and justice determined by his suffering love and overwhelming goodness in history and experience, the monarchical concept

---

[25] Ibid., 115.

[26] For example, in the Netherlands Christian political parties have gradually been 'greening' over the past decades.

[27] See Norman Wirzba, *From Nature to Creation: A Christian Vision for Understanding and Loving our World* (Grand Rapids: Baker Academic, 2013). It should be added, though, that when the earth is regarded as the Creator's gift it can just as well be treated as a warehouse.

[28] Here we concur with Hilda P. Koster, 'Questioning Eco-Theological Panentheisms: The Promise of Kathryn Tanner's Theology of God's Radical Transcendence for Ecological Theology', *Scriptura* 111 (2012), 385–94.

[29] See Willis Jenkins, *The Future of Ethics: Sustainability, Social Justice, and Religious Creativity* (Washington DC: Georgetown University Press, 2013), 68; also Jacques Schenderling, 'De Ecologische Paradox', *Radix* 43 (2017), 150–61 (159).

[30] See Cornelis van der Kooi and Gijsbert van den Brink, *Christian Dogmatics: An Introduction* (Grand Rapids: Eerdmans, 2017), 75–112, 113.

[31] Ibid., 701–8.

of God as all-powerful is an idol.'³² Conversely, if it is *this* God of grace and justice by whom we have been elected, the doctrine of election is a great comfort in the struggle against all kinds of injustice that we encounter. According to Reformation historian Heiko Oberman, the original setting in which notions like election and predestination came to flourish was that of persecuted Calvinist refugees. They found consolation in the knowledge that because of election they could never fall out of God's hands in the midst of all hardships and injustices they had to endure.³³ Here, it seems, we have an interpretation of the doctrine of election that is still relevant in times of such drastic climate change that we might easily become desperate.

This leads us to a final consideration. Recent reinterpretations of divine election try to overcome the individualism and dualism which were bound up with the traditional accounts, and they do so by retrieving some fundamentally biblical dimensions of God's work of election that have often been overlooked. In particular, biblical scholarship has brought about a twofold correction of traditional notions of election. First, both in the Old and New Testament election is much more a collective category than an individualistic one. In the Old Testament the people of Israel is the primary object of God's electing love whereas in the New Testament the Christian church is included into the people of God. And second, quite often God's election has a holistic purpose, namely to bring blessing to a world that is alienated from God as a result of sin. In other words, the election of both Israel and the church is in a profound way 'for service'. God chose the people of Abraham, culminating in the Messiah as its representative, to bring about the healing of a world fallen in sin.³⁴ Likewise, the elect community of the church exists for the sake of the other, in order to pass on God's blessing in Christ and bring his salvation and justice to the ends of the world. Teasing out the theological consequences of this biblical retrieval, Suzanne McDonald argues that '[e]lection can never simply be reduced to a vision of, or way of accounting for, personal salvation, but has in view the entire sweep of God's purposes for the whole created order.'³⁵

It is not far-fetched to apply this insight to the issue of human-induced climate change, as one of the most egregious contemporary expressions of human sin.³⁶ This is all the

---

[32] De Gruchy, *Liberating Reformed Theology*, 118; as his title indicates, De Gruchy develops his position especially in dialogue with Reformed theology (in particular John Calvin), but this clearly has a wider significance for Christian theology as a whole.

[33] See Heiko A. Oberman, *John Calvin and the Reformation of the Refugees* (Geneva: Droz, 2009), 46–9; only later, '[a]s the *réfugiés* became residents and citizens of new Reformed territories, the ... rock of faith [viz. the doctrine of predestination] changed into a stumbling stone' (48).

[34] See N. T. Wright, *The Climax of the Covenant: Christ and the Law in Pauline Theology* (Edinburgh: T&T Clark, 1991), 36.

[35] Suzanne McDonald, *Re-Imaging Election: Divine Election as Representing God to Others and Others to God* (Grand Rapids: Eerdmans, 2010), 130. Although McDonald develops this notion of 'election to representation' mainly in relation to humans, she realizes that it can also be applied to the created order, especially in light of the priestly role consigned to humans in the Genesis creation narratives.

[36] For a penetrating attempt to reinvigorate the doctrine of sin for our times of climate change, see Ernst M. Conradie, *Redeeming Sin? Social Diagnostics amid Ecological Destruction* (Lanham: Lexington, 2017).

more so when we realize that climate change first and foremost affects the weakest and most vulnerable people. As Michael Northcott argues, 'climate pollution, deforestation, groundwater depletion, local air and water pollution, soil erosion ... are all forms of environmental damage that directly impact the livelihoods and health *of the poor*.'[37] In this connection, we should remind ourselves that in the Bible God's work of election, far from being arbitrary, is often guided by God's partiality for the poor. According to Paul, God chose what is weak in the world to shame the strong; he elected what is low and despised in order to reduce to nothing what is viewed as something (1 Cor. 1.28). And James is even more straightforward when he chastises those who dishonour the poor, asking rhetorically: 'Didn't God elect the poor in this world to be rich in faith and heirs of the kingdom that He has promised to those who love him?' (James 2.5).

Conclusion

It follows from the above investigation that notions of election – firmly embedded as they are within Western Christianity – interact with attitudes towards global, human-induced climate change. First, we examined aspects and interpretations of election which hinder climate concerns. These have to do with individualistic and dualistic notions of human 'souls' being saved from the earth, notions which render the earth unworthy of deliberate preservation. Further, we might have genuine concerns about what kind of 'model' a monarchical God would present to humans, who might easily be tempted to regard themselves as sovereign over creation. As to notions of divine grace and forgiveness, there are problems as well: if these imply passive recipients of a divinely bestowed 'commodity' instead of partakers who somehow become active and involved in return, this may have detrimental ecological consequences.

However, we see no reasonable grounds to dismiss or totally redefine notions of divine election, since they also harbour 'creation friendly' perspectives that may open up fruitful avenues for contemporary climate ethics. For example, even Protestant doctrines of election do not necessarily conceive of grace as free from 'exchange'. An attitude of gratitude – as promulgated in the Heidelberg Catechism – is potentially very powerful in strengthening our ties with creaturely reality. Moreover, if we consider election as a function of God's steadfast love for us in Christ through the Spirit, we may gradually learn to adopt this attitude in our dealings with the created world and discover our environmental responsibilities in light of God's purposes. Finally, if God elects what is weak, vulnerable and lost (as the New Testament has it), we may be moved to look after the many contemporary victims of climate change and environmental degradation.

---

[37] Michael S. Northcott, 'Climate Change and Christian Ethics', in *The Wiley Blackwell Companion to Religion and Ecology*, John Hart (ed.) (Chichester: Wiley Blackwell, 2017), 286–300 (294; italics added).

Chapter 4.10
The story of God's work: An open-ended narrative

Ernst M. Conradie[1]

This main section of the volume is structured in terms of classic themes related to God's economy – that is, the narrative of God's work in the world. As is evident, this story can be told in rather different ways. It can also be messed up in many different ways. One crucial aspect of this story is that it is open-ended; we are telling the story as we are participating in it, with a sense of what has happened in the past, in order to make sense of the present in anticipation of what the future may hold.

In the context of climate change it would amount to a failure of nerve not to address the underlying question that those listening to the story will have: What is God doing? What is God up to, given what we know already about climate change? Where can signs of God's presence and creative engagement with the world be found (*vestigia Dei*)? This has always been an extremely dangerous question, as is well recognized by the South African theologian Jaap Durand in an essay on 'the finger of God' in history, with reference to apartheid theology.[2] Typically, narrow group interests are expressed in answering this question, thus serving as a theological legitimation of such interests. One may retort that there is only one thing that is more dangerous than raising this question and that is failing to raise it at all.

In the context of climate change, in particular, this is a question filled with anxiety: this message of salvation is confronted by a world clearly in need of salvation. Can we even speak about God's actions in the world? How is that to be discerned? Moreover, can this story change this world?

Storytellers need to hold listeners in suspense, but of course they do not really know the answer either. Yet, if they literally have no clue, they can hardly keep telling the story and should not be surprised if no one is listening any longer. They need not be surprised, then, that there are many others telling a different story without reference to the Triune

---

[1] Ernst M. Conradie is Senior Professor in the Department of Religion and Theology at the University of the Western Cape in South Africa, the leading historically black university in the country. He is situated in the Reformed tradition, teaches systematic theology and ethics and specializes in Christian ecotheology.
[2] See Jaap Durand, 'God in History: An Unresolved problem', in *The Meaning of History*, Adrio König and Marie Henri Keane (eds) (Pretoria: Unisa, 1980), 171–8.

God, if not without a whole array of new divinities, demons and monsters. Novelists, film-makers, poets and cartoonists seem perfectly capable of taking over the role of telling the story of where things are going and they do so in rather graphic apocalyptic imagery – the kind that the Hebrew prophets of old were not shy of adopting either.

Let us be bold, then, by making a few assumptions of where the world will be by a biblical seventy years from now by extending a few current trends, not allowing for dramatic (divine?) interventions (volcanic eruptions or asteroids). This could be deemed 'realistic'.

> It is very unlikely that sufficient political will can be mustered timeously to make drastic cuts in carbon emissions, despite the Paris Agreement, activist campaigns, many good intentions and ample scientific reports. The carbon budget for the rest of the century (arguably one trillion tons of CO_2) will therefore be spent long before the end of the century, if not already by 2050. The ideal of keeping global warming below 1.5 or even 2 degrees Celsius above pre-industrial levels will therefore have to be abandoned. If so, we are on course for a 4 degree world at best, while a 5 or 6 degree rise before the end of the century is also possible. Due to the lag effect of carbon cycles no one really knows where this will end up.

> Within this changing climate some trends may become irreversible: hundreds of millions humans could die from hunger and thirst due to crop failure and rivers no longer flowing; massive migrations of people may no longer be controlled; many low-lying areas would have to be evacuated due to hurricanes, flash floods and rising sea levels; stock exchanges may well collapse due to the sensitivity of markets to so many disasters; large parts of the Amazons could burn down; mass extinctions of species are already evident; the myth of endless economic growth would need to be abandoned; the planet's human populations may reach a peak around 2050 but could drop significantly after that – causing havoc to health services, pastoral care (all the funerals!), education, scientific research and property prices; organised crime will be rampant as people start looking after themselves; long-distance travel will become increasingly dangerous; mega-sport events will become few and far between. There may remain pockets of affluence but this will require militarised protection and the continued source of such wealth dubious; communication will still be possible but maintaining high-tech infrastructure across vast distances will be tricky.

Such a scenario requires theological interpretation. Again: Where can signs of God's work be found? What is God actually doing? How is divine action in the world to be understood?[3] How should the story of what God is doing now be told? Is the absence of evidence not evidence of absence? Should one follow Dante's *Divine Comedy* and abandon hope? For Christians this is only an option if we begin to believe that God has

---

[3] See, especially, Robert John Russell, Nancey Murphy and William R. Stoeger, *Scientific Perspectives on Divine Action: Twenty Years of Challenge and Progress* (Berkeley: Center for Theology and the Natural Sciences/Vatican City: Vatican Observatory Publications, 2008).

indeed abandoned us (and the covenant with Noah), is making other ominous long-term plans, or if we concur that the divine parent has actually passed away, perhaps for our sake, that our Father is dead – that is, 'in heaven' only. Or should one, instead of looking for a radically transcendent purposeful God, hope for an emergent yet all-powerful 'Thermostat' (Gaia) to self-regulate global temperatures? Even if 'God' is nothing more than a human construct, an idea (whether good or bad or ugly), a vision for the future, a way of talking about human agendas, then this question still has to be addressed.

The prophetic urge is not to predict the end times, but to speak truth to power in present, penultimate times, to recover the liberating, redeeming message of truth, reconciliation, justice and peace. Note that the question what God is doing now cannot be postponed as if this is only about the future, not also about the recent past, and most significantly the elusive present. Only in hindsight may we realize that the real catastrophe is not in what lies ahead, but in the failures of the present. Eschatology is not (only) about the future, but about the content and significance of hope – facing up to the present.

Instead of offering any affirmative answers, here are a few contrasting possibilities for provocation and discussion:

- God is waiting upon humans to change their hearts, habits and minds through mass-religious awakenings. Like in the days of Noah and after the Babylonian exile, there will be a severe crisis, but God promises to save a small remnant through a miracle that will revert global warming – for example, a series of volcanic eruptions, changes in the ocean currents, cooling off Europe, perhaps introducing a new ice age. Thus God will create a new humanity, one that has acquired a revised set of virtues.
- No mass conversion and no such miracle are to be expected. Instead, God is punishing the world's human population for their folly through a deadly plague that will wipe out most of the population. This allows God to start again with a small remnant in the twenty-second century. It may be expected that this will follow the pattern of the oasis of Eden and the expulsion into the desert, the destruction and rebuilding of Jerusalem, the exile and the return from exile. More pertinently, it will follow the dialectic of cross and resurrection, where all the followers of Jesus of Nazareth abandoned him but learned to follow the Way of the cross, inspired by the Spirit at Pentecost.
- God is asking us to do our best to help address climate change through mitigation and adaption efforts and especially to show solidarity with those struggling to cope with the adverse effects of climate change. We should not seek any higher purpose but live our lives before God in God's world as long as that may last – *etsi Deus non daretur*.
- This is way too timid. As secular commentators agree, only mass social movements can save us now from self-destruction. The current global economic system, based on profiteering through mass production and mass consumption, is

self-destructive. Only religion can provide the countervailing moral vision, moral energy and moral leadership to inspire people to resist industrialized capitalism. Indeed, a green conversion within Christianity is crucial, precisely given its historical impact. This is what the Triune God is calling for.
- God is asking humans to exercise responsible stewardship of God's good creation. We humans have been entrusted a habitable planet and are the heirs of the rich heritage bestowed on us through the Jewish-Christian-Muslim tradition. We are now called to safeguard human civilization (in every of its major forms) and should utilize the technologies available to adjust the earth's thermostat through geoengineering. We need to attend to our God-given duty to rule over the earth. This is God's command, for us, today.
- It is now clear, more than ever before, that God is not really the God of the poor, oppressed and marginalized. It is not the meek who will inherit the earth. God is favouring the brave and the clever and will help them to re-engineer themselves in order to escape from a doomed earth through colonizing other habitable planets.
- God is clearly not really concerned about the world after all. What is ultimately important is the salvation of the soul, becoming one with Absolute Spirit more than discerning the movement of the Spirit, gaining Enlightenment more than understanding the physical properties of light. Gnostic forms of Christianity understood God better than those who focus on what is material, bodily and earthly – that are subject to decay and futility anyway. The Anthropocene confirms that God is abandoning the Earth and invites those truly enlightened to escape from this earthly vale of tears. The first step may be to move from carbon-based to silicon-based intelligence.
- God has decided to abandon the covenant with Noah and will allow the human species to become extinct; but like in the past God will start again to renew God's creation with previously despised species such as rats and cockroaches taking the lead. This is after all just punishment for irresponsible human destruction.

It may be noted that God language is not required to raise these questions or to express these options. They arise no matter how secular one's orientation may be. There is also the postmodern claim that 'history' does not exist, that there is no grand all-encompassing narrative guaranteeing a sense of history in terms of meaning or direction. If so, not only the end of history is to be announced; there never has been any history. But even if there is no history, could there perhaps least be a story, or stories?

For Christian theology the question then remains: Can this story still be held together as one narrative or are there not only different versions of the story, but also different stories and indeed different gods? For Christians the different versions of the story, the different perspectives from which it may be told, even the nineteenth-century death of monotheism, need not be of any concern. They do not believe in God for the sake of believing in any available god. The question is which of these options is in line with the character of the triune God in whom they say they put their trust. This confession will be tested and this is what is at stake in working with others to address climate change.

From the biblical roots of the Christian tradition it seems unlikely that some form of dramatic divine intervention is to be expected that would miraculously avert a climate catastrophe. Despite the vehement cry from the crucified Christ that his Father has abandoned him, the Father did not intervene. This non-intervention made room for the slow power of God's Spirit to transform all things. It is unlikely that this is the message a world in need of salvation from self-destruction would wish to hear. Is this gospel then good news? This depends upon the way the story is told by Christian witnesses. Again, the authenticity of this confession will be tested in decades to come amidst a changing climate. It also prompts questions not merely about God's existence but also about the identity and character of this God. This is the theme of the next section.

The Christian story of God's work – a Brazilian response

Ivone Gebara[1]

Some current theological recollections

In this response I confine myself to some general considerations regarding the difficulties we are facing with climate change and its implications for Christian theology. My perspective in doing so is anthropological and theological, as well as ecofeminist. I adopt a phenomenological approach, aware that the complexity of the problem requires multiple approaches and methods of analysis.

My provocations are simply meant to reinforce the suspicions that many of us have regarding patriarchal and dualistic interpretations of Christian theology, as well as their current consequences in the formation of dualistic minds that reinforce the opposition between human life and the life of the planet.

In addition to the numerous interpretations of myths stemming from a variety of traditions (biblical and otherwise), today it can also be affirmed from science that our most remote origins included violent explosions and ruptures. Scientific rationality attempts a discourse that is somewhat different from myths and theologies. However, like myths, it does not decipher the human enigma in its most hidden secrets. It claims that we are the result of an initial explosion, the so-called Big Bang, which continuously generates other explosions. All of life, human life included, mysteriously stems from and, hence, somehow contains these originating explosive ruptures, which are therefore constitutive. In saying this, I am not only stating the recent contribution of astrophysical science, but also of phenomenological philosophy. Paul Ricoeur observed that there is a 'non coincidence'[2] learned and embedded in us, a disproportion between what we do and what we want, between the finitude of our reality and the infinity of our desire, and between our ambitions and our sharing. We can be lovers of the world and also its destroyers. This paradoxical constitution can be found in humans and, perhaps in a different way, in animals. It situates our origins, as far as we could historically describe

---

[1] Ivone Gebara is a Brazilian ecofeminist philosopher and theologian. She taught several years in the Institute of Theology of Recife and gave alternative theological formation to Christian Communities and Social Movements. She is presently living in São Paulo and lectures upon invitation at various universities and religious centres in Brazil and other countries.

[2] Paul Ricoeur, *Finitude et culpabilité I, l'homme faillible* (Paris: Aubier/Montaigne, 1960).

them, as belligerent. Despite this, we know only a fraction about our origins. We raise hypotheses, but they are very limited in light of what we do not know.

In the fourth century, Augustine wondered about the reasons for so much evil and suffering. He said humanity was marked by a kind of original stain, a crevice or constitutive imperfection, which led him to pose the concept of 'original sin'. In other words, it was as if all the causes of our evils could be found in our origin: the very advent of humanity is supposedly also creating our limit. This idea of 'original sin' has at times been interpreted in vulgar and mythological ways by some theologies and churches. However, in the line of Paul Ricoeur, I believe that the concept of 'original sin' should not only include the evil we do, but the *possibility* of evil that continually inhabits us. Remembering this doctrine centres us in our attempt to understand human limitations vis-à-vis the possibilities of life and the beings that constitute it. Moreover, it exposes us to the mystery of our emergence and the impossibility of detecting the first causes of all that exists in us and the actions we undertake. Do we find in ourselves a unique causality, an absolute reason to act as we are acting? Is 'original sin' the source of the evil we do? How do we understand it today? And where would be the cause of the good that we do? Would all good come from God? And if this is true, why are we experiencing destruction, cruelty and the disappearance of so many living species? Why do misery and hunger still plague us daily? Why do some have the right to take away the rights of others? Why do only a few take ownership of land, water and many other natural resources?

Rereading the tradition of sin

I believe that the Christian theological tradition marked by Platonic dualism has kept a radical opposition between the so-called principles of good and evil. Christianity has traditionally affirmed the victory of good over evil. It declared that all enemies of humankind will be overcome, even death. As such, if we want to continue with this vocabulary, we would say that 'original sin' is an expression of the fragility that constitutes us and the symbolic origin of the evil we do. It is one of the expressions of that mysterious evil that lives in us. In the same way, divine grace – an expression coined to affirm something that transcends us – would be both the primal source and possibility of the good we do and the good we are capable of. This is also a symbolic way to express that in the good we do there is something that escapes and transcends us.

We thus affirm that a binary force of multiple expressions and gradations lives and persists in us that feeds on its own opposition. It lives and feeds the fight between one side and the other to survive in a 'non-harmonious' way. And this has been verified in human history from its earliest days. From this point of view I can say that the origins of good and evil are the same in human beings throughout history and across cultures. There is no positive principle separate from a negative principle. The affirmation of the positive needs the negative. The good deeds we do probably have something to do with the bad things that have made us victims or the injustices and shortcomings we feel. The presence of light occurs in the negative along with the positive. Light is captured from obscurity and obscurity is recognized through light. In this sense the notion of God in an ethical and anthropological perspective must encompass good and evil, not as separate entities but as our constitutive reality.

This statement may seem to contradict what the Christian tradition has affirmed in relation to the infinite goodness of God, as it opens gaps for the modification of traditionally consecrated concepts and dogmas. I dare say that the Christian tradition separated both God and Jesus from evil. It created a world of perfections and goodness separate from the materiality of our world, and although we may understand the historical context of its emergence, today such a claim is problematic for us. Here lies a knot that would need to be untied. Traditionally it is affirmed that Jesus is equal to us except in sin. As the Son of God, sent by the Father, He fully took on our humanity minus the sin. But what kind of humanity is sinless? How do you sustain a humanity that would historically leave sin or evil in parentheses? And what kind of God would that be? How might we understand it from our current context?

It is precisely our experience of *effective* evil – that is, our experience of evil as pain, violence, robbery, destruction, injustice, lies or murder – that leads us to seek the elimination of forms of evil. I dare say that it is historical wickedness that makes the need for good and justice so urgent and great. Herein lies the principle of goodness and salvation that we seek. We not only commit evil and suffer its effects, but we are also continually exposed to it from our own ontological constitution. And when we are exposed or immersed in evil, we want to leave it, we want to establish the good in order to live. Our action is limited to our plural and current history.

What we call sin is a religious account of the consequences of this fallible ontological constitution. In other words, sin is not a fault, but implies the recognition of my responsibility that is not lived, not affirmed, not recognized. Sin, then, is consent to actions that are harmful to others in favour of myself and my equals. And finally, it implies a kind of recognition that one broke a collective pact of survival sealed from common convictions and values corroborated by something called the divine will or command. The latter could be translated as a covenant or a collective alliance between people who seek the common good. The destruction of peoples, forests, rivers and different groups that has been promoted in our day reveals the excesses, the imbalance in the forces of humanity and the breaking of our covenant of common life. It reveals that the opposing forces that live within us tend more towards the side of collective destruction than to construction and towards greed rather than sharing. It reveals that some become improperly owners of the assets of all.

In this line of thinking, one can affirm the mythological account that the gods are born of evil experiences and human fears in their various forms. They are born because injustice and violence on 'large plantations' of land become unbearable. And so we need to seek something beyond ourselves to get us out of the flood we are in. We appeal to the good, to saviours, to heavenly or earthly forces that we believe capable of helping us. We deify the good in order to make it a greater force upon us. We worship it so that he will not abandon us but will be generous in favours. To the extent that we surrender at least part of our lives to healing both the evils that afflict us and the evils that we have committed, we develop a belief in the dualistic distinction between good and evil. We construct metaphysical entities representing either supreme Good or supreme Evil. Yet it seems that God and the Devil go together. They talk and fight with each other and divide the world as we see in the book of Job. And in the Gospels, Jesus is led by the Devil at the beginning of his mission to the pinnacle of the Temple to be tempted. Jesus then insists that he defeated him.

We tend to create divine beings only as good, such as the Christian God and his only son Jesus. Roman Catholics also integrated the mother of Jesus, Mary, into the role of persons exempt from all sin. They proclaim her as the Mother of God, Virgin, without original sin and given over to the heavens in both body and soul. These dogmatic and mythical acrobatics no longer solve the challenges of our times, nor do they give reason for a hope of change. Our world blends order with disorder, evil with good, justice with injustice in a complex historical fabric that requires us to overcome the old dualisms and polarizations.

Today, we continue to reproduce the Manichaeism that was once criticized by the Christian theological tradition. And we create it in human relationships between different groups, each accusing the other of promoting good or evil. We need to go further and learn what is happening in our common history and in our everyday relationships through the lens of more ecological – that is, interdependent, references. A social ecology is needed to address the threats of destruction that certain human predators have been carrying out merely for their own benefit.

In the perspective that I am developing, good would not be possible if evil were not possible and real at the same time. The reality of evil in its manifold expressions of pain, lack of goods, destruction of nature, and cruelty seems to dwell more in our bodies and minds than the benefits of the good we receive and do to one another. As such, I affirm the 'real' as the *mixture* of all – the mixture of substances, of beings, of humans, of passions, of emotions and actions. Isolating good from evil is an artifice of our emotions, as if we were looking for perfect antidotes that could eliminate what we call the 'evil of the world' or the 'sin of the world'. Here, too, there is only a distinction between evil and sin, between the possibility and reality of evil, between good and evil, between personal responsibility and involuntary adhesion. After all, who defines the social good? And who accuses others of violence?

These statements that are often taught as clear and clean-cut are in reality obscure concepts when we examine them in light of the actual dramas affecting humanity as a whole. We are capable of creating prejudices, enemies and inventing colours that please or displease us. We are capable of creating divisions between ethnicities, determining superior and inferior beings and sexes. We are able to steal foreign lands, expel its inhabitants and generate conflicts and deadly massacres. Once again we open ourselves to the domain of unlimited passions and emotional reasoning whose foundation is merely *doxa*, the opinion of powerful groups and people about other people and situations. We enter the closed circle of the ego that is both violent and destructive where we find both reason and lack of reason. The selfish ego is capable of setting traps and capturing us in them.

Given all this, I believe there is a need to develop a Christian tradition around this issue that does not merely repeat what we have already been taught. We are in a new moment where we must construct meaning in the face of new perceptions of the world. Resuming the Christian ethical tradition also means updating it in light of insights from ecology and feminism. When we speak of climatic disasters and the harmful consequences resulting from human intervention, we are not only faced with problems of an immediate moral order, but with the conflict between old and new understandings of human beings in relation to themselves. Today, through the media we have greater access to an awareness of the pluralism that constitutes humanity as well as the disproportionate gap between our potentialities and achievements. We are facing a new set of powers from which some impose on others their 'admirable technological world', while others are only in search of bread to eat and a land on which to live. This social and political disproportion is our history. To recount history is to affirm the diversity of stages in the experience and understanding of humanity itself. It does not mean that some who repeat the past are wrong, and that those who voraciously flip to the novelties of the present are right. Moral concepts of right or wrong almost always announce a misjudgement. But who are the judges, and on what criteria do they judge one another? There is no need to fear the fact that we inadvertently end up judging each other's deeds. We are always judging each other based on the values we embrace or the interests we have. Even if we do not want to judge, by not judging we are still at some level passing judgement. As Kant put it in the *Fundamentals of the Metaphysics of Manners* (and as I remember in my own words), what I esteem in the other is the idea I hold of them and not the person themselves. And according to the idea of humankind that some groups have, the elimination of the majority – those who disrupt their own Pharaoh like projects – is part of the realization of their very own humanity. Perhaps, we could somehow broaden what we call judgement to include the words dialogue and understanding?

To dialogue with the diversity of our world is to understand this diversity without necessarily imposing on it a single model that we deem the most advanced and the best. We have to continually ask ourselves: better for whom?

To understand is to both know what is happening in the current history and to capture the complexity of the actions of multiple sides. What would be the criteria for judgement? Just look at the consequences in the current world. Thousands of people without a home! Thousands of people killed on the seas in an attempt to escape misery! Thousands of forests devastated to ensure private agro business! Thousands of fish and marine animals killed by the pollution of the seas! We increase hunger in the world! We have closed access to drinking water for thousands of people! There is no way to not judge or want to cease the actions of those who impose 'heavy taxes on mustard seeds' and then boast of their stolen riches believing that their prosperity is a sign of God's blessing.

The quest for radical causality

In the light of my brief reflection, I believe that it can be said that the quest for primary causality is always limited. In other words, causality is always found underneath the destructive consequences we experience today, especially in the lives of the majority impoverished population. There is a non-correspondence, an unmeasured relationship between causes and consequences. Even when we refer to the act that we would like to have not committed individually or collectively, causality appears surrounded by a thousand other reasons that do not allow us to clearly detect its origin. Causes reflect reasoning from past moments, those where we might have thought we were doing good. This does not excuse the atrocities, but serves only to affirm once again the 'mixture' that constitutes who we are, the fragility of the moment, the fear of the moment, the orders of the moment, the criminal disproportion of our desires. We are not fully lucid even though we speak as though we are. Our lucidity is the image of the shadows and lights that inhabit us.

The fallibility that constitutes who we are reveals the limits of all of our choices and denounces the excesses of certainty in affirming the causes of our evils. We seek a horizon of certainty perhaps to affirm new power and to point out that which we believe is to blame for our evil deeds. Once again we enter into the courts of judgement without realizing the contradictions that abide in us.

However, when it comes to coexistence, pointing out causes that are visible to the naked eye does not obliterate the invisible ones or our ontological constitution. Pointing out causes in relation to climate change issues also involves pointing out the limits of human actions, the limit of choices the limit of what is thought to be good and our common responsibility. Nefarious consequences are not always included in our good intentions and in our scientific discoveries. It is impossible to predict down to the smallest detail where the choices of technological development will take us in relation to an Earth that does not conform to the lifestyles of its inhabitants. Once again, affirming the limits of causality does not mean denying the obvious effects of certain initiatives, but rather shouting against the exclusionary policies and insanity of wars.

I would like to draw our attention to the complexity of our reflections and actions. Darkness surrounds us[3] and a lack of knowing envelops us. We must welcome them both as a space of freedom. The ethical view we assume to judge the world is itself limited to our tradition, our image and our likeness. Perhaps we still hide within us the same

---

[3] Catherine Keller, *Cloud of the Impossible: Negative Theology and Planetary Entanglement* (New York: Columbia University Press, 2015).

dualist structure of good and evil that characterizes so many religious traditions and especially Christianity. Trying to get out of it means affirming that we can do something different to collectively live a more worthy life.

A brief conclusion

Once again we see the need for dialogue and understanding others. We see the need for politicians to come down from their ivory towers, for intellectuals to let go of their fixed ideas about the world and for the religious to let go of their customary liturgies. We must go back to walking barefoot on the ground of uncertainties and differences and take a chance on the next step as if it were a fragile certainty.

From the collective consciousness of our fragility we invent something called politics – politics as the art of governing cities and the art of ruling the Earth in light of the life of its body, of all its inhabitants. Politics, the work of our hands, is undoubtedly marked by our fragility and the disproportion of our selfishness. But it is *here* that the possibility of establishing a more just coexistence among us resides; it is here where we must be formed to see the world beyond ourselves, to feel the pain of others as ours, and long for mutual recognition as a right we all share. It is necessary, therefore, to sink our feet firmly into the land of our time and to discover the *near causation*, the exclusionary and destructive choices that are made even when other choices could be better for all.

The Christian story of God's work – an African American response

Willie James Jennings[1]

A fragile planet and a weak word: Speaking theologically in a time of planetary wounding

How should Christian theologians speak at this moment of planetary ecological crisis? The essays in this section of this volume attempt to answer this difficult question by reminding us of the obligation of theologians to help all Christians articulate their lives of faith during ecological change and climate damage. Every theologian must now take up the task, as these theologians have, of asking how doctrine speaks to climate and how a life in God speaks to a life on earth, with plant and animal, wind and water, sky and soil. We Christians have had mixed success in such speaking due in large measure to the deep contradictions we have carried forward in our thought and practice since the emergence of colonial modernity in the fifteenth century. We have articulated great appreciation for the earth while simultaneously exploiting it in breathtaking ways. We Christians have spoken beautifully and elegantly of our love for the land while our pastoral and industrial practices have expressed deep hatred of it. Obviously, climate disaster affects everyone, and the problem cannot be laid exclusively at the feet of Christians. Christianity, however, bequeathed to the world a contradiction that we are yet to fully understand – a great appreciation and love for the world that did not thwart its exploitation or destruction – indeed it set the stage for planetary destruction. This aspect of Christianity's ecological legacy is a wider matter than the important observations along these lines expressed in Lynn White Jr's famous essay.[2] Christianity had a parenting role in creating a vision of the world that turned the world into a commodity form inside an abiding objectification.[3]

---

[1] Willie James Jennings is Associate Professor of Christian Systematic Theology and Africana Studies at Yale University, in New Haven, Connecticut, USA. He is an ordained Baptist minister who has served churches in North Carolina.
[2] Lynn White, Jr, 'The Historical Roots of Our Ecological Crisis', *Science* 155 (1967), 1203–7.
[3] See Willie James Jennings, *The Christian Imagination: Theology and the Origins of Race* (New Haven: Yale University Press), Chapter 2. Also see Willie James Jennings, 'Binding Landscapes: Secularism, Race, and the Spatial Modern', in *Race and Secularism in America,* Jonathan S. Kahn and Vincent W. Lloyd (eds) (New York: Columbia University Press, 2016), 207–38.

This response reflects on that wider colonial legacy in order to situate the redeployment of doctrinal logics in helping us cope with and address our impending planetary demise. A redeployment means that Christian doctrine and thought, speech and practice have already been used but in ways that turned Christian logics against the earth, against plant and animal and the many Indigenous peoples who found no need to see themselves alienated from the ways of the earth. Of course, my use of the generic term Indigenous is simply a placeholder for the many peoples who claimed and yet claim connection to specific places in ways that make self-knowledge and self-consciousness distorted without the precise contours of land and landscape, seasons and sounds and animals and water that constitute the living of life. Anyone who is from a place may call themselves Indigenous to that place, but the point of indigeneity is not announcing where someone is from but to name those who only know themselves in relation to these specifics of place. Christianity became an arsenal against such indigeneity as it formed in the unique situation of new world colonial power.

European Christian settlers who came to the new worlds came convinced and overwhelmed. They were overwhelmed by the vastness of the new worlds – the breadth of peoples, languages, customs and knowledge systems, the depth of the variety of foods, animals and landscapes, and the quantities of minerals, metals and woods. Christian theologians entered a struggle over the epistemological density of the new worlds, a struggle that we are yet to fully articulate to ourselves. Colonial Christian settlers entered worlds that were beyond their ability to adequately explain, but not beyond their ability to capture in theological narrative. These settlers were convinced that God had safely led them to the new worlds of sub-Saharan Africa, the Americas, the Pacific islands and other soon to be colonial sites because God wanted them to claim these new worlds for Christ. They imagined themselves blessed of God with a responsibility to bring these new worlds into maturity, the maturity of salvation and the maturity of proper use.[4] European Christian settlers saw themselves as teachers – instructors in the ways of God and in the right use of the world – and they saw indigenes as those held in a demonic captivity that clouded their minds and blinded them from seeing the true nature of the material reality of the world.

Christians articulated their theologies inside a greed that formed between an idea of providence and a vision of fear. As they overturned Indigenous worlds, reformatting them to make them extensions of European space, they enacted a new hermeneutic through which to look at the world, a hermeneutic of possession. The idea of land ownership was not the invention of the colonialists. Many peoples imagined themselves in possession of land, but that possession was reciprocal – the land possessed them as much as they possessed the land, holding them in an abiding intelligibility that pressed

---

[4] Willie James Jennings, 'Can White People Be Saved: Reflections on the Relationship of Missions and Whiteness', in *Can White People Be Saved: Triangulating Race, Theology, and Mission,* Love Sechrest, Johnny Ramirez-Johnson and Amos Yong (eds) (Downers Grove: IVP Academic, 2018), 27–43.

them towards living in balance with their specific environs.[5] This ancient sense of possessive reciprocity can be seen in its expansive reality in the Bible as Israel is called to live in covenantal relationship with God on the land that belongs to God as it belongs to them. Indeed, the land is presented to Israel as covenant partner, giving witness to Israel of its faithfulness or faithlessness in covenantal life (Lev. 20.22-26).[6] Christian colonialists, however, saw themselves as a new Israel and deformed this possessive reciprocity, creating a sense of absolute possession that turned the world – its plants, animals, rivers, minerals and so forth – into simply things to be owned and fragmented land into private property. Yet one of the most tragic aspects of this deformation is the creation of a theology of extraction. I have noted this in my work on the Jesuit missionary to Peru, José de Acosta (1570s), who in his famous text *Natural and Moral History of the Indies* gave witness to this theological vision.[7]

Acosta believed that God had hidden enormous riches in the most remote parts of the world in order to draw Christians to those places to do two things, evangelize the natives and extract the riches:

> But it is a circumstance worthy of much consideration that the wisdom of our Eternal Lord has enriched the most remote parts of the world, inhabited by the most uncivilized people, and has placed there the greatest numbers of mines that ever existed, in order to invite men [sic] to seek out and possess those lands and coincidentally to communicate their religion and the worship of the true God to men [sic] who do not know it ... Hence we see that the lands in the Indies that are riches in mines and wealth have been those most advanced in the Christian religion in our time; and thus the Lord takes advantage of our desires to serve his sovereign ends ... [God has endowed these rugged lands] ... with great wealth in mines so that whoever wished could find it by this means. Hence there is great abundance of mines in the Indies, mines of every metal: copper, iron, lead, tin, quicksilver, silver and gold.[8]

Acosta saw the work of extraction to be inside a gospel logic of disabusing Amerindians of any idea that the world was alive and communicative. Such a way of thinking was to Acosta and so many other missionaries not only demonically influenced confusion but showed a deep misunderstanding of the nature of the world which is a God-given resource for making things:

> Such is the diversity of metals that the Creator enclosed in the storage places and hollows of the earth that all of them are useful for human life. Man [sic] uses some to cure illnesses, others to provide him with weapons and a defense against his enemies,

---

[5] George E. Tinker, *American Indian Liberation: A Theology of Sovereignty* (Maryknoll: Orbis, 2008), 54; Linda Hogan, *Dwellings: A Spiritual History of the Living World* (New York: W.W. Norton, 1995).

[6] Gary M. Burge, *Jesus and the Land* (Grand Rapids: Baker Academic, 2010).

[7] Jennings, 'Binding Landscapes', 208–9. Jose de Acosta, *Natural and Moral History of the Indies* (Durham: Duke University Press, 2002).

[8] Acosta, *Natural and Moral History of the Indies*, 164.

others for the adornment and decoration of men's [sic] bodies and homes, and others for vessels and tools and various instruments invented by human ingenuity. But above all these uses, which are simple and natural, communication among men [sic] resulted in the use of money, which ... is the measure of all things.[9]

I quote Acosta at length here because he shows us a Christian logic that will inform theological discursive practice and that will grow over the centuries, forming the intellectual justification for changing the environment. Acosta is not the father of this formation. He is only an example of it. This Christian logic became the ground for the logic of environmental change for the sake of making the world more productive and bringing it to mature use – climate change grows out of this logic of change. Long after colonialism's Christian logic disappeared by going, conceptually speaking, subterranean, the theological power of this thrust remains unchallenged – seeing the world as a resource, extracting from it what we need, and transforming the materials of the earth into whatever we want is exactly what is normal and natural even if Westernized peoples no longer need to see it as God ordained. The point here is not that changing the environment was the new and terrible thing, but a vision of change, a sensibility of change that began with seeing the world as a raw thing – inanimate, non-communicative, lacking in any call to reciprocal respect – always ready to be made in something else. Christian theologians have since the emergence of colonial modernity built our discursive practices inside this sensibility, which means we have articulated Christian doctrine inside a sick logic of environmental change that leads irreversibly to climate catastrophe. Once the world is made an inanimate and non-communicative 'natural' resource, then what can be done with it and to it is only a matter of degrees.

How Christian doctrine relates to climate change must be articulated first in full recognition that we live in the wake of a Christian articulation of the world as resource. What follows then from this recognition? Doctrines must be articulated aiming at overturning that Christian-formed sensibility. Each of the doctrines outlined in this section seek to answer the questions of relevance and ramification of a doctrine to the destructive effects of environmental harm. At one level each author recognizes a form of futility in this exercise – how can any theological speech thwart what seems to be inevitable? Indeed, as Ernst Conradie suggest in his dystopic postscript, we must wrestle with the clear signs that the world is quickly moving to a reality of mass extinction of species and possibly of a significant portion of the planet or at the very least (or at the very best) a significant portion of the planet becoming almost inhabitable. The gravity of our situation must be respected in our theological speech, so we can ground doctrinal articulation in the reality of a wounded world needing intensive care intervention. Yet that grounding might mean a shattering of doctrinal loci logics.

Everyday more species go extinct, yet those extinctions do not occasion mourning or sorrow from most Christian communities, nor have we sufficiently reckoned within

---

[9] Ibid., 163.

our theological imaginations with this constantly encroaching presence of death further into ecologies of life. Have we reached a moment when the loci must be reconfigured to account for these matters? We know that the configuration of the loci is driven by a pedagogical concern and a desire for conceptual clarity. These are always important matters, but at a time of climate change there is wisdom in thinking from the site of disaster and wounding and in so doing to see how for example a doctrine of providence must open inside a soteriological vision of Christ's wounded body and this in turn must open inside the idea of a creation out of nothingness. Clive Pearson's insightful reading of the doctrine of providence could fruitfully speak more directly to Thomas Jay Oord's provocative denunciation of the doctrinal commitment to a creatio ex nihilo.

We must configure doctrines at the site of our environmental and human wreckage with a view to overcoming our hermeneutics of possession. We have naturalized a colonial vision of possession, reading it back through time into the biblical narrative itself and earlier, imagining a world permeated by the sensibilities of private property. Most scholars are aware at some level that private property is a recent development, but too many scholars function as though its ubiquity constitutes a natural theology and an aspect of the natural order of human development.[10] The privatization of land and space is more than just a geographical matter. It is also at the heart of the constitution of our spiritual and bodily senses, deeply affecting the ways we imagine communion and community, life together and our individual journeys. If there is any fault to these essays on doctrine and climate change, it is that they inhabit the geographic blindness that characterizes much of Western intellectual life. Modern possessive logics undermine any sense of deep connectivity across space and place that would yield a robust relationality that might move people to see and sense the shared affective dimensions of climate change. How might we write theology differently if we sensed our geographic connectivity more acutely?

Doctrinal articulation always reveals what I call a geographic unconscious (similar to what Frederic Jameson calls the political unconscious).[11] The geographic unconscious in this regard is the way ideas of possession insinuate themselves into how we talk about God's claim on us and the world or our claim on the world and on animals. Such claiming tends to move towards an individuation that belies a privatization. We have learned to see the world and our own lives in segmented, bordered and fragmented ways that shape how we understand the nature of human sovereignty and how we imagine the extent and reach of our actual moral and ethical concern. The privatization of land was a powerful engine in the formation of nationalist ways of viewing the world and modernist constructions of peoplehood. Our world has been formed through fragmentation and ownership and our

---

[10] Peter Garnsey, *Thinking about Property: From Antiquity to the Age of Revolution* (Cambridge: Cambridge University Press, 2007); Crawford Brough Macpherson (ed.), *Property: Mainstream and Critical Positions* (Toronto: University of Toronto Press, 1978).

[11] Frederic Jameson, *The Political Unconscious: Narrative as a Socially Symbolic Act* (New York: Cornell University, 1981).

explanations of doctrine need to reckon substantially with that formation. If we hope to reverse harmful environmental practices, even if reversal of the consequences may be beyond our reach, then we will need to show how doctrines like, for example, election and justification challenge possessive logics and reorient us away from fragmentation and bring important questions to ideas of geographic and human sovereignty.

Doctrinal articulations must also return to the site of original harm by reckoning with the forced silence and/or destruction of Indigenous epistemologies and the continued relegation of alternative ways of knowing and imagining knowledge as marginal to the Western cognitive empire.[12] Christian doctrine has played a crucial role in both this history of destruction and the continued denial of non-Western epistemologies and sciences. We are the inheritors of what I have termed a pedagogical imperialism that positioned Christians as always teachers and rarely learners *in the performance* of orthodox ways of thinking. This has always been a wider problem than simply the relentless Eurocentrism that dogs Christian doctrinal articulation. It has to do with how we frame our ecologies of knowing and who emerges as our interlocutors as Western theologians and intellectuals.

There is a poignancy to the loci's absence of Indigenous influence after centuries of non-white peoples' involvement with Christianity. Much like architecture, or music or food, there ought to be a long history of the cultural baroque where the inner cultural logics of multiple peoples should have shaped and reshaped the articulation of doctrine and formed new doctrines that would have given witness to a God who is the creator of all flesh. Sadly, this is not the case. Indeed, most articulations of doctrine exist as though the majority world does not exist as intellectual co-creators but only as recipients of European thought-forms. There is a direct connection to the possessive logics that turned the world into silent raw material and forms of doctrinal logics that yet render the majority world raw intellectual material that can be moulded and made to speak theologically. This does not have to be the case and should we wish not only to speak with a new depth about the problems of climate change, but also give insight into how we might live against a world turned into a thing, we will need to rethink the collaborative possibilities of speaking theologically about the climate.

There is a weakness to the Word, as Bonhoeffer so eloquently noted, that is appropriate to God's self-revealing in the world. Christian doctrine lives in that weakness, especially in a world that has been mangled by strong speech that determines what the world is and how it may be used. For too long Christian theology has lived inside that strong speech, misidentifying our word of witness with the world's words of control. At this moment we cannot hope to fight this strong speech by mimicking its ways. We must find our way of speaking in concert with a world that is speaking of its pain and wounding. Only then will doctrinal articulation matter to this world.

---

[12] Boaventura de Sousa Santos, *Epistemologies of the South: Justice Against Epistemicide* (Boulder: Paradigm Publishers, 2014). Also see Boaventura de Sousa Santos, *The End of the Cognitive Empire: The Coming of Age of Epistemologies of the South* (Durham: Duke University Press, 2018).

The Christian story of God's work – a Chinese Christian response

Lai Pan-chiu[1]

Introduction

The contributors in this section consciously adopt a contextual theological approach to climate change and characterize their perspective as 'North Atlantic Christian theology'. In order to enrich this contextual theological approach, the critical response that follows also adopts a contextual approach, but its perspective can be called 'Sino-Christian theology'.[2]

The Chinese Christian theological discourses on ecological issues are actually quite divergent, as they inherit different theological traditions and respond to different kinds of non-Christian ecological discourses in the Chinese context.[3] Among these non-Christian discourses, the most relevant is probably Confucianism. As some of the essays in this section mention, the earth has undergone several ice ages, but these radical climate changes in the past were not brought forth by human beings. By contrast, human beings play a key role in the climate change that threatens the survival of human beings as well as other forms of lives on this planet. For this reason, some scholars use the term 'Anthropocene' to characterize the present age. This emphasis on the key role of human beings in the universe echoes Confucianism more than Daoism and the other Chinese philosophical/religious traditions. In fact, some Chinese Christian theologians take the

---

[1] Lai Pan-chiu is Professor of Religious Studies at the Chinese University of Hong Kong. His research areas include inter-religious dialogue and modern Christian thought. He published *Confucian-Christian Dialogue and Ecological Concern* (with Lin Hongxing in Chinese, 2006).

[2] For a brief account of 'Sino-Christian theology', see Pan-chiu Lai and Jason Lam (eds), *Sino-Christian Theology: A Theological Qua Cultural Movement in Contemporary China* (Frankfurt-am-Main: Peter Lang, 2010); Pan-chiu Lai, 'Sino-Theology as a Non-Church Movement: Historical and Comparative Perspectives', *Christian Presence and Progress in North-East Asia*, Jan A. B. Jongeneel et al. (eds) (Frankfurt: Peter Lang, 2011), 87–103.

[3] For a brief survey of contemporary Chinese discourse on ecotheology, see Pan-chiu Lai, 'Ecological t\ Theology as Public Theology: A Chinese Perspective', *International Journal of Public Theology* 11:4 (2017), 477–500.

Confucian idea of unity between Heaven and humanity as a distinctive feature of Sino-Christian theology.[4]

Divine work in Confucian perspective

Before addressing the essays one by one, it may be useful to outline briefly the Confucian understanding of the relationship between divinity, humanity and nature. Confucianism's account of the divine work differs from the story of God's work offered by the mainstream of North Atlantic Christian theology in some crucial respects and yet exhibits certain similarities with some of its minor streams. Such similarities and dissimilarities make it possible to raise some critical questions regarding the essays in this section.

The Chinese religions regard the world as a living system.[5] According to this basic understanding of the world, the 'genesis' of the universe is often understood as analogous to the growth or development of an organism, rather than being created out of nothing by an external agent. According to the *Book of Changes*, which exercises tremendous influence on Confucianism, 'Production and reproduction is what is called Change,' and 'The great virtue of Heaven and Earth is to produce (or give birth).'[6] In other words, the production of life embodies the virtue of heaven and earth rather than demonstrating the intelligence of a divine designer or the omnipotence of a Creator God.

In Confucianism, this virtue of 'creativity' or 'life-loving' can also be interpreted in terms of 'benevolence' (*rén*),[7] which manifests itself not only in the production of life in the universe but also in human hearts (*xīn*). This virtue of benevolence constitutes some ontological continuity or unity between Heaven and humanity. According to Confucianism, the unity between Heaven and humanity (*tiān rén hé yī*) implies a distinctive and crucial role to be played by the human being in the universe, without denying or downplaying the role of Heaven.

There is no doubt that Confucianism affirms the primacy of divine action vis-à-vis human effort. *The Analects* 17.19 affirms that Heaven, without saying a word, makes the four seasons pursue their courses and give birth to all things continually.[8] Apart from the

---

[4] See Alexander Chow, *Theosis, Sino-Christian Theology and the Second Chinese Enlightenment: Heaven and Humanity in Unity* (New York: Palgrave Macmillan, 2013).

[5] Daniel L. Overmeyer, *Religions of China: The World as a Living System* (San Francisco: Harper San Francisco, 1991).

[6] The original Chinese verses read 'shēng shēng zhī wèi yì' (*Book of Changes*, Xi Ci, I.5) and 'tiān dì zhī dà dé yuē sheng' (*Book of Changes*, Xi Ci, II.1) respectively. For the Chinese text with an English translation by James Legge, see https://ctext.org/book-of-changes

[7] Wei-ming Tu, *Humanity and Self-Cultivation* (Berkeley: Asian Humanities Press, 1979), 8–9.

[8] The Chinese reads: 'tiān hé yán zāi? sì shí xíng yān, bǎi wù shēng yān, tiān hé yán zāi?' See https://ctext.org/analects/yang-huo/zh (accessed 20 April 2018).

divine providence embodied in the regular natural phenomena, Confucianism assumes the irregular natural phenomena – for example, natural disasters – can also result from the works of Heaven. In ancient China, the emperor was called Son of Heaven (*tiān zǐ*) and regarded as a sacral king who received the divine mandate (*tiān mìng*) from Heaven to govern. The divine mandate was supposed to be earned and maintained not by birth but by good deeds or merit, performing relevant religious rituals properly and governing the empire efficiently. If the emperor behaved badly or failed to govern his people properly, Heaven would show its disapproval, warning or even anger through some irregular or strange natural phenomena, especially natural disasters such as drought and flood. In this case, the emperor might have to perform a ritual and offer a prayer for his people, including making a confession to Heaven and a petition to bear the guilt on behalf of his people. Prolonged disasters therefore were interpreted as a sign that the emperor had lost the divine mandate and thus political legitimacy.[9] A typical case is Emperor Tāng of the Shāng Dynasty. According to one account, he attempted to offer himself as a human sacrifice in order to pray for rain and to end a drought for seven years, and Heaven was moved and extinguished the fire with rain on spot.[10] In *The Analects* 20.1, Confucius also praises Emperor Tāng for offering a sacrifice to Heaven, his prayer on behalf of his people and his willingness to bear the guilt of his people, without mentioning any human sacrifice.[11] This reflects how Confucianism inherited and transformed the Chinese tradition of shamanism as well as the belief in the interaction between Heaven and human beings.[12] In other words, for Confucianism, Heaven acts not only through the regular courses of nature, but also through the irregular natural phenomena in response to human activities. This makes the Confucian understanding of divine work significantly different from deism, which assumes that the Divine Being simply lets nature run its own course and will not respond to human behaviour or intervene in human affairs.

Confucianism affirms that the human being is ordained by Heaven to regulate, enhance and even complete the course of nature. In this sense, nature itself is incomplete without human beings. As *The Doctrine of the Mean* suggests,

> What Heaven has conferred is called 'The Nature'; an accordance with this nature is called 'The Path of duty'; the regulation of this path is called 'Instruction' … While there are no stirrings of pleasure, anger, sorrow, or joy, the mind may be said to be in the state of Equilibrium. When those feelings have been stirred, and they act in their due degree, there ensues what may be called the state of Harmony. This Equilibrium is the great root from which grow all the human actings in the world, and this Harmony

---

[9] See K. C. Chang, *Art, Myth, and Ritual: The Path to Political Authority in Ancient China* (Cambridge: Harvard University Press, 1983).

[10] See Chen Yongming, *Rú xué yǔ zhōng guó zōng jiào chuán tǒng* [Confucianism and the Chinese Religious Tradition] (Taipei: The Commercial Press of Taiwan, 2003), 41–52 (46).

[11] See https://ctext.org/analects/yao-yue/zh (accessed 21 April 2018).

[12] See Wu Wen-zhang, *Wū shī chuán tǒng hé rú jiā dí shēn céng jié gòu* [The Shaman Tradition and the Deep Structure of Confucianism] (Kaohsiung: Fu Wen Books, 2001).

is the universal path which they all should pursue. Let the states of equilibrium and harmony exist in perfection, and a happy order will prevail throughout heaven and earth, and all things will be nourished and flourish.[13]

In other words, the moral and spiritual cultivation of human beings is crucial for cosmic harmony.

It is only he who is possessed of the most complete sincerity that can exist under heaven, who can give its full development to his nature. Able to give its full development to his own nature, he can do the same to the nature of other men. Able to give its full development to the nature of other men, he can give their full development to the natures of animals and things. Able to give their full development to the natures of creatures and things, he can assist the transforming and nourishing powers of Heaven and Earth. Able to assist the transforming and nourishing powers of Heaven and Earth, he may with Heaven and Earth form a ternion.[14]

It is noteworthy that the Confucian affirmation of the distinctive role of human beings in the universe does not imply a rejection of the value of other forms of life. Because the uniqueness of human beings is based on humanity's participation in Heaven's virtue of benevolence, human beings have a responsibility to assist the works of Heaven in the production of life and in maintaining the cosmic harmony. These features render Confucian ecological ethics a middle path between anthropocentrism and eco-centrism.[15]

The crucial role of the human being assigned by *The Doctrine of the Mean* might refer primarily to the elitist sages, who could assist the transforming and nourishing operations of heaven and earth and therefore form a trinity with heaven and earth. However, in the subsequent development of Confucianism, it is emphasized that *all* human beings share the same human nature and that every human being has the potential to become sages. Neo-Confucianism particularly emphasizes that anyone can become a sage; and that, though the path of learning and self-cultivation is long and arduous, it remains an attainable goal because of the ontological unity between humanity and Heaven.[16] In other words, there is no significant difference in terms of essential nature shared by all human beings. The sage is not a supernatural being whose nature is entirely different from ordinary human beings. On the contrary, the sage is different simply because he or she has fully actualized his or her humanity through his or her own effort. In other words, the sage is merely the most authentic and genuine person.[17] In Neo-

---

[13] *The Doctrine of the Mean*, 1; https://ctext.org/liji/zhong-yong (accessed 21 April 2018).

[14] *The Doctrine of the Mean*, 23.

[15] Pan-chiu Lai, 'Beyond Anthropocentrism and Ecocentrism: Eco-Theology and Confucian-Christian Dialogue', *Ching Feng* 2:1–2 (2001), 35–55.

[16] Rodney Taylor, 'The Sage as Saint: The Confucian Tradition', in *Sainthood: Its Manifestations in World Religions*, Richard Kieckhefer and George D. Bond (eds) (Berkeley: University of California Press, 1988), 238–9.

[17] Tu, *Humanity and Self-Cultivation*, 72.

Confucianism, becoming a sage means not only the full realization of the potential of one's nature, but also achieving a sense of 'oneness' with all things. Many Neo-Confucians express in various ways the same idea that a person of benevolence (*rén*) can form one body with the myriad things of heaven and earth through 'enlarging' one's heart to sympathize all things. Displaying an extraordinary compassion for the life of others is an essential quality a sage must have.[18]

Responses to North Atlantic Christian theology

Based on the above sketch of Confucianism, one may consider articulating a Chinese Christian ecological theology informed by Confucianism[19] and giving responses to the 'North Atlantic Christian theology' embodied in the essays of this section.

Regarding Thomas Jay Oord's proposal to replace the traditional Christian theological concept of *creatio ex nihilo* with *creatio ex creation sempieternaliter en amore* (God creates out of creation, everlastingly in love), Confucianism may say emphatically 'Amen'. It is interesting to note that the Confucian emphasis on the virtue of 'creativity' or 'life-loving' is reminiscent of Wisdom of Solomon 11.24–12.1:

> Yes, you love all that exists, you hold nothing of what you have made in abhorrence, for had you hated anything, you would not have formed it. And how, had you not willed it, could a thing persist, how be conserved if not called forth by you? You spare all things because all things are yours, Lord, lover of life, you whose imperishable spirit is in all (Jerusalem Bible).

Based on such Jewish wisdom, Jürgen Moltmann developed a pneumatological conception of God as 'the lover of life'.[20] Furthermore, the Confucian ideas of the ontological continuity between humanity and Heaven as well as the cosmic role of human beings echo not only the traditional Christian concept of *imago Dei* but also Philip Hefner's proposal of recognizing the human being as 'created co-creator', assisting the *creatio continua* or the transformation of the universe.[21] Confucianism may also support John Wesley's (1703–91) understanding of the essential role played by human beings in cosmological salvation. In short, a Chinese Christian ecological theology may endorse most of the proposals made by Oord.

---

[18] Taylor, 'The Sage as Saint', 227–30.

[19] See Pan-chiu Lai, 'God of Life and Ecological Theology: A Chinese Christian Perspective', *The Ecumenical Review* 65:1 (2013), 67–82; Pan-chiu Lai, 'Christian Ecological Theology in Dialogue with Confucianism', *Ching Feng* 41:3–4 (1998), 309–44; reprinted as 'Ecological Theology in Dialogue with Confucianism', *Dialogue and Alliance* 17:1 (2003), 61–90.

[20] See Jürgen Moltmann, *God in Creation: An Ecological Doctrine of Creation* (London: SCM Press, 1985), xii.

[21] Philip Hefner, *The Human Factor: Evolution, Culture and Religion* (Minneapolis: Fortress, 1993).

In similar vein, the Confucian understanding of the distinctive human role ordained by Heaven and the Confucian ideal of forming one body with the myriad things of heaven and earth are very much in line with Peter Manley Scott's elaboration on the idea of the unity of all creatures and interpretation of human vocation as representative of all creatures. For Confucianism, the telos of human existence as well as moral or spiritual cultivation is to be a benevolent person who can embrace all lives in terms of both spirituality and ethical responsibility.

The Confucian position may differ slightly in emphasis from Ernst Conradie's analysis of sin. Different from the one-sided individualistic and moralistic account of sin, Conradie proposes a more comprehensive understanding of sin as power and as guilt and highlights the structural aspect of sin associated with the economic and political orders. In contrast, the Confucian tradition tends to emphasize the personal moral and spiritual cultivation, and this might have made many contemporary studies on Confucianism and ecology overlook the economic and political issues.[22] Chinese Christian theologians, including those who attempt to articulate ecological theology with a Confucian framework, tend to pay more attention to the structural aspect of sin. It is stressed that the ecological crisis has both historical as well as existential roots.[23] Underpinning the economic system that contributes to environmental degradation is not only consumerism but also human concupiscence.[24] In other words, the personal and structural aspects of sin may be intertwined rather than separate. Conradie's analysis of sin should be properly recognized as a rather distinctive contribution to be made by Christianity to the public discussion concerning environmental degradation. However, his mentioning of 'original sin' deserves further deliberation. Confucianism is very critical towards the Western Christian concept of original sin, which seems to be something inherited from human ancestors and therefore cannot be eliminated by human efforts. This concept of original sin provides a forceful support to the doctrine of salvation relying on 'Other-power' – a salvation to be established by the salvific work of Christ only. This understanding of salvation contradicts the Confucian emphasis on human moral effort.[25] Furthermore, this may also contradict the emphasis on the human role associated with the Anthropocene. As the concept of 'emergence' might have implied, human sin 'emerged' contingently and depended on human existence, rather than a permanent substance created by God eternally or in the very beginning before the emergence of human beings. Perhaps one may better take advice from Karl Barth (1886–1968), who highlights the nihilistic nature of sin and suggests viewing sin

---

[22] See the essays included in Mary Evelyn Tucker and John Berthrong (eds), *Confucianism and Ecology: The Interrelation of Heaven, Earth, and Humans* (Cambridge: Harvard University Center for the Study of World Religions, 1998).

[23] See Pan-chiu Lai, 'Paul Tillich and Ecological Theology', *The Journal of Religion* 79:2 (1999), 233–49.

[24] See for example: Lai Pinchao (=Pan-chiu Lai), 'zōng jiào yǔ shēng tài guān huái' [Religion and Ecological Concern], *Jiāng hǎi xué kān* [*Jianghai Academic Journal*] 219 (2002), 37–42.

[25] See Pan-chiu Lai, 'Christian-Confucian Dialogue on Humanity: An Ecological Perspective', *Studies in Interreligious Dialogue* 14:2 (2004), 202–15.

in the perspective of its being overcome.[26] Of course, overcoming human sin is the topic for another essay.

The essay by Clive Pearson, 'God's Continued Providence', raises an important question about divine providence, which may involve the question of whether the belief in a caring God is compatible with the prospect of massive extinction by apocalyptic or eschatological ecological catastrophe. Besides, the notion of the Anthropocene, which seems to highlight the human factor in the formation as well as resolution of ecological disasters, may challenge the Christian theological idea of providence, which seems to assume the regularity of seasons and the availability of what was required for the sustenance of life (*conservatio*), the wise governance and administration of continuing creation (*gubernatio*) and that the divine will might work secretly in collaboration with human freedom towards a teleological purpose (*concursus*). If one reconsiders the issues from a Confucian perspective, one may find that in addition to its emphasis on the human role in maintaining cosmic harmony, Confucianism does not have a doctrine of divine omnipotence or a doctrine of creation out of nothing. Furthermore, Confucianism observes divine providence both in regular and irregular natural phenomena. The challenge of massive extinction is therefore less serious for Confucianism than for North Atlantic Christian theology, but it remains relevant to Chinese Christian theology. The crucial issue remains whether and how the belief of divine love can be compatible with massive extinction. This question may lead to the question concerning election and eschatology.

As it is admitted by Gijsbert van den Brink and Eva van Urk, the theological discussion concerning climate change seldom mentions the doctrine of election or predestination largely because the traditional Western interpretation of this doctrine tended to be anthropocentric and individualistic in terms of the recipient of election, while theocentric and deterministic with regard to the agent of election. These features seem to make the doctrine irrelevant to climate change. In order to address the problem, Van den Brink and Van Urk propose four revisions. First, in line with the Finnish interpretation of Luther, God's grace is not just the divine forgiveness declared to us from an external point of view but includes union with Christ. Second, the notion of divine sovereignty underpins rather than diminishes human responsibility. Third, divine election and predestination should be interpreted within a Trinitarian framework, which includes the concrete revelation of God's love in Jesus Christ which is made known through the Holy Spirit. Fourth, the purpose of electing a particular group (Israel or the Church) is for the service of bringing blessing to the whole world. From a Confucian point of view, all these proposed revisions are to be endorsed. The Confucian emphasis on the unity between Heaven and humanity echoes the union with God in Christ. The Confucian idea of divine mandates highlights rather than diminishes human responsibility. The Confucian understanding of human

---

[26] See Pan-chiu Lai, 'Barth's Doctrines of Sin and Humanity in Buddhist Perspective', *Studies in Interreligious Studies* 16:1 (2006), 41–58.

uniqueness refers to the human role in maintaining cosmic harmony rather than focusing exclusively on the value of human beings per se. The Confucian concept of sanctification (becoming a sage) is compatible with the Orthodox understanding of deification which is the ultimate aim of salvation.[27] In fact, similar ideas have been suggested by Chinese Christian theologians.[28] However, even in these revisions, there is no explicit affirmation of the divine election of non-human creatures. The issue at stake is whether non-human creatures are also recipients of divine election and even key players in the story of God's work,[29] rather than merely the background for the drama of God's work for human salvation. This issue may lead to the question concerning how Christianity interprets the story of salvation.

Ernst Conradie's essay, 'God's Acts of Salvation for Us', examines three models of atonement, namely 'victory', 'reconciliation' and 'moral inspiration'. Conradie suggests that for ecotheology, all of these three are needed, and 'it is best to maintain the focus on the whole narrative of the incarnation, life, ministry, suffering, death, resurrection of Jesus Christ.' From a Confucian point of view, which characterizes the moral ideal of being a sage in terms of a benevolent person forming one body with the myriad things of heaven and earth, a more relevant Christological symbol is perhaps the concept of *anakephalaiosasthai* (Eph. 1.10), which refers to Jesus Christ as the one who unites all things in heaven and on earth. From a Chinese Christian point of view, *anakephalaiosasthai* may be recognized as the 'summary' of the life and work of Jesus Christ – the same Greek word used in Romans 13.9 for 'to summarize'. This symbol can combine the models of 'victory' (overcoming the 'enemies' of hatred, apartheid and alienation among creatures), 'moral inspiration' (inspiring creatures to follow Jesus Christ's moral example as a co-creator to love and care about all human and non-human creatures) and 'reconciliation' (achieving the universal and ultimate reconciliation between the Creator and the creation as well as that within the whole creation). It is perhaps important to note that a Chinese Christian reinterpretation of *anakephalaiosasthai* may also differ from the Confucian interpretation of forming one body with the myriad things of heaven and earth. The Confucian ideal assumes that the ultimate aim is to maintain the cosmic harmony of this world (which may be understood as the status quo) and tends to consider this harmony in terms of restoration – through restoring the cosmic order and making everything return to their proper or original places. This may sound similar to the ancient doctrine of *apokatastasis* (restoration

---

[27] See further Pan-chiu Lai, 'Chinese Explorations of Orthodox Theology: A Critical Review', *International Journal of Sino-Western Studies* 14 (2018), 27–41.

[28] See Pan-chiu Lai, 'Shaping Humanity with Word and Spirit: Perspectives East, West and Neither-East-Nor-West', in *Word and Spirit: Renewing Christology and Pneumatology in a Globalizing World*, Anselm K. Min and Christoph Schwöbel (eds) (Berlin: Walter de Gruyter, 2014), 131–49; and, 'Justification by Faith and Protestant Christianity in China: With Special Reference to the Finnish Interpretation of Luther', *International Journal of Sino-Western Studies* 16 (2019), forthcoming.

[29] See Lai, 'Paul Tillich and Ecological Theology', 233–49.

of all things).³⁰ The issue is whether *anakephalaiosasthai* should be considered merely in terms of restoration, and this may imply the continuation of the status quo – the prevalent natural order and the sustainability of the present environment. However, as the doctrine of *apokatastasis* may refer to an eschatological vision, rather than the mere continuation of the existing natural world, one may have to wonder whether the *anakephalaiosasthai* may also be considered in terms of 'new creation' (2 Cor. 5.17) to highlight that this is a creative transformation of the cosmos rather than merely a continuation or restoration. These two conceptions of the ultimate goal may have different practical implications for the strategies of environmental protection – one may be more open to imagining how a sustainable future can be achieved in an innovative way and the other may tend to focus on restoring everything to the pre-industrial period or returning to the scenario before the Anthropocene.

As Conradie notes, God's acts of salvation for us requires discourse on 'God's work of salvation in and through us' – which is the topic of Hilda Koster's essay, which shifts the focus to the human side and to the work of the Holy Spirit. The essay is focused on the concepts of grace, justification, sin, guilt and anxiety. The essay's retrieval of justifying grace against its 'ecological despisers' concurs with a Chinese Christian point of view, shaped by Confucianism, in that it considers the full humanity of Christ when thinking through 'God's work of salvation in and through us'. The essay furthermore highlights the Finnish interpretation of justification and its emphasis on the indwelling Christ and the transformation of the believer towards holiness. This emphasis relates to the Orthodox concept of 'deification', which indicates how God shared the divine life with human beings, and gave us the example as well as the ability to fulfil our roles as created co-creators.³¹ This line of thinking is very much in line with the Orthodox approach of combining 'ecological spirituality' with 'cosmic deification' pioneered by Maximus the Confessor (c.580–662).

Karen Bloomquist's essay, 'God's Work through the Church', reconsiders how the church, with its marks and practices, especially Eucharist, may challenge or counter the meta-framework of neoliberalism that contributes to climate change. From a Chinese Christian point of view (which remains a minority group in China), it is important to challenge the mainstream of current culture, whose practices lead towards environmental degradation. A similar approach is also proposed by Chinese Christian theologians.³² However, other than this countercultural approach, it is also important for Chinese Christian churches to explore possible partnerships with other organizations, including NGOs. Interpreted theologically, in renewing the universe, God the Spirit may work

---

[30] See Ilaria L. E. Ramelli, *The Christian Doctrine of Apokatastasis: A Critical Assessment from the New Testament to Eriugena* (Leiden: Brill, 2013).

[31] See Lai, 'Shaping Humanity with Word and Spirit', 131–49.

[32] For example Yik-pui Au, *The Eucharist as a Countercultural Liturgy: An Examination of the Theologies of Henri de Lubac, John Zizioulas, and Miroslav Volf* (Eugene: Pickwick, 2017).

not only in and through the Christian churches, but also beyond. In fact, some Chinese Christian theologians find such theological support in Paul Tillich (1886–1965).[33] With Tillich's idea of latent and manifested spiritual community, which recognizes the power of the New Being or Spiritual Presence outside the organized churches,[34] one may affirm that perhaps both the family (which, according to Confucianism, is the most important institution cultivating people's benevolence towards others) and environment organizations can be recognized as partners for the promotion of ecological awareness and action.

No matter how hard the church may work on environmental issues, it is undeniable that many lives or even species are becoming extinct due to climate change. One therefore has to address the inevitable question concerning 'Christian Eschatology in the Face of Climate Change'. Geiko Müller-Fahrenholz's essay attempts to address this issue with a proposal for an 'alternative eschatology', which highlights the universality of salvation and consummation of all things in the all-reconciling God, to replace the 'orthodox' position which is often associated with dualism, individualism, elitism and escapism. Müller-Fahrenholz's 'alternative eschatology', which includes the mentioning of 'in Christ, God reconciled the cosmos unto himself' and 'new creation', is very much in line with the Chinese Christian perspective described above. Compassion towards all life is adorable from Christian, Confucian and Buddhist perspectives. However, in comparison with Mahayana Buddhism, which is famous for its proclamation of universal salvation as its signature doctrine,[35] the Christian advocacy for universal salvation remains ambiguous. This is not only because the biblical evidence is ambivalent,[36] but also because a straightforward proclamation of universal salvation may have undesirable pastoral consequences – inhibiting one's motivation for evangelization and sanctification. This is the reason why those supportive of such an 'alternative eschatology', like Origen and Barth, would prefer to hold it privately or teach it cautiously to the right persons only.[37] In the present context, perhaps one may have to consider whether and how this 'alternative eschatology' is to be taught without the undesirable side effect of making people believe that 'we all will be saved by God anyway' and become too relaxed in our efforts to address the challenge of carbon mitigation.

---

[33] See Keith Ka-fu Chan, *Life as Spirit: A Study of Paul Tillich's Ecological Pneumatology* (Berlin: Walter de Gruyter, 2018).

[34] Paul Tillich, *Systematic Theology, Volume 3* (London: SCM, 1978), 152–5.

[35] See Pan-chiu Lai, 'Reconsidering the Christian Understanding of Universal Salvation in Mahayana Buddhist Perspective', *Ching Feng* 12 (2013), 19–42.

[36] According to Jürgen Moltmann, both universal salvation and a double outcome of judgement are well attested biblically. See Moltmann, *The Coming of God: Christian Eschatology* (London: SCM Press, 1996), 240–3.

[37] See Pan-chiu Lai, 'Karl Barth and Universal Salvation: A Mahayana Buddhist Perspective', in *Karl Barth and Comparative Theology,* Christian T. Collins Winn and Martha Moore-Keish (eds) (New York: Fordham University Press, forthcoming).

PART V

The Christian notion of God's identity and character

Introduction

Ernst M. Conradie and Hilda P. Koster

It is impossible to tell the story of God's work (the task of the previous main section of this volume) without a sense of God's identity and character. For Christians this constitutes the deepest mystery of history and offers the best available clues as to how a changing climate is to be interpreted.[1]

However, this is also where the Christian confession of faith in the triune God is most contested amidst a changing climate so that other rubrics such as religion, ultimate reality, culture or spirituality are preferred by some in order to refrain from giving offense and to facilitate collaboration with others. Accordingly, it needs to be recognized that 'God has many names' and that to privilege any one name (or for that matter three names) can only undermine collaborative efforts.

This may even lead to a refusal to name God or to explore God's identity and character. This cannot be a way forward if only because that would leave the suspicion that Christianity remains part of the problem unexplored. It would also not suffice to guard against idolatry, the many false gods that wreak havoc in legitimizing the current global economic order. Not every form of religion – certainly not every form of Christianity – is conducive to address climate change. Obvious examples include the Nazi God of 'blood and soil', the apartheid God who preserves ethnic identity and the purity of races, the patriarchal God who keeps male dominance in place, and also the God who could be bribed to ensure prosperity (for some), much like Ba'al in the biblical roots of Christianity. Today, a God who is narrowly defined in relation to human interest and images, or who is thought to be radically separated from the ecological web of life is or who is captured only by human related imaginary is being questioned.

For those inside the Christian tradition the triune confession is nothing but the doxological conclusion of their faith. This confession should be treated with some circumspection though. Apophatic theology serves as a constant reminder within the wider Christian tradition not to take God for granted, that one cannot presume to know God's identity and character. This is a recurring challenge throughout the Jewish–Christian tradition. Biblical figures such as Abraham, Moses, Gideon, Saul, David, Peter and Paul had to learn not to assume that they know what a divine being is like and on that basis only had to establish the true identity of this God. The biblical narratives

---

[1] For an exploration of naming the ultimate mystery of the world and indeed the mystery of history, see Ernst M. Conradie, *The Earth in God's Economy: Creation, Salvation and Consummation in Ecological Perspective* (Berlin: LIT Verlag, 2015).

constantly challenge such assumptions by not only helping the faithful to understand why Israel's God is different and unique but also to change their notions of divinity. The human tendency to identify God with a military commander, a mighty king, a wise judge, an emperor or a dispenser of goods and services is juxtaposed by the God of underdogs, of runaway slaves, of widows and orphans, of exiles, of suffering servants, of lepers and prostitutes, of one executed as a dangerous rebel and blasphemer, abandoned by his closest followers.

Beyond the biblical roots of Christianity this has remained a recurring theme: those who regard themselves as witnesses to God's identity and character have often failed to understand their own message while the (gentile, heathen, barbaric) recipients of the message seemed to get the point. Arguably, the gentiles understood the inclusiveness of God's love better than the Jews who initiated the message. The Indigenous tribes of Northern Europe accepted the message that they received from imperial Christianity even though the latter compromised the message in many ways. The colonized in countries of South America and Africa embraced the message that they received from colonizers who carried the 'flame' of Christianity across the world through voyages of exploration and exploitation. Slaves heard the message from slave owners and understood it much better than they did. Dalits in India are seeing the significance of the gospel clearer than others in higher classes and castes do. Does this apply to debates on sexual orientation too? What about non-human animals? The obvious danger is that Christians may become self-satisfied in naming God as triune through their own creeds and confessions. This is no guarantee for grasping who this God is, what this God is up to amidst a changing climate and what faith in God entails. In fact, for many North Atlantic Christians climate change raises the question of the plausibility of God's very existence and, hence, the very possibility of faith in God. These questions are perhaps not all that different from those raised by the death of God theology in the wake of the Holocaust.

The fifth main section of this volume includes essays on the Christian faith in God as Father, Son and Spirit. The traditional terms are maintained here precisely because they raise so many suspicions that Christianity remains part of the problem and far from the solution. Each of the core symbols does have anti-imperialist connotations: God is a Father not an emperor, the anointed Messiah emerges to bring a new dispensation, Winds of change are coming that cannot be controlled by the centres of power. However, subsequently these very symbols have often been used to reinforce imperial rule (*in hoc signo vinces!*), patriarchal authority and feudal/colonial lordship.

Either way, in order to stimulate some reflection, the traditional order is reversed. Instead of the logic of confession, a logic of coming to this confession is followed, starting (a) with experiences of God the Spirit, moving (b) to the ways in which the identity of this Spirit is exemplified in the Spirit of Christ, and then (c) to reflections on the 'Father' of whom we know mainly through the ministry of Jesus the Christ. In bringing this threefold confession together, this part of the volume concludes with (d) a reflection on faith in the triune God in the context of a changing climate. In each case there are major issues that need to be addressed.

The Christian confession of faith in the Holy Spirit is contested in several ways. On the one hand there are questions about the power of the Spirit to renew God's whole creation since this seems to be more hidden than overt. Some may question the power of love to make the world go round since it seems that it is instead money that makes the world go round. Other would contest the identification of the Holy Spirit as the Spirit of Christ while a vaguer sense of spirituality is endorsed. Yet others have little room for any spirits or ghosts since they focus only on what is visible and disregard the invisible. Yet, amidst climate change, there is an obvious need to discern the spirits. One cannot see the air or the climate but the effect of a changing climate is still evident. Whither, then, is this Wind blowing?

Christians confess that God was revealed in Jesus Christ in a special way and that he died and was risen 'for us and our salvation'. From the very beginning, both the person and the work of Jesus has been highly contested. Such contestation has never stopped so that climate change has become yet another site of struggle in this regard. One can raise questions about the formulation of Chalcedon, affirming a hypostatic union of a divine and a human nature, on the confession that Jesus Christ is 'Lord' (or that the Lord is Jesus?), on the particularity of Jesus as a Galilean man, on the accurate portrayal of his ministry, on the meaning of all the Christological symbols and on the theories of atonement. Each of these debates can be made relevant for climate change. But perhaps the core question is whether the person and work of Jesus Christ can really make a difference – whether this could be regarded as the decisive salvific event that can also inspire us, today, in addressing climate change. This is such an enormous claim that one would want to consider some supporting evidence to ascertain its plausibility. Where can such evidence be found in the Christian tradition in general and in North Atlantic Christianity in particular?

The identity and character of God the Father cannot be separated from the confession of faith in Jesus Christ and the Holy Spirit. We know about God as 'father' only through Jesus Christ. Moreover, the character of God as 'father' can only be established through the work of God as the one who creates, sustains, provides and cares. However, this confession is contested in multiple ways – for example, through the traditions of natural theology (knowing God independently from Christ and prior to the message of Christ), through multifaith collaboration and interfaith dialogue, including with Indigenous (or primal) religious traditions (in Africa, Australia, the Americas, Nordic countries) and of course also through feminist/womanist and queer theology. How is this relevant to climate change? Many ecofeminist voices have suggested that the logic of domination that is characteristic of patriarchal culture is the same logic of domination at work in modernity and in industrialized capitalism so that patriarchal culture lies at the root causes of anthropogenic climate change. Ecowomanists have further pointed out that the logic of both, patriarchy and modern capitalism, intersects with white privilege and racism. After all, climate-vulnerable communities are most often communities of colour, and among these communities women, especially, are suffering the negative effects of climate change. Although the historical and ideological roots of climate change may be contested, it is hard not to recognize the dangers related to the intersectionality of patriarchy, white supremacy and other logics of oppression, such as heteronormativity. Can Christians still confess their faith in God as Father in such a climate, one in which this confession seems to remain part of the underlying problem? Or, to the contrary, does climate change require that we do away once and for all with God the Father? Do female or gender-neutral metaphors for God fare better in a changing climate? What about the speciesism implied in our God-talk?

The Christian doctrine of the Trinity is sometimes regarded as so esoteric and speculative that it can scarcely be of any earthly use, not to mention in debates on climate change.[2] Even among Christian communities this trust in the Triune God is often underplayed – for example, wherever there is a need to collaborate with people of other living faiths. In the context of debates on decolonization and decoloniality, especially in Africa, it is underplayed in order to maintain continuity African traditional religion and culture.[3] Yet, other Christians have claimed that 'the Trinity is our social programme'. This is typically explained in terms of notions of communion, reciprocity, perichoresis and sociality. Does the so-called social Trinity offer us a much-needed ecological model for thinking about our relationship with one another and other-than-humans, or, to the contrary, does it draw on a rather idealized notion of interconnectedness? There are voices who have argued that the Trinity is best understood as the doxological conclusion of Christian liturgical praxis. To regard it as a starting point would tend to privilege the immanent trinity over the economic trinity. When the work of the triune God is considered, this begs many further questions: How can creation *and* salvation, Christ *and* the Spirit, the commission of the Spirit proceeding from the Father/Mother *and* Indigenous spiritualities be maintained in a creative tension?

Given such endless intra-Christian debates on the doctrine of the Trinity, is it not best, especially in the context of addressing climate change, to underplay this aspect of the Christian faith? At best, it may be regarded as an 'arcane discipline', to be treasured only by insiders. If not, how should the doctrine of the Trinity be expressed amidst a changing climate?

---

[2] For a helpful overview see Sallie McFague, 'Renaming the Triune God for a Time of Global Climate Change', in *Planetary Solidarity: Globa l Women's Voices on Christian Doctrine and Climate Justice*, Grace Ji-Sun Kim and Hilda P. Koster (eds) (Minneapolis: Fortress, 2017), 101–18.

[3] See Ernst M. Conradie and Teddy C. Sakupapa, '"Decolonising the Doctrine of the Trinity" or "The Decolonising Doctrine of the Trinity"'? *Journal of Theology for Southern Africa* 161 (2018), 37–53.

Chapter 5.1
The Spirit and climate change

Sigurd Bergmann[1]

Now the Spirit itself dwells among us, and supplies it with a clearer demonstration of it self.

— Gregory of Nazianz[2]

Clearly and aptly, Gregory of Nazianz summarized one of the central pillars of Christian faith in his homily. The Spirit has taken her/his dwelling among us.[3] The Creation now exists in the time of the Spirit. The Spirit reveals and creates liberating life.

The homily was probably held at the ecumenical council in Constantinople 381, where the consensus, still obligating today, characterizes the Spirit as 'the Giver of Life' (τὸ ζῳοποιόν), and the one who brings the 'life of the world to come' (ζωὴν τοῦ μέλλοντος αἰῶνος). Gregory claims that this now happens 'clearer' and that humans are able to become bodily aware of the Spirit in their life, on a local as well as on a cosmic scale. The ecumenical creed's formulation of faith in the Trinity and the Holy Spirit's central role herein synthesizes a long history of belief in the Spirit. With regard to the Hebrew Bible's emphasis on the Spirit's divinity and agency in the life-giving process of creation, and especially John's gospel and Paul's letters' emphasis on the Spirit's driving force in the history of salvation, it is hard to understand the marginal role of pneumatology in the history of Christian doctrine after the first ecumenical age. The art of pneumatology – reading and depicting the world through the lens and letters of faith in the Spirit – reposes as a hidden pearl with unimagined potential for constructive, contextual theology. Ambrose of Milan summarized this potential aptly:

Where the Spirit is, there is life; and where there is life, there, too, is the Holy Spirit.[4]

---

[1] Sigurd Bergmann is Professor emeritus in Religious Studies at the Norwegian University of Science and Technology in Trondheim and lives in Lund. Previous studies explored God and nature in late antiquity, contextual theology, Indigenous arts, architecture, and religion in climate change. He has initiated the European Forum for the Study of Religion and the Environment and serves as its secretary.

[2] Gregory of Nazianz, *Oratio* 31.26; See Sigurd Bergmann, *Creation Set Free: The Spirit as Liberator of Nature* (Grand Rapids: Eerdmans, 2005), 211.

[3] Literally εμπολιτευεται means 'becoming a citizen' and 'becoming local'.

[4] Ambrose 1983, book I, XV, 172, p. 113. Ambrose 1983, 'On the Holy Spirit'. In: *Some of the Principal Works of St. Ambrose*, translated by H. de Romestin, 93–158. Select Library of Nicene and Post-Nicene Fathers of the Christian Church, vol. 10. Grand Rapids.

What does it mean to believe in this Spirit as Giver of Life in a context where life itself is violated by anthropogenic climate change?

The Spirit dwelling in the homelessness of an unsustainable Anthropocene

Anthropogenic environmental change is, as science clearly states, at present turning into dangerous change, that is, an irreversible change of climatic and other conditions for life systems.[5] For vulnerable human ecologies such dangerous change implies substantial threats for survival, while it challenges wealthy nations to rebuild their infrastructure and change lifestyle extensively. Furthermore, dangerous environmental change increases economic, social and military conflicts in many regions of the planet, and it victimizes a large number of populations in economically weak and vulnerable zones. Species extinction is expected to increase rapidly, water scarcity will be exacerbated and ecological diversity reduced. In what we now call the Anthropocene,[6] that is, the whole biocene and universe impacted and transformed by human production and consumption patterns, in ways that destroy the conditions of life for humans and other species.

A well-known thesis claims that the intensification of pneumatology in the history of Christianity takes place in different kinds of crises, which it 'signals, interprets and tries to overcome productively'.[7] If the doctrine of the Spirit has been historically revitalized in times of social crisis, there is no doubt that the contemporary state of modernity mirrored in the lens of climatic change again offers such a critical threshold, an ecological *kairos*.

Questions like these are increasingly explored among theologians, although only few have yet recognized their spiritual depth.[8] Religious belief is always rooted in some belief of created, animated and sustained life, be it a God or other spiritual forces. Climate change appears in such a view as a second Copernican revolution, and climate science demands a new political theology critical to 'a hybrid of a human-centred

---

[5] See Colin N. Waters et al., 'The Anthropocene is Functionally and Stratigraphically Distinct from the Holocene', *Science* 351 (2016). DOI: 10.1126/science.aad2622.

[6] See Will Steffen, Jacques Grinevald, Paul Crutzen and John McNeill, 'The Anthropocene: Conceptual and Historical Perspectives', *Philosophical Transactions of the Royal Society* A 369:1938 (2011), 842–67.

[7] Wolf-Dieter Hauschild, 'Geist IV: Dogmengeschichtlich', *Theologische Realenzyklopädie* 12 (Berlin/New York: De Gruyter, 1984), 196–218 (196).

[8] See Anne Primavesi, *Gaia and Climate Change* (London: Routledge, 2008); Karen L. Bloomquist (ed.), *God, Creation, and Climate Change: Spiritual and Ethical Perspectives* (Geneva: Lutheran World Federation, 2009); Michael S. Northcott and Peter M. Scott (eds), *Systematic Theology and Climate Change: Ecumenical Perspectives* (London: Routledge, 2014).

cosmology and a Baconian, and post-Copernican, aspiration to technological control over the earth'.[9]

Reflection on what anthropogenic climate change does to our self-understanding as God's image in a good creation increases the existential alienation people experience in modern life, a widespread alienation and detachment which requires the acknowledgement 'of our existential need for a spiritual homecoming'.[10] Existential homelessness represents a crucial challenge, valid for the rich in the North, as well as for the many refugees and migrants in need of shelter and protected spaces to survive and rebuild in the South.

Late-modern homelessness has many faces, voices and places, and if the world is in a process of becoming, living in this world must also include the building and design of sheltered dwelling spaces for all, such that citizens have a home in heaven *and* on earth. Having a home in heaven then means being able to make oneself at home in God's flourishing creation which grows anew. How do we make ourselves at home on 'Earth, our home',[11] while we ourselves are spoiling it? How can we feel at home in the future? For Christians, continuing to believe in the Triune God as the good Creator and the Spirit as Giver of Life and Liberator of Nature,[12] such a discovery is radically painful and necessarily affects belief at the deepest level. How can the world be regarded as a good creation if God's own images, human beings, are destroying this world? Is God angry? Is climatic change with all its apocalyptic processes a God-given future which we plainly should accept? Should we interpret it as a heavenly sign that we are approaching the end times? Or is the promise sealed with the rainbow still valid, namely that this creation never again will be drowned and destroyed but renewed and successively turned into a liberated space, into 'a new heaven and a new earth' (Rev. 21.1, NIV)? To ask for faith in the Holy Spirit, who has taken dwelling 'among us' and 'became a citizen' in this world, appears in such a light as a central challenge to theology, and especially eschatology: Where does the Spirit take place, as Giver of new life and as driver for the new world to come? Can believers in the Spirit imagine, anticipate and move from an unsustainable Anthropocene towards a new creation, towards the Ecocene?

In the following I will explore two ways of developing Christian pneumatology in the so far depicted context. Firstly, I will depart from the approach of spatial eschatology and investigate how this also might become relevant for a pneumatology. Secondly, I will then sharpen the critical skill of faith in synergy with the Spirit by cultivating its

---

[9] Michael S. Northcott, *A Political Theology of Climate Change* (Grand Rapids: Eerdmans, 2013), 23.

[10] Juhani Pallasmaa, 'Existential Homelessness – Placelessness and Nostalgia in the Age of Mobility', in *Ethics of Mobilities: Rethinking Place, Exclusion, Freedom and Environment,* Sigurd Bergmann and Tore Sager (eds) (London: Routledge 2008), 143–56 (156).

[11] See http://earthcharter.org/discover/the-earth-charter (accessed 24 April 2013).

[12] See Bergmann, *Creation Set Free;* and 'The Legacy of Trinitarian Cosmology in the Anthropocene: Transcontextualising Late Antiquity Theology for Late Modernity', *Studia Theologica* 69:1 (2015), 32–44.

countervailing power in resistance against fetishizing money and technology. Finally, a sketch of what one might call an *ecocenic pneumatology* will be offered.[13]

Spatial eschatology of the Spirit's world to come

Continuing my earlier work on the Spirit as Liberator that sets creation free and about the spatiality of religion,[14] one should emphasize the liberating work of the Spirit within the dimension of space and place, motion and movement. The spatiality of the Spirit as all-embracing space would also then appear more clearly as the liberating movement in, for and within creation. The history of salvation as one common world history of all in need of liberation would then take place as interconnected and spatially mobile events of the life-giving Holy Spirit at work in the circular line that runs through many diverse places in creation. Earth and its many places would then – in accordance with biblical and traditional sources[15] – itself appear as an active partner in God's redemptive work.

Applying such a view to theology and climate change, theologians would need to put much more careful emphasis on the spatial dimension of Christian belief in the world to come. The rupture of the now and then would need to turn into an entanglement of the past and present for the sake of the future. The new creation dwells already in the original and continuing one. Time would need to turn into space.[16]

The inspiration for such an approach can come from Vítor Westhelle's extensive argument for reconstructing the lost dimension of space in eschatology.[17] Here we become aware of how spatiality from the position of those who lack both power and place appears as the most valuable tool to experience and interpret the presence of ongoing liberation that is still unseen. Michel de Certeau's distinction between 'strategy' and 'tactics' enables Westhelle to differentiate between strategy as 'maneuvering

---

[13] For a survey on pneumatology cf. Grace Ji-Sun Kim, *The Holy Spirit, Chi, and the Other: A Model of Global and Intercultural Pneumatology* (London: Palgrave Macmillan, 2011); F. LeRon Shults and Andrea Hollingsworth, *The Holy Spirit* (Grand Rapids: Eerdmans, 2008), Laurel Kearns and Catherine Keller (eds), *Ecospirit: Religions and Philosophies for the Earth* (New York: Fordham, 2007), George E. Tinker, *Spirit and Resistance: Political Theology and American Indian Liberation* (Minneapolis: Fortress, 2004), Mark Wallace, *Fragments of the Spirit* (London: T&T Clark, 2002) and Geiko Müller-Fahrenholz, *Gods' Spirit: Transforming a World in Crisis* (Geneva: WCC and New York: Continuum, 1995); cf. also the edition devoted to 'Ecumenical Discourse on Pneumatology and Ecology' of *The Journal of Reformed Theology* 6 (2012), 189–305.

[14] See Sigurd Bergmann, *Religion, Space and the Environment* (London: Transaction, 2014).

[15] See Elisabeth Moltmann-Wendel, 'Rückkehr zur Erde', *Evangelische Theologie* 53:5 (1993), 406–20.

[16] Sigurd Bergmann, 'Time Turned into Space – At Home on Earth: Wanderings in Eschatological Spatiality', in *Eschatology as Imagining the End: Faith between Hope and Despair*, Sigurd Bergmann (ed.) (London: Routledge, 2018), 88–112.

[17] Vítor Westhelle, *Eschatology and Space: The Lost Dimension in Theology Past and Present* (New York: Palgrave Macmillan, 2012).

technique to conquer the place of the other', while tactic works in the space of the other, taking place as the art of the weak. In the former we possess space; in the latter we are determined by the spaces that inhabit us as dispossessed.[18]

Applying such a distinction one can ask also if the producers of climatic change, that is the fossil-fuel-driven power constellations, are following a strategy of conquering the place of the other. Global space and many local spaces around the world are then transformed by the rich into *possessed space*. Climate change reveals how rich industrialized nations, as well as large 'developing' nations, possess space in order to continue their unsustainable modes of existing. Tactics, by contrast, take place as the art of the weak and dispossessed who need to survive in spaces that become increasingly uninhabitable. How then is the Triune Spirit as Giver of Life at work in these possessed spaces?

Another interesting analogy appears between eschatology and climate change if focusing on the long evolutionary time span of fossil resources. Following Westhelle we can aptly criticize reductionist time-centred eschatologies as representing strategies to conquer, expand and administer space. Eschatology as imagining the end only through the lens of linear time represents a deeply problematic way of mastering eschatology. Similarly, the distribution and usage of fossil-fuel-based energy systems represent a mastering reductionist strategy where time is simply regarded as a production factor that has allowed the accumulation of oil and gas deposits. These are brutally exploited and exhausted as so-called resources and they are priced for a world market totally without cognizance of the long scale bio-history that has made their emergence possible.[19] Fossil-fuel energy systems transform the gift of creation for all creatures into private and national commodities and enrich some with the help of fetishized money and technology.

What does it mean to believe in the Spirit as a Giver of Life in such a context? According to the biblical and patristic sources, the Spirit is not only blowing wherever he or she wants but also freely moving forth and back between the time forms. Past, future and presence are not, as for God's creatures, separated but rather open for each other and entangled in the Spirit's work. Reducing the Spirit's striving for 'the new time to come' simply to a linear timeline from the past to the future appears in such a view as questionable as approaching fossil deposits not as created gifts but as dead commodities for exploitation. A 'petro-eschatology' that, in Marion Grau's words, is 'mapping the end and ends of fossil dependency and possible ways through it'[20] might be able to produce efficient antidotes to fossil-fuel idolatry. Such an idolatry appears in this sense

---

[18] Ibid., 120. See also Sigurd Bergmann, 'Places of Encounter with the Eschata: Accelerating the Spatial Turn in Eschatology', in *Embracing the Ivory Tower and Stained Glass Windows: A Festschrift in Honor of Archbishop Antje Jackelén*, Jennifer Baldwin (ed.) (Heidelberg: Springer, 2015), 71–9.

[19] See Andreas Malm and Alf Hornborg, 'The Geology of Mankind? A Critique of the Anthropocene Narrative', *The Anthropocene Review* 1:1 (2014), 62–9.

[20] Marion Grau, 'The Revelations of Global Climate Change: A Petro-eschatology', in *Eschatology as Imagining the End: Faith between Hope and Despair*, Sigurd Bergmann (ed.) (London: Routledge, 2018), 45–60.

as a contradiction to belief in the Spirit, depicted by Hildegard of Bingen as *viriditas*, that is 'greening power' as 'the power of life, the dynamic energy nourishing the entire creation',[21] characterized in Paul's political ethics as freedom,[22] and in Gregory's Trinitarian cosmology as truth, as the power of consummating creation, as spring of the world, permeating all things and filling the world .[23]

In contrast to reductionist time-centred eschatology, Westhelle suggests 'latitudinal' thinking[24] and a 'choratic' eschatology where the understanding of 'choratic realms' makes it possible for those who have not much room to negotiate space to experience the eschaton.[25] 'Chora' denotes 'a space in between spaces, a place that is neither in nor out, a place that is between and betwixt. They are spaces of estrangement and intimacy; spaces of danger and possibilities, spaces of transition and therefore spaces of trial.'[26] Those who are suffering at non-places and have no history can here and now encounter the last things, the *eschata*.

In my view such a *choratic* eschatology also fits perfectly into the understanding of the Spirit as the Liberator of Nature, in a classical sense as well as in the frame of an ecological theology of liberation. The Spirit is then at work as the inner driving force of such a *choratic* process. In the context of climate change he or she takes place in the spaces between the spaces. Here he or she acts in synergy with those who are suffering at non-places and trying to survive in the dispossessed spaces caused by climate change.

The new world to come, as promised and depicted in the Creed, emerges in the midst of *choratic* realms where the experience of having no room to survive turns into hope and empowerment and moves towards a new creation. Hope and belief in and synergy with the Spirit create visions and practices for the new world to come. The spaces where climate change dispossess the poor turn into places shaped by a new heaven and earth. The Anthropocene turns into an Ecocene.

I here 'only' depict a vision, but I hope that the reader can grasp the enriching power of such a vision and narrative where spatial eschatology and pneumatology are embracing. Important here is to keep alive the perspective from below. In an unjust and unsustainable world it is necessary to cultivate one's 'ditch perspective',[27] that is, the lens from the underside of place and history. In the discourse about climate change this

---

[21] See Mary C. Grey, 'Creation and Salvation: Female Medieval Mystics', in *Creation and Salvation: A Mosaic of Essays on Selected Classic Christian Theologians*, Ernst M. Conradie (ed.) (Berlin: LIT, 2011), 82–99 (86).

[22] See 2 Cor. 3.17: 'Now the Lord is the Spirit, and where the Spirit of the Lord is, there is freedom' (NIV).

[23] See Bergmann, *Creation Set Free*, 103, 114, 160, 166.

[24] Westhelle, *Eschatology and Space*, 71–3.

[25] Ibid., 121.

[26] Mary Philip, 'Remembrance: A Living Bridge', in *Churrasco: A Theological Feast in Honor of Vítor Westhelle,* Mary Philip, John Nuenes and Charles M. Collier (eds) (Eugene: Pickwick, 2013), 94–104 (99).

[27] Antje Jackelén coined the Swedish term 'dikesperspektivet' (perspective from the roadside ditch) in her preaching on the Good Samaritan in Lk. 10. 25-37, http://www.svenskatal.se/20140930-antje-jackelen-predikan-vid-riksmotets-oppnande-2014/ (accessed 6 March 2015).

means that those who are existentially concerned and victimized have to be given the priority over the producers and profiteers of climatic change. The often-acknowledged option for the poor is highly relevant also as an ecological and climate-political demand.

The Spirit's countervailing power against money and machine fetishizing

Elaborating an ecological pneumatology in the frame of a *choratic* eschatology thus demands an option for the poor (in nature as well as in society) and this in turn demands a social analysis of the processes of impoverishment. Even if several instruments have proven successful in the fight against global poverty, the problem still exists and sharpens 'amid ecological destruction'.[28] Also climatic change, with all its facets of catalysing security conflicts, water scarcity, desertification, species extinction and more, functions as a driver of impoverishment of an increasing number of populations, in ecosystems as well as in human societies. In an unholy alliance with the injustice of a global finance system the impacts of ongoing climate change are even more intensified in threatening life.

The religiously loaded process of the fetishizing of money and technology appears as one of the central elements in this unholy, unsustainable and unjust world system. Faith in synergy with the Spirit therefore needs to unfold by cultivating its countervailing power in resistance against this force of fetishizing. It needs to reconstruct its history in a broader exchange with premodern animism, and maintain a creative dialogue with environmental neo-animism.

Modern technology is embedded in a cultural system of innovation for exchange processes, which are steered by economical driving forces. Monetary exchange systems operate through a commodification of things which are treated as lifeless objects on the one side and an adoration of money as the highest object with an intrinsic value on the other. While traditional animism departs from the gift of animated life in a larger relational system of interconnections between (personal) things and humans, fetishism moves the skill to animate to the human. Biblical pneumatology follows such a code as well; it is God's Holy Spirit who blows life into the creatures. Contemporary environmentalism strives for a neo-animistic revitalization of this code by developing beliefs about an inspired nature,[29] albeit without an assumption of one sole Spirit.

Fetishism makes it possible to decontextualize and delocalize objects, natural objects as well as artefacts, and to reconnect them anew across local and historical borders. Oil,

---

[28] See Ernst M. Conradie, *Redeeming Sin? Social Diagnostics amid Ecological Destruction* (Lanham: Lexington, 2017).

[29] See Graham Harvey, 'Animism – A Contemporary Perspective', in *Encyclopedia of Religion and Nature, Vol. 1*, Bron Taylor (ed.) (New York: Continuum, 2005), 81–3.

for example, grown from the earth's long history is turned into a commodity. Chinese landowners transfer profits and products from African lands cultivated by vulnerable local farmers to other parts of the world. Car companies hide and unravel the 'costs' of health and environmental damages caused by their products' emissions.

Modernity builds, as Karl Marx has shown clearly, on the commodified relations between humans and things, including the alienating split of human workers and the products of their labour. According to Marx, the shift from the perception of the 'physical relation between physical things' to fetishizing has its roots in the accelerating trading system, which in our age has been transferred to the global scale. For Marx, fetishism was 'the religion of sensuous appetites',[30] one more reason to regard it as highly relevant for critical theology.

The process of commodification and alienation of the relations between humans and things becomes understandable as a process of fetishizing. The superior fetish object in this process is money. Technology plays a central role herein and machine fetishism dispossesses in such a view the machines of their potential meaning of cooperating with humans and nature. Machines alienate humans from their labour and nature. Reification, alienation and machine fetishism characterize the central function of modern capitalism.

Undoubtedly, we need to unmask the capacity of technology to obscure global inequalities. According to Alf Hornborg, modern technological objects are basically inanimate things attributed with autonomous productivity or even agency, obscuring their own foundation in asymmetric global relations of exchange.[31] Global differences in the prices for labour and resources are part of a globally unjust asymmetry, where trade and economic exchange and the technological transfer of work and material into products to be traded represent a central driving force. So-called economic growth assisted by technological development must therefore in itself be unmasked as a part of the unjust resource flows and global power relations.

Money is not simply an artefact but presents in itself, following Marx, as 'the commodity par excellence'[32] and the 'common whore'[33] with a remarkable potential to impact on the production of life and to accelerate the asymmetry between poor and rich. As Ulrich Duchrow has shown, religions of different confessions resisted this production of inequality between humans and groups sometimes efficiently, but as capitalism develops into an at present global turbo capitalism, Marx's view of money as the steering superior fetish becomes true in a nearly uncanny way. Most likely the cultural shift of the so-called axial age also provoked the search for new answers in the Jewish, Christian, Greek, Islam and Buddhist faiths. Most likely one should understand

---

[30] Karl Marx and Friedrich Engels, *On Religion* (Atlanta: Scholars Press, 1982), 22.

[31] Alf Hornborg, 'Technology as Fetish: Marx, Latour, and the Cultural Foundations of Capitalism', *Theory Culture Society* 31:4 (2014), 119–40 (121).

[32] Adrian Johnston, 'The Cynic's Fetish: Slavoj Žižek and the Dynamics of Belief', *International Journal of Žižek Studies* 1 (2007), 65–111 (75).

[33] Marx quotes Shakespeare in *Economic and Philosophic Manuscripts of 1844,* https://www.marxists.org/archive/marx/works/1844/manuscripts/power.htm (accessed 19 February 2018).

the spiritual, religious and juridical innovations of the axial age as responses to the dangerous social developments where the money- and property-based economy was introduced.[34]

In such a long historical continuity money works as the dominant fetish which reifies our social relations, our relation to nature, our reproduction of daily life and our concepts of what (human) life is about. The old, wise personification of this power in the figure of Mammon serves as an intriguing visualization of a force with incredible skill to obscure its own efficiency over our life. Christ's clear unmasking statement that belief in money is repugnant to belief in God the Creator seems self-evident in this context.[35] Incredibly, faith communities have seldom reimagined their own mission in the light of this. Criticism of fetishized financial and machine systems therefore needs to move up to the spiritual and ethical agenda for religions of all kinds.

According to Hornborg, the money artefact, the root of all evil, must be 'redesigned so as to insulate local survival from the ravages of global capital flows'.[36] Nature nevertheless has no use for money. Following Hornborg and others, the most central option for post-capitalism is *degrowth*. This requires that we fundamentally transform our idea of money.

Globalization should therefore not be glorified as free trade but unmasked as global injustice, neocolonialism and unequal exchange, and growth is not a gift as in biology but rather an accumulation of limited goods for the disadvantage of some and the suffering of others. Technological so-called progress presupposes machine fetishism in a way that damages and destroys relations between the living.

It should be obvious why the analysis of modern capitalism and its fetishizing of technology and money represent a deep challenge to religious faith and especially to faith in the Holy Spirit as Giver of Life. Environmentalism tries to respond to this challenge by some kind of new animism. I will not discuss the political potential of such neo-animism in all its power and ambiguity here but rather focus on the challenge to pneumatology.

While fetishizing is a human process that transforms an unanimated being into an animated one, which is attributed with power over others in a larger cultural system, classical faith in the Holy Spirit is not situated in a *man*-made environment but in a world characterized by God-givenness. While a fetish receives its 'life' through the action of the human, the all-embracing Spirit breathes life. Fetishism and faith in the Spirit, following the older paths of animism, perform along contradictory codes. While

---

[34] Ulrich Duchrow and Franz Hinkelammert, *Transcending Greedy Money: Interreligious Solidarity for Just Relations* (New York: Palgrave Macmillan, 2012), 47.

[35] See Mt. 6.24: 'No one can serve two masters. Either you will hate the one and love the other, or you will be devoted to the one and despise the other. You cannot serve both God and money [mammon]' (NIV).

[36] Alf Hornborg, 'Post-capitalist Ecologies: Energy, "Value" and Fetishism in the Anthropocene', *Capitalism Nature Socialism* 27:4 (2016), 61–76.

the fetish is enchanted by humans, the created life is breathed by the Holy. When he or she sends her 'life-giving breath, they are created' (Ps. 104.30, NIV).

While the fetish works as an instrument for the power of the one over the other, the life-giving Spirit embraces all in one common world and history and nevertheless respects the face of every individual identity. While fetishism turns the given nature into a lifeless world, traditional animism and Christian pneumatology perceive the intrinsic value of all beings in their specific environments. While fetishism aggravates spatial and environmental injustices, faith in the Holy Spirit reveals the perfect, just and true community of the Trinity and opens a path to walk towards the (not yet seen) 'land that I will show you' (Gen. 12.1 NIV). The doctrine of the Spirit can in such a context be revisited and reconstructed as an animistic eco-pneumatology.[37]

Anthropogenic climatic change represents in such an analytical horizon nothing more than the outermost consequence of fetishizing as a cardinal human sin: the disenchantment of sacred earth and life as a gift of the Spirit and the unjust fragmentation of its life forms and artefacts into tools for power *over* each other. This conclusion necessarily moves to the demand to overcome the Anthropocene as 'capitalocene', and to unmask the unjust and unsustainable fetishizing of money and machines by the countervailing power of the vision of the Holy Spirit giving life and birth to a creation beyond this one that is 'groaning as in the pains of childbirth' (Rom. 8.22, NIV). The Triune's Spirit gives life and makes the new world to come as an Ecocene beyond the age of the humans.

The Spirit's new world to come – towards an *ecocenic* Pneumatology

Christian pneumatology, fertilized through its classical roots, has an enormous potential to contribute to the emergence of an animistic driving force that can resist and overcome the dominant world system of fetishizing. Faith in the Holy Spirit as the life-giving breath of the world to come allows the perception of our environment as a space populated by a manifold of created spiritual beings, a perception that is open for its own transformation towards a new creation. If the Holy Spirit reveals the face of the Triune Creator on Earth, She also performs in synergy with us as the one who brings the new world to come. As a liberating movement He takes place today in the struggle against fetishist idolatry at

---

[37] Sigurd Bergmann, 'Fetishism Revisited: In the Animistic Lens of Eco-Pneumatology', *Journal of Reformed Theology* 6 (2012), 195–215; also 'Millions of Machines are already Roaring' – Fetishized Technology Encountered by the Life-giving Spirit', in *Technofutures, Nature and the Sacred: Transdisciplinary Perspectives*, Celia E. Deane-Drummond, Sigurd Bergmann and Bronislaw Szerszynski (eds) (London: Routledge, 2015), 115–37.

those places on the planet where creatures groan and suffer from environmental and spatial injustice fuelled by the sin of modern fetishism.

The discourse on the Ecocene depicts a vision where human and other life forms cohabitate on Earth in fully just and peaceful entanglements. We might also partly understand it as a 'post-technocene' where the fetishizing of money and machines has been overcome and technical spaces have turned into lived spaces.[38]

In my view, the notion of Ecocene offers the most constructive term for a synthetic vision of an open and shared future. While terms like 'capitalocene' or 'post-technocene' operate with a limited focus, the notion of Ecocene can include entangled dimensions and envision 'an epoch in which not one single species determines the future of the Earth but the collective wisdom and interactions of all species and the bio- and geophysical world'.[39]

The term emerged recently, not so much in science but in other spheres such as architecture, design theory and also theology. It aims at a geological period beyond the Anthropocene, or rather a slow transformation from the one into the other, where the whole of the ecological sphere embraces and integrates the human. Design theorist Rachel Armstrong states, 'there is no advantage to us to bring the Anthropocene into the future … The myth of the Anthropocene does not help us … we must re-imagine our world and enable the Eocene.'[40]

While the contemporary discussion about the Anthropocene in my view suffers from a fatal lack of historical consciousness and a lack of including the future, the challenge in contrast is to imagine and negotiate the shared future,[41] a just and sustainable future that can be shared equally by all creatures. Probably it is this lack of a qualified reflection about potential sustainable and unsustainable futures that accelerates the triumphalist danger to celebrate this new period as a new period of human geo-management in spite of an accelerating dangerous climate change and increasing global warming.

While apocalyptic thinking imagines the end as a future of chaos and disaster, and manipulates and terrifies the contemporaries, eschatology operates with an integrated present and future dimension. It is not simply the interconnection of the Now and Then

---

[38] For the notion of 'technocene' see Alf Hornborg, 'The Political Ecology of the Technoscene: Uncovering Ecologically Unequal Exchange in the World-system', in *The Anthropocene and the Global Environmental Crisis: Rethinking Modernity in a New Epoch,* Clive Hamilton, Christopher Bonneuil, and Françoise Gemene (eds) (London: Routledge, 2015), 57–69.

[39] Arjen E. J. Wals, Joseph Paul Weakland and Peter Blaze Corcoran, 'Preparing for the Ecocene: Envisioning Futures for Environmental and Sustainability Education', *Japanese Journal of Environmental Education* 26:4 (2017), 71–6 (72).

[40] Rachel Armstrong, 'Architecture for the Ecocene', 31 July 2015, https://architectureukraine.org/rachel-armstrong-architecture-for-the-ecocene/ (accessed 20 November 2017). See also Joanne Boehnert, *Design, Ecology, Politics: Towards the Ecocene* (London: Bloomsbury, 2018).

[41] On the significance of 'shared future' in the context of *Beheimatung,* see John Rodwell and Peter M. Scott, 'Dialogues of Place and Belonging', in *At Home in the Future: Place & Belonging in a Changing Europe,* John Rodwell and Peter M. Scott (eds) (Berlin: LIT, 2016), 1–11 (9).

but develops as a spatial theory. The place of the encounter with the God of the Here and There and the God of the Now and Then transforms the places in the need of liberation. Climatic change represents such a place as it makes it necessary to encounter with the Life-giving Triune Spirit that takes place both now and then, and both here and there. Faith needs to be reconstructed, faith in in the Spirit breezing about the vibrating chaos waters in the beginning and the Spirit as the Giver of Life and as the source of the new creation to come.

In my view such a vision of the Ecocene fits perfectly with the biblical vision of a *creatio continua* that flows into a *creatio futura*. Biblical imaginaries for such an Ecocene are many, the heavenly Jerusalem as a truly eco-urban life sphere, peaceful pastoral gazing of wild and other animals in the meadows, the pastoral vision of God as good shepherd and the people and creatures as a herd, or the thanksgiving ritual after the flood and climate change disasters when the warrior's sign of the rainbow turns into a sign of peace between all created beings. Needless to say that such a vision does not allow for any anthropocentric understanding of the human as a simple "handmaid" (or superior steward) of the Creator Lord but as a co-creature in the web of Life. While scientists can circumscribe the 'Ecocene' quite soberly as the age where only some species and ecosystems have survived the Anthropocene, the environmental humanities including ecotheology might offer a broader understanding: the Ecocene partly as something that already takes place within the Anthropocene which it overcomes, and partly as new age that will finally supersede the imperial Anthropocene. Analogous to the mustard seed (Mk. 4.30-32), the Ecocene unfolds as a spatial process of the here and now for the sake of the there and then, for instance in composting, bioregional farming, eco-restoration or lived environmental and spatial justice.

Shortly, it is the vision of an age of nature beyond the age of the humans, accelerated by climate change that allows a transformation into another age where humans are no longer the masters of creation but subjects of the Creation, no longer herders but sheep in a flock, no longer alleged givers but true receivers of life from, with and in the Holy Spirit. The earth would then turn into a new inspired creation as an Ecocene and true home where the Life-giving Spirit is consummately taking place.

An African eco-woman's response to Sigurd Bergmann

Fulata L. Moyo[1]

God's Spirit brooding over the deep to facilitate interconnectedness, produce, protect, sustain and renew life. Brooding over Sigurd Bergmann's discourse on the Spirit and climate change is the question of how the intensification of pneumatology in the story of Christianity can signal, interpret and try to overcome the climate change crisis. Since the Spirit who is revealed to us as creator of life dwells among us, how can anthropogenic climate change still be a reality of the Anthropocene? What kind of self-understanding as God's image in a good creation does anthropogenic climate change unveil for us?

If the existential alienation and detachment that people experience is symptomatic of the marginal role of pneumatology in the life and story of the church, then the reality of anthropogenic climate change also provides evidence of a dysfunctional anthropocentric relationship of humans to the rest of creation – a relationship that is shaped by greed and selfishness based on the love of money and technological advances. For if the significance of the Holy Spirit would have been fully recognized, creation's interrelationships, human beings' respect of, care and protection for the environment would be an intrinsic expression of responsive love and compassion. Such love would be rooted in an understanding of creation as interconnected and interdependent. For 'Where the Spirit is, there is life; and where there is life, there, too, is the Holy Spirit'[2] – the life giver and driving force in the story of salvation.

Facing the living truth of social-economic disparities, maximizing the role of pneumatology also would mean that human beings commit to a preferential option for the poor – reflection and praxis against poverty – and to poverty, and the global disparity between the rich and the poor, as an injustice that begs to be resisted. The dichotomy of the 'rich industrialized nations, as well as so called large 'developing' nations, possess(ing) space in order to continue their unsustainable modes of existing', as Bergmann puts it, and the tactical art of survival by the exploited and dispossessed within spaces that are becoming increasingly uninhabitable falls short of the human

---

[1] Fulata L. Moyo is an eco-woman(ist) who interrogates religious resources for gender and eco-justice. She holds a PhD in Human Sciences with a focus in Gender and Sexual Ethics. She is a consultant in Trauma Transformation and Healing at the World Council of Churches.

[2] Ambrose 'On the Holy Spirit', Book I, XV, in *Some of the Principal Works of St. Ambrose, Select Library of Nicene and Post-Nicene Fathers of the Christian Church*, Volume 10, translated by H. de Romestin (Grand Rapids, 1983), 93–158 (113).

assumed knowledge of God's call as expressed by the prophet Micah: 'to do justice, and love kindness, and to walk humbly with (our) God!' (Micah 6.8b, NRSV). Bergmann therefore states that 'For vulnerable human ecologies such dangerous change implies substantial threats for survival, while it challenges wealthy nations to rebuild their infrastructures and change life style extensively.'

While this is not the common lived reality in the Anthropocene, Bergmann's vision of ecocenic pneumatology captures what I would call a 'prophetic' reimagining of a renewed Earth, that is more holistic as an 'open and shared future' governed by collective wisdom and the interaction of all species. Having said this, however, envisioning a post-Anthropocene/Capitalocene and post-Technocene still embodies our current anthropogenic reality with humanity dominating and determining the future of the Earth inspired by the fetishism of unshared power, money and technology. How does the convincing power of the Holy Spirit intervene to bring a transformation from fetishism to a more liberating, just coexistence where each species lives to its highest potential as created, sustained and guided by God?

This response takes an eco-African woman's perspective that is articulated within a postcolonial context that acknowledges gender and race as social markers that influence even one's social location whether in the rich and developing countries or in the so-called poor and exploited ones. First, I situate my African contextual conception of God as Completeness and the Great One. Second, I will critique the stewardship model of inter-creation relating, thus opting for the kinship model. This will also include a criticism of Bergmann's placing of the Holy Spirit's role within creation theology rather than within incarnational theology. As an African black woman, whose experience is often made invisible in the world that is still tarnished by gender injustice and racism, I argue for a focus on Mary's role in incarnation theology – acknowledging the importance of motherhood in both incarnation and ecological justice.

I argue that stewardship as an ecological response is still anthropocentric – with a hierarchical assumption that elevates humanity as the decider on a response to climate change. Locating the pneumatological response to climate change within creation theology still runs the danger of endorsing a stewardship model as the divinely mandated response to care for the earth.

My unsubstantiated thoughts about the African Christian conceptions of God[3] are based on common African discourse, most of it still transmitted orally. The Holy Spirit, *Mzimu Woyera* in Malawian Chichewa, can be conceived as a feminine divine power empowering creation's interconnected and interdependent reality of life. The *Umoya*

---

[3] Charles Nyamiti, John Mbiti, Josephus C. Chakanza and others have written on different aspects of the African conception of God, including reflections on Christ as an African ancestor (Nyamiti) and the Chewa concepts of God (Chakanza, Amanze). African Christianity has embraced a Trinitarian theology, yet it is mainly the articulation of the wholeness/completeness and greatness of God that is commonly articulated in African Christianity. There is an affirmation of the completeness and greatness of the self-existing God but not much on how the three-in-one relate. See J. Chaphadzika Chakanza, 'Some Chewa Concepts of God', *Religion in Malawi* 1:1 (1987), 4–8 (7).

Ongcwele[4] is the breath (life giver) of the church, the internal witness of God's revelation, the Ancestor that facilitates the daily communion between *Unkulunkulu*[5] as the great and wholly One (supreme Being) and God's creation – the divine interconnectedness with creation and 'intercreation interconnectedness'.[6]

The ecological ethical conceptions captured by ecofeminist and/or/ ecowomanist. theologians echo the deep Indigenous knowledge and wisdom that have existed orally and ritualistically for many generations. The Indigenous holistic perceptions of creation's embeddedness in their communitarianism embody the relational ethos that contextually articulate Micah's prophetic utterance referred to earlier. Would it be considered as an oversimplified analysis to argue that this Indigenous percipience, if taken seriously over the years, would have contributed to Bergmann's envisioned Ecocene as a lived reality?

In exploring Christian ecofeminism as kenotic ecology, Priscilla Eppinger[7] would argue against Sigurd Bergmann's locating the transforming role of the Holy Spirit within creation theology. Eppinger argues that incarnation theology, rather than creation theology, offers us an appropriate ecological relationship between humanity and the environment: a relationship rooted in a call to justice against anthropogenic climate change. As I suggested elsewhere,

> Seeing Christianity's entanglement with global capitalism, Eppinger critiques Christianity's embrace of the stewardship model, in which God relates to creation as an owner in a hierarchical, top-down manner. As stewards, human beings derive their mandate to care for the eco-community from God's hierarchical-patriarchal ownership. In this view, nonhuman nature is merely the recipient of care … To be a steward is to be a manager. While you can be a good or bad manager, stewards by definition retain power and authority over the resources entrusted to them. This … together with the creation theology in which it is rooted, has not been effective model for ecological justice and is in dire need of change.[8]

While, I agree with Bergmann that theologically the working of the Holy Spirit, and hence pneumatology, is important in envisioning the Ecocene, I do agree with Eppinger

---

[4] In Malawian Ngoni, *umoya* is a noun that can mean breath, soul, wind, air or spirit.

[5] In the Ngoni conception of God, the commonly used name is *Unkulunkulu* (the great Great One) followed by *Usomandla* (the all-powerful One), and *Usimakade* (the One who has always been there). *Umdali* (the Creator) is used less often. Yet when it comes to the Holy Spirit, it's the life-giving, creative, sustaining and renewing powers that are conceived holistically.

[6] Fulata Moyo, 'Holy Spirit in African Christianity', *The Cambridge Dictionary of Christianity*, Daniel Patte (ed.) (New York: Cambridge University Press, 2010), 556–7 (557).

[7] Priscilla Eppinger, 'Christian Ecofeminism as Kenotic Ecology: Transforming Relationships away from Environmental Stewardship', in 'Transforming Feminisms: Religion, Women, and Ecology', *Journal for the Study of Religion* 24:2 (2011), 47–63.

[8] Fulata Lusungu Moyo, '"Ukugqiba inkaba" – Burying the Umbilical Cord: An African Indigenous Ecofeminist Perspective on Incarnation', in *Planetary Solidarity: Global Women's Voices on Christian Doctrine and Climate Justice*, Grace Ji-Sun Kim and Hilda P. Koster (eds) (Minneapolis: Fortress, 2017), 177–90 (188).

that this vision can only be realized within the kinship relationship of creation's interconnectedness and interdependence, which is precluded by the theological imagery of stewardship. In her own exploration of kenotic incarnation theology, however, Eppinger focuses on Jesus's self-emptying (kenosis) without mentioning the importance of the role of Mary. Like Eboni Marshall Turman,[9] a womanist theologian, I argue in favour of an incarnational theology that does recognize the crucial role of Mary, the Holy Mother, in the process of God becoming human. Lifting up the role of Mary is significant especially today: it is a vehicle for making visible the life-saving resilience of poor, grass-root women who are faced with the catastrophic effects of anthropogenic climate change, yet are often made invisible by those in power.

If Bergmann's pneumatologically articulated vision of the Ecocene would have been located in incarnation theology and a relational model of kinship, it would allow for an ecowomanist envisioning of ecological justice. The incarnational focus on the role of the motherhood of Mary would also help make visible the existing disparities within communities that are categorized by certain social markers beyond the social-economic classifications of either rich or poor countries. This focus would further affirm the human agency and contribution of every person in each communal response to climate change. And, finally, this kind of acknowledgement would contribute to challenging and, ultimately, transforming the fetishism of money and technology.

---

[9] Eboni Marshall Turman uses the Greek term *homoousios*, which defines the being of Christ as a God-human-being as of same (*homo*) essence (*ousia*) with God to express Christian women's relationship with Christ – as being of the same essence. As an African American woman, her affirmation of female bodies aims at confronting the reality that often bodies, especially those that defy normativity, pose a theological problem. This theological affirmation is equally relevant in confronting anthropogenic climate change that often accumulate privileges for certain preferred bodies and exploit those considered expendable, especially women of colour. See Eboni Marshall Turman, 'Black and Blue: Uncovering the Ecclesial Cover-Up of Black Women's Bodies through Womanist Reimagining of the Doctrine of Incarnation', in *Reimagining with Christian Doctrines: Responding to Global Injustice*, Grace Ji-Sun Kim and Jenny Daggers (eds) (New York: Palgrave Macmillan, 2014), 71–89.

Chapter 5.2
Jesus the Christ and climate change

Sallie McFague[1]

Introduction

I believe there is a basic story that subconsciously or unconsciously dictates many of our actions, including those on climate change. The Western story, anchored by a monarchical, all-powerful, static God, is no longer functioning to give meaning to people's lives, nor to motivate their behaviour. We Western Christian folks have had a story of a supernatural God telling us how to behave and when we fail, he pays the price for our sins so we can have eternal life in heaven. However, this religious story is no longer credible in contemporary culture. But this does not mean that all stories are useless. For instance, when folks say that they no longer 'believe in God', it may mean, not that they don't believe in any God, but that the standard Western, supernatural picture of God as the all-powerful creator and controller of earthly life no longer works for them. It doesn't necessarily mean that no interpretation would work for them.

One of the tasks that theologians have is to suggest to people alternative interpretations of the God–world relationship. In this essay I am suggesting that the phenomenon of climate change, which is destabilizing all our hopes and plans for human and planetary well-being, needs a different story from the standard monarchical one. It needs one that is less individualistic and anthropocentric – one that is more social, relational and immanental than the monarchical one. It needs a story more in line with the secular, evolutionary story, for then the religious and the secular stories are mutually reciprocal and supportive.

The story of Jesus

A powerful candidate is one that begins with the story of Jesus, particularly the story that underscores the self-sacrificial or kenotic character of all Jesus's words and actions.

---

[1] Sallie McFague is Distinguished Theologian in Residence at the Vancouver School of Theology in Vancouver, Canada. For thirty years she taught at the Vanderbilt University Divinity School in Nashville, where she was the Carpenter Professor of Theology and for five years served as Dean of the School.

Such an interpretation is summed up in Philippians 2.5-8: 'Let the same mind be in you that was in Christ Jesus, who, though he was in the form of God, did not regard equality with God as something to be exploited, but emptied himself, taking the form of a slave, being born in human likeness, And being found in human form, he humbled himself and became obedient to the point of death – even death on a cross' (NRSV). Here we see an inversion of the power in the monarchical model in preference for a kenotic, sacrificial model, 'a joyous, kind and loving attitude that is willing to give up selfish desires and make sacrifices on behalf of others for the common good and the glory of God'.[2] This is both a salvation and a discipleship model – that is, it speaks to how God 'saves' the world and it tells us how we should act in the world. In this model, Jesus does not 'do it all', that is, suffer on the cross as a substitute for us, paying a price for our sins. Rather, it suggests that our salvation is patterned on Jesus's life and action: we join Jesus in living lives of sacrificial love for others, and as such, attain deification, that is, become like God. Made in the image of God, we become fully who we are, fully human, by participating in God's own life and love. Moreover, as some suggest (and I am among them), 'kenosis is not only an explanation of Jesus' real humanity, but it is also the pattern of all reality.'[3] The range of kenosis is understood here to be both broad and deep.

The story of evolution

For instance, we see our religious and secular lives coming together: the same proto-altruistic actions that we see in evolution reach an epitome in the Christian understanding of the Trinity. Kenosis as 'the pattern of all reality', from evolution to the Trinity, is a big assertion. How is this so? Holmes Rolston III refutes Richard Dawkins's assertion of the survival of the 'selfish gene', insisting instead that in evolution 'the survival of the fittest turns out to be the survival of the sharers'.[4] He asserts this position because in evolution 'fitness means dying to self for newness of life in a generation to come',[5] thus suggesting an unconscious kenosis at the most basic biological level. Rolston writes, 'the picture coming more and more into focus has a great deal of one kind of thing being sacrificed for the good of another. The lives of individuals are discharged into, flow into, "emptied into" these larger currents of life.'[6]

---

[2] George F. R. Ellis, 'Kenosis as a Unifying Theme for Life and Cosmology', in *The Work of Love: Creation as Kenosis*, John Polkinghorne (ed.) (Grand Rapids: Eerdmans, 2001), 107–26 (108).

[3] Lucien J. Richard, *A Kenotic Christology: In the Humanity of Jesus the Christ, The Compassion of God* (Lanham: University Press of America, 1982), 170.

[4] Holmes Rolston III, 'Kenosis and Nature', in *The Work of Love*, John Polkinghorne (ed.) (Grand Rapids: Eerdmans, 2001), 43–65 (49).

[5] Ibid., 50.

[6] Ibid., 56.

In fact, the process of evolution is nothing but this complex and continuous process of competition and interdependence. There is nothing mysterious about this process: all that is being claimed is that the upper levels of evolution depend on the lower levels in order for the complex, diverse world we actually have to exist. 'If the higher forms had to synthesize all the life materials from abiotic materials (also degrading their own wastes), they could never have advanced very far. The upper levels are freed for more advanced synthesis because they depend on syntheses (and decompositions) carried out by lesser organisms below.'[7] And this process is precisely the one of death for the purpose of new (and more complex, diverse) life that we see everywhere about us. It is the process of life preying on life, since advanced life requires food pyramids, eating and being eaten. Thus, while there is no kenosis in nature, there is limitation, struggle, sacrifice and death everywhere: it is the heart of the process. Take Rolston's comment on plants, for example: 'Seen in this more comprehensive scheme of things, plants function for the survival of myriads of others. We could say, provocatively, for our "kenosis" inquiry, that they are "emptied into", given over to, "devoted" to, or "sacrificed" for these others in their community.'[8] But of course it is not just a one-way scheme: the plants also 'benefit'. 'Plants become insects, which become chicks, which become foxes, which die to fertilize plants.'[9] We must keep in mind, however, that none of this is conscious, but is simply the way the system works: it works in a self-interested fashion but within a system of interdependencies that demands 'sharing'.

While it is not necessary for our purposes that we understand all the intricacies of the evolutionary process, it is essential that its major outlines, stressing both radical individuality and radical unity, be given full expression. Thus, while 'individualism' in the sense of existence by and for oneself is anathema in evolution, it is also the case that it works by 'individuality' – that is, each part, no matter how small or large, makes its contribution to the creation of more and more complex and diverse forms of life. Hence, were we to make a leap to the human scene, we could at least say that if reality is put together in this fashion, then it is impossible to imagine fulfilment for any individual apart from the whole. It is not as if individuality is added to the process when it reaches the human level; rather, we become the individuals we are only through the unimaginably old, complex, intricate and gradual process that has created all the individuals (of whatever species) in the world. At the very least, this new way of looking at individuality should make us open to contemplating the possibilities for the abundant life for human flourishing, not with terms such as me and mine, but us and ours.

---

[7] Ibid., 52.
[8] Ibid., 54.
[9] Ibid., 52.

Relational ontology

What we see in evolution we see also in the story of Jesus and the Trinity: radical relationality. In contrast to Descartes's 'I think; therefore I am', what we see emerging in evolution and in our interpretation of the Jesus story as well as its implications for understanding God, is a different mantra, 'I *relate*; therefore I am.' What we see, in other words, is a relational ontology, in which kenosis is a necessary first step at evolutionary, Christological, Triune and discipleship levels. Thus, kenosis, the unconscious or conscious sacrifice of one for the other(s), shows that there is a correlation between the Trinity and the basic structures of the universe. The new story that we are suggesting is not merely a religious or a secular one, but both, a story that stretches all the way from the most primitive one cell creature to an understanding of God. However, while the sacrifice of one for the others is unconscious at the pre-human level, it must be conscious at our level – and this is very challenging. As John Zizioulas tells us:

> Communion with the other requires the experience of the Cross. Unless we sacrifice our own will and subject it to the will of the other; repeating in ourselves what our Lord did in Gethsemane in relation to the will of his Father, we cannot reflect properly in history the communion and otherness that we see in the triune God. Since the Son of God moved to meet the other, his creation, by emptying himself through the kenosis of the Incarnation, the 'kenotic' way is the only one that befits the Christian in his or her communion with the other – be it God or one's 'neighbour'.[10]

In other words, there is no escape to 'let Jesus do it', if we accept this story of relational ontology as basic to our universe.

The stories unpacked

From this sketch of what is needed in the story with which to face climate change, we can see several features of this story. First, it must be anchored in an interpretation of the life and work of Jesus because Christians see God in the face of Jesus. Second, it must be in line with the understanding of reality current in our time. In other words, one criterion is that the religious and the secular stories of our time must be compatible. Third, it must be an engaging, powerful story in order to replace the monarchical, engaging powerful story. Do we have such a story? I believe we do, and I am trying to make a case for it.

First, the story of Jesus. There are many 'stories' of Jesus, but here I will sketch just one as a substitute for the standard one. This story takes as its primary biblical text

---

[10] John D. Zizioulas, *Communion and Otherness: Studies in Personhood and the Church*, edited by Paul McPartlan (New York: T&T Clark, 2006), 5–6.

Philippians 2.5-8, where the central movement is the self-emptying of God, becoming incarnate in a humble human being whose eventual end is death on a cross. Unlike the standard model where God is expressed as a powerful overlord, here we have the complete reversal: 'The self-emptying of Jesus is the revelation that to be God is to be unselfishness itself. Being God means to be the giver.'[11] Whereas the monarchical model underscores God's power at all levels – in the creation as the Creator ex nihilo and on the cross as the One who heroically takes our sins upon himself, the kenotic story is completely different. It is a mystery how the two stories could exist side by side for hundreds of years when their foundations and implications are exact opposites. The kenotic Jesus, as the incarnate God, is epitomized in the Sermon on the Mount and in the parables in which reversals of the powerful and the powerless are common.

But the story of Jesus is most powerfully expressed in the cross. Jürgen Moltmann could not be more emphatic: 'The death of Jesus on the cross is the centre of all Christian theology.'[12] The standard interpretation of the cross claims it is central because here Jesus, as our substitute, relieves us of punishment for our sins. 'Let Jesus do it all.' This mantra is the 'faith' we need in order to be 'saved', to inherit eternal life. A kenotic understanding of the cross is very different. To begin with it tells us who God is. As Moltmann writes:

> When the crucified Jesus is called the 'image of the invisible God', the meaning is that *this* is God, and God is like *this*. God is not greater than he is in this humiliation. God is not more glorious than he is in this self-surrender. God is not more powerful than he is in this helplessness. God is not more divine than he is in this humanity. The nucleus of everything that Christian theology says about 'God' is to be found in this Christ event. The Christ event on the cross is a God event.[13]

Because Christians see God in the life, teachings and death of Jesus, kenosis or self-sacrificing is not just the story of Jesus but also the story (interpretation) of God. Thus, theology (theos-logos), 'talk about God', begins with talk about Jesus. And it is talk about a kenotic Jesus or as John Caputo puts it, 'Suppose we think of God as someone who prowls the streets ... disturbs the peace ... Suppose we imagine God as a street person with a definite body odor.'[14] How shocking! The shock is necessary to save us from imagining Jesus and thus God in a sanitized, spiritualized way. The 'incarnation' is a messy business, or should be. It is about God as really, truly deeply being one of us, one who is with us in all the dark, dreary and shocking parts of our lives. As we have noted, Christians see God as both transcendent and immanent. However, Christians have

---

[11] Richard, *A Kenotic Christology*, 133.

[12] Jürgen Moltmann, *The Crucified God: The Cross of Christ as the Foundation and Criticism of Christian Theology* (New York: Harper and Row, 1974), 204.

[13] Ibid., 205.

[14] John D. Caputo, *The Weakness of God: A Theology of the Event* (Bloomington: Indiana University Press, 2006), 33.

emphasized, overemphasized, the transcendence of God. A kenotic theology demands that we start with and stay with immanence, that is, the worldly, fleshly, messy, despairing side of God. At the deepest level of 'immanence', of God being present with us, are the calls to a form of self-sacrifice, calls very apt for our consumer culture: 'If you wish to be perfect, go and sell all your possessions, and give to the poor … and come, follow me' (Mt. 19.21); 'Take nothing for your journey, neither staff nor knapsack, shoes, or money' (Lk. 9.3); 'If any man will come after me, let him renounce self, take up his cross and follow me' (Mt. 16.24).

Kenosis as an interpretation of reality

These typical sayings by Jesus have always been hard for well-off people to brush aside. Surely, God does not expect *us* to follow him to this extent! However, if a kenotic theology includes discipleship, then we must admit that it *does* include our lives as well. Apparently, what is becoming clear is that a kenotic theology moves in several directions to include what we say about God and what we say about ourselves. In other words, it is a total interpretation, a new, different way of being in and understanding the world. It is saying that in order to get a glimpse of what this new worldview is about, begin with the lowly story of a carpenter who lived in a strange, self-sacrificial way – a way totally different from our selfish, consumer-oriented way – and yet a way where glimpses of both evolutionary and Trinitarian reflection are present. How odd that the countercultural life of an insignificant peasant should touch on such seemingly esoteric topics as evolution and the Trinity? What is going on here? It seems to be saying that kenosis is both a form of knowledge and a way to live. Is it suggesting that in clear opposition to individual, human self-fulfilment (which is one twenty-first-century interpretation of the creed), a model of sacrificial love for the neighbour is not only 'good' for the other but close to 'reality' as understood by evolutionary theory and some interpretations of the Christian understanding of God. Does all this loosely hold together, that is, give us a different picture of how to live on planet earth in the twenty-first century than the consumer, individualistic model?

Kenosis and the model of friend

We will perhaps gain further insight into kenotic theology if we consider which model of God is most appropriate to express it. Of the most central and powerful relational models for expressing the God–world relationship, 'friend' is the richest and most suggestive. This may seem strange, since it is the least necessary when compared with parent or lover, since it does not have a biological base. As C.S. Lewis claims, 'rather, it is one of those things that gives value to survival.'[15] Since Aristotle, many have agreed with his comment, 'without friends no one would choose to live even though he possessed all other goods'.[16] And yet, the reason for its superiority to parent and lover is a strange backhanded compliment. Lewis writes that one need not hesitate to call God Father or Husband because 'only a lunatic' would take such models literally: 'But if Friendship was used for this purpose we might mistake the symbol for the thing symbolized.'[17] In other words, 'friend' is a metaphor for God that could be misinterpreted to be a description.

Hence, as a powerful candidate for expressing God's love for the world – as well as our response – it is composed of affection and respect and as such suggests that of all human loves it 'is the most free, the most reciprocal, the most adult, the most joyful, and most inclusive. Its range, from best friend to partner ... reveals it to be eminently suited to participate in the formation of a new sensibility for the conduct of our public life and not just for our private pleasures.'[18]

Kant's suggestion of affection and respect removes it from the intensity and potential individualism of parental love where the parent's eyes are fixated on the child or the lover's eyes that are obsessed with looking at each other. Rather, the friendship model suggests that God loves the world and all its creatures aesthetically – that is, loves each and every creature in appreciation of its uniqueness. Friendship is the purest, most disinterested kind of love, appreciating each life form in and for itself and what its diversity and specialness can contribute to the world. Likewise, with the friend model, we are called to love God because God is God and deserves our love, in fact, our adoration.

In the two places in the New Testament where the friendship model appears: Matthew 11.19, where Jesus is seen as 'the friend of tax collectors and sinners' and in John 15.12-15 where Jesus tells the disciples that they are no longer servants but friends, Jesus also claims 'No one has greater love than this, to lay down one's life for one's friends.' Here we see boldly and clearly the kenotic motif, for friends are called upon to sacrifice for others as the key to the life of discipleship. Here we also see clearly the call to friends to face outward towards a common goal and, surely, the well-being of the planet is such a goal. While the parent looks at the baby and lovers at each other, friends join hands and face outward, united in a common interest. Here we see lifted up both inclusiveness and public concern: one can be friends with anyone, even insentient objects such as mountains, libraries, gardens and organizations. Likewise, while friendship can be seen as an exclusive model (my best friend), it can also refer to acquaintances that can join together regardless of gender, sex, skin colour, nationality, disability, wealth or poverty.

---

[15] C. S. Lewis, *Four Loves* (New York: Harcourt, Brace and Co., 1960), 103.

[16] Aristotle, *Nicomachean Ethics*, edited and translated by John Warrington (London: J.M. Dent & Sons, 1963), 1155a.

[17] Lewis, *Four Loves*, 88.

[18] Sallie McFague, *Models of God: Theology for an Ecological, Nuclear Age* (Minneapolis: Fortress 1987), 178.

Yet, for all its plaudits from secular sources over the centuries, friendship has a particular importance to Christians due to its centrality as a Trinitarian model. As Simone Weil puts it, 'Pure friendship is an image of the original and perfect friendship that belongs to the Trinity and is the very essence of God.'[19] Friendship is both a source for understanding friendship and is most fully expressed by an Eastern Orthodox interpretation of the Trinity. Rather than the Western individualistic, substance view of the Trinity inherited from Augustine, the Eastern relational, dance-like view is both an illustration and an expression of kenosis. Unlike the Western view which has encouraged radical monotheism (and hence we find individualism reflected in ourselves), the *imago dei*, the Eastern view, underscoring the three 'persons' helps us to see God not as a static substance but as a constant activity of giving and receiving. The Trinity reveals that to be and to be in relation become identical and hence there is no God outside the Trinity and its characteristic is a constant giving and receiving in love.

Kenosis is not only best expressed by the model of friendship, but its typical ritual is table fellowship, the sharing of the basics (food, etc.) among all. While the Eucharist in the old monarchical story of Jesus fits with a substitutionary theory of the atonement – God in Jesus taking our sins upon himself and thus winning eternal life for us – here the bread and wine symbolize what 'companions' (meaning 'with bread') do. They eat together in order to renew their energy for working together for the well-being of the planet and all its creatures. The solidarity of friendship, its inclusivity and hospitality, are expressed in a kenotic view of the cross and resurrection as Jürgen Moltmann suggests in this comment: 'It is the eating and drinking in the kingdom of God which the Resurrected anticipates with everyone whom he has made a friend.'[20] To see the sharing of basic resources as a kenotic act in our time of climate change with its consequences of dire inequality is an essential commitment for us.

It relates also to another characteristic of friendship – that it is the most adult of all the God–world models. The model of God the Father, one of the favourite images for Christians, keeps us permanently as 'children', as most grateful to our all-powerful father and unable to contribute very much to the flourishing of the planet. Even the imperial models – lord, king, master – suggest our obedience, depriving us human beings of the responsibility that is rightfully ours, given that we are the only life form able to decide to share the planet's resources. Hence, the model of friendship between God and the world is especially powerful and appropriate for underscoring the adult nature of the relationship between God and human beings in our time. Let us recall John's comment suggesting our high calling, in Jesus's remark that we did not choose him, but he chose us to love one another as he now loves us, not as servants but as friends, laying down our lives for each other as he laid down his life for us (Jn 15.12-16).

---

[19] Simone Weil, *Waiting for God*, translated by Emma Craufurd (New York: Harper and Row, 1951), 208.
[20] Moltmann, *The Crucified God*, 73.

Kenosis and the great exchange

This high calling, the adult nature of the divine–human friendship is only possible because, and as, we participate in the life and love of God, in 'the great exchange'. Let us look more deeply into the kenotic track of interpretation. Michael Gorman summarizes it as 'cruciform theosis'.[21] What this phrase means is that divinity is qualified by the cross, that the cross takes place in, participates in, God. This kenotic track of interpretation suggests something entirely different from the standard Western story of Jesus, which, as we have seen, is a grim, negative one. The kenotic story suggests what the early church called 'the great exchange'. As Irenaeus puts it, 'our Lord Jesus Christ, who did, through His transcendent love, become what we are, that He might bring us to be even what He is Himself provided the most compelling and often-repeated form of the perennial *cur deus homo* for generations to come, even until today'.[22] In other words, God (in Jesus Christ) became incarnate in humanity, so that we, participating in Christ through the sacraments and our actions, might become God-like. The grand exchange is deep incarnation; it means that God is deeply, totally immanent in the flesh and, by implication, in all of creation – that the entire creation participates in, lives in, God. God lives in us, our world, and hence our world – and we humans by acknowledgement – live in God. This is an ontological statement about 'reality'; it is claiming that everything that is exists *because* it lives within God, and therefore has a certain character, a 'cruciform' character. Hence, the signs of sharing, symbiosis, life and death that we see in evolution *and* the pattern of give and take, of mutual reciprocity in the Trinity, are clues to the kenoticism inherent in the world. In other words, kenoticism, self-sacrificial behaviour, is not strange, but common; in fact, it is how the universe operates (says evolution) and it is how divinity operates (says the Trinity).

Hence, the goal of kenotic interpretation is not negative, but joyously positive, for it says this is the way both reality and God are. It does not say that everything will turn out as we wish, or that death (and sickness, wars, etc.) will not take place, but it does claim that we live kenotically in God – not on our own but with God and with reality. Hence, the grand exchange is indeed joyful for through it we participate in 'the way things are', according to both reality and God. It claims that God participates in (is incarnate in) the world and the world exists within God: this is the way kenotic interpretation works. Thomas Merton expresses it in a personal, powerful and persuasive way in the following passage. 'Christ Himself ... "breathes" in ... me divinely in giving me His Spirit ... The mystery of the Spirit is the mystery of selfless love. We receive Him in the "inspiration" of secret love, and we give Him to others in the outgoing of our own charity. Our love in

---

[21] Michael J. Gorman, *Inhabiting the Cruciform God: Kenosis, Justification, and Theosis in Paul's Narrative Soteriology* (Grand Rapids: Eerdmans, 2009), 161.

[22] As quoted by Jeffrey Finch, 'Irenaeus on the Christological Basis of Human Divinization', in *Theosis: Deification in Christian Theology*, Stephen Finlan and Vladimir Kharlamov (eds) (Eugene: Pickwick, 2006), 86.

Christ is then a life both of receiving and of giving. We receive from God in the Spirit, and in the same Spirit we return our love to God through our brothers.'[23] This wonderful passage expresses how the kenotic exchange works at the most basic, physical level – the level of each breath we take. With each incoming breath we receive Christ's selfless love into ourselves, making it possible, when we breathe out, to do so selflessly. So, Christ works *in* me, in my every breath (the ground of our physical existence) to make selfless love possible. Christ loves us selflessly with our intaking breath, empowering our physical being (our breath and our will) so that we *can* love selflessly.

A wonderful continuity is appearing here among various levels: personal, scientific and religious. What Merton expresses at the level of the individual Christian trying to do the impossible – be a disciple of the kenotic, self-sacrificing Jesus – expresses how this is possible. He is doing what religious folk have always done – use the deepest, most physical phenomenon of our lives (here the very breath that sustains us in life) – as a metaphor for the greatest conundrum of the religious life in most traditions: how to love the neighbour. This seemingly simple universal law has proven to be impossible for human beings, even the most saintly ones.[24] But the grand exchange – God becoming incarnate in the world – means that with each breath we take, God is in us doing what we cannot – love the neighbour. Hence, as we 'exhale' we *can* love the neighbour, not with our own love but with the only source of all life and love – God's. Therefore, the 'impossible' parables, the commands to 'take up one's cross' and follow Jesus, are not impossible, not because *we* are acting, but because God is. God, who first reached out to us in the incarnation, has given us the power to love. What we see at a personal level where the lonely Christian is trying to do the impossible – the saintly thing of loving the neighbour – she or he is now empowered to do so. Such persons are channels of divine love, breathing *in* God's love to empower them, and breathing God's love *out* in their actions.

What we see in the individual example we also see at scientific and religious levels. Thus, the glimmers of kenosis, albeit unconscious, are seen in evolution in the pattern of death for the purpose of new life and all the different forms of it: symbiosis, sharing, interdependence. In other words, the world works this way – what empowers the incredibly diverse, complex, intricate give and take of evolution is in continuity with Merton's personal experience of how faith in Jesus works. And it is also in continuity with the Christian Trinity: the movement of giving and receiving, the dance in which each 'person' takes the lead and then passes it on, and on and on.

---

[23] Thomas Merton, *New Seeds of Contemplation* (New York: New Directions, 1972), 159.

[24] For instance, for an analysis of saintly action, see Sallie McFague, *Blessed are the Consumers: Climate Change and the Practice of Restraint* (Minneapolis: Fortress, 2013).

Kenosis and discipleship

Certainly the way in which self-sacrificial love operates at these various levels is very different; yet, the pattern is similar. It is not a movement in which one succeeds while all the others fail (the triumph of the individual); rather, it is a movement in which through sacrifice new possibilities emerge. The 'sacrifice' is not always fair, just or pretty; in fact, it is often horrendously unfair and unbelievably painful for some. It is neither a just nor a pretty story; but its believers claim it is the way the world works; hence, it *must* be accepted. What religions such as Christianity claim is that the particular form of kenosis they practice is one that tries to take actions that help make up for the 'losers' to the ones who suffer most.

Here we see another difference between the levels of kenosis: at the level where science functions there are no operating agents who can attempt to make things more just. However, God's reaching out in the person of the Son (God incarnate in the world) offers the possibility of empowering love to even things out. So, Christians do not claim that evolution is just; rather, what they suggest is that by God working through us, things *can* turn out differently. While no creature but us can choose to be a participant in the grand exchange, we can so choose to be empowered by love. In other words, the individual Christian (as well as religious bodies) look for possibilities where sacrificial love can make a difference in worldly outcomes. Because we believe that God *is* kenotic love, self-sacrificial love, we have an ally in God for helping the grand exchange take place even in the worst of worldly realities: Holocaust, Hiroshima, Rwanda and Syria. The same power, sacrificial love that operates at the individual level can also be active at public and scientific levels, helping the realities at these levels 'bend' in the direction of kenotic love.

Are we assured of victory? Does God's will for sacrificial sharing always win? By no means. Ours is a 'minimal' faith, operating with eyes wide open to the negativities of existence at both personal and other levels, refusing to turn from inconvenient truths, naming them as objectively as possible. And yet, working with this faith, our hope remains open to the possibilities that God can bring about by working through us. We pray 'to him who by the power at work within us is able to accomplish abundantly far more than all we can ask or imagine' (Eph. 3.20, NRSV).

An African response to Sallie McFague

Robert Owusu Agyarko[1]

Sallie McFague's essay critiques the traditional Western Christian story about God–nature relations. For McFague, the model of God as father has slid over from being a model of God to a model of an idol. The story is anchored by a monarchical, all-powerful, static God that no longer gives meaning to people's lives. She argues that this traditional Christian story is not credible in contemporary culture. She also insists it is beyond any 'patch up'. And because it is inappropriate to allow dangerous notions of God to persist, it is the task of theologians to deconstruct and reconstruct talk about God.[2] McFague herself suggests the kenotic narrative from Philippians 2.5-8 and the friendship model that she finds in Matthew 11.19 and John 15.12-15 for envisioning the relationship between God and the world as fundamentally interrelated.[3] The kenotic concept depicts both salvation and discipleship. Kenosis or self-sacrificing is not just the story of Jesus but also the story (interpretation) of God and how Christians should live their lives. McFague's approach therefore differs from the traditional Western theology concerning God/world relations.

McFague's restorying of the traditional narrative of God–world relations is relevant for the African context. Africa has its own unique history. A significant part of the history is embedded with socio-economic and political hardship, which has placed the continent under the tutorship of the 'developed world' in the school of development for uncountable years to aid its 'development'. Injustices and evils such as slave trade, economic manipulation, military dictatorship and corruption are bedrocks of the problem and have awful socio-economic consequences for the majority of Africans. The kenotic narrative provides a firm theological foundation for addressing such social evils.

McFague encourages a recovery of the notion that God is beyond language and can never be captured by language. As such, the best way of speaking about God is metaphorical.[4] She insists that metaphors are open to critique, and if they fail to meet

---

[1] Robert Owusu Agyarko is a Ghanaian Pentecostal theologian who currently teaches at Central University in Kumasi, Ghana. He holds a PhD in Religion and Theology from the University of Western Cape, South Africa, where he is also a research fellow.
[2] Sallie McFague, 'Falling in Love with God and the World: Some Reflections on the Doctrine of God', *Ecumenical Review* 65:1 (2013), 17–34 (20).
[3] Ibid., 27.
[4] For McFague, a metaphor is seeing one thing *as* something else, pretending 'this' is 'that' because we do not know how to think or talk about 'this', so we use 'that' as a way of saying something about it. See Sallie McFague, *Metaphorical Theology: Models of God in Religious Language* (London: SCM, 1983), 15.

standards of helpfulness, they need to be altered or jettisoned. In Africa, talk about God are as a rule regarded as metaphorical. Creation stories and other God-related stories are also seen as myth. Among the Akan of Ghana the name for God, *OnyameKwame*, indicates that God is both male and born on a Saturday since males born on a Saturday are called Kwame and females Adwoa. However, God is frequently also referred to as *Onyamebatanpa* (God the good mother). It is obvious to the Akan that such depictions are metaphoric. It is very important to control the narrative of God–nature relations if we are to make a meaningful impact in our effort to address ecological degradation, as McFague insists. The impact of a theologian's contribution may be minimal, but it remains crucial for a transformative planetary agenda.

The kenotic narrative provokes us to develop a way of knowing that appreciates non-human nature for its intrinsic value instead of its instrumental value (seeing nature as a resource for human use). The kenotic narrative functions as a powerful transformative metaphor in this regard. McFague's essay stresses human responsibility for the environment in order to take eco-justice issues seriously. The essay also takes cognizance of the social reality that affects both human and non-human forms of life. Its strength is a clear discipleship orientation that takes Jesus's earthly life as point of departure. In this manner the historical Jesus is taken seriously. As a North Atlantic feminist theologian, McFague has a solid perspective on sin and salvation that draws some insights from liberation theology. The kenotic narrative functions as a transformative story that takes into account the social reality that affects the health of planet earth. Indeed, it is a necessary resource for Christian ecotheology.

Notwithstanding this, the concept of friendship as a model for God–nature relations is perhaps too light a word to express the religious bond between a worshipper and the object of worship. Some sense of companionship is needed between the human and his or her object of worship for the sake of mutual interdependence, but a sense of sacredness in religion demands a clear distinction between creator and creature. McFague's friendship metaphor to replace that of God as Father does not recognize a core feature of religion, namely an absolute dependence on the object of worship. The metaphor of friendship does not capture the key feature of awe and, more seriously, undermines the distinction between Creator and creature. The model of friendship could at best supplement the Father model, but it cannot stand alone as model for God–nature relations.

The father model of course entails domination especially in the childhood to adolescent stages where the father has to guide the minor into adult life. But in adulthood the father and his children become more like brothers and sisters or friends sharing ideas and taking mutual decisions. The father and child relation is not only about domination but of mutual respect. Of course, it remains hierarchical but after adolescence, such hierarchy requires deep mutual respect as fathers often relegate major decisions to adult children. In the Akan context fathers would not take major decisions without consulting their adult children. In this respect, to construe the model of father in terms of domination needs to be reconsidered. The father and child relationship has its limits and may indeed give way to deep friendship later in life. Yet it seems that McFague fails to see the model of father beyond the childhood/adolescent period. Comparing the models of father and friendship, the model of friendship lacks a sense of awe and reverence which is an integral part of worship. Religion without a 'Thou' and absolute dependence on the Thou reduces the relationship to being classmates.

Indeed, all discourse between 'Thou and I' may be seen as socially constructed by the 'I' based on his/her environment and thus become dangerous if the constructed narrative has negative implications. This is where theologians should guide the narratives or stories depicting God and nature relations. The Father model becomes dangerous if one fails to see such relationship beyond the period of adolescence. In the book of Exodus, Moses is seen dialoguing with God to avert His intention of destroying the Israelites when they grossly disobey God. This is an example of a father and son relationship that turns towards friendship but within the context of reverence and awe, which does not apply to friends on an equal level.

At least in an African context, deep respect and mutual trust are seen more in father–child relations than in friend–friend relations. This is affirmed by the Akan of Ghana in their saying, 'Mogya mu ye durusenensuo' (blood is thicker than water). These models are not perfect, but the model of father could be more suitable than the friendship model to depict religious relationships.

As a domineering character the father is placed in a position of power – this is the case also in traditional African culture. A father can be abusive and manipulative – the latter however also applies to friends and indeed to mothers and 'madams'. In Ghana and Nigeria, poor rural girls who serve as 'house maid' for middle-class and upper-class women are often maltreated by their 'madams'. Most of these girls do not even receive basic education. They do all the house chores, actually making sure their madam's children are free to study and prepare themselves for a better future. These girls are often not properly paid and readily fired. Naming God as 'SHE' or 'mother' becomes oppressive in the ears of these poor house maids.

The traditional Akan thought-form may be helpful here. In a matrilineal society the Akan refer to God both as father and as mother. The term mother is rarely used without the qualification 'good' (*Onyamebatanpa*). This is in recognition that the model of mother is not perfect. This also applies to God as a *good* father (*Agyapa*). Naming God as Mother therefore does not replace the metaphor of father, but qualifies and supplements it.

The kenotic narrative balances the other model that McFague offered previously, namely 'Earth as God's body'. The latter is open to the criticism of degree Christology where the two natures of Christ are not clarified. Both the motifs of kenosis and of God's body focus on Christ's earthly life and the cosmic scope of Christ's work is stressed on that basis. McFague's focus on Christopraxis is related to her anthropology; Jesus Christ is understood as the paradigm for human action towards the natural environment. Such a view correlates with her position on atonement in terms of moral influence.

Nonetheless, kenosis (which I do embrace) could also be meaningfully interpreted within the context of ransom and penal substitution theories that are more relevant in the African context, particularly where animal sacrifice and spiritual warfare against spirit beings are part of the cosmology.[5] As Father does not imply being a biological father, so the metaphors of penal substitution and ransom may also be seen as analogical (though such line of thinking may be contested).

McFague's essay differs from traditional anthropocentric forms of Western theology about God–world relations. She argues that no one has ever seen God, so all discourse about God is necessarily metaphorical. She therefore suggests that the traditional story of God–nature relations should be replaced with a kenotic narrative; the model of friendship should replace the model of father. McFague offers a cogent reformulation of God–nature relations, while her retelling of the Christian narratives provides a theoretical framework to handle ecological destruction. However, while the kenotic narrative is essential, it should rather add to but not replace the father model, because the Christian story is not merely Christocentric. The friendship model functions better if it does not stand alone but forms part of the larger Christian narrative.

---

[5] There are numerous contributions to an African Christology. For a discussion, see Robert Owusu Agyarko, 'God's unique priest (Nyamesofopreko): Christology within an Akan context' (PhD thesis, University of the Western Cape, 2010).

Chapter 5.3
God as Father: Patriarchy and climate change

Susan Rakoczy[1]

As the effects of global warming and climate change become ever more apparent with weather events such as very severe hurricanes and droughts, what was envisioned for the far distant future is happening now. Truly apocalyptic forecasts such as island nations being covered by rising sea waters are no longer unthinkable. How has humanity found itself in this crisis? For Christians, what role has traditional theological understandings of God in relation to creation – in particular, the language of domination used – played in bringing about this crisis? How has the 'father' language of the Christian tradition influenced attitudes towards creation? How has patriarchy shaped these attitudes? Are there resources in the Christian tradition which can reshape images of God in order that believers can experience what Pope Francis calls 'ecological conversion' (*LS* 217).[2]

This essay will discuss the influence and effects of patriarchal language of God as Father as a factor in humanity's attitudes towards creation. How have feminist scholars critiqued this view? It will source the Christian tradition for other images which offer perspectives more friendly to humanity's relationship to creation. Can 'God as Father' language be redeemed?

'Father' language

Human beings construct language and decide its use. Language for and about God developed from the need to articulate experience of the divine. Male dominated societies gave the Judeo-Christian tradition numerous masculine images for God – king, warrior, judge, ruler

---

[1] Susan Rakoczy is Professor of Christian Spirituality and Systematic Theology at St Joseph's Theological Institute, Cedara, and the School of Religion, Philosophy and Classics, University of KwaZulu-Natal in South Africa. Her research focuses on ecofeminism, mysticism and social justice and feminist theology. She writes from within the Roman Catholic tradition.

[2] Pope Francis, *Laudato Si': On Care for Our Common Home* (London: Catholic Truth Society, 2015). Cited as *LS*.

and more. Most significant is 'father' language seen mostly clearly in the 'Our Father', the prayer which Jesus taught his disciples (Mt. 6.9-13; Lk. 11.2-4). Christians hear an almost exclusive reference to God as 'he' in prayer and preaching. While the truth is that God is beyond all images, humanity must use language to express its experience. Use of exclusively male images of God has had the effect, over time, of impoverishing the religious imagination and experience of the Christian community and of individual believers. Augustine of Hippo cautioned that 'If you have understood God, what you have understood is not God.'[3]

All images of God are analogous; they both reveal and conceal. Analogy involves a threefold dynamic of affirmation, negation and eminence. A word such as 'father' is used to describe God; humans have experiences of 'father' and this word for God resonates within them – sometimes positively, sometimes negatively. Then the word is negated; God as father is utterly unlike human concepts of father. Then the negated is negated. Johnson states that 'every concept and symbol must go through this purifying double negation, negating the positive and negating the negative.'[4]

Images for God are depth symbols from limited human comprehension which point to the divine reality which is beyond all knowledge and images. The Christian spiritual tradition speaks of both kataphatic knowing – using images to speak of God – and apophatic knowing which is an 'unknowing' in darkness. 'God as Father' leads to theological reflection on how the Divine Mystery is father-like and to feelings both positive and negative which arise from a person's experience with 'father'. Thus, we must be very wary of sliding into univocal language for God: God is father as we know fathers and only 'father' language is an accurate image of God. The Scriptures tell us differently with their myriad names and images for God.

But since 'God as Father' is the predominant image in the Christian tradition, it has had profound effects on how believers relate to God. With its patriarchal connotations of 'over and against' women and creation, it continues to influence humanity's relationship to each other as persons and to all created reality.

Yet, to challenge this image makes many persons very uncomfortable. Brazilian theologian Ivone Gebara warns that when we do this we enter a dangerous space because it 'would force us to modify a centuries-old theological edifice ... Both conservatives and liberals show strong resistance to this kind of change.'[5]

White's critique of Christianity

In 1967 the historian Lynn White Jr launched a bold critique of Christianity as the dominant factor in the emerging ecological crisis. He asserted that the image of 'man'

---

[3] Augustine of Hippo, *Sermon* 52, 6.16.

[4] Elizabeth A. Johnson, *She Who Is: The Mystery of God in Feminist Theological Discourse* (New York: Crossroad, 1992), 113.

[5] Ivone Gebara, *Longing for Running Water: Ecofeminism and Liberation* (Minneapolis: Fortress, 1999), 128.

(1960s language) as 'superior to nature' is the root cause of this crisis since creation has an exclusively instrumental value. He wrote, 'No item in the physical creation had any purpose save to serve man's purposes.'[6] Thus humanity views itself as 'superior to nature' and 'contemptuous of it'.[7] The natural world exists only for humanity to use as it wishes.

This is a scathing criticism indeed and in the fifty years since his article White's position has been critiqued in many ways by many environmental ethicists and theologians.[8] Biblical scholars argue that he distorts the story of creation by blending the two stories in Genesis 1 and 2.[9] The Priestly (P) version is found in Genesis 1.1-2.4a and the Yahwist in Genesis 2.4b-25. Richard Huers cites Phyllis Bird who 'demonstrated that in the P story the terms for subduing (*kabash*) and having dominion over (*radah*) other creatures are to be read in connection with God's blessing of all creatures'.[10] White omits reference to the refrain in the P version that 'God saw that it was good', indeed 'very good'.

White's critique is directed at the biblical language of human domination of creation. His interpretation of Christianity raises the question of whether Christians 'have been overly anthropocentric in interpreting the biblical text as if only humans mattered'.[11] He did not address the question of patriarchy and patriarchal power in relation to nature. This is the core of the question around 'father' language and creation: How has patriarchy given humanity, specifically Christians, a framework for the domination of creation?

Patriarchy: Origin and power

Patriarchy, from the Greek *patēr* for 'father' and *archē* for 'power', is an ideology of male dominance in every aspect of life. The 'father rules'; thus men rule over women, children, society and all of creation. Gerda Lerner states that 'it implies that men hold power in all the important institutions of society ... as an institutionalized system of domination.'[12] The shadow side of this dominance is that those who are 'ruled over' are considered weak and inferior and thus unable to assume positions of power and authority in the family and society, including religious institutions. Sexism is the logical

---

[6] Lynn White, Jr, 'The Historical Roots of our Ecological Crisis', *Science* 155 (1967), 1203–7 (1205).
[7] Ibid.
[8] See especially Willis Jenkins, 'After Lynn White: Religious Ethics and Environmental Problems', *Journal of Religious Ethics* 37:2 (2009), 283–309.
[9] Richard H. Hiers, 'Ecology, Biblical Theology and Methodology: Biblical Perspectives on the Environment', *Zygon* 19 (1984), 43–59.
[10] Ibid., 45.
[11] Russell A. Butkus and Steven A. Kolme, *Environmental Science and Theology in Dialogue* (Maryknoll: Orbis, 2011), 34.
[12] Gerda Lerner, *The Creation of Patriarchy* (New York and Oxford: Oxford University Press, 1986), 239.

outcome of patriarchy because it structures male supremacy in concrete ways. Women's male-defined inferiority means that they cannot participate in social structures and roles, including leadership, as men do. But eventually the oppressed say 'no' and we see this in women's struggles since the nineteenth century in the West and in the latter part of the twentieth century in Africa to be recognized as fully human, not derived from men, and for their entry into the 'male space' of government, medicine, law and religious leadership.

Lerner has argued that 'the social subjugation of women is historically the original form of the oppressor-oppressed relationship, and thus the working paradigm for all others.'[13] Gradually 'the roles and behaviour deemed appropriate to the sexes were expressed in values, customs, laws, and social roles' and thus 'men-as-a-group had rights in women which women-as-a-group did not have in men.'[14] Lerner describes this process of using women who were 'acquired by men much as the land was acquired by men',[15] as a system of the commodification of women's reproductive and labour power.

Patriarchy as a social system became the 'natural', supposedly God-given structure for humanity. Males determined that they only were truly human and this allowed 'them to claim that they alone possess intrinsically the desirable qualities of spirit, initiative, reason, capacity for autonomy and higher virtue'.[16] Women became the 'other' who did not have these qualities. Any challenge by women was and is met with fierce resistance. The long history of women's efforts for education, for example, generated responses such as 'there is no need to educate a girl – she leaves the family to get married ... Women cannot be (fill in the blanks) because this is the way life is.' Johnson asserts that 'Religious patriarchy is one of the strongest forms of this structure, for it understands itself to be divinely established.'[17] Male religious authorities, chosen by other men, understand themselves to receive their power from a male God and rule in His name by divine mandate.

Male God language as oppressive – to women, to creation

Patriarchy's influence on Christian religious language is clear in the male dominant images that are used in the Hebrew Scriptures and the New Testament and in the language of community worship. Mary Daly has observed that although 'no theologian or biblical scholar believes that God literally belongs to the male sex ... the absurd idea

---

[13] Cited by Johnson, *She Who Is*, 27.
[14] Lerner, *The Creation of Patriarchy*, 212.
[15] Ibid., 212.
[16] Johnson, *She Who Is*, 28.
[17] Ibid., 23.

lingers on in the mind of theologians, preachers and simple believers.'[18] Both men and women act as if God is male. Gregory Baum clearly illustrated this in his early writings: 'To believe that God is Father is to become aware of oneself not as a stranger, not as an outsider or an alienated person, but as a son who belongs ... To believe that God is Father means to be able to say "we" in regards to all men.'[19]

Elizabeth Johnson names traditional male speech about God as both 'humanly oppressive and religiously idolatrous'.[20] It is oppressive because it uses male images and concepts for God which 'are almost exclusively drawn from the world of ruling men', thus serving to strengthen structures and ideologies which uphold men's 'right to rule' and to 'relegate women, children and other men to the deficient margins'.[21] This patriarchal language is religiously idolatrous because 'it absolutizes a single set of metaphors and obscures the height and depth and length and breadth of divine mystery.'[22] Efforts to make Christian liturgical and theological language inclusive derive from the realization that exclusively male language is spiritually detrimental to the human spirit, certainly for women, but this is also recognized by some men.

Although the actions of a father are not necessarily oppressive – some fathers are loving, kind, compassionate while others are absent, violent and abusive – because of the patriarchal nature of society the symbol of 'father' has power that 'mother' does not have. 'Mother' describes the back seat in a patriarchal family. Because a particular father may be oppressive and violent in the family, 'father God' images for both males and females of all ages may not be helpful in a person's relationship with God. To hear this language consistently can cause trauma as the person remembers the violence they experienced from their father, his abandonment of the family, his absence.

Use of Mother for God, while a minority image in Christian theology although with strong grounding in the literature of Christian spirituality,[23] certainly can be helpful in balancing the stress on the supposed 'maleness' of God.

However, Rosemary Radford Ruether critiques the use of both parent images for God because a parent model 'suggests a kind of permanent parent-child relationship to God ... Patriarchal theology uses the parent image for God to prolong spiritual infantilism as virtue.'[24]

---

[18] Mary Daly, *The Church and the Second Sex* (New York: Harper & Row, 1968, 1975), 180.

[19] Gregory Baum, *Man Becoming: God in Secular Experience* (New York: Herder and Herder, 1970), 195. Quoted in Mary Daly, *Beyond God the Father: Toward a Philosophy of Women's Liberation* (Boston: Beacon Press, 1973), 20. Baum, who died in 2016, grew in his consciousness of how language matters when we speak and write of human persons.

[20] Johnson, *She Who Is*, 18.

[21] Ibid.

[22] Ibid.

[23] See Julian of Norwich, *Revelations*, Chapters 60–1.

[24] Rosemary Radford Ruether, *Sexism and God-Talk: Toward a Feminist Theology* (Boston: Beacon Press, 1983), 69.

Father language and creation

Sallie McFague links the monarchical model of God and the world – a relation of control and obedience – with the father–child model of God and humanity. These models have been seen as '*the* way',[25] often the only way in a person's understanding. Her criticism of this language extends to the fact that they exclude the natural world except in terms of domination.

The 'father' language of power and dominance – against and over females both in the family, society and the church – is extended to creation. As women are subordinate to men by the power of patriarchy, creation in its diversity is also to be under male control. The power of patriarchy has led to the instrumentalization of creation: land, animals, birds, water and sea creatures, resources under the earth – are to be *used* by humanity with often little care or concern for the ecology of the whole. Our severe ecological challenges are the result of both human carelessness about creation ('throw the trash in the river – no one will ever notice') and greed such as overfishing, destruction of animal habitats, irresponsible mining and many other ecologically harmful acts.

Translations of Genesis 1.26 describe the understanding of human power that is male power in relation to creation: 'dominion' (Revised Standard Version), 'masters' (New Jerusalem Bible) or 'power' (Good News Version).

These words describe different dimensions of this over and against relationship with God's creation. 'Dominion' refers to possession: having dominion over creation thus describes humanity over and against creation. It also connotes 'rule': a king rules his dominion. 'Masters' recalls the abhorrent master–slave relationship with its inherent violence and abuse. 'Power' can have various meanings; power 'over' is similar to 'master' while power 'with' enables initiative and growth.

None of the translations use 'ownership' but humanity's relation to creation has frequently been thought of in terms of possession. Western relationship to land is that of ownership while many Indigenous cultures such as African peoples and the native peoples of the Americas understood that no one owns land – people use it, more specifically in community.

The category of ownership and possession of the natural world has led to the perspective that as humans we can do what we want with the air, water, land, animals, birds, fish and all reality outside of human beings. And so we have wreaked incredible ecological destruction on the earth and all its inhabitants, making it indeed a planet in peril.

So, was Lynn White right? Yes, in terms of drawing attention to Christianity's share of responsibility for ecological degradation although his critique is totally without

---

[25] Sallie McFague, *A New Climate for Theology: God, the World and Global Warming* (Minneapolis: Fortress, 2008), 69.

nuance. No, since his critique was too narrow and he did not understand the two strands of interpretation – the J and P traditions – in the Genesis stories of creation.

Ecofeminist theology and 'God as Father'

Ecofeminism is one dimension of the many ways in which women do theology: African women's theology, Western feminist theology, womanist theology, *mujerista* theology, Asian women's theology and more. The word was coined by Francoise d'Eaubonne in 1974. Linking analyses of class, race and culture together with critiques of patriarchy and sexism, it 'brings together feminism and ecology into a matrix which exposes the domination of women by men and the domination of the natural world by human beings'.[26] The goal of ecofeminism is 'a radical transformation of how we as human beings view ourselves, our relationships with other people and the earth itself'.[27] Laurie Zoloth asserts that 'climate change is a feminist issue',[28] an issue of eco-justice.

It is lamentable that *Laudato Si'*, the encyclical of Pope Francis on ecological issues, has not a single reference to how climate change and ecological degradation impact women, especially poor women. The signs of climate change such as 'the collapse of eco-systems, the spread of polluted water sources, and the lack of sustainable means of cooking (that) force women and girl children in Africa, Asia and Latin America to walk increasing distances to find water and firewood for their families'[29] are ignored. His use of names for God is entirely masculine, using 'Father' eighteen times. There are none for God as Mother. Mother language is used for the earth (following Francis of Assisi) and for Mary the Mother of God. In both the practical and theological senses. *Laudato Si'* ignores the gendered dimensions of the ecological crisis.

Brazilian theologian Ivone Gebara situates ecofeminism in reference to epistemology. She asserts: 'Philosophical theories of knowing created within the western tradition have always had an anthropocentric, or human-centered, and androcentric, or male-centered, bias … They refer to the experience of one part of humanity as though it were the experience of all.'[30] Gebara describes two types of knowledge: scientific, philosophical and theological knowledge generally attributed to men – thus judged as 'true' knowledge – and experiential knowledge of women and the poor, based on experience 'but this was not automatically recognized as real knowing.'[31]

---

[26] Susan Rakoczy, *In Her Name: Women Doing Theology* (Pietermaritzburg: Cluster Publications, 2004), 300.
[27] Ibid., 302.
[28] Laurie Zoloth, 'At the Last Well on Earth: Climate Change is a Feminist Issue', *Journal of Feminist Studies in Religion* 33 (2017), 139–52 (140).
[29] Susan Rakoczy, 'Is Pope Francis An Ecofeminist?', https://opendemocracy.net/transformation/susan-rakoczy/is-pope-francis-ecofeminist (accessed 16 February 2018).
[30] Gebara, *Longing for Running Water*, 25.
[31] Ibid., 25.

Patriarchal epistemology has shaped and continues to shape how people understand their world. Essentialism is one of its dimensions: each creature, each human being has an 'essence' that makes it what it is. Christian theology has understood this predetermined human essence as the state of humanity before the fall. Life is thus a search to recover who we really were 'in the beginning'.

When Gebara addresses the question of images of God as defined by the male tradition of theology down the centuries, she criticizes the 'pretentiously "objective" way in which it speaks, and the historical consequences of this speech and its influence on the lives of specific social groups',[32] especially women and the poor.

The image of God as Father is a striking example of male epistemology since it 'reveals the actions of men as expressions of the divine, and how much it veils and obscures all that falls outside patriarchal criteria'.[33] Women are excluded from fully sharing in the divine image. Augustine wrote:

> the woman with her husband is the image of God in such a way that the whole of that substance is one image, but when she is assigned her function of being an assistant, which is her concern alone, she is not the image of God; whereas in what concerns the man alone he is the image of God as fully and completely as when the woman is joined to him in one whole.[34]

Gebara argues that in the Bible 'human history is understood as absolutely dependent on the will of a Supreme Being whose historical image is masculine.'[35]

To use 'father' language for God is to assert that somehow God is like the fathers we know, the good fathers. But this is inadequate because the deepest strain of God language in the Christian tradition, apophatic theology, asserts that our language eventually stops in silence because God is not like us. From an ecofeminist perspective, Gebara argues that 'The notion of God as a person who is metaphysically asexual but historically identified with the male sex, and especially identified with the powerful of the world, is no longer adequate in dealing with the great issues of the survival of humanity and of life itself on this planet.'[36]

Because it reflects patriarchal values and structures and since it is often used univocally, Father language for God thus is problematic for believers and for all of creation: God as father is all powerful and human fathers and males in general in their power over others are thus like God. This is not to say that Father language for God and human fathers is necessarily oppressive and life-denying. In Western art, in, for example, Rembrandt's 'The Return of the Prodigal Son', the left hand of the father holding his son is larger and the right hand is smaller and softer, showing God as both father and mother.

---

[32] Ibid., 35.
[33] Ibid.
[34] Augustine of Hippo, *De Trinitate* 12.10.
[35] Gebara, *Longing for Running Water*, 38.
[36] Ibid., 116.

However people imagine 'father', the male patriarchal power which societies, cultures and religious institutions symbolize in a Father God needs much critical engagement.

African images of God and creation

African philosophy of nature and the insights of African ecofeminists provide helpful images of the relation of God and creation which are not dualistic or dominating. In general, African understandings of the relation of humanity and nature emphasize interconnection. The world is '"a living active and dynamic organism" in which "networks of interdependent forces" move in different directions'.[37] While a hierarchy of forces is recognized from inanimate objects to plants, animals and humanity, 'this philosophical interpretation of humanity and nature is much more positive than western hierarchical dualism.'[38]

The Shona people of Zimbabwe have developed the *Mutopo* principle of relationships between humanity and nature. They assert that all that exists has the same essence, is free and has the right to exist. God is named as *Mwari*, the author of creation who continues to create. All of creation is to be respected since everything radiates the energy of *Mwari*. Women are not the opposite of men since 'the two are intrinsically and permanently related.'[39]

West African insights also illustrate the positive relationship of humanity and nature. *Nyam* which is used in many West African languages 'connotes an enduring power and energy possessed by all life'.[40] The Fon people speak of *Da*, the energy in all of creation. Pulsing through all that exists is *Nommo*, a physical–spiritual life force.

These African insights echo a primary image of ecofeminist reflection: the web of life which affirms that all of creation is interconnected. To view a spider's web is to observe that there is no structured hierarchy of high and low – everything radiates from the centre.

However, even in the light of these positive images of God and creation, the patriarchy of African cultures continues to exert enormous power over African women who must provide for their families in environments which are increasingly degraded and depleted.

---

[37] E. A. Ruch and K. C. Anyanwu, *African Philosophy: An Introduction to the Main Philosophical Trends in Contemporary Africa* (Rome: Catholic Book Agency, 1981), 145, cited in Rakoczy, *In Her Name*, 311.

[38] Rakoczy, *In Her Name*, 311.

[39] Tumani Mutasa Nyajeka, 'Shona Women and the *Mutopo* Principle', in *Women Healing Earth: Third World Women on Ecology, Feminism and Religion,* Rosemary Radford Ruether (ed.) (Maryknoll: Orbis, 1996), 135–42 (141).

[40] Shamara Shantu Riley, 'Ecology is a Sistah's Issue Too: The Politics of Emergent Afrocentric Ecowomanism', in *Readings in Ecology and Feminist Theology,* Mary Heather MacKinnon and Moni McIntrye (eds) (Kansas City: Sheed & Ward, 1995), 214–30 (226).

How then shall we speak of God when our planet is in peril?

It is impossible to delete 'God as Father' language completely from Christian theology, worship and prayer. All efforts of women theologians to date have made only a limited impact on some people – mostly women, some men – to understand the negative effects 'God as Father' can and does have on the lives of individual persons – and in our perspective, on the earth.

Sallie McFague raises crucial questions about the language we use to describe the relationship between God and the world:

> How distant, how close, are God and the world? Is God only transcendent over the world or also immanent in it? ... Are we only externally related to God, or are we internally related? Is the world more like another 'subject' to God or more like an 'object'? ... Does God have all power over creation, or are human beings also responsible for creation? Are we puppets or partners?[41]

However, there are other ways to speak of God which draw attention to depth dimensions of the Divine which 'father' language does not encompass. The Scriptures contain more than patriarchal, monarchical images. Here we find Spirit and Sophia, Wisdom, a female figure of relatedness to humanity and creation. These images are much appropriate when we speak of the Divine and creation since they emphasize relatedness, not domination.

Spirit (*ruah* in Hebrew, *pneuma* in Greek, *spiritus* in Latin) connotes a myriad of activities which are life-giving, not dominating: creating the new, sustaining it, renewing it, imparting wisdom. Some Spirit language in Scriptures evokes the actions of women: knitting the baby in her womb (Ps. 139.13), as a midwife (Ps. 22. 9-10) and as washerwoman, making all things clean (Is. 4.4, Ps. 51.7).[42] Spirit language in the New Testament includes birth language when Jesus tells Nicodemus he must be born again of water and the Spirit (Jn 3:3).

Another strong female image for God is Sophia, Wisdom. Proverbs 8:22-31 describes how she is related to the act of creation; she is playful and joyful, taking delight in creation and humanity. Johnson comments that 'The scriptural tradition of creation theology here receives another dimension to the idea that creation is not simply the act of a solitary male deity.'[43] Celia Deane-Drummond concurs that Sophia is a very useful image for God and creation since it functions as 'a corrective to those male images of God that have existed in the past, while drawing explicitly on biblical thought.'[44]

---

[41] McFague, *A New Climate for Theology*, 63.
[42] Johnson, *She Who Is*, 83.
[43] Ibid., 88.
[44] Celia Deane-Drummond, *Eco-Theology* (Winona: Anselm Academic, 2008), 160.

Spirit–Sophia acts in creation including humanity in a variety of ways. She vivifies, renews, empowers, graces, 'shaping the world towards an ultimate end: the liberation of the world in God'.[45] Hers is an inclusive presence and action; all of humanity, all of created reality is within Her loving presence and action.

God as Father is an image of relationship, one that is not always helpful since it reinforces the patriarchal 'over and against' structures of society and the church and can be psychologically and spiritually harmful to persons whose experience of 'father' has been or is negative.

Gebara favours 'relatedness' as the most appropriate language with which to speak of God. It 'speaks of God as possibility, as opening, as the unexpected, the unknown … it is relatedness as a continual presence that is made explicit in different ways in different beings.'[46] Human experience of relatedness is diverse: parents, family, spouse, children, friends, colleagues. Relationships are essential for human flourishing and indeed the African sense of community – 'I am because we are and because we are I am' – describes not only a distinct cultural experience but that of humanity. Ecofeminists often use the image of the 'web of life' to describe the interrelatedness of all that is.

But some may object that 'relatedness' is too vague to describe God. On the one hand this is true since we can ask 'who or what is relating?', but its value is that we can expand it in various kinds of relatedness. The Scriptures provide many ways to make 'relatedness' concrete. This is seen most clearly in Jesus whose whole life was that of loving and healing relatedness.

God as Spirit is God as relatedness, dwelling in each person and all of creation. The book of Wisdom states: 'The Spirit of the Lord has filled the world' (Wis.1.7). The Spirit is closer to us than we are to ourselves in the depths of our being and 'creates community of all created things with God and with each other'.[47] This is a new community, a new creation of being with rather than being over.

God the Father as a difficult image

Can God as 'father' function as an image of relatedness in a time of ecological crisis?

On the one hand, it does function. Some believers find it good and helpful and would probably find this analysis disturbing. Others from their personal experience of absent, violent or abusive fathers find the image including the prayer 'Our Father' deeply disturbing.

Johnson stresses that Jesus used the father symbol, *abbâ,* as an image of loving relationship between himself and his *Abbâ*. His *Abbâ* 'is not a patriarchal figure who

---

[45] Johnson, *She Who Is*, 138.
[46] Gebara, *Longing for Running Water*, 103.
[47] Jürgen Moltmann, *God in Creation: An Ecological Doctrine of Creation* (London: SCM Press, 1985), 11.

can be used to legitimate systems of oppression, including patriarchal rule, but a God of the oppressed, a God of community and celebration'.[48] The experience of a 'good father' in a person's life allows that person to relate to God as Father as One whose relationship to humanity is infinite tenderness and love. And perhaps for persons who have not experienced life-giving paternal love the symbol can function in a positive way.

Yet, the questions remain because patriarchy still rules human structures including the church. Any use of 'God as Father' language as dominating and oppressive injures not only persons but also creation. Both consciously and subconsciously humanity, especially Christians, have learned that they can dominate and oppress each other and all of creation. God language can justify it; the structures of patriarchy remain strong.

So we live in an in-between time of awareness of how our religious language can be implicated in harming creation. The effects of climate change which we now confront daily challenge us to reflect on how religious language has effects far beyond private prayer and communal worship. Because images such as 'God as Father' are not going to disappear quickly and easily, we must be careful to deconstruct this image in order to challenge its power over humanity and creation while realizing that it is a symbol of divine relatedness that can be helpful to some persons in their religious searching.

---

[48] Johnson, *She Who Is*, 81.

A response to Susan Rakoczy

Whitney A. Bauman[1]

Since 'God as Father' is the predominant image in the Christian tradition, it has had profound effects on how believers relate to God. With its patriarchal connotations of 'over and against' women and creation, it continues to influence humanity's relationship to each other as persons and to all created reality (Rakoczy)

The queerness of theology

The omni-god of Christianity – all knowing, all powerful, eternal, omnipresent – has indeed been one of the major theological interpretative traditions within Christian thought. As Rakoczy points out in her essay, the male gender has often been used to describe this omni-god. Here I want to expand her critique of male metaphors in God-Talk, to the very category of maleness, and its intricate connection to gender/sex dimorphism, heteronormativity and human exceptionalism, which are all related.[2] As such I will utilize some of the work done in Lesbian and Gay Studies (LGS), and draw heavily on what has become known as Queer Theory (QT). One might assume that LGS and QT are synonymous, but the former deals more with identity and liberation of specific identities while the latter critiques how those identities get defined and stabilized. These are not mutually exclusive, and I argue that we need both: the critical, deconstructive bits from QT, and the liberative bits from LGS that focus on justice for specific, individual bodies. In the end, I argue that we must think queerly if we are going to open up God-talk to the multiplicity of the planetary community and all therein. In this sense, QT is a good partner in the struggle to end sexism in God-Talk,[3] and undo the hierarchical chain of reality attached to the omni-, male GOD. I will focus on three sources within Christianity for queer critiques of theology and the theological

---

[1] Whitney Bauman is Associate Professor of Religious Studies at Florida International University in Miami, also residing in Berlin, Germany, for half of the year. Growing up in a farming family in Arkansas, he developed an environmental sensibility at an early age. He identifies as a religious naturalist, taking a sense of wonder from studying the natural world.

[2] On gender-dimorphism, see Chris Gudorf, 'The Erosion of Sexual Dimorphism: Challenges to Religion and Religious Ethics', *Journal of the American Academy of Religion* 69:4 (2001), 863–91. On heteronormativity, see Adrienne Rich, 'Compulsory Heterosexuality and Lesbian Existence', *Signs* 5:4 (1980), 631–60.

[3] Rosemary Radford Ruether, *Sexism and God-Talk* (Boston: Beacon Press, 1983).

anthropologies derived from it: historical constructions, textual oddities and theological strangeness.

Historical constructions

As Rakoczy points out in her essay, there are other images for God beyond GOD the father found throughout scripture and the history of Christian theology. So, when we explore the history of a given text or tradition, we are not looking back into time to discover some sort of single, orthodox answer to our query. This would be impossible as all traditions are polydox: there are many given interpretations and theological assertions at any given point in history.[4] These traditions are living and changing, and they change as they come into contact with different cultures and places. We should not make the mistake, then, of thinking that 'Father' – or male, female, childhood, family or marriage – is a stable category across time and place.

We could take, for example, the writings of the Apostle Paul. When he is talking about sex and gender relations, he is doing so in the context of a Roman patriarchal context. Within this framework, wealthy, land-owning men were the patriarchs of a 'family' system that included women, children and slaves. These wealthy elite men were the only citizens with rights. The patriarch was virtually free to do what he wished with his own women, children and slaves. This is the context in which Paul argues that a 'man ought not to lie with another man as with a woman' (to paraphrase). What he meant here was a land-owning male should not have sex with another land-owning male: this didn't include the women, children and slaves of the elite male.[5]

This historical context – of the patriarchal, Roman system with its injustices – makes Jesus's mission seem a lot queerer. He is arguing for his disciples to leave their kin family and join him in starting a new family beyond kin, beyond religious boundaries (Jew and gentile), beyond male and female gender roles. He understood that the patriarchal system led to injustices for women, children and slaves, but also for the poor as property and wealth was passed down and accumulated over generations through kinship lines. In this sense, we might argue that Jesus would critique the Victorian 'family values' model argued for by some Christians.[6]

Another historically queer point is the existence in most cultures and traditions around the world of more than two genders. There are sometimes three or four genders,

---

[4] Catherine Keller and Laurel Schneider, *Polydoxy: Theology of Multiplicity and Relation* (New York: Routledge, 2010).

[5] See, e.g. Amy-Jill Levine and Marianne Blickenstaff (eds), *Feminist Companion to Paul: Authentic Pauline Writings* (Sheffield: Sheffield Academic Press, 2004).

[6] On the Victorian, modern family, see Rosemary Radford Ruether, *Christianity and the Making of the Modern Family* (Boston: Beacon, 2000).

and/or non-conformers, and/or gender androgynous options historically. The Waria of Indonesia, the Fa'afafine of Samoa, the 'third spirits' of some native traditions, and the Muxes of Zapotec cultural traditions are just a few examples. These genders undergo erasure under Western colonization and the colonizing attempt to force 'other cultures' into a monotheistic, gender dimorphic and heteronormative model.[7]

Textual oddities

In addition to historical construction of identities in different places over time, we can also look to hermeneutics for a much queerer reading of texts than is often considered. Note here, that 'queer' does not necessarily mean having to do with LGBTQ+ identities explicitly: a point that is often contentious between those who do LGBTQ+ liberation studies and those that would argue that even those identities are constructed over time. From my perspective these two important loci need not be at odds and should be taken together. We can practice what Gayatri Spivak calls a political 'strategic essentialism' without mistaking these strategies for stable essential identities.[8] Three examples of this come to mind in biblical hermeneutics.

Catherine Keller has been one of the main challengers to the concept of creation ex nihilo. She argues (correctly in my mind) that it is not an accurate reading of the Genesis 1 story, nor is it a theological assertion with 'orthodox' authority until around the fourth century. In the beginning was not 'nothing' but rather the *tehom* (the deep, or the watery chaos). This *tehom* is a transliteration of *Tiamat* from the older Babylonian *Enuma Elish*. This *tehom* according to Keller is more like a 'creation ex profundis', a creation out of the watery matrix of life (feminine) that is active and refuses our attempts to order all of life into human confines.[9]

In another queer reading of texts, the *Adam* created in the Genesis 2 'garden' narrative, is of the *adamah* (the earth). Adam is simply a genderless mud creature, created out of the dirt like other creatures. Gender is only created with Eve as a 'partner' so that Adam wouldn't be lonely. There is not really a heteronormative understanding of this text other than the obsession with the Jahwists in general over progeny and procreation. But something like the institution of heterosexual marriage is way too much to read back into this text.[10]

---

[7] Many of these 'third genders' are explored in Daniel Boisvert and Carly Daniel-Hughes, *The Bloomsbury Reader in Religion, Sexuality and Gender* (London: Bloomsbury, 2016).

[8] See the interview with Spivak in Elizabeth Gross, 'Criticism, Feminism, and the Institution', in *The Post-Colonial Critic: Interviews, Strategies and Dialogue*, Sarah Harasym (ed.) (New York: Routledge, 1990), 1–16.

[9] Catherine Keller, *Face of the Deep: A Theology of Becoming* (New York: Routledge, 2002).

[10] Theodore Hiebert, *The Yahwist's Landscape: Nature and Religion in Early Israel* (New York: Oxford University Press, 1996), 32–82.

Finally, as Mark Jordan and others have argued, the story of Sodom and Gomorrah does not have much to do with homosexuality and anal sex. Rather, it is a story about hospitality and how Yahweh gets angry when the rules of hospitality are broken. It is about perversion of kindness towards 'the other'. Jordan also reminds us that sodomy doesn't come to specifically mean anal sex between men until the nineteenth century (since 'homosexuality' was not even an identity category until that time).[11] Prior to this sodomy was a much broader category that meant something more like sex not for the purposes of reproduction.

Theological strangeness

If we can look at textual and historical per/versions, following Marcella Althaus-Reid – a term that means simply per (another) version – we should also be able to look at theological per/versions. For Reid, all theology that does not enter the bedroom is a problematic theology because we are human creatures and sex and sexuality is a part of our embodiment.[12] She argues that we need to think beyond the model of God as omni-god; within this model we can only be submissive bottoms because God must be the power top. This is not a problem, but it should be recognized and other theological models of sex and sexuality should proliferate. She argues, for instance, that we might think of the Trinity as a symbol for a divine threesome: based upon mutual respect, love and shared agency.[13]

Catherine Keller and Laurel Schneider argue for 'apophatic unknowing' in our epistemologies and in our theological constructions.[14] In other words, all of our knowledge is, in the end, surrounded by mystery, by that which we don't know. Rather than project certainty onto our unknowing, why not practice a bit of old-fashioned theological apophasis? There are always multiple interpretations at any given time, although not all interpretations are necessarily adequate.[15]

Part of such unknowing is part and parcel to LGBTQ+ experiences of embodiment. Judith/Jack Halberstam argues that there is a queer art of failure, which fails to perform heteronormative identities and habits in order for new identities, habits and ways of becoming to emerge in the world.[16] In many ways, this queer art of failure is

---

[11] Mark Jordan, *The Invention of Sodomy in Christian Theology* (Chicago: University of Chicago Press, 1996).

[12] Marcella Althaus-Reid, *Indecent Theology: Theological Perversions in Sex, Gender and Politics* (New York: Routledge, 2001).

[13] Marcella Althaus-Reid, *The Queer God* (New York: Routledge, 2003).

[14] Keller and Schneider, *Polydoxy*.

[15] Catherine Keller, *Cloud of the Impossible: Negative Theology and Planetary Entanglement* (New York: Columbia University Press, 2015).

[16] Judith/Jack Halberstam, *The Queer Art of Failure* (Durham: Duke University Press, 2011).

part and parcel of religious traditions: iconoclasm, apophasis, the emptiness and form of Buddhism, the Jain tradition of multiple perspectivalism and non-absolutism, and Indigenous models of the trickster figure are all a few examples. In all of these cases, the known is challenged so that a new way of becoming might emerge.

If, as Rakoczy argues, exclusive Male God-Talk (and I would add heteronormative) has indeed promoted a theological anthropology that understands humans as above nature then perhaps some theological failures of this metaphor might open us up to a much larger planetary community. Perhaps queering theology can open us to a planetary community in which humans emerge from and are part of the rest of the natural world, and in which identities and categories are constantly shifting over time.

Chapter 5.4
The triune God and climate change

Denis Edwards[1]

Does the Christian understanding of God as Trinity have anything to contribute to a twenty-first-century response to climate change? Many would see Trinitarian theology as a particularly speculative and obscure aspect of Christian faith, with no practical significance for the urgent issues facing the planetary community in the Anthropocene. Others find the Trinitarian language of Father and Son and Spirit as contributing to and reinforcing both sexism and anthropocentrism, and question its usefulness for a renewed theology of the natural world. For those who embrace evolutionary science, the concept of the Trinity can seem static, disengaged and otherworldly. For those committed to ecology, the doctrine of the Trinity can seem part of a religious cultural world that reinforces the idea that the planet is simply there for human exploitation.

In this essay, I will attempt to take account of these issues, and to propose that the theology of God as Trinity can offer vision, motivation and inspiration for Christians in addressing anthropogenic climate change. In making such a proposal, I see it as imperative that in responding to this issue Christians cooperate humbly and respectfully with those from various religious backgrounds and with those who profess no religious beliefs. But if Christian believers are to respond to the climate crisis from the deepest level of their being, it will involve a theological connection between the climate and their faith in God. Exploring this connection can be seen not simply as an in-house foundation for Christian participation in climate action, absolutely essential as this is, but also as a public theological act. It can offer a basis for genuine dialogue concerning the community of life on Earth between Christians and those of other faith traditions, such as Islam, Buddhism or Indigenous religions, and with those who do not identify with religious faith.

I am conscious of the partial nature of what follows and of my own context as a male, ordained and relatively wealthy Australian theologian. While some of my sources reflect my Roman Catholic tradition, my intentions are ecumenical, and my hope is that the breadth of this book will compensate for the limits of what I offer. I will discuss climate

---

[1] Denis Edwards (1943–2019) was Professorial Fellow in Theology at Australian Catholic University (Adelaide campus) and a member of the ACU Institute for Religion and Critical Inquiry. He was a priest of the Catholic Archdiocese of Adelaide. His writing focuses on the interrelationship between ecology, science and the heart of Christian faith.

change and the Trinity in five sections: (1) The Christian story of God; (2) Inclusive language for the Trinity; (3) Trinity in an evolutionary world; (4) Divine Communion and the community of creation; (5) Trinity and ecological conversion.

The Christian story of God

In this first section I will propose that a specific kind of Trinitarian theology is needed to engage meaningfully with climate change. What is required is a theology of the Trinity from below, a theology that begins from and is clearly determined by the biblical story of God, a narrative of a God who acts.

This kind of Trinitarian theology is a story of a God who creates a universe of creatures out of love, through the Word and in the Spirit. It tells of a God, who irrevocably binds God's very self to creatures, to all matter and flesh, in the Word incarnate. It describes a God who enters into the deepest place of creaturely suffering and human sin in the cross of Jesus, bringing liberation, radical forgiveness and hope and who, in the resurrection of the crucified Jesus, promises the transformation and fulfilment of the whole creation. It is a story of God's Spirit who, in Christ, is creatively present to all creatures enabling their existence and their becoming, and is given as pure grace to human beings, making them daughters and sons of God, as the first fruit of the new creation that will transfigure all things.

Such a narrative theology of the Trinity is in strong contrast to the everyday view of the Trinity held by many Christians in recent centuries. Based on what they had heard in sermons, and perhaps read in catechetical texts, the Trinity was for them a doctrine to be believed, but one that had little impact on life. It seemed abstract and speculative, an intellectual puzzle for the specialists. In this context it was not at all unusual for preachers and teachers to express despair at the thought of explaining the Trinity. By and large the doctrine, which nearly all acknowledged as the centre of Christian faith, had become a doctrine without practical effect in the life of the church, let alone in the wider world.

In the middle of the last century Karl Rahner summarized the situation: 'despite their orthodox confessions of the Trinity, Christians are, in their practical life, almost mere "monotheists" ... should the doctrine of the Trinity have to be dropped as false, the major part of religious literature could well remain virtually unchanged.'[2] One reason for this situation, Rahner proposed was that, after Thomas Aquinas, textbook (scholastic) theology in the West had dealt with the treatise *On the One God*, in philosophical mode focused on the divine essence, before turning to the second treatise, *On the Triune God*, informed by the Scriptures and the theological tradition. Rahner challenged the separation and sequence of the two treatises. He wanted to show that the Trinity is the

---

[2] Karl Rahner, *The Trinity* (New York: Seabury, 1974), 10–11.

God of creation and salvation. He proposed that the theology of the Trinity should be grounded in what we know of God from the biblical economy of salvation. He insisted that what we know of God from this economy (the economic Trinity) is true of God in God's self (the immanent Trinity). He proposed the axiom: 'The "economic" Trinity is the "immanent" Trinity and the "immanent" Trinity is the "economic" Trinity.'[3]

This axiom has since played a role in the work of many Trinitarian theologians. One example is Protestant theologian Jürgen Moltmann, who embraces the axiom, and then goes on to say something that Rahner does not, that the economic Trinity, above all in the event of the cross, not only reveals the immanent Trinity, but has a retroactive effect on it: 'the pain of the cross determines the inner life of the triune God from eternity to eternity.'[4] For Moltmann the doctrine of the immanent Trinity is 'the quintessence of doxology', and such doxology is an anticipation of the fullness of eschatological joy.[5] When God is all in all, Moltmann says, then 'the economic Trinity is raised into and transcended in the immanent Trinity'.[6]

A second example of a critical reflection on Rahner's axiom is found in the very different Trinitarian theology of Walter Kasper. He argues for the axiom, and points out that its original purpose was to overcome the 'non-functionality' of the doctrine of the Trinity, and to show its connection to the history of salvation. As such, he says, 'the axiom is correct, legitimate, and even necessary.'[7] He then goes on to point to possible misinterpretations of the axiom: where the work of the Trinity in the economy is stripped of its proper historical reality and newness and is seen merely as a revelation of the eternal immanent Trinity; where the immanent Trinity is dissolved in the economic, as if the Trinity only comes into existence in history; where the immanent Trinity is pushed out of the picture, so that the theological focus is only on the Trinity in the economy of salvation.

Other theologians have commented on this axiom, often raising the issues discussed by Kasper, or pointing to the way that the immanent Trinity far transcends what we can know through the economy or, like Moltmann, pointing to the eschatological experience of the Trinity where the distinction will no longer function. I have focused attention on this moment in the history of Christian theology because I see it as a turning point in Trinitarian theology, a moment of renewal, when this theology becomes again a story of God with us. It is this kind of renewed theology that can have meaning in the Anthropocene[8] and that can prove to be a practical theology.

---

[3] Ibid., 22.
[4] Jürgen Moltmann, *The Trinity and the Kingdom of God: The Doctrine of God* (London: SCM, 1981), 161.
[5] Ibid.
[6] Ibid.
[7] Walter Kasper, *The God of Jesus Christ* (London: SCM, 1983), 275.
[8] According to the International Union of Geological Sciences, we are officially in the Holocene epoch, which began 11,700 years ago, after the last ice age. Many, but not all scientists, have begun to use the word 'Anthropocene' for our current period. This word, popularized by Nobel laureate Paul Crutzen, points to the unprecedented and systemic way that humans are now impacting Earth, its systems and life-forms.

In emphasizing the importance of the story of God in the economy of creation and saving incarnation, I certainly do not mean that theology can leave aside the deep questions of the full divinity of the Spirit and of the Word, and their radical unity and interrelationships within the immanent Trinity. It matters greatly that it is the eternal Word of God who is made flesh, and that it is the eternal Spirit of God who breathes life into a world of creatures and is poured out upon the church. Theologians will always need to develop a coherent theology of God in God's self.

Athanasius is a prime example. He was, of course, a key player in the emergence and development of Nicaean faith in the eternal divinity of the Word and the Spirit, and of the radical unity of the Trinity in the divine being (*ousia*). But his theology remains biblical, a narrative theology of the Word and the Spirit actively engaged in the one economy of creation and salvation. Athanasius's theology is always a theology of the Trinity in act. However, he sees it as essential to defend the realism of the story of God creating and saving through the Word and in the Spirit. It is this concern for the truth of the narrative that motivates his strong defence of the full, eternal divinity of the Word and of the Holy Spirit. For Athanasius, the saving Word of the cross is the very same eternal Word *through* whom all things are created, and the Spirit at work in history and in the life of the church is the same eternal Spirit *in* whom all things are created.

The kind of Trinitarian theology that might speak to the issue of climate change, then, is not an abstract and highly speculative theology that seems disengaged from practical realities. It is, rather, first of all, the biblical story of a God of love who creates a universe of creatures, who embraces matter and flesh in the incarnation, enters into the place of sin, suffering and death, and brings glorious new life that promises to transform everything in God. It is also a theology that recognizes the importance of the Nicaean doctrine and systematic reflection on the Trinity in itself. However, this doctrinal reflection is necessarily grounded in the story of God. The claim made here is that *this* God, the God of this story, *is* the Trinity, even though God in God's self is far more than we know in this life.

Inclusive Trinitarian language

The exclusive use of Father–Son language in talk of the Trinity and the constant use of the male personal pronoun for each of the divine persons constitute a serious problem for many people today. They see it as functioning to maintain patriarchal culture in church and society and, because it is often understood literally, as functioning to limit and impoverish the understanding of God. While theologians have nearly always seen Father–Son language as analogical, this knowledge has been unavailable to the great majority of Christians, many of whom assume that God is literally male.

Feminist theologians have addressed this urgent issue, and they open up new pathways in our speech about the triune God. Sallie McFague sees all our language about God as metaphorical and proposes the metaphors of God as Mother, Lover and Friend.[9] Elizabeth Johnson addresses the issue by means of three strategies: she stresses the traditional theology of divine incomprehensibility, shows the limits of all analogies for the triune God, and then points to the importance of the use of many names in speech about God. She goes on to re-envision Trinitarian theology in wisdom language, as Spirit–Sophia, Jesus–Sophia and Mother–Sophia.[10] Catherine LaCugna has reflected on Rahner's axiom as a feminist theologian and developed a radically relational and participative theology of God as Persons in Communion. She defends the idea that there are different ways of naming God, and promotes the idea of a Christian community of praise as 'an inclusive community of person who in their communal life are the icon of the Trinity'.[11]

The image of God as mother is not a novelty in the biblical tradition. Like a mother God has borne us from the womb, and carried us from birth (Isa. 46.3-4), and will never abandon us: 'Can a woman forget her nursing child, or show no compassion for the child of her womb? Even if these forget, yet I shall not forget you' (Isa. 49.14-15). We can pray to God like a child on its mother's lap: 'But I have calmed and quieted my soul, like a weaned child with its mother' (Ps. 131.2). In our suffering God speaks tender words: 'As a mother comforts her child, so will I comfort you' (Isa. 66.13).

Johnson's feminist theology of God does not seek to replace male images with female images, but to think of and address God in a multitude of images. Jesus's use of *Abba*/Father for God, and his invitation to his followers is a precious and liberating part of our biblical and Christian heritage (Mk. 14.36; Gal. 4.6; Rom. 8.15). Taken in the context of the Kingdom message of Jesus, this *Abba*/Father language does not reinforce patriarchal domination, but challenges it with a vision of human beings as beloved daughters and sons of a God of limitless tender mercy and love. Maternal and paternal images can both speak of God, but as feminist theology also insists, we need more than parenting images for God, fundamental as they are.[12]

We need images taken from other aspects of the human, such as lover and friend, but for a Trinitarian theology that can deal with the natural world we need images from nature. To show how Trinitarian love embraces non-human creation we need to embrace language for the Trinity that is inclusive of the wider creation. Of course, such language, if it is to function in a Trinitarian way, needs to be correlational, able to express something of the dynamics of divine relations – the generation of the Word and the procession of

---

[9] Sallie McFague, *Models of God: Theology for an Ecological Nuclear Age* (Philadelphia: Fortress, 1987).

[10] Elizabeth A. Johnson, *She Who Is: The Mystery of God in Feminist Theological Discourse* (New York: Crossroad, 1992).

[11] Catherine Mowry LaCugna, *God for Us: The Trinity and Christian Life* (San Francisco: HarperSanFrancisco, 1991); 'God in Communion with Us: The Trinity', in *Freeing Theology: The Essentials of Theology in Feminist Perspective,* Catherine Mowry LaCugna (ed.) (San Francisco: HarperSanFrancisco, 1993), 83–114 (108).

[12] Johnson, *She Who Is*, 117–20.

the Spirit from the Source of All. I think it is worth noting that in the Christian tradition there are good examples of such inclusive Trinitarian language.

Athanasius (c. 297–373) is one of many such examples, insisting, on the one hand, that God is radically incomprehensible and beyond the limits of human language and, on the other, that we have a rich source of language for God in the biblical names or symbols (*paradeigmata*). Four of these biblical symbols of the Trinity found in his *Letters to Serapion* are The Light, Ever-lasting Radiance, Enlightening Spirit; The Spring, River of living Water, the Spirit of whom we drink; The Font of Wisdom, Wisdom, Gift of Wisdom; The Source of Life, Life, Life-Giving Spirit. Athanasius's Trinity is a dynamic God of endless life, a God who is fruitful by nature.[13]

A second example is Bonaventure (1221–74). He often speaks of the first person in the Trinity as the abundant flowing Spring, the *fontalis plenititudo* (Fountain Fullness), the fecund Source from which everything else springs. With regard to the second person, while he values the title *Son*, he sees *Image* as having a wider significance, because as perfect Image of the first person, the Image is the co-principle of the Spirit. *Word*, however, possesses a still wider meaning: As the Word is the expression of God's overflowing goodness, so creation is the external expression of the Word. The Word is not only the self-utterance within the divine life, but also this self-utterance in God's free choice to create a universe of creatures, and the incarnation of this Word is the radical creaturely embodiment of divine self-utterance.[14]

Feminist theologians have taught us the importance of having more than Father–Son language for the Trinity. Ecological theology points to the need for images and language that can include the natural world. There are good examples of such language in our tradition, which can point the way to renewed Trinitarian language that can speak in life-giving ways to the issues of climate change.

Trinity and evolution: The Spirit as the energy of love and the Word as the attractor

We now take it for granted that we are part of an observable universe that began from a tiny, dense hot state 13.8 billion years ago, which has been expanding, cooling and growing in complexity ever since. Not only human beings, but also all the living creatures of our reefs, rainforests and deserts have evolved from this first form of life that appeared on Earth about 3.7 billion years ago. How can Trinity be understood in this context? I will suggest that the Spirit can be thought of as the Energy of Love at work in

---

[13] Athanasius of Alexandria, *Letters to Serapion on the Holy Spirit* (= *Ser.*) 1.1.1; 1.33.1. See Mark DelCogliano et al., *Works on the Spirit: Athanasius and Didymus* (New York: St Vladimir's Seminary Press, 2011).

[14] Zachary Hayes, *The Hidden Center: Spirituality and Speculative Christology in St. Bonaventure* (New York: Paulist, 1981), 58–9.

evolutionary processes and the Word can be understood as the Attractor in evolutionary emergence.

In engaging with evolutionary science, Karl Rahner has proposed that the Creator not only confers on creatures their existence and their capacity to act, but also enables their active 'self-transcendence'.[15] God's closeness to creatures in self-bestowing love has the effect of setting them free to become what is new. The evolution of the new is completely open to explanation at the scientific level. But, theologically, this capacity can be understood as given in the relationship of continuous creation – 'When you send forth your spirit, they are created; and you renew the face of the ground' (Ps. 104.30). When Rahner's theology of self-transcendence is understood in a Trinitarian way, the Spirit of God can be seen as the Energy of Love that enables entities to exist, interact and to become in an interrelational world. The Spirit is the source of the new in evolutionary emergence, the Energy of Love at work in the emergence of the first particles of the early universe, in the birth of galaxies and stars, in the origin of the first microbial life on Earth, in the flourishing of life in all its diversity, and in the emergence of a climate on our planet that is hospitable to life in all its abundance and diversity.

How might we think of the Word of God in relation to an evolutionary world? Jósef Życiński (1948–2011) proposed the image of the attractor, found in the physics of non-linear systems. He sees God as the 'Cosmic Attractor' of evolution.[16] In a Trinitarian theology, the Word of God can be understood as the divine Attractor, who draws into existence galaxies, stars and planets and who, on Earth, calls into existence through evolutionary processes all the diverse species of microbes, insects, birds, fish, plants and animals, including the climate of Earth that is fundamental to the life of all these creatures.

The Word made flesh, Jesus crucified and risen, can be thought of as Attractor, not only of evolutionary emergence, but also of God's final transformation and fulfilment of the whole creation. The analogy of the Attractor can point to hope for the universe of creatures, but it can also be understood in a deeply personal way of the Jesus who attracts tax-collectors, sinners, disciples, crowds and children to himself. As the Wisdom of God in our midst he cries out: 'Come to me, all you that are weary and are carrying heavy burdens, and I will give you rest. Take my yoke upon you, and learn from me; for I am gentle and humble in heart, and you will find rest for your souls. For my yoke is easy, and my burden is light' (Mt. 11.28-30). An explicit theology of Jesus as the divine Attractor is found in the words from John's Gospel: 'And I, when I am lifted up from the earth, will draw all to myself' (Jn. 12.32). In the power of the creative indwelling Spirit, the crucified and risen Word is the Attractor who draws the whole creation to its new, transfigured state.

---

[15] Karl Rahner, *Foundations of Christian Faith: An Introduction to the Idea of Christianity* (New York: Seabury Press, 1978), 183–7.

[16] Jósef Życiński, *God and Evolution: Fundamental Questions of Christian Evolutionism* (Washington DC: Catholic University of America Press, 2006), 161–4.

Divine communion and the community of creation

Contemporary science has shown us how interconnected humans are with the rest of the natural world. We depend upon the climate, the atmosphere, the land, the glaciers, the rivers, the seas and upon the whole biosphere of our planet, including the bacteria at work in our soil and in our bodies. And we now know that all of these systems are changed by humanity. The human impact is changing the planet as a system, in ways that will accelerate the extinction of other species and cause enormous affliction for human beings, above all for those who already suffer extreme poverty. In this situation, the way humans choose to live will have enormous consequences for the whole planet.

But our interconnections extend way beyond our home planet. Everything is interconnected. We could not exist if it were not for the long, 13.8-billion-year history of our observable universe. We depend upon the hydrogen that has its origin in the Big Bang, upon the formation of the galaxies and stars and upon the synthesis in stars of elements such as the carbon atoms in our blood and in our brains. We are made from stardust.

Everything in the universe, from an atom, to a cell, to an organism, to a population, to the planetary system of life, to the observable universe itself, is interrelational. Entities are constituted by relationships, relationships between their constituents, and with the wider environment. The interrelationship of all things was already seen in the biblical tradition, where sun and moon, brilliantly shining stars, the highest heavens, the waters above the heavens, mountains and hills, fruit trees and cedars, wild animals and cattle and all creeping things and flying birds are united with human beings in a community of praise (Ps. 148). Richard Bauckham calls this biblical tradition, in which humans are united with all other creatures before God, the *Community of Creation* paradigm, and sees this as a tradition that Jesus himself inhabited: 'Jesus has very much made his own the Psalmist's understanding of creation as a common home for living creatures, in which God provides for all their needs.'[17] This biblically based paradigm has been taken up by ecological theologians, such as Elizabeth Johnson, who writes: 'We all share the status of creaturehood; we are all kin in the evolving community of life now under siege; our vision must be one of flourishing for all.'[18]

I believe that this theological vision of the community of creation is a fundamental theological foundation for a Christian response to climate change. And I am convinced that this vision is grounded at the deepest level in God. The interrelationships of creation are grounded in the interrelational God. This becomes apparent in theologies of the Trinity that see the unity of God in terms of profound communion, and in John Damascene's concept of *perichoresis*, which expresses the being-in-one-another, the

---

[17] Richard Bauckham, *The Bible and Ecology: Rediscovering the Community of Creation* (London: Darton, Longman & Todd, 2010), 73.

[18] Elizabeth A. Johnson, *Ask the Beasts: Darwin and the God of Love* (London: Bloomsbury, 2014), 285.

mutual indwelling of the divine persons. I will offer three examples of such theologies from Orthodox, Protestant and Roman Catholic theologians. The first is Greek Orthodox theologian John Zizioulas. He writes:

> The being of God is a relational being: without the concept of communion it would not be possible to speak of the being of God ... It would be unthinkable to speak of the 'one God' before speaking of the God who is 'communion', that is to say, of the Holy Trinity ... The substance of God, 'God', has no ontological content, no true being apart from communion.[19]

God's very being is to be in relationship. There is nothing more primordial than communion. At the deepest level the origin of all things, every star, every blue wren, the Great Barrier Reef with all is abundance and diversity, is the divine communion. Walter Kasper builds his view of the Trinity as a communion on the prayer of Jesus in John 17, where Jesus prays in profound unity with the Father, and implicitly with the Spirit, and then prays for the faithful, that they may 'be one even as we are one' (Jn. 17.22):

> The doctrine of the Trinity is the Christian form of monotheism. More accurately: the doctrine of the Trinity concretizes the initially abstract assertion of the unity and oneness of God by determining in what this oneness consists. The oneness of God is defined as a communion of Father and Son, but indirectly and implicitly also as a communion of Father, Son and Spirit; it is defined as a unity in love.[20]

This communion-unity is not the kind of monolithic unity that absorbs or suppresses otherness. God's unity is that of an overflowing fullness of self-giving love, of self-outpouring in love, a loving unity that does not exclude, but includes the other. Such a view of God as unity in love demands a different kind of politics in the church and in the world. Jürgen Moltmann develops this line of thought in terms of the open circle of *perichoresis*, which includes the whole creation:

> The Father exists in the Son, the Son in the Father, and both of them in the Spirit, just as the Spirit exists in both the Father and the Son. By virtue of their eternal love they live in one another to such an extent, and dwell in one another to such an extent, that they are one ... To throw open the circulatory movement of the divine light and the divine relationships, and to take men and women, with the whole of creation, into the life stream of the triune God: that is the meaning of creation, reconciliation and glorification.[21]

The mutual relations, and the *perichoretic* unity, of the divine persons are of such a kind as to be freely inclusive of a world of creatures. The story of this inclusion is what I have

---

[19] John D. Zizioulas, *Being as Communion: Studies in Personhood and the Church* (Crestwood: St Vladimir's Seminary Press, 1993), 17.
[20] Kasper, *The God of Jesus Christ*, 305.
[21] Moltmann, *The Trinity and the Kingdom of God*, 178.

been calling the story of God, a story that reaches it glorious fulfilment only when the whole creation is brought to its proper fulfilment in the life of the Trinity.

The abundance and diversity of the interrelated creatures of our planet give expression to the abundant goodness and beauty of the divine communion. Thomas Aquinas long ago wrote of God: And 'because one single creature was not enough, he produced many and diverse, so that what was wanting in one expression of the divine goodness might be supplied by another, for goodness, which in God is singular and all together, in creatures is multiple and scattered.'[22] The diversity of creatures represents the abundance of God.

Each of these creatures in our planetary community and beyond is the place of divine creative presence. Each is loved by the triune God. Each is meant to participate in ways known to God in the final fulfilment of all things in Christ. The loss of biodiversity brought about through human-induced climate change is not only a huge ethical issue, but also a radically theological one. The damage done to the Great Barrier Reef by rising sea temperatures is a profound theological issue.

The Trinity and ecological conversion

Towards the end of his *Laudato Si'*, Pope Francis reflects briefly on the Trinity in relation to the creation, suggesting that the interrelationships we find in nature can be seen as representing, however distantly, their model in the dynamic mutual relations of the Trinity. He then proposes a simple but profound view of the human as a radically interrelational creature:

> The human person grows more, matures more and is sanctified more to the extent that he or she enters into relationships, going out from themselves to live in communion with God, with others and with all creatures. In this way they make their own the Trinitarian dynamism which God imprinted in them when they were created.[23]

I see these few words as suggesting a fully Trinitarian anthropology. The human grows more, matures more and grows in holiness to the extent that he or she enters into relationships. Francis specifies these relationships as a threefold communion, with God, with our fellow human beings and with the natural world around us. He points out that when we embrace this threefold communion we are true to the Trinitarian dynamism that is imprinted on us as creatures made in the image of God. Learning to enter into this threefold communion we are true to ourselves at the very deepest level of our being. Conversely, when we close ourselves off from the natural world around us, or from the human person before us, or the living God, then we distort our own being and live in a

---

[22] Thomas Aquinas, *Summa Theologiae* (New York: Benziger, 1947), 1.47.1.
[23] Pope Francis, *Laudato Si'* (Vatican City: Libreria Editrice Vaticana, 2015), 209–10.

state of alienation – 'The external deserts in the world are growing, because the internal deserts have become so vast.'[24]

Pope Francis, along with many others, sees human beings in our time as called to an ecological conversion, a 'profound interior conversion'.[25] This involves learning to see everything as interrelated. It means learning to relate to trees, birds and animals, to rivers, seas and mountains, and to the climate, and in so doing, coming to our true selves. This conversion involves the continuous discovery of who we are in relation to Earth and its creatures, to our human sisters and brothers and to God. Ecological conversion means coming to see ourselves as part of a family of creatures before God, in a 'splendid universal communion'.[26] The conversion involves not only a radical transformation in the way we see the wider natural world, but also in the way we feel for it and with it. It involves a change in lifestyle, a new asceticism, new priorities and personal and communal action.

---

[24] Ibid., 190.
[25] Ibid.
[26] Ibid., 193.

A response to Denis Edwards

Teddy C. Sakupapa[1]

The essay 'Triune God and Climate Change' by Denis Edwards proposes a Trinitarian theology from below as a theological response to climate change. He offers an unashamedly Christian response that nevertheless recognizes the need for various voices in addressing the challenges posed by climate change. The significance of theology in addressing issues such as climate change is at times questioned. Edwards however observes that 'the theology of God as Trinity can offer vision, motivation, and inspiration for Christians in addressing anthropogenic climate change.' Edwards is categorical in stating that a Christian response to climate change may well stem from faith in God.

In my view, this self-reflexive approach is crucial. I find the three aspects of vision, motivation and inspiration absolutely necessary for any meaningful commitment to addressing aspects of climate change, irrespective of whether such endeavour is theological or not. Edwards's narrative approach in his essay is therefore apposite in illumining how the story of the Triune God may serve as the locus for a Christian response. His essay briefly discusses various aspects of renewed Trinitarian theology including the significance of inclusive Trinitarian language, the Trinity and evolution, the Trinity and the interrelatedness of all being, and a final section with a constructive proposal, namely, of ecological conversion.

In what follows, I will briefly engage with some of the insights in his essay, keeping in mind my own locus of enunciation. Edwards's point of departure is a discussion of Karl Rahner's diagnosis of the marginalization of the Trinity in Western theology. Locating the roots of the so-called Trinitarian renaissance in this manner, Edwards proceeds by highlighting how Rahners's distinctive theological heritage has been engaged by some of the most notable thinkers on the Trinity in modern times. Considering the bulk of work on the Trinity since the dawn of the Trinitarian renaissance, I found Edwards's succinct depiction of some of the crucial issues in rethinking Trinitarian theology remarkable. Edwards locates one of the significant turning points in Trinitarian theology with Rahner's famous axiom namely, 'The economic Trinity is the immanent Trinity and the immanent Trinity is the economic Trinity.' His brief discussion of two excellent

---

[1] Teddy Chalwe Sakupapa is a Zambian national and an ordained minister in the Reformed tradition. He teaches ecumenical studies and social ethics in the Department of Religion and Theology at the University of the Western Cape, South Africa. His current research focuses on decoloniality and the doctrine of the Trinity in African theology.

critical reflections on the axiom by the protestant Jürgen Moltmann and the Roman Catholic Walter Kasper illustrates his depth of insight into Rahner's axiom.

Given the author's ecumenical outlook in this essay, the absence of Catherine LaCugna's engagement of Rahner's axiom is understandable albeit unfortunate. Lacugna's *God for Us: The Trinity and Christian Life* is not only a crucial work on the revitalization of Trinitarian theology but also an example of an attempt to elucidate the Trinity as a doctrine with practical consequence for Christian life. Here, a crucial question that emerges is best captured in the title of Robert Jenson's essay 'What Is the Point of Trinitarian Theology?'[2] With respect to Rahner's axiom intimated above, LaCugna opined that the real difference between the economic Trinity and the immanent Trinity is not ontological but doxological.[3] The question whether or not Rahner's axiom must be understood as a methodological (epistemological – LaCugna) or ontological principle is debatable. For Zizoulas, what is needed is an apophatic theology in order not to draw sharp distinctions between ontology and epistemology.[4] Edwards's concern, however, is to navigate the terrain of Trinitarian thinking in search of a theology that may engage with climate change. In this vein, Edwards decries the merely abstract and speculative Trinitarian theologies. Such theologies are not apposite to a meaningful theology in the context of climate change. Therefore, his reading of Rahner's articulation of the Trinity as the God of creation and salvation is indeed attractive.

In the African context, the Western translation of the Trinity through missionary theologies introduced what is seen as an alien doctrine. While an earlier generation of African theologians worked out impressive Christologies, these did not sufficiently lead to thorough going Trinitarian theologies. This is not withstanding that many of them responded in the affirmative to the question of whether the God of creation in African Tradition religion is the same as the God of Christian proclamation, the Triune God.[5] Linked to this is the challenge of language. Some African theologians find the Trinitarian language of persons foreign. The work of some African women theologians has been helpful to address some of these challenges as well as the question of inclusive language. Pneumatology likewise is not fully developed in African theology. Some notable exceptions attempt to retrieve African traditional concepts to articulate African pneumatologies. This area has been fruitful particularly for African theologians engaging in ecological discourse. Instructive in this regard are the contributions by Kapya Kaoma, Teddy Sakupapa and Kuzipa Nalwamba which take the African communal context

---

[2] Robert W. Jenson, 'What is the Point of Trinitarian Theology?' in *Trinitarian Theology Today: Essays on Divine Being and Act*, Christoph Schwöbel (ed.) (London: T&T Clark, 1995), 31–43.

[3] Catherine Mowry LaCugna, *God for Us: The Trinity and Christian Life* (San Francisco: Harpercollins, 1991), 342–8.

[4] John Zizioulas, 'The Doctrine of God the Trinity Today: Suggestions for an Ecumenical Study', in *The Forgotten Trinity*, Alistair Heron (ed.) (London: BCC/CCBI, 1991), 23–4.

[5] For a detailed discussion on this see Ernst M. Conradie and Teddy Chalwe Sakupapa, '"Decolonising the Doctrine of the Trinity" or "The Decolonising Doctrine of the Trinity"'? *Journal of Theology for Southern Africa* 161 (2018), 37–53.

and the interrelatedness of being central in theological discourse.[6] These theologians contribute towards the articulation of language and vision for ecological discourse. Nevertheless, Edwards's deep insight, namely, the need for a 'coherent theology of God in God's self' that does justice to the full divinity of the word and spirit, is a crucial call, not least within the African context.

Being an ecumenical and intercultural theologian, I think that African contributions can fruitfully engage and draw on Edwards's appraisal of inclusive language for God-talk. Appreciative of the feminist critique of the irredeemably male language used to describe the Trinity, Edwards constructively urges for more than just parenting language. In his view, what is needed for a Trinitarian theology that deals with the natural world are images from nature. This move is significant in that it also goes over a number of binaries including the gender binary. For Edwards, one can draw from the Christian tradition from as far back as Athanasius and from, later, Bonaventure, both of whom employed inclusive language in their God-talk. Notably, several images drawn from Athanasius also resonate with a variety of African concepts that may be appropriated for a meaningful Trinitarian theology for the twenty-first century. However, what seems quite clear is that such wonderful insights remain deeply the theologies of men.

Edwards's appraisal of the feminist critique and his call to draw images from nature is best understood against the background of his large corpus of work on theology and evolution. Thus, it is no surprise, that drawing on Rahner's theology of self-transcendence and the ideas of Jósef Życiński, Edwards speaks of the Spirit as 'the Energy of Love at work in evolutionary processes' and of the Word as 'the Attractor in evolutionary emergence'. Accordingly, he accentuates the vision of interconnectedness of all reality and the diversity of creatures. He profoundly notes that 'God's very being is to be in relationship.' If the bulk of Edwards's essay provides a rich narrative of how the story of God the Trinity may provide motivation, inspiration and vision for a Christian response to climate change, the last section on ecological conversion drives the point home. It stresses Christian particularity and particularly draws on Pope Francis's *Laudato Si'* to accentuate a Trinitarian anthropology best captured in terms of a threefold communion namely with God, fellow humans and the natural world. Much of what is discussed under ecological conversion resonates with the deep insights on interrelatedness in African thought.

Edwards's essay illustrates how a renewed Trinitarian theology can indeed be a practical theology particularly in the context of climate change. It is a refreshing attempt that seeks to appropriate images from nature to articulate a practical theology predicated on the story of God. Comparatively, it is surprisingly that two of the notable books on the Trinity in Africa, namely by James Kombo and Ibrahim Bitrus completely neglect the

---

[6] See Kapya J. Kaoma, *God's Family, God's Earth: Christian Ecological Ethics of Ubuntu* (Blantyre: Kachere Series, 2014); Teddy Chalwe Sakupapa, 'Spirit and Ecology in the Context of African Theology', *Scriptura* 111 (2012), 422–30; Kuzipa Nalwamba, 'Mupasi as Cosmic s(S)pirit: The Universe as a Community of Life', *HTS Theological Studies* 73:3 (2017), 1–8.

ecological dimension.[7] To conclude, it is crucial to note that in my sub-Saharan African context, ecological discourse is at the same time a soteriological discourse. While reflections by Western theologians such as Denis Edwards are valuable, the question of differential justice emerges as a crucial one for the so-called Global South given that the poor are among the worst affected by climate change. This becomes manifest in the threat climate change poses to food security, health and in the stories of displacement. Here too, a narrative theology of the triune God may just be needed.

---

[7] See James Kombo, *The Doctrine of God in African Christian Thought: The Holy Trinity, Theological Hermeneutics, and the African Intellectual Culture* (Leiden: Brill, 2007); Ibrahim Bitrus, *Community and Trinity in Africa* (London: Routledge, 2017).

PART VI

The promise and perils of ecclesial praxis

Introduction

Hilda P. Koster

This section of the volume returns to the original question, namely whether North Atlantic Christian theology can help in addressing the challenges posed by climate change. Can Christians in the North Atlantic really work with others to address anthropogenic climate change? Or do they remain part of the problem? If not, what can they contribute that others, including Christians, elsewhere in the world cannot?

The logic of this section follows the model of theological reflection on praxis, namely one that involves an ongoing spiral of acting, seeing, judging and acting. Specifically, this section focuses on various aspects of ecclesial praxis, namely (a) liturgical praxis (dealing for instance with the carbon footprint of worship and finding creative ways of worshiping with the earth), (b) exegetical, hermeneutical and homiletical praxis (with specific reference to retrieving biblical wisdom against the grain), (c) Christian fellowship (with specific reference to the mitigating power of the sacraments and the prospects of eco-congregations), (d) pastoral praxis (dealing with the pastoral task of counselling Christians who experience deep sadness and anguish caused by the loss of species and living on the dark predictions of a climate change-induced apocalypse), and (e) ecclesial praxis in the light of social teaching (dealing for instance with the ecological impact of the ministries and missions of the church but also the very manner we think about what Christian mission on a planet in peril might mean).

The challenges faced by North Atlantic Christian theology in this regard are highly significant. Consider the following:

The Christian liturgy may be understood in cosmological terms as a way of seeing the world in the light of the Light of the world. It challenges other ways of looking at the world, for example in capitalist-utilitarian, social Darwinian, or romantic ways. The liturgy invites worshippers not to accept the ways in which the world is seen by 'the world'. It also elicits a powerful form of protest against principalities and powers. However, the reality is that worship often does not function in this way. This is already evident from the carbon footprint of worship services. In a consumerist society, the liturgy is easily commercialized, to provide services where people's spiritual needs can be met. This is epitomised by the prosperity gospel but all too often the liturgy is either archaic or merely a carbon copy (pun intended) of contemporary cultural expressions. There have been many attempts at liturgical innovation and reformation, for example around a 'Season of Creation' but this is necessarily slow work. In a rapidly changing climate such slow work may come too late. If so, if it is already too late, how does that affect liturgical practices?

How may an appeal to the Bible be made in response to the current climate crisis? Does the Bible offer resources for an environmental ethics and ecotheology for such a time as ours? What kind of ecological hermeneutics is necessary for such an engagement to be fruitful for exegetical and homiletical praxis? What are the interpretative choices required for a reading of the biblical text in light of human-made climate disruption? Similarly how may we develop a green homiletics, that is, a homiletics that places the current climate crisis and its victims, including its non-human casualties, at the centre of its hermeneutical praxis? Or to put it differently, how may we preach 'good news' in the face of environmental devastation, the climate crisis and extreme energy extraction? What would a climate-literate preaching look like? How can this type of preaching address climate justice while also attending towards congregational context, for instance due to geography, culture, political tensions and economics?

Yet another set of questions is raised when we consider Christian fellowship. How may we come together as the community of Christ in the face of anthropogenic climate change and its many human and non-human victims? How can churches in the high-carbon footprint world be in solidarity with churches in the low carbon footprint world, especially churches in low-lying countries in the Global South, who have very little responsibility for the current climate crisis and yet exponentially suffer its consequences? How may churches generate fellowship not just with fellow humans but also with the earth, its many creatures and the climate? How, moreover, may churches provide a space to engage with the cognitive, behavioural, and emotional conflicts inherent in confronting climate change and the consumerist lifestyles of climate-privileged congregants. And what may church communities learn from both Christians and non-Christians who feel the climate crisis as a sacred loss, and who are re-imagining their faith, spirituality and life through environmental advocacy?

The current climate crisis and its consequences make many people fearful about the future. We live in a day and age in which 'talk about the weather is filled with dread'. What are the challenges of this situation for pastoral care? How are people to be hopeful when faced with increases in violent and unpredictable weather events, the massive loss of species and the increase of social and political conflict due to climate-related droughts and sea-level rise? How may Christians in the high-carbon-footprint world deal with the guilt and shame they often feel about their contribution to climate change and the suffering of climate-vulnerable communities? Can confession and worship provide productive avenues for turning climate change-related guilt into earth-honouring and justice-seeking discipleship?

The climate crisis asks that we green the way we think about the ministries and missions of the Church. There have been numerous ecclesial experiments in this regard, for better and for worse. Yet these experiments in and of itself raise important questions: Are such efforts at greening ecclesial practices nearly enough? Do they make a difference that matters: a difference that leads to political change? Or, are these changes merely cosmetic and, worse still, lull us into complacency? When it comes to the ministries and missions of the church we also need to ask about the distinctive contribution that Christians can make that no other institution can make. To what extent do such ministries and missions allow and encourage collaboration with others? Is it true that the church should only initiative such missions if there is no one else to tackle that? How, then, may one assess current ecclesial praxis? Does it constitute a more than symbolic first step to address climate change?

Chapter 6.1
Climate change and liturgical praxis

Christina M. Gschwandtner[1]

Introduction

Christian faith is learnt and expressed in its worship practices. Although academia has tended to focus on doctrine as the most crucial identifying factor of faith, religion is lived and communicated through experience and practice. While this can obviously occur on very personal levels or in the semi-private context of family life, even such private practices flow out of and are inspired by communal settings. Religious experience and faith hence are always on some level *liturgical* even in contexts where such communal practices are not rigidly structured but characterized by greater impulsivity and creativity. If liturgy constitutes the time and place where habits of faith are acquired and find their most explicit expression, then it is absolutely crucial to ask how such practices impact life 'outside' the liturgical or ecclesial setting. Many liturgical scholars stress that liturgy is in some form on behalf of the 'world' and surely most pastors or priests wish for whatever occurs in worship to have an impact on how believers lead their 'regular' lives when they are not physically within the liturgical setting. As environmental destruction and climate change are the pressing issues of the 'world' that occupy us here, we must ask what liturgy has to say about this. Do worship practices endorse, perpetuate or contribute to climate change? Can liturgy provide resources for protecting creation or galvanize action on behalf of endangered species? What connection has liturgy with the life of *this* world, on *this* planet and its climate, at *this* moment in its (and our) history? Can liturgy challenge consumerist lifestyles or does it simply serve to endorse and perpetuate them?

While liturgy has not played a large role in the contemporary ecotheological discussion, which focuses more heavily on either concrete ethical or more theoretical doctrinal issues, on occasion comments are made about the possible potential for liturgy to transform practices in a more environmentally sensitive direction. Michael Northcott discusses the ecological dimensions of fasting and feasting practices,[2] Lawrence Micks

---

[1] Christina M. Gschwandtner teaches continental philosophy of religion at Fordham University. Her work is situated at the intersection of phenomenology, theology and ecology with a special interest in phenomenology of liturgy.

[2] Michael Northcott, *A Moral Climate: The Ethics of Global Warming* (Maryknoll: Orbis, 2007).

outlines some practical guidelines for integrating ecological concerns into liturgical practices,³ Norman Wirzba seeks to retrieve a more sacramental way of eating, and the Eucharist is occasionally considered to have 'ecological' potential.⁴ From the perspective of liturgical theology,⁵ Gordon Lathrop highlights the importance of place and the earth in liturgical patterns, occasionally hinting at ecological implications.⁶ Eastern Orthodox scholars (and, on a more popular level, Patriarch Bartholomew⁷) often point to the 'sacramental and liturgical worldview' of Eastern Orthodoxy or its 'cosmic liturgy' as especially suited to care for the planet,⁸ and sometimes Western scholars mention the potential of appropriating this 'Eastern' emphasis for Western contexts.⁹

Yet, many of the arguments cited for liturgy's ecological potential are ambiguous in their thrust: Does the cosmic scope of the patristic liturgical worldview show the value of all of creation or does it elevate invisible, incorporeal and intelligible reality over the visible, material and physical world in destructive ways? Does the 'sacramental' view of nature have concrete implications or benefits for non-human creatures or the planet as a whole, especially considering sacraments have traditionally only applied to humans? Does Christian anthropology as operative in liturgy – whether by worshippers or celebrants – call the human to responsibility for all creatures or elevate humans above other beings as the only ones worthy of redemptive concerns? Do concrete liturgical practices, such as the traditional cycles of fasting and feasting, encourage creation care or exploit nature? Does the manufacture of items for worship (e.g., icons, vestments, chalices, other material implements) and the building of churches value materiality

---

³ Lawrence E. Mick, *Liturgy and Ecology in Dialogue* (Collegeville: Liturgical Press, 1997); Charles Fensham and Sarah Travis, 'What on Earth is Liturgy (Leitourgia)? Liturgy and Ecology', in *The Church in God's Household: Protestant Perspectives on Ecclesiology and Ecology,* Clive W. Ayre and Ernst Conradie (eds) (Pietermaritzburg: Cluster Publications, 2016), 10–30.

⁴ See Lukas Vischer (ed.), *The Eucharist and Creation Spirituality* (Geneva: Centre Internationale Reformé John Knox, 2007).

⁵ Norman Wirzba, *Living the Sabbath: Discovering the Rhythms of Rest and Delight* (Grand Rapids: Brazos Press, 2006); Norman Wirzba, *Food and Faith: A Theology of Eating* (Cambridge: Cambridge University Press, 2011).

⁶ Gordon Lathrop, *Holy Ground: A Liturgical Cosmology* (Minneapolis: Fortress, 2003). See also Richard N. Fragomeni and John T. Pawlikowski, *The Ecological Challenge: Ethical, Liturgical, and Spiritual Responses* (Collegeville: Liturgical Press, 1994).

⁷ Patriarch Bartholomew, *On Earth as in Heaven: Ecological Vision and Initiatives of Ecumenical Patriarch Bartholomew*, John Chryssavgis (ed.) (New York: Fordham University Press, 2012).

⁸ Elizabeth Theokritoff, *Living in God's Creation: Orthodox Perspectives on Ecology* (Crestwood: St. Vladimir's Theological Seminary Press, 2009); John Chryssavgis and Bruce Foltz (eds), *Toward an Ecology of Transfiguration: Orthodox Christian Perspectives on Environment, Nature, and Creation* (New York: Fordham University Press, 2013). For a critical account of the Orthodox argument, see my 'Grounding Ecological Action in Orthodox Theology and Liturgical Practice? A Call for Further Thinking', *Journal for Orthodox Christian Studies* 1:1 (2018), 61–77.

⁹ See Celia Deane-Drummond, *A Handbook in Theology and Ecology* (London: SCM Press, 1996); Willis Jenkins, *Ecologies of Grace: Environmental Ethics and Christian Theology* (Oxford: Oxford University Press, 2008).

or does it constitute a merely instrumental use of matter? How wedded is Christian liturgical praxis to its emergence in the Northern hemisphere (particularly evident in the association of Easter with the coming of spring and Christmas with the winter solstice, very prevalent in the patristic homilies and often evoked by contemporary imagery)? Is liturgy necessarily aligned with the North's high-carbon footprint or can it sustain a more low-carbon lifestyle, possibly even inspiring life-saving and planet-preserving 'green' liturgies? How complicit is contemporary liturgical praxis in carbon-generating activities that contribute to climate change? Can liturgy challenge consumerist lifestyles or does it simply serve to endorse and perpetuate them?

Liturgy as pollution?

Indeed, in many contemporary contexts, especially in the Global North, worship can be a highly polluting activity. Especially in North America people frequently drive to worship services in gas-guzzling SUVs, employ sound systems or imaging technologies that can require huge amounts of energy to run, host social events with extensive use of plastic and other heavily polluting products, pay little attention to the sustainability or energy efficiency of their buildings and hold conventions that require air travel and other polluting activities, usually without any thought for the impact any of these have on the planet. Even worse, certain sectors of Christianity actively preach against environmental policies, exhort people from the pulpit to vote for candidates that deny climate change is occurring and actively encourage consumerist and capitalist lifestyles (e.g. the so-called prosperity gospel). Many conservative Christian parishes actively embrace and perpetuate the suburban capitalist and consumerist lifestyle that contributes so heavily to carbon emissions. The 'running' of worship – from care and maintenance of the building, investment in the implements employed for it, attendees' travel to and from the worship site, to all the other elements of 'fellowship' or education associated with liturgy – consumes often exorbitant amounts of resources that contribute significantly to climate change. Less use of technology and heavier use of traditional implements (rather than producing new ones) correspondingly reduce such contribution, but simply switching from plastic to paper products or other such minor adjustments are obviously not sufficient to address the looming crisis.

Worship did not always have a high-carbon footprint; this is a fairly recent phenomenon and may have more to do with the shifting of our lifestyles overall than anything insidious about liturgy itself. For example, is the consumerist approach to worship in many places due to something destructive within worship or liturgy itself or is it merely an expression of the larger consumerist lifestyle now also applied to church? Do people drive to church in big polluting cars because there is something wrong with worship or because there is something wrong with how we have structured our infrastructure and our larger consumerist habits? Yet, the resources necessary to repair (or even heat) crumbling and drafty medieval churches all over Europe – although built long before the current crisis – now also contribute their share. And the Western consumerist lifestyle with its ubiquity and accessibility of products has often been exported to developing nations via missionary activity: preaching the Gospel was often closely linked to perpetuating Western lifestyles. Christianity, 'progress', capitalism, consumerism and 'development' have frequently been presented as whole 'package', embodied in how Christianity became liturgically present in new environments, importing Western products and values and suppressing alternative ways of living or destabilizing subsistence economies.

More positively, the fluid worship styles in many contemporary traditions have allowed for the development of new liturgies that actively try to incorporate environmental concerns into the liturgical settings. In some contexts, older traditions of blessing animals are retrieved or new ones developed,[10] the sacral or sacramental character of all of creation stressed, specific ceremonies developed for the planting of trees or environmental restoration,[11] or fasting practices recommended as a more ascetic and less consumerist lifestyle.[12] These are obviously not sufficient to roll back climate change, but they do point to a shift in consciousness on this issue and the recognition that such a shift may require fostering different attitudes via liturgical habituation or ritual blessing. Is a broader retrieval of liturgical dimensions possible? Scripture scholars have increasingly developed an 'environmental hermeneutic' for reading Scripture in environmentally friendly ways and for retrieving aspects that may help us think differently about land and animals.[13] A similar approach could be applied to liturgy, especially in traditions where liturgy has an almost equivalent status with Scripture or employs texts with a long tradition that shape worldviews in ways similar to the biblical texts.[14]

---

[10] See Andrew Linzey, *Animal Rites: Liturgies of Animal Care* (London: SPCK, 1996). Some of these practices are ambivalent, however. The increasingly popular blessings of animals, for example, often become highly commercialized spectacles that feature pets or livestock – with all their problematic environmental implications – more than they have any positive effect on the preservation of species or restoration of habitats.

[11] See, for example, the worship resources for the 'season of creation': https://seasonofcreation.com/worship-resources/liturgies/ and https://www.oikoumene.org/en/what-we-do/climate-change/time-for-creation (accessed 9 April 2018) which contain a variety of other resources. Patriarch Bartholomew's predecessor Patriarch Demetrios designated September 1st, the beginning of the Orthodox liturgical year as a day of prayer for the environment. An English translation of the text for the vespers service can be found here: https://www.goarch.org/-/vespers-for-the-preservation-of-creation (accessed 9 April 2018).

[12] See, e.g., Kallistos Ware, 'Lent and the Consumer Society', in *Living Orthodoxy in the Modern World*, Andrew Walker and Costa Carras (eds) (London: SPCK, 1996), 64–84.

[13] E.g. Norman C. Habel and Peter Trudinger (eds), *Exploring Ecological Hermeneutics* (Atlanta: Society of Biblical Literature, 2008).

[14] In more heavily Scripture-oriented traditions, possibly the ways of applying Scripture environmentally might prove more useful than the liturgical retrieval. But as these traditions also tend to be much more fluid liturgically, they might well choose to appropriate some of these liturgical resources and adapt them to their own practices.

A retrieval of a liturgical vision

For this we have to step back for a moment to the early developments of liturgy and the context in which it emerged. Liturgical practices were part of Christian identity from its inception and to some extent precede the emergence of the Christian scriptures. Although we do not know much exactly about Jewish synagogue worship in the first century or the precise ways in which it might have influenced Christian worship practices, it is clear that Christians from early on assembled and prayed together, probably participating in Jewish Sabbath practices and continuing these in some form with an agape meal of fellowship that slowly developed into the Eucharistic liturgy.[15] Evidence for more elaborate liturgical practices and 'worship services' explodes in the fourth century, together with significant development of the liturgical year, often traceable via controversies for the dating of Pascha/Easter. While there were a diversity of liturgical practices in different areas of the Christian tradition (Latin, Byzantine, Syriac, Armenian, Georgian and others), certain common characteristics – like the centrality of the Eucharist and other sacramental practices (especially baptism), the importance of hymnody, reading of Scripture and rhetorical homily, architectural and artistic expressions, the use of material objects such as candles, chalices and vestments, the development of the liturgical year culminating in Great Lent and Easter/Pascha – are shared by most Christian traditions for most of Christian history.

In many ways liturgy was the central expression of Christian faith and the most important tool for formation of identity and the maintenance of social bonds in Christian communities. Christian life – from birth to death – centred on and was marked by liturgical practices. Liturgy for most of Christian history is not just some practical 'addendum' to Christian faith but constitutes and shapes Christian identity. Early Christian societies were thoroughly communal and their liturgy marked them as Christian societies in their beliefs and practices. Encounter with the divine, with the cosmos, and often even with each other occurred within the liturgical space and its extensions into the sacramental spaces of the household community. Doctrinal training and adhesion, reading and especially hearing of Scripture (in a mostly illiterate society without printed documents), even prayer and what we now call 'spirituality', as well as ethical, social and at times political formation occurred within liturgy and were fundamentally shaped by it. Christian identity and practice for much of Christian history is unthinkable without or outside of liturgy. We can thus ask whether liturgy still has the same potential to shape Christian worldviews or ethical practices today, whether such formation can be 'good for the planet' and whether such formative practices are instead predominantly harmful to the earth's habitats which we increasingly refuse to share with other creatures.

---

[15] Paul F. Bradshaw, *Reconstructing Early Christian Worship* (New York: Pueblo Books, 2010); Paul F. Bradshaw and Maxwell E. Johnson, *The Origins of Feasts, Fasts, and Seasons in Early Christianity* (New York: Pueblo Books, 2011).

In this respect, it is crucial that liturgy communicated a Christian worldview, both in the sense of expressing it and in the sense of transmitting it to future generations. And this worldview – deeply shaped by the Graeco-Roman worldview of late antiquity combined with the Jewish worldview of the Hebrew Scriptures and Christianity's early roots in first-century Jewish culture – was, like many ancient worldviews, fundamentally cosmic in nature. To a large extent Christianity adopted Greek philosophical presuppositions about the universe: the distinction between incorporeal, invisible, immutable and immaterial reality on the one hand and corporeal, visible, transitory and material reality on the other, the notion of the four elements (earth, water, air, fire) and their respective weight and density, of linear and cyclical motion and its respective cosmic significance, of a spherical universe revolving around the earth, of the relation of human soul and body as reflective of and as encapsulating these two realms. These presuppositions and convictions about the cosmos and the human person deeply influenced the development and meaning of liturgy (and obviously Christian theology more broadly). Implicitly and at times explicitly liturgy sought to bring together visible and invisible realms, corporeal and incorporeal reality, the earthly and the heavenly, body and soul. Liturgy not only organized time and space on all kinds of levels (architecturally, via the calendar, ritual practices for life's threshold experiences, etc.), but shaped affect and emotion, formed identity and community, moved to practice and expressed all this in corporeal form, inscribed it on the body and the senses.[16]

This cosmic worldview was deeply concerned about *phthora* (usually translated as corruption or defilement, but really meaning something like disintegration or passing out of being). In fact, *phthora* may well be *the* central problem of the patristic age. Redemption for the ancients is redemption from *phthora*. Life 'eternal' is a life without *phthora*. Christ 'tramples down death by death' because he redeems from *phthora* by undergoing death without corruption or decomposition, undoing it by nullifying its consequences. *Phthora* is a characteristic of the created order, which is subject to change and disintegration, which comes to be and goes out of being. It is first of all a fairly neutral term that applies to that part of the cosmos that is constructed of the four elements, moves in linear fashion and undergoes change. Change always comes with disintegration and corruption, because only the eternal and immutable remains unchanging. These are basic presuppositions of ancient cosmology, already articulated in Plato and Aristotle, appropriated by Philo, and taken up to a large extent by the Christian tradition, especially in the East. These cosmological presuppositions undergird not only the central claims of Christian faith, but any number of Christian practices, like the veneration of relics, and of course most centrally the practice of the Eucharist – taken to confer immortality and hence save from *phthora*. The early liturgies are full of language and imagery describing such turning from death to life, from disintegration

---

[16] See Christina M. Gschwandtner, *Welcoming Finitude: Toward a Phenomenology of Orthodox Liturgy* (New York: Fordham University Press, 2019).

to healing, from corruption to incorruptibility. Liturgy both conveyed this worldview – from highly intellectual to profoundly visceral levels – and shaped Christian convictions and practices on a subconscious level to create moral expectations that accorded with this worldview.

For manifold reasons we have abandoned this larger worldview and think of faith, spirituality and even liturgy primarily on private and personal levels. We no longer take our liturgical practice to reflect or mirror the scientific presuppositions about the universe – as they did for the ancients – much less to have cosmic significance. Rather, spiritual and liturgical actions are generally presumed to confer only private redemptive benefits. Even more clearly our thinking about ethical theory and moral practice – whether on religious or secular levels – is explicated primarily if not exclusively in personal terms: actions require individual agents and are evaluated in terms of the particular consequences of single actions often in isolation from broader contexts. We have individual rights, bear individual responsibility, and are judged as individual culprits for our own personally willed actions (presuppositions shared by both deontological and utilitarian approaches). One of the greatest challenges of environmental destruction and especially of the phenomenon of climate change is precisely that the modern ethical theories that we employ to evaluate moral actions are utterly inadequate to deal with them or even to understand our failure to act.[17] Most environmental problems transcend local and national boundaries and take on a life of their own that cannot be neatly traced to one perpetrator. Air and water pollution do not dissipate at national borders; pesticides do not heed the edge of the field but seep into groundwater that kills far from the original source; acidic clouds rain off over virgin forests where no one lives or pollutes; toxins travel up the food chain in complex ways, etc. Climate change exacerbates this problem in exponential fashion; it is truly a global, planetary problem. And while it is clear that human carbon emission is the primary culprit for the increasing greenhouse effect, this recognition does not make it easy to assign concrete responsibility or to hold individuals responsible, especially as the effects are often delayed by several decades. People do not feel like they ought to engage in or refrain from practices that disproportionately affect people they do not know and who may not yet even be born, nor do they sense culpability for something of such scope that it far transcends any of their specific individual actions. Our moral thinking and feeling is restricted to very narrow personal terms and thus utterly inadequate to deal with environmental destruction on a global scale.

It is hence environmental scientists, ethicists and policy makers who are calling for a larger scope in our thinking, for a global rather than individual perspective. Can we retrieve the cosmic dimension of ancient liturgy – that is still preserved in the contemporary liturgical language at least in the Orthodox tradition and also in

---

[17] James Garvey, *The Ethics of Climate Change: Right and Wrong in a Warming World* (London: Continuum, 2008); Hans Jonas, *The Imperative of Responsibility: In Search of an Ethics for the Technological Age* (Chicago: University of Chicago Press, 1984).

some Western rites – to address this need for a larger scope? Can we reinvigorate and reappropriate the language and imagery of *phthora* and its pernicious effect to fight the corruption and defilement we are currently visiting on the planet and to recover a more cosmic vision that sees all of creation as intimately connected and wrapped up together in a larger cosmic struggle? Although such cosmic 'battle' was often read traditionally in terms of Christ's victory over the 'devil' or demonic forces (such as those expelled in liturgies for baptism and Theophany), there is little reason why such imagery could not be evoked for confronting and combatting the hostile and evil powers threatening the planet and life as a whole – including our own complicity in this destruction. The ancient worldview held in tension personal culpability and larger cosmic forces in a way that often makes very little sense to us today on *theological* terms, but actually captures quite accurately their enmeshment on *ecological* levels where individual responsibility and systemic structures are tightly interwoven and cannot be neatly separated from each other. Redemption and sin for much of Christian history were understood – and exercised liturgically – in much broader cosmic and communal fashion than they are often read today. A problem like climate change precisely requires such a larger vision, because it is not easily traceable to single, individual responsibility, it crosses personal and national boundaries, it is long-term in its effect and it concerns the planet and all its species as a whole. We have to stop thinking of faith and redemption as purely personal experiences that we can appropriate for individual use and instead retrieve the ways in which liturgy at least until quite recently presupposed and practiced communal and corporate redemption, recognizing that we are not saved without each other and the entire cosmos.

In this respect liturgy has great potential for communal repentance that is not separate from personal contrition, but encourages, models and enfolds it. Climate change urgently requires a genuine recognition of the tremendous damage – and evil – perpetrated not just by individuals but by whole societies, especially those in the Northern hemisphere. It calls for radical repentance and genuine metanoia, but doing so on personal levels is simply not enough: entire structures have to be acknowledged as sinful and evil, as requiring a total 'turn-around'. A slight (or even major) shift in personal lifestyle is utterly insufficient – and often does not happen precisely because people feel that it will make no difference. For change to occur, repentance and contrition have to happen on both personal and communal levels, and those levels have to be connected with each other in meaningful ways. They have to touch individuals, become inscribed on minds and hearts via deeply affective corporeal expression, but do so in a setting where we recognize that we are part of a larger story, that our personal failures are always part of larger patterns of consumption and exploitation. Such communal rites then have to translate explicitly into communal action; they cannot remain purely symbolic. At the same time, the symbolism matters: genuine change of lifestyle usually requires a change of worldview, not merely different actions, because consistent actions that result in truly changed practices have to be motivated and habituated. Ritual is precisely one of the most significant ways in which human societies traditionally motivated and habituated patterns of conduct, including creating the deep sense of obligation that comes with such ritualized behaviour reinforced by frequent repetition and the weight of presumed sanctity.[18] A sense of moral responsibility is inculcated at a 'gut' level only when it is acquired sufficiently early and cemented by deeply ingrained habits, so that it comes to function at semi-automatic levels. The repetitiveness of liturgical practices contributes to such deep formation of habits that can sustain practices over time.

Furthermore, despite its ambivalence about the value of the human body or, more broadly, the material world, it might also be worth considering a recovery of the ascetic practices that accompanied liturgy in the past (and still do in some settings). Many patristic homilies rail against wealth and luxury or counsel abstinence and moderation. Traditional liturgical cycles call for fasting from meat or other animal products for much of the year and in general encourage simplicity in lifestyle. Exorbitant use of resources was always seen as antithetical to a Christian lifestyle. Although liturgical spaces, implements and decoration could become luxurious at times, such abundance was often accompanied by criticisms of indulgence and excess. Care for the poor was always a moral requirement, even when it was not put into practice sufficiently. Given how poverty and indigence are now often directly linked to climate change – something sure to increase exponentially in the coming years – these obligations become even more pressing today. We must return – maybe via creative adaptation – to ascetic and liturgical practices of abstinence, simplicity and care for others with generosity and hospitality. At the same time we must urge even more strongly that these are not isolated personal choices, but that they are communal lifestyles that we must practice together, that the very structures of our lives affect the lives of all others on this planet, human and non-human.[19]

Conclusion

Much more remains to be done to work this out fully and surely the ancient worldview cannot be retrieved wholesale. Many questions remain: clearly the possibility of the overcoming of *phthora* in the patristic and liturgical sources applied only to humans, its solution was framed in terms of immortality, and its precise relationship to ascetic living and liturgical practice was never worked out in its entirety. Yet, one might at least suggest that practices that wreak destruction, defilement and corruption on the planet and increase death – not just personal death but wholesale destruction – for all

---

[18] Such inculcation of moral responsibility and habitual action must occur as early as possible. Teaching children environmental values in school is simply too late. Values of simplicity and habits of sustainable living have to be cultivated and ingrained much earlier if they are to shape life effectively. This is another reason why ritual shaping – if communities actively pursue it – can be a crucial contributing factor.

[19] As Gandhi famously said, we must 'live more simply', so that others may 'simply live'.

species are incompatible with the Christian ideas of redemption and theosis at their most fundamental levels. Ecological engagement can flow out of liturgical practice, because it is about combatting *phthora* and living into life, because – to use the title of Alexander Schmemann's popular liturgical text – liturgy is 'for the life of the world'.[20] If Christianity is life-giving, then it cannot be death-dealing. The two are incompatible. And it is liturgy that teaches us this, liturgy that seeks to live this out, liturgy that attempts to shape us in pursuing such a life-giving kind of life, a life that turns away from *phthora* – especially through its penitential and ascetic practices – and turns towards life, most exorbitantly at Pascha.

It obviously remains a question whether ritual or symbolism can ever be recovered once they have become lost. Even if we recognize that rites play an important function in shaping minds and hearts, forming emotions and deepening commitments, do newly invented or individually fabricated symbols have the same power or carry the same weight? Will they not always feel arbitrary and somehow 'fake'? Can we invent new 'green' liturgies and can they function on a 'cosmic' scale that actually affirms life on this earth, rather than abandoning it for some other reality? Do tree-planting ceremonies, for example, remain recognizably Christian or must Christian symbolism or content be abandoned for ritual that genuinely embraces the earth and this life? Will such ritual enable a deep shaping of worldview and practices and will it do so quickly enough to have an impact today?[21] The 'resources' of liturgy may be too little, too late and too slow.[22] And, yet, what choice do we have? If we are to have any hope of transforming hearts, minds, actions and lifestyles, liturgy surely must be one of the ways to pursue such transfiguration.

---

[20] Alexander Schmemann, *For the Life of the World: Sacraments and Orthodoxy* (Crestwood: St. Vladimir's Seminary Press, 1973).

[21] Maybe liturgy is most useful for the 'follow-up' of supporting and sustaining a more 'ascetic' lifestyle, while other measures (legal, political, policy changes, etc.) are first needed for the most immediate and urgent changes.

[22] Admittedly, if scientists are right about current prognoses for the warming trends, *any* claim to 'solve' climate change is utopian. Even if all emission of carbon were to stop today, we would already have committed ourselves to an unsustainable rise in temperatures with unpredictable dire consequences for all of life on earth. Obviously that does not mean that we should give up or not do anything.

A response to Christina Gschwandtner

Ezra Chitando[1]

How may liturgy and liturgical theology contribute to the theological and religious response to the vagaries of climate change? What is it in liturgical formulae and expressions that can be enhanced, tweaked or reformulated to address climate distortion? Should liturgy even feature in a discourse on climate change at all? The foregoing essay by Christina Gschwandtner touches on these questions and addresses some of them in appreciable detail, although it ends on a rather pessimistic note. Although I subscribe to the realist school of thought and contend that utopian approaches are counterproductive, I am also a firm believer in the human capacity to turn the tide against climate change. Religion, or at least its Christian version, is in the business of peddling realistic hope. Therefore, I remain convinced that there is hope yet in the overall response to climate change.

Gschwandtner's essay provides valuable insights into the meaning and deployment of liturgy. Indeed, liturgy can be a powerful resource in changing perceptions and attitudes. In the area in which I have worked for many years, namely, the theological, religious and ecclesial response to HIV and AIDS, we have experienced the power of liturgy in transformation. In the face of extreme levels of stigma and discrimination against people living with HIV, theologians developed creative and powerful liturgies that reminded the church that solidarity with people living with HIV was critical. Using confessions, proclamations and declarations, the church began to change negative attitudes towards people living with HIV. The publication and wide circulation of HIV-sensitive sermon guidelines and liturgy contributed immensely.[2]

The transformative power of liturgy in mobilizing responses to climate change is confirmed by the work that Marthinus Daneel undertook with African Independent and Initiated Churches (AICs) in Southern Zimbabwe in the mid-1980s to the early 2000s. The liturgy that was developed within the AICs precipitated a shift in the concept of healing, now turning the church to embrace the idea of being an 'environmental hospital' that cares for the wounded earth.[3] For me, the challenge lies with the churches

---

[1] Ezra Chitando is Professor of History and Phenomenology of Religion at the University of Zimbabwe and Theology Consultant on HIV and AIDS for the World Council of Churches. He studies different dimensions of religion in Africa.

[2] Musa W. Dube (ed.), *Africa Praying: A Handbook of HIV/AIDS Sensitive Sermon Guidelines and Liturgy* (Geneva: World Council of Churches, 2003).

[3] Marthinus L. Daneel, *African Earthkeepers – Wholistic Interfaith Mission* (Maryknoll: Orbis, 2001).

in the Global North and mission-derived churches in the Global South to reflect on the liturgy developed by AICs and find ways of adapting them in their settings. The tree-planting Eucharist within the AIC movement represents a highly creative and powerful intervention that can be appropriated in different contexts.

Liturgy must not be the last resort in the theological response to climate change; it must be the first! Liturgy has the capacity to influence action. Adherents who are conscientized about their responsibility towards nature and how their actions have precipitated climate change can be mobilized to change their way of life. Gschwandtner's essay does very well in outlining the extent to which religious activities in the Global North have had a deleterious impact on the environment. This is quite informative. However, what is required is greater prophetic action, inspired by transformative liturgy, in order to bring about repentance and conversion. This will not be an easy process, since lifestyles appear normal and divinely ordained. Powerful liturgy has the ability to move people from their comfort zones into new spaces where new experiences become possible.

The tendency to downplay the role of liturgy in responding to climate change lies in the emphasis on reason in Western theology. One very negative outcome has been to regard movement and emotion as belonging to a lower rung of human existence. Yet, the distinction between liturgy and theology is palpably false. Effective liturgy must be preceded by serious and thorough theological reflection. Therefore, it is vital for theologians in the Global North and within mainstream churches in the Global South to invest in developing liturgy that engages the reality of climate change. Thus, the liturgy must be informed by deep theological reflections (necessarily informed by the best available scientific knowledge).

Gschwandtner is at pains to draw attention to the reality of climate change and the seeming futility of liturgy in responding to it. For example, 'These are obviously not sufficient to roll back climate change' and that the recourse to liturgy 'may be too little, too late, too slow'. I do like the realistic evaluation of all our interventions. But, the world has never been changed by people who are 'realistic'. It takes, 'revolutionary madness' to change the status quo.[4] That is, it is those individuals who engage in acts that do not confirm to reason as understood within their context who transform the world. Similarly, there is need to initiate radical action – no matter how unpromising it might seem to those without faith – to address climate change. Careful consideration of the potentially limited impact of our interventions on climate change will generate paralysis, a point well noted in Gschwandtner's essay.

If I have highlighted a few points where I see matters from an angle different from the one where Gschwandtner is positioned, it is precisely because I am in agreement with the major issues she addresses. Yes, current consumption patterns in the Global North are unsustainable. Developing and embracing liturgy that reinforces a theology

---

[4] Emmanuel Katongole, *The Sacrifice of Africa: A Political Theology for Africa* (Grand Rapids: Eerdmans, 2011).

of enough,⁵ particularly in the Global North, is an urgent undertaking. However, the Global South is not a shining example of moderation either. Due to globalization, the unsustainable consumption patterns have been introduced and have found some enthusiastic takers. Therefore, the call for repentance and transformation must address the whole people of God. With the assault on Indigenous spirituality in different parts of the world increasing in intensity, theologians in every part of the world must employ the creative spirit in developing new liturgies to address climate change.

I completely agree that liturgy needs to stir more than individuals and instigate community transformation if the response to climate change is to have a fighting chance. While individual lifestyle changes are important, much more is required in order for the response to be effective. This is where the African concept of Ubuntu ('I am because you are') can be quite helpful. Through Ubuntu, the community realizes that there is no separation between humans and other beings, including nature. Ubuntu has the capacity to mobilize the community to provide effective and holistic responses to climate change.⁶ It is critical, therefore, for liturgy to reflect the basic tenets of Ubuntu in order to generate community responses to climate change.

Faith communities are strategically placed to play a critical role in responding to climate change. Recognizing the ambivalence of religion,⁷ it is vital for theologians to create liturgy that energizes communities to express the positive side of religion. Religion can be a vital resource in community transformation in the face of climate change. Yet, liturgy has the potential to drive religion, only if its true value is appreciated. Therefore, powered by transformative liturgy, religion can be the spark plug that animates communities to provide effective responses to the challenge of climate change.

---

⁵ Shane Clairborne, *The Irresistible Revolution: Living as an Ordinary Radical* (Grand Rapids: Zondervan, 2006).

⁶ Danford T. Chibvongodze, 'Ubuntu is Not Only about the Human! An Analysis of the Role of African Philosophy and Ethics in Environment Management', *Journal of Human Ecology* 53:2 (2016), 157–66.

⁷ R. Scott Appleby, *The Ambivalence of the Sacred: Religion, Violence, and Reconciliation* (Lanham: Rowman & Littlefield, 2000).

Chapter 6.2
Climate change and exegetical, hermeneutical and homiletical praxis

Barbara R. Rossing[1]

Holy ground: Reading the Bible for our urgent *kairos* moment

This essay interprets the Bible in an environmentally positive way, with an ethical commitment to climate justice. The crisis of climate change represents not only an environmental crisis, but a 'profound narrative crisis for Western civilization ... linked to questions of worldview and spirituality', as Naomi Klein describes. In order to challenge the narrative of extractive carbon-consuming capitalism we need a different story, a different social imaginary.[2] The Bible can help us with that alternative story.

Ecologically, the dilemma is that the Bible contains both wonderful and problematic texts, open to multiple competing interpretations. There is no direct link between the Bible and climate change, we must be clear. The Bible does not 'predict' this crisis as punishment for sin – although that is sometimes how it gets interpreted, even by victims of floods or climate disasters, who did the least to cause the problem. Depending on interpretative choices, the very same biblical narratives – the creation stories, human dominion, Noah and the Flood, the prophets, Jesus, end times and more – can be used by climate-change deniers and environmentalists.

Two major projects, the *Earth Bible Project* and the Exeter Project, have brought together collaborative teams of biblical scholars to develop ecological principles for biblical interpretation.[3] For climate justice, their goals are to counter anthropocentric

---

[1] Barbara Rossing is Professor of New Testament at the Lutheran School of Theology of Chicago, where she directs the Environmental Ministry Emphasis and teaches in the Zygon Center for Religion and Science. She served as pastor at Holden Village Retreat Center in the Cascade Mountains, and Chair of the Society of Biblical Literature Ecological Hermeneutics section.
[2] Sam Mowe, Interview of Naomi Klein, 'Spiritual Questions and Climate Change', *Tricycle* 25 (2015), https://tricycle.org/magazine/capitalism-vs-climate/ (accessed 22 December 2018). See also Naomi Klein, *This Changes Everything: Capitalism vs the Climate* (New York: Simon & Schuster, 2014).
[3] See the multivolume *Earth Bible* series and various commentaries and, for the Exeter Project, David Horrell et al. (eds), *Ecological Hermeneutics: Biblical, Historical and Theological Perspectives* (London: T&T Clark, 2010).

bias and to retrieve sometimes-submerged voices in biblical texts, including the voices of earth communities. Ecowomanist and feminist interpretative communities lift up justice and liberation insights, as do Indigenous scholars. Interconnectedness becomes a key interpretative principle. All of Earth's living systems – oceans, atmosphere, biological and human communities – suffer consequences of climate disruption and greed. All cry out together for justice.

This essay examines some key biblical texts and scholarship important to discussions of climate change and homiletics.[4] I will propose ways to draw on the Bible for hope and healing at this crucial 'hinge moment' in human history.

Creation's beauty: God saw how beautiful it was (Genesis 1)

We start with the Bible's own starting point: God's love for the beauty and goodness of the created world. Earth, with all living creatures, its oceans and atmosphere, its biological and physical systems, its communities of organisms, is fundamentally declared 'good'. This entire world is 'a burning bush of God's energies', as Gregory Palamas claimed in the fourteenth century.[5] The entire cosmos is holy ground (Exod. 3.5).

Genesis 1 is liturgical poetry, showing us the beauty of each element of creation in its ecological niche. The poetic refrain 'God saw that it was good' anchors this creation story. Repeated six times, with variation, the refrain culminates in the declaration of 'very good' on the sixth day (Gen. 1.31). The Hebrew conjunction *ki* can also be translated adverbially as 'how': 'God saw *how* (*ki*) good it was' (Common English Bible). 'How good' evokes God's delight in discovering each element of the world as good.

'Good' is the key word. *Tov* in Hebrew expresses joy and relationship. One rabbinic commentary translates *tov* as 'beautiful'.[6] By calling each creature good, God initiates an ongoing relationship of love with each new creature and with Earth. God 'is *affected* by what is seen'.[7] As Norman Habel notes, a similar exclamation of 'good' is used to

---

[4] For homiletics, see David Rhoads (ed.), *Earth and Word: Classic Sermons on Saving the Planet* (New York: Continuum, 2007); Norman Habel, David Rhoads and H. Paul Santmire (eds), *Season of Creation: A Preaching Commentary* (Minneapolis: Fortress, 2011); Leah Schade, *Creation-Crisis Preaching: Ecology, Theology, and the Pulpit* (St Louis: Chalice Press, 2015).

[5] John Chryssavgis, 'A New Heaven and a New Earth: Orthodox Christian Insights for Theology, Spirituality and the Sacraments', in *Toward and Ecology of Transfiguration: Orthodox Christian Perspective on Environment, Nature, and Creation*, John Chryssavgis and Bruce Foltz (eds) (Fordham University Press, 2013), 152–62 (156).

[6] Ellen Bernstein, 'Creation Theology: A Jewish Perspective', in *The Green Bible*, Michael S. Maudlin and Marlene Baer (eds) (San Francisco: HarperOne, 2008), 1–53.

[7] Terrence Fretheim, *God and World in the Old Testament: A Relational Theology of Creation* (Nashville: Abingdon Press, 2005), 40.

describe the response of Moses's mother when her child is born. Moses's mother 'sees he is good' (Exod. 2.1). Similarly, in Genesis 1, 'Elohim beholds Earth emerge from the waters below and "sees Earth is good".'[8] Earth is God's living child.

With amazing scientific insight the Priestly author (P) of Genesis 1 describes Earth and Oceans as co-creators with God in creating more life forms. Written before a scientific worldview, Genesis's appreciation of earth's ongoing creativity coheres with our understanding of the biological processes of evolution and speciation. Earth itself brings forth creatures of its own on the third and sixth days ('Let the earth bring forth living creatures of every kind' Gen. 1.24; 1.12). Waters, too, bring forth animals and living creatures in a bounty of life (Gen. 1.20). God calls this entire process of ongoing creation 'good'. Important to underscore is that creatures are good *for their own intrinsic value*. Utilitarian value for humans is not the meaning of 'good'.

Moreover, the superlative 'very good' (*tov ma'ov,* Gen. 1.31) on the sixth day is not reserved for humans alone, as some anthropocentric interpretations have claimed. Rather, it is when God sees how the whole creation works together as an interconnected living ecological system, that God declares everything to be very, very good. Goodness includes physical and chemical processes and laws, and even the physics of the 'greenhouse effect' that causes carbon dioxide to trap some of the sun's infrared heat rays. Goodness includes the perfectly calibrated thinness and vulnerability of the earth's atmosphere relative to the rest of the planet – thinner than the peel of an apple relative to the apple. This protective layer of atmosphere is what Genesis calls 'firmament'. The crisis today is that humans' burning of fossil fuels is endangering the planet's very firmament, endangering the lives of people and all living communities, especially the poorest and most vulnerable.

The creation stories of the Bible hold deep truths about who we are, who God is and about our human vocation in relation to creation. In the Priestly account, humans – both male and female – are equally created in the 'image of God'. As image bearers, humans are commanded to 'have dominion' (*radah,* Gen. 1.26) – a difficult word, invoked through history to justify capitalist expansion and unrestrained consumption. Dominion's dangerous legacy is especially problematic because it is paired with the command to 'subdue' (*kabash*) the earth. The model given by God's own royal dominion shows that dominion carries responsibility to exercise care, like a priest.[9] However, many scholars make the case that the Genesis 1:26 vocation to 'subdue and have dominion' must be replaced by the more ecological understanding of humans' vocation as farmers in Genesis 2.

---

[8] Norman Habel, *The Birth, the Curse and the Greening of Earth: An Ecological Reading of Genesis 1-11* (Sheffield: Phoenix Press, 2011), 32.
[9] Theodore Hiebert, 'The Human Vocation', in *Christianity and Ecology: Seeking the Well-Bring of Earth and Humans,* Dieter Hessel and Rosemary Radford Ruether (eds) (Cambridge: Harvard University Center for the Study of World Religions, 2000), 135–54 (137).

Restraint: Limits as part of God's good creation (Genesis 2)

The second creation story, Genesis 2, authored by the Yahwist (J), pictures an agrarian world of subsistence farming. God causes the rain to fall on the dry earth so that plants and crops can grow. God forms the human out of the humus, 'from the topsoil of the fertile land' (Gen. 2.7, CEB), *adam* from *adamah*. God plants a garden with 'every beautiful tree bearing edible fruit' (Gen. 2.9, CEB), and sets humankind in the garden 'to till it and to keep it' (Gen. 2.15, NRSV) and 'to farm it and take care of it' (CEB).

What does to 'keep' the garden mean? In English 'keeping' can have multiple meanings. One extreme meaning in our ownership society is that of hoarding. 'I'm keeping that garden for myself.' But the Hebrew word *shamar* is used most of all of God: God keeps covenants. God keeps people, in the sense of protecting their life.[10] When that same word is used for the human role in creation – 'to till and to keep' – it means first of all protecting creation's life, for its long-term flourishing.

Ellen Davis gives yet another meaning to the verb *shamar*, namely of observing and respecting limits:

> [F]requently the verb translates 'observe', with a variety of nuances: ... to acquire wisdom by observing the workings of the world (Ps. 107.43); to abide by moral guidelines ... or even the rhythms of nature (Jer. 8:7)... So it may be that the human is charged to 'keep' the garden and at the same time to 'observe' it, to learn from it and respect the limits that pertain to it.[11]

Respect for limits is a crucial aspect of the creation stories. We are to eat and consume with restraint, 'mindful of limits that are built into the created order'.[12] God creates the limit in the very middle of the garden, in the form of the tree of the knowledge of good and evil (Gen. 2.9, 17). As Dietrich Bonhoeffer points out, the limit is not out at the edge, as something we are to push up against and strive to overcome. We are to respect and even love the limit in the middle of our world. Bonhoeffer argues that our limit is the essence of human creatureliness:

> The very fusion of freedom and creaturehood is expressed in the picture language of the Bible by the fact that the tree of knowledge, the forbidden tree that denotes the limit of the human, stands in the middle. The limit is grace because it is the basis of creatureliness and freedom; the limit is the middle.[13]

---

[10] As the Psalmist says, 'The Lord will keep your going out and your coming in from this time forth and forevermore' (Psalm 121.8).

[11] Ellen Davis, *Scripture, Culture, and Agriculture: An Agrarian Reading of the Bible* (Cambridge: Cambridge University Press, 2009), 30.

[12] Ibid., 31.

[13] Dietrich Bonhoeffer, *Creation and Fall: A Theological Interpretation of Genesis 3,* translated by John C. Fletcher, revised by SCM Press (London: Macmillan Publishing, 1976), 50–1. Note that in this edition the

Acknowledgement of the goodness of limits may offer the most radical biblical insight for climate justice today. For the Israelites in Genesis, 'keeping' meant caring for their little farms for future generations, not plowing to the margins, not taking too much water, living in harmony with a delicate ecosystem and its constraints. Today, respecting atmospheric limits may be the most urgent mandate of 'keeping'. Scientists warn that crossing limits or tipping points beyond 400 parts per million of carbon dioxide in the atmosphere will become increasingly dangerous for our world's life. Climatologist Raymond Pierrehumbert proposes an analogy between the Genesis tree of the knowledge of good and evil in the garden, and fossil fuels today.[14] Just as Adam and Eve had to walk around the tree and refrain from consuming it, so we must resist the temptation to consume the cheap, abundant, low-hanging 'fruit' of coal and petroleum. Fossil fuels are 'good'; they are God's creation. But that does not mean they are created for humans to consume. Whereas in the nineteenth and twentieth centuries the 'good' of oil-rich sedimentary rocks was seen as the energy they provided for humans to burn to fuel economic growth, we now know that those same rock formations perform an even greater 'good', serving as storehouses for vast amounts of sequestered carbon, kept safely in the ground.

Genesis 2 creates a limit in the centre of our lives, and declares the limit good.

The flood: Covenant with creation and future generations (Genesis 8-9)

The story of Noah and the Flood can be interpreted either problematically or hopefully for climate change, depending on the interpreter. One of the most extreme climate change deniers in the US Congress, Rep. John Shimkus, quoted Genesis 8.21-23 to argue against the science of global warming. Government should not regulate carbon emissions, he testified, because God promised never to destroy the Earth after the flood: 'As long as the Earth endures, seedtime and harvest, cold and heat, summer and winter, day and night, will never cease ... Man will not destroy this Earth.'[15]

On the other hand, for ecologically minded Jews and Christians, the Flood story – especially the 'eco-covenant' God makes with every living creature – embodies environmental truths. Ecological interpreters read God's promise never again to destroy the earth as an imperative for healing and saving creation, not as cavalier license to

---

German *Mitte* is translated as 'middle' and not 'centre' as in the latest edition in the Dietrich Bonhoeffer Works.

[14] Based on a private conversation.

[15] 25 March 2009 hearing of the US House Subcommittee on Energy and Environment, website https://www.youtube.com/watch?v=_7h08RDYA5E (accessed 22 December 2018).

ignore global warming. For homileticians, 'Shabbat Noach' – the Sabbath when the Noah cycle is read in worship – proclaims God's will to preserve creation.

Vivid narrative details communicate ecological insights:

- The accelerating destruction ('corruption') of Earth caused by human violence, including violence against the creation (Gen. 6.11-13). As Australian Indigenous commentator Wali Fejo says of the flood story, Earth is 'sick – corrupted by human evils – and in need of healing ... so that it can be renewed.'[16]
- God's grieving heart (Gen. 6.6), a heart that is first moved to destroy the Earth because of human sin, but then declares 'never again' to any future destruction;
- The image of an 'Ark' that saved Noah's family together with all the creatures, an apt image for our Earth when we and all living things inhabit the planet's fragile 'Ark' together;
- God's repeated command to bring living creatures of every kind into the ark and 'keep them alive', a divine 'endangered species act', mandating that no species become extinct through human negligence. In the 1990s the Evangelical Environmental Network invoked the Noah story to support the Endangered Species Act, calling the legislation a 'modern-day Noah's Ark', and lobbying the US Congress not to overturn it.[17]

Theodore Hiebert points out that the promise of Genesis 8.22 lists all the major seasons of the Israelite agricultural year for hill-country farmers.[18] By preserving the rhythm of seasons, God promises to preserve a future for sustainable agriculture 'as long as the earth shall endure'.

In Genesis 9.8-17, God makes covenant with more than humans. God's first covenant in the Bible is a covenant with birds, animals and 'every living creature'. The covenant is for 'all future generations' (Gen. 9.12). This is the most important aspect of the Noah story in our time of climate change, as Rabbi Jonathan Sacks, the chief rabbi of Great Britain, points out. The call of God in our times is that 'we have to honour our covenant with future generations that they will be able to live.'[19]

While God will never break the everlasting covenant (*berit olam*, 9.16) with all creation and future generations, there remains the possibility of humans' breaking the

---

[16] Wali Fejo, 'The Voice of the Earth: An Indigenous Reading of Genesis 9', in *The Earth Story in Genesis*, Norman Habel and Shirley Wurst (eds) (Sheffield: Sheffield Academic Press, 2000), 140–6 (142).

[17] Peter Steinfels, 'Evangelical Group Defends Laws Protecting Endangered Species as a Modern "Noah's Ark:"', *New York Times*, 31 January 1996.

[18] Agricultural seasons include 'the sowing of grain in the fall (*zera'*) and its harvesting the spring (*qasir*), the harvest of summer fruit, including primarily grapes and figs (*qayis*) and the autumn harvest of olives (*horep*)'. See Theodore Hiebert, *The Yahwist's Landscape: Nature and Religion in Early Israel* (Oxford: Oxford University Press, 1996), 45.

[19] Jonathan Sacks, 'The Relationship Between the People and God', *Lambeth Conference*, 28 July 2008, http://justus.anglican.org/~edmondto/pdf/Sacks_The_Relationship_between_280708.pdf (accessed 22 December 2018).

everlasting covenant from our side. We humans are the ones altering the very climatic patterns of seasonal rainfall, cold and heat, summer and winter (Gen. 8.22) that God promised never to destroy. The prophet Isaiah warns that when humans break that 'everlasting covenant' (*berit olam,* Isa. 24.5), the consequences lead to destruction, to the undoing of creation.

Exodus and holy ground: Healing from the economic sicknesses of Egypt

'The Earth is ill': This stark diagnosis begins Brazilian liberation theologian Leonardo Boff's *Cry of the Earth, Cry of the Poor.* If we frame the climate crisis today as an illness of empire from which we and the Earth need healing, then we can draw on prophetic critiques and visions of hope. Biblical authors use imagery of sickness to describe ancient empires' exploitation of people and the earth. Boff uses the language of 'bleeding wounds'. Poor people and nature voice parallel cries, recalling the Exodus story:

> Liberation theology and ecological discourse have something in common: they start from two bleeding wounds. The wound of poverty breaks the social fabric of millions and millions of poor people around the world. The other wound, systematic assault on the Earth, breaks down the balance of the planet … Both lines of reflection and practice have as their starting point a cry: The cry of the poor for life, freedom, and beauty (cf. Exodus 3.7) and the cry of the earth (cf. *Romans* 8. 22-23). Both seek liberation of the poor … and a liberation of the Earth.[20]

Ecologically, the call of Moses (Exod. 3.1-12) to lead the Exodus begins with holy ground – Earth ablaze with God's radiant presence. The story anticipates the prophet Isaiah's 'Holy, holy, holy is the Lord of hosts; the whole Earth is full of God's glory!' Moses must remove his shoes. God's statement to Moses: 'You are standing on holy ground' sets up God's response to the people's cry for relief from their suffering, as well as God's revelation of the divine name. As William Brown notes, 'a bush burns because God has "heard their cry" (Exod. 3.7) … The cry for deliverance kindles God's holy heart.'[21]

The Egyptian economic system shows the connection between food insecurity, ecological injustice and slavery. Ellen Davis interprets the Exodus in terms of contesting economics and ideologies of food production. She draws stunning parallels between the oppressive Egyptian economic system and today's system of industrial agriculture. Both

---

[20] Leonardo Boff, *Cry of the Earth, Cry of the Poor* (Maryknoll: Orbis, 1997), 104.
[21] William Brown, *Sacred Sense: Discovering the Wonder of God's Word and World* (Louisville: Westminster John Knox, 2015), 53.

are globalized large-scale agricultural systems, producing a surplus for trade on the international market. Both are unsustainable.

In contrast to the sick food system of Egypt, God gives a vision for an agrarian 'manna economy', a counter-narrative that 'outlines a new moral economy of food production and distribution.' God aims to form the people with a new mindset, that will 'enable them to be free of all the sickness of Egypt' (Exod. 15:26).[22]

Davis' language of sickness and healing, drawing on Exodus 15:26, provides a biblical frame to interpret today's climate crisis: We and our world are sick, as Boff diagnoses. We need healing. Biblical writers aptly called Egypt 'the Iron Furnace' (cf. Deut. 4.20; Jer. 11.4; or 'iron-smelting furnace', NIV). Egypt was 'the biblical archetype of the industrial society: burning, ceaseless in its demand for slave labor (the cheapest fuel of the ancient industrial machines), consuming until it is itself consumed'.[23] The Exodus liberated people from that system, healing them from all the sicknesses of Egypt (Exod. 15.26) – 'for I am the Lord who heals you.'

Medical experts tell us that the climate crisis is now the most urgent public health crisis facing our world.[24] The climate crisis is a sickness of agriculture, forests, watersheds and our entire economic system.[25] In this situation of peril to our health, the Bible's many stories of healing can help.

The ten plagues against Pharaoh are part of the Exodus's liberating vision – 'ecological signs'. Terence Fretheim argues that the Exodus plagues 'function in a way not unlike certain ecological events in contemporary society, portents of unmitigated historical disaster.'[26] In our time, it is important to frame the threats of rising seas, drought and other calamities not as predictions but as wake-up calls – portents of disaster, warnings of consequences while there is still time to avert the disaster. The world is ill, in need of liberation. But this is not a sickness unto death (Jn 11.4). The remedy is to call upon industrial nations to change course before it is too late.

---

[22] Davis, *Scripture, Culture, and Agriculture*, 72, 68. For homiletical insight and art, see also Daniel Erlander, *Manna and Mercy: A Brief History of God's Unfolding Promise to Mend the Entire Universe* (Mercer Island: The Order of St. Martin and Theresa, 1992). Erlander whimsically draws Moses's chalkboard and the Israelites sitting at little desks at 'Wilderness School', learning manna economy lessons ('hoarding stinks').

[23] Davis, *Scripture, Culture, and Agriculture*, 69. For the description of 'the sick society that is Egypt', see Ibid., 71.

[24] So *The Lancet* and University College London Institute for Global Health Commission, *Managing the Health Effects of Climate Change*, 16 May 2009, http://www.ucl.ac.uk/global-health/ucl-lancet-climate-change.pdf (accessed 22 December 2018).

[25] Transforming agriculture and restoring soil health will be vital for sequestering the enormous amounts of carbon necessary to avert disaster. See Paul Hawken and Tom Steyer (eds), *Drawdown: The Most Comprehensive Plan Ever to Reverse Global Warming* (New York: Penguin, 2017), 110. Project Drawdown proposes the 100 most effective ways to 'draw down' carbon dioxide out of the atmosphere in order to reverse the increase in global temperatures. See its homepage at https://www.drawdown.org/.

[26] Terence Fretheim, 'The Plagues as Ecological Signs of Historical Disaster', *Journal of Biblical Literature* 110:3 (1991), 385–96 (387).

Jonah: How A grassroots people's movement can turn an empire in forty days

To envision how governments can lead a just transition to a clean energy economy, we turn to the story of Jonah. Jonah is a parable. With humour and grace, it communicates the message that God wants the biggest empire on earth to turn towards healing, while there is yet time. Nineveh's repentance inspires hope that a notorious global empire can abandon its destructive course in time to avert a catastrophe.

'In just forty days this city will be destroyed,' Jonah preached to Nineveh. The prophet Nahum lists Nineveh's many sins: a predatory economic and military system that devoured its neighbours and its own people. Nineveh was a 'city of bloodshed, utterly deceitful ... that enslaves nations' (Nah. 3.1). Its economic violence seemed invincible: 'You increased your merchants more than the stars of heaven' (Nah. 3.16).

Nineveh, the capital of the Assyrian world trading empire, has come to God's attention. The prophet Jonah expected to see his prediction of destruction in forty days come true. But to Jonah's astonishment, 'The people of Nineveh believed God, and proclaimed a fast' (Jon. 3.5). Change happened! The empire turned! Radical 'turning' (the meaning of the biblical word 'repentance') started from the people in the streets, a kind of populist 'Occupy' movement. People's grassroots action pressured the king into embarking on a fast-track campaign, in response to public will: 'All shall turn from their evil ways and from the violence that is in their hands.' Amazingly, the whole empire turned, in under forty days. Jonah's parable enlists even animals in sackcloth, and a Jack-in-the-Beanstalk-like plant, to humorously illustrate the grace of turning.

Several elements of the story can help us. First, biblical prophecy is not prediction, but warning. Scientists function like prophets today, warning of the future consequences of inaction. Scientific reports of the Intergovernmental Panel on Climate Change are not predictions of inevitable doom, but wake-up calls, modelling an alternative path while there is yet time to turn. Second, when people mobilize, leaders will respond. Leadership for climate justice requires societal and governmental action. Third, God's compassion embraces all: 'Shall I not be concerned about Nineveh, that great city, in which there are more than a hundred and twenty thousand persons ... and also many animals?'

Homiletically, if we draw upon Jonah to address climate change today, the lesson is hopeful: that grassroots community movements can wake up a large-scale empire. Biblically speaking, our moment – like Jonah's – is a moment when unjust political economies have come to God's attention, and God hears the cries of the poorest and most vulnerable. Our challenge is to galvanize daring prophetic actions, mobilizing a mass movement, in order to persuade governments to enact fast-track change.

God with us: The kingdom of heaven as renewal of creation (Gospel of Matthew)

Within the emerging discipline of ecological hermeneutics, New Testament scholarship has opened up new insights on familiar texts. Rereading even a word or phrase ecologically can overcome anthropocentric bias – for example, Joseph Sittler's 1961 broadening of redemption to include not only humans but 'all things' (*ta panta*) in Colossians 1,[27] and Niels Gregersen's 'deep incarnation' reading of John 1.14 (the Word became flesh) as Jesus's sharing in the flesh of all animals. The Apostle Paul's description of human communities and creation 'groaning' together for liberation (Rom. 8.22, 23) reflects profound ecological interconnectedness.[28] The whole cosmos suffers birth pangs and waits together in hope. We live at a turning of the ages, Paul and other New Testament authors proclaim – a turning inaugurated in Jesus's death and resurrection. The urgency of our present time (*kairos*) calls communities of Jesus's followers to 'wake from sleep' (Rom. 13.11). Such biblical descriptions of our time as a *kairos* can help us frame our urgent moment today as a moment for transformative climate action and hope.[29]

Jesus's preaching of the Kingdom of God means first of all the 'renewal of creation', underscores Richard Bauckham. The entire New Testament presupposes Jewish creation traditions:

> We must 're-enter God's creation' ... The modern project, as an ideology of progress that supposedly liberates us from nature and gives us godlike power over it, has been an exercise in forgetting our creatureliness ... But the kingdom of God is the renewal of creation. We can seek the kingdom of God only by first understanding the world as God's creation and finding our place within it.[30]

---

[27] Joseph Sittler, 'Called to Unity', *Ecumenical Review* 14 (1962), 177–87; Niels Henrik Gregersen, 'Deep Incarnation: The Logos Became Flesh', in *Transformative Theological Perspectives,* Karen Bloomquist (ed.) (Geneva: Lutheran World Federation, 2009), 167–81.

[28] On Romans 8, see Sylvia Keesmaat and Brian Walsh, *Romans Disarmed: Resisting Empire, Demanding Justice* (Grand Rapids: Brazos Press, 2019); Jonathan Moo and Robert White, *Let Creation Rejoice: Biblical Hope and Ecological Crisis* (London: IVP Academic Press, 2014), 101–14; Sygve Tonstad, *The Letter to the Romans: Paul among the Ecologists* (Sheffield: Sheffield Phoenix Press, 2017).

[29] Ecumenical Patriarch Bartholomew I, archbishop of Constantinople, calls the climate change crisis a 'kairos moment' for churches and for the world: As individuals we are often conscious of a kairos, a moment when we make a choice that will affect our whole lives. For the human race as a whole, there is now a kairos, a decisive time in our relationship with God's creation. We will either act in time to protect life on earth from the worst consequences of human folly, or we will fail to act. See Ecumenical Patriarch Bartholomew, 'Symposium on the Arctic', 7–12 September 2007, Greenland, http://orth-transfiguration.org/library/orthodoxy/mirros (accessed 22 December 2018).

[30] Richard Bauckham, *Living With Other Creatures: Green Exegesis and Theology* (Waco: Baylor University Press, 2011), 144.

The promise of 'I am with you always' (Mt. 28.20) roots the Gospel of Matthew on Earth. Unlike Luke, Matthew does not portray Jesus as ascending up to heaven. Matthew presents Jesus as 'Emmanuel, God-with-us', who never leaves the earth behind. 'God with us' (Mt. 1.23) means God is with not only humans but also, as Elaine Wainwright notes, with 'Earth and all earth's constituents … all who participate in the biotic and abiotic Earth community'.[31] Similarly, Matthew's Easter story underscores the horizontal dimension. 'Jesus is going ahead – not going away,' notes Elisabeth Schüssler Fiorenza. The empty tomb 'does not signify absence but presence: it announces the Resurrected One's presence on the road ahead, in a particular space of struggle and recognition'.[32] We find the power of resurrection in transformative community struggle for life, on earth.

Vicky Balabanski's 'Earth Bible Reading of the Lord's Prayer' addresses the question that is perhaps most important for reading Matthew's Gospel ecologically – namely, how to read the vocabulary of 'heaven' (the same word as 'sky', *ouranos*). Matthew's systematic changing of Mark's 'kingdom of God' to 'kingdom of heaven' can make Matthew seem less earthly, and can even contribute to what Norman Habel calls 'heavenism'.[33] Matthew has eighty-two occurrences of the word *ouranos*, more frequent than in any other New Testament work. Heaven serves as a circumlocution for the name of God. The Lord's Prayer should be read in the context of Jewish prayer, drawing on the Psalms. If there is a spatial heaven/earth dualism in the prayer, the prayer 'takes a stand against its own cosmology by praying that the distinction between heaven and earth will be collapsed'.[34]

There is nothing about 'going to heaven' in Matthew – and certainly nothing about escaping Earth. Christians have sometimes embraced dualism, individualizing salvation into a picture of going away from the earth, up to heaven, after death. But that is not biblical. In Matthew, the kingdom of heaven constitutes an alternative to the kingdom of Rome. This counter-imperial perspective helps us understand the apocalyptic discourse (Mt. 24-25) and other aspects of Matthew's eschatology. Older studies of Matthaean eschatology tended to focus on the question of the supposed delay of the *parousia*, and Jesus's 'second coming', a term not found in the Bible.[35] But we need to contextualize Matthew's eschatology more in terms of Roman imperial eschatology, and the aftermath of the Roman–Jewish War of 67–70 CE. Brutal military campaigns had

---

[31] Elaine M. Wainwright, *Habitat, Human, and Holy: An Eco-rhetorical Reading of the Gospel of Matthew* (Sheffield, Phoenix, 2016), 42–3.

[32] Elisabeth Schüssler Fiorenza, *Jesus: Miriam's Child, Sophia's Prophet* (New York: Continuum, 1995), 126.

[33] Habel defines 'heavenism' as 'the belief that heaven as God's home is also the true home of Christians, the place where they are destined to dwell for eternity'. See Norman Habel and Vicky Balabanski (eds), *The Earth Story in the New Testament* (London: Sheffield Academic Press, 2002), 3.

[34] Vicky Balabanski, 'An Earth Bible Reading of the Lord's Prayer', in *Readings from the Perspective of Earth,* Norman Habel (ed.) (Sheffield: Sheffield Academic Press, 2000), 151–61 (155).

[35] See the overview in Vicky Balabanski, *Eschatology in the Making: Mark, Matthew and the Didache* (Cambridge: Cambridge University Press, 1997).

assaulted villages and lands, inflicting great suffering. Matthew employs vivid imagery of fleeing the desolating sacrilege, as well as traditional Day of the Lord imagery from the Hebrew prophets, in order to speak to present-time trauma of his community. In Matthew 24, '[t]he immediacy of the Matthaean community's experience of the Roman war projected into the future imaginary is almost palpable.'[36] Matthew's eschatology, like the eschatology of Daniel and early Jewish apocalypses, functions more as a critique of hostile occupying empires' violence than a vision of the end of the physical created world. As Jürgen Moltmann reminds us, eschatology announces not the end of the world, but 'the end of the system of this world'.[37]

Revelation and God's future on Earth

The book of Revelation, like Matthew's Gospel, was written in the aftermath of the trauma of the Roman–Jewish war. Biblical apocalypses galvanize scriptural imagination, to help people recognize God's future breaking into the present when hope seems impossible. Creation plays a central role throughout Revelation's story. When the Lamb Jesus is introduced, a whole chorus of animals, sea creatures and creatures under the earth burst into songs of praise (Rev. 5.13).

Revelation's apocalyptic call to renounce empire and participate in God's healing and renewal gives a model for responding to the climate change crisis as a crisis of 'empire'. A strong sense of an impending end pervades the entire book of Revelation. However, the end that the book envisions is not primarily the destruction of earth or the end of the created world. Rather, Revelation envisions an end to the imperial order of oppression and destruction. The message of Revelation is not that the world is about to *end*, but 'the world is about to *turn*'.[38]

Crucial to such an anti-imperial reading of Revelation is God's proclamation that the time (*kairos*) has come 'for destroying those who destroy the earth' (Rev. 11.18). This statement attributes blame for the destruction of Earth not to God but to unjust 'destroyers'.[39] What God plans to destroy, according to this crucial verse, is not the earth itself but rather the idolatrous 'destroyers' of earth – that is, Rome, with its entire economy of exploitation and domination.

---

[36] Wainwright, *Habitat Human and Holy*, 193.
[37] Jürgen Moltmann, 'Liberating and Anticipating the Future', in *Liberating Eschatology: Essays in Honor of Letty M. Russell,* Margaret Farley and Serene Jones (eds) (Louisville: Westminster, 1999) 189–208 (189).
[38] The quote is from the hymn 'Canticle of the Turning' by Rory Cooney, based on Mary's Magnificat in Luke 1. See Barbara Rossing, 'The World is About to Turn: Preaching Apocalyptic Texts for a Planet in Peril', in *Eco-Reformation: Grace and Hope for a Planet in Peril,* Lisa Dahill and James Martin-Schramm (eds) (Eugene: Wipf and Stock, 2016), 140–59 (140).
[39] Micah Kiel, *Apocalyptic Ecology: The Book of Revelation, the Earth, and the Future* (Collegeville: Liturgical Press, 2018).

Revelation's laments, 'Alas for the earth' (*ouai*, Rev. 12.12), concede that Rome's imperial claims of domination over the earth have temporarily come to pass. Such laments can help us voice our own laments for climate losses today. But Revelation does not allow despair. The book puts great emphasis on the present as a moment for decision and repentance. The audience is drawn into 'an abiding sense of the imminent' – extending the urgency of the present moment, as Harry Maier describes.[40] Revelation places the Christian community at an ethical crossroads – a *kairos* moment – facing a choice between the doomed empire of Babylon/Rome or citizenship in God's New Jerusalem.

How will the liberation and healing come about for Earth and its peoples? Revelation suggests a parallel to the Exodus journey out of Egypt. The Lamb's followers are to 'come out' of Babylon (Rev. 18.4). As Pablo Richard suggests, the book of Revelation gives a 're-reading of the Exodus, now being experienced not in Egypt but in the heart of the Roman Empire'.[41] John of Patmos applied the biblical critique of Egypt as a 'sick society' to diagnose as toxic the Roman imperial system of his day.

Understanding the profound ways that Revelation borrows from the Exodus story can also help interpret the most ecologically difficult imagery of the book – the plague sequences in the middle chapters (Rev. 6-16). The plagues serve as wake-up calls – not predictions – projecting into the future the logical consequences of the trajectory the Roman Empire is on, so that people can see in advance where the dangerous imperial path is taking them. The plague visions of Revelation function like the nightmarish visions of Ebenezer Scrooge in Charles Dickens's *A Christmas Carol*, which show a terrifying future that will happen if Scrooge does not change his life.[42] They also make clear that there is still time for change, and that disaster is not inevitable.

Pablo Richard interprets Revelation's plagues as imperial assaults on the poor, arguing that it is inaccurate even to call the plagues of Revelation 'natural' disasters: the plagues of the trumpets and bowls in Revelation refer not to 'natural' disasters, but to the agonies of history that the empire itself causes.[43]

Threats of dire consequences await oppressors if they continue in their unjust ways. As the messenger of the waters in Revelation 16.5-6 says, it is axiomatic or 'fitting' (*axioi eisin*) that the consequences of oppression will come back around in boomerang-like fashion upon empires that commit injustices. We may apply a similar logic of consequences today. Global warming is not punishment from God, but rather a consequence of the physical fact that in a finely tuned atmosphere, certain actions cause other things to happen. In terms of a biblical logic of consequences, what may

---

[40] Harry Meier, *Apocalypse Recalled: The Book of Revelation After Christendom* (Minneapolis: Fortress, 2002), 147.

[41] Pablo Richard, *Apocalypse: A People's Commentary on the Book of Revelation* (Maryknoll: Orbis, 1995), 77.

[42] See Barbara Rossing, *The Rapture Exposed: The Message of Hope in the Book of Revelation* (Boulder: Westview Press, 2004).

[43] Richard, *Apocalypse*, 86.

be 'axiomatic' is that humans cannot continue on this trajectory of carbon consumption without heating up the planet to dangerous levels. God calls on people to withdraw from participation in an unjust economy and participate instead in the world-healing vision of renewal: God's New Jerusalem. Revelation seeks to make God's vision of beauty so persuasive that the audience will 'come out' of the evil empire (Rev. 18.4) and enter into the promise of blessing and healing.

The heart of Revelation is New Jerusalem, Revelation 21-22, the most wonderfully earth-centred future vision in all of Scripture. Contrary to the 'heavenism' or 'Rapture theology' that dominates some fundamentalist interpretations today, Revelation envisions our future dwelling and God's on a radiant earth – a 'Rapture in reverse'. Green space and a river of life fill the city. The tree of life's medicinal leaves 'for the healing of the nations' offer an alternative political economy in which the essentials of health and life are available for all, even those without money. The tree provides food for the hungry each month of the year. The invitation to 'take the water of life as a gift' (*dorean,* Rev. 21.6; 22.17), underscores economic transformation.

The biblical book of Revelation holds out great hope for the future. The two witnesses of Revelation 11, symbolically representing God's people, model the public testimony and witness that John wants the Christian community of his own time to emulate. As Brian Blount describes, 'John is calling for a witness of active, nonviolent resistance to Rome's claim of lordship over human history.'[44] Testimony makes a difference. Today, we are called to give our testimony against carbon-fuels' claim to lordship. The hope John proclaims is that unjust empires and systems will soon come to an end – in fact, they have already been defeated by Lamb power and the community's bold testimony (Rev. 12.11). Revelation's message of hope assures communities thirsting for justice that change is coming. God hears their cries. God dwells with them on Earth. The hope of Revelation opens our eyes to see God's river of life already in our midst and a healing tree of life that renews our world.

---

[44] Brian K. Blount, *Can I Get a Witness? Reading Revelation through African American Culture* (Louisville: Westminster John Knox, 2005), 40.

A response to Barbara Rossing from South Asia

Monica Jyotsna Melanchthon[1]

Climate change is a global issue but it has different effects on communities, exacerbating poverty and existing inequalities. In India, the impact of climate change and the ecological crisis has animated the anxieties of the poor, the tribal/adivasi communities and especially those at the bottom of the caste ladder, who have to constantly negotiate their lives to access opportunities for work, food and water. This has reinforced an organic link between the destruction of the environment and social, economic and political injustice. Hence, as Leonardo Boff says,

> Ecological injustice is transformed into social injustice by producing social oppression, exhaustion of resources, contamination of the atmosphere and the deteriorating quality of life that touches all human beings and all of society.[2]

The dominant in India have co-opted nature to create a social ecology founded on notions of impurity, pollution and dirt that render Dalits as untouchables. Natural spaces such as riverbanks and water sources, and places such as temples, sacred groves and churches are restricted to them through imaginaries of danger and pollution posed by the presence of Dalits, resulting in 'environmental othering'.[3] Environmental degradation is intricately intertwined with the Dalit experience of discrimination, humiliation, fear, violence, deprivation, death, displacement and exploitation. Dalit reverence of and dependence on the soil, especially agriculture, is vital for their subsistence. Their proximity to nature and their dependence on it has evoked the imagination of Dalit poets and writers who are expending effort to articulate their environmental imagination.

---

[1] Monica Melanchton is a Hebrew Bible scholar from India currently teaching at the Pilgrim Theological College, University of Divinity, Melbourne (Australia). She has contributed towards developing Dalit and Indian feminist hermeneutics, drawing on insights from the social biographies of women, Dalits and other marginalized communities.

[2] Leonardo Boff, 'Social Ecology: Poverty and Misery', in *Ecotheology: Voices from the South and the North*, David G. Hallman (ed.) (Maryknoll: Orbis / Geneva: WCC, 1995), 235–7 (244).

[3] Mukul Sharma, *Caste and Nature: Dalits and Indian Environmental Politics* (Oxford: Oxford University Press, 2017), xviii.

Betrayed by culture and its discriminatory constructions, Dalit imagination goes back to the very state of nature – non-casteist ground zero of culture, a pre-civilizational site bereft of artificial distortions.[4]

Conscious of the fact that the eco-balance is being destroyed by the hierarchical relationship between humanity and nature, their poetic reflection is making serious ecological interventions to resist the abuse of nature by the dominant repositories of culture. Inherent in their poetry[5] is the belief that nature offers a landscape 'of primitive communism of refulgent pre-historical co-existence of non-institutionalized and non-hierarchized humanity'.[6]

The Dalit experiences of the environment and climate change and their perspective on these problems should thus be the starting point of our discussion. It is integral to their struggle for justice and liberation, and it is about preserving the integrity of creation. Might the Hebrew Scriptures and the New Testament offer insights that would accompany Dalits in their efforts to address 'eco-casteism'[7] and its impact both on nature and the Dalit community?

Rossing's emphasis that we can draw on the traditions within the Bible to offer hope and healing at this rather crucial moment in human history is beyond debate. Rossing's essay is helpful in that it stresses several significant issues through her treatment of select texts, including themes such as 'The goodness and beauty of creation', now endangered by human action (Genesis 1). She states that 'Limitations are at the core of human creatureliness and part of God's good creation.' Acknowledgement of these limits would help in addressing the abuse of earth's resources (Gen. 2). 'God makes a covenant with Creation and with Coming Generations.' This covenant and promise is not a license to ignore the signs of climate change. The text is actually highlighting 'environmental truths'. God's promise and covenant is an assurance that God will continue to work alongside human beings to preserve and nurture creation for the sake of future generations (Gen. 8-9). Rossing states that 'Earth and economically oppressed humanity together voice their cry for liberation.' The relationship between the oppressed earth and the oppressed of the earth are exemplified in the stories of the Hebrews in

---

[4] Akshaya Kumar, *Poetry, Politics and Culture: Essays on Indian Texts and Contexts* (London: Routledge, 2009), 291.

[5] 'There is this law in the world of jungle:
   Lion and jackal
   Elephant and deer
   Small-big
   Weak-mighty—
   All drink water from the same riverbank.'
   See Satnam Singh, in *Dalit Sahitya Varshiki* (2004–2005), Jaiprakash Kardam (ed.), Vol 6, No. #6 and 7 (2005), 355, cited by Kumar, *Poetry, Politics and Culture: Essays on Indian Texts and Contexts*, 291.

[6] Ibid.

[7] Sharma defines this term as 'the interrelationship between environment and caste' in Sharma, *Caste and Nature*, xix.

Egypt. The abuse of the earth and the oppression of the poor are realized through the establishment of economic systems for the profit of some. God hears the cries of the oppressed earth and humanity and comes down to deliver by revealing Godself through holy ground, and a burning bush (Exodus). Indeed, 'We can bring required changes and transform the empire through repentance and a radical turning initiated by grassroots movements, the poorest and the most vulnerable.' And, 'The Kingdom of heaven is a renewed creation' – the groaning cosmos inclusive of both humanity and the earth are in pain and wait in hope (Rom. 8.22-23) for a turning initiated by Jesus through his death and resurrection. For Rossing, 'Liberation and healing will come to the earth and humanity by withdrawing from the sin of empire' – through non-violent resistance and participation in the establishment of the New Jerusalem, renewed and healed (Revelation).

The present ecological predicament lies in the particular vision of reality, which considers the human being at the centre of reality and reason at the centre of being human.[8] Rossing's emphasis on the correlation between the oppression of the earth and peoples and the fact that empire can be awakened by 'grassroots community movements' to 'turn away from a path of destruction' is appreciated in the light of two issues. First, the incessant and significant call for liberation hermeneutics to strive beyond the sociopolitical dimensions of liberation (human alone) and include the neglected cultural and ecological aspects of liberation. Second, the epistemological framework of Dalit theology, poetry and Dalit interpretations of Scripture, the category of experience and 'pathos' can actually enable the realization of the interrelation of the groaning of nature and the cry of the Dalit/tribal poor in India. Its reliance on oral tradition and the absence of historical determinism,[9] its enormous wealth of ecologically significant myths and poetic reflections could help in the development of a Christian ecological doctrine of creation.

Although Rossing does not identify the hermeneutical principles she uses, one can discern the earth bible principles of intrinsic worth, of interconnectedness, of voice, of purpose, of mutual custodianship and of resistance guiding her analysis of these texts.[10] Norman Habel writes that these principles are not exhaustive or definitive and can be used 'broadly across traditions'.[11] This is encouraging since the cultures and the traditions of the tribal and marginalized communities of India contain within them resources and insights that are liberative. More than dogma and beliefs, they embody the relationship of peoples to the ecosystem in their day-to-day lives.[12] The *Muria hond*

---

[8] Vandana Shiva, *Staying Alive: Women, Ecology and Survival in India* (Delhi: Kali for Women, 1988).

[9] George Matthew Nalunnakkal, *Green Liberation: Towards an Integral Ecotheology* (New Delhi: ISPCK / NCCI India, 1999), 193, 201.

[10] For explanation of these principles, see Norman Habel, 'Ecological Criticism', in *New Meanings for Ancient Texts: Recent Approaches to Biblical Criticisms and Their Applications,* Steven L. McKenzie and John H. Kaltner (eds) (Louisville: Westminster John Knox, 2013), 39–58 (46–7).

[11] Ibid., 47.

[12] Felix Wilfred, *Asian Public Theology: Critical Concerns in Challenging Times* (New Delhi: ISPCK, 2010), 308–14.

tribes of Bastar in North India, for example, as cited by Nalunnakkal, consider human beings to be the crops of God, raised by Mother Earth. As the crops depend on the soil, all human beings rely on Mother Earth.[13] This is a powerful image for Dalits. The recurrent insights in such myths of creation consistently interrelate God, humanity and nature. Commenting on how humans and the earth are held together in God, Dalit theologian, Arvind P. Nirmal writes,

> Both God and human then share in earthliness. The earth is the common bond between God and humans. May I say, both of them smell earth and dust.[14]

The challenge before us is to bring native texts into conversation with biblical texts that would help critique and enhance our understanding of both. Christian theology on its own will not go far enough in influencing the religiously pluralistic Asian context on ecological issues. The theological, moral and spiritual insights on ecology in various religions such as Hinduism, Buddhism, Jainism and Islam and tribal religions and their immanent dimensions of the divine need to be integrated so that it may foster an interfaith dialogue, specifically from the perspective of eco-justice in Asia.[15]

George Zachariah, ethicist and Indian theologian, writes that there is a need to transform our communities into eco-just congregations, which means that we need to green the pulpit. The ecological bankruptcy or our theological and doctrinal traditions and ecological abuses of the Christian scriptures might be a starting point for such an endeavour.[16] Greening the pulpit would perhaps require the following: that we apply the six eco-justice guidelines named above for the purposes of preaching. The methodological approach that involves the hermeneutic of suspicion of inherent anthropomorphism in our interpretations and preaching, empathetic identification with the earth and members of the earth community and a retrieval of non-human voices in the text are important to engage the Bible amidst the ecological crisis. Rossing's interpretations shows us how the Bible (from Genesis to Revelation) is replete with evidence of God's love and concern for all of creation, God's revelation through nature and God's call to us to not just be stewards of nature, but to be in a *kinship* relationship with non-human creation. Rossing's reflections thus provide homiletic insights for strengthening our spiritual kinship connections to the earth.

---

[13] Nalunnakkal, *Green Liberation: Towards an Integral Ecotheology*, 203.
[14] Arvind P. Nirmal, 'Ecology, Ecumenics, and Economy in Relation: A New Theological Paradigm', in *Ecology and Development: Theological Perspectives*, Daniel Chetti (ed.) (Madras: Gurukul Lutheran Theological College/BTESSC, 1991), 17–28 (23).
[15] Wilfred, *Asian Public Theology*, 308–9.
[16] George Zachariah, *Alternatives Incorporated: Earth Ethics from the Grassroots* (London: Equinox, 2011).

Chapter 6.3
Climate change and Christian fellowship

Erin Lothes Biviano[1]

America the beautiful: Creation care and the choirs of two cultures

It's no secret that the American public is deeply polarized and divided.[2] The same holds true for the US Catholic church in particular ways. It's also no secret that our earth is far from healthy. In the face of these challenges, ecclesial polarization is a sad fact with division between 'liberals' and 'conservatives' damaging Church unity. While the highly oversimplified terms 'liberal' and 'conservative' have grave limitations, nonetheless they point to a reality few would deny.

Without wishing to analyse the differences that mark 'liberal' and 'conservative' groups in the church in their full complex political and social dimensions, a task that is beyond the scope of this essay,[3] I will address the ecclesial polarization that takes particular and pointed form in the sphere of environmental concern. Famously framed in *Laudato Si'* as the Church's mission to care for our common home, this is a mission that arouses passion and support, but also division, within the ecclesial community.

To state the problem plainly, the polarization within the Catholic Church in the United States is sharply revealed in differences over environmentalism and the embrace of her ecological mission primarily by progressives. Bill Patenaude, author of the well-regarded blog *Catholic Ecology*, asks incisively: can half the Church carry the whole

---

[1] Erin Lothes is Associate Professor of Religious Studies, Theology and Philosophy at the College of St. Elizabeth in Morristown, New Jersey, USA. The author of two books, she researches energy ethics from a Catholic perspective and is a scholar of the interfaith environmental movement.
[2] Stephen Hawkins and Tommy Flint, 'Two Stories: One America: How Political Narratives Shape Our Understanding of Reality', http://ksr.hkspublications.org/2016/07/20/two-stories-one-america-how-political-narratives-shape-our-understanding-of-reality/ (accessed 21 January 2019).
[3] John Gehring, *The Francis Effect: A Radical Pope's Challenge to the American Catholic Church* (Lanham: Rowman & Littlefield, 2015).

church's ecological mission?[4] The answer is, no! In his words, 'growing ideological divides are inhibiting Catholic eco-activity.'[5] Given the political power of US Catholics,[6] the family feud of polarized US Catholics in regards to environmentalism carries grave cost to all the earth.

Ecclesial polarization has been theorized not as the existence of diametrically opposed groups on extreme ends of a pole, but as the inability to enter into communion with the centre.[7] It is a problem of relating to the core of the Church. Polarization is painful. Indeed, Bishop Flores offers the searing insight that the wound of polarization is 'a loss of confidence that the members of the household of faith actually love one another'.[8] Tending to relationships, and healing relational divisions, would seem to offer a way forward. Kindness and fairness towards all in the broadest circles of relationships is at the core of Christian faith: such 'kinship' is embedded in the great command to 'love one's neighbour', and in the very interpretation of the Trinitarian God as a mystery of divine relationality.

Yet a sociological theory of culture shows that it is precisely the characteristic patterns of relationship that mark differing groups that intensify their polarization. If ecclesial polarization is understood as a failure of relationships in the Church community, analysing characteristic patterns of relationship as cultures may clarify the ecclesial ecological divide, identify the differences in their values, and offer an interpretation that reframes these differences as diversity within a common experience of being a US Catholic. Accepting diversity of perspectives may lead to embracing diverse solutions to the environmental crisis as well.

Reframing the conflict model using cultural theory

Analysing polarization using cultural theory can perhaps reframe the disagreements, shifting the model of the polarized landscape from ideological conflict to contrasting cultures. In so doing the landscape of debate is reframed as an arena for intercultural dialogue – almost as if conducting interfaith dialogue within the one communion of US Catholics. Then differences that appear to be impassable boulders, as landmarks

---

[4] Charles C. Camosy, 'Activist Says Pope's Eco-Message Can't Be Carried by "Half the Church"', *Crux*, 10 April 2017.

[5] Bill Patenaude, 'Learning from the Left', *Catholic Ecology*, 16 May 2017, https://catholicecology.net/blog/learning-left. See also 'Conversations with Conservatives', *Catholic Ecology*, 6 May 2017, https://catholicecology.net/blog/conversations-conservatives (accessed 19 May 2018).

[6] Russell R. Reno, 'No More Tirades', *First Things*, 29 September 2015, 1.

[7] Annie Selak, 'Inheriting Climate Controversies: Reception in a Polarized Church', unpublished conference paper presented at the *Catholic Theological Society of America* (Albuquerque, 2017).

[8] Mary Ellen Konieczny, Charles C. Camosy, and Tricia A. Bruce (eds), *Polarization in the US Catholic Church: Naming the Wounds, Beginning to Heal* (Collegeville: Liturgical Press, 2016), 6.

of conflict, may be reframed as contrasting but comprehensible aspects of different cultures, and instead become manageable stepping stones, perhaps not flagstones, on a single narrow path, but navigable aspects of a shared landscape. Alternately, the metaphor of a complex chorus divided into choirs singing different verses of the same song invites the effort to find a way forward into harmony.

Thus this essay will begin by identifying the characteristics of both choirs using the cultural theory developed by anthropologists Mary Douglass and Aaron Wildavsky. I will trace the dissonant interpretations of *Laudato Si'* in the voices of prominent Catholic commentators that seem to align with the (admittedly oversimplified) popular understanding of the liberal and conservative choirs today. I will then propose a reassessment of how each group evaluates the social priorities of the other, while reconsidering ways each can return to the core ecclesial communion. This reassessment may enable a more complex harmonization of the identities of the choirs in one hymn – let us say, *America the Beautiful* – for the sake of creation.

Cultural theory and constructions of value

Cultural theory diagrams the characteristic patterns of relationships preferred by different persons, patterns that correlate with core values about society, the individual, nature, and the economy. Culture refers to groups with shared, socially constructed belief systems, or worldviews, in which 'the view of the universe and a particular kind of society holding this view are closely interdependent'.[9] Differing cultures construe different meanings upon situations, events, groups and relationships between individuals and society. Such worldviews can even filter the evidence of our eyes and shape persons' own recollections of the weather they themselves experienced. Katherine Hayhoe, an evangelical climate scientist who is a leading voice for creation care, relates that people surveyed about the temperatures they experienced reported different temperatures according to their political affiliation.[10] Incredibly, self-reported accounts of perceived temperatures in one's own backyard are politically filtered. This striking example shows why worldviews matter so much to environmental polarization, and thus why analysis of the cultures that generate them is critical.

Douglas and Wildavsky's cultural theory identifies four types of groups, or cultures, which represent different personal preferences for characteristic patterns of social relationship. These four cultures result from the intersection of preferences regarding the extent of collectivization in social and political groupings, with preferences

---

[9] Karl Dake, 'Myths of Nature: Culture and the Social Construction of Risk', *Journal of Social Issues* 48:4 (1992), 21–37 (27).

[10] Katherine Hayhoe and Daniel DiLeo, webinar, 'Communicating Climate Change to People of Faith', Catholic Climate Covenant, 22 February 2018, http://www.catholicclimatecovenant.org/resource/communicating-climate-change-to-people-of-faith (accessed 18 April 2018).

for the extent of individual autonomy. Hence a four-way grid results. Rather than placing individualism and collectivism on opposite ends of a continuum, this cultural theory offers a more complex view. It recognizes that social identity is one aspect of collectivism, and some persons will identify more or less strongly with social groups, boundaries and roles. Autonomy is another dimension of one's preference for social belonging, and here also different persons have stronger and weaker identification with strong social prescriptions or greater autonomy. Thus four 'cultures' emerge, identified as the hierarchical, egalitarian, individualistic and fatalist patterns of social relations. A description of these four types follows:

> People in *individualistic* and *fatalistic* social relations *are not* part of a collective undertaking, but individualists retain their autonomy, while fatalists do not. People in *egalitarian* and *hierarchical* social relations, meanwhile, *are* part of a collective undertaking, but egalitarians retain much more of their autonomy than hierarchs. Hierarchical social relations are highly structured, with everyone and everything having his, her, and its place-represented by a pyramid here. Individualistic social relations, by contrast, are highly fluid, and are subject to individual choice, represented by a network ... Egalitarian social relations retain their autonomy by giving all members an equal voice in (and thus the power to veto) collective decisions.[11]

I suggest that initially this diagram of cultures maps onto the (admittedly simplified) US Catholic landscape such that conservative Catholics are perceived as hierarchical (strong social identity and strong social prescriptions) and liberal Catholics as egalitarians (strong social identity and high preference for autonomy). Note that the term 'hierarchical' here is unrelated to the Catholic hierarchy, but expresses a highly structured view of social roles. (For simplicity's sake, I am omitting discussion of fatalists, who do not map neatly onto this analysis of US Catholics.)

Characteristic cultural values regarding nature

Characteristic values correlate with these patterns of social relations:

> Hierarchs value order, propriety, and whatever collectivity gives them their station; egalitarians value equality (of result), and freedom to the extent that it can be reconciled with community; individualists value liberty, autonomy, and personal space.[12]

Hierarchs value the traditional family and compliance with established rules, respect strong group boundaries and accept high levels of social prescription. Egalitarians want equal outcomes above all. Their resultant ethical concern for the environmental and

---

[11] Brendon Swedlow, 'Toward Cultural Analysis in Policy Analysis: Picking up Where Aaron Wildavsky Left Off', *Journal of Comparative Analysis, Research and Practice* 4:3 (2002), 267–85 (269).
[12] Ibid., 271.

the social, political and health impacts of technology creates the willingness to critique society's managing institutions.[13]

The different cultures also correlate with diverse views of nature. Hierarchs view nature as both fragile and resilient, requiring experts with specialized knowledge to address environmental problems. Egalitarians construe nature as vulnerable, an interpretation which justifies limits upon corporate activity and promotes smaller and egalitarian communities. Finally, individualists see nature as robust, comprising resources available for commercial activity and best engaged without regulation.[14] For individualists, nature is in fact benign and abundant, and social sanctions should defend the freedom to enact options in self-regulating systems.[15] Naturally, such views correlate with different interpretations of what maximizes happiness, what ends are to be sought, and thus what policies are effective.

These interpretations of what makes for good policy are coloured by what Yuval Levin identifies as the differing nostalgias of today's conservatives and liberals, who have variously construed memories of America's past greatness. In his analysis, conservative or Republican nostalgia yearns for the cultural and moral consensus of mid-century, the perceived social solidarity that exploded with the assassination of John F. Kennedy. A more recently focused conservative nostalgia looks back to the Reagan years, the optimism and economic reforms that spurred growth without inflating the welfare state.[16] Meanwhile, liberal or Democratic nostalgia seeks to 'add more rooms to the mansion of the Great Society', to manage the economy to ensure more social benefits for all, and to recapture the energy of the protest movements that also expanded rights and broad social participation – the classic egalitarian aim.[17]

How then does this cultural map play out in the environmental debate? Unless violently opposed or illegitimately unorthodox, diverse values can be all well and good – until they frustrate expectations and undermine familial communication. Employing cultural theory prompts a diagnosis of the perhaps unexpected way that individualism functions for both choirs because different patterns of relationship engage in different contexts, further complexifying attempts to interpret characteristic dynamics.[18] That is, persons who might seem to identify the most with hierarchical culture in fact *engage individualist* patterns of relationship in the context of climate change *taken as an economic issue*. Conservatives thus appear to be more closely aligned with individualists in the economic sphere – which is determinative

---

[13] Dake, 'Myths of Nature', 29.
[14] Swedlow, 'Toward Cultural Analysis in Policy Analysis', 272.
[15] Dake, 'Myths of Nature', 29.
[16] Yuval Levin, *The Fractured Republic: Renewing America's Social Contract in the Age of Individualism* (New York: Basic Books, 2016), 21–2.
[17] Ibid., 20.
[18] Anna L. Peterson, 'Talking the Walk: A Practice-Based Environmental Ethic as Grounds for Hope', in *Ecospirit: Religions and Philosophies for the Earth*, Laurel Kearns and Catherine Keller (eds) (New York: Fordham University Press, 2007), 45–62 (53).

for their environmental beliefs. In a different way, liberals engage individualist patterns in the sphere of personal freedom of conscience, and sometimes frustrate conservative expectations of hewing to traditional values. In fact, neither group is fully traditional – and in the divergences of both camps from Catholic tradition, there erupts the potential for a mutual sense of betrayal.

The individualistic dynamic in the personal morality sphere is perceived by conservatives as the pitfall of secular progressivism and represents a major neuralgic point in the polarization of liberals and conservatives. To this strong sense of individualism in the personal sphere, a person with hierarchical values might reply with a line from *America the Beautiful*: 'confirm thy soul in self-control, and liberty in law.' This imagined retort overlooks that conscience partakes of the nature of a rule of law; nonetheless emphasis on personal conscience may lack the social cohesion of a strongly shared moral consensus favoured by social conservatives. And to the competitiveness of a hierarchical-turned-economic individualist, liberals might reply with a paraphrased line from the hymn: 'love mercy more than [one's own] life.'

In the case of environmental ecclesial polarization, these diverse values have the effect of shifting the reading of *Laudato Si'* by conservative and liberal commentators. Though both are reading the same text, their interpretative lenses result in different glosses and diverging conclusions about how the text frustrates or supports their key values.

Comparing readings of *Laudato Si'* among liberal and conservative commentators

Comparing prominent commentators on *Laudato Si'* reveals the different motifs for environmental–social crisis that each choir sings out the strongest. In listening to *Laudato Si'*, both sides hear the same lyrics yet render them differently.

Human ecology or suffering creation?

First, David Cloutier has compared the commentaries of two priests who wrote in anticipation of the release of *Laudato Si'*: Father Robert Sirico, co-founder of the Acton Institute, a group identified on its website as 'a think-tank whose mission is to promote a free and virtuous society characterized by individual liberty and sustained by religious principles', and Father Thomas Reese, SJ, former editor of *America Magazine* and columnist for the *National Catholic Reporter*. In Cloutier's analysis, while both affirm that creation is an ordered gift from God, Father Siroco emphasizes nature as subject to humanity's unique dignity and stewardship, whereas Father Reese highlights the suffering of creation 'groaning for redemption'.[19]

Their anticipation of the encyclical's moral message likewise shows distinct emphases. Father Reese focuses on the intense human suffering climate change will create, evidencing the 'liberal' concern for equality and impacts, while Father Sirico emphasizes the necessary respect between natural ecology and human ecology, or the natural moral law. Cloutier points out that both highlight Catholic values, but each overlooks the full picture. Conservatives must realistically acknowledge the significant dangers of climate change, refrain from claiming that prudential judgement enables us to put scientific consensus in doubt, and avoid the stereotypical straw dog that environmentalists 'worship nature'. Liberals must take seriously the critique that the 'throwaway culture' and 'culture of waste' pose to sexual and relational ethics as well as to consumerism. Thus, neither section of the choir sings the full range of the traditional teachings.

Both liberal and conservatives honour strong social identities and social boundaries in the religious sphere, which grounds their loyalty to Catholic identity. Yet as American Catholics, there is undoubtedly a strong strain of independence in both choirs. The hymn *America the Beautiful* captures this: 'O beautiful for pilgrim feet, whose stern impassioned stress / A thoroughfare of freedom beat across the wilderness!' Both choirs have their feet firmly set on the thoroughfare of freedom in their own ways, but their paths diverge over hidden fault lines. Individualism shifts full expression of traditional Catholic differently for both choirs, who are left wondering, why aren't we in sync?

One explanation comes from comparing Cloutier's analysis of the values highlighted by the two priests with the values identified by cultural theory. Liberals, unsurprisingly, are individualists in the personal and social spheres. Liberals value equal outcomes in society and thus lament 'the suffering of all creation', while valuing individual freedom of conscience and an individually tuned social progressivism. However, while the liberal reading supplied by Father Reese coheres with the egalitarian culture, a neat pairing of conservatives and hierarchists begins to break down. Conservatives who might be expected to identify with hierarchical cultural patterns are in fact individualists precisely in the environment sphere. Conservative Catholics value strong social identity and consensus in moral matters within the personal and social spheres, while preferring freedom in the market and limited government, thus demonstrating economic and political individualism.

---

[19] David Cloutier, 'Frs. Reese and Sirico on the Encyclical: What We Can Learn', *Catholic Moral Theology*, 1 June 2015.

Economic emphases

A second pair of commentators further underscores the way individualism becomes the dominant 'cultural' mode of conservatives in the economic sphere, as the influence of economic views is evident in their interpretations of *Laudato Si'*. Here I compare Father James Martin, SJ, editor-at-large of *America Magazine*, and Russell Reno, editor of *First Things*.

Where Francis writes of 'a politics which is farsighted and capable of a new, integral and interdisciplinary approach', Reno sees a nightmare of 'armies of technocrats' in a 'global bureaucracy of unprecedented size and power'.[20] For Martin, the fact that 'everything is connected' means that protecting nature, justice, society and inner peace calls for worldwide dialogue.[21] Egalitarian inclusion is the tone here, opposed to apocalyptic bureaucratic hegemony feared by small-government conservatives. Reno acknowledges that he agrees with Pope Francis's main point that the 'triumph of global capitalism poses significant and fundamental challenges', though he puts the 'substantive issues differently'. This difference is reflected in another interview, in which Reno observes that a 'conservative tends to think the dynamism of capitalism helps ameliorate these inequalities over time and the cost to human freedom of over-regulation is a perilous thing'. Here the individualist themes emerge strongly.

In addition, where Pope Francis seeks to humanize capitalism in the name of a preferential option for the poor, Reno reads an 'uncritical', if well-intentioned, acceptance of the 'intellectual and moral framework of secular progressivism' which is easily manipulated by power elites and the 'rich secular world'.[22] On the other hand, in the pope's critique of indifference and selfishness which neglects the dignity and worth of the poor, Martin sees legitimate and theologically grounded critiques of the limits of the market when maximized profit provides the sole criterion of its function.[23]

The point for the aim of advancing communion is that traditional Catholicism embraces a range of social, economic and personal values that do not map neatly onto either right or left. Catholics cannot identify wholesale with either caricature of liberal Democrats or conservative Republicans. The social and political commitments of what may be called 'traditional' Catholicism bridge the polarized reduction of the liberal and conservative platforms to hot-button issues. As John Carr, former director of the Department of Justice and Peace for the U.S. Conference of Catholic Bishops, asked, 'Who left Planned Parenthood in charge of Democrats and the Tea Party in charge of Republicans?'[24]

---

[20] Russell R. Reno, 'The Weakness of Laudato Si", *First Things*, 1 July 2015, 3.
[21] James Martin, SJ, 'Top Ten Takeaways from 'Laudato Si"', *America Magazine*, 18 June 2015.
[22] Russell R. Reno, 'First Things Editor R.R. Reno Responds to Pope Francis' Visit to the United States', *America Magazine*, 26 September 2015, 6.
[23] Martin, 'Top Ten Takeaways from 'Laudato Si".
[24] John Carr, 'The Francis Factor', *America Magazine*, 21 October 2013, 11.

It is true that sometimes persons on the left champion causes not supported by the traditional church – notably, for egalitarian reasons. As Bill Patenaude notes, liberals can be 'unfettered by the realities like natural law – which are seen as restrictions'. Yet as a young pro-life advocate, Erin Stoyell-Mulholland writes, showing the interconnection of all life issues sends a powerful message that can lessen the polarization surrounding pro-life and environmental issues. Liberals could more strongly underscore the interconnection of all life issues to increase cross-choir unity regarding the life issue of caring for the creation, the primordial origin of every living person and creature.[25]

But Patenaude further observes:

> the left is right sometimes, too. I'm convinced that the often dismissive attitude toward eco-protection and the downright denial of climate change is, for many on the right, largely rooted in the lazy reaction of simply opposing anything the left supports ... It makes no sense to deny science – even if voices on the left use ecology for political, anti-life ends ... The right should instead charge in, find common ground where it is to be found, and add its voice to the solutions being offered – all in defense of innocent life.[26]

Communion calls both to the ecclesial centre where the common good and defence of life transcends these political binaries. As Bishop McElroy states, affirming the necessary cross-choir complexity of Catholic social teaching:

> There is no single category of sin or evil, social good or virtue, that is the filter for discerning the priorities of the church in the public order. The concept of the common good is multidimensional in its very nature, and any reductionist effort to minimize this quality is a distortion of our heritage and teaching.[27]

For precisely this reason, the diocese of Camden states that life and justice issues are 'impossible to separate', and thus has one office of 'Life and Justice Ministries.' This inseparability offers a way to harmonize the sometimes differing ways the very phrase 'life ethic' is engaged by liberal (environmental) Catholics and conservative Catholics (here traditionalist life advocates).

While a diversity of prudential judgements may enliven 'intercultural dialogue', resolving ecclesial polarization requires a return to the centre. Asked if American conservatives have become 'cafeteria Catholics', Reno observes that in a certain sense, 'we're all at odds with some aspect of the Church's leadership.' Yet he captures the essential spirit of unity by continuing, 'what matters most is our spiritual disposition. Are we willing to see and learn what [our bishops and pope] want to teach us? We're in

---

[25] Erin Stoyell-Mulholland, 'Polarization and Abortion: Living out Our Pro-Life Beliefs', in *Polarization in the US Catholic Church: Naming the Wounds, Beginning to Heal*, Mary Ellen Konieczny, Charles C. Camosy and Tricia A. Bruce (eds) (Collegeville: Liturgical Press, 2016), 119–29 (128).

[26] Patenaude, 'Learning from the Left'.

[27] Robert W. McElroy, 'A Church for the Poor', *America*, 21 October 2013, 13–16 (15).

this American project together. We need to accompany each other, even as we contest for the future.'[28] Contestation for the future evokes the 'liberating strife' of the hymn *America the Beautiful*, a contestation of healthy debate and dialogue through which the choirs can share a common vision, and join forces to care for the 'fruited plains' with which we have been entrusted in our prior identity as fellow creatures, as stewards and caretakers of creation.

'Freedom' for environmental mistrust

As important as trust is to allow diverse groups to join forces, ecclesial environmental polarization is intensified not only by differently individualized, 'conservative/liberal' choirs, but by a striking phenomenon of *ecologically particularized mistrust* conveyed by survey findings. The Center for Applied Research in the Apostolate in 2017 confirmed that regular Mass-goers are the most likely to see little conflict between their faith and science. Yet it is precisely weekly Mass-goers who are *least likely* to say that climate change is a very important or the most important problem. This is also the group *least likely* to agree they have a moral responsibility to respond to climate change.[29]

This targeted mistrust exists against a background of very strong general support for Pope Francis as an environmental communicator. According to a before-and-after *Laudato Si'* study, 72 per cent of Catholics trust Francis as a source of information on global warming.[30] Thus, despite generally robust support for Pope Francis, and very strong tendency to see faith and science as compatible by regular Mass-goers, a small portion of these Mass-goers diverges specifically on the topic of climate change such that they fail to see climate change as a very important problem for which they have moral responsibility. This reversal of trust seems to further confirm a felt sense of freedom to dissent from Pope Francis's ecological teaching, an individualist dynamic in the environmental sphere specifically among otherwise traditional Catholics – defined here as traditional because of their regular Mass-going habits.

The 'rhetoric of crisis' which Reno highlights as problematic in *Laudato Si'* corroborates this ecclesial mistrust and offers another clue as to why conservatives often dismiss environmentalist warnings.[31] Climate communication experts recognize that the narratives of warning don't always communicate. The 'scientists say' that the 'crisis' story fail to inspire participation and even backfire by overwhelming people with

---

[28] Reno, 'No More Tirades', 3.

[29] Mark M. Gray and Jonathon L. Wiggins, *Catholics' Opinions About Faith and Science*, (Washington DC: Center for Applied Research in the Apostolate, 2017), 4.

[30] Edward W. Maibach, Anthony Leiserowitz, Connie Roser-Renouf, Teresa Myers and Geoff Feinberg, *The Francis Effect: How Pope Francis Changed the Conversation About Global Warming* (Fairfax: George Mason University Center for Climate Change Communication and Yale University, 2015), 8.

[31] Reno, 'The Weakness of Laudato Si'', 2.

negativity and despair.[32] Others perceive the 'crisis' story as deliberately and dishonestly overstated in order to manipulate them. This politically filtered interpretation of science results from an emotional dismissal of climate warnings that seem overblown. Climate psychologist Anthony Leiserowitz has found that this dismissal which rejects climate apocalypticism is the most powerful of all the emotional responses to climate images. Survey research found that doom-and-gloom warnings evoked what he calls a 'naysayer response' – a response which is even more significant than the correlation of political affiliation with environmental attitudes.[33] Such intense rejection of climate apocalypticism may be at work to increase the phenomenon of particularized, ecclesial environmental distrust.

At the worst, mistrust fosters stereotypes which replace sincere dialogue. Sister Simone Campbell, the progressive activist and 'nun on the bus', emphasizes that care for our common home calls for an individual and communal conversion of the heart – a spiritual and religious renewal.[34] But she has been criticized with the stereotype that environmentalists 'worship nature', ignoring her stated focus on religious renewal.[35] Dialogue that avoids caricature is needed: there is more common ground in shared commitment to a religious perspective on climate change. To reach that common ground, both choirs need to move towards the centre.

I have employed cultural theory in tandem with analysis of readings of *Laudato Si'* by diverse commentators to suggest that Catholic 'liberals' and 'conservatives' in fact form individualist subcultures. These subcultures express identities in some ways dissonant to orthodox Catholicism: liberal egalitarianism permits secular ethics to predominate, and conservatives engage their individualist leanings in the economic sphere to embody the American civil religion of capitalism. For both sections of the choir, this divergence from orthodoxy is a breach from which bitter resentment and betrayal can seep out, a wound that makes polarization so painful while the stakes for the environment grow higher.

Pragmatically, cultural theory affirms that *both* liberals and conservatives value high collectivism and high individualism: only, they do so in different spheres. This reflects the 'differing nostalgias' which Levin highlights: nostalgia for a moral and social consensus on the one hand, and nostalgia for shared commitments to economic equality on the other.

---

[32] Climate Access Webinar, 'From People to Policies: Best Practices in Advocacy Storytelling', https://climate access.org/resource/webinar-recording-people-policies-best-practices-advocacy-storytelling (accessed 8 November 2017).

[33] Anthony Leiserowitz and Nicholas Smith, 'The Rise of Global Warming Skepticism: Exploring Affective Image Associations in the United States over Time', *Risk Analysis* 32:6 (2012), 1021; Jürgen Moltmann, 'Liberating and Anticipating the Future', in *Liberating Eschatology: Essays in Honor of Letty M. Russell*, Margaret Farley and Serene Jones (eds) (Louisville: Westminster, 1999), 1032 (1028).

[34] Simone Campbell, 'We Need an Integral Ecology, Not an Economy of Exclusion', *Global Sisters Report*, 19 June 2015.

[35] Marian T. Horvat, 'Progressivist Sisters Rejoice over Laudato Si'', *Tradition in Action*, 1 July 2015.

Commonalities within difference

This zeal for union is desperately needed. All the 'alabastor cities and fruited plains' are facing serious impacts, now and in the future, in the United States and around the world. Efforts to move away from 'business-as-usual' are not keeping pace with the energy shift needed to keep temperature increases below 1.5 degrees Celsius. And the costs in terms of economic damage, displacement of families, rising mortality and loss of agricultural productivity are extraordinary. The world has grown tragically accustomed to the sights of climate refugees losing their traditional homelands, and their displacement increases tensions in many parts of the world. Analysts find that as temperatures go up, costs in terms of GDP go up:

> The combined value of market and nonmarket damage across analyzed sectors – agriculture, crime, coastal storms, energy, human mortality, and labor – increases quadratically in global mean temperature, costing roughly 1.2% of gross domestic product per +1°C on average.[36]

A conservative's characteristic concern for robust economics, farming communities and immigration needs to reckon seriously with the impact of climate change on these issues. Part of the challenge for political conservatives is finding solutions to climate change that cohere with their preference for market mechanisms. Conservatives often reject an ecological agenda because the proposed solutions (more regulation, more taxation) seem unpalatable and intolerable, and part of an overall liberal agenda. Yet distinct connections exist between traditional conservative values and liberal 'caring for creation'. Clean energy is one such shared value, given impact of mercury from coal plants on developing foetuses.[37] A commitment to the environment as a life issue gains credibility from partners on the right when joined to support for conditions that ensure the well-being of all life from its beginnings. Other primarily economic solutions are points of connection as well. The Green Tea Party is a case in point of right-wing environmentalist activists campaigning on small government and personal freedom in energy issues. Offered the 'right' solutions, many become true believers.

Both choirs can fruitfully attend to the direction coming from decades of magisterial teaching. Celia Deane-Drummond's essay reviews the deep tradition of Catholic magisterial teaching. The more fundamental unity as Catholics precedes the identity of the choirs, who are both called to honour care for creation as central to social stability and the well-being that undergirds human dignity. Pope Emeritus Benedict wrote, 'If you want to cultivate peace, care for creation.'[38]

---

[36] Solomon Hsiang et al., 'Estimating Economic Damage from Climate Change in the United States', *Science* 356:6345 (2017), 1362–9 (1362).

[37] 'Blood Mercury Levels Rising among Us Women', *US News and World Report*, 24 August 2009.

[38] Benedict XVI, 'Message of His Holiness Pope Benedict Xvi for the Celebration of the World Day of Peace, 1 January 2010' (Rome: Vatican, 2010).

And crown thy good with brotherhood (and sisterhood)

US Catholics can acknowledge a larger pattern to their life as church, the complexity of the fully orchestrated hymn. What love enlivens this song? Family life is a shared concern for many, while also a source of differing nostalgias or family values. Solutions for one's family are a driving motivation for conservatives, Republicans, Green Tea Party members and many on the hierarchical–individualist choir, which suggests family as a unifying theme with the solidarity emphasis of egalitarians.

The family motif enlarges in concentric circles from the nuclear family, citizens, global neighbours and the entire family of creation – all living creatures – extending throughout the cosmic family. In the words of *America the Beautiful* and Francis's *Canticle of Creation,* all are brothers and sisters, echoed by the spirituality of the Indigenous First People which centres on 'all my relations' and calls the world's powers to humility and repentance for the exploitation done to the earth and many of her peoples. The hymn echoes the praising choir of spacious skies and purple majestic mountains. In these themes of the family and the neighbour who is to be cared for as family within a shared and beautiful home, there are magnetically attractive centres strong enough to re-align the charged environmental polarities within American Catholicism.

Consider a parable.

> Two siblings were responsible for a sick parent but they didn't believe the parent was sick, partly because they didn't believe any cure would work. They didn't agree on what cures to try. They couldn't cooperate because of their own disagreements. In fact the siblings had not been communicating well for a while. As the parent grew very sick, the siblings grew fearful, and they prayed to Jesus for a miracle. Jesus told them, 'You don't need a miracle. You need a partner. All your cures will work. Use them!'

The many points of agreement among US Catholics are a strong point, even in relationship to the environment. After the promulgation of *Laudato Si'*, a key study shows that 35 per cent of US Catholics report that the pope changed their views on global warming; 53 per cent are more concerned; 62 per cent believe that global warming will harm the worlds' poor – a twenty-percentage point increase – and 74 per cent believe future generations will be harmed.[39]

By attempting to reframe the divide as cultural differences, this essay seeks to centre upon that which unites us as one family, a family which embraces the home, the church and the family of creation, united by the growing consensus that Catholics need to be concerned about the environment for the sake of the vulnerable and the future.

---

[39] Maibach et al., 'The Francis Effect', 15–23.

US Catholics have the opportunity to sing a new song that praises our God and Creator together, bringing the distinct gifts, perspectives and solutions of the entire choir into harmony. Reframing conflict as a diversity of family cultures affirms the moral strength of a family eager to care for its common home. The hymn prays that God 'prosper our work and defend us', and this prayer can lift up the necessary 'liberating strife' that seeks fair societies within a green and fruitful America the Beautiful, and an abundant and peaceful Earth.

A response to Erin Lothes

Kuzipa Nalwamba[1]

Koinonia: The universe as cosmic communion

In her essay, Erin Lothes applies the lens of sociological theory of culture to reframe the causes of ecclesial polarization around environmental concerns in the Roman Catholic Church in America. She analyses the response of progressives and conservatives to *Laudato Si'*, the papal statement on the Catholic Church's mission to care for the earth. She concludes that the passion and support as well as the division within the ecclesial community around eco-activity and the declarations of *Laudato Si'* are not undergirded by grounding beliefs of the Christian faith. They are rather a function of the broader cultural divide that exists within American society.

The causal relationship is however not necessarily consistent along the obvious fault lines. Lothes illustrates that by showing how the culture that separates the 'two choirs' in the Catholic Church does not confine them to specific positions as she indicates in the example of conservatives being hierarchical in the social sphere and individualist in the economic sphere, particularly in relation to ecological discourse.

Lothes thus accentuates the contextual nature of the responses of both sides to climate change. Reframing the divide minimizes the differences to focuses on the centrality of shared core Christian commitments. She puts forward the family as a reorienting metaphor for relationships – spanning from home, to church and to the entire cosmos – that will bring about reconciliation in the Catholic Church in the United States of America.

Lothes's observation that both choirs have departed from the core of Christianity provides a natural entry point for my response. She advances that tending to relationships is a Christian imperative that finds its orientation from the Trinity. I appreciatively engage with those from an African Protestant standpoint.

The largely affluent United States suffers relatively less from climate change effects than its less affluent global 'neighbours' like African and other poorer economies in the world. For Americans to live in relationship it requires consideration of such neighbours. The ecological crisis has made our interrelatedness more apparent. Christians therefore

---

[1] Kuzipa Nalwamba is an ordained minister of the United Church of Zambia, residing in Pretoria, South Africa, and works part-time at the Council for World Mission (CWM) as Project Consultant. She is situated within the Reformed/Evangelical tradition and does research in dogmatics and Christian ethics, with a focus on ecotheology.

are called to go beyond mere pragmatic reasons for caring. We need to retrieve resources from our faith that commit us to care for all creation at a deeper theological level.

Lothes asserts that ecclesial polarization in the Catholic Church in America is not a result of diametrically opposed inability to enter into communion with the centre. It is rather that ideological considerations loom larger in shaping attitudes towards environmental concerns. This suggests that the task is to define what the orienting Christian centre is.

Koinonia understood from an ecological perspective enriches our perception of cosmic relatedness. As a hermeneutical tool it unlocks and undergirds a renewed vision of the universe as a cosmic community. In this interrelated and interconnected universe of which humans are only a part, everything that is relates. It centres relationship and contributes to earth care discourse. Although I have nothing against Lothes's preference for the notion of family, when family is understood strictly in terms of blood relationship it could potentially be cliquish, less open to 'non-family' members and be the basis for discrimination of 'non-family' in the case of 'blended' and adoptive families and by extension on ethnic and nationalistic terms. The idea of *koinonia* is arguably more inclusive and lends itself towards accommodation of other(kind)s.[2]

Koinonia originates from the Greek root *koinon*, denoting what is communal or held in common as opposed to what is private (or individual). It evokes ideas of reciprocity, togetherness and commonality. Though Greek in origin, *koinonia* is biblical in its religious usage. It is rooted in the Jewish experience of covenant, which underpins the understanding of ecclesial relationships and social ethics. In that view, the church is understood as the global human fellowship in relationship with the triune God. *Koinonia* is therefore foundational to the identity and nature of the Church. The *perichoretic* nature of the triune God, which is inherently relational, undergirds the understanding of relationships. From that standpoint, interdependency and interrelatedness are at the core of the church's being and self-understanding as participation of Christians in the Spirit of Christ.[3] Thus, the Trinity is the prototype of Christian community. *Koinonia* is, theologically speaking, the equivalent of the mutuality that exists in the Godhead. This orientates interdependence and belonging in the Christian community and is an amplification of what Lothes asserts as an important reorientation towards the Christian centre.

According to Lothes, then, kindness and fairness to all in ever-widening concentric circles of relationships is the kinship that love of one's neighbour entails. As a theological term, *koinonia* evokes *being* rather than action, even though action is implied. The common life in the church calls for solidarity which issues in common witness and

---

[2] See Kuzipa Nalwamba and Teddy C. Sakupapa, 'Ecology and Fellowship (*Koinonia*): A Fellowship of Life', in *The Church in God's Household: Protestant Perspectives on Ecclesiology and Ecology,* Clive W. Ayre and Ernst M. Conradie (eds) (Pietermaritzburg: Cluster Publications, 2016), 75–93.

[3] See Jean-Marie Tillard, 'Koinonia', in *Dictionary of the Ecumenical Movement*, Nicholas Lossky et al. (eds) (Geneva: WCC, 2002), 646–53.

service to all creation, not just fellow human beings. It has the potential to reform Christian understanding. The inclination towards *being*, primarily denoting relationship, which prioritizes participation in the common life as bearer of the gospel of Christ. It is primarily lived out in relationship with God, fellow humans and the rest of creation. The ministry of reconciliation is futile if it does not arise from and take into consideration the full range of relationships.

If relationships matter, then the common good is what determines where the church directs its service. A global emergency like climate change should signal the direction of service to address the common ill that threatens all of life. When it is cast in relational terms, it is more than an overstated 'crisis' story intended to scare. The common life is under threat and the whole people of God is summoned to service. The values of sharing and participation define what church is (ecclesiology) and what the church does (ethics).

The church as God's alternative community must therefore respond to the ethical challenge of ecological destruction from its standpoint as a *koinonia* working towards the common good and a theological orientation where, as David Bosch notes, 'new relationships take shape, (and) the *Church* automatically becomes a challenge to society'.[4]

Drawing upon cosmology, palaeontology and biological sciences, Catholic theologian Denis Edwards argues that human beings 'are intimately linked to life-forms of our planet and to the atmosphere, the soil, and the oceans. Our existence is encompassed by the mystery of God revealed in all the variety of creatures that surround us. We are part of them and they are part of us.'[5]

The Orthodox idea of the 'liturgy after the liturgy' where the Eucharist is the climax of the church's life is instructive in this regard. Liturgy as 'a celebration of God's presence in the midst of creation'[6] enhances the church's ability to distil its deepest commitments into a meaningful ethos that could become a lived reality and manifest in relationships and values.

The church, though set apart as the 'intangible, interpersonal dynamic of human community and faith in God',[7] is not apart from the ecosystem. Theological reflection and unrelenting experiential liturgical moments have the potential to shape Christian theology and practice, taking earth care into account as a tenet of faith. Theological appropriation of the ecological wisdom embedded in the cultural values of Africa[8] and first-nation people in America are a gift to the global church in this regard.

---

[4] David Bosch, 'The Church as the "Alternative Community"', *Journal of Theology for Southern Africa* 13 (1975), 3–11 (9).

[5] Denis Edwards, *Ecology at the Heart of Faith* (Maryknoll: Orbis, 2006), 26.

[6] See Ernst M. Conradie, *Christianity and Ecological Theology: Resources for Further Research* (Stellenbosch: Sun Press, 2006), 188.

[7] H. Paul Santmire, *The Travail of Nature: The Ambiguous Ecological Promise of Christian Theology* (Minneapolis: Fortress, 1985), 13.

[8] I have explored that in Kuzipa Nalwamba, 'Mupasi as Cosmic s(S)pirit: The Universe as a Community of Life', *HTS Theological Studies* 73:3 (2016), 1–8; also Kuzipa Nalwamba, 'A Cosmic Perspective of Pneumatheology', *Asia Journal of Theology* 32:1 (2018), 60–70.

An African sense of cosmic relatedness

The African stamp on Christianity may find its expression in the interrelatedness of the divine, the ancestors, the living and nature. In the ritual of the lifecycle from an African standpoint, all living beings – including God, spirits and ancestors – share in the ontological life-principle that binds them together. That life force imbues the African universe with potency. Thus, everything is potentially a religious *symbol* that connects human beings to the unseen and points to a transcendent realm. In Christian parlance we could say that in the African universe every object is potentially sacramental, if sacrament refers to external objects that become a medium or realm in which an encounter with God is possible. When we construe the life force in inorganic objects as 'sacramental presence', we secure the argument against any pantheistic connotations. Such a unified vision in African metaphysical conception, which transcends matter–spirit dichotomies, emphasizes the biocentric focus which regards the universe as sacred. It 'is the creative force behind all human and non-human action'.[9] And according to Setiloane it is an 'interpenetrating and permeating'[10] influence that saturates the community of life. Setiloane asserts that in African thought all creation emanates from a single source, therefore:

> [T]he term community is inclusive of all life (*bios*): animals, the habitat (the land), flora, and even the elements. The success of life is found in the ability to maintain a healthy relationship with all.[11]

Setiloane's cosmological asserts this by framing relational inclusivity in terms that confirm that an ecological ethic may emanate from African cosmology.

Koinonia as communion implies more than kinship with God – it is the grounding principle for Christian unity that entails the Church's participation in God's mission. Ecologically responsible ecclesial faith and witness is fellowship-based and communion-inspired. The church in America is part of the problem of ecological destruction. Acknowledging its place in the cosmic communion must take into account both the common ills and the potential common good that could emanate from a dialogue beyond the two choirs to include global voices like the African worldview.

---

[9] Philip J. Nel, 'Morality and Religion in African Thought', *Acta Theologica* 2 (2008), 33–47 (40).

[10] Gabriel Setiloane, 'Towards a Biocentric Theology and Ethic – via Africa', in *Faith, Science and African Culture: African Cosmology and Africa's Contribution to Science*, Cornel W. du Toit (ed.) (Pretoria: Unisa, 1998), 73–84 (80).

[11] Ibid., 79.

Chapter 6.4
Climate change and pastoral theology

Storm Swain[1]

Pastoral theology in North America has been iconically anthropocentric, which has limited the field's ability to view climate change from an eco-systemic perspective. The focus has often been on the suffering person, and suffering in local contexts, rather than on a planetary level. Nevertheless, the field of pastoral theology in North America has evolved through various paradigm shifts towards intercultural[2] and communal-contextual[3] models, which point to both suffering and flourishing in increasingly global ways. However, humanity, whether as individuals, family systems or communities, is often still the primary focus of care.

Traditionally, such care most often reflected theological anthropologies grounded in creation narratives that saw humanity as the pinnacle of creation, and the human person as made in the image of God. Despite Larry Graham's psycho-systemic approach to pastoral praxis in the early 1990s, which acknowledged an 'increasing awareness of the ecological or systemic connection between all living things',[4] his call for an 'ecological partnership' has largely gone unheard. Similarly, Howard Clinebell's call for an 'ecological spirituality' moving from 'ecological alienation' to 'ecological bonding' has also gone mostly unheard.[5] Only recently have pastoral theologians, such as Emmanuel Yartekwei Lartey and Joretta Marshall,[6] included ecological care in their broad view, or delved deeper to address this systemically as Genny Carin Rowley, who argues for a 'A Planetary Pastoral Theology',[7] or Ryan LaMothe have done. The latter argues that such

---

[1] Storm Swain is Associate Professor of Pastoral Care and Theology, and Director of Anglican Studies, at United Lutheran Seminary, Gettysburg and Philadelphia. An Episcopal priest, originally from New Zealand, she teaches and writes primarily on pastoral theology, disaster spiritual care and Anglicanism.
[2] See Emmanuel Y. Lartey, *In Living Color: An Intercultural Approach to Pastoral Care and Counseling*, (New York: Jessica Kinsley, 2003).
[3] See John Patton, *Pastoral Care in Context: An Introduction to Pastoral Care* (Louisville: Westminster John Knox, 2005).
[4] Larry K. Graham, *Care of Persons, Care of Worlds: A Psychosystems Approach to Pastoral Care and Counseling* (Nashville: Abingdon, 1992).
[5] Howard J. Clinebell, *Ecotherapy: Healing Ourselves, Healing the Earth* (New York: Haworth Press, 1996).
[6] Joretta L. Marshall, 'Collaborating Hope: Joining the In-between Spaces', *Journal of Pastoral Theology* 26:2 (2016), 77–90.
[7] Genney C. Rowley, 'Practicing Hope: Congregational Environmentalism as Intersystemic Care' (PhD Dissertation, Brite Divinity, School, 2013), https://repository.tcu.edu/bitstream/handle/116099117/4495/R

a planetary consciousness must change pastoral theology's teaching, research and even organization as a guild.

This essay will argue in favour of thinking about our ecological location in an intersectional way as the next step for a 'ecological' pastoral theology. Drawing on the intersection of three major paradigms in current pastoral theology – postmodernism, postcolonialism and a post-traumatic perspective – the essay shows movement in the field towards a systemic pastoral approach that takes account of the anthropogenic nature of climate change which decentres the human species, while recentring the ecological body that continues to suffer.

Postmodern pastoral care and its relation to climate change

While not discarding an approach informed by Scripture, Christian communities that are engaged in climate change initiatives often draw on a postmodern approach to knowledge that acknowledges a multiplicity of approaches to authoritative truth, the scriptural metanarrative being a guiding but not singular authority. In beginning to pay attention to a postmodern approach, twenty years ago, editors of the *Journal of Pastoral Theology*, Larry Graham and Nancy Ramsey, noted that postmodernism 'includes a rejection of earlier modern confidence in a universal viewpoint, and represents a turn to the other as a recognition that the human community is constituted by radical difference, all knowing is inevitably perspectival, and the negotiation of competing perspectives and rights makes power a primarily relational and intellectual category'.[8]

Such an approach builds a community of concern where the voices of scientists can be heard alongside those of evangelical, conservative and liberal Christians. In such a community the contextual concerns from the margins, such as the disappearing islands of Svalbard in Norway, or Shishmaref in Alaska, where the ice is melting, as Tuvalu and Kiribati in the South Pacific where the sea level is rising, are seen as equally if not more important to the concerns coming from the centres of power and privilege in North America – the offices of Washington and New York, where issues of climate change may be seen through the lens of political expediency and the rising level of neoliberal economic goals. Those seen as speaking from the margins of power are recentred as 'legitimate experts on the experience of suffering',[9] especially as the Church in those

---

owley_tcu_0229D_10413.pdf?sequence=1&isAllowed=y (accessed 31 July 2018).

[8] Larry K. Graham and Nancy Ramsey, 'Editorial', *Journal of Pastoral Theology* 8 (1998), iii–viii (iii).

[9] Pamela Cooper-White, '"I do not Do the Good I Want, but the Evil I Do not Want is what I Do": The Concept of the Vertical Split in Self Psychology in Relation to Christian Concepts of Good and Evil', *Journal of Pastoral Theology* 13:1 (2003), 63–84 (72).

places moves from local engagement with suffering to policy papers on climate change to prevent or ameliorate such.

A postmodern approach which decentralizes a sole locus of authority leads to an approach on climate change in faith communities that is slowly beginning to parallel the urgency in the scientific community. The 2016 statement of the Evangelical Climate Initiative describes that shift well:

> For most of us, until recently this has not been treated as a pressing issue or major priority. Indeed, many of us have required considerable convincing before becoming persuaded that climate change is a real problem and that it ought to matter to us as Christians. But now we have seen and heard enough to offer the following moral argument related to the matter of human-induced climate change.[10]

While claiming a biblically based approach, the Evangelical initiative goes forward to profess four claims:

- CLAIM 1: Human-Induced Climate Change is Real
- CLAIM 2: The Consequences of Climate Change Will Be Significant, and Will Hit the Poor the Hardest
- CLAIM 3: Christian Moral Convictions Demand Our Response to the Climate Change Problem
- CLAIM 4: The need to act now is urgent. Governments, businesses, churches and individuals all have a role to play in addressing climate change starting now.

Such urgency may be seen as coming rather late to the table in some faith communities, but a collective consensus is building. It appears that once a faith community accepts or knows the first three of these claims, it is difficult to 'unknow' them and not be impelled to the fourth claim – that of action. However, getting to those first three claims may take faith communities varying lengths of time. Seven years earlier than the Evangelical Climate Initiative, the 218th Assembly of the Presbyterian Church (USA) not only expressed the urgency of the Evangelical Partnerships fourth claim, but specified what that action may be:

> The Presbyterian Church (U.S.A.) supports comprehensive, mandatory, and aggressive emission reductions that aim to limit the increase in Earth's temperature to 2 degrees Celsius or less from pre-industrial levels. Legislation should focus on the short-term goal of reducing U.S. greenhouse gas emissions 20% from 1990 levels by 2020, and 80% from 1990 levels by 2050.[11]

---

[10] Evangelical Climate Initiative, 'Climate Change'.
[11] Office of the General Assembly PCUSA, *The Power To Change: U.S. Energy Policy and Global Warming* (Advisory Committee on Social Witness Policy, PCUSA, 2008), 3. This built on their 1981 initiative. See http://www.pcusa.org/media/uploads/acswp/pdf/ energyreport.pdf (accessed 22 July 2018).

By 2014, Interfaith Power and Light were able to say, 'Most faith communities have released statements on Climate Change and the need to care for creation.'[12]

Drawing on the work of Elizabeth Kolbert,[13] pastoral theologian Ryan LaMothe captures the urgency well in his charge to the Society of Pastoral Theology in 2015: 'This Changes Everything: The Sixth Extinction and its Implications for Pastoral Theology.'[14] He asks, 'How do we construct a pastoral theology that can address both the global and local issues of suffering associated with climate change, while also considering global and contextually sensitive pastoral interventions?'[15] Two decades earlier pastoral theologian Howard Clinebell argued, 'The human species must now be included on the endangered species list. That is the bottom-line health challenge we all face.'[16] LaMothe seems to be moving from Clinebell's possibility to probability. If LaMothe's urgency and use of the word 'extinction' seems alarmist in 2015, Nathaniel Rich's must-read *New York Times* article on climate change in 2018, makes it feel tame: 'Long term disaster is now the best case scenario.'[17] Here the immediate urgency is seen to be about delaying the inevitable rather than the (lost) opportunity for prevention. Such an urgency, combined with a postmodern critique of dominant metanarratives, leads to a shift in where we must look for other narratives that help us address the realities of climate change, the consequent suffering on the most marginalized, and the reality that we are not only seeking to prevent something in the future but dealing with an experience that has already happened. Such a shift leads us to postcolonial and post-traumatic perspectives in pastoral theology and care.

Postcolonialism and climate change from a pastoral theology perspective

North America lives with two deep and variably un/conscious scars of colonization: (1) the historic enslavement of African persons from another continent – denied their freedom, liberty, and pursuit of happiness, and (2) the slaughter and disavowal of the rights, land, culture and self-determination of the first peoples (at least in the United States). Such un/consciousness leads to a vertical split in the national psyche, where

---

[12] Interfaith Power and Light, 'Religious Statements on Climate Change', https://www.interfaithpowerand light.org/religious-statements-on-climate-change/ (accessed 2 August 2018).
[13] Elizabeth Kolbert, *The Sixth Extinction: An Unnatual History* (New York: Henry Holt, 2014).
[14] Ryan LaMothe, 'This Changes Everything: The Sixth Extinction and Its Implications for Pastoral Theology', *Journal of Pastoral Theology* 26:3 (2016), 178–94.
[15] Ibid., 185.
[16] Clinebell, *Ecotherapy*, 1.
[17] Nathaniel Rich, 'Losing Earth: The Decade We Almost Stopped Climate Change', *New York Times*, 1 August 2018.

America can see itself simultaneously as imbuing the idealistic identity of the American Revolution, the successful underdog in the fight against the colonizing British Empire, *and* as the global empire, 'the most powerful nation on earth' which will not tolerate being told what to do by any other, even a global coalition. Colonial consciousness and settlement, whether as an expansion of empire, hope for new opportunities and freedom from oppression, or simply the establishment of penal colonies on other shores, all begs the question of what or who was there first.

In the expansion of the British Empire in the 1700 and 1800s, one can see the full range of attitudes to first peoples: from Australia, which was seen as an uninhabited 'empty country', *terra nullis* in 1770,[18] where the approximately 500 aboriginal tribes, were not only given no voice, but technically only classified as citizens in 1949,[19] to New Zealand, where the Crown signed the Treaty of Waitangi with most of the Maori tribes in 1840, with a tribunal set up to settle treaty claims in 1975. Despite the debates in countries, such as Canada or New Zealand, as to whether treaties are about 'sovereignty' or 'partnership' between Indigenous persons and colonial government, it is interesting that countries such as New Zealand, that continue to (re)value such treaties as part of their national identity, are those who are leading the way in discussions on the implications of climate change. Concerned for climate-change related displacement and migration of populations in the Pacific, the New Zealand action plan affirms core values that uphold the desire of climate refugees to retain their 'social and cultural identity', the desire to 'continue to live in their own countries where possible' and 'respect and uphold the ... countries' sovereignty and right to self-determination'.[20]

In North America, treaties with the first peoples have a variable history but one that does not appear to have current value in public consciousness. This is well described by G. Peter Jemison in his discussion of the Canandaigua Treaty of 1794 'between the Haudenosaunee (Six Nations Iroquois Confederacy) and the United States of America'.

> Treaties, when and if they are known, remain vaguely understood by many Americans, often regarded as obsolete relics of a distant past. The most vociferous critics of treaties made with Native Americans wish to view them all as invalid because they were made a long time ago. Treaties with Native Americans belong in the past, best forgotten and certainly no longer legitimate after all these years.[21]

---

[18] Aboriginal Heritage Office, 'A Brief Aboriginal History', (N.S.W.) See http://www.aboriginalheritage.org/history/history/ (accessed 2 August 2018).

[19] Nationality and Citizen Act, 1948; with all entitled to vote in 1962 (Commonwealth Electoral Act, 1962), and be counted in the census in 1967 (Australian referendum, 1967).

[20] Office of the Minister of Foreign Affairs, New Zealand Government, 'Pacific Climate Change-related Displacement and Migration: a New Zealand Action Plan', https://www.mfat.govt.nz/assets/Uploads/Redacted-Cabinet-Paper-Pacific-climate-migration-2-May-2018.pdf (accessed 21 August 2018).

[21] G. Peter Jemison and Anna M. Schein (eds), *Treaty of Canandaigua 1794: 200 Years of Treaty Relations Between the Iroquois Confederacy and the United States* (Santa Fe: Clear Light Publishers, 2000).

Jemison goes on to suggest that such treaties should be treated with the same historical honour and current legitimacy as other contemporary documents (signed by or on behalf of Washington) such as the US Constitution, and the Declaration of Independence (1776), not just as matters of law but of recognition. Like the 1752 Halifax Treaty in Canada,[22] this early treaty was signed for 'peace and friendship' between the six nations and the Administration, affirming not only the land, but also the sovereignty of these Native American nations. The over 300 ratified (and largely broken) treaties[23] that followed with other tribes were less to do with honouring sovereignty and self-determination and more to do with land grabs in the face of expanding colonial fervour. Consequently, the ecological consciousness of the first peoples is less a part of the United States mentality, than it would be in countries with a developed bi-cultural relationship between first peoples and those that followed:

> Teach your children what we have taught our children, the earth is our mother. This we know. The earth does not belong to humans, humans belong to the earth. This we know. All things are connected like the blood that unites one family … Whatever befalls the earth befalls the children of the earth. People did not weave the web of life, they are merely a strand of it. Whatever they do to the web, they do to themselves.[24]

One can see, however, from the use of the above statement attributed to (but not actually by) Chief See-ath (Seattle), in the speech of then vice president Al Gore (1993–2001), at the twenty-fifth anniversary of the Clean Water Act in 1997,[25] that when discussing climate change, we have to reach both forward and back to the voices of first peoples to help us find values that affirm a relationality to the planet and her peoples that is representative of dominion and partnership rather than domination, overuse and abuse of the earth's resources. Ironically, it is from Dr. Henry Smith's remembering of Chief Seath's actual words in 1887 that we learn that rather than ecological connectedness it is suffering and death that may bring Indigenous and those with a colonial heritage together:

> A few more moons, a few more winters, and not one of all the mighty hosts that once filled this broad land or that now roam in fragmentary bands through these

---

See https://archive.nytimes.com/www.nytimes.com/books/first/j/jemison-treaty.html?_r=1 (accessed 21 August 2018).

[22] The Canadian Encyclopedia, 'Treaties with Indigenous Peoples in Canada', https://www.thecanadianencyclopedia.ca/en/article/aboriginal-treaties/ (accessed 21 August 2018).

[23] National Museum of the American Indian, 'Nation to Nation: Treaties between the United States and American Indian Nations' (Washington DC: Smithsonian, 2016) See http://nmai.si.edu/nationtonation/ (accessed 21 August 2018).

[24] Al Gore, 'The 25th Anniversary of the Clean Water Act', (18 October 1997), https://clintonwhitehouse3.archives.gov/WH/EOP/OVP/speeches/clean.html (accessed 21 August 2018). This quote was actually written by screenwriter Ted Perry in a film script for *Home*, Southern Baptist Radio and Television Commission, 1972.

[25] Ibid.

vast solitudes will remain to weep over the tombs of a people once as powerful and as hopeful as your own ... Even the white man, whose God walked and talked with him, as friend to friend, is not exempt from the common destiny. We may be brothers after all. We shall see.[26]

In challenging the dominant society to turn from a 'pollution based economy', and 'change what it is doing to Mother Earth and our peoples', and highlighting the risks of the common destiny of climate change today which will affect all peoples, Tom Goldtooth, the Navajo/Lakota executive director of the Indigenous Environmental Movement, notes,

> Populations such as ours that have a close relationship with nature, that still have traditional practices off the land and waterways, are experiencing these real effects, from Alaska to many of our tribal people here in the lower 48 ... Climate change is real. It's not, as some believe, just some conspiracy theory ... When we have a U.S. administration that is a denier of science and the facts, we have a serious problem that violates our treaty rights to fish and hunt and gather ... These aren't just rights that we negotiated in treaties with the United States. These are inherent rights.[27]

The question of 'inherent rights' brings us to listen to the other intersubjective narrative, or oft-silenced voice in the American story, those among us who are African American, whose history of slavery and subjugation in the United States has included not only being stripped of dignity, liberty and a sense of (full) humanity, but also stripped of a relationship to the land and earth as their own. Arguably, although slavery has long been abolished, the legacy of brutality and racism still persists in pernicious ways in the United States today. That the 'Black Lives Matter' movement is necessary, points to this shameful reality. Listening to African (American) pastoral theologians who point to values based on relationship to land and community forged in the African continent, rather than being co-opted into an economic relationship with the land forged by colonial migration and slavery, has been an important contribution to the field of pastoral theology and public theology in general. Where Bonnie Miller-McLemore shifted us from pastoral theology's early focus on Boisen's 'living human document', to the 'living human web',[28] pastoral theologians such as Emmanuel Yartekwei Amugi Lartey and

---

[26] Dr. Henry A. Smith, 'Hail to the Chief: "My Words are Like Stars that Never Set"', *Seattle Sunday Star*, 29 October 1887. See http://www.skagitriverjournal.com/WA/Indians/SealthSpeech-Smith.html (accessed 21 August 2018).

[27] Reported by Cecily Hilleary, 'Native Americans Most at Risk from Impact of Climate Change', *Voice of America*, 19 April 2017, https://www.voanews.com/a/native-americans-most-at-risk-from-impact-of-climate-change/3816564.html (accessed 21 August 2018).

[28] Bonnie Miller-McLemore, 'The Living Human Web: Pastoral Theology at the Turn of the Century', in *Through the Eyes of Women: Insights for Pastoral Care*, Jeanne Stevenson Moessner (ed.) (Minneapolis: Fortress, 1996), 9–26.

M. Fulgence Nyengele help us to see how a postcolonial communal contextuality goes beyond human justice and relationality. Lartey argues that 'Postcolonizing approaches re-adopt this African sense and engage the spiritual essence of persons, recognizing that this essence has divine as well as psychological, social, and *ecological* dimensions to its complexity.'[29]

Drawing on this postcolonizing approach that not only builds community across diverse perspectives but seeks to transform culture, Lartey and other pastoral theologians from Africa affirm the African value of *ubuntu* to counter North American individualism, building a global rather than local consciousness that not only affirms the cultural heritage of African Americans within North America but seeks to transform the consciousness of *all* involved in engaging complex concerns in pastoral theology. M. Fulgence Nyengele notes,

> *Ubuntu* is an embodiment of a communal worldview in which we are all interdependent and interconnected. As such it is an antidote to extreme individualism that isolates and diminishes people's vitality and flourishing, causing them to live in oppressive loneliness. Stressing the importance of mutual commitment, belonging, and participating in the communal life, *ubuntu* as a worldview advocates for a profound sense of group solidarity and emphasizes the fact that our true human potentials can only be realized in partnership with others.[30]

Through an affirmation of the communality that *ubuntu* embodies, we can begin (or continue) to listen beyond economic interests to humanitarian and ecological sensibilities, not just within our own national identities, but again, through a decentring and recentring around a common goal, a global partnership, such as was manifest in the Paris Accord.

The Paris Climate Agreement was not just significant in terms of climate change, but also signified a 'paradigm shift' in global relationships. While not explicitly using postcolonial language, such a partnership, which functioned as a voluntary mutual compact, exemplifies Nyengele's description of *ubuntu*. Such a relationality is perhaps more true for climate change action than almost anything else, an *interdependent* approach which needs 'a profound sense of group solidarity and emphasizes the fact that our true human potentials can only be realized in partnership with others'.[31] Here, 'I am because we are' (*ubuntu*) not only explicates a human relationality, but also an ecological relationality that we deny at our peril.

---

[29] Emmanuel Y. Lartey, *Postcolonializing God: New Perspectives on Pastoral and Practical Theology*, (London: SCM Press, 2013), 120, italics mine.

[30] M. Fulgence Nyengele, 'Cultivating Ubuntu: An African Postcolonial Pastoral Theological Engagement with Positive Psychology', *Journal of Pastoral Theology* 24:2 (2014), 4–19.

[31] Ibid.

Post-traumatic pastoral theology

'As 2017 gets going we find ourselves in the midst of intercultural, political, and ecological trauma,' write Emmanuel Lartey and Melinda McGarrah Sharp, editors of the *Journal of Pastoral Theology*.[32] In designating the state of the planet as being in 'trauma', they are recognizing that the field needs to see this in the context of its overall approach to trauma, and expand our thinking to include planetary or ecological trauma. Again, it also highlights that we are not simply focused on mitigation, preventing a planetary crisis, but we are focusing on something that has already happened. These pastoral theologians are aligning themselves with climate change scientists who are not simply saying, as did James Hansen, in 1988, 'it is happening', but 'it *has* happened'. This speaks to an important issue in trauma theory about the differences between an acute trauma, and 'drip' or 'strain trauma', which, like sexual abuse, may continue over years, and even decades, without one particular event being that which overwhelms the ability of the entity to cope. This ecological trauma has both happened, and continues to happen, both globally and locally. Rather than feeling hopeless, helpless or horrified, a post-traumatic approach calls us to recognize and respond to a traumatic reality, with agency and empathy towards those most affected. The editors of the journal move us beyond an anthropocentric understanding of suffering to include the suffering Earth.

Likewise, in his essay, 'Elegy for a Lost World', ecotheologian Mark Wallace, counters the neoliberal economic worldview where 'Earth is no longer a "living being" or "feeling organism" who can undergo traumatic suffering.' Instead of treating Earth as 'a "resource," a commodity to be bought and sold in the financial marketplace', he posits that 'Earth suffers' at the hands of human oppressors, who do harm to the vital organisms and processes that make our common planetary system of life both generative and sustainable. Such suffering is near 'ecocidal'.[33] While the idea of Earth suffering may strike religious people as odd, Wallace argues that 'Religiously speaking, the model of Earth as an inherently valuable living organism with the capacity to feel and suffer is a green thread that ties together the Biblical texts in the Jewish and Christian traditions.'[34]

Here, as did the *Journal of Pastoral Theology* editors, Wallace is urging us to reclaim a tradition we may have lost in a modernist worldview, but that can impel us to see the traumatic realities of not just human but ecological suffering. Along with the usual associations of climate change to temperature, sea-level carbon-dioxide emissions levels, increasing severity and frequency of climate-related extreme weather events, Wallace alerts us to the impact on ecosystems, which is akin to a 'biocidal runaway train, with

---

[32] Emmanuel Y. Lartey and Melinda A. McGarrah Sharp, 'Seeking Steadiness in Storms: Pastoral Theology in the Midst of Intercultural, Political and Ecological Trauma', *Journal of Pastoral Theology* 26:3 (2016), 149–51.

[33] Mark Wallace, 'Elegy for a Lost World', in *Post-Traumatic Public Theology*, Stephanie N. Arel and Shelly Rambo (eds) (Cham: Palgrave McMillan, 2016), 135–54 (138).

[34] Ibid., 138–9.

biologists conservatively estimating that 30,000 plant and animal species are now being driven to extinction every year'.³⁵ In seeing the Earth as suffering or traumatized, we not only focus on the threat to life or self of the ecological body, but the disruptions of the ability to adapt, and the rupture of the sense of time, which is characteristic of trauma.

Such disruption of time can be seen in the revisions of caps on carbon dioxide emission from 450 to 350 ppm, and the exponentially increasing effects of emissions on the planet. Although 2013 was the year that the 400 ppm point was reached, 2016 signalled the movement into a '400 ppm world', where even the lowest monthly readings no longer dropped below that level. Known for its alarmist headlines, perhaps the *New York Post* captured this traumatic reality accurately, 'This Is The Worst News For Life On Earth.'³⁶ A little over six months after this realization of this annual threshold mark, a scant four years after the 400 ppm threshold was breached, the *Scientific American* declared, 'We Just Breached the 410 PPM Threshold for CO_2: Carbon dioxide has not reached this height in millions of years.'³⁷

Although a distinction is made in pastoral theology between a disaster and its potentially traumatizing effect, dependent upon the experience of the person, whether they are overwhelmed or able to adapt in response to the disaster, like many marginalized persons whose voices are silenced, the Earth cannot speak for itself. Yet these emissions readings, the extinction of species, acidification of the world's coral reefs, the incrementally rising sea levels and consequent displaced populations, droughts that affect the national, if not global, food infrastructure, wildfires and seeming trend towards more intense hurricanes with higher and more devastating rainfall rates can be seen as symptoms of the trauma to the earth that can speak for itself.

In the face of such trauma, rather than continuing to avoid distressing reminders, dissociating and disavowing the reality of climate change, we need to work through to a place of agency where we can recognize and respond to the suffering of our planet and its peoples affected by climate change, and, if it is still possible, recover not only life-giving practices, but the life of our planet, itself. From a perspective of pastoral theology, this includes not only our attention to the created world, but to God.

Response to climate change through the eyes of pastoral theology

In pastoral methodology, attention to climate change is not disconnected from our thinking about God as continuing to be involved in creation. Graham, in writing on

---

[35] Ibid., 137.

[36] Lauren Tousignant, 'This Is the Worst News for Life On Earth', *The New York Post*, 29 September 2016.

[37] Brian Kahn, Climate Central, *The Scientific American*, 21 April 2017, https://www.scientificamerican.com/article/we-just-breached-the-410-ppm-threshold-for-co2/ (accessed 25 August 2018).

catastrophic disaster, opines that 'God suffers loss, when the world suffers catastrophe, and laments human and ecological destructiveness.'[38] For Graham, in the face of climate change and other catastrophic disaster, 'the power of life to reclaim life from catastrophic disasters is the compassion and vitalizing power of God made palpable in lamentation, interrogation, and reclamation.'[39] The way forward is to recognize and lament the incessant traumatic drip of the destruction of our ecosystem, using our anger and aggression to rigorously interrogate the causes and our own actions in this destructiveness, and, turning that anger and despair into hope and corporate action, to reclaim practices of goodness for our planet and ourselves.

Drawing on a Trinitarian model of God as 'Earth-maker, Pain-bearer, Life-giver', we are called to these three movements in our care of others, which includes our care of the Earth.[40] Rather than beginning with lament, we begin from a position of responsibility and resilience, creating space for our Earth and its creatures to flourish, and it is from that space that we can attend to our suffering planet. Here economics and earth care are interrelated, as we begin with practices of care rather than see them as a last resort. Following on from this place, we are called to attend to the suffering of both the individual and ecological body, limiting and stopping practices, such as the production and over-reliance on fossil fuels which increase our emissions levels, and caring for those displaced by climate change and weather-related disasters. From earth-making and pain-bearing processes, we may then discover that which is life-giving for our planet and its inhabitants, in a living ecological web.

For LaMothe, this means as pastoral theologians in a globally interconnected way, we must not just focus on 'care of persons, families, communities, and societies, all of which are dependent on the care of the Earth',[41] but that 'Global and local realties of climate change demand that we alter our stance and become public-political theologians and, as a guild act, politically.'[42] Thinking systemically, LaMothe suggests proactively that this is a pastoral task, as we in the field of pastoral theology need to not just attend to pastoral praxis in the here and now, but prepare the next generation of pastoral theologians that will have to deal with the unfolding realities of climate change as scholar–activists in a way that current generations may think they have the luxury of avoiding.

---

[38] Larry K. Graham, 'Pastoral Theology and Catastrophic Disaster', *Journal of Pastoral Theology* 16:2 (2006), 1–17 (12).

[39] Ibid., 14–15.

[40] Storm K. Swain, *Trauma and Transformation at Ground Zero: A Pastoral Theology* (Minneapolis: Fortress, 2011), 41.

[41] LaMothe, 'This Changes Everything', 189.

[42] Ibid., 191.

Final words

In drawing not only on post-traumatic theology but also on postmodern and postcolonial perspectives, a pastoral theology responds to climate trauma by looking to the margins for life-giving signs of hope. Hope may come from energy producers as well as activists, from scientists and statesnot and statesmen, from congregational earth-care teams and coalitions. In May 2018, in Massachusetts, such a group coalesced with over 500 lead scientists and religious leaders coming together to sign a 'Faith and Science Joint Appeal for Climate Action.' This document reframes 'climate change' as an urgent 'climate crisis':

> Climate change is an ecological and moral emergency that impacts all other aspects of our shared lives and requires us to work together to protect our common home … All of us … must do our utmost to reduce greenhouse gas emissions and to protect our communities from the catastrophic impacts of climate change. We especially call upon our political representatives to address the climate crisis with the boldness and urgency it requires, with substantive and immediate action … We now have an opportunity and an obligation to be leaders in protecting our common home. We are called to be a beacon to the nation and the world. There is still time to take action and that time is now.[43]

Public witness in word and deed needs to flow not simply from the centres of powers, but from an eco-ethic of care, that pastorally connects care of person, to care of planet, embodied by 'the living human document in a living ecological web', exemplified by the aforementioned intersection of those in pastoral practice coming together in solidarity with the scientific community. Such a solidarity recognizes the 'climate crisis' and acts with a trauma-informed approach to the Earth, which may not halt the global crisis but may build both psychological and ecological systems of responsibility and resilience which enable us to act from a place of informed solidarity rather than idealistic denial. This is a resurrection reality which does not deny the woundedness of our planet but seeks a way forward into what can only be a 'new normal'.

---

[43] See https://www.episcopalnewsservice.org/wp-content/uploads/2018/05/Faith-and-Science-Joint-Appeal-for-Climate-Action.pdf (accessed 25 August 2018).

A response to Storm Swain from the Philippines

Elizabeth Tapia[1]

My name is Elizabeth Tapia, born and raised in the Philippines, a country vulnerable to climate change. I belong to the native groups called Taga-Ilog, or Tagalog, which means 'people of the river'. I am a fisherman's daughter, pastor, missionary and a practical theologian. My field of study is missiology and constructive theology but I am also interested to learn how pastoral theology relates to climate change.

In her essay 'Climate Change and Pastoral Theology', Storm Swain argues that pastoral theology in North America needs to view climate change in an intersectional way, so as to be able to draw wisdom from postmodern, postcolonial and post-traumatic perspectives and move beyond its current anthropocentric view. Why so?

Swain observes that 'pastoral theology in North America has been iconically anthropocentric' in which the focus of discussion and care are centred on the suffering of humans, not on the suffering Earth. The scope of North Atlantic pastoral theology further is local rather than planetary. According to her, anthropomorphic readings of creation stories in the Bible have led to a 'decentring' of 'an ecological relationship of which humanity is only a part'.

Despite the call of several pastoral theologians for a creation-centred perspective, she laments that a human-centred ecological perspective still persists in North America. She wants to engage pastoral theologians in an 'ecosystemic perspective' by showing how practical theology could use the triple paradigms of postmodern, postcolonial and post-traumatic thought in relation to climate change. She describes these approaches under the subtitles 'Postmodern Pastoral Care and Its Relation to Climate Change', 'Postcolonialism and Climate Change from a Pastoral Theology Perspective', and lastly, 'Posttraumatic Pastoral Theology'.

Swain concludes that pastoral theology done in an intersectional way – drawing on postcolonial, postmodern and post-traumatic perspectives – also needs the perspective of those from the margins who can provide 'life-giving signs of hope' amidst climate catastrophe.

---

[1] Elizabeth S. Tapia is a missionary pastor and teacher in the United Methodist Church, Philippines. She serves as Resident Theologian and Curriculum Consultant in Baguio Episcopal Area, Northern Philippines. Based in the mountain city of Baguio, she participates in grass roots seminars on missiology, gender justice and climate change.

Storm Swain's essay gave me an important update on pastoral theology in North America from the perspectives of North American, African and New Zealand pastoral theologians. Working in the mountain town Baguio City, I have no access to books on this subject, a lack that is compounded by intermittent power failures due to recent typhoons.

Swain's essay raises two issues that are interrelated: First it helps me to understand better how pastoral theology takes on the global issue of climate change. Second, I wonder how pastoral theology practitioners can meaningfully engage in solidarity with Indigenous peoples in North America, and people from the Global South who are most affected by climate change? Let me briefly share our context.

I believe that Indigenous peoples can teach us a great deal about caring for life and embracing Mother Earth. Pastoral theologians (including lay and church leaders) can learn greatly from Indigenous communities and the marginalized communities in the Global South and can working together for the healing of the creation.

I fully agree with Swain when she reiterates the importance of listening to the voices of Indigenous and marginalized peoples. She rightfully recognizes their moral agency. In Baguio City, both the United Methodist Church and Roman Catholic Church (Maryknoll Ecological Center) have conducted seminars on 'Climate Change & Environmental Action Plan' with Indigenous folks and poor urban dwellers. The Roman Catholic sponsored seminar was attended by over 300 persons from 108 different organizations, while the United Methodist seminar was attended mostly by fifty youth from churches and universities. Participants were asked to reflect on the United Methodist Church's 'Social Principles on The Natural World' and Pope Francis's Encyclical *Laudato Si'*. In a country visited by twenty typhoons each year, we lament and condemn the unabated deforestation, mining, displacement of communities and animals.

I value the way Swain connects a postmodern approach of multiple voices to the 'urgency in the scientific community', even though her essay does not elaborate much on these urgent voices coming from the scientific community.

The section on the postmodern and post-traumatic paradigm reminds me of the theme 'Rise Up for Abundant Life' at a conference in response to typhoon Yolanda/Hayan, organized by the National Council of Churches in the Philippines (9 November 2016) in Tacloban, the 'ground zero' of the typhoon. This conference, which was attended by representatives from churches, people's organizations, survivors, disaster risk managers and others, reiterated that 'global warming primarily affects the poor and vulnerable in countries like the Philippines … and that the wealthy's greed for resources and rapacious consumption have overwhelmingly contributed to climate change.'[2] This is not shaming, this is naming the reality.

Drawing on her model of God as 'Earth-maker, Pain-bearer, Life-giver', Swain powerfully reiterates that because as human beings we are made in God's image, we are called to (a) 'begin from a position of responsibility and resilience' as we 'create space

---

[2] See www.nccphilippines.org/2016/11/09/rise-up-for-abundant-life/ (accessed 2 November 2018).

for our Earth and its creatures to flourish'; (b) attend to the suffering of ecological body; and (c) care for those displaced by climate change and weather-related disasters'. I agree and would want us to ask how these callings might be reflected in our daily life, worship, social justice campaigns and missional priorities.

Quoting Ryan LaMothe, Swain suggests that this means pastoral theologians must not only focus on care of persons or communities, but also on care of the Earth. This implies that we must become 'public-political theologians and, as a guild, act politically'.

I wish to offer a few points for further reflection:

- What will it take to generate a new generation of 'scholar-activists?', or 'public-political theologians' in North America. Is this happening now?
- What preventative action and healing rituals can we use in a post-traumatic pastoral theology in relation to climate change?
- What measures can we take to halt the extinction of species?
- Wherein lies our hope? Part of the ecological trauma is that the United States administration withdrew from the Paris Agreement on climate change. Nevertheless, Swain is hopeful that because thirty-eight states in the United States will forge ahead by 'working to lower emissions', there is hope. The practical question is: Will people in North America be willing to, as the saying goes, 'live simply so others may simply live?' Swain describes Aotearoa/New Zealand's 'action plan' in response to the plight of Pacific Islanders who are facing rising sea level, displacement and forced migration. May other nations follow! The world needs to be more aware of the who, why and where to of climate change refugees.
- How we can learn from the Ubuntu principle described in Swain's essay? Can this be a beginning of our ecological praxis? How can Ubuntu be appropriated by an individualistic and consumerist society? How do we advance what Swain calls 'ecological relationality' in a digital and throw-away society?

Whereas Swain's essay is primarily written for academics and professional, pastoral theologians, my hope is that concrete proposals will follow as to how pastoral theologians can be effective 'scholar-activists' in relation to climate change advocacy work.

Reflecting further on Swain's 'intersectional' process, the following questions come to my mind:

- How does the academy support collaborative research between scientists and agriculturists, between social ethicists and botanists, between environmental planners and policy makers in addressing climate change?
- Is practical theological research being done on issues of 'power and authority', 'dominion or domination' as applied to land use, the role of transnational corporations, environmental racism, militarization of seas, skies and forests? Is attention being paid to climate change migrants? And, finally, is scholarly

attention given to developing an ecological path based on Indigenous people's spirituality and self-determination?

Swain's essay contributes greatly to ongoing academic pastoral theological research into climate change studies. By moving from an anthropocentric view of life and suffering to a 'planetary view' as she suggests, pastoral theology's approach to climate change must take into account postcolonial, postmodern and post-traumatic, and Indigenous perspectives.

I believe that Indigenous peoples all over the world can teach us a great deal about caring for life, embracing the Earth. As an Indigenous song has it, 'The Earth is our Mother, let us take care of her.'

Finally, I dedicate this space to honour all living creatures, and to all who believe that the earth is the Lord's, and all that is in it, the world and those who live in it (Psalm 24.1, NRSV).

Chapter 6.5
Climate change, ecclesial praxis and social teaching

Seán McDonagh, SSC[1]

Climate change poses a grave threat to humans, to other creatures and to the natural environment. It will affect the lives of all people around the world, especially the poorest and most vulnerable.

At the COP 23 Climate Conference in Bonn, Germany, in November 2017, environmental and development groups made it clear that partnerships around the world must be developed as quickly as possible in the global effort to achieve a smooth transition to low carbon.

Since the Paris Agreement on Climate Change which was signed at COP 21 in December 2015, climate change is seen as one of the most important ethical issues of the twenty-first century. As of November 2017, 195 countries have signed the agreement and many people are aware of the efforts of the United Nations Framework Convention on Climate Change (UNFCCC) to address climate change through global treaties. They are also aware of the work done by scientists, especially those on climate change for the Intergovernmental Panel on Climate Change (IPCC) which is published every few years.

Much of our understanding of climate change comes from the media and environmental and developmental organizations such as Friends of the Earth, Greenpeace, An Taisce (the Natural Trust), Trocaire in Ireland and CAFOD in England and Wales. They have done a remarkable job in educating people about climate change in recent years.

The World Council of Churches

But even church-going Christians might not be aware of what the churches have been doing during the past forty years. It is clear that the World Council of Churches

---

[1] Seán McDonagh is a Columbian missionary priest. He worked in the Philippines from 1969 to 1992 where he witnessed the devastation of tropical deforestation. He was involved in helping to draft the Philippines' Catholic Bishops pastoral letter on the environment in 1988. He is now Researcher for JPIC Priorities for the Columbian missionaries.

(WCC) has given the most courageous leadership on a wide range of ecological issues, especially climate change.[2] As far back as 1988, the WCC sponsored a consultation on global warming in Geneva. This was attended by church members, environmental groups, scientists, politicians and theologians.

WCC observers took part in the meetings which led to the adoption of the UN treaty on Climate Change which was ratified at the Earth Summit in Rio de Janeiro in 1992. In the wake of the Rio Summit, the WCC observers prepared an assessment of the UN Treaty and made a number of recommendations. Firstly, it felt that it was important to deepen theological and ethical reflections on climate change. Secondly, it highlighted the importance of informing people that responding to climate change would involve profound changes in all spheres of life. Thirdly, it pointed out that the ecological, economic and political aspects of climate change ought to be assessed from a justice perspective, especially in the light of the growing gap between the minority rich world and the majority poor world.[3] Finally, the WCC believed that it was crucial to make resources available to individual churches so that these can be used to develop educational, advocacy and lifestyle programmes to stabilize the global climate.

The publication of *Sign of Peril, Test of Faith* in 1994 addressed these issues.[4] After first evaluating the scientific evidence for global warming and sketching the future consequences of climate change, this document develops a theological and ethical framework to help Christians understand the implications of climate change for their faith. These reflections are understood as flowing from the basic tenets of the Christian faith. This includes God's love and concern for creation and for the poor of the earth. Reflecting on God's care for and sovereignty over creation, Christians are reminded that our behaviour is not merely confined to actions which affect other human beings; to harm other species and destroy creation is also a sin.

Sign of Peril, Test of Faith further looks at what a positive response to climate change might mean for the various sectors of society. It spells out what might be involved for industry, and especially transnational corporations, as they trade in goods and

---

[2] See also the essay by Wesley Granberg-Michaelson in this volume.

[3] There is a real problem here with the language used by different groups to describe rich and poor countries. The official UN documents use the term developed nations to refer to countries which are financially well off and developing nations to those who are not well off financially. I find these terms quite problematic and unhelpful. In terms of global warming it is the so-called developed nations which are emitting so much carbon dioxide that they are causing major climate change across the globe. We would need six planets like the earth if everyone on earth had the same standard of living as citizens of the United States or Europe. The meaning inherent in developing nations is that these should move in the direction of developed nations and further add to our climate woes. In NGO meetings one hears the terms North and South, but again these are problematic as Australia and New Zealand is in the North (financially) but in the South geographically. I tend to use the terms majority and minority world. These are basically demographic terms. The majority world refers to most of the people living in Asia, Africa and Latin America. Numerically, they are in a majority in terms of the world's population. Minority refers to people living in Europe, North America, Australia, Japan and New Zealand. It could also include affluent minorities in relatively poor countries.

[4] *Sign of Peril, Test of Faith* (Geneva: World Council of Churches, 1994).

services around the world. The document is adamant that any comprehensive response to global warming will involve profound changes at a social, political and economic level, especially in the minority world. The document is remarkably ahead of its time by discussing which countries might reduce their output of greenhouse gases through developing a realistic timetable which would involve incentives to change and penalties for not changing. It recognizes that the responses from the affluent world will need to be different from and make provisions for poor nations and communities. Governments and industry must pursue policies which promote energy efficiency and accelerate the shift from burning fossil fuel to energy use derived from renewable sources – wind, wave, tidal, solar, micro-hydro and biomass.

Sign of Peril, Test of Faith also raises the crucial question of economic growth. Can the targets for greenhouse gas emissions be met within the present global sociopolitical system where economic growth is extolled as the panacea for all problems, especially overcoming poverty in the majority world? The document challenges the validity of this growth model by pointing out that unlimited economic growth is manifestly impossible in a finite world. It challenges people in the minority rich world to live more simply, so that energy will be available for the poor who need it badly just to improve their basic standard of living. Reducing the threat of global warming will require a new vision of what constitutes the 'good life'. The 'good life' today is understood as having wealth, ownership of property and a huge carbon footprint. Transforming this vision will not be easy, but it will open up the possibility for an abundance for all life, both human and more-than-human.

The final chapters of this visionary document examine the potential role of the churches in addressing the crisis of human-induced climate change. In line with the churches' prophetic vocation which is to denounce evil and empower Christians to seek the path of reconciliation and harmony, the report insists that churches must actively campaign on climate change and cooperate with independent environmental organisations such as Friends of the Earth.

In March 1996, the then president of the Pontifical Council for Justice and Peace, Cardinal Roger Etchegaray, wrote to the presidents of the Episcopal Conferences of industrial countries and acknowledged that the World Council of Churches has taken a leading role in drawing the attention of its member churches to the relationship between climate change and human activity, particularly the burning of fossil fuels. He encouraged local churches to examine ways in which they could cooperate with any WCC-inspired initiative in their country. Unfortunately, very few in the Catholic Church took up this challenge.

In 2002, the WCC followed up with another excellent document on climate change entitled *Solidarity with Victims of Climate Change*. This document pointed out that the extreme weather conditions caused by climate change are enormously costly. Insurance companies claim that very soon the cost of these events will reach $300 billion annually. Once again, poor countries will be most vulnerable. But even in the United States costs are mounting. According to the U.S. National Oceanic and Atmospheric Administration

(NOAA), in 2017 the United States experienced a record year of losses from fires, hurricanes and other weather-related disasters amounted to $306 billion, $90 billion more than the previous record which was set in 2005.[5]

Solidarity with Victims of Climate Change recognized that the Kyoto Protocol was only the beginning of a response. At that time scientists associated with the Intergovernmental Panel on Climate Change (IPCC) called for a reduction of between 60 per cent and 80 per cent of greenhouse gas emissions by the year 2050. This reduction would be needed to stabilize the global weather system. The countries involved in the Kyoto Protocol were only committing themselves to reduce their greenhouse gas emissions by 5.2 per cent. The document does point out that, with the vast array of technologies and policy measures on energy supply and demand, the targets are achievable, if there is strong political leadership.[6] The document further discusses the World Trade Organisation (WTO) Conference in Doha which was held in November 2001. The authors make the point that it is almost impossible to insert binding ecological criteria into the WTO. The system is basically incapable of integrating the environmental dimension into trade negotiations. The market mechanisms being proposed by the WTO seem fine, but they don't take account of the scale and limits of trade in relationship with the wider global environment.

One of the driving forces behind the WCC's engagement with climate change was the theologian Lukas Vischer (1926–2008). He joined the staff of the WCC as a young theologian in 1961. He participated in the 1961 New Delhi Assembly of the WCC with staff responsibility for the statement on church unity, and he was sent as an observer to the Second Vatican Council. He developed a deep understanding of the new dynamics in the ecumenical movement, both at the professional level of theology and in terms of personal friendship with people from other churches. He was the person who guided the two WCC documents which I discussed above through the WCC.

The Catholic Church and climate change

The Vatican had been slow to embrace climate change. Scientists have known about the deleterious effects of global warming for decades. In my book, *To Care for the Earth,* written in the early 1980s,[7] I quoted *The Global 2000 Report to the President,* commissioned by US president Jimmy Carter in the late 1970s. It discussed the greenhouse effect and predicted that the warming of the Earth's atmosphere would lead to extreme weather patterns and a rise in the level of the oceans, causing flooding in

---

[5] Matt McGrath, 'Most Expensive Year on Record for US Natural Disasters', http://www.bbc.com/news/science-environment-42608161 (accessed 8 January 2018).

[6] World Council of Churches, *Solidarity with Victims of Climate Change* (Geneva: WCC, 2002), 11.

[7] Seán McDonagh, *To Care for the Earth: A Call to a New Theology* (London: Chapman, 1986).

many of the world's most densely populated areas. The report identified the emissions of carbon dioxide mainly from industrial societies as the main cause of climate change. At that time religious leaders should have drawn attention to the precautionary principle which stresses that, even if the science is not certain, the ethical thing to do where serious destruction could happen is to err on the side of caution.

In 2002, Sister Marjorie Keenan wrote a book drawing together the papal teachings on the environment. Her book was published by the Pontifical Council for Justice and Peace and is entitled *Care for Creation: Human Activity and the Environment*. The book is a very slim volume because the papal magisterium had published very little on the destruction of creation.[8]

The *Compendium of the Social Doctrine of the Church,* published in 2004, has one very slim chapter (chapter 10) on the safeguarding the environment.[9] It runs for a mere fifteen pages. In contrast, the chapter on human work (chapter 6) has twenty-seven pages. Only one paragraph in the whole book is devoted to climate change. Paragraph 470 states that:

> every economic activity making use of natural resources must also be concerned with safeguarding the environment and should foresee the costs involved, which are an essential part of the actual cost of economic activity. In this context, one considers relations between human activity and climate change which, given their extreme complexity, must be opportunely and constantly monitored at the scientific, political and juridical, national and international level. The climate is a good that must be protected.

This paragraph fails to capture either the magnitude of climate change or the urgency with which it must be faced. In 2004, there was a growing consensus among climate scientists that we had, at the most, twenty years to take decisive, mitigating action, otherwise we will have reached an irreversible 'tipping point'.

One of the most extraordinary talks on environmental degradation was delivered by Pope John Paul II and took place on 17 January 2001. It was not included in the *Compendium of the Social Doctrine of the Church*. At that General Audience the pope said that when we scan the regions of our planet, we immediately see that humanity has disappointed God's expectations. Man, especially in our time, has without hesitation devastated wooded plains and valley, polluted waters, disfigured the earth's habitat, and made the air unbreathable, disturbed the hydrogeological and atmospherics spheres and turned luxuriant areas into deserts and undertaken forms of unrestrained industrialization, humiliating the flower-garden of the universe, to use the image of Dante Alighieri (Paradiso XXII, 151). We must therefore encourage and support the 'ecological conversion' that in recent decades has made humanity more sensitive to the

---

[8] Sister Marjorie Keenan, RSHM, *Care for Creation, Human Activity and the Environment* (Vaticana: Libreria Editrice, 2000).
[9] *The Compendium of the Social Doctrine of the Church* (Vatican: Veritas, 2004).

catastrophe to which it has been heading. Man is no longer the Creator's steward, but an autonomous despot, who is finally beginning to understand that he must stop at the edge of the abyss.[10]

One of the first references to global warming in the papal teaching by Pope John Paul II papal teaching is found in *Peace with God the Creator: Peace with all Creation*, published in 1990. The document states that 'the gradual depletion of the ozone layer and the related "greenhouse" gas effect have now reached crisis proportions as a consequence of industrial growth, massive urban concentration and vastly increased energy needs.'[11]

Even as the warning from scientists became more alarming, the Vatican and most Episcopal Conferences have had very little to say about the various reports from the Intergovernmental Panel on Climate Change (IPCC) which were published during the 1990s and 2000s. There has been a richness within Catholic Society Teaching (CST), however, which can form the ethical basis for dealing with climate change. I developed some of these in my book, *Climate Change: The Challenge to All of Us*.[12] They include viewing climate change in the context of the protection of the common good, which now must include, protecting habitats, ecosystems and the entire biosphere. The preferential option for the poor is hugely important because those who were least responsible for causing climate change, such as the people in Bangladesh, are destined to suffer most. Equitable ways must be found to compensate and accommodate them. Climate change points to the ethical issues involved in intergenerational justice. The irresponsible use of fossil fuel by two or three generations can have irreversible consequences for all future generations. Concern for the wider earth community also enters into this new moral context. Scientists estimate that climate change will push one million species over the precipice of extinction.

But despite reports from the Intergovernmental Panel on Climate Change (IPCC), the Vatican has been almost silent on climate change. In May 2007, the Pontifical Council for Justice and Peace organized a two-day seminar on climate change. While there were excellent presentations from credible scientists, whose writings have been peer reviewed, the organizers also gave a platform to at least four participants who were in denial about climate change or believe it is a good thing. One of these was Craig Idso, adjunct professor at the Office of Climatology at Arizona State University. He is the chairman of the Center for the Study of Carbon Dioxide and Global Change. The stated purpose of this institute was to separate reality from rhetoric in the emotionally charged on carbon dioxide and global change. Together with his father, Sherwood, and his brother, Keith, he co-authored a report entitled 'Enhanced or Impaired? Human Health in a CO_2-Enriched World'. The report argues that global warming and an increase in atmospheric CO_2 would benefit humanity.

---

[10] Pope John Paul II, 'God Made Man the Steward of Creation', *L'Observatore Romano* 24 (January 2001), 11
[11] Pope John Paul II, *Peace with God the Creator, Peace with All Creation* (Vatican City: Libreria Editrice Vatican, 1990).
[12] Seán McDonagh, *Climate Change: The Challenge to All of Us* (Dublin: Columba, 2006).

Bishops' conferences and climate change

The Australian Catholic bishops' conference addressed this issue of climate change at a conference in Canberra in November 2005. Bishop Christopher Toohey, the then chair of Catholic Earthcare Australia, spoke about the responsibility to sustain God's creation. He said that rapid climate change as a result of human activity is now recognized by the global scientific community as a reality. He made the point that the well-being of the human community and the well-being of the earth are intertwined.[13]

In September 2006, the German Bishops' Commission for Society and Social Action published a document entitled *Climate Change: A Focal Point for Global Intergenerational and Ecological Justice*.[14] The bishops saw that coming generations will be victims of our present-day action. It is one of the first documents to discuss how climate change affects other creatures. Climate change fundamentally changes the living conditions of non-human nature. Habitats and environments for plant and animal species are disappearing, which in turn reduces biological diversity on earth. Hence, climate change is also a problem for justice for creation.[15]

In 2009 the Irish bishops also published a pastoral reflection on climate change entitled *The Cry of the Earth*. The bishops stated that 'every action taken in favour of a just and more sustainable environment, no matter how small, has an intrinsic value. Action at a global level as well as every individual action that contributes to integral human development and global solidarity, helps to construct a more sustainable environment and, therefore, a better world.'[16]

Laudato Si'

Climate change has been a central concern of Pope Francis's pontificate. In 2009, Pope Benedict published a social encyclical, *Cartias in Veritate* (Charity in Truth). Climate change was not mentioned in this text.

Right from the beginning of his pontificate in 2013, Pope Francis has constantly called attention to the reality of climate change and its impact on the poor,

---

[13] Catholic Earthcare Australia, *Climate Change; Our Responsibility to Sustain God's Earth* (2015), 4, 7, http://catholicearthcare.org.au/wp-content/uploads/2015/02/Climate-Change-Our-Responsibility-To-Sustain-God%E2%80%99s-Earth-.pdf (accessed 23 January 2019).

[14] German Bishops: Commission for Society and Social Affairs and Commission for International Church Affairs, *Climate Change; A Focal Point of Global, Intergenerational and Ecological Justice* (2006), 7, https://catholicclimatecovenant.org/files/inline-files/German-Bishops-Report_0.pdf (accessed 23 January 2019).

[15] Ibid.

[16] Irish Catholic Bishops' Conference, *The Cry of the Earth: Pastoral Reflections on Climate Change from the Irish Catholic Bishops* (2009), 27, https://www.catholicbishops.ie/wp-content/uploads/2014/09/The-Cry-of-the-Earth-A-Call-to-Action-for-Climate-Justice-2014.pdf (accessed 23 January 2019).

Laudato Si': On Care for Our Common Home by Pope Francis which appeared on 15 June 2015 is the most important Catholic document ever issued on the environment and global warming. The two words *Laudato Si'* (Be Praised or Praised be) is taken from a popular prayer of St. Francis of Assisi. In the prayer, Francis gave thanks to God for the creation of the different creatures on earth and the elements of creation 'Brother Fire', 'Sister Moon' and 'Mother Earth'.

Laudato Si' is attempting to redefine the relationship between humans and the rest of creation so that we can soon reach a point where human needs are met in a way that does not endanger the rest of creation or irreversibly damage it. Many issues such as climate change and the destruction of habitat and biodiversity are treated very competently. *Laudato Si'* is the first encyclical to capture the extent of the modern ecological crisis – across land, air and oceans in every part of the planet. It also understands the urgency of dealing with the crisis now, before humans do irreversible damage to the life systems of the planet.

Today, care for the earth is still only at the periphery of Catholic experience. For example, there are very few 'care of the earth' ministries in dioceses or parishes worldwide. Pope Francis, who was bishop of Buenos Aires in 1998, has much more experience of wretched poverty and ecological devastation than his predecessors. *Laudato Si'* is very clear that climate change is happening and that it affects the poorest people on earth. Paragraph twenty-three states:

> The climate is a common good, belonging to all and meant for all. At the global level, it is a complex system linked to many of the essential conditions for human life. A very solid scientific consensus indicates that we are presently witnessing a disturbing warming of the climatic system. In recent decades this warming has been accompanied by a constant rise in sea levels and, it would appear, by an increase of extreme weather events, even if a scientifically determinable cause cannot be assigned to each particular phenomenon. Humanity is called to recognise the need for changes of lifestyle, production and consumption, in order to combat this warming or at least the human causes which produce or aggravate it.

In paragraph twenty-four the pope continues:

> Things are made worse by the loss of tropical forests which would otherwise help to mitigate climate change. Carbon dioxide pollution increases the acidification of the oceans and compromises the marine food chain. If present trends continue, this century may well witness extraordinary climate change and an unprecedented destruction of ecosystems, with serious consequences for all of us.

In paragraph 25, the pope points out that the poor will suffer most:

> Many of the poor live in areas particularly affected by phenomena related to warming, and their means of subsistence are largely dependent on natural reserves and ecosystemic services such as agriculture, fishing and forestry. They have no

other financial activities or resources which can enable them to adapt to climate change or to face natural disasters, and their access to social services and protection is very limited.

It is clear that Pope Francis understands the science behind climate change and the consequences of climate change for the poor and other species. In November 2017, Pope Francis sent a letter to the COP 23 climate conference which was taking place in Bonn. The letter was sent to Prime Minister Frank Bainimarama of the Fiji Islands, who was officially hosting the event, and it was read out to COP-23 participants.

The fact that *Laudato Si'* appeared six months before the crucial COP 21 meeting in Paris was very helpful. Memories of the abortive Copenhagen Conference in 2009 haunted those preparing for the Paris COP. Another failure would have done enormous damage to the UN efforts to get a global treaty in place. According to John Sweeney (National University of Ireland, Maynooth), the detailed choreography involving the United Nations, the Intergovernmental Panel on Climate Change (JPIC), the Vatican, and the tireless efforts of the French diplomatic system was undertaken. This paid off and, despite some last-minute hitches, the first legally binding global agreement on climate change – requiring action by both developing and developed countries – was adopted and will enter into force in 2020.[17]

Pope Francis congratulated the world leaders present at COP 23 and invited them to maintain a high level of cooperation. He renewed his urgent call for renewed dialogue on how we are building the future of the planet. 'We need an exchange that unites us all,' he said, 'because the environmental challenge we are experiencing, and its human roots, and affects us all'. The pope warned participants not to fall into four perverse attitudes regarding the future of the planet: denial, indifference, resignation and trust in inadequate solutions. Finally, Pope Francis hoped that COP 23 would be inspired by the same collaborative and prophetic spirit manifested during COP 2, the event at which the historic Paris Agreement was signed.[18]

Some island leaders from the Pacific Ocean area took time out from the COP 23 to pay a visit to Pope Francis in the Vatican. The president of the tiny island of Nauru, Baron Waqa, told the pope they are on the frontline of climate change. The devastating impact of cyclones has caused enormous losses to their fragile economies and matters have not ended there.[19] Highlighting the moral authority of Pope Francis on ecological issues, the Pacific leaders noted that the significance of the encyclical, *Laudato Si'*, which they said had re-dynamized the discussion on the recognition above all, of the vulnerable, in the face of climate change.[20]

---

[17] John Sweeney, 'Walking the Road from Paris', in *Laudato Si': An Irish Response,* Seán McDonagh (ed.) (Dublin: Veritas, 2017), 137–8.
[18] For these quotations, see Pope Francis's letter to COP 23 in Bonn, http://en.radiovaticana.va/news/2017/11/16/pope_francis_sends_letter_to_cop23_climate_conference_in_bon/1349337 (accessed 12 June 2018).
[19] 'Threatened Islands Appeal to Pope', *Sunday Examiner,* 26 November 2017, 4.
[20] Ibid.

In October 2017, Pope Francis implicitly criticized the United States for pulling out of the Paris Agreement on Climate Change. The United States is the only country out of 195 signatories to have withdrawn from the accord, which aims to cut emissions blamed for the rise in temperatures. US President Donald Trump announced the decision in June shortly after visiting the pope, a strong supporter of the Paris deal. At the time a Vatican official said the move was a slap in the face for the pope and the Vatican.[21]

In his address to the Diplomatic Corps on 8 January 2018, Pope Francis called on humans to care for the earth. He is particularly concerned about the devastating impact of climate changes. According to him,

> there is a need to take up, in a united effort, the responsibility of leaving to coming generations a more beautiful and liveable world, and to work, in the light of the commitments agreed upon in Paris in 2015. The spirit that must guide individuals and nations in this effort can be compared to that of the builders of the medieval cathedrals that dot the landscape of Europe, who knew that they would not see the completion of their work. Yet they worked diligently, in the knowledge that they were part of a project that would be left to their children to enjoy.[22]

In June 2018, Pope Francis and Vatican officials met with some of the world's leading oil executives in June 2018 to lobby the industry to take the dangers of climate change more seriously. Attendees included the CEOs of Exxon Mobil, Eni, BP, Royal Dutch Shell and Norway's Equinor. The meeting further underscores the importance of climate change for Pope Francis and the Vatican.[23]

Global Catholic climate movement

The notion of an 'ecological conversion' first articulated by John Paul II is central to Pope Francis's teaching. The Global Catholic Climate Movement (GCCM), which was founded in June 2015 during a visit of Pope Francis to the Philippines, has responded to his call. In the run-up to the COP 21 in Paris, GCCM gathered 900,000 signatures calling for the 1.5 degrees Celsius target, which in itself required major emissions reductions. The signatures were presented to President Francoise Hollande and to the UN climate chief Christiana Figueres at an interfaith event in Paris.

---

[21] Philip Pullella, 'Pope Implicitly Criticizes U.S. for Leaving Paris Climate Accord', 15 October 2017, https://www.aol.com/article/news/2017/10/16/pope-implicitly-criticizes-us-for-leaving-paris-climate-accord/23244500/ (accessed 12 June 2018).

[22] Andre Tornielli, 'Defending the Right to Freedom and Physical Integrity of Every Human Person', *Vatican Insider*, 8 January 2018.

[23] Brian Roewe and Joshua J. McElwee, 'Big Oil to Meet with Vatican Officials, Pope Francis', *National Catholic Reporter*, 5 June 2018.

Tomás Insua who comes from Argentina is co-founder and executive director of the Global Catholic Climate Movement. This organization is working across the globe helping the Catholic Church turn the *Laudato Si'* call into bold action for climate justice. GCCM has set itself high targets. Between 2018 and 2020, the organization plans to bring the teaching of Laudato Si' to 120 million Catholics. They plan to recruit 1.2 million people to bring this teaching into their parishes. GCCM emphasizes the fact that the Church's teaching on the environment, and especially tackling climate change, as a moral issue. Now is the opportune moment for Catholics to 'walk-the-walk' and bring the encyclical to life in order to change our economy and develop a society which is in service of life everywhere.

One of the very positive fruits of GCCM is the divestment programme which it and other Catholic organizations such as Trocaire and CAFOD supports. The guide encourages the leadership of faith-based institutions to withdraw their investments in fossil-fuel companies. The guide recognizes that many Catholic institutions already have ethical investment guidelines and policies. These policies should be regularly updated to ensure that they cover important ethical areas such as climate changes. The guide highlights the fact that climate change is a clear and direct risk to human well-being and to the environment

The Global Catholic Climate Movement (GCCM) has set itself a challenging task over the next few years, as they hope that their programmes will inspire Catholics to tackle climate change and other environmental problems. They hope to work with religious communities, conferences of bishops and the Vatican in educating people about the moral challenge of climate changes. Many of their people are young and idealists and certainly seem to have the energy for this long hard battle ahead.

A response to Seán McDonagh, SSC

Meehyun Chung[1]

Father Seán McDonagh's essay provides a helpful overview of recent Christian documents regarding climate change. I will respond to Father McDonagh's essay from my perspective as a Korean protestant theologian, educated in Korea and Europe, yet living and teaching in South-Korea.

Let me start with two observations. First, I believe that it is important to counter Christianity's human-centred tendencies and retrieve the cosmic, albeit often marginalized, orientation articulated by visionaries such as Hildegard of Bingen and John Amos Comenius.[2] Such marginalized views are valuable to counter an age of anthropocentrism. Second, while ecclesial documents are important first steps towards addressing our climate crisis, their significance ultimately depends on their implementation in daily praxis.

Let me share a personal experience concerning a friend of mine who was studying botany and lived next to me in the dormitory when I was studying in Switzerland. This friend was only nominally Christian and yet she was very cautious regarding the preservation of the life of all creatures. Whenever I tried to catch a mayfly, she grabbed my wrist and said, 'What are you doing? Why do you want to cease the life of God's creature?' Ever since I have tried not to kill insects. But to be honest, I still cannot stop catching those small insects when they are annoying me or are disturbing my sight, although my friend's advice has not left my mind.

When I returned to Korea, I moved into a studio apartment that had a problem with ants. Because the ants made my day-to-day life difficult, especially around my food, I asked my landlady how I could solve this problem quickly with chemicals. She answered, 'I am a Buddhist and we don't kill any living creature.' Her answer impressed me deeply, so I learnt to have more respect for living creatures from my landlady.

These two experiences have led me to rethink what I am doing to protect and preserve the life of God's creatures. What kind of Christian am I? This past year Korea experienced an extremely cold winter and faced micro-dust problems. This led to a greater awareness of the problem of climate change and ecological destruction. But I wonder whether on

---

[1] Meehyun Chung is Professor of Systematic Theology at Yonsei University, Seoul, and serves as the first female Chaplain of Yonsei University. She is an ordained minister in the Presbyterian Church in the Republic of Korea and holds a doctorate degree in theology from Basel University in Switzerland.

[2] Meehyun Chung, 'No More Flight: Gender and Eco-Justice', in *Mission and Power: History, Relevance and Perils*, Atola Longkumer (ed.) (Oxford: Regnum, 2016), 227–35.

average Christians are concerned about this matter and raise the question: How does Christianity affect today's ecology, climate change and environmental crisis?

In a now famous article Lynn White Jr gave a very concise answer to this question: Christianity has been the culprit in destroying the ecosystem and cannot avoid its responsibility.³ His article finds the cause of the ecological crisis in the history of Christianity, most notably its anthropocentric worldview. I have found his argument convincing. The problem is not only with the Bible, however, but rather with the *history* of biblical interpretation and the way these interpretations have subsequently given rise to an anthropocentric and egocentric worldview.

The main message of the Bible is that all things exist by the power and love of God. Every time God creates, God expresses the beauty and goodness of creation. But the wonders God has given us are disappearing today. Every corner of the globe is suffering. God's very beautiful, original and ongoing blessing has been distorted by humankind, especially since the Enlightenment era. Christianity contributed to this distortion in part because people interpreted the scriptures literally and without considering the historical and cultural context in which they were written.

From the Enlightenment onwards Western civilization, building on the Protestant turn to the self, relied entirely on the potential of human reason. Yet its infinite optimism about the capacity of humans to understand and shape the world strengthened the dualism between culture and nature, making non-human nature the passive recipient of utilitarian schemes. This has become the ideological basis of the development of modern capitalism, which develops resources without taking sustainability into consideration. This means that Christianity is not free from the accusation that it is a factor in the ecological destruction, most notably climate-related destruction, we are witnessing today.

Today, Christians are demanding a paradigm shift to overcome the dualism of this arrogant and hostile scheme. While human beings are precious subjects, we must approach more than human nature as subjects in their own right, which means that we need to recognize and respect their unique and intrinsic value.

The problem with the literal interpretation of the Bible manifested itself not only in anthropocentric attitudes towards nature, but has also influenced Euro-American white male-centric missions. While many good fruits have been born through missions, we must also take a critical look at the many dysfunctions that missions have brought. Christian missionary work has gone hand in hand with orientalism and the promotion of Western supremacy. The Christianity that was preached often ignored the unique cultures and characteristics of the Global South. Christian mission was one-directionally: from the Global North to the Global South. Indeed, it is an uncomfortable historical truth that Christian mission was in tune with colonial expansion and Western imperialist proliferation. The legacy of the entanglement of mission with colonial imperialism can still be found in many parts of the Global South.

---

³ Lynn White, Jr, 'The Historical Roots of Our Ecological Crisis', *Science* 155 (1967), 1203–7.

The concept 'missio Dei' is based on the words of Jesus: 'Just as God sent me, I also send you' (Jn 20.21). This was the message of the resurrected Jesus, when sending his disciples into the world. The disciples' ministry extends not only to the restoration of broken relationships between humans and humans, but also helps restore the broken relationship between humans and other creatures.

The human being is a precious being created in the image of God. Yet the human is not divine: the human being is a creature from the earth (*adamah*). This is true even in our era of the fourth Industrial Revolution, in which humans have almost become God's equal. It is important therefore that we practice our God-given mission to be an earth creature in our day-to-day life. Precisely because we should pursue the abundant life for all creatures, including our future descendants, we need to reflect on our daily behaviour and its influence on our environment. Indeed, I believe that publications concerning eco-justice, such as the ones discussed in McDonagh's essay, will be ineffective when it comes to increasing awareness of people if we fail to implement eco-justice within our daily praxis. Many environmental problems, including the micro-dust issues we are facing in Korea, pose very serious challenges to our economy, culture and society. However, Korean Protestant churches are still predominantly human-centred. Instead of a universal 'green' salvation, they are preaching a narrow anthropocentric and individualistic 'red' salvation.

The World Council of Churches has produced fine publications on environmental matters, such as *Together towards Life: Mission and Evangelism in Changing Landscapes,* which also introduces a new perception of mission.[4] Unfortunately, this document has not generated much interest at the level of local churches in Korea. Because of the hierarchical structure of the Catholic Church, Pope Francis's encyclical *Laudato Si'* may very well have more of an impact in Korea. The Orthodox Church is still generally relatively unknown in Korea. Its cosmic theology may however help correct the lack of ecological awareness in Protestant Korean churches.

In conclusion I offer an inspiring example of a green Christian practice of earth care in Korea. Hansalim[5] is a federation of Korean organic farmers. This movement is rooted in a Catholic movement which was initiated by Park Jaeil, who served as the president of an association of Catholic farmers. The organization was founded in 1986 as a small-scale grain store, selling organic product like grain, sesame oil, egg and rice. Today, Hansalim is the largest and most profitable organic consumer cooperative in Korea: they have reached annual sales of over USD 300 million and serve over 1.2 million individual consumers through internet sales, shops and nationwide branches. Hansalim promotes integrated farming systems and sustainability by preserving Korean traditional farming techniques and organic farming methods, avoiding the use of GMO's.

---

[4] Jooseop Keum (ed.), *Together Towards Life: Mission and Evangelism in Changing Landscapes* (Geneva: World Council of Churches, 2013).

[5] See http://orgprints.org/24218/7/24218.pdf (accessed 1 June 2018).

There have been various forms of networking among interfaith-based movements for joint action against government projects that have disastrous environmental impacts. For instance when the Korean government launched the four major rivers restoration project as a so-called "multi-layered green growth project" in 2009, faith communities came together and organized demonstrations protesting it.

These are just small examples showing how we can move away from being despots over and against nature. Whereas nature can exist without us, we cannot live without nature. Thus, we should give up our arrogance and pretend we can somehow manage nature. We are just guests on Earth.[6]

---

[6] Christoph Stückelberger, *Umwelt und Entwicklung: eine sozialethische Orientierung* (Stuttgart: Kohlhammer, 1997), 230–9.

PART VII

Concluding observations

Introduction

Hilda P. Koster

As editors of this volume we have opted to structure the volume in such a way that the main essays are written by authors situated in what we call 'North Atlantic Christian theology'. Such authors are asked to address primarily readers who are situated in the same context. The assumption here is that the North Atlantic region is mainly responsible for historic carbon emission while North Atlantic Christian theology is often regarded, especially from the outside, as being part of the problem. Of course, Christian theologians would tend to believe that Christianity forms a necessary part of the solution too and they may well be right if this is where the main problem lies! The volume may therefore be understood as an exercise in self-conscious contextual theology.

While the 'main' essays in this volume focus on the 'North Atlantic', we have invited responses from leading scholars and theologians who come from outside of North Atlantic Christian theology – because they are situated in other geographic regions, because they represent voices that have been marginalized in Christian theology, because they are not standing in the Christian tradition, or because their main discipline is not theology. The purpose has been to give those situated *outside* North Atlantic theology an opportunity to react to the way those *within* North Atlantic theology phrase the problem and articulate the solution. Are North Atlantic theologians and ethicists who are writing and thinking about climate change asking the right questions, that is, questions that really matter to scientists, policy makers and/or communities adversely impacted by climate change? Do their theological proposals make sense to those from outside North Atlantic theology? For instance, do the solutions raised by North Atlantic theologians carry any weight when it comes to discussions on carbon mitigation and adaptation? Do they interpret the science adequately? Does the way theologians frame the challenges raised by a changing climate correspond to the way scientists interpret the data? How do economists evaluate the discussions on climate justice within theology? What can theologians learn from ecological–economists when it comes to climate justice?

We further have been interested to hear from theologians and ethicists from outside 'the North Atlantic' whether North Atlantic theology speaks to the climate change-related struggles within their communities? Do efforts by North Atlantic theologians to 'purge' North Atlantic theology from 'toxic' teachings – teachings that have contributed to our current climate predicament – address the needs of those at/on the margins? Or, are these attempts still rather abstract when it comes to climate change-related violence, suffering, debt and in/justice? We may also ask whether North Atlantic theologians grasp onto climate change and ecology in order to rescue Western Christianity from its own growing irrelevance vis-à-vis a secularizing world. And, finally, how do theologians from outside the North Atlantic make theology matter for life on an endangered planet? Is North Atlantic theology capable of self-criticism in light of these contributions? Or, is North Atlantic theology ultimately too much beholden to colonial and neocolonial forms of Christianity, as some authors have argued, for it to be challenged in a fundamental and unsettling manner?

It has been our hope that these and other critical questions and responses have made this handbook more interesting and provocative, also as a teaching source.

However, we realize that much more can be said when one takes issues of class, gender, race, geographic divides and religious diversity into consideration. In this concluding section of the handbook we have therefore invited a number of senior scholars to survey the introductions, essays and responses found in the volume and to critically assess these from a particular perspective. The question is whether and to what extent the contributions gathered together in this volume are doing justice to the following concerns: (a) issues of class, (b) issues of gender, (c) issues of race, (d) issues of religious diversity, (e) issues related to geographic divides, and (f) issues related to non-human animals. Finally we also raise the obvious question, namely whether such a volume will make any difference to carbon mitigation and adaptation. We asked the contributors to this section to be frank in their assessment. Thus in case we have not sufficiently foregrounded questions raised by, for instance, critical animal studies, as David Clough suggests in his contribution, we asked authors to not mince words. Yet we asked also that authors indicate constructive ways forward. How may we do better when it comes to foregrounding perspectives and concerns related to gender, race, class, animal rights and so on. How may we more effectively integrate these perspectives in the very questions we ask, the methodologies we follow and the sources we use.

Finally, it important to note that this handbook is complemented by other recent volumes that give voice to theological perspectives coming from outside North Atlantic theology on issues of climate justice. Examples of such works are *Making Peace with the earth: Action and advocacy for Climate Justice* edited by Grace Ji-Sun Kim and Guillermo Kerber (WWC); *Planetary Solidarity: Global Women's Voices on Christian Doctrine and Climate Justice* edited by Hilda P. Koster and Grace Ji-sun Kim (Fortress); *Justice and Food Security: Theological Education and Christian Leadership* edited by Dietrich Werner (Globethics); and an edition of *Ecumenical Review* on 'Praying for Rain? Religion and Climate Change in Africa' edited by Ezra Chitando and Ernst Conradie. This final section, then, joins voices these volumes and, we hope, offers critical perspectives for future work in Christian theology and climate change.

Chapter 7.1
Doing justice to issues of class?

Kwok Pui-lan[1]

The discussion of class, religion and climate change must attend to the interconnection between modernity and colonialism in the modern West. Colonialism included the exploitation of natural resources for Europe's industrial development and for the fulfilment of the desires of the colonizers. The growth of tea, sugar cane, spices, cotton and other 'cash crops' in former colonies enabled the rising European bourgeois to enjoy a middle-class lifestyle and taste. Colonial difference was maintained through the social worlds and distinctions that were constructed based on class, race and gender.

Today, the neoliberal market's global reach has challenged national and geographical boundaries. A new transnational capitalist class has risen, who are the owners of worldwide means of production through transnational corporations and private financial institutions. This new class has amassed enormous wealth. In 2017, the top 1 per cent of citizens globally owned half of all household wealth.[2] This transnational capitalist class and their big corporations exert pressure on governments to pass laws protecting business interests and loosening regulations protecting the environment.

Because of the history of colonialism and the widening economic inequity between the Global North and Global South, discussion on climate change and environmental issues often take divergent turns. Annika Rieger and Joerg Rieger, in their essay, point out that climate change, capitalism and Christianity are imbricated and that the emphasis on economic growth contributes to the environmental crisis.[3] People in the Global South may respond in a different way. Many are eager to – or have no other choice but to – jump onto the bandwagon of the neoliberal market to make a living or to attain middle-class status. China is a case in point. Emerging from a rigid Communist system in the late 1970s, the introduction of a market economy has brought phenomenal economic growth. The so-called capitalism with Asian characteristics has lifted more than 500 million Chinese people out of extreme poverty. It is true that economic

---

[1] Kwok Pui-lan is the former William F. Cole Professor of Christian Theology and Spirituality at Episcopal Divinity School, USA, and has published extensively in Asian feminist theology, biblical interpretation and postcolonial criticism. She has served as President of the American Academy of Religion (2011).
[2] Aimee Picchi, 'World's Richest 1% Control More Than Half of All of Wealth', *Moneywatch*, 14 November 2017, https://www.cbsnews.com/news/richest-1-percent-control-more-than-half-of-all-wealth/ (accessed 26 September 2018).
[3] Annika Rieger and Joerg Rieger, 'Working with Environmental Economists', in this volume.

growth was accompanied by pollution, environmental disasters and economic inequity, but it would be unthinkable for China to go back to the old Communist system. It is challenging to balance economic growth and environmental protection, and even more so for 'developing' countries, which must feed a growing population while coming out from a long period of colonial underdevelopment.

The problem is exacerbated by the globalization of production, which entails the fragmentation of production into many steps and segments all over the world to maximize profits. Asia has become the factory of the world because of its relatively lower cost of labour. As the rich countries shift their industries overseas, they also 'outsource' their climate pollution to poorer countries. Even though carbon dioxide emissions have been falling in the US and Europe for years, emissions in developing countries such as China and India have been growing at a very rapid rate, partly due to 'emissions transfers'.[4] But the capitalist class's responsibility for the pollution produced overseas has not been taken seriously in international negotiations. For example, under the Paris climate deal, countries are generally held accountable for the emissions produced within their own borders.

As the environment has worsened in developing countries, corporations in rich countries have seen an opportunity to make profits by introducing green technology or other expansive solutions. As geochemist Asfawossen Asrat has said, the Global South is suspicious of efforts such as climate engineering, which aims to overturn the effects of climate change. The Global South wants the rich countries in the North to first address the historical causes of climate injustice. Poorer countries complain that they have been under-represented in the deliberations of these new technologies and that their values and belief systems have seldom been considered in finding solutions to mitigate climate change.[5]

Climate change is a serious peril affecting the whole planet and there is no presumed innocence, as both the rich and the poor contribute to the anthropogenic causes of our environmental crisis, though to a different degree. Ivone Gebara encourages us to avoid thinking about good and evil in a binary way. She insists that we have the potential to do both good and evil.[6] Today the transnational capitalist class is found in both the Global North and the South. The rising middle class in developing countries has caught onto global consumerism. Class is a relational term and must be understood in a global context.

Climate change presents challenges and opportunities to rethink the relation between class, economics and Christian theology. An important area to reconsider is theological anthropology. Classical economists understood the human nature of *homo economicus*

---

[4] Brad Plumer, 'A Closer Look at How Rich Countries "Outsource" Their CO_2 Emissions to Poorer Ones', *Vox*, 18 April 2017, https://www.vox.com/energy-and-environment/2017/4/18/15331040/emissions-outsourcing-carbon-leakage (accessed 26 September 2018).

[5] Asfawossen Asrat, 'A Response to Forrest Clingerman', in this volume.

[6] Ivone Gebara, 'The Christian Story of God's Work – A Response', in this volume.

as being concerned with self-interest and wealth-making. Capitalism is predicated upon individualism, competitiveness, maximizing utility and profit-making. Several authors in this volume emphasize the social dimension of existence as well as human beings' capacity for love, care and compassion for others. Such care must be extended to the whole of creation, as humans exert pervasive influence in the earth system. Larry Rasmussen writes about the need to develop a moral world of Anthropocene which includes not just humans but extends to planetary boundaries.[7]

Theologians have condemned the greed of capitalism and provided theological or moral principles to judge the economy or to suggest correctives to social ills. Theologians contrast the worship of God with the worship of Mammon and denounce capitalism, or the market economy, as a false religion or idol. Theology is often treated as separate or distinct from the economy, to the extent that it is unclear how theological or ethical principles can be translated into concrete social and economic practices. For example, theologians have criticized the problems associated with commodity exchange and suggested gift exchange as a model for mutuality and building relationships. They interpret Christian redemption and God's grace in terms of gifts and argue that Christian theology can point to bonds and relationships established by gift-giving as alternatives to capitalistic exploitation.[8] But it is unclear how the principles of gift exchange, based on studies of simpler societies in Asia and Pacific, can be applicable to modern complex societies. From an East Asian perspective, gift-giving can also be used to reinforce hierarchical positions (gifts are determined by people's social positions) or to establish relationships outside of formal channels through briberies and corruption.

Newer works on theology and economics pay attention to money and finance, which play critical roles in post-industrial capitalism. Devin Singh discusses ways in which money, debt, and economic exchange in the Roman Empire had structured the ways that early Christian theologians thought about God, the image of Christ and salvation. God was seen as an economic administrator and Christ as divine currency to exchange for humanity's redemption. The classic ransom theory of atonement imagined God paying a ransom or debt to the devil for human sin. Singh argues that this long-standing association of money and theology has shaped Christian imagination and has been used to justify colonialism and conquest in later centuries.[9] Kathryn Tanner argues that today's capitalism is very different from the capitalism being practised when Max Weber wrote his *Protestant Ethic and the Spirit of Capitalism*.[10] Today's capitalism is finance-dominated, which is built upon a highly competitive work ethic that treats workers as dispensable assets. This work ethic is incompatible with Christian commitments, as

---

[7] Larry Rasmussen, 'Introduction – A Moral Anthropocene', in this volume.

[8] John Milbank, 'Can a Gift Be Given? Prolegomena to a Future Trinitarian Metaphysic', *Modern Theology* 11:1 (1995), 119–61; Kathryn Tanner, *Economy of Grace* (Minneapolis: Fortress, 2005).

[9] Devin Singh, *Divine Currency: The Theological Power of Money in the West* (Stanford: Stanford University Press, 2018).

[10] Max Weber, *The Protestant Ethic and the Spirit of Capitalism,* Talcott Parsons (trans.) (New York: Scribner, 1958).

God does not treat humans according to their achievements. Although Christians cannot dissociate themselves from this world, they can exploit the nodes of vulnerabilities in the unjust system and work towards an alternative cooperative project.[11]

Humans' economic activities have contributed to climate change, and this impact is disproportionately borne by Indigenous people, women, children and other marginalized groups.

Unusually hot temperatures and severe hurricanes, typhoons and floods have caused large-scale migration and created refugees. In discussing economics and theology, we can no longer leave out the question of environmental costs. There have been conversations about developing a global or planetary ethic, and more exchanges between scholars and activists in the Global North and South are needed. We look forward to a time when God will renew the creation, as Second Isaiah says: 'For you will go out in joy, and be led back in peace; the mountains and hills before you shall burst into song, and all the trees of the field shall clap their hands' (Isa. 55.12).

---

[11] Kathryn Tanner, *Christianity and the New Spirit of Capitalism* (New Haven: Yale University Press, 2019).

Chapter 7.2
Doing justice to issues of gender?

Sharon A. Bong[1]

This *T&T Clark Handbook of Christian Theology and Climate Change* is a highly reflexive endeavour. Its internal critique of the North Atlantic Christian theology undergirds all six prime sections with the explicit standpoint that such a theology emanating from the world's most developed nations with a culpably high-carbon footprint has been more of a problem rather than a solution to climate change. The concluding observations of the *Handbook* doing justice to issues of gender along with other key indexes such as class, race, religious diversity, animal issues, geographic divides and carbon mitigation are intended as an external critique of North Atlantic Christian theology in relation to climate change.

The *Handbook* is also highly inclusive. This underlined ethos is evident particularly in Part One – working with others that necessarily and commonsensically foregrounds contributions from evolutionary biologists, environmental economists, political players, geoengineers, social scientists, artists, climate activists in civil society and other religious traditions to complement theologizing in a North Atlantic Christian context. This list of stakeholders is of course not exhaustive. Such an ethos of inclusivity is also evident in Part Three – working with and against others from within; Orthodox, Catholic, Anglican, Lutheran, Reformed, Baptist, Pentecostal forms of Christianity that are potentially divisive on issues related and unrelated to climate change and ecumenical fellowships that strive towards negotiating the tensions of these divisiveness.

The *Handbook* is also highly conversational: each essay (of an approximate total of forty) is assigned a respondent. The iterative process of articulation-response (Parts One to Six) and observations (Part Seven) in aspiring towards a 'common good, a common vision, common values and principles' as stated in the main introduction to the *Handbook*, is a highly uncommon practice, not the least because it is not expedient albeit fruitful. It is fruitful, even ethical, because it privileges the principle of relationality among all who are committed from within and without the Christian framework to climate justice and hold themselves accountable for (as opposed to denying) anthropogenic climate change.

---

[1] Sharon A. Bong is Associate Professor of Gender Studies at the School of Arts and Social Sciences, Monash University, Malaysia. She works in the intersection of genders, sexualities and religions with a focus on Southeast Asia, for example, queer ecofeminisms, feminist theologies and sexual and reproductive health and rights.

The *Handbook* is, however, highly ungendered or put more simply, gender-blind. On the one hand, one could posit that the principles of reflexivity, inclusivity and relationality broadly resonate as gendered even feminist principles in a collaborative bid to manage – neither reconciling nor eliding – differences that matter: disciplinary, ideological, denominational, geographical and so forth. The intersectionality of Part Seven (concluding observations) holds particular promise as this is the section dedicated to the voices of the other; disciplinary, ideological, denominational and geographical. These voices of the other in relation to North Atlantic-based Christian theologians, represent voices of minorities but not necessarily subjugated others as that would include Indigenous persons, displaced persons, refugees, migrant workers, gender and sexual minorities, the dispossessed (e.g. children, the infirm, the elderly, differently abled and altered bodies), ecosystem and non-humans who are first and last casualties of not only climate change but also ecological degradation that are exacerbated by systemic poverty and violence.

On the other hand, these principles are neither overtly claimed nor framed as gendered or feminist. Therein lies the gap. More fundamental than gender issues – which suggests ad hoc considerations, for example regarding gender representation among contributors – is a gender lens that underlies disciplinary, ideological, denominational and geographical differences. Such a gender lens is often framed as feminist and queer theoretical and theological approaches and when applied, potentially gives rise to a critique of androcentric and heterosexist ways of thinking and being that often run counter to principles of reflexivity, inclusivity and relationality. A gender lens as such would make visible the different and disproportionate impact of climate change on women in relation to men, among women, among men in different social-political contexts, rather than a gender-neutral approach which presupposes a similar and undifferentiated impact. A gender lens would also make apparent what Jacqui True, a feminist political scientist, deems as 'masculinist logics'[2] in drawing a parallel between male heads of households and male heads of states and markets (hence political economy) that not only sustains unsustainable development but also the violence of systemic discrimination. At its most basic, a gender lens, in making visible (de-naturalizing) the constructs of gender binaries that undergird the structural sin of gender inequality and gender inequity, seeks to deconstruct and reconstruct such 'masculinist logics'.

With regard to climate justice, ecofeminists would show, for instance, how hurting women and the girl-child – as a consequence of upholding 'masculinist logics' – invariably hurts the environment, and vice versa. The intimate relationality of women and nature – as a counterpoint to men and culture – is claimed and celebrated by an ecofeminist such as Vandana Shiva who in her seminal text *Staying Alive*, sacralizes 'Purusha-Prakriti' which embodies 'duality in unity'; the male and female principles of creation within Hindu cosmology. Such 'dialectical unity' runs counter to Cartesian

---

[2] Jacqui True, 'A Tale of Two Feminisms in International Relations? Feminist Political Economy and the Women, Peace and Security Agenda', *Politics and Gender* 11:2 (2015), 419–24 (420).

thought that dwells on dualities and the consequential disconnect between human and nature resulting in the former's mechanistic treatment of the latter[3] that, in turn, begets anthropocentric climate change. Although ecofeminists have been critiqued for a gender bias in their (seemingly reductionist) postulation that the domination of nature by men externalizes the domination of women by men, in retrospect they now become prophetic witnesses of the interconnectedness of climate justice and gender justice. This interconnectedness finds expression in the globally-endorsed seventeen Sustainable Development Goals.

Ecofeminists are thus uncommon witnesses (rather than the 'common witness' that is called for in this *Handbook*) also to 'heterosexist logic' which complements a 'masculinist logics'. A similar construction, deconstruction and reconstruction of 'heterosexist logics' are consequences of applying a gender lens to climate change by queer ecofeminists. As many remain perplexed and ask, 'What's gender got to do with it (climate change)?' others, no less befuddled, ask, 'What's (hetero)sexuality got to do with it (climate change)?' Queer ecofeminists, start by making the connection between sexual diversity and species diversity or biodiversity. Where differences proliferate in sexual diversity and species diversity, the flattening of differences becomes an extension of 'heterosexist logic' that seeks to suppress 'radical pluralism'.[4] The othering of women, non-heteronormative sexualities or differently abled bodies, akin to the depletion of species diversity, become legitimized: women are commodified (even consumed) as the 'preservable body', most animals and plants (as non-humans) are marked as the 'consumable body' (for humans), while queer (non-heteronomative or LGBTQI+) bodies naturally become the 'disposable body'.[5] The ecological implications of such 'heterosexist logic' is made apparent through its corollary 'logic of disposability' that renders certain bodies and not others as preservable, consumable and disposable. Who decides this and for whom?

What would be the consequences of following through such construction, deconstruction and reconstruction of masculinist-heterosexist logics of Christian theology in relation to climate change? The large corpus of feminist theologies from North Atlantic, Asian, African, South American contexts, as successor and subjugated knowledge (to male theologizing), have now been mainstreamed in secular and sacred spaces, as these intergenerational feminists engage in reflection from the lived realities of the disenfranchised, beginning with women's narratives. Reimagining God the Father, reclaiming Jesus as the first feminist, embracing Sophia which amalgamates the Holy Spirit with the spirit of all beings, sentient and non-sentient, are somewhat elided in this *Handbook*. In my view some of the essays promisingly manifest a challenge to a masculinist-heterosexist logics of Christian theology. Inhabiting the tension between

---

[3] Vandana Shiva, *Staying Alive: Women, Ecology and Development* (London: Zed Books, 2002), 40.

[4] Danne Polk, 'Ecologically Queer: Preliminaries for a Queer Ecofeminist Identity Theory', *Journal of Women and Religion* 19&20 (2001/2002), 72–89 (88).

[5] Ibid., 80.

'Christian particularity' and 'common ground' that this *Handbook* aspires towards may arguably be realized with the preparedness to decentre the human in creation, in order to better embrace the sacredness of all beings, human and non-human. As humans are created in the image of God, such decentring of the highest form of creation, renders fuzzy the hierarchical and oppositional differences and boundaries between Creator and created.

In looking to Christian theology as an ecological resource of hope, the 'spirit of humility' finds expression in decentring the human which is not necessarily a post-Christian endeavour. Decentring the human is inspired by the ecological wisdom and fortitude of ecofeminist theologians who challenged androcentrism and anthropocentrism in secular and religious discourses alike. In doing so, they show the way in embodying the principles of reflexivity, inclusivity and relationality that weave through this *Handbook*, most notably through Sallie McFague's conceptualization of 'kenosis' or emptying of the self (Chapter 5.2). The profound relationality of God, human and nature may then be experienced as unconditional (selfless) love for self and all others.

Chapter 7.3
Doing justice to issues of race?

Melanie L. Harris[1]

Ecowomanism

Ecowomanism is an approach to environmental ethics that centres the voices, perspectives and epistemologies of women of African descent. Ecowomanism is distinctive in that it combines theoretical frameworks from religion and ecology discourse and womanist theological ethics. Ecowomanist ties to the womanist tradition are especially important because of the legacy of womanist scholarship that unashamedly disrupts 'normative' ways of doing ethics. Following womanist scholarship in theology and ethics, ecowomanism employs intersectional analyses using race–class–gender analysis when engaging conversations about Christian theology, religion and climate justice. Rather than moving from the assumption that all in the Christian faith operate, understand and honour the theological presupposition of *imago dei*, womanist, black liberationist and other forms of liberation theology point to countless examples within Christian history and history itself when the precept that all are created in the image of God, and, hence are sacred, was not honoured. The divine within Trayvon Martin was not honoured when he was murdered based on the racial bias and beliefs held by his killer. Nor was 'the divine within' honoured during the arrest and later 'unexplained' death of Sandra Bland, a Black Lives Matter' activist and educator. The list goes on. Whether in life or death the theological assumption of *imago dei* is all too often not being honoured (even by those who claim to be Christians) when it comes to people of colour.

One origin of this sin is explained by critical race theorists and black liberationists as the sin of white supremacy. The sin of white supremacy systematically views some human life (white people) as more valuable in God's and in humans' eyes than other lives (people of colour). According to womanist and black liberationist perspectives, racism eats away at one's connection to God, other humans and ultimately all of creation. The social, individual and communal sin of racism shows up in churches, church history, as well as in the history of the faith.

---

[1] Melanie L. Harris is Visiting Professor of Global Ethical Leadership and Environmental Studies at the University of Denver. She is also Professor of Religion and Founding Director of African American and Africana Studies at TCU. A graduate from the Harvard Leadership Program, her research focuses on womanist ethics and ecology.

It also shows up in climate change. That is, there is a connection between racism and climate injustice. As many authors in this volume point out, there is an eerie history to the claims of white supremacy and the theological claim that humans have more worth and value to God than the rest of creation. These flawed theological claims need to be corrected. In order to do this corrective work, theology needs a critical framework or lens which brings into focus the significance of the interconnected sin of devaluing certain beings – most notably black women and black women's bodies – and the earth.[2] From an ecowomanist perspective, to truly repent the sins of climate change requires a deep, and critical understanding of the multiple ways the abuse of the earth and the abuse and exploitation of black bodies intersect. Only when this is acknowledged can we turn away and is transformation possible.

Yet at times analyses of climate injustice brush aside the effects of climate change on black women caught in the middle of structural evils and social realities of racism, classism, sexism, hetero-sexism ... Black women, their experiences as well as the experiences of their communities are too often made invisible by environmental and climate scientist. This problem demonstrates the need for a different kind of correction. An ecowomanist method of analysis offers such a critical corrective lens for climate justice analysis. The remainder of this essay, therefore, briefly outlines the different aspects of an ecowomanist method for climate justice analysis; most notably it describes how ecowomanist method offers a practical tool for shaping theological and practical activist work, as well as provides theoretical links to other disciplines.

Ecowomanist method

Ecowomanism combines an intersectional approach to environmental ethics and adopts an environmental justice paradigm. That is, it uses intersectional analysis to environmental ethics while simultaneously uncovering the eco-wisdom of women of colour, specifically women of African descent. This helps to 'shift the gaze' of environmental talk from culturally normative speech flowing from classical (read: white) theory to an inclusive conversation engaging women and communities of colour. Rather, than solely featuring the theories of white men of European descent, ecowomanism draws its inspiration, theory and reflection from the practice, reflection and creative climate work of black women. In light of the fact that these ideas have often been heralded in black communities as life-giving and sustaining but ignored or devalued by non-black scholars, this starting point is significant. Similar to the black liberation theology and womanist thought of its day, ecowomanism responds to the attempt to erase the contributions of people and communities of colour from the environmental movement. Correcting the

---

[2] Delores S. Williams, 'Sin, Nature and Black Women's Bodies', in *Ecofeminism and the Sacred*, Carol Adams (ed.) (New York: Continuum, 1993), 24–9 (24).

institutional and sometimes structural racism that is embedded within certain forms of environmental ethics, ecowomanism dismantles approaches to environmental ethics that hide the experiences and contributions of black women.

There are seven steps to an ecowomanist method that makes it distinctive. The method begins with an acknowledgement of the presence of the work of ecowomanism as prophetic. Ecowomanism calls for the ethical work that is required to respond to climate injustice and recognizes the systemic violence rooted in theologies and histories that needs to be carefully remembered in order to act more justly. By examining these 'eco-memories' as counter memories (African American environmental history) ecowomanism calls us to resist the subjugation of peoples of colour and the Earth.

Step one of an ecowomanist method thus begins with *honouring experience, eco-story and eco-narratives*. In the case of many peoples of African descent living in a North American context these stories also uncover the reality of migration due to the influence of often legalized and accepted white supremacist norms held throughout the United States.

The second movement is *to reflect on experience*. This move allows for the posing of questions of history to tell us the truth about systemic oppressions and structural evil that has been used to repress the voices of peoples of colour and violate the earth.

Step three invites the *application of womanist analysis* to examine environmental degradation. It uses race, class, gender and intersectional analysis to highlight cases of environmental racism and climate injustice.

The *deep questioning of history and tradition* prompted by the previous analysis takes place in step four. This step promotes deep questioning of history and tradition and examines the parallel examples of what Delores Williams calls the 'sin of defilement' that devalues the lives and bodies of black women and the body of the earth.[3] Ecowomanism helps to examine intersecting nature of oppressions that work to undermine wholeness in the self, as well as planetary wholeness.

Building upon womanist social analysis that insists that the structural evil be exposed, ecowomanist method turns to a fifth step of *engaging transformation*. This step introduces ecowomanist spirituality as a response to climate change. It focuses on the praxis, and spiritual activism alive in ecowomanism by exploring new resources for eco-justice work based on the experiences of African and African American women. It also examines the ethical imperative for earth justice interwoven in African cosmology. Here, interconnectedness, interconnectivity and inter-relationality are primary keys towards building new 'earth honouring faiths', thus opening the door to interfaith dialogue about climate change.

Stepping into this new door is step six of the method: sharing *dialogue with multiple religious perspectives and earth-honouring faith traditions* that also honour African and African American women's eco-spirituality. Using the third wave womanist

---

[3] Ibid.

hallmarks and approach that I have articulated in my previous work,[4] this step is crucial in that it incorporates attention to globalization, postcolonial theory, interdisciplinary approaches and inter-religious dialogue as important aspects of ecowomanism. These three hallmarks of third wave womanism widen the sources of ecowomanist refection and analysis, giving way for constructing new methods of analysis that connect theory with praxis, and break new ground in inter-religious dialogue about earth justice.

Step seven is to *take action for earth justice* by making the link between social justice and earth justice. This involves building mutual approaches to share in work of exposing what Emilie M. Townes calls the 'production of evil',[5] protest the logic of domination and abuse in all of its forms, naming and resisting structural and individual forms of violence and replacing it with 'truth force' and love.

Ecowomanist method is useful to multiple discourses and can be taught and applied to a variety of disciplines; however, its origins to the womanist tradition remain vital to the method as well as the voices it seeks to lift up.

---

[4] Melanie L. Harris, *Gifts of Virtue, Alice Walker and Womanist Ethics* (New York: Palgrave McMillan, 2010).
[5] Emilie M. Townes, *Womanist Ethics and the Cultural Production of Evil* (New York: Palgrave MacMillan, 2006).

Chapter 7.4
Doing justice to religious diversity?

Kim Yong-Bock[1]

Eco-justice in an East Asian spirituality of life: Working with other religions

The current discourse on ecology is part of the modern scientific and philosophical discourse that pervades the present global academic order. Such ecological discourse will be problematic, however, if it does not take seriously the relationships among all living beings, as well as the relations of living beings with their environments. This is clear particularly in the light of Asian and other integral cosmologies of life. But there can be a new, alternative discourse to the current, merely scientific understanding of ecology. In fact the ecological crisis is deeply intertwined with science and technology, as they have come to dominate nature and the ecological environment.

The crisis is thoroughly embedded in modern Western civilization, and is a central symptom of the crisis of that civilization. It is now commonly understood that the current environmental destruction has its roots in Western industrial civilization and its engine, modern technocracy – that is, modernity in the form of science and technology.

The recent context for our common action as stewards of life for all living beings is defined by the experience of the clash of civilizations, the confrontation between East and West, between modern and 'pre-modern' cultures. Over the past two centuries, Asia has been trapped in the vortex of these violent cultural, spiritual and religious confrontations.[2]

The impact of Western technocracy upon Asia, arriving as colonizer with the modern nation state and the capitalist industrial economy, has been the deep erosion of Asian civilizations, especially during the past two or three centuries. During this time, Asia has been profoundly affected by Western civilization in the form of Western Christianity

---

[1] Kim Yong-Bock is Founder and Chancellor of the Asia Pacific Center for Integral Study of Life and Endowed Professor at the Hanshin University, Seoul. He is a widely respected Korean Minjung Theologian who graduated from Princeton Theological Seminary with a PhD on 'Historical Transformation, People's' Movement and Christian Koinonia' (1976).

[2] Arnold Joseph Toynbee, *The World and the West* (Oxford: Oxford University Press, 1953).

and the Western technocracy, that is, the symbiotic convergence of the industrial and military economy, communications, and the scientific culture including technetronics, artificial intelligence (AI) and nano-technology.[3]

The impact of modernity has come through violent modes: commercial and economic encroachments, colonial invasions and domination, the introduction of the modern nation state, the globalization of a capitalist economy – most recently the neoliberal economic regime – and the global military regime that has waged hegemonic geopolitical confrontations in the form of hot and cold wars over the last century. This process is likely to accelerate.

The corrosion of Asian societies and nations has been integrated into a global symbiosis of Westernization with Asian religions, as in Japan (Shinto religion), the Indian continent (Hinduism) and Indonesia and other Islamic nations (Islam). Our human community is searching for ways to overcome the ecological crisis, including climate change and the destruction of the biosphere itself. The basic framework of modernity now dominates the globe and is aggressing against all life.

In the context of the Christian faith community, two interrelated questions should be asked: (1) In what ways have Christian faith traditions in the West promoted the ecological crisis by eroding the spiritual foundation of the 'zoe-sphere' of humans and other beings? (2) In what ways can the Christian faith participate in transformative, prophetic action to overcome this crisis of the destruction of life in the ecosphere and zoe-sphere?

The Christian faith has destroyed Indigenous and other non-Christian spiritualities during the rise of Western modernity, through the influence of science and technology, modern nation states, global economic capitalism, and technocratic convergence including even 'transhumanism' in the military, political, social and cultural spheres. Secularized 'messianic' triumphalism, as expressed in technocratic secularism and in political power obtained through colonial and imperial domination and cultural hegemony, has been embraced by the Christian faith.

Christianity needs a spiritual conversion that will allow it to foster a convivial community among all living beings. A radical, critical reorientation and creative self-transformation of the Christian faith is needed, if it is going to confront and overcome the current civilization of violence caused by technocratic, political, economic and cultural greed and hegemony.

Lynn White Jr. has argued that Christian cosmology, expressed in the doctrine of creation, is one of the chief factors in modern Western civilization with its industrialization and technocracy.[4] This poses a critical challenge to the whole of Christianity, which – in Asia and elsewhere – has been deeply implicated in the history of destruction of life on

---

[3] Mihail C. Roco and William Sims Bainbridge (eds), *Converging Technologies for Improving Human Performance Nanotechnology, Biotechnology, Information Technology And Cognitive Science*, NSF/DOC-sponsored report (Sims Bainbridge, National Science Foundation, June 2002).

[4] Lynn White, Jr, 'The Historical Roots of Our Ecological Crisis', *Science* 155 (1967), 1203–7.

earth. The charge is made that the Christian doctrine of creation, which enjoins humans to exert dominion over all other living beings, has opened the way to the secularization and de-spiritualization of the whole of creation, including humans. Earth's ecological crisis is at the centre of this process. Admittedly, some Western theologians and ecologists, such as Thomas Berry, see Asian traditions as undergirding the ethics of ecological integrity and preservation.

One way to respond to this situation is through the radical convergence of the religious wisdom of all the world religions and popular religions, in the process of which the Christian faith will experience transformation. Modern Christianity within the framework of Western civilization alone has little hope for such transformation. Actually, the missiology of Western Christianity, along with cultural colonialism, has been destructive of Asian spiritualities. Even the programme of 'indigenizing' Christianity in the non-Western world has been marked by profound suspicion from non-Christian religions.[5]

It is in this sense that Jesus of Galilee must be rescued and liberated from the modern Western cultural, political and economic configurations of power under the colonial hegemony of the global market and empire. I believe Christianity can be transformed through a process of creative convergence with other spiritualities. In this creative, transformative convergence for a holistic spirituality of life, there is no room for fragmentation into different dimensions, thus isolating the ecosphere from the lives of all living beings. That is, there is no way we can isolate ecological discourse from an integral discourse of life. I believe that the East Asian philosophical perspective can be developed and converged with its Western counterpart. This may be a good way to construct an integral discourse on ecology and life for all living beings.

Integral study of life as a framework to relate ecology and spirituality

A universal crisis of life is taking place for all beings, and it is not limited to the ecological dimension. This serious, ongoing ecological disruption has broad implications for the whole of life. It is closely related to the economy, culture and all other dimensions of life. It therefore forms a central part of the integral study of life, which searches for 'zoesophia', wisdom of life.

The integral study of life is holistic and integral. This study is not fragmented, compartmentalized or specialized, nor is it merely a biological study. It takes a

---

[5] See www.bu.edu/missiology/missionary-biography/i-k/kraemer-hendrik-1888-1965/ (accessed 24 March 2019).

multidisciplinary approach. Rather than being a composite of specialized studies, it is the convergent integration of all aspects of life. In East Asia we may call it 'wisdom of life'. It affirms that life is a subjective agency, not an object: living beings live actively as the subject of their own existence. Living beings live together, forming the community of conviviality on earth. Integral and holistic study sees life together in all its dimensions: as the spirit of the body and community of all living beings, and as the body and community of the living spirit of all living beings.

As an academic study, the integral study of life (生命學) rejects the reductionism and fragmented specialization of modern natural science. It therefore undertakes a multidisciplinary study of the whole of life in all its dimensions. I have been exploring the convergence of diverse and even divergent studies of life. In this convergence process there appears a new horizon that goes beyond every dimension of life or the sum of those dimensions. The emergence of the new horizon points to life constantly evolving into new living beings. Beings living together give birth to the next generation of living beings. As subjects, they are born, grow into mature beings, feed themselves, heal themselves and seek to fulfil themselves. They live in a universe of conviviality, not as mere individual beings. The integral study of life cannot happen outside of the convivial context of living beings in the cosmos.

I propose that ecology should be seen in the context of the integral study of life, not as a separate issue from life as a whole. At times the ecological crisis is being treated as a separate issue, which is misguided and dangerous. We can clarify this holistically from the perspective of the integral study of life.

Religions form the spiritual foundation of life for all living beings

Indigenous religions as well as the so-called world religions affirm the proposition that all living beings are spiritual subjects both singularly and in community, and that they are spiritually intertwined with one another and with the natural environment. The global community of life on earth has a spiritual foundation, a spiritual 'arche' (*T'aegeuk*: the Ultimate Pivot: 태극 太極), which has sustained the life of all living beings in every part of earth.

The religions of Asia are enshrined in the community of all living beings. Religious faiths should be seen as expressions of the spirituality that is the foundation of life of all living beings. For when we accept that all living beings are spiritual subjects we will start to see the communities of life as *spiritual* communities. This is radically different from the modern scientific worldview. The celebration of secularization within modern theological discourse should be re-evaluated. The spirit of secularity may be regarded as a different form of spirituality. Likewise, modern political ideologies as well as imperial ideologies have spiritual underpinnings, just as each world religion has its own spirituality. Therefore it is natural to reflect upon the issue of ecology in relation to religions and their spiritualities.

Shamanism believes that all the world is alive, and by learning from plants and animals, rocks and mountains, winds and waters, from the sun, moon and stars, shamans have helped their people to live in balance with the universe. Spiritual ecology teaches us how all living things, visible and invisible, are connected. Seen from the shaman's perspective, many current environmental difficulties are related to being out of balance, both with the world and within ourselves. By reawakening a feeling of connection, we come to remember that the Earth is our home, and that we are all part of life on earth.[6]

Let me illustrate the co-participation of all the different religions, major religions as well as Indigenous (original) religions in every corner of the earth, as the spirituality of life of all living beings, starting with the Korean peninsula.

The Korean peninsula is on the eastern edge of the Eurasian continent. This peninsula has been very much a spiritual community of all its living beings. The archaic 'gestalt' is called *Seon* (선仙), which is the saga of a shamanic spirituality. It is manifested in the communal framework of the peninsula: the all-embracing, comprehensive well-being of human beings, the conviviality ('convivencia') of all living beings, and great peace (*T'aiping*) on earth. The spiritual foundation of *Seon* forms a matrix of spiritual convergence in the Korean peninsula. Buddhist faith, Confucian teaching and Taoist wisdom all converge with the spiritual base of *Seon*. Once we see the history of Korean religions as a process of spiritual convergence of different religions centred in Korean *Seon* spirituality, a Korean brand of Shaman spirituality, an 'Indigenous' Korean Christian faith should be understood in terms of this process of spiritual convergence as well.[7]

Towards a new discourse on ecology?

A new discourse on ecology rejects fragmentation of the order of life into spirit, body, society and cosmos. Life forms an integral whole. Zhang Hwe Ik, a Korean physical scientist, has introduced the concept of 'global life' to help us think about life as a whole community.[8] The concept of 'global life' examines the position and role of humanity in the world of life in light of the ontological structure of life itself. Following Zhang Hui-

---

[6] See for instance the work of the Scandinavian Center for Shamanic Studies http://www.shamanism.dk/ (accessed 24 March 2019).
[7] Spencer J. Palmer, *Korea and Christianity, the Problem of Identification with Tradition* (Seoul: Royal Asiatic Society, 1986).
[8] Zhang Hwe Ik, 'Global Life and the Significance of the Human Being', *Cogito* 60 (2006).

ik's insights I argue that the only meaningful unit of life is 'global life', framed in a star-planet system. Any other possible unit of life exhibited by various kinds of individuals is conditional in the sense that it would leave out an essential part of 'global life'. The relationship between human beings and global life should be understood in this general scheme. It is emphasized, however, that the human being occupies a unique position in global life in the sense that humanity can promote either a cancerous situation or a healthy higher-order enhancement of global life.

Life as a whole is the fundamental framework in the East Asian tradition of cosmology. This framework rejects any form of reductionism or fragmentation in epistemology as found in the modern West. The cosmos is understood neither on a linear timescale nor as a Cartesian extension of space. The Alpha and Omega of time and space is one and the same point which embraces the whole at all times. This is illustrated by the *Book of Changes*, which permeates East Asian religious and philosophical thinking and popular culture. Unfortunately, this understanding has been neglected during the last two centuries, especially during the last century, due to modernization. This should be corrected; much study is needed to restore the wisdom of life and consequently to search for a new discourse on ecology.

In East Asian philosophy the cosmos is the house of life. All living beings and their house are organically interconnected. The cosmic order is the very order of conviviality. It is not that there are no contradictions in the order of conviviality, but that contradictions and conflicts are subsumed and integrated in the order of convivial community. Naturally, knowledge of life is the integral wisdom of life.

East Asian wisdom of life

East Asian civilization has a long history of rich wisdom about life. But there has been a serious lack of study and development in recent centuries. Particularly since the time of the Western onslaught on the East and the rest of the world, the development of East Asian wisdom has been discarded or neglected. The Westernization and modernization drive of the East Asian nations caused this historical disaster. East Asian philosophy and religion, along with their practical dimensions, took a back seat in the history making of the nations of East Asia. The tragic consequence has been the downplaying of Asian wisdom, especially during the last two centuries.

Thus we need to revive East Asian studies to the level that they are given equal importance with Western studies and make decisive differences. What I hope for is a convergence of East and West in the search for wisdom of life. East Asian studies in the West were initiated to serve the interests of Western political, economic and cultural power. Some of the authentic studies on East Asia were done to complement the West, rather than find ways of coming together in a deep and meaningful way.

The convergence of East Asian wisdom and spirituality

The Taoist universe is one, but infinitely diverse. Its unity is implied by the fact that all dimensions of existence, from the budding of a flower to the orbit of the stars, may be denominated in terms of *Qi (ch'i)* the fundamental energy-matter of the universe whose dynamic pattern is a cosmic heartbeat of expansion *(yang)* and contraction *(yin)*. Its diversity is a function of the complex interaction of the myriad cosmic processes, both light and fluid and heavy and dense. The universe is a single, vital organism, not created according to some fixed principle but spontaneously regenerating itself.

East Asian Buddhism affirms compassion as the central value in the universe, caring for all living beings as well as overcoming the dichotomy of subject and object in its epistemology. It is interesting to investigate the convergence of East Asian religions on this point. Even East Asian Christianity, differentiating itself from Western theologies, converges with East Asian religions, as illustrated in K.H. Ting's notion of the 'Cosmic Love of Christ'.[9]

Another example of the attempt to explore ecological discourse in Buddhist terms is found in the notion of 'Dharma Gaia', or 'earth consciousness'. A volume with that title edited by Allan Hunt Badiner brings together ecologists and Buddhists to examine the spiritual roots of the ecological crisis.[10] This suggests the need to restore human powers of perception and to understand that humans are interconnected with each other and the cosmos. The essays in the volume are grouped together as 'Green Buddhism', 'Shifting Views of Perception', 'Experiencing Extended Mind', 'Becoming Sangha', 'Meditations', and a 'Call to Action'. Badiner advocates the transformation of egocentricity into eco-centricity and recalls the Buddhist concepts of *paticca samuppada* (dependent co-origination) and *sunyata* (emptiness) to emphasize the interdependence of reality.

A Confucian view of ecology rooted in an organic view of the universe

The worldview of Confucianism is characterized by four key elements: an anthropocosmic rather than an anthropocentric perspective, an organic holism of the continuity of being, a dynamic vitalism of material force *(ch'i, qi)*, and a comprehensive ethics embracing

---

[9] See K. H. Ting (Ding Guangxun), *God is Love: Collected Writings of Bishop K. H. Ting* (Cook Communications Ministries International, 2004).

[10] Allan Hunt Badiner (ed.), *Dharma Gaia: A Harvest of Essays in Buddhism and Ecology* (Berkeley: Parallax Press, 1990).

both humans and nature. 'Anthropocosmic' refers to the great triad of heaven (a guiding force), earth (nature), and humans. This idea is central to Confucian thought from its earliest expressions in the classical texts to its later developments in neo-Confucianism, which arose in the eleventh century. The seamless interaction of these three forces contrasts markedly with the more human-centred orientation of Western traditions, where personal salvation in relation to a divine figure is central.

The sense of holism is characterized by the view that there is no Creator God behind the universe. Chinese thought is less concerned with theories of origin or with concepts of a personal God than with the perception of an ongoing reality of a self-generating, interconnected universe, described by Tu Wei-Ming as a 'continuity of being'.[11] 'Dynamic vitalism' refers to the underlying unity of reality which is constituted of *ch'i*, the material force of the universe. This is the unifying element of the cosmos and creates the basis for a profound reciprocity between humans and the natural world. Material force *(ch'i)* as the substance of life is the basis for the continuing processes of change and transformation in the universe. The term *sheng-sheng* – 'production and reproduction' – is repeatedly used in Confucian texts to illustrate the creativity of nature. This recognition of the ceaseless movement of the cosmos arises from a profound meditation on the fecundity of nature in continually giving birth to new life. Furthermore, it constitutes a sophisticated awareness that change is the basis of the web of life systems – mineral, vegetable, animal and human. Finally, it celebrates transformation as the clearest expression of the creative processes of life with which humans should harmonize their own actions. In essence, human beings are urged to 'model themselves on the ceaseless vitality of the cosmic process'.[12]

East Asian accounts of the universe (宇宙 = household) have profound implications for discourses on life and ecology. There can be no separation between living beings and ecology, which is an integral part of the cosmic household of all living beings. Accordingly, there is a radical difference between modern Western cosmology, which tends to be dualistic, and the Eastern organic view of the cosmos as the abode of all living beings.

The East Asian philosophy of ecology and life as an integral whole entails an ethics of cosmic compassion as an organic part of the cosmology. Confucians advocate compassionate care (惻隱之心) for all living beings. This was the philosophical ethics of the Korean Confucian sage Yi T'oe Gye. Other than in Western thought, then, here is no separation between ethics and cosmology in Eastern philosophy.

The unity of theory and practice, science and ethics, in the organic cosmology of East Asia provides a possibility for convergence of East and West in developing a new, fresh discourse on ecology in the context of integral study of life.

---

[11] Tu Wei-Ming, *Confucian Thought: Selfhood as Creative Transformation* (Albany: SUNY, 1985).
[12] Ibid.

Convergence of East and West for new discourse of life and ecology

Western thinkers on the issue of ecology are beginning to appreciate Eastern religious, philosophical and cultural wisdom, even of 'primitive' societies. This is good progress. However, the engagement with Eastern and Indigenous worldviews is still being taken as a corrective to Western discourse on ecology. While many Eastern scholars are taking their traditional wisdom on ecology seriously, at the same time it is still secondary to the prevailing understanding and discourse of the West on ecology. The reason is that Eastern wisdom is regarded as insufficient to overcome the current ecological crisis. Eastern wisdom needs to be studied and developed to discover practical ways to deal with the ecological crisis.

One example of a theological paper that attempts to fuse the East and the West is Wioleta Polinska's article 'Ecology and Art: East Asian Traditions Meet West'.[13] It argues that 'aesthetic cosmologies in the Daoist and certain Buddhist traditions (Zen Buddhist) as well as their respective artistic traditions can provide Christianity with helpful ecological resources.'[14] In addition, examples of contemporary environmental art in the West are examined for their ecologically sensitive messages. The aesthetic traditions of East Asia display well the vision of nature in which every element of the universe is celebrated for its particular contribution. According to this model, humanity's role is not to dominate nature; rather, as members of the cosmic community, humanity needs to align (itself) with the rest of the universe. Since our culture is deeply visual, East Asian aesthetic traditions together with contemporary ecological art provide important insight (into) how to envision an environmental ethics of care.

This means that there are attempts to forge a convergence of ecological thinking and, therefore, the discourses of East and West. What will be the nature of this convergence? This is a complex question. In fact the convergence may be an open process, radically open to the ultimate 'Omega point'. Such a convergence would bring about a new horizon that would conceive new discourse on a new plane. This convergence would not nullify the diversity, or the divergence, of East and West, but would be inclusive of the diverse and divergent wisdoms with their identity and integrity.

Then we will be free from the problems of Westernization, modernization, Orientalism, acculturation, indigenization, contextualization and even hybridization in Asia, for we will seek a convergence for justice, peace and conviviality among all living beings. This is what the integral study of life (Zoe-sophia) seeks for conviviality of life in the cosmos:

1) Ecological discourse rises out of the organic cosmic order of life, which is holistic and integral. It cannot be reductionist, fragmentary, subject-object splitting, or

---

[13] Wioleta Polinska, https://www.questia.com/library/journal/1G1-168513020/ecology-and-art-east-asian-traditions-meet-west (accessed 24 March 2019).
[14] Ibid.

human–nature separating. Ecology is the cosmos (house) of convivial life for its fullness. Ecological discourse cannot be the simple scientific discourse of physics, biology or biochemistry.

2) Political discourse of life establishes the right to life for all living beings. There should be ecological rights for all living beings in heaven and earth. The polity of nation states cannot exclude the rights of all living beings.

3) The whole society becomes the cosmos (oikos) and the whole universe the society of all living beings. Discourses of justice, harmony, reconciliation, cooperation and care form an integral part of ecology. Physical and scientific laws converge with ethical principles as shown in the cosmic love of Christ among all living beings.

4) Economic discourse is easy to understand in ecological terms. *Oikonomia*, as in agriculture, is closely related to ecology. The aim of economy is the common prosperity of all living beings, not just human survival. It is a common life (*SangSaeng*: 相生 = conviviality), that is, an economy of life. So-called natural beings cannot be seen simply as natural resources, but must be regarded as living beings. The UN protocol on preservation of species needs to be reformulated to recognize all living beings as subjects.

5) Wholesomeness of life is not an isolated condition or event of the human body. Discourse on the body and spirit in health and disease is macro- and micro-cosmic and biological, religious and cultural. The ecological environment is the womb of the overall health of all living beings. Eastern medicine demonstrates this clearly; and it can be converged with Western medicine.

6) Nor can cultural and spiritual discourse be separated from ecological discourse. All of life longs to participate in an inclusive fiesta with a cosmic orchestra of music and dance. Cultural and social anthropology has been moving in this direction. Culture is not human artifice; it is co-creation among all living beings.

7) Religious and ethical discourse cannot be separated from the discourse of sciences such as physics and biology. Discourse on life ethics is cosmic, social, biological and spiritual. Spirituality and faith is the soul of the oikos (the household of life).

8) Geopolitical discourse on war and peace is seen in the context of the convivial life of all living beings, not merely in the context of nation states and geopolitical groups. In East Asia, peace means great peace, cosmic peace (T'aiping 太平). This is the complete opposite of the existing regime of military weapons systems with the capability of destroying not just human beings but all living beings in the entire ecosystem.

As I have indicated above, the ecological concern permeates the entire discourse of life, which is multidimensional. All the above eight (and more) dimensions converge at the 'Omega point' of the cosmos, just as they emerge from the 'Alpha point'. Omega and Alpha points are one in convergence as expressed in the Asian notion of *T'aeguk* (태극 = 太極 = the Great Absolute) of the universal Oikos of life of all living beings.

Spiritual hermeneutics of convergence for cosmic life in history

In the process of creative convergence with religious spiritualities, philosophies, scientific propositions and all other wisdoms, the Christian faith can be a catalytic agency to trigger a creative transformation towards a process of revitalization and even creative 'evolution' of the life of all living beings. This will bring about the self-transformation of its own faith and spirituality into a higher and richer plane.

Today the ecological crisis, and the crisis of life as a whole, is due to the symbiotic convergence of powers for political and military hegemony, uncontrolled economic greed, social discrimination, and the cultural (scientific) conquest of life. There is always the danger of a religious or spiritual symbiosis with these power realities. On the other hand, both religious and secular spiritualities have the possibility of converging with the communities of living beings for creative transformation of the 'zoesphere' so as to overcome the ecological crisis, including the challenges related to climate change.

Chapter 7.5
Doing justice to animals?

David L. Clough[1]

Human impacts on fellow animal creatures are extraordinary in scale with multiple linkages to climate change. According to estimates by Vaclav Smil by the year 1900, the combined biomass of domesticated animals had grown to exceed the biomass of all wild land mammals by three and a half times. That resulted from a combination of big increases in livestock numbers, and big decreases in wild land animals, significantly driven by the need to make space for all the livestock. Humans displaced wild animals in order to make space for raising domesticated animals for food. During the twentieth century humans quadrupled the biomass of domesticated animals, which was a major factor in the halving of wild land mammal biomass, so that by 2000 the biomass of domesticated animals was twenty-four times greater than that of all wild land mammals. Domesticated chickens alone are three times the biomass of all wild birds. And in the same one hundred years we reduced numbers of fish in the oceans by 89 per cent.[2] Raising livestock in these numbers is a major contributor to an anthropogenic mass extinction of animals comparable with those found in the geological record. If we continue on this trajectory there will be virtually no wild animals to be concerned about. If we combine this with the realization of the cruelly impoverished lives we inflict on farmed animals, the vast majority of which are raised in novel industrial environments, it is clear that attending to the impact of human activity on other animals is an urgent demand.[3]

Human practice in relation to other animals has multiple and complex linkages to the catastrophic climate change that is the theme of this volume. The raising of livestock for food on the current unprecedented scale is one of the major sources of anthropogenic carbon emissions yet is missing from many climate change strategies. Changes in animal populations resulting from global warming, especially in the oceans, will interact to

---

[1] David L. Clough is Professor of Theological Ethics at the University of Chester. His current research is on the place of animals in Christian theology and ethics. In 2015 he founded CreatureKind (http://becreaturekind.org), a project aiming to engage Christians with farmed animal welfare.
[2] Vaclav Smil, 'Harvesting the Biosphere: The Human Impact', *Population and Development Review* 37:4 (2011), 613–36 (619); Yinon M. Bar-On, Rob Phillips and Ron Milo, 'The Biomass Distribution on Earth', *Proceedings of the National Academy of Sciences, USA* (2018), 1–6 (3); Heike K. Lotze and Boris Worm, 'Historical Baselines for Large Marine Animals', *Trends in Ecology and Evolution* 24:5 (2009), 254–62 (259).
[3] For discussion of the human use of other animals for food, see David L. Clough, *On Animals*, Volume II: *Theological Ethics* (London: T&T Clark, 2019), Chapter 2, 35–90.

precipitate further climatic changes. The catastrophic impacts of climate change are already imperilling vulnerable wild animal populations and will accelerate the human-caused mass extinction event currently in process, with a majority of wild animals at risk of extinction in many climate scenarios.[4] Human populations displaced by climate change will contribute to further habitat loss and extinctions. Non-human animals are in the frontline of the effects of climate change and paying attention to their plight is a crucial component of formulating adequate theological and policy responses. Failing to attend sufficiently to the more-than-human animal world in the context of our climate catastrophe is therefore self-defeating in terms of addressing its causes and unjust in ignoring a large proportion of its victims.

Attending to other-than-human animals is also crucial for theological method, in this and most other contexts. Presenting Christian understandings of the world as concerned with only one of God's myriad creaturely kinds is in danger of failing to give an account consistent with doctrinal claims as fundamental as monotheism. If God is not merely the local deity of *Homo sapiens* but the creator of an entire vast universe of diverse creatures, living and non-living, theologies unable to interpret the meaning of the existence of more-than-human creatures in non-anthropocentric terms are obviously lacking. Other-than-human animals are one small part of this great creaturely expanse but paying attention to these close relatives is a valuable first step in opening ourselves to the wider creaturely world. Doing theology and theological ethics with attention to animals helps us escape problematic anthropocentric patterns of thinking that many contributors to this volume diagnose as a key part of addressing climate change in a theological context.[5]

Animals are not entirely missing from this volume. A number of the contributors mention problematic human attitudes and practice in relation to other animals: most notably the contributions from Lisa Sideris, Celia-Deane-Drummond, Steven Bouma-Prediger, Barbara Rossing and Tinyiko Maluleke. The structure of the volume means, however, that across seven parts and thirty-eight main essays it is only at this late stage that animals are the direct focus of attention. As a result, much of the preceding analysis remains stuck in an unhelpful human/environment binary that rushes from consideration of the single species *Homo sapiens* to consideration of everything without pausing to consider the situation of our nearest neighbours. The editors note in the introduction that engaging climate change requires attention to a wide range of cross-cutting ethical issues of which animals are but one. No doubt the champions of the other issues mentioned might also complain at the absence of essays devoted to those topics. Overlooking the importance of attending directly to animals, however, makes the task

---

[4] See, for example, IPCC, *Summary for Policymakers of the Synthesis Report of the IPCC Fourth Assessment* (Geneva: IPCC, 2007), 13–14.

[5] My attempt to set out a framework for a Christian theology and ethics of animals is the two-volume monograph *On Animals* Volume I: *Systematic Theology* (London: T&T Clark, 2012); Volume II: *Theological Ethics* (2019).

of the volume harder in particular ways: it is an obstacle to adequate analysis of causal factors leading to climate change, an obstacle to an adequate appreciation of its impacts, and an obstacle to formulating a theological and ethical methodology capable of an appropriate constructive response.

Christian theological engagement with our current situation of catastrophic climate change has a strong claim to be the most urgent priority for theologians, yet is still receiving far too little attention. In this problematic context we should warmly welcome all efforts such as this one to consider seriously how Christians may bring resources from their traditions to join with others in addressing this global emergency. This volume makes a substantial contribution to this crucial common task and does so with particular and much-needed attention to the context of theology. It will hopefully resource a new generation of scholarship and activism in this area. To be sufficient to the task, and to do justice to their fellow animal creatures, however, it will be vital for this new generation of theologians and activists to attend directly and systematically to one more issue of context – that of being humans among other animals – as a core part of their theological methodology.

Chapter 7.6
Doing justice to geographic divides?

Jesse N. K. Mugambi[1]

The Earth without borders

Viewed from Space, planet earth appears like a huge, coloured balloon, without any artificial borders – except for the mountains, volcanoes, hills and valleys; rivers, lakes and oceans; forests, deserts and polar glaciers. Artificial borders are more for self-aggrandisement than necessary. Roads, railways, canals, dams and other human additions appear rather odd in contrast with nature's own design. Cities, dams, stadia, power transmission lines; wind power turbines; solar power panels; skyscrapers; palaces; motor-racing tracks, highways, railways – all these appear rather awkward in the midst of nature's unique arrangement. Human encroachment on nature is glaringly unmistakeable. Along the coastlines the ports are identifiable – with cargo and passenger ships docked, departing or arriving. Airports appear from space like black strips of plastic stuck on flat ground, but the planes betray the purpose thereof. The farmland is distinguishable from natural forests, especially where humans have encroached. Tropical and arctic deserts are also visible. Administrative borders are invisible, except where the Global Positioning System (GPS) coordinates have been specified.

Humans are endowed with the capacity to enhance natural processes, and also to interfere with them. Apparently, humans find greater satisfaction in destroying nature, rather than enhancing it. When the extreme limit of such interference is reached, a downward spiral begins, oftentimes irreversibly. Such has been the tragedy on every continent. Human civilizations are not eternal. To reckon with this, every civilization has a religion offering an 'eternal' dimension for temporal achievements and failures. The competition within and between religions arises from the quest for plausible explanations for the inexplicable – about ultimate origin; ultimate purpose; and ultimate destiny.

Any attempt in doing away with institutionalized religion results in alternative, or substitute religiosity. This is because the inexplicable demands explication, which has

---

[1] Jesse N. K. Mugambi is Professor of Philosophy and Religious Studies at the University of Nairobi. His specializations include philosophy of religion, phenomenology of religion, ecology and applied ethics. He is an ecumenist, and for many years has been involved in the World Council of Churches' Working Group on Climate Change.

to be rationalized outside the scope of experimental or 'measurable' science. Humans are fascinated by imagination and creativity, especially in times of extreme abundance and scarcity; happiness and sorrow; wealth and destitution; life and death. From this 'religious' perspective, humans have a great deal in common, across races, ethnicities, nationalities, religions, rationalities, ideologies and civilizations. John Mbiti in his books *Concepts of God in Africa* and *Prayers of African Religion* has documented the deep respect for nature that pervaded pre-colonial African communities.[2]

Destruction of the environment was regarded as ungodly, and would accordingly be punished as warning to others. Whether in the Equatorial Forest that stretched from the shores of the Indian the Atlantic Oceans, or on the slopes of the mountains and hills across Africa, the African attitude to nature was one of care and stewardship. The European colonizers, having depleted their temperate forests in Europe, 'discovered' plenty more to squander, and much of the virgin tropical forests were converted into settlers' farms and ranches. The Christian missionary enterprise was not helpful in conserving Africa's natural ecology. On the contrary, evangelization was presented as 'civilization', which, in practice, meant the destruction of the natural environment and replacing it with 'cash crops' – for exporting to European markets. For example, in Central Kenya Christian missionaries (both Protestant and Catholic) introduced and promoted the planting of cash crops such as coffee and tea for export to Europe, replacing the natural vegetation. This interference with the natural environment had an adverse impact on the ways of life among the communities affected and a devastating impact on the economic sustainability of Tropical Africa.[3] This pattern is exacerbated by climate change.

Colonial borders versus ecological zones

Africa's national and internal administrative boundaries, inherited from the colonial era, are largely the outcome of the Berlin Conference (November 1884 to February 1885), drawn according to the political and military prowess of the fourteen nations that participated. At the Berlin Conference ecological zones were not of primary concern, except for the natural and strategic resources at stake in the negotiations – including the inhabitants that became subjects of the respective empires. A few boundaries were defined along rivers, but most were straight lines drawn on maps, without any regard for the communities on the ground. Consequently, throughout the continent of Africa

---

[2] John S. Mbiti, *Concepts of God in Africa* (Nairobi: Acton, 2012); *The Prayers of African Religion* (New York: Orbis, 1976).

[3] See, for example, Serena Belligoli, 'EU, China and the Environmental Challenge in Africa: A Case Study from Timber Industry in Gabon', https://www.ies.be/files/Belligoli-F5.pdf (accessed 6 March 2019); Godfrey F. Njimated and Nkwetta A. Aquilas, 'Impact of Timber Exports on Economic Growth in Cameroon: An Economic Investigation', https://www.ies.be/files/Belligoli-F5.pdf (accessed 6 March 2019).

there are awkward cases of families that were separated, with some relatives becoming subjects of two or more imperial powers.

This imperial legacy still lingers on.[4] The European Christian missionary enterprise enjoyed patronage of the imperial powers that occupied Africa, and often blessed conquest and occupation as divinely ordained for conversion of the 'pagan natives' to Christianity. From an ethical perspective there was no justification for invasion and conquest; no justification for drawing inter-colonial and intra-colonial boundaries completely overlooking the governance structures of the vanquished African peoples; no justification for plunder. Might never justifies right. The aftermath of the Berlin Conference still reverberates in the politics, economy and religiosity of African nations. The African Union (AU) has pledged to consolidate Africa as a political and economic block by the deadline of 2063 – the year when Africa commemorates the first centenary since the inauguration of the Organization of African Unity (OAU).[5]

The region called 'Europe' did not exist as a political entity until the eighth century CE, during the Imperium of Charlemagne. European Christianity is implicated in the popularization of 'Europe' – a term which was to distinguish the 'Christian' Empire from its 'Islamic' rival. It is ironic that the continent that for centuries boasted of being the defender of Christianity derives its name from the Greek goddess *Europa*, It is equally ironic, perhaps, for Europe to bear its name from a myth – Europa – and also to boast of secularism as the most commendable worldview. These European shifts – from paganism through Christianity to secularism – correspond with another shift, from peasantry to mechanized, urbanite economy. The industrialization of Europe, from the eighteenth century onwards, progressively distanced individuals and communities from religiosity towards scientific and also technological determinism, relegating theistic belief to the level of myth and superstition. The impact of this transformation of European social consciousness was lucidly articulated by Paul van Buren in his book *The Secular Meaning of the Gospel*, which sparked much controversy during the 1970s.[6] Hopefully, Africa will not follow the same trajectory.

---

[4] See for example, Basil Davidson, *The Black Man's Burden: Africa and the Curse of the Nation State* (London: James Currey, 1992); Walter Okumu, 'Resources & Border Disputes in Eastern Africa', *Journal of Eastern African Studies* 4:4 (2010), 279–97; Valentine A. Tellen, Juliana A. Anchang and Martin Shu, *Conflicts over Land and Pasture in North West Cameroon: Listening to the Voices of Farmers and Grazers* (Pan African Institute for Development – West Africa, 2016); Carola Lentz, 'Land Conflicts on a West African Border', *American Ethnologist* 30:2 (May 2003), 273–89; Maina Waruru, 'Two Worlds Collide', *New Internationalist,* April 2018; Joshua Craze, *Contested Borders: Continuing Tensions over the Sudan-South Sudan Border* (Geneva: Graduate Institute of International and Development Studies, 2014).

[5] African Union, *Agenda 2063: The Africa We Want* (Addis Ababa, 2013).

[6] Paul van Buren, *The Secular Meaning of the Gospel* (New York: Macmillan, 1966).

Sub-Sahara Africa and Sub-Tundra Europe?

The name of this continent called 'Africa' is derived not from such a myth as *Europa* – after which the European Continent is named.[7] Rather, Africa's name is an extension of that narrow strip of coastland along the southern shores of the Mediterranean Sea, which in 46 BC was named *Africa Proconsularis* under the Roman emperor Julius Caesar. The headquarters of *Africa Proconsularis* was at Carthage near the present city of Tunis in Tunisia and included all the territory stretching from the Atlas Mountains to the Red Sea.

However, by the fifteenth century the label 'Africa' had long ceased to be applicable exclusively for the former *Africa Procosularis* of Julius Caesar. An African contemporary of Martin Luther (1483–1546) called Leo Africanus (c.1485–c.1554) was commissioned by Pope Leo X (1475–1521) to write a report on 'Africa', which is perhaps the oldest known documentary about the peoples and cultures between the Niger River and the Sahara Desert. Leo Africanus reported that the Kingdom of 'Tombukto' was a prosperous reign founded by King Mense Suleiman, on the northern banks of the Niger, in the present-day Republic of Mali. According to Leo Africanus, it was so prosperous as to attract scholars and merchants from as far as Europe, with flourishing trading in gold, fabrics, foods and jewels. His report, written in the mid-sixteenth century, sounds contemporary in the twenty-first. At Sankore there was a university with as many as 25,000 scholars, dating from the thirteenth century.

In the twentieth century CE it has become fashionable among Europeans to separate the northern part of Africa from the rest of the continent, perhaps on recollection that the imperium of Julius Caesar included all of southern Europe; the lands on the southern shores of the Mediterranean Sea from the Atlantic Ocean to the Red Sea; and all the lands along the eastern shores of the Mediterranean and around the Black Sea.[8] It is from this European legacy that label 'Africa' has remained when referring to the extension of European hegemony southwards across the Mediterranean.

During the last quarter of the twentieth-century attempts were made in the media to popularize the phrase 'Sub-Saharan Africa', as if the Sahara Desert was conceptually more important than the Mediterranean Sea and the African continent.

Grammatically, the label 'Sub-Sahara' Africa gives cognitive prominence to the Sahara Desert, with desolation and barrenness that the word connotes. The popularization of this label in Western Media and Academia has the impact of shifting cognitive attention from the positive innovations in Tropical Africa, towards the negative impact of imperial rule in this continent. If the label 'Sub-Sahara Africa' is valid, then perhaps the phrase 'Sub-Tundra Europe' should also become normative for all the nations north of the Mediterranean Sea. Europe lies south of the Arctic Desert called the Tundra, in the same

---

[7] See https://www.britannica.com/story/where-does-the-name-europe-come-from (accessed 14 February 2019).

[8] On this point see https://www.bible-history.com/maps/romanempire/Africa.html (accessed 14 February 2019).

way that Tropical Africa lies south of the Tropical Desert called the Sahara. Such abuse of language, however, is irresponsible and unethical – both for Europe and for Africa.

A similar attempt was made to separate the Southern Cone of Africa from the rest of Africa, whereby 'Dutch South Africa' was portrayed as an outpost of Europe and European culture – 'home away from home'. Throughout the twentieth century the Pan-Africanist movement campaigned for a different self-understanding involving African intellectuals within Africa, Europe, North America and also in the Caribbean. Through their campaign, and the struggles within Africa, national sovereignty was finally achieved, and in 1963 the Organization of African Unity (OAU) was born – transformed into the African Union (AU) in 2013. The AU's first centenary, in 2063, will commemorate at least two important events: the inauguration of the OAU (1963), and the Second Vatican Council – during which the anathema against Protestant Christianity was lifted (1962-65).

In 1959 the American anthropologist George Murdock published a map of Africa, illustrating the inexplicable inconsistency between ethnic identities and administrative boundaries. There can be no justification for the straight-line administrative boundaries that respected neither geographical features nor ethnic identities. Postcolonial Africa has to contend with this ridiculous colonial legacy. Through Agenda 2063, the African Union aspires to transcend this mess, not by redrawing the boundaries, but by transcending them.[9]

Rivers, streams, valleys, hills and mountains are often used as landmarks for internal, national and regional borders. There is no intrinsic correlation between national borders and ecological zones. It often happens that a mountain is shared between multiple nations, and that a river is shared by many nations both along and across. In Africa, the Nile River Basin is shared by eleven nations: Egypt; Sudan; South Sudan; Ethiopia; Uganda; DRC; Rwanda Burundi; Eritrea; Kenya; Tanzania The Zambezi is shared by eight nations: Angola; Namibia; Botswana; Zambia; Zimbabwe; Malawi; Tanzania and Mozambique. The Niger River Basin is shared by nine nations: Benin; Burkina Faso; Cameroon; Chad, Côte d'Ivoire, Guinea, Mali, Niger. Six countries share the Rhine: Switzerland, Principality of Liechtenstein, Austria, Germany, France and the Netherlands. The Amazon borders nine South American nations, the largest of which is Brazil. The others are Ecuador, Venezuela, Suriname, Peru, Columbia, Bolivia, Guyana and French Guiana.

Interestingly, the Amazon is to South America as the Congo, the Nile and the Niger are to Africa; the Euphrates and Tigris to West Asia; and the Rhine to Western Europe. Only in colonial (and postcolonial) Africa do most administrative borders run in straight lines, completely ignoring anthropological, linguistic and religious considerations. This imperial legacy is indicative of the dehumanising impact of imperialism in Africa.

---

[9] For this map, see https://peterslarson.com/2011/01/19/african-conflict-and-ethnic-distribution/ (accessed 15 January 2019).

Concluding observations

The World Happiness Index seems to confirm the insights outlined above. Consistently, the nations with the highest degree of happiness have been those which accord highest priority to sustainable ecological management – the nations outside the Tropics, including those near the Arctic Circle.[10]

There is a glaring paradox here, namely that the nations of Tropical Africa, endowed with the most favourable ecological habitat, also seem to be the most miserable! Perhaps the explanation for this paradox is to be found in the imperial history of Africa, and its postcolonial aftermath. Internal and external national boundaries of African nations were externally imposed, for convenience of the conquerors – not that of the vanquished. Consequently, administrative borders within and across African territories ripped families apart, without the possibility of re-unification. Tanzania resolved the problem through the national unitary policy of *Ujamaa,* while Kenya has taken the opposite route of 'devolution' into forty-seven Counties. Any meaningful discussion of climate mitigation and adaptation with reference to the African context needs to take this imperial history and its postcolonial aftermath into account.

During the Fourth United Nations Environment Assembly (UNEA 4) in Nairobi (11-15 March 2019) many governmental and non-governmental agencies re-affirmed the necessity for action – at local, national, regional and global levels – to take such measures as will stabilize, and also begin to reduce the adverse human impact on the Environment at all levels. All three strategies are essential – precaution, adaptation and mitigation. Only a few days after UNEA 4, on 18 March 2019, Cyclone Idai inundated coastal Mozambique, eastern Zimbabwe and southern Malawi, causing many deaths, destroying infrastructure and making thousands of people homeless. The 'extreme weather events' predicted by climate scientists will cause more devastation in years to come.

According to NASA and the National Oceanic and Atmospheric Administration (NOAA), the year 2018 was the fourth warmest since 1880 –especially in the Arctic region. Such extreme weather events devastate whole regions, across national borders. National environment policies in one country or region result in ecological disaster in other countries and regions, both far and near. The current global ecological crisis is a clarion call for all nations – especially those with the highest carbon dioxide emission per capita, to rethink their policies, and commit themselves to mitigate for the damage already caused, while reorienting their industrial policies towards low-carbon economies and arranging for mitigation for the damage already caused – both at home and abroad. Exemplary leadership at the global level is essential for any such commitment to become self-evident and self-explanatory. Nations with the highest per capita emissions also have the means and capability for alternatives, which can provide the cue for the rest.

---

[10] See https://countryeconomy.com/demography/world-happiness-index (accessed 6 March 2019).

Global warming is a *global* challenge. Some nations have contributed more or less than others. Some have been more adversely affected than others. The crisis is cross-national and cross regional. It is in recognition of this complexity that the UN Framework Convention on Climate Change (UNFCCC) recognizes the principle of Common but Differentiated Responsibilities and Respective Capabilities (CBDR–RC). Ideally, those who pollute more should pay more for mitigation and adaptation across borders and regions. The challenge is that there are no mechanisms to enforce compliance, with the consequence that the weakest and the poorest bear the brunt of the richer and the more powerful.

Chapter 7.7
Doing justice to carbon mitigation?

Hans Diefenbacher[1]

In this impressive volume, in accordance with about 97 per cent of the scientists dealing with this issue, there is no doubt that climate change influenced by the activity of humanity is seen as one of the major dangers of the twenty-first century, and that we are confronted with the realization that climate change is already happening. Connected with climate change, there is a fundamental problem of justice: the impacts of greenhouse gas emissions are very unequally distributed, on a global scale and also within countries. This holds true in two different ways: the inequality concerns the positive and, separated from it, the negative external effects of carbon emissions – people enjoy the benefits of the use of such energy to a very different extent, while people suffer from the negative external effects of climate change in very different ways, as Kevin O'Brien shows, for example, very clearly in the case of Bolivia, in his contribution. This is one of the core issues that the present volume addresses in a dialogue involving Christian ethicists and theologians as well as economists and scientists from other disciplines.

This fundamental inequality is deeply rooted in history. One side of it can be described by what the editors call the 'North Atlantic' – rich Western countries with an economic orientation towards exploitation not only of nature connected with a Christianity that is 'the most anthropocentric religion the world has seen'.[2] Within these countries, 'nearly everyone participates in the systemic production of a planetary problem, no matter their own intentions or desires', as Willis Jenkins maintains. To understand how capitalist economics is tied to ecology and religion is a central question, also for understanding the dynamics of climate change. On the one hand, there are fundamental debates in economics, namely on the question whether the current economic system is dependent on growth or more or less open to de-growth strategies, and on the role of technological solutions to environmental problems and the possibility of de-coupling growth from resource and energy consumption. Could dematerialization of consumption solve the

---

[1] Hans Diefenbacher, born in Mannheim, Germany (1954), studied economics at the universities of Heidelberg, Freiburg and Kassel, and is Deputy Director of the Protestant Institute for Interdisciplinary Research and Extraordinary Professor of Economics at the Alfred-Weber-Institute of the University of Heidelberg. His main research interests include the relation between ecology and economy and the history of economic thought.

[2] Lynn White, Jr, 'The Historical Roots of Our Ecologic Crisis', *Science* 155:3767 (1967), 1203–7 (1205).

ecological problem, especially in rich countries? For a possible answer, it is necessary to assess the probability of de-growth, the probability of a wide acceptance and radical change in lifestyle, a new orientation around social and ethical values, maybe even the success of transnational social movements. A theological position corresponding to these findings can be seen in liberation theology.[3] The present volume shows a richness of theological approaches underlining the necessity of carbon mitigation as a core issue in the transition to a sustainable future.

What can be done to promote the idea that action on carbon mitigation might be more urgent than is commonly adhered to today? The first conclusion that can be drawn from the present volume is far from being trivial: We have to maintain the consensus within the global society that climate change has to be seen as a cause for immediate and urgent action: any carbon reduction plan until 2050, requiring a reduction by 95 per cent for affluent countries, can be reached only if we act today.

Mitigation can be realized mainly through two different options: (1) by substituting carboniferous fuels by others, and (2) by reducing energy consumption either by increasing energy efficiency or by a reduction of energy consuming activities, and all of these activities have to be put to the test: housing, mobility, agriculture, just to name a few of them.

How far should carbon mitigation go? There are the results of the COP conference in Paris (2015), that breathe a spirit of pragmatic optimism: on the one hand there is an attempt not to formulate goals that are unrealistic, on the other hand, the message is spread that an intelligent climate protection is feasible and even not too expensive if started timeously. But virtually every international debate on the speed and extent of climate protection is inevitably intertwined with differences in perceptions of international justice – and with the failure of neoclassical economic theory that is evidently not prepared to even address this dimension of the question in any meaningful way. Therefore, environmental economics has to go beyond the standard paradigm of economics, and it must be open for an interdisciplinary discussion – where theology has a place.

Can we describe the criteria for a globally effective strategy for carbon mitigation? The Paris Agreement, indeed, gives a few beacons for orientation:

First, we need to know for every year to come the maximum amount of greenhouse gas that might be emitted. This maximum amount should be reduced by a certain safety margin to take scientific uncertainties into consideration that still exist.

- This amount of greenhouse gas emissions has to be distributed globally; this could be done by using a so-called grandfathering principle, reflecting the ideas of justice that are common to the participating nations: Either every person on earth should receive the same right to pollute, or the right to pollute in a given year could, as a possible point of starting the process, be oriented at the pollution of the year before, but should reflect the necessity to reduce global emissions.

---

[3] See, for example, Leonardo Boff, *Cry of the Earth, Cry of the Poor* (Maryknoll: Orbis Books, 1997).

- All the emissions rights for a certain year could be offered at a special stock exchange; the total revenue could be evenly distributed among all participants, or it could be used to finance additional mitigation actions.
- If there are no such common visions of justice, a compromise has to be found that could be commonly accepted. The rules quoted above could be combined as desired.

Even if there is a version of the grandfathering principle that could be accepted globally, it remains of course the question whether grandfathering *within* nations could be regarded by the majority of their citizens as just. The problem is that international and national trading of emission rights is questioning the justice of trade systems and monetary systems in general far beyond the justice of the emissions trade itself: just consider the difference between the trading positions of 'soft currency' and 'hard currency' countries. International trade prices will be influenced much more by hard currency countries.

Climate policy on a global level can only succeed if:

- poor countries get an appropriate weight in international bargaining procedures on climate mitigation schemes;
- if there will be a global distribution of emission rights that can be accepted as just by all the participants in COP conferences;
- if the path of the reduction of greenhouse gas emissions is demanding enough to get to a nearly carbon free economy by 2050;
- if structural imbalances on the world financial markets do not outweigh by far the influence of a global emission trading scheme.

Currently, there is no global structure that can legally enforce carbon obligations. But there is some common ground on universal human responsibility that is widely recognized by humankind. A global policy on climate protection to promote mitigation is not possible without appealing to criteria of international justice. The polluters pay principle and the principle of a complete internalization of external costs are widely accepted – as normative and regulatory ideas that are valid *theoretically*. In global climate negotiations, any attempt to put these principles into practice has failed thus far. Important questions of monetarization and assignment are still unsolved, while the inequality of the current emissions per capita is so big that the main emitters substitute discussions of the problem of justice with debates that address many details of emissions trading schemes, bypassing the basic problem of unjust distribution.

It is not uncommon to hear people express a sense of feeling powerless, especially insofar as they feel unable to influence climate politics in a meaningful and relevant way. People also often express a sense of helplessness stemming from being overwhelmed by the way the structural complexity of the problem intersects with their daily life. In his essay Willis Jenkins describes how our everyday activities – cooking a meal, lighting a room – that were 'never intrinsically wrong and would remain innocent if performed under different conditions … are now caught up in wrong only because of their aggregation with trillions of other acts contribute – in a non-linear way across vast scales of time and space – to cumulative dangers'. Yet while there are serious reasons to be overwhelmed, there are signs of hope in the pages of this Companion. There is some optimism in the conviction expressed by the editors that what has been part of the problem in mitigating climate change can become part of the solution. It might be possible to change the basic orientation of technological development – towards people and nature, instead of capital profits. It may be possible to create a network of new alliances, a new form of togetherness centred around care of creation. All of this will require 'swimming counter to a rising tide', as Terra Schwerin Rowe puts it in her contribution, but it is not impossible. International climate politics will benefit a lot from such a movement countering a rising tide.

Select bibliography

This select bibliography includes only entries referred to in contributions to this volume that are directly relevant for both climate change and Christian theology. Exceptions are allowed for monographs and edited volumes in ecotheology that address ecological concerns more generally. Except for significant statements by church leaders and ecclesial publications on climate change, references to websites are not included.

Abramides, Elias C. and Juan A. Taffi, 'WCC Participation in UN Conferences on Climate Change', in *Spiritual Values for Earth Community*, David G. Hallman (ed.) (Geneva: WCC, 2012), 153–60.
Anglican Consultative Council and the Anglican Environmental Network, *The World is our Host: A Call to Urgent Action for Climate Justice* (Cape Town, 2015).
Aquino, María Pilar (ed.), 'Laudato Sí' and Ecology', *Voices* 39:2 (2016), 1–199.
Atkinson, David, *Renewing the Face of the Earth* (Norwich: Canterbury Press, 2008).
Ayre, Clive W. and Ernst M. Conradie (eds), *The Church in God's Household: Protestant Perspectives on Ecclesiology and Ecology* (Pietermaritzburg: Cluster Publications, 2016).
Bartholomew (Patriarch), *On Earth as in Heaven: Ecological Vision and Initiatives of Ecumenical Patriarch Bartholomew*, John Chryssavgis (ed.) (New York: Fordham University Press, 2012).
Bartholomew (Patriarch) and Justin Welby, 'Climate Change and Moral Responsibility', https://www.nytimes.com/2015/06/20/opinion/climate-change-and-moral-responsibility.html (accessed 4 December 2018).
Bauckham, Richard, *The Bible and Ecology: Rediscovering the Community of Creation* (London: Darton, Longman, and Todd, 2010).
Bauckham, Richard, *Living With Other Creatures: Green Exegesis and Theology* (Waco: Baylor University Press, 2011).
Bauman, Whitney A., *Religion and Ecology: Developing a Planetary Ethic* (New York: Columbia Press, 2014).
Bauman, Whitney A., *Theology, Creation and Environmental Ethics* (London: Routledge, 2014).
Bedford-Strohm, Heinrich, 'Tilling and Caring for the Earth: Public Theology and Ecology', *International Journal of Public Theology* 1 (2007), 230–48.
Bergmann, Sigurd, 'Climate Change Changes Religion: Space, Spirit, Ritual, Technology – Through a Theological Lens', *Studia Theologica* 63 (2009), 98–118.
Bergmann, Sigurd, 'The Legacy of Trinitarian Cosmology in the Anthropocene: Transcontextualising Late Antiquity Theology for Late Modernity', *Studia Theologica* 69:1 (2015), 32–44.
Bergmann, Sigurd, 'Time Turned into Space – At Home on Earth: Wanderings in Eschatological Spatiality', in *Eschatology as Imagining the End: Faith between Hope and Despair*, Sigurd Bergmann (ed.) (London: Routledge, 2018), 88–112.
Bernstein, Ellen, *The Splendor of Creation: A Biblical Ecology* (Cleveland: Pilgrim, 2005).
Berry, Thomas, *The Dream of the Earth* (San Francisco: Sierra Club, 1988).
Blanchard, Kathryn and Kevin J. O'Brien, *An Introduction to Christian Environmentalism* (Waco: Baylor, 2014).

Bloomquist, Karen L. (ed.), *God, Creation and Climate Change: Spiritual and Ethical Perspectives* (Geneva: Lutheran World Federation, 2009).
Boff, Leonardo and Virgilio P. Elizondo (eds), *Ecology and Poverty: Cry of the Earth, Cry of the Poor, Concilium*, 1995/5 (Maryknoll: Orbis, 1995).
Boff, Leonardo, *Cry of the Earth, Cry of the Poor* (Maryknoll: Orbis, 1997).
Bong, Sharon A., 'Not Only for the Sake of Man: Asian Feminist Theological Responses to *Laudato Si*'', in *Planetary Solidarity: Global Women's Voices on Christian Doctrine and Climate Justice*, Grace Ji-Sun Kim and Hilda P. Koster (eds), (Minneapolis: Fortress, 2017), 81–96.
Bookless, Dave, 'Jesus is Lord … of All? Evangelicals, Earth Care and the Scope of the Gospel', in *Creation Care in Christian Mission*, Kapya J. Kaoma (ed.) (Oxford: Regnum Studies in Mission, 2016), 105–20.
Bouma-Prediger, Steven, *For the Beauty of the Earth: A Christian Vision for Creation Care* (Grand Rapids: Baker Academic, 2007).
Bouma-Prediger, Steven, *Earthkeeping and Character: Exploring a Christian Ecological Virtue Ethic* (Grand Rapids: Baker Academic, 2019).
Brown, William P., *Sacred Sense: Discovering the Wonder of God's Word and World* (Louisville: Westminster John Knox, 2015).
Brunner, Daniel, Jennifer Butler and Andrew J. Swoboda, *Introducing Evangelical Ecotheology* (Grand Rapids: Baker Academic, 2014).
Buckingham, Susan and Virginie Le Masson (eds), *Understanding Climate Change through Gender Relations* (London: Routledge, 2019).
Butkus, Russell A. and Steven A. Kolme, *Environmental Science and Theology in Dialogue* (Maryknoll: Orbis, 2011).
Carbine, Rosemary, 'Imagining and Incarnating an Integral Ecology: A Critical Ecofeminist Public Theology', in *Planetary Solidarity: Global Women's Voices on Christian Doctrine and Climate Justice*, Grace Ji-Sun Kim and Hilda Koster (eds) (Minneapolis: Fortress, 2017), 47–66.
Catholic Earthcare Australia, *Climate Change; Our Responsibility to Sustain God's Earth*, (2015), 4, 7, http://catholicearthcare.org.au/wp-content/uploads/2015/02/Climate-Change-Our-Responsibility-To-Sustain-God%E2%80%99s-Earth-.pdf (accessed 23 January 2019).
Chekwony, Adam K. Arap (ed.), 'Ecological Vision in a Groaning World', *Voices* 36:2–3 (2013), 1–147.
Chibvongodze, Danford T., 'Ubuntu is Not Only about the Human! An Analysis of the Role of African Philosophy and Ethics in Environment Management', *Journal of Human Ecology* 53:2 (2016), 157–66.
Chitando, Ezra and Ernst M. Conradie (eds), 'Praying for Rain? African perspectives on Religion and Climate Change', *The Ecumenical Review* 69:3 (2017), 311–435.
Chow, Alexander, *Theosis, Sino-Christian Theology and the Second Chinese Enlightenment: Heaven and Humanity in Unity* (New York: Palgrave Macmillan, 2013).
Chryssavgis, John (ed.), *Cosmic Grace, Humble Prayer: The Ecological Vision of the Green Patriarch Bartholomew I* (Grand Rapids: Eerdmans, 2003).
Chryssavgis, John and Bruce Foltz (eds), *Toward an Ecology of Transfiguration: Orthodox Christian Perspectives on Environment, Nature, and Creation* (New York: Fordham University Press, 2013).
Chung, Meehyun, 'No More Flight: Gender and Eco-Justice', in *Mission and Power: History, Relevance and Perils*, Atola Longkumer (ed.) (Oxford: Regnum, 2016), 227–35.
Church of Sweden, *A Bishops' Letter about the Climate* (Uppsala: Ineko, 2014).
Clinebell, Howard J., *Ecotherapy: Healing Ourselves, Healing the Earth* (New York: Haworth Press, 1996).

Clingerman, Forrest, 'Between Babel and Pelagius: Religion, Theology and Geoengineering', in *Engineering the Climate: The Ethics of Solar Radiation Management*, Christopher Preston (ed.) (Lanham: Lexington, 2012), 201–19.
Clingerman, Forrest, 'Theologians as Interpreters – Not Prophets – In a Changing Climate', *Journal of the American Academy of Religion* 83 (2015), 336–55.
Clingerman, Forrest, 'Theologies of the Climate', *Religious Studies Review* 42:2 (2016), 71–6.
Clingerman, Forrest and Kevin J. O'Brien, 'Playing God: Why Religion Belongs in the Geoengineering Debate', *Bulletin of the Atomic Scientists* 70 (2014), 27–37.
Clough, David, *On Animals* Volume I: *Systematic Theology* (London: T&T Clark, 2012).
Clough, David, *On Animals* Volume II: *Theological Ethics* (London: T&T Clark, 2019).
Cobb, John B., Jr, *Sustaining the Common Good: A Christian Perspective on the Global Economy* (Cleveland: Pilgrim Press, 1994).
Cobb, John B., Jr, 'Christianity, Economics, and Ecology', in *Christianity and Ecology*, Dieter T. Hessel and Rosemary Radford Ruether (eds) (Cambridge: Harvard, 2000), 497–511.
Cobb, John B., Jr and Herman E. Daly, *For the Common Good*: *Redirecting the Economy toward Community, the Environment, and a Sustainable Future* (Boston: Beacon Press, 2nd edn., 1994).
Conradie, Ernst M., 'Reformed Perspectives from the South African Context on an Agenda for Ecological Theology', *Ecotheology: The Journal of Religion, Nature, and the Environment* 10:3 (2005), 281–314.
Conradie, Ernst M., *Christianity and Ecological Theology: Resources for Further Research* (Stellenbosch: Sun Press, 2006).
Conradie, Ernst M., *The Church and Climate Change* (Pietermaritzburg: Cluster Publications, 2008).
Conradie, Ernst M., *Christianity and a Critique of Consumerism: A Survey of Six Points of Entry* (Wellington: Bible Media, 2009).
Conradie, Ernst M., 'Confessing Guilt in the Context of Climate Change: Some South African Perspectives', *Scriptura* 103 (2010), 134–52.
Conradie, Ernst M., 'The Salvation of the Earth from Anthropogenic Destruction: In Search of Appropriate Soteriological Concepts in an Age of Ecological Destruction', *Worldviews: Global Religions, Culture, Ecology* 14:2–3 (2010), 111–40.
Conradie, Ernst M., *Saving the Earth? The Legacy of Reformed Views on 'Re-creation'* (Berlin: LIT Verlag, 2013).
Conradie, Ernst M., 'What on Earth Did God Create? Overtures to an Ecumenical Theology of Creation', *The Ecumenical Review* 6:4 (2014), 433–53.
Conradie, Ernst M., *The Earth in God's Economy: Creation, Salvation and Consummation in Ecological Perspective* (Berlin: LIT Verlag, 2015).
Conradie, Ernst M., 'Epilogue: Theological Reflections on Ecumenical Action and Advocacy on Climate Change', in *Making Peace with the Earth: Action and Advocacy for Climate Justice*, Grace Ji-Sun Kim (ed.) (Geneva: WCC, 2016), 234–47.
Conradie, Ernst M., 'Penultimate Perspectives on the Root Causes of Environmental Destruction in Africa', *Scriptura* 115 (2016), 1–19.
Conradie, Ernst M., '*Laudato Si*' and the Root Causes of Ecological Destruction', *Journal of Theology for Southern Africa* 157 (2017), 138–45.
Conradie, Ernst M., *Redeeming Sin? Social Diagnostics amid Ecological Destruction* (Lanham: Lexington, 2017).
Conradie, Ernst M., Sipho Mtetwa and Andrew Warmback (eds), *The Land is Crying for Justice: A Discussion Document on Christianity and Environmental Justice in South Africa* (Stellenbosch: Ecumenical Foundation of Southern Africa, 2002).

Conradie, Ernst M., Charity Majiza, Jim Cochrane, Welile T. Sigabi, Victor Molobi and David Field, 'Seeking Eco-justice in the South African Context', in *Earth Habitat: Eco-Injustice and the Church's Response*, Dieter T. Hessel and Larry L. Rasmussen (eds) (Minneapolis: Fortress, 2001), 135–57.

Conradie, Ernst M., Sigurd Bergmann, Celia Deane-Drummond and Denis Edwards, *Christian Faith and the Earth: Current Paths and Emerging Horizons in Ecotheology* (New York: Bloomsbury T&T Clark, 2014).

Daly, Herman E. and John B. Cobb, Jr, *For the Common Good: Redirecting the Economy Toward Community, the Environment, and a Sustainable Future* (Boston: Beacon Press, 1989).

Daneel, Marthinus, *African Earthkeepers*, Volume 1 and 2 (Maryknoll: Orbis, 2001).

Dankelman, Irene, *Gender and Climate Change: An Introduction* (London: Routledge, 2010).

Davies, Kate, 'Greening Christian Institutions and Practices An Emerging Ecclesial Reform Movement', in *Ecclesial Reform and Deform Movements in the South African Context*, Ernst M. Conradie and Miranda N. Pillay (eds) (Stellenbosch: Sun Press, 2015), 40–60.

Davis, Ellen, *Scripture, Culture, and Agriculture: An Agrarian Reading of the Bible* (Oxford: Oxford University Press, 2009).

Deane-Drummond, Celia, 'Joining in the Dance: Ecology in Roman Catholic Social Teaching', *New Blackfriars*, 93:1044 (2012), 193–212.

Deane-Drummond, Celia, *A Primer in Ecotheology: Theology for a Fragile Earth* (Eugene: Cascade Books, 2017).

Deane-Drummond, Celia, *Eco-Theology* (London: Darton, Longman and Todd, 2008).

Deane-Drummond, Celia and Heinrich Bedford-Strohm (eds), *Religion and Ecology in the Public Sphere* (London: Continuum, 2011).

Deane-Drummond, Celia and Rebecca Artinian-Kaiser (eds), *Theology and Ecology Across Disciplines* (New York: Bloomsbury, 2018).

Delgado, Sharon, *Love in the Time of Climate Change* (Minneapolis: Fortress, 2017).

DeWitt, Calvin B., *Earth-Wise: A Biblical Response to Environmental Issues* (Grand Rapids: CRC Publications, 1994).

DeWitt, Calvin B., 'Earth Stewardship and *Laudato Si*", *Quarterly Review of Biology* 91:3 (2016), 271–84.

Diakonia Council of Churches, *The Oikos Journey: A Theological Reflection on the Economic Crisis in South Africa* (Durban: Diakonia, 2006).

Dombek, Kristin, 'Swimming Against the Rising Tide: Secular Climate-Change Activists Can Learn from Evangelical Christians', *New York Times*, 9 August 2014.

Doran, Chris, *Hope in the Age of Climate Change* (Eugene: Cascade, 2017).

Dorr, Donald, *Option for the Poor and for the Earth: Catholic Social Teaching* (Maryknoll: Orbis, 2012).

Dorr, Donald, 'Themes and Theologies in Catholic Social Teaching Over Fifty Years', *New Blackfriars*, 93:1044 (2012), 137–54.

Duchrow, Ulrich and Franz Hinkelammert, *Transcending Greedy Money: Interreligious Solidarity for Just Relations* (New York: Palgrave Macmillan, 2012).

Ecumenical Patriarch Bartholomew, 'Statement on Climate Change', 12 August 2005.

Ecumenical Patriarch Bartholomew, Symposium on the Arctic', 7–12 September 2007, Greenland, http://orth-transfiguration.org/library/orthodoxy/mirros (accessed 22 December 2018).

Edwards, Denis, *Ecology at the Heart of Faith* (Maryknoll: Orbis, 2006).

Erhard, Nancy, *Moral Habitat: Ethos and Agency for the Sake of Earth* (Albany: SUNY Press, 2007).

Erlander, Daniel, *Manna and Mercy: A Brief History of God's Unfolding Promise to Mend the Entire Universe* (Mercer Island: The Order of St. Martin and Theresa, 1992).

Select Bibliography

Fowler, Robert, *The Greening of Protestant Thought* (Chapel Hill: University of North Carolina Press, 1995).
Francis (Pope), *Laudato Si'*: *On Care for Our Common Home* (Vatican City: Encyclical Letter, 2015).
Fredericks, Sarah, 'Ritual Responses to Climate Engineering', in *Theological and Ethical Responses to Climate Engineering*, Forrest Clingerman and Kevin J. O'Brien (eds) (Lanham: Lexington, 2016), 165–85.
Fretheim, Terence E., 'The Plagues as Ecological Signs of Historical Disaster', *Journal of Biblical Literature* 110:3 (1991), 385–96.
Fretheim, Terence E., *God and the World: A Relational Theology of Creation* (Nashville: Abingdon, 2005).
Gardiner, Stephen, *A Perfect Moral Storm: The Ethical Tragedy of Climate Change* (New York: Oxford University Press, 2011).
Garvey, James, *The Ethics of Climate Change: Right and Wrong in a Warming World* (London: Continuum, 2008).
Gebara, Ivone, *Longing for Running Water: Ecofeminism and Liberation* (Minneapolis: Fortress, 1999).
Gebara, Ivone, 'Women's Suffering, Climate Injustice, God, and Pope Francis's Theology: Some Insights from Brazil', in *Planetary Solidarity: Global Women's Voices on Christian Doctrine and Climate Justice*, Grace Ji-Sun Kim and Hilda P. Koster (eds) (Minneapolis: Fortress, 2017), 67–79.
General Assembly PCUSA, *The Power To Change: U.S. Energy Policy and Global Warming* (Advisory Committee on Social Witness Policy, PCUSA, 2008).
German Bishops: Commission for Society and Social Affairs and Commission for International Church Affairs, *Climate Change; A Focal Point of Global, Intergenerational and Ecological Justice* (2006), https://catholicclimatecovenant.org/files/inline-files/German-Bishops-Report_0.pdf (accessed 23 January 2019).
Granberg-Michaelson, Wesley, *Ecology and Life* (Waco: Word, 1988).
Granberg-Michaelson, Wesley, *Redeeming the Creation, The Rio Earth Summit: Challenges for the Churches* (Geneva: WCC, 1992).
Grau, Marion, 'The Revelations of Global Climate Change: A Petro-eschatology', in *Eschatology as Imagining the End: Faith between Hope and Despair*, Sigurd Bergmann (ed.) (London: Routledge, 2018), 45–60.
Gregorios, Paulos Mar, *The Human Presence: Ecological Spirituality and the Age of the Spirit* (New York: Amity, 1978).
Gschwandtner, Christina M., 'Grounding Ecological Action in Orthodox Theology and Liturgical Practice? A Call for Further Thinking', *Journal for Orthodox Christian Studies* 1:1 (2018), 61–77.
Gustafson, James M., *A Sense of the Divine: The Natural Environment from a Theocentric Perspective* (Cleveland: Pilgrim Press, 1994).
Hamilton, Clive, *Requiem for a Species: Why We Resist the Truth about Climate Change* (New York: Routledge, 2014).
Hamilton, Clive, 'The Theodicy of the "Good Anthropocene"', *Environmental Humanities* 7 (2015), 233–8.
Hamilton, Clive, *Defiant Earth: The Fate of Humans in the Anthropocene* (Cambridge: Polity Press, 2017).
Harker, Ryan and Janeen Bertsche Johnson (eds), *Rooted and Grounded* (Eugene: Pickwick, 2016).
Hart, John, *What Are They Saying About Environmental Theology?* (New Jersey: Paulist Press, 2004).

Hartman, Laura M., 'Healing the Climate? Christian Ethics and Medical Models for Climate Engineering', in *Theological and Ethical Responses to Climate Engineering*, Forrest Clingerman and Kevin J. O'Brien (eds) (Lanham: Lexington, 2016), 129–48.

Hefner, Philip, *The Human Factor: Evolution, Culture, and Religion* (Minneapolis: Fortress, 1993).

Horrell, David et al. (eds), *Ecological Hermeneutics: Biblical, Historical and Theological Perspectives* (London: T&T Clark, 2010).

Hulme, Mike, *Why We Disagree about Climate Change: Understanding Controversy, Inaction and Opportunity* (New York: Cambridge University Press, 2009).

Ingram, Paul O., *You Have Been Told What is Good: Interreligious Dialogue and Climate Change* (Eugene: Cascade Books, 2016).

Irish Catholic Bishops' Conference, *The Cry of the Earth: Pastoral Reflections on Climate Change from the Irish Catholic Bishops* (2009), 27, https://www.catholicbishops.ie/wp-content/uploads/2014/09/The-Cry-of-the-Earth-A-Call-to-Action-for-Climate-Justice-2014.pdf (accessed 23 January 2019).

Jenkins, Willis, 'After Lynn White: Religious Ethics and Environmental Problems', *Journal of Religious Ethics* 37:2 (2009), 283–309.

Jenkins, Willis, *Ecologies of Grace: Environmental Ethics and Christian Theology* (Oxford: Oxford University Press, 2008).

Jenkins, Willis, *The Future of Ethics: Sustainability, Social Justice, and Religious Creativity* (Washington DC: Georgetown University Press, 2013).

Jenkins, Willis, Evan Berry and Luke Beck Kreider, 'Religion and Climate Change', *Annual Review of Environment and Resources* 43 (2018), 85–108.

Jennings, Willie James, *The Christian Imagination: Theology and the Origins of Race* (New Haven: Yale University Press, 2010).

John Paul II (Pope), *Peace with God the Creator, Peace with All Creation* (Vatican City: Libreria Editrice Vatican, 1990).

Johnson, Elizabeth A., *Ask the Beasts: Darwin and the God of Love* (London: Bloomsbury, 2014).

Kaoma, Kapya J., *God's Family, God's Earth: Christian Ecological Ethics of Ubuntu* (Blantyre: Kachere Series, 2014).

Katongole, Emmanuel, *The Sacrifice of Africa: A Political Theology for Africa* (Grand Rapids: Eerdmans, 2011).

Kearns, Laurel, 'Climate Change', in *Grounding Religion: A Field Guide to the Study of Religion and Ecology*, Whitney Bauman, Richard Bohannon and Kevin J. O'Brien (eds) (London: Routledge, 2nd edn., 2017), 141–6.

Kearns, Laurel and Catherine Keller (eds), *Ecospirit: Religions and Philosophies for the Earth* (New York: Fordham, 2007).

Keenan, Marjorie (Sister) RSHM, *Care for Creation, Human Activity and the Environment* (Vatican City: Libreria Editrice Vaticana, 2000).

Keller, Catherine, *Face of the Deep: A Theology of Becoming* (London: Routledge, 2003).

Keller, Catherine, *Cloud of the Impossible – Negative Theology and Planetary Entanglement* (New York: Columbia University Press, 2015).

Kempf, Wolfgang, 'The Rainbow's Power: Climate Change, Sea Level Rises and Reconfiguration of the Noah Story in Oceania', in *Pacific Voices. Local Governments and Climate Change*, Ropate Qalo (ed.) (Suva: USP Press, 2014), 68–84.

Kerber, Guillermo, 'International Advocacy for Climate Justice', in *How the World's Religions are Responding to Climate Change: Social Scientific Investigations*, Robin Globus Veldman, Andrew Szasz and Randolph Haluza-Delay (eds) (London/New York: Routledge, 2014), 278–93.

Kerber, Guillermo, 'Ecumenical Background and Reactions to Laudato Si", *Voices* 39:2 (2016), 63–75.
Keum, Jooseop (ed.), *Together Towards Life. Mission and Evangelism in Changing Landscapes* (Geneva: World Council of Churches, 2013).
Kim, Grace Ji-Sun (ed.), *Making Peace with the Earth: Action and Advocacy for Climate Justice* (Geneva: WCC, 2016).
Kim, Grace Ji-Sun and Hilda Koster, *Planetary Solidarity: Global Women's Voices on Christian Doctrine and Climate Justice* (Minneapolis: Fortress, 2017).
Koster, Hilda P., 'Questioning Eco-Theological Panentheisms: The Promise of Kathryn Tanner's Theology of God's Radical Transcendence for Ecological Theology', *Scriptura* 111 (2012), 385–94.
Koster, Hilda P., 'Tanner's Theology of God's Ongoing Gift-Giving as an Ecological Theology', in *The Gift of Theology: The Contribution of Kathryn Tanner*, Rosemary P. Carbine and Hilda P. Koster (eds) (Minneapolis: Fortress, 2015), 257–85.
Lai, Pan-chiu, 'Beyond Anthropocentrism and Ecocentrism: Eco-Theology and Confucian-Christian Dialogue', *Ching Feng* 2:1–2 (2001), 35–55.
Lai, Pan-chiu, 'Christian-Confucian Dialogue on Humanity: An Ecological Perspective', *Studies in Interreligious Dialogue* 14:2 (2004), 202–15.
Lai, Pan-chiu, 'God of Life and Ecological Theology: A Chinese Christian Perspective', *The Ecumenical Review* 65:1 (2013), 67–82.
Lai, Pan-chiu, 'Ecological Theology as Public Theology: A Chinese Perspective', *International Journal of Public Theology* 11:4 (2017), 477–500.
LaMothe, Ryan, 'This Changes Everything: The Sixth Extinction and its Implications for Pastoral Theology', *Journal of Pastoral Theology* 26:3 (2016), 178–94.
Latin American Theological Commission (ed.), 'Ecology and Religion: In this Hour of Planetary Emergency', *Voices* 34:1 (2011), 1–326.
Latour, Bruno, *Facing Gaia: Eight Lectures on the Climactic Regime* (New York: Polity, 2017).
Linzey, Andrew, *Love the Animals: Meditations and Prayers* (New York: Crossroad Press, 1989).
Linzey, Andrew, *Animal Rites: Liturgies of Animal Care* (London: SPCK, 1996).
Lusama, Tafue, 'Punishment of the Innocent: The Problem of Global Warming with Special Reference to Tuvalu' (Master's Thesis, Tainan Theological Seminary and College, 2004).
Maibach, Edward W., *The Francis Effect: How Pope Francis Changed the Conversation about Global Warming* (Fairfax: George Mason University Center for Climate Change Communication, 2015).
Martin-Schramm, James B., *Climate Justice: Ethics, Energy, and Public Policy* (Minneapolis: Fortress, 2010).
Maseno, Loreen, 'Prayer for Rain: A Pentecostal Perspective from Kenya', *The Ecumenical Review* 69 (2016), 436–41.
McDaniel, Jay B., 'Ten Ideas for Saving the Planet', in *Replanting Ourselves in Beauty: Toward an Ecological Civilization*, Jay B. McDaniel and Patricia Adams Farmer (eds) (Anoka: Process Century Press, 2015), 200–36.
McDonagh, Seán, *To Care for The Earth: A Call to a New Theology* (London: Chapman, 1986).
McDonagh, Seán, *Climate Change: The Challenge to All of Us* (Dublin: Columba, 2006).
McFague, Sallie, 'An Earthly Theological Agenda', in *Ecofeminism and the Sacred*, Carol J. Adams (ed.) (New York: Continuum, 1993), 84–98.
McFague, Sallie, *Super, Natural Christians: How We Should Love Nature* (Minneapolis: Fortress, 1997).
McFague, Sallie, *Life Abundant: Rethinking Theology and Economy for Planet in Peril* (Minneapolis: Fortress, 2001).

McFague, Sallie, *A New Climate for Theology: God, the World and Global Warming* (Minneapolis: Fortress, 2008).
McFague, Sallie, *Blessed are the Consumers: Climate Change and the Practice of Restraint* (Minneapolis: Fortress, 2013).
McFague, Sallie, 'Renaming the Triune God for a Time of Global Climate Change', in *Planetary Solidarity: Global Women's Voices on Christian Doctrine and Climate Justice*, Grace Ji-Sun Kim and Hilda P. Koster (eds) (Minneapolis: Fortress, 2017), 101–18.
McLaren, Duncan, 'Framing Out Justice: The Post-politics of Climate Engineering Discourses', in *Climate Justice and Geoengineering: Ethics and Policy in the Atmospheric Anthropocene*, Christopher J. Preston (ed.) (Lanham: Lexington, 2016), 139–60.
Meeks, Douglas M., *God the Economist: The Doctrine of God and Political Economy* (Grand Rapids: Eerdmans, 1989).
Mick, Lawrence E., *Liturgy and Ecology in Dialogue* (Collegeville: Liturgical Press, 1997).
Moe-Lobeda, Cynthia D., *Resisting Structural Evil: Love as Ecological-Economic Vocation* (Minneapolis: Fortress, 2013).
Moe-Lobeda, Cynthia D., 'The Spirit as Moral-Spiritual Power for Earth-Honoring, Justice Seeking Ways of Shaping Our Life in Common', in *Planetary Solidarity: Global Women's Voices on Christian Doctrine and Climate Justice*, Grace Ji-Sun Kim and Hilda P. Koster (eds) (Minneapolis: Fortress, 2017), 249–73.
Moltmann, Jürgen, *God in Creation: An Ecological Doctrine of Creation* (London: SCM Press, 1985).
Moltmann, Jürgen, *The Coming of God. Christian Eschatology* (Minneapolis: Fortress, 1996).
Moo, Jonathan and Robert White, *Let Creation Rejoice: Biblical Hope and Ecological Crisis* (London: IVP Academic Press, 2014).
Moyo, Fulata Lusungu, '"Ukugqiba inkaba" – Burying the Umbilical Cord: An African Indigenous Ecofeminist Perspective on Incarnation', in *Planetary Solidarity: Global Women's Voices on Christian Doctrine and Climate Justice*, Grace Ji-Sun Kim and Hilda P. Koster (eds) (Minneapolis: Fortress, 2017), 177–90.
Müller-Fahrenholz, Geiko, *God's Spirit: Transforming a World in Crisis* (New York: Continuum, 1995), 59–77.
Myers, Ched, 'From "Creation Care" to "Watershed Discipleship": Re-Placing Ecological Theology and Practice', *Conrad Grebel Review* 32:3 (2014), 250–75.
Nalwamba, Kuzipa and Teddy C. Sakupapa, 'Ecology and Fellowship (*Koinonia*): A Fellowship of Life', in *The Church in God's Household: Protestant Perspectives on Ecclesiology and Ecology*, Clive W. Ayre and Ernst M. Conradie (eds) (Pietermaritzburg: Cluster Publications, 2016), 75–93.
Nash, James A., *Loving Nature: Ecological Integrity and Christian Responsibility* (Nashville: Abingdon Press, 1991).
Nash, James A., 'Toward the Ecological Reformation of Christianity', *Interpretation* 50:1 (1996), 5–15.
Niles, D. Preman (ed.), *Between the Flood and the Rainbow* (Geneva: WCC, 1992).
Northcott, Michael S., 'Climate Change and Christian Ethics', in *The Wiley Blackwell Companion to Religion and Ecology*, John Hart (ed.) (Chichester: Wiley Blackwell, 2017), 286–300.
Northcott, Michael S., *A Moral Climate: The Ethics of Global Warming* (Maryknoll: Orbis, 2007).
Northcott, Michael S., *A Political Theology of Climate Change* (Grand Rapids: Eerdmans, 2013).
Northcott, Michael S. and Peter M. Scott (eds), *Systematic Theology and Climate Change: Ecumenical Perspectives* (London: Routledge, 2014).

O'Brien, Kevin J., '"First to be Reconciled": The Priority of Repentance in the Climate Engineering Debate', in *Theological and Ethical Responses to Climate Engineering*, Forrest Clingerman and Kevin J. O'Brien (eds) (Lanham: Lexington, 2016), 187–203.

O'Brien, Kevin J., *The Violence of Climate Change: Lessons of Resistance From Nonviolent Activists* (Washington, DC: Georgetown University Press, 2017).

Oord, Thomas Jay (ed.), *Theologies of Creation: Creation Ex Nihilo and its New Rivals* (New York: Routledge, 2015), 79–86.

Pearson, Clive, 'The Purpose and Practice of a Public Theology in a Time of Climate Change', *International Journal of Public Theology* 4 (2010), 356–72.

Peters, Ted, *Sin Boldly! Justifying Faith for Fragile and Broken Souls* (Minneapolis: Fortress, 2015).

Pihkala, Panu, 'Eco-Anxiety, Tragedy, and Hope: Psychological and Spiritual Dimensions of Climate Change,' *Zygon* 53:2 (2018), 545–69.

Philip, Mary, 'Remembrance: A Living Bridge', in *Churrasco: A Theological Feast in Honor of Vítor Westhelle*, Mary Philip, John Nuenes and Charles M. Collier (eds) (Eugene: Pickwick, 2013), 94–104.

Polk, Danne, 'Ecologically Queer: Preliminaries for a Queer Ecofeminist Identity Theory', *Journal of Women and Religion*, 19–20 (2001/2002), 72–89.

Primavesi, Anne, *Gaia and Climate Change* (London: Routledge, 2008).

Purdy, Jedediah, *After Nature: A Politics for the Anthropocene* (Cambridge: Harvard University Press, 2015), 47–8.

Rakoczy, Susan, *In Her Name: Women Doing Theology* (Pietermaritzburg: Cluster Publications, 2004), 300.

Rasmussen, Larry L., *Earth-Honoring Faith: Religious Ethics in a New Key* (New York: Oxford University Press, 2013).

Redekop, Calvin (ed.), *Creation and the Environment: An Anabaptist Perspective on a Sustainable World* (Baltimore: Johns Hopkins University Press, 2000).

Rhoads, David (ed.), *Earth and Word: Classic Sermons on Saving the Planet* (New York: Continuum, 2007).

Rieger, Joerg, *No Rising Tide: Theology, Economics, and the Future* (Minneapolis: Fortress, 2009).

Rieger, Joerg and Rosemarie Henkel-Rieger, *Unified We Are a Force: How Faith and Labor Can Overcome America's Inequalities* (St. Louis: Chalice Press, 2016).

Rieger, Joerg and Edward Waggoner (eds), *Religious Experience and New Materialism: Movement Matters* (New York: Palgrave Macmillan, 2016).

Riley, Shamara Shantu, 'Ecology is a Sistah's Issue Too: The Politics of Emergent Afrocentric Ecowomanism', in *Readings in Ecology and Feminist Theology*, Mary Heather MacKinnon and Moni McIntrye (eds) (Kansas City: Sheed & Ward, 1995), 214–30.

Robinson, Mary, *Climate Justice: Hope, Resilience, and the Fight for a Sustainable Future* (London: Bloomsbury, 2018).

Rohr, Richard, *Spiritual Ecology: The Cry of the Earth* (Point Reyes: The Golden Sufi Center, 2014).

Rolston, Holmes III, 'Kenosis and Nature', in *The Work of Love*, John Polkinghorne (ed.) (Grand Rapids: Eerdmans, 2001), 43–65.

Rossing, Barbara, 'The World is About to Turn: Preaching Apocalyptic Texts for a Planet in Peril', in *Eco-Reformation: Grace and Hope for a Planet in Peril*, Lisa Dahill and James Martin-Schramm (eds) (Eugene: Wipf and Stock, 2016), 140–59.

Rowe, Terra S., 'Grace and Climate Change: The Free Gift in Capitalism and Protestantism', in *Eco-Reformation: Grace and Hope for a Planet in Peril*, Lisa E. Dahill and James B. Martin-Schramm (eds) (Eugene: Cascade Books, 2016), 253–71.

Rowe, Terra S., *Toward a Better Worldliness: Ecology, Economy, and the Protestant Tradition* (Minneapolis: Fortress, 2017).
Sakupapa, Teddy Chalwe, 'Spirit and Ecology in the Context of African Theology', *Scriptura* 111 (2012), 422–30.
Santmire, H. Paul, *The Travail of Nature: The Ambiguous Ecological Promise of Christian Theology* (Minneapolis: Fortress Press, 1985).
Schade, Leah, *Creation-Crisis Preaching: Ecology, Theology, and the Pulpit* (St Louis: Chalice Press, 2015).
Schor, Juliet, *Plenitude: The New Economics of True Wealth* (New York: Penguin Press, 2010).
Scott, Dane, 'The Temptations of Climate Engineering', in *Theological and Ethical Responses to Climate Engineering*, Forrest Clingerman and Kevin J. O'Brien (eds) (Lanham: Lexington, 2016), 39–58.
Scott, Peter M., *A Political Theology of Nature* (Cambridge: Cambridge University Press, 2003).
Scott, Peter M., *Anti-human Theology* (London: SCM Press, 2010).
Setiloane, Gabriel, 'Towards a Biocentric Theology and Ethic – via Africa', in Faith, Science & African *Culture: African Cosmology and Africa's Contribution to Science*, Cornel W. du Toit (ed.) (Pretoria: Unisa, 1998), 73–84.
Silva, Rohan, Marlene Perera and Shirley Lal Wijesinghe (eds), 'Eco-Crisis: Theological Visions', *Voices from the Third World* (2019), 1–135.
South African Council of Churches, *Climate Change – A Challenge to the Churches in South Africa* (Braamfontein: SACC, 2009).
Southgate, Christopher B., *The Groaning of Creation: God, Evolution, and the Problem of Evil* (Louisville: Westminster John Knox, 2008).
Standing Conference of the Canonical Orthodox Bishops in the Americas, 'Global Climate Change: A Moral and Spiritual Challenge', *New York City*, 25 May 2007. See http://assembly ofbishops.org/news/scoba/2007-05-25-global-climate-change (accessed 15 June 2017).
Stuckelberger, Christoph and Guillermo Kerber (eds), *Religions for Climate Justice: International Interfaith Statements 2008–2014* (Geneva: Globethics, 2014).
Sung Park, Andrew, *The Triune Atonement: Christ's Healing for Sinners, Victims, and the Whole Creation* (Louisville: Westminster John Knox, 2009).
Suzuki, David, *Sacred Balance: Rediscovering Our Place in Nature* (Seattle: Mountaineers Books, 2002).
Swoboda, Aaron J. (ed.), *Blood Cries Out: Pentecostals, Ecology, and the Groans of Creation* (Eugene: Pickwick, 2014).
Talia, Maina, 'Towards a *Fatele* Theology: A Contextual Theological Response in Addressing Threats of Global Warming in Tuvalu' (Master's Thesis, Tainan Theological Seminary and College, 2009).
Tanner, Kathryn, *Economy of Grace* (Minneapolis: Fortress, 2005).
Tanner, Kathryn, *Christianity and the New Spirit of Capitalism* (New Haven: Yale University Press, 2019).
Theokritoff, Elizabeth, *Living in God's Creation: Orthodox Perspectives on Ecology* (Crestwood: St. Vladimir's Theological Seminary Press, 2009).
Tinker, George E., *Spirit and Resistance: Political Theology and American Indian Liberation* (Minneapolis: Fortress, 2004),
Turman, Eboni Marshall, 'Black and Blue: Uncovering the Ecclesial Cover-Up of Black Women's Bodies through Womanist Reimagining of the Doctrine of Incarnation', in *Reimagining with Christian Doctrines: Responding to Global Injustice*, Grace Ji-Sun Kim and Jenny Daggers (eds) (New York: Palgrave Macmillan, 2014), 71–89.
Tutu, Desmond M., *God Has a Dream: A Vision of Hope for Our Time* (New York: Doubleday, 2004).

Veldman, Robin Globus, 'An Inconvenient Faith? Conservative Christianity, Climate Change and the End of the World' (PhD Dissertation, University of Florida, 2014).
Vélez Caro, Olga Consuelo, 'The Ecological Conversion Encyclical and its Accessibility to the Impoverished of this World', *Voices* 39:2 (2016), 38–49.
Vigil, José María (ed.), 'Deep Ecology: Spirituality and Liberation', *Voices* 37:2–3 (2014), 1–414.
Vischer, Lukas (ed.), *The Eucharist and Creation Spirituality* (Geneva: Centre Internationale Reformé John Knox, 2007).
Wainwright, Elaine M., *Habitat, Human, and Holy: An Eco-rhetorical Reading of the Gospel of Matthew* (Sheffield: Sheffield Phoenix Press, 2016).
Wallace, Mark, 'Elegy for a Lost World', in *Post-Traumatic Public Theology*, Stephanie N. Arel and Shelly Rambo (eds) (Cham: Palgrave McMillan, 2016), 135–54.
Wallace, Mark, *Fragments of the Spirit* (London: T&T Clark, 2002).
Ware, Kallistos, 'Lent and the Consumer Society', in *Living Orthodoxy in the Modern World*, Andrew Walker and Costa Carras (eds) (London: SPCK, 1996), 64–84.
Welby, Justin, 'Our Moral Opportunity on Climate Change', https://www.nytimes.com/2017/11/03/opinion/faith-climate-change-justin-welby.html (accessed 3 December 2018).
Westhelle, Vítor, *Eschatology and Space: The Lost Dimension in Theology Past and Present* (New York: Palgrave Macmillan, 2012).
White, Lynn, Jr, 'The Historical Roots of Our Ecological Crisis', *Science* 155 (1967), 1203–7.
Wirzba, Norman, *Living the Sabbath: Discovering the Rhythms of Rest and Delight* (Grand Rapids: Brazos Press, 2006).
Wirzba, Norman, *Food and Faith: A Theology of Eating* (Cambridge: Cambridge University Press, 2011).
Wirzba, Norman, *From Nature to Creation: A Christian Vision for Understanding and Loving our World* (Grand Rapids: Baker Academic, 2013).
World Communion of Reformed Churches, *The Accra Confession: Covenanting for Justice in the Economy and the Earth* (Geneva: WCRC, 2004).
World Council of Churches, *Solidarity with Victims of Climate Change* (Geneva: WCC, 2002).
Yong, Amos, *Spirit Renews the Face of the Earth* (Eugene: Wipf and Stock, 2009).
Zachariah, George, *Alternatives Unincorporated: Earth Ethics from the Grassroots* (New York: Routledge, 2015).
Zaleha, Bernard D. and Andrew Szasz, 'Keep Christianity Brown! Climate Denial on the Christian Right in the United States', in *How the World's Religions Are Responding to Climate Change: Social Scientific Investigations*, Robin Globus Veldman, Andrew Szasz, and Randolph Haluza-DeLay (eds) (New York and Abingdon: Routledge, 2014), 209–28.
Zaleha, Bernard D. and Andrew Szasz, 'Why Conservative Christians Don't Believe in Climate Change', *Bulletin of the Atomic Scientists* 71:5 (2015), 19–30.
Zoloth, Laurie, 'At the Last Well on Earth: Climate Change is a Feminist Issue', *Journal of Feminist Studies in Religion* 33 (2017), 139–52.

Index

Abelard, Peter 413
acidification (of oceans) 141, 624, 638
Acosta, José 476, 477
adaptation 6, 21, 29, 38, 39, 42, 49, 50, 51, 76, 77, 92, 93, 96, 99, 101–5, 128, 183, 202–3, 211, 384, 386–7, 402–3, 415, 574, 649–50, 682–3. *See also* climate adaptation
Africa 1, 3, 83, 84, 85, 86, 87, 89, 102–4, 132–5, 164, 171, 189, 246, 247, 259, 260, 261, 262–9, 272–5, 291, 294, 298, 308, 336–8, 349, 355, 384, 385, 387, 394, 406, 409, 411, 430, 462, 475, 494–6, 524, 525, 528, 531, 534, 536, 556–9, 576, 577, 611, 613, 614, 622, 632, 650, 678, 679, 680–2
African American 431, 512, 592, 621, 659, 661
African American environmental history 661
African Christianity 510–11
African cosmology 614, 661
African culture 526
African theology 7, 556–8
African traditional roots 132, 496, 557
Alaska 140, 616, 621
All African Conference of Churches 3, 87, 133, 135, 342
Ambrose of Milan 497, 509
America (Latin) 211
America (North) 1, 78, 87, 129, 160, 164, 171, 273, 308, 311–15, 320, 328, 336, 393, 422, 434, 435, 443, 445, 474, 568, 597, 599, 602–3, 606, 609–10, 613–19, 622, 627–9, 632, 681
America (South) 273, 308, 314, 494, 681
Amish 308–11, 321
Anabaptism 308, 311, 313
Anabaptist(s) 7, 228, 308, 309–23
Anglican Church 259, 262, 265–70, 393
   eco-Anglicanism 272, 275
   evangelical Anglicans 262, 269
   Green Anglicans 266–9

animals 9, 19, 21, 27, 36, 38, 40, 41, 83–5, 110, 137, 186, 203, 231, 232, 234, 253, 271, 315, 319, 364, 368, 390, 391, 448, 449, 467, 471, 475, 476, 478, 483, 494, 508, 533, 536, 551, 552, 555, 569, 581, 584, 587–8, 590, 614, 628, 650, 657, 667, 674–6
animal studies 15, 650
animism 503, 505, 506
Anthropocene 31, 35, 37, 40–6, 48, 54, 69, 76, 92, 93, 99, 100, 148, 153–6, 209, 291, 373, 375, 376, 382, 383, 399, 401–4, 465, 480, 485–8, 498–9, 501–2, 505–10, 545, 547, 653
anthropocentric 47, 54, 79, 83, 84, 86, 89, 125, 148, 166, 167, 174, 177, 255, 304, 305, 326, 345, 347, 371, 373, 378, 382, 418, 455, 486, 509–10, 513, 527, 530, 534, 579, 581, 588, 615, 623, 627, 630, 643, 644, 657, 669, 675, 684
anthropocentrism 125, 133, 135, 153, 180, 215, 244, 251, 303, 326, 336, 338, 364, 365, 374–7, 381, 383, 385, 418, 423, 483, 545, 642, 658
anthropology (moral) 161–2
anthropology (theological) 32, 35–7, 43, 48, 99, 240, 242, 256, 291, 374, 381, 402, 526, 544, 554, 558, 567, 652
Apartheid 4, 85, 87, 133, 293, 346, 388–9, 394, 409, 462, 487, 493
apocalypse 563, 590, 591
apocalyptic 122, 123, 130, 297, 329, 385, 403–4, 442–5, 463, 486, 499, 507, 528, 589, 590, 604
apophatic theology 493, 535, 557
Aquinas, Thomas 183, 191–2, 453, 546, 554
Aristotelian 183, 190–2, 283
Aristotle 183–5, 283, 305, 519, 571
art 111–16, 118, 232, 442, 482, 497, 501, 509, 535, 543, 586, 671
ascesis 232
ascetic 191, 231, 451, 569, 574, 575

asceticism 231, 555
Asia 4, 136, 164, 171, 273, 275, 308, 480, 534, 593, 596, 614, 632, 652–5, 663–6, 668, 670, 671–2, 681
Asian feminist theology 250, 651
astrobiology 37, 45, 46, 298, 373, 375, 380
Athanasius of Alexandria 230, 548, 550, 558
atonement 99, 408–11, 413, 415, 487, 495, 520, 526, 653
Augustine of Hippo (Saint) 368, 391, 453, 468, 520, 529, 535
Aulén, Gustaf 409
Australia 142, 229, 252, 265, 395, 495, 593, 619, 632, 637

Bangladesh 109, 388, 636
baptism 312, 339, 570, 573
Barth, Karl 294, 440, 446, 454, 485, 489
Bartholomew (Ecumenical Patriarch) 229, 232–3, 235–8, 249, 273, 274, 347, 352, 567, 588
Bauckham, Richard 364, 552, 588
Bauman, Whitney A. 53, 61, 62, 311, 378, 540
Beisner, Calvin 129, 130, 328
Benedict XVI (Pope) 244, 245, 247, 251, 609, 637
Bergmann, Sigurd 90, 301, 412, 497, 499–502, 506, 509, 510, 512
Berry, Thomas 178, 665
Berry, Wendell 180
biocentrism 373, 377
biodiversity 6, 31, 79, 88, 185, 190, 206, 209, 352, 374, 386, 416, 554, 638, 657
black theology 4
Boff, Leonardo 60, 305, 315, 585, 586, 593, 685
Bolivia 211–15, 217–20, 222, 314, 681, 684
Bonaventure 453, 550, 558
Bonhoeffer 5, 156, 304, 419, 479, 582, 583
Bookless, David (Dave) 271–2, 274–5
Bosch, David 86, 613
Bouma-Prediger, Steven 178–80, 182, 184, 189–91, 297, 298, 332, 675
Brazil 60, 75, 216, 217, 235, 250, 277, 354, 356, 467, 681
Buddha 136, 138, 144, 406
Buddhism 136, 284, 489, 544, 545, 596, 669
Buddhist–Christian dialogue 136, 138, 140, 144

Calvin, John 294–6, 298–303, 454, 460
Canada 15, 27, 312, 314, 321, 342, 513, 619, 620
capitalism 1, 2, 54–9, 62, 63, 66–8, 76, 77, 136–9, 158, 170, 171, 190–1, 209, 242–3, 374, 384, 388–9, 417–19, 425, 451–2, 456, 465, 495, 504–5, 511, 569, 579, 604, 607, 643, 651, 653–4, 664. *See also* global capitalism
carbon emissions 1, 2, 6, 7, 9, 29, 55, 163, 171, 186, 227, 280, 289, 388, 393, 407, 412, 463, 568, 572, 583, 649, 674, 684
carbon footprint 2–4, 9, 187, 199, 227, 253, 267, 269, 280, 426, 563, 564, 568, 633
carbon sequestration 91, 95, 583, 586
Carson, Rachel 41, 373
Carter, Jimmy (President) 634
Catholic social teaching 244, 245, 255–8, 605
China 75, 123, 141, 142, 198, 206, 434, 436, 480–2, 487, 488, 651–2, 678
Chipko movement 250, 283
Christology 99, 282, 487, 514, 517, 526, 527, 550
Chryssavgis, John 182, 240, 242, 243, 352, 567, 580
Church 1, 8, 9, 20, 27, 70–2, 81, 82, 87, 102, 107, 126, 127, 130–5, 138, 147, 153, 156–9, 163, 168, 180–2, 191–3, 216, 228–32, 234, 237, 239, 240, 244–6, 248–52, 254–5, 257–61, 263, 265–74, 276, 279–81, 283, 284, 291, 297, 299, 301–3, 308–11, 320, 332, 338, 340–4, 348, 350, 352, 354, 361, 389, 393–5, 416, 417, 424, 431–40, 442, 446, 452–5, 460, 486, 488, 489, 497, 509, 511, 516, 521, 532, 533, 538, 539, 546, 548, 553, 563–5, 567–8, 576, 597–8, 605, 609–14, 616–17, 627–8, 632–7, 641–2, 644, 659
civil society 2, 4, 6, 13, 120, 131–2, 173, 194, 206, 267, 284, 290, 344, 354, 431–5, 655
Clayton, Phillip 139, 144
climate adaptation 3, 128, 198, 205, 207. *See also* adaptation
climate agreement 74, 199, 205, 622
climate anxiety 426

Index

climate colonialism 157, 158, 164, 166. *See also* colonialism
climate debt 64, 212, 412, 415, 653
climate denialism 13, 78, 207. *See also* denialism
climate engineering 47, 90–106, 402, 652
climate injustice 93, 104–5, 161, 163, 167, 172–3, 216, 240, 250, 329, 429, 652, 660–1
climate justice 2–4, 77, 92, 102, 132, 134, 148–50, 157–8, 162, 164, 186, 193, 195, 198, 204, 206, 209, 210, 216, 243, 250, 258, 266, 274, 324, 325, 329–31, 334, 335, 351, 353–5, 384, 402, 403, 412, 419, 427–9, 437, 496, 511, 564, 579, 583, 587, 649, 650, 655–7, 659, 660
climate mitigation 164, 386, 388, 682, 686
climate policy 71, 76, 77, 95, 127, 194–7, 199, 686
  privilege 163, 169, 405
climate refugees 3, 246, 297, 412, 432, 608, 619
climate science 1, 15, 17, 20, 26, 28–30, 64, 81, 106, 109, 128, 135, 325, 335, 397
climate sin 101, 105–6, 162, 368, 384, 420–3, 426. *See also* sin
Clinebell, Howard J. 615, 618
Clingerman, Forrest 90, 91, 97–9, 101–3, 458, 652
Clough, David 650, 674
Cobb, John B., Jr 22, 56, 60, 62, 66, 67, 137–9, 141, 142
co-creator(s) (created) 365–7, 479, 484, 487–8, 581
colonialism 77, 78, 84, 89, 99, 117, 133, 157, 158, 164, 166, 173–5, 260, 263, 270, 271, 278, 314, 315, 388, 389, 408, 417, 420, 433, 651, 653, 665
coloniality 175, 176
colonization 177, 217, 219, 260, 423, 542, 618
commodification of nature 270, 325, 419
commodity (earth/nature as) 271, 294, 474, 623, 653
common good 5, 6, 17, 62, 137, 139, 140, 145, 146, 159, 215, 223, 250, 257, 284, 304, 367, 403, 469, 514, 605, 613, 614, 636, 638, 655
common home 35, 134, 138, 183, 185, 191, 214, 250, 307, 352, 366, 403, 528, 552, 597, 607, 610, 626, 638

commons 131, 242, 251, 259, 271
communion 68, 69, 79, 240, 254, 279, 294, 423–5, 439, 457, 478, 496, 511, 516, 546, 549, 552–5, 588–98, 599, 604, 605, 611, 612, 614. *See also* Trinitarian communion
  cosmic communion 240, 254, 555, 611, 612, 614
  divine communion 546, 552–4,
conciliar process 340, 341, 343, 349, 350, 353
Confucian–Christian dialogue 480, 483
Confucianism 480–6, 488–9, 669
Confucius 136, 138, 140, 482
Conradie, Ernst M. 1–11, 86, 102, 134, 182, 227–8, 247, 259–62, 272, 291–7, 301, 337, 359–61, 371, 384–94, 406–16, 421, 430, 434, 460, 462–6, 477, 485, 487, 493–6, 503, 557, 613, 650
consumerism 6, 58, 60, 99, 116, 118, 135–6, 141, 144–5, 147, 190, 191, 231, 260–3, 272, 294, 385–6, 437, 445, 485, 569, 603, 652
consumerist 141, 143–4, 227, 384, 386, 393, 414, 563–4, 566, 568–9, 629
  lifestyles 564, 566, 568
  society 384, 414, 563, 629
consummation 8, 295, 334, 360–1, 407, 440, 447, 489, 493
contextual 3, 21, 87, 223, 241, 257, 290, 294, 395, 396, 480, 497, 510, 611, 616, 649
contextual theology 3, 395, 497, 649
Copenhagen summit (2009) 197, 204, 268, 347, 639
Cornwall Alliance 120, 129, 328
cosmological 80, 88, 123, 189, 230, 234, 366, 372, 446, 484, 563, 571, 614
  salvation 372, 484 (*see also* cosmic salvation)
cosmology 22, 25, 80, 124, 144, 387, 392, 413, 418, 499, 502, 514, 527, 567, 571, 589, 613, 614, 656, 661, 664, 668, 670
cosmos 16, 45, 46, 121, 164, 174, 189, 231, 305, 322, 360, 378, 446, 488, 489, 570, 571, 573, 580, 588, 595, 611, 666–72
Council of Chalcedon 282
Council of Trent 425
creation, doctrine of 8, 18, 25, 26, 158, 167, 169, 181, 189, 191, 194, 229–38, 240, 242, 248, 269, 284–6, 289, 290,

702

293–301, 303–7, 314, 316–17, 322, 326–7, 332–4, 336–8, 340–52, 355, 360–72, 374–9, 381–3, 392, 394–7, 400–4, 409, 411, 418, 421, 428, 431, 433–5, 437, 439, 442, 444, 446–9, 457–61, 465, 476, 478, 484, 486–9, 493, 495–502, 506, 508–11, 514–17, 521, 525, 528–31, 533–40, 542, 546–54, 557, 563, 566, 567, 569, 573, 579–85, 588, 590, 594–7, 599, 602, 603, 605, 606, 612–15, 618, 624, 627, 628, 632, 635–8, 643, 653, 654, 656, 658–60, 664, 665, 687
creation care   229, 240, 241, 265, 269, 273–6, 297, 317, 322, 332–4, 364, 567, 597, 599, 608
creation ex nihilo   363, 364, 542
creationist/creationism   22, 35–6, 51, 127
creation theology   296, 510, 511, 537, 580
cross   16, 282, 287, 311, 320, 401, 404, 410–13, 415–16, 419, 428, 434, 446, 464, 514, 516–18, 520–2, 546–8, 683
Crutzen, Paul J.   96, 498, 547
cry of the earth   60, 241, 305, 307, 315, 339, 352, 372, 585, 637, 685
cultural theory   598, 599, 601, 603, 607
cultural values   600, 613
Cyprian (Saint)   453

Dalits   416, 494, 593, 594, 596
Dalit theology   595
Daly, Herman E.   56, 62, 66, 67, 139
Daly, Mary   531, 532
Daneel, Marthinus   86, 576
Daoism   480
Daoist   138, 141–2, 671
  sages   138
  traditions   141
  way   142
Darwin, Charles   51, 68, 124, 428, 552
Darwinian evolution   68, 124
Dawkins, Richard   514
Deane-Drummond, Celia   35, 36, 43, 44, 48, 147, 244, 250, 255–8, 301, 506, 537, 567
decentering   373, 382, 383, 627, 658
  decentering of the human   373, 658
decolonial epistemologies   177
decoloniality   496, 556
decolonization   175, 176, 496

deep incarnation   305, 363, 428, 521, 588. *See also* incarnation
deforestation   6, 38, 78, 140, 201–3, 270, 278, 280, 289, 436, 448, 461, 628, 631
De Gruchy, John W.   134, 296, 300–1, 456, 458–60
deification   234, 417, 424, 426, 487, 488, 514, 521. *See also* divinization
Delgado, Susan   97, 98, 418, 427
denialism   13, 71, 72, 78, 81, 132, 135, 207, 227. *See also* climate denial
deontological   572
deontology   191
despair   46, 169, 187–8, 291, 297, 334, 371, 437, 442, 445, 500–1, 546, 591, 607, 625
DeWitt, Calvin B.   125–6, 324, 332
divine action   360, 391, 463, 481
divine communion   546, 552–4. *See also* communion
divine economy   401
divine election   14, 279, 418, 451, 452, 459–61, 486, 487. *See also* election
divine image   229, 233, 535
divine immanence   459. *See also* immanence
divine love   400, 486
divine mystery   529, 532
divine power   123, 364, 365, 372, 445, 511
divine providence   397, 404, 482, 486
divine sovereignty   402, 458, 486
divine transcendence   399, 459. *See also* transcendence
divine will   400, 402–4, 469, 486
divinization   234, 521
domination   100, 114, 208, 242, 303, 366, 368, 386, 419, 432, 438–9, 456, 495, 525, 528, 530, 533, 534, 537, 549, 590, 591, 620, 629, 657, 662, 664
dualism   122, 182, 242, 260–1, 420, 444–5, 447, 454, 460–1, 467–8, 470, 489, 536, 589, 643, 670
  hierarchical dualism   122, 242, 536
  human/humanity and nature dualism   242, 261, 536
Durand, Jaap   294, 462

earth-care   625–6
Earth Charter   134, 213–15, 286, 287, 344
Earth community   22, 161, 166, 589, 596, 636
earth-honouring, justice   419

earth-honouring faith   6, 154, 182, 213, 368
earthkeeping   86, 125, 182–4, 188
Eastern Orthodox   82, 182, 239, 424, 520, 567
ecclesial   4, 9, 133, 244, 295, 311, 334, 449, 457, 512, 561, 563–6, 576, 597–9, 602, 605–7, 611–12, 614, 631, 642
  polarization   597, 598, 602, 605, 611, 612
  praxis   4, 9, 244, 561, 563, 565, 631
ecclesiology (doctrine of the Church)   272, 350, 355, 434, 454, 567, 612, 613
eco-anxiety   422, 423
Ecocene   499, 502, 506–8, 511, 512
eco-congregations   356, 563
ecofeminism   60, 217, 365, 511, 528, 529, 534, 660
ecojustice   15, 20, 23, 25, 72, 134, 135, 197, 222, 224, 242, 330–2, 336, 509, 525, 596, 642, 644, 661, 663. *See also* ecological justice
ecological awareness   273, 282, 412, 489, 644
ecological civilization   137, 142
ecological communities   317–19
ecological conversion   246, 248, 249, 257, 258, 528, 546, 554–6, 558, 635, 640
ecological destruction   2, 58, 191, 241, 247, 288, 296, 367, 384, 460, 503, 527, 533, 613, 614, 642, 643
ecological-economics   74, 100, 166, 313, 368, 386, 437
ecological ethics   272, 298, 440, 483, 558
ecological hermeneutics   121, 564, 569, 579, 588
ecological integrity   142, 143, 195, 296, 665
ecological justice   65, 85, 186, 193–5, 206, 209, 337, 355, 418, 510–12, 637. *See also* ecojustice
ecological reformation   272, 273, 293, 295, 296, 304
ecological spirituality   2, 134–5, 242, 488, 615
ecological sustainability   170, 171. *See also* sustainability
ecological theology   1, 164, 178, 255, 291, 295, 297, 304, 308, 317, 355, 373, 417, 433, 459, 484, 485, 487, 502, 550, 613
ecological trauma   623, 629
ecological virtues   7, 178, 188; 248
ecological wisdom   2, 6, 133, 135, 185, 613, 658

Ecowomanism   536, 659–62
Ecowomanist   511–12, 580, 659, 660–2
  method   660–2
  spirituality   661
  theologians   511
ecumenical   3, 7, 81, 100, 223, 227–9, 232, 233, 235–8, 244–4, 249, 256–7, 265, 269, 273, 287, 293, 301, 302, 308, 326, 337, 340–56, 362, 388, 392, 415, 417, 423–5, 429, 440, 443, 448–9, 451, 456, 484, 497–8, 500, 524, 545, 556–8, 567, 588, 612, 634, 650, 655
  community   256, 345, 348, 349
  movement   228, 257, 340, 341, 346, 347, 351, 352, 355, 356, 612, 634
  studies   429, 556
  theology   342
Ecumenical Association of Third World Theologians (EATWOT)   256, 355
Ecumenical Patriarch (Bartholomew)   229, 232, 233, 235–8, 244, 273, 347, 352, 567, 588
Edwards, Denis   301, 545, 556–9, 613
Einstein, Albert   15, 441
Ellis, Erle   40–4, 46, 514
Empire   99, 122, 163, 259, 263, 301, 386, 388, 393, 416, 428, 437–9, 479, 482, 585, 587–8, 590–2, 595, 619, 653, 665, 679
England (Great Britain)   65, 259–61, 263, 267–9, 631
Enlightenment   80, 88, 229, 260–1, 274, 279, 452, 465, 481, 643
environmental activism   1, 283, 291, 302
environmental degradation   53–6, 58, 63, 87, 125, 133–4, 142, 193, 213, 220, 229, 244, 262, 324, 329–30, 362, 365, 372, 461, 485, 593, 635
environmental destruction   56, 137, 258, 289, 385, 422, 566, 572, 663
environmental economists   6, 13, 53, 55, 651, 655. *See also* ecological economy
environmental education   27, 179, 507
environmental ethics   1, 31, 32, 65, 182, 186, 192, 211, 217, 224, 308, 325, 332, 355, 378, 417, 418, 564, 567, 659–61, 671
environmental humanities   19, 43, 69, 70, 120, 404, 508
environmentalism   43, 123, 125, 183, 324, 328, 329, 335, 503, 505, 597, 598, 615

environmental justice   3, 186, 243, 255, 258, 325, 328, 330, 333, 432, 433, 660
environmental problems   57, 181, 222, 331, 366, 530, 572, 601, 641, 644, 684
environmental racism   7, 167, 318, 419, 433, 629, 661
environmental refugees   20, 27, 272, 331. *See also* climate refugees; refugees
environmental restoration   569
environmental rights   211, 212, 214, 220, 221
environmental studies   120, 126, 178, 206, 332, 659
environmental sustainability   209, 223, 263, 327, 348. *See also* sustainability
environmental theology   90, 303, 304. *See also* ecological theology
epistemology   25, 88, 177, 256, 376, 380, 479, 534–5, 543, 557, 659, 668–9
Eppinger, Priscilla   511–12
eschatology   99, 182, 297, 304, 326, 329, 336–7, 369, 377, 403–4, 440–9, 464, 486, 489, 499–503, 507, 589, 590, 607
eschaton   371, 502
Eurocentric Christianity   177
Eurocentrism   175, 479
Europe   1, 21, 57, 87, 89, 93, 97, 121, 123, 171, 175–6, 273, 277, 279, 308, 320, 342, 355, 387, 389, 443, 464, 494, 507, 569, 632, 640, 642, 652, 678–81
Evangelical   1, 7, 15, 65, 66, 71, 81, 82, 120–1, 123–9, 131, 133, 135, 138, 178, 182, 193, 222, 223, 228, 246, 262, 264–5, 269, 273–6, 296, 324–38, 330–3, 335, 336, 342, 417, 584, 599, 611, 616–17
  Christians   15, 65, 128, 131
  ecotheology   182, 332
  environmentalism   125
  forms of Christianity   7, 228, 324, 336
Evangelical Environmental Network (EEN)   120, 332
Evangelicalism   2, 66, 71, 126, 270, 274–6, 324, 328, 331, 336, 337, 388
Evangelical Lausanne Movement   82, 265, 270, 274
Evangelical Lutheran Church of America (ELCA)   1, 138, 193, 417
evolution   17, 22, 31, 33–6, 43–5, 47–52, 60, 61, 68, 124, 127, 130, 252, 298, 359, 361, 366, 369, 375, 391, 392, 484, 514–15, 518, 521–3, 550–1, 556, 558, 581, 673–4
evolutionary biology   13, 14, 36, 48, 253, 451
evolutionary emergence   252, 551, 558
evolutionary history   32, 251, 369, 374, 391
evolutionary psychology   37, 40, 43
evolutionary science   124, 130, 252, 545, 551
evolutionary theory   32–4, 49, 51, 392, 518
extinction   3, 113, 122, 141, 211, 395, 440, 444, 448, 477, 486, 629, 636, 674–5
  species   31, 40, 79, 89, 113, 141, 145, 154, 179, 183, 215, 235, 362, 369, 374, 382–3, 391, 392, 403, 440–1, 444, 448, 477, 486, 498, 503, 552, 624, 629, 636, 674–5
extinction, the sixth   3, 47, 403, 618
extinction studies   374

faith and science   194, 606, 626
Fall (into sin/evil)   156, 374, 376–7, 383, 391, 453
feminist theology   4, 528, 532, 534, 536, 549, 651
fetishizing   500, 503–7
fifth mark of Christian mission   264, 270, 274
Fiji   267, 356, 639
Finnish School of Lutheran Theology   420, 424–6, 430, 458, 486–8
fossil-fuel   73, 74, 81, 129, 141, 162, 195, 265, 501
  divestment   267
  gospel   81
  propaganda   81
  reserves   141
Fourth National Climate Assessment (USA)   28, 29
Fox, Matthew   368
Francis (Pope)   134, 138, 145, 191, 214–16, 219, 220, 222, 238, 244–54, 258, 307, 352, 366, 403, 528, 534, 554, 555, 558, 604, 606, 637–40, 644
Francis of Assisi (Saint)   248, 253, 534, 638
Fuentes, Agustin   36, 43–6
fundamentalism   121, 126–7, 130–3, 135, 326, 443, 592
future generations   27, 40, 78, 79, 145, 195, 206, 213, 239, 243, 261, 266, 291, 296, 307, 427, 459, 571, 583, 584, 594, 609, 636

Gaia   18, 80, 255, 464, 498, 669
Gardiner, Stephen   72, 79
Gebara, Ivone   60, 212, 216–23, 250, 467, 529, 534, 535, 538, 652
gender inequality   423, 656
gender justice   85, 419, 627, 657
Genesis 1.1–2.4a   530
Genesis (creation)   123, 284, 285, 460
geoengineering   6, 90, 97–103, 105, 384, 402, 445, 465. *See also* climate engineering
Germany   57, 98, 208, 277, 294, 349, 356, 440, 540, 631, 681, 684
Ghana   114, 115, 524–6
Gilkey, Langdon   181
global capitalism   2, 170, 171, 511, 604. *See also* capitalism
global Christianity   2, 14, 270, 289
global Evangelicalism   274–6. *See also* evangelicalism
globalization   56, 145, 154, 293, 294, 448, 505, 578, 652, 662, 664
global market   247, 301, 320, 422, 423, 665
Global North   105, 164, 166, 172, 222, 253, 277, 280, 281, 286, 288, 289, 393, 394, 441, 568, 577, 578, 643, 651, 652, 654
Global South   1, 25, 75, 76, 82, 104, 105, 132, 134, 162, 164, 223, 277–81, 286, 288–90, 341, 342, 348, 393, 418, 443, 559, 564, 577, 578, 628, 643, 651, 652. *See also* the South
global warming   29, 91, 97, 102, 107–9, 111, 112, 118, 119, 129, 130, 136, 138–44, 146, 147, 179, 183, 192, 195, 196, 198, 201, 202, 207, 235, 273, 292, 293, 295, 301, 349, 392, 395, 396, 463, 464, 507, 528, 533, 566, 583, 584, 586, 591, 606, 607, 609, 617, 628, 632–4, 636, 638, 674, 683
God as Creator   181, 381. *See also* creation
God as Father   8, 496, 524, 525, 528–9, 534–5, 537–40
God as Mother   526, 534, 549
God as Trinity   545, 556
God-language   465
God-talk   63, 241, 496, 532, 540, 544, 558
God-world relation   513, 518, 520, 524
goodness of creation   18, 246, 643. *See also* creation
goodness of God   301, 345, 469

grace (doctrine of)   68, 279, 281, 289, 374, 395, 401, 417–20, 423–6, 429, 446, 453, 454, 456–8, 461, 488
Graham, Larry K.   615, 616, 624, 625
Granberg-Michaelson, Wesley   180–1, 340, 342–3, 345, 350–5, 632
greenhouse effect   218, 572, 581, 634
greenhouse gas (GHG) emissions   28, 29, 90–3, 95, 96, 141, 159, 194, 197, 199, 203–6, 212, 237, 268, 295, 349, 359, 399, 617, 626, 633–4, 684–6
Greenland   108, 111, 395, 588
Greenpeace   631
Gregersen, Niels Henrik   305, 322, 428, 588
Gregory of Nazianz   497
Gregory of Nyssa   232, 580
growth   55, 56, 59, 61, 66–8, 79, 127, 136, 170, 193, 194, 203, 234, 247, 251, 271–2, 294, 318, 326, 335, 338, 384–5, 388, 399, 412, 441, 463, 481, 504, 505, 533, 583, 601, 633, 636, 645, 651, 652, 678, 684. *See also* limitless growth
Gustafson, James M.   124

Habel, Norman C.   123, 242, 364, 366, 569, 580, 581, 584, 589, 595
Hamilton, Clive   43, 153, 402–4, 507
Haraway, Donna   68, 69
Hartman, Laura M.   98, 100
Hartshorne, Charles   125
Hayhoe, Katharine   27, 28, 126, 332, 599
heaven   122, 123, 129, 158, 180–2, 230, 232, 236, 282, 327, 334, 442, 444, 446, 449, 452, 455, 464, 481–7, 499, 502, 513, 567, 580, 587–9, 595, 670, 672
heaven and earth   181, 232, 282, 442, 481, 483–5, 487, 502, 589, 672
heavenism   589, 592
Hefner, Philip   366, 484
Heidelberg Catechism   397, 455, 458, 461
hermeneutics   4, 24, 121, 242, 253, 559, 564, 569, 579, 588, 593, 595, 673. *See also* ecological hermeneutics
heteronormative   542–4
heteronormativity   496, 540
Hildegard von Bingen   502, 642
Hinduism   596, 664
Hinkelammert, Franz   505
Holocene   153, 155, 402, 498, 547
homelessness   179, 498, 499

hope 4, 25, 27, 46, 59, 63, 111, 118, 133, 142–4, 147, 150, 157, 164–5, 168, 174, 178–9, 183, 186–8, 190, 204–5, 209, 224, 238, 247, 257, 263, 268, 274, 302, 329, 335, 343, 356, 371, 372, 397, 404, 419, 422–3, 442, 444–9, 456, 463–4, 470, 479, 500–2, 523, 545, 546, 551, 575, 576, 580, 585, 587, 588, 590–2, 594, 595, 601, 615, 619, 625–7, 629, 641, 650, 658, 665, 668, 687–9
hope and despair 500–1
hope and love 183, 190, 209
hopelessness 164, 187, 442, 445, 447
Hornborg, Alf 148, 501, 504, 505, 507
human creatureliness 582, 594
human creatures 158, 162, 167–8, 543
human dignity 171, 214, 245, 257, 295, 609
human distinctiveness 32, 36, 380
human ecology 145, 245, 578, 602–3
human evolution 36, 40, 43, 47, 392
human exceptionalism 31, 45, 47, 79, 540
human flourishing 36, 326, 515, 538
human freedom 399, 401–5, 486, 604
human responsibility 32, 153, 214, 244, 392, 431, 445, 458, 486, 525, 686
human rights 6, 213, 215, 223, 258, 346, 352
human sinfulness 282, 285, 289
human species 32, 38, 40, 42, 44, 46, 118, 173, 216, 246, 303, 385, 402, 440, 616, 618
humility (as ecological virtue) 183, 184, 188, 192, 239, 240, 609, 658

ice 19, 40, 111, 112, 114, 141, 155, 293, 359, 395, 464, 480, 547, 616
  caps 114, 155
  sheets (Arctic and/or Antarctic) 141
  watch 111
image of God 90, 105, 123, 299, 372, 381, 456, 514, 517, 520, 529, 535, 538, 549–51, 554, 581, 615, 635, 644, 653, 658, 659
Imago dei 366, 377, 380, 381, 451, 484, 520, 659
imperialism 3, 142, 388, 408, 479, 643, 681
incarnation (doctrine of) 236, 305, 322–3, 363, 364, 377, 410–13, 415, 416, 428, 487, 510–12, 516–17, 521–2, 548, 550, 588. *See also* deep incarnation

incarnation theology 510–12
inclusivity 416, 520, 614, 655, 656, 658
India 48, 75, 147, 164, 243, 250, 269, 271, 342, 416, 431, 436, 494, 593, 595, 596, 652
indigenous 3, 7, 22, 77, 78, 80, 82, 87, 88, 107, 132, 149, 155, 164, 165, 175–7, 211–14, 216, 219, 222, 224, 241, 248–9, 253–4, 260, 262, 264, 269, 313–15, 318, 320, 342, 347, 348, 353, 395, 418, 431, 433–4, 475, 479, 494–7, 511, 533, 544, 545, 578, 580, 584, 609, 619–21, 628, 630, 654, 656, 664, 666–7, 671
  communities 78, 80, 82, 88, 149, 216, 222, 248, 253, 313, 628
  cosmovisions 80, 88
  epistemologies 177, 479
  knowledge 88, 511
  peoples 3, 7, 77, 78, 82, 176, 211–14, 262, 313, 353, 395, 418, 475, 620, 628, 630
  religions 177, 545, 666
  rights 78, 318
  spirituality 176, 578
  theologians 78
  wisdom 155, 224
integrity of creation 194, 224, 234, 264, 270, 340–52, 458, 594
interfaith 14, 65, 136, 147–8, 150, 223, 224, 238, 248, 266, 269, 273, 353, 354, 495, 576, 596–8, 618, 640, 661
  dialogue 136, 147–8, 495, 596, 598, 661
interfaith Lambeth Declaration (2015) 273
Interfaith Power and Light 14, 266, 618, 661
Interfaith Summit on Climate Change (2014) 238, 354
Intergovernmental Panel Climate Change (IPCC) 13, 29, 91, 92, 95, 104, 163, 178, 237, 346, 631, 634, 636, 675
intrinsic value 22, 186, 189, 191, 246, 249, 251, 367, 503, 525, 643
Ireland 631, 639
Irenaeus of Lyons (Saint) 43, 363, 365, 521
Islam 190, 191, 284, 505, 545, 596, 664
Islamic-Christian dialogue 136
Islamic Declaration of Global Climate Change (2015) 136, 138
Islamic environmental ethics 189, 191, 192, 664, 679

Index

Jainism 596
Jamieson, Dale 80
Jenkins, Willis 70, 73, 79, 83, 87–8, 153, 194, 382, 418, 443–5, 459, 530, 567, 684, 686
Jennings, Willie James 474–6
Jenson, Robert 458, 557
John Paul II (Pope) 244, 245, 247, 249, 352, 635–6, 640
Johnson, Elizabeth 322, 380, 428, 529, 531–2, 537–9, 549, 552
Justice, Peace and the Integrity of Creation (JPIC) 153, 194, 340–3, 349, 350, 352
justification (doctrine of) 8, 279, 288–9, 418–21, 423–30, 458, 479, 487–8, 521
justifying grace 417, 419, 423–30, 488. *See also* grace

Kant, Immanuel 471, 519
Kärkäinen, Veli-Matti 424, 426
Kaufman, Gordon 310, 375
Kearns, Laurel 53, 57, 500, 601
Keller, Catherine 142, 362, 363, 419, 472, 500, 541–3, 601
kenosis 512, 514–18, 520–4, 526, 527, 658
kenotic 511–14, 516–27
Kenotic Christology 514, 517
kenotic ecology 511
Kenya 250, 337, 338, 678, 681, 682
King, Martin Luther 138, 196
Kingdom 169, 181, 236, 264, 311, 382, 461, 520, 547–9, 553, 588–9, 595, 680
Kingdom of God 181, 520, 547, 553, 588–9
Kiribati 395, 410, 616
Klein, Naomi 62, 63, 68, 243, 452, 579
Koinonia 350, 611–14, 663
Kolbert, Elizabeth 403, 618
Koster, Hilda P. 3, 216, 250, 295, 419, 459, 496, 512, 650

Lamb of God 590, 592
LaMothe, Ryan 615, 618, 625, 629
land 3, 41, 78, 84, 86, 110–11, 116–18, 159, 160, 181, 233–6, 246, 259–63, 267, 269–72, 280, 285, 311, 313–18, 320, 360, 366, 386, 406, 409, 431–2, 436, 441, 448, 468–9, 471, 473–6, 478, 506, 531, 533, 552, 569, 582, 614, 618, 620–1, 629, 638, 674, 679
conflicts 679
degradation 270, 272
grabs 271, 272, 620
landless movement, 59
landscape 6, 46, 84, 116, 131, 132, 249, 254, 338, 475, 542, 584, 594, 598, 599, 600, 640
Latin American theology 351, 354
Latour, Bruno 79, 80, 504
Laudato Si': On Care for Our Common Home 134, 138, 145, 183, 191, 212, 214–16, 219, 221–3, 244–7, 249, 250, 256–8, 273, 307, 352, 355, 366, 403, 528, 534, 554, 558, 597, 599, 602, 604, 606–9, 611, 628, 637–9, 641, 644
Lausanne Conference 265, 274–5
Lerner, Gerda 530–1
LGBTQ 328, 416, 542, 543, 657
liberation theology 4, 59, 63, 88, 248, 257, 315, 380, 525, 585, 659–60, 685
limitations 166, 171, 190, 210, 223, 258, 441, 468, 594, 597
limitless growth 271–2. *See also* growth
liturgy 156, 188, 230, 232–4, 248, 268, 488, 563, 566–78, 613
Luther, Martin 101, 279, 281–7, 289–90, 419, 424–7, 458, 486–7, 680
Lutheran theology 277–8, 290, 420, 424
Lutheran World Federation (LWF) 138, 158, 268, 278–9, 295, 431, 435, 588

Maathai, Wangari 250
McDaniel, Jay B. 137–8, 141–3
McDonagh, Seán 244–5, 249, 631, 634–6, 639, 642
McFague, Sallie 58, 60, 66, 164, 272, 304–7, 365, 433, 456, 496, 513, 519, 522, 524–7, 533, 537, 548–9
McKibben, Bill 143
Makgoba, Thabo (Archbishop) 273–4
Malawi 34, 272, 510, 681–2
Mannermaa, Tuomo 424
Margulis, Lynn 68
Marshall islands 198, 340, 395, 398
Martin Luther King 138, 196
Martin-Schramm, James B. 186, 193, 195, 206, 208–10, 419, 456, 590
Marx, Karl 374, 504
Maximus the Confessor 234–5, 488

Mbiti, John   510, 678
Mennonites   308, 310–12, 314–17, 321–2
Merton, Thomas   138, 521, 522
Metanoia   238, 240, 573
migration   19, 246, 297, 403, 619, 621, 629, 654, 661
　of climate refugees/displaced people   246, 297, 403, 619, 654
Missio Dei   644
Mission (Christian)   4, 8, 86, 87, 244, 261–4, 266, 267, 270, 271, 273–6, 310, 355, 394, 398, 414, 475, 563, 597, 598, 611, 614, 642–4
missionaries   84, 176, 260–2, 270, 271, 476, 631, 678
mitigation. *See* climate mitigation
modernity   1, 55, 57, 100, 105, 175, 176, 180, 331, 386, 387, 399, 474, 477, 495, 498, 499, 504, 507, 651, 663, 664
Moe-Lobeda, Cynthia   74, 100, 157, 166, 170, 174–6, 313–14, 386, 419, 421, 425–9, 437
Moltmann, Jürgen   4, 363, 378, 380–2, 434, 440, 443, 446, 484, 489, 517, 520, 538, 547, 553, 557, 590, 607
moral agency   157, 164, 167, 421–2, 628
moral anthropology   161, 162
moral climate   292, 301, 566
moral paralysis   423, 429
moral vision   154, 157–8, 160–2, 165–75, 177, 223, 317, 385, 465
Muers, Rachel   339
Muhammad (Prophet)   136, 138, 189, 191, 406

Naess, Arne   305
narrative theology   360, 546, 548, 559
Nash, James A.   195, 293, 295, 296
Nasr, Seyyed H.   190
natural disasters   295, 482, 634, 639
natural environment   27, 124, 189, 191–2, 238, 319, 336, 338, 352, 666, 678
natural evil   391–2, 394
natural sciences   18, 22, 25, 124, 136–9, 144, 146–8, 255, 299, 375, 376, 391
natural selection   14, 34, 37, 39, 49–51, 124, 298, 392
natural suffering   253
natural theology   294, 478

neo-liberalism   64, 166, 170, 431–3, 488
Neo-platonism   455
Netherlands (The)   57, 109, 116, 681
new materialism, 18, 62
New Testament   236, 345, 416, 435, 460–1, 519, 531, 588–9, 594
New Zealand   267, 615, 619, 628–9, 632
Nicene Creed   409, 413
Niche construction theory (NCT)   32–5, 37–52
Niebuhr, Reinhold   101
Nigeria   526
Noah narrative/covenant   396, 398, 584
nonviolence   15, 211, 308–12, 315–21, 323
nonviolent activists   73, 102, 220
nonviolent resistance   413, 592, 595
Non-Western Christianity   176, 479, 665
North-Atlantic Christians   421, 436, 494
North-Atlantic theology   419, 481, 627, 649, 650
Northcott, Michael S.   79, 80, 98, 100, 199, 200, 291–4, 301, 373, 451, 457, 461, 498–9, 566
Nyamiti, Charles   510
Nyengele, M. Fulgence   622

Obama, Barack (President)   198
O'Brien, Kevin J.   53, 73, 90, 91, 98, 101–3, 183, 211, 220, 222, 420, 684
ocean currents   20, 464
Oceania   396
oceans   19, 85, 124, 141, 155, 170–1, 206, 293, 441, 580–81, 613, 634, 638, 674, 677–8
Origen of Alexandria   446, 489
original sin   166, 247, 279, 391, 453, 460, 468–70, 485, 659

Pacific, The   349, 355, 616, 619, 639, 653, 663
Pacific Islands/Islanders   340, 348, 410, 629
panentheism/s   125, 260, 363, 459
Paris Climate Agreement (COP 21)   30, 70, 71, 90–2, 95, 96, 98, 103, 108, 111, 117, 126, 193, 197–209, 267, 268, 344, 349, 463, 467, 622, 629, 631, 639, 640, 652, 685
pastoral   9, 122, 248, 297, 300, 345, 385, 463, 474, 489, 508, 563, 564, 615, 616, 618, 621–31, 637

care 463, 564, 615, 616, 621, 627
praxis 9, 563, 615, 625
theology 615, 616–18, 621–9, 630
patriarchal 122, 216, 222, 250, 258, 345, 467, 494, 495, 528–30, 532, 535–41, 548, 549
ideology 258
language 528, 532
power 530, 536
symbolic 216, 222
theology 532
patriarchy 7, 388, 389, 417, 495, 496, 528, 530, 531, 533, 534, 536, 539
Pentecostal 7, 133, 182, 227, 228, 324–8, 330–2, 334–9, 524, 655
churches 334, 338
communities 326, 328, 335
ecotheology 337–9
theology 326, 330, 337–8
Pentecostalism 324, 326, 328, 334–8, 388, 416
Peters, Ted F. 385, 424, 426–8
petro-eschatology 501
petroleum 112, 119, 141, 237, 583
Philippines, The 627–8, 631, 640
Pihkala, Panu 422–3, 426
planetary 3, 15, 17, 19, 22, 31, 38, 43–6, 61, 73, 74, 89, 91, 93, 120, 141, 153, 155, 157, 159, 173, 216, 250, 256, 326, 355, 375, 380, 386, 396, 399, 404, 412, 419, 422, 428, 472, 474, 475, 496, 511, 513, 525, 540, 543–5, 552, 554, 572, 615, 616, 623, 627, 630, 650, 653–4, 661, 684
community 540, 544, 545, 554
ethic 61, 654
health 22, 428
solidarity 3, 216, 250, 419, 496, 511, 564, 576, 601, 615–16, 622, 650
Plato/Platonism 125, 285, 571
pneumatology 334, 337–8, 487–9, 497–500, 502–3, 505–6, 509, 510–11, 557
polarization 330, 434, 597–9, 602, 605–7, 611, 612
political ecology 78, 121, 208, 507
political economy 77, 295, 592, 656
political theology 72, 79, 80, 98, 291, 373, 377–9, 444, 457, 498–500, 577
Pondo Populus 138
Pope Francis. *See* Francis

population growth 193, 251, 272, 399
postcolonial, theology 176, 618, 622, 626–7, 630, 651
postcolonialism 399, 616, 618, 627
postmodern/postmodernism 142, 360, 399, 465, 616–18, 626–8, 630
post-natural 378, 379
post-traumatic 616, 618, 623, 626–30
theology 623
pragmatism 76, 459
predestination (doctrine of) 67, 451–5, 457–60, 486
process philosophy/theology 125
process theologians 138, 141–2
prophetic 6, 107, 137–8, 144, 147, 165, 176–7, 191, 209, 329, 339, 343–6, 385, 434, 464, 510, 511, 577, 585, 587, 633, 639, 657, 661, 664
imagination 165
tradition 339
visions 6
vocation 633
voices 107, 339
Pui-lan, Kwok 64, 272, 345, 651
Purdy, Jedediah 76, 79

queer 495, 540–3, 655–7
ecofeminisms 655
ecofeminist identity theory 657
theology 495
theory (QT) 540, 542, 656, 657
quotidian 73, 88
Qur'an 140, 189, 190, 192

Rahner, Karl 546, 547, 551
Rancière, Jacques 305
Rapture 591, 592
Rasmussen, Larry L. 6, 134, 153–4, 167, 182, 213–14, 345, 368, 385, 653
reconciliation 8, 85, 86, 89, 91, 99, 100, 102, 105–6, 156, 183, 264, 406, 410–11, 417, 447–9, 464, 487, 553, 578, 611, 613, 633, 672
Redekop, Calvin 310, 311, 313–14, 316
redemption 25, 67–9, 181, 282, 301, 334, 367, 374, 376–7, 407, 417, 425, 446, 459, 571, 573, 575, 588, 603, 653
reformation (ecological) 272, 273, 293, 295, 296, 304

reformation (Protestant)   272, 277, 279, 286, 289, 293, 308, 328, 420, 454
Reformed churches   294, 342, 423,
Reformed theology   178, 292–4, 296, 299, 301, 303–5, 451, 454, 456, 458, 460, 500
Reformed tradition   1, 292, 294, 297, 299, 302–4, 306, 454, 462, 556
refugees (climate/environmental)   3, 20, 27, 246, 272, 297, 315, 412, 432, 499, 608, 619, 629, 654, 656
Republican Party (USA)   28, 126–9
Republicans   128, 129, 604, 609
resurrection   67, 182, 187, 360, 409–15, 416, 434–5, 464, 487, 520, 546, 588–9, 595, 626
  of the body/bodily   67, 182, 410, 413
  and the cross   434, 464, 487, 520, 546, 588, 595
  of Jesus Christ   67, 360, 409, 410, 413, 435, 487, 546, 588, 595
Ricoeur, Paul   467, 468
Rieger, Joerg   53, 58, 59, 62, 64–6, 68, 651
Rolston, Holmes (III)   186, 514
Rossing, Barbara   579, 590–1, 593–5, 675
Rowe, Terra Schwerin   65–8, 419, 420, 425, 429–30, 456, 458, 687
Ruether, Rosemary Radford   60, 532, 536, 540–1, 581

sacramental   22, 68, 69, 230, 240, 248, 254, 363, 404, 567, 569, 570, 614
sacraments   229, 304, 454, 521, 563, 567, 575, 580
salvation (doctrine of)   8, 47, 100, 167, 175, 232, 241, 260–1, 279, 293, 295–6, 298, 303, 334, 360–1, 371, 372, 394, 406–9, 411, 413–15, 417, 418, 424, 439, 442, 446–9, 453, 455, 460–2, 465, 466, 469, 475, 484–5, 487–9, 493, 495–7, 500, 502, 509, 514, 524–5, 547, 548, 557, 589, 644, 653, 670. *See also* universal salvation
  and consummation   295, 361, 489, 493
  of humanity   293, 303, 406, 455
  for us   8, 361, 406, 487–8
sanctification   8, 69, 232, 418, 425, 487, 489
sanctifying grace   417, 425, 429. *See also* grace
Santmire, H. Paul   293, 367–8, 580, 613

Schaeffer, Francis   125
Schor, Juliet   60–2
Scott, Peter Manley   100–1, 207, 293–4, 301, 310, 373–5, 377–81, 451, 498, 507, 578
sea   40, 67, 76, 104, 108–9, 138, 141, 159, 203, 232–3, 246, 271, 280, 293, 395–7, 404–5, 436, 463, 528, 533, 554, 564, 616, 624, 629, 638, 680
  ice   40, 395
  levels   67, 76, 104, 141, 159, 246, 280, 395, 404–5, 463, 624, 638
Setiloane, Gabriel   614
sexism   389, 419–20, 530, 532, 534, 540, 545, 660
Shinto religion   664
Shiva, Vandana   283, 595, 656, 657
sin (doctrine of)   8, 14, 25, 27, 67, 91, 99–102, 105–6, 162, 166, 231, 241, 247, 279, 280, 282, 285, 290, 297, 304, 313, 334, 361, 368, 384–94, 402, 407, 409, 415, 420–8, 453, 458, 460, 468–70, 485, 486, 488, 503, 506, 507, 525, 546, 548, 573, 579, 584, 595, 605, 632, 653, 656, 659–61. *See also* climate sin; original sin
Sittler, Joseph   588
social evil   391, 392. *See also* evil
social holiness   333, 427
solar   77, 91, 93, 94, 101, 105, 139, 201, 239, 633, 677
  power   77, 139, 201, 239
  radiation   91, 93, 94,
  radiation management   91, 93, 94, 101
solidarity   3, 25, 27, 60, 62, 63, 72, 145, 193–5, 197, 209, 216, 245, 250, 256, 257, 273, 318, 352, 353, 386, 413, 416, 419, 427, 428, 438, 447, 464, 496, 505, 511, 520, 564, 576, 601, 609, 612, 622, 626, 628, 633, 634, 637, 650. *See also* planetary solidarity
  deep solidarity   62
  intergenerational solidarity   3, 145, 256
South (The)   1, 3, 25, 75, 76, 82–9, 102–5, 109, 120, 126, 128, 132–5, 147, 149, 162, 164, 175, 177, 182, 189, 207, 209, 223, 228, 259, 261, 263, 265, 268, 269, 273, 275, 277–81, 286, 288–92, 294, 298, 301, 308, 314, 336–7, 341, 342, 348, 384, 387, 393, 406, 409, 411–12, 418, 430, 443, 462, 479, 494, 499, 524,

528, 556, 559, 564, 577, 578, 593, 611, 616, 628, 632, 643, 651–4, 657, 680–1. *See also* Global South

South Africa 1, 3, 83–5, 87, 102, 132–5, 189, 259, 261, 263, 265, 268, 291, 294, 298, 336–7, 384, 387, 406, 409, 411, 430, 462, 524, 528, 556, 681

Southgate, Christopher 369, 372, 392

South-Korea 642

spatial eschatology 499, 500, 502. *See also* eschatology

Spirit, (God the Spirit/God's Spirit) 323, 334, 345, 381, 441, 466, 488, 494, 497, 499, 502, 503, 509, 522, 538, 546, 551, 553, 558

Spirit, Holy 230, 232, 334, 337–9, 343, 379, 407, 416, 417, 424–6, 429, 459, 464, 486, 488, 495, 497–500, 503, 505, 506, 509–12, 521, 548, 550, 657

Spirit-Sophia 538, 549

structural evil 74, 100, 166, 170, 313, 314, 368, 386, 421, 429, 437, 661

structural sin 101, 162, 247, 656. *See also* sin

structural violence 93, 100–2, 314, 319, 386, 388–90, 420–2, 428, 429. *See also* violence

survival 15, 17, 36, 53, 61, 64, 108, 159, 167, 213, 215, 233, 250, 291, 315, 368, 392, 419, 469, 480, 498, 505, 509, 510, 514, 515, 519, 535, 595, 672

sustainability 41, 55–9, 73, 94, 121, 142–3, 149, 153, 170–2, 193, 194, 197, 208–9, 223, 243, 247, 258, 263, 298, 318, 322, 327, 347–8, 385, 396–7, 403, 417, 459, 488, 507, 568, 643, 644, 678
  ecological/environmental 56, 58, 170–2, 209, 223, 263, 327, 348
  norm of 193, 194, 197, 209

sustainable 7, 29, 55, 56, 58, 59, 61, 91, 116, 134, 137, 139, 142, 143, 145, 149, 159, 168, 173–5, 177, 193, 194, 199, 200, 202, 203, 205, 208, 209, 223, 244, 247, 258, 262, 272, 314, 316, 341, 355, 386, 419, 429, 431, 449, 488, 507, 534, 564, 574, 584, 623, 637, 657, 682, 685,

sustainable development 29, 56–9, 91, 137, 145, 149, 159, 199, 200, 202–3, 209, 244, 247, 272

Sustainable Development Goals (SDGs) 247

Swoboda, Aaron 182, 332–4, 337–9

Synod of Dordt (1618–19) 454

Szerszynski, Bronislaw 97, 101, 506

Tanner, Kathryn 295, 417, 453, 653, 654

technology 6, 31, 47, 55–9, 66, 88, 90, 97–100, 102, 105, 181, 183, 187, 203–4, 209, 231, 236, 247, 260, 384, 420, 497, 500–1, 503–6, 510–12, 568, 601, 652, 663–4

theodicy 43, 296, 361, 375, 394, 398, 404

Theokritoff, Elizabeth 567

theology of nature 367, 377–9

Thomas Aquinas 191, 453, 546, 554

Ting, K. H. (Ding Guangxun) 669

Tinker, George E. 78, 177, 476, 500

Toynbee, Arnold Joseph 663

transcendence 60, 300, 303, 399, 401–5, 439, 459, 518. *See also* divine transcendence

transformation 38, 40, 45, 86, 89, 139, 141, 144, 176–7, 183, 207–9, 229, 236, 248, 255, 257, 275, 285, 306–7, 309, 320, 333, 366, 386, 390, 422, 425, 438, 484, 488, 506–10, 534, 546, 551, 555, 576, 578, 592, 625, 660–1, 663, 665, 669, 670, 673, 679

tree of knowledge 284, 582–3

trees 19, 34, 167, 179, 231, 232, 236, 243, 297, 337, 338, 395, 436, 552, 555, 569, 654

Trinitarian 370, 379, 442, 456, 459, 486, 499, 502, 510, 518, 520, 545–51, 554, 556–8, 598, 625, 653
  anthropology 554, 558
  cosmology 499, 502
  doctrine of creation 379; 510, 545–9, 556–8

Trinity, (doctrine of) 131, 143, 240, 370, 379, 440, 441, 444, 448, 483, 496, 497, 506, 514, 516, 518, 520–2, 543, 545–50, 552, 553–4, 556, 557–9, 611–12

Triune (God) 8, 9, 370, 387, 396, 400, 411, 462, 465–6, 493, 495, 496, 499, 516, 545–9, 553, 554, 556–7, 559, 612

Trump, administration 126, 127, 393

Trump, Donald (President) 127, 128, 135, 205, 640

Truth and Reconciliation Commission (South Africa) 85

Tucker, Mary Evelyn 138, 214, 485

Tutu, Desmond (Archbishop) 85, 262, 267–8, 271, 274
Tuvalu 243, 395–9, 404, 410, 616

Ubuntu 272, 436, 558, 578, 622, 629
uncertainty (scientific) 28–30, 128
uniqueness (human) 14, 31, 215, 483, 487.
 See also human
United Nations 90, 197–9, 201–4, 206, 207, 213, 233, 247, 321, 341, 344, 353, 631, 639, 682
United States (of America) 15, 29, 40, 66, 70, 71, 73–5, 81, 93, 97, 107, 116, 120–1, 123–8, 131–3, 135, 157–60, 163, 166, 169, 173, 198, 203–6, 212–13, 218–19, 229, 237, 238, 252, 266, 267, 313, 321, 324, 332, 336, 342, 349, 356, 362, 432, 436, 441, 443, 597, 604, 607–8, 611, 619–21, 629, 632–4, 640, 661
Universal Declaration of Human-Rights 213
Universal salvation /universality of salvation 8, 167, 295, 334, 372, 409, 442, 446–9, 484, 489, 493, 644

values 2, 5–7, 24, 28, 47, 58, 66, 72, 148, 150, 161, 168, 175, 193, 236, 249, 257, 258, 260, 263, 274, 296, 308, 311, 312, 315, 317–19, 323, 328, 330–1, 336, 353, 387, 437, 469, 471, 531, 535, 541, 550, 569, 574, 598–604, 608, 609, 613, 619–21, 652, 655, 685
vespers-for-the-preservation-of-creation 569
violence 73, 102, 161, 163, 169, 173, 174, 220, 264, 420, 421, 427, 649. *See also* climate violence; structural violence
virtue ethics 182, 183, 189–92, 297
virtues 6, 7, 178, 183, 184, 186, 188, 464.
 See also ecological virtues
Vischer, Lukas 567, 634
vocation 74, 100, 166, 229, 233, 242, 248, 274, 313, 368, 380, 382, 386, 417, 421, 427, 437, 456, 485, 581, 633
vulnerability, climate 76, 109, 163, 202

Wallace, Mark 500, 623
waters 56, 65, 76, 107–9, 118, 140, 233, 301, 398, 498, 508, 528, 552, 581, 591, 635, 667
watershed discipleship 317, 320, 322

Weber, Max 67, 388, 423, 451, 653
Weil, Simone 520
Welby, Justin (Archbishop of Canterbury) 138, 264, 273, 274
Welker, Michael 299, 302
Wesley, John 333, 334, 371
Westhelle, Vitor 277, 288–90, 418, 500–2
White, Lynn, Jr. 66, 125, 133, 242, 270, 292, 324–6, 366, 388, 418, 474, 529, 530, 533, 643, 664, 684
Whitehead, Alfred North 125, 145
white supremacy 71, 125, 160, 166, 388, 417, 495, 496, 621, 659–61
White US Evangelicals (WUSE) 71
Williams, Delores S. 660, 661
Williams, Rowan (Archbishop) 115, 264, 268, 272–3
Wirzba, Norman 180, 181, 366, 459, 567
wisdom 2, 6, 17, 25–7, 42, 108, 114, 118, 133, 135, 142, 143, 155, 161–2, 168, 183, 185–6, 188, 190, 192, 194, 224, 230–3, 243, 366–7, 369, 385, 387, 406, 413, 415, 476, 478, 484, 507, 510–11, 537–8, 549–51, 563, 582, 613, 627, 658, 665–9, 671
Wolterstorff, Nicholas 186, 456
World Alliance of Reformed Churches (WARC) 68, 294, 423
World Christianity 174, 175, 177, 342
World Council of Churches (WCC) 82, 153, 193, 194, 228, 268, 270, 273, 276, 310, 340, 351, 414, 449, 509, 576, 631–4, 644, 677
World Parliament of Religions 142, 148
worldview 43, 124, 136, 143, 175, 177, 180, 208, 223, 238–40, 326–7, 336, 338, 518, 567, 571–5, 579, 581, 614, 622, 623, 643, 666, 669, 679
worship 27, 134, 187, 229, 232, 235, 241, 248, 259, 261, 284, 363, 369, 379, 470, 476, 525, 526, 531, 537, 539, 563–4, 566–70, 584, 603, 607, 629, 653

Zachariah, George 149, 212, 217–21, 240, 596
Zachman, Randall 299–301
Zambia 270, 611, 681
Zen-Buddhism 136, 144, 671
Zimbabwe 85, 265, 536, 576, 681, 682

www.ingramcontent.com/pod-product-compliance
Lightning Source LLC
Chambersburg PA
CBHW052107010526
44111CB00036B/1543